Lecture Notes in Computer Science 1443

Edited by G. Goos, J. Hartmanis and J. van Leeuwen

Springer
Berlin
Heidelberg
New York
Barcelona
Budapest
Hong Kong
London
Milan
Paris
Singapore
Tokyo

Kim G. Larsen Sven Skyum
Glynn Winskel (Eds.)

Automata, Languages and Programming

25th International Colloquium, ICALP'98
Aalborg, Denmark, July 13-17, 1998
Proceedings

Springer

Volume Editors

Kim G. Larsen
Department of Computer Science, Aalborg University
Fredrik Bajersvej 7E, DK-9220 Aalborg, Denmark
E-mail: kgl@cs.auc.dk

Sven Skyum
Glynn Winskel
Department of Computer Science, University of Aarhus
Ny Munkegade, Bldg. 540, DK-8000 Aarhus C, Denmark
E-mail: {sskyum, gwinskel}@daimi.aau.dk

Cataloging-in-Publication data applied for

Die Deutsche Bibliothek - CIP-Einheitsaufnahme

Automata, languages and programming : 25th international colloquium ; proceedings / ICALP '98, Aalborg, Denmark, July 13 - 17, 1998. Kim G. Larsen (ed.). - Berlin ; Heidelberg ; New York ; Barcelona ; Budapest ; Hong Kong ; London ; Milan ; Paris ; Singapore ; Tokyo : Springer, 1998
(Lecture notes in computer science ; Vol. 1443)
ISBN 3-540-64781-3

CR Subject Classification (1991): F, E.1, I.3.5, C.2, I.2.3

ISSN 0302-9743
ISBN 3-540-64781-3 Springer-Verlag Berlin Heidelberg New York

Typesetting: Camera-ready by author
SPIN 10638067 06/3142 – 5 4 3 2 1 0 Printed on acid-free paper

Foreword

The International Colloquium on Automata, Languages, and Programming (ICALP) is the annual conference series of the European Association for Theoretical Computer Science (EATCS). It is intended to cover all important areas of theoretical computer science, such as computability, automata, formal languages, new computing paradigms, term rewriting, analysis and design of algorithms, computational geometry, computational complexity, symbolic and algebraic computation, cryptography and security, data types and data structures, theory of data bases and knowledge bases, semantics of programming languages, program specification and verification, foundations of functional and logic programming, parallel and distributed computation, theory of concurrency, theory of robotics, theory of logical design and layout.

ICALP'98 was hosted by Basic Research in Computer Science (BRICS) and Department of Computer Science at Aalborg University, Denmark, from July 13 to July 17, 1998. ICALP'98 was accompanied by the four satellite events: Software Tools for Technology Transfer (STTT), INFINITY'98, Semantics of Objects as Processes (SOAP), and APPROX'98 as well as a summer school in Cryptology and Data Security.

Previous colloquia were held in Bologna (1997), Paderborn (1996), Szeged (1995), Jerusalem (1994), Lund (1993), Vienna (1992), Madrid (1991), Warwick (1990), Stresa (1989), Tampere (1988), Karlsruhe (1987), Rennes (1986), Nafplion (1985), Antwerp (1984), Barcelona (1983), Århus (1982), Haifa (1981), Amsterdam (1980), Graz (1979), Udine (1978), Türkü (1977), Edinburgh (1976), Saarbrücken (1974), and Paris (1972). ICALP'99 will be held in Prague, Czech Republic, during the second week of July, 1999.

The Program Committee selected 70 papers from a total of 182 submissions. Authors of submitted papers came from 35 countries covering all continents. Each submitted paper was sent to at least four Program Committee members, who were often assisted by subreferees. The Program Committee meeting took place at BRICS, Aarhus University, on March 14 and 15, 1998. This volume contains the 70 papers selected at the meeting plus 8 invited papers.

We would like to thank all the Program Committee members and the subreferees who assisted them in their work. Also, members of the Organizing Committee and further members of BRICS deserve our gratitude for their contributions throughout the preparations. A special thanks to Vladimiro Sassone who created the WWW software used for electronic submission and reviewing.

We gratefully acknowledge support from Bosch-Telecom, Beologic, Department of Computer Science at Aalborg University, BRICS, and the City of Aalborg.

May 1998

Kim Guldstrand Larsen, Sven Skyum, and Glynn Winskel
BRICS

Invited Speakers

Martín Abadi, DEC
Gilles Brassard, Montréal
Thomas A. Henzinger, Berkeley
Mark Overmars, Utrecht
Andrew Pitts, Cambridge
Amir Pnueli, Weizmann Institute
Leslie G. Valiant, Harvard
Avi Wigderson, Jerusalem

Program Committee

Kim G. Larsen, Aalborg (chair)

Sven Skyum, Aarhus (vice-chair)
Susanne Albers, Saarbrücken
Mark de Berg, Utrecht
Ronald Cramer, Zürich
Faith Fich, Toronto
Burkhard Monien, Paderborn
Mike Paterson, Warwick
Arto Salomaa, Türkü
Mikkel Thorup, Copenhagen
Ugo Vaccaro, Salerno
Shmuel Zaks, Haifa

Glynn Winskel, Aarhus (vice-chair)
Gerard Boudol, INRIA Sophia-Antipolis
Julian Bradfield, Edinburgh
Pierpaolo Degano, Pisa
Jean-Pierre Jouannaud, Paris
Edmund Robinson, QMW, London
Bernhard Steffen, Passau
Andrzej Tarlecki, Warsaw
Frits Vaandrager, Nijmegen

Organizing Committee

Kim G. Larsen (chair)
Helle Andersen
Hans Hüttel
Ole H. Jensen
Lene Mogensen
Arne Skou

Referees

N. Abiteboul
L. Aceto
N. Alon
S. Alstrup
R. Alur
D. Amsterdam
A. Andersson
D. Angluin
S. Arora
A. Bac
E. Bach
E. Badouel
C. Baier
R. Barbuti
M. A. Bednarczyk
M. Benke
A. Benveniste
P. Berenbrink
M. Bernardo
G. Berry
A. Berthiaume
E. Best
S. Bezrukov
M. Bidoit
B. Bieber
S. Bistarelli
P. van Emde Boas
C. Bodei
H. L. Bodlaender
F. de Boer
M. Bonsangue
M. Bonuccelli
M. Boreale
E. Boros
A. Borzyszkowski
A. Bouali
A. Bouhoula
F. van Breugel
G. Brodal
V. Bruyere
A. Bucciarelli
P. Burton
N. Busi
C. Cachin
L. Cai
C. Calcagno
L. Cardelli
I. Castellani
G. Luca Cattani
D. Caucal
G. Cece
B. Chlebus
P. Chrzastowski-Wachtel
J. Chrzaszcz
G. Clark
M. Clavel
H. Comon
A. Compagnoni
R. Di Cosmo
G. Costa
P. Crescenzi
G. Di Crescenzo
K. Culik
A. Czumaj
F. d'Amore
P. R. D'Argenio
S. Dal-Zilio
W. van Dam
I. Damgaard
O. Danvy
J. Dassow
M. Rettelbach
T. Decker
N. Dershowitz
M. Devillers
R. Diekmann
M. Dietzfelbinger
K. Diks
W. Drabent
T. Ehrhard
T. Eilam
J. Engelfriet
A. Eppendahl
F. Ergun
M. Escardó
J. Esparza
F. Fages
T. Fahle
A. Fantechi
R. Feldmann
C. De Felice
S. Fenner
G. Ferrari
M. C. F. Ferreira
P. Flocchini
W. Fokkink
M. Fraenzle
L. Fredlund
S. Fröschle
X. Fu
B. Gärtner
A. Gal
N. Galli
J. A. Garay
P. Gardner
L. Gargano
J. von zur Gathen
A. Geser
G. Ghelli
P. Di Giannantonio
P. Gibson
S. Gilmore
S. Gnesi
P. Godefroid
M. Goemans
H. Goguen
P. Goldberg
M. Goldwurm
R. Gorrieri
J. Goubault-Larrecq
S. Graf
D. Griffioen
M. Grigni
G. Grudzinski
S. Guerrini
P. Habermehl
C. Hankin
T. Harju
M. Hennessy
M. Hermann
N. Higham
T. Hildebrandt

B. Hilken
M. Hirvensalo
J. Honkala
J. Hooman
J. Hromkovic
H. Hüttel
L. Ilie
A. Ingolfsdottir
P. Inverardi
S. Ishtiaq
B. Jacobs
K. Jansen
D. Janssens
A. Jeffrey
M. Jerrum
M. Kaminski
S. Kannan
G. Kant
D. Kapur
B. von Karger
J. Karhumki
J. Kari
J. Katoen
D. Kesner
S. Khanna
R. Klasing
J. Kleist
U. Kohlenbach
B. Konikowska
G. Kortsarz
M. van Kreveld
K. Kristoffersen
D. Krizanc
R. Kubiak
E. Kushilevitz
Y. Lakhnech
C. Laneve
S. Lasota
U. Lechner
M. Lenisa
S. Leonardi
A. Lepist
P. Blain Levy
M. Li
H. Lin
M. Liskiewicz
R. Loader
J. Longley
L. Longpre
U. Lorenz
R. Lueling
G. Luettgen
D. Lugiez
M. Müller-Olm
I. Mackie
A. Mader
J. Maluszynski
V. Manca
Y. Mansour
D. Marchignoli
L. Margara
T. Margaria
A. Marzetta
A. Masini
A. Mateescu
O. Matz
M. Mauny
A. Mazurkiewicz
P. McKenzie
P. Mellis
M. Mendler
N. Mery
S. Merz
J. Meseguer
K. Meyer
M. Miculan
P. Bro Miltersen
E. Moggi
F. Moller
B. Monate
C. Mongenet
U. Montanari
S. Moran
P. D. Mosses
M. Mukund
S. Muthukrishnan
M. Napoli
M. Nesi
U. Nestmann
F. Neugebauer
R. De Nicola
J. Niehren
F. Nielson
R. Nieuwenhuis
P. O'Hearn
M. Okada
T. Okamoto
M. Overmars
L. Pagli
J. Pagter
C. Palamidessi
J. Palsberg
D. Panario
A. Panconesi
M. Papatriantafilou
M. Parente
J. Parrow
C. Paulin
W. Pawlowski
M. Nicolaj Pedersen
A. Pekec
S. Pelagatti
D. Pelleg
M. Pellegrini
W. Penczek
A. Philippou
J. E. Pin
M. Pistore
W. Plandowski
V. Pratt
R. Preis
C. Priami
R. De Prisco
D. Pym
O. Rüthing
A. Rabinovich
C. Rackoff
R. Raman
R. Ramanujam
D. Ranjan
J. Rathke
R. Ravi
A. Razborov
L. Regnier
J. Rehof

K. Reinert
D. Remy
A. Rensink
A. Renvall
M. Rettelbach
M. Reynolds
M. Riedel
J. Riely
I. Rieping
S. Riis
M. Roettger
L. Rosaz
G. Rosolini
F. Rossi
P. Ružička
M. Rusinowitch
G. Sénizergues
C. Sahinalp
L. Salvail
D. Sangiorgi
D. Sannella
V. Sassone
V. Scarano
C. Scheideler
G. Schied
E. M. Schmidt
B. Schoenmakers
U. Schroeder
A. Schubert
J. Schulze
M. Schwartzbach
R. Segala
L. Segoufin
P. Selinger
G. Senizergues
N. Sensen
C. Series
P. Sewell
J. Sgall
P. Shor
R. Shore
H. U. Simon
R. de Simone
A. Simpson
A. Skou
M. Smid
G. Smolka
S. Sokolowski
S. Soliman
A. Marchetti Spaccamela
M. Srebrny
F. van der Stappen
P. Stevens
C. Stirling
M. Stoelinga
A. Szepietowski
G. Sénizergues
G. Tel
J. Arne Telle
H. Thielecke
W. Thomas
Y. Toyama
L. Trevisan
S. Tschoeke
P. Tsigas
F. Turini
D. N. Turner
J. Tyszkiewicz
W. Unger
P. Urzyczyn
S. Varricchio
E. Varvarigos
M. Veldhorst
B. Victor
E. de Vink
P. Vitany
P. Vitanyi
H. Vollmer
I. Vrto
P. Wadler
D. Walker
D. Walukiewicz
J. van Wamel
P. Weil
J. Wein
C. Weise
J. Winkowski
D. Wotschke
H. Wupper
H. Yoo
N. Young
H. Zantema
M. Zawadowski
G. Zhang
M. Venturini Zilli
D. Zuckerman
O. Østerby

Table of Contents

Automata and Temporal Logic:

Algorithms:

Infinite State Systems:

Invited Lecture:

Complexity:

Verification:

Complexity:

Concurrency:

Algorithmic Verification of Linear Temporal Logic Specifications *

Yonit Kesten**, Amir Pnueli***, and Li-on Raviv

Abstract. In this methodological paper we present a coherent framework for symbolic model checking verification of linear-time temporal logic (LTL) properties of reactive systems, taking full fairness into consideration. We use the computational model of a *fair Kripke structure* (FKS) which takes into account both *justice* (weak fairness) and *compassion* (strong fairness). The approach presented here reduces the model checking problem into the question of whether a given FKS is *feasible* (i.e. has at least one computation).

The contribution of the paper is twofold: On the methodological level, it presents a direct self-contained exposition of full LTL symbolic model checking without resorting to reductions to either CTL or automata. On the technical level, it extends previous methods by dealing with compassion at the algorithmic level instead of adding it to the specification, and providing the first symbolic method for checking feasibility of FKS's (equivalently, symbolically checking for the emptiness of Streett automata).

The presented algorithms can also be used (with minor modifications) for symbolic model-checking of CTL formulas over fair Kripke structures with compassion requirements.

1 Introduction

Two brands of temporal logics have been proposed over the years for specifying the properties of reactive systems: the *linear time* brand LTL [GPSS80] and the *branching time* variant CTL [CE81]. Also two methods for the formal verification of the temporal properties of reactive systems have been developed: the *deductive approach* based on interactive theorem proving, and the fully automatic *algorithmic approach*, widely known as *model checking*. Tracing the evolution of these ideas, we find that the deductive approach adopted LTL as its main vehicle for specification, while the model-checking approach used CTL as the specification language [CE81], [QS82].

This is more than a historical coincidence or a matter of personal preference. The main advantage of CTL for model checking is that it is *state-based* and, therefore, the process of verification can be performed by straightforward *labeling*

* This research was supported in part by an infra-structure grant from the Israeli Ministry of Science and Art and a gift from Intel.

** Dept. of Com. Sys. Eng., Ben Gurion University, ykesten@bgumail.bgu.ac.il

*** Weizmann Institute of Science, amir@wisdom.weizmann.ac.il

of the existing states in the Kripke structure, leading to no further expansion or unwinding of the structure. In contrast, LTL is *path-based* and, since many paths can pass through a single state, labeling a structure by the LTL sub-formulas it satisfies necessarily requires splitting the state into several copies. This is the reason why the development of model-checking algorithms for LTL always lagged several years behind their first introduction for the CTL logic.

The first model-checking algorithms were based on the enumerative approach, constructing an explicit representation of all reachable states of the considered system [CE81], and were developed for the branching-time temporal logic CTL. The LTL version of these algorithms was developed in [LP85] for the future fragment of propositional LTL (PTL), and extended in [LPZ85] to the full PTL. The basic fixed-point computation algorithm for the identification of fair computations presented in [LP85], was developed independently in [EL85] for FCTL (fair CTL). Observing that upgrading from justice to full fairness (i.e., adding compassion) is reflected in the automata view of verification as an upgrade from a Buchi to a Street automaton, we can view the algorithms presented in [EL85] and [LP85] as algorithms for checking the emptiness of Street automata [VW86]. An improved algorithm solving the related problem of emptiness of Street automata, was later presented in [HT96]. The development of the impressively efficient symbolic verification methods and their application to CTL [BCM+92] raised the question whether a similar approach can be applied to PTL. The first satisfactory answer to this question was given in [CGH94], which showed how to reduce model checking of a future PTL formula into CTL model checking. The advantages of this approach is that, following a preliminary transformation of the PTL formula and the given system, the algorithm proceeds by using available and efficient CTL model checkers such as SMV.

A certain weakness of all the available symbolic model checkers is that, in their representation of fairness, they only consider the concept of *justice* (weak fairness). As suggested by many researchers, another important fairness requirement is that of *compassion* (strong fairness) (e.g., [GPSS80], [LPS81], [Fra86]). This type of fairness is particularly useful in the analysis of systems that use semaphores, synchronous communication, and other special coordination primitives. A partial answer to this criticism is that, since compassion can be expressed in LTL (but not in CTL), once we developed a model-checking method for LTL, we can always add the compassion requirements as an antecedent to the property we wish to verify. A similar answer is standardly given for symbolic model checkers that use the μ-calculus as their specification language, because compassion can also be expressed as a μ-calculus formula [SdRG89]. The only question remaining is how practical this is.

In this methodological paper (summarizing an invited talk), we present an approach to the symbolic model checking of LTL formulas, which takes into account full fairness, including both justice and compassion. The presentation of the approach is self-contained and does not depend on a reduction to either CTL model checking (as in [CGH94]) or to automata. The treatment of the LTL component is essentially that of a symbolic construction of a tableau by assigning a new auxiliary variable to each temporal sub-formula of the property we wish to verify. In that, our approach resembles very much the reduction method used in [CGH94] which, in turn, is an extension of the *statification* method used in [MP91a] and [MP95] to deal with the past fragment of LTL.

Another work related to the approach developed here is presented in [HKSV97], where a BDD-based symbolic algorithm for bad cycle detection is presented. This algorithm solves the problem of finding all those cycles within the computation graph, which satisfy some fairness constraints. However, the algorithm of [HKSV97] deals only with *justice*, and does not deal with *compassion*. According to the automata-theoretic view, [HKSV97] presents a symbolic algorithm for the problem of emptiness of Buchi automata while the algorithms presented here, provide a symbolic solution to the emptiness problem of Street automata.

The symbolic model-checking algorithms presented here are not restricted to the treatment of LTL formulas. With minor modifications they can be applied to check the CTL formula $\mathbf{E}_{fair}\mathbf{G}p$, where the *fair* subscript refers now to full fairness.

2 Fair Kripke Structure

As a computational model for reactive systems, we take the model of *fair kripke structure* (FKS). Such a system $K : \langle V, \Theta, \rho, \mathcal{J}_K, \mathcal{C}_K\rangle$ consists of the following components.

- $V = \{u_1, ..., u_n\}$: A finite set of typed *state variables*. For the case of finite-state systems, we assume that all state variables range over finite domains. We define a *state* s to be a type-consistent interpretation of V, assigning to each variable $u \in V$ a value $s[u]$ in its domain. We denote by Σ the set of all states.
- Θ : The *initial condition*. This is an assertion characterizing all the initial states of an FKS. A state is defined to be *initial* if it satisfies Θ.
- ρ : A *transition relation*. This is an assertion $\rho_\tau(V, V')$, relating a state $s \in \Sigma$ to its K-successor $s' \in \Sigma$ by referring to both unprimed and primed versions of the state variables. An unprimed version of a state variable refers to its value in s, while a primed version of the same variable refers to its value in s'. For example, the transition relation $x' = x + 1$ asserts that the value of x in s' is greater by 1 than its value in s.
- $\mathcal{J}_K = \{J_1, \ldots, J_k\}$: A set of *justice* requirements (also called *weak fairness requirements*). Intuitively, the justice requirement $J \in \mathcal{J}_K$ stipulates that every computation contains infinitely many J-state (states satisfying J).
- $\mathcal{C}_K = \{\langle p_1, q_1\rangle, \ldots \langle p_n, q_n\rangle\}$: A set of *compassion* requirements (also called *strong fairness requirements*). Intuitively, the compassion requirement for $\langle p, q\rangle \in \mathcal{C}_K$ stipulates that every computation containing infinitely many p-states also contains infinitely many q-states.

The transition relation $\rho(V, V')$ identifies state s' as a K-*successor* of state s if

$$\langle s, s'\rangle \models \rho(V, V'),$$

where $\langle s, s' \rangle$ is the joint interpretation which interprets $x \in V$ as $s[x]$, and interprets x' as $s'[x]$.

Let $\sigma : s_0, s_1, s_2, ...,$ be an infinite sequence of states, φ be an assertion (state formula), and let $j \geq 0$ be a natural number. We say that j is a φ-position of σ if s_j is a φ-state.

Let K be an FKS for which the above components have been identified. We define a *computation* of K to be an infinite sequence of states $\sigma : s_0, s_1, s_2, ...,$ satisfying the following requirements:

- *Initiality:* s_0 is initial, i.e., $s_0 \models \Theta$.
- *Consecution:* For each $j = 0, 1, ...,$ the state s_{j+1} is a K-successor of the state s_j.
- *Justice:* For each $J \in \mathcal{J}_K$, σ contains infinitely many J-positions
- *Compassion:* For each $\langle p, q \rangle \in \mathcal{C}_K$, if σ contains infinitely many p-positions, it must also contain infinitely many q-positions.

For an FKS K, we denote by $\mathit{Comp}(K)$ the set of all computations of K.

3 Parallel Composition of FKS's

Fair Kripke structures can be composed in parallel. Let $K_1 = \langle V_1, \Theta_1, \rho_1, \mathcal{J}_1, \mathcal{C}_1 \rangle$ and $K_2 = \langle V_2, \Theta_2, \rho_2, \mathcal{J}_2, \mathcal{C}_2 \rangle$ be two fair Kripke structures. We consider two versions of parallel composition.

3.1 Asynchronous Parallel Composition

We define the *asynchronous parallel composition* of two FKS's to be

$$\langle V, \Theta, \rho, \mathcal{J}, \mathcal{C} \rangle \quad = \quad \langle V_1, \Theta_1, \rho_1, \mathcal{J}_1, \mathcal{C}_1 \rangle \parallel \langle V_2, \Theta_2, \rho_2, \mathcal{J}_2, \mathcal{C}_2 \rangle,$$

where,

$$\begin{aligned} V &= V_1 \cup V_2 \\ \Theta &= \Theta_1 \wedge \Theta_2 \\ \rho &= (\rho_1 \wedge \mathit{pres}(V_2 - V_1)) \;\vee\; (\rho_2 \wedge \mathit{pres}(V_1 - V_2)) \\ \mathcal{J} &= \mathcal{J}_1 \cup \mathcal{J}_2 \\ \mathcal{C} &= \mathcal{C}_1 \cup \mathcal{C}_2. \end{aligned}$$

The asynchronous parallel composition of systems K_1 and K_2 is a new system K whose basic actions are chosen from the basic actions of its components, i.e., K_1 and K_2. Thus, we can view the execution of K as the *interleaved execution* of K_1 and K_2, and can use asynchronous composition. in order to construct big concurrent systems from smaller components.

As seen from the definition, K_1 and K_2 may have different as well as common state variables, and the variables of K are the union of all of these variables. The initial condition of K is the conjunction of the initial conditions of K_1 and K_2. The transition relation of K states that at any step, we may choose to perform a step of K_1 or a step of K_2. However, when we select one of the two systems, we should also take care to preserve the private variables of the other system. For example, choosing to execute a step of K_1, we should preserve all variables in $V_2 - V_1$.

The justice and compassion sets of K are formed as the respective unions of the justice and compassion sets of the component systems.

3.2 Synchronous Parallel Composition

We define the *synchronous parallel composition* of two FKS's to be

$$\langle V, \Theta, \rho, \mathcal{J}, \mathcal{C} \rangle \quad = \quad \langle V_1, \Theta_1, \rho_1, \mathcal{J}_1, \mathcal{C}_1 \rangle \ ||| \ \langle V_2, \Theta_2, \rho_2, \mathcal{J}_2, \mathcal{C}_2 \rangle,$$

where,

$$\begin{aligned} V &= V_1 \cup V_2 \\ \Theta &= \Theta_1 \wedge \Theta_2 \\ \rho &= \rho_1 \ \wedge \ \rho_2 \\ \mathcal{J} &= \mathcal{J}_1 \cup \mathcal{J}_2 \\ \mathcal{C} &= \mathcal{C}_1 \cup \mathcal{C}_2. \end{aligned}$$

The synchronous parallel composition of systems K_1 and K_2 is a new system K, each of whose basic actions consists of the joint execution of an action of K_1 and an action of K_2. Thus, we can view the execution of K as the *joint execution* of K_1 and K_2.

In some cases, in particular when considering hardware designs which are naturally synchronous, we may also use synchronous composition to assemble a system from its components. However, our primary use of synchronous composition is for combining a system with a *tester* for a temporal property (described in Section 5) which continuously monitor the behavior of the system and judges whether the system satisfies the desired property.

4 Linear Temporal Logic

As a requirement specification language for reactive systems we take the propositional fragment of *linear temporal logic* [MP91b].

Let $\mathcal{P}$ be a finite set of propositions. A *state formula* is constructed out of propositions and the boolean operators $\neg$ and $\vee$. A *temporal formula* is constructed out of state formulas to which we apply the boolean operators and the following basic temporal operators:

$\bigcirc$ – Next $\ominus$ – Previous

$\mathcal{U}$ – Until $\mathcal{S}$ – Since

A *model* for a temporal formula p is an infinite sequence of states $\sigma : s_0, s_1, \ldots$, where each state s_j provides an interpretation for the variables mentioned in p.

Given a model σ, as above, we present an inductive definition for the notion of a temporal formula p holding at a position $j \geq 0$ in σ, denoted by $(\sigma, j) \models p$.

- For a state formula p,
  $(\sigma, j) \models p \quad \iff s_j \models p$
  That is, we evaluate p locally, using the interpretation given by s_j.
- $(\sigma, j) \models \neg p \quad \iff (\sigma, j) \not\models p$
- $(\sigma, j) \models p \vee q \iff (\sigma, j) \models p$ or $(\sigma, j) \models q$
- $(\sigma, j) \models \bigcirc p \iff (\sigma, j+1) \models p$
- $(\sigma, j) \models p \mathcal{U} q \iff$ for some $k \geq j, (\sigma, k) \models q$,
  and for every i such that $j \leq i < k, (\sigma, i) \models p$
- $(\sigma, j) \models \ominus p \iff j > 0$ and $(\sigma, j-1) \models p$
- $(\sigma, j) \models p \mathcal{S} q \iff$ for some $k \leq j, (\sigma, k) \models q$,
  and for every i such that $j \geq i > k, (\sigma, i) \models p$

We refer to the set of variables that occur in a formula p as the *vocabulary of* p. For a state formula p and a state s such that p holds on s, we say that s is a *p-state*.

If $(\sigma, 0) \models p$, we say that p *holds* on σ, and denote it by $\sigma \models p$. A formula p is called *satisfiable* if it holds on some model. A formula is called *temporally valid* if it holds on all models.

The notion of validity requires that the formula holds over *all* models. Given an FKS K, we can restrict our attention to the set of models which correspond to computations of K, i.e., *Comp*(K). This leads to the notion of K-validity, by which a temporal formula p is K-*valid* (valid over FKS K) if it holds over all the computations of P. Obviously, any formula that is (generally) valid is also K-valid for any FKS K. In a similar way, we obtain the notion of K-satisfiability.

5 Construction of Testers for Temporal Formulas

In this section, we present the construction of a *tester* for a PTL formula φ, which is an FKS T_φ characterizing all the sequences which satisfy φ.

For a formula ψ, we write $\psi \in \varphi$ to denote that ψ is a sub-formula of (possibly equal to) φ. Formula ψ is called *principally temporal* if its main operator is a temporal operator. The FKS T_φ is given by

$$T_\varphi: \quad \left\langle V_\varphi, \Theta_\varphi, \rho_\varphi, \mathcal{J}_\varphi, \mathcal{C}_\varphi \right\rangle,$$

where the components are specified as follows:

System Variables The system variables of T_φ consist of the vocabulary of φ plus a set of auxiliary boolean variables

$$X_\varphi: \quad \{x_p \mid p \in \varphi \text{ a principally temporal sub-formula of } \varphi\},$$

which includes an auxiliary variable x_p for every p, a principally temporal sub-formula of φ. The auxiliary variable x_p is intended to be true in a state of a computation iff the temporal formula p holds at that state.

We define a mapping χ which maps every sub-formula of φ into an assertion over V_φ.

$$\chi(\psi) = \begin{cases} \psi & \text{for } \psi \text{ a state formula} \\ \neg\chi(p) & \text{for } \psi = \neg p \\ \chi(p) \vee \chi(q) & \text{for } \psi = p \vee q \\ x_\psi & \text{for } \psi \text{ a principally temporal formula} \end{cases}$$

The mapping χ distributes over all boolean operators. When applied to a state formula it yields the formula itself. When applied to a principally temporal sub-formula p it yields x_p.

Initial Condition The initial condition of T_φ is given by

$$\Theta_\varphi:\quad \chi(\varphi) \wedge \bigwedge_{\ominus p \in \varphi} \neg x_{\ominus p} \wedge \bigwedge_{p\mathcal{S}q \in \varphi} (x_{p\mathcal{S}q} \leftrightarrow \chi(q)).$$

Thus, the initial condition requires that all initial states satisfy $\chi(\varphi)$, and that all auxiliary variables encoding "Previous" formulas are initially false. This corresponds to the observation that all formulas of the form $\ominus p$ are false at the first state of any sequence. In addition, Θ_φ requires that the truth value of $x_{p\mathcal{S}q}$ equals the truth value of $\chi(q)$, corresponding to the observation that the only way to satisfy the formula $p\mathcal{S}q$ at the first state of a sequence is by satisying q.

Transition Relation The transition relation of T_φ is given by

$$\rho_\varphi:\quad \left(\begin{array}{l} \wedge \bigwedge_{\ominus p \in \varphi} (x'_{\ominus p} \leftrightarrow \chi(p)) \wedge \bigwedge_{p\mathcal{S}q \in \varphi} (x'_{p\mathcal{S}q} \leftrightarrow (\chi'(q) \vee (\chi'(p) \wedge x_{p\mathcal{S}q}))) \\ \wedge \bigwedge_{\bigcirc p \in \varphi} (x_{\bigcirc p} \leftrightarrow \chi'(p)) \wedge \bigwedge_{p\mathcal{U}q \in \varphi} (x_{p\mathcal{U}q} \leftrightarrow (\chi(q) \vee (\chi(p) \wedge x'_{p\mathcal{U}q}))) \end{array}\right)$$

Note that we use the form x_ψ when we know that ψ is principally temporal and the form $\chi(\psi)$ in all other cases. The expression $\chi'(\psi)$ denotes the primed version of $\chi(p)$. The conjuncts of the transition relation corresponding to the *Since* and the *Until* operators are based on the following expansion formulas:

$$p\mathcal{S}q \iff q \vee (p \wedge \ominus(p\mathcal{S}q)) \qquad\qquad p\mathcal{U}q \iff q \vee (p \wedge \bigcirc(p\mathcal{U}q))$$

Fairness Requirements The justice set of T_φ is given by

$$\mathcal{J}_\varphi:\quad \{\chi(q) \vee \neg x_{p\mathcal{U}q} \mid p\mathcal{U}q \in \varphi\}.$$

Thus, we include in $\mathcal{J}_\varphi$ the disjunction $\chi(q) \vee \neg x_{p\mathcal{U}q}$ for every *until* formula $p\mathcal{U}q$ which is a sub-formula of φ. The justice requirement for the formula $p\mathcal{U}q$ ensures that the sequence contains infinitely many states at which $\chi(q)$ is true, or infinitely many states at which $x_{p\mathcal{U}q}$ is false. The compassion set of T_φ is always empty.

Correctness of the Construction For a set of variables U, we say that sequence $\widetilde{\sigma}$ is a *U-variant* of sequence σ if σ and $\widetilde{\sigma}$ agree on the interpretation of all variables, except possibly the variables in U. The following claim states that the construction of the tester T_φ correctly captures the set of sequences satisfying the formula φ.

Claim. A state sequence σ satisfies the temporal formula φ iff σ is an X_φ-variant of a computation of T_φ.

6 Checking for Feasibility

An FKS $K : \langle V, \Theta, \rho, \mathcal{J}, \mathcal{C} \rangle$ is called *feasible* if it has at least one computation. In this section we present a symbolic algorithm for checking feasibility of a finite-state FKS.

We define a *run* of K to be a finite or infinite sequence of states which satisfies the requirements of initiality and consecution but not necessarily any of the justice or compassion requirements. We say that a state s is *K-accessible* if it appears in some run of K. When K is understood from the context, we simply say that state s is accessible.

The symbolic algorithm presented here, is inspired by the full state-enumeration algorithm originally presented in [LP85] and [EL85] (for full explanations and proofs see [Lic91] and [MP95]). The enumerative algorithm constructs a *state-transition graph* G_K for K. This is a directed graph whose nodes are all the K-accessible states, and whose edges connect node s to node s' iff s' is a K-successor of s. If system K has a computation it corresponds to an infinite path in the graph G_K which starts at a K-initial state. We refer to such paths as *initialized paths*.

Subgraphs of G_K can be specified by identifying a subset $S \subseteq G_K$ of the nodes of G_K. It is implied that as the edges of the subgraph we take all the original G_K-edges connecting nodes (states) of S. A subgraph S is called *just* if it contains a J-state for every justice requirement $J \in \mathcal{J}$. The subgraph S is called *compassionate* if, for every compassion requirement $(p, q) \in \mathcal{C}$, S contains a q-state, or S does not contain any p-state. A subgraph is *singular* if it is composed of a single state which is not connected to itself. A subgraph S is *fair* if it is a non-singular strongly connected subgraph which is both just and compassionate.

For π, an infinite initialized path in G_K, we denote by $Inf(\pi)$ the set of states which appear infinitely many times in π. The following claims, which are proved in [Lic91], connect computations of K with fair subgraphs of G_K.

Claim. The infinite initialized path π is a computation of K iff $Inf(\pi)$ is a fair subgraph of G_K.

Corollary 1. *A system K is feasible iff G_K contains a fair subgraph.*

The Symbolic algorithm The symbolic algorithm, aimed at exploiting the data structure of OBDD's, is presented in a general set notation. Let Σ denote the set of all states of an FKS K. A *predicate* over Σ is any subset $U \subseteq \Sigma$. A (binary) *relation* over Σ is any set of pairs $R \subseteq \Sigma \times \Sigma$. Since both predicates and relations are sets, we can freely apply the set-operations of union, intersection, and complementation to these objects. In addition, we define two operations of composition of predicates and relations. For a predicate U and relation R, we define the operations of pre- and post-composition as follows:

$$R \circ U = \{s \in \Sigma \mid (s, s') \in R \text{ for some } s' \in U\}$$
$$U \circ R = \{s \in \Sigma \mid (s_0, s) \in R \text{ for some } s_0 \in U\}$$

If we view R as a transition relation, then $R \circ U$ is the set of all R-predecessors of U-states, and $U \circ R$ is the set of all R-successors of U-states. To capture the set of all states that can reach a U-state in a finite number of R-steps (including zero), we define

$$R^* \circ U \quad = \quad U \;\cup\; R \circ U \;\cup\; R \circ (R \circ U) \;\cup\; R \circ (R \circ (R \circ U)) \;\cup\; \cdots .$$

It is easy to see that $R^* \circ U$ converges after a finite number of steps. In a similar way, we define

$$U \circ R^* \quad = \quad U \;\cup\; U \circ R \;\cup\; (U \circ R) \circ R \;\cup\; ((U \circ R) \circ R) \circ R \;\cup\; \cdots,$$

which captures the set of all states reachable in a finite number of R-steps from a U-state. For predicates U and W, we define the relation $U \times W$ as

$$U \times W \quad = \quad \{(s_1, s_2) \in \Sigma^2 \mid s_1 \in U, s_2 \in W\}.$$

For an assertion φ over V_K (the system variables of FKS K), we denote by $\|\varphi\|$ the predicate consisting of all states satisfying φ. Similarly, for an assertion ρ over (V_K, V_K'), we denote by $\|\rho\|$ the relation consisting of all state pairs $\langle s, s' \rangle$ satisfying ρ.

The algorithm FEASIBLE presented in fig. 1, consists of a main loop which converges when the values of the predicate variable *new* coincide on two successive visits to line 4. Prior to entry to the main loop we place in R the transition relation implied by ρ_K, and compute in *new* the set of all accessible states.

The main loop contains three inner loops. The inner loop at lines 6–7 removes from *new* all states which are not R^*-successors of some J-state for all justice requirements $J \in \mathcal{J}$.

The loop at lines 8–10, removes from *new* all p-states which are not R^*-successors of some q-state for some $(p, q) \in \mathcal{C}$. Line 10 restricts again R to pairs (s_1, s_2) where s_2 is currently in *new*.

Finally, the loop at lines 11–12, successively removes from *new* all states which do not have a predecessor in *new*. This process is iterated until all states in the set *new* have a predecessor in the set.

Algorithm FEASIBLE (K) : **predicate** — Check feasibility of an FKS

new, old : **predicate**
R : **relation**

1. $old := \emptyset$
2. $R := \|\rho_K\|$
3. $new := \|\Theta_K\| \circ R^*$
4. **while** $(new \neq old)$ **do**
   begin
5. $\quad old := new$
6. $\quad$ **for each** $J \in \mathcal{J}$ **do**
7. $\qquad new := (new \cap \|J\|) \circ R^*$
8. $\quad$ **for each** $(p, q) \in \mathcal{C}$ **do**
   $\quad$ **begin**
9. $\qquad new := (new - \|p\|) \cup (new \cap \|q\|) \circ R^*$
10. $\qquad R := R \cap (\Sigma \times new)$
    $\quad$ **end**
11. $\quad$ **while** $(new \neq new \cap (new \circ R))$ **do**
12. $\qquad new := new \cap (new \circ R)$
    end
13. **return**(new)

Fig. 1. Algorithm FEASIBLE

Correctness of the Set-Based Algorithm Let K be an FKS and U_K be the set of states resulting from the application of algorithm FEASIBLE over K. The following sequence of claims establish the correctness of the algorithm

Claim (Termination). The algorithm FEASIBLE terminates.

Let us denote by new_i^4 the value of variable new on the i'th visit $(i = 0, 1, \ldots)$ to line 4 of the algorithm. Since new_0^4 is closed under R-succession, i.e. $new_0^4 \circ R^* = new_0^4$, it is not ddificult to see that $new_1^4 \subseteq new_0^4$. From this, it can be established by induction on i that $new_{i+1}^4 \subseteq new_i^4$, for every $i = 0, 1, \ldots$. It follows that the sequence $|new_0^4| \geq |new_1^4| \geq |new_2^4| \cdots$, is a non-increasing sequence of natural numbers which must eventually stabilize. At the point of stabilization, we have that $new_{i+1}^4 = new_i^4$, implying termination of the algorithm.

Claim (Completeness). If K is feasible then $U_K \neq \emptyset$.

Assume that K is feasible. According to Corollary 6, G_K contains a fair subgraph S. By definition, S is a non-singular strongly-connected subgraph which contains a J-state for every $J \in \mathcal{J}$, and such that, for every $(p, q) \in \mathcal{C}$, S contains a q-state or contains no p state. Following the oprtations performed by Algorithm FEASIBLE, we can show that S is contained in the set new at all locations beyond the first visit to line 4. This is because any removal of states from new which is carried out in lines 7, 9, and 12, cannot remove any state of S. Consequently, S must remain throughout the process and will be contained in U_K, implying the non-emptiness of U_K.

Claim (Soundness). If $U_K \neq \emptyset$ then K is feasible.

Assume that U_K is non-empty. Let us characterize the properties of an arbitrary state $s \in U_K$. We know that s is K-accessible. For every $J \in \mathcal{J}$, s is reachable from a J-state by a path fully contained within U_K. For every $(p, q) \in \mathcal{C}$, either s is not a p-state, or s is reachable from a q-state by a U_K-path.

Let us decompose U_K into maximal strongly-connected subgraphs. At least one subgraph S_0 is *initial* in this decomposition, in the sense that every U_K-edge entering an S_0-state also originates at an S_0-state. We argue that S_0 is fair. By definition, it is strongly connected. It cannot be singular, because then it would consist of a single state s that would have been removed on the last execution of the loop at lines 11-12. Let s be an arbitrary state within S_0. For every $J \in \mathcal{J}$, s is reachable from some J-state $\tilde{s} \in U_K$ by a U_K-path. Since S_0 is initial within U_K, this path must be fully contained within S_0 and, therefore, $\tilde{s} \in S_0$. In a similar way, we can show that S_0 satisfies all the comapssion requirements. Thus, if $U_K \subseteq G_K$ is non-empty, it contains a fair subgraph which, by Corollary 1, establishes that K is feasible.

The Claims *Completeness* and *Soundness* lead to the following conclusion:

Corollary 2. *K is feasible iff the set $U_K \neq \emptyset$.*

The original enumerative algorithms of [EL85] and [LP85] were based on recursive exploration of strongly connected subgraphs. Strongly connected subgraphs require closure under both successors and predecessors. As our algorithm (and its proof) show, it is possible to relax the requirement of bi-directional closure into either closure under predecessors and looking for terminal components, or symmetrically requiring closure under successors and looking for initial components which is the approach taken in Algorithm FEASIBLE. This may be an idea worth exploring even in the enumerative case, and to which we can again apply the *lock-step search* optimization described in [HT96].

6.1 How to Model Check?

Having presented an algorithm for checking whether a given FKS is feasible, we outline our proposed algorithm for model checking that an FKS K satisfies a temporal formula φ. The algorithm is based on the following claim:

Claim. $K \models \varphi$ iff $K|||T_{\neg\varphi}$ is not feasible.

Thus, to check that $K \models \varphi$ we apply algorithm FEASIBLE to the composed FKS $K|||T_{\neg\varphi}$ and declare success if the algorithm finds that $K|||T_{\neg\varphi}$ is infeasible.

7 Extracting a Witness

To use formal verification as an effective debugging tool in the context of verification of finite-state reactive systems checked against temporal properties, a most useful information is a computation of the system which violates the requirement, to which we refer as a *witness*. Since we reduced the problem of checking $K \models \varphi$ to checking the feasibility of $K \mid\mid\mid T_{\neg\varphi}$, such a witness can be provided by a computation of the combined FKS $K \mid\mid\mid T_{\neg\varphi}$.

In the following we present an algorithm which produces a computation of an FKS that has been declared feasible. We introduce the **list** data structure to represent a linear list of states. We use Λ to denote the empty list. For two lists $L_1 = (s_1, \ldots, s_a)$ and $L_2 = (s_a, \ldots, s_b)$, we denote by $L_1 * L_2$ their *fusion*, defined by $L_1 * L_2 \quad = \quad (s_1, \ldots, s_a, \ldots, s_b)$ Finally, for a list L, we denote by *last*(L) the last element of L. For a non-empty predicate $U \subseteq \Sigma$, we denote by *choose*(U) a consistent choice of one of the members of U.

The function *path*(*source*, *destination*, R), presented in Fig. 2, returns a list which contains the shortest R-path from a state in *source* to a state in *destination*. In the case that *source* and *destination* have a non-empty intersection, *path* will return a state belonging to this intersection which can be viewed as a path of length zero.

```
Function path(source, destination : predicate; R : relation) : list —
                    — — Compute shortest path from source to destination
 start, f : predicate
 L        : list
 s        : state
 start := source
 L := Λ
 while (start ∩ destination = ∅) do
 begin
     f := R ∘ destination
     while (start ∩ f = ∅) do
         f := R ∘ f
     s := choose(start ∩ f)
     L := L * (s)
     start := s ∘ R
 end
 return L * (choose(start ∩ destination))
```

Fig. 2. Function *path*.

Finally, in figure 3 we present an algorithm which produces a computation of a given FKS. Although a computation is an infinite sequence of states, if K is feasible, it always has an *ultimately periodic* computation of the following form:

$$\sigma: \quad \underbrace{s_0, s_1, \ldots, s_k,}_{prefix} \; \underbrace{s_{k+1}, \ldots, s_k,}_{period} \underbrace{s_{k+1}, \ldots, s_k,}_{period} \cdots, \underbrace{s_{k+1}, \ldots, s_k,}_{period} \cdots$$

Based on this observation, our witness extracting algorithm will return as result the two finite sequences *prefix* and *period*.

Algorithm WITNESS (K) : **[list, list]** — Extract a witness for a feasible FKS.

final : **predicate**
R : **relation**
prefix, *period* : **list**
s : **state**

1. *final* := FEASIBLE (K)
2. **if** (***final*** $= \emptyset$) **then return** (Λ, Λ)
3. $R := \|\rho_K\| \cap (\mathit{final} \times \Sigma)$
4. $s := \mathit{choose}(\mathit{final})$
5. **while** $(R^* \circ \{s\} - \{s\} \circ R^* \neq \emptyset)$ **do**
6. $\quad s := \mathit{choose}(R^* \circ \{s\} - \{s\} \circ R^*)$
7. $\mathit{final} := R^* \circ \{s\} \;\cap\; \{s\} \circ R^*$
8. $R := R \cap (\mathit{final} \times \mathit{final})$
9. $\mathit{prefix} := \mathit{path}(\|\Theta_K\|, \mathit{final}, \|\rho_K\|)$
10. $\mathit{period} := (\mathit{last}(\mathit{prefix}))$
11. **for each** $J \in \mathcal{J}$ **do**
12. $\quad$ **if** $(\textit{list-to-set}(\mathit{period}) \cap \|J\| = \emptyset)$ **then**
13. $\quad\quad \mathit{period} := \mathit{period} * \mathit{path}(\{\mathit{last}(\mathit{period})\}, \mathit{final} \cap \|J\|, R)$
14. **for each** $(p, q) \in \mathcal{C}$ **do**
15. $\quad$ **if** $(\textit{list-to-set}(\mathit{period}) \cap \|q\| = \emptyset \;\wedge\; \mathit{final} \cap \|p\| \neq \emptyset)$ **then**
16. $\quad\quad \mathit{period} := \mathit{period} * \mathit{path}(\{\mathit{last}(\mathit{period})\}, \mathit{final} \cap \|q\|, R)$
17. $\mathit{period} := \mathit{period} * \mathit{path}(\{\mathit{last}(\mathit{period})\}, \{\mathit{last}(\mathit{prefix})\}, R)$
18. **return** (***prefix***, ***period***)

Fig. 3. Algorithm WITNESS.

The algorithm starts by checking whether FKS K is feasible. It uses Algorithm FEASIBLE to perform this check. If K is found to be infeasible, the algorithm exits while providing a pair of empty lists as a result.

If K is found to be feasible, we store in *final* the graph returned by FEASIBLE. This graph contains all the fair SCS's reachable from am initial state. We restrict the transition relation R to depart only from states within *final*. Next, we perform a search for an initial *maximal strongly connected subgraph* (MSCS) within *final*. The search starts at $s \in \mathit{final}$, an arbitrarily chosen state within *final*. In the loop at lines 5 and 6 we search for a state s satisfying $R^* \circ \{s\} \quad \subseteq \quad \{s\} \circ R^*$. i.e. a state all of whose R^*-predecessors are also R^*-successors. This is done by successively replacing s by a state $s \in R^* \circ \{s\} - \{s\} \circ R^*$ as long as the set of s-predecessors is not contained in the set of s-successors. Eventually, execution of the loop must terminate when s reaches an initial MSCS within *final*. Termination is guaranteed because each such replacement move the state from one MSCS to a preceding MSCS in the canonical decomposition of *final* into MSCS's.

A central point in the proof of correctness of Algorithm FEASIBLE established that any initial MSCS within *final* is a fair subgraph. Line 7 computes the MSCS containing s and assigns it to the variable *final*, while line 8 restricts the transition relation to edges connecting states within *final*. Line 9 draws a (shortest) path from an initial state to the subgraph *final*.

Lines 10 – 17 construct in *period* a traversing path, starting at *last*(*prefix*) and returning to the same state, while visiting on the way states that ensure that an infinite repetition of the period will fulfill all the fairness requirements.

Lines 11–13 ensure that *period* contains a J-state, for each $J \in \mathcal{J}$. To prevent unnecessary visits to state, we extend the path to visit the next J-state only if the part of *period* that has already been constructed did not visit any J-state. Lines 14–16 similarly take care of compassion. Here we extend the path to visit a q-state only if the constructed path did not already do so and the MSCS *final* contains some p-state. Finally, in line 17, we complete the path to form a closed cycle by looping back to *last*(*prefix*).

8 Implementation and Experimental Results

The algorithms described in the paper have been implemented within the TLV system [PS96]. Since the novel features of the approach concern systems which rely on compassion for their correctness, we chose as natural test cases several programs using semaphores for coordination between processes.

A simple solution to the dining philosophers problem is presented as program DINE in Fig. 4.

$$
\begin{array}{l}
\textbf{in} \quad n : \textbf{integer where } n \geq 2 \\
\textbf{local } c : \textbf{array } [1..n] \textbf{ where } c = 1 \\
\\
\overset{n}{\underset{j=1}{\Big\|}} \; P[j] :: \left[\begin{array}{l} \ell_0 : \textbf{loop forever do} \\ \quad \left[\begin{array}{l} \ell_1 : \textbf{noncritical} \\ \ell_2 : \textbf{request } c[j] \\ \ell_3 : \textbf{request } c[j \oplus_n 1] \\ \ell_4 : \textbf{critical} \\ \ell_5 : \textbf{release } c[j] \\ \ell_6 : \textbf{release } c[j \oplus_n 1] \end{array} \right] \end{array} \right]
\end{array}
$$

Fig. 4. Program DINE: a simple solution to the dining philosophers problem.

While satisfying the safety requirement that no two neighboring philosophers can dine at the same time, this naive algorithm fails to satisfy the liveness requirement of *accessibility* by which every philosopher who wishes to dine will eventually do so.

To guarantee the property of accessibility, we must use better algorithms. However, we prefer to model check the incorrect program DINE in order to test the ability of our algorithms to produce appropriate counter-examples.

In the table of Fig. 5, we present the results of running our verification algorithms checking the property of accessibility over program DINE for different numbers of processes. The numbers are given in seconds of running time over a *Sun* 450.

n	Time to Analyze	Time to produce A witness	Witness size
7	7	19	22
8	15	62	25
9	28	183	28
10	51	513	31
11	93	1227	34
12	174	2695	37
13	303	5589	40

Fig. 5. Results for model checking program DINE using the algorithms with builtin compassion.

To examine the efficiency of our approach versus the possibility of including the compassion requirement as part of the property to be verified, we ran the same problem but this time added the compassion requirements to the specification and ran our algorithm with an empty compassion set. The results are summarized in the table of Fig. 6. As can be seen from comparing these tables, the algorithms with the compassion requirements incorporated within the FKS model are far superior to the runs in which the compassion requirements were added to the property to be verified.

n	Time to Analyze	Time to produce A witness	Witness size
3	4	4	11
4	25	25	14
5	133	139	17
6	612	651	20
7	2279	2473	23

Fig. 6. Results for model checking program DINE using the algorithms with the compassion requirement added to the property.

References

[BCM+92] J.R. Burch, E.M. Clarke, K.L. McMillan, D.L. Dill, and J. Hwang. Symbolic model checking: 10^{20} states and beyond. *Information and Computation*, 98(2):142–170, 1992.

[CE81] E.M. Clarke and E.A. Emerson. Design and synthesis of synchronization skeletons using branching time temporal logic. In *Proc. IBM Workshop on Logics of Programs*, volume 131 of *Lect. Notes in Comp. Sci.*, pages 52–71. Springer-Verlag, 1981.

[CGH94] E.M. Clarke, O. Grumberg, and K. Hamaguchi. Another look at LTL model checking. In D. L. Dill, editor, *Proc. 6th Conference on Computer Aided Verification*, volume 818 of *Lect. Notes in Comp. Sci.*, pages 415–427. Springer-Verlag, 1994.

[EL85] E.A. Emerson and C.L. Lei. Modalities for model checking: Branching time strikes back. In *Proc. 12th ACM Symp. Princ. of Prog. Lang.*, pages 84–96, 1985.

[Fra86] N. Francez. *Fairness.* Springer-Verlag, 1986.

[GPSS80] D. Gabbay, A. Pnueli, S. Shelah, and J. Stavi. On the temporal analysis of fairness. In *Proc. 7th ACM Symp. Princ. of Prog. Lang.*, pages 163–173, 1980.

[HKSV97] R. H. Hardin, R. P. Kurshan, S. K. Shukla, and M. Y. Vardi. A new heuristic for bad cycle detection using BDDs. In O. Grumberg, editor, *Proc. 9th Intl. Conference on Computer Aided Verification (CAV'97)*, Lect. Notes in Comp. Sci., pages 268 – 278. Springer-Verlag, 1997.

[HT96] M. R. Henzinger and J. A. Telle. Faster algorithms for the nonemptiness of street automata and for communication protocol prunning. In *Proceedings of the 5th Scandinavian Workshop on Algorithm Theory*, pages 10–20, 1996.

[Lic91] O. Lichtenstein. *Decidability, Completeness, and Extensions of Linear Time Temporal Logic.* PhD thesis, Weizmann Institute of Science, 1991.

[LP85] O. Lichtenstein and A. Pnueli. Checking that finite state concurrent programs satisfy their linear specification. In *Proc. 12th ACM Symp. Princ. of Prog. Lang.*, pages 97–107, 1985.

[LPS81] D. Lehmann, A. Pnueli, and J. Stavi. Impartiality, justice and fairness: The ethics of concurrent termination. In *Proc. 8th Int. Colloq. Aut. Lang. Prog.*, volume 115 of *Lect. Notes in Comp. Sci.*, pages 264–277. Springer-Verlag, 1981.

[LPZ85] O. Lichtenstein, A. Pnueli, and L. Zuck. The glory of the past. In *Proc. Conf. Logics of Programs*, volume 193 of *Lect. Notes in Comp. Sci.*, pages 196–218. Springer-Verlag, 1985.

[MP91a] Z. Manna and A. Pnueli. Completing the temporal picture. *Theor. Comp. Sci.*, 83(1):97–130, 1991.

[MP91b] Z. Manna and A. Pnueli. *The Temporal Logic of Reactive and Concurrent Systems: Specification.* Springer-Verlag, New York, 1991.

[MP95] Z. Manna and A. Pnueli. *Temporal Verification of Reactive Systems: Safety.* Springer-Verlag, New York, 1995.

[PS96] A. Pnueli and E. Shahar. A platform for combining deductive with algorithmic verification. In R. Alur and T. Henzinger, editors, *Proc. 8th Intl. Conference on Computer Aided Verification (CAV'96)*, Lect. Notes in Comp. Sci., pages 184–195. Springer-Verlag, 1996.

[QS82] J.P. Queille and J. Sifakis. Specification and verification of concurrent systems in *cesar*. In M. Dezani-Ciancaglini and M. Montanari, editors, *International Symposium on Programming*, volume 137 of *Lect. Notes in Comp. Sci.*, pages 337–351. Springer-Verlag, 1982.

[SdRG89] F.A. Stomp, W.-P. de Roever, and R.T. Gerth. The μ-calculus as an assertion language for fairness arguments. *Inf. and Comp.*, 82:278–322, 1989.

[VW86] M.Y. Vardi and P. Wolper. An automata-theoretic approach to automatic program verification. In *Proc. First IEEE Symp. Logic in Comp. Sci.*, pages 332–344, 1986.

On Existentially First-Order Definable Languages and Their Relation to NP

Bernd Borchert[1], Dietrich Kuske[2], and Frank Stephan[1]

[1] Universität Heidelberg, {bb,fstephan}@math.uni-heidelberg.de
[2] Technische Universität Dresden, kuske@math.tu-dresden.de

Abstract. Under the assumption that the Polynomial-Time Hierarchy does not collapse we show that a regular language L determines NP as an unbalanced polynomial-time leaf language if and only if L is existentially but not quantifierfree definable in FO$[<, \min, \max, -1, +1]$. The proof relies on the result of Pin & Weil [PW97] characterizing the automata of existentially first-order definable languages.

1 Introduction

NP is the set of languages L for which there is a nondeterministic polynomial-time Turing machine (NPTM) M such that a word x is in L iff some computation path of the computation tree $M(x)$ accepts. It is easy to see that for example the following definition also yields the class NP (note that an NPTM defines in an obvious way an order on the computation paths): NP is the set of languages A for which there is an NPTM M such that a word x is in A iff there is an accepting path p of the computation tree of $M(x)$ and the next path $p+1$ in that computation tree does not accept. Yet another example of a characterization of NP is the following: NP is the set of languages A for which there is an NPTM M such that a word x is in A iff there is an accepting path p of the computation tree of $M(x)$ and some later path $p' > p$ in that computation tree of $M(x)$ does not accept.

The reader will notice that by writing a 1 for acceptance and a 0 for rejection the above three examples of definitions of NP can easily be described by languages: the language corresponding to the first standard definition is $\Sigma^* 1 \Sigma^*$, the language corresponding to the second example is $\Sigma^* 10 \Sigma^*$, and the language corresponding to the third is $\Sigma^* 1 \Sigma^* 0 \Sigma^*$. This concept is the so-called *leaf language approach* of characterizing complexity classes, more precisely: the polynomial-time unbalanced one, see Borchert [Bo95] (the first paper about leaf languages by Bovet et al. [BCS92] used the balanced approach).

We had three examples of languages such that the complexity class characterized by it equals NP. Now an obvious question is of course: which are exactly the languages that characterize NP? – at least we would like to know which *regular* languages characterize NP. Because the regular language $1\Sigma^*$ characterizes the complexity class P we would, with an answer to that question, solve the P=NP? question. Therefore, we cannot expect a perfect answer. But under the assumption that the Polynomial-Time Hierarchy (PH) does not collapse we are able to give the following answer (see Theorem 3).

> Assume that PH does not collapse. Then a regular language L characterizes NP as an unbalanced polynomial-time leaf language if and only if L is existentially but not quantifierfree definable in $\mathrm{FO}[<, \min, \max, -1, +1]$.

The proof heavily relies on the results of Pin & Weil [PW97] characterizing the ordered syntactic monoids and the finite automata of the existentially definable languages.

Borchert [Bo95] showed that under the assumption that PH does not collapse there is no class characterized by a regular leaf language properly between P and NP and neither between P and co-NP. In this paper we will prove such an emptiness result for the intervals between NP and co-1-NP and between NP and NP⊕co-NP (see Theorem 5).

Finally, we will show a *union-style* result for a correlation of the Boolean Hierarchy over NP and the Boolean Hierarchy over the set of first-order existentially definable languages (see Theorem 6).

A full paper is available from the authors and as ECCC-Report TR97-013.

2 Language-Theoretic Results

Let in this paper languages be over the alphabet $\Sigma = \{0, 1\}$. We consider the usual model of defining languages by formulas, see for example [MP71,St94]. In addition to the usual predicates Q (unary) and $<$ (binary) we allow the constants min and max and the unary successor and predecessor functions $+1$ and -1. These additional functions are first-order definable in $\mathrm{FO}[<]$ but on the level of existential definability the extended logic $\mathrm{FO}[<, \min, \max, +1, -1]$ is strictly more powerful. We will call this extended first-order logic FOX. We will not define formally how a formula in this logic defines a language, for that see for example [Th82,St94]. Note that a variable x indicates a position in a word and $Q(x)$ is true if there is a 1 at that position. We will give some intuitive examples. The quantifier-free formula "$Q(\min) \wedge \neg Q(\min+1) \wedge Q(\max)$" defines the language $10\Sigma^*1$ because it expresses formally "there is a 1 at the first, a 0 at the second and a 1 at the last position in the word". A language L is *existentially (universally)* FOX-*definable* if there is an existentially (universally) quantified FOX-formula in prenex normal form defining L. The three existentially quantified formulas "$\exists x(Q(x))$", "$\exists x(Q(x) \wedge \neg Q(x+1))$", and "$\exists x \exists y(x < y \wedge Q(x) \wedge \neg Q(y))$" express formally "there is a 1 in the word", "there is a 1 followed by a 0 in the word", and "there is a 1 and later a 0 in the word", respectively. Therefore, the three formulas define the languages $\Sigma^*1\Sigma^*$, $\Sigma^*10\Sigma^*$, and $\Sigma^*1\Sigma^*0\Sigma^*$, respectively, which were mentioned in the introduction as examples of leaf languages for NP. An example of a universally quantified formula is "$\forall x(Q(x))$", defining the language 1^*. It should be mentioned that the set of FOX-definable languages (with any number of quantifier alternations) is a proper subset of the set of regular languages, namely the set of star-free regular languages, see for example [MP71,St94].

A language L is *generalized definite* iff there exists a natural number n such that $xyz \in L \iff xy'z \in L$ for any words x, y, y', and z with $|x| = |z| = n$, i.e. the membership of a word in L depends only on the n first and the n last letters of w. According to the terminology in [PW97] a language has *dot-depth 1/2* if it is the finite union of languages of the form $w_1\Sigma^* w_2\Sigma^* w_3 \ldots \Sigma^* w_n$ where $w_1, \ldots, w_n$ are words, i.e. it is the finite union of products of generalized definite languages. Finite automata are defined as usually, see for example [MP71,St94], we consider them to be deterministic. We say that a finite automaton *contains the* co-UP-*pattern* if there are two reachable states p, q, a nonempty word $v \in \Sigma^+$ and two words $w, z \in \Sigma^*$ such that $p.v = p$, $q.v = q$, $p.w = q$, and $p.z$ is an accepting state and $q.z$ is not an accepting state, see Figure 1 where F denotes the accepting states of the automaton (we will explain the strange name for this pattern later, see Lemma 1).

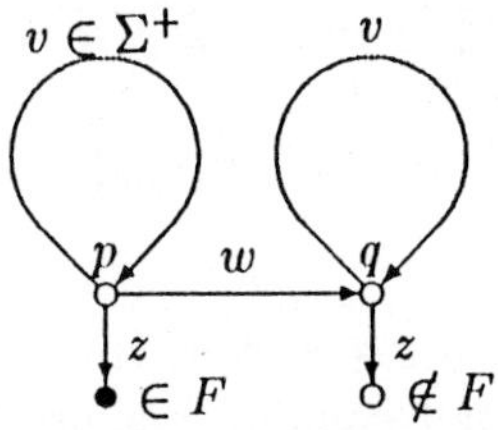

Fig. 1. co-UP-pattern

The part (a) $\iff$ (b) in the following theorem is due to Thomas [Th82]. The equivalence (b) $\iff$ (c) is not stated by Pin & Weil [PW97] the way we present it but easily follows from their Proposition 8.14. The UP-pattern occuring in the following theorem is defined like the co-UP-pattern by exchanging "$\in F$" and "$\notin F$".

Theorem 1 (Thomas [Th82], Pin & Weil [PW97]). *For a language L it is equivalent:*

(a) *L is existentially (universally, quantifier-free) definable in* FOX,

(b) *L has dot-depth 1/2, (the complement of L has dot-depth 1/2, L is generalized definite)*

(c) *L is accepted by a finite automaton which does not contain the* co-UP-*pattern (the* UP-*pattern, neither the* co-UP- *nor the* UP-*pattern).*

We define some more patterns: the co-NP-pattern, the co-1-NP-pattern and the counting pattern (Figures 2 and 3). The co-NP-*pattern* looks like the co-UP-pattern, with an additional w-loop at q, i.e. $q.w = q$. In the co-1-NP-*pattern*, $v \neq \epsilon$ and $p.v = p$, $q.v = q$ and $q_i.v = q_i$. Furthermore, $p.w = q$, $q.w = q_1$ and $q_i.w = q_{i+1}$ for $i = 1, 2, \ldots, n-1$ and $q_n.w = q_n$. Finally, $p.z \in F$, $q.z \notin F$ and $q_i.z \in F$ for $i = 1, 2, \ldots, n$. An automaton contains the *counting pattern (for the number n)* if there are two reachable states p, q and two words w, z such that $p.w =$

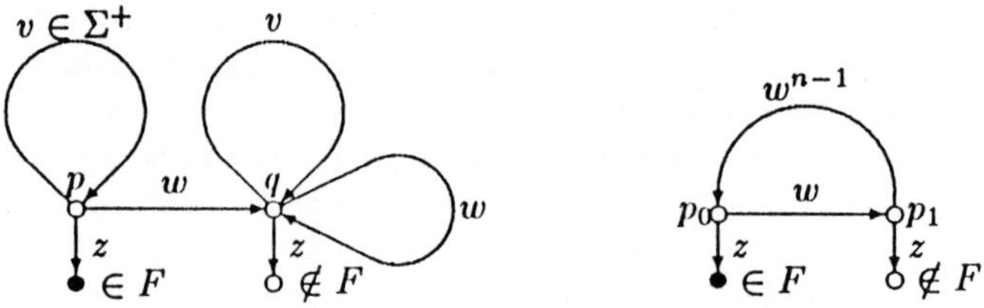

Fig. 2. co-NP-pattern and n-counting pattern

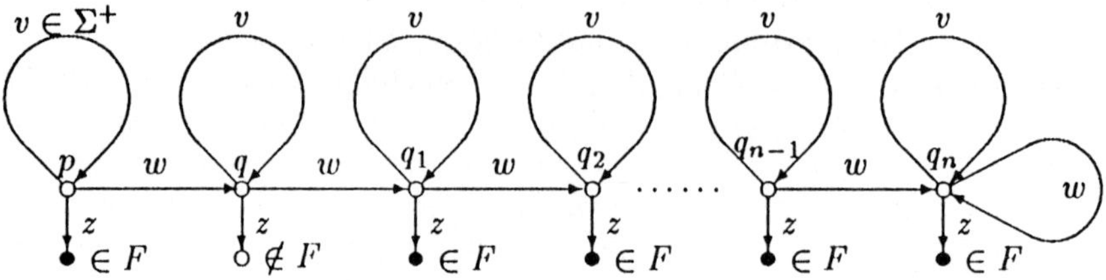

Fig. 3. co-1-NP-pattern

$q, q.w^{n-1} = p$ and $p.z \in F$ and $q.z \notin F$. Note that a minimal automaton contains the counting pattern iff it is not counter-free, see for example [MP71,St94] for that notion. Finally, the NP-pattern and the 1-NP-pattern are defined like the co-NP-pattern and the co-1-NP-pattern, respectively, by exchanging "$\in F$" and "$\notin F$". Note that the co-NP-pattern, the 1-NP-pattern, the co-1-NP-pattern, and the counting pattern contain the co-UP-pattern as a subpattern (with $v := w^n$ in the counting pattern).

The following Corollary 1 will be the bridge from Theorem 1 to the results about complexity classes presented in the next section.

Corollary 1. *Let $\mathcal{A}$ be the minimal automaton accepting the regular language L. Then L is not existentially (universally) definable in* FOX *iff $\mathcal{A}$ contains at least one of the following patterns:*

(1) the counting pattern,
(2) the co-NP*-pattern (the* NP*-pattern),*
(3) the co-1-NP*-pattern (the* 1-NP*-pattern).*

Proof. We give the proof for the case of not existentially definable languages: Suppose the automaton $\mathcal{A}$ contains one of these patterns. Then it contains the co-UP-pattern, too. Hence, by Theorem 1, L is not existentially definable in FOX.

For the other direction let L be a regular language which is not existentially definable in FOX. If $\mathcal{A}$ contained the counting pattern it was not counter-free. Hence L was not first-order definable, see for example [MP71,St94]. Therefore, from now on we can assume that $\mathcal{A}$ is counter-free.

Because L is not existentially definable in FOX the automaton $\mathcal{A}$ contains the co-UP-pattern, i.e. there is a state p and words v, w, z with $v \in \Sigma^+$ such that $p.v = p$, $p.wv = p.w$, $p.z \in F$ and $p.wz \notin F$. With $x := wv^n$ where n is the number of states of the minimal automaton $\mathcal{A}$ one gets $p.x^n = p.x^{n+1}$ since the automaton is counter-free. Then some state $p.x^i$ with $0 \leq i < n$ together with $p.x^n$ and the words v, x^{n-i} and z forms the co-NP- or the co-1-NP-pattern depending on $p.x^n z \notin F$ or $p.x^n z \in F$. □

3 A Leaf Language Characterization of NP

In this section we will give an application of the results from the previous section to the question which leaf languages characterize the complexity class NP. An informal idea of the leaf language concept was already given in the introduction. Let us be a bit more formal (for a detailed definition and more examples and motivation see [Bo95]). Consider the computation tree given by a nondeterministic polynomial-time Turing machine (NPTM) M which runs on an input x. Note that by the original definition of nondeterminism the tree is not necessarily balanced. Also note that there is a natural order on the paths of the tree: if at some configuration there appears nondeterminism the Turing machine M gives a natural linear order on the different possible following configurations: this order is given by the order of the commands in the list representing the transition table. Given the computation tree, label every accepting final configuration with 1 and each rejecting final configuration with 0. This way one gets an ordered tree in which the leaves are labeled by 0 and 1, see Figure 4. The word consisting of the

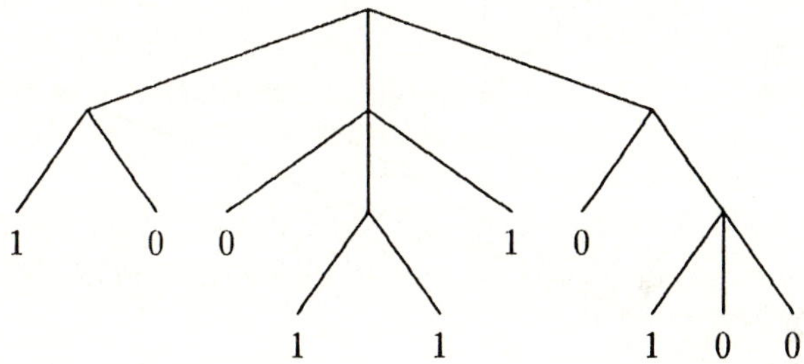

Fig. 4. Computation tree (whose yield is 1001110100)

leaf labels read from left to right is called the *yield* of the tree. Let any language $L \subseteq \Sigma^+$ over the alphabet $\Sigma = \{0,1\}$ be given (because the yield has always positive length we ignore the empty word). Let M be a NPTM. A word x is in the language $M[L]$ iff the yield of the computation tree of M running on input x is in L. Then the *(unbalanced polynomial-time) leaf language class* $L-$ P is the set of all languages $M[L]$ for some NPTM M.

Examples. In the introduction we already mentioned that NP $= \Sigma^* 1 \Sigma^* -$ P $=$ $\Sigma^* 10 \Sigma^* -$ P $= \Sigma^* 1 \Sigma^* 0 \Sigma^* -$ P. As another example, $0^* -$ P $=$ co-NP. It is easy to see that $1\Sigma^* - \mathrm{P} = \mathrm{P}$. The classes $\mathrm{MOD}_n\mathrm{P}$ for each $n \geq 2$ are defined as $C_n - \mathrm{P}$ where C_n is the set of words w such that the number of 1's in w is not a multiple of n. The two *trivial* leaf languages are $\emptyset$ and Σ^+, it holds $\emptyset - \mathrm{P} = \{\emptyset\}$ and $\Sigma^+ - \mathrm{P} = \{\Sigma^*\}$. The *join of* NP *and* co-NP, NP $\oplus$ co-NP, is characterized as $J - \mathrm{P}$ where $J = 0\overline{0^*} \cup 10^*$, it is the smallest class among all classes $L - \mathrm{P}$ containing both NP and co-NP, see [Bo95, Proof of Prop. 2(c)]. Another example is the class UP, a so-called *promise class*: It is the set of all languages A for which there is an NPTM M such that the yield of the computation tree $M(x)$ is in 0^* or 0^*10^* for every x, and a word x is in A iff the yield of the computation tree is in 0^*10^*. We give the definition of UP and its set of complements co-UP just in order to explain the name of the corresponding pattern (see Lemma 1); we do not use them for our results. The class 1-NP $= 0^*10^* - \mathrm{P}$ and its class of complements co-1-NP $= \overline{0^*10^*} - \mathrm{P}$ will be crucial for our main result. Note that co-NP $\subseteq$ 1-NP $\subseteq$ DP and NP $\subseteq$ co-1-NP $\subseteq$ co-DP, where DP and co-DP are the two classes of the second level of the Boolean Hierarchy over NP, see [CG*88] or Chapter 4. It should be mentioned that the Boolean Hierachy over NP is contained in both Σ_2^p and Π_2^p. Figure 5 gives an idea about the location of 1-NP and co-1-NP.

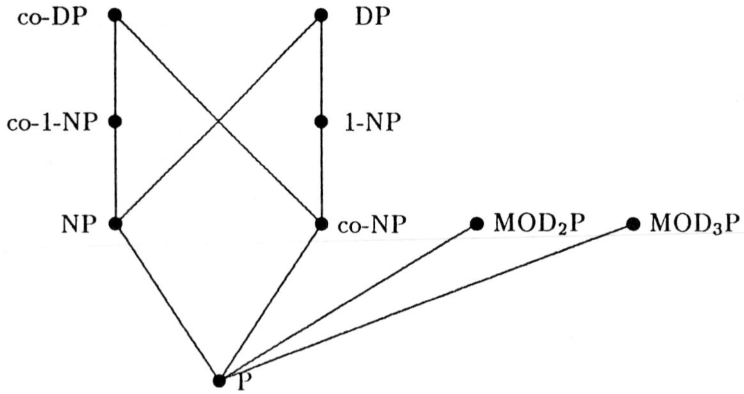

Fig. 5. 1-NP and co-1-NP

Theorem 2. **(Blass & Gurevich [BG82], Chang, Kadin & Rohatgi [CKR95], Toda [To91])**
Assume that PH does not collapse. Then 1-NP (co-1-NP) *is not contained in neither* NP, co-NP, *nor* co-1-NP (1-NP). *Furthermore,* $\mathrm{MOD}_n\mathrm{P}$ *for* $n \geq 2$ *is not contained in* PH.

The following Lemma 1 gives the main connex between patterns in automata and complexity classes, it also explains the names of the patterns.

Lemma 1. *Let L be the language accepted by a finite automaton $\mathcal{A}$ where any state is reachable from the initial state.*

(a) *Let* X *be in* {NP,co-NP,1-NP,co-1-NP,UP,co-UP}. *If $\mathcal{A}$ contains the* X-*pattern then* X *is a subset of $L-$* P.

(b) *If $\mathcal{A}$ contains a counting pattern, then* $\mathrm{MOD}_p\mathrm{P}$ *is a subset of $L-$* P *for some prime p.*

(c) *If $\mathcal{A}$ contains both the* NP- *and the* co-NP-*pattern, then* NP $\oplus$ co-NP *is a subset of $L-$* P.

Proof. (a) Let the automaton $\mathcal{A}$ contain the co-NP-pattern, see Figure 2. Let the state p be reachable from the initial state by the word a. We want to show that co-NP is included in $L-$ P. It suffices to construct for every NPTM M an NPTM M' such that an input x is accepted by M via the leaf language 0^* iff x is accepted by M via the leaf language L. Given M, let M' be the following machine. On input x, M' produces first of all $|a|$ leftmost computation paths with a written on them, this way the yield of the computation tree $M'(x)$ will have the prefix a. Then it simulates the computation of M including the nondeterministic branchings. Everytime M accepts (rejects) it produces the word w (the word v) by extending that computation path of M by $|w|$ (by $|v|$) new computation paths. Finally it produces $|z|$ rightmost computation paths for z. By this construction, $M'(x)$ has a similar computation tree as $M(x)$, besides that every 0 is replaced by a tree for v and every 1 is replaced by a tree for w, and at the leftmost and rightmost part there are computation paths for a and z, respectively. Looking at Figure 2 one can verify: if $M(x)$ does not accept on any computation path then the yield of the computation tree of $M'(x)$ reaches the state $p.z$, i.e. the yield is in L, and if $M(x)$ does accept on at least one computation path then the yield of the computation tree of $M'(x)$ reaches $q.z$, i.e. the yield is not in L. In other words: The yield of the computation tree of $M'(x)$ is in L iff the yield of the computation tree of $M(x)$ is in 0^*. This means that we have the desired inclusion: Let A be a language in co-NP witnessed by a machine M. Then it is witnessed by the machine M' that $A \in L-$ P. In other words, co-NP $\subseteq L-$ P. For the other patterns the proof including the construction of M' is the same.

(b) If the minimal automaton for a language contains a counting pattern for the number n then it contains a counting pattern for a prime p, see [Bo95, Lemma 6]. Now [Bo95, Lemma 7] (using the methods of [BG92]) together with the construction from (a) completes the proof.

(c) This follows immediately from (a) and the fact that NP$\oplus$co-NP is the smallest class $L-$ P containing both NP and co-NP. □

The following Lemma 2 implies one direction of Theorem 3. Note that it does not use the assumption that PH does not collapse.

Lemma 2. *Let L be existentially definable in* FOX. *If L is quantifier-free definable in* FOX *then $L-$* P *equals one of the classes* $\{\emptyset\}$, $\{\Sigma^*\}$, *or* P, *otherwise* $L-$ P $=$ NP.

Proof. If L is quantifier-free definable then L is generalized definite (Theorem 1) and the claim above is shown in [Bo95, Lemma 11].

Now let L be existentially but not quantifier-free definable in FOX. Let $\mathcal{A}$ be the minimal automaton accepting L. By Theorem 1, $\mathcal{A}$ does not contain the co-UP-pattern (because L is existentially definable) By Corollary 1, $\mathcal{A}$ does contain the counting pattern, the NP-pattern or the 1-NP-pattern (because L it is not quantifier-free definable and therefore not universally definable). But the counting pattern and the 1-NP-pattern contain the co-UP-pattern as a subpattern. Therefore, $\mathcal{A}$ has to contain the NP-pattern, and by Lemma 1 the class NP is contained in $L-$ P.

It remains to show that if a language L is existentially definable in FOX then $L-$ P is a subset of NP (this was actually already shown in [BV96]). Let L consist of all words satisfying the existential sentence f in prenex normal form that contains m existential quantifiers. Let M be a NPTM. One has to construct a NPTM M' that accepts via the leaf language $\overline{0^\star}$ those inputs that are accepted by M via the leaf language L. This machine M' simulates M m times and memorizes the nondeterministic choices, i.e. the corresponding paths in the computation tree of M. Since these paths represent positions in the yield of M it is then possible to compute the truth value of f in polynomial time. □

The following lemma implies the other direction of our main Theorem 3 below. It relies mainly on Corollary 1 which itself is a consequence of the characterization (cf. Theorem 1) by Pin & Weil [PW97]. Note that like in Lemma 2 (for the other direction of the main theorem) we do not need the assumption that PH does not collapse.

Lemma 3. *Let L not be existentially definable in* FOX. *Then* $L-$ P *contains at least one of the classes* co-NP, co-1-NP, *or* MOD_pP *for some prime* p.

Proof. By Corollary 1 the minimal automaton for L contains the counting pattern, the co-NP-pattern, or the co-1-NP-pattern. Therefore, by Lemma 1, $L-$ P contains at least one of the classes co-NP, co-1-NP, or MOD_pP for some prime p. □

Figure 6 depicts the situation. All the classes $L-$ P with L regular but not existentially definable in FOX are situated somewhere in the gray area.

Now, finally, we can state the following theorem about the close relation of existentially definable languages and NP.

Theorem 3 (Main Result). *Assume that* PH *does not collapse and let L be a regular language. Then* $L-\text{P} = \text{NP}$ $(L-\text{P} = \text{co-NP})$ *iff L is existentially (universally) but not quantifier-free definable in* FOX.

Proof. Let L be existentially but not quantifier-free definable in FOX. Then, by Lemma 2 $L-\text{P} = \text{NP}$. If L is quantifier-free definable, then $L-\text{P} \subseteq \text{P}$, and by the assumption that PH does not collapse we have $L-\text{P} \neq \text{NP}$. Finally, let L be not existentially definable in FOX. Then, by Lemma 3, $L-$ P contains at least one of the classes co-NP, co-1-NP, or MOD_pP for some prime p. If PH does not collapse none of these classes is a subset of NP, see Theorem 2. Therefore, also $L-$ P is not a subset of NP. It follows that $L-\text{P} \neq \text{NP}$. The dual claim for co-NP follows immediately. □

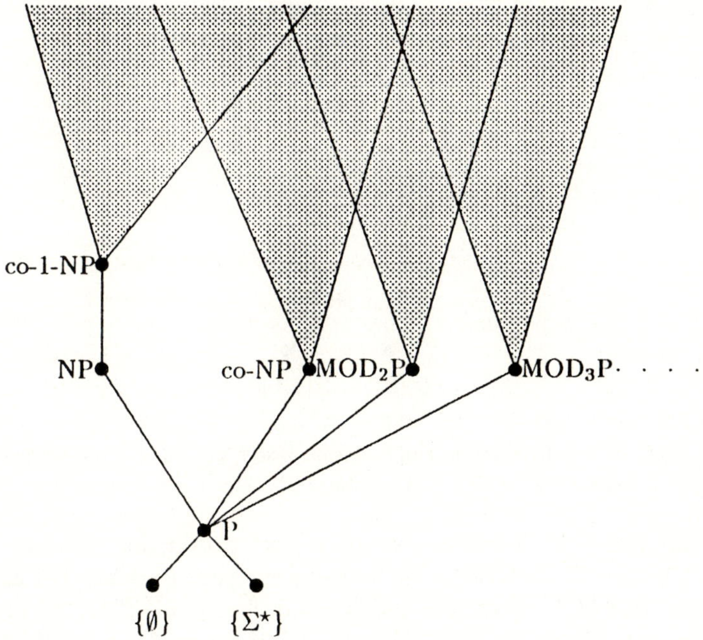

Fig. 6. cf. Theorem 3

Under the assumption that PH does not collapse we characterized in Theorem 3 the regular languages which characterize NP and co-NP, respectively, as leaf languages. The following result solves this question for the class P.

Theorem 4. *Assume that* PH *does not collapse and let L be a regular language. Then $L-\mathrm{P}=\mathrm{P}$ iff L is quantifier-free definable in* FOX *but not trivial.*

In [Bo95] it was shown that under the assumption that PH does not collapse there are no classes $L-\mathrm{P}$ properly between P and NP and neither between P and co-NP. Here we have the following extension of that result, it is depicted in Figure 7.

Theorem 5. *Assume that* PH *does not collapse. Then* $\{\emptyset\}$, $\{\Sigma^*\}$, P, NP, co-NP, 1-NP, co-1-NP *and* NP$\oplus$co-NP *are eight different classes. Moreover, each of the intervals depicted as a line between two inclusion-comparable classes in Fig. 7 represents a nondensity in the sense that both classes are a class $L-\mathrm{P}$ with L regular but no class of that kind is located properly between them.*

4 On the Boolean Hierarchy over NP

So far, we addressed the question what classes are characterized by *single* leaf languages, see for example the main result Theorem 3. But there is a different approach which asks about the union of the classes characterized by a *set*

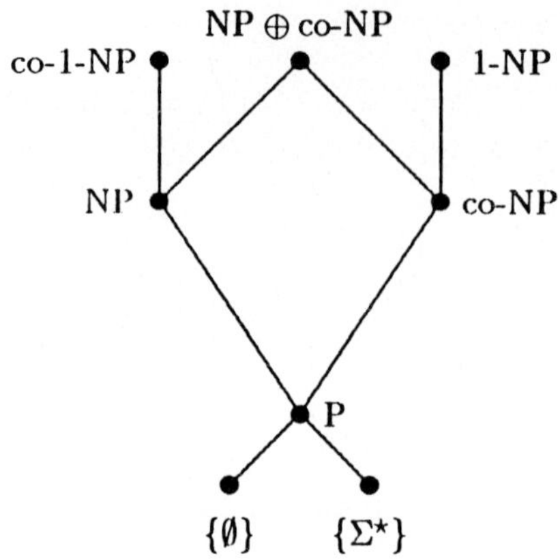

Fig. 7. Nondensities in the inclusion order $\{L - P \mid L \text{ regular}\}$.

of leaf languages. The following examples were proven for balanced leaf languages but they hold likewise for the unbalanced case: Hertrampf et al. [HL*93] showed that PSPACE equals the *union* of all classes $L - \mathrm{P}$ for L regular, and that the Boolean closure of Σ_k^p is the union of all classes $L - \mathrm{P}$ for the languages L of dot-depth k. This in particular implies that PH is the union of all classes $L - \mathrm{P}$ where L is definable in first-order logic. These results have been refined by Burtschick & Vollmer [BV96]: Remember that a language is Σ_k-definable if there is a defining sentence in prenex normal form that has k blocks of equal quantifiers starting with existential ones (Σ_1-definability equal existential definability), see [Th82,St94,PW97] for details.

$$\Sigma_k^p = \bigcup \{L - \mathrm{P} \mid L \text{ is } \Sigma_k\text{-definable in FOX}\}.$$

In this paper we present a union-style result for the classes of the Boolean Hierarchy over NP, see [CG*88]. Let NP(n) denote the level n of the Boolean Hierarchy over NP, i.e. NP(1) = NP,

$$\begin{aligned}\mathrm{NP}(2n) &= \{A \setminus B \mid A \in \mathrm{NP}, B \in \mathrm{NP}(2n-1)\},\\ \mathrm{NP}(2n+1) &= \{\overline{A \setminus B} \mid A \in \mathrm{NP}, B \in \mathrm{NP}(2n)\}.\end{aligned}$$

Let $\Gamma(1) = \Gamma$ denote the set of languages of dot-depth 1/2, and define the Boolean Hierarchy over this class by

$$\begin{aligned}\Gamma(2n) &= \{L_1 \setminus L_2 \mid L_1 \in \Gamma, L_2 \in \Gamma(2n-1)\},\\ \Gamma(2n+1) &= \{\overline{L_1 \setminus L_2} \mid L_1 \in \Gamma, L_2 \in \Gamma(2n)\}.\end{aligned}$$

We can prove the following union-style result.

Theorem 6. *For every $n \geq 1$ it holds the following:*

$$\mathrm{NP}(n) = \bigcup \{L - \mathrm{P} \mid L \in \Gamma(n)\}.$$

5 Open Problems

Under the assumption that PH does not collapse the authors could characterize the regular leaf languages which characterize P, NP, and co-NP, respectively. They would have liked to extend their result to other classes, for example to higher classes of the Polynomial-Time Hierarchy like Σ_k^p. The (unproven) claim for these classes would be the following: If PH does not collapse then a regular language L characterizes Σ_k^p as an unbalanced polynomial-time leaf language if and only if L is Σ_k-definable but not Π_k-definable in FOX. This claim is motivated and supported by the union-style result of Burtschick & Vollmer [BV96] mentioned above. But Pin & Weil [PW97] remark that no (at least no easy) automata criterion like the co-UP-pattern criterion is known for dot-depth 3/2, 5/2, etc. But such a criterion seems to be necessary.

Acknowledgements

The authors are grateful for comments by Klaus Ambos-Spies, Jean-Eric Pin, Wolfgang Thomas and Heribert Vollmer. Thanks to Heinz Schmitz and Heribert Vollmer for pointing out a mistake in a former version of Theorem 2.

References

[BG92] R. BEIGEL, J. GILL: *Counting classes: thresholds, parity, mods, and fewness*, Theoretical Computer Science **103**, 1992, pp. 3–23.

[BG82] A. BLASS, Y. GUREVICH: *On the unique satisfiability problem*, Information and Control **55**, 1982, pp. 80-88.

[Bo95] B. BORCHERT: *On the acceptance power of regular languages*, Theoretical Computer Science **148**, 1995, pp. 207–225.

[BCS92] D. P. BOVET, P. CRESCENZI, R. SILVESTRI: *A uniform approach to define complexity classes*, Theoretical Computer Science **104**, 1992, pp. 263-283.

[BV96] H.-J. BURTSCHICK, H. VOLLMER: *Lindström Quantifiers and Leaf Language Definability*, ECCC Report TR96-005, 1996.

[CG*88] J.-Y. CAI, T. GUNDERMANN, J. HARTMANIS, L. A. HEMACHANDRA, V. SEWELSON, K. WAGNER, G. WECHSUNG: *The Boolean Hierarchy I: structural properties*, SIAM Journal on Computing **17**, 1988, pp. 1232-1252

[CKR95] R. CHANG, J. KADIN, P. ROHATGI: *On unique satisfiability and the threshold behavior of randomized reductions*, Journal of Computer and System Science **50**, 1995, pp. 359-373.

[HL*93] U. HERTRAMPF, C. LAUTEMANN, T. SCHWENTICK, H. VOLLMER, K. WAGNER: *On the power of polynomial-time bit-computations*, Proc. 8th Structure in Complexity Theory Conference, 1993, pp. 200-207

[MP71] R. MCNAUGHTON, S. PAPERT: *Counter-Free Automata*, MIT Press, Cambridge, MA, 1971.

[PP86] D. PERRIN, J.-E. PIN: *First-order logic and Star-free sets*, J. of Computer and System Sciences **32**, 1986, pp. 393-406.

[PW97] J.-E. PIN, P. WEIL: *Polynomial closure and unambiguous product*, Theory of Computing Systems **30**, 1997, pp. 1-39.

[St94] H. STRAUBING: *Finite Automata, Formal Logic, and Circuit Complexity*, Birkhäuser, Boston, 1994.

[Th82] W. THOMAS: *Classifying regular events in symbolic logic*, Journal of Computer and System Sciences **25**, 1982, pp. 360-376.

[To91] S. TODA: PP *is as hard as the Polynomial-Time Hierarchy*, SIAM Journal on Computing **20**, 1991, pp. 865-877.

An Algebraic Approach to Communication Complexity

Jean-François Raymond, Pascal Tesson, and Denis Thérien*

School of Computer Science, McGill University, 3480 rue University, Montréal (PQ) H3A 2A7, Canada,
raymond,ptesso,denis@cs.mcgill.ca

Abstract. Let M be a finite monoid: define $C^{(k)}(M)$ to be the maximum number of bits that need to be exchanged in the k-party communication game to decide membership in any language recognized by M. We prove the following:
a) If M is a group then, for any k, $C^{(k)}(M) = O(1)$ if M is nilpotent of class $k-1$ and $C^{(k)}(M) = \Theta(n)$ otherwise.
b) If M is aperiodic, then $C^{(2)}(M) = O(1)$ if M is commutative, $C^{(2)}(M) = \Theta(\log n)$ if M belongs to the variety **DA** but is not commutative and $C^{(2)}(M) = \Theta(n)$ otherwise.
We also show that when M is in **DA**, $C^{(k)}(M) = O(1)$ for some k and conjecture that this algebraic condition is also necessary.

1 Introduction

In [20], Yao introduced a communication game where two players try to collaboratively evaluate a function $f(x)$. Each receives half the input bits, and their goal is to compute f by exchanging a minimal amount of information. This model was motivated by questions in distributed computing and VLSI. It has been well studied [11, 12] and variants of the original game have found deep applications in complexity [10, 16, 17].

One interesting extension was proposed by Chandra, Furst and Lipton in [5]. They introduced multiparty games where k-players try to compute a k-argument function. Each player has part of the input written on his forehead so that this information is available to all but himself. This model is stronger than the 2-party game, hence lower bounds for it are difficult to prove [1, 5]. Results that have been obtained have many applications in the study of bounded width branching programs [5], pseudorandomness [1], and circuit complexity [7–9].

In this paper, we will discuss the communication complexity of finite monoids. Since the 50's, algebra has provided powerful tools to analyze and classify languages that can be recognized by finite-state machines (See [6, 14] for comprehensive surveys). More recently, using the formalism of programs over monoids, deep

* Research supported by FCAR and NSERC grants. We would like to thank Peter Bro Miltersen of the University of Aarhus, Denmark for his ideas and comments, that helped us improve some of our lower bounds.

connections have been uncovered between algebraic properties of finite monoids and several natural classes of boolean circuits [2,4,13]. There are reasons to suspect the existence of interesting links between monoids and communication complexity. In [17], Szegedy provided an algebraic characterization of languages for which membership can be decided in constant communication by two players: they are exactly the sets recognized by programs over finite commutative monoids.

It thus seems worthwhile to investigate further how the algebraic structure of a finite algebraic system influences the communication complexity of the languages that can be recognized, using morphisms or programs. Our results indicate several interesting connections. We first show that the complexity classes that are defined in the communication framework induce in a natural way "varieties" of monoids (the notion of variety being the relevant one to classify monoids in terms of their computing power). We then study what varieties arise in this way, first if we restrict to groups, then to aperiodic structures. In the group case, we find that for any fixed k, languages recognized by the group G can be decided in constant communication in the k-player game if and only if the group is nilpotent of class $k-1$, and require linear communication otherwise. In the aperiodic case, we show that, for the two-player game, languages recognized by the monoid M will be decided in $O(1)$ communication if M is commutative, in $\Theta(\log n)$ if M belongs to the variety $\mathbf{DA}$ but is not commutative, and in $\Theta(n)$ otherwise. Furthermore, when M is in $\mathbf{DA}$, there exists some k such that corresponding languages can be done in $O(1)$ communication in the k-party game and we conjecture that this condition is also necessary. This points to a natural conjecture on how to extend Szegedy's theorem from 2 players to $O(1)$ players.

Our paper is organized as follows: in section 2, we summarize the needed background on communication complexity and algebra. In section 3, we show that complexity classes defined in the communication complexity framework give rise to varieties of monoids. In section 4 and 5, we discuss our results about groups and aperiodic structures respectively. In the conclusion, we will discuss our conjecture to extend Szegedy's theorem.

2 Background and definitions

2.1 Communication complexity

We give here some formal definitions together with basic results in communication complexity. For a more detailed introduction, we refer the reader to chapters 1, 2 and 6 of [11].

2-party model In the 2-party game, two players P_1 and P_2, each having unlimited computational power try to jointly compute a function $f : X^n \to Y$, where X and Y are finite alphabets. The set A of input variables is partitioned in two, $A = A_1 \dot\cup A_2$, so that each player sees only variables assigned to him.

They exchange bits according to a fixed protocol and when the communication stops, both players should know the value of f on the given input.

The cost of a protocol is the maximum number, taken over all possible inputs, of bits exchanged between P_1 and P_2. The communication complexity of f with respect to the partition (A_1, A_2), denoted $C^{(2)}_{(A_1,A_2)}$ is the cost of the cheapest protocol computing f given this partition. The symetric communication complexity (or just the communication complexity) of f, denoted $C^{(2)}(f)$ is the maximum, taken over all possible partitions of the input variables, of f's communication complexity. That is: $C^{(2)}(f) = \max_{A=A_1\dot{\cup}A_2} C^{(2)}_{(A_1,A_2)}(f)$

Among the many lower bound techniques known for 2-party communication complexity, we will use the so-called fooling-set method. A fooling set for the function $f(x_1, x_2)$ is a set F of input pairs (x_1, x_2) such that for all $(x_1, x_2) \in F$, $f(x_1, x_2) = v$ and for any two distinct (x_1, x_2), $(x'_1, x'_2) \in F$, either $f(x'_1, x_2) \neq v$ or $f(x_1, x'_2) \neq v$.

Lemma 1. *If f has a size $|F|$ fooling set, then $C^{(2)}(f) \geq \log |F|$*

Multiparty model The two-party model can be generalized to k-party in the following way. We have k players $P_1, \ldots, P_k$. The input variables are partitioned in k sets: $A = A_1\dot{\cup}\ldots\dot{\cup}A_k$, and player P_i knows all the variables except those in A_i. There is a considerable overlap of information since each variable is known to (k-1) players.

The players now communicate by writing bits on a blackboard seen by all players.The protocol should specify which player writes the next bit. This should be a function of the communication thus far, and not of the input. What a party writes depends on the information on the board and on the parts of the input it sees. Protocol cost, communication complexity with respect to a given partition and symetric communication complexity are defined in the obvious way. We denote the k-party communication complexity of f as $C^{(k)}(f)$. As usual, we will be interested in studying the complexity of functions $f : X^* \to Y$ and consequently consider $C^{(k)}(f)$ as a function from $\mathbf{N}$ to $\mathbf{N}$. We define $CC^{(k)}(g(n))$ as the class of functions f such that $C^{(k)}(f) = O(g(n))$.

We state two easy facts about k-party complexity.

Fact 1. If $k < k'$ then $C^{(k)}(f) \geq C^{(k')}(f)$

Fact 2. $C^{(k)}(f) \leq \frac{n}{k} + 1$

2.2 Algebra

Monoids and morphisms We refer the reader to [6] or [14] for more details on the material sketched here. A monoid is a set together with a binary associative operation and a distinguished identity element. All monoids considered are finite, except for X^*, the free monoid generated by the set X.

Given two monoids M and N, we say that M divides N, and write $M \prec N$, if M is a morphic image of a submonoid of N. The natural unit to classify finite monoids is given by the notion of pseudo-variety (or variety for short). A class **V** of finite monoids forms a variety iff it is closed under division and finite direct product.

We say that a language $L \subseteq X^*$ is recognized by the monoid M if there is a morphism $\phi : X^* \to M$ such that $L = \phi^{-1}(F)$ for some subset $F \subseteq M$. It is well known that L is regular iff it can be recognized by some finite monoid M.

Given a regular language $L \subseteq X^*$, define for any word x the set $Y_x = \{(u, v) : uxv \in L\}$. We get a congruence of finite index on X^* by declaring $x \sim_L y$ iff $Y_x = Y_y$. The monoid $X^*/\sim_L$ is called the syntactic monoid of L, and is denoted $M(L)$. This monoid $M(L)$ recognizes L and for any N also recognizing L, $M(L) \prec N$.

Monoid M is a group iff it satisfies the equation $m^q = 1$ for some $q \geq 1$: it is aperiodic iff it satisfies $m^t = m^{t+1}$ for some $t \geq 0$. Groups and aperiodic monoids form varieties. Given a group G, form the sequence $G_0 = G$ and $G_i = [G_{i-1}, G]$ where $[H, G]$ is defined as the subgroup of G generated by all commutators $[h, g] = h^{-1}g^{-1}hg$, $h \in H$ $g \in G$. We say that G is nilpotent of class k if $G_k = \{1\}$: for any $k \geq 0$, nilpotent groups of class k form a variety. We will also mention the variety of commutative monoids, i.e. those satisfying the equation $st = ts$, and the variety **DA** which is defined as the class of monoids satisfying $(stu)^n t (stu)^n = (stu)^n$, for some $n \geq 0$.

Monoids and programs The concept of recognition of a language by a morphism can be extended using programs over monoids. Formally, given an input alphabet A, an n-input program of length l over a monoid M is a sequence of instructions $(i_1, f_1), (i_2, f_2) \ldots, (i_l, f_l)$ with $i_j \in \{1, \ldots, n\}$ and $f_j : A \to M$, together with an accepting subset $F \subseteq M$. The program accepts the input $x_1 x_2 \ldots x_n$ iff the sequence $f_1(x_{i_1}) \ldots f_l(x_{i_l})$ evaluates to an element of F.

We say that $L \subseteq A^*$ is P-recognized by M if there is a sequence $(\varphi_1, \varphi_2, \ldots)$ where φ_n is an n-input program over M, of length $l(n)$ with $l(n)$ polynomial in n, such that the program φ_n accepts $L \cap A^n$.

We say that the monoid M P-divides monoid N and write $M \prec_{\wp} N$ if any language recognized by a morphism over M can be recognized by a polynomial length program over N. If $M \prec N$ then $M \prec_{\wp} N$ since morphisms are just special cases of programs. We say that a class **V** of monoids is a P-variety if it is closed under finite direct product and P-division.

We state (without proof) the following :

Fact 3. Let S, T be finite monoids, with $S \prec_{\wp} T$. Suppose T is commutative, then S is commutative.

3 Communication complexity of finite monoids

In this section we define the communication complexity of a monoid and relate communication complexity classes to monoid varieties. For this section, we fix k, the number of players, to some arbitrary finite value.

3.1 Complexity of monoids

We define the communication complexity of a monoid M as the maximum complexity of any language recognized by M.

The operation on a monoid defines a canonical surjective morphism $eval_M$: $M^* \to M$

$$eval_M(m_1 m_2 \dots m_n) = m$$

where $m = m_1 \cdot m_2 \cdot \dots \cdot m_n$ is the product in M of this sequence of monoid elements.

We say that a regular language $L \subseteq A^*$ has an identity letter if there exists $e \in A$ such that $\phi(e) = 1_M$, where ϕ is the recognizing morphism.

Theorem 1. *Let $L \subseteq A^*$ be a regular language and let $M = M(L)$ be its syntactic monoid. Let c_L and c_{eval_M} be the k-party communication complexity of L and $eval_M$ respectively. Then $c_L = O(c_{eval_M})$.*

Moreover, if L has an identity letter then $c_{eval_M} = O(c_L)$ and so $c_L = \Theta(c_{eval_M})$.

Proof. First, we give a $O(c_{eval_M})$-bit k-party protocol for L.

Let $\phi : A^* \to M$ be the recognizing morphism. Given a length n input in A^*, each player privately applies ϕ to each letter of the input. They now have a word of length n in M^*. Using the c_{eval_M}-bit protocol they can evaluate this product. Finally, each player privately checks whether or not the result is in F, where $\phi^{-1}(F) = L$.

For the other direction, we know that each monoid element is an equivalence class of the syntactic congruence of L. Since M is finite, there are only $|M|$ equivalence classes of $\sim_L$. Moreover, each such class corresponds to some unique Y_x, and two different Y's must disagree on some pair (u, v). We can thus choose minimal length pairs $(u_1, v_1), (u_2, v_2), \dots, (u_t, v_t)$, $t \leq |M|^2$, such that $x \sim_L y$ iff Y_x and Y_y contain exactly the same pairs (u_i, v_i).

Using this fact, we can now build a $O(c_L)$ protocol for $eval_M$.

The players have agreed beforehand on a choice of pairs (u_i, v_i) and, for each $m \in M$ on a word $w \in A^*$ of length q such that $\phi(w) = m$. (Note that this can be done because of the identity letter)

The players are given an input in M^*, say $m_1, \dots, m_t$. Privately, the players translate this input to a word x of length qt in A^*. Note that

$$eval(m_1, \dots, m_t) = m \equiv [x]_{\sim L}$$

Now for each pair (u_i, v_i) the players can use the c_L-bit protocol to determine if (u_i, v_i) is in Y_x. Finally, each player knows Y_x and there is a unique $m \in M$ corresponding to it.

Also, since $c_L = O(n)$, we have $c_L(qt) = O(c_L(t))$. Hence $c_{eval_M} = O(c_L)$. □

This theorem shows that $C^{(k)}(M) = \Theta(C^{(k)}(eval_M))$. This is very convenient as $eval_M$ provides an explicit representation for $C^{(k)}(M)$. In fact, any language L having an identity letter and such that $M(L) = M$ will have the same property.

Lemma 2. *Let M, N be finite monoids. Let c_M, c_N and $c_{M\times N}$ be the communication complexity of M, N and $M \times N$ respectively. Then* $\max\{c_M, c_N\} \leq c_{M\times N} \leq c_M + c_N$

Proof. First we can obviously build a protocol of cost $c_{M\times N}$ for $eval_M$, using the identity in N for the N-coordinate. This shows the first inequality.

To show $c_{M\times N} \leq c_M + c_N$, we build a cost $(c_M + c_N)$ protocol for $eval_{M\times N}$ by evaluating the product coordinate-wise using the c_M and c_N-bit protocols. □

Lemma 3. *Let M, N be finite monoids such that $M \prec N$. Then $c_M \leq c_N$*

Proof. There is a submonoid $T \subseteq N$ and a surjective morphism $\phi : T \to M$. Given a word in M^*, the k players want to evaluate the product $m_1 m_2 \dots m_l$ in M. Since ϕ is a surjective morphism, we have

$$m_1 m_2 \dots m_l = \phi[\phi^{-1}(m_1) \dots \phi^{-1}(m_l)]$$

Note that ϕ^{-1} is not necessarily defined uniquely, but any choice will do since ϕ is a morphism.

So, on any input in M^*, the players privately translate the input to a word in T^* using a previously agreed upon scheme. (i.e. for every $m \in M$ they have chosen some $t \in T$ such that $\phi(t) = m$)

Now, using the c_N-bit protocol, they can evaluate in T the product

$$\phi^{-1}(m_1) \dots \phi^{-1}(m_l) = t_0$$

and privately compute $\phi(t_0)$. Note that t_0 is in T, since T is a submonoid and is therefore closed under the operation of N. □

Lemma 4. *Let $L \subseteq A^*$ be such that L can be recognized by a $O(l(n))$-length program over a finite monoid M. Let c_L and c_M be the communication complexities of L and M respectively, then $c_L(n) = O(c_M(l(n)))$. In particular, if $l(n) = n$ then $c_L = O(c_M)$.*

Proof. Given a length n input in A^*, the players can use that program and then evaluate a string of length $O(l(n))$ in M^*, which they can do using $c_M(O(l(n)) = O(c_M(l(n)))$ bits of communication. □

Corollary 1. *Suppose $M \prec_{\wp} N$ and $c_N = O(\log^r(n))$, for some r; then $c_M = O(c_N)$.*

As a direct consequence of these lemmas, we get the following theorem:

Theorem 2. *The monoids in $CC^{(k)}(f(n))$, that is monoids whose k-party communication complexity are $O(f(n))$, form a monoid variety. Moreover they form a P-variety if $f(n)$ is polylogarithmic.*

We are interested here in the varieties defined by the following communication complexity classes:

$$CCC^{(k)} = CC^{(k)}(O(1)) \text{ and } CCC = \bigcup_{k\geq 2} CCC^{(k)}$$

3.2 Szegedy's result

In [17], Szegedy proved an algebraic characterization for the class $CCC^{(2)}$. His main theorem is:

Theorem 3 (Szegedy). *A language L has bounded 2-party communication complexity iff L can be recognized by an M-program over a commutative monoid M.*

Combining this with theorem 2 and fact 3, we get the following corollary.

Corollary 2. *A finite monoid N has constant communication complexity iff N is commutative.*

Our goal now is to investigate the varieties defined by communication complexity classes. We study separately the cases of groups and aperiodic monoids.

4 The case of groups

In this section, we characterize exactly groups having constant communication complexity in the k-party game, for every $k \geq 2$. In order to do this, we need the combinatorial description of the languages recognized by nilpotent groups of class k that was presented in [18].

We say that $u = u_1 u_2 \dots u_m$ is a subword of x if x can be factorized as $x = A^* u_1 A^* u_2 A^* \dots u_m A^*$. Let $u \in A^*$, $q \geq 1$. Define $|x|_u$ as the number of occurrences of u as a subword of x. Also, define $[u, i, q] = \{x; |x|_u \equiv i \pmod{q}\}$

Denote by $\mathbf{G_{nil,m}}$ the variety of finite nilpotent groups of class $\leq m$.

It is known that $L \subseteq A^*$ is recognized by $G \in \mathbf{G_{nil,m}}$ iff L is in the boolean algebra generated by $\{[u, i, q]; |u| \leq m, q \geq 1\}$. Equivalently, $\mathbf{G_{nil,m}}$ is generated by the syntactic monoids of the languages $[u, i, q]$ where $|u| \leq m$.

Of course in an $(m+1)$-party game, every subword of size m is seen entirely by at least one player, so clearly, if $G \in \mathbf{G_{nil,m}}$ then the $(m+1)$-party communication complexity of G is $O(1)$.

Groups in $\mathbf{G_{nil,m}}$ are actually the only groups in $CCC^{(m+1)}$. To show this, we will use lemma 4 together with the powerful lower bound obtained in [1] and generalized by Grolmusz in [7]:

Theorem 4 (Grolmusz). *Let $GIP_{k,p} : \{0,1\}^{n \times k} \to \{0,1\}$ be the function defined as $GIP_{k,p}(A) := 1$ iff the number of all 1 rows of A is congruent to 0 (mod p).*

$C^{(k)}(GIP_{k,p}) = \Omega(n/4^k)$ for any prime p.

Let $L_{k,p}$ be the regular language defined by $x \in L$ iff $|x|_{a_1} \equiv 0 \pmod{p}$, $|x|_{a_1 a_2} \equiv 0 \pmod{p}$, $\dots$ $|x|_{a_1 a_2 \dots a_k} \equiv 0 \pmod{p}$.

Let $G_{k,p}$ be the syntactic monoid of $L_{k,p}$. $G_{k,p}$ is a class k nilpotent group.

Lemma 5. *For any $t \leq k$, there is a t-input program $B(t)$ over $G_{k,p}$ which outputs an element of order p if all t input bits are on and e otherwise. The length of $B(t)$ is less than 2^{t+1}.*

Proof. For any $i \leq k$, the commutator $[[\dots[a_1, a_2], a_3], \dots, a_i]$ has order p in $G_{k,p}$. Indeed, an easy induction shows that this word contains no subwords (mod p) of the form $a_1a_2\dots a_j$ for $j < i$ and contains (mod p) exactly one subword $a_1a_2\dots a_i$.

Now, let $C(i)$ be the single instruction outputting a_i if the ith bit is on and e otherwise. We define inductively

$B(1) = C(1)$

$B(i+1) = B(i)C(i+1)B(i)^{-1}C(i+1)^{-1}$

If some bit is off, $B(t)$ will output e. Otherwise it produces the commutator $[[\dots[a_1, a_2], a_3], \dots, a_t]$. which is an element of order p. □

Theorem 5. *Let G be a nilpotent group of class k. $C^{(k)}(G) = \Omega(n)$.*

Proof. It is sufficient to show that $C^{(k)}(G_{k,p}) = \Omega(n)$ for any k, p.

By concatenating n copies of the $B(k)$'s defined in the previous lemma, we can get a length $2^{k+1}.n$ program over $G_{k,p}$ recognizing $GIP_{k,p}$. Indeed, $GIP_{k,p}$ counts (mod p) the results of n k-wise AND's.

By lemma 4, this shows that $C^{(k)}(G_{k,p}) = \Omega(n)$ for any k, p. □

Theorem 6. *Let G be a non-nilpotent group. $C^{(k)}(G) = \Omega(n)$ for any k.*

Proof. Since G is not nilpotent, there is a normal subgroup $H \triangleleft G$ such that $[G, H] = H$, and $|H| \neq 1$.

It was shown in [3] (Theorem 5) that for any $h \in H$, there is a k-input program of length at most $(4 \cdot |H|)^k$ which outputs h if all input bits are on and outputs e otherwise.

Let $h \in H$ be an element of order p, where p divides $|H|$. It is now clear how one can construct a program of length at most $n \cdot (4|H|)^k$ which recognizes $GIP_{k,p}$. Finally, lemma 4 yields the result. □

Hence, we have proved the following theorem :

Theorem 7. *Let G be a finite group. G is in $CCC^{(k)}$ if and only if G is nilpotent of class $< k$. Otherwise $C^{(k)}(G) = \Omega(n)$.*

5 The case of aperiodic monoids

We now investigate the communication complexity of aperiodic monoids. In the 2-party game, we provide a complete characterization for all aperiodic monoids. We then present some results for the situation where $O(1)$ players are involved.

The case with 2 players By corollary 2, we know that any monoid, hence any aperiodic monoid, has constant communication complexity iff it is commutative. We now proceed to show that every non-commutative aperiodic monoid has communication complexity of either $\Theta(\log n)$ or $\Theta(n)$, depending if the monoid belongs to the variety **DA** or not. Recall that the variety **DA** is defined as the class of monoids that satisfy $(stu)^n t(stu)^n = (stu)^n$ for some n. It is known that $L \subseteq A^*$ is recognized by M in **DA** iff L is a disjoint union of languages of the form $A_0^* a_1 A_1^* \ldots a_k A_k^*$ where $a_i \in A$, $A_i \subseteq A$ and the concatenation is unambiguous [15], which means that whenever we have w in L, the factorization $w = w_0 a_1 w_1 \ldots w_{k-1} a_k w_k$ where $w_i \in A_i^*$, is unique.

Lemma 6. *Let $L = A_0^* a_1 A_1^* a_2 \ldots a_k A_k^*$ be an unambiguous concatenation.* $C^{(2)}(L) = O(\log n)$.

Proof (Sketch). We will show by induction on k, the number of bookmarks, that an $O(\log n)$ protocol exists for any such language.

For $k = 1$, notice that the only non-trivial unambiguous concatenations $A_0^* a_1 A_1^*$ are $c^* a A^*$ and $A^* a c^*$, where $A = \{a, b, c\}$. The $O(\log n)$ bound is simple in this case: each player gives the position of the first a it sees. Now, that they know where the first a is, they check if every letter preceding it is a c.

For the induction step, notice that if $A_0^* a_1 A_1^* a_2 \ldots a_k A_k^*$ is an unambiguous concatenation, then so is $A_{i-1}^* a_i A_i^* a_{i+1} \ldots a_j A_j^*$, for any $1 \leq i < j \leq k$.

We say that the players have identified the bookmark a_i at position p if they know that if the input w is in L, then the bookmark a_i is at position p.

By taking advantage of the unambiguity, it is possible to show that the players will always be able to identify one of the bookmarks, using only $O(\log n)$ communication. Thus they can reduce the problem for k bookmarks to two problems of less than k bookmarks.□

Hence, monoids in **DA** have logarithmic 2-party communication complexity. We state the following fact whose proof will be given in the full paper:

Fact 4. Let M be a finite non-commutative aperiodic monoid. Then M is divided by one of the following aperiodic monoids:

1. BA_2, the syntactic monoid of $(c^* ac^* bc^*)^*$
2. U, the syntactic monoid of $((b+c)^* a(b+c)^* b(b+c)^*)^*$
3. The syntactic monoid of $A^* a A^* b A^*$
4. The syntactic monoid of either $c^* a A^*$ or $A^* a c^*$

Moreover, if $M \notin$ **DA**, M is divided by BA_2 or U.

The next two lemmas show that the upper bound proved for monoids in **DA** is tight for non-commutative monoids in this variety.

Lemma 7. *Let $L = A^* a A^* b A^*$, we have $C^{(2)}(L) = \Theta(\log n)$.*

Proof. Consider the partition where player 1 gets odd-indexed bits and player 2 gets even-indexed bits. The following is a size $\frac{n}{2}$ fooling set for L: $F = \{b^{2i} a^{n-2i}\}$ None of these words are in L, but for any two words of this set, one of the words in the rectangle they define is of the form $b^j (ab)^l a^{(n-j-2l)}$, which is in L. □

Lemma 8. *The unambiguous concatenation $K = c^* a A^*$ on the alphabet $A = \{a, b, c\}$ requires $\Theta(\log n)$ communication for two players.*

Proof. For the partition where player 1 gets only odd-indexed bits, one can provide a size n fooling set of similar nature: $F = \{c^i bac^{n-2-i}\}$. □

Note that the languages $L = (c^*ac^*bc^*)^*$ and $K = ((b+c)^*a(b+c)^*b(b+c)^*)^*$ used in fact 4 to define the monoids BA_2 and U respectively have similarities: L requires that a's and b's alternate while K only requires that there be a b between any two a's. So it is easy to see that BA_2 divides $U \times U$.

Both monoids have linear 2-party communication complexity. Because of the preceeding remark, it is sufficient to establish this lower bound for BA_2.

First, we need a result from [12]

Fact 5. Let $DISJ(x, y)$ be the Disjointness function, defined as

$$DISJ(x, y) = 1 \text{ iff } x_i = 0 \vee y_i = 0, \text{ for all } 1 \leq i \leq n$$

We have $C^{(2)}(DISJ) = n$.

Lemma 9. $C^{(2)}(BA_2) = \Omega(n)$.

Proof. Disjointness can be recognized by the following linear length program over BA_2. For every pair x_i, y_i, we build a four letter string w. Let $w_1 = a$ if $x_i = 1$ $w_2 = a$ if $y_i = 1$ $w_3 = b$ if $x_i = 1$ $w_4 = a$ if $y_i = 1$. Any letter of w is c otherwise. One can easily check that the concatenation of the w's corresponding to each pair x_i, y_i is a program over BA_2 recognizing $DISJ$. □

Summing up the bounds proved in lemmas 6, 7, 8 and 9, we get :

Theorem 8. *Let M be a finite aperiodic monoid,*

1. $C^{(2)}(M) = \Theta(1)$ *iff M is commutative.*
2. $C^{(2)}(M) = \Theta(\log n)$ *iff M is in* **DA** *and non-commutative.*
3. $C^{(2)}(M) = \Theta(n)$ *iff M is not in* **DA**.

The case with $O(1)$ players By the results of the previous section, we know that any monoid in **DA** has $O(\log n)$ complexity for $O(1)$ players. However, we can do better and for any monoid $M \in$ **DA**, there is a k such that $C^{(k)}(M) = O(1)$ as the next theorem shows.

Theorem 9. *Let $L = A_0^* a_1 A_1^* \ldots A_{k-1}^* a_k A_k^*$ be an unambiguous concatenation, then $L \in CCC^{(k+2)}$.*

Proof. We exhibit a constant cost protocol for L.

Each player in turn verifies if the input he sees is in L. If so he outputs a 1 followed by the identities of the players who see each letter he identified as one of the bookmarks in his factorization. Otherwise, he outputs 0.

The protocol accepts the input if two players outputted a 1 and subsequently identified each other. We claim that this protocol is valid.

First, if the input w is in L, then w can be uniquely factorized as $w = w_0 a_1 w_1 \ldots w_{k-1} a_k w_k$. Two players, at least, see the bookmarks $a_1, \ldots, a_k$. The letters they ignore are taken from the w_i's so they both receive an input which is in L. Moreover, since the concatenation is unambiguous, they must choose these same bookmarks when they factorize their input. Therefore, the protocol will accept.

Conversely, if the protocol accepts, then two players, say P1 and P2, received inputs w^1, w^2 such that $w^1, w^2 \in L$.

Let w^0 be the word obtained from w by erasing letters unknown to either P1 or P2. Since the protocol accepted, w^0 contains the bookmarks of w^1. It can therefore be factorized using these bookmarks. Similarly, w^0 can be factorized using w^2's bookmarks. But by the uniqueness of the factorization, it follows that w^1 and w^2 have the same bookmarks.

Finally, since w^1 and w^2 are in L, and since P1 and P2 collectively know the whole input, w is in L.

The protocol is simultaneous and has cost at most $(k+2)\cdot(1+\log(k+2))$ □

It is not known whether one can, in general, reduce the number of players and keep the communication complexity constant.

Not all aperiodic monoids are in the variety defined by CCC:

Theorem 10. *For any fixed k, $C^{(k)}(U) = \Omega(\log n)$*

Proof. It is shown in [19] that U is universal, that is any boolean function can be recognized by a program of length $O(c^n)$ over U, corresponding to the function's conjunctive normal form.

For any k, we know there exists a language L such that $C^{(k)}(L) = \Omega(n)$. So lemma 4 completes the proof. □

6 Conclusion

In this paper, we have established a number of bridges between communication complexity and algebraic structure of finite monoids. A first question that remains, concerns the communication complexity of the language $(c^*ac^*bc^*)^*$ in the case where $O(1)$ players are involved : we conjecture that its communication complexity is $\Theta(n)$. But the real challenge would be to extend Szegedy's result to constant number of players: we are thus looking for a theorem of the form "language L can be decided in constant communication by $O(1)$ players iff L can be recognized by a program over a monoid that belongs to the variety $\mathbf{V}$". We conjecture that $\mathbf{V}$ should be $\mathbf{DA} \vee \mathbf{G_{nil}}$, the smallest variety that contains $\mathbf{DA}$ and all nilpotent groups. This conjecture is consistent with all results that we have obtained. There is also some combinatorial intuition to support that claim : this variety is the largest one for which all languages can be characterized by subwords (order of appearance and counting with respect to a finite index congruence). A detailed discussion of this idea will be presented in the full paper.

References

1. L. Babai, N. Nisan, and M. Szegedy. Multiparty protocols, pseudorandom generators for logspace, and time-space trade-offs. *J. Comput. Syst. Sci.*, 45(2):204–232, Oct. 1992.
2. D. A. Barrington. Bounded-width polynomial-size branching programs recognize exactly those languages in NC^1. *J. Comput. Syst. Sci.*, 38(1):150–164, Feb. 1989.
3. D. A. M. Barrington, H. Straubing, and D. Thérien. Non-uniform automata over groups. *Information and Computation*, 89(2):109–132, Dec. 1990.
4. D. A. M. Barrington and D. Thérien. Finite monoids and the fine structure of NC^1. *Journal of the ACM*, 35(4):941–952, Oct. 1988.
5. A. K. Chandra, M. L. Furst, and R. J. Lipton. Multi-party protocols. In *Proc. 15th ACM STOC*, pages 94–99, 1983.
6. S. Eilenberg. *Automata, Languages and Machines*, volume B. Academic Press, 1976.
7. V. Grolmusz. Separating the communication complexities of MOD m and MOD p circuits. In *Proc. 33rd IEEE FOCS*, pages 278–287, 1992.
8. V. Grolmusz. A weight-size trade-off for circuits and MOD m gates. In *Proc. 26th ACM STOC*, pages 68–74, 1994.
9. J. Håstad and M. Goldmann. On the power of small-depth threshold circuits. In *Proc. 31st IEEE FOCS*, volume II, pages 610–618, 1990.
10. M. Karchmer and A. Wigderson. Monotone circuits for connectivity require super-logarithmic depth. In *Proc. 20th ACM STOC*, pages 539–550, 1988.
11. E. Kushilevitz and N. Nisan. *Communication Complexity.* Cambridge University Press, 1997.
12. L. Lovász. Communication complexity: a survey. Technical Report CS-TR-204-89, Princeton University, 1989.
13. P. McKenzie, P. Péladeau, and D. Thérien. NC^1: The automata theoretic viewpoint. *Computational Complexity*, 1:330–359, 1991.
14. J.-E. Pin. *Varieties of formal languages.* North Oxford Academic Publishers Ltd, London, 1986.
15. J.-É. Pin, H. Straubing, and D. Thérien. Locally trivial categories and unambiguous concatenation. *J. Pure Applied Algebra*, 52:297–311, 1988.
16. R. Raz and P. McKenzie. Separation of the monotone NC hierarchy. In *Proc. 38thth IEEE FOCS*, 1997.
17. M. Szegedy. Functions with bounded symmetric communication complexity, programs over commutative monoids, and ACC. *J. Comput. Syst. Sci.*, 47(3):405–423, 1993.
18. D. Thérien. Subword counting and nilpotent groups. In L. Cummings, editor, *Combinatorics on Words: Progress and Perspectives*, pages 195–208. Academic Press, 1983.
19. D. Thérien. Programs over aperiodic monoids. *Theoretical Computer Science*, 64(3):271–280, 29 May 1989.
20. A. C. Yao. Some complexity questions related to distributive computing. In *Proc. 11th ACM STOC*, pages 209–213, 1979.

Deciding Global Partial-Order Properties

Rajeev Alur* Ken McMillan** Doron Peled***

Abstract. Model checking of asynchronous systems is traditionally based on the interleaving model, where an execution is modeled by a total order between events. Recently, the use of partial order semantics that allows independent events of concurrent processes to be unordered is becoming popular. Temporal logics that are interpreted over partial orders allow specifications relating global snapshots, and permit reduction algorithms to generate only one representative linearization of every possible partial-order execution during state-space search. This paper considers the satisfiability and the model checking problems for temporal logics interpreted over partially ordered sets of global configurations. For such logics, only undecidability results have been proved previously. In this paper, we present an EXPSPACE decision procedure for a fragment that contains an eventuality operator and its dual. We also sharpen previous undecidability results, which used global predicates over configurations. We show that although our logic allows only local propositions (over events), it becomes undecidable when adding some natural *until* operator.

1 Introduction

The *model checking* problem is to decide whether a finite-state description of a reactive system satisfies a temporal-logic specification. The solutions to this problem have been implemented, and the resulting tools are increasingly being used as debugging aids for industrial designs. All of these solutions employ the so-called *interleaving* semantics in which a single execution of the system is considered to be a totally-ordered sequence of events. The (linear) semantics of the system is, then, a set of total-order executions that the system can possibly generate. The specifications are written in the linear temporal logic LTL. The model checker checks if every execution of the system satisfies the LTL-specification[4].

In contrast to the interleaving semantics, the *partial order semantics* considers a single execution as a partially ordered set of events. The partial order semantics does not distinguish among total-order executions that are *equivalent* up to reordering of independent events, thereby, resulting in a more abstract and faithful representation of concurrency, and has attracted researchers in concurrency theory for many years [8, 12].

* University of Pennsylvania and Bell Laboratories, Email: alur@cis.upenn.edu

** Cadence Berkeley Labs, Email: mcmillan@cadence.com

*** Bell Laboratories and CMU, Email: doron@research.bell-labs.com

[4] In the alternative branching-time paradigm, the semantics of the system is a labeled state-transition graph, and the specification is given as a formula of the *Computation tree logic* (CTL) [2]. Branching-time versions of partial-order semantics are possible (see, for instance, [4]), but are not studied in this paper.

Partial-order semantics, unlike the interleaving semantics, distinguishes between nondeterminism and concurrency. Consequently, specification languages over partial orders can permit a direct representation of properties involving causality and concurrency, for example, serializability.

Partial order specifications are also interesting due to their compatibility with the so-called partial order reductions. The partial-order equivalence among sequences can be exploited to reduce the state-space explosion problem: the cost of generating at least one representative per equivalence class is typically significantly less than the cost of generating all interleavings [5, 9, 10, 15]. If the specification could distinguish between two sequences of the same equivalence class, as is the case with LTL, the above equivalence cannot be used: the same equivalence class may contain both a sequence that satisfies the specification and a sequence that does not. It is possible to refine the equivalence relation, providing more representatives at the expense of using a bigger state space [10]. The alternative solution is to use a specification logic that is directly interpreted over partial orders. This latter approach demands study of decision problems for partial order logics.

How does one define a temporal logic over partial orders? Two approaches have been proposed to write temporal requirements over a model consisting of a set of partially ordered events, or local states of processes. In *local* partial order logics, the truth of a formula is evaluated at a local state, and the temporal modalities relate causal precedences among local states. Examples of such logics include TRPTL [13] and TLC [1]. In *global* partial order logics, the truth of a formula is evaluated in a *global* state, also called a configuration or a slice, which consists of a consistent set of local states. The temporal modalities of a global logic, such as ISTL [6], relate causal precedences among configurations. Global partial order logics are strictly more general than the local ones. In a partial order, unlike in a total order, there are many ways to proceed from one state to the next, and consequently, the syntax of partial order logics, uses path quantifiers as in CTL. For example, if p is a global state predicate asserting that states of all processes are consistent with one another, then the ISTL-formula $\exists\Diamond p$ asserts that p is a possible global snapshot. A system satisfies $\exists\Diamond p$ if every partial-order execution has some linearization containing a p-state. It should be noted that this property cannot be specified in LTL or CTL or any local partial-order logic.

Before we consider the model checking for partial order logics, let us briefly review the solution to the model checking problem for LTL. A system M is viewed as an ω-automaton A_M that generates all possible total-order executions of M. To check whether the system satisfies an LTL-formula φ, the model-checking algorithm first constructs an ω-automaton $A_{\neg\varphi}$ that accepts all the satisfying models of $\neg\varphi$, and tests emptiness of the intersection of the languages of the two automata A_M and $A_{\neg\varphi}$ [16]. For algorithmic verification of partial order logics, the solution is to construct, given a partial order specification φ, an ω-automaton $A_{\neg\varphi}$ that accepts the linearizations of the partial order models of $\neg\varphi$. To check whether the system M satisfies a partial order formula φ, we need to test emptiness of the the intersection of $A_{\neg\varphi}$ and the automaton A_M. Since we know that the automaton $A_{\neg\varphi}$ does not distinguish among the linearizations of the same partial order, the above approach yields a correct result even if A_M generates only one linearization of each partial order execution of M.

Thus, the verification problem for partial order logics can be solved if a partial order specification can be translated to an ω-automaton accepting the linearizations of its models. Consequently, the main challenge in this approach is to translate the modal operators interpreted over a partial-order to requirements on its linearizations. In other words, by examining one linearization, the automaton needs to infer a property of all equivalent linearizations. This goal has already been met for local partial order logics TRPTL and TLC [13, 1]. Unfortunately, the technique used in these constructions does not lead to similar constructions for global partial order logics. Some simple global specification formalisms were even shown to be undecidable [11, 7].

In this paper, we identify a global partial order logic for which the model checking problem is decidable by presenting a tableau construction. This logic is ISTL$^\diamond$, a subset of the logic ISTL obtained by retaining the modalities $\exists\diamond$ and $\exists\bigcirc$, and their duals, but disallowing the modalities $\exists\Box$ or $\exists\mathcal{U}$. The complexity of verifying that a finite state program satisfies a specification in ISTL$^\diamond$ is linear in the number of global states of the program, and doubly exponential in the size of the specification. We also refine the undecidability result of [11] by establishing that the modality $\exists\mathcal{U}$ is sufficient, by itself, to render undecidability.

The decidability for ISTL$^\diamond$ can also be established by translating its formulas to a first-order language of [3] that has variables ranging over local states, monadic predicates, and a binary partial-order relation. However, this approach leads to a decision procedure of nonelementary complexity. Indeed, the translation from requirements on global cuts to linear sequences of local states is difficult due to various factors. We overcome these problems by showing that every ISTL$^\diamond$ formula can be rewritten to a special form such that for each of its eventuality subformulas ψ, there exists a maximal configuration that contains exactly those configurations satisfying ψ. The decision procedure, then, builds on this key insight.

It should be noted that, while the decision procedure for local partial-order logics such as TLC is PSPACE, the decision procedure for the global logic ISTL$^\diamond$ is EXPSPACE. A recent result by Walukiewicz shows a lower bound of EXPSPACE for ISTL$^\diamond$ [17]. The decidability in presence of the operator $\exists\Box$ that is useful in specifying properties such as serializability, is an open problem.

2 A Global Partial-Order Logic

We begin with a model theory for the logic ISTL. Our models can be viewed in one of two ways: either as a partially ordered set of local states (states of individual processes), or as a branching structure (a Kripke model). The Kripke model represents all possible sequences of global states that may be derived from the partial order.

Causal Structures. We will consider first the partially ordered view, which we refer to as a *causal structure*, and then define its relation to a Kripke model. In a causal structure, a state is "local", in the sense that it is occupied by some subset of the processes in the system, which are, in effect, synchronized at that state. All of the states occupied by a given process are totally ordered, but no further ordering is imposed on the structure. Each atomic proposition of the logic is associated with a particular process, and may only label states that are occupied by that process. As an example, the causal structure in Figure 1 shows two concurrent processes that synchronize at a common state.

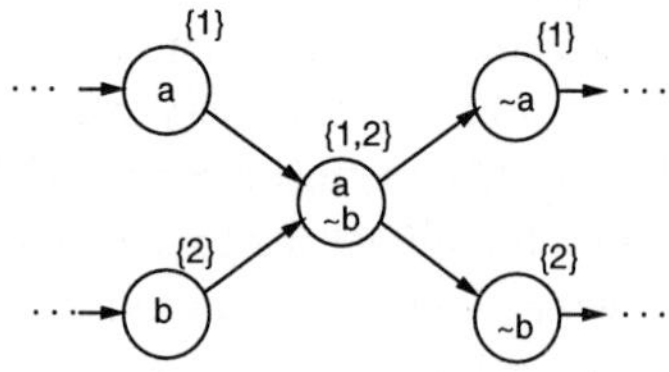

Fig. 1. A two-process causal structure, where $P_1 = \{a\}$ and $P_2 = \{b\}$.

To be more precise, let a *concurrent alphabet* be a set P of propositions that is partitioned into disjoint sets, P_x, for $x = 1 \ldots n$. We use N to denote the set $\{1 \ldots n\}$ of processes. A *causal structure* Γ over a concurrent alphabet P consists of:

- *State-space:* For each process x, a countable infinite set S_x of states. These are the states occupied by x. The set $\cup_x S_x$ of all states is denoted S.
- *Causality relation:* For each process x, a total, well founded order $\preceq_x$ on S_x, whose minimal element is a unique state denoted s^I (the global initial state). The relation $(\cup_x \preceq_x)^*$, is denoted $\preceq$, and must be a partial order.
- *State labeling:* For each process x, a mapping v_x that assigns each state $s \in S_x$, a set $v_x(s) \subseteq P_x$ of propositions true in s.

Causal structures to Kripke models. Now we define the correspondence between causal structures and a restricted class of Kripke models. To do this, we use *configurations* (or *slices*) as our global states. A configuration is a set of states of the causal structure that is left-closed under $\preceq$. This may be thought of as a "partial run" of the structure. Any set of states $\Theta \subseteq S$ can be extended to a configuration $pre(\Theta)$ by simply taking its left closure under $\preceq$. The notion of configuration is illustrated in Figure 2. For

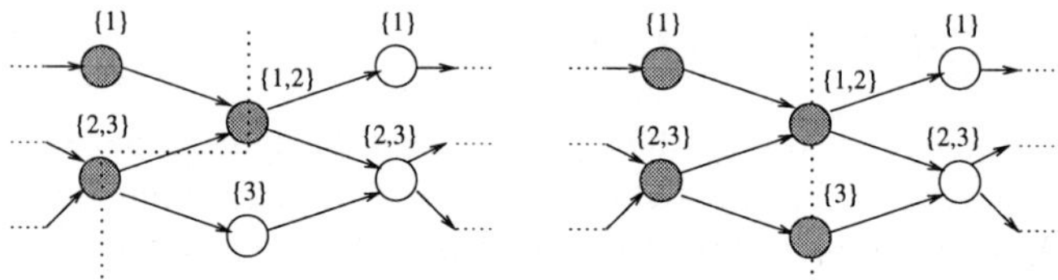

Fig. 2. Two configurations. Each one is a left-closed set of states. The associated cut (dashed line) comprises the elements maximal w.r.t. each process.

a configuration Θ, let fin_Θ be the set of processes x such that $\Theta \cap S_x$ is finite. For any nonempty configuration Θ and any process x in fin_Θ, there is a unique maximal state under the local order $\preceq_x$, we denote this state by Θ^x. If $\Theta \cap S_x$ is infinite, then no such maximal state exists, and let us define $\Theta^x = \perp$ in that case. The tuple $(\Theta^1, \ldots \Theta^n)$ is called the *cut* of the configuration Θ. The notion of a cut is illustrated in Figure 2. We note that any nonempty configuration (finite or infinite) is uniquely defined by its cut.

Configurations are ordered by the subset relation: if $\Theta \subseteq \Delta$ then the configuration Δ is in the future of the configuration Θ. The ordering $\subseteq$ is a partial order over the set of configurations, and is called the *global partial order*. This leads to the definition of a Kripke model of a causal structure. Given a causal structure $\Gamma = (S, \preceq, v)$ over a concurrent alphabet P, let the Kripke model $K_\Gamma = (T, R, L)$, where

- T, the state set, is the set of finite, nonempty, configurations of Γ.
- R, the transition relation, is the transitive reduction of the partial order $(T, \subseteq)$, that is, $\Theta \, R \, \Delta$ if $\Theta \subset \Delta$ and there is no configuration Θ' such that $\Theta \subset \Theta' \subset \Delta$.
- L, the labeling function, maps any configuration $\Theta \in T$ to the set of propositions $\cup_x v_x(\Theta^x)$. That is, a local proposition of a process x is true in Θ iff it is true in the maximal state Θ^x.

The left and right configurations in Figure 2 are related by R. Figure 3 shows a causal structure and the associated Kripke model.

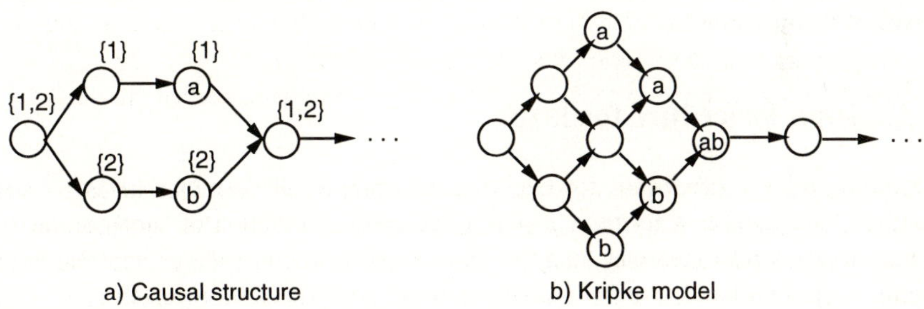

Fig. 3. Causal structure and associated Kripke model.

Syntax and Semantics. The formulas of ISTL are defined inductively by the grammar

$$\varphi \ := \ p \mid \neg\varphi \mid \varphi \wedge \varphi \mid \exists\Diamond\varphi \mid \exists\bigcirc\,\varphi \mid \varphi\,\exists\mathcal{U}\,\psi \mid \exists\Box\varphi$$

where p is an atomic proposition. Given a causal structure Γ, the formulas of ISTL are interpreted over configurations of Γ. The interpretation of modalities is as in CTL interpreted over the Kripke structure K_Γ.

Let φ be a ISTL-formula, Γ be a causal structure, and Θ be a configuration of Γ. Then, the satisfaction relation $(\Gamma, \Theta) \models \varphi$ is defined inductively below

$\Theta \models p$ iff $p \in L(\Theta)$ for an atomic proposition p;
$\Theta \models \neg\varphi$ iff $\Theta \not\models \varphi$;
$\Theta \models \varphi \wedge \psi$ iff $\Theta \models \varphi$ and $\Theta \models \psi$;
$\Theta \models \exists\Diamond\varphi$ iff $\Theta \subseteq \Delta$ and $\Delta \models \varphi$ for some configuration Δ;
$\Theta \models \exists\bigcirc\varphi$ iff $\Theta R \Delta$ and $\Delta \models \varphi$ for some configuration Δ;
$\Theta \models \varphi \exists\mathcal{U} \psi$ iff there exists a finite sequence $\Theta_0 \ldots \Theta_n$ of configurations such that (i) $\Theta_0 = \Theta$, (ii) $\Theta_i R \Theta_{i+1}$ for $0 \leq i < n$, (iii) $\Theta_n \models \psi$, and (iv) $\Theta_i \models \varphi$ for all $0 \leq i < n$;
$\Theta \models \exists\Box\varphi$ iff there exists an infinite sequence $\Theta_0\Theta_1 \ldots$ of configurations such that (i) $\Theta_0 = \Theta$, (ii) $\Theta_i R \Theta_{i+1}$ for all i, and (iii) $\Theta_i \models \varphi$ for all i.

Denote $\Gamma \models \varphi$ iff $(\Gamma, \{s^I\}) \models \varphi$. As in CTL, we can define a variety of auxiliary logical (e.g. disjunction) and temporal (e.g. $\forall\Box$) operators. We use $\wedge_k \varphi_k$ to denote the conjunction of finitely many formulas. We will consider various fragments of ISTL by restricting the syntax to a subset of the temporal modalities: the fragment ISTL$^\Diamond$ allows only $\exists\Diamond$ modality, the fragment ISTL$^{\Diamond,\bigcirc}$ allows $\exists\Diamond$ and $\exists\bigcirc$, and the fragment ISTL$^{\mathcal{U}}$ allows only $\exists\mathcal{U}$ (note that $\exists\Diamond$ is definable from $\exists\mathcal{U}$). All these fragments are closed under boolean operations.

A typical ISTL$^\Diamond$-formula is $\forall\Box(p \rightarrow \exists\Diamond q)$, where p and q are assertions about global snapshots. It means that no matter how the system evolves, if p is a possible snapshot at some time, then q is a possible snapshot at a later time. No formula of LTL or TLC is equivalent to this formula.

3 Decision Procedure for ISTL$^\Diamond$

We now describe a procedure for deciding satisfiability of formulas of ISTL$^\Diamond$. The procedure first rewrites a formula φ into a boolean combination of subformulas that use negation in a restricted way, and the second step is to construct an automaton that recognizes the set of all linearizations of models of such special formulas.

Normal Form. We consider formulas of a special type, namely, the ones in which negation is not applied to a conjunction. The set of *normal-form* ISTL$^\Diamond$-formulas is the least set such that:

(1) Every atomic proposition is a normal-form formula.
(2) $\exists\Diamond \wedge_k \varphi_k$ is a normal-from formula whenever all φ_k are.
(3) If φ is a normal-form formula then so is $\neg\varphi$.

For example, the formula $\exists\Diamond(a \wedge \neg\exists\Diamond b)$ is in normal form, whereas the formulas $\exists\Diamond(a \vee \exists\Diamond b)$ and $a \wedge \exists\Diamond b$ are not.

An *eventuality* formula of ISTL$^\Diamond$ is a formula of the form $\exists\Diamond\varphi$. For an eventuality formula $\varphi = \exists\Diamond\wedge_k\varphi_k$, the formulas φ_k are called *conjuncts* of φ. Next, we establish that we do not lose any expressive power by restricting ourselves to normal-form formulas: each ISTL$^\Diamond$ formula is equivalent to a boolean combination of normal-form formulas.

Proposition 1 *For every eventuality-formula φ of* ISTL$^\Diamond$*, there exists a* ISTL$^\Diamond$*-formula ψ such that (1) φ and ψ are equivalent, (2) ψ is a disjunction of at most $2^{|\varphi|}$ normal-form* *eventuality-formulas, and (3) the number of distinct eventuality-subformulas of ψ is at most* $2^{|\varphi|+1}$.

Proof: The proof is by induction on the size of φ. Let $\varphi_1, \ldots \varphi_k$ be the top-level eventuality-subformulas of φ (i.e. each φ_i is a subformula of φ, and there is no eventuality-subformula ψ of φ such that φ_i is a (strict) subformula of ψ). Let m be the length of φ, counting each φ_i to be of size 1, and let m_i be the actual size of φ_i. Then, $|\varphi| \geq m + m_1 + \cdots + m_k$ (assuming that the formula is fully parenthesized). Rewrite φ in disjunctive normal form while treating each φ_i as a proposition. Since $\exists\Diamond$ distributes over disjunction, we have φ equivalent to $\bigvee_l \psi_l$ with at most 2^m disjuncts ψ_l. Each disjunct ψ_l is of the form $\exists\Diamond \bigwedge_j \chi_j$ with at most m conjuncts χ_j. Each such conjunct χ_j is either a proposition, a negated proposition, some φ_i, or some negated φ_i. Rewrite each φ_i as a disjunction of normal-form formulas using induction: each φ_i is equivalent to a disjunction of at most 2^{m_i} normal-form formulas. It follows that $\neg\varphi_i$ is also equivalent to a disjunction of at most 2^{m_i} normal-form formulas. Let us revisit $\psi_l = \exists\Diamond \bigwedge_j \chi_j$. We need to do additional rewriting to get rid of the newly introduced disjunctions. It follows that ψ_l is equivalent to a disjunction of at most $2^{m_1+\cdots+m_k}$ normal-form formulas. Hence, φ is equivalent to at most $2^m 2^{m_1+\cdots+m_k}$ normal-form formulas. Using $|\varphi| \leq m + m_1 + \cdots + m_k$, we have the number of disjuncts bounded by $2^{|\varphi|}$.

To count the number of eventuality-subformulas, observe that the number of eventuality-subformulas after rewriting equals the number of disjuncts at the top-level plus the number eventuality-subformulas generated by rewriting each φ_i. This is bounded by $2^{|\varphi|} + 2^{m_1+1} + \cdots + 2^{m_k+1}$. Using $|\varphi| \geq m + m_1 + \cdots + m_k$, we can bound this number by $2^{|\varphi|+1}$. □

Maximal configurations. We now show that every normal form eventuality formula φ has a maximal configuration max_φ, such that a configuration satisfies φ exactly when it is contained in max_φ. Figure 4 shows a formula and its maximal configuration in two different causal structures. We note that the maximal configuration need not be finite (and may also be empty, in the case where the formula is false everywhere). Also, note that such unique maximal configurations may not exist for formulas other than eventuality formulas in normal form. For instance, for the left causal structure of Figure 4, there is no unique maximal configuration satisfying the formula $\exists\Diamond(a \vee b)$.

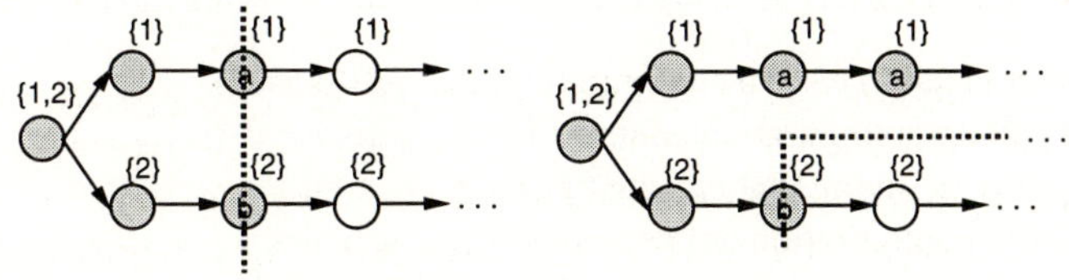

Fig. 4. Maximal configuration for the formula $\exists\Diamond(a \wedge b)$ in two different causal structures. Note that in one case, the maximal configuration is infinite for process 1.

In the following, we identify every formula φ with the set $\{\Theta \mid \Theta \models \varphi\}$ of configurations satisfying that formula. We also note that a set of configurations is "$\subseteq$-closed" if every subset of a member is also in the set, "$\supseteq$-closed" if every superset of a member is also in the set, and "$\cup$-closed" if the union of any two members is also in the set. First, if φ and ψ are $\cup$-closed then $\varphi \wedge \psi$ is $\cup$-closed. Second, for $\varphi = \exists\Diamond\psi$, φ is $\subseteq$-closed, $\neg\varphi$ is $\supseteq$-closed, and if ψ is $\cup$-closed then so is φ.

Lemma 2 *If φ is an eventuality formula in normal form then φ is $\cup$-closed.*

Proof: The satisfaction of an atomic proposition depends upon the corresponding local state. Hence, if φ is a proposition or a negated proposition, then φ is $\cup$-closed. If φ is a negated eventuality-formula, then φ is $\supseteq$-closed, and hence, $\cup$-closed. Now consider $\varphi = \exists\Diamond \bigwedge_k \varphi_k$, with each φ_k in normal-form. By induction, φ_k are $\cup$-closed. Then so is $\bigwedge_k \varphi_k$, and hence, so is φ. □

Proposition 3 *Let φ be an eventuality-formula in normal form. For every causal structure, there exists a configuration max_φ such that $\Theta \models \varphi$ iff $\Theta \subseteq max_\varphi$.*

Tableau constraints. We now transform the problem of satisfiability of a normal form eventuality formula φ by augmenting the causal structure with a set of new atomic propositions (each labeling the maximal configuration of some subformula) and formulating a set of "tableau" constraints, such that there exists an augmented structure satisfying the tableau constraints exactly when there exists a structure satisfying φ.

Given a concurrent alphabet P and a normal form formula φ, let P^φ be P augmented by introducing a special proposition c_ψ for every eventuality-subformula ψ. The propositions c_ψ differ from ordinary propositions in that they are allowed to label any subset of the state space S, rather than just the states of one process. In particular, the states labeled with c_ψ are intended to represent max_ψ, the maximal configuration satisfying ψ. We will say that ψ is "correctly labeled" in a given causal structure if c_ψ labels exactly the states in the maximal configuration of ψ. If the maximal configuration max_ψ contains only finitely many states of a process x, then the maximal local state of x that is labeled with c_ψ is denoted c_ψ^x.

We now wish to formulate a set of constraints that guarantee that a formula is correctly labeled, given that its own subformulas are correctly labeled. Suppose ψ is an arbitrary eventuality-subformula of φ. It must be of the form $\psi = \exists\Diamond(\psi_1 \wedge \cdots \wedge \psi_k)$. We note that c_ψ is a correct labeling exactly when the following three conditions hold:

(1) (the set labeled) c_ψ is a configuration (*i.e.*, left-closed),

(2) every finite configuration contained in c_ψ satisfies ψ (if c_ψ is finite, this is the same as saying that c_ψ satisfies $\psi_1 \wedge \cdots \wedge \psi_k$),

(3) no finite configuration not contained in c_ψ satisfies $\psi_1 \wedge \cdots \wedge \psi_k$ (else c_ψ is not maximal).

Let condition 1 above be denoted C_ψ^1. Condition 2, assuming all of the subformulas of ψ are correctly labeled, is equivalent to the following condition, which we denote C_ψ^2: If c_ψ is nonempty, then

(i) for all $i = 1, \ldots k$, if ψ_i is an eventuality formula, then $c_\psi \subseteq c_{\psi_i}$,
(ii) for all $i = 1, \ldots k$, if ψ_i is a negated eventuality formula, then $c_\psi \not\subseteq c_{\psi_i}$,
(iii) for all $i = 1, \ldots k$, if ψ_i is an atomic (resp. a negated atomic) formula in P_x and $x \in fin_{c_\psi}$ then $\psi_i \in L(c_\psi^x)$ (resp. $\psi_i \notin L(c_\psi^x)$),
(iv) There exists an infinite sequence of configurations $\Theta_1 \subset \Theta_2 \subset \cdots$, such that for every process x if $S_x \subseteq c_\psi$ then $S_x \subseteq \cup_j \Theta_j$ and for every atomic (or negated atomic) formula ψ_i in P_x, $\Theta_j \models \psi_i$ (resp. $\Theta_j \not\models \psi_i$) for all j.

The last condition guarantees that if c_ψ is infinite, then every configuration contained in c_ψ is contained in some finite configuration satisfying $\psi_1 \wedge \cdots \wedge \psi_k$. Finally we deal with condition 3, which guarantees that c_ψ is in fact maximal. Assuming subformulas of ψ are correctly labeled, it is equivalent to the following, which we denote C_ψ^3: There does not exist a finite configuration $\Theta \not\subseteq c_\psi$ such that, for all ψ_i, $i = 1 \ldots k$:

(i) if ψ_i is an eventuality formula, then $\Theta \subseteq c_{\psi_i}$,
(ii) if ψ_i is an atomic (resp. a negated atomic) proposition in P_x, then $\psi_i \in L(\Theta_x)$ (resp. $\psi_i \notin L(\Theta_x)$).

Observe that, in C_ψ^3, there is no requirement that Θ satisfy negated eventuality conjuncts. Now, let C_ψ denote the condition that ψ and all its subformulas are correctly labeled. We then have following by induction on the structure of ψ and the semantics of the logic:

Lemma 4 *A normal form formula φ is satisfiable exactly when there exists a causal structure over P^φ, satisfying C_φ, where c_φ is true in the initial state.*

In the following, we show how to determine satisfiability of φ algorithmically, by coding causal structures as infinite strings, and constructing an ω-automaton that exactly characterizes C_φ.

Causal structures as ω-words. Let Σ be an alphabet consisting of truth assignments to the propositions $P^\varphi \cup \{at_1, \ldots, at_n\}$. The new propositions at_x will be used to encode the set of processes synchronized at a given state. We say that the causal structure Γ *generates* an ω-word $\overline{a} \in \Sigma^\omega$ iff there exists an enumeration $s_1 s_2 \ldots$ of the state-space S such that (1) for all processes x, $at_x \in \overline{a}_i$ iff $s_i \in S_x$, (2) for all $p \in P$, $p \in \overline{a}_i$ iff $p \in L(s_i)$, and (3) for all $k < l$, it is not the case that $s_l \preceq s_k$. That is, the ω-words generated by Γ are exactly its linearizations, appropriately encoded. Since the partial order $\preceq$ on a causal structure is exactly characterized by the set of total orders on the process state spaces S_x, it follows that:

Lemma 5 *For an ω-word $\overline{a}$ over Σ, there is at most one (up to isomorphism) causal structure $\Gamma_{\overline{a}}$ such that $\Gamma_{\overline{a}}$ generates $\overline{a}$.*

Thus, for a fixed concurrent alphabet P, causal structures can be represented by ω-words over Σ. In this sense, we can say that an ω-automaton A over Σ "recognizes" a set of causal structures, which are exactly those that generate some word accepted by A. By building a finite recognizer for each "tableau constraint" C_ψ^i, and constructing the product of these automata, we obtain a recognizer for C_φ. Testing satisfiability of φ then reduces to testing non-emptiness of this automaton.

Lemma 6 *For any normal form formula φ, there exists a nondeterministic Büchi automaton recognizing C_φ of $O(2^{O(m^2+m2^n)})$ states, where m is the size of φ.*

Proof: For any eventuality subformula ψ, there exists a deterministic Büchi automaton recognizing C^1_ψ of $O(2^n)$ states. This is because left-closure of c_ψ can be tested by a product of n 2-state automata, each of which tests closure w.r.t. $\preceq_x$.

Now consider verification of C^2_ψ for an eventuality subformula ψ. Testing containment of configurations (for the eventuality subformula cases) requires no information to be remembered about previous states. For each negated eventuality subformula, a two-state automaton with a Büchi acceptance condition is needed to ensure non-containment. For the atomic subformulas, the automaton guesses initially for each process whether c_ψ contains a finite or infinite number of states. For the finite case, it must guess the last state in the configuration. For the infinite case it must guess an infinite number of configurations Θ. However, only one configuration Θ need be "remembered" at any given time. This yields one 4-state machine per process. A Büchi acceptance condition requires that a new configuration Θ be completed infinitely often. Hence, there exists a nondeterministic Büchi automaton recognizing C^2_ψ of $O(4^n 2^k)$ states, where k is the number negated eventuality formulas appearing as conjuncts of ψ.

Now consider the requirement C^3_ψ for an eventuality subformula ψ. This condition states that there *does not exist* a finite configuration satisfying $\psi_1 \ldots \psi_k$, but strictly containing c_ψ (ensuring maximality of c_ψ). The automaton guesses such a configuration. Verifying that the guess is a configuration requires 2^n states. Remaining checks require no additional state. *Complementing* this automaton, by the subset construction, increases the size to $O(2^{2^n})$ states.

The automaton recognizing C_φ is just the product of the above automata for all eventuality subformulas of φ. □

Given the automaton for C_φ, we finally need to determine whether it recognizes any causal structures where φ is true in the initial state. This requires an automaton to accept those ω-words which are in fact generated by some causal structure.

Lemma 7 *There is a Büchi automaton G_n accepting exactly those words generated by some causal structure over P^φ, of size $O(1)$.*

Theorem 8 *Satisfiability of any* ISTL$^\diamond$ *formula φ can be tested in $O(2^{2^{O(m+n)}})$ time, where m is the size of φ.*

Proof: The formula φ can be translated to boolean combination of normal form formulas containing a total of $O(2^m)$ eventuality-subformulas. The product of the automata for C_ψ for each of these subformulas has $O((2^{O((2^m)^2+2^m 2^n)})) = O(2^{2^{O(m+n)}})$ states. Take the product of this automaton with G_n and a 2-state automaton that checks the boolean combination at the initial state, and check emptiness of this automaton. □

By a standard argument, it is possible to establish that the decision procedure can be implemented in space exponential in the size of the input, and thus, the problem is in EXPSPACE. Walukiewicz has recently shown an EXPSPACE lower bound [17].

4 Extensions

Next-time operator. The fragment ISTL$^{\Diamond,\bigcirc}$ contains the modalities $\exists\Diamond$ and $\exists\bigcirc$. The construction of the previous section for ISTL$^{\Diamond}$ relies on (1) it suffices to consider only boolean combinations of normal form formulas, and (2) the set of configurations satisfying a normal form formula can be characterized by a maximal configuration. Both these properties continue to hold even after the introduction of the next-time operator: satisfiability of an ISTL$^{\Diamond,\bigcirc}$ formula is decidable is EXPSPACE.

Undecidability of ISTL$^{\mathcal{U}}$. In [11] it was shown that ISTL is undecidable. We sharpen the result of [11] by showing that the until operator $\exists\mathcal{U}$ is sufficient to prove undecidability, even in the absence of global propositions.

Theorem 9 *The logic* ISTL$^{\mathcal{U}}$ *is undecidable.*

Proof Sketch: By reduction from the HALTING problem. It is possible to show that one can encode in ISTL$^{\mathcal{U}}$ two processes which never interact. Each process represents a sequence of instantaneous descriptions (IDs) of a Turing machine tape. We can assert that each processes consists of a sequence of IDs, the first ID contains an initial state, and the last ID contains an accepting state. Next, we can assert that the two sequences of IDs are the same. To do this, we assert that there exists an interleaving that alternates between the events of the two processes. Then we can compare each event of the first process with the one that follows it (and belongs to the other process) on this interleaving sequence. Finally, we assert that there exists an interleaving that alternates between the events of the two processes after completing the events corresponding to the first ID in the first process. Thus, this is an interleaving that differ from the previous one by shifting the second process by one ID. We can now assert that the transformation from one ID to its successor follow the execution of a transition of the Turing machine by comparing adjacent events on the latter interleaving. Alternation is not strict here, to allow some IDs to be longer than their predecessors. □

Relation to monadic first-order logic of partial order. The decidability of the logic ISTL$^{\Diamond,\bigcirc}$ can be seen directly by the fact that one can encode a formula of the type $\exists\Diamond\varphi$ and $\exists\bigcirc\varphi$ in first order language with the causal order $\preceq$. Specifically, consider the language $\mathcal{L}$ that contains first-order variables, second-order monadic variables (sets or propositions), logical connectives, quantification over first-order variables, and the binary relation $\preceq$. The formulas of $\mathcal{L}$ are interpreted over causal structures. When the relation $\preceq$ is generated by the union of total orders $\preceq_x$, one per each process, the set of linearizations of causal structures satisfying a formula of $\mathcal{L}$ is ω-regular, and can be characterized by a Büchi automaton [3].

While the logic ISTL$^{\Diamond,\bigcirc}$ can be translated to $\mathcal{L}$, the undecidability of the logic ISTL$^{\mathcal{U}}$ implies that the until operator $\exists\mathcal{U}$ is not definable using second order formulas over partial orders. It is possible to define a different until operator $\mathcal{U}$: $\Theta \models \varphi\mathcal{U}\psi$ iff for some $\Theta \subseteq \Delta$, $\Delta \models \psi$, and for each $\Theta \subseteq \Theta' \subset \Delta$, $\Theta' \models \varphi$. This version is decidable, but has nonelementary complexity [17].

Model checking. A system M of concurrently executing processes generates a set of causal structures. The system M satisfies a requirement given as a formula φ of ISTL, if every causal structure generated by A satisfies φ. The decision procedure outlined in the previous section can be employed to obtain an automata-theoretic solution to the model checking problem of ISTL$^{\diamond}$. From M, we first construct an automaton A_M that accepts linearizations of the causal structures of M. Then, we construct the automaton $A_{\neg\varphi}$ that accepts the linearizations of the causal structures satisfying $\neg\varphi$. The system M satisfies the specification φ iff the intersection of the languages of the two automata A_M and $A_{\neg\varphi}$ is empty. Model checking using representatives outlined in [5, 10, 15] can now be used as a heuristic improvement: The automaton A_M need not generate all linearizations, but at least one linearization of every causal structure.

References

1. R. Alur, W. Penczek, and D. Peled. Model-checking of causality properties. *10th Symposium on Logic in Computer Science*, 90–100, 1995.
2. E.M. Clarke and E.A. Emerson. Design and synthesis of synchronization skeletons using branching time temporal logic. *Workshop on Logic of Programs*, LNCS 131, 52–71, 1981.
3. W. Ebinger. Logical definability of trace languages. In V. Diekert, G. Rozenberg (Eds.) *The Book of Traces*, World Scientific, 382–390, 1995.
4. J. Esparza. Model checking using net unfolding. *Science of Computer Programming* 23, 1994.
5. P. Godefroid and P. Wolper. A partial approach to model checking. *Information and Computation* 110 (2), 305–326, 1994.
6. S. Katz and D. Peled. Interleaving set temporal logic. *Theoretical Computer Science* 75, 21–43, 1992.
7. K. Lodaya, R. Parikh, R. Ramanujam, and P.S. Thiagarajan. A logical study of distributed transitions systems. *Information and Computation* 119, 91–118, 1985.
8. A. Mazurkiewicz. Trace Theory. In W. Brauer, W. Reisig, G. Rozenberg (eds.), *Advances in Petri Nets 1986*, LNCS 255, 279–324, 1987.
9. K.L. McMillan. Using unfoldings to avoid the state explosion problem in the verification of asynchronous circuits. *Fourth CAV*, LNCS 663, 164-177, 1992.
10. D. Peled. Combining partial order reductions with on-the-fly model checking. *Sixth Conference on Computer Aided Verification*, LNCS 818, 377–390, 1994.
11. W. Penczek. On undecidability of propositional temporal logics on trace systems. *Information Processing Letters* 43, 147–153, 1992.
12. V.R. Pratt. Modeling concurrency with partial orders. *Intl. J. of Parallel Programming* 15 (1), 33–71, 1986.
13. P.S. Thiagarajan. A trace based extension of linear time temporal logic. *Ninth Symposium on Logic in Computer Science*, 1994.
14. P.S. Thiagarajan and I. Walukiewicz. An expressively complete linear time temporal logic for Mazurkiewicz traces. *12th Symposium on Logic in Computer Science*, 1997.
15. A. Valmari. A Stubborn attack on state explosion. *Proc. 2nd Conference on Computer-Aided Verification*, LNCS 531, 156–165, 1990.
16. M.Y. Vardi and P. Wolper. An automata-theoretic approach to automatic program verification. *First Symposium on Logic in Computer Science*, 332–344, 1986.
17. I. Walukiewicz. Difficult configurations – on the complexity of LTrL. *25th International Colloquium on Automata, Languages, and Programming*, 1998.

Simple Linear-Time Algorithms for Minimal Fixed Points*
(Extended Abstract)

Xinxin Liu and Scott A. Smolka

Department of Computer Science
State University of New York at Stony Brook
Stony Brook, NY 11794 USA

{xinxin,sas}@cs.sunysb.edu

Abstract. We present global and local algorithms for evaluating minimal fixed points of dependency graphs, a general problem in fixed-point computation and model checking. Our algorithms run in linear-time, matching the complexity of the best existing algorithms for similar problems, and are simple to understand. The main novelty of our global algorithm is that it does not use the counter and "reverse list" data structures commonly found in existing linear-time global algorithms. This distinction plays an essential role in allowing us to easily derive our local algorithm from our global one. Our local algorithm is distinguished from existing linear-time local algorithms by a combination of its simplicity and suitability for direct implementation.
We also provide linear-time reductions from the problems of computing minimal and maximal fixed points in Boolean graphs to the problem of minimal fixed-point evaluation in dependency graphs. This establishes dependency graphs as a suitable framework in which to express and compute alternation-free fixed points.
Finally, we relate HORNSAT, the problem of Horn formula satisfiability, to the problem of minimal fixed-point evaluation in dependency graphs. In particular, we present straightforward, linear-time reductions between these problems for both directions of reducibility. As a result, we derive a linear-time local algorithm for HORNSAT, the first of its kind as far as we are aware.

1 Introduction

Model checking [CE81, QS82, CES86] is a verification technique aimed at determining whether a system specification possesses a property expressed as a temporal logic formula. Model checking has enjoyed wide success in verifying, or finding design errors in, real-life systems. An interesting account of a number of these success stories can be found in [CW96].

Model checking has spurred interest in evaluating *fixed points*, as these can be used to express basic system properties, such as safety and liveness. Probably, the most canonical temporal logic for expressing fixed-point properties of systems is the

* Research supported in part by NSF grants CCR-9505562 and CCR-9705998, and AFOSR grants F49620-95-1-0508 and F49620-96-1-0087.

modal mu-calculus [Pra81, Koz83], which makes explicit use of the dual fixed-point operators μ (least or minimal fixed point) and ν (greatest or maximal fixed point).

Model-checking algorithms come in two types: global and local. In a *global* algorithm, the entire transition system representing the system to be analyzed is constructed in advance of the model-checking computation; this can sometimes lead to exceedingly large memory requirements due to the ***state explosion*** problem. An alternative is *local* model checking [Lar88, SW91, Lar92], in which the state space is constructed incrementally, as the model-checking computation proceeds. An advantage of local model checking is that pruning is often possible: how much of the state space actually has to be explored depends on how much of it turns out to be relevant to establishing satisfaction of the formula to be verified.

In this paper, we present linear-time algorithms for global and local evaluation of minimal fixed points of *Dependency Graphs*, an abstract framework for fixed-point computation. Dependency graphs are a special case of the Partitioned Dependency Graphs (PDGs) presented in [LRS98]. We later provide linear-time reductions from both the problems of evaluating maximal and minimal fixed points of Boolean Graphs [And94] to that of evaluating minimal fixed points of dependency graphs. Thus, the generality of the problem of minimal fixed-point evaluation in dependency graphs subsumes that of many other problems of maximal and minimal fixed-point computation, such as those found in Boolean graphs [And94], Boolean equation systems [VL94], the alternation-free modal mu-calculus, and the alternation-free equational mu-calculus [CKS92, BC96].

Our algorithms are very simple in nature, perhaps deceptively so, and this is partially a consequence of the abstractness of the dependency graph framework. We describe our algorithms both at an abstract level of dependency-graph computation, and at a lower level in terms of arrays and lists, suitable for direct implementation.

Several linear-time global [CS93, AC88, And94] and local [And94, VL94] algorithms for similar fixed-point computation problems have previously appeared in the literature. The global algorithms in [CS93, AC88, And94] all use counters and "reverse list" data structures. In terms of the minimal fixed point of a Boolean equation system, the counter of a variable v keeps track of the number of remaining zero-valued variables in the right-hand side of v's conjunctive defining equation, while a reverse list records, for each variable v, the equation right-hand sides in which v appears. Reverse lists enable fast access to counters when modification is required. Counters and reverse lists are first seen in an algorithm for deciding the satisfiability of Horn Formulae [DG84].

A main novelty of our global algorithm is that it does not use counters and reverse lists. This distinction plays an essential role in allowing us to easily derive our local algorithm from our global one.

Our local algorithm is distinguished from existing linear-time local algorithms as follows. The local algorithm of [VL94] is expressed at an abstract level only; no implementation-level description is provided and the details of such an implementation, particularly one that is linear-time, are not obvious. The local algorithm of [And94] is considerably more complex than our local algorithm, involving mutually recursive calls between procedures ***visit*** ("visit a node") and ***fwtn*** ("find a witness").

In this paper, we also clarify the relationship between minimal fixed-point evaluation of dependency graphs and HORNSAT, the problem of Horn formula satisfiability (see, for example, [HW74]). In particular, we present straightforward, linear-time reductions between these problems for both directions of reducibility. As a result, we derive a linear-time local algorithm for HORNSAT, the first of its kind as far as we are aware.

Relatedly, Shukla et al. [SHIR96] consider the reduction of model checking in the alternation-free modal mu-calculus to HORNSAT, but not the other direction. They further mention that they "have developed HORNSAT-based methods to capture the tableau based local model checking in [Cle90] and [SW91]," but provide no details. In any event, a local algorithm for HORNSAT based on a tableau method is unlikely to be linear-time.

In [LRS98], a local algorithm for computing fixed points of arbitrary alternation depth is presented. Although in this paper we treat the problem of computing alternation-free fixed points, which is a special case of the problem solved by the algorithm in [LRS98], the algorithm presented here is based on completely different ideas, and as a result runs faster than the algorithm of [LRS98] on instances of alternation-free fixed points (linear vs cubic). We comment more in the Conclusions about how to combine the ideas of the two algorithms, in search for faster algorithms for arbitrary fixed points.

The structure of the rest of this paper is as follows. Section 2 presents our dependency-graph framework. Our linear-time global and local algorithms are the subject of Section 3. Section 4 contains our reductions from minimal and maximal Boolean graph fixed-point computation to dependency graph evaluation, while the interreducibility results involving HORNSAT are presented in Section 5. Finally, Section 6 concludes.

2 Dependency Graphs

A *dependency graph* is a pair (V, E), where V is a set of *vertices* and $E \subseteq V \times \wp(V)$ is a set of *hyper-edges*. For a hyper-edge $e = (v, S)$ of a dependency graph G, we call v the *source* of e and S the *target set* of e.

Example 1. $G_0 = (V_0, E_0)$ is a dependency graph where $V_0 = \{u, v, w\}$, $E_0 = \{(u, \emptyset), (u, \{v, w\})(v, \{u, w\}), (w, \{u, v\})\}$. ■

Let $G = (V, E)$ be a dependency graph. An *assignment* A of G is a function from V to $\{0, 1\}$. A *post-fixed-point assignment* F of G is an assignment such that, for every $v \in V$, whenever $(v, S) \in E$ such that for all $v' \in S$ it holds that $F(v') = 1$, then $F(v) = 1$. If we take the standard partial order $\sqsubseteq$ between assignments of dependency graph G such that $A \sqsubseteq A'$ just in case $A(v) \leq A'(v)$ for all $v \in V$ (using the usual order $0 < 1$), then by a straightforward application of the Knaster-Tarski fixed-point theorem, there exists a unique minimum post-fixed-point assignment which we will write as $F^G_{\min}$.

Our aim is to find efficient algorithms which, for a given $G = (V, E)$, computes $F^G_{\min}$ or $F^G_{\min}(v)$, for some $v \in V$. The former problem is one of *global* fixed-point computation, and the latter is one of *local* fixed-point computation.

For the reader familiar with *boolean equation systems* [VL94], a dependency graph (V, E) can be viewed as a boolean equation system with $x \in V$ having the equation $x = \bigvee_{(x,S)\in E} \bigwedge_{y\in S} y$, and $F^G_{\min}$ corresponding to the minimal solution of the boolean equation system. For the dependency graph of Example 1, the boolean equation system is $u = \mathbf{true} \vee (v \wedge w), v = u \wedge w, w = u \wedge v$. Subsequently, in Section 4, we also discuss the relationship between dependency graphs and *boolean graphs* [And94].

3 Algorithms

In this section, we present our two algorithms, a global algorithm that computes $F^G_{\min}$, and a local algorithm that computes $F^G_{\min}(v)$, where G is the input dependency graph and v is a vertex of G. We first describe the global algorithm using mathematical entities of functions and sets, without considering the detailed implementation data structures. The correctness of the algorithm is easy to see from such a description. Later we will furnish the global algorithm with more efficient data structures. We then modify the global algorithm to obtain the local algorithm.

3.1 The Global Algorithm

The high-level description of the global algorithm is given in Figure 1. The algorithm takes as input a dependency graph $G = (V, E)$ and computes an assignment A that is an approximation of $F^G_{\min}$ and such that upon termination $A = F^G_{\min}$.

```
W := E;
for v ∈ V do
    A(v) := 0; D(v) := ∅;
od
while W ≠ ∅ do
    let e = (v, S) ∈ W;
    W := W − {e};
    if ∀v' ∈ S. A(v') = 1 then
                        A(v) := 1; W := W ∪ D(v);
                    else
                        let v' ∈ S & A(v') = 0;
                        D(v') := D(v') ∪ {e};
    fi
od
```

Fig. 1. Algorithm Global1

Besides A, the algorithm also maintains a set W containing all of the hyper-edges waiting to be processed, and a function $D : V \to \wp(E)$ that, for each $v \in V$, records in $D(v)$ the hyper-edges which have been processed under the assumption that $A(v) = 0$. Here we adopt the common idea of using A to approximate $F^G_{\min}$ from below. Thus, in the initialization phase, $A(v)$ is set to 0, $D(v)$ to $\emptyset$, for every $v \in V$, and W to E, the hyper-edge set of G. The main part of the algorithm consists of a single while-loop that repeatedly processes the hyper-edges remaining in W. The algorithm terminates upon completion of the while-loop.

The intuition behind the processing of each $e = (v, S) \in W$ in the body of the while-loop is as follows. There are two cases. If $A(v') = 1$ for all $v' \in S$ (a special case is $e = (v, \emptyset)$), then since A approximates $F^G_{\min}$, which is a post-fixed point assignment of G, $A(v)$ is now forced to be updated to 1. At the same time, each $e' \in D(v)$ must be re-processed since the assumption of $A(v) = 0$ no longer holds. The second case is that there exists a $v' \in S$ such that $A(v') = 0$. In this case $A(v)$ will not be forced to become 1 and we add e to $D(v')$ to indicate that e has not been used to force $A(v)$ to be 1 assuming $A(v') = 0$. As such, if $A(v')$ is later forced to be 1, then all $e \in D(v')$ depending on the now false assumption can be re-processed.

Lemma 1. *The while-loop of algorithm Global1 has the following invariant properties:*

1. $A \sqsubseteq F^G_{\min}$*;*
2. *For all* $v \in V$ *with* $A(v) = 0$*, whenever* $(v, S) \in E$ *then either* $(v, S) \in W$ *or* $(v, S) \in D(v')$ *for some* $v' \in S$ *with* $A(v') = 0$.

Proof Upon entering the while-loop the first invariant property holds trivially. The only place at which A is updated in the while-loop is the *true* branch of the if-statement. In this case, $A(v)$ is changed from 0 to 1, for some $v \in V$, and the condition is that there exists $(v, S) \in E$ such that $\forall v' \in S.\ A(v') = 1$. Assume that the invariant property holds before the update; we are left to show that $A(v) \leq F^G_{\min}(v)$ after the update. By the condition of the update and the inductive assumption, $\forall v' \in S.\ F^G_{\min}(v') = 1$, and since $F^G_{\min}$ is a post-fixed-point assignment, $F^G_{\min}(v) = 1$. Thus, after the update, the invariant property is maintained. The second invariant property is easy to verify. ∎

Theorem 2. *Upon termination of running algorithm Global1 on a given dependency graph* $G = (V, E)$*, it holds that* $F^G_{\min} = A$.

Proof By 1. of Lemma 1, it certainly holds that $A \sqsubseteq F^G_{\min}$ upon termination. To conclude the proof we show that A is a post-fixed-point assignment of G upon termination, so $A \sqsupseteq F^G_{\min}$ since $F^G_{\min}$ is the minimum post-fixed-point assignment of G. Suppose $(v, S) \in E$ with $\forall v' \in S.\ A(v') = 1$. We show that $A(v) = 1$ and hence A is a post-fixed-point assignment. If $A(v) = 0$, then by 2. of Lemma 1 (coupled with the fact that $W = \emptyset$ upon termination), there exists $v' \in S$ with $A(v') = 0$. Contradiction. ∎

```
W := nil;
for k = 1 to n do
        A[k] := 0;  D[k] := nil;  Load(W, H, k);
od
while W ≠ nil do
        (k, l) := hd(W);  W := tl(W);
        if A[k] = 0 then
                        while A[hd(l)] = 1 & l ≠ nil do l := tl(l);  od
                        if l = nil then
                                        A[k] := 1;  W := W@D[k];
                                    else
                                        D[hd(l)] := (k, tl(l)) :: D[hd(l)];
                        fi
        fi
od
proc Load(W, H, k) ≡
  l := H[k];
  while l ≠ nil do
          W := (k, hd(l)) :: W;  l := tl(l)
  od
end
```

Fig. 2. Algorithm Global2

We now describe the implementation of our global algorithm using concrete data structures. We first discuss the representation of the input dependency graph $G = (V, E)$. Suppose G has n nodes, then to represent V we can use the first n positive integers $\{1, \ldots, n\}$, and to represent E we can use an array H with indexing set $\{1, \ldots, n\}$ such that for each $k \in \{1, \ldots, n\}$, $H[k]$ lists the hyper-edges of G having k as the source. Since the source has been fixed to k, to list the hyper-edges in $H[k]$ we only need to list the target sets, which are again represented by lists. Thus $H[k]$ is a list of lists, with each sublist corresponding to a target set of a hyper-edge of the form (k, S). Now W is represented as a list of hyper-edges, with each hyper-edge represented as a pair consisting of a number and a list of numbers.

The functions A and D in the algorithm can now be implemented as two arrays of length n, with A having elements from $\{0, 1\}$ and D having elements of lists of hyper-edges. The refined algorithm, Global2, is given in Figure 2. Here we use some common notations for list operations. For a list l, $hd(l), tl(l)$ are the head and tail of l, respectively. Also $a :: l$ is a list with head a and tail l, and $l@l'$ is the concatenation of two lists l and l'.

Compared with Global1, there are some minor changes in Global2. W here is initialized by repeatedly executing procedure *Load*. Also, there is an extra test to see whether $A[k] = 0$ before processing each hyper-edge (k, l) in W, since if $A[k]$ is already 1 (set as the result of processing other hyper-edges), then there is no need to process (k, l). Finally, the testing of the condition whether $\forall v' \in S.\ A(v') = 1$ is implemented by a combination of while- and if-statements; it is easy to see why this is a faithful implementation of this test.

Since Global1 is just a high-level presentation of the algorithm, without detail to the data structures, it is only meaningful to study the precise complexity of the algorithm presented as Global2. For a dependency graph $G = (V, E)$, let $|G|$ be the size of G defined by $|G| = |V| + \sum_{(v,S)\in E}(|S| + 1)$ where $|V|$ and $|S|$ denote, as usual, the size of the sets V and S, respectively.

Theorem 3. *When executed on input dependency graph $G = (V, E)$, algorithm Global2 takes $O(|G|)$ time.*

Proof The execution of Global2 can be clearly divided into two phases: the *initialization phase*, consisting of the assignment of nil to W and the for-loop, and the *iteration phase*, consisting of the main while-loop. For the initialization phase, the assignment to W takes constant time and it is not difficult to see that the for-loop takes $O(|G|)$ time. Next we show that the iteration phase also takes $O(|G|)$ time.

Let $M = n + \sum_{(k,l)\in W}(len(l) + 1) + \sum_{1\leq i\leq n, A[i]=0} \sum_{(k,l)\in D[i]}(len(l) + 1)$, where $len(l)$ is the length of the list l, and for a list l we write $a \in l$ to mean that a is an element of list l. Clearly at the beginning of the main while-loop, it holds that $\sum_{(k,l)\in W}(len(l) + 1) = \sum_{(v,S)\in E}(|S| + 1)$ and $D[i] =$ nil for all $1 \leq i \leq n$, so $M = |V| + \sum_{(v,S)\in E}(|S| + 1)$. That is, M has the initial value of $|G|$ upon entering the iteration phase. Suppose that during one iteration, i.e. one execution of the body of the main while-loop, the inner while-loop takes t iterations. Note that after each such single iteration, M decreases by at least $1 + t$, while the time spent on this iteration is $c + t * d$ where c, d are some constant natural numbers. Thus, the execution time spent on the main while-loop is proportional to the decrease in M. Since M has an initial value of $|G|$ and lower bound of 0, the total execution time of the main while-loop is $O(|G|)$. ∎

In the Section 4 we will show that any instance of a usual maximal or minimal fixed-point problem in the form of a *boolean graph* can be reduced to a dependency graph of linear size in linear time. Thus the complexity measure given by Theorem 3 matches the complexity of the best global linear algorithms based on boolean graphs and boolean equation systems.

3.2 The Local Algorithm

In many model checking applications, the answer we are looking for is just the value of $F^G_{\min}$ at a given node $v \in V$, not the entire $F^G_{\min}$. In this case, of course, we can still run the global algorithm to obtain $F^G_{\min}$ and then look up the value at v. Local model checking, however, is likely to be a more efficient strategy. Fortunately, the global algorithm presented above can be easily made into a local one. The key observation is that there is no need to assume that all hyper-edges will have to be examined in deciding the value at a particular node. So there is no need to include all the hyper-edges in W in the beginning of the algorithm. Suppose that we want to know $F^G_{\min}(v_0)$ for $v_0 \in V$. Then W will initially include all hyper-edges having v_0 as the source, and will expand later when there is the need to investigate other nodes.

The local algorithm is presented in Figure 52 at the abstract level of sets and dependency-graph hyper-edges. It takes as input a dependency graph $G = (V, E)$,

```
for v ∈ V do A(v) := ⊥; od
A(v₀) = 0; D(v₀) := ∅; W := {e ∈ E | e = (v₀, S)};
while W ≠ ∅ do
      let e = (v, S) ∈ W;
      W := W − {e};
      case of
          ∀v' ∈ S.A(v') = 1: A(v) := 1; W := W ∪ D(v);
          v' ∈ S.A(v') = 0: D(v') := D(v') ∪ {e};
          v' ∈ S.A(v') = ⊥: A(v') := 0; D(v') := ∅;
                                       W := W ∪ {e' ∈ E | e' = (v', S)};
      esac
od
```

Fig. 3. Algorithm Local1

with $v_0 \in V$ the vertex whose minimal fixed-point value we are interested in computing. We assume that the execution of the case-statement is such that the conditions are tested in the order they are written, until one of them is satisfied. The corresponding statement is then executed, and only one of the cases is executed. We use $\perp$ to represent value *unknown*; thus, A is unknown everywhere initially. Whenever a node v is being investigated, it is assumed that $A(v) = 0$, and later it may be forced to 1. Also, at the same time, all hyper-edges having v as the source are added into W.

The processing of hyper-edges in W is very much like in the global algorithm, except that now we have a third case, in which the node under examination can neither be evaluated to 1 nor to 0, and the only way to proceed is to investigate a new node that has not been investigated yet. This happens in the last case of the case-statement. The rigorous proof of the correctness of algorithm Local1 is provided by the following lemma and theorem.

Lemma 4. *The while-loop of algorithm Local1 has the following invariant properties:*

1. *For all $v \in V$, if $A(v) = 1$ then $F^G_{\min}(v) = 1$;*
2. *For all $v \in V$ with $A(v) = 0$, whenever $(v, S) \in E$ then either $(v, S) \in W$ or $(v, S) \in D(v')$ for some $v' \in S$ with $A(v') = 0$.*

Proof Similar to the proof of Lemma 1. ■

Theorem 5. *Upon termination of running algorithm Local1 on a given dependency graph $G = (V, E)$, for all $v \in V$, if $A(v) = 0$ then $F^G_{\min}(v) = 0$, and if $A(v) = 1$ then $F^G_{\min}(v) = 1$.*

Proof By 1. of Lemma 4, it certainly holds that if $A(v) = 1$ then $F^G_{\min}(v) = 1$ after termination. To show that if $A(v) = 0$ then $F^G_{\min}(v) = 0$, we construct an assignment B of G such that $B(v) = 0$ just in case $A(v) = 0$ (thus $B(v) = 1$ if $A(v) = 1$ or $A(v) = \perp$). We show in the following that B is a post fixed point of G, so $F^G_{\min} \sqsubseteq B$, and if $A(v) = 0$ then $B(v) = 0$ and $F^G_{\min}(v) = 0$. Suppose $(v, S) \in E$ with $\forall v' \in S.B(v') = 1$. We will show that $B(v) = 1$ so B is a post-fixed-point assignment. If $B(v) = 0$ then $A(v) = 0$, since in this case $W = \emptyset$. By 2. of Lemma 4, there exists $v' \in S$ with $A(v') = 0$. Contradiction. ■

The implementation of the local algorithm with array and list data structures is given in Figure 4. It is not difficult to see that the total execution time of the local algorithm cannot exceed that of the global algorithm, and, hence, Local2 still takes $O(|G|)$ time in the worst case.

```
for k = 1 to n do A[k] := ⊥; od
A[m] := 0; D[m] := nil; W := nil; Load(W, H, m);
while W ≠ nil do
      (k, l) := hd(W); W := tl(W);
      if A[k] = 0 then
           while A[hd(l)] = 1 & l ≠ nil do l := tl(l); od
           case of
             l = nil: A[k] := 1; W := W@D[k];
             A[hd(l)] = 0 : D[hd(l)] := (k, tl(l)) :: D[hd(l)];
             A[hd(l)] = ⊥ : A[hd(l)] := 0; D[hd(l)] := nil;   Load(W, H, hd(l));
           esac
      fi
od
```

Fig. 4. Algorithm Local2

4 Boolean Graphs and Dependency Graphs

In [And94], *Boolean graphs* were introduced as a general framework for model checking problems. A boolean graph is a triple (V, E, L) where V is a set of vertices, $E \subseteq V \times V$ a set of edges, and $L \to \{\vee, \wedge\}$ is a function labeling the vertices as disjunctive or conjunctive. We say $v \in V$ is a *disjunctive node* (*conjunctive node*) if $L(v) = \vee$ ($L(v) = \wedge$).

Let $G = (V, E, L)$ be a boolean graph. An *assignment* A of G is a function from V to $\{0, 1\}$. A *pre-fixed-point assignment* F of G is an assignment such that for every disjunctive node $v \in V$, if $F(v) = 1$ then there exists $(v, v') \in E$ such that $F(v') = 1$, and for every conjunctive node $v \in V$, if $F(v) = 1$ then $F(v') = 1$ for all $(v, v') \in E$. A *post-fixed-point assignment* F of G is an assignment such that for every disjunctive node $v \in V$, if there exists $(v, v') \in E$ such that $F(v') = 1$ then $F(v) = 1$, and for every conjunctive node $v \in V$, if $F(v') = 1$ for all $(v, v') \in E$ then $F(v) = 1$. A *fixed-point assignment* F of G is both a pre-fixed point assignment and a post-fixed point assignment.

If we take the standard partial order $\sqsubseteq$ between assignments of boolean graphs G such that $A \sqsubseteq A'$ just in case $A(v) \leq A'(v)$ for all $v \in V$ (using the usual order $0 < 1$), then according to the Knaster-Tarski fixed-point theorem, for a given boolean graph G, there exists a unique maximum pre-fixed-point assignment, which we will write as $F^G_{\max}$, and also a unique minimum post-fixed point-assignment, which we will write as $F^G_{\min}$, and both of them are fixed points.

It turns out that many fixed-point computation problems in model checking, especially the problem of model checking the alternation-free modal mu-calculus, can be reduced to a series of problems involving the computation of $F^G_{\max}$ or $F^G_{\min}$ on some boolean graph G. In this section we present direct linear time reductions from both maximal and minimal fixed-point evaluation of boolean graphs to the problem of minimal fixed-point evaluation on dependency graphs. Thus our algorithms presented in the previous section represent both local and global linear-time algorithms for alternation-free fixed-point evaluation.

Theorem 6. *Let $G = (V, E, L)$ be a boolean graph, and $G_1 = (V, E_1)$ be the dependency graph having the same vertex set as G, and whose set of hyper-edges E_1 is the minimum set satisfying the following:*

1. *each $(v, v') \in E$ with $L(v) = \vee$ induces a hyper-edge $(v, \{v'\}) \in E_1$;*
2. *each $v \in V$ with $L(v) = \wedge$ induces a hyper-edge $(v, \{v' \mid (v, v') \in E\}) \in E_1$.*

With G_1 thus constructed, it holds that $F^G_{\min} = F^{G_1}_{\min}$.

Proof It is easy to see that an assignment of G (which must also be an assignment of G_1) is a post-fixed-point assignment of G if and only if it is at the same time a post-fixed-point assignment of G_1. Thus $F^G_{\min}$ is a post-fixed-point assignment of G_1. Since $F^{G_1}_{\min}$ is the minimum post-fixed-point assignment of G_1, $F^{G_1}_{\min} \sqsubseteq F^G_{\min}$. Similarly, to show $F^G_{\min} \sqsubseteq F^{G_1}_{\min}$ just note that $F^{G_1}_{\min}$ is a post-fixed-point assignment of G, and $F^G_{\min}$ is the minimum post-fixed-point assignment of G. The two inequality give us $F^G_{\min} = F^{G_1}_{\min}$. ■

For an assignment F of a (dependency or boolean) graph G, we write $\neg F$ for the assignment of G obtained under componentwise-complement of F.

Theorem 7. *Let $G = (V, E, L)$ be a boolean graph, and $G_0 = (V, E_0)$ be the dependency graph having the same vertex set as G, and whose set of hyper-edges E_0 is the minimum set satisfying the following:*

1. *each $(v, v') \in E$ with $L(v) = \wedge$ induces a hyper-edge $(v, \{v'\}) \in E_0$;*
2. *each $v \in V$ with $L(v) = \vee$ induces a hyper-edge $(v, \{v' \mid (v, v') \in E\}) \in E_0$.*

With G_0 thus constructed, it holds that $F^G_{\max} = \neg F^{G_0}_{\min}$.

Proof It is easy to see that if F is a pre-fixed-point assignment of G then $\neg F$ is a post-fixed-point assignment of G_0, and if F is a post-fixed-point assignment of G_0 then $\neg F$ is a pre-fixed-point assignment of G. So $\neg F^G_{\max}$ is a post-fixed-point assignment of G_0. Since $F^{G_0}_{\min}$ is the minimum post-fixed-point assignment of G_0, $F^{G_0}_{\min} \sqsubseteq \neg F^G_{\max}$, and so $F^G_{\max} \sqsubseteq \neg F^{G_0}_{\min}$. On the other hand, $\neg F^{G_0}_{\min}$ is a pre-fixed-point assignment of G. Since $F^G_{\max}$ is the maximum pre-fixed-point assignment of G, $\neg F^{G_0}_{\min} \sqsubseteq F^G_{\max}$. Hence $F^G_{\max} = \neg F^{G_0}_{\min}$. ■

5 Horn Formulae and Dependency Graphs

A *literal* is either a propositional letter P (a positive literal) or the negation $\neg P$ of a propositional letter P (a negative literal). A *basic Horn formula* is a disjunction of literals, with at most one positive literal. A basic Horn formula will also be called a Horn clause, or simply a clause. A *Horn formula* is a conjunction of basic Horn formulae. A Horn formula is satisfiable if there is a boolean assignment under which the Horn formula evaluates to true.

[DG84] is the earliest work to present linear-time algorithms for HORNSAT, the problem of Horn formula satisfiability. Shukla et al. [SHIR96] demonstrated effective reductions from model checking in the alternation-free modal mu-calculus and related problems to HORNSAT, thereby establishing an early link between HORNSAT and fixed-point computation. Interestingly, the idea of counter and "reverse list" data structures found in linear-time global model checking algorithms such as [CS93, AC88, And94] was already present in [DG84]. This suggests closer connection between the structure of the two problems.

In this section, we present reductions between these problems for both directions of reducibility. The reductions are straightforward, and should help further clarify the connections between model-checking-based fixed-point computation and HORNSAT. The reductions are linear-time with suitable representations of the problem instances. As a result, we derive a linear-time local algorithm for HORNSAT, the first of its kind as far as we are aware.

Theorem 8. *Let $G = (V, E)$ be a dependency graph, $v_0 \in V$, $\{P_v \mid v \in V\}$ a set of propositional letters in one-to-one correspondence with vertices in V, and $H_G^{v_0}$ the following Horn formula:*

$$H_G^{v_0} = \bigwedge_{(v_0,S)\in E} \Big(\bigvee_{v'\in S} \neg P_{v'}\Big) \wedge \bigwedge_{(v,S)\in E, v\neq v_0} \Big(P_v \vee \bigvee_{v'\in S} \neg P_{v'}\Big).$$

Then $F_{\min}^G(v_0) = 0$ if and only if $H_G^{v_0}$ is satisfiable.

Proof Let A be an assignment of $H_G^{v_0}$ under which $H_G^{v_0}$ evaluates to 1. From A we construct an assignment F of G such that $F(v_0) = 0$ and for all other $v \in V$, $F(v) = A(P_v)$. It is easy to verify that F is a post-fixed-point assignment of G, hence $F_{\min}^G(v_0) \leq F(v_0) = 0$. For the other direction, from $F_{\min}^G$ we construct an assignment A for $H_G^{v_0}$ such that for all $v \in V$, $A(P_v) = F_{\min}^G(v)$. Since $F_{\min}^G$ is a post-fixed-point assignment, it is easy to see that under A, $H_G^{v_0}$ evaluates to $\bigwedge_{(v_0,S)\in E}(\bigvee_{v'\in S} \neg F_{\min}^G(v'))$ which should be 1 when $F_{\min}^G(v_0) = 0$ (otherwise there exists $(v_0, S_0) \in E$ such that $\forall v' \in S_0.\ F_{\min}^G(v') = 1$, which contradicts $F_{\min}^G(v_0) = 0$ and $F_{\min}^G$ being a post-fixed-point assignment). ■

Theorem 9. *Let H be a Horn formula, and $G_H = (V, E)$ a dependency graph, where V consists of all the propositional letters occurring in H plus a special node v_0, and E contains exactly the hyper-edges obtained by one of the follow rules:*

1. *for each Horn clause* C *of the form* $\neg P_1 \vee \ldots \vee \neg P_m$ *without a positive literal, there is a hyper-edge* $(v_0, \{P_1, \ldots, P_m\}) \in E$*;*
2. *for each Horn clause* C *of the form* $P_0 \vee \neg P_1 \vee \ldots \vee \neg P_m$*, there is a hyper-edge* $(P_0, \{P_1, \ldots, P_m\}) \in E$ *(a special case here is a Horn clause* P_0 *which corresponds to a hyper-edge* $(P_0, \emptyset) \in E$*).*

Then H *is satisfiable if and only if* $F_{\min}^{G_H}(v_0) = 0$*.*

Proof Similar to the proof of Theorem 8. ∎

Observe that Theorem 9 presents a reduction from the problem of satisfiability of H to the problem of whether $F_{\min}^{G_H}(v_0) = 0$, a local model checking problem. With array representations of instances of HORNSAT, it is not difficult to see that the reduction can be carried out in linear-time.

6 Conclusions

We have presented simple linear-time algorithms for minimal fixed-point evaluation in dependency graphs. The algorithms also have simple and clear proofs of correctness and complexity. We also demonstrated that dependency graphs represent a suitable framework for expressing and computing alternation-free fixed-points, an important problem in model checking. Finally, we clarified the relationship between minimal fixed-point evaluation and horn-formula satisfiability, deriving a linear-time local algorithm for HORNSAT in the process. To our knowledge, this is the first such linear-time local algorithm to appear in the literature.

In [LRS98], a local algorithm LAFP for computing fixed points of arbitrary alternation depth is presented. Like most fixed-point algorithms, LAFP computes fixed points iteratively. By using a "recovery strategy" that carefully accounts for the effects of value changes of a more dominant fixed point — thus avoiding unnecessary recomputation of fixed points nested inside it — the number of iterations required by LAFP to evaluate fixed points of an instance with size N and alternation depth ad is $O((N-1) + (\frac{N+ad}{ad})^{ad})$. Asymptotically, this matches the iteration complexity of the best existing global algorithms. However, the *total* execution time of LAFP (in which the time taken during iterations of the while-loop is taken into account) introduces an additional factor of N^2, making the total execution time worse than that of the best global algorithms. This additional factor is due to the lack of an efficient data structure that works well with the recovery strategy. As future work, we plan to extend the local algorithm presented in this paper to the the case of alternating fixed points, in the hope that the complexity matches that of the best global algorithms. We believe that this would lead to optimal algorithms for the problem.

References

[AC88] A. Arnold and P. Crubille. A linear algorithm to solve fixed-point equations on transition systems. *Information Processing Letters*, 29:57–66, September 1988.

[And94] H. R. Andersen. Model checking and boolean graphs. *Theoretical Computer Science*, 126(1), 1994.

[BC96] G. S. Bhat and R. Cleaveland. Efficient model checking via the equational μ-calculus. In E. M. Clarke, editor, *11th Annual Symposium on Logic in Computer Science (LICS '96)*, pages 304–312, New Brunswick, NJ, July 1996. Computer Society Press.

[CE81] E. M. Clarke and E. A. Emerson. Design and synthesis of synchronization skeletons using branching-time temporal logic. In D. Kozen, editor, *Proceedings of the Workshop on Logic of Programs*, Yorktown Heights, volume 131 of *Lecture Notes in Computer Science*, pages 52–71. Springer-Verlag, 1981.

[CES86] E. M. Clarke, E. A. Emerson, and A. P. Sistla. Automatic verification of finite-state concurrent systems using temporal logic specifications. *ACM TOPLAS*, 8(2), 1986.

[CKS92] R. Cleaveland, M. Klein, and B. Steffen. Faster model checking for the modal mu-calculus. In G.v. Bochmann and D.K. Probst, editors, *Proceedings of the Fourth International Conference on Computer Aided Verification (CAV '92)*, Vol. 663 of *Lecture Notes in Computer Science*, pages 410–422. Springer-Verlag, 1992.

[Cle90] R. Cleaveland. Tableau-based model checking in the propositional mu-calculus. *Acta Informatica*, 27:725–747, 1990.

[CS93] R. Cleaveland and B. U. Steffen. A linear-time model checking algorithm for the alternation-free modal mu-calculus. *Formal Methods in System Design*, 2:121–147, 1993.

[CW96] E. M. Clarke and J. M. Wing. Formal methods: State of the art and future directions. *ACM Computing Surveys*, 28(4), December 1996.

[DG84] W. F. Dowling and J. H. Gallier. Linear-time algorithms for testing the satisfiability of propositional horn formulae. *Journal of Logic Programming*, 3:267–284, 1984.

[HW74] L. Henschen and L. Wos. Unit refutations and horn sets. *Journal of the ACM*, 21:590–605, 1974.

[Koz83] D. Kozen. Results on the propositional μ-calculus. *Theoretical Computer Science*, 27:333–354, 1983.

[Lar88] K.G. Larsen. Proof systems for Hennessy–Milner logic with recursion. *Lecture Notes In Computer Science, Springer Verlag*, 299, 1988. in Proceedings of 13th Colloquium on Trees in Algebra and Programming 1988.

[Lar92] K.G. Larsen. Efficient local correctness checking. *Lecture Notes In Computer Science, Springer Verlag*, 663, 1992. in Proceedings of the 4th Workshop on Computer Aided Verification, 1992.

[LRS98] X. Liu, C. R. Ramakrishnan, and S. A. Smolka. Fully local and efficient evaluation of alternating fixed points. In *Proceedings of the Fourth International Conference on Tools and Algorithms for the Construction and Analysis of Systems (TACAS '98), Lecture Notes in Computer Science*. Springer-Verlag, 1998.

[Pra81] V.R. Pratt. A decidable mu-calculus. In *Proceedings of the 22nd IEEE Ann. Symp. on Foundations of Computer Science,* Nashville, Tennessee, pages 421–427, 1981.

[QS82] J. P. Queille and J. Sifakis. Specification and verification of concurrent systems in Cesar. In *Proceedings of the International Symposium in Programming*, volume 137 of *Lecture Notes in Computer Science*, Berlin, 1982. Springer-Verlag.

[SHIR96] S. K. Shukla, H. B. Hunt III, and D. J. Rosenkrantz. HORNSAT, model checking, verification and games. In R. Alur and T. A. Henzinger, editors, *Computer Aided Verification (CAV '96)*, volume 1102 of *Lecture Notes in Computer Science*, pages 99–110, New Brunswick, New Jersey, July 1996. Springer-Verlag.

[SW91] C. Stirling and D. Walker. Local model checking in the modal mu-calculus. *Theoretical Computer Science*, 89(1), 1991.

[VL94] B. Vergauwen and J. Lewi. Efficient local correctness checking for single and alternating boolean equation systems. In *Proceedings of ICALP'94*, pages 304–315. LNCS 820, 1994.

Hardness Results for Dynamic Problems by Extensions of Fredman and Saks' Chronogram Method*

Thore Husfeldt[1,2] and Theis Rauhe[1]

[1] BRICS, Department of Computer Science, University of Aarhus
[2] Department of Computer Science, Lund University

Abstract We introduce new models for dynamic computation based on the cell probe model of Fredman and Yao. We give these models access to nondeterministic queries or the right answer ± 1 as an oracle. We prove that for the dynamic partial sum problem, these new powers do not help, the problem retains its lower bound of $\Omega(\log n / \log \log n)$.

From these results we easily derive a large number of lower bounds of order $\Omega(\log n / \log \log n)$ for conventional dynamic models like the random access machine. We prove lower bounds for dynamic algorithms for reachability in directed graphs, planarity testing, planar point location, incremental parsing, fundamental data structure problems like maintaining the majority of the prefixes of a string of bits and range queries. We characterise the complexity of maintaining the value of any symmetric function on the prefixes of a bit string.

1 Introduction

Update versus query time. For dynamic problems, two trivial solutions are immediate: Either the algorithm spends time after each update reorganising the data structure to anticipate every future query, or the algorithm spends time after each query to read the entire history of updates. However, a crucial property of many hard problems is that these two cannot be optimised simultaneously. This tradeoff between *update time* and *query time* was studied using the *chronogram method* by Fredman and Saks [13], a result that has proved extremely useful for lower bounds for dynamic algorithm and data structures.

The method of [13] is an information-theoretic argument formalising the idea that not all relevant information about the updates can be passed on to a typical query. The present paper takes a closer look at this information, asking what kind of information is responsible for the hardness of the problem. Our approach is to provide the query algorithm with well-defined aspects of the information for free, e.g., we consider nondeterministic query algorithms.

Example: Range queries. We can illustrate our approach using range query problems. The object is to maintain a set $S \subseteq \{1, \ldots, n\}^2$ of points in the plane, the updates insert and remove points from S. An *existential* range query asks whether a given rectangle R contains a point from S. This problem requires time $\Omega(\log \log n / \log \log \log n)$ [4, 20].

* See [15] for a full version of this paper, with all proofs included. This work was supported by the ESPRIT Long Term Research Programme of the EU, project number 20244 (ALCOM-IT). The first author was partially supported by a grant from TFR. BRICS (Basic Research in Computer Science) is a Centre of the Danish National Research Foundation.

With nondeterministic queries, this problem becomes trivial: guess a point and verify that it is in $S \cap R$. In other words, the sole reason for the hardness of this problem lies in maintaining precisely the kind of information that nondeterminism provides for free. However, this is not true for all problems; our main result implies that reporting the *parity* of $|R \cap S|$ remains just as hard as without nondeterminism, so the hardness of this problem hinges on information of a fundamentally different kind.

Main contribution. We state our two main results in terms of the *signed partial sum problem*. The problem is to maintain a string $x \in \{-1, 0, +1\}^n$ under updates that change the letters of x and queries of the form

query(i): return $x_1 + \cdots + x_i \mod 2$.

We prove two theorems about this problem. Theorem 1 shows that even in models with nondeterministic queries, the partial sum problem requires time $\Omega(\log n / \log\log)$ per operation with logarithmic cell size. It is known that this is also the deterministic complexity of the problem [7, 13], so nondeterminism does not help.

Our second main result studies the same problem in a *promise* setting, where the query algorithm receives almost the correct answer for free. The updates are as before, and the query is

parity(i, s): return $x_1 + \cdots + x_i \mod 2$ provided that $|s - \sum_{j=1}^{i} x_j| \leq 1$ (otherwise the behaviour of the query algorithm is undefined).

Theorem 2 shows that this problem still requires $\Omega(\log n / \log\log n)$ per operation.

We reason within the cell probe model of Fredman [10] and Yao [28], with some extensions to cope with our stronger modes of computation. This can be viewed as a nonuniform version of the random access computer with arbitrary register instructions. Especially, our lower bounds are valid on random access machines with unit-cost instructions on logarithmic cell size. The success of this model is partly due to the validity of these bound in light of schemes like hashing, indirect addressing, bucketing, pointer manipulation, or recent algorithms that exploit the parallelism inherent in unit-cost instructions. For these reasons the cell probe model has arguably become the model of choice for lower bounds for dynamic computation.

Theorems 1 and 2 are proved by extending the chronogram method, which was introduced by Fredman and Saks [13] and got its name in [5].

Lower bounds for dynamic algorithms. Our results suggest a new general technique for proving lower bounds for dynamic algorithm and data structure problems. Because Thms. 1 and 2 hold in very strong models of computation, we can exploit these strengths in our reductions—this yields simple proofs. We support our claims about the versatility of this technique by exhibiting a number of new lower bounds for well-studied problems, including planar point location, reachability in upward planar digraphs and in grid graphs, incremental parsing of balanced parentheses, and partial sum problems.

Limitations of the chronogram method. A large number of hardness results for dynamic problems employ the chronogram method, usually by constructing a reduction from a partial sum problem. Our results imply in some precise sense that this method is unable to distinguish deterministic from nondeterministic computation. In particular, this method cannot prove lower bounds for a problem that are better than the best nondeterministic algorithm. This is an important guide in the search for lower bounds for a large class of problems, including for example existential range searching and convex hull.

Outline of paper. Section 2 introduces dynamic algorithms with nondeterministic queries and contains the statement of Thm. 1; the proof of this result, which is the main technical contribution of this paper, is sketched in Sect. 3. Our lower bounds for dynamic algorithms and partial sum problems are presented in Sect. 4. Finally, Sect. 5 introduces the notion of refinement and presents Thm. 2. Many proofs are omitted due to space limitations, they can be found in the full version [15].

2 Nondeterminism in Dynamic Algorithms

2.1 Nondeterministic query algorithms. We now introduce our notion of nondeterministic query algorithms for dynamic decision problems. We allow query algorithms to nondeterministically load a value into a memory cell. The semantics is as usual: The value returned by a nondeterministic query is 1 unless all nondeterministic choices return 0. For example, the following program solves the existential range query problem from the introduction, storing all points from S in a two-dimensional array M:

update(i, j):	*query*(R):
$M[i,j] := \neg M[i,j]$	**guess** $(i,j) \in R$
	return $M[i,j]$

We should mention that we have not defined the *side-effects* of a nondeterministic query algorithm, i.e., the effect of its assignments to memory. This can be done in a number of ways; for example we might say that if there are computations (i.e., sequences of nondeterministic choices) that result in '1', the algorithm will execute one of these computations; otherwise it will execute a computation leading to '0'. We mention that our lower bound is immune to precisely how these effects are defined, since the hard operation sequence constructed in the proof needs only a single query, which happens at the very end.

Nondeterministic queries are a powerful tool for a number of well-studied problems. A good example from Computational Geometry is *dynamic convex hull*, the problem of maintaining the convex hull of a set of points S, where points are inserted and removed. The query operation asks whether the query point q lies inside or outside the convex hull of S. Again, we can solve this problem with a trivial update algorithm that simply stores S in a large table (in the cell probe model we do not worry about memory space, otherwise we can use standard dictionaries). The nondeterministic query guesses three points from S and verifies that the query point lies in the triangle spanned by these points—a well known result in plane geometry asserts that this is necessary and sufficient.

Note that the complement of this problem (answer 'yes' iff q lies outside the convex hull) does not seem to allow such an algorithm. In contrast, the complement of the existential range query problem in one dimension does, since we can maintain a doubly linked list of the inserted points, and the query can guess both the immediate predecessor and immediate successor of a query interval and verify that they are neighbours is S.

In general, a problem is amenable to nondeterminism, if the outcome of each query depends on only a bounded number of updates. Contrast this with the problems identified in [13], where each update affects only a bounded number of queries, e.g., dictionary problems.

2.2 Signed partial sum. The *signed partial sum* problem is to maintain a string $x \in \{-1, 0, +1\}^n$, initially 0^n, under updates that change the letters of x and queries about the parity of the prefix sums of x

update(i, a): change x_i to $a \in \{-1, 0, +1\}$,

query(i): return $x_1 + \cdots + x_i \mod 2$.

The data structure of Dietz [7] solves this problem, deterministically, in time $O(\log n/\log\log n)$ per operation with logarithmic cell size. The next theorem states that nondeterministic queries can do no better. We state theorem as a trade-off between update and query time.

Theorem 1 *Every nondeterministic algorithm for the signed partial sum problem with cell size b, update time t_u, and query time t_q must satisfy*

$$t_q = \Omega\Big(\frac{\log n}{\log(bt_u \log n)}\Big). \tag{1}$$

The lower bound holds even if the algorithm requires

$$0 \le x_1 + \cdots + x_i \le \Big\lceil \frac{\log n}{\log(bt_u \log n)} \Big\rceil \tag{2}$$

for all i after each update.

The balancing condition (2) continues previous work [16] on extending the chronogram method, which is implicit in the constructions in the present paper. In Sect. 4.2 we state a further generalisation of Thm. 1, relating the terms in (1) and (2).

3 Proof of Theorem 1

We consider a specific sequence of operations that consists of a number of updates followed by a single query. The update sequence is chosen at random from a set U defined in Sect. 3.5.

3.1 Model of computation. The computational model is an extension of the cell-probe model [10, 28]; since there is only a single query in the hard sequence of operations constructed in our proof, which happens at the very end of the sequence, we can model query algorithms by nondeterministic decision trees.

More precisely, a *cell probe* algorithm consists of a family of trees, one for each operation, and a memory $M \in \{0, \ldots, 2^b - 1\}^*$. We refer to the elements of M as *cells*, each of which can store a b-bit number. To each update we associate a decision–assignment tree as in [13]. There are two types of nodes: *Read* nodes are 2^b-ary and labelled by a memory address, computation proceeds to the child identified at that address; *write* nodes are unary and labelled by a memory address and a b-bit value, with the obvious semantics.

To each query we associate a nondeterministic decision tree of arity 2^b whose internal nodes are labelled by a memory address or by '$\exists$'. The leaves are labelled 0 or 1 to represent the possible answers to the query. We define the value $qM \in \{0, 1\}$ computed by a query tree q on memory M to be 1 if there exists a path from the root to a leaf with label 1. A witness of such an accepting computation is the description of the choices for the $\exists$ nodes. We let q_i denote the query tree corresponding to *query*(i). The query time t_q is the height of the largest query tree and the update time t_u is the height of the largest update tree; we account only for memory reads and writes and for nondeterministic choices, all other computation is for free.

3.2 Updates and epochs. Each update sequence in U is described by a binary string $u \in \{0, 1\}^*$. Each bit represents an update *update*(j, a). The parameters for these updates will be specified in Sect. 3.5. The update sequences $u \in U$ are split into d substrings each corresponding to an *epoch*. It turns out to be convenient that time flows backwards, so epoch 1 corresponds to the end of u. In general the update string is an element in $U = U_d U_{d-1} \cdots U_1$ where $U_t = \{0,1\}^{e(t)}$, and where $e(t)$ is the length of epoch t is such that $e(t)+\cdots+e(1) = \lfloor n^{t/d}/d \rfloor$. The length of the entire update sequence is $\lfloor n/d \rfloor$. The size of d and hence the growth rate of $e(t)$ is $d = \lceil \log n / \log(bt_{\mathrm{u}} \log n) \rceil$. The goal is to establish that $t_{\mathrm{q}} \in \Omega(d)$.

3.3 Time stamps and nondeterminism. To each cell we associate a time stamp when it is written. A cell receives time stamp t if some update during epoch t writes to it, and none of the subsequent updates during epochs $t-1$ to 1 write to it.

For an update sequence $u \in U$ let M^u denote the memory resulting from these updates (recall that updates are restricted to perform deterministically), starting with some arbitrary initial contents corresponding to the initial instance 0^n.

For index i and update string u let $T(i,u)$ denote the set of time stamps that are found on every accepting computation path of q_i on M^u. If there are no accepting computations, the set is empty. More formally, let w denote a witness for a computation path of q_i on M^u, and let $A(i,u)$ denote the set of witnesses that lead to accepting computations of q_i on M^u. Let for a moment $T(i,u,w)$ denote the set of time stamps encountered by the computation of q_i on M^u that is witnessed by w. Then $T(i,u) = \bigcap\{\, T(i,u,w) \mid w \in A(i,u) \,\}$ if $A(i,u) \neq \emptyset$, and $T(i,u) = \emptyset$ otherwise.

The simple lemma below is the tool to identify a read of a cell with time stamp t by nondeterministic queries.

Lemma 1 *If M^u and M^v differ only on cells with time stamp t then $q_i M^u \neq q_i M^v$ implies $t \in T(i,u) \cup T(i,v)$.*

3.4 Lower bound on query time. The update sequences are chosen such that even if two sequences differ only in a single epoch, they still result in very different instances. To each update sequence $u \in U$ we associate the query vector $q^u = (q_1 M^u, q_2 M^u, \ldots, q_n M^u) \in \{0,1\}^n$. Update sequences that differ only in epoch t are called *t-different.*

Lemma 2 *No Hamming ball of diameter $\frac{1}{8}n$ can contain more than $|U_t|^{9/10}$ query vectors from t-different update sequences, for large n.*

The difficult part is constructing a set of update sequences for which the statement is true, which we present in Sect. 3.5. The proof itself is as in [13].

Write $U_{>t}$ for $U_d \cdots U_{t+1}$, the set of updates sequences prior to epoch t, and $U_{<t}$ for $U_{t-1} \cdots U_1$, the set of update sequences in epoch t to epoch 1. Assume for the rest of this section that $t_{\mathrm{q}} = \mathrm{O}(\log n)$, else there is nothing to prove. The worst-case query time t_{q} is at least the average of $|T(i,u)|$ over choices of $i \in \{1,\ldots,n\}$ and $u \in U$, so

$$|U| n t_{\mathrm{q}} \geq \sum_{u \in U} \sum_{i=1}^{n} |T(i,u)| = \sum_{t=1}^{d} \sum_{u \in U_{>t}} \sum_{w \in U_{<t}} \sum_{v \in U_t} \sum_{i=1}^{n} \big(t \in T(i,uvw)\big).$$

The next lemma tells us how many $v \in U_t$ fail to make the last sum exceed $\frac{1}{16}n$.

Lemma 3 *Fix any epoch $1 \leq t \leq d$ and past and future updates $x \in U_{<t}$, $y \in U_{>t}$. For large n, at least half of the update sequences $u \in xU_t y$ satisfy $\big|\{\, 1 \leq i \leq n \mid t \in T(i,u) \,\}\big| \geq \frac{1}{16}n$, if $t_{\mathrm{q}} = \mathrm{O}(\log n)$.*

By this lemma we obtain for large n:

$$|U| n t_{\mathrm{q}} \geq \sum_{t=1}^{d} |U_{>t}| \cdot |U_{<t}| \cdot \tfrac{1}{16} n \cdot \tfrac{1}{2} |U_t| = \tfrac{1}{32} n d |U|,$$

and hence $t_{\mathrm{q}} \geq \frac{1}{32} d$ as desired.

3.5 Update scheme. The technical part that remains is to exhibit a set of update sequences U satisfying Lem. 2. There are a number of ways to do this; the following construction is one which simultaneously anticipates our needs in Sect. 5 and satisfies the balancing condition (2).

To alleviate notation we assume that n/d is an integer. Consider the updates in epoch t and index them as $u_1 \cdots u_{e(t)} \in U_t$. If $u_i = 0$ then nothing happens in the ith update. Else it performs *update*(j, a), where the update position j is given below. The new value is $a = (-1)^r$, where $r = 1 + u_1 + \cdots + u_i \bmod 2$, so the nonzero updates in u alternate between -1 and $+1$, starting with $+1$. The position of the affected letter is defined as follows. Write x as a table of dimension $d \times n/d$ like this:

$$\begin{bmatrix} x_1 & x_{d+1} & & x_{n-d+1} \\ \vdots & \vdots & \cdots & \vdots \\ x_d & x_{2d} & & x_n \end{bmatrix}.$$

All updates in epoch t will affect only the letters in row t. The updates of an epoch are spread out evenly from left to right across that row, so the distance between two of them is $\lfloor (n/d)/e(t) \rfloor$. In summary, the ith update in epoch t affects the letter in row t and the column given by $(i-1) \cdot \lfloor (n/d)/e(t) \rfloor + 1$.

This update scheme satisfies the statement in Lem. 2, we omit the proof. Also, the prefix sums of instances resulting from our scheme are small: Let x denote an instance resulting from our scheme from the initial instance 0^n. Let x^t denote the string resulting from only the updates in epoch t and write x as $x^1 + \cdots + x^d$; this works because no two epochs write in the same positions. Then

$$\sum_{j=1}^{i} x_j = \sum_{j=1}^{i} \sum_{t=1}^{d} x_j^t = \sum_{t=1}^{d} \sum_{j=1}^{i} x_j^t \in \{0, \ldots, d\},$$

because the prefix sum of every x^t is 0 or 1 by construction. It can be checked that the balancing bound (2) holds at all times.

Another important feature of this update scheme, which is used to prove Thm. 2, is that if x and y result from t-different updates then $x^r = y^r$ for $r \neq t$ and hence $\left| \sum_{j=1}^{i} x_j - \sum_{j=1}^{i} y_j \right| \leq 1$ for all i.

4 Lower Bounds for Dynamic Algorithms and Partial Sum Problems

Theorem 1 suggests a new approach for proving lower bounds by employing nondeterminism in the reduction from signed partial sum. We demonstrate this with a number of examples in this section. The results are presented for cell size $b = \log n$ for concreteness. Some of the reductions extend previous work of the authors with Søren Skyum [16].

4.1 Nested brackets. Consider the problem of maintaining a nested structure, i.e., a string x with round and square brackets under the following operations:

change(i, a): change x_i to a, where a is a round or square opening or closing bracket, or whitespace.

balance: return 'yes' if and only if the brackets in x are properly nested.

This problem was studied in [9], where an algorithm with polylogarithmic update time is presented.

Proposition 1 *Maintaining a string of nested brackets requires time* $\Omega(\log n / \log\log n)$ *per operation.*

Proof. Consider a deterministic algorithm for this problem and let $x \in \{0, -1, +1\}^n$ be an instance to signed partial sum. Let b_i be an encoding of x_i given by:

$$+1 \mapsto))\sqcup, \quad 0 \mapsto)\sqcup\sqcup, \quad -1 \mapsto \sqcup\sqcup\sqcup,$$

where '$\sqcup$' stands for space. Let c be the string '$\sqcup($'. We maintain a balanced string of brackets uvw, where $u = c^{2n}$, $v = b_1\, b_2 \, \ldots \, b_n$ and $w =)^{n-s}\sqcup^s$, where $s = x_1 + \cdots + x_n$. It is easy to see that uvw balances and can be maintained by a constant number of updates per update in x. For any prefix size i this construction enables efficient verification of a nondeterministic guess g of the prefix sum $x_1 + \cdots + x_i$: Place a closing square bracket on the last $\sqcup$ of b_i and an opening square bracket on the $\sqcup$ of the first c of suffix c^{i+g} of u. This modification keeps uvw balanced iff g is the right guess of prefix sum $x_1 + \cdots + x_i$. Conclusion by Thm. 1. ∎

4.2 Dynamic graph algorithms. Our techniques improve the lower bounds of a number of well-studied graph problems considered in [16].

Tamassia and Preparata [26] present an algorithm for the class of *upward planar source–sink graphs* that runs in time $O(\log n)$ per operation. These digraphs have have a planar embedding where all edges point upward (meaning that their projection on some fixed direction is positive) and where exactly one node has indegree 0 (the source) and exactly one node has outdegree 0 (the sink). The updates are:

insert(u, v): insert an edge from u to v
delete(u, v): delete the edge from u to v if it exists
reachable(u, v): return 'yes' iff there is a path from u to v.

The updates have to preserve the topology of the graph, including the embedding.

Proposition 2 *Dynamic reachability in upward planar source–sink graphs requires time* $\Omega(\log n/ \log\log n)$ *per operation.*

Planarity testing is to maintain a planar graph where the query asks whether a new edge violates the planarity of the graph. Italiano *et al.* [18] present an efficient algorithm for a version of this problem, and a strong lower bound is exhibited by Henzinger and Fredman [12]. Our lower bound holds also for *upward* planarity testing, where the topology is further restricted to upward planar graphs. The updates insert and delete edges as above, and the query is

planar(u, v): return 'yes' if and only if the graph remains upward planar after insertion of edge (u, v).

This problem was studied by Tamassia [25], who found an $O(\log n)$ upper bound.

Proposition 3 *Upward planarity testing requires time* $\Omega(\log n/ \log\log n)$ *per operation.*

A classical problem in Computational Geometry is *planar point location*: given a subdivision of the plane, i.e., a partition into polygonal regions induced by the straight-line embedding of a planar graph, determine the region of query point $q \in \mathbf{R}^2$. An important restriction of the problem considers only *monotone* subdivisions, where the subdivision consists of polygons that are monotone (so no horizontal line crosses any polygon more than twice). In the dynamic version of this problem updates manipulate the geometry of the subdivision. Preparata and Tamassia [24] give an algorithm that runs in time $O(\log^2 n)$ per operation, this was improved to query time $O(\log n)$ by Baumgarten, Jung, and Mehlhorn [3]. The lower bound for this problem in [16] applies only to algorithms returning the name of the region containing the queried point. The techniques of the present paper extend this bound to work for simpler decision queries like

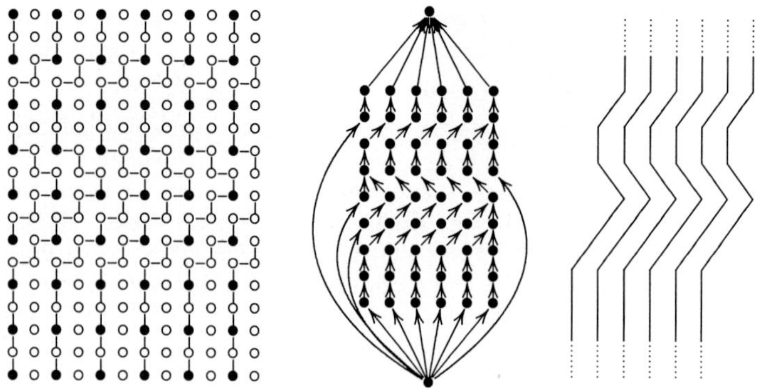

Fig. 1. Planar graphs corresponding to $x = (0,\ 0,\ +1,\ +1,\ -1,\ 0,\ +1,\ 0)$. Left: grid graph. Even grid points are marked $\bullet$, odd grid points are marked $\circ$. Middle: upward planar source–sink graph. Right: monotone planar subdivision.

query(x): return 'yes' if and only if x is in the same polygon as the origin.

Proposition 4 *Planar point location requires time* $\Omega(\log n/\log\log n)$ *per operation, even in monotone subdivisions.*

Traditionally, lower bounds in Computational Geometry are proved in an algebraic, comparison-based model (see [23] for a textbook account) that is broken by standard RAM operations like indirect addressing, bucketing, hashing, etc. Cell probe lower bounds for that field are lacking.

To explain our reduction we turn to the conceptually very simple class of *grid graphs*. The vertices of a grid graph of width w and height h are integer points (i, j) in the plane for $1 \leq i \leq w$ and $1 \leq j \leq h$. All edges have length 1 and are parallel to the axes. The dynamic reachability problem for these graphs is the following:

flip(x, y): add an edge between $x \in [w] \times [h]$ and $y \in [w] \times [h]$ or remove it if it exists,

reachable(x, y): return 'yes' if and only if there is a path from x to y.

There are several well-known constructions that prove a lower bound for this problem [8, 12, 14, 21], but our proof translates to the other problems in Props. 2 to 4. The details in these constructions are omitted, Fig. 1 illustrates the structures arising in the reductions.

Proposition 5 *Dynamic reachability in grid graphs requires time* $\Omega(\log n/\log\log n)$ *per operation.*

Proof. From an instance $x \in \{0, \pm 1\}^n$ to signed partial sum we build a grid graph on the points $\{0, \ldots, 2w\} \times \{0, \ldots, 2n\}$, where $w = \lceil \log n/\log\log n \rceil$. We will exploit the balancing constraint (2) of Thm. 1 to keep the instance within this width.

For every i and j, consider any point with even coordinates $(2i, 2j-2)$, drawn as $\bullet$ in Fig. 1, and connect it to one of the three even grid points above it using 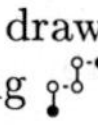, , or 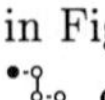, depending on whether $x_j = +1$, 0, or -1, respectively. The idea is that the path from $(0, 0)$ mimics the prefix sums of x in that it passes through $(2s, 2j)$ if and only if

$x_1 + \cdots + x_j$ equals s. Hence a guess of the sum can be verified by a single reachability query in the graph.

It remains to note that the graph can be maintained efficiently. Any changed letter in x incurs $O(w)$ edges to be inserted or deleted. So if the update time of the graph algorithm is polylogarithmic then the graph can be maintained in polylogarithmic time. The bound follows from Thm. 1. ∎

The width of the hard graph above is logarithmic in the height, while the graphs constructed in [8, 12, 14, 21] are square. Hence narrow grid graphs are as hard as square ones. However, this is not true for *very* narrow graphs: It is known that the reachability problem for grid graphs of *constant* width can be solved in time $O(\log\log n)$ by [2], an exponential improvement. This leaves open the question of what happens for graphs of sublogarithmic width. To answer this, we introduce a subtler statement of Thm. 1.

Theorem 1 (Parameterised) *Let $d = O\big(\log n/\log(bt_{\mathrm{u}}\log n)\big)$ be an integer function. Every nondeterministic algorithm for signed partial sum with cell size b, update time t_{u}, and query time t_{q} must satisfy $t_{\mathrm{q}} = \Omega(d)$. The lower bound holds even if the algorithm requires $0 \leq x_1 + \cdots + x_i \leq d$ for all i after each update.*

This result implies a lower bound for grid graphs that smoothly connects the two extremes between linear and constant width. A similar parameterisation can be done for all our problems.

Proposition 6 *For every $w = O(\log n/\log\log n)$, dynamic reachability in grid graphs of width w requires time $\Omega(w)$ per operation.*

4.3 Partial sum problems. The partial sum problem [11, 29] is to maintain a bit string $x \in \{0,1\}^n$ under the following operations

update(i): change x_i to $1 - x_i$,

sum(i): return $x_1 + \cdots + x_i$.

It was shown in [13] that the parity query

parity(i): return $x_1 + \cdots + x_i \mod 2$,

requires time $\Omega(\log n/\log\log n)$, so even the least significant bit is hard to maintain. We turn to two other natural variants, *prefix majority* and *prefix equality* whose query operations are

majority(i): return 1 iff $x_1 + \cdots + x_i \geq \lceil \frac{1}{2}n \rceil$,

equality(i): return 1 iff $x_1 + \cdots + x_i = \lceil \frac{1}{2}n \rceil$.

These problems arise in many data structures, e.g. when following paths towards heavy subtrees in balanced search trees. We can also dress up these problems as database queries like 'did as many male as female guests arrive before noon?' or 'are more French than English talks scheduled between Tuesday and Friday?' Similarly, these problems can be viewed as natural *range query* problems in Computational Geometry.

No nontrivial lower bounds for these two problems follow from [13]. The results from [4, 19, 20, 27] can be seen to imply $\Omega(\log\log n/\log\log\log n)$ lower bounds using an entirely different technique based on Ajtai's result [1]; and [16] reports $\Omega((\log n/\log\log n)^{1/2})$ for equality and $\Omega(\log n/(\log\log n)^2)$ for the majority.

The next result shows that these problems are just as hard as the parity query from [13]. The proof is again a simple application of Thm. 1.

Proposition 7 *The prefix equality and prefix majority problems require time $\Omega(\log n/\log\log n)$ per operation.*

There are other partial sum problems that are far easier. Consider the query

or(i): return 'yes' iff $x_1 + \cdots + x_i \geq 1$.

This problem, *prefix-or*, can be solved in time $O(\log\log n)$ per operation by a van Emde Boas tree. To study this kind of problem in a general, let the *threshold* ϑ be an integer function such that $\vartheta(i) \in \{0, \ldots, \lceil \frac{1}{2} i \rceil\}$. The query in the *prefix threshold problem for* ϑ is

threshold(i): return 'yes' iff $x_1 + \cdots + x_i \geq \vartheta(i)$.

Prefix majority is the special case $\vartheta(i) = \lceil \frac{1}{2} i \rceil$, prefix-or is $\vartheta(i) = 1$. Now for our lower bound. Our assumption on ϑ is that there are integers $p(1) < p(2) < \cdots < p(i) < \cdots$ such that $\vartheta(p(i)) = i$. We call such functions *nice* for lack of a better word. It is reasonable to assume that ϑ is monotonically increasing, the niceness assumption also prevents it from skipping points.

Proposition 8 *Let $t_u = t_u(n)$ and $t_q = t_q(n)$ denote the update and query time of any cell size b implementation of the prefix threshold problem for a nice threshold ϑ. Then $t_q = \Omega(\log\vartheta / \log(t_u b \log\vartheta))$.*

The proof is not difficult but tedious. The idea is to stretch an instance for a threshold problem, padding it with sufficiently many 0s or 1s to turn it into a majority problem.

To gauge the strength of this result we mention that the problem can be solved on the unit-cost RAM with logarithmic cell-size in time $O\big((\log\vartheta / \log\log n) + \log\log n\big)$ per update (if $\vartheta(1), \ldots, \vartheta(n)$ can be computed in the preprocessing stage of the algorithm). The left term in the expression stems from a search tree, the right term from a priority queue, which vanishes for cell size $b = \Omega(\log^2 n)$; details are omitted. Comparison with Prop. 8 shows that the lower bound is tight for logarithmic cell size and $\vartheta = \Omega(\log^{\log\log n} n)$. For smaller thresholds, the bounds leave a gap of size $O(\log\log n)$. We consider a more general problem in Sect. 5.1.

5 Refinement

We now take a somewhat subtler approach to our basic question than in Sect. 2. Instead of nondeterminism, we study the performance of query algorithms in a *promise* setting. We assume that the query algorithm for signed partial sum receives a value s that is promised to be *close to* (but not known to be equal to) the right sum and then decides between right and wrong values.

The *partial sum refinement* problem can be phrased as follows: Maintain a string $x \in \{0, \pm 1\}^n$, initially 0^n, under the following operations:

update(i, a): change x_i to $a \in \{-1, 0, +1\}$,

parity(i, s): return $x_1 + \cdots + x_i \mod 2$ provided that $|s - \sum_{j=1}^{i} x_j| \leq 1$ (otherwise the behaviour of the query algorithm is undefined).

The problem gets its name from the following alternative definition, where the query operation is replaced by

refine(i, s): return 1 if $s = \sum_{j=1}^{i} x_j$ and 0 if $s \neq \sum_{j=1}^{i} x_j$, provided that $|s - \sum_{j=1}^{i} x_j| \leq 1$. For other values of s, the answer is undefined.

The two problems reduce to each other.

Theorem 2 *Let d be an integer function such that $d = O(\log n / \log(t_u b \log n))$. Every algorithm for partial sum refinement with cell size b, update time t_u and query time t_q must satisfy $t_q = \Omega(d)$. Moreover, this is true even for algorithms that require $0 \leq x_1 + \cdots + x_i \leq d$ for all i after each update.*

5.1 The dynamic prefix problem for symmetric functions. Thm. 2 acts as an important ingredient in characterising the dynamic complexity of all the *symmetric functions*, generalising the results for the threshold functions of last section. A Boolean function is *symmetric* if it depends only on the number of 1s in the input $x = (x_1, \ldots, x_n)$. The symmetric functions include some of the most well-studied functions in complexity theory, like parity, majority, and the threshold functions.

In general, we can describe every symmetric function f in n variables by its *spectrum*, a string in $\{0,1\}^{n+1}$ whose ith letter is the value of f on inputs where exactly i variables are 1. The *boundary* of a spectrum s is the smallest value ϑ such that $s_{\lfloor\vartheta\rfloor} = s_{\lfloor\vartheta\rfloor+1} = \cdots = s_{\lfloor n-\vartheta\rfloor}$. For instance the boundary of the parity or majority functions is $\frac{1}{2}n$, and for the threshold functions with threshold ϑ, the boundary is $\min(\vartheta, n-\vartheta)$.

Let $\langle f_n \rangle = (f_1, \ldots, f_n)$ be a sequence of symmetric Boolean function where the ith function f_i takes i variables. The *dynamic prefix problem for* $\langle f_n \rangle$ is to maintain a bit string $x \in \{0,1\}^n$ under the following operations:

update(i): change x_i to $\neg x_i$,

query(i): return $f_i(x_1, \ldots, x_i)$.

For example, taking f_i to be the parity function on i variables we have the prefix parity problem of [13], and taking f_i to be the threshold function for $\vartheta(i)$ we have the problem from Prop. 8.

Proposition 9 *Let ϑ be a nice function and let $\langle f_n \rangle$ be a sequence of symmetric functions where $f_i\colon \{0,1\}^i \to \{0,1\}$ has boundary $\vartheta(i)$. Let t_u and t_q denote the update and query time of any cell size b implementation of the dynamic prefix problem for $\langle f_n \rangle$. Then $t_q = \Omega(\log\vartheta / \log(t_u b \log\vartheta))$.*

Intriguingly, the bound in the proposition is precisely the same bound as for the size–depth trade-off for Boolean circuits for these functions [17, 6, 22].

Acknowledgements

The authors thank Arne Anderson, Gerth Stølting Brodal, Faith Fich, Peter Bro Miltersen, and Sven Skyum for valuable comments about various aspects of this work.

References

1. M. Ajtai. A lower bound for finding predecessors in Yao's cell probe model. *Combinatorica*, 8(3):235–247, 1988.
2. D. Mix Barrington, C. Lu, P. Bro Miltersen, and S. Skyum. Searching constant width mazes captures the AC^0-hierarchy. In *STACS*, 1998.
3. H. Baumgarten, H. Jung, and K. Mehlhorn. Dynamic point location in general subdivisions. In *Proc. 3rd SODA*, pages 250–258, 1992.
4. P. Beame and F. Fich. On searching sorted lists: A near-optimal lower bound. Manuscript, 1997.
5. A.M. Ben-Amram and Z. Galil. Lower bounds for data structure problems on RAMs. In *Proc. 32nd FOCS*, pages 622–631, 1991.
6. B. Brustmann and I. Wegener. The complexity of symmetric functions in bounded-depth circuits. *Inf. Proc. Letters*, 25(4):217–219, 1987.
7. P.F. Dietz. Optimal algorithms for list indexing and subset rank. In *Proc. 1st WADS*, volume 382 of *LNCS*, pages 39–46. 1989.
8. D. Eppstein. Dynamic connectivity in digital images. *Inf. Proc. Letters*, 62(3):121–126, 1997.

9. G.S. Frandsen, T. Husfeldt, P. Bro Miltersen, T. Rauhe, and S. Skyum. Dynamic algorithms for the Dyck languages. In *Proc. 4th WADS*, volume 955 of *LNCS*, pages 98–108. Springer, 1995.
10. Michael L. Fredman. Observations on the complexity of generating quasi-Gray codes. *SIAM J. Comput.*, 7(2):134–146, 1978.
11. Michael L. Fredman. The complexity of maintaining an array and computing its partial sums. *J. ACM*, 29:250–260, 1982.
12. M.L. Fredman and M. Rauch Henzinger. Lower bounds for fully dynamic connectivity problems in graphs. *Algorithmica.* To appear.
13. M.L. Fredman and M.E. Saks. The cell probe complexity of dynamic data structures. In *Proc. 21st STOC*, pages 345–354, 1989.
14. T. Husfeldt. Fully dynamic transitive closure in plane dags with one source and one sink. In *Proc. 3rd ESA*, volume 955 of *LNCS*, pages 199–212. 1995.
15. T. Husfeldt and T. Rauhe. Hardness results for dynamic problems by extensions of Fredman and Saks' chronogram method. Full version of this paper, available at http://www.brics.dk/RS/97/32/.
16. T. Husfeldt, T. Rauhe, and S. Skyum. Lower bounds for dynamic transitive closure, planar point location, and parentheses matching. *Nordic J. Comp.*, 3(4):323–336, 1996.
17. J.T. Håstad. Almost optimal lower bounds for small depth circuits. In *Proc. 18th STOC*, pages 6–20, 1986.
18. G.F. Italiano, J.A. La Poutré, and M.H. Rauch. Fully dynamic planarity testing in planar embedded graphs. In *Proc. 1st ESA*, volume 726 of *LNCS*, pages 212–223. 1993.
19. P. Bro Miltersen. Lower bounds for union–split–find related problems on random access machines. In *Proc. 26th STOC*, pages 625–634, 1994.
20. P. Bro Miltersen, N. Nisan, S. Safra, and A. Wigderson. On data structures and asymmetric communication complexity. In *Proc. 27th STOC*, pages 103–111, 1995.
21. P. Bro Miltersen, S. Subramanian, J.S. Vitter, and R. Tamassia. Complexity models for incremental computation. *TCS*, 130:203–236, 1994.
22. S. Moran. Generalized lower bounds derived from Hastad's main lemma. *Inf. Proc. Letters*, 25:383–388, 1987.
23. F.P. Preparata and M.I. Shamos. *Computational Geometry.* Springer, 1985.
24. F.P. Preparata and R. Tamassia. Fully dynamic point location in a monotone subdivision. *SIAM J. Comp.*, 18(4):811–830, 1989.
25. R. Tamassia. On-line planar graph embedding. *J. Algorithms*, 21(2):201–239, 1996.
26. R. Tamassia and F.P. Preparata. Dynamic maintenance of planar digraphs, with applications. *Algorithmica*, 5:509–527, 1990.
27. B. Xiao. *New bounds in cell probe model.* Doctoral dissertation, University of California, San Diego, 1992.
28. A.C. Yao. Should tables be sorted? *J. ACM*, 28(3):615–628, July 1981.
29. A.C. Yao. On the complexity of maintaining partial sums. *SIAM J. Comput.*, 14(2):277–288, 1985.

Simpler and Faster Dictionaries on the AC^0 RAM*

Torben Hagerup

Max-Planck-Institut für Informatik, D–66123 Saarbrücken, Germany
torben@mpi-sb.mpg.de

Abstract. We consider the static dictionary problem of using $O(n)$ w-bit words to store n w-bit keys for fast retrieval on a w-bit AC^0 RAM, i.e., on a RAM with a word length of w bits whose instruction set is arbitrary, except that each instruction must be realizable through an unbounded-fanin circuit of constant depth and $w^{O(1)}$ size. We improve the best known upper bound for moderate values of w relative to n. If $w/\log n = (\log\log n)^{O(1)}$, query time $(\log\log\log n)^{O(1)}$ is achieved, and if additionally $w/\log n \geq (\log\log n)^{1+\epsilon}$ for some fixed $\epsilon > 0$, the query time is constant. For both of these special cases, the best previous upper bound was $O(\log\log n)$. A new lower bound is also observed.

1 Introduction

The *static dictionary problem* is one of the most fundamental data-structuring problems. Informally, an instance of the problem is given by a set X of *keys*, each with associated *satellite data*, and the task is to store X in a way that allows rapid retrieval of the satellite data of a given key. Formally, we fix a *universe* U of possible key values and consider an instance of the problem to be given by a finite subset $X \subseteq U$, called the *key set*. A *static dictionary* for the key set X is a data structure $\mathcal{D}$ that supports *searches* for elements of U, as follows: If $x \in X$, a search for x in $\mathcal{D}$ returns $\pi(x)$, called the *index* of x, where π is an arbitrary but fixed bijection from X to $\{1, \ldots, |X|\}$; if $x \in U \setminus X$, a search for x in $\mathcal{D}$ may return an arbitrary element of $\{1, \ldots, |X|\}$. The *static dictionary problem* is to realize a static dictionary $\mathcal{D}$ for a given key set X, parameters of interest being the space occupied by $\mathcal{D}$ and the *query time*, the time needed to carry out a search in $\mathcal{D}$, but not the time needed to construct $\mathcal{D}$ from X.

Since our formal definition of the static dictionary problem is somewhat nonstandard and, at first glance, may appear rather different from the informal description, we argue that the two are, in fact, quite close. In order to obtain a static dictionary in the formal sense from one in the informal sense, we can simply store the index of each key as its associated satellite data. And to go the other way, we can support satellite data by interpreting each index as a pointer into a table of satellite data or, if the keys have different amounts of associated

* Part of this work was carried out while the author held a visiting position at the Department of Computer Science, University of Copenhagen, Denmark.

satellite data, as a pointer into a table that in turn contains pointers to the satellite data (see Fig. 1).

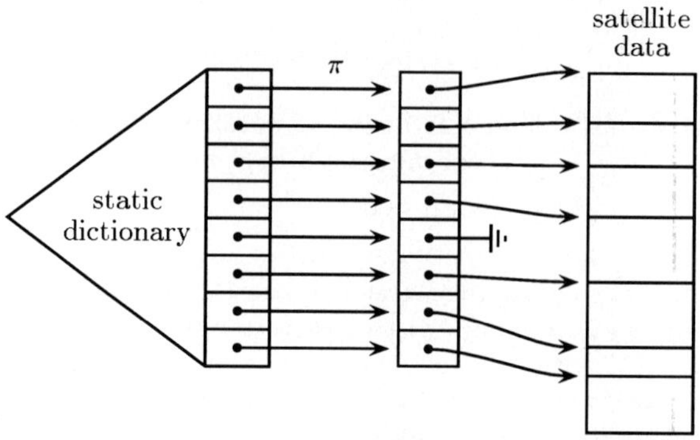

Fig. 1. A static dictionary augmented with satellite data

The model of computation used in this paper is the *word RAM.* This model is related to the classic unit-cost RAM of Cook and Reckhow [4], the main difference being that, for a certain integer parameter $w \geq 1$ called the *word length*, all values stored in memory cells are nonnegative w-bit integers (i.e., elements of $\{0, \ldots, 2^w - 1\}$), sometimes identified with strings of w bits each and called *words.* As for the classic RAM, we assume a word RAM to have constant-time instructions for executing direct and indirect loads and stores as well as conditional and unconditional jumps. In addition, the instruction set of a word RAM contains a finite number of constant-time *arithmetic instructions*, each of which maps a constant number of operand words (usually two words) to a single result word. We always assume the arithmetic instruction set to be a superset of the *restricted instruction set*, which comprises addition and subtraction modulo 2^w, left and right shift (with zero filling) by a variable number of bit positions, as well as the bitwise boolean operations AND, OR, and NOT. Additional instructions will be specified in the following. Specializing the static dictionary problem to the word RAM with word length w, we fix the universe U of possible keys to be the set $\{0, \ldots, 2^w - 1\}$. We focus on *linear-space* dictionaries, ones that store n keys using $\Theta(n)$ w-bit words. We will assume that $w \geq 2 \log n$ (all logarithms in the paper are to base 2), so that we can actually address $\Theta(n)$ words of storage.

A class $\mathcal{H}$ of functions from U to a finite set S is said to be *universal* if there is a constant $c > 0$ such that for all $x, y \in U$ with $x \neq y$, $|\{h \in \mathcal{H} : h(x) = h(y)\}| \leq c|\mathcal{H}|/|S|$ (several related definitions are common). In a celebrated result, Fredman et al. [6] showed that if for each integer $s \geq 1$ there is a universal class $\mathcal{H}_s$ of functions from U to $\{0, \ldots, s-1\}$ (such that the classes share a common value of the implicit constant c), each of whose functions can be represented in a constant number of words and evaluated in constant time when s is bounded by the size of the key set, then the static dictionary problem has a linear-space solution with constant query time. Such families of universal classes actually exist. E.g., the original formulation of Fredman et al. used $\mathcal{H}_s = \{x \mapsto (kx \bmod p) \bmod s \mid 1 \le k < p\}$, for $s = 1, 2, \ldots$, where p is an arbitrary prime larger than 2^w. While the resulting static dictionary is a very appealing data structure, it yields constant query time only under the assumption that constant-time multiplication and integer division are available. It has been argued that this assumption is not realistic for large word lengths because the operations of multiplication and integer division are not *AC^0 operations* [7, 9], i.e., they cannot be realized with unbounded-fanin circuits of constant depth and polynomial size (which, in the present context, means $w^{O(1)}$ size). Motivated by such concerns, Andersson et al. [1] studied the problem of implementing *static AC^0 dictionaries*, static dictionaries whose search operations use only AC^0 instructions. We continue this study, requiring the set of AC^0 instructions used to be finite and independent of the key set stored. All instructions in the restricted instruction set are AC^0 instructions.

Many families of universal classes of functions other than the one described above have been proposed; in particular, Dietzfelbinger et al. [5] showed how to eliminate the need for integer division and get by with multiplication as the only instruction outside the restricted instruction set. However, none of these classes consists of functions that can be evaluated in constant time using only AC^0 instructions and, indeed, Mansour et al. [10, Theorem 6.3(1)] proved that such a class cannot exist (for a slightly different notion of universality). While this does not in itself imply anything about the existence of fast static AC^0 dictionaries, it does suggest that maybe universal classes are not the way to go. It turns out, however, that a modification of a well-known universal class yields an efficient construction.

Carter and Wegman, who introduced the concept of a universal class, proved that for any two finite-dimensional vector spaces V and W over the two-element field, the class of all linear mappings from V to W is universal [3, Proposition 9]. Thus if r and b are positive integers and $\mathcal{M}^{r \times b}$ is the set of all $r \times b$ matrices with entries in $\{0, 1\}$, then the class $\mathcal{H} = \{x \mapsto Ax \bmod 2 \mid A \in \mathcal{M}^{r \times b}\}$ is universal. (Recall that we identify integers with bit strings, which here in turn are identified with 0-1 column vectors in the obvious way.) Premultiplication with arbitrary matrices in $\mathcal{M}^{r \times b}$ modulo 2 is not an AC^0 operation. However, Andersson et al. [1] constructed a static AC^0 dictionary based on the following two observations: (1) If A is *sparse*, i.e., if each row of A contains only a small number of entries equal to 1, then premultiplication with A may be easy (depending on the representation of A). (2) Although two keys may be very likely to collide (be mapped to the same value) under premultiplication with a randomly chosen sparse matrix, this happens only for keys whose binary representations largely coincide, and collisions between such keys are easier to handle. The static AC^0 dictionary of Andersson et al. has query time

$$O\left(\min\left\{\frac{\log w \cdot \max\{\log\log\log n - \log\log\log w, 1\}}{\log\log w}, \sqrt{\frac{\log n}{\log\log n}}\right\}\right)$$

and uses linear or near-linear space (a linear space bound is claimed, but does not appear obvious from the (recursive) construction).

We reuse some of the building blocks of Andersson et al. [1], in particular, those underlying what is here called sampling and block compression, but implement one of them more efficiently and put them together in a simpler and cleaner way that achieves a stronger result. Taking $z = w/\log n$, we achieve a query time of

$$O\left(\min\left\{(\log z)^{\log 3/\log(3/2)}, \left(1 + \frac{\log z}{\log\log w}\right) \cdot 2^{2\log z/\log(2+z/\log w)}, 1 + \frac{\log n}{\log w}\right\}\right)$$

together with a linear space bound. The exponent $\log 3/\log(3/2)$ is approximately 2.71.

For moderate values of w, namely as long as $w = 2^{(\log n)^{o(1)}}$, the new bound is stronger than the bound of Andersson et al. [1], and it is never weaker. E.g., for $z = (\log\log n)^{O(1)}$, the new query time is always $O((\log\log\log n)^{2.71})$, and if additionally $z \geq (\log\log n)^{1+\epsilon}$ for some fixed $\epsilon > 0$, the query time is constant. In both cases, the bound of Andersson et al. is $O(\log\log n)$. For this range of w of arguably greatest practical relevance—in realistic situations, w is larger than $\log n$, but not much larger—we thus achieve what is sometimes called an "exponential improvement". If we eliminate the parameter w to obtain a bound that depends only on n (thus, for every value of n, w is chosen in a worst-case manner), the bound of Andersson et al. and the new bound both simplify to $O(\sqrt{\log n/\log\log n})$, which matches a lower bound of $\Omega(\sqrt{\log n/\log\log n})$ of Andersson et al. Proposition 28 and Theorem 34 of [1], the latter used with $\mathrm{B} = w^{O(1)}$ and $\mathrm{S} = O(\log(nw))$, in fact show that every linear-space static dictionary for n w-bit keys that uses only AC^0 instructions must have query time $\Omega(\min\{\log w/\log\log n, \log n/\log w\})$, which generalizes the bound of Andersson et al. and shows the new static dictionary to be optimal for $w = 2^{(\log n)^{\Omega(1)}}$. The new upper bound thus improves the upper bound of [1] everywhere except where the bound of [1] was already optimal.

Just as for the data structure of Andersson et al., standard methods can be used to derive from our static dictionary a *dynamic* randomized dictionary with the same query time and insertion and deletion times of the same order, except that an update may take longer with probability at most n^{-c}, where n is the current number of keys and c is an arbitrary constant. We can also obtain a deterministic dynamic *neighbor dictionary*, additionally supporting predecessor and successor queries, with operation times of $O((\log n)^{2/3}/(\log\log n)^{1/3})$, except that for insertion the bound applies only in the amortized sense. This slightly improves the bound of $O((\log n)^{2/3})$ of [2], derived in the same way.

2 Overview

In this section we first cite two previous results to which we will appeal repeatedly and then give an overview over our construction.

Multiplication and integer division of b-bit integers can be carried out by looking up the result in tables of $O(2^{2b}b)$ bits, and multiplication and integer division of $O(b)$-bit integers reduce to multiplication and integer division of b-bit integers via standard algorithms for multiple-precision arithmetic. The result of Fredman et al. [6] discussed in the introduction therefore implies the following.

Lemma 1 ([1]). *For $w = O(\log n)$, there is a linear-space static AC^0 dictionary for n keys with constant query time.*

The following result, in contrast, provides a linear-space static dictionary with constant query time for sufficiently large values of w relative to n.

Lemma 2. *There is a linear-space static AC^0 dictionary for n keys with query time $O(1 + \log n / \log w)$.*

Proof. It was shown in [8, Theorem 6] that there is even a linear-space *dynamic* AC^0 dictionary with the stated time bound. □

In light of Lemma 2, we can assume without loss of generality that $w \le n$. In particular, a pointer into a block of $O(nw)$ bits can be stored in $O(\log n)$ bits. We shall frequently need such pointers to locate various parts of a static dictionary. Since $O(\log n)$ bits will always be a negligible amount of storage, however, these pointers will not be mentioned explicitly.

Suppressing a few details, we can describe the task of a static dictionary as that of mapping a key set X injectively to the set $\{1, \ldots, |X|\}$. We solve this problem by first mapping $X = X_0$ injectively to a set X_1 of keys of fewer bits, then mapping X_1 to a set X_2 of still shorter keys, and so on, until finally X_k is mapped injectively to $\{1, \ldots, |X|\}$, for some $k \ge 0$. For $i = 1, \ldots, k$, the mapping of X_{i-1} to X_i is called a *reduction*, and each reduction will access its own auxiliary data stored as part of the complete static dictionary.

Each reduction is composed of three mappings that are applied successively to the keys under consideration, the *sampling*, the *block compression*, and the *cleanup mapping*. We next describe these three mappings in turn, assuming that we are dealing with a key set X of n keys of $b \le w$ bits each. Let s and t be parameters that will be fixed later as squares of positive integers and take $r = 8t\lceil \log n \rceil$.

The sampling maps each b-bit key to an r-bit *signature* concatenated with a b-bit *offset*. Call a matrix with entries in $\{0, 1\}$ a *sampling pattern*. The r-bit signature of a b-bit key x is obtained as $Ax \bmod 2$, where A is an $r \times b$ sampling pattern, bit strings are identified with column vectors, and the modulo operation is applied separately to each component. In the context of a particular $r \times b$ sampling pattern A, we define a *cluster* (with respect to X and A) to be an equivalence class of the equivalence relation $\sim$ on X defined by $x \sim y \Leftrightarrow Ax \equiv Ay \pmod 2$; i.e., two keys belong to the same cluster if and only if they have the same signature. In general, the signature alone will not be enough to distinguish all keys in X; i.e., some clusters may contain more than one key. The offset serves to distinguish the keys within each cluster and simply measures the bitwise difference, modulo 2, to a fixed key in the cluster called the *representative* of the cluster. If the representative of a cluster containing a key x is the key x', the b-bit offset of x is thus computed as $x \oplus x'$, where $\oplus$ denotes the bitwise exclusive-or operation, i.e., bitwise addition modulo 2. The sampling is clearly injective.

In order to compute the offset of a given key, we need to know the representative of the cluster defined by the signature of the key. We therefore store all signatures of keys in X in a separate static dictionary—realized either recursively or according to Lemma 1—and store the representatives as their satellite data. We can also use this to replace each signature by a *signature index* of $\lceil \log n \rceil$ bits, another obviously injective mapping.

The sampling replaces the original keys by longer keys, which may seem counterproductive. The point is, however, that the offsets will have small *Hamming norms*, where the Hamming norm of a bit string x, denoted $||x||$, is the number of occurrences of a 1 in x. Informally, the reason for this is that if two keys x and y belong to the same cluster and thus fail to be distinguished by their signatures, x and y will agree on many bits, so that their *Hamming distance*, $||x \oplus y||$, will be small; in particular, the Hamming distance of each key x from the representative of its cluster, which is the Hamming norm of the offset of x, will be small. More precisely, we will ensure that the Hamming norm of each offset is bounded by $b/(st)$. The block compression capitalizes on this fact.

The block compression operates on the transformed keys consisting of signature indices and offsets. It leaves the signature indices unchanged, but replaces each offset by a *directory* concatenated with a *compressed offset.* The details are as follows (see Fig. 2): The b-bit offset is viewed as a sequence of $\lceil b/\sqrt{st} \rceil$ *blocks* of

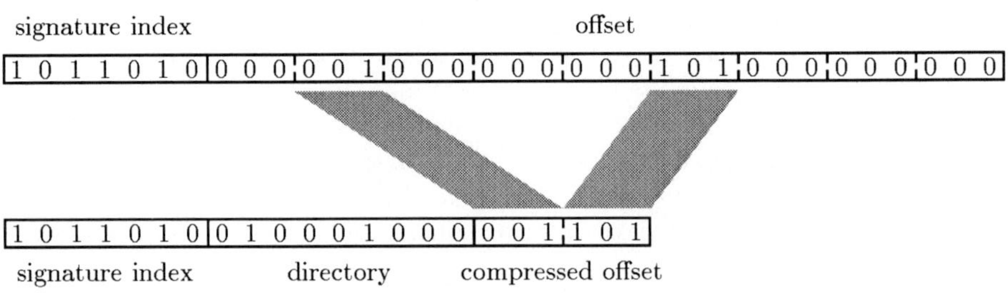

Fig. 2. The block compression

$\sqrt{st}$ consecutive bits each, except that the last block may be smaller (recall that st is a perfect square). The directory consists of $\lceil b/\sqrt{st} \rceil$ bits, the ith of which, for $i = 1, \ldots, \lceil b/\sqrt{st} \rceil$, has the value 1 if and only if the ith block is nonzero, i.e., contains at least one bit with a value of 1. The directory thus specifies the set of nonzero blocks in a straightforward manner, and the compressed offset is simply the concatenation of the nonzero blocks in their original order. The block compression is clearly injective. Since the Hamming norm of each offset is bounded by $b/(st)$, the number of nonzero blocks is bounded by the same quantity, and thus each compressed offset consists of at most $b/(st) \cdot \sqrt{st} = b/\sqrt{st}$ bits; we append zeros as necessary to make the number of bits be exactly $\lfloor b/\sqrt{st} \rfloor$.

It turns out that we can compute a compressed offset efficiently from the corresponding offset only if we have access to certain "magic numbers" that depend on the relevant directory. For this reason we store the directories in yet another separate static dictionary—realized recursively—and store the "magic numbers" as their satellite data. As above, we can then replace each directory by a *directory index* of $\lceil \log n \rceil$ bits.

The sampling and block compression together replace each b-bit key by a signature index of $\lceil \log n \rceil$ bits, a directory index of $\lceil \log n \rceil$ bits, and a compressed offset of $\lfloor b/\sqrt{st} \rfloor$ bits, a total of $q = 2\lceil \log n \rceil + \lfloor b/\sqrt{st} \rfloor$ bits. The cleanup mapping reduces the number of bits in the keys further to $\max\{\lfloor b/\sqrt{st} \rfloor, \lceil \log n \rceil\}$ by replacing the leftmost $\min\{3\lceil \log n \rceil, q\}$ bits of each key by an index of $\lceil \log n \rceil$ bits by means of a static dictionary realized according to Lemma 1. The net effect of the three parts of a reduction is to reduce the number of bits in the keys from b to $\lfloor b/\sqrt{st} \rfloor$ or, in the case of the last reduction, to $\lceil \log n \rceil$. As part of the reduction we must realize two auxiliary static dictionaries, each of which contains at most n keys. One of these dictionaries (for the signatures) contains r-bit keys, while the other (for the directories) contains keys of $\lceil b/\sqrt{st} \rceil$ bits, which we can reduce to $\lfloor b/\sqrt{st} \rfloor$ bits as in the cleanup mapping. In addition, we must deal with the transformed keys of $\lfloor b/\sqrt{st} \rfloor$ bits each. When executing a query, we must carry out one search in each of the two auxiliary dictionaries and one search for the transformed key.

In the following sections we will argue the existence of sampling patterns that cause the Hamming norms of all offsets to be sufficiently small, discuss the implementation of the sampling and block compression, realize a complete static dictionary as a cascade of successive reductions, and finally estimate the query time and the space requirements of the complete static dictionary.

3 A Reduction: The Details

For $s \geq 0$, let us call a sampling pattern A *s-sparse* if no row in A contains more than s bits with a value of 1. We will employ only s-sparse sampling patterns for relatively small values of s because such sampling patterns can be stored and applied efficiently. The following lemma is instrumental in showing the existence of suitable s-sparse sampling patterns.

Lemma 3. *Let Z be binomially distributed with parameters s and p, where s is odd. Then* $\Pr(Z \textit{ is odd}) \geq \frac{1}{2}(1 - \Pr(Z = 0))$.

Proof. Omitted. □

A lemma similar to Lemma 4 below was stated without proof by Andersson et al. [1, Lemma 12].

Lemma 4. *Let n, b, s and t be positive integers, where s is odd, take $r = 8t\lceil\log n\rceil$, and let X be a set of n strings of b bits each. Then there is an s-sparse $r \times b$ sampling pattern A with the property that for all $x, y \in X$ with $||x \oplus y|| \geq b/(st)$, we have $Ax \not\equiv Ay \pmod 2$.*

Proof. We use the *probabilistic method* and exhibit a random process that, with nonzero probability, yields a sampling pattern with the property mentioned in the lemma. The random process is simple: Starting from an all-zero sampling pattern, we process the r rows independently of each other. For each row, we s times in succession choose a position in the row at random from the uniform distribution over the set of all b positions and independently of all other such choices and invert the bit stored in that position.

Fix two arbitrary elements x and y of X with $||x \oplus y|| \geq b/(st)$ and consider a particular row a of A, viewed as a random quantity. Since $(ax + ay) \bmod 2 = a(x \oplus y) \bmod 2$, we will have $ax \not\equiv ay \pmod 2$ and hence $Ax \not\equiv Ay \pmod 2$ if a contains an *odd* number of bits equal to 1 in positions in which $x \oplus y$ holds a 1. The latter is the case exactly if the number Z of inversions of bits of a carried out in such positions is odd (even though the two odd numbers may not coincide, due to cancellations). The random variable Z is binomially distributed with parameters s and $||x \oplus y||/b \geq 1/(st)$, and we can apply Lemma 3. $\Pr(Z = 0) \leq (1 - 1/(st))^s \leq e^{-1/t} \leq 1 - \frac{1}{2t}$, where in the last step we used the inequality $e^{-u} \leq 1 - u/2$, valid for $0 \leq u \leq 1$. Thus $\Pr(Z \text{ is odd}) \geq \frac{1}{4t}$. In other words, a fixed row of A distinguishes between x and y with probability at least $\frac{1}{4t}$, and the probability that none of the $r = 8t\lceil\log n\rceil$ rows of A distinguishes between x and y is bounded by $(1 - \frac{1}{4t})^r \leq e^{-(8/4)\lceil\log n\rceil} < 1/n^2$. The number of pairs $x, y \in X$ with $||x \oplus y|| \geq b/(st)$ is bounded by n^2, and therefore the probability that some such pair is not distinguished by A is strictly smaller than 1. □

Choosing the sampling pattern A employed by the sampling mapping of a reduction in accordance with Lemma 4 guarantees that the Hamming norm of each offset of the reduction is bounded by $b/(st)$, as anticipated in the previous section.

We next discuss the implementation of the sampling in terms of AC^0 instructions. We will represent sampling patterns in two different ways, the *bit-vector representation* and the *sparse-row representation*, which we consider separately.

The bit-vector representation. The suitability of a sampling pattern, its having the property mentioned in Lemma 4, is not affected by an arbitrary permutation of its rows or by the replacement of all but one occurrence of a particular row by all-zero rows. We can therefore assume without loss of generality that the rows of a sampling pattern are sorted in nonincreasing lexicographic order and that the nonzero rows are all distinct. This is useful in the case of a 1-sparse $r \times b$ sampling pattern A, which, if it is of this restricted kind, can be represented simply by a b-bit vector whose ith bit is 1, for $i = 1, \ldots, b$, exactly if the ith column of A contains a (single) 1. We will call a bit vector used in this way a *sampling vector* and speak of the bit-vector representation (see Fig. 3).

$$\begin{pmatrix}
0&0&1&0&0&0&0&0&0&0&0&0&0&0&0\\
0&0&0&0&1&0&0&0&0&0&0&0&0&0&0\\
0&0&0&0&0&0&0&0&1&0&0&0&0&0&0\\
0&0&0&0&0&0&0&0&0&1&0&0&0&0&0\\
0&0&0&0&0&0&0&0&0&0&0&0&0&0&1\\
0&0&0&0&0&0&0&0&0&0&0&0&0&0&0\\
0&0&0&0&0&0&0&0&0&0&0&0&0&0&0
\end{pmatrix}$$

0	0	1	0	1	0	0	0	1	1	0	0	0	0	1

Fig. 3. A sorted 1-sparse sampling pattern and the corresponding sampling vector

The mapping represented by a sampling vector can be visualized in a particularly simple way (see Fig. 4): The sampling vector specifies a set of bit positions

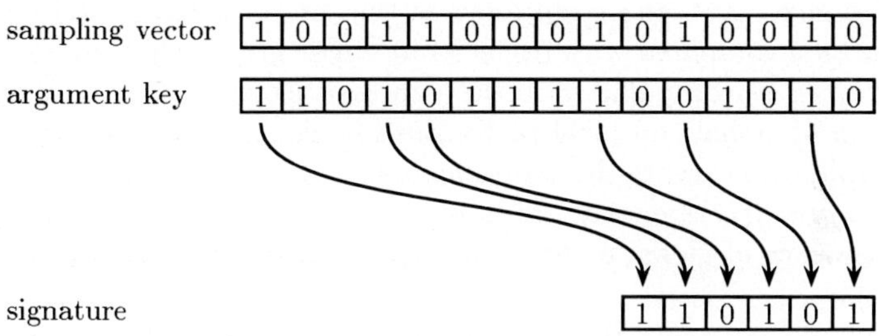

Fig. 4. The mapping represented by a sampling vector

to be "sampled", and the bits of the argument key in these positions are extracted and concatenated in their original order. In order to realize this operation by means of AC^0 instructions, we begin by connecting each input "conditionally" to each output. More precisely, we consider a circuit that maps the b bits of a key to the r bits of its signature and in which each of the r output bits is obtained as the disjunction of b bits, each of which is the conjunction of a different input bit and a *control bit*. What is still missing is circuitry to compute values for the br control bits that precisely establish the desired connections from input bits to output bits. Let us number the input and output bits as well as the bits of the sampling vector from the right starting at 1 and denote the ith bit of the sampling vector by v_i, for $i = 1, \ldots, b$. It is easy to see that the control bit that establishes a connection from the ith input bit to the jth output bit should have the value 1 exactly if $(v_i = 1) \wedge (d_i = j)$, where $d_i = \sum_{l=1}^{i} v_l$, for $i = 1, \ldots, b$ and $j = 1, \ldots, r$. Provided that $d_1, \ldots, d_b$ are available, the control bits are very easy to compute with an AC^0 circuit. The prefix sums $d_1, \ldots, d_b$ cannot be computed from $v_1, \ldots, v_b$ with an AC^0 circuit; however, just as we store the sampling vector as part of the static dictionary, we can store also its prefix sums. One complication is that we need $\Theta(b \log b)$ bits to represent all of

$d_1, \ldots, d_b$, whereas we want to get by with $O(b)$ bits—in particular, the prefix sums should fit in a single word. We can get around this complication by using the following well-known fact.

Lemma 5. *Every boolean function of* $\lceil \log(w+1) \rceil$ *bits can be computed with an unbounded-fanin circuit of constant depth and* $w^{O(1)}$ *size.*

To see that the fact is true, simply imagine a circuit that directly reflects the truth table of the function under consideration. We use the fact as follows: We divide the bits of the sampling vector into *groups* of $\lceil \log(w+1) \rceil$ consecutive bits each, except that the leftmost group may be smaller, and record only the prefix sums of the groups. In more detail, if the number of groups is g, we store as part of the static dictionary a sequence of $g-1$ *global prefix sums* of $\lceil \log(w+1) \rceil$ bits each, where the ith global prefix sum is the total number of bits equal to 1 in the i rightmost groups, for $i = 1, \ldots, g-1$. The number of bits needed to store the sequence of global prefix sums is clearly bounded by b, and each of the b original prefix sums can be obtained as the sum of a global prefix sum and a *local prefix sum* computed with respect to a single group. By Lemma 5, the local prefix sums can be computed from the sampling vector with an AC^0 circuit, and the addition of global and local prefix sums is also an AC^0 operation. We have thus shown how to execute the sampling mapping with a single AC^0 instruction, the *sampling instruction*, that takes as arguments a key, the sampling vector, and the sequence of global prefix sums. The storage required is at most $2b$ bits.

The sparse-row representation. In the sparse-row representation, also used by Andersson et al. [1], we store an s-sparse sampling pattern A as a sequence of r groups of s integers of $m = \lceil \log(w+1) \rceil$ bits each. For $i = 1, \ldots, r$, the s integers in the ith group specify the at most s positions in the ith row of A that contain a 1, a special bit pattern reserved to denote "no position" (in case the row contains fewer than s occurrences of a 1). We will later ensure that $rsm = O(w)$, so that the entire sampling pattern fits in a constant number of words, and we analyze the time needed to apply the sampling pattern under this assumption.

The application of the sampling pattern can be decomposed into two subtasks: Extracting the at most rs bits specified in the sampling pattern from the argument key and storing them in consecutive positions of a word (they will fit, except for n bounded by a constant); and forming the sum, modulo 2, of the bits within each of the r groups of s consecutive bits. The first subtask can be carried out in constant time using a "multiselect" circuit that is easy to devise and shown explicitly in [8, Fig. 11]. If $s = m^k$ for some integer $k \geq 1$, the second subtask can be carried out by k successive applications of a one-argument operation that views its argument as composed of segments of m bits each and replaces the bits in each segment by their sum, modulo 2 (storing the resulting bits in consecutive positions); by Lemma 5, this operation can be realized via an AC^0 instruction. If s is not a power of m, it is necessary first to reduce the number of bits within each group to the nearest smaller power of m. For each fixed value of s, this can be done with an AC^0 circuit C_s, much as above, and the circuits $C_1, \ldots, C_w$ can be combined into a single circuit that takes s as a second argument and uses the value of s to select the output of the correct circuit C_s. The combined circuit still realizes an AC^0 operation. Summing up, we can execute the sampling using the sparse-row representation in $O(1 + \log s/\log m) = O(1 + \log s/\log\log w)$ time.

Having dealt with the sampling, we turn to the block compression. First, the directory is very easy to compute with an AC^0 instruction. As for the computation of the compressed offset, it is similar to the sampling according to a sampling vector and can be carried out in constant time in the same way, provided that a suitable b-bit "sampling vector" and its global prefix sums are available as satellite data of the relevant directory (these are the "magic numbers" alluded to earlier). The "sampling vector" should have a 1 precisely in each position belonging to a block that is nonempty in the relevant keys.

4 The Main Result

Theorem 1. *For all integers $n \geq 4$ and $w \geq 2\log n$ and for all sets X of n w-bit integers, there is a static dictionary for the key set X that works on a word RAM with a word length of w bits and a finite and fixed instruction set containing only AC^0 instructions, uses $O(n)$ w-bit words of storage, and has query time*

$$O\left(\min\left\{(\log z)^{\log 3/\log(3/2)}, \left(1 + \frac{\log z}{\log\log w}\right) \cdot 2^{2\log z/\log(2+z/\log w)}, 1 + \frac{\log n}{\log w}\right\}\right),$$

where $z = w/\log n$.

Proof. We consider the three parts of the bound one by one. In order to show the validity of the first bound, $O((\log z)^{\log 3/\log(3/2)})$, we take $s = 1$ and represent all sampling patterns according to the bit-vector representation. For a reduction that inputs keys of $b \geq \log n$ bits each, we choose t as the square of a positive integer such that $t = \Theta((b/\log n)^{2/3})$. The reduction spawns three new instances of the static dictionary problem (for brevity: *instances*), and the value of t was chosen to make all three instances involve keys of $O(b^{2/3}(\log n)^{1/3})$ bits each. For a suitable constant $c > 0$, this implies that the derived quantity $\log(cb/\log n)$ is reduced by a factor of at least $3/2$ from each level of recursion to the next. Since the derived quantity starts out at $O(\log(w/\log n)) = O(\log z)$ and we can end the recursion according to Lemma 1 when it reaches 1, the depth of recursion will be $\log\log z/\log(3/2) + O(1)$. But then both the total number of instances spawned and the query time will be $O(3^{\log\log z/\log(3/2)}) = O((\log z)^{\log 3/\log(3/2)})$.

A reduction that inputs keys of $b \geq \log n$ bits needs $O(nb)$ bits of storage. Each new level of recursion triples the number of instances, but except for a constant number of levels just before the recursion bottoms out, each recursive level reduces the number of bits per key by a factor of more than 6. This can be seen to imply that the total space requirements are $O(nw)$ bits or $O(n)$ words of w bits each.

In order to show the validity of the second bound of Theorem 1, observe first that we can assume that $z/\log w \geq 16$, since otherwise the first bound is surely no larger than the second bound. We take $t = 1$, choose s as a square of an odd integer with $s \geq 2 + z/\log w$, but $s = O(z/\log w)$, and represent all sampling patterns according to the sparse-row representation. The condition $rsm = O(w)$, imposed in the discussion of the sparse-row representation, now takes the form $\lceil \log n \rceil \lceil \log(w+1) \rceil s = O(w)$ and is easily seen to be satisfied, so that each reduction can be executed in $O(1 + \log z/\log\log w)$ time. The choice $t = 1$ implies that the static dictionaries storing signatures can be implemented directly using Lemma 1, for which reason each reduction now spawns only two new instances. Each recursive level reduces the number of bits in the keys under consideration by a factor of at least $\sqrt{s}$, so that the required depth of recursion is $\log z/\log \sqrt{s} + O(1) = 2\log z/\log(2 + z/\log w) + O(1)$. The total number of instances spawned is therefore $O(2^{2\log z/\log(2+z/\log w)})$, and the query time is $O((1 + \log z/\log\log w) \cdot 2^{2\log z/\log(2+z/\log w)})$, as claimed.

A space bound of $O(nw)$ bits follows essentially as in the case of the first bound, noting that $\sqrt{s} \geq 4$. One difference is that each reduction now needs a negligible $O(w)$ bits to store its sampling pattern. The third bound of Theorem 1, finally, is just a restatement of Lemma 2. □

References

1. A. Andersson, P. B. Miltersen, S. Riis, and M. Thorup, Static dictionaries on AC^0 RAMs: Query time $\Theta(\sqrt{\log n/\log\log n})$ is necessary and sufficient, in Proc. 37th Annual IEEE Symposium on Foundations of Computer Science (FOCS 1996), pp. 441–450.
2. A. Andersson, P. B. Miltersen, S. Riis, and M. Thorup, Dictionaries on AC^0 RAMs: Query time $\Theta(\sqrt{\log n/\log\log n})$ is necessary and sufficient, Tech. Rep. No. RS-97-14, BRICS, Dept. of Computer Science, Univ. of Aarhus, 1997.
3. J. L. Carter and M. N. Wegman, Universal classes of hash functions, *J. Comput. System Sci.* **18** (1979), pp. 143–154.
4. S. A. Cook and R. A. Reckhow, Time bounded random access machines, *J. Comput. System Sci.* **7** (1973), pp. 354–375.
5. M. Dietzfelbinger, T. Hagerup, J. Katajainen, and M. Penttonen, A reliable randomized algorithm for the closest-pair problem, *J. Algorithms* **25** (1997), pp. 19–51.
6. M. L. Fredman, J. Komlós, and E. Szemerédi, Storing a sparse table with $O(1)$ worst case access time, *J. Assoc. Comput. Mach.* **31** (1984), pp. 538–544.
7. M. Furst, J. B. Saxe, and M. Sipser, Parity, circuits, and the polynomial-time hierarchy, *Math. Syst. Theory* **17** (1984), pp. 13–27.
8. T. Hagerup, Sorting and searching on the word RAM, in Proc. 15th Annual Symposium on Theoretical Aspects of Computer Science (STACS 1998), Lecture Notes in Computer Science, Springer-Verlag, Berlin, Vol. 1373, pp. 366–398.
9. J. Hastad, Almost optimal lower bounds for small depth circuits, in Proc. 18th Annual ACM Symposium on Theory of Computing (STOC 1986), pp. 6–20.
10. Y. Mansour, N. Nisan, and P. Tiwari, The computational complexity of universal hashing, *Theoret. Comput. Sci.* **107** (1993), pp. 121–133.

Partial-Congruence Factorization of Bisimilarity Induced by Open Maps*

Sławomir Lasota

Institute of Informatics, Warsaw University, Banacha 2, 02-097 Warszawa, Poland, phone: +48 22 658-31-65, fax: +48 22 658-31-64, e-mail: sl@mimuw.edu.pl

Abstract. We investigate some relationships between bisimilarity defined by open maps and behavioural equivalence *factorized* by indistinguishability relations. This is done in the setting of a concrete category supporting algebraic constructions of subobject and quotient. Some sufficient condition is found for bisimilarity to be factorizable by the greatest *open congruences.* We also find a necessary and sufficient condition for a factorization of bisimilarity: quotients by all maximal open congruences are isomorphic. The general results are motivated and illustrated by important examples: transition systems, event structures and presheaves.

Introduction

The concept of *a behavioural equivalence* is a fundamental notion in programming methodology. It instantiates to a behavioural equivalences of sequential programs or data types [Rei81,GGM76,BHW95], as well as to various bisimulation equivalences of concurrent processes [Par81,Miln89,VGG89,JNW93].

Recently a categorical generalisation of bisimulation was proposed, by means of *open maps* (*open morphisms*) [JNW93], enabling a uniform definition of bisimulation equivalence across a range of different models for parallel computations. This setting turned out appropriate for defining, among others, strong and weak bisimilarity [Miln89], trace and testing equivalence and a bisimilarity of event structures (see [CN95], [JNW93] for an overview). Open maps can be understood as arrows witnessing a bisimulation, hence two objects A and B in a category are bisimilar if they are related by a span of open maps, representing abstractly a bisimulation.

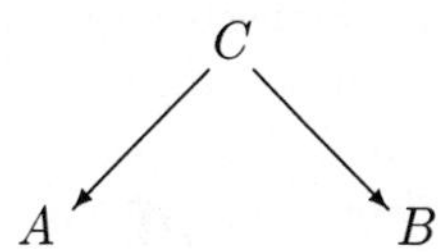

A dual approach was used for defining the behavioural equivalence for algebras. Roughly speaking, two algebras A and B are *behaviourally equivalent* if their quotients by *indistinguishability relations* $\sim_A$ and $\sim_B$ are isomorphic [BHW95], that is if they are related by a cospan of quotient projections. We say that behavioural equivalence is *factorized* by the family of indistinguishability relations.

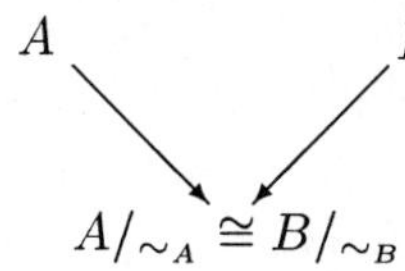

* This work was supported by the KBN grant 8 T11C 046 14.

This scheme is appropriate for various categories of algebras, and more generally for an arbitrary *concrete category* [BT96].

The undeniable conceptual analogies (despite technical differences) between both approaches are well recognised and much work was done in linking the two notions, mainly in applying methods based on bisimulation to sequential programs [AO93,Gor95]. In this paper, roughly speaking, we investigate the opposite direction, namely we show that algebraic techniques are applicable to bisimulation of processes as well. This is a completion of [Las97], where the author (re-)defined observational equivalences for standard, partial and regular algebras ([BT95]) by means of open maps.

The main problem investigated in this paper is to find a family of relations factorizing open-map bisimilarity. Our motivation was the observation that for strong bisimilarity of transition systems such a factorization exists and is given by the greatest bisimulations (Section 2). In Section 4 we present an attempt to imitate these properties in an arbitrary concrete category. We find general conditions sufficient, under some mild assumptions, for the greatest congruences induced by open maps (the greatest *open congruences*) to factorize bisimilarity. Most interestingly, these very general results apply to some important examples: transition systems (which fit into the general scheme) and presheaf models [JM94], proposed in [JNW93] as a uniform model for concurrency (Section 6).

In some relevant cases the greatest open congruences need not exist. In Section 4.1 we prove that for factorization it suffices to have a weaker property: the quotients by all maximal open congruences to be isomorphic. Moreover, this condition turns out to be necessary too, which gives a characterisation of factorizable bisimilarities. The crucial example is the category of event structures [NW95] (studied in detail in Section 5), failing to have greatest open congruences, but satisfying the weaker requirement.

This paper is not the only attempt to define bisimilarity by means of cospans. An observation central to [C85,BB88] is that two transition systems are strongly bisimilar precisely when they are related by a cospan of open maps (zig-zag maps). Our work is hence a generalisation of this development, specific for transition systems. Moreover, our results on event structures give a response to the negative statement from [JNW93] that the "open cospan" approach can not be applied to the bisimilarity of *transition systems with independence* [NW95], generalising both transition systems and event structures.

After preliminary definitions in Section 1, we start in Section 2 with some intuition based on strong bisimilarity between transition systems. This should be a preparation before Sections 3 and 4, being more general and abstract, hence unavoidably less understandable. Proofs omitted here together with some further details can be found in the full version of this paper [Las98].

1 Preliminaries

Transition systems ([NW95]) Throughout the paper let L be a fixed set of labels. A *labelled transition system* (over L) is a structure $T = (S, i, t)$, where S

is a set of *states* with an initial state $i \in S$ and $t \subseteq S \times L \times S$ is a *transition relation.* We write $s \stackrel{a}{\to} s'$ for $(s, a, s') \in t$. A morphism between two systems $T_1 = (S_1, i_1, t_1)$, $T_2 = (S_2, i_2, t_2)$, is a function $f : S_1 \to S_2$, such that $f(i_1) = i_2$ and $s \stackrel{a}{\to} s'$ implies $f(s) \stackrel{a}{\to} f(s')$. This defines a category TS_L (morphisms compose as functions). Following [Par81,Miln89], we say that systems T_1 and T_2 are *strongly bisimilar* if there exists a strong bisimulation between them; bisimulation is defined as usual, with the only additional requirement to relate initial states.

Event structures The following definitions are cited from [JNW93,NW95] and specialised for a fixed set of labels. A *labelled event structure* (over L) is a structure $E = (|E|, \leq_E, Con_E, l_E)$ consisting of a set $|E|$ of events partially ordered by $\leq_E$, the *causal dependency relation*, a family $Con_E \subseteq \mathcal{P}^{fin}(|E|)$ of finite subsets of events (the *consistency relation*), and a labelling function $l_E : |E| \to L$ satisfying:

- $\lceil e \rceil = \{e' : e' \leq_E e\}$ is finite, for every $e \in |E|$,
- $\{e\} \in Con_E$,
- $Y \subseteq X \in Con_E \Rightarrow Y \in Con_E$,
- $X \in Con_E \wedge e \leq_E e' \in X \Rightarrow X \cup \{e\} \in Con_E$.

A *configuration* of E, representing a state of computation, is any subset C of events being: *downward closed* ($e' \in C \wedge e \leq_E e' \Rightarrow e \in C$) and *consistent* ($\forall X \subset^{fin} C . X \in Con_E$). A morphism of event structures $h : E \to F$ is a labels-preserving function $h : |E| \to |F|$, such that whenever C is a configuration of E then $h(C)$ is a configuration of F and $h \rceil C$ is 1-1. For configurations C, C' of E and any $a \in L$, by $C \stackrel{a}{\to} C'$ we mean $e \notin C, C' = C \cup \{e\}$ and $l_E(e) = a$. Note that morphisms of event structures preserve transitions ($C \stackrel{a}{\to} C'$ in E implies $h(C) \stackrel{a}{\to} h(C')$ in F) and concurrency of events.

Definition 1.1. A *history preserving bisimulation* (hp-bisimulation in short) between event structures E_1, E_2 is a set H of triples (C_1, ξ, C_2), where C_1 is a finite configuration of E_1, C_2 is a finite configuration of E_2 and ξ is an isomorphism of pomsets between them, such that $(\emptyset, \emptyset, \emptyset) \in H$, and whenever $(C_1, \xi, C_2) \in H$,

- if $C_1 \stackrel{a}{\to} C_1'$ then $C_2 \stackrel{a}{\to} C_2'$ and $(C_1', \xi', C_2') \in H$, for some C_2', $\xi' \supseteq \xi$,
- if $C_2 \stackrel{a}{\to} C_2'$ then $C_1 \stackrel{a}{\to} C_1'$ and $(C_1', \xi', C_2') \in H$, for some C_1', $\xi' \supseteq \xi$.

(C_1' and C_2' stay for finite configurations of E_1 and E_2, respectively.) A hp-bisimulation H is *strong* (shp-bisimulation in short) if whenever $(C_1, \xi, C_2) \in H$,

- $C_1' \subseteq C_1$ implies $(C_1', \xi', C_2') \in H$, for some $\xi' \subseteq \xi$ and $C_2' \subseteq C_2$,
- $C_2' \subseteq C_2$ implies $(C_1', \xi', C_2') \in H$, for some $\xi' \subseteq \xi$ and $C_1' \subseteq C_1$.

E_1 and E_2 are *shp-bisimilar* if there exists a shp-bisimulation between them.

In [JNW93] infinite configurations are also allowed in bisimulations. We stick here only to finite ones, following [VGG89], as this has no influence on induced bisimilarity.

Behavioural equivalence in a concrete category

We introduce here a categorical setting, borrowed from [BT96], in which we are going to work in the following sections. All abstract definitions presented below follow usual algebraic intuitions – we identify abstractly some constructions, like quotients and subobjects, sufficient for dealing with behavioural equivalence.

Let $\mathcal{M}$ be an arbitrary category, equipped with a concretization functor $|\_| : \mathcal{M} \to \mathit{Set}^S$ to the category of sets indexed by a set S (category of S-sorted sets and functions), which we require to be faithful (although in most of examples S will be a singleton set). For an object A, $|A|$ can be seen as a carrier of A, hence we can think of objects of $\mathcal{M}$ as "sets with structure". Moreover, faithfulness of $|\_|$ allows us to treat morphisms as (structure preserving) functions between carrier sets. For instance, category TS_L of transition systems can be equipped with the forgetful functor $|\_| : TS_L \to \mathit{Set}$, defined on objects by $|(S, i, t)| = S$ and on morphisms by $|f| = f$. A natural choice for a concretization functor for events structures is $|\_| : ES_L \to \mathit{Set}$, taking an event structure E to the set $|E|$ of its events and a morphism h to its underlying function $|h|$.

Subobjects For an object[1] $A \in |\mathcal{M}|$, a *full subobject* of A is an object B together with a morphism $\iota_{B \hookrightarrow A} : B \to A$ such that $|\iota_{B \hookrightarrow A}|$ is an inclusion and for any morphism $f : C \to A$ with $|f|(|C|) \subseteq |B|$, there exists a (necessarily unique) morphism $\widehat{f} : C \to B$ satisfying $\widehat{f}; \iota_{B \hookrightarrow A} = f$. Intuitively speaking, the full subobject inherits the whole "structure" of A restricted to $|B|$. Given an object A and a set $X \subseteq |A|$, a *full subobject of A generated by X*, denoted by $\langle X \rangle_A$, is a full subobject B of A such that $X \subseteq |B|$ and such that for any other subobject C of A either $|B| \subseteq |C|$ or $X \not\subseteq |C|$. $\mathcal{M}$ *has full subobjects* if for each object A and a set $X \subseteq |A|$, there exists a full subobject generated by X.

Congruences and quotients For any morphism $f : A \to B$ in $\mathcal{M}$, by a *kernel* of f we mean an equivalence $\{(a, a') \in |A| \times |A| : |f|(a) = |f|(a')\}$, denoted by $\mathbf{ker}(|f|)$. Given an object A in $\mathcal{M}$, by a *congruence* on A we mean the kernel $\mathbf{ker}(|f|)$ of some morphism $f : A \to B$.

A *quotient* of an object A is an object B together with an epimorphism $\pi : A \to B$, called the *quotient projection*, such that for any morphism $f : A \to C$ with $\mathbf{ker}(|\pi|) \subseteq \mathbf{ker}(|f|)$ there exists a (necessarily unique) morphism $\bar{f} : B \to C$ satisfying $\pi; \bar{f} = f$. For a congruence $\sim$ on A, a quotient of A by $\sim$ is a quotient B of A whose projection satisfies $\mathbf{ker}(|\pi|) = \sim$. Given $\sim$, this quotient projection will be also denoted by $\pi_{A/\sim}$, and B will be written as $A/\sim$. We say that $\mathcal{M}$ *has surjective quotients* if for any A and any congruence $\sim$ on A, the quotient $A/\sim$ exists and the projection $|\pi_{A/\sim}|$ is surjective.

Indistinguishability structures By a *partial congruence* on an object A we mean a congruence on a full subobject of A, called its *domain subobject.* In the sequel we often deal with a family of partial congruences consisting, for

[1] We use a (deliberately overloaded) notation $|\mathcal{M}|$ for the class of objects of $\mathcal{M}$.

each object A in $\mathcal{M}$, of a partial congruence $\simeq_A \subseteq |A| \times |A|$. We will write $\simeq$ for $\{\simeq_A\}_{A \in |\mathcal{M}|}$, and then, for each object A, we will write $A_{\simeq}$ for a domain subobject of $\simeq_A$. When no danger of confusion arises we will omit subscripts and write $A/\simeq$ instead of $A_{\simeq}/\simeq_A$. Such a family $\simeq$ we call an *indistinguishability structure*, since $\simeq_A$ is meant to represent a (behavioural) indistinguishability in A. We say that two objects A and B are *behaviourally equivalent* (w.r.t. $\simeq$), which we denote by $A \equiv_{\simeq} B$, if $A/\simeq$ and $B/\simeq$ are isomorphic. For a justification of this abstract setting and some concrete examples we refer to [BT96].

Bisimulation from open maps

Let $\mathcal{M}$ be a category of models of computation, in which we choose a subcategory $\mathcal{P}$ (not necessarily full) of *observation objects*. Any morphism $p : O \to A$ from an observation object $O \in |\mathcal{P}|$ is understood as an observable *computation* in A. A morphism $h : A \to B$ between models can be intuitively thought of as a simulation of A in B since h transforms every computation $p : O \to A$ in A to a computation $p; h : O \to B$ in B. Moreover any morphism $m : O \to O'$ in $\mathcal{P}$ making $p = m; p'$ means intuitively that a "larger" computation p' is an extension of p (via m).

Definition 1.2 (Open maps and bisimilarity). A morphism $h : A \to B$ in $\mathcal{M}$ is *$\mathcal{P}$-open* if for any morphism $m : O \to O'$ in $\mathcal{P}$ and two computations $p : O \to A$ and $p' : O' \to B$, whenever the square

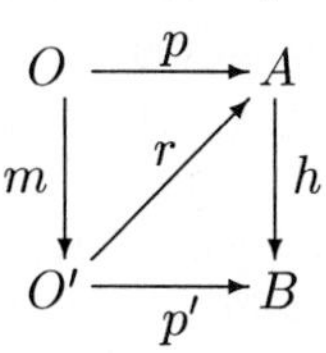

commutes, i.e. $p; h = m; p'$, there exists a *diagonal* morphism $r : O' \to A$ in $\mathcal{M}$ making two triangles commute, i.e. $p = m; r$ and $p' = r; h$. Two models A and B are *$\mathcal{P}$-bisimilar*, denoted by $A \sim_{\mathcal{P}} B$, if there exists in $\mathcal{M}$ a span of $\mathcal{P}$-open maps: $A \longleftarrow C \longrightarrow B$.

We omit the prefix $\mathcal{P}$- when it is obvious from a context. The notion of $\mathcal{P}$-bisimilarity generalises the strong bisimilarity, which was shown in [JNW93] to coincide with $Bran_L$-bisimilarity, where $Bran_L$ is the full subcategory of transition systems consisting of finite sequences of actions: $i \xrightarrow{a_1} s_1 \xrightarrow{a_2} \ldots \xrightarrow{a_n} s_n$. $Bran_L$-open morphisms $f : (S_1, i_1, t_1) \to (S_2, i_2, t_2)$, called also *zig-zag morphisms*, are those satisfying the following *zig-zag* property: for each reachable $s \in S_1$, whenever $f(s) \xrightarrow{a} s'$, then $s \xrightarrow{a} s''$, for some $s'' \in S_1$ satisfying $f(s'') = s'$.

To obtain a shp-bisimilarity of event structures we need some branching structure in observation objects: shp-bisimilarity coincides with Pom_L-bisimilarity [JNW93], where Pom_L is the full subcategory of ES_L consisting of finite *pomsets*, i.e. finite event structures with consistency relation containing all finite subsets of events. A morphism $f : E \to F$ is Pom_L-open iff it satisfies similar zig-zag property and moreover reflects concurrency of events.

2 Motivating Example

Let us focus for a while on the category of transition systems, and try to find out an indistinguishability structure $\simeq = \{\simeq_T\}_{T \in |TS_L|}$ factorizing strong bisimilarity. Transition systems are intended to serve as an intuitive example and a justification for the considerations in the following sections. For a domain subobject of a transition system T it is reasonable to choose its part "observable" by means of computations; the good candidate is the subobject consisting of all reachable states of T and inheriting all the transitions between reachable states. Observe that $T_{\simeq}$ defined in this way is precisely the full subobject generated by the union of all images of computations in T (compare with (2) in Section 3).

As the indistinguishability relation $\simeq_T$ on $T_{\simeq}$ take the greatest bisimulation between $T_{\simeq}$ and $T_{\simeq}$ itself. The following lemma justifies this choice and implies that $\simeq_T$ is actually a congruence.

Lemma 2.1. *An equivalence $\sim \subseteq |T_{\simeq}| \times |T_{\simeq}|$ is a bisimulation iff it is a kernel of a zig-zag morphism from $T_{\simeq}$.*

Due to this lemma, $\simeq_T$ is the greatest *zig-zag congruence*, that is the greatest kernel of a zig-zag morphism. One can check that strong bisimilarity $\sim_{Bran_L}$ is factorized by $\simeq$, i.e.

$$T_1 \sim_{Bran_L} T_2 \;\text{ iff }\; T_1/_{\simeq} \cong T_2/_{\simeq}. \tag{1}$$

Equivalently spelled out, strong bisimilarity $\sim_{Bran_L}$ coincides with the behavioural equivalence $\equiv_{\simeq}$ in the category of transition systems.

In Section 4 we redo this scheme in the framework of an arbitrary concrete category and find some conditions which are necessary and sufficient for the factorization analogous to (1) to hold. Moreover, (1) is an immediate corollary from Theorem 4.3, applicable due to the fact that transition systems have the greatest zig-zag congruences.

3 Open Congruences and Subobjects

In the sequel let $\mathcal{M}$ be an arbitrary category of models of computation with some fixed subcategory $\mathcal{P}$ of observation objects. We assume throughout the rest of this paper that:

- category $\mathcal{M}$ has pullbacks[2],
- $\mathcal{M}$ is equipped with a faithful functor $|\_| : \mathcal{M} \to Set^S$, for some set S,
- the concrete category $(\mathcal{M}, |\_|)$ has full subobjects and surjective quotients.

We state here some general properties of open maps, useful in the sequel. We say that $\mathcal{M}$ is *initialized* if for any $\mathcal{P}$-open morphism $f : A \to B$ and a computation $q : O \to B$ there exists a computation $p : O \to A$ such that $p; f = q$. The most

[2] This requirement could be replaced by any other property forcing $\mathcal{P}$-bisimilarity to be an equivalence, which is needed in Lemma 4.1.

usual situation is when $\mathcal{M}$ has the initial object $\mathcal{I}$ being also initial in $\mathcal{P}$, which forces $\mathcal{M}$ to be initialized. In such a case, the unique morphism from $\mathcal{I}$ can be thought of as the empty (initial) computation.

Proposition 3.1. *For any $\mathcal{P}$-open morphism $f : A \to B$, the quotient projection $\pi_{A/\mathbf{ker}(|f|)}$ is open. Moreover, when $\mathcal{M}$ is initialized, then for any $\mathcal{P}$-open morphism $g : A \to C$ meeting $\mathbf{ker}(|f|) \subseteq \mathbf{ker}(|g|)$, the unique morphism $\bar{g}$ satisfying $g = \pi_{A/\mathbf{ker}(|f|)}; \bar{g}$ is also $\mathcal{P}$-open.*

Let $\mathbb{COMP}_A \subseteq |A|$ stand for the union of images of all computations in A:

$$\mathbb{COMP}_A := \bigcup_{O \xrightarrow{p} A,\ O \in |\mathcal{P}|} |p|(|O|). \tag{2}$$

Proposition 3.2. *For any $A \in |\mathcal{M}|$ and any full subobject $\iota_{B \hookrightarrow A} : B \to A$ including $\mathbb{COMP}_A$ (i.e. $\mathbb{COMP}_A \subseteq |B|$), the inclusion $\iota_{B \hookrightarrow A} : B \to A$ is $\mathcal{P}$-open. Moreover, for any open $g : C \to A$ meeting $|g|(|C|) \subseteq |B|$, the unique morphism $\hat{g}$ satisfying $\hat{g}; \iota_{B \hookrightarrow A} = g$ is also $\mathcal{P}$-open.*

By the above facts, quotients by kernels of open maps as well as subobjects including $\mathbb{COMP}_A$ are also quotients and subobjects in the subcategory of open maps. They will play an important role in the following sections, hence for convenience we introduce the following naming convention:

open congruence on A = a kernel of an open map from A,
open quotient = a quotient by an open congruence,
open subobject of A = a full subobject including $\mathbb{COMP}_A$.

4 Factorization by Open Congruences

In this section we address the following problem, for an arbitrary category $\mathcal{M}$ under the same assumptions as in the previous section, and for its arbitrary subcategory $\mathcal{P}$:

> *Find a family of partial congruences $\simeq\ = \{\simeq_A\}_{A \in |\mathcal{M}|}$, inducing the same equivalence as spans of $\mathcal{P}$-open morphisms:*

$$A/_{\simeq} \cong B/_{\simeq} \ \Leftrightarrow\ A \sim_{\mathcal{P}} B, \quad \text{for all } A, B \in |\mathcal{M}| \quad (\text{i.e. } \equiv_{\simeq}\ =\ \sim_{\mathcal{P}}).$$

In the following we prove that under some assumptions the family of the greatest open congruences on the smallest open subobjects (cf. Assumption 4.2) is the solution to this problem (Theorem 4.3). The domain subobjects will be defined as the full subobjects $\langle \mathbb{COMP}_A \rangle_A$ generated by the set-theoretic sum of images of all computations. We denote the subobject $\langle \mathbb{COMP}_A \rangle_A$ in short by $\widetilde{A}$, as it will be often mentioned in the sequel.

Why do we choose the smallest open subobjects and the greatest open congruences? Restricting to open maps is suggested by Propositions 3.1 and 3.2, stating that subcategory of open maps inherits all the relevant algebraic structure of $\mathcal{M}$, i.e. open subobjects and surjective quotients. The choice of *the smallest* open subobjects follows the intuition that a domain of an indistinguishability relation (i.e. the observable part of an object) should be equal to its part "visible" via computations. An argument for considering only open quotients is our aim to have $A/\simeq$ bisimilar to A. Another justification for *the smallest* subobjects and *the greatest* quotients is given by the observation that any of indistinguishability structures under consideration is finer than bisimilarity:

Lemma 4.1. *Let $\approx$ be an indistinguishability structure in $\mathcal{M}$ consisting, for each object A, of an open congruence $\approx_A$ on an open subobject of A. Then $\equiv_\approx \subseteq \sim_\mathcal{P}$.*

Thus, choosing the smallest open subobjects and the greatest open congruences we aim, intuitively speaking, at staying as close as possible to the bisimilarity. Now we are going to introduce formally the indistinguishability structure $\simeq$ to factorize $\mathcal{P}$-bisimilarity. We need in the sequel the following assumption, justified by some important examples, like transition systems or presheaves (Section 6):

Assumption 4.2. *For each object A in $\mathcal{M}$, there exists the greatest (w.r.t. inclusion) open congruence on $\widetilde{A}$.*

These greatest open congruences make up an indistinguishability structure $\simeq = \{\simeq_A\}_{A\in\mathcal{M}}$, whose domain subobjects are $A_\simeq := \widetilde{A}$.

Before stating the main result (Theorem 4.3), we need some more definitions. First, we say that *computations create subobjects* in $\mathcal{M}$ if $|\widetilde{A}| = \mathbb{COMP}_A$, for any A in $\mathcal{M}$. Second, we say that the concretization functor $|\_|$ *lifts isomorphisms* if for any open morphism $f : \widetilde{A} \to \widetilde{B}$, f is iso whenever $|f|$ is bijection. This means, roughly speaking, that open maps are powerful enough to transport and reflect the whole structure of observable parts of objects. In the following theorem we formulate conditions to guarantee a factorization of $\mathcal{P}$-bisimilarity. All these requirements are verified in Sections 5 and 6 to be satisfied by standard models.

Theorem 4.3 (Factorization). *If $|\_|$ lifts isomorphisms, computations create subobjects in $\mathcal{M}$ and $\mathcal{M}$ is initialized, then $\equiv_\simeq = \sim_\mathcal{P}$.*

4.1 Maximal Open Congruences

The requirement of existence of the greatest open congruences in Theorem 4.3 is slightly too strong – a weaker, but still sufficient assumption is formulated in Theorem 4.4 below. On the other hand, it also turns out to be necessary, hence we obtain a characterisation of open-map bisimilarities which are factorizable by open congruences. This result is applied in the following section to event structures, failing to have the greatest open congruences.

Let $\approx$ be an indistinguishability structure with $A_\approx = \widetilde{A}$, for all objects A. The consideration below are done under the assumption that the posets of open congruences on $\widetilde{A}$ are *bounded*, that is every increasing chain of such congruences has an upper bound. Note that this guarantees, for each open congruence, some maximal open congruence including it. We say that $\mathcal{M}$ *is normalized by* $\approx$ if quotients of $A_{\approx}$ by all maximal open congruences are isomorphic to $A/_{\approx}$ (for all A in $\mathcal{M}$). This intuitively means that there is essentially only one way to quotient any object.

Theorem 4.4. *Assume, together with assumptions from Theorem 4.3, that posets of open congruences on $\widetilde{A}$ are bounded, for all objects A in $\mathcal{M}$. Then*

$$\equiv_{\approx} = \sim_{\mathcal{P}} \quad \textit{iff} \quad \mathcal{M} \textit{ is normalized by } \approx.$$

5 Shp-bisimilarity

Now our aim is to apply results from the previous section to shp-bisimilarity in the category ES_L of event structures (over a fixed, throughout this section, labelling set L). This bisimilarity is induced by Pom_L, the full subcategory of finite pomsets. We omit prefixes Pom_L- and shp-, obvious in the context. Recall from Section 1 that category of event structures is equipped with a concretization functor $|\_|$ returning the set of events. Event structures satisfy all assumptions needed in previous sections: ES_L has pullbacks [JNW93], is initialized, has full subobjects and surjective quotients; moreover computations create subobjects in ES_L ($\mathbb{COMP}_E = E$) and $|\_|$ lifts isomorphisms (for details see [Las98]).

Event structures fail to have greatest open congruences. A counter-example is given in Figure 1: an event structure with a set of events $\{1, \ldots, 6, 1', \ldots, 6'\}$ labelled by a, b, c, build up of two identical six-event components. Its consistency relation contains all pairs of events connected in the picture by edges as well as of all triples of events forming a triangle; it has trivial, discrete causality relation. One can easily check that no open congruence can identify events from the same component and that there are two maximal open congruences: $\{1 \leftrightarrow 1', 2 \leftrightarrow 2', 3 \leftrightarrow 3', 4 \leftrightarrow 4', 5 \leftrightarrow 5', 6 \leftrightarrow 6'\}$ and $\{1 \leftrightarrow 3', 2 \leftrightarrow 4', 3 \leftrightarrow 1', 4 \leftrightarrow 2', 5 \leftrightarrow 6', 6 \leftrightarrow 5'\}$. But not everything is lost: one can check that both maximal open congruences give isomorphic quotients. In this case it follows from auto-symmetry, but the observation generalises to all events structures (Theorem 5.3). Before proving this fact, we need to know that every open congruence is included in a maximal one:

Lemma 5.1. *The poset of open congruences on an event structure is bounded.*

The crucial role in the proof of this lemma is played by Lemma 5.2, formulated below after some preparation. By *the concretization* of a shp-bisimulation H

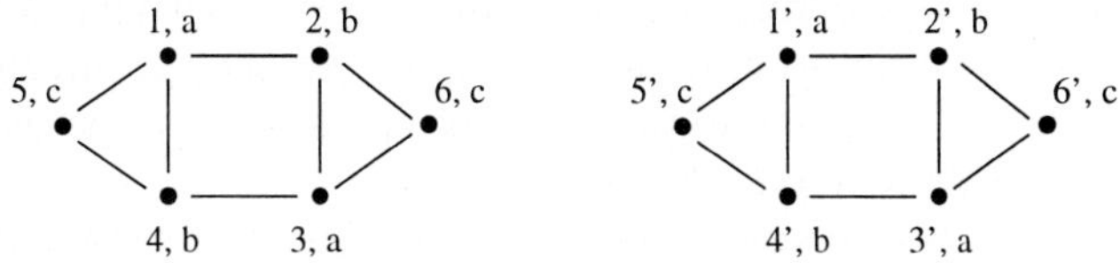

Fig. 1. An event structure with two different maximal open congruences.

between two event structures E_1 and E_2 we mean a relation $|H| \subseteq |E_1| \times |E_2|$ containing all pairs of events related by any of pomset-isomorphisms from H. Formally $(e_1, e_2) \in |H| \Leftrightarrow_{\text{def}} \exists\ (C_1, \xi, C_2) \in H \,.\, \xi(e_1) = e_2$.

It is not possible, in general, to recover unambiguously a bisimulation from its concretization. By a *lifting* $\text{Lift}(\sim)$ of a relation $\sim \subseteq |E_1| \times |E_2|$ we mean a relation consisting (similarly as shp-bisimulations) of triples (C_1, ξ, C_2), where C_1 and C_2 are finite configurations of E_1 and E_2, respectively, and ξ is an isomorphism of pomsets between them, defined by $(C_1, \xi, C_2) \in \text{Lift}(\sim) \Leftrightarrow_{\text{def}} \xi \subseteq \sim$. Intuitively, $\text{Lift}(\sim)$ is the greatest possible candidate to have a concretization $\sim$, but $\text{Lift}(\sim)$ needs not necessarily be a bisimulation, even if $\sim$ is a concretization of some bisimulation. We call a bisimulation H *recoverable* if $H = \text{Lift}(|H|)$.

Now we are ready to state a correspondence between shp-bisimulations and open congruences. Unlike in the case of transition systems, where all bisimulation equivalences are congruences, open congruences on an event structure correspond to recoverable bisimulations, that do not identify consistent pairs of events:

Lemma 5.2. *Let $\sim$ be an equivalence on the set of events of an event structure E; $\sim$ is an open congruence on E iff it is a concretization of some recoverable bisimulation and* respects consistency *$(e_1 \sim e_2 \wedge e_1 \neq e_2 \Rightarrow \{e_1, e_2\} \notin Con_E)$.*

The main result of this section follows, allowing together with Lemma 5.1 to apply Theorem 4.4 so that to obtain factorization of shp-bisimilarity.

Theorem 5.3. *The quotients of an event structure by all maximal open congruences are isomorphic.*

Corollary 5.4. *Shp-bisimilarity is factorized by any indistinguishability structure consisting of maximal open congruences.*

6 Presheaves

Category of presheaves, proposed as a general and uniform model for concurrency [JNW93,CW96], is another example of application of results from previous sections. For an arbitrary category $\mathcal{P}$, category $\widehat{\mathcal{P}}$ of presheaves consists of all contravariant functors $\mathcal{P}^{op} \to Set$, with natural transformations as morphisms.

For any category $\mathcal{M}$ and an observation subcategory $\mathcal{P}$, consider a canonical functor $\mathcal{M} \to \widehat{\mathcal{P}}$, transforming an object X of $\mathcal{M}$ to the representable functor $\mathcal{M}(\_, X)$. It is suitable to study presheaves over $\mathcal{P}$: for example, category $\widehat{Bran_L}$ corresponds via the canonical functor to synchronisation forests, i.e. collections of *synchronisation trees* (unfoldings of transition systems) [JNW93]. Moreover, the subcategory of synchronisation trees is equivalent to the subcategory of *rooted* presheaves, i.e. those assigning to the initial object in $Bran_L$ (or generally in $\mathcal{P}$, if it has the initial object) a singleton set.

From now on we consider presheaves over an arbitrary fixed small category $\mathcal{P}$ and bisimilarity induced by $\mathcal{P}$-open morphisms (we can treat $\mathcal{P}$ as a subcategory of $\widehat{\mathcal{P}}$ as it embeds fully and faithfully into $\widehat{\mathcal{P}}$).

A concretization functor $||\_||$ from $\widehat{\mathcal{P}}$ to $Set^{|\mathcal{P}|}$, category of sets indexed by the set $|\mathcal{P}|$ of objects of $\mathcal{P}$, essentially forgets about values of presheaves on morphisms and assigns to F a family $||F|| = \{F(C)\}_{C \in |\mathcal{P}|}$.

Motivated by synchronisation trees and even structures, which correspond to rooted presheaves, we restrict our attention in the sequel to the subcategory of rooted presheaves over $\mathcal{P}$, assumed to have the initial object – this enables to rule out unique morphisms from the empty initial presheaf, being always open. As usual two rooted presheaves are bisimilar if they are related by a span of open maps.

We are going to show that every presheaf has the greatest open congruence. To this aim we establish a correspondence between open congruences and bisimulation equivalences (Lemma 6.1), where by ($|\mathcal{P}|$-sorted) *bisimulation relation* we mean any relation represented by a span of open maps; for a span $F \xleftarrow{f} H \xrightarrow{g} G$, the relation which it *represents* is $\{(||f||(s), ||g||(s)) : s \in ||H||\}$.

Lemma 6.1. *An ($|\mathcal{P}|$-sorted) equivalence $\sim \subseteq ||F|| \times ||F||$ is a bisimulation iff it is an open congruence on F, for any presheaf F.*

Since between any two presheaves there exists the greatest bisimulation [Las98], above lemma ensures existence of the greatest open congruences $\simeq_F$. Moreover, rooted presheaves satisfy all assumptions needed in previous sections (while $\widehat{\mathcal{P}}$ needs not be initialized), hence we can apply Theorem 4.3:

Corollary 6.2. *Bisimilarity of rooted presheves is factorized by the greatest bisimulations.*

7 Conclusions

In the paper we analysed necessary and sufficient conditions for factorization of bisimilarity by partial open congruences. The general results give an interesting conclusion that a wide class of bisimilarities (including those for transition systems, event structures and presheaves) can be equivalently defined by cospans of open quotient projections, similarly as algebraic behavioural equivalences.

The natural continuation of this work is to check whether the results can be applied to other equivalences of processes, like testing or weak equivalence (captured in [CN95] in the setting of open maps). Our approach offers still some potentials for future investigations, for instance Lemmas 2.1 and 6.1 suggest some general line of establishing coincidence between bisimulations and open congruences, giving automatically the greatest open congruences. Another challenge is to generalise the proof of Theorem 5.3, specific for event structures.

The crucial role is played in our development by the subobjects $\widetilde{A}$. We have found another possibility to define a domain subobject of A, as a canonical colimit (if it exists!) of all computations in A. This construction, being more natural in category theory, ensures without any special assumptions that open maps between domain subobjects are quotient projections (the key fact needed in the proof of Theorem 4.3). Resulting subobjects need not be full in general, however they are in all examples considered in this paper.

Acknowledgements The author is very grateful to Andrzej Tarlecki for fruitful discussions and helpful comments during this work.

References

[AO93] S. Abramsky, C.-H. Luke Ong. Full Abstraction in the Lazy Lambda Calculus. *Information and Computation* 105(2), 159-267, 1993.

[BB88] Benson, D.B., Ben-Schachar, O. Bisimulation of automata. *Information and Computation*, 79, 60-83, 1988.

[BHW95] Bidoit, M., Hennicker, R., Wirsing, M. Behavioural and abstractor specifications. *Science of Computer Programming* 25(2-3):149-186, 1995.

[BT95] Bidoit, M., Tarlecki, A. Regular algebras: a framework for observational specifications with recursive definitions. Report LIENS-95-12, Ecole Norm. Sup., 1995.

[BT96] Bidoit, M., Tarlecki A. Behavioural satisfaction and equivalence in concrete model categories. *Proc. 20th CAAP'96*, Linköping, Springer-Verlag.

[C85] Castellani, I. Bisimulation and abstraction homomorphisms. *Proc. of CAAP'85*, Springer-Verlag LNCS, 1985.

[CW96] Cattani, G.L., Winskel, G. Presheaf models for concurrency. *Computer Science Logic* CSL'96, LNCS 1258. Preliminary version: BRICS Report RS-96-35.

[CN95] Cheng, A., Nielsen, M. Open maps (at) work. Research series RS-95-23, BRICS, Department of Comp. Sc., University of Aarhus, 1995.

[GGM76] Giarratana, V., Gimona, F., Montanari, U. Observability concepts in abstract data type specification. *Proc. 5th Intl. Symp. Mathematical Foundations of Computer Science*, Gdańsk 1976, LNCS 45, Springer-Verlag 1976, 576-587.

[VGG89] Van Glabeek, R.J., Goltz, U. Equivalence notions for concurrent systems and refinement of actions. *Proc. of MFCS*, Springer-Verlag LNCS vol. 379, 1989.

[Gor95] Gordon, A. A tutorial on co-induction and functional programming. *Proc. of the 1994 Glasgow Workshop on Functional Programming*, Springer Workshops in Computing, 1995, 78-95.

[JM94] Joyal, A., Moerdijk, I. A completeness theorem for open maps. *Annals of Pure and Applied Logic* 70(1994), 51-86.

[JNW93] Joyal, A., Nielsen, G. Winskel, Bisimulation and open maps. *Proc. 8th Annual Symposium on Logic in Computer Science* LICS'93, 1993, 418-427.

[Las97] Lasota, S. Open Maps as a Bridge between Algebraic Observational Equivalence and Bisimilarity. *Proc. 12th Workshop on Algebraic Developement Techniques, Tarquinia, 1997, LNCS 1376.*

[Las98] Lasota, S. Partial-Congruence Factorization of Bisimilarity Induced by Open Maps. The full version of this paper, available at `http://zls.mimuw.edu.pl/~sl`.

[Miln89] Milner, R. *Communication and concurrency.* Prentice-Hall International Series in Computer Science, C. A. R. Hoare series editor, 1989.

[NW95] Nielsen, M., Winskel, G. *Models for concurrency.* Chapter 1 of *The Handbook of Logic in Computer Science*, vol. 4, Oxford University Press, 1995.

[Par81] Park, D.M.R. Concurrency and Automata on Infinite Sequences. *Proc. 5th G.I. Conference*, Lecture Notes in Computer Science 104, Springer-Verlag, 1981.

[Rei81] Reichel, H. Behavioural equivalence – a unifying concept for initial and final specification methods. *Proc. 3rd Hungarian Computer Science Conference, Mathematical Models in Computer Systems*, M. Arato, L. Varga, eds., Budapest, 1981.

Reset Nets Between Decidability and Undecidability

C. Dufourd, A. Finkel, and Ph. Schnoebelen

Lab. Specification and Verification,* ENS de Cachan & CNRS URA 2236.

Abstract. We study Petri nets with Reset arcs (also Transfer and Doubling arcs) in combination with other extensions of the basic Petri net model. While Reachability is undecidable in all these extensions (indeed they are Turing-powerful), we exhibit unexpected frontiers for the decidability of Termination, Coverability, Boundedness and place-Boundedness. In particular, we show counter-intuitive separations between seemingly related problems. Our main theorem is the very surprising fact that boundedness is undecidable for Petri nets with Reset arcs.

1 Introduction

> *"In general, it seems that any extension which does not allow zero testing will not actually increase the modeling power (or decrease the decision power) of Petri nets but merely result in another equivalent formulation of the basic Petri net model. (Modeling convenience may be increased.)"* [Pet81], page 203.

Extensions of Petri nets. The above quote from [Pet81] is a fair summary of current beliefs in the Petri net community regarding extensions of the basic Petri net model: extensions are either Turing-powerful or they are not real extensions. It explains why there exist very few studies of decidability issues for small extensions of Petri nets (with the notable exception of Valk's Post-SM nets) compared to the hundreds of papers investigating subclasses of Petri nets (free-choice nets, conflict-free nets, 1-safe nets, ...).

Reset arcs. Reset arcs from a transition t to a place p are a new kind of arcs used to reset p (i.e. to empty it) whenever t fires. Their modeling convenience has been investigated e.g. in [Bil91,LC94].

There are some obvious connections between "reseting" and "testing for emptiness" (see the proof of Theorem 11). It is widely known that Petri nets with inhibitory (or "zero test") arcs are Turing-powerful. By contrast, the study of decidability issues for Petri nets with Reset arcs only started in [AK77] where the Reachability problem is shown undecidable. Then, language-theoretical properties and extensions of p-semi flows techniques were studied in [Cia94] for Reset

* 61, av. Pdt Wilson; 94235 Cachan Cedex; FRANCE. email: {dufourd, finkel, phs}@lsv.ens-cachan.fr.

(and other) arcs. Recently, [KCK+97] announced that the Boundedness problem is decidable for Petri nets extended with Reset arcs (actually for their more general PCN model).

It turns out that Reset arcs push Petri nets closer towards the frontiers of decidability. The scarcity of results in this domain is partly explained by the difficulty of the remaining open questions. But the study of such borderline models is an important topic. Indeed there exists an annual conference, "Verification of Infinite State Systems", devoted to the algorithmic aspects of decision methods for such models.

Our contribution. In this paper, we study decidability issues for Reset arcs (and related extensions) in a general framework, aiming at a better understanding of the situation. We introduce G-nets, a general framework containing in a natural way all the extensions we are interested in, and where we can smoothly isolate relevant subclasses. We study in a systematic way the decidability of the Coverability, the Termination, the Reachability, and the two Boundedness problems for G-nets and several relevant subclasses. Our three most important results are:

- The decidability of the Coverability problem for a very large extension of Petri nets, using a surprisingly simple new algorithm.
- The undecidability of the Boundedness problem for Petri nets with Reset arcs, a deep result countering our earlier intuitions (and the decidability proof from [KCK+97]).
- The proof that the Coverability, Boundedness and place-Boundedness problems can be separated in counter-intuitive ways.

Related Works. Valk introduced and studied Self-Modifying nets (that contain Reset Petri nets) and Post Self-Modifying nets [Val78b,Val78a]. He showed that SM-nets can simulate two-counters machines with inhibitor arcs, and then that almost all properties (like Reachability, Boundedness or Termination) are undecidable. He also proved that Reachability is undecidable for Post SM-nets and that the place-Boundedness problem is decidable (with the non-primitive-recursive Karp and Miller algorithm) for Post SM-nets. Lakos and Christensen [LC94] compared different sets of primitives for extended arcs, essentially from a modelization point of view. Billington modelized the Cambridge Ring Network using Reset arcs [Bil91]. See the bibliographies in [Cia94,LC94] for other *applications* of Petri nets with Reset and Transfer arcs. Because we are not concerned with true concurrency issues, we see Read arcs [Vog97] as classical arcs.

Plan of the paper. We define G-nets and relevant subclasses in Sections 2 and 3. Then we study Coverability and Termination (Section 4), Boundedness (Section 5), place-Boundedness (Section 6), and Reachability (Section 7) in turn.

2 Generalized Self-Modifying Nets

Let $P = \{p_1, \ldots, p_k\}$. We write $\mathbb{N}[P]$ or $\mathbb{N}[p_1, \cdots, p_k]$ the set of polynomials over k variables with coefficients from $\mathbb{N}$. We adopt the usual convention $P \cup \mathbb{N} \subseteq \mathbb{N}[P]$.

All the Petri nets extensions studied in this paper will be subclasses of *Generalized Self-Modifying nets*, a very general new class of extended nets. A Generalized Self-Modifying net (a G-net for short), with k places $p_1, \ldots, p_k$, is a net where each arc is labeled by a polynomial Q from $\mathbb{N}[p_1, p_2, \ldots, p_k]$ of the special form $\Sigma_{j \in J} \lambda_j p_{i_j}^{n_j}$ (J finite, λ_j, $n_j \in \mathbb{N}$ and $1 \leq i_j \leq k$). Generalized Self-Modifying nets naturally extend Self-Modifying nets defined twenty years ago by Valk [Val78b,Val78a] where only polynomials of the form $\Sigma_{i=1}^{k} \lambda_i p_i$ are considered.

Why we use this notion of G-nets is mostly a matter of clarity and convenience. It has convenience because computing with simple polynomials is easy. It has clarity because we wanted to show that our approach is quite general and smoothly go beyond the simple linear functions used in Self-Modifying nets.

Definition 1. A Generalized Self-Modifying net (shortly a G-net) is a 4-tuple $N = \langle P, T, F, m_0 \rangle$ where
- $P = \{p_1, \cdots, p_{|P|}\}$ is a finite set of *places*,
- T is a finite set of *transitions* (with $P \cap T = \emptyset$),
- $F : (P \times T) \cup (T \times P) \longrightarrow \mathbb{N}[P]$ is a *flow function* such that : $\forall x, y \in P \cup T$, $F(x, y)$ has the form $\Sigma_{j \in J} \lambda_j p_{i_j}^{n_j}$ where J is a finite set, $\lambda_j \in \mathbb{N}$, $n_j \in \mathbb{N}$ and $1 \leq i_j \leq |P|$,
- $m_0 \in \mathbb{N}^{|P|}$ is the *initial marking.*

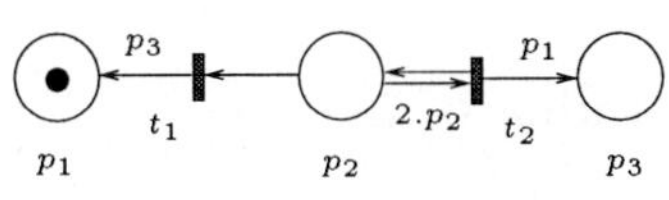

Fig. 1. A G-net computing Fibonacci numbers

Figure 1 shows a G-net computing the Fibonacci numbers. We follow the usual convention that arcs with omitted labels have a weight of 1, a constant polynomial. We use vector notation to denote markings: in the example $m_0 = (1, 0, 0)$. Given a marking m, we write $m(p)$ to denote the number of tokens in place p. We write $m \leq m'$ when $m(p) \leq m'(p)$ for all p.

A transition t is *firable* from a marking $m \in \mathbb{N}^{|P|}$, written $m \xrightarrow{t}$, if for any place p_i :

$$m(p_i) \geq \Sigma_j \lambda_j m(p_{i_j})^{n_j} \text{ where } F(p_i, t) = \Sigma_j \lambda_j p_{i_j}^{n_j}$$

In the example we have $F(p_2, t_2) = 2p_2$ so that $m \xrightarrow{t_2}$ only if $m(p_2) \geq 2m(p_2)$, i.e. iff p_2 is empty in m. This shows how inhibitory arcs are a special case of our extended arcs.

When $m \xrightarrow{t}$, firing t from m leads to a new marking m' where for any place p_i, $m'(p_i) = m(p_i) - \Sigma_j \lambda_j m(p_{i_j})^{n_j} + \Sigma_j \mu_j m(p_{i_j})^{n_j}$ where $F(p_i, t) = \Sigma_j \lambda_j p_{i_j}^{n_j}$ and $F(t, p_i) = \Sigma_j \mu_j p_{i_j}^{n_j}$.

In our example, t_2 is firable from $(1, 0, 0)$. Firing it leads to add 1 token into p_2 and to add the current content of p_1 into p_3. We have $m_0 = (1, 0, 0) \xrightarrow{t_2} (1, 1, 1)$. Now t_1 is firable.

An *execution* of N is a sequence of markings $m_0 \xrightarrow{t_{i_1}} m_1 \xrightarrow{t_{i_2}} m_2 \ldots$ successively reachable from m_0. An execution of the Fibonacci net is $m_0 \xrightarrow{t_2} (1, 1, 1) \xrightarrow{t_1} (2, 0, 1) \xrightarrow{t_2} (2, 1, 3) \xrightarrow{t_1} (5, 0, 3) \ldots$. For odd k, we reach the marking $m_k = (\mathit{fib}(k + 1), 0, \mathit{fib}(k))$.

A net *terminates* if there exists no infinite execution (*Termination Problem*). E.g. the Fibonacci net does not terminate. A marking m' is *reachable* from m, written $m \xrightarrow{*} m'$, if there exists a sequence $\sigma \in T^*$ such that $m \xrightarrow{\sigma} m'$ (*Reachability Problem*). The *reachability set* of N, denoted $RS(N)$,is $\{m | m_0 \xrightarrow{*} m\}$. A marking $m \in \mathbb{N}^{|P|}$ is *coverable* in N, if there exists a marking $m' \in RS(N)$ such that $m' \geq m$ (*Coverability Problem*). A G-net is *bounded* if its reachability set is finite (*Boundedness Problem*). A place $p \in P$ is *bounded* if there exists a $k \in \mathbb{N}$ such that $\forall m \in RS(N), m(p) \leq k$ (*place-Boundedness Problem*). In our example, place p_2 is bounded, but places p_1 and p_3 are not.

These five problems are crucial for verification. The finiteness of the behavior (Termination) or the finiteness of the reachability set (Boundedness) are among the first properties of interest. When some places are used to model buffers or files, implementation issues may require to check Boundedness for these places only. The Coverability and the Reachability Problems are key notions for decidability of temporal logics. Coverability is an abstract problem containing Determinism, Quasi-Liveness, Control-State Reachability, ...

3 Some Relevant Families of G-nets

Our Fibonacci example already illustrates several common kinds of arcs. A flow function $F(p, t) = 2p$ is in fact an inhibitory arc from p to t. A flow function $F(p, t) = p$ is a Reset arc: firing t will set p to zero. We usually draw such arcs with a crossed edge from t to p to emphasize the postcondition side of such arcs. See figure 3. A Transfer arc is used to transfer all tokens from p into some p' when t is fired. Because it empties p, there is an obvious connection with Reset arcs. With $F(p, t) = F(t, p') = p$, G-nets allow Transfer arcs.

We can now define formally how well-known families of extended nets are subclasses of G-nets (see also figure 3).

- Valk's Self-Modifying nets (*SM-nets*) are G-nets such that the flow function F uses polynomials of degree at most 1.
- A *Post G-net* is a G-net where only post-arcs are extended arcs: $\forall p \in P$, $\forall t \in T$, $F(p, t) \in \mathbb{N}$.
- Similarly, a *Post-SM* net is a SM-net such that for every $p \in P$, $t \in T$, $F(p, t) \in \mathbb{N}$.

- A *Petri net* is a G-net with only classical arcs: for every x, y, $F(x,y) \in \mathbb{N}$.
- A *Reset Post G-net* is a G-net where pre-arcs are Reset arcs or classical Petri arcs: for all $p \in P$ and $t \in T$, $F(p,t) = p$ or $F(p,t) \in \mathbb{N}$.
- A *Reset Petri net* is a Reset Post G-net such that all post-arcs are classical: $F(t,p) \in \mathbb{N}$.
- A *Transfer Post G-net* is a Reset Post G-net such that whenever there is a reset arc $F(p,t) = p$ then there is a p' with $F(t,p') = p$. (As a whole, the two arcs (p,t) and (t,p') are what we call a Transfer arc.)
- A *Transfer Petri net* is a Transfer Post G-net such that all arcs are classical arcs or Transfert arcs.
- A *Double Petri net* is a Post G-net such that for every $p \in P$, $t \in T$, $F(t,p) = p$ or $F(t,p) \in \mathbb{N}$. When $F(t,p) = p$, (t,p) is called a *Doubling arc*.

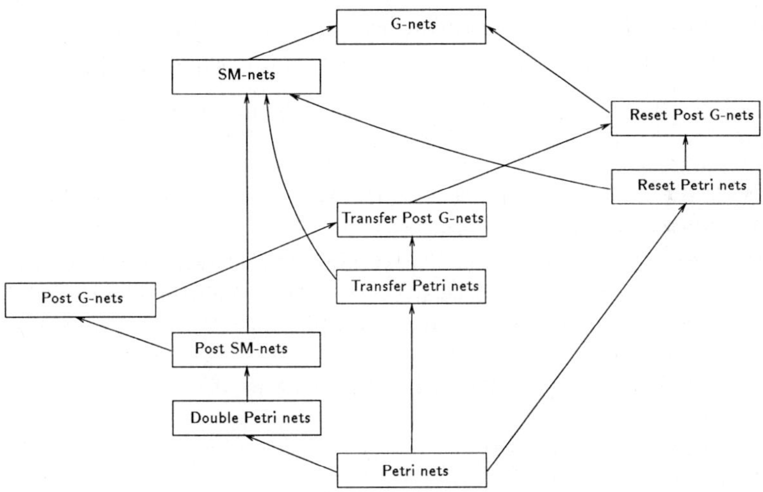

Fig. 2. Subclasses of G-nets and inclusions between them

Self-Modifying nets were defined in 1978 by Valk in [Val78a]. Reset Petri nets were introduced in 1977 by Araki and Kasami in [AK77]. Transfer Petri nets are defined in [Cia94]. Post-SM nets are a subclass of SM-nets defined and studied by Valk in [Val78a]. Petri nets have been defined in 1962 by Petri! The other classes are natural extensions of the previous one.

4 Decidability of Coverability and Termination

The Coverability problem has usually been associated with the coverability tree algorithms [Rac78,KM69,Hac76,Fin90] and then with the Boundedness (and place-Boundedness) problems. Recently, Abdulla *et al.* [AČJY96] and Finkel and Schnoebelen [FS98] have proposed another algorithm for the Coverability problem. This algorithm works on general so-called Well-Structured Transition Systems. It works "backward" (computes predecessors of states), contrasting the earlier "forward" algorithm for coverability trees.

Definition 2. [Fin90,AČJY96] A *well-structured transition system* (a WSTS) is a structure $S = \langle Q, \rightarrow, \leq \rangle$ such that:
- $Q = \{m, \ldots\}$ is a set of states,
- $\rightarrow \subseteq Q \times Q$ is a set of transitions,
- $\leq \subseteq Q \times Q$ is a well-quasi-ordering (a wqo) on the set of states, satisfying the *simple monotonicity* property

$$m \rightarrow m' \text{ and } m_1 \geq m \text{ imply } m_1 \rightarrow m'_1 \text{ for some } m'_1 \geq m' \qquad (1)$$

Thus a WSTS is a transition system where the transitions have the monotonicity property w.r.t. some wqo. (Recall that a wqo is any reflexive and transitive relation such that for any infinite sequence $m_1, m_2, \ldots$, there exists two indexes $i < j$ s.t. $m_i \leq m_j$.)

Theorem 3. [AČJY96,FS98] *For WSTS's with an effective wqo and effective pred-basis, Coverability is decidable.*

(This result is called "decidability of control-state reachability" in [AČJY96].) Here we give the ideas of the algorithm.

Pred-basis is related to one-step coverability: to any $m \in Q$, we associate $pb(m)$, a finite set $\{m_1, \ldots, m_k\}$ such that it is possible to cover m from m' in one step iff m' covers some $m_i \in pb(m)$. Formally,

$$(\exists m_i \in pb(m), m' \geq m_i) \text{ iff } (\exists m'' \geq m, m' \rightarrow m'')$$

The set pb is well-defined because $\{m' \mid \exists m'' \geq m, m' \rightarrow m''\}$ is upward-closed (a consequence of monotonicity) and upward-closed sets have finite basis (a property of well-quasi-orderings). When pb is effective, it is possible to build a sequence $K_0 \subseteq K_1 \subseteq K_2 \subseteq \cdots$ of finite sets with $K_0 \stackrel{\text{def}}{=} \{m\}$, $K_{j+1} \stackrel{\text{def}}{=} K_j \cup pb(K_j)$. Because $\leq$ is a well-quasi-ordering, the sequence eventually stabilizes, i.e. there exists an index n s.t. $\forall m_i \in K_{n+1}, \exists m_j \in K_n, m_j \leq m_i$. Because $\leq$ is effective, stabilization can be detected effectively, hence n can be computed. At stabilization, K_n answers the coverability problem: it is possible to cover m from m' iff m' covers some $m_i \in K_n$.

This algorithm applies to all effective WSTS's, including Petri nets, lossy channels systems, normed BPA processes, ... see [AČJY96,FS98].

Now Reset Post G-nets enjoy simple monotonicity w.r.t. "$\leq$", the usual ordering between markings. Further, $\leq$ is an effective wqo, effectivity of pb is clear (see example below), hence Reset Post G-nets are effective WSTS's. The corollary is

Theorem 4. *Coverability is decidable for Reset Post G-nets.*

Let us illustrate the algorithm with the Reset Petri net from figure 3. Assume we are interested into covering the target marking $m = (1, 2, 0, 0)$. We start with $K_0 = \{(1, 2, 0, 0)\}$. Now let us compute $pb(\{(1, 2, 0, 0)\})$.

With t_1, we can cover $(1, 2, 0, 0)$ in one step if we start from $(1, 3, 0, 0)$ or any larger marking. With t_2 is is impossible to cover m in one step because t_2 resets p_2. With t_3, we can cover m if we start from $(1, 1, 1, 1)$ or above. With t_4, we need to start from $(0, 1, 1, 0)$ or above. Eventually, we end up with $K_1 = \{(1, 2, 0, 0), (1, 3, 0, 0), (1, 1, 1, 1), (0, 1, 1, 0)\}$. For convenience, we remove non-minimal elements, writing $K_1 = \{(1, 2, 0, 0), (0, 1, 1, 0)\}$, before going on with the computation of K_2.

Eventually we reach $K_5 = \{(1, 0, 0, 0), (0, 0, 1, 0)\}$ and notice that $K_6 = K_5$. We have reached stabilization: it is possible to cover m from some m_0 iff m_0 has at least one token in p_1 or p_3. Hence m is coverable in N.

Theorem 5. *Termination is decidable for Reset Post G-nets.*

Proof. Again we can apply a general decidability result (from [Fin90]) for WSTS's with effective $\leq$ and effective one-step successors mapping. □

Theorems 4 and 5 cannot be extended beyond Reset Post G-nets:

Theorem 6. [Val78b,Val78a] *Coverability and Termination are undecidable for SM-nets (and hence for G-nets).*

Proof. Strictly speaking, undecidability of Coverability and Termination for SM-nets is not considered in [Val78b,Val78a] but his encoding of Minsky's counter machines into SM-nets can be reused with no difficulty. □

Theorem 4 generalizes a result of Valk [Val78b,Val78a] who decides Coverability for Post SM-nets by using the Karp and Miller coverability tree algorithm on Post SM-nets. His proof cannot be extended because *there does not exist effective coverability trees* (nor finite coverability sets) for Reset Post G-nets, as a consequence of Theorem 8.

5 Decidability of Boundedness

Transfer Post G-nets are Well-Structured Transition Systems with additional structure. They enjoy *strict monotonicity*:

$$m \rightarrow m' \text{ and } m_1 > m \text{ imply } m_1 \rightarrow m'_1 \text{ for some } m'_1 > m' \tag{2}$$

(while Reset Petri nets only enjoy simple monotonicity). With strict monotonicity, boundedness is decided by searching for a sequence $m_0 \xrightarrow{*} m_1 \xrightarrow{\sigma} m_2$ with $m_1 < m_2$. Then σ is iterated: $m_1 \xrightarrow{\sigma} m_2 \xrightarrow{\sigma} m_3 \cdots$ yielding $m_1 < m_2 < m_3 < \cdots$ and the net is unbounded. This gives

Theorem 7. *Boundedness is decidable for Transfer Post G-nets.*

Proof. Strict monotonicity makes Transfer Post G-nets 1'-well-structured transition systems in the sense of [Fin90], hence boundedness is decidable. □

Reset Petri nets do not enjoy strict monotonicity, making the situation less comfortable: in a Reset Petri net, when $m_1 \xrightarrow{\sigma} m_2$, with $m_2 > m_1$, σ can be iterated, but $m_{i+1} = m_i$ is possible in the sequence $m_1 \xrightarrow{\sigma} m_2 \xrightarrow{\sigma} m_3 \xrightarrow{\sigma} m_4 \cdots$. [KCK+97] thought they could overcome this difficulty by claiming that a Reset Petri net is unbounded iff there is a $m_0 \xrightarrow{*} m_1 \xrightarrow{\sigma} m_2$ with $m_1 < m_2$ and more precisely with $m_1(p) < m_2(p)$ for some place p that is not reset by any transition in σ (see Theorem 7 from [KCK+97]). They conclude that Boundedness is decidable for Reset Petri nets.

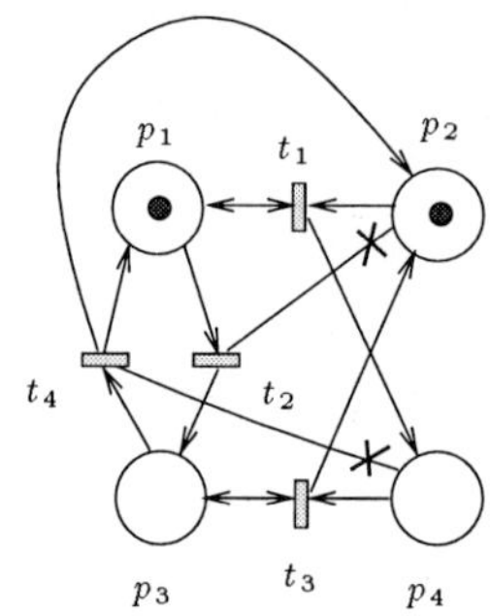

Fig. 3. An unbounded Reset Petri net with no iterated sequence

It turns out their claim is false. Consider the net from figure 3. This net is unbounded but its only unbounded behaviour has the form:

$$(1,1,0,0) \xrightarrow{t_1t_2t_3t_4} (1,2,0,0) \xrightarrow{t_1{}^2t_2t_3{}^2t_4} (1,3,0,0) \ldots (1,i,0,0) \xrightarrow{t_1{}^it_2t_3{}^it_4} (1,i{+}1,0,0) \ldots$$

and no $m_1 \xrightarrow{\sigma} m_2$ can be found with $m_1 < m_2$ and $m_1(p) < m_2(p)$ for a p that is not reset.

In fact, we cannot extend theorem 7 beyond Transfer Post G-net. Surprisingly

Theorem 8. *Boundedness is undecidable for Reset Petri nets.*

Proof. A full proof of this result can be found in the longer version of this paper [1]. The details take several pages but it is possible to explain the main ideas here.

1. We prove a main lemma, stating that Reset nets can compute polynomials in a weak sense: given Q in $\mathbb{N}[x_1, \ldots, x_n]$, there exists a Reset net N_Q computing Q. Here *computing* Q means that, starting from a vector of $\bar{v} \in \mathbb{N}^n$ of tokens in its input places $p_1^{\text{in}}, \ldots, p_n^{\text{in}}$, N_Q can transfer all tokens in the corresponding output places $p_1^{\text{out}}, \ldots, p_n^{\text{out}}$ by a sequence of exactly $Q(\bar{v})$ visible transitions. (Note that this is different from the more usual notion of gathering $Q(\bar{v})$ tokens in some

[1] available from the authors.

result place.) N_Q does not create new tokens (hence it is bounded), it only moves them around. Now it is not possible to enforce this exact behaviour in a Reset net, and other transitions sequences are possible. However, N_Q is such that (1) *it is not possible to fire more than* $Q(\bar{v})$ *visible transitions*, and (2) *when* N_Q *terminates properly after less than* $Q(\bar{v})$ *transitions, then some tokens have been lost in the transfer from the input to the output places* (this uses Reset arcs).
2. Then we show how to compare two polynomials Q and R. Clearly it is possible to check in a weak sense whether $Q(\bar{v}) = R(\bar{v})$: one synchronizes N_Q and N_R on their visible transitions and feed them with $\bar{v}$ tokens. If Q and R do not agree on $\bar{v}$, then necessarily some tokens will be lost. We use a similar construction checking for non-equality: if the two polynomials agree, then necessarily some tokens will be lost in the transfer.
3. Then we wrap this in an enumeration scheme. We enumerate all vectors $\bar{v}_1, \bar{v}_2, \bar{v}_3, \ldots$ in such a way that (1) *there exists a Reset net outputting (again in a weak sense)* $\bar{v}_i$ *when given* $\bar{v}_{i-1}$, and (2) *whenever some token is lost from some* $\bar{v}_i$*, we end up into a* $\bar{v}_j$ *with* $j < i$. This too uses Reset arcs. When we connect the "check $Q \neq R$" net and the tuple-enumeration net, we end up with a Reset net having the following potential behaviour: check that $Q(\bar{v}_0) \neq R(\bar{v}_0)$, compute $\bar{v}_1$ from $\bar{v}_0$, check that $Q(\bar{v}_1) \neq R(\bar{v}_1)$, compute $\bar{v}_2$ from $\bar{v}_1$, etc. This behaviour is unbounded. Two conditions make it possible: (1) *the net picks the correct behaviour for evaluating polynomials and enumerating tuples*, and (2) *for any* $i \in \mathbb{N}$, $Q(\bar{v}_i)$ *and* $R(\bar{v}_i)$ *really differ so that the comparison does not loose tokens*. Any other behaviour is bounded.
4. Thus, given Q and R, we have constructed a Reset net which is bounded iff the diophantine equation $Q(x_1, \ldots, x_n) = R(x_1, \ldots, x_n)$ has no solution. This is an effective reduction of Hilbert's Tenth Problem to our Boundedness Problem for Reset nets. □

Hence Coverability is decidable for Reset Petri nets but Boundedness is not. As far as we know, this is the first published instance of an extension of Petri nets where Coverability and Boundedness are separated from a decidability viewpoint. Because Coverability has always been associated with coverability trees, because Boundedness is decidable for Transfer Petri nets, the natural conjecture had always been that the Boundedness problem must be decidable for Reset nets.

6 Decidability of Place-Boundedness

When it is possible to extend the procedure of Karp and Miller, place-Boundedness is decidable:

Theorem 9. *Place-Boundedness is decidable for Post G-nets.*

Proof. Post G-nets are 1'-well-structured in the sense of [Fin90]. Further, they enjoy the continuity conditions required for theorem 4.16 in [Fin90]. Hence, a (generalized) Coverability tree can be built effectively for Post G-nets. This tree is used to answer place-Boundedness. □

We cannot extend this beyond Post G-nets

Theorem 10. *Place-Boundedness is undecidable for Transfer Petri nets.*

Proof. A Reset Petri net N may be simulated by a Transfer Petri net N' which mimics resets of places by transferring their contents into a (new) dummy place. N is unbounded iff one place different from the dummy place is unbounded in N'. Thus decidability of place-Boundedness for Transfer Petri nets would imply decidability of Boundedness for Reset Petri nets. □

Hence Boundedness is decidable for Transfer Petri net but place-Boundedness is not. As far as we know, this is the first time Boundedness and place-Boundedness are separated from a decidability viewpoint. (What is more, in most papers where place-Boundedness is involved, the name "Boundedness" is used, showing how the two problems have always been seen as one single general problem.)

7 Undecidability of Reachability

Reachability is an important problem. It is decidable for Petri nets and it often becomes undecidable as soon as the power of Petri nets is increased. In this section, we show that for any of the smallest extended classes of Petri nets we defined, *two* extended arcs suffice to make the Reachability Problem undecidable.

Theorem 11. *Reachability is undecidable for Double Petri nets, Reset Petri nets and Transfer Petri nets having two extended (Doubling, Reset or Transfer) arcs.*

Proof. We reduce reachability for nets with inhibitory arcs into reachability for nets with extended (Doubling, Reset or Transfer) arcs. Consider a net N with inhibitory arcs. Any place which is the input place of an inhibitory arc is called an *inhibitory place.* We build a Reset Petri net N^+ by modifying N. In N^+ we add a *twin place* p' for every inhibitory place p. The idea is that p and p' will always have the same number of tokens as long as N^+ correctly simulates N. We extend the flow relation of N^+ by setting $F(p',t) \stackrel{\text{def}}{=} F(p,t)$ and $F(t,p') \stackrel{\text{def}}{=} F(t,p)$ for every t and every inhibitory p. Finally we replace every inhibitory arc from some p to some t by a Reset arc from t to p'. See diagram:

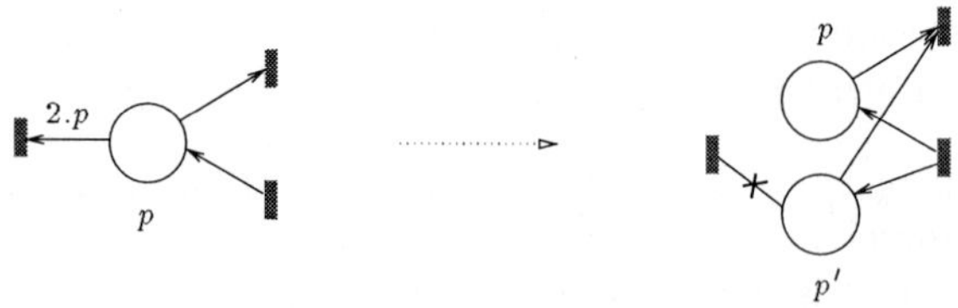

Consider any step $m_1 \to m_2$ in N^+. The construction ensures that, for any inhibitory p, if $m_1(p) \geq m_1(p')$ then $m_2(p) \geq m_2(p')$. Furthermore, if $m_1(p) > m_1(p')$ then $m_2(p) > m_2(p')$. These two properties are summarized by "N^+ *preserves imbalances*".

Now let m be a marking of N and write m^+ for the marking of N^+ obtained by extending m to twin places: $m^+(p') \stackrel{\text{def}}{=} m(p)$. We claim that $m_0 \stackrel{*}{\to} m$ in N iff $m_0^+ \stackrel{*}{\to} m^+$ in N^+. This uses a simple induction over the length of executions. The crucial case in the induction is when N^+ erases for the first time some non empty p' with a Reset arc. This introduces an imbalance that can never be recovered. In N, this step is not possible because p is not empty and inhibits the transition.

The construction also works if we use a Transfer arc from p' to a new dummy place instead of a Reset arc.

The same construction works if we use a doubling arc from t to p' instead of a Reset arc, but this time imbalance means $M(p') > M(p)$. □

It does not seem possible to go beyond Theorem 11 because Reachability is decidable for Petri nets with only one inhibitor arc [Rei95], hence also for Petri nets with at most one Reset arc or one Transfer arc. We conjecture Reachability is decidable when only one Doubling arc is allowed.

Conclusion

In this paper we answered all the decidability questions concerning Coverability, Termination, Reachability, Boundedness and place-Boundedness for all the relevant subclasses of G-nets we gave in figure 3. These results are summarized in figure 4. Let us stress the most important ones:

- A very surprising result is that Boundedness is undecidable even for the very small class of Reset Petri nets. This is the main technical result of the paper. It is highly non-trivial and has been open for several years. That it is counter-intuitive is underlined by the fact that an (erroneous) decidability proof was published recently. Our proof required inventing a new, more faithful, way of weakly-evaluating polynomials with Reset Petri nets. A corollary is that, for Transfer Petri nets, Boundedness is decidable but place-Boundedness is not. Again, this came as a surprise. To the best of our knowledge, this is the first time these two problems are separated.
- It is possible to generalize the Karp and Miller coverability tree algorithm for Post G-nets (and then to decide place-Boundedness), but not for Reset Post G-nets, an extension of Valk's Post SM-nets. Now, for Reset Post G-nets, the Termination problem is decidable using a partial construction of coverability tree; and Coverability is decidable, using a backward algorithm, which computes sets of predecessors of markings, instead of computing sets of successors (as it is done in the coverability tree construction).

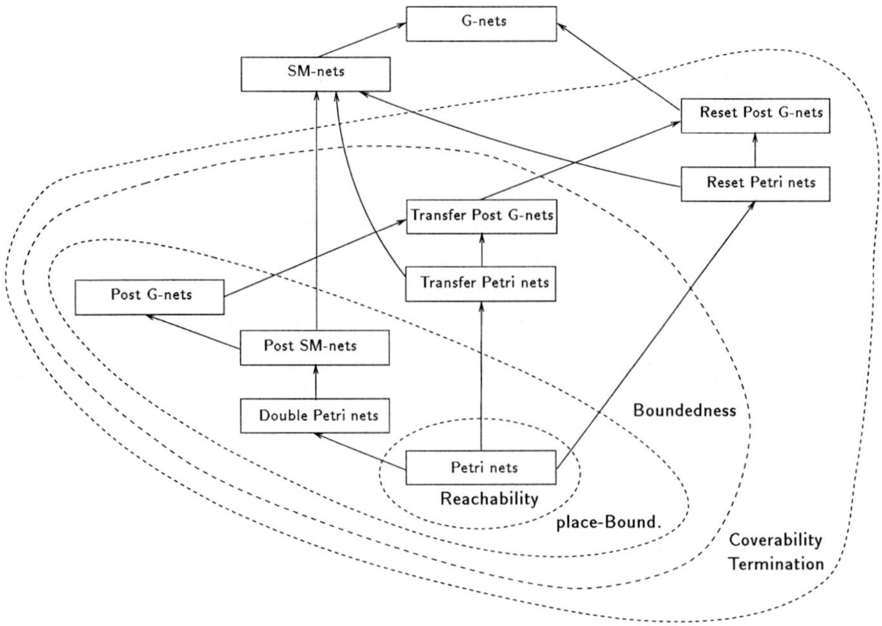

Fig. 4. What's decidable where.

Finally, we may update the opening quote:
There exist extensions of Petri nets which do not allow zero testing but that will actually increase the modeling power (e.g. in term of terminals and covering languages) and decrease the decision power (e.g. Boundedness becomes undecidable). In fact, when one considers a collection of various decision problems (not just Reachability), there are many layers between mere reformulations of the basic Petri net model (at one end), and at the other end Petri nets with inhibitory arcs (i.e. counter machines).

References

[AČJY96] P. A. Abdulla, K. Čerāns, B. Jonsson, and T. Yih-Kuen. General decidability theorems for infinite-state systems. In *Proc. 11th IEEE Symp. Logic in Computer Science (LICS'96), New Brunswick, NJ, USA, July 1996*, pages 313–321, 1996.

[AK77] T. Araki and T. Kasami. Some decision problems related to the reachability problem for Petri nets. *Theoretical Computer Science*, 3(1):85–104, 1977.

[Bil91] J. Billington. *Extensions to coloured Petri nets and their applications to protocols*. PhD thesis, University of Cambridge, UK, May 1991. Available as Tech. Report No.222.

[Cia94] G. Ciardo. Petri nets with marking-dependent arc cardinality: Properties and analysis. In *Proc. 15th Int. Conf. Applications and Theory of Petri Nets, Zaragoza, Spain, June 1994*, volume 815 of *Lecture Notes in Computer Science*, pages 179–198. Springer-Verlag, 1994.

[Fin90] A. Finkel. Reduction and covering of infinite reachability trees. *Information and Computation*, 89(2):144–179, 1990.

[FS98] A. Finkel and Ph. Schnoebelen. Fundamental structures in well-structured infinite transition systems. In *Proc. 3rd Latin American Theoretical Informatics Symposium (LATIN'98), Campinas, Brazil, Apr. 1998*, volume 1380 of *Lecture Notes in Computer Science.* Springer-Verlag, 1998.

[Hac76] M. Hack. Decidability questions for Petri nets. PhD Thesis MIT/LCS/TR-161, Massachusetts Institute of Technology, Lab. for Computer Science, June 1976.

[KCK+97] M. Kishinevsky, J. Cortadella, A. Kondratyev, L. Lavagno, A. Taubin, and A. Yakovlev. Coupling asynchrony and interrupts: Place chart nets. In *Proc. 18th Int. Conf. Application and Theory of Petri Nets, Toulouse, France, June 1997*, volume 1248 of *Lecture Notes in Computer Science*, pages 328–347. Springer-Verlag, 1997.

[KM69] R. M. Karp and R. E. Miller. Parallel program schemata. *Journal of Computer and System Sciences*, 3(2):147–195, 1969.

[LC94] C. Lakos and S. Christensen. A general approach to arc extensions for coloured Petri nets. In *Proc. 15th Int. Conf. Applications and Theory of Petri Nets, Zaragoza, Spain, June 1994*, volume 815 of *Lecture Notes in Computer Science*, pages 338–357. Springer-Verlag, 1994.

[Pet81] J. L. Peterson. *Petri Net Theory and the Modeling of Systems.* Prentice Hall Int., 1981.

[Rac78] C. Rackoff. The covering and boundedness problems for vector addition systems. *Theoretical Computer Science*, 6(2):223–231, 1978.

[Rei95] K. Reinhardt. Reachability in Petri nets with inhibitor arcs, November 1995. Unpublished manuscript. See `www-fs.informatik.uni-tuebingen.de/~reinhard`.

[Val78a] R. Valk. On the computational power of extended Petri nets. In *Proc. 7th Symp. Math. Found. Comp. Sci. (MFCS'78), Zakopane, Poland, Sep. 1978*, volume 64 of *Lecture Notes in Computer Science*, pages 526–535, 1978.

[Val78b] R. Valk. Self-modifying nets, a natural extension of Petri nets. In *Proc. 5th Int. Coll. Automata, Languages, and Programming (ICALP'78), Udine, Italy, Jul. 1978*, volume 62 of *Lecture Notes in Computer Science*, pages 464–476. Springer-Verlag, 1978.

[Vog97] W. Vogler. Partial order semantics and read arcs. In *Proc. 22nd Int. Symp. Math. Found. Comp. Sci. (MFCS'97), Bratislava, Slovakia, Aug. 1997*, volume 1295 of *Lecture Notes in Computer Science*, pages 508–517. Springer-Verlag, 1997.

Geometric Algorithms for Robotic Manipulation

Mark H. Overmars

Department of Computer Science, Utrecht University, P.O.Box 80.089, 3508 TB, Utrecht, the Netherlands. Email: markov@cs.uu.nl.

As product life cycles shrink in the face of global competition, new methods are required to facilitate rapid design and production. In particular, it is widely recognized that products must be designed using CAD systems: methods are needed to automatically evaluate CAD models during the design cycle to faciliate manufacture.

Most automated manufacturing, assembly, and inspection operations require specialized part feeders, grippers, and fixtures to orient, locate, and hold parts. Given part shape and desired position and orientation, mechanisms are usually custom-designed by manufacturing engineers and machinists using intuition and trial-and-error. A science base is required to replace this "black art" with efficient tools that start from CAD models.

Although part handling is widely recognized as one of the most crucial problem areas in industrial manufacture, there are currently only general guidelines in handbooks. Recent results suggest, however, that it is possible to develop systematic algorithms for automatically designing part handling mechanisms based on CAD part models.

Techniques from Computational Geometry can provide the basis for such algorithms. Clearly, part feeding deals with geometric objects. Computational Geometry has, over the 20 years of its existence, developed a huge base of general algorithmic techniques and data structures that are at our disposal. Also combinatorial geometry has provided us with a rich collection of results that should be useful in making provable statements about the feasibility of certain part handling tasks. The application of Computational Geometry to part handling is though still a largely unexplored domain.

In this talk I will give some examples of the use of geometric algorithms for automatic design of part handlers. I will concentrate on two problems: fixturing and orienting parts.

Fixturing

In modular fixturing a family of interchangeable components is used and re-used to fixture a broad class of parts. Commercially-available systems typically include a square lattice of tapped and dowelled holes with closely toleranced spacing and an assortment of precision locating and clamping elements that can be rigidly attached to the lattice. Brost and Goldberg presented the first systematic algorithm for the design of such fixtures. Given a polygonal part description, the algorithm returns a list of all planar form-closure fixtures that require 3 locators and one clamp. Since that paper, algorithms have been designed for various types of fixturing devices. I will give an overview of a number of these results and indicate some promising directions for further research.

Fence design

The second topic is the sensorless manipulation of parts. In particular, I will focus on sensorless orientation. Here the initial pose of a part is unknown and the goal is to orient the part into a known orientation using passive mechanical compliance. I will concentrate on two models: orientating by pushing or squeezing the object, and orienting by using a number of passive fences along a conveyor belt. In particular the model with fences is very practical but not much was known about it. I will show that any polygonal part without certain rotational symmetry can be oriented in a unique orientation using a finite number of fences and I will give efficient algorithms to compute such fence designs.

Further reading

Over the past few years, a large number of papers have appeared on geometric algorithms for problems in robotics. An excellent source are the proceedings of the three workshops on algorithmic foundations of robotics (WAFR), held in 1994, 1996 and 1998, published by A.K. Peters[2, 3, 1]. Most likely, the next workshop will be held in the year 2000.

References

1. Agarwal, P., L. Kavraki, and M. Mason, *Proc. WAFR'98,* A.K. Peters, Wellesley, 1998, to appear.
2. Goldberg, K., D. Halperin, J-C. Latombe, and R. Wilson, *Algorithmic Foundations of Robotics,* A.K. Peters, Wellesley, 1995.
3. Laumond, J-P., and M.H. Overmars, *Algorithms for Robotic Motion and Manipulation,* A.K. Peters, Wellesley, 1997.

Compact Encodings of Planar Graphs via Canonical Orderings and Multiple Parentheses

Richie Chih-Nan Chuang[1], Ashim Garg[2], Xin He[2*], Ming-Yang Kao[3**], and Hsueh-I Lu[1]

[1] Department of Computer Science and Information Engineering, National Chung-Cheng University, Chia-Yi 621, Taiwan, {cjn85, hil}@cs.ccu.edu.tw

[2] Department of Computer Science, State University of New York at Buffalo, Buffalo, NY 14260, USA, {agarg,xinhe}@cs.buffalo.edu

[3] Department of Computer Science, Yale University, New Haven, CT 06250, USA, kao-ming-yang@cs.yale.edu

Abstract. We consider the problem of coding planar graphs by binary strings. Depending on whether $O(1)$-time queries for adjacency and degree are supported, we present three sets of coding schemes which all take linear time for encoding and decoding. The encoding lengths are significantly shorter than the previously known results in each case.

1 Introduction

This paper investigates the problem of encoding a graph G with n nodes and m edges into a binary string S. This problem has been extensively studied with three objectives: (1) minimizing the length of S, (2) minimizing the time needed to compute and decode S, and (3) supporting queries efficiently.

A number of coding schemes with different trade-offs have been proposed. The adjacency-list encoding of a graph is widely useful but requires $2m\lceil\log n\rceil$ bits. (All logarithms are of base 2.) A folklore scheme uses $2n$ bits to encode a rooted n-node tree into a string of n pairs of balanced parentheses. Since the total number of such trees is at least $\frac{1}{2(n-1)}\cdot\frac{(2n-2)!}{(n-1)!(n-1)!}$, the minimum number of bits needed to differentiate these trees is the log of this quantity, which is $2n-o(n)$. Thus, two bits per edge up to an additive $o(1)$ term is an information-theoretic tight bound for encoding rooted trees. Works on encodings of certain other graph families can be found in [7, 12, 4, 17, 5, 16].

Let G be a plane graph with n nodes, m edges, f faces, and no self-loop. G need not be connected or simple. We give coding schemes for G which all take $O(m+n)$ time for encoding and decoding. The bit counts of our schemes depend on the level of required query support and the structure of the encoded graphs.

For applications that require support of certain queries, Jacobson [6] gave an $\Theta(n)$-bit encoding for a simple planar graph G that supports traversal in $\Theta(\log n)$ time per node visited. Munro and Raman [15] recently gave schemes to encode a planar graph using $2m+8n+o(m+n)$ bits while supporting adjacency and degree queries in $O(1)$ time. We reduce this bit count to $2m+5\frac{1}{k}n+o(m+n)$ for any

* Research supported in part by NSF Grant CCR-9205982.

** Research supported in part by NSF Grant CCR-9531028.

	adjacency and degree		adjacency		no query	
	[15]	ours	old	ours	[13]	ours
self-loops					$3.58m$	
general	$2m + 8n$	$2m + 5\frac{1}{k}n$		$2m + 4\frac{2}{3}n$		
simple		$\frac{5}{3}m + 5\frac{1}{k}n$		$\frac{4}{3}m + 5n$		
degree-one free					$3m$	
triconnected		$2m + 3n$		$2m + 3n$		
simple & triconnected		$2m + 2n$		$2m + 2n$		$\frac{3}{2}(\log 3)m$
triangulated		$2m + 2n$		$2m + 2n$		
simple & triangulated		$2m + n$		$2m + n$	$1.53m$	$\frac{4}{3}m$

Fig. 1. This table compares our results with previous ones, where k is a positive constant. The lower-order terms are omitted. All but row 1 assume that G has no self-loop.

constant $k > 0$ with the same query support. If G is triconnected or triangulated, our bit count decreases to $2m+3n+o(m+n)$ or $2m+2n+o(m+n)$, resp. With the same query support, we can encode a simple G using only $\frac{5}{3}m + 5\frac{1}{k}n + o(n)$ bits for any constant $k > 0$. If a simple G is also triconnected or triangulated, the bit count is $2m + 2n + o(n)$ or $2m + n + o(n)$, resp. If only $O(1)$-time adjacency queries are supported, our bit counts for a general G and a simple G become $2m + 4\frac{2}{3}n + o(m + n)$ and $\frac{4}{3}m + 5n + o(n)$, resp.

If we only need to reconstruct G with no query support, the code length can be substantially shortened. For this case, Turán [19] used $4m$ bits. This bound was improved by Keeler and Westbrook [13] to $3.58m$ bits. They also used $1.53m$ bits for a triangulated simple G, and $3m$ bits for a connected G free of self-loops and degree-one nodes. For a simple triangulated G, we improve the count to $\frac{4}{3}m + O(1)$. For a simple G that is free of self-loops, triconnected and thus free of degree-one nodes, we improve the bit count to $1.5(\log 3)m + O(1)$. Figure 1 summarizes our results and compares them with previous ones.

Our coding schemes employ two new tools. One is new techniques of processing strings of multiple types of parentheses. The other tool is new properties of canonical orderings for plane graphs which were introduced in [3, 8]. These concepts have proven useful also for drawing plane graphs [10, 11, 18]. §2 discusses the new tools. §3 describes the coding schemes that support queries. §4 presents the more compact coding schemes which do not support queries. Due to space limitation, the proofs of most lemmas are omitted.

2 New Encoding Tools

A *simple* (resp., *multiple*) graph is one that does not contain (resp., may contain) multiple edges between two distinct vertices. A multiple graph can be viewed as a simple one with positive integral edge weights, where each edge's weight indicates its multiplicity. The *simple version* of a multiple graph is one obtained from the graph by deleting all but one copy of each edge. In this paper, all graphs are multiple unless explicitly stated otherwise. The *degree* of a node v in a graph is the number of edges, counting multiple edges, incident to v in the graph. A node v is a *leaf* of a tree T if v has exactly one neighbor in T. Since T may have multiple edges, a leaf of T may have a degree greater than one.

2.1 Multiple Types of Parentheses

Let S be a string. S is *binary* if it contains at most two kinds of symbols. Let $S[i]$ be the symbol at the i-th position of S, for $1 \le i \le |S|$. Let $\text{select}(S, i, \Box)$ be the position of the i-th $\Box$ in S. Let $\text{rank}(S, k, \Box)$ be the number of $\Box$'s that precede or at the k-th position of S. Clearly, if $k = \text{select}(S, i, \Box)$, then $i = \text{rank}(S, k, \Box)$. Let $S_1 + \cdots + S_k$ denote the concatenation of strings $S_1, \ldots, S_k$. (In this paper, the encoding of G is usually a concatenation of several strings. For simplicity, we ignore the issue of separating these strings. This can be handled by using well-known data compression techniques with $\log n + O(\log \log n)$ bits [1].)

Let S be a string of multiple types of parentheses. Let $S[i]$ and $S[j]$ be an open and a close parenthesis with $i < j$ of the same type. $S[i]$ and $S[j]$ *match* in S if every parenthesis enclosed by $S[i]$ and $S[j]$ that is the same type as $S[i]$ and $S[j]$ matches a parenthesis enclosed by $S[i]$ and $S[j]$. Here are some queries defined for S:

- Let $\text{match}(S, i)$ be the position of the parenthesis in S that matches $S[i]$.
- Let $\text{first}_k(S, i)$ (resp., $\text{last}_k(S, i)$) be the position of the first (resp., last) parenthesis of the k-th type that succeeds (resp., precedes) $S[i]$.
- Let $\text{enclose}_k(S, i_1, i_2)$ be the positions (j_1, j_2) of the closest matching parenthesis pair of the k-th type that encloses $S[i_1]$ and $S[i_2]$.

S is *balanced* if every parenthesis in S belongs to a matching parenthesis pair. Note that the answer to a query above may be undefined. If there is only one type of parentheses in S, the subscript k in $\text{first}_k(S, i)$, $\text{last}_k(S, i)$, and $\text{enclose}_k(S, i, j)$ may be omitted; thus, $\text{first}(S, i) = i + 1$ and $\text{last}(S, i) = i - 1$. If it is clear from the context, the parameter S may also be omitted.

Fact 1 ([2, 14, 15]) *1. Let S be a binary string. An auxiliary binary string $\mu_1(S)$ of length $o(|S|)$ can be obtained in $O(|S|)$ time such that* $\text{rank}(S, i, \Box)$ *and* $\text{select}(S, i, \Box)$ *can be answered from $S + \mu_1(S)$ in $O(1)$ time.*
2. Let S be a balanced string of one type of parentheses. An auxiliary binary string $\mu_2(S)$ of length $o(|S|)$ can be obtained in $O(|S|)$ time such that $\text{match}(S, i)$ *and* $\text{enclose}(S, i, j)$ *can be answered from $S + \mu_2(S)$ in $O(1)$ time.*

The next theorem generalizes Fact 1 to handle a string of multiple types of parentheses that is not necessarily balanced.

Theorem 1. *Let S be a string of $O(1)$ types of parentheses that may be unbalanced. An auxiliary $o(|S|)$-bit string $\alpha(S)$ can be obtained in $O(|S|)$ time such that* $\text{rank}(S, i, \Box)$, $\text{select}(S, i, \Box)$, $\text{match}(S, i)$, $\text{first}_k(S, i)$, $\text{last}_k(S, i)$, *and* $\text{enclose}_k(S, i, j)$ *can be answered from $S + \alpha(S)$ in $O(1)$ time.*

Proof. The statement for $\text{rank}(S, i, \Box)$ and $\text{select}(S, i, \Box)$ is a straightforward generalization of Fact 1(1). The statement for $\text{first}_k(S, i)$ can be shown as follows. Let $f(S, i, \Box)$ be the position of the first $\Box$ that succeeds $S[i]$. Clearly,

$$f(S, i, \Box) = \text{select}(S, 1 + \text{rank}(S, i, \Box), \Box); \;\; \text{first}_k(S, i) = \min\{f(S, i, (), f(S, i,))\}$$

where (and) are the open and close parentheses of the k-th type in S, resp. The statement for $\text{last}_k(S,i)$ can be shown similarly.

To prove the statement for $\text{match}(S,i)$ and $\text{enclose}_k(S,i,j)$, first we ca show that Fact 1 can be generalized to an unbalanced binary string S (proof omitted). Suppose S has ℓ types of parentheses. Let S_k ($1 \leq k \leq \ell$) be the string obtained from S as follows.

- Every open (resp., close) parenthesis of the k-th type is replaced by two consecutive open (resp., close) parentheses of the k-th type.
- Every parenthesis of any other type is replaced by a matching parenthesis pair of the k-th type.

Each S_k is a string of length $2|S|$ consisting of one type of parentheses and each symbol $S_k[i]$ can be determined from $S[\lfloor i/2 \rfloor]$ in $O(1)$ time. For example,

$$\begin{aligned} S &= \texttt{[[(\{)] (\{ \} \} ( ])} \\ S_1 &= \texttt{()()((()))()((()()()((()))} \\ S_2 &= \texttt{[[[[[][][]]][][][][][]]][]} \end{aligned}$$

The queries for S can be answered by answering the queries for S_k as follows.

- $\text{match}(S,i) = \lfloor \text{match}(S_k, 2i)/2 \rfloor$, where $S[i]$ is a parenthesis of the k-th type.
- Given i and j, let $A = \{2i, 2i+1, \text{match}(S_k, 2i), \text{match}(S_k, 2i+1)\} \cup \{2j, 2j+1, \text{match}(S_k, 2j), \text{match}(S_k, 2j+1)\}$. Let $i_1 = \min A$, $j_1 = \max A$, and $(i_2, j_2) = \text{enclose}(S_k, i_1, j_1)$. Then: $\text{enclose}_k(S,i,j) = (\lfloor i_2/2 \rfloor, \lfloor j_2/2 \rfloor)$.

Note that each of the above queries on some S_k can be answered in $O(1)$ time by $S_k + \mu_2(S_k)$. Since each symbol $S_k[i]$ can be determined from $S[\lfloor i/2 \rfloor]$ in $O(1)$ time, the theorem holds by letting $\alpha(S) = \mu_2(S_1) + \mu_2(S_2) + \cdots + \mu_2(S_\ell)$. □

Let $S_1, \ldots, S_k$ be k strings, each of $O(1)$ types of parentheses. For the remainder of the paper, let $\alpha(S_1, S_2, \ldots, S_k)$ denote $\alpha(S_1) + \alpha(S_2) + \cdots + \alpha(S_k)$.

2.2 Encoding Trees

An encoding for a graph G is *weakly convenient* if it takes linear time to reconstruct G; $O(1)$ time to determine the adjacency of two nodes in G; $O(d)$ time to determine the degree of a node; and $O(d)$ time to list the neighbors of a node of degree d. A weakly convenient encoding for G is *convenient* if it takes $O(1)$ time to determine the degree of a node.

The folklore encoding $F(T)$ of a simple rooted unlabeled tree T of n nodes uses a balanced string S of one type of parentheses to represent the preordering of T. Each node of T corresponds to a matching parenthesis pair in S.

Fact 2 *Let v_i be the i-th node in the preordering of a rooted simple tree T. The following properties hold for the folklore encoding S of T.*

1. *The parenthesis pair for v_i encloses the parenthesis pair for v_j in S if and only if v_i is an ancestor of v_j.*
2. *The parenthesis pair for v_i precedes the parenthesis pair for v_j in S if and only if v_i and v_j are not related and $i < j$.*

3. The i-th open parenthesis in S belongs to the parenthesis pair for v_i.

Fact 3 ([15]) *Let T be a simple rooted tree of n nodes. $F(T) + \mu_2(F(T))$ is a weakly convenient encoding for T of $2n + o(n)$ bits, obtainable in $O(n)$ time.*

We show Fact 3 holds even if S is mixed with other $O(1)$ types of parentheses.

Theorem 2. *Let T be a simple rooted unlabeled tree. Let S be a string of $O(1)$ types of parentheses such that a given type of parentheses in S gives the folklore encoding of T. Then $S + \alpha(S)$ is a weakly convenient encoding of T.*

Proof. Let the parentheses, denoted by (and), in S used by the encoding of T be the k-th type. Let $v_1, \ldots, v_n$ be the preordering of T. Let $p_i = \text{select}(S, i, ()$ and $q_i = \text{match}(S, p_i)$. By Theorem 1, p_i and q_i can be obtained from $S + \alpha(S)$ in $O(1)$ time. The index i can be obtained from p_i or q_i in $O(1)$ time by $i = \text{rank}(S, p_i, () = \text{rank}(S, \text{match}(S, q_i), ()$. The queries for T are as follows.

Case: adjacency queries. Suppose $i < j$. Then, $(p_i, q_i) = \text{enclose}_k(p_j, q_j)$ if and only if v_i is adjacent to v_j in T, i.e., v_i is the parent of v_j in T.

Case: neighbor queries. Suppose that v_i has degree d in T. The neighbors of v_i in T can be listed in $O(d)$ time as follows. First, if $i \neq 1$, output v_j, where $(p_j, q_j) = \text{enclose}_k(p_i, q_i)$. Then, let $p_j = \text{first}_k(p_i)$. As long as $p_j < q_i$, we repeatedly output v_j and update p_j by $\text{first}_k(\text{match}(p_j))$.

Case: degree queries. Since T is simple, the degree d of v_i in T is simply the number of neighbors in T, which is obtainable in $O(d)$ time. □

We next improve Theorem 2 to obtain convenient encodings for multiple trees. For a condition P, let $\delta(P) = 1$, if P holds; let $\delta(P) = 0$, otherwise.

Theorem 3. *Let T be a rooted unlabeled tree of n nodes, n_1 leaves and m edges. Let $S + \alpha(S)$ be a weakly convenient encoding of T_s (the simple version of T).*

1. *A string D of $(2m - n + n_1)$ bits can be obtained in $O(m+n)$ time such that $S + D + \alpha(S, D)$ is a convenient encoding for T of $2m + n + n_1 + o(m)$ bits.*
2. *If T is simple, a string D of n_1 bits and a string Y of n bits can be obtained in $O(m+n)$ time such that $S + D + \alpha(S, D, Y)$ is a convenient encoding for T and has $2n + n_1 + o(n)$ bits.*

Proof. Let $v_1, \ldots, v_n$ be the preordering of T_s. Let d_i be the degree of v_i in T. We show how to use a string D to store the information required to obtain d_i in $O(1)$ time. We only prove Statement 1.

Let $\delta_i = \delta(v_i \text{ is internal in } T_s)$. Since $S + \alpha(S)$ is a weakly convenient encoding for T_s, each δ_i can be obtained in $O(1)$ time from $S + \alpha(S)$. Initially, D is just n copies of 1. Let $b_i = d_i - 1 - \delta_i$. We add b_i copies of 0 right after the i-th 1 in D for each v_i. Since the number of internal nodes in T_s is $n - n_1$, the bit count of D is $n + \sum_{i=1}^{n}(d_i - 1 - \delta_i) = n + 2m - n - (n - n_1) = 2m - n + n_1$. D can be obtained from T in $O(m + n)$ time. The number b_i of 0's right after the i-th 1 in D is $\text{select}(D, i+1, 1) - \text{select}(D, i, 1) - 1$. Since $d_i = 1 + \delta_i + b_i$, the degree of v_i in T can be computed in $O(1)$ time from $S + D + \alpha(S, D)$. □

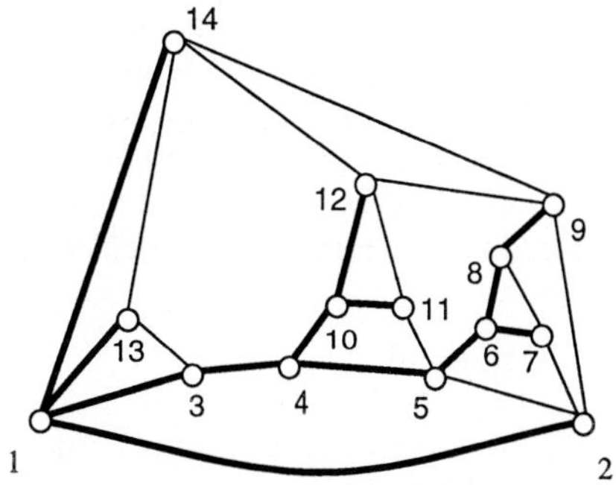

step j:	interval I_j:
1	3, 4, 5
2	6, 7
3	8
4	9
5	10, 11
6	12
7	13
8	14

Fig. 2. A triconnected plane graph G and a canonical ordering of G.

2.3 Canonical Orderings

In this subsection, we describe the *canonical ordering* of plane graphs. It was first introduced for plane triangulations in [3], and extended to triconnected plane graphs in [8]. We prove some new properties of this ordering. Let G be a simple triconnected plane graph. Let $v_1, \ldots, v_n$ be a node ordering of G. Let G_i be the subgraph of G induced by $v_1, v_2, \ldots, v_i$. Let H_i be the exterior face of G_i.

Definition 1. Let $v_1, v_2, \ldots, v_n$ be a node ordering of a simple triconnected plane graph $G = (V, E)$, where (v_1, v_2) is an arbitrary edge on the exterior face of G. The ordering is *canonical* if there exist ordered intervals $I_1, \ldots, I_K$ that partition the interval $[3, n]$ such that the following properties hold for every $1 \le j \le K$: Suppose $I_j = [k, k+q]$. Let C_j be the path $(v_k, v_{k+1}, \ldots, v_{k+q})$.

- The graph G_{k+q} is biconnected. Its boundary H_{k+q} contains the edge (v_1, v_2) and the path C_j. C_j has no chords in G.
- If $q = 0$, v_k has at least two neighbors in G_{k-1}, each of them is on H_{k-1}.
- If $q > 0$, the path C_j has exactly two neighbors in G_{k-1}, each of them is on H_{k-1}. The leftmost neighbor v_ℓ is incident only to v_k and the rightmost neighbor v_r is incident only to v_{k+q}.
- For each v_i ($k \le i \le k+q$), if $i < n$, v_i has at least one neighbor in $G - G_{k+q}$.

Figure 2 shows a canonical ordering of G. Every triconnected plane graph has a canonical ordering which can be constructed in $O(n)$ time [8].

Given a canonical ordering of G with interval partition $I_1, I_2, \ldots, I_K$, we can obtain $G = G_n$ from G_2, which consists of the single edge (v_1, v_2), through the following K steps: Suppose $I_j = [k, k+q]$. The j-th step obtains G_{k+q} from G_{k-1} by adding $q+1$ nodes $v_k, v_{k+1}, \ldots, v_{k+q}$ and their incidental edges in G_{k+q}.

Let T be the edge (v_1, v_2) plus the union of the paths $(v_\ell, v_k, v_{k+1}, \ldots, v_{k+q})$ over all intervals $I_j = [v_k, v_{k+q}]$, $1 \le j \le K$, where v_ℓ is the leftmost neighbor of v_k on H_{k-1}. One can easily see that T is a spanning tree of G rooted at v_1. T is called a *canonical spanning tree* of G. In Figure 2, T is indicated by thick lines.

We show every canonical spanning tree T has the following property.

Lemma 1. *Let T be the canonical spanning tree rooted at v_1 corresponding to a canonical ordering $v_1, v_2, \ldots, v_n$ of G.*

1. *Let $(v_i, v_{i'})$ be an edge in $G - T$. Then v_i and $v_{i'}$ are not related in T.*
2. *For each node v_i, the edges incident to v_i show the following pattern around v_i in counterclockwise order: The edge from v_i to its parent in T; followed by a block of nontree edges from v_i to lower-numbered nodes; followed by a block of tree edges from v_i to its children in T; followed by a block of nontree edges from v_i to higher-numbered nodes. (Any of these blocks maybe empty).*

3 Schemes with Query Support

In this section we present our coding schemes that support queries. We give a weakly convenient encoding for a simple triconnected graph G in §3.1, which illustrates our basic techniques. We give the schemes for triconnected plane graphs in §3.2. We state our results for triangulated and general plane graphs in §3.3.

3.1 Basis

Let T be a canonical spanning tree of a simple triconnected plane graph G. We encode G using a balanced string S of two types of parentheses. The first type (*parentheses*) is for the edges of T. The second type (*brackets*) is for the edges of $G - T$.

The encoding Let S be the folklore encoding for T. Let v_i be the i-th node in the counterclockwise preordering of nodes of T. Let $(_i$ and $)_i$ be the parenthesis pair corresponding to v_i in S. We augment S by inserting a pair $[_e$ and $]_e$ of brackets for every edge $e = (v_i, v_j)$, where $i < j$, of $G - T$ as follows: we place $[_e$ right after $)_i$ and $]_e$ right after $(_j$.

Suppose that v_i is adjacent to ℓ_i (resp., h_i) lower- (higher-, resp.) numbered nodes in $G-T$. Then S has the following pattern for every $1 \le i \le n$: The open parenthesis $(_i$ is immediately followed by ℓ_i close brackets. The close parenthesis $)_i$ is immediately followed by h_i open brackets. The following properties are clear.

Fact 4 *Let $e = (v_i, v_j)$ be an edge of $G - T$, where $i < j$. Then*

1. *$[_e$ is located between $)_i$ and the first parenthesis that succeeds $)_i$ in S;*
2. *$]_e$ is located between $(_j$ and the first parenthesis that succeeds $(_j$ in S.*

The following property for S is immediate from Fact 4:
Property A: The last parenthesis that precedes an open bracket is close. The last parenthesis that precedes a close bracket is open.

Let $e = (v_i, v_j)$ be an edge of $G - T$, where $i < j$. By Lemma 1 and Fact 2, $)_i$ precedes $(_j$ in S. By Fact 4, S has the following property:

Fact 5 *Let e be an edge of $G - T$. Then $[_e$ precedes $]_e$ in S.*

Lemma 2. *Let e and f be two edges in $G - T$ with no common end vertex. Suppose that $[_e < [_f$. Then either $[_e <]_e < [_f <]_f$ or $[_e < [_f <]_f <]_e$.*

($[_e < [_f$ indicates $[_e$ precedes $[_f$.) The above lemma implies that $]_e$ and the bracket that matches $[_e$ in S are in the same block of brackets. From now on, we rename the close brackets by redefining $]_e$ to be the close bracket that matches $[_e$ in S. It is clear that Property A and Facts 4, 5 still hold for S.

The queries We show $S + \alpha(S)$ is a weakly convenient encoding for G. Since T is simple, then by Theorem 2, $S+\alpha(S)$ is a weakly convenient encoding for T. It remains to show that $S + \alpha(S)$ is also a weakly convenient encoding for $G - T$. Let p_i and q_i be the positions of $(_i$ and $)_i$ in S, resp.

- *Adjacency.* Suppose $i < j$. Note that v_i and v_j are adjacent in $G - T$ if and only if $q_i < p < q < \text{first}_1(p_j)$, where $(p, q) = \text{enclose}_2(\text{first}_1(q_i), p_j)$, as indicated by the following figure:

$$\begin{array}{cccccc})_i & [& & (_j &] & \\ \uparrow & \uparrow & \uparrow & \uparrow & \uparrow & \uparrow \\ q_i & p & \text{first}_1(q_i) & p_j & q & \text{first}_1(p_j) \end{array}$$

- *Neighbors and degree.* The neighbors, and thus the degree, of a degree-d node v_i in $G - T$ can be obtained in $O(d)$ time as follows.
  - For every position p such that $q_i < p < \text{first}_1(q_i)$, we output v_j, where $p_j = \text{last}_1(\text{match}(p))$. ($(v_i, v_j)$ is an edge in $G - T$ with $j > i$.)
  - For every position q such that $p_i < q < \text{first}_1(p_i)$, we output v_j, where $q_j = \text{last}_1(\text{match}(q))$. ($(v_i, v_j)$ is an edge in $G - T$ with $j < i$.)

The bit count. Clearly $|S| = 2n+2(m-n) = 2m$. Since there are four symbols in S, S can be encoded by $4m$ bits. We can improve the bit count by the following:

Lemma 3. *Let S be a string of p parentheses and b brackets that satisfies Property A. Then S can be encoded by a string of $2p + b + o(p + b)$ bits, from which each $S[i]$ can be determined in $O(1)$ time.*

Proof. Let S_1 and S_2 be two binary strings defined as follows.

- $S_1[i] = 1$ if and only if $S[i]$ is a parenthesis, $1 \le i \le p + b$.
- $S_2[j] = 1$ if and only if the j-th parenthesis in S is open, $1 \le j \le p$.

Each $S[i]$ can be determined from $S_1 + S_2 + \alpha(S_1)$ in $O(1)$ time as follows. Let $j = \text{rank}(S_1, i, 1)$. If $S_1[i] = 1$, $S[i]$ is a parenthesis. Whether it is open or close can be determined from $S_2[j]$. If $S_1[i] = 0$, $S[i]$ is a bracket. Whether it is open or close can be determined from $S_2[\text{select}(S_1, \text{rank}(S_1, i, 1), 1)]$ by Property A. □

We summarize the above arguments as follows.

Lemma 4. *A simple triconnected plane graph of n nodes and m edges has a weakly convenient encoding that has $2m + 2n + o(n)$ bits.*

3.2 Triconnected Plane Graphs

We adapt all notation of §3.1 to this subsection. We first show that the weakly convenient encoding for a simple triconnected plane graph G given in §3.1 can be further shortened to $2(m + n - n_1) + o(n)$, where n_1 is the number of leaves in T. We then give a convenient encoding for G that has $2m + 2n + o(n)$ bits. Finally we augment both encodings to handle multiple edges.

Let v_i be a leaf of T, where $2 < i < n$. By definition of T and Definition 1, v_i is adjacent to a higher-numbered node and a lower-numbered node in $G - T$. This implies that $(_i$ is immediately succeeded by a], and $)_i$ is immediately succeeded by a [, for every such v_i. Let P be the string obtained from S by removing a] that immediately succeeds $(_i$, and removing a [that immediately succeeds $)_i$ for every leaf v_i of T, where $2 < i < n$. If each $S[j]$ were obtainable in $O(1)$ time from $P + \alpha(P)$, the string S could then be replaced by $P + \alpha(P)$. This does not seem likely. However, we can show that there exists a string Q of length $|P|$, each $Q[i]$ can be obtained from $P + \alpha(P)$ in $O(1)$ time, such that $P + \alpha(P, Q)$ is a weakly convenient encoding for G. Since S satisfies Property A and P is obtained from S by removing some brackets, P also satisfies Property A. Since P has $2n$ parentheses and $2(m - (n - 1) - n_1)$ brackets, by Lemma 3 G has a weakly convenient encoding of $2(m + n - n_1) + o(n)$ bits.

Next we augment our weakly convenient encoding for G to a convenient one. Note that the degree of v_i in $G - T$ can be obtained in $O(1)$ time from $P + \alpha(P, Q)$. It remains to supply $O(1)$-time degree query for T. By Theorem 3 we know that $n_1 + o(n)$ more bits suffices. Therefore there exists a $(2m + 2n - n_1 + o(n))$-bit convenient encoding for G that can be obtained in $O(m + n)$ time.

The above convenient encoding can be extended to handle multiple edges as follows. Let G_a be a multiple graph obtained from G by adding some multiple edges between nodes that are adjacent in $G - T$. Note that the above arguments in this subsection also hold for G_a exactly the same way. Suppose that G_a has m_a edges. Then G_a has a weakly convenient encoding of $2(m_a + n - n_1) + o(m_a + n)$ bits, from which the degree of a node in $G_a - T$ can actually be determined in $O(1)$ time. Let G_b be a multiple graph obtained from G_a by adding some multiple edges between nodes that are adjacent in T. Suppose that G_b has m_b edges. Let T_b be the union of multiple edges of G_b between the nodes that are adjacent in T. In order to obtain a convenient encoding for G_b, it remains to supply $O(1)$-time query for the degree of a node in T_b. Clearly T_b has $m_b - m_a + n - 1$ edges. By Theorem 3, $2(m_b - m_a + n - 1) - n + n_1 + o(m_b)$ more bits suffice.

We summarize the subsection as follows.

Lemma 5. *Let G be a triconnected plane graph of n nodes and m edges. Let G_s be the simple version of G, which has m_s edges. Let n_1 be the number of leaves in a canonical spanning tree of G_s. Then G (resp., G_s) has a convenient encoding of $2m + 3n - n_1 + o(m + n)$ (resp., $2m_s + 2n - n_1 + o(n)$) bits. All these encodings can be obtained in linear time.*

3.3 Plane Triangulations and General Plane Graphs

Lemma 6. *Let G be a plane triangulation of $n \geq 3$ nodes and m edges. Let G_s be the simple version of G, which has $m_s = 3n - 6$ edges. Then G (resp., G_s) has a convenient encoding of $2m + 2n + o(m + n)$ (resp., $2m_s + n + o(n)$) bits. All these encodings can be obtained in linear time.*

Lemma 7. *Let G be a plane graph of n nodes and m edges. Let G_s be the simple version of G, which has m_s edges. Let k be a positive constant. Then G has a convenient encoding of $2m + 5\frac{1}{k}n + o(m + n)$ bits and a weakly convenient encoding of $2m + 4\frac{2}{3}n + o(m + n)$ bits. G_s has a convenient encoding of $\frac{5}{3}m_s + 5\frac{1}{k}n + o(n)$ bits and a weakly convenient encoding of $\frac{4}{3}m_s + 5n + o(n)$ bits.*

4 More Compact Schemes

In some applications, the only requirement for the encoding is to reconstruct the graph, no queries are needed. In this case, we can obtain even more compact encodings for simple triconnected and triangulated plane graphs.

Let G be a simple triconnected plane graph. Let T be a canonical spanning tree of G. Let $v_1, \ldots, v_n$ be the counterclockwise preordering of T. By using techniques in [8], it can be shown that this ordering is also a canonical ordering of G. (In Figure 2, the canonical ordering shown is the counterclockwise preordering of T.) This special canonical ordering is used in our encoding.

Let $I_1, \ldots, I_K$ be the interval partition corresponding to the canonical ordering. G can be constructed from a single edge (v_1, v_2) through K steps. The j-th step corresponds to the interval $I_j = [k, k+q]$. There are two cases:

Case 1: A single node v_k is added.

Case 2: A chain of $q+1$ $(q > 0)$ nodes $v_k, \ldots, v_{k+q}$ is added.

The last node added during a step is called a *type a* node. Other nodes are *type b* nodes. Thus the single node v_k added during a Case 1 step is of type a. For a Case 2 step, the nodes $v_k, \ldots, v_{k+q-1}$ are of type b and v_{k+q} is of type a.

Consider the interval $I_j = [k, k+q]$. Let $c_1(=v_1), c_2, \ldots, c_t(=v_2)$ be the nodes of the exterior face H_{k-1} ordered consecutively along H_{k-1} from left to right above the edge (v_1, v_2). We define the following terms.

Case 1. Let c_ℓ and c_r $(1 \le \ell < r \le t)$ be the leftmost and rightmost neighbors of v_k in H_{k-1}, resp. The edge (c_ℓ, v_k) is in T. The edge (c_r, v_k) is called an *external edge*. The edges (c_i, v_k) where $\ell < i < r$, if present, are *internal edges*.

Case 2. Let c_ℓ and c_r $(1 \le \ell < r \le t)$ be the neighbors of v_k and v_{k+q} in H_{k-1}, resp. The edges $(c_\ell, v_k), (v_k, v_{k+1}), \ldots, (v_{k+q-1}, v_{k+q})$ are in T. The edge (c_r, v_k) is called an external edge.

For each v_k $(1 \le k \le n-1)$, let $B(v_k)$ denote the edge set $\{(v_k, v_j) \mid k < j\}$. By Definition 1 and Lemma 1, the edges in $B(v_k)$ show the following pattern around v_k in counterclockwise order: A block (maybe empty) of tree edges; followed by at most one internal edge; followed by a block (maybe empty) of external edges. Next, we show that if we know the sets $B(v_k)$ $(1 \le k \le n-1)$ and the type of v_k $(3 \le k \le n)$, then we can uniquely reconstruct G.

First the edge (v_1, v_2) is drawn. Then we perform the following K steps. The j-th step processes $I_j = [k, k+q]$. Before the j-th step, the graph G_{k-1} and its exterior face H_{k-1} has been constructed. We need to determine the leftmost neighbor c_ℓ and the rightmost neighbor c_r of the nodes added in this step. We know (c_ℓ, v_k) is a tree edge in T. Since $v_1, \ldots, v_n$ is the counterclockwise preordering of T, c_ℓ is the rightmost node that has a remaining tree edge and c_r is the leftmost node that is to the right of c_ℓ and has a remaining external edge. There are two cases:

If v_k is of type a, this is a Case 1 step and v_k is the single node added during this step. We add the edges (c_ℓ, v_k) and (c_r, v_k). For each c_i with $\ell < i < r$, if $B(c_i)$ contains an internal edge, we also add the edge (c_i, v_k).

If v_k is of type b, this is a Case 2 step. Let q be the integer such that $v_k, v_{k+1}, \ldots, v_{k+q-1}$ are of type b and v_{k+q} is of type a. The chain $v_k, \ldots, v_{k+q}$ is added between c_ℓ and c_r.

This completes the j-th step. When the process terminates, we obtain the graph G. Thus, if we can encode the type of each v_k and the sets $B(v_k)$ $1 \le$

$k \le n-1$, then we get an encoding of G. We first define the *type* of a set $B(v_k)$, which tells us the types of the edges contained in $B(v_k)$. We use T to denote the tree edges, X the external edges, and I the internal edges. The type of $B(v_k)$ is a combination of the symbols T, X, I. For examples, if $B(v_k)$ has type TXI, then $B(v_k)$ contains tree edges, external edges and an internal edge, and so on.

We further divide type a nodes v_k into two subtypes: If $B(v_k)$ contains no tree edges, then v_k is a *type a1* node. If $B(v_k)$ contains tree edges, then v_k is a *type a2* node. For a type b node v_k, since v_k is not the last node added during a Case 2 step, by the definition of T, $B(v_k)$ contains at least one tree edge.

Our encoding of G uses two strings S_1 and S_2 both using three symbols $0, 1, *$. The length of S_1 is n. $S_1[k]$ $(1 \le k \le n)$ indicates whether v_k is of type a1, a2, or b. S_2 encodes the sets $B(v_k)$ $(1 \le k \le n-1)$. Each $B(v_k)$ is specified by a *code word*, denoted by Code$[v_k]$. S_2 is the concatenation of Code$[v_k]$ $(1 \le k \le n-1)$. The length of Code$[v_k]$ equals to the number of the edges in $B(v_k)$. Depending on the type of v_k and the type of $B(v_k)$, Figure 3 gives the format of Code$[v_k]$. In the table, the number of the tree edges (external edges, resp.) in $B(v_k)$ is denoted by α (β, resp). 1^α denotes a string of α copies of 1, and so on. A symbol T (resp., X or I) under Code$[v_k]$ denotes the portion in Code$[v_k]$ corresponding to the tree (resp., external or internal) edges.

Type of v_k	Type of $B(v_k)$	Code$[v_k]$	Type of v_k	Type of $B(v_k)$	Code$[v_k]$
a1	XI	$\underbrace{1^\beta}_{X}\ \underbrace{0}_{I}$	a2 or b	T	$\underbrace{0^{\alpha-1}*}_{T}$
	I	$\underbrace{0}_{I}$		TXI	$\underbrace{1^\alpha}_{T}\ \underbrace{0^\beta}_{X}\ \underbrace{*}_{I}$
	X	$\underbrace{1^{\beta-1}*}_{X}$		TX	$\underbrace{1^{\alpha-1}0}_{T}\ \underbrace{0^{\beta-1}1}_{X}$
				TI	$\underbrace{1^\alpha}_{T}\ \underbrace{*}_{I}$

Fig. 3. Code Word Table.

From S_1, S_2 and the Code Word Table, we can easily recover the type of each v_k and the sets $B(v_k)$. It is straightforward to implement the encoding and decoding procedures in $O(n)$ time. The length of S_1 is n. The length of S_2 is m. We use the binary representation S of S_1 and S_2 to encode G. Since both S_1 and S_2 use 3 symbols, $|S| = \log 3(n+m)$. Thus we have the following:

Lemma 8. *Any simple triconnected plane graph with n nodes and m edges can be encoded using at most* $\log 3(n+m)$ *bits. Both encoding and decoding procedures take $O(n)$ time.*

We can improve Lemma 8 as follows. Let G^* be the dual of G. G^* has f nodes, m edges and n faces. Since G is triconnected, so is G^*. Furthermore, if $n > 3$, then $f > 3$ and G^* has no self-loop or multiple edge. Thus, we can use the coding scheme of Lemma 8 to encode G^* with at most $\log 3(f+m)$ bits. Since G can be uniquely determined from G^*, to encode G, it suffices to encode

G^*. To make S shorter, if $n \leq f$, we encode G using at most $\log 3(n+m)$ bits; otherwise, we encode G^* using at most $\log 3(f+m)$ bits. This new encoding uses at most $\log 3(\min\{n,f\}+m)$ bits. Since $\min\{n,f\} \leq \frac{n+f}{2}$, the bit count is at most $\log 3(1.5m+1)$ by Euler's formula $n+f=m+2$. We use one extra bit to denote whether we encode G or G^*. Thus we have proved the following:

Theorem 4. *Any simple triconnected plane graph with n nodes, m edges and f faces can be encoded using at most* $\log 3(\min\{n,f\}+m)+1 \leq 1.5(\log 3)m+3$ *bits. Both encoding and decoding take* $O(n)$ *time.*

Theorem 5. *Any simple plane triangulation of n nodes and m edges can be encoded using* $4n-7=\frac{4m}{3}+1$ *bits. Both encoding and decoding take* $O(n)$ *time.*

References

1. T. Bell, J. G. Cleary, and I. Witten, *Text Compression*, Prentice-Hall, 1990.
2. D. R. Clark, *Compact Pat Tree*, PhD thesis, University of Waterloo, 1996.
3. H. D. Fraysseix, J. Pach, and R. Pollack, *How to draw a planar graph on a grid*, Combinatorica, 10 (1990), pp. 41–51.
4. H. Galperin and A. Wigderson, *Succinct representations of graphs*, Information and Control, 56 (1983), pp. 183–198.
5. A. Itai and M. Rodeh, *Representation of graphs*, Acta Informatica, 17 (1982), pp. 215–219.
6. G. Jacobson, *Space-efficient static trees and graphs*, in proc. 30th FOCS, 30 Oct.–1 Nov. 1989, pp. 549–554.
7. S. Kannan, N. Naor, and S. Rudich, *Implicit representation of graphs*, SIAM Journal on Discrete Mathematics, 5 (1992), pp. 596–603.
8. G. Kant, *Drawing planar graphs using the lmc-ordering (extended abstract)*, in proc. 33rd FOCS, 24–27 Oct. 1992, pp. 101–110.
9. ——, *Algorithms for Drawing Planar Graphs*, PhD thesis, Univ. of Utrecht, 1993.
10. G. Kant and X. He, *Regular edge labeling of 4-connected plane graphs and its applications in graph drawing problems*, TCS 172 (1997), pp. 175–193.
11. M. Y. Kao, M. Fürer, X. He, and B. Raghavachari, *Optimal parallel algorithms for straight-line grid embeddings of planar graphs*, SIAM Journal on Discrete Mathematics, 7 (1994), pp. 632–646.
12. M. Y. Kao and S. H. Teng, *Simple and efficient compression schemes for dense and complement graphs*, in Fifth Annual Symposium on Algorithms and Computation, LNCS 834, Beijing, China, 1994, Springer-Verlag, pp. 201–210.
13. K. Keeler and J. Westbrook, *Short encodings of planar graphs and maps*, Discrete Applied Mathematics, 58 (1995), pp. 239–252.
14. J. I. Munro, *Tables*, in proc. of 16th Conf. on Foundations of Software Technology and Theoret. Comp. Sci., LNCS 1180, 1996, Springer-Verlag, pp. 37–42.
15. J. I. Munro and V. Raman, *Succinct representation of balanced parentheses, static trees and planar graphs*, in proc. 38th FOCS 20–22 Oct. 1997.
16. M. Naor, *Succinct representation of general unlabeled graphs*, Discrete Applied Mathematics, 28 (1990), pp. 303–307.
17. C. H. Papadimitriou and M. Yannakakis, *A note on succinct representations of graphs*, Information and Control, 71 (1986), pp. 181–185.
18. W. Schnyder, *Embedding planar graphs on the grid*, in Proceedings of the First Annual ACM-SIAM Symposium on Discrete Algorithms, 1990, pp. 138–148.
19. G. Turán, *On the succinct representation of graphs*, Discrete Applied Mathematics, 8 (1984), pp. 289–294.

Reducing Simple Polygons to Triangles - A Proof for an Improved Conjecture -

Thorsten Graf[1] and Kamakoti Veezhinathan[2]

[1] Research Center Jülich, 52425 Jülich, Germany
t.graf@fz-juelich.de
[2] Institute of Mathematical Sciences, CIT Campus, Chennai - 600 113, India
kama@imsc.ernet.in

Abstract. An edge of a simple closed polygon is called *eliminating* if it can be translated in parallel towards the interior of the polygon to eliminate itself or one of its neighbor edges without violating simplicity. [3] presents an algorithm that reduces a polygon P with n vertices to a triangle by a sequence of $O(n)$ parallel edge translations, of which $n-3$ translate an eliminating edge; the algorithm is used in [3] for computing morphs between polygons. It is conjectured in [3] that in each simple closed polygon there exists *at least one* eliminating edge, i.e. $n-3$ edge translations are sufficient for the reduction of P. Also the computation of eliminating edges remains an open problem in [3].
In this paper we prove that in each simple closed polygon there exist *at least two* eliminating edges; this lower bound is tight since for all $n \geq 5$ there exists a polygon with only two eliminating edges. Furthermore we present an algorithm that computes in total $O(n \log n)$ time using $O(n)$ space an eliminating edge for each elimination step. We thus obtain the first non-trivial algorithm that computes for P a sequence of $n-3$ edge translations reducing P to a triangle.

1 Introduction

The paper [3] entitled "Morphing Simple Polygons" presents a Lemma, due to Emo Welzl, that shows that each simple polygon P can be reduced to a triangle by a linear number of parallel edge translations towards the inner of P:

Lemma 1. *Given a simple polygon P with n vertices, we can reduce it to a triangle by a sequence of $O(n)$ edge translations, each of which preserves simplicity and $n-3$ of which shorten some edge to zero length.*

We call an edge of P *eliminating* if it can be translated in parallel towards the interior of P such that the edge itself or one of its neighbor edges is eliminated without violating simplicity.

The eliminating edges of the polygon P in Figure 1 are denoted by a, b, and c. The edges a and c eliminate a neighbor edge, whereas the edge b eliminates itself. The portions of the plane that are swept over during the eliminations appear dark.

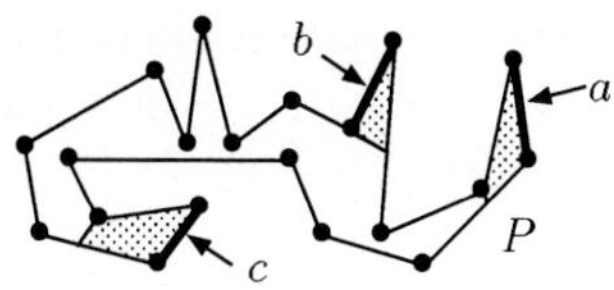

Fig. 1. Eliminating edges a, b, and c of polygon P

Conjecture 1. [3] At least one edge of any simple closed polygon P is an eliminating edge.

The following Theorem, which gives the main result of this paper, proves an improved version of the conjecture:

Theorem 1. *At least two edges of any simple closed polygon P are eliminating edges. There exists an algorithm that computes in $O(n \log n)$ time using $O(n)$ space for P a sequence of $n-3$ eliminating edges that reduces P to a triangle.*

Before we give the technical details of the proof (section 2) we give a brief non-technical outline: Imagine igniting all boundary points of the polygon P and assume that the flame burns inward with a uniform rate. The points where the flame meets and extinguishes itself define the *medial axis* (Fig. 4 middle). We cut off all branches of the medial axis that are connected to vertices of P. (Fig. 4 right). Two endpoints of the remaining structure - which exist since the medial axis contains no cycles - can be identified, such that for each of them there exists an eliminating edge of P from which the flame burnt towards the endpoint. Furthermore, these two eliminating edges can be chosen to be different from each other.

We have thus improved Lemma 1 as follows:

Lemma 2. *Given a simple polygon P with n vertices, we can reduce it to a triangle by a sequence of $n-3$ edge translations, each of which preserves simplicity and shortens some edge to zero length.*

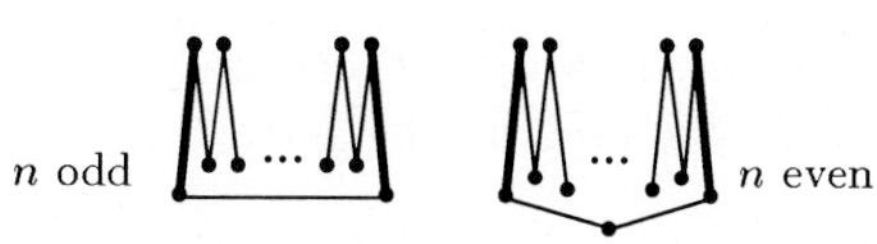

Fig. 2. Only the two thick edges are eliminating, $n \geq 5$

This lower bound on the number of eliminating edges is tight since for arbitrary $n \in \mathbb{N}$, $n \geq 5$, a simple closed polygon with n edges, of which only two are eliminating, can be easily constructed (Fig. 2).

Section 2 gives the proof for the existence of two eliminating edges, section 3 presents our algorithm for computing the sequence of $n-3$ eliminating edges.

2 A proof of the improved conjecture

2.1 Preliminaries

Given two different points $p, q \in \mathbb{R}^2$ we denote by $s(p,q)$ the open line segment connecting p and q. Throughout the paper, let P denote a simple closed polygon given by its vertices in counterclockwise cyclic order; denote by V_P the set of its vertices and by E_P the set of its open edges. Since Theorem 1 is trivial for triangles, we assume that $|V_P| \geq 4$ in the following.

For a vertex $p \in V_P$ we denote by $e(p)$ the open edge in E_P that is incident to p and extends counterclockwise from p. A vertex $p \in V_P$ is a *convex* vertex if the two edges incident on p form a left turn at p when traversed counterclockwise, otherwise p is called a *reflex* vertex.

An edge $e \in E_P$ is called *convex* if e is incident on two convex vertices of P. An edge $e \in E_P$ is called *weak convex* if only one vertex of e is convex and the supporting lines of the predecessor edge and the successor edge of e intersect on the left side of e (where e is oriented counterclockwise). If both vertices of e are reflex or the supporting lines intersect on the right side of e then the edge e is called *reflex*. Figure 3 gives some illustrations.

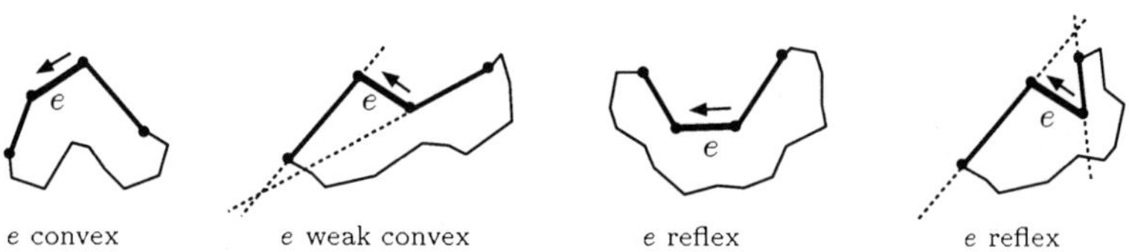

Fig. 3. Convex / weak convex / reflex edge e

An *arc* of ∂P is a connected part of ∂P oriented counterclockwise along ∂P, where the endpoints of the arc need not be vertices of P.

The *medial axis* $M(P)$ of a simple closed polygon P is the locus of all centers of circles entirely contained in P that touch the boundary ∂P in at least two points ([1,4]). Figure 4 gives an illustration.

The medial axis can be interpreted as the embedding of an acyclic connected graph with vertex set V_M and edge set E_M. To obtain V_M and E_M we first construct the Voronoi diagram of $V_P \cup E_P$, i.e. the *inner Voronoi diagram* of P (Fig. 4 left), and remove those bisectors corresponding to an edge and an incident vertex ([1,2,4], Fig. 4 middle) . Note that the convex vertices of P are contained in V_M. For a vertex $v \in V_M$ denote by $E_M(v)$ the set of edges in E_M that are adjacent to v. For a point q on $M(P)$ denote by $C_{max}(q)$ the unique circle with center q and maximal radius $r_{max}(q)$ that touches ∂P in at least two points. The *generators* of an edge $e \in E_M$ are the two sites in $V_P \cup E_P$ which touch $C_{max}(q)$ for all points $q \in e$; by definition of $M(P)$, the generators of $e \in E_M$ are well-defined and unique. The edges in E_M are embedded in different ways: If e is generated by two vertices in V_P or by two edges in E_P, then the edge e is embedded as a straight line segment; if e is generated by a vertex in V_P and an edge in E_P, then e is embedded as a parabolic curve ([1,4]).

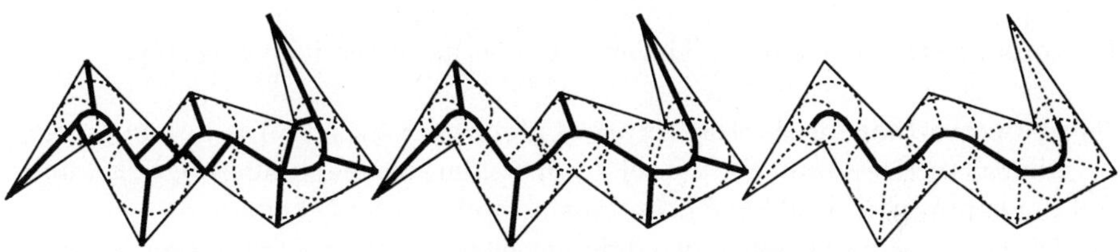

Inner Voronoi diagram of P Medial axis $M(P)$ Reduced medial axis $m(P)$

Fig. 4. Three structures on polygon P

We obtain the *reduced medial axis* $m(P)$ from $M(P)$ by removing all edges from $M(P)$ ending in a vertex of P (Fig. 4 right). For a vertex v of $m(P)$ we denote by $E_P(v)$ the set of edges of P that are connected with v in $M(P)$ by one of the edges we removed from $M(P)$; in Figure 4 we have $|E_P(v)| \in \{0, 2\}$ for all vertices v of $m(P)$.

A point w on $m(P)$ is a *waist point* of $m(P)$ if the radius $r_{max}(w)$ of $C_{max}(w)$ is locally minimal, i.e. inside a small neighborhood of w no point exists on $m(P)$ with a value $r_{max}(\cdot)$ that is equal to or smaller than $r_{max}(w)$, and w is not a leaf of $m(P)$ (Fig. 5).

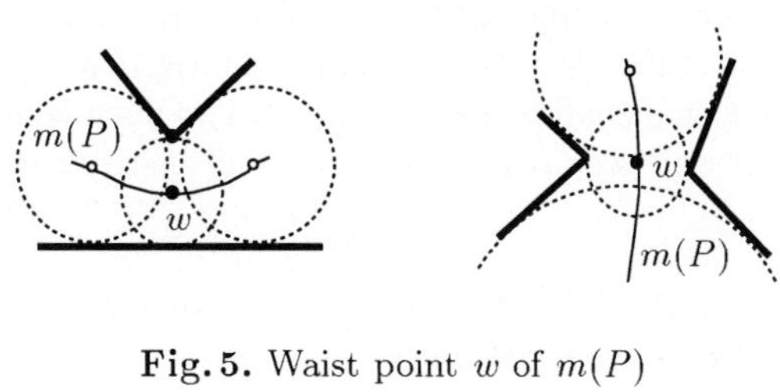

Fig. 5. Waist point w of $m(P)$

Since each edge of $m(P)$ is generated by two elements of $E_P \cup V_P$, the values $r_{max}(\cdot)$ on an edge of $m(P)$ behave bitonic, i.e. when traversing the edge from vertex to vertex in $m(P)$ the values $r_{max}(\cdot)$ can be broken into an increasing sequence and a decreasing sequence; it follows that each edge of $m(P)$ contains at most one waist point of $m(P)$.

We assume that the vertices and the edges of the polygon P are in general position which can be simulated by actual or conceptual perturbation of the input. Here, we mean by general position that all vertices of $m(P)$ have degree three in the inner Voronoi diagram of P, and that all edges of P have different slopes. Under this assumption, each elimination step eliminates only one edge of P, and the number $n-3$ of edge translations given in Lemma 2 is optimal.

2.2 Proof outline

Our proof of the first part of Theorem 1 consists of the following steps:

(1) We prove that for the leaf vertex $v^\star$, for which $r_{max}(v^\star)$ is minimal among all leaf vertices of $m(P)$, the set $E_P(v^\star)$ contains an eliminating edge, under the assumption that $m(P)$ contains no waist points (Lemma 3).
(2) We show, using (1), that two different edges of P are eliminating; again, we assume that $m(P)$ contains no waist points (Lemma 4).
(3) We prove that if $m(P)$ contains waist points, then P can be divided into open subpolygons that contribute no waist points to $m(P)$, but all waist points are generated at the border of neighbored subpolygons. We show that among the edges that are eliminating in any of the subpolygons, at least two are also eliminating in P (Lemma 5).

Finally, in section 3 we present the algorithm for computing a sequence of $n-3$ edge eliminations which proves the second part of Theorem 1.

2.3 The proof

For each leaf vertex v of $m(P)$ the set $E_P(v)$ contains two or three edges of P, depending on whether the single edge in $m(P)$ incident to v is embedded as a parabolic curve, or is embedded as a straight line segment, respectively. For the moment we assume that for all leaves v of $m(P)$ two such edges in $E_P(v)$ can be chosen such that not both edges are reflex; we will justify this assumption later.

Lemma 3. *Let $v^\star$ denote the leaf vertex of $m(P)$ such that $r_{max}(v^\star)$ is minimal among all leaf vertices of $m(P)$. If $m(P)$ contains no waist points then $E_P(v^\star)$ contains an eliminating edge of P.*

Proof. The vertex $v^\star$ is well-defined since $m(P)$ contains at least two leaf vertices due to our assumption that the polygon P has $n \geq 4$ edges. Denote by $p_0, \ldots, p_4$ subsequent vertices of P such that the edges $e(p_1)$ and $e(p_2)$ are contained in $E_P(v^\star)$ and p_2 is a convex vertex of P (see Figure 6). Denote by $e^\star$ the single edge in $m(P)$ that is incident on $v^\star$.

If $e^\star$ is embedded as a parabolic curve (Fig. 6 left and middle), then due to our assumption of general position not both vertices p_1 and p_3 lie on $C_{max}(v^\star)$. W.l.o.g. we assume that p_3 does not lie on $C_{max}(v^\star)$; hence p_1 is reflex and lies on $C_{max}(v^\star)$. W.l.o.g. we assume that $e(p_2)$ is convex or weak convex. Assume that the shaded parallelogram that we obtain by translating the edge $e(p_2)$ parallely towards the inner of P is not entirely contained in P (Fig. 6 left and middle), which is equivalent to say that $e(p_2)$ is not eliminating. Then there exists a vertex $p_m \in V_P$ such that $e(p_m)$ intersects the parallelogram, and the edges $e(p_m)$ and $e(p_2)$ generate a point c of $m(P)$ such that $r_{max}(c) < r_{max}(v^\star)$. The arc from p_3 to p_m generates at least one leaf vertex v' of $m(P)$, and $r_{max}(v')$ is not smaller than $r_{max}(v^\star)$ by our choice of $v^\star$. Since there exists a path in $m(P)$ from $v^\star$ over c to v' we obtain that $m(P)$ contains a waist which is a contradiction. It follows that $e(v_2)$ is an eliminating edge.

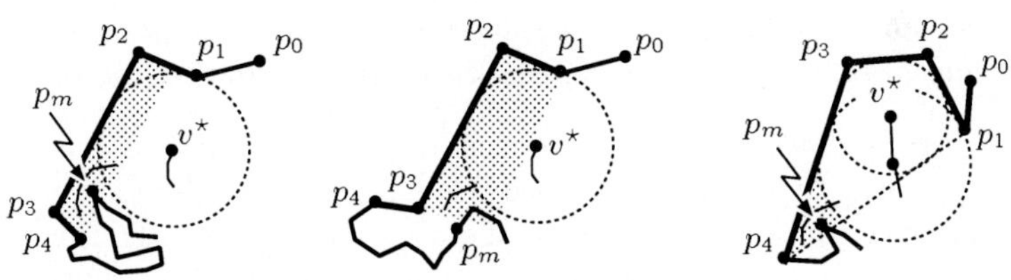

Fig. 6. $E_P(v^\star)$ contains eliminating edge $e(p_2)$

If $e^\star$ is embedded as a straight line segment (Fig. 6 right) then p_2 is convex and does not lie on $C_{max}(v^\star)$. By our choice of $v^\star$ we see that either p_1 or p_4 lies on $C_{max}(\cdot)$ of the second vertex of $e^\star$. A similar argument as for the case that $e^\star$ is embedded as a parabolic curve now shows that the line segment $s(p_1, p_4)$ is entirely contained in P. It follows that $e(p_2)$ is an eliminating edge. □

Lemma 4. *If $m(P)$ contains no waist points, then two different edges of P are eliminating.*

Proof. Choose v to be the leaf vertex with the second-smallest value $r_{max}(v)$. Applying Lemma 3 to v we see that if none of the edges in $E_P(v)$ is eliminating then the arc from p_3 to p_m must contribute the leaf vertex $v^\star$ to $m(P)$ (see Lemma 3 for the notations).

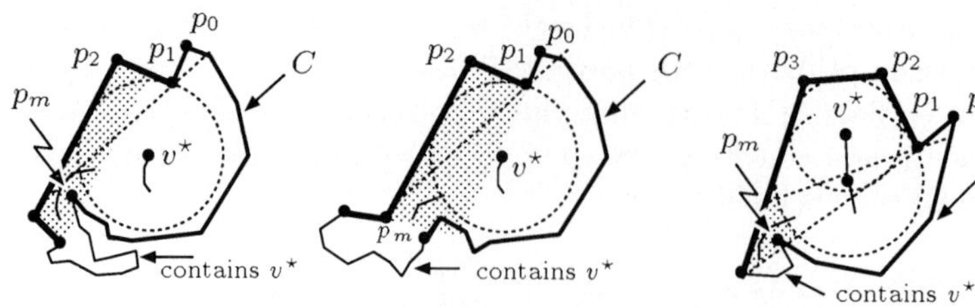

Fig. 7. $E_P(v^\star)$ and C contain an eliminating edge each

If the edge $e(v_0)$ is eliminating then nothing remains to be shown. We therefore assume that $e(v_0)$ is not eliminating. It follows that the arc C from v_m to v_0 contains more than one edge one of which must be convex or weak convex. Since C does not contribute a waist point to $m(P)$ the same argument as in the proof or Lemma 3 shows that C contains an eliminating edge of P. The lemma follows. □

Lemma 5. *If $m(P)$ contains waist points, then P can be divided into open subpolygons that contribute no waist points to $m(P)$, but all waist points are generated at the border of neighbored subpolygons. Among the edges that are eliminating in any of the subpolygons, at least two are also eliminating in P.*

Proof. Let v be a waist point of $m(P)$. Assume that the circle $C_{max}(v)$ touches ∂P in three points; these touch points divide $C_{max}(v)$ into three circular arcs of which at most one contains more than half of $C_{max}(v)$ (Fig. 8 left). Hence $r_{max}(\cdot)$ is increasing only in at most one direction starting from v; in Figure 8 arrows indicate the direction of increasing $r_{max}(\cdot)$ values. It follows that $r_{max}(v)$ is not locally minimal which contradicts our choice of v as waist point of $m(P)$. Hence $C_{max}(v)$ touches ∂P in two points and the two touch points have Euclidean distance $2r_{max}(v)$, i.e. they can be connected by a diameter line segment of $C_{max}(v)$.

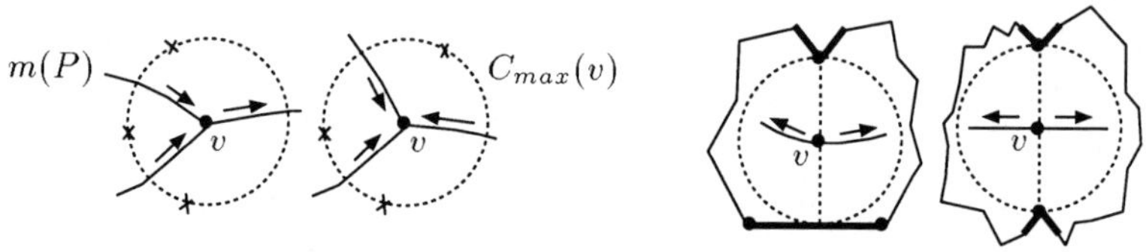

Fig. 8. Waist node v of $m(P)$

Imagine dividing the polygon P at all waist points in the sense that no polygon edge is actually split, but a polygon edge defining a waist point belongs to two open subpolygons (Fig.8 right). It can be seen easily that each of the subpolygons that we obtain contains at least three edges of E_P, but may consist of two connectivity components. If a subpolygon is neighbor of only one other subpolygon then its edges are connected. There exist at least two such subpolygons. We easily see that each these two subpolygons contributes an eliminating edge to P; obviously these edges are different from each other. □

We assumed that for all leaves v of $m(P)$ two edges in $E_P(v)$ can be chosen such that not both edges are reflex. Leaves v of $m(P)$, for which all edges in $E_P(v)$ are reflex, can be neglected since they do not contribute anything to the left-curvature of arcs which is a crucial point in our arguments (see proofs of Lemmas 3-5); it can be verified easily that all arguments remain valid in the presence of such leaves.

3 Computing eliminating edges

In this section we prove the second part of Theorem 1, i.e. we present our algorithm for computing the sequence of $n-3$ eliminating edges.

First, we compute the inner Voronoi diagram of P using the algorithm in [2], from which we then obtain the reduced medial axis $m(P)$. Then we compute all waist points of $m(P)$ which gives us the open subpolygons that are considered in Lemma 5.

Algorithm Reduce_Polygon_To_Triangle
    / Input: Polygon P with n vertices */*
    / Output: Sequence of $n-3$ eliminating edges */*
    begin
1.   Compute $m(P)$;
2.   Compute the waist points of $m(P)$;
3.   Use waist points to divide P into subpolygons;

        for $i = 1$ **to** $n-3$ **do begin**
4.   Select connected subpolygon C;
5. $m(C)$:= portion of $m(P)$ that is generated by C;
6. $v^\star$:= leaf vertex of $m(P)$ with smallest $r_{max}(v^\star)$ in $m(C)$;
7.   Select and output eliminating edge e in $E_P(v^\star)$;
8.   Execute elimination step for e which gives P'; */* see [3] */*
9.   Compute $m(P')$;
10.   Update the waist points of $m(P')$;
11.   Update the subpolygons of P';
12. $P := P'$;

        end;
    end.

Using Lemma 3 we select a connected subpolygon, i.e. a subpolygon with only one connectivity component, and compute an eliminating edge inside this subpolygon. We execute the elimination step and update the data structures that maintain $m(P)$, the waist points of $m(P)$ and the subpolygons obtained by the splitting.

Lemma 6. *The algorithm given above computes a sequence of $n-3$ eliminating edges in $O(n \log n)$ time using $O(n)$ space, that reduces the polygon P to a triangle.*

Proof. We start with an important fact: The only elements in $V_P \cup E_P$ that can be modified or removed during the elimination process of an eliminating edge out of $E_P(v^\star)$, where $v^\star$ is chosen as in the algorithm above, are the edges in $E_P(v^\star)$, the successor edge and the predecessor edge of the arc formed by the edges in $E_P(v^\star)$, and the vertices of all these edges. In total these are not more than $O(1)$ elements out of $V_P \cup E_P$. It follows that only the edges of a connected subgraph of $m(P)$ with size $O(1)$ are modified or deleted during the elimination process.

From this fact we obtain immediately:

- Selecting an eliminating edge from $E_P(v^\star)$ in step 7 can be done in $O(1)$ time by trivial computations since only a subpolygon of P with $O(1)$ edges needs to be considered for this.
- The new reduced medial axis $m(P')$ can be computed in step 9 from $m(P)$ in $O(1)$ time by trivial computations.
- Updating the waist points in step 10 can be done in $O(1)$ time.
- Given the subpolygons of P, computing the subpolygons of P' in step 11 can be done in $O(1)$ time.

Selecting the leaf vertex $v^\star$ in $m(C)$, which is also a leaf vertex of $m(P)$ and has minimal $r_{max}(v^\star)$ in $m(C)$, requires total $\Omega(n \log n)$ time (step 6); by maintaining all leaves of $m(C)$ in sorted order according to their values $r_{max}(\cdot)$, step 6 can be implemented to use total $O(n \log n)$ time.

The time analysis of the remaining steps of the algorithms is straightforward: Computing the inner Voronoi diagram of P and the reduced medial axis $m(P)$ in step 1 can be done in $O(n)$ time ([2]). From $m(P)$ all waist points can be computed in step 2 in $O(n)$ time since the continuous function given by $r_{max}(\cdot)$ on $m(P)$ is bitonic on each edge of $m(P)$. By maintaining the connected subpolygons in a separate list such a polygon can be selected in step 4 in $O(1)$ time. Obviously step 5 and step 12 can be done in $O(1)$ time. Executing the $n-3$ eliminations (step 8) can be implemented using total $O(n)$ time.

Obviously, all data structures used in the algorithm can be implemented using $O(n)$ space, which completes the proof. q.e.d.

4 Conclusions

We have shown that at least two edges of a simple closed polygon are eliminating edges, i.e. can be translated in parallel towards the interior of P without violating simplicity such that the edge itself or one of its neighbor edges is eliminated; this lower bound is tight since there exist polygons with only two eliminating edges. This improves and proves the conjecture given in [3], and improves the result of Lemma 1. Furthermore we have presented the first non-trivial algorithm for computing a sequence of $n-3$ edge translations that reduces the polygon P having n edges to a triangle. The algorithm runs in $O(n \log n)$ time and uses $O(n)$ space.

We thank the anonymous referees for their comments that helped to considerably improve the technical content and the quality of the paper.

References

1. F. Aurenhammer. Voronoi diagrams: A survey of a fundamental geometric data structure. *ACM Comput. Surv.*, 23:345–405, 1991.
2. Francis Chin, Jack Snoeyink, and Cao-An Wang. Finding the medial axis of a simple polygon in linear time. In *Proc. 6th Annu. Internat. Sympos. Algorithms Comput. (ISAAC 95)*, volume 1004 of *Lecture Notes in Computer Science*, pages 382–391. Springer-Verlag, 1995.
3. L. Guibas and J. Hershberger. Morphing simple polygons. In *Proc. 10th Annu. ACM Sympos. Comput. Geom.*, pages 267–276, 1994.
4. Atsuyuki Okabe, Barry Boots, and Kokichki Sugihara. *Spatial Tessellations: Concepts and Applications of Voronoi Diagrams.* John Wiley & Sons, Chichester, England, 1992.

Difficult Configurations – On the Complexity of *LTrL*

(Extended Abstract)

Igor Walukiewicz*

Institute of Informatics, Warsaw University
Banacha 2, 02-097 Warsaw, POLAND
igw@mimuw.edu.pl

Abstract. The complexity of *LTrL*, a global linear time temporal logic over traces is investigated. The logic is global because the truth of a formula is evaluated in a global state, also called configuration. The logic is shown to be non-elementary with the main reason for this complexity being the nesting of until operators in formulas. The fragment of the logic without the until operator is shown to be EXPSPACE-complete.

1 Introduction

Infinite words, or linear orders on *events*, are often used to model executions of systems. Infinite *traces*, or partial orders on events, are often used to model concurrent systems when we do not want to put some arbitrary ordering on actions occurring concurrently. A *state* of a system in the linear model is just a prefix of an infinite word; it represents the actions that have already happened. A state of a system in the trace model is a *configuration*, i.e., a finite downwards closed set of events that already happened.

Temporal logics over traces come in two sorts: a *local* and a *global* one. The truth of a formula in a *local logic* is evaluated in an event, the truth of the formula in a *global logic* is evaluated in a configuration. Global logics have the advantage of talking directly about configurations but, as we show here, have high complexity.

In this paper we investigate the complexity of *LTrL*, a global temporal logic over traces proposed in [13]. We show that the full logic is non-elementary. As it turns out, it is the nesting of until operators that gives such a high complexity. This makes it natural to ask what is the complexity of the logic without the until operator. We investigate a global logic, $LTrL^{-}$, containing only "for some configuration in the future" modality and "next step" modalities. We show that this logic is EXPSPACE-complete. These results give also the bounds on the model checking problem for the logics in question.

Our results show that the complexity of global logics is bigger than the complexity of local logics. It is well known that LTL, a linear temporal logic

* Supported by Polish KBN grant No. 8 T11C 002 11

over infinite words, is PSPACE-complete. It is still PSPACE-complete if we have just "some time in the future" operator instead of the until operator [11]. Local temporal logics for traces proposed in [2, 10, 12] have also PSPACE complexity. It is not known what kinds of global properties are expressible in these local logics. Our results show that expressing global trace properties in these logics, if at all possible, will require big formulas.

There are not many results known about the complexity of global logics. Some undecidability results were obtained in [6, 9]. The most relevant here is the paper by Alur, McMillan and Peled [1]. In this paper an EXPSPACE upper bound is shown for a fragment of ISTL [8]. A modification of their argument shows an EXPSPACE upper bound for $LTrL^-$.

Let us finish this introduction with some remarks showing a more general context of this paper. From the verification point of view, traces are interesting for at least two reasons. First, as the development of the trace theory shows [3], they are "like words" because most of the properties of words have their counterparts in traces. The generalisation from words to traces is interesting because it is far from trivial and it requires new methods and new insights. Next, traces can model systems more faithfully than words as they do not introduce ad hoc dependencies. Because of this, traces also seem to be of some help in coping with the state explosion problem [14, 5, 7].

If we agree that modelling systems with traces is a good enough idea to try then the immediate question is: how to express properties of traces. For this we must understand the complexity of checking properties over traces. Instead of talking about particular properties it is often better to design a logic and talk about a set of properties definable in this logic. A twenty year long development of temporal logics seems to indicate a strong candidate for the class of properties we want to express – the class of properties expressible in first order logic over traces represented as dependence graphs. This class of properties has many different characterisations [4] and is a natural counterpart of the class of properties expressible in *LTL* over words. The next question then is: with what kinds of operators we want to express this class of properties. *LTL* and first order logic can express exactly the same properties of infinite words but, often, *LTL* is preferred because of its low complexity. This low complexity would be useless if it was not often the case that the properties we want to express can be written as small *LTL* formulas. To have this feature in the trace world it seems agreeable to base a logic on configurations and not events. Unfortunately, the present paper shows that one has to be very careful with operators one allows unless one is willing to cope with very high complexity.

This paper is organised as follows. We start with the necessary definitions and notations. In Section 3 we describe the proof of the non-elementary lower bound for *LTrL*. In Section 4 we sketch the proof of the EXPSPACE lower bound for the fragment, $LTrL^-$, of *LTrL*. Because of the lack of space we will not present the proof of the containment of $LTrL^-$ in EXPSPACE. It follows from some modifications of the argument in [1].

2 Preliminaries

A (Mazurkiewicz) *trace alphabet* is a pair (Σ, I) where Σ is a finite set of actions and $I \subseteq \Sigma \times \Sigma$ is an irreflexive and symmetric *independence relation*. $D = (\Sigma \times \Sigma) - I$ is called the dependency relation.

We shall view (Mazurkiewicz) trace, over an alphabet (Σ, I), as a restricted Σ-labelled poset. Let $(E, \leq, \lambda)$ be a Σ-labelled poset. In other words, $(E, \leq)$ is a poset and $\lambda : E \to \Sigma$ is a labelling function. For $Y \subseteq E$ we define $\downarrow Y = \{x : \exists y \in Y.\ x \leq y\}$ and $\uparrow Y = \{x : \exists y \in Y.\ y \leq x\}$. In case $Y = \{y\}$ is a singleton we shall write $\downarrow y$ ($\uparrow y$) instead of $\downarrow \{y\}$ ($\uparrow \{y\}$). We also let $\lessdot$ be the relation: $x \lessdot y$ iff $x < y$ and for all $z \in E$, $x \leq z \leq y$ implies $x = z$ or $z = y$.

A *trace* (over (Σ, I)) is a Σ-labelled poset $T = (E, \leq, \lambda)$ satisfying:

(T1) $\forall e \in E.\quad \downarrow e$ is a finite set.
(T2) $\forall e, e' \in E.\quad e \lessdot e' \Rightarrow \lambda(e) D \lambda(e')$.
(T3) $\forall e, e' \in E.\quad \lambda(e) D \lambda(e') \Rightarrow e \leq e'$ or $e' \leq e$.

We shall refer to members of E as *events*. All our traces will be infinite, i.e., will have infinitely many events. The set of infinite traces over (Σ, I) is denoted by $TR(\Sigma, I)$.

Let $T = (E, \leq, \lambda)$ be a trace. A *configuration* is a finite subset $C \subseteq E$ such that $C = \downarrow C$. We let $\mathrm{Conf}(T)$ be the set of configurations of T and let C, C', C'' range over $\mathrm{Conf}(T)$. Note that $\emptyset$, the empty set, is a configuration and $\downarrow e$ is a configuration for every $e \in E$. Finally, the transition relation $\to_T \subseteq \mathrm{Conf}(T) \times \Sigma \times \mathrm{Conf}(T)$ is given by: $C \xrightarrow{a}_T C'$ iff there exists $e \in E$ such that $\lambda(e) = a$ and $e \notin C$ and $C' = C \cup \{e\}$. It is easy to see that if $C \xrightarrow{a}_T C'$ and $C \xrightarrow{a}_T C''$ then $C' = C''$.

The set of formulas of our linear time temporal logic of traces ($LTrL$) is defined as follows:

$$LTrL(\Sigma, I) ::= \underline{\mathrm{tt}} \mid \neg\alpha \mid \alpha \wedge \beta \mid \langle a \rangle \alpha \mid \alpha \mathbin{\mathrm{U}} \beta \mid \langle a^{-1} \rangle \underline{\mathrm{tt}}$$

Thus the next state modality is indexed by actions. There is also a very restricted version of the previous state modality. This modality will play no role in our considerations, we just mention it in order to be consistent with the original definition.

A model of $LTrL$ is a trace $T = (E, \leq, \lambda)$. The relation $T, C \models \alpha$ will denote that $\alpha \in LTrL(\Sigma, I)$ is satisfied at the configuration $C \in \mathrm{Conf}(T)$. This notion is defined via:

- $T, C \models \underline{\mathrm{tt}}$. Furthermore $\neg$ and $\wedge$ are interpreted in the usual way.
- $T, C \models \langle a \rangle \alpha$ iff $\exists C' \in \mathrm{Conf}(T).\ C \xrightarrow{a}_T C'$ and $T, C' \models \alpha$.
- $T, C \models \alpha \mathbin{\mathrm{U}} \beta$ iff $\exists C' \in \mathrm{Conf}(T).\ C \subseteq C'$ and $T, C' \models \beta$ and $\forall C'' \in \mathrm{Conf}(T).\ C \subseteq C'' \subset C'$ implies $T, C'' \models \alpha$.
- $T, C \models \langle a^{-1} \rangle \underline{\mathrm{tt}}$ iff $\exists C' \in \mathrm{Conf}(T).\ C' \xrightarrow{a}_T C$.

We will write $T \models \alpha$ for $T, \emptyset \models \alpha$. The definition of until allows us to have also derived "sometime" and "always" modalities:

$$\mathbb{E}\alpha \equiv \underline{tt}\ \mathbb{U}\ \alpha \qquad \mathbb{A}\alpha \equiv \neg\mathbb{E}\neg\alpha$$

with the expected semantics:

- $T, C \models \mathbb{E}\alpha$ iff $\exists C' \in \mathrm{Conf}(T).\ C \subseteq C'$ and $T, C' \models \alpha$.
- $T, C \models \mathbb{A}\alpha$ iff $\forall C' \in \mathrm{Conf}(T).\ C \subseteq C'$ implies $T, C' \models \alpha$.

3 The complexity of *LTrL*

In this section we show an non-elementary lower bound for the complexity of deciding satisfiability of *LTrL* formulas. Let Tower stand for the "tower of exponentials" function, i.e., $\mathrm{Tower}(0, n) = n$ and $\mathrm{Tower}(k+1, n) = 2^{\mathrm{Tower}(k,n)}$.

Given a $\lambda x.\mathrm{Tower}(m, x)$ space bounded Turing machine M and a word w, we will construct a $\mathcal{O}(|w|2^{\mathcal{O}(m)} + |w| + |M|)$ size formula that is satisfiable iff w is accepted by M. This will show that the satisfiability problem for *LTrL* cannot be solved in time bounded by the function $\lambda x.\mathrm{Tower}(m, x)$ for any fixed m. On the other hand the satisfiability problem can be solved in time $\lambda m.\mathrm{Tower}(m, 2)$. This follows from the translation of *LTrL* into first order logic over infinite words [13].

The plan of this section is the following. Our first goal is to show, on an example, how to construct big counters with small formulas. Even before the example we will introduce some extensions to our logic and show how to code these extensions in the basic language. After the example we will formally define what a big counter is and we will say what kind of formulas we can write. Finally, we will explain how to use big counters to code long computations of Turing machines.

Counters: an example

For $i = 0, 1, 2$ let $\Sigma_i = \{a_i, b_i\}$ and let $\overline{\Sigma}_i = \{\bar{a}_i, \bar{b}_i\}$. Let $\Delta = \Sigma_0 \cup \Sigma_1 \cup \Sigma_2$ and similarly for $\overline{\Delta}$. Our trace alphabet will be $(\Delta \cup \overline{\Delta}, I)$ where I says that two letters are independent iff one has a bar and the other does not, i.e., $I = (\Delta \times \overline{\Delta}) \cup (\overline{\Delta} \times \Delta)$.

In the formulas below we will use the construction $\langle\Sigma\rangle\alpha$ for a set of letters $\Sigma \subseteq \Delta$ or $\Sigma \subseteq \overline{\Delta}$. This just an abbreviation for $\bigvee_{\sigma \in \Sigma}\langle\sigma\rangle\alpha$. Of course if we want to replace $\langle\Sigma\rangle\alpha$ with what it stands for, we may obtain an exponentially bigger formula. This is not a problem for us because we want to show a non-elementary lower bound. Anyway, below we will show how to code $\langle\Sigma\rangle\alpha$ more efficiently if we have traces of a special form.

We will also use the construction $\langle\Sigma^*\rangle\alpha$ for a set of letters $\Sigma \subseteq \Delta$ or $\Sigma \subseteq \overline{\Delta}$. The meaning of such a formula is that $\langle v\rangle\alpha$ holds for some $v \in \Sigma^*$. We need to require some special form of a trace to encode this formula with the constructions we have in *LTrL*. Every trace over the alphabet we have defined above consists of two, independent from each other, sequences of events (one over Δ and one over $\overline{\Delta}$). Assume that we have two more letters $e, \overline{e}$. Letter e depends only on letters from Δ and $\overline{e}$ depends only on letters from $\overline{\Delta}$. We will force our traces to have e on every even position of the Δ sequence and $\overline{e}$ on every even position of the $\overline{\Delta}$ sequence. So traces we will consider will look as follows:

$$e\sigma_0 e\sigma_1 \cdots e\sigma_i \cdots$$
$$\overline{e}\rho_0\overline{e}\rho_1 \cdots \overline{e}\rho_i \cdots$$

where $\sigma_0, \sigma_1, \ldots \in \Delta$ and $\rho_0, \rho_1, \ldots \in \overline{\Delta}$. It is easy to write a formula forcing the trace to be of this shape. Over such traces the formula $\langle(\Sigma \cup \{e\})^*\rangle\alpha$ is equivalent to $(\langle\overline{e}\rangle\underline{\mathrm{tt}} \wedge \langle\Sigma \cup \{e\}\rangle\underline{\mathrm{tt}})\ \mathbb{U}\ \alpha$. Strictly speaking it is equivalent in configurations satisfying $\langle\overline{e}\rangle\underline{\mathrm{tt}}$. We could avoid this problem but anyway we will be interested only in configurations satisfying $\langle e\rangle\langle\overline{e}\rangle\underline{\mathrm{tt}}$. Let us also mention that if we have this form of trace then there is a more efficient way to code $\langle\Sigma\rangle\alpha$. In case $\Sigma \subseteq \Delta$, we can define it with the formula: $\langle e\rangle\big(\big(\langle\overline{e}\rangle\underline{\mathrm{tt}} \wedge \neg\langle e\rangle\underline{\mathrm{tt}} \wedge \bigwedge_{a\notin(\Delta-\Sigma)} \neg\langle a\rangle\underline{\mathrm{tt}}\big)\ \mathbb{U}\,(\alpha \wedge \langle e\rangle\underline{\mathrm{tt}}\big)$. Because α appears only once in this formula, we avoid an exponential blowup caused by the previous translation.

To make the presentation easier we will forget about the e and $\overline{e}$ letters and use $\langle\Sigma^*\rangle\alpha$ construct as if we had it in our language. To translate what we will write into the language without $\langle\Sigma^*\rangle\alpha$ construct one has to add the formula forcing occurrences of e and $\overline{e}$, replace each $\langle\Sigma^*\rangle\alpha$ by its definition and then replace each $\langle a\rangle\beta$ by $\langle ea\rangle\beta$; moreover some care is also needed with the until operator (we skip the details).

After this preliminary remarks about the formulas we can write, let us start with the description of the construction. A word $l \in (\Sigma_0)^n$ can be considered as a counter when we identify a_0 with 0 and b_0 with 1. The value of such a counter $\sigma_0 \ldots \sigma_{n-1} \in (\Sigma_0)^n$ is $\sum_{i=0,\ldots,n-1} \sigma_i 2^i$. (Please note that the most significant digit is to the right.) Similarly an element of $(\overline{\Sigma}_0)^n$ can be considered as a counter.

Consider the following formulas:

$$\begin{aligned} \mathrm{counter}_0 \equiv & \langle\Sigma_0\rangle^n\langle\overline{\Sigma}_0\rangle^n\langle\Sigma_1\rangle\langle\overline{\Sigma}_1\rangle\underline{\mathrm{tt}} \\ \mathrm{same}_0 \equiv & \bigwedge_{i=0,\ldots,n-1} \langle\Sigma_0\rangle^i\langle\overline{\Sigma}_0\rangle^i(\langle a_0\rangle\langle\overline{a}_0\rangle\underline{\mathrm{tt}} \vee \langle b_0\rangle\langle\overline{b}_0\rangle\underline{\mathrm{tt}}) \\ \mathrm{first}_0 \equiv & \langle a_0\rangle^n\langle\overline{a}_0\rangle^n\langle\Sigma_1\rangle\langle\overline{\Sigma}_1\rangle\underline{\mathrm{tt}} \end{aligned}$$

Please recall that the letters from Δ are independent from the letters from $\overline{\Delta}$ so, for example, $\langle a_0\rangle\langle\overline{a}_0\rangle\underline{\mathrm{tt}}$ is equivalent to $\langle\overline{a}_0\rangle\langle a_0\rangle\underline{\mathrm{tt}}$. The formula $\mathrm{counter}_0$ says that a trace starts with two counters, one over Σ_0 and one over $\overline{\Sigma}_0$. After these counters, there are letters from Σ_1 and $\overline{\Sigma}_1$ which will be used for defining bigger counters. The formula same_0 says that the counters at the beginning of a trace represent the same values. One can also write, a slightly longer, formula next_0 saying that the value of the Σ_0 counter is one plus the value of the $\overline{\Sigma}_0$ counter. Finally, the formula first_0 just says that the values of the two counters are 0. Similarly we can write a formula last_0 saying the that values of the two counters are $2^n - 1$.

Now we want to write a formula counter_1 forcing the beginning of a trace to consist of two exponentially long counters, i.e., the beginning of a trace will have the form

$$\begin{array}{l} l_0\sigma_0 l_1\sigma_1 \ldots l_k\sigma_k\sigma \\ \bar{l}_0\rho_0\bar{l}_1\rho_1 \ldots \bar{l}_k\rho_k\rho \end{array} \tag{1}$$

where $k = 2^n - 1$; $l_0, \ldots, l_k \in (\Sigma_0)^n$ and $\bar{l}_0, \ldots, \bar{l}_k \in (\overline{\Sigma}_0)^n$ are counters representing successive numbers; $\sigma_i \in \Sigma_1$, $\rho_i \in \overline{\Sigma}_1$, $\sigma \in \Sigma_2$, $\rho \in \overline{\Sigma}_2$ (for $i = 0, \ldots, k$).

$$\begin{aligned} \text{counter}_1 &\equiv \text{first}_0 \wedge (\alpha \ \mathbb{U} \ \langle \Sigma_2 \rangle \langle \overline{\Sigma}_2 \rangle \underline{\text{tt}}) \\ \alpha &\equiv \text{same}_0 \Rightarrow (\text{last}_0 \wedge \beta_1) \vee (\neg \, \text{last}_0 \wedge \beta_2) \\ \beta_1 &\equiv \langle \Sigma_0 \rangle^n \langle \overline{\Sigma}_0 \rangle^n \langle \Sigma_1 \rangle \langle \overline{\Sigma}_1 \rangle \langle \Sigma_2 \rangle \langle \overline{\Sigma}_2 \rangle \underline{\text{tt}} \\ \beta_2 &\equiv \langle \Sigma_0 \rangle^n \langle \Sigma_1 \rangle \big(\text{next}_0 \wedge \langle \overline{\Sigma}_0 \rangle^n \langle \overline{\Sigma}_1 \rangle \, \text{same}_0 \big) \end{aligned}$$

The formula counter_1 says that a trace should begin with two counters representing 0 followed by σ_0 and ρ_0; the rest of the formula says that α should be true until we reach (uniquely determined) configuration from which it is possible to do $\langle \Sigma_2 \rangle \langle \overline{\Sigma}_2 \rangle$. Formula α says that whenever we are in a configuration ahead of which there are two counters with the same values then either these counters represent the maximal values and β_1 holds or otherwise β_2 holds. Formula β_1 says that after the counters we should have $\sigma_k, \rho_k, \sigma, \rho$. Formula β_2 says that the value of the next Σ_0 counter is bigger by one than the value of the current $\overline{\Sigma}_0$ counter and is equal to the value of the next $\overline{\Sigma}_0$ counter.

A counter as in (1) represents the number $\sum_{i=0,\ldots,k} \sigma_i 2^i$. We can force the value of the counter consisting of ρ's, i.e., the lower line of the trace (1), to have the same value as the σ counter. This can be done using the formula same_1:

$$\begin{aligned} \text{same}_1 &\equiv \delta \ \mathbb{U} \ \langle \Sigma_2 \rangle \langle \Sigma_2 \rangle \underline{\text{tt}} \\ \delta &\equiv \text{same}_0 \Rightarrow \langle \Sigma_0 \rangle^n \langle \overline{\Sigma}_0 \rangle^n (\langle a_1 \rangle \langle \overline{a}_1 \rangle \underline{\text{tt}} \vee \langle b_1 \rangle \langle \overline{b}_1 \rangle \underline{\text{tt}}) \end{aligned}$$

The formula says that whenever a configuration starts with two counters representing the same value then these counters are followed by either two letters representing 0 or two letters representing 1.

With a slightly more elaborate formula, next_1, we can force the value of the counter represented by σ's to be bigger by one than the value of the counter represented by ρ's.

This way we have obtained exponentially bigger counters than the ones we have started with. We have also means to compare and add one to these counters. Clearly we can also write formulas saying that the value of such a counter is 0 or the maximal possible. At this point we can iterate the whole construction to get even bigger counters.

Counters: definition

For describing inductive construction of bigger and bigger counters we need a precise definition what a counter is. To simplify matters a counter of level 0 does not count to n as in our example above but just to 1. A *counter of level* $n \geq 0$ is a trace of the form:

$$\begin{gathered} l_0\sigma_0 l_1\sigma_1 \ldots l_k\sigma_k\sigma \\ \bar{l}_0\rho_0\bar{l}_1\rho_1 \ldots \bar{l}_k\rho_k\rho \end{gathered} \tag{2}$$

Where $k = \text{Tower}(n-1,2)-1$. For each $i = 0,\ldots,k$, a trace $l_i\sigma_i\bar{l}_i\rho_i$ is a counter of level $n-1$ representing the number i; these counters are over the alphabets $\Delta_{n-1} = \bigcup_{i=1,\ldots n-1}\Sigma_i$ and $\overline{\Delta}_{n-1}$. Letters σ_i are from $\Sigma_n = \{a_n, b_n\}$, letters ρ_i are from $\overline{\Sigma}_n$. Finally $\sigma \in \Sigma_{n+1}$, $\rho \in \overline{\Sigma}_{n+1}$.

We can construct formulas: (i) counter(n) saying that a trace starts with the counter of level n; (ii) same(n) saying that if a trace is of the form (2) then $\sigma_0,\ldots,\sigma_k$ and $\rho_0,\ldots,\rho_k$ represent the same numbers; (iii) next(n) saying that the number represented by $\sigma_0,\ldots,\sigma_k$ is one plus the number represented by $\rho_0,\ldots,\rho_k$. Due to the lack of space we present only the counter formula:

$$\begin{aligned} \text{counter}(n) &\equiv \text{first}(n-1) \land \alpha \; \mathbb{U} \, \langle\Sigma_{n+1}\rangle\langle\overline{\Sigma}_{n+1}\rangle\underline{\text{tt}} \\ \alpha(n) &\equiv \text{same}(n-1) \land \text{counter}(n-1) \Rightarrow \\ &\qquad\qquad \big[(\text{last}(n-1) \land \beta_1) \lor (\neg\,\text{last}(n-1) \land \beta_2)\big] \\ \beta_1(n) &\equiv \langle(\Delta_{n-1} \cup \overline{\Delta}_{n-1})^*\rangle\langle\Sigma_n\rangle\langle\overline{\Sigma}_n\rangle\langle\Sigma_{n+1}\rangle\langle\overline{\Sigma}_{n+1}\rangle\underline{\text{tt}} \\ \beta_2(n) &\equiv \langle\Delta^*_{n-1}\rangle\langle\Sigma_n\rangle\big(\text{next}(n-1) \land \langle\overline{\Delta}^*_{n-1}\rangle\langle\overline{\Sigma}_n\rangle\,\text{same}(n-1)\big) \end{aligned}$$

We have:

Lemma 1. *For every trace T and $n \in \mathbb{N}$. Prefix of T is a counter of level n iff* $T \vDash \text{counter}(n)$. *The size of the formula* counter(n) *is* $2^{\mathcal{O}(n)}$.

Encoding of Turing Machines

Let $m \geq 0$ and let M be a $\lambda x.\,\text{Tower}(m,x)$ space bounded Turing machine. For a given word $w \in \{0,1\}^*$ we are going to write a formula Accept that is satisfiable iff $w \in L(M)$. Configurations of M on w can be of length Tower($m,|w|$), so we need counters able to count up to this number. Let n be the smallest number such that $\text{Tower}(n,2) \geq \text{Tower}(m,|w|)$. Clearly $n \leq m + \log(|w|)$. We will write a formula Accept such that:

$$\text{Accept is satisfiable} \quad \text{iff} \quad w \in L(M) \tag{3}$$

Let Q be the set of states of M, Γ its tape alphabet, q_I, q_F its initial and finial sates respectively. The blank symbol is denoted by B. A configuration is a word $\vdash vqv' \dashv$ with v representing symbols to the left of the head, v' representing symbols to the right, and the head looking at the first symbol of v'. We use $\vdash$ and $\dashv$ as end markers. Let $\Omega = Q \cup \Gamma \cup \{\vdash, \dashv\}$ be the alphabet needed to write down configurations.

We can define our trace alphabet. Recall that Δ_n stands for $\bigcup_{i=0,\ldots,n} \Sigma_n$ and $\overline{\Delta}_n$ denotes the appropriate set of letters with bars. Our trace alphabet is $(\Delta_n \cup \Omega \cup \overline{\Delta}_n \cup \overline{\Omega} \cup \{\$, \overline{\$}\}, I)$, where I says that two letters are independent iff one has a bar and the other doesn't.

First step in constructing the formula Accept is to write a formula Conf saying that a prefix of a trace is of the form as in (2) but the letters σ_i come from Ω, letters ρ_i come from $\overline{\Omega}$, σ is the symbol \$, and ρ is the symbol $\overline{\$}$. This formula can be obtained by a simple modification of the formula counter$(n+1)$ (replace Σ_{n+1} by Ω and Σ_{n+2} by $\{\$\}$).

To write the formula Accept we will need tools to compare two configurations, to define initial configuration and to say that one configuration is obtained from the other in one step of M.

$$
\begin{aligned}
\text{Same} &\equiv \text{Conf} \wedge (\delta \ \mathbb{U} \ \langle \$\overline{\$} \rangle \underline{\text{tt}}) \\
\delta &\equiv \text{same}(n) \Rightarrow \langle \Delta_n^* \rangle \langle \overline{\Delta}_n^* \rangle \bigvee_{\sigma \in \Omega} \langle \sigma \rangle \langle \overline{\sigma} \rangle \underline{\text{tt}} \\
\text{Init} &\equiv \text{Conf} \wedge \text{Same} \\
&\quad \wedge \langle (\Delta_n)^* \vdash (\Delta_n)^* q_I (\Delta_n)^* w_1 \ldots (\Delta_n)^* w_{|w|} (\Delta_n)^* \dashv \rangle \, \text{Blanks} \\
\text{Blanks} &\equiv \langle \Delta_n \cup \{B\} \rangle \underline{\text{tt}} \ \mathbb{U} \ \langle \$ \rangle \underline{\text{tt}} \\
\text{Comp} &\equiv \alpha \ \mathbb{U} \, (\text{Conf} \wedge \langle \Delta_n^* \rangle \langle q_F \rangle \underline{\text{tt}}) \\
\alpha &\equiv \text{Same} \Rightarrow \langle (\Delta_n \cup \Omega)^* \rangle \langle \$ \rangle \big(\text{Step} \wedge \langle (\overline{\Delta}_n \cup \overline{\Omega})^* \rangle \langle \overline{\$} \rangle (\text{Conf} \wedge \text{Same}) \big)
\end{aligned}
$$

The formula Step, that we have not presented, looks at the three consecutive letters of the lower configuration (i.e., the configuration written in $\overline{\Omega}$) and decides what letters should there be in the upper configuration. We need to look at three letters at the time because a letter may change at some position if and only if it is adjacent to a state.

The formula Accept is: Init $\wedge$ Comp. It can be shown that it satisfies the property (3)

In the construction of Accept we have used the alphabet depending on the machine. Fortunately the traces we are interested in consist always of two independent sequences of events. Hence we can code big alphabets that we have used, with a four letter alphabet – two letters for each of the sequences.

Finally, let us calculate the size of the formula Accept. By Lemma 1 the formula Conf is of the same size as counter$(n+1)$ hence of the size $2^{\mathcal{O}(n)}$. Also same(n) is of the size $2^{\mathcal{O}(n)}$. This makes the size of Init to be $\mathcal{O}(|w| + 2^{\mathcal{O}(n)})$. The only new element in the formula Comp is the formula Step. This formula encodes the transition function of the machine and uses same(n). Hence the size of Comp is $\mathcal{O}(|M| + 2^{\mathcal{O}(n)})$. This makes the whole formula Accept to be of the size $\mathcal{O}(2^{\mathcal{O}(n)} + |w| + |M|)$. Finally comes the duty of removing $\langle \Delta \rangle \alpha$ and $\langle \Delta^* \rangle \alpha$ constructs but this causes only linear blowup.

Summarising, for a $\lambda x.\text{Tower}(m, x)$ space bounded machine M and a word w we construct a $\mathcal{O}(|w| 2^{\mathcal{O}(m)} + |w| + |M|)$ size formula Accept that is satisfiable iff $w \in L(M)$. This implies:

Theorem 1. *Let (Σ, I) be a trace alphabet containing four letters $a, b, \overline{a}, \overline{b}$ with the only dependencies among them being that between a and b and between $\overline{a}$ and $\overline{b}$. The satisfiability of LTrL over (Σ, I) is non-elementary.*

4 A lower bound for the fragment of *LTrL*

As the previous section shows, it is until operator that gives us the power to reach non-elementary complexity. In this section we will deal with *LTrL* without until. Instead of until we will allow "sometime" and "always" modalities ($\mathbb{E}$ and $\mathbb{A}$ respectively) and a new next step modality $\langle\cdot\rangle\alpha$ with the semantics:

$T, C \vDash \langle\cdot\rangle\alpha$ iff $T, C \vDash \langle a\rangle\alpha$ for some action a

We call this logic $LTrL^-$. The addition of the new modality requires some justification. One good justification is that we don't know the complexity of $LTrL^-$ without this modality. We don't know its complexity even in the case when all the letters dependent on each other. In this case we obtain *LTL*, a linear time temporal logic, but without until, propositional constants and arbitrary next time modality; what is left are $\langle a\rangle$ modalities and sometimes in the future modality. Of course $\langle\cdot\rangle\alpha$ is equivalent to $\bigvee_{a\in\Sigma}\langle a\rangle\alpha$ but this definition shows that the formulas using $\langle\cdot\rangle$ may be exponentially more succinct. Finally, let us say that if we add any form of "trace independent" propositional constants to $LTrL^-$ then we don't need $\langle\cdot\rangle$ modality to obtain the EXPSPACE lower bound.

To encode computations of EXPSPACE Turing machines in traces we will use similar ideas as in the previous section although we will not be able to construct as huge counters as before because for this we need the until operator. Here we will use counter alphabets: $\{a, b\}$, $\{c, d\}$, $\{\overline{a}, \overline{b}\}$ and $\{\overline{c}, \overline{d}\}$. A counter is a word over one of these four alphabets. The interpretation is that a and c stand for 0 and b and d stand for 1.

Let M be a 2^n space bounded Turing machine. Let Q be its set of states, Γ its tape alphabet, q_I and q_F its initial and final states respectively. Let $w \in \Gamma^*$ be a word, let n be the length of w and let $k = 2^n - 1$. We are going to write a formula Accept having the property:

$$\text{Accept is satisfiable} \quad \text{iff} \quad w \in L(M) \tag{4}$$

The configuration of M is, as before, a string $\vdash vqv' \dashv$, with $v, v' \in \Gamma^*$ and $q \in Q$. We write $\Omega = Q \cup \Gamma \cup \{\vdash, \dashv\}$ for the alphabet needed to write down configurations. Let $\Delta = \{a, b, c, d\}$ be the counter alphabet and let $\overline{\Omega}$ and $\overline{\Delta}$ stand for appropriate sets of letters with bars over them.

Our trace alphabet is $(\Omega \cup \Delta \cup \overline{\Omega} \cup \overline{\Delta} \cup \{\downarrow, \nearrow\}, I)$ where I is the smallest symmetric relation containing:

$$((\Omega \cup \Delta) \times (\overline{\Omega} \cup \overline{\Delta})) \cup (\{\downarrow\} \times (\overline{\Omega} \cup \overline{\Delta})) \cup (\{\nearrow\} \times (\Omega \cup \Delta))$$

In words: letters with bars are independent from the letters without bars; the symbol $\downarrow$ depends only on letters without bars and $\nearrow$; the symbol $\nearrow$ depends only on letters with bars and $\downarrow$.

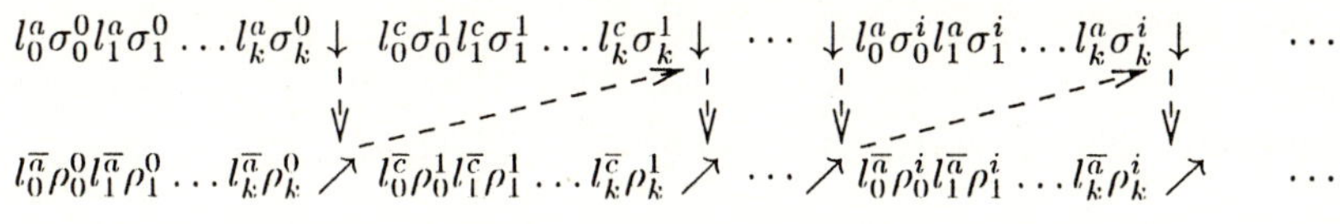

Fig. 1. The trace shape

The shape of traces we are after is depicted in Figure 1. The dashed arrows represent additional dependencies and the meanings of the components is the following. For every $i = 1, \ldots, k$, $l_i^a \in \{a, b\}^n$ is a counter representing number i; similarly for $l_i^{\overline{a}}$, l_i^c $l_i^{\overline{c}}$. Letters $\sigma_j^i, \rho_j^i \in \Omega$ are used to describe configurations. Letters $\downarrow, \nearrow$ are used to force synchronisation and their role we will explain later.

In our formulas we will use the construction $\langle\Sigma\rangle\alpha$, for some set of letters $\Sigma \subseteq (\Omega \cup \Delta)$. To have a translation of this construction into our core language without causing an exponential blowup we need once again to use the trick with e, $\overline{e}$ actions. To the shape of trace presented in Figure 1 we should add that every second action in the upper sequence is e and every second action in the lower sequence is $\overline{e}$. Having this we can define $\langle\Sigma\rangle\alpha$ construction by $\langle\cdot\rangle(\alpha \wedge \langle\overline{e}\rangle\underline{\mathrm{tt}}) \wedge \bigwedge_{a \notin \Sigma} \neg\langle a\rangle\underline{\mathrm{tt}}$. Once again this long formula is equivalent to $\langle\Sigma\rangle\alpha$ only in configurations satisfying $\langle\overline{e}\rangle\underline{\mathrm{tt}}$ but these will be the only configurations we will be interested in. Also following the previous section, we forget about the complication caused by adding $e, \overline{e}$ letters and pretend that we have $\langle\Sigma\rangle\alpha$ construct from the start. So in the formulas we will write, we will never mention $e, \overline{e}$ letters.

We can write $\mathcal{O}(n)$ size formula Shape forcing a trace to be of the form presented in Figure 1. We can also write a formula Init saying that $\sigma_0^0 \ldots \sigma_{n+3}^0$ form the initial configuration of M on w. With a formula of size $\mathcal{O}(n)$, and no until, we cannot say that every σ_i^0 for $i > |w| + 3$ is blank. This is not a problem as we will always look only at the prefix up to the first $\dashv$.

For every $i \in \mathbb{N}$, we would like to force $\sigma_0^{i+1} \ldots \sigma_k^{i+1}$ to represent the next configuration after $\sigma_0^i \ldots \sigma_k^i$. First consider the formulas:

$$\mathrm{same}(a, \overline{a}) \equiv \bigwedge_{i=0,\ldots,n-1} \langle\Delta\rangle^i \langle\overline{\Delta}\rangle^i (\langle a\rangle\langle\overline{a}\rangle\underline{\mathrm{tt}} \vee \langle b\rangle\langle\overline{b}\rangle\underline{\mathrm{tt}})$$

$$\beta(a, \overline{a}) \equiv \mathbb{A}\big(\,\mathrm{same}(a, \overline{a}) \Rightarrow \langle\Delta\rangle^n \langle\overline{\Delta}\rangle^n \bigvee_{\sigma \in \Omega} \langle\sigma\rangle\langle\overline{\sigma}\rangle\underline{\mathrm{tt}}\big)$$

The formula $\mathrm{same}(a, \overline{a})$ says that from the current configuration we see two counters, one over $\{a, b\}$ and one over $\{\overline{a}, \overline{b}\}$, representing the same numbers. Now, we can explain the role of the synchronisation letters $\downarrow, \nearrow$. Because of the structure of the trace forced by these letters, if some configuration satisfies $\mathrm{same}(a, \overline{a})$ then this configuration must be necessary of the form symbolised by the thick vertical line:

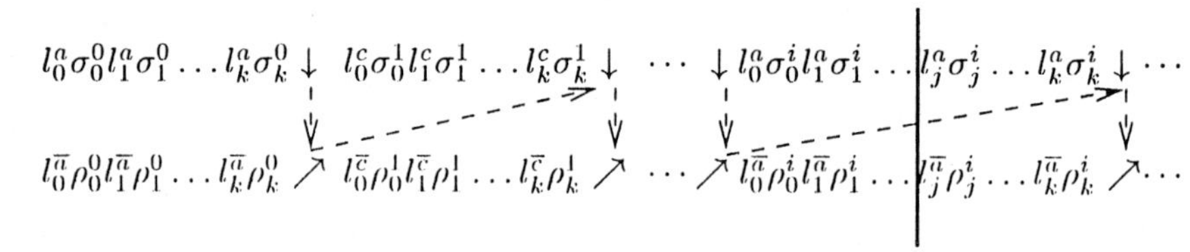

for some i and j. That the j's in σ^i_j and ρ^i_j are the same is due to the fact that the counters represent the same value. That the i's are the same is due to the fact that if $i' \neq i''$ then the positions of $\sigma^{i'}_j$ and $\rho^{i''}_j$ are comparable in the dependency ordering of the above trace.

Formula $\beta(a, \overline{a})$ says that whenever we see two counters representing the same numbers then the letters after them are the same. This way we have $\sigma^i_j = \rho^i_j$ for all even i and all $j \in \{0, \ldots, k\}$.

Similarly one can write the formulas $\mathrm{same}(c, \overline{c})$ and $\beta(c, \overline{c})$ forcing $\sigma^i_j = \rho^i_j$ for all odd i and all $j \in \{0, \ldots, k\}$.

Now, we want to write a formula saying that $\sigma^{i+1}_0 \ldots \sigma^{i+1}_k$ represents the next configuration after $\rho^i_0 \ldots \rho^i_k$. For this observe that in order to decide what σ^{i+1}_j should be it is enough to know $\rho^i_{j-1}, \rho^i_j, \rho^i_{j+1}$. We define the formula:

$$Ls(\sigma_1, \sigma_2, \sigma_3) \equiv \langle \Delta \rangle^n \langle \sigma_1 \rangle \langle \Delta \rangle^n \langle \sigma_2 \rangle \langle \Delta \rangle^n \langle \sigma_3 \rangle \underline{\mathrm{tt}}$$

checking that the three consecutive letters in the upper sequence (i.e., the one written with letters without bars) are $\sigma_1, \sigma_2, \sigma_3$. Similarly we can define $\overline{Ls}$ talking about the lower sequence. Consider the formulas:

$$\begin{aligned}
\mathrm{Step}(c, \overline{a}) &\equiv \mathrm{same}(c, \overline{a}) \Rightarrow \gamma_1 \wedge \gamma_2 \wedge \gamma_3 \wedge \gamma_4 \\
\gamma_1 &\equiv \bigwedge_{\sigma_1, \sigma_2, \sigma_3 \in \Omega - Q} \overline{Ls}(\overline{\sigma}_1, \overline{\sigma}_2, \overline{\sigma}_3) \Rightarrow \langle \Delta \rangle^n \langle \Omega \rangle \langle \Delta \rangle^n \langle \sigma_2 \rangle \underline{\mathrm{tt}} \\
\gamma_2 &\equiv \bigwedge_{\sigma_1, \ldots, \sigma_6 \in \Omega} (\overline{Ls}(\overline{\sigma}_1, \overline{\sigma}_2, \overline{\sigma}_3) \wedge \mathrm{trans}(\sigma_1, \ldots, \sigma_6)) \Rightarrow Ls(\sigma_4, \sigma_5, \sigma_6) \\
\gamma_3 &\equiv \langle \overline{\Delta} \rangle^n \langle \overline{\Omega} - \overline{Q} \rangle \langle \overline{\Delta} \rangle^n \langle \overline{\dashv} \rangle \Rightarrow \langle \Delta \rangle^n \langle \Omega \rangle \langle \Delta \rangle^n \langle \dashv \rangle \\
\gamma_4 &\equiv \mathrm{first}(\overline{a}) \Rightarrow \langle \Delta \rangle^n \langle \vdash \rangle
\end{aligned}$$

Formula γ_1 says that for every position not containing a state on the neighbouring positions the letters should be the same. Formula γ_2 takes care of the case when there is a state: we consult the transition function of M encoded in the formula trans. Formula γ_3 assures that the end of configuration marker is copied correctly, similarly γ_4 but for the starting marker. Once again the shape of the trace guarantees that the only configurations satisfying $\mathrm{same}(c, \overline{a})$ are those ending in ρ^i_j and σ^{i+1}_j for some $i \in \mathbb{N}$, $j \in \{0, \ldots, k\}$.

Finally we can write a formula Finish saying that the automaton has reached the final state and its head is at the leftmost position:

$$\mathrm{Finish} \equiv \langle \downarrow \rangle \langle \Delta \rangle^n \langle \vdash \rangle \langle \Delta \rangle^n \langle q_F \rangle \underline{\mathrm{tt}}$$

Of course we can assume that if M accepts then it does so with the head at the leftmost position. Our main formula is:

$$\text{Accept} \equiv \text{Shape} \wedge \text{Init} \wedge \beta(a, \overline{a}) \wedge \beta(c, \overline{c}) \wedge \text{Step}(c, \overline{a}) \wedge \text{Step}(\overline{c}, a) \wedge \text{Finish}$$

It can be checked that this formula satisfies property (4). As the size of Accept is linear in the size of $|M| + |w|$ we obtain:

Theorem 2. *Let (Σ, I) be a trace alphabet containing six letters $\{a, b, c, d, \downarrow, \nearrow\}$ with the only dependencies between these letters being those between: (a, b), (c, d), $(\downarrow, a)$, $(\downarrow, b)$, $(\nearrow, c)$, $(\nearrow, d)$, $(\downarrow, \nearrow)$. The satisfiability problem for LTrL$^-$ over (Σ, I) is EXPSPACE-hard.*

A modification of the argument from [1] shows:

Theorem 3. *For arbitrary trace alphabet, LTrL$^-$ is in EXPSPACE.*

Acknowledgements

I thank Doron Peled for giving me his paper [1]. I also thank Manfred Droste for an invitation to a very inspiring workshop on traces.

References

1. R. Alur, K. McMillan, and D. Peled. Deciding global parial-order properties. submitted, 1997.
2. R. Alur, D. Peled, and W. Penczek. Model-checking of causality properties. In *LICS '95*, pages 90–100, 1995.
3. V. Diekert and G. Rozenberg, editors. *The Book of Traces*. World Scientific, 1995.
4. W. Ebinger and A. Muscholl. Logical definability on infinite traces. In *ICALP '93*, volume 700, pages 335–346, 1993.
5. P. Godefroid. *Partial-order methods for the verification of concurrent systems*, volume 1032 of *LNCS*. Springer-Verlag, 1996.
6. K. Lodaya, R. Parikh, R. Ramanujam, and P. Thiagarajan. A logical study of distributed transition systems. *Information and Computation*, 119:91–118, 1985.
7. D. Peled. Partial order reduction : model checking using representatives. In *MFCS'96*, volume 1113 of *LNCS*, pages 93–112, 1996.
8. D. Peled and A. Pnueli. Proving partial order properties. *Theoretical Computer Science*, 126:143–182, 1994.
9. W. Penczek. On udecidability of propositional temporal logics on trace systems. *Information Processing Letters*, 43:147–153, 1992.
10. R. Ramanujam. Locally linear time temporal logic. In *LICS '96*, pages 118–128, 1996.
11. A. Sistla and E. Clarke. The complexity of propositional linear time logic. *J. ACM*, 32:733–749, 1985.
12. P. S. Thiagarajan. A trace based extension of linear time temporal logic. In *LICS*, pages 438–447, 1994.
13. P. S. Thiagarajan and I. Walukiewicz. An expressively complete linear time temporal logic for mazurkiewicz traces. In *LICS'97*, pages 183–194. IEEE, 1997.
14. A. Valmari. A stubborn attack on state explosion. *Formal Methods in System Design*, 1:297–322, 1992.

On the Expressiveness of Real and Integer Arithmetic Automata (Extended Abstract)

Bernard Boigelot*, Stéphane Rassart and Pierre Wolper

Université de Liège
Institut Montefiore, B28
B-4000 Liège Sart-Tilman, Belgium
{boigelot,rassart,pw}@montefiore.ulg.ac.be

Abstract. If read digit by digit, a n-dimensional vector of integers represented in base r can be viewed as a word over the alphabet r^n. It has been known for some time that, under this encoding, the sets of integer vectors recognizable by finite automata are exactly those definable in Presburger arithmetic if independence with respect to the base is required, and those definable in a slight extension of Presburger arithmetic if only a specific base is considered.
Using the same encoding idea, but moving to infinite words, finite automata on infinite words can recognize sets of real vectors. This leads to the question of which sets of real vectors are recognizable by finite automata, which is the topic of this paper. We show that the recognizable sets of real vectors are those definable in the theory of reals and integers with addition and order, extended with a special base-dependent predicate that tests the value of a specified digit of a number. Furthermore, in the course of proving that sets of vectors defined in this theory are recognizable by finite automata, we show that linear equations and inequations have surprisingly compact representations by automata, which leads us to believe that automata accepting sets of real vectors can be of more than theoretical interest.

1 Introduction

The ability to represent and manipulate sets of integers and/or reals is a fundamental tool that has many applications. The specific problems motivating this paper come from the algorithmic verification of reactive systems where manipulating sets of integers or reals is important for verifying protocols [BW94], real-time systems [AD94] or hybrid systems [ACH+95, Hen96, BBR97]. Of course, many well-established approaches exist for manipulating such sets, for instance using symbolic equations or various representations of polyhedra. However, each of these approaches has its limits and usually copes better with sets of reals than

* "Chargé de Recherches" (Post-Doctoral Researcher) for the National Fund for Scientific Research (Belgium).

with sets of integers or sets involving both reals and integers. This situation has prompted an effort to search for alternative representations, with Ordered Binary Decision Diagrams [Bry86, Bry92], a very successful representation of very large finite sets of values, as a leading inspiration.

An ordered binary decision diagram is a representation of a set of fixed-length bit-word values. It is a layered DAG in which each level corresponds to a fixed-position bit and separates between words in which this bit has value 0 and value 1. Abstractly, it is just a representation of a Boolean function, but one for which an effective algorithmic technology has been developed. A BDD can of course represent a set of fixed-length binary represented integers or reals, but in this context it has an interesting and powerful generalization. Indeed, observing that a BDD is just an acyclic finite automaton, one is naturally led to considering lifting this acyclicity restriction, i.e., to consider finite automata accepting the binary encoding of numbers. Actually, it is more than worthwhile to go one step further and consider automata operating on the encoding of vectors of numbers. For doing so, one makes the encoding of the numbers in the vector of uniform length and reads all numbers in the vector in parallel, bit by bit. An n-dimensional vector is thus seen as a word over the alphabet 2^n.

For integers, the representation of each integer is a finite word and one is thus dealing with traditional languages of finite words. The subject of finite automata accepting binary (or more generally base-r) encodings of integer vectors has been well studied, going back to work of Büchi [Büc60]. Indeed, this use of finite automata has applications in logic. For instance, noticing that addition and order are easily represented by finite automata and that these are closed under the Boolean operations as well as projection, it is very easy to obtain a decision procedure for Presburger arithmetic. Going further, the question of which sets of integer vectors can be represented by finite automata has been remarkably answered by Cobham [Cob69] for 1-dimensional vectors and Semenov [Sem77] for n-dimensional vectors. The result is that sets that are representable independently of the chosen base (≥ 2) are exactly those that are Presburger definable. If one focuses on a given base, a predicate relating a number and the largest power of the base dividing it has to be added in order to capture the sets recognizable by finite automata (see [BHMV94] for a survey of these results).

When considering the reals, the situation is somewhat more complex. Indeed, to be able to represent all reals, one has to consider infinite representations, a natural choice being the infinite base-r expansion of reals. A number or vector of numbers is thus now an infinite word and an automaton recognizing a set of reals is an automaton on infinite words [Büc62]. This idea was actually already familiar to Büchi himself and leads very simply to a decision procedure for the theory of reals and integers with addition and order predicates. We are, however, not aware of any further study of the subject since then.

This paper delves into this topic with the dual goal of understanding the theoretical limits of representing sets of reals and integers by automata on infinite words and of investigating the pragmatic algorithmic aspects of this approach. On the first of these topics, we settle the question of which sets of real vectors are representable by nondeterministic Büchi automata operating on base-r encodings, i.e., by ω-regular languages of base-r encodings. The result is that the representable sets are those definable in the theory of the integers and reals with addition and order predicates, as well as with a special predicate $X_r(x, u, k)$. This predicate is true if and only if u is a positive or negative integer power of the base r, k belongs to $\{0, \ldots, r-1\}$ (i.e., is a digit in base r), and the value of the digit of the representation of x appearing in the position corresponding to the power of the base u is k. In simpler terms, the predicate X_r lets one check which digit appears in a given position of the base-r encoding of a number x. The proof of this result, inspired by [Vil92], relies on an interesting encoding of the possible computations of a Büchi automaton by an arithmetic formula.

On the second topic, we will show that the sets representable by linear equations and inequations have remarkably simple and easy to construct representations by automata. Furthermore, in many cases, an optimal deterministic representation can be directly constructed. This improves on the results of [BBR97] and extends those of [BC96], which are limited to the positive integers.

2 Recognizing Sets of Real Vectors with Automata

In this section, we recall the encoding of real vectors by words introduced in [BBR97] and define the type of finite automata that will be used for recognizing sets of such encodings.

Let $x \in \mathbf{R}$ be a real number and $r > 1$ be an integer. We encode x in base r, most significant digit first, using r's complement for negative numbers. The result is a word of the form $w = w_I \star w_F$, where w_I encodes the integer part x_I of x as a finite word over the alphabet $\{0, \ldots, r-1\}$, the symbol "$\star$" is a separator, and w_F encodes the fractional part x_F of x as an infinite word over the alphabet $\{0, \ldots, r-1\}$. We do not fix the length p of w_I, but only require it to be nonzero and large enough for $-r^{p-1} \leq x_I < r^{p-1}$ to hold. Hence, the most significant digit of a number will be "0" if this number is positive or equal to zero, and "$r-1$" otherwise. The length $|w_I|$ of w_I will be called the *integer-part length* of the encoding of x by w. For simplicity, we require that the length of w_F always be infinite (this is not a real restriction, since an infinite number of "0" symbols can always be appended harmlessly to w_F).

It is important to note that some numbers $x \in \mathbf{R}$ have two distinct encodings with the same integer-part length. For example, in base 10, the number $x = 11/2$ has the following two encodings with integer-part length 3 : $005 \star 5(0)^\omega$ and $005 \star 4(9)^\omega$ ($^\omega$ denotes infinite repetition). Such encodings are said to be *dual*. The encoding which ends with an infinite succession of "0" digits is said to be a *high* encoding of x. The encoding which ends with an infinite succession of "$r-1$" digits is said to be a *low* encoding of x. If there is only one encoding of x that has a given integer-part length, this encoding is said to be both high and low.

To encode a vector of real numbers, we encode each of its components with words of identical integer-part length. This length can be chosen arbitrarily, provided that it is sufficient for encoding the vector component with the highest magnitude. It follows that any vector has an infinite number of possible encodings. An encoding of a vector of reals $\mathbf{x} = (x_1, \ldots, x_n)$ can indifferently be viewed either as a tuple $(w_1, \ldots, w_n)$ of words of identical integer-part length over the alphabet $\{0, \ldots, r-1, \star\}$, or as a single word w over the alphabet $\{0, \ldots, r-1\}^n \cup \{\star\}$. For convenience, the real vector represented by a word w interpreted in base r is denoted $[w]_r$.

Since a real vector has several possible encodings, we have to choose which of these the automata we define will recognize. A natural choice is to accept all encodings. This leads to the following definition.

Definition 1 *Let $n > 0$ and $r > 1$ be integers. A* Real Vector Automaton (RVA) *$\mathcal{A}$ in base r for vectors in $\mathbf{R}^n$ is a Büchi automaton [Büc62] over the alphabet $\{0, \ldots, r-1\}^n \cup \{\star\}$, such that:*

- *Every word w accepted by $\mathcal{A}$ is of the form $w = w_I \star w_F$, with $w_I \in (\{0, r-1\}^n)(\{0, \ldots, r-1\}^n)^*$ and $w_F \in (\{0, \ldots, r-1\}^n)^\omega$.*
- *For every vector $\mathbf{x} \in \mathbf{R}^n$, $\mathcal{A}$ accepts either all the encodings of $\mathbf{x}$ in base r, or none of them.*

An RVA is said to *represent* the set of vectors encoded by the words belonging to its accepted language. Note that this notion of representation is not canonical since different Büchi automata may accept the same language. Any subset of $\mathbf{R}^n$ that can be represented by an RVA in base r is said to be *r-recognizable.*

3 The Expressive Power of Real Vector Automata

In this section, we introduce a logical theory in which all sets of real vectors that are recognizable by Real Vector Automata can be defined. Precisely, we prove that for any base $r > 1$, the r-recognizable subsets of $\mathbf{R}^n$ are definable in the first-order theory $\langle \mathbf{R}, +, \leq, Z, X_r \rangle$, where Z is a unary predicate that tests whether its argument belongs to $\mathbf{Z}$, and X_r is a ternary predicate that tests the value of the digit occurring at a given position in the development of a real number in base r (see below). As will be shown in Section 6, the converse translation also holds and thus the theory $\langle \mathbf{R}, +, \leq, Z, X_r \rangle$ exactly characterizes the r-recognizable sets of real vectors.

The predicate X_r over $\mathbf{R}^3$ is such that $X_r(x, u, k) = \mathbf{T}$ if and only if u is a (positive or negative) integer power of r, and there exists an encoding of x such that the digit at the position specified by u is k (which implies that $k \in \{0, \ldots, r-1\}$). Formally, $\mathbf{N}_0$ denoting the strictly positive integers, we have

$$\begin{aligned} X_r(x, u, k) \equiv (\exists p \in \mathbf{N}_0, a_p \in \{0, r-1\}, a_{p-1}, a_{p-2}, \ldots \in \{0, 1, \ldots, r-1\}) \\ (x = -(a_p/(r-1))r^p + a_{p-1}r^{p-1} + a_{p-2}r^{p-2} + \cdots \\ \wedge (\exists q \in \mathbf{Z})(q \leq p \wedge r^q = u \wedge a_q = k)). \end{aligned}$$

A subset of $\mathbf{R}^n$ that can be defined in the theory $\langle \mathbf{R}, +, \leq, Z, X_r \rangle$ is said to be *r-definable.*

We are now ready to show that every set of real vectors that is r-recognizable is definable in the theory $\langle \mathbf{R}, +, \leq, Z, X_r \rangle$.

Theorem 2. *Let $n > 0$ and $r > 1$ be integers. Every r-recognizable subset of $\mathbf{R}^n$ is r-definable.*

Proof sketch The idea of the proof is that a computation of an RVA can be encoded by an infinite word that can itself be seen as the encoding of a real vector. This makes it possible to express the existence of a computation of an RVA on a real vector within our target language.

Consider a r-recognizable set $U \subseteq \mathbf{R}^n$. By definition, there exists a Büchi automaton $\mathcal{A} = (\Sigma, S, \Delta, s_0, F)$ accepting all the encodings in base r of the elements of U. Let us show that U can be defined in $\langle \mathbf{R}, +, \leq, Z, X_r \rangle$. We take $m \in \mathbf{N}$ such that $r^m > |S| + 1$, where $|S|$ denotes the number of states of $\mathcal{A}$. Each state $s \in S$ can be encoded by a tuple

$$E(s) = (e_1(s), e_2(s), \ldots, e_m(s)) \in \{0, 1, \ldots, r-1\}^m.$$

Without loss of generality, we can assume that there is no $s \in S$ such that $e_1(s) = e_2(s) = \cdots = e_m(s) = 0$ or such that $e_1(s) = e_2(s) = \cdots = e_m(s) = r-1$.

Using this encoding of states, a vector $(y_1, y_2, \ldots, y_m)$ of reals can be seen as representing, by means of its base-r encoding, a run $s_0, s_1, s_2, \ldots \in S^\omega$ of $\mathcal{A}$. However, given the multiplicity of encodings, this representation is ambiguous. There are two causes of ambiguity. The first is the fact that one can have various integer-part lengths. This is actually of no consequence since, if one restricts the y_i's to be positive or 0, going from one integer-part length to another just implies adding to the beginning of the encoding a number of tuples $\{0\}^m$ that by convention do not represent a state of $\mathcal{A}$.

The second cause of ambiguity is the existence of dual encodings. To solve this, we append to the vector $(y_1, y_2, \ldots, y_m)$ a second vector $(a_1, a_2, \ldots, a_m)$ whose elements are restricted to values in the set $\{1, 2\}$, with the convention that the value 1 for a_i expresses the fact that y_i should be represented using a low encoding and the value 2 specifies a high encoding. In summary, a vector

$$(y_1, y_2, \ldots, y_m, a_1, a_2, \ldots, a_m) \in \mathbf{R}_+^m \times \{1, 2\}^m$$

represents a run $s_0, s_1, s_2, \ldots \in S^\omega$ of $\mathcal{A}$ as follows.

- Let l be the shortest integer-part length that allows the base-r encoding of the real vector $(y_1, y_2, \ldots, y_m)$.
- For $i \in \{1, \ldots, m\}$ let w_i be the (low if $a_i = 1$ or high if $a_i = 2$) integer-part length l base-r encoding of y_i.
- The represented run is then the one such that, for all $j \geq 0$, the state s_j is the one whose encoding $E(s_j) = (e_1(s_j), e_2(s_j), \ldots, e_m(s_j))$ is given by the digits of the words $w_1, \ldots, w_m$ at the position corresponding to $r^{l-(j+1)}$. If at a given position the digits of the w_i do not represent a state, then the vector $(y_1, y_2, \ldots, y_m, a_1, a_2, \ldots, a_m)$ does not represent a run of $\mathcal{A}$.

To prove our theorem, it is sufficient to show that the predicate $R_{\mathcal{A}}(x_1, x_2, \ldots, x_n, y_1, y_2, \ldots, y_m, a_1, a_2, \ldots, a_m)$ which is satisfied if and only if the tuple $(y_1, y_2, \ldots, y_m, a_1, a_2, \ldots, a_m)$ encodes an execution of $\mathcal{A}$ which accepts an encoding in base r of the real vector $(x_1, x_2, \ldots, x_n)$ is expressible in $\langle \mathbf{R}, +, \leq, Z, X_r \rangle$. Indeed, using this predicate $R_{\mathcal{A}}$, the set U of real vectors whose encodings are accepted by $\mathcal{A}$ can be expressed as follows

$$U = \{(x_1, x_2, \ldots, x_n) \in \mathbf{R}^n \mid (\exists y_1, y_2, \ldots, y_m, a_1, a_2, \ldots, a_m \in \mathbf{R}) \\ (R_{\mathcal{A}}(x_1, x_2, \ldots, x_n, y_1, y_2, \ldots, y_m, a_1, a_2, \ldots, a_m))\}.$$

We now turn to expressing $R_{\mathcal{A}}$ in $\langle \mathbf{R}, +, \leq, Z, X_r \rangle$. The idea is to express that $R_{\mathcal{A}}(x_1, x_2, \ldots, x_n, y_1, y_2, \ldots, y_m, a_1, a_2, \ldots, a_m) = \mathbf{T}$ if and only if there exist $z \in \mathbf{R}$ and $b_1, b_2, \ldots, b_n \in \{1, 2\}$ satisfying the conditions expressed below (z is used to represent the highest significant position used in the y_i's and the $b_1, b_2, \ldots, b_n$ to make explicit the fact that the encoding of the x_i's is high or low).

- The y_i's are positive, and the number z is the highest power of r appearing in the encodings in base r of the y_i's (with the convention that the encoding of a y_i is supposed to be low if $a_i = 1$, and high otherwise).
- In the encodings of the y_i's, the digits at the position specified by z correspond to the encoding of the initial state s_0 of $\mathcal{A}$.
- There exists an accepting state of $\mathcal{A}$ whose encoding as a tuple of digits appears infinitely often in the digits of the y_i's.
- At any two successive positions, the digits of the y_i's encode two states of $\mathcal{A}$ linked together by a transition. The label of the transition is given by the corresponding digits of an encoding of the x_i's, except that reading the separator $\star$ introduces a shift. Precisely, for a transition whose origin is encoded at position $u \geq 1$, the label is given by the digits of the x_i's at position u. For a transition whose origin is encoded at position $u = r^{-1}$, the label is the separator $\star$. Finally, for a transition whose origin is encoded at position $u < r^{-1}$, the label is given by the digits of the x_i's at position ru. The encoding of a x_i is supposed to be low if $b_i = 1$, and high otherwise. □

4 Representing Linear Equations by Automata

The problem addressed in this section consists of constructing an RVA that represents the set S of all the solutions $\mathbf{x} \in \mathbf{R}^n$ of an equation of the form $\mathbf{a}.\mathbf{x} = b$, given $n \geq 0$, $\mathbf{a} \in \mathbf{Z}^n$ and $b \in \mathbf{Z}$.

4.1 A Decomposition of the Problem

The basic idea is to build the automaton corresponding to a linear equation in two parts : one that accepts the integer part of solutions of the equation and one that accepts the part of the solution that belongs to $[0, 1]^n$.

More precisely, let $\mathbf{x} \in S$, and let $w_I \star w_F$ be an encoding of $\mathbf{x}$ in a base $r > 1$, with $w_I \in \Sigma^*$, $w_F \in \Sigma^\omega$, and $\Sigma = \{0, \ldots, r-1\}^n$. The vectors $\mathbf{x}_I$ and $\mathbf{x}_F$ respectively encoded by the words $w_I \star \mathbf{0}^\omega$ and $\mathbf{0} \star w_F$, where $\mathbf{0} = (0, \ldots, 0)$, are such that $\mathbf{x}_I \in \mathbf{Z}^n$, $\mathbf{x}_F \in [0,1]^n$, and $\mathbf{x} = \mathbf{x}_I + \mathbf{x}_F$. Since $\mathbf{a}.\mathbf{x} = b$, we have $\mathbf{a}.\mathbf{x}_I + \mathbf{a}.\mathbf{x}_F = b$. Moreover, writing $\mathbf{a}$ as $(a_1, \ldots, a_n)$, we have $\alpha \leq \mathbf{a}.\mathbf{x}_F \leq \alpha'$, where $\alpha = \sum_{a_i<0} a_i$ and $\alpha' = \sum_{a_i>0} a_i$, which implies $b - \alpha' \leq \mathbf{a}.\mathbf{x}_I \leq b - \alpha$. Another immediate property of interest is that $\mathbf{a}.\mathbf{x}_I$ is divisible by $\gcd(a_1, \ldots, a_n)$.

From those results, we obtain that the language L of the encodings of all the elements of S satisfies

$$L = \bigcup_{\varphi(\beta)} \{w_I \in \Sigma^* \mid \mathbf{a}.[w_I \star \mathbf{0}^\omega]_r = \beta\} \cdot \{\star\} \cdot \{w_F \in \Sigma^\omega \mid \mathbf{a}.[\mathbf{0} \star w_F]_r = b - \beta\},$$

where "$\cdot$" denotes concatenation and $\varphi(\beta)$ stands for $b - \alpha' \leq \beta \leq b - \alpha \wedge (\exists m \in \mathbf{Z})(\beta = \gcd(a_1, \ldots, a_n) \times m)$.

This decomposition of L reduces the computation of an RVA representing S to the following problems:

- building an automaton on finite words accepting all the words $w_I \in \Sigma^*$ such that $[w_I \star \mathbf{0}^\omega]_r$ is a solution of a given linear equation;
- building a Büchi automaton accepting all the words $w_F \in \Sigma^\omega$ such that $[\mathbf{0} \star w_F]_r$ is a solution of a given linear equation.

These problems are addressed in the two following sections.

4.2 Recognizing Integer Solutions

Our goal is, given an equation $\mathbf{a}.\mathbf{x} = b$ where $\mathbf{a} \in \mathbf{Z}^n$ and $b \in \mathbf{Z}$, to construct a finite automaton $\mathcal{A}_{\mathbf{a},b}$ that accepts all the finite words encoding in a given base r the integer solutions of that equation.

The construction proceeds as follows. The initial state of $\mathcal{A}_{\mathbf{a},b}$ is denoted s_0. All the other states s are in one-to-one correspondence with an integer $\beta(s)$, with the property that the vectors $\mathbf{x} \in \mathbf{Z}^n$ accepted by the paths leading from s_0 to s are exactly the solutions of the equation $\mathbf{a}.\mathbf{x} = \beta(s)$. The only accepting state s_F of $\mathcal{A}_{\mathbf{a},b}$ is the one such that $\beta(s_F) = b$.

The next step is to define the transitions of $\mathcal{A}_{\mathbf{a},b}$. Consider moving from a state s to a state s' while reading a tuple $\mathbf{d} = (d_1, \ldots, d_n)$ of digits. This has the effect of appending these digits to the number that has been read so far and thus the number $\mathbf{x}'$ read when reaching s' is related to the number $\mathbf{x}$ that had been read when reaching s by $\mathbf{x}' = r\mathbf{x} + \mathbf{d}$. Therefore, for states s and s' other than s_0 to be linked by a transition labeled d, the number $\beta(s')$ associated with the state s' has to be given by

$$\beta(s') = \mathbf{a}.\mathbf{x}' = r\,\mathbf{a}.\mathbf{x} + \mathbf{a}.\mathbf{d} = r.\beta(s) + \mathbf{a}.\mathbf{d}.$$

For transitions from s_0, the relation is similar, except that the bits that are read can only be sign bits (0 or $r-1$), that a bit $r-1$ has to be interpreted as -1 when computing $\mathbf{a}.\mathbf{d}$, and that the fictitious $\beta(s_0)$ is taken to be 0.

In practice, we will compute the automaton $\mathcal{A}_{\mathbf{a},b}$ backwards, starting from the accepting state and moving backwards along transitions. Thus, the transition reaching a given state s' and labeled by a vector of bits $\mathbf{d}$ will originate from the state s such that

$$\beta(s) = \frac{\beta(s') - \mathbf{a}.\mathbf{d}}{r}.$$

Note that $\beta(s)$ must be an integer, and must be divisible by $\gcd(a_1, \ldots, a_n)$, otherwise there would be no integer solution to $\mathbf{a}.\mathbf{x} = \beta(s)$. If this requirement is not satisfied, then there is no ingoing transition to s' labeled by $\mathbf{d}$.

From an algorithmic perspective, the automaton $\mathcal{A}_{\mathbf{a},b}$ can be constructed by starting from the state s_F such that $\beta(s_F) = b$, and then repeatedly computing the ingoing transitions to the current states until stabilization occurs (we will shortly show that it always does). If one wishes to construct k automata $\mathcal{A}_{\mathbf{a},b_1}, \mathcal{A}_{\mathbf{a},b_2}, \ldots, \mathcal{A}_{\mathbf{a},b_k}$, with $b_1, \ldots, b_k \in \mathbf{Z}$ (for instance, as an application of the method presented in Section 4.1, in which the b_i are all the integers satisfying φ), then a technique more efficient than repeating the construction k times consists of starting from the set $\{s_1, \ldots, s_k\}$ such that $\beta(s_i) = b_i$ for each $i \in \{1, \ldots, k\}$, rather than from a set containing a single state. The states and transitions computed during the construction will then be shared between the different $\mathcal{A}_{\mathbf{a},b_i}$, and each s_i will be the only accepting state of the corresponding $\mathcal{A}_{\mathbf{a},b_i}$.

Let us now show that the computation terminates. The immediate predecessors $s \neq s_0$ of a state $s' \neq s_0$ are such that $(\beta(s') - (r-1)\alpha')/r \leq \beta(s) \leq (\beta(s') - (r-1)\alpha)/r$, where α and α' are as defined in Section 4.1. As a consequence, if there exists a path of length $k \geq 0$ from a state s to the accepting state s_F, we have

$$\frac{1}{r^k}\beta(s_F) - (r-1)\alpha' \sum_{1 \leq i \leq k} \frac{1}{r^i} \leq \beta(s) \leq \frac{1}{r^k}\beta(s_F) - (r-1)\alpha \sum_{1 \leq i \leq k} \frac{1}{r^i}.$$

It follows that if k is such that $r^k > \beta(s_F)$, then we have $-(r-1)\alpha' \leq \beta(s) \leq -(r-1)\alpha$. Thus during the construction of the automaton, the only non-initial states s that have to be considered are those belonging to the finite union of intervals

$$\bigcup_{0 \leq k \leq l} [\frac{1}{r^k}\beta(s_F) - (r-1)\alpha', \frac{1}{r^k}\beta(s_F) - (r-1)\alpha],$$

where $l = \log_r(\beta(s_F)) + 1$. The total number of states of the automaton is then bounded by $l(r-1)(\alpha' - \alpha) + 1$. If as described above, the construction is done simultaneously for a set $b_1, \ldots, b_k \in \mathbf{Z}$ of right-hand side values for the equation, the computation above should be reworked taking into account the maximum β_{max} and the minimum β_{min} of these values and the bound on the number of states of the automaton becomes $l(r-1)(\alpha' - \alpha) + (\beta_{max} - \beta_{min} + 1)$ with $l = \log_r(\max(|\beta_{min}|, |\beta_{max}|)) + 1$.

4.3 Recognizing Fractional Solutions

We now address the computation of a Büchi automaton $\mathcal{A}'_{\mathbf{a},b}$ that accepts all the infinite words $w \in \Sigma^\omega$ such that $\mathbf{0} \star w$ encodes a solution $\mathbf{x} \in [0,1]^n$ of the equation $\mathbf{a}.\mathbf{x} = b$.

The construction is similar to the one of Section 4.2, except that we are now dealing with the expansion of fractional numbers. All the states s of $\mathcal{A}'_{\mathbf{a},b}$ are in a one-to-one correspondence with an integer $\beta'(s)$, such that the vectors $\mathbf{x} \in \mathbf{Z}^n$ accepted by the infinite paths starting from s are exactly the solutions of the equation $\mathbf{a}.\mathbf{x} = \beta'(s)$. The initial state s_0 is the one such that $\beta'(s_0) = b$. All the states are accepting.

The transitions of $\mathcal{A}'_{\mathbf{a},b}$ are defined as follows. Consider moving from a state s to a state s' while reading a tuple $\mathbf{d} = (d_1, \ldots, d_n)$ of digits. This amounts to prefixing the tuple $\mathbf{d}$ to the word that will be read from s'. The value $\mathbf{x}$ of the word read from s is thus related to the value of the word read from s' by $\mathbf{x} = (1/r)(\mathbf{x}' + \mathbf{d})$. Therefore, for states s and s' to be linked by a transition labeled $\mathbf{d}$, the number $\beta'(s')$ associated with the state s' has to be given by

$$\beta'(s') = \mathbf{a}.\mathbf{x}' = r\mathbf{a}.\mathbf{x} - \mathbf{a}.\mathbf{d} = r\beta'(s) - \mathbf{a}.\mathbf{d}.$$

This expression allows one to compute the value of $\beta'(s')$ given $\beta'(s)$ and $\mathbf{d}$, i.e., to determine the outgoing transitions from the state s. Note that $\beta'(s')$ must belong to the interval $[\alpha, \alpha']$, where α and α' are as defined in Section 4.1, otherwise there would be no solution in $[0,1]^n$ to $\mathbf{a}.\mathbf{x}' = \beta'(s')$. If this requirement is not satisfied, then there is no outgoing transition from s labeled by $\mathbf{d}$.

The automaton $\mathcal{A}'_{\mathbf{a},b}$ can be constructed by starting from the state s such that $\beta'(s) = b$, and then repeatedly computing the outgoing transitions from the current states until stabilization occurs. Like in Section 4.2, the construction of k automata $\mathcal{A}'_{\mathbf{a},b_1}, \mathcal{A}'_{\mathbf{a},b_2}, \ldots, \mathcal{A}'_{\mathbf{a},b_k}$, with $b_1, \ldots, b_k \in \mathbf{Z}$ (for instance, as an application of the method presented in Section 4.1) can simply be done by starting from the set $\{s_1, \ldots, s_k\}$ such that $\beta'(s_i) = b_i$ for each $i \in \{1, \ldots, k\}$, rather than from a set containing a single state. The computation terminates, since for every state s, the integer $\beta'(s)$ belongs to the bounded interval $[\alpha, \alpha']$. The number of states of the resulting automaton is thus bounded by $\alpha' - \alpha + 1$.

4.4 Complexity

If the decomposition proposed in Section 4.1 and the algorithms presented in Sections 4.2 and 4.3 are used to build an RVA $\mathcal{A}$ representing the set of all the solutions of the equation $\mathbf{a}.\mathbf{x} = b$, with $n \geq 0$, $\mathbf{a} \in \mathbf{Z}^n$ and $b \in \mathbf{Z}$, then the number of states N_S of $\mathcal{A}$ is bounded by $l(r-1)(\alpha' - \alpha) + (\beta_{max} - \beta_{min} + 1) + \alpha' - \alpha + 1$, where α, α' and l are as defined in Sections 4.2 and 4.3, $\beta_{min} = b - \alpha'$, and $\beta_{max} = b - \alpha$. As a consequence, we have $N_S = 0(\sum_{1 \leq i \leq n} |a_i| \log_r |b|)$. The numbers of ingoing and of outgoing transitions of each state are bounded independently of $\mathbf{a}$ and of b by r^n. The total size of $\mathcal{A}$ is thus asymptotically linear in the magnitude of the multiplicative coefficients a_i of the equation, and logarithmic in the magnitude of the additive constant b. The cost of the construction is linear in the size of $\mathcal{A}$.

It is worth mentioning that the automaton $\mathcal{A}$ is deterministic and minimal. Indeed, by construction, any pair of transitions outgoing from the same state and labeled by the same tuple of digits lead to the same state. Moreover, the sets of words labeling the paths that are accepted from two distinct states s_1 and s_2 correspond to the sets of solutions of two equations $\mathbf{a}.\mathbf{x} = \beta_1$ and $\mathbf{a}.\mathbf{x} = \beta_2$ such that $\beta_1 \neq \beta_2$, and are thus different.

5 Representing Linear Inequations by Automata

The method presented in Section 4 can be easily adapted to linear inequations. The problem consists of computing an RVA representing the set of all the solutions $\mathbf{x} \in \mathbf{R}^n$ of an inequation of the form $\mathbf{a}.\mathbf{x} \leq b$, given $n \geq 0$, $\mathbf{a} \in \mathbf{Z}^n$ and $b \in \mathbf{Z}$.

The decomposition of the problem into the computation of representations of the sets of integer solutions and of solutions in $[0,1]^n$ of linear inequations is identical to the one proposed for equations in Section 4.1.

Given an inequation of the form $\mathbf{a}.\mathbf{x} \leq b$, where $\mathbf{a} \in \mathbf{Z}^n$ and $b \in \mathbf{Z}$, the definition of an automaton $\mathcal{A}_{\mathbf{a},b}$ that accepts all the finite words $w \in \Sigma^*$ such that $w \star \mathbf{0}^\omega$ encodes an integer solution of $\mathbf{a}.\mathbf{x} \leq b$ is very similar to the one given for equations in Section 4.2. The only difference with the case of equations, is that we do not discard the states s for which the computed $\beta(s)$ is not an integer or is not divisible by $\gcd(a_1, \ldots, a_n)$. Instead, we round the value of $\beta(s)$ to the nearest lower integer β'' that is divisible by $\gcd(a_1, \ldots, a_n)$. This operation is correct since the sets of integer solutions of $\mathbf{a}.\mathbf{x}' \leq \beta(s')$ and of $\mathbf{a}.\mathbf{x}' \leq \beta''$ are in this case identical.

The construction of an automaton $\mathcal{A}_{\mathbf{a},b}$ that accepts all the infinite words $w \in \Sigma^\omega$ such that $\mathbf{0} \star w$ encodes a solution of $\mathbf{a}.\mathbf{x} \leq b$ that belongs to $[0,1]^n$ is again very similar to the one developed for equations in Section 4.3. The difference with the case of equations, in that we do not discard here the states s' for which the computed $\beta'(s')$ is greater than α'. Instead, we simply replace the value of $\beta'(s')$ by α', since the sets of solutions in $[0,1]^n$ of $\mathbf{a}.\mathbf{x}' \leq \beta'(s')$ and of $\mathbf{a}.\mathbf{x}' \leq \alpha'$ are in this case identical. On the other hand, we still discard the states s' for which the computed $\beta'(s')$ is lower than α, since this implies that the inequation $\mathbf{a}.\mathbf{x}' \leq \beta'(s')$ has no solution in $[0,1]^n$.

The size of the resulting RVA and the cost of the construction are similar to those obtained for equations. However, in general, the constructed RVA is neither deterministic nor minimal in this case.

6 RVA Representing Arbitrary Formulas

RVA are not restricted to representing the set of solutions of linear equations and inequations. We have the following result [BBR97].

Theorem 3. *Let V_1, V_2 be sets of real vectors of respective arities (number of components per vector) n_1 and n_2, and A_1, A_2 be base-r RVA representing respectively V_1 and V_2. There exist algorithms for computing a base-r RVA representing:*

- *The union $V_1 \cup V_2$ and intersection $V_1 \cap V_2$, provided that $n_1 = n_2$;*
- *The complement $\overline{V_1}$;*
- *The Cartesian product $V_1 \times V_2 = \{(\mathbf{x}_1, \mathbf{x}_2) \mid \mathbf{x}_1 \in V_1 \wedge \mathbf{x}_2 \in V_2\}$;*
- *The projection $\exists x_i V_1 = \{(x_1, \ldots, x_{i-1}, x_{i+1}, \ldots, x_{n_1}) \mid (\exists x_i)(x_1, \ldots, x_{n_1}) \in V_1\}$;*
- *The reordering $\pi V_1 = \{(x_{\pi(1)}, \ldots, x_{\pi(n_1)}) \mid (x_1, \ldots, x_{n_1}) \in V_1\}$, where π is a permutation of $\{1, \ldots, n_1\}$.*

Furthermore, we can also prove the following.

Theorem 4. *Given a base $r > 1$, there exist RVA representing the sets $\{(x, u, k) \in \mathbf{R}^3 \mid X_r(x, u, k)\}$ as well as the sets $\mathbf{R}^n$ and $\mathbf{Z}^n$.*

Proof sketch The RVA accepting $\mathbf{R}^n$ and $\mathbf{Z}^n$ are immediate to construct. The one representing the set $\{(x, u, k) \in \mathbf{R}^3 \mid X_r(x, u, k)\}$, though simple in its principle is rather lengthy due to the necessity to deal with dual encodings. It will be given in the full paper. □

As a consequence of the results of Sections 4 and 5 as well as of Theorems 3 and 4, one can build for every formula ψ of $\langle \mathbf{R}, +, \leq, Z, X_r \rangle$ an RVA representing the set of real vectors that satisfies ψ. From this and the fact that RVA can be algorithmically tested for nonemptiness, we can establish the following results.

Theorem 5. *Let $n, r \in \mathbf{N}$ with $r > 1$. Every subset of $\mathbf{R}^n$ is r-recognizable if and only if it is r-definable.*

Theorem 6. *The first-order theory $\langle \mathbf{R}, +, \leq, Z, X_r \rangle$ is decidable.*

7 Conclusions

At first glance, studying the representation of sets of real vectors by Büchi automata might seem to be a rather odd idea. Indeed, real vectors are such a well studied subject that questioning the need for yet another representation is natural. However, the appeal of automata is their ability to deal easily with integers as well as reals, their simplicity and, foremost, the fact that they are a representation that is easily manipulated by algorithms, which for instance makes the existence of decision procedures almost obvious. The results of this paper show furthermore that the expressiveness of Büchi automata accepting the encodings of real vectors can be characterized quite naturally.

The procedures that were given for building automata corresponding to linear equations and inequations are not needed from a theoretical point of view (a direct expression of basic predicates would be sufficient), but show that the most commonly used description of sets of real vectors can be quite efficiently expressed by automata. This opens the path towards the actual use for practical purposes of this representation. From this point of view, a likely objection is that the size of the alphabet increases exponentially with the number of components of the vectors. However, this problem can be solved by sequentializing the reading of the digits of the vector components. That is, rather than reading a tuple of digits $\mathbf{d} = (d_1, \ldots, d_n)$ at each transition, one cycles through transitions reading in turn d_1, d_2, $\ldots d_n$, which is actually what would be done in a BDD.

References

[ACH+95] R. Alur, C. Courcoubetis, N. Halbwachs, T. A. Henzinger, P. H. Ho, X. Nicollin, A. Olivero, J. Sifakis, and S. Yovine. The algorithmic analysis of hybrid systems. *Theoretical Computer Science*, 138(1):3–34, 1995.

[AD94] R. Alur and D. L. Dill. A theory of timed automata. *Theoretical Computer Science*, 126(2):183–235, April 1994.

[BBR97] B. Boigelot, L. Bronne, and S. Rassart. An improved reachability analysis method for strongly linear hybrid systems. In *Proc. CAV'97*, volume 1254 of *Lecture Notes in Computer Science*, pages 167–177, Haifa, Israel, June 1997. Springer-Verlag.

[BC96] A. Boudet and H. Comon. Diophantine equations, Presburger arithmetic and finite automata. In *Proc. CAAP'96*, volume 1059 of *Lecture Notes in Computer Science*, pages 30–43. Springer-Verlag, 1996.

[BHMV94] V. Bruyère, G. Hansel, C. Michaux, and R. Villemaire. Logic and p-recognizable sets of integers. *Bulletin of the Belgian Mathematical Society*, 1(2):191–238, March 1994.

[Bry86] R. E. Bryant. Graph based algorithms for boolean function manipulation. *IEEE Transactions on Computers*, 35(8):677–691, 1986.

[Bry92] R. E. Bryant. Symbolic Boolean manipulation with ordered binary decision diagrams. *ACM Computing Surveys*, 24(3):293–318, September 1992.

[Büc60] J. R. Büchi. Weak second-order arithmetic and finite automata. *Zeitschrift Math. Logik und Grundlagen der Mathematik*, 6:66–92, 1960.

[Büc62] J. R. Büchi. On a decision method in restricted second order arithmetic. In *Proceedings of the International Congress on Logic, Method, and Philosophy of Science*, pages 1–12, Stanford, CA, USA, 1962. Stanford University Press.

[BW94] B. Boigelot and P. Wolper. Symbolic verification with periodic sets. In *Proc. CAV'94*, volume 818 of *Lecture Notes in Computer Science*, pages 55–67, Stanford, June 1994. Springer-Verlag.

[Cob69] A. Cobham. On the base-dependence of sets of numbers recognizable by finite automata. *Mathematical Systems Theory*, 3:186–192, 1969.

[Hen96] T. A. Henzinger. The theory of hybrid automata. In *Proc. LICS'96*, pages 278–292, New Brunswick, New Jersey, July 1996. IEEE Comp. Soc. Press.

[Sem77] A. L. Semenov. Presburgerness of predicates regular in two number systems. *Siberian Mathematical Journal*, 18:289–299, 1977.

[Vil92] R. Villemaire. The theory of $\langle \mathbf{N}, +, V_k, V_l \rangle$ is undecidable. *Theoretical Computer Science*, 106:337–349, 1992.

Distributed Matroid Basis Completion via Elimination Upcast and Distributed Correction of Minimum-Weight Spanning Trees
(Extended Abstract)

David Peleg[1] *

Department of Applied Mathematics and Computer Science, The Weizmann Institute, Rehovot 76100, Israel.

Abstract. This paper proposes a time-efficient distributed solution for the *matroid basis completion* problem. The solution is based on a technique called *elimination upcast*, enabling us to reduce the amount of work necessary for the upcast by relying on the special properties of matroids. As an application, it is shown that the algorithm can be used for correcting a minimum weight spanning tree computed for a D-diameter network, after k edges have changed their weight, in time $O(k + D)$.

1 Introduction

1.1 Motivation

The theory of matroids provides a general framework allowing us to handle a wide class of problems in a uniform way. One of the main attractive features of matroids is that their associated optimization problems are amenable to greedy solution. The greedy algorithm is simple and elegant, and its runtime is linear in the number of elements in the universe, which is perfectly acceptable in the sequential single-processor setting. In the parallel and distributed settings, however, one typically hopes for faster solutions. Unfortunately, direct implementations of the greedy algorithm are inherently sequential. Hence the problem of designing time-efficient distributed algorithms for handling matroid optimization problems (particularly, problems involving the computation of the minimum / maximum cost basis of a given matroid) may be of considerable interest.

This paper focuses on situations where a partial solution is already known, and it is only necessary to modify or complete it. In such cases, one may gain considerably from applying a *matroid basis completion* algorithm, rather than solving the entire optimization problem from scratch. Hence the paper considers time-efficient distributed solutions for the optimal matroid basis completion problem, and some of its applications. The problem is defined as follows. Given an independent but non-maximal set R in the universe, find a completion of R

* E-mail: peleg@wisdom.weizmann.ac.il. Supported in part by grants from the Israel Science Foundation and from the Israel Ministry of Science and Art.

into a maximum-weight basis assuming such completion exists. (Precise definitions are given in Sections 2.2 and 3.) In particular, applied with $R = \emptyset$, the problem reduces to the usual matroid optimization problem.

1.2 MST correction

The main application we present for matroid basis completion involves the problem of maintaining and correcting an MST in a distributed network. Maintenance of dynamic structures in a distributed network is a problem of considerable significance, and was handled in various contexts (cf, e.g., [1, 11, 12]). The specific problem of MST correction can be described as follows. Suppose that a minimum-weight spanning tree M has been computed for the (weighted) network G. Moreover, suppose that each node stores a description of the edge set of M (but not of the entire network G). At any time, certain edges of the tree M may significantly increase their weight, indicating the possibility that they should no longer belong to the MST, and certain other edges may reduce their weight, possibly enabling them to join the MST.

Suppose that a central vertex v_0 in the graph accumulates information about such deviant edges. This can be done over some shortest paths tree T spanning the network. At some point (say, after hearing about a set W_{bad} of $|W_{\text{bad}}| = k_{\text{bad}}$ edges of M whose weight has deteriorated and a set W_{good} of $|W_{\text{good}}| = k_{\text{good}}$ edges outside M whose weight has improved, where $k_{\text{bad}} + k_{\text{good}}$ or the accumulative change in weights exceeds some predetermined limit), v_0 may decide to initiate a recomputation of the MST. The question studied in this paper is whether such a recomputation can be performed in a cheaper way than computing an MST from scratch.

Let us observe the following facts concerning the problem. First, note that as collecting the information at v_0 takes $\Omega(k_{\text{bad}} + k_{\text{good}} + Diam(G))$ time, we may as well distribute the information throughout the entire network, at the same (asymptotic) time, by broadcasting it on the tree T in a pipelined fashion.

Secondly, note that the two problems of taking W_{bad} and W_{good} into account can be dealt with separately, one after the other. In particular, suppose first that $W_{\text{good}} = \emptyset$. In this case, we only need to find a way to discard those edges of W_{bad} that should no longer be in M, and replace them by other edges. Similarly, supposing $W_{\text{bad}} = \emptyset$, we only need to find a way to add those edges of W_{good} that should be in M, and throw away some other edges currently in M. Now, assuming we have two separate procedures for handling these separate problems, applying them one after the other to the general case would result in a correct MST.

Our next observation is that, as every vertex stores a description of the entire tree M, checking the possibility of incorporating the edges of W_{good} can be done locally at each vertex (ignoring the set W_{bad} or assuming it is empty). Hence the second of our two problems is easy, and can be solved in time $\Omega(k_{\text{good}} + Diam(G))$. However, solving our first problem is not as straightforward, as possible modifications involving the elimination of some of the edges of W_{bad} from the tree M may require some knowledge about all other edges currently not in M, and this knowledge is not available at all vertices.

Two natural approaches are the following. First, it is possible to keep at each vertex the entire topology of the graph. The disadvantage of this solution is that it involves large ($\Omega(|E|)$) amounts of storage, and therefore may be unacceptable in certain cases.

A second approach is to employ the well-known GHS algorithm for distributed MST computation [4], but invoke it only from the current stage. Specifically, once v_0 has broadcasted the set W_{bad} throughout the graph, every vertex in G can (tentatively) throw these edges from M, and remain with a partition of M into a spanning forest $\mathcal{F}$ composed of $k \leq k_{\text{bad}} + 1$ connected subtrees (or "fragments" in the terminology of [4]), $M_1, \ldots, M_k$. A standard rule can be agreed upon (say, based on vertex ID's) for selecting a responsible vertex in each of these fragments. These vertices can now initiate an execution of the GHS algorithm, starting from the current fragments. The disadvantage of this solution is that the last few phases of the GHS algorithm are often the most expensive ones. In particular, it may be the case that some of the fragments M_i have large depth (even if G has low diameter), thus causing the fragment-internal communication steps to be time consuming. As a result, the correction process may take $\Omega(n)$ time.

The approach proposed in this paper is the following. We first discard the edges of W_{bad} from M, remaining with the forest $\mathcal{F}$. We now view the problem as a matroid basis completion problem, and look for a completion of M into a full spanning tree. Our approach yields an $O(k + Diam(G))$ time MST correction algorithm.

1.3 Model

The network is modeled as an undirected unweighted graph $G = (V, E)$, where V is the set of nodes, and E is the set of communication links between them. The nodes can communicate only by sending and receiving messages over the communication links connecting them.

In this paper we concentrate on time complexity, and ignore the communication cost of our algorithms (i.e., the number of messages they use). Nevertheless, we still need to correctly reflect the influence of message size. Clearly, if messages of arbitrary unbounded size are allowed to be transmitted in a single time unit, then any computable problem can be trivially solved in time proportional to the network diameter, no matter how many information items need to be collected. We therefore adopt the more realistic (and more common) model in which a single message can carry only a limited amount of information (i.e., its size is bounded), and a node may send at most one message over each edge at each time unit.

For simplicity of presentation, it is assumed that the network is synchronous, and all nodes wake up simultaneously at time 0. Let us note, however, that all the results hold (with little or no change) also for the fully asynchronous model (without simultaneous wake up).

It is also assumed that we are provided with a shortest paths spanning tree, denoted T, rooted at v_0. Otherwise, it is possible to construct such a tree in time $Diam(G)$.

1.4 Contribution

The main result of this paper is a time-efficient distributed solution for the optimal matroid basis completion problem. Specifically, in a tree T of depth D, given a partial basis R of size r in a matroid of rank t over an m-element universe, the optimal basis completion problem is solved in time $O(D + t - r)$. (Hence in particular, a matroid optimization problem of rank t over an m-element universe is solved from scratch in time $O(D + t)$, as opposed to the $O(D + m)$ time complexity achieved, say, by a naive use of upcast.)

Let us briefly explain the basic components of our solution. The reason why the greedy algorithm is inherently sequential is that it is global in nature, and has to look at all the edges. This difficulty can be bypassed by using a dual approach for matroid problems, which is more localized. The idea is to work top-down rather than bottom-up, i.e., instead of building the basis by gradually *adding* elements to it, one may gradually *eliminate* some elements from consideration. This is known in the context of MST construction as the "red rule" (cf. [17]).

One source of difficulty encountered when working with the basis completion problem, rather than solving the matroid optimization problem from scratch, is that the usual version of the red rule is not applicable. Consequently, the first component in our solution is a generalized form of the red rule, applicable to basis completion problems.

It should be clear that if restricted to sequential computation, the use of the dual algorithm based on the red rule would still yield linear complexity, despite its more local behaviour. Consequently, the second component of our algorithm is geared at exploiting the generalized red rule in a distributed fashion, in order to enable us to reduce the time complexity of the algorithm in the distributed setting, relying on the special properties of matroids. This is done via a technique called *elimination upcast*. This technique in fact implements a combination of the two dual approaches discussed above. Its main operation is a greedy upcasting process on a tree, collecting the best elements to the root. This operation is sped up by accompanying it with the complementary operation of eliminating elements known for certain to be out of the optimal solution. This elimination process is carried out locally at the various nodes, relying on the generalized red rule.

The elimination upcast technique is a variant of the procedure used in [5, 10] as a component in a fast distributed algorithm for computing a minimum-weight spanning tree (MST), but it applies to a wider class of problems (namely, all matroid optimization problems), and it deals with the more general setting of basis completion. Moreover, its correctness proof and analysis are (perhaps surprisingly) somewhat simpler.

For the MST correction problem, our matroid basis completion algorithm enables us to perform the second phase of the solution, replacing the edges of

W_{bad}, in time $\Omega(k_{\mathrm{bad}} + Diam(G))$. The result is an MST correction algorithm solving the entire problem in time $\Omega(k_{\mathrm{bad}} + k_{\mathrm{good}} + Diam(G))$.

2 Basics

2.1 Upcasts

This section reviews known or straightforward background concerning upcasts on a tree T rooted at v_0. Let $Depth(T)$ denote T's depth, i.e., the maximum distance from v_0 to any vertex of T. Define the *level* of a vertex v in T as the depth of the subtree T_v rooted at v, denoted by $\hat{L}(v) = Depth(T_v)$. More explicitly, $\hat{L}(v)$ is defined as follows:

$$\hat{L}(v) = \begin{cases} 0 & \text{if } v \text{ is a leaf;} \\ 1 + \max_{u \in child(v)}(\hat{L}(u)) & \text{otherwise.} \end{cases}$$

Suppose that m data items $\mathcal{A} = \{\alpha_1, \ldots, \alpha_m\}$ are initially stored at some of the vertices of the tree T. Items can be replicated, namely, each item is stored in one or more vertices (and each vertex may store zero or more items). The goal is to end up with all the items stored at the root of the tree. We refer to this operation as *upcast*. (Note, that this task is not really a "convergecast" process, since the items are sent up to the root individually, and are "combined" only in the sense that a vertex sends only a single copy of a replicated item.)

It is easy to verify that upcasting m distinct messages on the tree T requires $\Omega(\max\{m, Depth(T)\})$ time in the worst case. It turns out that a simple algorithm guarantees this optimal bound on the upcast operation. For every v, let M_v denote the set of items initially stored at some verex of T_v. The only rule that each vertex has to follow is to upcast to its parent in each round *some* item in its possession that has not been upcast in previous rounds. One can show that for every $1 \leq i \leq |M_v|$, at the end of round $\hat{L}(v) + i - 1$, at least i items are stored at v. Hence at the end of round $Depth(T) + m$, all the items are stored at the root of the tree.

Let us remark that similar results hold also in much more general settings, without the tree structure. In particular, the bounds hold even when the m messages are sent from different senders to different (possibly overlapping) recipients along arbitrary shortest paths, under a wide class of conflict resolution policies (for resolving collisions in intermediate vertices between messages competing over the use of an outgoing edge), so long as these policies are consistent (namely, if item α_i is preferred over item α_j at some vertex v along their paths, then the same preference will be made whenever their paths intersect again in the future). This was first shown in [2, 16] for two specific policies, and later extended to any consistent greedy policy in [14].

2.2 Matroid problems and greedy algorithms

Let us continue with a brief presentation of matroid problems. (See [15] for more on the subject.) A *subset system* is specified as a pair $\Phi = \langle \mathcal{A}, \mathcal{S} \rangle$, where $\mathcal{A}$ is a universe of m elements, and $\mathcal{S}$ is a collection of subsets of $\mathcal{A}$, closed under inclusion (namely, if $A \in \mathcal{S}$ and $B \subseteq A$ then also $B \in \mathcal{S}$). The sets in $\mathcal{S}$ are called the *independent sets* of the system. A maximal independent set is called a *basis*. The optimization problem associated with the system Φ is the following: given a weight function ω assigning nonnegative weights to the elements of $\mathcal{A}$, find the basis of maximum total weight. This problem may be intractable in general.

A natural approach for solving the optimization problem associated with Φ is to employ a greedy approach. Two types of greedy approaches may be considered. The *best-in* greedy algorithm is based on starting with the empty set and adding at each step the heaviest element that still maintains the independence of the set. Its dual, the *worst-out* greedy algorithm, starts with the entire universe, and discards at each step the lightest element whose removal still leaves us with a set containing some basis of Φ. Unfortunately, these algorithms do not necessarily yield an optimal solution.

A subset system Φ is said to be a *matroid* if it satisfies the following property.

Replacement property: If $A, B \in \mathcal{S}$ and $|B| = |A| + 1$, then there exists some element $\alpha \in B \setminus A$ such that $A \cup \{\alpha\} \in \mathcal{S}$[2].

One of the most well-known examples for matroids is the *minimum weight spanning tree (MST)* problem, where the universe is the edge set of a graph, the independent sets are cycle-free subsets of edges, and the bases are the spanning trees of the graph. (The goal here is typically to find the spanning tree of *minimum* weight, rather than maximum weight, but this can still be formalized as a matroid optimization problem.) Another fundamental example is that of vector spaces, where the universe is the collection of vectors in d-dimensional space, and the notions of dependence in set of vectors and bases are defined in the usual algebraic sense. The common representation of matroids is based not on explicit enumeration of the independent sets, but on a *rule*, or procedure, deciding for every given subset of $\mathcal{A}$ whether or not it is independent.

One important property of matroids is that both the best-in greedy algorithm and the worst-out greedy algorithm correctly solve every instance of the optimization problem associated with Φ. (In fact, these properties hold for a somewhat wider class of problems, named *greedoids*, which were thoroughly treated in [6, 7, 9, 8].)

Here is another well-known property of matroids that we will use later on.

Proposition 1. *All bases of a given matroid Φ are of the same cardinality, denoted rank(Φ).*

One source of difficulty in trying to adapt the greedy algorithms for solving matroid problems fast in a distributed fashion is that both algorithms are inher-

---

[2] There are in fact a number of other equivalent definitions for matroids, [15].

ently "global" and sequential. First, they require going over the elements in order of weight, and secondly, they require us to be able to decide, for each element, whether after eliminating it we still have a basis (namely, an independent set of cardinality $rank(\Phi)$) in our set of remaining elements. It is therefore useful to have a variant of the greedy algorithm which is more localized in nature. Such a variant was given for the MST problem [17]. This algorithm makes use of the so-called *red rule*, which is based on the following fact.

Lemma 2. [17] *Consider an instance of the MST problem on a graph $G = (V, E, \omega)$, with a solution of (minimum) weight ω^*. Consider a spanning subgraph G' of G (with all the vertices and some of the edges), and suppose that G' still contains a spanning tree of weight ω^*. Let C be a cycle in G', and let e be the heaviest edge in C. Then $G' \setminus \{e\}$ still contains a spanning tree of weight ω^*.* ▮

The lemma leads to a localized version of the worst-out greedy algorithm, avoiding both difficulties discussed above. This localized algorithm starts with the entire graph G, and repeatedly applies the *red rule* (stated next), until remaining with a spanning tree.

The "red rule": Pick an *arbitrary* cycle in the remaining graph, and erase the heaviest edge in that cycle.

Lemma 2 guarantees that once the process halts, the resulting tree is an MST of the graph G. Indeed, this localized greedy algorithm was previously used as a component in a fast distributed algorithm for computing MST [5, 10].

The proof of Lemma 2 relies on some specific properties of the MST problem, and therefore it is not immediately clear that a similar general rule applies to every matroid problem. Nonetheless, it turns out that a rule of this nature exists for all matroids (cf. [13]).

2.3 Matroid problems in distributed systems

Let us illustrate the relevance of matroid problems in distributed systems via two examples.

Distributed resource allocation: Suppose that our distributed system features t types of resources, with a set $\mathcal{R}_i$ of r_i resource units of each type i. At any given moment, some of the units are occupied and only $m_i \le r_i$ are readily available. There is also a cost $c(u)$ associated with each resource unit u. At a given moment, a process residing in node v decides to perform some task which requires it to get hold of some k_i resource units of each type $1 \le i \le t$ (where possibly $k_i \ll m_i$). Naturally, the process would prefer to identify the k_i cheapest free units of each type i. Assume that there is a spanning tree T (rooted at v, for the sake of this example), so v can broadcast its needs to all nodes over T. We would now like to collect the necessary information (namely, the ID's of the k_i cheapest available resource units of each type i) from all nodes to v. Note that the necessary information (concerning the free units of each type and their costs) is scattered over the different nodes of the system, and is not readily available in one place. Hence a naive solution based on collecting all the information to v over the tree T might cost $O(\sum_i m_i + Depth(T))$ time.

This problem can be solved by casting it as a simple kind of matroid problem, where the independence of any particular set in the universe is determined solely by counting the number of elements of each type. The methods developed in this paper for handling matroid problems are thus applicable, and yield a solution of optimal time $O(\sum_i k_i + Depth(T))$. We note that in this particular case, the problem can also be optimally solved directly, through a technique based on a careful pipelining of the separate upcast tasks involved. However, things become more involved once certain inter-dependencies and constraints are imposed among different types of resources (for example, suppose that the cheapest available processor is incompatible with the cheapest available disk, so they cannot be used together.) In such a case, it is not possible to neatly separate and pipeline the treatment of the different resource types. Yet in some cases, these more intricate dependencies can still be formulated as matroids, and hence are still solvable by our algorithm. □

Task scheduling: Our next example concerns optimally scheduling unit-time tasks on a single processor. Suppose that the sites of our system generate a (distributed) collection S of m tasks $1 \leq i \leq m$, all of which must be executed on the same processor in the system, with each requiring exactly one time unit to execute. The specification of task i includes a *deadline* d_i by which it is supposed to finish, and a *penalty* p_i incurred if task i is not finished by time d_i. The goal is to find a schedule for the collection S on the processor, minimizing the total penalty incurred by the tasks for missed deadlines. In particular, we would like to decide on a maximal set of $k \leq m$ tasks that can be scheduled without violating their deadlines. Collecting all the information to the root of the tree T spanning the system and computing the schedule centrally may require $O(m + Depth(T))$ time.

This problem is discussed in a number of places (cf. [13, 3]), and again, it is known that it can be formulated as a matroid problem. Hence our methods can be applied, yielding an $O(k + Depth(T))$ time solution. □

3 Optimal matroid basis completion

We now consider the following slightly more general problem. Consider an instance ω of the optimization problem associated with the matroid $\Phi = \langle \mathcal{A}, \mathcal{S} \rangle$, with a solution of (maximum) weight ω^*, and two disjoint sets $A, R \subseteq \mathcal{A}$, where R is a non-maximal independent set. A *completion* for R in A is a set $W \subseteq A$ such that $R \cup W$ is a basis. W is said to be an *optimal completion* if $\omega(R \cup W) = \omega^*$. The problem is to find an optimal completion for R in A, assuming such a completion exists. (Note that in particular, if $R = \emptyset$ then the problem reduces to the basic question of finding an optimal basis.) This is again doable in a localized manner by a generalized variant of the red rule.

We need the following definition. Consider an instance ω of the optimization problem associated with the matroid $\Phi = \langle \mathcal{A}, \mathcal{S} \rangle$, with a solution of (maximum) weight ω^*. Consider two disjoint sets $A, R \subseteq \mathcal{A}$, where R is a non-maximal independent set. Suppose that A contains an optimal completion for R. Let $\varepsilon \in A$ and $D \subseteq A \setminus \{\varepsilon\}$. Then the pair (ε, D) is called an *elimination pair* for R if it satisfies the following:
(1) $R \cup D$ is independent,
(2) $R \cup D \cup \{\varepsilon\}$ is dependent, and
(3) ε is no heavier than any element in D.

Lemma 3. *For an instance ω, Φ and disjoint sets A, R as above, if (ε, D) is an elimination pair for R then $A \setminus \{\varepsilon\}$ still contains an optimal completion for R.*

We thus get a modified greedy algorithm, based on the following rule.

The "generalized red rule": Pick an element ε in the remaining set A for which there exists a set $D \subseteq A \setminus \{\varepsilon\}$ such that (ε, D) is an elimination pair, and erase ε from A.

Of course, the rule in itself does not specify how such ε can be found systematically; our distributed algorithm addresses precisely this point.

4 A distributed algorithm for optimal matroid basis completion

We now describe a distributed algorithm for solving the optimal matroid basis completion problem on a tree T. In the distributed setting, it is assumed that the elements of the (non-maximal) independent set R are known to all the vertices of the system (connected by a tree T), and that each of the elements of the set $\mathcal{A}$ is stored at some vertex of T. (We make no a-priori assumptions on the precise distribution of the elements.) An element can be sent in a single message.

Recall that $m = |\mathcal{A}|$ and $r = |R|$. Denote the number of elements missing from R by $\pi = rank(\Phi) - r$. In order to solve the problem, we require that the elements of the maximum-weight independent set be gathered at the root of the tree T. (The π completion elements added to R can then be broadcast by the root over the tree T in a pipelined manner in $O(\pi + Depth(T))$ additional steps.)

A straightforward approach to solving this problem would be to upcast all the elements of $\mathcal{A}$ to the root, and solve the problem locally using one of the greedy algorithms. However, this solution would require $O(m - r + Depth(T))$ time for completing the upcast stage. Our aim in this section is to derive an algorithm requiring only $O(\pi + Depth(T))$ time. The algorithm uses elimination upcast,

4.1 The Elimination Upcast Algorithm

The algorithm presented next for the problem is a distributed implementation of the localized greedy algorithm for matroid basis completion. It is based on upcasting the elements toward the root in a careful way, attempting to eliminate as many elements as we can along the way, relying on the generalized red rule.

Our elimination upcast procedure operates as follows. During the run, each vertex v on T maintains a set Q_v of all the elements of $\mathcal{A}$ it knows of, including both those stored in it originally and those it learns of from its children, but not including the elements of R, which are kept separately. The elements of Q_v are ordered by non-increasing weight. The vertex v also maintains a set A_v of all the elements it has already upcast to its parent. Initially $A_v = \emptyset$.

A leaf v starts upcasting elements at pulse 0. An intermediate vertex v starts upcasting at the first pulse after it has heard from all its children. At each pulse i, v computes the set

$$Dep_v \leftarrow \{\alpha \in Q_v \setminus A_v \mid R \cup A_v \cup \{\alpha\} \text{ is dependent}\}$$

and the set of candidates

$$C_v \leftarrow Q_v \setminus (A_v \cup Dep_v).$$

If $C_v \neq \emptyset$ then v upcasts to its parent the heaviest element α in C_v. Else, it stops participating in the execution. Finally, once the root r_0 stops hearing from its children, it locally computes the solution to the problem, based on the elements in $R \cup Q_{r_0}$.

4.2 Analysis

The correctness proof proceeds by showing that the elements upcast by each vertex v to its parent are in nonincreasing weight order, and that v upcasts elements continuously, until it exhausts all the elements from its subtree. It follows that once $C_v = \emptyset$, v will learn of no new elements to report.

We use the following straightforward observations.

Lemma 4. *(1) For every vertex v, $R \cup A_v$ is independent.*
(2) Every vertex v starts upcasting at pulse $\hat{L}(v)$. ∎

Call a node *t-active* if it upcasts an element to its parent on round $t-1$.

Lemma 5. *(a) For each t-active child u of v, the set C_v examined by v at the beginning of round t contains at least one element upcast by u.*
(b) If v upcasts to its parent an element of weight ω_0 at round t, then all the elements v was informed of at round $t-1$ by its t-active children were of weight ω_0 or smaller.
(c) If v upcasts to its parent an element of weight ω_0 at round t, then any later element it will learn of is of weight ω_0 or smaller.
(d) Node v upcasts elements to its parent in nonincreasing weight order.

Lemma 6. *A vertex v that has stopped participating will learn of no new candidate elements.*

Lemma 7. *The algorithm requires $O(\pi + Depth(T))$, and the resulting set is a solution for the optimal basis completion problem.*

Theorem 8. *(1) There exists a distributed algorithm for computing the optimal completion for a partial basis of cardinality r on a tree T in time $O(\text{rank}(\Phi) - r + Depth(T))$.*
(2) There exists a distributed algorithm for solving a matroid optimization problem on a tree T in time $O(\text{rank}(\Phi) + Depth(T))$.

4.3 Distributed MST correction

Let us now explain how our algorithm enables us to correct an MST fast in the distributed setting. Suppose that we start with a weighted graph $G = (V, E, \omega)$ and a spanning BFS tree T. As discussed earlier, the subproblem of taking into account the edges in W_{good} is easily solved in time $\Omega(k_{\text{good}} + Diam(G))$. The other subproblem, of taking into account the edges in W_{bad}, can now be solved by first removing those edges from the MST M, resulting in a partial edge set M', and then completing M' into a minimum weight spanning tree using the elimination upcast algorithm.

Observe that the assumptions necessary for the elimination upcast procedure are satisfied in our case, namely, each node stores the entire current MST and every edge e is stored at some node (in the obvious way, namely, each node knows the edges incident to itself.) As mentioned earlier, despite the fact that we seek the minimum-weight solution rather than the maximum-weight one, this problem is still a matroid optimization problem, so the same algorithm applies (flipping the ordering in the procedure, or redefining the edge weights by setting $\omega'(e) = W - \omega(e)$, where $W = \max_e \omega(e)$).

Hence by Corollary 8, this part can be solved in time $\Omega(k_{\text{bad}} + Diam(G))$, and thus the entire problem is solvable in time $\Omega(k_{\text{bad}} + k_{\text{good}} + Diam(G))$.

Acknowledgement

I am grateful to Guy Kortsarz for helpful comments.

References

1. Baruch Awerbuch, Israel Cidon, and Shay Kutten. Communication-optimal maintenance of dynamic trees. Unpublished manuscript, September 1988.
2. Israel Cidon, Shay Kutten, Yishay Mansour, and David Peleg. Greedy packet scheduling. In *Proc. 4th Workshop on Distributed Algorithms*, pages 169–184, 1990. LNCS Vol. 486, Springer Verlag.
3. T.H. Cormen, C.E. Leiserson, and R.L. Rivest. *Introduction to Algorithms*. MIT Press/McGraw-Hill, 1990.
4. Robert G. Gallager, Pierre A. Humblet, and P. M. Spira. A distributed algorithm for minimum-weight spanning trees. *ACM Trans. on Programming Lang. and Syst.*, 5(1):66–77, January 1983.

5. J. Garay, S. Kutten, and D. Peleg. A sub-linear time distributed algorithm for minimum-weight spanning trees. *SIAM J. on Computing*, 1998. To appear. Extended abstract appeared in *34th IEEE Symp. on Foundations of Computer Science*, pages 659–668, November 1993.
6. B. Korte and L. Lovász. Mathematical structures undelying greedy algorithms. *in: Fundamentals of Computation Theory, Lecture Notes in Computer Science*, 117:205–209, 1981.
7. B. Korte and L. Lovász. Structural properties of greedoids. *Combinatorica*, 3:359–374, 1983.
8. B. Korte and L. Lovász. Greedoids-a structural framework for the greedy algorithms. *in: W. Pulleybank editor, Progress in Combinatorial Optimization*, pages 221–243, 1984.
9. B. Korte and L. Lovász. Greedoids and linear objective functions. *SIAM J. Alg. and Disc. Meth.*, 5:229–238, 1984.
10. Shay Kutten and David Peleg. Fast distributed construction of k-dominating sets and applications. In *Proc. 14th ACM Symp. on Principles of Distributed Computing*, 1995.
11. Shay Kutten and David Peleg. Fault-local distributed mending. In *Proc. 14th ACM Symp. on Principles of Distributed Computing*, August 1995.
12. Shay Kutten and David Peleg. Tight fault-locality. In *Proc. 36th IEEE Symp. on Foundations of Computer Science*, October 1995.
13. E.L. Lawler. *Combinatorial Optimization: Networks and Matroids*. Holt, Rinehart and Winston, 1976.
14. Y. Mansour and B. Patt-Shamir. Greedy packet scheduling on shortest paths. In *Proc. 10th ACM Symp. on Principles of Distributed Computing*, August 1991.
15. C.H. Papadimitriou and K. Steiglitz. *Combinatorial Optimization: Algorithms and Complexity*. Prentice-Hall, Inc., 1982.
16. P. I. Rivera-Vega, R. Varadarajan, and S. B. Navathe. The file redistribution scheduling problem. In *Data Eng. Conf.*, pages 166–173, 1990.
17. Robert E. Tarjan. *Data Structures and Network Algorithms*. SIAM, Philadelphia, 1983.

Independent Sets with Domination Constraints

Magnús M. Halldórsson[1,3], Jan Kratochvíl[2,*], and Jan Arne Telle[3]

[1] University of Iceland, Reykjavik, Iceland. mmh@hi.is
[2] Charles University, Prague, Czech Republic. honza@kam.ms.mff.cuni.cz
[3] University of Bergen, Bergen, Norway. telle@ii.uib.no

Abstract. A ρ-independent set S in a graph is parameterized by a set ρ of non-negative integers that constrains how the independent set S can dominate the remaining vertices ($\forall v \notin S : |N(v) \cap S| \in \rho$.) For all values of ρ, we classify as either $\mathcal{NP}$-complete or polynomial-time solvable the problems of deciding if a given graph has a ρ-independent set. We complement this with approximation algorithms and inapproximability results, for all the corresponding optimization problems.
These approximation results extend also to several related independence problems. In particular, we obtain a $\sqrt{m}$ approximation of the Set Packing problem, where m is the number of base elements, as well as a $\sqrt{n}$ approximation of the maximum independent set in power graphs G^t, for t even.

1 Introduction

A large class of well-studied domination and independence properties in graphs can be characterized by two sets of nonnegative integers σ and ρ. A (σ, ρ)-set S in a graph has the property that the number of neighbors every vertex $u \in S$ (or $u \notin S$) has in S, is an element of σ (of ρ, respectively) [9]. This characterization facilitates the common algorithmic treatment of problems defined over sets with such properties. Previous papers on classification of the complexity of problems from an infinite class include [5, 8]. Unfortunately, the investigations of uniform complexity classification for subclasses of (σ, ρ)-problems have so far been incomplete [7, 10]. In this paper we give a complete complexity classification of the cases where $\sigma = \{0\}$, which constitute maybe the most important subclass of (σ, ρ)-problems.

In this class of problems the chosen vertices are pairwise non-adjacent, forming an independent set. Independent (stable) sets in graphs are a fundamental topic with applications wherever we seek a set of mutually compatible elements. It is therefore natural to study the solvability of finding independent sets with particular properties, as in this case, where the independent set is constrained in its domination properties.

Assume that we have an oracle for deciding membership in $\rho \subset \mathbb{N} = \{0, 1, ...\}$. Let $N(v)$ denote the set of neighbors of a vertex v. Consider the following decision problem:

* Research support in part by Czech research grants GAUK 194 and GAČR 0194/1996.

ρ-IS Problem
Given: A graph G
Question: Does G have an independent set of vertices $S \neq \emptyset$ with $|S| \geq \min\{k : k \notin \rho\}$ such that $\forall v \notin S : |N(v) \cap S| \in \rho$?

When ρ is the set of all positive integers the ρ-IS problem is asking for an independent dominating set, a problem which is easy since any maximal independent set is also a dominating set. When $\rho = \{1\}$ the ρ-IS problem is asking for the existence of a perfect code, a problem which is $\mathcal{NP}$-complete even for planar 3-regular graphs [6] and for chordal graphs [7]. The natural question becomes: For what values of ρ is the ρ-IS problem solvable in polynomial time? In the next section we resolve this question for all cases, up to $\mathcal{P}$ vs. $\mathcal{NP}$.

Theorem 1 *The ρ-IS problem is $\mathcal{NP}$-complete if there is a positive integer $k \notin \rho$ with $k+1 \in \rho$, and otherwise it is solvable in polynomial time.*

Approximation algorithms Even for the cases when the decision problem is solvable in polynomial time, the corresponding optimization problem, finding a minimum or maximum size ρ-IS, is hard. In Section 3 we give on the one hand approximation algorithms for these optimization problems, and on the other hand strong inapproximability results.

The class of problems that we can approximate is that of finding an independent set where vertices outside the set are adjacent to at most a given number k vertices inside. We obtain performance ratios of $O(\sqrt{n})$ for the maximization versions of these problems. This is significantly better than what is known for the ordinary Independent Set problem, where the best performance ratio known is $O(n/\log^2 n)$ [1], a mere $\log^2 n$ factor from trivial. In fact, it is known that obtaining a performance ratio that is any fixed root of n factor better than trivial is highly unlikely [4].

We find that the same algorithmic technique extends to a number of related independence problems, for which no non-trivial bounds had been given before. Given a base set with m elements and a collection of n subsets of the base set, the Set Packing problem is to find the largest number of disjoint sets from the collection. There is a standard reduction from Independent Set to Set Packing [2] where the number of sets n equals the number of vertices of the graph and the number of base elements m equals the number of edges of the graph. Thus, the hardness results of [4] translates to a $n^{1-\epsilon}$ lower bound for Set Packing, as a function of n, but only a $m^{1/2-\epsilon}$ lower bound in terms of m. The only previous upper bound in terms of m (to our best of knowledge) was the trivial bound m. This left a considerable gap in our understanding of the approximability of the problem, e.g. when m is linear in n.

We resolve this issue by showing that a simple and practical greedy algorithm yields a performance ratio of $\sqrt{m}$. It also yields an $O(\sqrt{m})$ performance ratio for the Maximum k-Matching of a set system (see definition in Section 3), and a $\sqrt{n}$ ratio for the maximum collection of vertices of a graph of mutual distance at least t, for odd t. In all of these cases, the bounds are essentially best possible.

2 Decision Problems

In this section we prove Theorem 1. The polynomial cases are summarized in the following result:

Lemma 2. *The ρ-IS problem is solvable in polynomial time if $\rho = \emptyset$, $\rho = \mathbb{N}^+$ or $\rho = \{0, 1, ..., k\}$ for some $k \in \mathbb{N}$.*

Proof. The cases $\rho = \emptyset$ and $\rho = \mathbb{N}^+$ are trivial. When $\rho = \{0, 1, ..., k\}$ for some $k \in \mathbb{N}$, we are asking if the input graph G has an independent set S of at least $k+1$ vertices such that every vertex not in S has at most k neighbors in S. The algorithm simply tries all subsets S of size $k+1$, and if none of them satisfy the conditions the answer is negative. ∎

We remark that when restricted to chordal graphs the ρ-IS problem is solvable in polynomial time whenever $\min\{k : k \in \rho\} \geq 2$ [7]. We turn to the $\mathcal{NP}$-complete cases, and first state two earlier results. When $\rho = \{1\}$, a ρ-IS set is also known as a perfect code.

Theorem 3 *[6] Deciding if a 3-regular graph has a perfect code is $\mathcal{NP}$-complete.*

Theorem 4 *[10] The ρ-IS problem is $\mathcal{NP}$-complete whenever ρ is a finite non-empty subset of positive integers or when $\rho = \{k, k+1, ...\}$ for some $k \geq 2$.*

Our first result, whose proof is omitted from this extended abstract, is an $\mathcal{NP}$-completeness reduction from the above problem.

Lemma 5. *The $\{0, k+1, k+2, \ldots\}$-IS problem is $\mathcal{NP}$-complete for $k \geq 1$.*

Let EVEN be the set of all even and ODD be the set of all odd non-negative integers. As is often the case with parity problems, e.g. Chromatic Index of 3-regular graphs, the cases of EVEN-IS and ODD-IS require a special reduction for their $\mathcal{NP}$-completeness. These reductions, from the problem EXACT 3-COVER [2], are again left out of this extended abstract.

Lemma 6. *The EVEN-IS and ODD-IS problems are $\mathcal{NP}$-complete.*

We now prove the remaining cases, completing the proof of Theorem 1

Lemma 7. *The ρ-IS problem is $\mathcal{NP}$-complete if there is a positive integer $k \notin \rho$ with $k+1 \in \rho$.*

Proof. Let $t = \min\{x : (x \geq 1) \wedge (x \in \rho) \wedge (x+1 \notin \rho)\}$. If such t does not exist then either $\rho = \{k+1, k+2, ...\}$ and ρ-IS problem is $\mathcal{NP}$-complete by Theorem 4, or $\rho = \{0, k+1, k+2, ...\}$ and is $\mathcal{NP}$-complete by Lemma 5. Let $z = \min\{x : (x > t) \wedge (x \notin \rho) \wedge (x+1 \in \rho)\}$. If such z does not exist then $\rho = \{1, 2, ..., k\}$ and is $\mathcal{NP}$-complete by Theorem 4.

For any 3-regular graph G we construct a graph G' which has a ρ-IS if and only if G has a perfect code. We shall be assuming that G is sufficiently large, e.g. contain at least z^2 vertices.

Let $V(G) = \{v_1, ..., v_n\}$. The derived graph G' will consist of $z+1$ copies $G^1, ..., G^{z+1}$ of G, with vertices $V(G^k) = \{v_1^k, ..., v_n^k\}$, along with a large collection of nodes connected into a clique. For each edge $v_iv_j \in E(G)$ add edges $v_i^k v_j^{k'}$ for $1 \le k, k' \le z+1$. This ensures that for any independent set S in G', its projection S_G ($u_i \in S_G$ iff $\exists k : u_i^k \in S$) onto G is also an independent set.

A *claw* is a set of four vertices, consisting of a *center* vertex v_i^k and its three neighbors in a particular copy of G. Thus, G' contains $n(z+1)$ claws. Note that an independent set contains at most three vertices of a claw, and if the center vertex is in the independent set then the other three are not. Our construction will ensure that for any ρ-IS S of G', each claw contains exactly one vertex of S. This will imply that for each $v_i \in V(G)$, either all copies of v_i or no copies of v_i are in S, as all copies have the same neighbors. Moreover, it will imply that the projection S_G of S onto the 3-regular graph G is a perfect code, since a subset of vertices containing exactly one vertex from the closed neighborhood of each vertex is a perfect code. Henceforth, when we refer to claws, we always mean claws as described above.

There is a clique node for every group of $z+1$ vertex-disjoint claws in G' and also one clique node for every group of t vertex-disjoint claws in G'. These clique nodes are connected to all the vertices of those claws in G', and to no other vertex in the copies of G. Note that both $t \in \rho$ and $z+1 \in \rho$, but $\{t+1, ..., z\} \cap \rho = \emptyset$ and $t+1 \le z$.

It remains to show that for any ρ-IS S of G', each claw contains exactly one vertex of S. To ease the presentation, we first prove a weaker property, and then complete the specification of G' by adding some more vertices to the clique, which will allow us to prove the main property.

Claim. Any ρ-IS S in G' contains either one or three vertices from each claw.

Proof. Recall that by definition S must contain at least $t+1$ nodes, and at most one of these could be a clique node. But if S contains a clique node y, we could arbitrarily pick t other vertices of S, and some clique node $x \neq y$ would be adjacent to exactly t vertex-disjoint claws having these t vertices from S as centers. We ensure that the claws are vertex-disjoint by choosing the neighbors of the centers from separate copies of G. The clique node x would have a total of $t+1$ neighbors in S, but $t+1 \notin \rho$. Thus, S contains no clique node.

Moreover, if $t+1 \le |S| \le z$, then we can find $|S|$ vertex-disjoint claws with vertices of S as centers, chosen as above, and some clique node will be adjacent to these $|S|$ vertices, but $\{t+1, ..., z\} \cap \rho = \emptyset$. Thus $|S| \ge z+1$.

If some claw X has $X \cap S = \emptyset$, we can take z vertices from S, cover them by z vertex-disjoint claws centered at these vertices, as above, and a clique node x will be adjacent to these claws and to X. But then x would have z neighbors in S, and $z \notin \rho$. Thus X has at least one vertex in S.

Moreover, X cannot have two vertices in S, since we can pick $t-1$ vertices from S and cover them, as above, by $t-1$ vertex-disjoint claws that do not intersect the neighborhood of X. A clique node x is adjacent to these claws and to X and it would have $t+1$ neighbors in S if X had two vertices in S. However, $t+1 \notin \rho$. ∎

Claim 2 already establishes that either all or none of the copies of a vertex $v_i \in V(G)$ must be in a ρ-IS S, since any pair v_i^k and $v_i^{k'}$ are centers of distinct claws sharing the three other claw vertices. When $v_i^k \in S$ the three other claw vertices are not in S so that $v_i^{k'} \in S$ also, and vice-versa.

We complete the construction of G' in three different manners depending on which of the following three cases holds:

- (i) 0 and 1 are in ρ, but 2 is not.
- (ii) For some $w \geq 3$, $w-2$ is in ρ, but w is not.
- (iii) For some $w \geq 2$, w is in ρ but $w-2$ is not.

If none of these cases hold, then for each $w \in \mathbb{N}$ either both or none of w and $w+2$ would have to be in ρ, and $\rho \subset \mathbb{N}$ would be equal to EVEN or ODD. Note that if any pair of non-center vertices of a claw are adjacent, then by Claim 2 we already know the claw has exactly one vertex in any ρ-IS set.

In case (i) we add a node to the clique for each pair of vertices in G^1 which are copies of vertices at distance 2 in G, and make the node adjacent to the pair.

In case (ii) we add a node to the clique for each group of $w-2$ vertex disjoint claws, and make the node adjacent to these claws.

In case (iii) we add for each set Y of $w-2$ vertex-disjoint claws a new clique node Y_i for each $v_i \in G$ whose neighbors form an independent set. We make Y_i adjacent to v_i^1 and to v_i^2 and to all copies of vertices in G^1 at distance two from v_i. There are between three and six such vertices in G^1, since if only two then this would be the whole graph G. Let v_i have neighbors v_a, v_b, v_c and let these latter three have additional neighbors a' and a'', b' and b'', c' and c'', respectively. We make Y_i adjacent to the copy in G^2 of some of these vertices, depending on the common identities of this multiset of six vertices (see Figure 1):

- A: six singletons- adjacent to no further vertices,
- B: one triple and three singletons- adjacent to no further vertices,
- C: one pair and four singletons- adjacent to copy in G^2 of the pair,
- D: two pairs and two singletons- adjacent to copies in G^2 of both pairs,
- E: three pairs- adjacent to copies in G^2 of all three pairs,
- F: one triple, pair and singleton- adjacent to copy in G^2 of the pair.

Claim. Any ρ-IS S in G' contains exactly one vertex from each claw.

Proof. Let X be any claw in G^1. We show that in none of the cases (i),(ii) or (iii) does X contain three vertices in S. The claim then follows for all claws in G', since either all or no copies of a vertex must be in S.

In case (i) we have $2 \notin \rho$. No two vertices in G^1 at distance two in G can both be in S since then the corresponding newly added clique node would have exactly two neighbors in S. Hence no claw in G^1 can contain more than one vertex in S.

In case (ii) we can find a set of $w-3$ vertex-disjoint claws in G whose centers are all in S. We ensure that such vertex-disjoint claws can always be found by assuming, without loss of generality, that G is large, say with at least w^2 vertices, so that by Claim 2 the center vertices can be chosen to be copies of vertices in

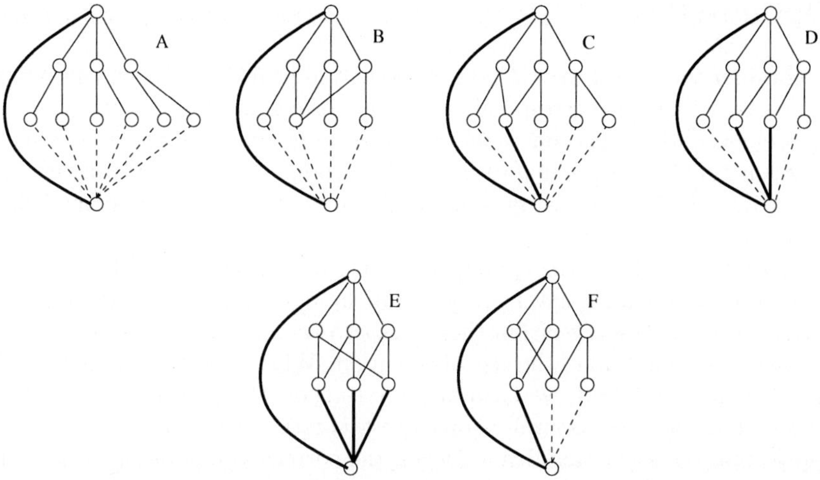

Fig. 1. The six cases, showing the center vertex of the claw on top, the clique vertex on bottom, with a thick edge indicating that the clique vertex is adjacent to copies in both G^1 and G^2 and a dotted edge indicating adjacency only to the copy in G^1. In each case, if the top claw has three vertices in S the clique vertex has no S-neighbors in the figure, whereas if each claw has exactly one vertex in S the clique vertex has exactly two S-neighbors in the figure (counting thick edges twice).

G whose pairwise distance in G is at least three. If X had three neighbors in S, the clique node adjacent to X and these claws would have exactly w neighbors in S. However, $w \notin \rho$.

In case (iii) a set Y of $w - 2$ vertex-disjoint claws has the central vertex chosen. Let X have center node v_i^1. The clique node Y_i added for v_i^1 and these $w-2$ claws has at least $w-2$ neighbors in S. If the claw X has three vertices in S then these are all the three neighbors of v_i^1 and none of the remaining neighbors of Y_i is in S. On the other hand, if X and all other claws all have one vertex in S, then it is easy to check, in each of the separate cases of common identities above, that exactly two of the remaining neighbors of Y_i is in S. For example, if Y_i has an extra neighbor v_j^2 in G^2 then in each case v_j^2 is adjacent to exactly two (a pair) of the neighbors of v_i^1 and the third neighbor of v_i^1 must be in S whenever $v_j^2 \in S$ so that the remaining neighbors of Y_i could then not be in S. We conclude that, since $w - 2 \notin \rho$ but $w \in \rho$, the claw X must have exactly one vertex in S. ∎

A perfect code in G gives rise to a ρ-IS in G' consisting of all copies of nodes in the perfect code. For every ρ-IS S in G', either all or no copies of a vertex from G must be in S and no clique node is in S. Hence it follows from Claim 2 that the projection of S onto G is a perfect code. ∎

3 Optimization

Let us consider the complexity of ρ-IS optimization problems. Clearly optimization is no easier than the corresponding decision problem, thus we are interested in the problems where the decision version is polynomial solvable. When an optimization problem turns out to be hard to compute, we would further like to know how hard it is to compute approximate solutions by polynomial-time algorithms.

We say that an algorithm *approximates* a problem *within* r if the solution computed on any instance never strays from the optimal by more than a multiplicative factor r. The algorithm then has *performance ratio* r. Note that the factor r may be a function of the size of the input. When a better approximation algorithm cannot be found, we naturally try to show that no better algorithm can be found given some natural complexity-theoretic assumption.

Approximation is not well defined when the corresponding decision problem is not polynomial solvable. If an algorithm cannot produce a feasible value for a solvable problem, the approximation ratio for that problem is not defined. Attempts to deal with this by modifying the definition of a performance ratio seldom meet with success. Thus, we consider only the approximation of the ρ-IS optimization problems, either minimization or maximization, whose decision version is in P, namely: $\rho = \mathbb{N}^+$, $\rho = \{0\}$, and $\rho = \{0, 1, \ldots, k\}$, for some $k \in \mathbb{N}^+$.

Minimization problems are trivial when ρ contains zero, which leaves only the case $\rho = \mathbb{N}^+$. This is the *Minimum Independent Dominating Set* problem, which is known to be $\mathcal{NP}$-hard to approximate within $n^{1-\epsilon}$, for any $\epsilon > 0$ [3]. The reduction holds even if the graph is sparse, thus it is hard within $m^{1-\epsilon}$. In fact, no sub-linear performance ratio is known for this problem.

The maximization problem with $\rho = \{0\}$ is trivial, whose solution consists of all isolated vertices. When $\rho = \mathbb{N}^+$ we have the *Maximum Independent Set* problem, for which the best performance ratio known is $O(n/\log^2 n)$ [1]. Håstad has recently improved a sequence of deep results to show that this problem is hard to approximate within $n^{1-\epsilon}$, for any $\epsilon > 0$ [4]. This result is modulo the assumption that $\mathcal{NP} \neq \mathcal{ZPP}$, namely that zero-error randomized polynomial algorithms do not exist for all problems in $\mathcal{NP}$. This is highly expected, while slightly weaker hardness results are known under the stronger assumption that $\mathcal{P} \neq \mathcal{NP}$. We shall use this result in this paper, with the knowledge that weaker assumptions will then also transfer to our results. In particular, our reductions do give the $\mathcal{NP}$-hardness of the exact optimization problems considered.

The only remaining maximization problems are when $\rho = \{0, 1, \ldots, k\}$, for some $k \in \mathbb{N}^+$. We focus on these problems for the remainder of this section. We show them to be $\mathcal{NP}$-hard, and obtain nearly tight bounds on their approximabilities. The results are summarized in the following theorem. Let *opt* denote the size of the optimal solution of the instance.

Theorem 8 *The $\{0, 1, \ldots, k\}$-IS maximization problem, for $k \in \mathbb{N}^+$, can be approximated within $O(\sqrt{n})$ in polynomial time, but not within $O(n^{1/(k+1)-\epsilon})$ nor $O(opt^{1-\epsilon})$, for any fixed $\epsilon > 0$, unless $\mathcal{NP} = \mathcal{ZPP}$.*

3.1 Approximation algorithm

We now give an algorithm that approximates some important problems on set systems. These results are interesting in their own right. Simple reductions then imply the same approximation for the $\{0, 1, \ldots, k\}$-IS problems.

Definition 9 *The* Set Packing *problem is the following: Given a base set S and a collection $\mathcal{C}$ of subsets of S, find a collection $\mathcal{C}' \subseteq \mathcal{C}$ of disjoint sets that is of maximum cardinality.*

Set Packing and Maximum Independent Set can be shown to be mutually reducible by approximation-preserving reductions. Given a graph, form a set system with a base element for each edge and a set corresponding to a vertex containing the elements corresponding to incident edges. Then independent sets in the graph are in one-to-one correspondence with packings of the set system. Thus, the $O(n/\log^2 n)$ approximation of Independent Set carries over to Set Packing. This approximation is in terms of n, the number of sets in the set system.

An alternative would be to measure the approximation in terms of m, the size of the base system. For this, there is an obvious upper bound of m, since that is the maximum size of any solution. Another easy upper bound is the maximum cardinality k of a set in the solution, since any maximal solution will find a solution of size at least m/k. However, k can be as large as m, and no better bounds were known in terms of m, to the best of our knowledge.

Theorem 10 *Set Packing can be approximated within $\sqrt{m}$, where m is the size of the base set, in time linear in the input size.*

Proof. A greedy algorithm is given in Fig. 2. In each step, it chooses a smallest set and removes from the collection all sets containing elements from the selected set.

```
Greedy(S,C)
t ← 0
repeat
  t ← t + 1
  X_t ← C ∈ C of minimum cardinality
  Z_t ← {C ∈ C : X ∩ C ≠ ∅ }
  C ← C − Z_t
until |C| = 0
Output {X_1, X_2, ..., X_t}
```

Fig. 2. Greedy set packing algorithm

Let $M = \lfloor \sqrt{m} \rfloor$. Observe that $\{Z_1, \ldots, Z_t\}$ forms a partition of $\mathcal{C}$. Let i be the index of some iteration of the algorithm, i.e. $1 \leq i \leq t$. All sets in Z_i

contain at least one element of X_i, thus the maximum number of disjoint sets in Z_i is at most the cardinality of X_i. On the other hand, every set in Z_i is of size at least X_i, so the maximum number of disjoint sets in Z_i is also at most $\lfloor m/|X_i|\rfloor$. Thus, the optimal solution contains at most $\min(|X_i|, \lfloor m/|X_i|\rfloor) \leq \max_{x\in\mathbb{N}} \min(x, \lfloor m/x\rfloor) = M$ sets from Z_i.

Thus, in total, the optimal solution contains at most tM sets, when the algorithm finds t sets, for a ratio of at most M. ∎

The *Strong Stable Set* problem is the $\{0,1\}$-IS maximization problem. A strong stable set, also known as a *2-packing*, corresponds to a set of vertices of pairwise distance at least three. The Strong Stable Set problem reduces to Set Packing in the following way. Recall that $N[v] = N(v) \cup \{v\}$. Given a graph $G = (V, E)$, construct a set system $(S, \mathcal{C})$ with $S = V$ and $\mathcal{C} = \{N[v] : v \in V\}$. Then, a strong stable set corresponds to a set of nodes whose closed neighborhoods do not overlap, thus forming a set packing of $(S, \mathcal{C})$.

Corollary 11 *Strong Stable Set can be approximated within* $\sqrt{n}$.

The *Distance-t Set* problem is that of finding a maximum cardinality set of vertices of mutual distance at least t in a given graph G. It corresponds to finding a maximum independent set in the power graph G^{t-1}. If A is the adjacency matrix of G and I is the identity matrix, then the adjacency matrix of G^{t-1} is obtained by computing $(A+I)^{t-1}$, replacing non-zero entries by ones, and eliminating self-loops. The Strong Stable Set problem on G is the Distance-3 Set problem, or that of finding a maximum independent set in G^2. Since the Distance-$2q+1$ Set problem is that of finding a maximum independent set in $(G^q)^2$, the odd case is a restricted case of the Strong Stable Set problem.

Corollary 12 *The Distance-t Set problem can be approximated within* $\sqrt{n}$ *for any odd t.*

We now extend the application of the greedy set packing algorithm.

Definition 13 *A* k-matching *of a set system* $(S, \mathcal{C})$ *is a collection* $\mathcal{C}' \subseteq \mathcal{C}$ *such that each element in* S *is contained in at most* k *sets in* $\mathcal{C}'$.

In particular, a 1-matching is precisely a set packing. The *k-Matching* problem is that of finding a k-Matching of maximum cardinality, i.e. containing the greatest number of sets.

Observe that the sizes of maximum set packings and maximum k-matchings can vary widely. Consider the set system that is the dual of a complete graph, namely $S = \{e_{i,j} : 1 \leq i < j \leq n\}$, $\mathcal{C} = \{C_x : 1 \leq x \leq n\}$ and $C_x = \{e_{i,x} : 1 \leq i < x\} \cup \{e_{x,j} : x < j \leq n\}$. Then, the whole system is a 2-matching while any set packing is of unit size. Thus, the ratio between the two can be as much as $\sqrt{m}$. We nevertheless find that the algorithm for Set Packing still yields $O(\sqrt{m})$ approximations for k-Matching.

Theorem 14 *The greedy set packing algorithm approximates the k-Matching problem within* $k\sqrt{m}$.

Proof. The sum of the sizes of sets in a k-matching is at most km. Thus, if each set contains at least q elements, then the matching contains at most $\lfloor \frac{km}{q} \rfloor$ sets.

Consider any iteration i. Each set in Z_i is of size at least $|X_i|$. Thus, the optimal k-matching OPT contains at most $\lfloor \frac{km}{|X_i|} \rfloor$ sets from Z_i. On the other hand, OPT never contains more than $k|X_i|$ sets from Z_i, since it contains at most k sets containing a particular element from X_i. Thus,

$$|OPT \cap Z_i| \leq k \min(|X_i|, m/|X_i|) = k\sqrt{m}.$$

Hence, the optimal k-matching contains at most $tk\sqrt{m}$ sets,

$$|OPT| = \sum_{i=1}^{t} |OPT \cap Z_i| \leq tk\sqrt{m}.$$

while the algorithm obtains t sets, for a performance ratio of $k\sqrt{m}$. ∎

This also translates to a similar ratio for the other $\{0, 1, \ldots, k\}$-IS problems. While we can again show that the size of a maximum strong stable set and a maximum $\{0, 1, 2\}$-IS can differ by a factor of as much as $\Omega(\sqrt{n})$, the analysis nevertheless works out.

Corollary 15 *The $\{0, 1, \ldots, k\}$-IS problem, for $k \geq 1$ is approximable within $O(\sqrt{n})$.*

Proof. Given an instance G to $\{0, 1, \ldots, k\}$-IS, form the set system of closed neighborhoods, as in the reduction of Strong Stable Set to Set Packing. Recall that the number of base elements m now equals the number of sets n. Clearly the solution output by the greedy set packing solution is a feasible solution, since it forms a $\{0, 1\}$-IS.

Observe that any solution to the $\{0, 1, \ldots, k\}$-IS problem of G corresponds to a k-matching in the derived set system (while the converse is not true). Hence, by Theorem 14 the size of the algorithm's solution is also within $O(\sqrt{n})$ of the optimal $\{0, 1, \ldots, k\}$-IS solution. ∎

3.2 Approximation lower bound

A set system is also sometimes referred to as a hypergraph, where the hypervertices correspond to the base elements and hyperedges correspond to the sets of the set system. A *t-uniform hypergraph* is a set system where the cardinality of all edges is t. A subset S of V is an *independent set* if no hyperedge is fully contained in S.

Our lower bound rests on the following reduction from the problem of finding an approximately maximum independent set in a hypergraph.

Lemma 16. *If the $\{0, 1, \ldots, k\}$-IS maximization problem can be approximated within $f(n)$, then the Maximum Independent Set problem in $(k+1)$-uniform hypergraphs can be approximated within $O(f(n)^{k+1})$.*

Also, if the former problem can be approximated within $g(opt)$, as a function of the optimal solution value opt, so can the latter.

Proof. Given a hypergraph H, construct a graph G as follows. G contains a vertex for each node and each hyperedge of H. The hyperedge-vertices form a clique, while the node-vertices are independent. A hyperedge-vertex is adjacent precisely to those node-vertices that correspond to nodes incident on the hyperedge.

We first claim that any independent set S in the hypergraph H is a $\{0,1,\ldots,k\}$-IS in G. Clearly it is an independent set in G since it consists only of node-vertices. Each node-vertex thus has a ρ-value of 0. Hyperedge-vertices have exactly k node-vertices as neighbors and not all of those can be in S given the independence property of S in H. Thus, hyperedge-vertices have a ρ-value of at most $k-1$.

Any $\{0,1,\ldots,k\}$-IS S in G can contain at most one hyperedge-vertex, and if we eliminate that possible vertex from S, it can be verified that the remainder corresponds to an independent set in H.

Taken together, any approximate solution to $\{0,1,\ldots,k\}$-IS gives an equally approximate independent set of H, within an additive one. Hence, ratios in terms of *opt* carry over immediately. For approximations in terms of the input size, we must factor in that $|V(G)| = |V(H)| + |E(H)| = O(|V(H)|^{k+1})$. ∎

To obtain the theorem, we need to show that Maximum Independent Set in hypergraphs is hard to approximate. We sketch here how the $n^{1-\epsilon}$ inapproximability result of [4] translates to the same bound for the case of uniform hypergraphs. Given a graph G, form a hypergraph H on the same vertex set, with hyperedges for any $(k+1)$-tuples such that some pair of vertices in the tuple form an edge in G. Then, we have a one-to-one correspondence between independent sets (of cardinality at least k) in G and in H.

Observe that in the case $k=1$, the Strong Stable Set problem, we obtain a lower bound of $\Omega(n^{1/2-\epsilon})$ which is essentially tight in light of the upper bound given. The lower bound can be generalized for Set Packing to show that the $O(\sqrt{m})$ approximation in terms of the number of base elements is essentially the best possible.

We also obtain tight lower bounds for the Distance-t Set problems defined earlier.

Theorem 17 *For any $\epsilon > 0$, the Distance-t Set problem is hard to approximate within $n^{1-\epsilon}$ when t is even, and within $n^{1/2-\epsilon}$ when t is odd, $t \geq 3$.*

Proof. First consider the even case, $t = 2q+2$. Given a graph G, construct a graph H that contains a copy of G, a vertex u adjacent to every vertex of G, and a distinct path of q edges attached to each vertex of G. That is, $V(H) = \{v_i, w_{i,j} : v_i \in V(G), 1 \leq j \leq q\} \cup \{u\}$, and $E(H) = E(G) \cup \{uv_i, v_i w_{i,1}, w_{i,j}w_{i,j+1} : v_i \in V(G), 1 \leq j < q\}$. All pairs of vertices in H are of distance at most $2q+2 = t$. The only vertices of distance t are pairs $w_{i,q}, w_{j,q}$ of leaves on paths where (v_i, v_j) are non-adjacent. Hence, a Distance-t Set in H is in one-to-one correspondence with an independent set in G. Further, the size of H is linear in the size of G. Thus, the Distance-t Set problem, for t even, is no easier to approximate than the IS problem.

For the lower bound for the odd case, we similarly append paths to each vertex of the construction for the Strong Stable Set problem. We invite the reader to verify the details. ∎

4 Conclusion

We have investigated the complexity of decision and optimization problems over independent sets with domination constraints. These problems belong to the framework of (σ, ρ)-problems. Our results constitute a complete complexity classification for the cases when $\sigma = \{0\}$, up to $\mathcal{P}$ vs. $\mathcal{NP}$ for the decision problems, and with tight approximability bounds for the optimization problems. The approximation results extended also to several related independence problems. The complexity of problems for other cases of $\sigma \subseteq \mathbb{N}$ remain to be investigated in detail.

Acknowledgement

A comment by Hiroshi Nagamochi prompted us to greatly improve an early algorithm.

References

1. R. B. Boppana and M.M. Halldórsson, Approximating maximum independent sets by excluding subgraphs, *BIT*, 32 (1992), 180–196.
2. M. R. Garey and D. S. Johnson, *Computers and Intractability* (Freeman, New York, 1979).
3. M.M. Halldórsson, Approximating the minimum maximal independence number, *Information Processing Letters* 46 (1993), 169–172.
4. J. Håstad, Clique is hard to approximate within $n^{1-\epsilon}$, In *Proc. 37th IEEE Symp. on Found. of Comput. Sci.*, (1996), 627–636.
5. S. Khanna, M. Sudan and D. P. Williamson, A complete classification of the approximability of maximization problems derived from boolean constraint satisfaction. in *Proc. 29th ACM Symp. on Theory of Computing*, (1997), 11–20.
6. J. Kratochvíl, Perfect codes in general graphs, monograph, Academia Praha (1991).
7. J. Kratochvíl, P. Manuel and M. Miller, Generalized domination in chordal graphs, *Nordic Journal of Computing* 2 (1995), 41–50
8. T.J. Schaefer, The complexity of satisfiability problems, In *Proc. 10th ACM Symp. on Theory of Computing* (1978), 216–226.
9. J.A. Telle, Characterization of domination-type parameters in graphs, *Proceedings of 24th Southeastern International Conference on Combinatorics, Graph Theory and Computing -Congressus Numerantium* Vol.94 (1993), 9–16.
10. J.A. Telle, Complexity of domination-type problems in graphs, *Nordic Journal of Computing* 1 (1994), 157–171.

Robust Asynchronous Protocols Are Finite-State

Madhavan Mukund[1]*, K Narayan Kumar[1]**,
Jaikumar Radhakrishnan[2], and Milind Sohoni[3]

[1] SPIC Mathematical Institute, 92 G.N. Chetty Road, Madras 600 017, India.
E-mail: {madhavan,kumar}@smi.ernet.in

[2] Computer Science Group, Tata Institute of Fundamental Research, Homi Bhabha Road, Bombay 400 005, India. E-mail: jaikumar@tcs.tifr.res.in

[3] Department of Computer Science and Engineering, Indian Institute of Technology, Bombay 400 076, India. E-mail: sohoni@cse.iitb.ernet.in

Abstract. We consider networks of finite-state machines which communicate over reliable channels which may reorder messages. Each machine in the network also has a local input tape. Since channels are unbounded, the network as a whole is, in general, infinite-state.

An asynchronous protocol is a network equipped with an acceptance condition. Such a protocol is said to be *robust* if it never deadlocks and, moreover, it either accepts or rejects each input in an unambiguous manner. The behaviour of a robust protocol is insensitive to nondeterminism introduced by either message reordering or the relative speeds at which components read their local inputs.

Using an automata-theoretic model, we show that, at a global level, every robust asynchronous protocol has a finite-state representation. To prove this, we establish a variety of pumping lemmas. We also demonstrate a distributed language which does not admit a robust protocol.

1 Introduction

We analyze message-passing systems from a language-theoretic point of view. In such systems, computing agents run *protocols* to collectively process distributed inputs, using messages for coordination. These messages may undergo different relative delays and hence arrive out of order. Protocols need to be "robust" with respect to the irregular behaviour of the transmission medium.

Most protocols assume that the transmission medium has an unlimited capacity to hold messages—undelivered messages are assumed to be stored in a transparent manner in intermediate buffers. Can the unlimited capacity of the medium enhance the power of message passing protocols?

Unfortunately, the answer is *no*; we show that even for a benign medium which does not lose messages, a "robust" protocol cannot use unbounded buffers to its advantage. However, if a protocol need not always gracefully halt, then the medium can be exploited to accept a larger class of "distributed languages".

* Partly supported by IFCPAR Project 1502-1.

** Currently on leave at Department of Computer Science, State University of New York at Stony Brook, NY 11794-4400, USA. E-mail: kumar@cs.sunysb.edu.

Consider then a system of processes which interact independently with the environment and communicate internally via message-passing. The communication between the processes and the programs which they run impose restrictions on the distributed input—some interactions with the environment are valid and some are not. For instance, consider a banking network which is connected to the external world via a set of automated teller machines. The protocol may enforce a limit on the number of withdrawals by an individual across the network.

We are interested in finite-state processes, so we assume that the number of different types of messages used by the system is finite. This is not unreasonable if we distinguish "control" messages from "data" messages. In our model, channels may reorder or delay messages. For simplicity, we assume that messages are never lost. Since messages may be reordered, the state of each channel can be represented by a finite set of counters which record the number of messages of each type which have been sent along the channel but are as yet undelivered.

We say that an asynchronous protocol is *robust* if it never deadlocks on any distributed input and every distributed input is either accepted or rejected in a consistent manner. In other words finite delays, reordering of messages and nondeterministic choices made by the protocol do not affect the outcome of a robust protocol on a given distributed input.

Our main result is that every language of distributed inputs accepted by a robust asynchronous protocol can be "represented" by a regular sequential language. In other words, a robust asynchronous protocol always has a globally finite-state description. This implies that robust protocols essentially use messages only for "handshaking". Since robust protocols can be modelled as finite-state systems, they may, in principle, be verified using automated tools [5].

The paper is organized as follows. In the next section, we define message-passing networks. In Section 3 we state some basic results about these networks, including a Contraction Lemma which leads to the decidability of the emptiness problem. Section 4 develops a family of pumping lemmas which are exploited in Section 5 to prove our main result about robust protocols. We also describe a simple language for which no robust protocol exists. In the final section, we discuss the connection between our results and those in Petri net theory and point out directions for future work. We have had to omit detailed proofs in this extended abstract. Full proofs and related results can be found in [10].

2 Message-Passing Networks

Natural numbers and tuples As usual, $\mathbb{N}$ denotes the set $\{0,1,2,\ldots\}$ of natural numbers. For $i,j \in \mathbb{N}$, $[i..j]$ denotes the set $\{i, i+1, \ldots, j\}$, where $[i..j] = \emptyset$ if $i > j$. We compare k-tuples of natural numbers component-wise. For $\overline{m} = \langle m_1, m_2, \ldots, m_k \rangle$ and $\overline{n} = \langle n_1, n_2, \ldots, n_k \rangle$, $\overline{m} \leq \overline{n}$ iff $m_i \leq n_i$ for each $i \in [1..k]$.

Message-passing automata A *message-passing automaton* $\mathcal{A}$ is a tuple $(S_a, S_t, \Sigma, \#, \Gamma, T, s_{\text{in}})$ where:

- S_a and S_t are disjoint, non-empty, finite sets of *active* and *terminal states*, respectively. The *initial state* s_{in} belongs to S_a.

- Σ is a finite *input alphabet* and $\#$ is a special end-of-tape symbol which does *not* belong to Σ. Let $\Sigma^{\#}$ denote the set $\Sigma \cup \{\#\}$.
- Γ is a finite set of *counters*. With each counter C, we associate two symbols, C^{+} and C^{-}. We write $\Gamma^{\pm}$ to denote the set $\{C^{+} | C \in \Gamma\} \cup \{C^{-} | C \in \Gamma\}$.
- $T \subseteq (S_a \times (\Sigma \cup \Gamma^{\pm}) \times S_a) \cup (S_a \times \{\#\} \times S_t) \cup (S_t \times \Gamma^{\pm} \times S_t)$ is the *transition relation*.

A message-passing automaton begins reading its input in an active state. It remains within the set of active states until it reads the special end-of-tape symbol. At this point, the automaton moves into the set of terminal states where the only moves possible are those which increment or decrement counters.

Networks A *message-passing network* is a structure $\mathcal{N} = (\{\mathcal{A}_i\}_{i \in [1..n]}, Acc, Rej)$ where:

- For $i \in [1..n]$, $\mathcal{A}_i = (S_a^i, S_t^i, \Sigma_i, \#_i, \Gamma_i, T_i, s_{\text{in}}^i)$ is a message-passing automaton. As before, for $i \in [1..n]$, $\Sigma_i^{\#}$ denotes the set $\Sigma_i \cup \{\#_i\}$.
- For $i, j \in [1..n]$, if $i \neq j$ then $\Sigma_i \cap \Sigma_j = \emptyset$.
- A *global state* of $\mathcal{N}$ is an n-tuple $\langle s_1, s_2, \ldots, s_n \rangle$ where $s_i \in (S_a^i \cup S_t^i)$ for $i \in [1..n]$. Let $Q_{\mathcal{N}}$ denote the set of global states of $\mathcal{N}$. If $q = \langle s_1, s_2, \ldots, s_n \rangle$ is a global state, then q_i denotes the ith component s_i.
  The *initial state* of $\mathcal{N}$ is given by $q_{\text{in}} = \langle s_{\text{in}}^1, s_{\text{in}}^2, \ldots, s_{\text{in}}^n \rangle$. The *terminal states* of $\mathcal{N}$, denoted $Q_{\mathcal{N}}^t$, are given by $\prod_{i \in [1..n]} S_t^i$. The sets Acc and Rej are disjoint subsets of $Q_{\mathcal{N}}^t$; Acc is the set of *accept states* of $\mathcal{N}$ while Rej is the set of *reject states*. We do not insist that $Q_{\mathcal{N}}^t = Acc \cup Rej$—there may be terminal states which are neither accepting nor rejecting.

Counters may be shared across the network—shared counters represent channels along which components send messages to each other. Strictly speaking, a point-to-point channel would consist of a set of counters shared by two processes, where one process only increments the counters and the other only decrements the counters. Our definition permits a more generous notion of channels.

The assumption that local alphabets are pairwise disjoint is not critical—we can always tag each input letter with the location where it is read.

Let $\Sigma_{\mathcal{N}}$ denote $\bigcup_{i \in [1..n]} \Sigma_i^{\#}$ and $\Gamma_{\mathcal{N}}$ denote $\bigcup_{i \in [1..n]} \Gamma_i$.

Global transitions For a network $\mathcal{N}$, we can define a *global transition relation* $T_{\mathcal{N}}$ as follows. For $q, q' \in Q_{\mathcal{N}}$ and $d \in \Sigma_{\mathcal{N}} \cup \Gamma_{\mathcal{N}}^{\pm}$, (q, d, q') belongs to $T_{\mathcal{N}}$ provided:

- For some $i \in [1..n]$, $d \in \Sigma_i^{\#} \cup \Gamma_i^{\pm}$ and $(q_i, d, q_i') \in T_i$.
- For $j \neq i$, $q_j = q_j'$.

Configurations A *configuration* of $\mathcal{N}$ is a pair (q, f) where $q \in Q_{\mathcal{N}}$ and $f : \Gamma \to \mathbb{N}$ records the values stored in the counters. If the counters are $C_1, C_2, \ldots, C_k$ then we represent f by an element $\langle f(C_1), f(C_2), \ldots, f(C_k) \rangle$ of $\mathbb{N}^k$. By abuse of notation, the k-tuple $\langle 0, 0, \ldots, 0 \rangle$ is uniformly denoted $\overline{0}$, for all values of k.

We use χ to denote configurations. If $\chi = (q, f)$, $Q(\chi)$ denotes q and $F(\chi)$ denotes f. Further, for each counter C, $C(\chi)$ denotes the value $f(C)$.

Moves The network *moves* from configuration χ to configuration χ' on $d \in \Sigma_{\mathcal{N}} \cup \Gamma^{\pm}_{\mathcal{N}}$ if $(Q(\chi), d, Q(\chi')) \in T_{\mathcal{N}}$ and one of the following holds:

- $d \in \Sigma_{\mathcal{N}}$ and $F(\chi) = F(\chi')$.
- $d = C^+$, $C(\chi') = C(\chi) + 1$ and $C'(\chi) = C'(\chi')$ for every $C' \neq C$.
- $d = C^-$, $C(\chi') = C(\chi) - 1 \geq 0$ and $C'(\chi) = C'(\chi')$ for every $C' \neq C$.

Such a move is denoted $\chi \stackrel{(q,d,q')}{\longrightarrow} \chi'$—that is, transitions are labelled by elements of $T_{\mathcal{N}}$. Given a sequence of transitions $t_1 t_2 \ldots t_m = (q_1, d_1, q_2)(q_2, d_2, q_3) \ldots (q_m, d_m, q_{m+1})$, the corresponding sequence $d_1 d_2 \ldots d_m$ over $\Sigma_{\mathcal{N}} \cup \Gamma^{\pm}_{\mathcal{N}}$ is denoted $\alpha(t_1 t_2 \ldots t_m)$.

Computations and runs A *computation* of $\mathcal{N}$ is a sequence $\chi_0 \stackrel{t_1}{\longrightarrow} \chi_1 \stackrel{t_2}{\longrightarrow} \ldots \stackrel{t_m}{\longrightarrow} \chi_m$. We also write $\chi_0 \stackrel{t_1 t_2 \ldots t_m}{\Longrightarrow} \chi_m$ to indicate that there is a computation labelled $t_1 t_2 \ldots t_m$ from χ_0 to χ_m. Notice that χ_0 and $t_1 t_2 \ldots t_m$ uniquely determine all the intermediate configurations $\chi_1, \chi_2, \ldots, \chi_m$. If the transition sequence is not relevant, we just write $\chi_0 \Longrightarrow \chi_m$. As usual, $\chi \stackrel{t_1 t_2 \ldots t_m}{\Longrightarrow}$ and $\chi \Longrightarrow$ denote that there exists χ' such that $\chi \stackrel{t_1 t_2 \ldots t_m}{\Longrightarrow} \chi'$ and $\chi \Longrightarrow \chi'$, respectively.

For $K \in \mathbb{N}$, a *K-computation* of $\mathcal{N}$ is a computation $\chi_0 \Longrightarrow \chi_m$ where $C(\chi_0) \leq K$ for each $C \in \Gamma_{\mathcal{N}}$.

If w is a string over a set X and $Y \subseteq X$, we write $w\!\restriction_Y$ to denote the subsequence of letters from Y in w.

An input to the network $\mathcal{N}$ is an n-tuple $\overline{w} = \langle w_1, w_2, \ldots, w_n \rangle$—each component w_i is a word over the local alphabet Σ_i. As we shall see when we define the notion of a run, each component w_i of the input $\overline{w}$ is assumed to be terminated by the end-of-tape symbol $\#_i$ which is not recorded as part of the input.

A *run of $\mathcal{N}$ over $\overline{w}$* is a 0-computation $\chi_0 \stackrel{t_1 t_2 \ldots t_m}{\Longrightarrow} \chi_m$ where $Q(\chi_0) = q_{\text{in}}$, $Q(\chi_m) \in \mathit{Acc} \cup \mathit{Rej}$ and $\alpha(t_1 t_2 \ldots t_m)\!\restriction_{\Sigma_i^\#} = w_i \#_i$ for each $i \in [1..n]$. The run is said to be *accepting* if $Q(\chi_m) \in \mathit{Acc}$ and *rejecting* if $Q(\chi_m) \in \mathit{Rej}$. The input $\overline{w}$ is *accepted* by $\mathcal{N}$ if $\mathcal{N}$ has an accepting run over $\overline{w}$.

A 0-computation starting from the initial state which reads the entire input is not automatically a run—a run *must* end in an accept or a reject state. As usual, an input $\overline{w}$ is *not* accepted if all runs on $\overline{w}$ end in reject states—in particular, if the network does not admit any runs on $\overline{w}$, then $\overline{w}$ is not accepted by $\mathcal{N}$.

Languages A *tuple language* over $\langle \Sigma_1, \Sigma_2, \ldots, \Sigma_n \rangle$ is a subset of $\prod_{i \in [1..n]} \Sigma_i^*$. The *language accepted* by $\mathcal{N}$, denoted $L(\mathcal{N})$, is the set of all inputs accepted by $\mathcal{N}$. A tuple language L is said to be *message-passing recognizable* if there is a network $\mathcal{N} = \{\mathcal{A}_i\}_{i \in [1..n]}$ with input alphabets $\{\Sigma_i\}_{i \in [1..n]}$ such that $L = L(\mathcal{N})$.

We will also be interested in the connection between sequential languages over $\Sigma_{\mathcal{N}}$ and tuple languages accepted by message-passing networks. We say that a word w over $\Sigma_{\mathcal{N}}$ *represents* the tuple $\langle w_1, w_2, \ldots, w_n \rangle$ if $w\!\restriction_{\Sigma_i^\#} = w_i \#_i$ for each $i \in [1..n]$. We call the word $\langle w\!\restriction_{\Sigma_1}, w\!\restriction_{\Sigma_2}, \ldots, w\!\restriction_{\Sigma_n} \rangle$ represented by w the *$\mathcal{N}$-projection* of w. Let $L_s \subseteq \Sigma_{\mathcal{N}}^*$ and $L \subseteq \prod_{i \in [1..n]} \Sigma_i^*$. We say that L_s *represents* L if the following conditions hold:

– For each word w in L_s, the $\mathcal{N}$-projection of w belongs to L.
– For each tuple $\overline{w} = \langle w_1, w_2, \ldots, w_n \rangle$ in L, there is a word w in L_s which represents $\overline{w}$.

Example 2.1. Let $\Sigma_1 = \{a\}$ and $\Sigma_2 = \{b\}$. Let L_{ge} denote the language $\{\langle a^\ell, b^m \rangle \mid \ell \geq m\}$. Figure 1 shows a network which accepts L_{ge}. The initial state of each component is marked $\Downarrow$ while the terminal states are marked by double circles. There is one accept state, $\langle s, s \rangle$, and no reject state.

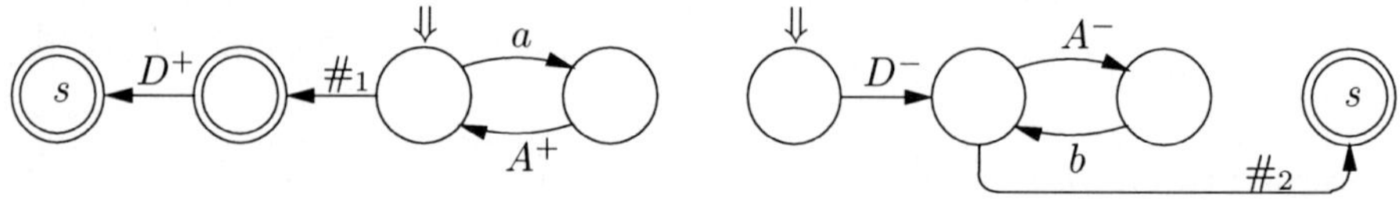

Fig. 1.

Each time the second process reads b it has to consume a message generated by the first process after reading a. Thus, the second process can read at most as many b's as the first process does a's. The counter D is used to signal that the first process's input has been read completely.

Robustness
In general, an asynchronous protocol may process the same distributed input in many different ways because of variations in the order in which components read their local inputs, reordering of messages due to delays in transmission as well as local nondeterminism at each component. Intuitively, a protocol is *robust* if its behaviour is insensitive to these variations—for each distributed input, all possible runs lead either to acceptance or rejection in a consistent manner. Further, a robust protocol should never deadlock along any computation—in other words, every input is processed fully and clearly identified as "accept" or "reject". This motivates following definition.

Robust networks Let $\mathcal{N}$ be a message-passing network. We say that $\mathcal{N}$ is *robust* if the following hold:

– For each input $\overline{w} = \langle w_1, w_2, \ldots, w_n \rangle$, $\mathcal{N}$ admits at least one run over $\overline{w}$. Moreover, if ρ and ρ' are two different runs of $\mathcal{N}$ over $\overline{w}$, either both are accepting or both are rejecting.
– Let $\overline{w} = \langle w_1, w_2, \ldots, w_n \rangle$ be any input and $\rho : \chi_0 \overset{t_1 t_2 \ldots t_m}{\Longrightarrow} \chi_m$ a 0-computation of $\mathcal{N}$ such that $Q(\chi_0) = q_{\text{in}}$. If $\alpha(t_1 t_2 \ldots t_m)\lceil_{\Sigma_i^\#}$ is a prefix of $w_i\#_i$ for each $i \in [1..n]$, then ρ can be extended to a run on $\overline{w}$.

It is easy to observe that if we interchange the accept and reject states of a robust network $\mathcal{N}$, we obtain a robust network for the complement of $L(\mathcal{N})$.

The network in Example 2.1 is not robust—if the number of b's exceeds the number of a's, the network hangs.

Example 2.2. We can make the network of Example 2.1 robust by changing the interaction between the processes. Rather than having the first process send a count of the number of inputs it has read, we make the processes read their inputs alternately, with a handshake in-between.

As before, let $\Sigma_1 = \{a\}, \Sigma_2 = \{b\}$ and $L_{\text{ge}} = \{\langle a^\ell, b^m\rangle \mid \ell \geq m\}$. Figure 2 shows is a robust network for L_{ge}. The initial states are marked $\Downarrow$ and the terminal states of each component are marked by double circles. There is one accept state, $\langle s, s\rangle$, and one reject state $\langle s, r\rangle$. The terminal states $\langle s, t\rangle$, $\langle t, r\rangle$, $\langle t, s\rangle$ and $\langle t, t\rangle$ are neither accepting nor rejecting.

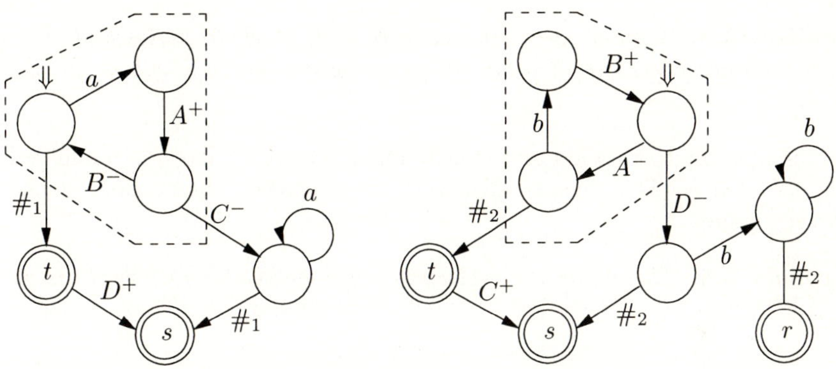

Fig. 2.

The loops enclosed by dashes represent the phase when the processes read their inputs alternately. This phase ends either when either process reads its end-of-tape symbol. If the loop ends with first process reading $\#_1$, the second process must immediately read $\#_2$. If the loop ends with the second process reading $\#_2$, the first process can go on to read any number of a's.

3 Analyzing Message-Passing Networks

The next two sections contain technical results about message-passing networks that we need to prove our main theorem. Many of these results have analogues in Petri net theory [13]—a detailed discussion is presented in the final section.

The following result is basic to analyzing the behaviour of message-passing networks. It follows from the fact that any infinite sequence of N-tuples of natural numbers contains an infinite increasing subsequence. We omit the proof.

Lemma 3.1. *Let X be a set with M elements and $\langle x_1, f_1\rangle, \langle x_2, f_2\rangle, \ldots, \langle x_m, f_m\rangle$ be a sequence over $X \times \mathbb{N}^N$ such that each coordinate of f_1 is bounded by K and for $i \in [1..m-1]$, f_i and f_{i+1} differ on at most one coordinate and this difference is at most 1. There is a constant ℓ which depends only on M, N and K such that if $m \geq \ell$, then there exist $i, j \in [1..m]$ with $i < j$, $x_i = x_j$ and $f_i \leq f_j$.*

Weak pumping constant We call the bound ℓ for M, N and K from the preceding lemma the *weak pumping constant* for (M, N, K), denoted $\pi_{M,N,K}$.

Using the weak pumping constant, we can identify when a run of a network can be contracted by eliminating a sequence of transitions. We omit the proof.

Lemma 3.2 (Contraction). *Let $\mathcal{N}$ be a message-passing network with M global states and N counters. For any K-computation $\chi_0 \stackrel{t_1 t_2 \ldots t_m}{\Longrightarrow} \chi_m$ with $m > \pi_{M,N,K}$, there exist i and j, $m - \pi_{M,N,K} \leq i < j \leq m$, such that $\chi'_0 \stackrel{t_1 \ldots t_i t_{j+1} \ldots t_m}{\Longrightarrow} \chi'_{m-(j-i)}$ is also a K-computation of $\mathcal{A}$, with $\chi'_\ell = \chi_\ell$ for $\ell \in [0..i]$ and $Q(\chi_\ell) = Q(\chi'_{\ell-(j-i)})$ for $\ell \in [j..m]$.*

Corollary 3.3. *A message-passing network with M global states and N counters has an accepting run iff it has an accepting run whose length is bounded by $\pi_{M,N,0}$.*

It is possible to provide an explicit upper bound for $\pi_{M,N,K}$ for all values of M, N, and K. This fact, coupled with the preceding observation, yields the following result.

Corollary 3.4. *The emptiness problem for message-passing networks is decidable.*

4 A Collection of Pumping Lemmas

Change vectors For a string w and a symbol x, let $\#_x(w)$ denote the number of times x occurs in w. Let v be a sequence of transitions. Recall that $\alpha(v)$ denotes the corresponding sequence of letters. For each counter C, define $\Delta_C(v)$ to be $\#_{C^+}(\alpha(v)) - \#_{C^-}(\alpha(v))$. The *change vector* associated with v, denoted Δv, is given by $\langle \Delta_C(v) \rangle_{C \in \Gamma_N}$.

Pumpable decomposition Let $\mathcal{N}$ be a message-passing network with N counters and let $\rho : \chi_0 \stackrel{t_1 t_2 \ldots t_m}{\Longrightarrow} \chi_m$ be a computation of $\mathcal{N}$. A decomposition $\chi_0 \stackrel{u_1}{\Longrightarrow} \chi_{i_1} \stackrel{v_1}{\Longrightarrow} \chi_{j_1} \stackrel{u_2}{\Longrightarrow} \chi_{i_2} \stackrel{v_2}{\Longrightarrow} \chi_{j_2} \stackrel{u_3}{\Longrightarrow} \cdots \stackrel{u_y}{\Longrightarrow} \chi_{i_y} \stackrel{v_y}{\Longrightarrow} \chi_{j_y} \stackrel{u_{y+1}}{\Longrightarrow} \chi_m$ of ρ is said to be *pumpable* if it satisfies the following conditions:

(i) $y \leq N$.
(ii) For each $k \in [1..y]$, $Q(\chi_{i_k}) = Q(\chi_{j_k})$.
(iii) For each v_k, $k \in [1..y]$, Δv_k has at least one positive entry.
(iv) Let C be a counter and $k \in [1..y]$ such that $\Delta_C(v_k)$ is negative. Then, there exists $\ell < k$ such that $\Delta_C(v_\ell)$ is positive.

We refer to $v_1, v_2, \ldots, v_y$ as the *pumpable blocks* of the decomposition. We say that C is a *pumpable counter* if $\Delta_C(v_k) > 0$ for some pumpable block v_k. The following lemma shows that all the pumpable counters of a pumpable decomposition are simultaneously unbounded. We omit the proof. (This is similar to a well-known result of Karp and Miller in the theory of vector addition systems [7].)

Lemma 4.1 (Counter Pumping). *Let $\mathcal{N}$ be a network and ρ a K-computation of $\mathcal{N}$, $K \in \mathbb{N}$, with a pumpable decomposition of the form* $\chi_0 \stackrel{u_1}{\Longrightarrow} \chi_{i_1} \stackrel{v_1}{\Longrightarrow} \chi_{j_1} \cdots \stackrel{u_y}{\Longrightarrow} \chi_{i_y} \stackrel{v_y}{\Longrightarrow} \chi_{j_y} \stackrel{u_{y+1}}{\Longrightarrow} \chi_m$. *Then, for any $I, J \in \mathbb{N}$, with $I \geq 1$, there exist $\ell_1, \ell_2, \ldots, \ell_y \in \mathbb{N}$ and a K-computation ρ' of $\mathcal{N}$ of the form* $\chi'_0 \stackrel{u_1}{\Longrightarrow} \chi'_{i'_1} \stackrel{v_1^{\ell_1}}{\Longrightarrow} \chi'_{j'_1} \cdots \stackrel{u_y}{\Longrightarrow} \chi'_{i'_y} \stackrel{v_y^{\ell_y}}{\Longrightarrow} \chi'_{j'_y} \stackrel{u_{y+1}}{\Longrightarrow} \chi'_p$ *such that ρ' satisfies the following properties:*

(i) $\chi_0 = \chi'_0$.
(ii) $Q(\chi'_p) = Q(\chi_m)$.
(iii) *For* $i \in [1..y]$, $\ell_i \geq I$.
(iv) *For every counter C,* $C(\chi'_p) \geq C(\chi_m)$.
(v) *Let Γ_{pump} be the set of pumpable counters in the pumpable decomposition of ρ. For each counter $C \in \Gamma_{\text{pump}}$,* $C(\chi'_p) \geq J$.

Having shown that all pumpable counters of a pumpable decomposition can be simultaneously raised to arbitrarily high values, we describe a sufficient condition for a K-computation to admit a non-trivial pumpable decomposition.

Strong pumping constant For each $M, N, K \in \mathbb{N}$, we define the *strong pumping constant* $\Pi_{M,N,K}$ by induction on N as follows (recall that $\pi_{M,N,K}$ denotes the weak pumping constant for (M, N, K)):

$$\begin{aligned} \forall M, K \in \mathbb{N}. \quad & \Pi_{M,0,K} = 1 \\ \forall M, N, K \in \mathbb{N}. \ & \Pi_{M,N+1,K} = \Pi_{M,N,\pi_{M,N+1,K}+K} + \pi_{M,N+1,K} + K \end{aligned}$$

Lemma 4.2 (Decomposition). *Let $\mathcal{N}$ be a network with M global states and N counters and let $K \in \mathbb{N}$. Let* $\rho : \chi_0 \stackrel{t_1 t_2 \ldots t_m}{\Longrightarrow} \chi_m$ *be any K-computation of $\mathcal{N}$. Then, there is a pumpable decomposition* $\chi_0 \stackrel{u_1}{\Longrightarrow} \chi_{i_1} \stackrel{v_1}{\Longrightarrow} \chi_{j_1} \cdots \stackrel{u_y}{\Longrightarrow} \chi_{i_y} \stackrel{v_y}{\Longrightarrow} \chi_{j_y} \stackrel{u_{y+1}}{\Longrightarrow} \chi_m$ *of ρ such that for every counter C, if $C(\chi_j) > \Pi_{M,N,K}$ for some $j \in [0..m]$, then C is a pumpable counter in this decomposition.*

Proof Sketch: The proof is by induction on N, the number of counters. In the induction, the key step is to identify a prefix ρ' of ρ containing two configurations χ_r and χ_s such that $Q(\chi_r) = Q(\chi_s)$, $F(\chi_r) < F(\chi_s)$ and, moreover, no counter value exceeds $\pi_{M,N,K} + K$ within ρ'.

Having found such a prefix, we fix a counter C which increases between χ_r and χ_s and construct a new network $\mathcal{N}'$ which treats $\{C^+, C^-\}$ as input letters. Since $\mathcal{N}'$ has $N-1$ counters, the induction hypothesis yields a decomposition $u_2 v_2 u_3 v_3 \ldots u_y v_y u_{y+1}$ of the suffix of ρ after ρ'. We then set u_1 to be the segment from χ_0 to χ_r and v_1 to be the segment from χ_r to χ_s and argue that the resulting decomposition $u_1 v_1 u_2 v_2 \ldots u_y v_y u_{y+1}$ of ρ satisfies the conditions of the lemma. □

The Decomposition Lemma plays a major role in the proof of our main result.

5 Robustness and Regularity

The main technical result of this paper is the following.

Theorem 5.1. *Let $\mathcal{N}$ be a robust message-passing network. Then, there is a regular sequential language L_s over $\Sigma_{\mathcal{N}}$ which represents the tuple language $L(\mathcal{N})$.*

This means that at a global level, any robust asynchronous protocol can be substituted by an equivalent finite-state machine. To prove this result, we need some technical machinery.

Networks with bounded counters Let $\mathcal{N} = (\{\mathcal{A}_i\}_{i\in[1..n]}, Acc, Rej)$ be a message-passing network. For $K \in \mathbb{N}$, define $\mathcal{N}[K] = (Q[K], T[K], Q[K]_{\rm in}, F[K])$ to be the finite-state automaton over the alphabet $\Sigma_{\mathcal{N}} \cup \Gamma_{\mathcal{N}}^{\pm}$ given by:

- $Q[K] = Q_{\mathcal{N}} \times \{f \mid f : \Gamma \longrightarrow [0..K]\}$, with $Q[K]_{\rm in} = (q_{\rm in}, \overline{0})$.
- $F[K] = Acc \times \{f \mid f : \Gamma \longrightarrow [0..K]\}$.
- If $(q, d, q') \in T_{\mathcal{N}}$, then $((q, f), d, (q', f')) \in T[K]$ where:
  - If $d \in \Sigma_{\mathcal{N}}$, $f' = f$.
  - If $d = C^+$, $f'(C') = f(C')$ for $C' \neq C$ and $f'(C) = \begin{cases} f(C){+}1 & \text{if } f(C) < K \\ K & \text{otherwise.}\end{cases}$
  - If $d = C^-$, $f'(C') = f(C')$ for $C' \neq C$, $f(C) \geq 1$ and $$f'(C) = \begin{cases} f(C){-}1 & \text{if } f(C) < K \\ K & \text{otherwise.}\end{cases}$$

Each transition $t = ((q, f), d, (q', f')) \in T[K]$ corresponds to a unique transition $(q, d, q') \in T_{\mathcal{N}}$, which we denote t^{-1}. For any sequence $t_1 t_2 \ldots t_m$ of transitions in $T[K]$, $\alpha(t_1 t_2 \ldots t_m) = \alpha(t_1^{-1} t_2^{-1} \ldots t_m^{-1})$. Moreover, if $(q_0, f_0') \overset{t_1 t_2 \ldots t_m}{\Longrightarrow} (q_m, f_m')$ and $(q_0, f_0) \overset{t_1^{-1} t_2^{-1} \ldots t_m^{-1}}{\Longrightarrow} \chi_m$, then $Q(\chi_m) = q_m$.

Thus, the finite-state automaton $\mathcal{N}[K]$ behaves like a message-passing network except that it deems any counter whose value attains a value K to be "full". Once a counter is declared to be full, it can be decremented as many times as desired. The following observations are immediate.

Proposition 5.2. *(i) If $(q_0, f_0') \overset{t_1'}{\longrightarrow} \cdots \overset{t_m'}{\longrightarrow} (q_n, f_m')$ is a computation of $\mathcal{N}$ then, $(q_0, f_0) \overset{t_1}{\longrightarrow} \cdots \overset{t_m}{\longrightarrow} (q_m, f_m)$ is a computation of $\mathcal{N}[K]$ where*
- *$t_1' \ldots t_m' = t_1^{-1} \ldots t_m^{-1}$.*
- *$\forall C \in \Gamma.\ \forall i \in [1..m].\ f_i(C) = \begin{cases} f_i'(C) & \text{if } f_j'(C) < K \text{ for all } j \leq i \\ K & \text{otherwise.}\end{cases}$*

(ii) Let $(q_0, f_0) \overset{t_1}{\longrightarrow} \cdots \overset{t_m}{\longrightarrow} (q_m, f_m)$ be a computation of $\mathcal{N}[K]$. There is a maximum prefix $t_1 \ldots t_\ell$ of $t_1 \ldots t_m$ such that $\mathcal{N}$ has a computation $(q_0, f_0') \overset{t_1^{-1}}{\longrightarrow} \cdots \overset{t_\ell^{-1}}{\longrightarrow} (q_\ell, f_\ell')$ with $f_0 = f_0'$. Moreover, if $\ell < m$, then for some counter C, $\alpha(t_{\ell+1}^{-1}) = C^-$, $f_\ell'(C) = 0$ and for some $j < \ell$, $f_j'(C) = K$.

(iii) Let $L_{seq}(\mathcal{N})$ denote the set of all words over $\Sigma_{\mathcal{N}}$ which arise in accepting runs of $\mathcal{N}$—in other words, $w \in L_{seq}(\mathcal{N})$ if there is an accepting run $\chi_0 \stackrel{t_1 t_2 \ldots t_m}{\Longrightarrow} \chi_m$ of $\mathcal{N}$ such that $w = \alpha(t_1 t_2 \ldots t_m)\restriction_{\Sigma_{\mathcal{N}}}$. Let $L_{\Sigma_{\mathcal{N}}}(\mathcal{N}[K]) = \{w\restriction_{\Sigma_{\mathcal{N}}} \mid w \in L(\mathcal{N}[K])\}$. Then, $L_{seq}(\mathcal{N}) \subseteq L_{\Sigma_{\mathcal{N}}}(\mathcal{N}[K])$.

We can now prove our main result.

Proof Sketch: (of Theorem 5.1)
Let $\mathcal{N}$ be a robust network with M global states and N counters. By interchanging the accept and reject states, we obtain a robust network $\overline{\mathcal{N}}$ for $\overline{L(\mathcal{N})}$ with the same state-transition structure as $\mathcal{N}$. Let K denote $\Pi_{M,N,0}$, the strong pumping constant for $\mathcal{N}$ (and $\overline{\mathcal{N}}$). Consider the finite-state automaton $\mathcal{N}[K]$ generated from $\mathcal{N}$ by ignoring all counter values above K.

We know that $L_{seq}(\mathcal{N})$ is a subset of $L_{\Sigma_{\mathcal{N}}}(\mathcal{N}[K])$. We claim that there is no word $w \in L_{\Sigma_{\mathcal{N}}}(\mathcal{N}[K])$ which represents an input $\langle w_1, w_2, \ldots, w_n\rangle$ from $L(\overline{\mathcal{N}})$.

Assuming the claim, it follows that for every word w in $L_{\Sigma_{\mathcal{N}}}(\mathcal{N}[K])$, the $\mathcal{N}$-projection $\langle w\restriction_{\Sigma_1}, w\restriction_{\Sigma_2}, \ldots, w\restriction_{\Sigma_n}\rangle$ belongs to $L(\mathcal{N})$. On the other hand, since $L_{seq}(\mathcal{N})$ is a subset of $L_{\Sigma_{\mathcal{N}}}(\mathcal{N}[K])$, every tuple $\langle w_1, w_2, \ldots, w_n\rangle$ in $L(\mathcal{N})$ is represented by some word in $L_{\Sigma_{\mathcal{N}}}(\mathcal{N}[K])$. Thus, $L_{\Sigma_{\mathcal{N}}}(\mathcal{N}[K])$ represents the language $L(\mathcal{N})$. Since $\mathcal{N}[K]$ is a finite-state automaton, the result follows.

To complete the proof, we must verify the claim. Suppose that there is a word w in $L_{\Sigma_{\mathcal{N}}}(\mathcal{N}[K])$ which represents a tuple $\langle w_1, w_2, \ldots, w_n\rangle$ in $L(\overline{\mathcal{N}})$. There must be a run $\rho : \chi_0 \stackrel{t_1 t_2 \ldots t_m}{\Longrightarrow} \chi_m$ of $\mathcal{N}[K]$ on w which leads to a final state (q, f), where q is an accept state of $\mathcal{N}$ and hence a reject state of $\overline{\mathcal{N}}$.

Since $\overline{\mathcal{N}}$ has the same structure as $\mathcal{N}$, by Proposition 5.2 it is possible to mimic ρ in $\overline{\mathcal{N}}$. However, since $\langle w_1, w_2, \ldots, w_n\rangle \in L(\overline{\mathcal{N}})$ and $\overline{\mathcal{N}}$ is robust, it is not possible to mimic all of ρ in $\overline{\mathcal{N}}$—otherwise, $\overline{\mathcal{N}}$ would admit both accepting and rejecting runs on $\langle w_1, w_2, \ldots, w_n\rangle$. So, $\overline{\mathcal{N}}$ must get "stuck" after some prefix $\rho_1 : \chi_0 \stackrel{t_1 t_2 \ldots t_\ell}{\Longrightarrow} \chi_\ell$ of ρ—for some counter C, $t_{\ell+1}$ is a C^- move with $C(\chi_\ell) = 0$.

We call the residual computation $\rho_2 : \chi_\ell \stackrel{t_{\ell+1} t_{\ell+2} \ldots t_m}{\Longrightarrow} \chi_m$ the *stuck suffix* of ρ. Without loss of generality, assume that ρ has a stuck suffix of minimum length among all accepting runs over words in $L_{\Sigma_{\mathcal{N}}}(\mathcal{N}[K])$ representing tuples in $L(\overline{\mathcal{N}})$.

Let u be the prefix of w which has been read in ρ_1 and v be the suffix of w which is yet to be read. Let $\langle u_1, u_2, \ldots, u_n\rangle$ and $\langle v_1, v_2, \ldots, v_n\rangle$ be the $\mathcal{N}$-projections of u and v, respectively. Clearly, u_i is a prefix of $w_i\#_i$ for each $i \in [1..n]$. Since $\overline{\mathcal{N}}$ is robust, there must be an extension of ρ_1 to a run over $\langle w_1, w_2, \ldots, w_n\rangle$—this run must be accepting since $\langle w_1, w_2, \ldots, w_n\rangle \in L(\overline{\mathcal{N}})$.

Since $\mathcal{N}[K]$ can decrement C after ρ_1 while $\overline{\mathcal{N}}$ cannot, C must have attained the value K along ρ_1. By Lemmas 4.1 and 4.2, we can transform ρ_1 into a computation ρ_1' of $\overline{\mathcal{N}}$ which reaches a configuration $\chi_{\rho_1'}$ with $Q(\chi_{\rho_1'}) = Q(\chi_\ell)$, $C(\chi_{\rho_1'}) > 0$ and $F(\chi_{\rho_1'}) \geq F(\chi_\ell)$.

Let $\langle u_1', u_2', \ldots, u_n'\rangle$ be the input read along ρ_1'. Since ρ_1 could be extended to an accepting run of $\overline{\mathcal{N}}$ over $\langle u_1 v_1, \ldots, u_n v_n\rangle$, ρ_1' can be extended to an accepting run of $\overline{\mathcal{N}}$ over $\langle u_1' v_1, \ldots, u_n' v_n\rangle$. On the other hand, we can extend ρ_1' in $\mathcal{N}[K]$ to a successful run over $u'v$, where u' is the sequentialization of $\langle u_1, u_2, \ldots, u_n\rangle$ along ρ_1'. This means that $u'v \in L_{\Sigma_{\mathcal{N}}}(\mathcal{N}[K])$ represents a tuple in $L(\overline{\mathcal{N}})$.

Since the counter C has a non-zero value after ρ'_1, we can extend ρ'_1 in $\overline{\mathcal{N}}$ to execute some portion of the stuck suffix ρ_2 of ρ. If this extension of ρ'_1 gets stuck, we have found a run which has a shorter stuck suffix than ρ, contradicting our assumption that ρ had a stuck suffix of minimum length.

On the other hand, if we can extend ρ'_1 to mimic the rest of ρ, we find that $\overline{\mathcal{N}}$ has an accepting run on $\langle u'_1v_1, \ldots, u'_nv_n \rangle$ as well as a rejecting run on $\langle u'_1v_1, \ldots, u'_nv_n \rangle$. This contradicts the robustness of $\overline{\mathcal{N}}$.

Thus it must be the case that there is no word w which is accepted by $\mathcal{N}[K]$ but which represents a tuple in $L(\overline{\mathcal{N}})$.

□

Example 5.3. Consider a network with two processes where $\Sigma_1 = \{a, c\}$ and $\Sigma_2 = \{b, d\}$. Let $L = \{\langle a^i c^k, b^j d^\ell \rangle \mid i \geq \ell \text{ and } j \geq k\}$. We can modify the network in Example 2.1 to accept L—we use two counters A and B to store the number of a's and b's read, respectively. We then decrement B each time c is read and A each time d is read to verify if the input is in L.

However, there is no robust protocol for L. If L has a robust protocol, there must be a regular language L_s which represents L. Let $\mathcal{A}$ be a finite-state automaton for L_s with n states. Choose a string $w \in L_s$ which has at least n occurrences each of c and d. It is easy to see that either all d's in w occur after all a's or all c's in w occur after all b's. We can then pump a suffix of w so that either the number of d's exceeds the number of a's or the number of c's exceeds the number of b's, thereby generating a word $u \in L_s$ with $\langle u\lceil_{\Sigma_1}, u\lceil_{\Sigma_2} \rangle \notin L$.

6 Discussion

Other models for asynchronous commmunication Many earlier attempts to model asynchronous systems focus on the infinite-state case—for instance, the port automaton model of Panangaden and Stark [12] and the I/O automaton model of Lynch and Tuttle [8]. Also, earlier work has looked at issues far removed from those which are traditionally considered in the study of finite-state systems.

Recently, Abdulla and Jonsson have studied decision problems for distributed systems with asynchronous communication [1]. However, they model channels as unbounded, fifo buffers, a framework in which most interesting questions become undecidable. The results of [1] show that the fifo model becomes tractable if messages may be lost in transit: questions such as reachability of configurations become decidable. While their results are, in general, incomparable to ours, we remark that their positive results hold for our model as well.

Petri net languages Our model is closely related to Petri nets [3, 6]. We can go back and forth between labelled Petri nets and message-passing networks while maintaining a bijection between the firing sequences of a net N and the computations of the corresponding network $\mathcal{N}$.

There are several ways to associate a language with a Petri net [4, 6, 13]. The first is to examine all firing sequences of the net. The second is to look at firing sequences which lead to a set of *final markings*. A third possibility is to identify firing sequences which reach markings which *dominate* some final marking. The third class corresponds to message-passing recognizable languages.

A number of positive results have been established for the first class of languages—for instance, regularity is decidable [2, 14]. On the other hand, a number of negative results have been established for the second class of languages—for instance, it is undecidable whether such a language contains *all* strings [14]. However, none of these results, positive or negative, carry over to the third class—ours is one of the few tangible results for this class of Petri net languages.

Directions for future work A challenging problem is to synthesize a distributed protocol from a description in terms of global states. In systems with synchronous communication, this is possible using an algorithm whereby each process maintains the latest information about the rest of the system [11, 15]. This algorithm has been extended to message-passing systems and could help in solving the synthesis problem [9]. Another important question is to be able to decide whether a given protocol is robust. We believe the problem is decidable.

References

1. P.A. Abdulla and B. Jonsson: Verifying programs with unreliable channels, in *Proc. 8th IEEE Symp. Logic in Computer Science*, Montreal, Canada (1993).
2. A. Ginzburg and M. Yoeli: Vector addition systems and regular languages, *J. Comput. System. Sci.* **20** (1980) 277–284
3. S.A. Greibach: Remarks on blind and partially blind one-way multicounter machines, *Theoret. Comput. Sci* **7** (1978) 311–324.
4. M. Hack: Petri Net Languages, *C.S.G. Memo 124*, Project MAC, MIT (1975).
5. G.J. Holzmann: *Design and validation of computer protocols*, Prentice Hall (1991).
6. M. Jantzen: Language theory of Petri nets, in W. Brauer, W. Reisig, G. Rozenberg (eds.), *Advances in Petri Nets, 1986, Vol 1*, Springer LNCS **254** (1986) 397–412.
7. R.M. Karp and R.E. Miller: Parallel program schemata, *J. Comput. System Sci.*, **3** (4) (1969) 167–195.
8. N.A. Lynch and M. Tuttle: Hierarchical correctness proofs for distributed algorithms, *MIT/LCS/TR-387*, Laboratory for Computer Science, MIT (1987).
9. M. Mukund, K. Narayan Kumar and M. Sohoni: Keeping track of the latest gossip in message-passing systems, *Proc. Structures in Concurrency Theory (STRICT)*, Berlin 1995, Workshops in Computing Series, Springer-Verlag (1995) 249–263.
10. M. Mukund, K. Narayan Kumar, J. Radhakrishnan and M. Sohoni: Counter automata and asynchronous communication, *Report TCS-97-4*, SPIC Mathematical Institute, Madras, India (1997).
11. M. Mukund and M. Sohoni: Gossiping, asynchronous automata and Zielonka's theorem, *Report TCS-94-2*, School of Mathematics, SPIC Science Foundation, Madras, India (1994).
12. P. Panangaden and E.W. Stark: Computations, residuals, and the power of indeterminacy, *Proc. ICALP '88*, Springer LNCS **317** (1988) 439–454.
13. J.L. Peterson: *Petri net theory and the modelling of systems*, Prentice Hall (1981).
14. R. Valk and G. Vidal-Naquet: Petri nets and regular languages, *J. Comput. System. Sci.* **23** (3) (1981) 299–325.
15. W. Zielonka: Notes on finite asynchronous automata, *R.A.I.R.O.—Inf. Théor. et Appl.*, **21** (1987) 99–135.

Deciding Bisimulation-Like Equivalences with Finite-State Processes*

Petr Jančar[1], Antonín Kučera[2], and Richard Mayr[3]

[1] Dept. of Computer Science FEI, Technical University of Ostrava, 17. listopadu 15, 708 33 Ostrava, Czech Republic, Petr.Jancar@vsb.cz
[2] Faculty of Informatics MU, Botanická 68a, 602 00 Brno, Czech Republic, tony@fi.muni.cz
[3] Institut für Informatik, Technische Universität München, Arcisstr. 21, D-80290 München, Germany, mayrri@informatik.tu-muenchen.de

Abstract. We design a general method for proving decidability of bisimulation-like equivalences between infinite-state processes and finite-state ones. We apply this method to the class of PAD processes, which strictly subsumes PA and push-down (PDA) processes, showing that a large class of bisimulation-like equivalences (including e.g. strong and weak bisimilarity) is decidable between PAD and finite-state processes. On the other hand, we also demonstrate that no 'reasonable' bisimulation-like equivalence is decidable between state-extended PA processes and finite-state ones. Furthermore, weak bisimilarity with finite-state processes is shown to be undecidable even for state-extended BPP (which are also known as 'parallel pushdown processes').

1 Introduction

In this paper we study the decidability of bisimulation-like equivalences between infinite-state processes and finite-state ones. First we examine this problem in a general setting, extracting its core in a form of two rather special subproblems (which are naturally not decidable in general). A special variant of this method which works for strong bisimilarity has been described in [10]; here we extend and generalize the concept, obtaining a universal mechanism for proving decidability of bisimulation-like equivalences between infinite-state and finite-state processes. Then we apply the designed method to the class of PAD processes (defined in [16]), which properly subsumes all PA and push-down processes. We prove that a large class of bisimulation-like equivalences (including e.g. strong and weak bisimilarity) is decidable between PAD and finite-state processes, utilizing previously established results on decidability of the model-checking problem for EF logic [15,17]. We also provide several undecidability results to complete the picture—we show that any 'reasonable' bisimulation-like equivalence is undecidable between state-extended PA processes and finite-state ones. Moreover, even for state-extended BPP processes (which are a natural subclass of Petri nets) weak bisimilarity with finite-state processes is undecidable.

* The first author is supported by the Grant Agency of the Czech Republic, grant No. 201/97/0456. The second author is supported by a Post-Doc grant GA ČR No. 201/98/P046 and by a Research Fellowship granted by The Alexander von Humboldt Foundation.

Decidability of bisimulation-like equivalences has been intensively studied for various process classes (see e.g. [19] for a complete survey). The majority of the results are about the decidability of strong bisimilarity, e.g. [3,6,5,22,4,13,8].

Strong bisimilarity with finite-state processes is known to be decidable for (labelled) Petri nets [12], PA and pushdown processes [10]. Another positive result of this kind is presented in [14], where it is shown that weak bisimilarity is decidable between BPP and finite-state processes. However, weak bisimilarity with finite-state processes is undecidable for Petri nets [9]. In [21] it is shown that the problem of equivalence-checking with finite-state systems can be reduced to the model-checking problem for the modal μ-calculus. Thus, in this paper we obtain original positive results for PAD (and hence also PA and PDA) processes, and an undecidability result for state-extended BPP processes. Moreover, all positive results are proved using the same general strategy, which can also be adapted to previously established ones.

2 Definitions

Transition systems are widely accepted as a structure which can exactly define the operational semantics of processes. In the rest of this paper we understand processes as (being associated with) nodes in transition systems of certain types.

Definition 1. *A transition system (TS) $\mathcal{T}$ is a triple $(S, Act, \rightarrow)$ where S is a set of* states, *Act is a finite set of* actions *(or* labels*) and $\rightarrow \subseteq S \times Act \times S$ is a* transition relation.

We defined *Act* as a finite set; this is a little bit nonstandard, but we can allow this as all classes of processes we consider generate transition systems of this type. As usual, we write $s \xrightarrow{a} t$ instead of $(s, a, t) \in \rightarrow$ and we extend this notation to elements of Act^* in an obvious way (we sometimes write $s \rightarrow^* t$ instead of $s \xrightarrow{w} t$ if $w \in Act^*$ is irrelevant). A state t is *reachable* from a state s if $s \rightarrow^* t$.

Let $Var = \{X, Y, Z, \ldots\}$ be a countably infinite set of *variables*. The class of *process expressions*, denoted $\mathcal{E}$, is defined by the following abstract syntax equation:

$$E ::= \lambda \mid X \mid E \| E \mid E.E$$

Here X ranges over *Var* and λ is a constant that denotes the empty expression. In the rest of this paper we do not distinguish between expressions related by *structural congruence* which is the smallest congruence relation over process expressions such that the following laws hold: associativity for '.' and '$\|$', commutativity for '$\|$', and 'λ' as a unit for '.' and '$\|$'.

A *process rewrite system* [16] is specified by a finite set Δ of *rules* which are of the form $E \xrightarrow{a} F$, where E, F are process expressions and a is an element of a finite set *Act*. Each process rewrite system determines a unique transition system where states are process expressions, *Act* is the set of labels, and transitions are defined by Δ and the following inference rules (remember that '$\|$' is commutative):

$$\frac{(E \xrightarrow{a} F) \in \Delta}{E \xrightarrow{a} F} \qquad \frac{E \xrightarrow{a} E'}{E.F \xrightarrow{a} E'.F} \qquad \frac{E \xrightarrow{a} E'}{E\|F \xrightarrow{a} E'\|F}$$

The classes of BPA, BPP, PA, and PAD systems are subclasses of process rewrite systems obtained by certain restrictions on the form of the expressions which can appear at the left-hand and the right-hand side of rules. To specify those restrictions, we first define the classes of *sequential* and *parallel* expressions, composed of all process expressions which do not contain the '$\|$' and the '.' operator, respectively. BPA, BPP, and PA allow only a single variable at the left-hand side of rules, and a sequential, parallel, and general process expression at the right-hand side, respectively. Note that each transition $E \xrightarrow{a} F$ is due to some rule $X \xrightarrow{a} G$ of Δ (i.e. X is rewritten by G within E, yielding the expression F). Generally, there can be more than one rule of Δ with this property—if e.g. $\Delta = \{X \xrightarrow{a} X\|Y, Y \xrightarrow{a} Y\|Y\}$, then the transition $X\|Y \xrightarrow{a} X\|Y\|Y$ can be derived in one step in two different ways. For each transition $E \xrightarrow{a} F$ we denote the set of all rules of Δ which allow to derive the transition in one step by *Step*$(E \xrightarrow{a} F)$.

The PA class strictly subsumes BPA and BPP systems; a proper extension of PA is the class of PAD systems (see [16]), where sequential expressions are allowed at the left-hand side and general ones at the right-hand side of rules. The PAD class strictly subsumes not only PA but also PDA processes (see below). This is demonstrated in [16].

Another way how to extend a PA system is to add a finite-state control unit to it. A *state-extended PA system* is a triple (Δ, Q, BT) where Δ is a PA system, Q is a finite set of *states*, and $BT \subseteq \Delta \times Q \times Q$ is a set of *basic transitions*. The transition system generated by a state-extended PA system (Δ, Q, BT) has $Q \times \mathcal{E}$ as the set of states (its elements are called *state-extended PA processes*, or *StExt(PA)* processes for short), *Act* is the set of labels, and the transition relation is determined by

$$(p, E) \xrightarrow{a} (q, F) \text{ iff } E \xrightarrow{a} F \text{ and } (X \xrightarrow{a} G, p, q) \in BT \text{ for some } X \xrightarrow{a} G \in Step(E \xrightarrow{a} F)$$

Natural subclasses of *StExt(PA)* systems are *StExt(BPA)* and *StExt(BPP)*, which are also known as pushdown (PDA) and parallel pushdown (PPDA) systems, respectively. Each *StExt(BPA)* system can also be seen as a PAD system; however, the classes of *StExt(BPP)* and PAD systems are semantically incomparable (w.r.t. *strong bisimilarity*, which is defined in the next section—see also [16]).

3 A General Method for Bisimulation-Like Equivalences

In this section we design a general method for proving decidability of bisimulation-like equivalences between infinite-state processes and finite-state ones.

Definition 2. *Let $R : Act \rightarrow 2^{Act^*}$ be a (total) function, assigning to each action its corresponding set of* responses. *We say that R is* closed under substitution *if the following conditions hold:*

- *$a \in R(a)$ for each $a \in Act$*
- *If $b_1 b_2 \ldots b_n \in R(a)$ and $w_1 \in R(b_1), w_2 \in R(b_2), \ldots, w_n \in R(b_n)$, then also $w_1 w_2 \ldots w_n \in R(a)$.*

In order to simplify our notation, we adopt the following conventions in this section:

- $\mathcal{G} = (G, Act, \rightarrow)$ always denotes a (general) transition system.
- $\mathcal{F} = (F, Act, \rightarrow)$ always denotes a finite-state transition system with k states.
- R always denotes a function from *Act* to 2^{Act^*} which is closed under substitution.
- N always denotes a decidable binary predicate defined for pairs (s,t) of nodes in transition systems (which will be clear from the context). Moreover, N is reflexive, symmetric, and transitive.
- We write $s \stackrel{a}{\Rightarrow} t$ if $s \stackrel{w}{\rightarrow} t$ for some $w \in R(a)$.

Note that $\mathcal{G}$ and $\mathcal{F}$ have the same set of actions *Act*. All definitions and propositions which are formulated for $\mathcal{G}$ should be considered as general; if we want to state some specific property of finite-state transition systems, we refer to $\mathcal{F}$. We also assume that $\mathcal{G}$, $\mathcal{F}$, R, and N are defined in a 'reasonable' way so that we can allow natural decidability assumptions on them (e.g. it is decidable whether $g \stackrel{a}{\rightarrow} g'$ for any given $g, g' \in G$ and $a \in Act$, or whether $w \in R(a)$ for a given $w \in Act^*$, etc.)

Definition 3. *A relation $P \subseteq G \times G$ is an* R-N-bisimulation *if whenever $(s,t) \in P$, then $N(s,t)$ is true and for each $a \in Act$:*

- *If $s \stackrel{a}{\rightarrow} s'$, then $t \stackrel{a}{\Rightarrow} t'$ for some $t' \in G$ such that $(s', t') \in P$.*
- *If $t \stackrel{a}{\rightarrow} t'$, then $s \stackrel{a}{\Rightarrow} s'$ for some $s' \in G$ such that $(s', t') \in P$.*

States $s, t \in G$ are R-N-bisimilar, *written $s \stackrel{RN}{\sim} t$, if there is an R-N-bisimulation relating them.*

Various special versions of *R-N*-bisimilarity appeared in the literature, e.g. *strong* and *weak* bisimilarity (see [20,18]). The corresponding versions of R (denoted by S and W, respectively) are defined as follows:

- $S(a) = \{a\}$ for each $a \in Act$
- $W(a) = \begin{cases} \{\tau^i \mid i \in \mathbb{N}_0\} & \text{if } a = \tau \\ \{\tau^i a \tau^j \mid i, j \in \mathbb{N}_0\} & \text{otherwise} \end{cases}$

The 'τ' is a special (silent) action, usually used to model an internal communication. As the predicate N is not employed in the definitions of strong and weak bisimilarity, we can assume it is always true (we use T to denote this special case of N).

The concept of *R-N*-bisimilarity covers many equivalences, which have not been explicitly investigated so far; for example, we can define the function R like this:

- $K(a) = \{a^i \mid i \in \mathbb{N}_0\}$ for each $a \in Act$.
- $L(a) = \{w \in Act^* \mid w \text{ begins with } a\}$.
- $M(a) = \begin{cases} Act^* & \text{if } a = \tau \\ \{w \in Act^* \mid w \text{ contains at least one } a\} & \text{otherwise} \end{cases}$

The predicate N can also have various forms. We have already mentioned the 'T' (always true). Another natural example is the I predicate: $I(s,t)$ is true iff s and t have the same sets of initial actions (the set of initial actions of a state $g \in G$ is $\{a \in Act \mid g \stackrel{a}{\rightarrow} g' \text{ for some } g' \in G\}$). It is easy to see that e.g. $\stackrel{ST}{\sim}$ coincides with $\stackrel{SI}{\sim}$, while $\stackrel{WI}{\sim}$ refines $\stackrel{WT}{\sim}$.

To the best of our knowledge, the only bisimulation-like equivalence which cannot be seen as *R-N*-bisimilarity is *branching bisimilarity* introduced in [23]. This relation also places requirements on 'intermediate' nodes that extended transitions pass through, and this brings further difficulties. Therefore we do not consider branching bisimilarity in our paper.

R-N-bisimilarity can also be defined in terms of the so-called *R-N-bisimulation game*. Imagine that there are two tokens initially placed in states s and t such that $N(s,t)$ is true. Two players, Al and Ex, now start to play a game consisting of a (possibly infinite) sequence of rounds, where each round is performed as follows:

1. Al chooses one of the two tokens and moves it along an arbitrary (but single!) transition, labelled by some $a \in Act$.
2. Ex has to respond by moving the other token along a finite sequence of transitions in such a way that the corresponding sequence of labels belongs to $R(a)$ and the predicate N is true for the states where the tokens lie after Ex finishes his move.

Al wins the *R-N*-bisimulation game, if after a finite number of rounds Ex cannot respond to Al's final attack. Now it is easy to see that the states s and t are *R-N*-bisimilar iff Ex has a universal defending strategy (i.e. Ex can play in such a way that Al cannot win).

A natural way how to approximate *R-N*-bisimilarity is to define the family of relations $\overset{RN}{\sim}_i \subseteq G \times G$ for each $i \in \mathbb{N}_0$ as follows: $s \overset{RN}{\sim}_i t$ iff $N(s,t)$ is true and Ex has a defending strategy within the first i rounds in the *R-N*-bisimulation game. However, $\overset{RN}{\sim}_i$ does not have to be an equivalence relation. Moreover, it is not necessarily true that $s \overset{RN}{\sim} t \iff s \overset{RN}{\sim}_i t$ for each $i \in \mathbb{N}_0$. A simple counterexample is the weak bisimilarity (i.e. *W-T*-bisimilarity) and its approximations.

Now we show how to overcome those drawbacks; to do this, we introduce the *extended R-N*-bisimulation relation:

Definition 4. *A relation $P \subseteq G \times G$ is an* extended *R-N-bisimulation if whenever $(s,t) \in P$, then $N(s,t)$ is true and for each $a \in Act$:*

- *If $s \overset{a}{\Rightarrow} s'$, then $t \overset{a}{\Rightarrow} t'$ for some $t' \in G$ such that $(s',t') \in P$.*
- *If $t \overset{a}{\Rightarrow} t'$, then $s \overset{a}{\Rightarrow} s'$ for some $s' \in G$ such that $(s',t') \in P$.*

States $s,t \in G$ are extended R-N-bisimilar *if there is an extended R-N-bisimulation relating them.*

Naturally, we can also define the extended *R-N*-bisimilarity by means of the extended *R-N*-bisimulation game; we simply allow Al to use the 'long' moves (i.e. Al can play the same kind of moves as Ex). Moreover, we can define the family of approximations of extended *R-N*-bisimilarity in the same way as in case of *R-N*-bisimilarity—for each $i \in \mathbb{N}_0$ we define the relation $\overset{RN}{\simeq}_i \subseteq G \times G$ as follows: $s \overset{RN}{\simeq}_i t$ iff $N(s,t)$ is true and Ex has a defending strategy within the first i rounds in the extended *R-N*-bisimulation game where tokens are initially placed in s and t.

Lemma 1. *Two states s,t of $\mathcal{G}$ are R-N-bisimilar iff s and t are extended R-N-bisimilar.*

Lemma 2. *The following properties hold:*

1. *$\overset{RN}{\simeq}_i$ is an equivalence relation for each $i \in \mathbb{N}_0$.*
2. *Let s,t be states of $\mathcal{G}$. Then $s \overset{RN}{\sim}_i t$ for each $i \in \mathbb{N}_0$ iff $s \overset{RN}{\simeq}_i t$ for each $i \in \mathbb{N}_0$.*

Now we examine some special features of *R-N*-bisimilarity on finite-state transition systems (remember that $\mathcal{F}$ is a finite-state TS with k states).

Lemma 3. *Two states s, t of $\mathcal{F}$ are R-N-bisimilar iff $s \overset{RN}{\simeq}_{k-1} t$.*

Proof. As $\mathcal{F}$ has k states and $\overset{RN}{\simeq}_{i+1}$ refines $\overset{RN}{\simeq}_i$ for each $i \in \mathbb{N}_0$, we have that $\overset{RN}{\simeq}_{k-1} = \overset{RN}{\simeq}_k$, hence $\overset{RN}{\simeq}_{k-1} = \overset{RN}{\sim}$.

Theorem 1. *States $g \in G$, $f \in F$ are R-N-bisimilar iff $g \overset{RN}{\simeq}_k f$ and for each state g' reachable from g there is a state $f' \in F$ such that $g' \overset{RN}{\simeq}_k f'$.*

Proof.
'$\Longrightarrow$': Obvious.
'$\Longleftarrow$': We prove that the relation $P = \{(g', f') \mid g \rightarrow^* g' \text{ and } g' \overset{RN}{\simeq}_k f'\}$ is an extended *R-N*-bisimulation. Let $(g', f') \in P$ and let $g' \overset{a}{\Rightarrow} g''$ for some $a \in \mathit{Act}$ (the case when $f' \overset{a}{\Rightarrow} f''$ is handled is the same way). By definition of $\overset{RN}{\simeq}_k$, there is f'' such that $f' \overset{a}{\Rightarrow} f''$ and $g'' \overset{RN}{\simeq}_{k-1} f''$. It suffices to show that $g'' \overset{RN}{\simeq}_k f''$; as $g \rightarrow^* g''$, there is a state $\overline{f}$ of $\mathcal{F}$ such that $g'' \overset{RN}{\simeq}_k \overline{f}$. By transitivity of $\overset{RN}{\simeq}_{k-1}$ we have $\overline{f} \overset{RN}{\simeq}_{k-1} f''$, hence $\overline{f} \overset{RN}{\simeq}_k f''$ (due to Lemma 3). Now $g'' \overset{RN}{\simeq}_k \overline{f} \overset{RN}{\simeq}_k f''$ and thus $g'' \overset{RN}{\simeq}_k f''$ as required. Clearly $(g, f) \in P$ and the proof is complete. □

Remark 1. We have already mentioned that the equivalence $s \overset{RN}{\sim} t \Longleftrightarrow s \overset{RN}{\simeq}_i t$ *for each* $i \in \mathbb{N}_0$ is generally invalid (e.g. in case of weak bisimilarity). However, as soon as we assume that t is a state in a finite-state transition system, the equivalence becomes true. This is an immediate consequence of the previous theorem. Moreover, the second part of Lemma 2 says that we could also use the $\overset{RN}{\sim}_i$ approximations in the right-hand side of the equivalence.

The previous theorem in fact says that one can use the following strategy to decide whether $g \overset{RN}{\sim} f$:

1. Decide whether $g \overset{RN}{\simeq}_k f$ (if not, then $g \overset{RN}{\not\sim} f$).
2. Check whether g can reach a state g' such that $g' \overset{RN}{\not\simeq}_k f'$ for *any* state f' of $\mathcal{F}$ (if there is such a g' then $g \overset{RN}{\not\sim} f$; otherwise $g \overset{RN}{\sim} f$).

However, none of these tasks is easy in general. Our aim is to examine both subproblems in detail, keeping the general setting. Thus we cannot expect any 'universal' (semi)decidability result, because even the problems $g \overset{WT}{\simeq}_1 f$ and $g \overset{WT}{\not\simeq}_1 f$ are not semidecidable in general (see Section 5).

As $\mathcal{F}$ has finitely many states, the extended transition relation $\Rightarrow$ is finite and effectively constructible. This allows us to "extract" from $\mathcal{F}$ the information which is relevant for the first k moves in the extended *R-N*-bisimulation game by means of branching trees with depth at most k, whose arcs are labelled by elements of *Act* and nodes are labelled by elements of $F \cup \{\perp\}$, where $\perp \notin F$. The aim of following definition is to describe all such trees up to isomorphism (remember that *Act* is a *finite* set).

Definition 5. *For each $i \in \mathbb{N}_0$ we define the set of* Trees *with* depth *at most i (denoted Tree_i) inductively as follows:*

- *A Tree with depth 0 is any tree with no arcs and a single node (the root) which is labelled by an element of $F \cup \{\perp\}$.*

- *A Tree with depth at most $i + 1$ is any directed tree with root r whose nodes are labelled by elements of $F \cup \{\bot\}$, arcs are labelled by elements of Act, which satisfies the following conditions:*
  - *If $r \xrightarrow{a} s$, then the subtree rooted by s is a Tree with depth at most i.*
  - *If $r \xrightarrow{a} s$ and $r \xrightarrow{a} s'$, then the subtrees rooted by s and s' are not isomorphic.*

It is clear that the set $Tree_j$ is finite and effectively constructible for any $j \in \mathbb{N}_0$. As each Tree can be seen as a transition system, we can also speak about *Tree-processes* which are associated with roots of Trees (we do not distinguish between Trees and Tree-processes in the rest of this paper).

Now we introduce special rules which replace the standard ones whenever we consider an extended *R*-*N*-bisimulation game with initial state (g, p), where $g \in G$ and p is a Tree process (formally, these rules determine is a new (different) game—however, it does not deserve a special name in our opinion).

- Al and Ex are allowed to play only 'short' moves consisting of exactly one transition whenever playing within the Tree process p (transitions of Trees correspond to extended transitions of $\mathcal{F}$).
- The predicate $N(g', p')$, where $g' \in G$ and p' a state of the Tree process p, is evaluated as follows:
  - if $label(p') \neq \bot$, then $N(g', p') = N(g', label(p'))$
  - if $label(p') = \bot$ and $N(g', f) = true$ for some $f \in F$, then $N(g', p') = false$
  - if $label(p') = \bot$ and $N(g', f) = false$ for any $f \in F$, then $N(g', p') = true$

Whenever we write $g \overset{RN}{\simeq}_i p$, where $g \in G$ and p is a Tree process, we mean that Ex has a defending strategy within the first i rounds in the 'modified' extended *R*-*N*-bisimulation game. The importance of Tree processes is clarified by the two lemmas below:

Lemma 4. *Let g be a state of $\mathcal{G}$, $j \in \mathbb{N}_0$. Then $g \overset{RN}{\simeq}_j p$ for some $p \in Tree_j$*

Lemma 5. *Let f be a state of $\mathcal{F}$, $j \in \mathbb{N}_0$, and $p \in Tree_j$ such that $f \overset{RN}{\simeq}_j p$. Then for any state g of $\mathcal{G}$ we have that $g \overset{RN}{\simeq}_j f$ iff $g \overset{RN}{\simeq}_j p$.*

Now we can extract the core of both subproblems which appeared in the previously mentioned general strategy in a (hopefully) nice way by defining two new and rather special problems—the Step-problem and the Reach-problem:

The Step-problem

Instance: (g, a, j, p) where g is a state of $\mathcal{G}$, $a \in Act$, $0 \leq j < k$, and $p \in Tree_j$.

Question: Is there a state g' of $\mathcal{G}$ such that $g \overset{a}{\Rightarrow} g'$ and $g' \overset{RN}{\simeq}_j p$?

The oracle which for any state g'' of $\mathcal{G}$ answers whether $g'' \overset{RN}{\simeq}_j p$ can be used.

The Reach-problem

Instance: (g, p) where g is a state of $\mathcal{G}$ and p is a Tree-process of depth $\leq k$.

Question: Is there a state g' of $\mathcal{G}$ such that $g \rightarrow^* g'$ and $g' \overset{RN}{\simeq}_k p$?

The oracle which for any state g'' of $\mathcal{G}$ answers whether $g'' \overset{RN}{\simeq}_k p$ can be used.

Formally, the transition system $\mathcal{F}$ should also be present in instances of both problems, as it determines the sets $Tree_j$ and the constant k; we prefer the simplified form to make the following proofs more readable.

Theorem 2. *If the Step-problem is decidable (with possible usage of the mentioned oracle), then $\overset{RN}{\simeq}_k$ is decidable between any states g and f of $\mathcal{G}$ and $\mathcal{F}$, respectively.*

Proof. We prove by induction on j that $\overset{RN}{\simeq}_j$ is decidable for any $0 \leq j \leq k$. First, $\overset{RN}{\simeq}_0$ is decidable because the predicate N is decidable. Let us assume that $\overset{RN}{\simeq}_j$ is decidable (hence the mentioned oracle can be used). It remains to prove that if the Step-problem is decidable, then $\overset{RN}{\simeq}_{j+1}$ is decidable as well. We introduce two auxiliary finite sets:

- The set of **C**ompatible **S**teps, denoted CS_j^f, is composed exactly of all pairs of the form (a, p) where $a \in Act$ and $p \in Tree_j$, such that $f \overset{a}{\Rightarrow} f'$ for some f' with $f' \overset{RN}{\simeq}_j p$.
- The set of **INC**ompatible **S**teps, denoted $INCS_j^f$, is a complement of CS_j^f w.r.t. $Act \times Tree_j$.

The sets CS_j^f and $INCS_j^f$ are effectively constructible. By definition, $g \overset{RN}{\simeq}_{j+1} f$ iff $N(g, f)$ is true and the following conditions hold:

1. If $f \overset{a}{\Rightarrow} f'$, then $g \overset{a}{\Rightarrow} g'$ for some g' with $g' \overset{RN}{\simeq}_j f'$.
2. If $g \overset{a}{\Rightarrow} g'$, then $f \overset{a}{\Rightarrow} f'$ for some f' with $g' \overset{RN}{\simeq}_j f'$.

The first condition in fact says that (g, a, j, p) is a positive instance of the Step-problem for any $(a, p) \in CS_j^f$ (see Lemma 4 and 5). It can be checked effectively due to the decidability of the Step-problem.

The second condition does *not* hold iff $g \overset{a}{\Rightarrow} g'$ for some g' such that $g' \overset{RN}{\simeq}_j p$ where (a, p) is an element of $INCS_j^f$ (due to Lemma 4 and 5). This is clearly decidable due to the decidability of the Step-problem again. □

It is worth mentioning that the Step-problem is generally semidecidable (provided it is possible to enumerate all finite paths starting in g). However, it does not suffice for semidecidability of $\overset{RN}{\simeq}_i$ or $\overset{RN}{\not\simeq}_i$ between states of $\mathcal{G}$ and $\mathcal{F}$.

Theorem 3. *Decidability of the Step-problem and the Reach-problem (with possible usage of the indicated oracles) implies decidability of the problem whether for each g' reachable from a given state g of $\mathcal{G}$ there is a state f' of $\mathcal{F}$ with $g' \overset{RN}{\simeq}_k f'$.*

Proof. First, the oracle indicated in the definition of Reach-problem can be used because we already know that decidability of the Step-problem implies decidability of $\overset{RN}{\simeq}_k$ between states of $\mathcal{G}$ and $\mathcal{F}$ (see the previous theorem). To complete the proof, we need to define one auxiliary set:

- The set of **INC**ompatible **T**rees, denoted $INCT$, is composed of all $p \in Tree_k$ such that $f \overset{RN}{\not\simeq}_k p$ for each state f of $\mathcal{F}$.

The set *INCT* is finite and effectively constructible. The state g can reach a state g' such that $g' \overset{RN}{\not\simeq}_k f$ for any state f of $\mathcal{F}$ (i.e. g is a *negative* instance of the problem specified in the second part of this theorem) iff (g, p) is a positive instance of the Reach problem for some $p \in \mathit{INCT}$ (due to Lemma 4 and 5). □

4 Applications

In this section we show that the Step and Reach problems can be reduced to the model checking problem for the branching-time temporal logic EF. In this way we elegantly prove that a large class of *R*-*N*-bisimulation equivalences is decidable between PAD processes and finite-state ones (the class includes all versions of *R*-*N*-bisimulation equivalences we defined in this paper and many others). First we define the logic EF (more exactly an extended version of EF with constraints on sequences of actions). The formulae have the following syntax:

$$\Phi ::= \mathit{true} \mid \neg\Phi \mid \Phi_1 \wedge \Phi_2 \mid \langle a\rangle\Phi \mid \Diamond_C\Phi$$

where a is an atomic action and C is a unary predicate on sequences of atomic actions. Let $\mathcal{T} = (S, \mathit{Act}, \rightarrow)$ be a transition system. The denotation $[\![\Phi]\!]$ of a formula Φ is a set of states of $\mathcal{T}$, which is defined as follows (sequences of actions are denoted by w):

$$[\![\mathit{true}]\!] := S,\ [\![\neg\Phi]\!] := S - [\![\Phi]\!],\ [\![\Phi_1 \wedge \Phi_2]\!] := [\![\Phi_1]\!] \cap [\![\Phi_2]\!]$$
$$[\![\langle a\rangle\Phi]\!] := \{s \in S \mid \exists s' \in S.\ s \overset{a}{\rightarrow} s' \in [\![\Phi]\!]\}$$
$$[\![\Diamond_C\Phi]\!] := \{s \in S \mid \exists w, s'.\ s \overset{w}{\rightarrow} s' \ \wedge\ C(w)\ \wedge\ s' \in [\![\Phi]\!]\}$$

The predicates C are used to express constraints on sequences of actions. For every *R*-*N*-bisimulation we define predicates C_a s.t. for every action a and every sequence w we have $C_a(w) \iff w \in R(a)$. Let EF_R be the fragment of EF that contains only constraints C_a for R and the *true* constraint.

An instance of the *model checking problem* is given by a state s in S and an EF_R-formula Φ. The question is whether $s \in [\![\Phi]\!]$. This property is also denoted by $s \models \Phi$.

Let us fix a general TS $\mathcal{G} = (G, \mathit{Act}, \rightarrow)$ and a finite-state TS $\mathcal{F} = (F, \mathit{Act}, \rightarrow)$ with k states in the same way as in the previous section. We show how to encode the Step and the Reach problems by EF_R formulae. The first difficulty is the N predicate. Although it is decidable, this fact is generally of no use as we do not know anything about the strategy of the model-checking algorithm. Instead, we restrict our attention to those predicates which can be encoded by EF_R formulae in the following sense: for each $f \in F$ there is an EF_R formula Ψ_f such that for each $g \in G$ we have that $g \models \Psi_f$ iff $N(g, f)$ is true. In this case we also define the formula $\Psi_\perp := \bigwedge_{f \in F} \neg\Psi_f$. A concrete example of a predicate which can be encoded by EF_R formulae is e.g. the 'I' predicate defined in the previous section. Now we design the family of $\Phi_{j,p}$ formulae, where $0 \leq j \leq k$ and $p \in \mathit{Tree}_j$, in such a way that for each $g \in G$ the equivalence $g \overset{RN}{\simeq}_j p \iff g \models \Phi_{j,p}$ holds. Having these formulae, the Step and the Reach problems can be encoded in a rather straightforward way:

- (g, a, j, p) is a positive instance of the Step problem iff $g \models \Diamond_{C_a}(\Phi_{j,p})$
- (g, p) is a positive instance of the Reach problem iff $g \models \Diamond(\Phi_{k,p})$

The family of $\Phi_{j,p}$ formulae is defined inductively on j as follows:

– $\Phi_{0,p} := \Psi_f$, where $f = label(p)$

– $\Phi_{j+1,p} := \Psi_f \wedge \left(\bigwedge_{a \in Act} \bigwedge_{p' \in S(p,a)} \diamond_{C_a} \Phi_{j,p'} \right) \wedge \left(\bigwedge_{a \in Act} (\neg \diamond_{C_a} (\bigwedge_{p' \in S(p,a)} \neg \Phi_{j,p'})) \right)$,

where $f = label(p)$ and $S(p,a) = \{p' \mid p \xrightarrow{a} p'\}$. If the set $S(p,a)$ is empty, any conjunction of the form $\bigwedge_{p' \in S(p,a)} \Theta_{p'}$ is replaced by *true*.

The decidability of model checking with the logic EF_R depends on the constraints that correspond to R. It has been shown in [15] that model checking PA-processes with the logic EF is decidable for the class of *decomposable constraints*. This result has been generalized to PAD processes in [17]. These constraints are called decomposable, because they can be decomposed w.r.t. sequential and parallel composition. The formal definition is as follows: A set of decomposable constraints $\mathcal{DC}$ is a finite set of unary predicates on finite sequences of actions that contains the predicates *true* and *false* and satisfies the following conditions.

1. For every $C \in \mathcal{DC}$ there is a finite index set I and a finite set of decomposable constraints $\{C_i^1, C_i^2 \in \mathcal{DC} \mid i \in I\}$ s.t.
$$\forall w, w_1, w_2.\ w_1 w_2 = w \Rightarrow (C(w) \iff \bigvee_{i \in I} C_i^1(w_1) \wedge C_i^2(w_2))$$
2. For every $C \in \mathcal{DC}$ there is a finite index set J and a finite set of decomposable constraints $\{C_i^1, C_i^2 \in \mathcal{DC} \mid i \in J\}$ s.t.
$$\forall w_1, w_2.(\ (\exists w \in interleave(w_1, w_2).\ C(w)) \iff \bigvee_{i \in J} (C_i^1(w_1) \wedge C_i^2(w_2)))$$
Here $w \in interleave(w_1, w_2)$ iff w is an arbitrary interleaving of w_1 and w_2.

It is easy to see that the closure of a set of decomposable constraints under disjunction is again a set of decomposable constraints. All the previously mentioned examples of functions R can be expressed by decomposable constraints. However, there are also functions R that are closed under substitution, but which yield non-decomposable constraints. For example, let $Act = \{a, b\}$ and $R(a) := \{w \mid \#_a w > \#_b w\}$ and $R(b) := \{b\}$, where $\#_a w$ is the number of actions a in w. On the other hand, there are decomposable constraints that are not closed under substitution like $R(a) := \{a^i \mid 1 \leq i \leq 5\}$. Now we can formulate a very general decidability theorem:

Theorem 4. *The problem $g \overset{RN}{\sim} f$, where R yields a set of constraints contained in a set $\mathcal{DC}$ of decomposable constraints, N is expressible in EF_R, g is a PAD processes, and f is a finite-state process, is decidable.*

5 Undecidability Results

Intuitively, any 'nontrivial' equivalence with finite-state processes should be undecidable for a class of processes having 'full Turing power', which can be formally expressed as e.g. the ability to simulate Minsky counter machines. Any such machine $\mathcal{M}$ can be easily 'mimicked' by a *StExt(PA)* process $P(\mathcal{M})$. A construction of the $P(\mathcal{M})$ process is described in [10]. If we label each transition in $P(\mathcal{M})$ by an action a then it is can either perform the action a boundedly many times and stop (its behaviour can be defined as a^n for some n) or do a forever (its behaviour being a^ω); this depends on whether the corresponding counter machine $\mathcal{M}$ halts or not. Notice that a^ω is the behaviour of the 1-state transition system $(\{s\}, \{a\}, \{(s, a, s)\})$. When we declare as *reasonable* any equivalence which distinguishes between (processes with) behaviours a^ω and a^n, we can conclude:

Theorem 5. *Any reasonable equivalence between StExt(PA) processes and finite-state ones is undecidable.*

It is obvious that (almost) any *R-N*-bisimilarity is reasonable in the above sense, except for some trivial cases. For weak bisimilarity, we can even show that none of the problems $g \overset{WT}{\simeq}_1 f$, $g \overset{WT}{\not\simeq}_1 f$ is semidecidable when g is a *StExt(PA)* process.

Once seeing that *StExt(PA)* are strong enough to make our equivalences undecidable, it is natural to ask what happens when we add finite-state control parts to processes from subclasses of PA, namely to BPA and BPP. The *StExt(BPA)* (i.e. PDA) processes have been examined in the previous section. In the case of *StExt(BPP)*, strong bisimilarity with finite-state processes is decidable [12]. Here we demonstrate that the problem for weak bisimilarity is undecidable; the proof is obtained by a modification of the one which has been used for labelled Petri nets in [9].

It can be easily shown that a labelled Petri net where each transition t has exactly one input place is equivalent to a BPP process (the corresponding transition systems are isomorphic)—see e.g. [7]. Similarly, if any transition has at most one unbounded place among its input places, then it is easy to transform the net into an equivalent *StExt(BPP)* process (the marking of bounded places is modelled by finite control states); let us call such nets as *StExt(BPP)*-nets.

The idea of the mentioned construction from [9] looks as follows. First, a 7-state transition system $\mathcal{F}$ is fixed. Then it is shown how to construct a net $N_\mathcal{M}$ for any two-counter machine $\mathcal{M}$ such that $N_\mathcal{M}$ is weakly bisimilar to $\mathcal{F}$ iff $\mathcal{M}$ does not halt for zero input. Therefore, if the net $N_\mathcal{M}$ were always a *StExt(BPP)*-net, we would be done. In fact, it is not the case but $N_\mathcal{M}$ can be suitably transformed. The description of the transformation is omitted due to the lack of space; it can be found in [11]. Now we can conclude:

Theorem 6. *Weak bisimilarity is undecidable between StExt(BPP) processes and finite-state ones.*

6 Conclusions, Future Work

A complete summary of the results on decidability of bisimulation-like equivalences with finite-state processes is given in the table below. As we want to make clear what results have been previously obtained by other researchers, our table contains more columns than it is necessarily needed (e.g., the positive result for PAD and $\overset{RN}{\sim}$, where R and N have the above indicated properties, 'covers' all positive results for BPA, BPP, PA, and PDA). The results obtained in this paper are in boldface. We also add a special row which indicates decidability of the model-checking problem for EF. Note that although model-checking EF logic is undecidable for *StExt(BPP)* processes and Petri nets, strong bisimilarity with finite-state systems is decidable. The original proof in [12] in fact demonstrates decidability of the Reach problem (the Step problem is trivially decidable), hence our general strategy applies also in this case.

	BPA	BPP	PA	*StExt(BPA)*	*StExt(BPP)*	*StExt(PA)*	PAD	PN
$\overset{ST}{\sim}$	Yes [6]	Yes [5]	Yes [10]	Yes [10]	Yes [12]	No [10]	**YES**	Yes [12]
$\overset{WT}{\sim}$	**YES**	Yes [14]	**YES**	**YES**	**NO**	No [10]	**YES**	No [9]
$\overset{RN}{\sim}$	**YES**	**YES**	**YES**	**YES**	**NO**	No [10]	**YES**	No [9]
EF	Yes	Yes	Yes	Yes	No	No	Yes	No

References

1. *Proceedings of CONCUR'96*, volume 1119 of *LNCS*. Springer-Verlag, 1996.
2. *Proceedings of CONCUR'97*, volume 1243 of *LNCS*. Springer-Verlag, 1997.
3. J.C.M. Baeten, J.A. Bergstra, and J.W. Klop. Decidability of bisimulation equivalence for processes generating context-free languages. *JACM*, 40:653–682, 1993.
4. I. Černá, M. Křetínský, and A. Kučera. Bisimilarity is decidable in the union of normed BPA and normed BPP processes. *ENTCS*, 6, 1997.
5. S. Christensen, Y. Hirshfeld, and F. Moller. Bisimulation is decidable for all basic parallel processes. In *Proceedings of CONCUR'93*, volume 715 of *LNCS*, pages 143–157. Springer-Verlag, 1993.
6. S. Christensen, H. Hüttel, and C. Stirling. Bisimulation equivalence is decidable for all context-free processes. *Information and Computation*, 121:143–148, 1995.
7. J. Esparza. Petri nets, commutative context-free grammars, and basic parallel processes. In *Proceedings of FCT'95*, volume 965 of *LNCS*, pages 221–232. Springer-Verlag, 1995.
8. P. Jančar. Undecidability of bisimilarity for Petri nets and some related problems. *Theoretical Computer Science*, 148(2):281–301, 1995.
9. P. Jančar and J. Esparza. Deciding finiteness of Petri nets up to bisimilarity. In *Proceedings of ICALP'96*, volume 1099 of *LNCS*, pages 478–489. Springer-Verlag, 1996.
10. P. Jančar and A. Kučera. Bisimilarity of processes with finite-state systems. *ENTCS*, 9, 1997.
11. P. Jančar, A. Kučera, and R. Mayr. Deciding bisimulation-like equivalences with finite-state processes. Technical report TUM-I9805, Technische Universität München, 1998.
12. P. Jančar and F. Moller. Checking regular properties of Petri nets. In *Proceedings of CONCUR'95*, volume 962 of *LNCS*, pages 348–362. Springer-Verlag, 1995.
13. A. Kučera. How to parallelize sequential processes. In *Proceedings of CONCUR'97* [2], pages 302–316.
14. R. Mayr. Weak bisimulation and model checking for basic parallel processes. In *Proceedings of FST&TCS'96*, volume 1180 of *LNCS*, pages 88–99. Springer-Verlag, 1996.
15. R. Mayr. Model checking PA-processes. In *Proceedings of CONCUR'97* [2], pages 332–346.
16. R. Mayr. Process rewrite systems. *ENTCS*, 7, 1997.
17. R. Mayr. *Decidability and Complexity of Model Checking Problems for Infinite-State Systems*. PhD thesis, TU-München, 1998.
18. R. Milner. *Communication and Concurrency*. Prentice-Hall, 1989.
19. F. Moller. Infinite results. In *Proceedings of CONCUR'96* [1], pages 195–216.
20. D.M.R. Park. Concurrency and automata on infinite sequences. In *Proceedings* 5th *GI Conference*, volume 104 of *LNCS*, pages 167–183. Springer-Verlag, 1981.
21. B. Steffen and A. Ingólfsdóttir. Characteristic formulae for processes with divergence. *Information and Computation*, 110(1):149–163, 1994.
22. C. Stirling. Decidability of bisimulation equivalence for normed pushdown processes. In *Proceedings of CONCUR'96* [1], pages 217–232.
23. R.J. van Glabbeek and W.P. Weijland. Branching time and abstraction in bisimulation semantics. *Information Processing Letters*, 89:613–618, 1989.

Do Probabilistic Algorithms Outperform Deterministic Ones?

Avi Wigderson
Computer Science Institute
The Hebrew University
Jerusalem, Israel

Summary

The introduction of randomization into efficient computation has been one of the most fertile and useful ideas in computer science. In cryptography and asynchronous computing, randomization makes possible tasks that are impossible to perform deterministically. For function computation, many examples are known in which randomization allows considerable savings in resources like space and time over deterministic algorithms, or even "only" simplifies them.

But to what extent is this seeming power of randomness over determinism real? The most famous concrete version of this question regards the power of BPP, the class problems solvable by probabilistic polynomial time algorithms making small constant error. We know nothing beyond the trivial relation $P \subseteq BPP \subseteq EXP$, so both $P = BPP$ (read "randomness is useless") or $BPP = EXP$ (read "randomness is all-powerful") are currently equally possible. A major problem is shrinking this gap in our knowledge, or at the very least eliminating the (proposterous) second possibility.

A fundamental discovery (that emerged in the early 80's in the sequence of seminal papers [18, 4, 19]) regarding this problem is the "hardness versus randomness" paradigm. It relates this major problem to another equally important one: are there natural hard functions? Roughly speaking, "computationally hard" functions can be used to construct "efficient pseudo-random generators". These in turn lower the randomness requirements of any efficient probabilistic algorithm, allowing for a nontrivial deterministic simulation. Thus, under various complexity assumptions, randomness is weak or even "useless", and the challenge becomes to use the weakest possible assumption, at the hope of finally removing it altogether.

Only two methods are known for converting hard functions into pseudo-random sequences: the BMY-generator (introduced by Blum, Micali and Yao) and the NW-generator (introduced by Nisan and Wigderson). The BMY-generator [4, 19, 8, 9], in which the hardness versus randomness paradigm first appeared, uses one-way functions. Its construction facilitates using either nonuniform or uniform hardness assumptions. The results are (informally) summarized below, for nonuiniform assumptions. We use $SIZE(s(n))$ to denote all functions computable with a family of Boolean circuits of size $s(n)$, and $P/poly = SIZE(n^{O(1)})$. Also, $SUBEXP = \cap_{\delta>0} DTIME(2^{n^\delta})$, and $\tilde{P} = DTIME(exp(\log n)^{O(1)})$, namely quasi-polynomial time.

Theorem 1 *[4, 19, 8, 9]*

If there are one-way functions not in $P/poly$, then $BPP \subset SUBEXP$.

If there are one-way functions not in $SIZE(exp(n^{o(1)})$, then $BPP \subset \tilde{P}$.

The NW-generator [16, 17, 3] considerably weakened the hardness assumption needed in the nonuniform setting. It achieves the same deterministic simulation of BPP, from any function in EXP. The (wide ?) belief that $EXP \not\subseteq P/poly$ makes easy the belief in its corolarry $BPP \neq EXP$.

Theorem 2 *[16, 17, 3]*

If $EXP \neq P/poly$, then $BPP \subset SUBEXP$

If $EXP \neq SIZE(exp(n^{o(1)})$, then $BPP \subset \tilde{P}$

While this already supplies considerable evidence to the weakness of probabilistic polynomial time algorithms, it leaves much room for progress. Recently significant steps were made in two different directions - tighter trade-offs and uniform assumptions.

The first deals with finding natural assumptions under which randomness is really "useless", namely $BPP = P$. The major obstacle was the fact that various "hardness amplification" techniques, most notably the XOR-lemma, which are key in the hardness to pseudorandomness conversion, significantly increased the input size. The combination of two papers, [10, 11] give much more efficient versions of the XOR lemma, and yield the following. Here $E = DTIME(exp(O(n)))$.

Theorem 3 *[10, 11] If $E \not\subseteq SIZE(exp(o(n))$ then $BPP = P$.*

The same consequence was obtained, under the considerably stronger assumption $E \not\subseteq SIZE(o(2^n/n))$, but via totally different and interesting techniques, in [1, 2].

The second direction deals with the possible use of a uniform of Theorem 2, i.e. requiring the hard function be hard for probabilistic Turing machines rather than Boolean circuits. While this presents no major problems if the function is one-way and we are using the BMY-generator (as was pointed out in the original papers), for 10 years since the introduction of the NW-generator no way was found to "uniformize" that conversion of hardness to randomness. Very recently, this was achieved in [12], and is stated (informally) below. Note that the simulation of BPP here is only in $Av - SUBEXP$, namely requires deterministic subexponential time on average whenever the inputs are drawn from an efficiently samplable distribution [13].

Theorem 4 *[12] If $BPP \neq EXP$, then $BPP \subseteq Av - SUBEXP$*

This result is naturally interpreted as a gap theorem on derandomization - either no derandomization of BPP is possible at all (BPP is "all-powerful"), or otherwise a highly nontrivial dernadomization is possible.

We believe that the basic question of the power of BPP deserves more attention, and that an unconditional result is possible. The challenge is to prove the weakest such statement:

Conjecture 5 $EXP \neq BPP$

To conclude, we refer the reader to some general surveys that contain some of this material in an organized fashion - the three surveys of Oded Goldreich [5, 6, 7] and the monograph of Mike Luby [14].

References

[1] A. Andreev, A. Clementi and J. Rolim, "Hitting Sets Derandomize BPP", in *XXIII International Colloquium on Algorithms, Logic and Programming (ICALP'96)*, 1996.

[2] A. Andreev, A. Clementi, and J. Rolim, "Hitting Properties of Hard Boolean Operators and its Consequences on BPP", manuscript, 1996.

[3] L. Babai, L. Fortnow, N. Nisan and A. Wigderson, "BPP has Subexponential Time Simulations unless EXPTIME has Publishable Proofs", *Complexity Theory*, Vol 3, pp. 307–318, 1993.

[4] M. Blum and S. Micali. "How to Generate Cryptographically Strong Sequences of Pseudo-Random Bits", *SIAM J. Comput.*, Vol. 13, pages 850–864, 1984.

[5] O. Goldreich, *Modern Cryptography, Probabilistic Proofs and Pseudorandomness*, to be published by *Springer*.

[6] O. Goldreich, "Randomness, Interaction, Proofs and Zero-Knowledge", *The Universal Turing Machine: A Half-Century Survey*, R. Herken (ed.), Oxford University Press, 1988, London, pp. 377–406. A revised version of the section on pseudorandomness is available from `http://theory.lcs.mit.edu/pub/people/oded/prg88.ps`.

[7] O. Goldreich. "Pseudorandomness", Chapter 3 of *Foundation of Cryptography – Fragments of a Book*, February 1995. Available from `http://theory.lcs.mit.edu/~oded/frag.html`.

[8] O. Goldreich and L.A. Levin. "A Hard-Core Predicate for all One-Way Functions", in *ACM Symp. on Theory of Computing*, pp. 25–32, 1989.

[9] J. Hastad, R. Impagliazzo, L.A. Levin and M. Luby, "Construction of Pseudorandom Generator from any One-Way Function", to appear in *SICOMP*. (See preliminary versions by Impagliazzo et. al. in *21st STOC* and Hastad in *22nd STOC*.)

[10] R. Impagliazzo, "Hard-core Distributions for Somewhat Hard Problems", in *36th FOCS*, pages 538–545, 1995.

[11] R. Impagliazzo and A. Wigderson, "P=BPP unless E has sub-exponential circuits: Derandomizing the XOR Lemma", in *29th STOC*, pp. 220–229, 1997.

[12] R. Impagliazzo and A. Wigderson, "A Gap Theorem for Derandomization", In preparation.

[13] L.A. Levin, "Average Case Complete Problems", *SIAM J. Comput.*, 15:285–286, 1986.

[14] M. Luby, *Pseudorandomness and Cryptographic Applications*, Princeton Computer Science Notes, Princeton University Press, 1996.

[15] R. Lipton, "New directions in testing", In J. Fegenbaum and M. Merritt, editors, *Distributed Computing and Cryptography*, DIMACS Series in Discrete Mathematics and Theoretical Computer Science Volume 2, pp. 191-202. American Mathematical Society, 1991.

[16] N. Nisan, "Pseudo-random bits for constant depth circuits", *Combinatorica 11* (1), pp. 63-70, 1991.

[17] N. Nisan, and A. Wigderson, "Hardness vs Randomness", *J. Comput. System Sci.* 49, 149-167, 1994

[18] A. Shamir, "On the generation of cryptographically strong pseudo-random sequences", *8th ICALP, Lecture Notoes in Computer Science* 62, Springer-Verlag, pp. 544–550, 1981.

[19] A.C. Yao, "Theory and Application of Trapdoor Functions", in *23st FOCS*, pages 80–91, 1982.

A Degree-Decreasing Lemma for (MOD q, MOD p) Circuits

Vince Grolmusz

Department of Computer Science
Eötvös University, Budapest
Múzeum krt.6-8, H-1088 Budapest, HUNGARY
E-mail: grolmusz@cs.elte.hu

Abstract. Consider a $(\mathrm{MOD}_q, \mathrm{MOD}_p)$ circuit, where the inputs of the bottom MOD_p gates are degree-d polynomials of the input variables (p, q are different primes). Using our main tool — the Degree Decreasing Lemma — we show that this circuit can be converted to a $(\mathrm{MOD}_q, \mathrm{MOD}_p)$ circuit with *linear* polynomials on the input-level with the price of increasing the size of the circuit. This result has numerous consequences: for the Constant Degree Hypothesis of Barrington, Straubing and Thérien [3], and generalizing the lower bound results of Yan and Parberry [21], Krause and Waack [13] and Krause and Pudlák [12]. Perhaps the most important application is an exponential lower bound for the size of $(\mathrm{MOD}_q, \mathrm{MOD}_p)$ circuits computing the n fan-in AND, where the input of each MOD_p gate at the bottom is an *arbitrary* integer valued function of cn variables ($c < 1$) plus an arbitrary linear function of n input variables.
We believe that the Degree Decreasing Lemma becomes a standard tool in modular circuit theory.

1 Introduction

Boolean circuits are perhaps the most widely examined models of computation. They are used in VLSI design, in general computability theory and in complexity theory context as well as in the theory of parallel computation.

Many from the strongest and deepest lower bound results for the computational complexity of finite functions were proved using the Boolean circuit model of computation (for example [14], [22], [10], [15], [16], or see [20] for a survey).

Unfortunately, lots of questions — even for very restricted circuit classes — have been unsolved for a long time.

Bounded depth and polynomial size is one of the most natural restrictions. Ajtai [1], Furst, Saxe, and Sipser [6] proved that no polynomial sized, constant depth circuit can compute the PARITY function. Yao [22] and Håstad [10] generalized this result for sub-logarithmic depths.

Since the modular gates are very simple to define, and they are immune to the random restriction techniques in lower bound proofs for the PARITY function, the following natural question was asked by Barrington, Smolensky and others:

How powerful will become the Boolean circuits if — beside the standard AND, OR and NOT gates — MOD_m gates are also allowed in the circuit? Here a MOD_m gate outputs 1 iff the sum of its inputs is in a set $A \subset \{0, 1, 2, \ldots, m-1\}$ modulo m.

Razborov [15] showed that for computing MAJORITY with AND, OR, NOT and MOD_2 gates, exponential size is needed with constant depth. This result was generalized by Smolensky [16] for MOD_p gates instead of MOD_2 ones, where p denotes a prime.

Very little is known, however, if both MOD_p and MOD_q gates are allowed in the circuit for different primes p, q, or, if the modulus is a non-prime power composite, e.g., 6. For example, it is consistent with our present knowledge that depth-3, linear-size circuits with MOD_6 gates *only*, recognize the Hamiltonian graphs (see [3]). The existing lower bound results use diverse techniques from Fourier-analysis, communication complexity theory, group-theory and several forms of random restrictions (see [3], [12], [18], [19], [17], [9], [7], [8], [2], [11]).

It is not difficult to see that constant-depth circuits with MOD_p gates only, (p prime), cannot compute even simple functions: the n-fan-in OR or AND functions, since they can only compute constant degree polynomials of the input variables over GF_p (see [16]).

But depth-2 circuits with MOD_2 and MOD_3 gates, or MOD_6 gates can compute the n-fan-in OR and AND functions [11], [3]. Consequently, these circuits are more powerful than circuits with MOD_p gates only. For completeness, we give here the sketch of the construction: take a MOD_3 gate at the top of the circuit, and 2^n MOD_2 gates on the next level, and each subset of the n input variables is connected to exactly one MOD_2 gate, then this circuit computes the n-fan-in OR, since if at least one of the inputs is 1, then exactly half of the MOD_2 gates evaluate to 1.

By the famous theorem of Yao [23] and Beigel and Tarui [4], every polynomial-size, constant-depth circuit with AND, OR, NOT and MOD_m gates can be converted to a depth-2 circuit with a SYMMETRIC gate at the top and quasi-polynomially many AND gates of poly-logarithmic fan-in at the bottom. This result would allow an excellent tool for bounding the power of circuits containing modular gates. Unfortunately, the existing lower bound techniques are not strong enough to bound the computational power of these circuits.

Our main contribution here is a lemma, the Degree Decreasing Lemma, which yields a tool for dealing with low-fan-in AND gates at the bottom of (MOD_q, MOD_p) circuits. We believe that – in the light of the result of Yao, Beigel and Tarui – our result may have important consequences in modular circuit theory.

2 Preliminaries

Definition 1. *A fan-in n gate is an n-variable Boolean function. Let* $G_1, G_2, \ldots, G_\ell$ *be gates of unbounded fan-in. Then a*

$$(G_1, G_2, \ldots, G_\ell; d) - \textit{ circuit}$$

denotes a depth-ℓ circuit with a G_1-gate on the top, G_2 gates on the second level, G_3 gates on the third level from the top,..., and G_ℓ gates on the last level. Multi-linear polynomials of input-variables $x_1, x_2, \ldots, x_n$ of degree at most d are connected to G_ℓ gates on the last level. The size of a circuit is defined to be the total number of the gates $G_1, G_2, \ldots, G_\ell$ in the circuit.

All of our gates are of unbounded fan-in, and we allow to connect inputs to gates or gates to gates with multiple wires.

Let us note, that we get an equivalent definition, if we allow AND gates of fan-in at most d on the bottom level, instead of degree d multi-linear polynomials.

In the literature MOD_m gates are sometimes defined to be 1, iff the sum of their inputs is divisible by m, and sometimes they are defined to be 1, iff the sum of their inputs is not divisible by m. The following, more general definition covers both cases.

Definition 2. *We say that gate G is a* MOD_m-gate, *if there exists a non-empty $A \subset \{0, 1, \ldots, m-1\}$, $A \neq \{0, 1, \ldots, m-1\}$ such that*

$$G(x_1, x_2, \ldots, x_n) = \begin{cases} 1, & \text{if } \sum_{i=1}^n x_i \bmod m \in A \\ 0 & \text{otherwise.} \end{cases}$$

$A \subset \{0, 1, \ldots, m-1\}$ is called the 1-set of G. MOD_m gates with 1-set A are denoted by MOD_m^A.

Definition 3. *Let p and q be two different primes, and let d be a non-negative integer. Then*

$$(\text{MOD}_q, \text{MOD}_p; d - \text{AND})$$

denotes a $(\text{MOD}_q, \text{MOD}_p; d+1)$ circuit, where the input of each MOD_p-gate is a polynomial, which can be computed by an arithmetic circuit with arbitrarily many ADDITION gates of unbounded fan-in and with at most d fan-in 2 MULTIPLICATION gates.

For example, the determinant (or the permanent) of a $t \times t$ matrix with entries z_{ij} can be computed by $t^2 - 1$ MULTIPLICATION-gates, each with fan-in 2.

Each polynomial, which can be computed by arbitrarily many ADDITION gates and at most d fan-in 2 MULTIPLICATION gates has degree at most $d+1$. However, the converse is not true. This can be seen by considering the degree-2 polynomial $x_1y_1 + x_2y_2 + \cdots + x_ny_n$ over GF(2), which has high communication complexity [5], while polynomials which are computable by d fan-in 2 MULTIPLICATION gates have low communication complexity for small d's .

3 The Degree-Decreasing Lemma

The following lemma is our main tool. It exploits a surprising property of $(\text{MOD}_p, \text{MOD}_q)$-circuits, which lacks in $(\text{MOD}_p, \text{MOD}_p)$ circuits, since constant-depth circuits with MOD_p gates are capable only to compute a constant degree polynomial of the inputs, and this constant depends on the depth, and not on the size.

Remark 1. Generally, the inputs of the modular gates are Boolean variables. Here, however, for wider applicability of the lemma, we allow input x for a general MOD_m gate to be chosen from set $\{0, 1, \ldots, m-1\}$.

Remark 2. The output of the general MOD_m gates depend only on the sum of the inputs. In the next lemma it will be more convenient to denote $MOD_m^A(y_1, y_2, \ldots, y_\ell)$ *i.e.*, gate MOD_m^A with inputs $y_1, y_2, \ldots, y_\ell$, by $MOD_m^A(y_1 + y_2 + \cdots + y_\ell)$.

Lemma 1. *(Degree Decreasing Lemma) Let p and q be different primes, and let x_1, x_2, x_3 be variables with values from $\{0, 1, \ldots, p-1\}$. Then*

$$MOD_q^B(MOD_p^A(x_1 x_2 + x_3)) = MOD_q^B(H_0 + H_1 + \cdots + H_{p-1} + \beta),$$

where H_i abbreviates

$$H_i = \alpha \sum_{j=0}^{p-1} MOD_p^A(i x_2 + x_3 + j(x_1 + (p-i)))$$

for $i = 0, 1, \ldots, p-1$, where α is the multiplicative inverse of p modulo q: $\alpha p \equiv 1 \pmod q$, and β is a positive integer satisfying $\beta = -|A|(p-1)\alpha \bmod q$.

In the special case of $(MOD_3, MOD_2^{\{1\}})$ circuit, the statement of Lemma 1 is illustrated on Figure 1.

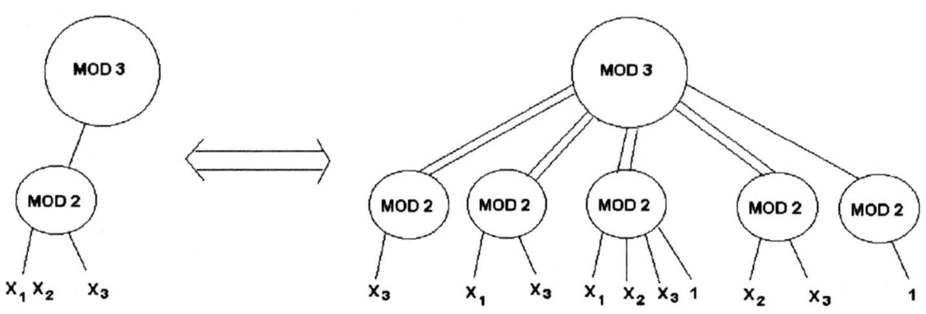

Fig. 1. Degree-decreasing in the $(MOD_3, MOD_2^{\{1\}})$ case: on the left the input is a degree two polynomial, on the right the inputs are linear polynomials.

Proof. Let $x_1 = k$ and let $0 \le i \le p-1,\ k \ne i$. Then

$$H_k = \alpha \sum_{j=0}^{p-1} \mathrm{MOD}_p^A(kx_2+x_3) = \alpha p \mathrm{MOD}_p^A(kx_2+x_3) \equiv \mathrm{MOD}_p^A(x_1x_2+x_3) \pmod q,$$

and

$$H_i = \alpha \sum_{j=0}^{p-1} \mathrm{MOD}_p^A(ix_2 + x_3 + j(k-i)) = \alpha|A|,$$

since for any fixed x_2, x_3, i, k expression $kx_2 + x_3 + j(k-i)$ takes on every value exactly once modulo p while $j = 0, 1, \ldots, p-1$; so $\mathrm{MOD}_p^A(ix_2 + x_3 + j(k-i))$ equals to 1 exactly $|A|$ times. Consequently,

$$\mathrm{MOD}_q^B(H_0+H_1+\cdots+H_{p-1}+\beta) = \mathrm{MOD}_q^B(\mathrm{MOD}_p^A(x_1x_2+x_3)+(p-1)\alpha|A|+\beta) =$$

$$= \mathrm{MOD}_q^B(\mathrm{MOD}_p^A(x_1x_2 + x_3)).$$

4 Applications of the Degree Decreasing Lemma

4.1 Constant Degree Hypothesis

Barrington, Straubing and Thérien in [3] conjectured that any $(\mathrm{MOD}_q^B, \mathrm{MOD}_p^A; d)$ circuit needs exponential size to compute the n fan-in AND function. They called it the *Constant Degree Hypothesis* (CDH), and proved the $d = 1$ case, with group-theoretic techniques.

Yan and Parberry [21] – using Fourier-analysis – proved also the $d = 1$ case for $(\mathrm{MOD}_q^{\{1,2,\ldots,q-1\}}, \mathrm{MOD}_2^{\{1\}}; 1)$ circuits, but their method also works for the special case of the CDH where the sum of the degrees of the monomials g_i on the input-level satisfies:

$$\sum_{\deg(g_i)\ge 1} (\deg(g_i) - 1) \le \frac{n}{2(q-1)} - O(1).$$

Our Theorem 4 yields the following generalization of this result:

Theorem 1. *There exist* $0 < c < 1$ *and* $0 < c' < 1$, *such that if a* $(\mathrm{MOD}_q^B, \mathrm{MOD}_p^A, cn - \mathrm{AND})$ *circuit computes the n-fan-in AND function, then its size is at least* $2^{c'n}$.

Proof. From the result of [3] and from Theorem 4 the statement is immediate.

We should add, that Theorem 1 does not imply the CDH, but it greatly generalizes the lower bounds of [21] and of [3], and it works not only for the constant degree, but degree cn polynomials as well.

Corollary 1. *There exist* $0 < c < 1$ *and* $0 < c' < 1$, *such that if the n fan-in AND function is computed by a circuit with a* MOD_q^B *gate at the top,* MOD_p^A *gates at the next level, where the inputs of each* MOD_p^A *gate is* an arbitrary integer-valued function *of cn variables plus an arbitrary linear polynomial of n variables, then the circuit must contain at least* $2^{c'n}$ MOD_p^A *gates.*

Proof. First we convert the integer-valued function of cn variables into a polynomial over GF(p), for each MOD_p^A gates. These polynomials have degree at most cn, and depend on at most cn variables. Consequently, the circuit is a (MOD_q^B,MOD_p^A,($cn - 1$)-AND) circuit, and Theorem 1 applies.

We should mention, that Corollary 1 is much stronger than Yan and Parberry's result [21], since here the degree-sum of the inputs of each MOD_p^A gate can be even exponentially large in n, *vs.* the small linear upper bound of [21].

4.2 The ID function

Krause and Waack [13], using communication-complexity techniques, showed that any ($\text{MOD}_m^{\{1,2,\ldots,m-1\}}$, SYMMETRIC; 1) circuit, computing the ID function:

$$\text{ID}(x, y) = \begin{cases} 1, & \text{if } x = y, \\ 0 & \text{otherwise,} \end{cases}$$

for $x, y \in \{0,1\}^n$, should have size at least $2^n/\log m$, where SYMMETRIC is a gate, computing an arbitrary symmetric Boolean function.

Using this result, we prove:

Theorem 2. *Let p and q be two different primes. If a*

$$(\text{MOD}_q^{\{1,2,\ldots,m-1\}}, \text{MOD}_p^A, (1-\varepsilon)n - \text{AND})$$

circuit computes the 2n-fan-in ID *function, then its size is at least* $2^{c\varepsilon n}$, *where* $0 < c < 1$ *depends only on p.*

Proof. From the result of [13] and from Theorem 4 the statement is immediate.

Unfortunately, the methods of [13] do not generalize for MOD_q^B gates with unrestricted B's.

4.3 The MOD r function

Krause and Pudlák [12] proved that any ($\text{MOD}_{p^k}^{\{0\}}$, $\text{MOD}_q^{\{0\}}$; 1) circuit which computes the $\text{MOD}_r^{\{0\}}$ function has size at least $2^{c''n}$, for some $c > 0$, where p, q and r are different primes. We also generalize this result as follows:

Theorem 3. *There exist* $0 < c' < c < 1$ *for different primes* p, q, r, *and positive integer k, if circuit* ($\text{MOD}_{p^k}^{\{0\}}$, $\text{MOD}_q^{\{0\}}$; cn − AND) *computes* $\text{MOD}_r^{\{0\}}(x_1, x_2, \ldots, x_n)$, *then its size is at least* $2^{c'n}$.

Proof. From the result of [12] and from Theorem 4 the statement is immediate.

Unfortunately, the methods of [12] do not generalize for MOD_m^B gates with unrestricted B's.

4.4 The Proof of Theorem 4

Theorem 4. *Suppose, that function* $f : \{0,1\}^n \rightarrow \{0,1\}$ *can be computed by a* $(\mathrm{MOD}_q^B, \mathrm{MOD}_p^A; d - \mathrm{AND})$ *circuit of size* s*, where* p *and* q *are two different primes, and* d *is a non-negative integer. Then* f *can also be computed by a* $(\mathrm{MOD}_q^B, \mathrm{MOD}_p^A; 1)$ *circuit of size*

$$(p^{2d} + 1)s.$$

Proof. We first show, that our $(\mathrm{MOD}_q^B, \mathrm{MOD}_p^A; d - \mathrm{AND})$ circuit of size s can be converted into a $(\mathrm{MOD}_q^B, \mathrm{MOD}_p^A; (d-1) - \mathrm{AND})$ circuit of size at most $p^2 s + 1$. Repeating this conversion $d - 1$ times, the statement follows.

We know that the input of every MOD_p^A-gate can be constructed with at most d multiplication in an arithmetic circuit. Lets consider a fixed MOD_p^A-gate. Suppose, that the last multiplication, which computes its input-polynomial is $\Phi\Psi + \Xi$, where Φ, Ψ, Ξ are multi-linear polynomials of n variables. This MOD_p^A-gate, using the Degree Decreasing Lemma (Lemma 1), can be converted to at most p^2 MOD_p^A-gates, each with inputs, constructible with at most $d-1$ multiplications, plus (possibly) a leftover MOD_p^A-gate with input 1 (which may be connected to the MOD_q^B gate with multiple wires) such that the sum of these gates give the same output modulo q as the original one. If the conversion is done for all MOD_p^A-gates, the result is a $(\mathrm{MOD}_q^B, \mathrm{MOD}_p^A; (d-1) - \mathrm{AND})$ circuit of size at most $p^2 s + 1$, since the "leftover" MOD_p^A-gate with input 1 should be counted once.

Acknowledgment. The author is indebted to Dániel Varga for suggesting an improvement on the original version of Definition 3, and for Katalin Friedl, Zoltán Király, and Gábor Tardos for fruitful discussions on this work. Supported in part by grants OTKA F014919, FKFP 0835.

References

[1] M. Ajtai. $\sum_1^1$ formulae on finite structures. *Annals of Pure and Applied Logic*, 24:1–48, 1983.

[2] D. A. M. Barrington, R. Beigel, and S. Rudich. Representing Boolean functions as polynomials modulo composite numbers. *Comput. Complexity*, 4:367–382, 1994. Appeared also in *Proc. 24th Ann. ACM Symp. Theor. Comput.*, 1992.

[3] D. A. M. Barrington, H. Straubing, and D. Thérien. Non-uniform automata over groups. *Information and Computation*, 89:109–132, 1990.

[4] R. Beigel and J. Tarui. On ACC. In *Proc. 32nd Ann. IEEE Symp. Found. Comput. Sci.*, pages 783–792, 1991.

[5] B. Chor and O. Goldreich. Unbiased bits from sources of weak randomness and probabilistic communication complexity. In *Proc. 26th Ann. IEEE Symp. Found. Comput. Sci.*, pages 429–442, 1985. Appeared also in SIAM J. Comput. Vol. 17, (1988).

[6] M. L. Furst, J. B. Saxe, and M. Sipser. Parity, circuits and the polynomial time hierarchy. *Math. Systems Theory*, 17:13–27, 1984.

[7] V. Grolmusz. A weight-size trade-off for circuits with mod m gates. In *Proc. 26th Ann. ACM Symp. Theor. Comput.*, pages 68–74, 1994.

[8] V. Grolmusz. On the weak mod m representation of Boolean functions. *Chicago Journal of Theoretical Computer Science*, 1995(2), July 1995.

[9] V. Grolmusz. Separating the communication complexities of MOD m and MOD p circuits. *J. Comput. System Sci.*, 51(2):307–313, 1995. also in Proc. 33rd Ann. IEEE Symp. Found. Comput. Sci., 1992, pp. 278–287.

[10] J. Håstad. Almost optimal lower bounds for small depth circuits. In *Proc. 18th Ann. ACM Symp. Theor. Comput.*, pages 6–20, 1986.

[11] J. Kahn and R. Meshulam. On mod p transversals. *Combinatorica*, 10(1):17–22, 1991.

[12] M. Krause and P. Pudlák. On the computational power of depth 2 circuits with threshold and modulo gates. In *Proc. 26th Ann. ACM Symp. Theor. Comput.*, 1994.

[13] M. Krause and S. Waack. Variation ranks of communication matrices and lower bounds for depth-two circuits having nearly symmetric gates with unbounded fan-in. *Mathematical Systems Theory*, 28(6):553–564, Nov./Dec. 1995.

[14] A. Razborov. Lower bounds for the monotone complexity of some Boolean functions. *Sov. Math. Dokl.*, 31:354–357, 1985.

[15] A. Razborov. Lower bounds on the size of bounded depth networks over a complete basis with logical addition, (in Russian). *Mat. Zametki*, 41:598–607, 1987.

[16] R. Smolensky. Algebraic methods in the theory of lower bounds for Boolean circuit complexity. In *Proc. 19th Ann. ACM Symp. Theor. Comput.*, pages 77–82, 1987.

[17] R. Smolensky. On interpolation by analytic functions with special properties and some weak lower bounds on the size of circuits with symmetric gates. In *Proc. 31st Ann. IEEE Symp. Found. Comput. Sci.*, pages 628–631, 1990.

[18] M. Szegedy. Functions with bounded symmetric communication complexity and circuits with MOD m gates. In *Proc. 22nd ANN. ACM SYMP. THEOR. COMPUT.*, pages 278–286, 1990.

[19] G. Tardos and D. A. M. Barrington. A lower bound on the MOD 6 degree of the OR function. In *Proceedings of the Third Israel Symosium on the Theory of Computing and Systems (ISTCS'95)*, pages 52–56, 1995.

[20] J. van Leeuwen, editor. *Handbook of Theoretical Computer Science*, volume A, chapter 14. The complexity of finite functions, by R.B. Boppana and M. Sipser. Elsevier-MIT Press, 1990.

[21] P. Yan and I. Parberry. Exponential size lower bounds for some depth three circuits. *Information and Computation*, 112:117–130, 1994.

[22] A. C. Yao. Separating the polynomial-time hierarchy by oracles. In *Proc. 26th Ann. IEEE Symp. Found. Comput. Sci.*, pages 1–10, 1985.

[23] A. C. Yao. On ACC and threshold circuits. In *Proc. 31st Ann. IEEE Symp. Found. Comput. Sci.*, pages 619–627, 1990.

Improved Pseudorandom Generators for Combinatorial Rectangles

Chi-Jen Lu

Computer Science Department
University of Massachusetts at Amherst
cjlu@cs.umass.edu

Abstract. We explicitly construct a pseudorandom generator which uses $O(\log m + \log d + \log^{3/2} 1/\epsilon)$ bits and approximates the volume of any combinatorial rectangle in $[m]^d = \{1, \ldots, m\}^d$ to within ϵ error. This improves on the previous construction by Armoni, Saks, Wigderson, and Zhou [4] using $O(\log m + \log d + \log^2 1/\epsilon)$ bits. For a subclass of rectangles with at most $t \geq \log 1/\epsilon$ nontrivial dimensions and each dimension being an interval, we also give a pseudorandom generator using $O(\log \log d + \log 1/\epsilon \log^{1/2} \frac{t}{\log 1/\epsilon})$ bits, which again improves the previous upper bound $O(\log \log d + \log 1/\epsilon \log \frac{t}{\log 1/\epsilon})$ by Chari, Rohatgi, and Srinivasan [5].

1 Introduction

Pseudorandom generators for combinatorial rectangles have been actively studied recently, because they are closely related to some fundamental problems in theoretical computer science, such as derandomizing RL, DNF approximate counting, and approximating the distributions of independent multivalued random variables.

Let U be a finite set with uniform distribution. The *volume* of a set $A \subseteq U$ is defined as

$$vol(A) = P_{x \in U}[x \in A].$$

Let $\mathcal{A}$ be a family of subsets from U. We want to sample from a much smaller space, instead of from U, and still be able to approximate the volume of any subset $A \in \mathcal{A}$. We call a function $g : \{0,1\}^l \to U$ an *ϵ-generator* using l bits for $\mathcal{A}$, if for all $A \in \mathcal{A}$,

$$|P_{y \in \{0,1\}^l}[g(y) \in A] - vol(A)| \leq \epsilon.$$

For positive integers m and d, a *combinatorial rectangle* of type (m, d) is a subset of $[m]^d = \{1, \ldots, m\}^d$ of the form $R_1 \times \cdots \times R_d$, where $R_i \subseteq [m]$ for all $i \in [d]$. Let $\mathcal{R}(m, d)$ denote the family of all such rectangles. The volume of a rectangle $R \in \mathcal{R}(m, d)$ is now $\prod_{i \in [d]} \frac{|R_i|}{m}$. Our goal is to find explicit ϵ-generators with small l for $\mathcal{R}(m, d)$ and its subclasses.

As observed by Even, Goldreich, Luby, Nisan, and Veličković [6], this is a special case of constructing pseudorandom generators for RL. Nisan's generator for RL [11] is currently the best, using $O(\log^2 n)$ bits. Because it has many important applications and no improvement has been made for several years, one might hope that solving this special case could shed some light on the general problem.

It's easy to show that a random function mapping from $O(\log m + \log d + \log 1/\epsilon)$ bits to $[m]^d$ is very likely to be an ϵ-generator for $\mathcal{R}(m,d)$. However, the efficient construction of an explicit one still remains open. Even, Goldreich, Luby, Nisan, and Veličković [6] gave two ϵ-generators. One uses $O((\log m + \log d + \log 1/\epsilon)\log 1/\epsilon)$ bits based on k-wise independence, and the other uses $O((\log m + \log d + \log 1/\epsilon)\log d)$ bits based on Nisan's generator for RL. Armoni, Saks, Wigderson, and Zhou [4] observed that the generator of Impagliazzo, Nisan, and Wigderson [8] for communication networks also gives an ϵ-generator for $\mathcal{R}(m,d)$ using $O(\log m + (\log d + \log 1/\epsilon)\log d)$ bits, which is good when d is small. They then reduced the original problem to the case when d is small (a formal definition of reductions will be given in the next section), and used the INW-generator to get an ϵ-generator for $\mathcal{R}(m,d)$ using $O(\log m + \log d + \log^2 1/\epsilon)$ bits.

When m, d, and $1/\epsilon$ are polynomially related, say all $n^{\Theta(1)}$, all previous generators still use $\Theta(\log^2 n)$ bits, which is the current barrier for its generalized problem — constructing generators for RL. We break this barrier for the first time, and give an ϵ-generator for $\mathcal{R}(m,d)$ using $O(\log m + \log d + \log^{3/2} 1/\epsilon)$ bits. Our construction is based on that of Armoni, Saks, Wigderson, and Zhou [4], and uses two more reductions to further reduce the dimension before applying the INW-generator. The overall construction can be seen as a composition of several generators for rectangles. Independently, Radhakrishnan and Ta-shma [14] have a slightly weaker result using a very similar idea.

We also observe that further improvements can be made if one can do better for a special case. Let $\mathcal{R}(m,d,k)$ be the set of rectangles from $\mathcal{R}(m,d)$ with at most k nontrivial dimensions (those not equal to $[m]$). We show that if an explicit ϵ-generator using $O(k + \log m + \log d + \log 1/\epsilon)$ bits for $\mathcal{R}(m,d,k)$ exists, we can construct an explicit ϵ-generator using $O(\log m + \log d + \log 1/\epsilon \log\log 1/\epsilon)$ bits for $\mathcal{R}(m,d)$. Unfortunately we still don't know how to construct such a generator for $\mathcal{R}(m,d,k)$.

Another interesting special case is for rectangles where each dimension is an interval. Let $\mathcal{B}(m,d,k)$ be the set of rectangles from $\mathcal{R}(m,d,k)$ with each dimension being an interval. Even, Goldreich, Luby, Nisan, and Veličković [6] observed that the problem of approximating the distribution of independent multivalued random variables can be reduced to this case. They gave a generator using $O(k + \log d + \log 1/\epsilon)$ bits. This is good when $k = O(\log 1/\epsilon)$. For the case $k \geq \log 1/\epsilon$, Chari, Rohatgi, and Srinivasan [5] gave a generator using $O(\log\log d + \log 1/\epsilon \log \frac{k}{\log 1/\epsilon})$ bits. Here, we improve this again to $O(\log\log d + \log 1/\epsilon \log^{1/2} \frac{k}{\log 1/\epsilon})$.

We will not emphasize the efficiency of our generators, but one can easily check that all the generators can be computed in simultaneous $(md/\epsilon)^{O(1)}$ time and $O(\log m + \log d + \log 1/\epsilon)$ space.

It's worth mentioning that the hitting version of our problem has already been settled. Linial, Luby, Saks, and Zuckerman [9] gave an explicit generator using $O(\log m + \log\log d + \log 1/\epsilon)$ bits that can hit any rectangle in $\mathcal{R}(m, d)$ of volume at least ϵ. In fact the work of Armoni, Saks, Wigderson, and Zhou [4] followed closely this result, and so does ours. Andreev, Clementi, and Rolim [1] have a related result on hitting sets for systems of linear functions.

2 Preliminaries

2.1 Notations

For a set U, we let 2^U denote the family of subsets of U. For a rectangle $R \in \mathcal{R}(m, d)$ and a set of indices $I \subseteq [d]$, we let R_I denote the subrectangle of R restricted to those dimensions in I. Similarly, for a vector $v \in [m]^d$ and $I \subseteq [d]$, we define v_I to be the subvector of v restricted to those dimensions in I.

Let $\mathcal{H}_k(n_1, n_2)$ denote the standard family of k-wise independent hash functions from $[n_1]$ to $[n_2]$. It can be identified with $[|\mathcal{H}_k(n_1, n_2)|]$ in the sense that there is a one-to-one mapping from $[|\mathcal{H}_k(n_1, n_2)|]$ onto $\mathcal{H}_k(n_1, n_2)$ that can be efficiently computed. Whenever we can identify a class $\mathcal{F}$ of functions with $[|\mathcal{F}|]$, we can use numbers in $[|\mathcal{F}|]$ to represent functions in $\mathcal{F}$.

There is a natural correspondence between functions from A to B and vectors in $B^{|A|}$. So $\mathcal{H}_k(n_1, n_2)$ can be seen as $|\mathcal{H}_k(n_1, n_2)|$ vectors in $[n_2]^{n_1}$. For a function $f : A \to [m]^d$, an element $x \in A$, and an index $y \in [d]$, we will use $f(x)(y)$ to denote the yth dimension in the vector $f(x) \in [m]^d$.

When we sample from a finite set, the default distribution is the uniform distribution over that set. All the logarithms throughout this paper will have base 2.

2.2 Reductions

We adopt the notion of reduction introduced by Armoni, Saks, Wigderson, and Zhou [4]. It enables us to reduce a harder problem to an easier one, and then focus our attention to solving the easier problem. A class $\mathcal{F}$ of functions from a set U_2 to a set U_1 defines a reduction from U_1 to U_2. Let $\mathcal{A}_1 \subseteq 2^{U_1}$ and $\mathcal{A}_2 \subseteq 2^{U_2}$. $\mathcal{F}$ is said to be $(\mathcal{A}_1, \mathcal{A}_2, \epsilon)$-good, if for each $R \in \mathcal{A}_1$ the following hold:

1. $\forall f \in \mathcal{F}, f^{-1}(R) \in \mathcal{A}_2$, and
2. $|E_{f\in\mathcal{F}}[vol(f^{-1}(R))] - vol(R)| \leq \epsilon$.

Suppose now that $\mathcal{F}$ is $(\mathcal{A}_1, \mathcal{A}_2, \epsilon_1)$ good and $g : \{0,1\}^s \to U_2$ is an ϵ_2-generator for $\mathcal{A}_2$. Armoni, Saks, Wigderson, and Zhou [4] showed that the function $g' : \{0,1\}^s \times \mathcal{F} \to U_1$, defined as $g'(y, f) = (f \circ g)(y)$, is an $(\epsilon_1 + \epsilon_2)$-generator for $\mathcal{A}_1$. The *reduction cost* of $\mathcal{F}$ is $\log |\mathcal{F}|$, which is the number of extra bits needed for the new generator. The following lemma follows immediately.

Lemma 1. *For each i, $0 \leq i \leq l$, let U_i be a set and $\mathcal{A}_i \subseteq 2^{U_i}$. Suppose that $\mathcal{F}_i$ is $(\mathcal{A}_{i-1}, \mathcal{A}_i, \epsilon_{i-1})$-good for $1 \leq i \leq l$, and $g : \{0,1\}^s \to U_l$ is an ϵ_l-generator for $\mathcal{A}_l$. Then the function $g' : \{0,1\}^s \times \mathcal{F}_1 \times \cdots \times \mathcal{F}_l \to U_0$ defined as $g'(x, f_1, \ldots, f_l) = (f_1 \circ \cdots \circ f_l \circ g)(x)$, is a $(\sum_{i=0}^{l} \epsilon_i)$-genertor for $\mathcal{A}_0$.*

So to construct a generator for $\mathcal{A}_0$, it suffices to find a series of reductions from $\mathcal{A}_0$ to $\mathcal{A}_l$, and then find a generator for $\mathcal{A}_l$.

Notice that an $(\mathcal{A}_1, \mathcal{A}_2, \epsilon)$-good reduction $\mathcal{F}$ actually corresponds to a special kind of ϵ-generator for $\mathcal{A}_1$. Let $h : U_2 \times \mathcal{F} \to U_1$ be defined as $h(y, f) = f(y)$. Then the second condition guarantees that for all $R \in \mathcal{A}_1$,

$$\begin{aligned} |P_{(y,f)\in U_2\times\mathcal{F}}[h(y,f) \in R] - vol(R)| &= |E_{f\in\mathcal{F}}[P_{y\in U_2}[f(y) \in R]] - vol(R)| \\ &= |E_{f\in\mathcal{F}}[vol(f^{-1}(R))] - vol(R)| \\ &\leq \epsilon. \end{aligned}$$

The first condition guarantees that one part of h's input, U_2, can come from the output of a generator for $\mathcal{A}_2$, and makes the composition of generators possible. So one way of finding a reduction is to use some generator that might use many bits but can be composed with other generators.

3 The Pseudorandom Generator for $\mathcal{R}(m, d)$

3.1 The Overview of the Construction

The INW-generator uses $O(\log m + (\log d + \log 1/\epsilon) \log d)$ bits, which is good when d is small. The idea of Armoni, Saks, Wigderson, and Zhou [4] is to reduce the dimension of rectangles first to $d' = (1/\epsilon)^{O(1)}$ before applying the INW-generator.

In addition to that, we also reduce m to $m' = (1/\epsilon)^{O(1)}$. The INW-generator for $\mathcal{R}(m', d')$ needs $O(\log m' + (\log d' + \log 1/\epsilon) \log d') = O(\log 1/\epsilon + \log^2 1/\epsilon)$ bits. Observe that we do not lose by letting m' increase a little. By allowing m' to grow to $m'' = (1/\epsilon)^{O(\sqrt{\log 1/\epsilon})}$, we are able to reduce d' to $d'' = 2^{O(\sqrt{\log 1/\epsilon})}$. The INW-generator now uses $O(\log^{3/2} 1/\epsilon)$ bits for $R(m'', d'')$. The total reduction cost is $O(\log m + \log d + \log^{3/2} 1/\epsilon)$, and we have the desired generator for $\mathcal{R}(m, d)$.

More precisely, we will use the following three reductions.

- $\mathcal{F}_1$ is called the first dimension reduction family, and is used to reduce d to $d_1 = (1/\epsilon)^{O(1)}$. It is $(\mathcal{R}(m, d), \mathcal{R}(m_1, d_1), \epsilon/4)$-good, where $m_1 = (md)^{O(1)}$. The reduction cost is $O(\log d)$.
- $\mathcal{F}_2$ is called the range reduction family, and is used to reduce m_1 to $m_2 = (1/\epsilon)^{O(1)}$. It is $(\mathcal{R}(m_1, d_1), \mathcal{R}(m_2, d_2), \epsilon/4)$-good, where $d_2 = d_1$. The reduction cost is $O(\log m + \log d + \log 1/\epsilon)$.
- $\mathcal{F}_3$ is called the second dimension reduction family, and is used to reduce d_2 to $d_3 = 2^{(3 \log \frac{12}{\epsilon})/(k-1)}$, with k a parameter to be chosen to optimize our construction. It is $(\mathcal{R}(m_2, d_2), \mathcal{R}(m_3, d_3), \epsilon/4)$-good, where $m_3 = |\mathcal{H}_k(d_2, m_2)| = (1/\epsilon)^{O(k)}$. The reduction cost is $\log |\mathcal{H}_k(d_2, d_3)| = O(k \log 1/\epsilon)$.

Together with the $\epsilon/4$-generator for $\mathcal{R}(d_3, m_3)$ from the INW-generator, we have an ϵ-generator for $\mathcal{R}(m, d)$. The number of bits used depends on k, and choosing $k = \log^{1/2} 1/\epsilon$ results in the minimum $O(\log m + \log d + \log^{3/2} 1/\epsilon)$.

3.2 The First Dimension Reduction Function Family

Let $\mathcal{F}_1$ be the reduction family used by Armoni, Saks, Wigderson, and Zhou [4], which is the composition of three reduction families. $|\mathcal{F}_1| = d^{O(1)}$, and $\mathcal{F}_1$ is $(\mathcal{R}(m,d), \mathcal{R}(m_1, d_1), \epsilon/4)$-good, where $m_1 = (dm)^{O(1)}$, $d_1 = (1/\epsilon)^{O(1)}$, and each is a power of 2. Let $V_1 = [m_1]^{d_1}$.

3.3 The Range Reduction Function Family

We will use a generator of Nisan and Zuckerman [13], based on an extractor of Goldreich and Wigderson [7]. The idea of using extractors for range reduction was inspired by that of Radhakrishnan and Ta-Shma [14]. We choose a more appropriate extractor and get a better reduction.

Definition 1 *A function $E : \{0,1\}^s \times \{0,1\}^t \to \{0,1\}^l$ is an (s, r, t, l, δ)-extractor if for x chosen from a distribution over $\{0,1\}^s$ with min-entropy[1] r, and y chosen from the uniform distribution over $\{0,1\}^t$, the distribution $E(x, y)$ has distance[2] at most δ to the uniform distribution over $\{0,1\}^l$.*

Extractors are used to extract randomness from weakly random sources, and have many other applications. For more details, please refer to an excellent survey by Nisan [12]. We use an extractor due to Goldreich and Wigderson [7].

Lemma 2. *There are constants c_1 and c_2 such that for any s, γ, and δ with $s > \gamma$, $s - \gamma > l$, and $\delta > 2^{-(s-l-c_1\gamma)/c_2}$, an explicit $(s, s-\gamma, O(\gamma + \log \frac{1}{\delta}), l, \delta)$-extractor exists.*

Choose $\delta = \epsilon/(4d_1) = \epsilon^{O(1)}$, $\gamma = \lceil \log 1/\delta \rceil$, $t = O(\gamma)$, and $l = \log m_1$. Choose $s = l + c\gamma = O(\log(md) + \log 1/\epsilon) = O(\log(md/\epsilon))$ for some constant c, such that $2^{-(s-l-c_1\gamma)/c_2} = 2^{-((c-c_1)/c_2)\log 1/\delta} < 2^{\log \delta} = \delta$. We have the following extractor for this setting.

Corollary 1 *There exists an explicit $(s, s-\gamma, t, l, \delta)$-extractor A.*

The building block of Nisan and Zuckerman's generator for space bounded Turing machines [13], when using the extractor A, has the form $G : \{0,1\}^s \times \{0,1\}^{td_1} \to [m_1]^{d_1}$, where

$$G(x, y_1, \ldots, y_{d_1}) = (A(x, y_1), \ldots, A(x, y_{d_1})).$$

---

[1] The min-entropy of a distribution D on a set S is $\min_{a \in S} \log \frac{1}{D(a)}$.

[2] The distance of two distributions D_1 and D_2 over a set S is defined as $\max_{A \subseteq S} |D_1(A) - D_2(A)|$

For $R = R_1 \times \cdots \times R_{d_1} \in \mathcal{R}(m_1, d_1)$, one can easily modify the proof of Nisan and Zuckerman [13] to show the following:

$$|P_{x,y_1,\ldots,y_{d_1}}[G(x, y_1, \ldots, y_{d_1}) \in R] - vol(R)| \leq \frac{\epsilon}{4}.$$

Now let $m_2 = 2^t = (1/\delta)^{O(1)} = (d_1/\epsilon)^{O(1)} = (1/\epsilon)^{O(1)}$, $d_2 = d_1$, and $V_2 = [m_2]^{d_2}$. Consider the reduction $\mathcal{F}_2 = \{f_x \mid x \in \{0,1\}^s\}$, where $f_x : V_2 \to V_1$ is defined as follows

$$f_x(y_1, \ldots, y_{d_2}) = G(x, y_1, \ldots, y_{d_1}).$$

Then $f_x^{-1}(R) = R'_1 \times \cdots \times R'_{d_2} \in \mathcal{R}(m_2, d_2)$, where $R'_i = \{y_i \mid A(x, y_i) \in R_i\}$. Also,

$$\begin{aligned}|E_x[vol(f_x^{-1}(R))] - vol(R)| &= |P_{x,y_1,\ldots,y_{d_1}}[G(x, y_1, \ldots, y_{d_1}) \in R] - vol(R)| \\ &\leq \epsilon/4.\end{aligned}$$

So we have the following lemma.

Lemma 3. *$\mathcal{F}_2$ is $(\mathcal{R}(m_1, d_1), \mathcal{R}(m_2, d_2), \epsilon/4)$-good.*

3.4 The Second Dimension Reduction Function Family

Let $R = R_1 \times \cdots \times R_{d_2} \in \mathcal{R}(m_2, d_2)$. We want to partition the d_2 dimensions of R into d_3 parts using some function $h : [d_2] \to [d_3]$ in the natural way. For $q \in [d_3]$, those dimensions of R that are mapped to q form a subrectangle $R_{h^{-1}(q)} = \prod_{i \in h^{-1}(q)} R_i$. Based on the idea of Even, Goldreich, Luby, Nisan, and Veličković [6], its volume can be approximated by sampling from the k-wise independent space $G = \mathcal{H}_k(d_2, m_2)$. We use d_3 copies of G, one for each subrectangle. The corresponding rectangle $R^{(h)} = R'_1 \times \cdots \times R'_{d_3}$, where $R'_q = \{p \in G : p_{h^{-1}(q)} \in R_{h^{-1}(q)}\}$, should have a volume close to that of R. The error depends on the choice of k and h. We will show that for $k = O(\log^{1/2} 1/\epsilon)$ and h chosen uniformly from $H = \mathcal{H}(d_2, d_3)$, the expected error is at most $\epsilon/4$.

More formally, let $d_3 = 2^{(3 \log \frac{12}{\epsilon})/(k-1)}$, $m_3 = |G|$, $V_3 = [m_3]^{d_3}$, and $\mathcal{F}_3 = \{f_h : h \in H\}$, where $f_h : V_3 \to V_2$ is defined as follows

$$f_h(p_1, \ldots, p_{d_3}) = (p_{h(1)}(1), \ldots, p_{h(d_2)}(d_2)).$$

Then for $R \in \mathcal{R}(m_2, d_2)$ and $f_h \in \mathcal{F}_3$, $f_h^{-1}(R) = R^{(h)} \in \mathcal{R}(m_3, d_3)$.

We also need the following notation for the proofs below. For $R = R_1 \times \cdots \times R_{d_2} \in \mathcal{R}(m_2, d_2)$, let $\tilde{R}$ denote the rectangle $\overline{R}_1 \times \cdots \times \overline{R}_{d_2} \in \mathcal{R}(m_2, d_2)$, where $\overline{R}_i = [m_2] \setminus R_i$. For $i, j \in [d_2]$, and $I \subseteq [d_2]$, denote

$$\delta_i = \frac{|\overline{R}_i|}{m_2},$$

$$\pi(I) = vol(\tilde{R}_I) = \prod_{i \in I} \delta_i,$$

$$\gamma(I) = P_{p\in G}[p_I \in \tilde{R}_I], \text{ and}$$
$$\tau_j(I) = \sum_{J\subseteq I, |J|=j} \pi(I).$$

The approximation error of each subrectangle can be bounded in the following way.

Proposition 1 $\forall I \subseteq [d_2], |P_{p\in G}[p_I \in R_I] - vol(R_I)| \leq \tau_k(I)$

Proof: Because G is a k-wise independent space, for $J \subseteq I$ with $|J| \leq k$, $\pi(J) = \gamma(J)$. From the principle of inclusion and exclusion, we have the following.

$$vol(R_I) = \prod_{i\in I}(1-\delta_i) = \sum_{J\subseteq I}(-1)^{|J|}\pi(J) = \sum_{j=0}^{k}(-1)^j\tau_j(I) + \sum_{j=k+1}^{|I|}(-1)^j\tau_j(I).$$

$$P_{p\in G}[p_I \in R_I] = \sum_{J\subseteq I}(-1)^{|J|}\gamma(J) = \sum_{j=0}^{k}(-1)^j\tau_j(I) + \sum_{j=k+1}^{|I|}(-1)^j \sum_{J\subseteq I, |J|=j}\gamma(J).$$

Now the proposition follows as $\sum_{j=0}^{k-1}(-1)^j\tau_j(I) \leq vol(R_I), P_{p\in G}[p_I \in R_I] \leq \sum_{j=0}^{k}(-1)^j\tau_j(I)$. □

The approximation error of any partition can be bounded by the following.

Lemma 4. $\forall h : [d_2] \to [d_3], |vol(R^{(h)}) - vol(R)| \leq \sum_{q\in[d_3]} \tau_k(h^{-1}(q))$

Proof:

$$vol(R) = \prod_{q\in[d_3]} vol(R_{h^{-1}(q)}).$$
$$vol(R^{(h)}) = \prod_{q\in[d_3]} P_{p\in G}[p_{h^{-1}(q)} \in R_{h^{-1}(q)}].$$

This lemma follows from the previous proposition and the known fact that $|\prod_{i=1}^{l} x_i - \prod_{i=1}^{l} y_i| \leq \sum_{i=1}^{l} |x_i - y_i|$ when $0 \leq x_i, y_i \leq 1$ for all $i \in [l]$. □

Finally, we can bound the expected approximation error.

Lemma 5. *For* $R \in \mathcal{R}(m_2, d_2)$, $|E_{h\in H}[vol(R^{(h)})] - vol(R)| \leq \frac{\epsilon}{4}$.

Proof:

$$\begin{aligned}
|E_{h\in H}[vol(R^{(h)})] - vol(R)| &\leq E_{h\in H}[|vol(R^{(h)}) - vol(R)|] \\
&\leq E_{h\in H}[\sum_{q\in[d_3]} \tau_k(h^{-1}(q))] \\
&= \sum_{q\in[d_3]} E_{h\in H}[\sum_{I\subseteq h^{-1}(q), |I|=k} \pi(I)] \\
&= \sum_{q\in[d_3]} \sum_{I\subseteq[d_2], |I|=k} P_{h\in H}[\forall i \in I\ h(i) = q]\pi(I) \\
&= \sum_{q\in[d_3]} \sum_{I\subseteq[d_2], |I|=k} (1/d_3)^k\pi(I) \\
&= (1/d_3)^{k-1}\tau_k([d_2])
\end{aligned}$$

Let $\alpha = \sum_{i\in[d_2]} \delta_i$. There are two cases depending on the value of α.

– $\alpha \le \log \frac{12}{\epsilon}$:
$\tau_k([d_2])$ gets it maximum value when $\delta_i = \frac{\alpha}{d_2}$ for all $i \in [d_2]$. So $\tau_k([d_2]) \le (\frac{ed_2}{k})^k(\frac{\alpha}{d_2})^k \le (\frac{e\log\frac{12}{\epsilon}}{k})^k$, which is again maximized when $k = \log \frac{12}{\epsilon}$. So for $d_3 = 2^{(3\log\frac{12}{\epsilon})/(k-1)}$, we have

$$\begin{aligned}|E_{h\in H}[vol(R^{(h)})] - vol(R)| &\le 2^{-3\log\frac{12}{\epsilon}} e^{\log\frac{12}{\epsilon}} \\ &= 2^{-(3-\log e)\log\frac{12}{\epsilon}} \\ &= (\frac{\epsilon}{12})^{3-\log e} \\ &\le \frac{\epsilon}{12}.\end{aligned}$$

– $\alpha > \log \frac{12}{\epsilon}$:
In this case, both $E_{h\in H}[vol(R^{(h)})]$ and $vol(R)$ are small, so their difference is small. First, $vol(R) = \prod_{i\in[d_2]}(1-\delta_i) \le 2^{-\sum_{i\in[d_2]}\delta_i} < \frac{\epsilon}{12}$.
Next, we show that $E_{h\in H}[vol(R^{(h)})] \le \frac{\epsilon}{3}$. Let d' be the smallest integer such that $\log\frac{12}{\epsilon} - 1 < \sum_{i\in[d']}\delta_i \le \log\frac{12}{\epsilon}$. Let $R' = R_{[d']} \times [m_2]^{d_2-d'}$. From the previous case $E_{h\in H}[vol(R'^{(h)})] \le vol(R') + \frac{\epsilon}{12}$. So

$$\begin{aligned}E_{h\in H}[vol(R^{(h)})] &\le E_{h\in H}[vol(R'^{(h)})] \\ &\le vol(R') + \frac{\epsilon}{12} \\ &\le 2^{-\sum_{i\in[d']}\delta_i} + \frac{\epsilon}{12} \\ &\le 2^{-\log\frac{12}{\epsilon}+1} + \frac{\epsilon}{12} \\ &= \frac{2\epsilon}{12} + \frac{\epsilon}{12} \\ &= \frac{\epsilon}{4}\end{aligned}$$

Then $0 \le E_{h\in H}[vol(R^{(h)})], vol(R) \le \frac{\epsilon}{4}$, and $|E_{h\in H}[vol(R^{(h)})] - vol(R)| \le \frac{\epsilon}{4}$. □

So we have the following lemma.

Lemma 6. *$\mathcal{F}_3$ is $(\mathcal{R}(m_2,d_2), \mathcal{R}(m_3,d_3), \frac{\epsilon}{4})$-good.*

Theorem 1 *There is an explicit ϵ-generator for $\mathcal{R}(m,d)$, using $O(\log m + \log d + \log^{3/2} 1/\epsilon)$ bits.*

Proof: $|\mathcal{F}_1| = d^{O(1)}$, $|\mathcal{F}_2| = 2^s = (md/\epsilon)^{O(1)}$, and $|\mathcal{F}_3| = |\mathcal{H}_k(d_2,d_3)| \le d_2^k = (1/\epsilon)^{O(k)}$.

The INW-generator gives us an $\frac{\epsilon}{4}$-generator for $\mathcal{R}(m_3,d_3)$ using $O(\log m_3 + (\log d_3 + \log 1/\epsilon)\log d_3) = O(k\log 1/\epsilon + 1/k\log^2 1/\epsilon)$ bits. From Lemma 1, we have an ϵ-generator for $\mathcal{R}(m,d)$ using $O(\log m + \log d + k \log 1/\epsilon + 1/k \log^2 1/\epsilon)$ bits. When $k = O(\log^{1/2} 1/\epsilon)$, the number of bits used gets its minimum value $O(\log m + \log d + \log^{3/2} 1/\epsilon)$. □

4 A Potential Improvement

For $\mathcal{F}_3$, we can replace the k-wise independent space H by an approximate k-wise independent space H', over $[d_3]^{d_2}$, such that for any $I \subseteq [d_2]$ with $|I| \leq k$ and for any $y \in [d_3]^{d_2}$,

$$|P_{x \in H'}[x_I = y_I] - (\frac{1}{d_3})^{|I|}| \leq O(\frac{\epsilon}{d_3}).$$

A simple generalization from the constructions of Alon, Goldreich, Hastad, and Peralta [2], or Naor and Naor [10] gives us $|H'| = (\frac{k \log d_2}{\epsilon})^{O(1)} = (\frac{1}{\epsilon})^{O(1)}$. H' can also be identified efficiently with $|H'|$. One can easily verify that only an additional $O(\epsilon)$ error is introduced in Lemma 5, and now the reduction cost for $\mathcal{F}_3$ is $O(\log 1/\epsilon)$. From now on we will use H' instead of H in $\mathcal{F}_3$.

Recall from the previous section that $m_3 = |\mathcal{H}_k(d_2, m_2)| = (1/\epsilon)^{O(k)}$ and $d_3 = 2^{(3 \log 1/\epsilon)/(k-1)}$. Larger k implies smaller d_3 but larger m_3. The optimum is attained at $k = \Theta(\log^{1/2} 1/\epsilon)$. If we can replace $\mathcal{H}_k(d_2, m_2)$ by a smaller space, we might be able to choose a larger k and get a smaller d_3. Remeber that d_3 copies of $\mathcal{H}_k(d_2, m_2)$ are used to approximate the volumes of the d_3 subrectangles of R partitioned by a function $h : [d_2] \to [d_3]$. The approximation is guaranteed by the fact that for $R \in \mathcal{R}(m_2, d_2)$ and for $J \subseteq [d_2]$ with $|J| \leq k$,

$$|\pi(J) - \gamma(J)| = |vol(\tilde{R}_J) - P_{p \in G}[p_J \in \tilde{R}_J]| = 0.$$

We want to use a smaller space by allowing a small error ϵ' instead of 0 above. The approximate k-wise independent space does not help here, because it needs $\Omega(k \log m_2 + \log 1/\epsilon')$ bits to achieve an error ϵ' here, no better than G. However, observe that what we need here is to approximate the volume of a rectangle with at most k nontrivial dimesions. This turns out to be a special case of our original problem — constructing a pseudonrandom generator for $\mathcal{R}(m, d, k)$.

Suppose that $g : \{0,1\}^s \to [m_2]^{d_2}$ is an ϵ'-generator for $\mathcal{R}(m, d, k)$. In $\mathcal{F}_3$, we replace $\mathcal{H}_k(d_2, m_2)$ by the space generated by g. Let $m_3 = 2^s$. For $h \in H'$, let $f_h : [m_3]^{d_3} \to [m_2]^{d_2}$ be defined as follows

$$f_h(x_1, \ldots, x_{d_3}) = (g(x_{h(1)})(1), \ldots, g(x_{h(d_2)})(d_2)).$$

For $R = R_1 \times \cdots \times R_{d_2} \in \mathcal{R}(m_2, d_2)$, $f_h^{-1}(R) = R^{(h)} = R'_1 \times \cdots \times R'_{d_3} \in \mathcal{R}(m_3, d_3)$, where $R'_q = \{x \in [m_3] : g(x)_{h^{-1}(q)} \in R_{h^{-1}(q)}\}$. Then for $J \subseteq h^{-1}(q)$ with $|J| \leq k$, $|P_{x \in [m_3]}[g(x)_J \in \tilde{R}_J] - vol(\tilde{R}_J)| \leq \epsilon'$. So, for any $h : [d_2] \to [d_3]$,

$$\begin{aligned} |vol(R) - vol(R^{(h)})| &\leq \sum_{q \in [d_3]} ((\sum_{J \subseteq h^{-1}(q), |J| \leq k} \epsilon') + \tau_k(h^{-1}(q))) \\ &\leq d_2^{k+2} \epsilon' + \sum_{q \in [d_3]} \tau_k(h^{-1}(q)), \end{aligned}$$

and $|E_{h\in H'}[vol(R^{(h)})] - vol(R)| \leq d_2^{k+2}\epsilon' + \frac{\epsilon}{4} = \epsilon/2$, for $\epsilon' = \frac{\epsilon}{4d_2^{k+2}}$.

So if we have a better ϵ'-generator for $\mathcal{R}(m_2, d_2, k)$, we can choose a larger k and thus a smaller d_3.

Theorem 2 *If there exists an explicit ϵ-generator for $\mathcal{R}(m, d, k)$ using $O(k + \log d + \log m + \log 1/\epsilon)$ bits, then there exists an explicit ϵ-generator for $\mathcal{R}(m, d)$ using $O(\log d + \log m + \log \frac{1}{\epsilon} \log\log \frac{1}{\epsilon})$ bits.*

Proof: Using the ϵ'-generator for $\mathcal{R}(m_2, d_2, k)$ in $\mathcal{F}_3$ gives $m_3 = (\frac{2^k d_2 m_2}{\epsilon/d_2^k})^{O(1)} = (\frac{d_2^k}{\epsilon})^{O(1)}$. We want to repeatedly reduce the dimensions of rectangles. Notice that each time the dimension is reduced, we can choose a larger next k.

For $3 \leq i \leq l = \log\log \frac{12}{\epsilon} - \log\log\log \frac{12}{\epsilon}$, let

$$\begin{aligned} k_i &= 2^i, \\ d_i &= 2^{O((\log \frac{1}{\epsilon})/k_i)} = 2^{O((\log \frac{1}{\epsilon})/2^i)}, \\ \epsilon_i &= \frac{\epsilon}{4d_{i-1}^{k_i+2}} = \epsilon^{O(1)}, \text{ and} \\ m_i &= (\frac{2^{k_i} m_{i-1} d_{i-1}}{\epsilon_i})^{O(1)} = (\frac{1}{\epsilon})^{O(i)} \end{aligned}$$

For $3 \leq i \leq l$, let $\mathcal{F}_i$ be the dimension reduction discussed before, using the assumed ϵ_i-generator for $\mathcal{R}(m_{i-1}, d_{i-1}, k_i)$. One can check that each $\mathcal{F}_i$ is $(\mathcal{R}(m_{i-1}, d_{i-1}), \mathcal{R}(m_i, d_i), \epsilon)$-good. Using the INW-generator as an ϵ-generator for $\mathcal{R}(m_l, d_l)$, we have an $O(\epsilon \log\log \frac{1}{\epsilon})$-generator for $\mathcal{R}(m, d)$. The total number of bits used is

$$\begin{aligned} & O(\log m + \log d + \log \frac{1}{\epsilon} + \log\log \frac{1}{\epsilon} \log \frac{1}{\epsilon} + \log m_l + (\log d_l + \log \frac{1}{\epsilon}) \log d_l) \\ &= O(\log m + \log d + \log \frac{1}{\epsilon} \log\log \frac{1}{\epsilon}). \end{aligned}$$

So we have an ϵ-generator for $\mathcal{R}(m, d)$ using $O(\log m + \log d + \log \frac{1}{\epsilon^2} \log\log \frac{1}{\epsilon^2}) = O(\log m + \log d + \log \frac{1}{\epsilon} \log\log \frac{1}{\epsilon})$ bits. □

We don't know yet how to construct such an explicit ϵ-generator for $\mathcal{R}(m, d, k)$ using $O(\log k + \log d + \log m + \log 1/\epsilon)$ bits. Using an idea of Auer, Long, and Srinivasan [3], we can derive one using $O(\log k + \log m + \log^{3/2} 1/\epsilon)$ bits, which improves their upper bound, but does not serve our purpose here.

5 The Pseudorandom Generator for $\mathcal{B}(m, d, t)$

Recall that $\mathcal{B}(m, d, t)$ denote the class of rectangles from $\mathcal{R}(m, d)$ with at most t nontrivial dimensions and each dimension being an interval. For $\mathcal{B}(m, d, t)$, Even, Goldreich, Luby, Nisan, and Veličković [6] have an ϵ-generator using $O(t + \log\log d + \log 1/\epsilon)$ bits. Unfortunately, we cannot apply the iterative procedure in the previous section to $\mathcal{B}(m,d,d)$ because after applying the dimension reduction once, each dimension is no longer an interval.

For $t \geq \log 1/\epsilon$, Chari, Rohatgi, and Srinivasan [5] had an ϵ-generator for $\mathcal{B}(m,d,t)$ using $O(\log\log d + \log 1/\epsilon \log \frac{t}{\log 1/\epsilon})$ bits, a significant improvement in the dependence on t. This is improved again by the following theorem.

Theorem 3 *For $t \geq \log 1/\epsilon$, there is an explicit ϵ-generator for $\mathcal{B}(m,d,t)$, using $O(\log\log d + \log 1/\epsilon \log^{1/2} \frac{t}{\log 1/\epsilon})$ bits.*

Proof: Here we use only one reduction, the modified dimension reduction discussed in the previous section. Let $k \leq t$ be a parameter to be chosen later. For $\epsilon' = \epsilon(\frac{k}{t})^{O(k)}$, let $g : \{0,1\}^s \to [m]^d$ be the ϵ'-generator of Even, Goldreich, Luby, Nisan, and Veličković for $\mathcal{B}(m,d,k)$. Let $m' = 2^s$ and $d' = 2^{(3\log\frac{12}{\epsilon})/(k-1)}$. Given $R = R_1 \times \cdots \times R_d \in \mathcal{B}(m,d,t)$, assume w.o.l.g. that the first t dimensions are nontrivial. For $h \in H'$ let $R^{(h)} = f_h^{-1}(R) = R'_1 \times \cdots \times R'_{d'}$, where $R'_q = \{x \in [m'] : g(x)_{h^{-1}(q)} \in R_{h^{-1}(q)}\}$.

For $J \not\subseteq [t]$,

$$|vol(\tilde{R}_J) - P_{x\in[m']}[g(x)_J \in \tilde{R}_J]| = 0,$$

because $\overline{R}_j = \emptyset$ for $j \notin [t]$. For $J \subseteq [t]$ with $|J| \leq k$,

$$|vol(\tilde{R}_J) - P_{x\in[m']}[g(x)_J \in \tilde{R}_J]| \leq 2^{|J|}\epsilon',$$

as each $\tilde{R}_J$ is the union of at most $2^{|J|}$ rectangles from $\mathcal{B}(m,|J|,|J|)$. Then

$$\begin{aligned} |E_{h\in H'}[vol(R^{(h)})] - vol(R)| &\leq \sum_{j=0}^{k} \sum_{J\subseteq[t],|J|=j} 2^j\epsilon' + E_{h\in H'}[\sum_{q\in[d']} \tau_k(h^{-1}(q))] \\ &\leq (\frac{t}{k})^{O(k)}\epsilon' + O(\epsilon) \\ &\leq O(\epsilon). \end{aligned}$$

Combined with the INW-generator, we get an ϵ-generator using $O(\log\{\frac{k\log d}{\epsilon} + k\log\frac{t}{k} + \log\frac{1}{\epsilon}\frac{\log 1/\epsilon}{k}) = O(\log k + \log\log d + \log 1/\epsilon + k\log\frac{t}{k} + \frac{\log^2 1/\epsilon}{k})$ bits. Choosing $k = (\log 1/\epsilon)/\log^{1/2}\frac{t}{\log 1/\epsilon}$ results in $O(\log\log d + \log 1/\epsilon \log^{1/2}\frac{t}{\log 1/\epsilon})$.

□

6 Acknowledgements

We would like to thank David Barrington for correcting some mistakes and making useful suggestions. We would like to thank Shiyu Zhou for telling us the result in [14] and for some helpful comments. We would also like to thank Amnon Ta-Shma, Jaikumar Radhakrishnan, and Avi Wigderson for reading this paper.

References

1. A.E. Andreev, A.E.F. Clementi, and J.D.P. Rolim, Efficient constructions of hitting sets for system of linear functions, In *Proceedings of the 14th Annual Symposium on Theoretical Aspects of Computer Science*, pages 387-398, 1997
2. N. Alon, O. Goldreich, J. Hastad, and R. Peralta, Simple constructions of almost k-wise independent random variables, *Random Structures and Algorithms*, 3(3), pages 289-303, 1992.
3. P. Auer, P. Long, and A. Srinivasan, Approximating hyper-rectangles: learning and pseudo-random sets, In *Proceedings of the 29th Annual ACM Symposium on Theory of Computing*, 1997.
4. R. Armoni, M. Saks, A. Wigderson, and S. Zhou, Discrepancy sets and pseudo-random generators for combinatorial rectangles, In *Proceedings of the 37th Annual IEEE Symposium on Foundations of Computer Science*, pages 412-421, 1996.
5. S. Chari, P. Rohatgi, and A. Srinivasan, Improved algorithms via approximations of probability distributions, In *Proceedings of the 26th Annual ACM Symposium on Theory of Computing*, pages 584-592, 1994.
6. G. Even, O. Goldreich, M. Luby, N. Nisan, and B. Velicković, Approximations of general independent distributions. In *Proceedings of the 24th Annual ACM Symposium on Theory of Computing*, pages 10-16, 1992.
7. O. Goldreich and A. Wigderson, Tiny families of functions with random properties: a quality-size trade-off for hashing, In *Proceedings of the 26th Annual ACM Symposium on Theory of Computing*, pages 574-583, 1994.
8. R. Impagliazzo, N. Nisan, and A. Wigderson, Pseudorandomness for network algorithms, In *Proceedings of the 26th Annual ACM Symposium on Theory of Computing*, pages 356-364, 1994.
9. N. Linial, M. Luby, M. Saks, and D. Zuckerman, Efficient construction of a small hitting set for combinatorial rectangles in high dimension, In *Proceedings of the 25th Annual ACM Symposium on Theory of Computing*, pages 258-267, 1993.
10. J. Naor and M. Naor, Small-bias probability spaces: efficient constructions and applications, *SIAM Journal on Computing*, 22(4), pages 838-856, 1990.
11. N. Nisan, Pseudorandom generators for space-bounded computation, *Combinatorica*, 12, pages 449-461, 1992.
12. N. Nisan, Extracting randomness: how and why - a survey, In *Proceedings of the 11th Annual IEEE Conference on Computational Complexity*, pages 44-58, 1996.
13. N. Nisan and D. Zuckerman, Randomness is linear in space, *Journal of Computer and System Sciences*, 52(1), pages 43-52, 1996.
14. J. Radhakrishnan and A. Ta-shma, Private communication.

Translation Validation for Synchronous Languages

A. Pnueli O. Shtrichman M. Siegel

Weizmann Institute of Science, Rehovot, Israel

Abstract. *Translation validation* is an alternative to the verification of translators (compilers, code generators). Rather than proving in advance that the compiler always produces a target code which correctly implements the source code (compiler verification), each individual translation (i.e. a run of the compiler) is followed by a validation phase which verifies that the target code produced on this run correctly implements the submitted source program. In order to be a practical alternative to compiler verification, a key feature of this validation is its *full automation*.
Since the validation process attempts to "unravel" the transformation effected by the translators, its task becomes increasingly more difficult (and necessary) with the increase of sophistication and variety of the optimizations methods employed by the translator. In this paper we address the feasibility of translation validation for highly optimizing, industrial code generators from DC+, a widely used intermediate format for synchronous languages, to C.

1 Introduction

Compiler verification is an extremely complex task and every change to the compiler requires redoing the proof. Thus, compiler verification tends to "freeze" the compiler design and discourages any future improvements and revisions which is not acceptable in an industrial setting. This drawback can be avoided by a well designed translation validation approach, first introduced in [10], which compares the input and the output of the compiler for each individual run mostly independent of *how* the output is generated from the input.

In this paper we consider translation validation for synchronous languages. Synchronous languages [8], such as Esterel [3], Argos [9], Signal [2] and Lustre [5], are mainly used in industrial applications for the development of safety critical, reactive systems. In particular, they are designed to be translatable into code which is as time/space efficient as handwritten code. This code is generated by sophisticated code generators which perform various analyses/calculations on the source code in order to derive highly efficient implementations in languages such as C and ADA. In order to share code generation tools (and silicon compilers, simulators, verification tools etc.) for synchronous languages, the DC+ format has been developed. DC+ [7] is an equational representation for both imperative and declarative synchronous languages.

In this paper we explain the theory underlying translation validation for two industrial compilers from DC+ to C. These compilers – which apply more than 100 optimization rules during code generation [11] – are developed in the ESPRIT project SACRES by the French company TNI and by Inria (Rennes) and are used by Siemens, SNECMA and British Aerospace. Their formal verification is prohibitive due to their size (more than 20.000 lines of code each) and the fact that they are constantly improved/extended.

We present a common semantic model for DC+ and C, introduce the applied notion of *being a correct implementation*, formulate the correctness of the generated C code as proof obligations in first order logic and present efficient decision procedures to check the correctness of the generated proof obligations. All translations and constructions which are presented in the course of the paper have been implemented in a tool called TVT (Translation Validation Tool).

Related work: In [10] we addressed translation validation for a non-optimizing compiler from Signal to C . The revision of this work to deal with the optimizing compilers from TNI and Inria is the topic of this paper.

The work in [6] performs translation validation on a purely syntactic level. Their method is based on finding a bijection between abstract and concrete instruction sets (resp. variables) because they are considering a *structural* translation of one sequential program into another sequential program. Since we are dealing with optimizing compilers we have to employ a far more involved *semantic* approach.

The paper is organized as follows. In Section 2 we give a brief introduction to DC+. Section 3 presents the concepts which underly the generation of the proof obligations. In Section 4 we present the decision procedures to check the validity of these proof obligations. Section 5 contains some conclusions.

2 The DC+ Format

A DC+ program describes a reactive system whose behavior along time is an infinite sequence of *instants* which represent reactions, triggered by external or internal events. The main objects manipulated by a DC+ program are *flows*, which are sequences of values synchronized with a *clock*. A flow is a typed object which holds a value at each instant of its clock. The fact that a flow is currently absent is represented by the bottom symbol $\perp$ (cf. [2]). Clocks are boolean flows, assuming the values $\{T, \perp\}$. A clock has the value T if and only if the flow associated with the clock holds a value at the present instant of time. Actually, any expression *exp* in the language has its corresponding clock *clk*(*exp*) which indicates whether the value of the expression at the current instant is different from $\perp$.

Besides *external* flows (input/output flows), which determine the interface of the DC+ program with its environment, also *internal* flows are used and manipulated by the program.

2.1 DC+ and Its Semantics

In order to present the formal semantics of DC+ we introduce a variant of *synchronous transition systems* (STS) [10]. STS is the computational model of our translation validation approach.

Let V be a set of typed variables. A *state* s over V is a type-consistent interpretation of the variables in V. Σ_V denotes the set of all states over V. A *synchronous transition system* $A = (V, \Theta, \rho)$ consists of a finite set V of typed variables, a satisfiable assertion Θ characterizing the initial states of system A, and a transition relation ρ. This is an assertion $\rho(V, V')$, which relates a state $s \in \Sigma_V$ to its possible successors $s' \in \Sigma_V$ by referring to both unprimed and primed versions of variables in V. Unprimed variables are interpreted according to s, primed variables according to s'. To the state space of an STS A we refer to as Σ_A. We will also use the term "system" to abbreviate "synchronous transition system". Some of the variables in V are identified as *volatile* while the others are identified as *persistent*. Volatile variables represent flows of DC+ programs, thus their domains contain the designated element $\perp$ to indicate absence of the respective flow.

A *computation* of $A = (V, \Theta, \rho)$ is an infinite sequence $\sigma = \langle s_0, s_1, s_2, \ldots \rangle$, with $s_i \in \Sigma_V$ for each $i \in \mathbb{N}$, which satisfies $s_0 \models \Theta$ and $\forall i \in \mathbb{N}.\ (s_i, s_{i+1}) \models \rho$. Denote by $\|A\|$ the set of computations of the STS A.

For the purpose of translation validation, DC+ programs are translated into the STS formalism. A brief introduction to DC+ and details of its translation to STS are given next.

A DC+ program consists of a set of constraints which determine the transition relation of the system. At each instant of time all constraints have to be satisfied by the values that the flows have at this instant. The constraints are expressed as *equation* and *memorization* statements. The equation $v = exp$ [1] defines the flow v to be equal to the expression exp at any instant, which implies that also their clocks coincide. Formally this equation contributes the following clause to the transition relation of the STS which represents the DC+ source:

$$v' = \text{if } clk(exp') \text{ then } exp' \text{ else } \perp .$$

The second kind of constraints are memorization statements $r \overset{m}{=} exp$ which defines r to hold the last (*not* including the present) non-bottom value of exp. Also memorizations imply that the arguments have the same clocks. Whereas equations are used to specify *instantaneous reactions* of the system, memorizations are used to define the *internal state* of the system, i.e. its registers when the DC+ program is considered as an operator network [7]. The formal semantics of memorizations is

$$\begin{aligned} \wedge\ x.r' &= \text{if } clk(exp') \text{ then } exp' \text{ else } x.r \\ \wedge\ r' &= \text{if } clk(exp') \text{ then } x.r \text{ else } \perp . \end{aligned}$$

[1] we omit an optional activation condition to simplify the presentation

This definition introduces an auxiliary variable $x.r$ which stores the last (including the present) non-bottom value of exp. Variable $x.r$ is initialized in Θ of the STS representing the DC+ source to define the first non-bottom value of r (an init-construct in DC+ defines such initial values). From now on we refer to flows defined by memorizations as *register flows*. Variables in an STS which represent register flows will typically be denoted by r, corresponding memorization variables by $x.r$.

There are two kinds of functions which can be used in DC+ expressions: *monochronous* functions, such as $+, -, div, \ldots$, are standard operators on flows whose results share the same clock as their arguments while *polychronous* functions, such as $\mathsf{when}(w, cond)$ and $\mathsf{pcond}(cond, exp_1, exp_2)$, introduce and handle flows with different clocks. The latter operators can be used for under/oversampling of flows. They are translated as follows:

$$\mathsf{when}(exp, cond) \stackrel{\text{def}}{=} \text{if } \ cond = \mathrm{T} \text{ then } \ exp \text{ else } \ \bot$$

$$\mathsf{pcond}(cond, exp_1, exp_2) \stackrel{\text{def}}{=} \begin{pmatrix} \text{if} & & cond = \mathrm{T} \wedge clk(exp_1) \text{ then } & exp_1 \\ \text{else} & \text{if} & cond = \mathrm{F} \wedge clk(exp_2) \text{ then } & exp_2 \\ & \text{else} & \bot & \end{pmatrix}$$

Based on these definitions we can define the semantics of a DC+ program D by an STS $S = (V, \Theta, \rho)$ as follows. Set V is identical to the set of flows in D plus the memorization variables $x.r$ which are introduced by the semantics above. Assertion Θ defines all variables to be initially absent [7] except memorization variables which are initialized as stated in the DC+ source. Finally, ρ is obtained as the conjunction of the predicates which define the semantics of equation and memorization statements.

In the following sections we assume that the type definitions for variables also specify the "DC+ type" of variables, i.e. whether they are input, output, register, memorization or local variables. The respective sets of variables are denoted by I, O, R, M, L. Combinations of these letters stand for the union of the respective sets; e.g. IOR stands for the set of input/output/register variables of some system.

2.2 Compilation of Multi-clocked Synchronous Languages

```
DC+:   r_in ≞ in
       out = when(2*r_in,in>10)

C:     WHILE true DO
      {read(in);
        c_out = (in>10);
        IF c_out { out = 2*r_in;
                   write(out);}
       r_in = in;}
```

Fig. 1. translation of DC+

The compilation scheme for multi-clocked synchronous languages (s.a. Signal, DC+) to imperative, sequential languages (s.a. C, ADA) looks as follows. The set of equation and memorization statements of a program D form a *linear equation system LES* on the flows of D and their associated clocks. Solutions of LES for a given set of input/register values determine the next state of the system. The compiler derives from D an imperative program C which consists of one main loop whose task is to repeatedly compute such solutions of the LES.

In order to do so, the compiler computes from LES a *conditional* dependency graph on flows and another linear equation system – the, so called, *clock calculus* [2] – which records the dependencies amongst clocks. The produced code contains statements originating from the clock calculus and assignments to variables (representing the flows of D) whose order must be consistent with the dependency graph. These assignments are performed if the corresponding flow is currently present in the source program, i.e. the clocks of flows determine the control structure of the generated program. For the translation validation process also the C programs are translated into the STS formalism. Since the generated C code uses in the body of the main loop only a small fragment of ANSI C (e.g. no pointers, no loops), the translation is straightforward. Note, however that the C programs use *persistent* variables (i.e. variables which are never absent) to implement DC+ programs which use volatile variables. This has to be taken into account when defining the notion of "correct implementation" in the next section.

3 Correct Implementation: Refinement

Our approach to establish that "the C-code correctly implements the DC+ source" is based on the notion of *refinement*. The presented concepts have been approved by TNI and Inria.

3.1 Refinement and Refinement Mappings

Consider the two STSs $A = (V_A, \Theta_A, \rho_A)$ and $C = (V_C, \Theta_C, \rho_C)$, with $IO_A = IO_C$, to which we refer as the *abstract* and *concrete* system, respectively. We say that *C refines A*, denoted by $C \,\mathsf{ref}\, A$, if for any $\sigma = \langle s_0, s_1, s_2, \ldots \rangle$ in $\|C\|$ there exists a $\tau = \langle t_0, t_1, t_2, \ldots \rangle$ in $\|A\|$ such that

$$\forall x \in IO_A . \forall i \in \mathbb{N}.\ s_i[x] = t_i[x] \text{ or } \ t_i[x] = \bot.$$

In order to establish this notion of refinement for two given systems we have to *construct* for each concrete computation $\sigma \in \|C\|$ the corresponding abstract computation $\tau \in \|A\|$ such that the above property is satisfied. Such constructions are usually done by means of *refinement mappings* [1]. Rather than the standard static correspondence between concrete and abstract variables, we need a more general mechanism which relates *persistent* variables of the STS-representation of the C-code (denoted C-STS from now on) to *volatile* variables of the STS-representation of the DC+ program (DC+STS).

Definition 1. *Given systems $A = (V_A, \Theta_A, \rho_A)$ and $C = (V_C, \Theta_C, \rho_C)$ with $IO_A = IO_C$. A mapping $f : \Sigma_C \to \Sigma_A$ is a* clocked refinement mapping *from C to A if it satisfies the requirements of*

- *Initiation: $s \models \Theta_C$ implies $f(s) \models \Theta_A$, for all $s \in \Sigma_C$.*
- *Propagation: $(s, s') \models \rho_C$ implies $(f(s), f(s')) \models \rho_A$, for all $s, s' \in \Sigma_C$.*
- *Preservation of Observation: $\forall x \in IO_A . \forall s \in \Sigma_C.\ f(s)[x] = s[x]$ or $f(s)[x] = \bot$.*

The idea of this definition is, that in each time instant and for each observable variable $x \in IO_A = IO_C$ either x is present in the abstract system and $f(s)[x]$ coincides with $s[x]$ or x is absent in $f(s)$. In the following presentation we omit the qualifier "clocked" if it is clear from the context.

Theorem 1. *If there exists a clocked refinement mapping from C to A then C* ref *A.*

Usually, finding such a mapping f is left to the ingenuity of the verifier. In the context of translation validation it is essential that f can be *automatically constructed* from the source and target programs.

The main idea in [10] was to generate refinement mappings which reconstruct the values of *all* abstract variables. In order to do so, it was necessary to extract from the structure of the C-code the information whether an abstract variable is currently present/absent, i.e. we reconstructed the clocks of these variables. With this information about clocks we could define the correct values of abstract variables from the values of their concrete counterparts. Such a reconstruction of all abstract variables is not possible in the case of the optimizing code generators, because:

1. Internal abstract variables are possibly eliminated for space efficiency during compilation; so there are no corresponding variables in the C-code from which we could automatically reconstruct their values.
2. The reconstruction of the clocks of abstract variables was based in [10] on the assumption that an abstract variable is present iff the corresponding concrete variable has been updated in the current iteration (cf. Fig. 2.2). The optimizing compilers *move assignments* between if-blocks in the C-code such that neither the fact that a concrete variable is written implies that its abstract counterpart is actually present nor does the presence of an abstract variable implies that its concrete counterpart is written in the current iteration.

Since the code generators cannot eliminate IOR variables without producing incorrect code, we can exploit the property of *determinacy* – which is a central property of synchronous programs [2] – to *implicitly* reconstruct local abstract variables.

Definition 2. *An* STS *$S = (V, \Theta, \rho)$ is* determinate in *$V \subseteq V_S$ if:*

$$\forall s_1, s_2, s_3 \in \Sigma_S . ((s_1, s_2) \models \rho \wedge (s_1, s_3) \models \rho \wedge s_2[V] = s_3[V]) \Rightarrow s_2[V_S \backslash V] = s_3[V_S \backslash V]$$

Determinacy of S in V says that, after a transition, the values of variables in set $V_S \setminus V$ are uniquely determined once the values for the variables in V have been fixed. The considered compiler exclusively accept DC+ programs which are determinate in their IRM variables. Determinacy of DC+ programs is assumed from now on.

In order to determine corresponding abstract states it thus suffices to reconstruct these IRM variables by the refinement mapping. Besides this we have to reconstruct the values of abstract output variables to check whether the generated abstract and concrete outputs indeed coincide. For these IORM variables the clock generation scheme as presented in [10] can still be applied[11].

Technically we eliminate all local variables in DC+STS $= (V, \Theta, \rho)$ by removing them from V, removing their initializations from Θ and hiding them from ρ by existential quantification. The result of applying this transformation to some STS A is denoted by $A^{\exists}$. Determinacy of A in IRM_A implies that it suffices to construct an inductive refinement mapping from C to $A^{\exists}$ to actually prove that C correctly implements A, i.e. C ref A.

However, there is one remaining problem with the reconstruction of the values of register variables. Registers are updated during one iteration of the main loop *after* they have been used in assignments of other variables, cf. Fig. 2.2. Thus, at the end of an iteration, register variables are already updated for the *next* iteration. So, the values of abstract register variables have to be reconstructed from the values of the corresponding variables at the *beginning* of the iteration while input/output/memorization variables can be reconstructed from the values of corresponding variables at the *end* of the iteration. This situation is handled by automatically inserting a *history variable* $h.r$ into the C-code for each register variable r.

3.2 Syntactic Representation and Proof Rule for Refinement

In the quest for automating the translation validation process, we present in this section a *syntactic representation* of clocked refinement mappings and an associated proof rule. Then, we describe how the components used in the proof rule can be computed, so that the translation validation process can be carried out fully automatically.

Consider two STSs A and C with $IO_A = IO_C$. Let $\alpha : V_A \longrightarrow \mathcal{E}(V_C)$ be a *substitution* that replaces each abstract variable $v \in V_A$ by an expression $\mathcal{E}_v$ over the concrete variables V_C. Such a substitution α induces a mapping between states, denoted by f_α. For $s_C \in \Sigma_C$ the abstract state $s_A \stackrel{\text{def}}{=} f_\alpha(s_C)$ corresponding to s_C under substitution α assigns to each variable $v \in V_A$ the value of expression $\mathcal{E}_v$ evaluated in s_C. In this way, a refinement mapping can be syntactically defined by means of an appropriate substitution α. Such a substitution α is defined to be *observation preserving* if $\forall v \in IO_A .\ \models (v)[\alpha] = v \vee (v)[\alpha] = \bot$, cf. Definition 1.

Let $\alpha : V_A \longrightarrow \mathcal{E}(V_C)$ be an observation preserving substitution
R1. $\Theta_C \Rightarrow \Theta_A[\alpha]$ Initiation
R2. $\rho_C \Rightarrow \rho_A[\alpha]$ Propagation
C ref A
Rule ref: Proving Refinement

Note, that no auxiliary invariant is needed in **R2.** since code generators can not exploit reachability information for optimizations.

In order for rule ref to be useful in a fully automatic translation validation process, an appropriate substitution α has to be generated automatically. Based on the previous explanations we can define the following generic substitutions α.

Definition 3. *Given $A \in$ STS, representing the DC+ program where local variables have been eliminated, and $C \in$ STS, representing the C-code. We define $\alpha : V_A \longrightarrow \mathcal{E}(V_C)$ by:*

$$\begin{array}{llll} \alpha(v) = & \textit{if} \ \ \mathrm{clk}_c(v) \ \ \textit{then} \ \ v \ \ \textit{else} \ \ \bot & & \textit{for all } v \in IO_A (= IO_C) \\ \alpha(r) = & \textit{if} \ \ \mathrm{clk}_c(r) \ \ \textit{then} \ \ h.r \ \ \textit{else} \ \ \bot & & \textit{for all } r \in R_A (= R_C) \\ \alpha(x.r) = r & & & \textit{for all } x.r \in M_A \end{array}$$

This specific definition of α automatically yields observation preserving substitutions. The algorithm for computing the clock expressions $clk_c(.)$ above can be found in [10]. Intuitively, $clk_c(v)$ is computed from conditions of if-statements such that $clk_c(v)$ is true if and only if variable v is written in the current iteration of the C-loop.

The combination of the techniques and constructions mentioned above allow us to automatically extract two first order logic formulas (corresponding to **R.1.** and **R.2.** in rule **ref**) which state the correctness of the generated code if these formulas can be shown to be valid.

The presented approach is immune against the optimizations performed by the industrial code generators that we consider. The proof technique exploits, in contrast to our previous work [10], only minimal knowledge about the code generation process. We only assume that *IORM* variables are reconstructible which is the minimal requirement for the C-code to be a correct implementation of the DC+ source [11].

4 Checking the Proof Obligations

The generated proof obligations are infinite state assertions. Directly supplying them to a theorem prover such as PVS and starting proof strategies turned out to be far too slow.

In this section we explain the theoretical basis for an efficient BDD-based evaluation of the proof obligations on the basis of *uninterpreted functions*.

All the generated proof obligations are of the form $\varphi_C \Rightarrow \exists y_1, \ldots, y_n . \, (\varphi_A \wedge \bigwedge_{i=1}^{i=n} y_i = exp_i)$ where φ_C is the left hand side of the implications in Rule **ref**. The right hand side consists of the abstract local variables which are hidden by existential quantification and a conjunct φ_A which deals with the other variables. (We assume that the substitution α in Rule **ref** has already been performed.) In case of a determinate DC+ program, the set of equalities $y_1 = exp_1, \ldots, y_n = exp_n$ uniquely determine the values of $y_1, \ldots, y_n$ in terms of the other abstract variables. Thus we can use the following transformation in order to remove the existential quantifications from the proof obligations.

$$\varphi_C \Rightarrow \exists y. \, (y = exp \wedge \varphi_A) \quad \text{iff} \quad \forall y. \, (\varphi_C \wedge y = exp) \Rightarrow \varphi_A$$

The second formula is validity equivalent to the quantifier-free implication $(\varphi_C \wedge y = exp) \Rightarrow \varphi_A$. So, from now on we can concentrate on quantifier-free formulas with free variables. In order to simplify the presentation we consider formulas φ with variables of type boolean and integer and functions over these domains. Predicates are treated as boolean valued functions.

In the rest of this section we use a validity relation which is parameterized by a *declaration* D and an *interpretation* I, denoted by $\models_I^D \varphi$. Here, the declaration D determines the type of the variables in φ and I interprets (possibly a subset of) the function symbols occurring in φ. We say that φ is *valid w.r.t.* (I, D), denoted by $\models_I^D \varphi$, if φ is valid in every model M where function symbols are interpreted according to I and variables according to D. Note, that M may interpret in an arbitrary way those function symbols whose interpretation is not fixed by I.

For interpretations I_1, I_2 we define $I_1 \preceq I_2$ if I_1 and I_2 coincide on those function symbols interpreted by I_1, but I_2 possibly interprets more function symbols. Obviously, we have for $I_1 \preceq I_2$ that $\models_{I_1}^D \varphi$ implies $\models_{I_2}^D \varphi$.

The idea of the forthcoming abstractions is as follows. We have to check the validity of formula φ (the proof obligation) w.r.t. a declaration D which assigns integer/boolean types to variables and an interpretation J which gives (a standard) interpretation to all function symbols in φ.

As a sufficient condition for $\models_J^D \varphi$ we check $\models_I^D \varphi$ where $I \preceq J$ only interprets a subset of the function symbols in φ. Moving from interpretation J to I means relaxing the constraints on the interpretation of some function symbols and treating them logically as *uninterpreted*. In a second step we apply the technique of *function encoding*, described below, in order to substitute uninterpreted functions by fresh variables.

The encoded formulas belong to a fragment of first order logic which has a *small model* property [4]. This means that the validity of these formulas can be established by solely inspecting models up to a certain finite cardinality. In order to make these finite domains as small as possible we apply another techniques called *constant encoding*.

The final step of the abstraction is to determine the finite domains over which the variables of the encoded formulas need to be interpreted in order to check their validity.

4.1 The function encoding scheme

Assume we are given a formula φ, an interpretation I, and a declaration D. Furthermore, let f be a function symbol occuring in φ which is not interpreted by I. Then the function encoding scheme for f looks as follows.

- Replace each occurrence of the form $f(t_1, \ldots, t_k)$ in φ by a new variable v_f^i of a type equal to that of the value returned by f. Occurrences $f(t_1, \ldots, t_k)$ and $f(u_1, \ldots, u_k)$ are replaced by the same v_f^i iff t_j is identical to u_j for every $j = 1, \ldots, k$.
- Let $\hat{t}$ denote the result of replacing all outer-most occurrences of the form $f(t_1, \ldots, t_k)$ by the corresponding new variable v_f^i in a sub-term t of φ. For every pair of newly added variables v_f^i and v_f^j, $i \neq j$, corresponding to the non-identical occurrences $f(t_1, \ldots, t_k)$ and $f(u_1, \ldots, u_k)$, add the implication $(\hat{t_1} = \hat{u_1} \wedge \cdots \wedge \hat{t_k} = \hat{u_k}) \Rightarrow v_f^i = v_f^j$ as antecedent to the transformed formula.

Example 1. For $\varphi \stackrel{\text{def}}{=} (f(x, f(y, y)) = z \wedge x = y \wedge f(x, x) = x) \Rightarrow x = z$ the function encoding results in:

$$\begin{pmatrix} \wedge((x = y \wedge v_2 = y) \Rightarrow v_1 = v_2) \\ \wedge((x = x \wedge v_2 = x) \Rightarrow v_1 = v_3) \\ \wedge((y = x \wedge x = y) \Rightarrow v_2 = v_3) \end{pmatrix} \Rightarrow [(v_1 = z \wedge x = y \wedge v_3 = x) \Rightarrow x = z]$$

Let f-enc(φ) denote the result of applying the function encoding to φ.

Theorem 2. *Given a formula φ, an interpretation I, and a declaration D. Let f be a function symbol which is not interpreted by I. Then φ is valid w.r.t. (I, D) iff* f-enc(φ) *is valid w.r.t. (I, D).*

4.2 Level-zero abstraction

In Level-zero abstraction we consider the validity of the generated proof obligation w.r.t. an interpretation I which only gives interpretations to (polymorphic) equality, boolean functions (i.e. functions with boolean domain and range) and if-then-else. All remaining function symbols are left uninterpreted and are successively removed by the above scheme. Let F-enc(φ) denote the resulting formula after elimination.

F-enc(φ) belongs to a fragment of first order logic formulas which have a small model property [4] which we exploit to check the validity of $\models_I^D$ F-enc(φ). In order to limit the domains over which we have to interpret the integer variables in F-enc(φ) we apply a constant encoding scheme where the integer constants appearing in F-enc(φ) replaced by smaller integer constants. Such an encoding is possible since no ordering information can be expressed in the considered fragment of first order logic (note that we treat at Level-zero also comparison functions as being uninterpreted).

Let C denote the set of integer constants appearing in F-enc(φ), and let $|C|$ denote the size of C. Let π be any bijection from C to $\{0, \ldots, |C|-1\}$.

The constant encoding consists of replacing each constant $c \in C$ by its encoding $\pi(c)$. Let CF-enc(φ) denote the result of applying the constant encoding transformation to F-enc(φ). The following claim, where interpretation I, declaration D, F-enc(φ) and CF-enc(φ) are defined as above, justifies this encoding.

Theorem 3. *Formula* F-enc(φ) *is valid w.r.t. (I, D) iff* CF-enc(φ) *is valid w.r.t. (I, D).*

Finally, in order to check the validity of CF-enc(φ) w.r.t. (I, D) we alter the standard declaration D to a declaration D^* which associates *finite* types with all variables previously declared to be integers.

Let N denote the number of distinct variables appearing in CF-enc(φ) and, as before, let $|C|$ denote the number of distinct integer constants appearing in CF-enc(φ). Since CF-enc(φ) has been obtained by applying the constant-encoding transformation, we know that all of these constants lie in the range $\{0, \ldots, |C| - 1\}$. Let D^* denote the modified declaration in which all integer variables are redeclared to belong to the integer sub-type $\{0, \ldots, |C|+N-1\}$.

In the following claim let I, D, D^* and CF-enc(φ) be as defined as above.

Theorem 4. CF-enc(φ) *is valid w.r.t. (I, D) iff it is valid w.r.t. (I, D^*).*

Now, validity of CF-enc(φ) w.r.t. (I, D^*) is a sufficient condition for the validity of φ w.r.t. the original interpretation J and the original declaration D. However, as in all abstraction approaches, if $\models_I^{D^*}$ CF-enc(φ) does not hold we can not conclude anything for the validity of the original formula. Thus we suggest to use a more refined abstraction if the Level-zero abstraction failed.

4.3 Level-one abstraction

In Level-one we keep the interpretation of equality, boolean functions, if-then-else and additionally of comparison operators.

The formulas F-enc(φ) – resulting from function encoding of all uninterpreted function symbols – again possess the small model property. However, a different constant encoding scheme than in the Level-zero has to be used since now ordering information amongst variables and constants can be expressed and thus has to be preserved.

Let $C = \{c_1, \ldots, c_m\}$ be the set of constants appearing in F-enc(φ) where $c_1 < \cdots < c_m$. We introduce new variables $v_{c_1}, \ldots, v_{c_m}$ and transform F-enc(φ) by replacing all constant symbols by their respective new variables. Then we define for a pair (c_1, c_2), $c_1 < c_2$, of constants the following clause (N denotes again the number of distinct variables appearing in F-enc(φ)):

$$\mathsf{const}(c_1, c_2) = \begin{cases} v_{c_1} < v_{c_2} \wedge v_{c_2} - v_{c_1} \leq (c_2 - c_1) & \text{if } c_2 - c_1 \leq N \\ v_{c_2} > v_{c_1} & \text{if } c_2 - c_1 > N \end{cases}$$

Then, we add the predicate $\mathsf{const}(c_1, c_2) \wedge \ldots \wedge \mathsf{const}(c_{m-1}, c_m)$ as antecedent to the transformed formula. The result is again denoted by CF-enc(φ). Let interpretation I, declaration D, F-enc(φ) and CF-enc(φ) be as defined above.

Theorem 5. F-enc(φ) *is valid w.r.t.* (I, D) *iff* CF-enc(φ) *is valid w.r.t.* (I, D).

Finally, the standard declaration D is altered. Let N denote the number of distinct variables appearing in CF-enc(φ). Let D^* denote the modified declaration in which all integer variables are redeclared to belong to the integer sub-type $\{0, \ldots, N-1\}$. The following theorem justifies this transformation where I, D, D^*, and CF-enc(φ) are defined as above.

Theorem 6. CF-enc(φ) *is valid w.r.t.* (I, D) *iff it is valid w.r.t.* (I, D^*).

Obviously, Level-one yields more faithful abstractions than Level-zero. However, what do we do in case that also Level-one fails? Currently we are elaborating a hierarchy of abstractions by removing less interpretations of function symbols from the original formula. However, for the purpose of translation validation our experience suggests that Level-zero and Level-one will be sufficient to establish validity of the proof obligations if the generated code is indeed a correct implementation of its DC+ source.

5 Conclusion

We have presented the theory which underlies our translation validation approach for optimizing industrial compilers from DC+ to C. The insertion of history variables into the C code, the translation of DC+ and C programs to STS, the generation of the substitution α and the final assembling of the proof obligations according to Rule **ref** are implemented in TVT (Translation Validation Tool). TVT uses the decision procedures explained in Section 4 in order to check the validity of the generated proof obligations. A report on translation validation by means of TVT for industrial case studies is in preparation.

References

[1] M. Abadi and L. Lamport. The existence of refinement mappings. *Theoretical Computer Science*, 82(2), 1991.

[2] A. Benviniste, P. Le Guernic, and C. Jacquemot. Synchronous programming with events and relations: the SIGNAL language. *Science of Computer Programming*, 16, 1991.

[3] G. Berry and G. Gonthier. The ESTEREL synchronous programming language: Design, semantics, implementation. *Science of Computer Programming*, 19(2), 1992.

[4] E. Börger, E. Grädel, and Y. Gurevich. *The Classical Decision Problem*. Springer, 1996.

[5] P. Caspi, N. Halbwachs, P. Raymond, and D. Pilaud. The synchronous dataflow programming language LUSTRE. *Proceedings of the IEEE*, 79(9), 1991.

[6] A. Cimatti, F. Giunchiglia, and P. Pecchiari et al. A provably correct embedded verifier for the certification of safety critical software. In *CAV*, number 1254 in LNCS. Springer, 1997.

[7] The declarative code DC+. ESPRIT Project: SACRES, Project Report, 1997. Version 1.3.

[8] *Another look at real-time programming*, volume 79 of *Special Issue in Proc. of the IEEE*, September 1991.

[9] F. Maraninchi. Operational and compositional semantics of synchronous automata compositions. In *Proceedings CONCUR*, volume 630 of *LNCS*. Springer, 1992.

[10] A. Pnueli, M. Siegel, and E. Singermann. Translation validation. In *TACAS 98: Tools and Algorithms for the Construction and Analysis of Systems*, LNCS. Springer-Verlag, 1998.

[11] private communications with TNI (BREST), Siemens (Munich) and Inria (Rennes).

An Efficient and Unified Approach to the Decidability of Equivalence of Propositional Programs

Vladimir A. Zakharov

Faculty of Computational Mathematics and Cybernetics,
Moscow State University, Moscow, RU-119899, Russia
(zakh.cs.msu.su)

Abstract. The aim of this paper is to present a unified and easy-to-use technique for deciding the equivalence problem for propositional deterministic programs. The key idea is to reduce this problem to the well-known group-theoretic problems by revealing an algebraic nature of program computations. By applying the main theorems of this paper to some traditional computational models we demonstrate that the equivalence problem for these models is decidable by the simple algorithms in polynomial time.

The study of the equivalence problem for models of computation is of basic interest in computer science since the very beginning of formal methods in programming is related to this topic [13, 17, 25]. Informally, the equivalence problem is to find out whether two given programs have the same behavior. Taking various formalisms for the terms "program" and "behavior", we get numerous variants of this problem.

The equivalence problem significantly influences the programming practice. Tackling this problem, we comprehend better to what extent the specific changes in the structure of a program affect its behavior. The understanding of relationship between the syntactic and semantic components of programs is very important for specification, verification and optimization of programs, partial computations, reusing of programs, etc.

The decidability of the equivalence problem essentially depends on the expressive power of a computational model and the exact meaning of the term "the same behavior". When programs under consideration are deterministic, it is usually assumed that two programs have the same behavior if for every valid input they output identical results (if any), i.e. the programs realize the same mapping of the input data to the output data. Obviously, the functional equivalence thus defined is undecidable for the universal computational models such as Turing machine, RAM, rewriting system, etc. whose programs are capable to compute all recursive functions. At the same time it is decidable for the less powerful models such as Yanov's schemata [25], multi-tape and push-down deterministic automata [8, 20], monadic functional schemata [2], and some others. Sometimes, changing a little the syntax of computational models, we jump from decidable cases of the equivalence problem to the undecidable ones. Thus, the equivalence problem is decidable for deterministic multi-tape automata [8], one-counter automata [24], and RAMs without nested loops [5], whereas it is undecidable for nondeterministic multi-tape automata [17], multi-counter automata [9], and for RAMs having nested loops [4].

In most cases [2, 3, 10, 12, 14, 15, 17, 22–24] the algorithms solve the equivalence problem by taking an advantage of the specific phenomenon which is the very nature of some models of computation. It is as follows. Suppose that, given a pair of programs π_1, π_2, the results of some "long" runs of π_1 and π_2 detect the difference between the functions realized by these programs. Then some "short" runs distinguish π_1 and π_2 as well. The equivalence problem is effectively solvable when the boundary between the "long" and the "short" computations depends recursively on some syntactic characteristics of π_1 and π_2. In this case one needs only to check the behavior of programs on the finitely many runs to decide if they are equivalent or not. However, this approach to the equivalence problem is of little use for practice since the number of "short" runs to be checked is very large (as a rule, it is exponential of the size of programs π_1 and π_2 under consideration).

To overcome this difficulty we offer a novel decision technique for the equivalence relation on the formalized sequential programs. The key idea is to reduce the equivalence problem for deterministic programs to some known algebraic problems (such as the identity problem for semigroups) by revealing an algebraic nature of program computations. When the corresponding algebraic problems are efficiently solvable, this method yields efficient decision procedures as a result. To demonstrate the capability of the algebraic machinery some usual computational models are embedded in the framework of propositional deterministic programs. By applying the main theorems of this paper we prove the polynomial time complexity of the equivalence problem for these models, assuming that the alphabets of basic actions and propositions are finite and fixed.

We would like to emphasize that our approach advances and corroborates the ideas and hypothesis suggested in [10, 12, 22, 23]. The proof of Theorem 2 is omitted due to space limitations.

1 Preliminaries

In this section we introduce the concept of a propositional deterministic program (PDP), its syntax, and semantics. We define some basic properties of PDP computations, set up formally the equivalence problem for PDPs, and discuss some known decision results expressed in terms PDPs.

1.1 Syntax of PDP

Fix two finite alphabets $\mathcal{A} = \{a_1, \dots, a_N\}$ and $\mathcal{P} = \{p_1, \dots, p_M\}$.

The elements of $\mathcal{A}$ are called *basic actions*. Intuitively, the basic actions stand for the elementary program statements such as assignment statements and procedure calls. A finite sequence of basic actions is called an $\mathcal{A}$-sequence. The set of all $\mathcal{A}$-sequences is denoted by $\mathcal{A}^*$. We write λ for the empty $\mathcal{A}$-sequence, $|h|$ for the length of h, and hg for the concatenation of h and g.

The symbols of $\mathcal{P}$ are called *basic propositions*. We assume that basic propositions denote the primitive relations on program data. Each basic proposition may be evaluated either by 0 (falsehood) or by 1 (true). A binary M-tuple $\delta = \langle d_1, \ldots, d_M \rangle$ of truth-values of all basic propositions is called a *condition*. We write $\mathcal{C}$ for the set of all conditions.

A *propositional deterministic program* (PDP) over alphabets $\mathcal{A}$, $\mathcal{P}$ is a tuple $\pi = \langle V, \mathbf{entry}, \mathbf{exit}, \mathbf{loop}, B, T \rangle$, where

- V is a finite set of *internal program nodes*;
- **entry** is an *initial node*, $\mathbf{entry} \notin V$,
- **exit** is a *terminal node*, $\mathbf{exit} \notin V$,
- **loop** is a *dead node*, $\mathbf{loop} \notin V$,
- $B : V \rightarrow \mathcal{A}$ is a *binding function*, associating every internal node with some basic action;
- $T : (V \cup \{\mathbf{entry}\}) \times \mathcal{C} \rightarrow (V \cup \{\mathbf{exit}, \mathbf{loop}\})$ is a total *transition function.*

In essence, a PDP may be thought of as a finite-state labelled transition system representing the control structure of a sequential program. By the size $|\pi|$ of a given PDP π we mean the number $|V|$ of its internal nodes. It should be noted that the alphabets $\mathcal{A}$, $\mathcal{P}$ are finite and fixed. Hence, the number of transitions in π is $2^{|\mathcal{P}|}|\pi|$, where $2^{|\mathcal{P}|} = 2^M$ is a constant which depends on the alphabet $\mathcal{P}$ only.

We say that a node v'' is *accessible* from a node v' in a PDP π if one of the following equalities holds: $v'' = v'$ or $v'' = T(\ldots T(T(v', \delta_1), \delta_2), \ldots, \delta_n)$, for some finite sequence of conditions $\delta_1, \delta_2, \ldots, \delta_n$, $n \geq 1$. A PDP π is said to be *reduced* if the terminal node is accessible from every internal node, and each internal node is accessible from the initial one.

1.2 Dynamic Frames

The semantics of PDP is defined by means of dynamic Kripke structures (frames and models) (see [6, 7]).

A *dynamic deterministic frame* (or simply a *frame*) over alphabet $\mathcal{A}$ is a triple $\mathcal{F} = \langle S, s_0, R \rangle$, where

- S is a non-empty set of *data states*,
- s_0 is an *initial state*, $s_0 \in S$,
- $R : S \times \mathcal{A} \rightarrow S$ is an *updating function.*

$R(s, a)$ is interpreted as a result of the application of an action a to a data state s. It is assumed that each basic action $a \in \mathcal{A}$ transforms deterministicaly one state into another; therefore, the dynamic frames under considerations are both functional and serial relative to every action $a \in \mathcal{A}$.

An updating function R can be naturally extended to the set $\mathcal{A}^*$ as follows

$$R^*(s,\lambda) = s,\ R^*(s,ha) = R(R^*(s,h),a).$$

We say that a state s'' is *reachable* from a state s' ($s' \preceq_{\mathcal{F}} s''$ in symbols) if $s'' = R^*(s',h)$ for some $h \in \mathcal{A}^*$. Denote by $[h]_{\mathcal{F}}$ the state $s = R^*(s_0,h)$ reachable from the initial state by means of $\mathcal{A}$-sequence h. As usual, the subscript $\mathcal{F}$ will be omitted when the frame is understood. We will deal only with data states reachable from the initial state. Therefore, we may assume without loss of generality that every state $s \in S$ is reachable from the initial state s_0, i.e. $S = \{[h] : h \in \mathcal{A}^*\}$.

A frame $\mathcal{F}_s = \langle S', s, R' \rangle$ is called a *subframe* of a frame $\mathcal{F} = \langle S, s_0, R \rangle$ generated by a state $s \in S$ if $S' = \{R^*(s,h) : h \in \mathcal{A}^*\}$ and R' is the restriction of R to S'. We say that a frame $\mathcal{F}$ is

- *semigroup* if $\mathcal{F}$ can be mapped homomorphically onto every subframe $\mathcal{F}_s$,
- *homogeneous* if $\mathcal{F}$ is isomorphic to every subframe $\mathcal{F}_s$,
- *ordered* if $\preceq$ is a partial order on the set of data states S,
- *length-preserving* if $[h] = [g]$ implies $|h| = |g|$ for every pair h, g of $\mathcal{A}$-sequences,
- *universal* if $[h] = [g]$ implies $h = g$ for every pair h, g of $\mathcal{A}$-sequences.

Taking the initial state $s_0 = [\lambda]$ for the unit, one may regard a semigroup frame $\mathcal{F}$ as a finitely generated monoid $\langle S, * \rangle$ such that $[h] * [g] = [hg]$. Clearly, the universal frame $\mathcal{U}$ corresponds to the free monoid generated by $\mathcal{A}$. Consequently, an ordered semigroup frame is associated with a monoid whose unit $[\lambda]$ is irresolvable, i.e. $[\lambda] = [gh]$ implies $g = h = \lambda$, whereas a semigroup corresponding to a homogeneous frame is a left-contracted monoid, i.e. $[gh'] = [gh'']$ implies $[h'] = [h'']$. In this paper we deal mostly with the ordered semigroup frames.

1.3 Dynamic Models

A *dynamic deterministic model* (or simply a *model*) over alphabets $\mathcal{A}$, $\mathcal{P}$ is a pair $M = \langle \mathcal{F}, \xi \rangle$ such that

- $\mathcal{F} = \langle S, s_0, R \rangle$ is a frame over $\mathcal{A}$,
- $\xi : S \rightarrow \mathcal{C}$ is a *valuation function*, indicating truth-values of basic propositions at every data state.

Let $\pi = \langle V, \mathbf{entry}, \mathbf{exit}, \mathbf{loop}, B, T \rangle$ be some PDP and $M = \langle \mathcal{F}, \xi \rangle$ be a model based on the frame $\mathcal{F} = \langle S, s_0, R \rangle$. A finite or infinite sequence of quadruples

$$r = (v_0, \delta_0, s_0, \lambda), (v_1, \delta_1, s_1, a_1), \ldots, (v_m, \delta_m, s_m, a_m), \ldots \qquad (1)$$

is called a *run* of π on M if (1) meets the following requirements:

1. $v_0 = \mathbf{entry}$, λ is the empty $\mathcal{A}$-sequence,
2. $s_i \in S$, $\delta_i \in \mathcal{C}$ for every $i \geq 0$, and $v_j \in V$, $a_j \in \mathcal{A}$, for every $j \geq 1$,

3. for every i, $i \geq 0$,
   $\delta_i = \xi(s_i)$,
   $v_{i+1} = T(v_i, \delta_i)$,
   $a_{i+1} = B(v_i)$,
   $s_{i+1} = R(s_i, a_{i+1})$,
4. (1) is a finite sequence iff $T(v_m, \delta_m) \in \{\mathbf{exit}, \mathbf{loop}\}$ for some $m \geq 0$.

When a run r ends with a quadruple $(v_m, \delta_m, s_m, a_m)$ as its last element and $T(v_m, \delta_m) = \mathbf{exit}$ we say that r *terminates*, having the data state s_m as the *result*. Otherwise, when r is an infinite sequence, or it is finite and $T(v_m, \delta_m) = \mathbf{loop}$, we say that it *loops* and has no result. Since all PDPs and frames under consideration are deterministic, every propositional program π has a unique run $r(\pi, M)$ on a given model M. We write $[r(\pi, M)]$ for the result of $r(\pi, M)$, assuming $[r(\pi, M)]$ is undefined when the run loops.

1.4 The Equivalence Problem for PDPs

Let π' and π'' be some PDPs and $\mathcal{F}$ be a frame. Then π' and π'' are called *equivalent on* $\mathcal{F}$ ($\pi' \sim_{\mathcal{F}} \pi''$ in symbols) if $[r(\pi', M)] = [r(\pi'', M)]$ for every model $M = \langle \mathcal{F}, \xi \rangle$ based on $\mathcal{F}$.

For a given frame $\mathcal{F}$ the *equivalence problem* w.r.t. $\mathcal{F}$ is to check for an arbitrary pair π_1, π_2 of PDPs whether $\pi' \sim_{\mathcal{F}} \pi''$ holds. Since we are interested in decidability and complexity of the equivalence problem, it is assumed that the frame $\mathcal{F}$ we deal with is effectively characterized in logic or algebraic terms (say, by means of dynamic logic formulae or semigroup identities). The following propositions illustrate some useful properties of the equivalence relations on PDPs.

Proposition 1. *Suppose that a frame $\mathcal{F}_1$ is a homomorphic image of some frame $\mathcal{F}_2$. Then for every pair of PDPs π_1, π_2 we have*

$$\pi_1 \sim_{\mathcal{F}_2} \pi_2 \Rightarrow \pi_1 \sim_{\mathcal{F}_1} \pi_2 \ .$$

Clearly, every frame $\mathcal{F}$ is a homomorphic image of some universal frame $\mathcal{U}$. Therefore, $\pi_1 \sim_{\mathcal{U}} \pi_2 \Rightarrow \pi_1 \sim_{\mathcal{F}} \pi_2$ holds for each pair of PDPs π_1, π_2.

Proposition 2. *For every PDP π there exists a reduced PDP π' such that $|\pi'| \leq |\pi|$ and $\pi \sim_{\mathcal{U}} \pi'$.*

Proof. Suppose $\pi = \langle V, \mathbf{entry}, \mathbf{exit}, \mathbf{loop}, B, T \rangle$. Let V' be the set of all internal nodes v, $v \in V$, which are accessible from **entry** and have an access to **exit**. Let us consider a PDP $\pi' = \langle V', \mathbf{entry}, \mathbf{exit}, \mathbf{loop}, B', T' \rangle$, where B' is a restriction of B to V' and

$$T'(v, a) = \begin{cases} T(v, a), \text{ if } T(v, a) \in V' \cup \{\mathbf{exit}, \mathbf{loop}\}, \\ \mathbf{loop}, \text{ otherwise} \end{cases}$$

Clearly, π and π' have the same set of terminal runs on the models based on $\mathcal{U}$, and hence $\pi \sim_{\mathcal{U}} \pi'$. □

1.5 Decidable Cases of the Equivalence Problem

Now we can give a brief survey of some traditional computational models for which the equivalence problem is decidable.

The computational model of Yanov's schemata [25] was the first attempt to provide a precise mathematical basis for the common activities involved in reasoning about computer program. A few years later an advanced concept of finite automaton was developed in [17]. The close relationship between Yanov's schemata and finite automata was established in [18]. Both models of programs correspond to the universal frame semantics of PDP. The equivalence problem for Yanov's schemata and deterministic finite automata was proved to be decidable [25, 17]. In fact, it is decidable in polynomial time when the alphabets of basic symbols $\mathcal{A}, \mathcal{P}$ are finite.

Another algebraic concept of computer program was introduced in [3]. It corresponds to the semigroup frame semantics of PDP. The equivalence problem for automata over semigroups was studied in [3, 10–12, 21]. The most remarkable results are as follows

1. Suppose $\mathcal{F}$ is a homogeneous frame such that the identity problem "$[g] = [h]$?" is decidable. Then the equivalence problem w.r.t. $\mathcal{F}$ is decidable.
2. Suppose $\mathcal{F}$ is a homogeneous frame associated with a right-contracted monoid and the identity problem "$[g] = [h]$?" is decidable on $\mathcal{F}$. Then the equivalence problem w.r.t. $\mathcal{F}$ is decidable iff it is decidable w.r.t. $\mathcal{F}'$, where $\mathcal{F}'$ is the maximal subgroup of $\mathcal{F}$.

It was proved also that the equivalence problem is decidable for free commutative semigroups [3, 12], free groups [11], an Abelian groups of rank 1 [10]. But in all these cases the complexity of the decision procedures is at least exponential of the size of programs (automata).

The first-order concept of formalized computer programs was introduced in [13–15]. The relationship between the equivalence of first-order program schemata and that of PDPs is as follows.

Let $Var = \{x_1, \ldots, x_n\}$ be a finite set of variables and $Term$ be a set of terms over Var. A substitution on Var is a map $\theta : Var \to Term$. A composition of substitutions is defined in the usual way (see [1]). Associating with every basic action $a \in \mathcal{A}$ a substitution θ_a (which is called a *basic substitution*), we define the frame $\mathcal{F} = \langle Subst, \epsilon, R \rangle$, where $Subst$ is the set of all finite compositions of basic substitutions, ϵ stands for the empty substitution, and $R(\theta, a) = \theta_a \theta$ holds for every $\theta \in Subst$, $a \in \mathcal{A}$. The frame $\mathcal{F}$ is said to be a *substitution frame*. Clearly, $\mathcal{F}$ is a semigroup frame. The semantics of the first-order program schemata [13, 14] corresponds to the substitution frame semantics of PDPs. It was established in [13] that the equivalence problem for the first-order schemata is undecidable in general case. At the same time this problem was proved to be decidable (see [15, 19]) for some specific classes of program schemata.

Assume that each basic action $a \in \mathcal{A}$ is associated with a non-empty basic substitution θ_a such that every variable x_i occurs in some term $t_j = \theta_a(x_j)$. A substitution frame $\mathcal{F}$ of this kind corresponds to the semantics of *conservative* program schemata [15]. The equivalence problem was proved to be decidable for some sets of models based on conservative frames. But nevertheless no complexity results for the decidable cases are known.

2 Deciding the Equivalence Problem in Poly-time

In this section we present a novel approach to the equivalence problem for PDPs. The key idea is to reduce the equivalence problem "$\pi_1 \sim_{\mathcal{F}} \pi_2$?" to the well-known identity problem "$w_1 = w_2$?" on some specific semigroup W related with $\mathcal{F}$. A uniform technique thus developed makes it possible to construct polynomial time decision procedures for the equivalence problem w.r.t. some ordered semigroup frames and models. We first consider the case for length-preserving frames in some details, and then we show the changes needed to extend the results obtained to the ordered frames. Using the computational models discussed in the previous section as the examples, we illustrate how the main theorems of the paper may be put in practice.

Let $\mathcal{F}$ be a semigroup frame. Considering it as a monoid, we write $\mathcal{F} \times \mathcal{F}$ for the direct product of the monoids. When $\mathcal{F}$ is a length-preserving frame we denote by $\mathcal{E}(\mathcal{F})$ the submonoid of $\mathcal{F} \times \mathcal{F}$ whose elements are all pairs $\langle [g], [h] \rangle$, such that $|g| = |h|$.

Suppose W is a finitely generated monoid, U is a submonoid of W, and w^+, w^* are two distinguished elements in W. Denote by $\circ$ and e a binary operation on W and the unit of W respectively. Given a semigroup frame (a length-preserving semigroup frame) $\mathcal{F}$ we say that the quadruple $K = \langle W, U, w^+, w^* \rangle$ is a k_0-*criterial system* for $\mathcal{F}$, where k_0 is some positive integer, if K and $\mathcal{F}$ meet the following conditions:

($C1$) there exists a homomorphism φ of $\mathcal{F} \times \mathcal{F}$ (of $\mathcal{E}(\mathcal{F})$, respectively) in U such that
$$[h] = [g] \Leftrightarrow w^+ \circ \varphi(\langle [g], [h] \rangle) \circ w^* = e$$
holds for every pair g, h (for every pair g, h, such that $|g| = |h|$) in $\mathcal{A}^*$

($C2$) for every element w in the coset $U \circ w^*$ the equation $X \circ w = e$ has at most k_0 pairwise different solutions X in the coset $w^+ \circ U$.

It is worth noting that if W is a group then ($C2$) is always satisfied with $k_0 = 1$. Since the alphabet $\mathcal{A}$ of basic actions is finite, the criterial homomorphism φ is, clearly, computable.

2.1 The Length-Preserving Frames

Theorem 1. *Suppose $\mathcal{F}$ is a length-preserving semigroup frame over the alphabets $\mathcal{A}$ and $\mathcal{P}$. Suppose also $K = \langle W, U, w^+, w^* \rangle$ is a k_0-criterial system for $\mathcal{F}$ such that the identity problem "$w_1 = w_2$?" on W is decidable in time $t(m)$, where $m = \max(|w_1|, |w_2|)$. Then the equivalence problem "$\pi_1 \sim_{\mathcal{F}} \pi_2$?" is decidable in time $c_1 n^2 (t(c_2 n^2) + \log n)$, where $n = \max(|\pi_1|, |\pi_2|)$. The constants c_1, c_2 depend on k_0, $|\mathcal{A}|$, $|\mathcal{P}|$, and the homomorphism φ.*

Proof. We first describe the decision procedure and then prove its correctness.

For a given pair of PDPs $\pi_i = \langle V_i, \mathbf{entry}, \mathbf{exit}, \mathbf{loop}, B_i, T_i \rangle$, $i = 1, 2$, define a labelled directed graph Γ. The vertices of Γ are the triples of the form $(\mathbf{entry}, \mathbf{entry}, w^+)$ or (v_1, v_2, w), such that $v_i \in V_i \cup \{\mathbf{exit}, \mathbf{loop}\}$, $i = 1, 2$, and w is in coset $w^+ \circ U$. The vertex $(\mathbf{entry}, \mathbf{entry}, w^+)$ is called the *root* of Γ. The set of vertices is divided into three subsets X_1, X_2, and X_3 such that
$X_1 = \{(v_1, v_2, w) : \ w \circ w^* \neq e, \ v_i \in V_i, \ i = 1, 2\}$,
$X_2 = \{(v_1, v_2, w) : \ w \circ w^* = e, \ v_i \in V_i, \ i = 1, 2\} \cup \{(\mathbf{entry}, \mathbf{entry}, w^+)\}$,
and all other vertices are in X_3.

The arcs of Γ are marked with pairs (δ_1, δ_2) in $\mathcal{C} \times \mathcal{C}$. For every vertex x in Γ we define the set Δ_x as follows:

$$\Delta_x = \begin{cases} \{(\delta_1, \delta_2) : \ \delta_i \in \mathcal{C}, \ i = 1, 2\}, \text{ if } x \in X_1, \\ \{(\delta, \delta) : \delta \in \mathcal{C}\}, \text{ if } x \in X_2, \\ \emptyset, \text{ if } x \in X_3. \end{cases}$$

Each vertex x in X_1 has $4^{|\mathcal{P}|}$ outgoing arcs, and each vertex x in X_2 has $2^{|\mathcal{P}|}$ outgoing arcs, marked with pairs in Δ_x. The vertices in X_3 have no outgoing arcs. The arcs connect the vertices in Γ as follows.

Let $x = (v_1, v_2, w)$ be a vertex in $X_1 \cup X_2$, and (δ_1, δ_2) be a pair in Δ_x. Then the arc marked with (δ_1, δ_2) leads from x to the vertex $x' = (v_1', v_2', w')$, where $v_1' = T_1(v_1, \delta_1)$, $v_2' = T_2(v_2, \delta_2)$, and the element w' is such that $w' = w \circ w^*$ if $\mathbf{exit} \in \{v_1', v_2'\}$, and $w' = w \circ \varphi(\langle [B_1(v_1')], [B_2(v_2')] \rangle)$ otherwise.

If a vertex $x = (v, u, w)$ is such that either $u = v = \mathbf{exit}$ and $w \neq e$, or $\{u, v\} \cap \{\mathbf{exit}, \mathbf{loop}\} \neq \emptyset$ and $u \neq v$ then x is called a *rejected* vertex. To check the equivalence $\pi_1 \sim_{\mathcal{F}} \pi_2$ it suffices to certain that Γ satisfies the following requirements:

($R1$) the rejected vertices are inaccessible from the root,
($R2$) for every pair of internal nodes $v_1 \in V_1$, $v_2 \in V_2$ no more then k_0 vertices of the form (v_1, v_2, w) are accessible from the root.

Clearly, both ($R1$) and ($R2$) can be checked in time $c_1 n^2 (t(c_2 n^2) + \log n)$. To prove the correctness of the checking algorithm observe the following lemmas.

Lemma 1. *Suppose $\delta_1^0, \delta_1^1, \ldots \delta_1^{m_1}$ and $\delta_2^0, \delta_2^1, \ldots \delta_2^{m_2}$ are two arbitrary sequences of conditions, and α_1, α_2 are two finite sequences*

$$\alpha_j = (v_j^0, \delta_j^0, s_j^0, \lambda), (v_j^1, \delta_j^1, s_j^1, a_j^1), \ldots, (v_j^{m_j}, \delta_j^{m_j}, s_j^{m_j}, a_j^{m_j}) ,$$

such that $v_j^0 = \mathbf{entry}$, $s_j^0 = [\lambda]$, and $v_j^{i+1} = T_j(v_j^i, \delta_j^i)$, $a_j^{i+1} = B_j(v_j^i)$, $s_j^{i+1} = [a_j^1 \ldots a_j^{i+1}]$, $1 \leq i \leq m_j$, $j = 1, 2$. Then the sequences α_1, α_2 are prefixes of runs $r(\pi_1, M)$, $r(\pi_1, M)$ of π_1, π_2 on some model $M = \langle \mathcal{F}, \xi \rangle$ based on the frame $\mathcal{F}$ iff for every i, $0 \leq i \leq \min(m_1, m_2)$, the equality of states $s_1^i = s_2^i$ implies the equality of the corresponding conditions $\delta_1^i = \delta_2^i$.

Proof. It suffices to consider a valuation function ξ such that $\xi(s_j^i) = \delta_j^i$, $0 \leq i \leq m_j$, $j = 1, 2$, and use the inherent property of length-preserving frames. □

Lemma 2. *Suppose $x_0, x_1, \ldots, x_m, x_{m+1}$, $m \geq 0$ is a finite sequence of vertices in Γ such that x_0 is the root of Γ and $x_i = (v_1^i, v_2^i, w_i)$, $1 \leq i \leq m+1$. Then*

$$x_0 \overset{(\delta_1^0,\delta_2^0)}{\longrightarrow} x_1 \overset{(\delta_1^1,\delta_2^1)}{\longrightarrow} \cdots \overset{(\delta_1^{m-1},\delta_2^{m-1})}{\longrightarrow} x_m \overset{(\delta_1^m,\delta_2^m)}{\longrightarrow} x_{m+1}$$

is a directed path in Γ iff for some model M based on $\mathcal{F}$ the runs $r(\pi_j, M)$, $j = 1, 2$, have the prefixes

$$(\mathbf{entry}, \delta_j^0, s_0, e), (v_j^1, \delta_j^1, s_j^1, a_j^1), \ldots, (v_j^m, \delta_j^m, s_j^m, a_j^m),$$

such that $v_j^{i+1} = T_j(v_j^i, \delta_j^i)$ and $w_i = w^+ \circ \varphi(s_1^i, s_2^i)$, $0 \leq i \leq m$, $j = 1, 2$.

Proof. By induction on m using definition of Γ, Lemma 1, condition $(C1)$ of criterial system and the length-preserving property of $\mathcal{F}$. □

Lemma 3. *Suppose $\delta^0, \delta^1, \ldots, \delta^m$, $m \geq 0$ is a finite sequence of conditions, and $v_j^0, v_j^1, \ldots, v_j^m, v_j^{m+1}$ are two sequences of nodes in π_j, $j = 1, 2$, such that $v_j^{i+1} = T_j(v_j^i, \delta^i)$ for every i, $0 \leq i \leq m$. Then for every vertex $x_0 = (v_1^0, v_2^0, w_0)$ in Γ there exists a directed path*

$$x_0 \overset{(\delta^0,\delta^0)}{\longrightarrow} x_1 \overset{(\delta^1,\delta^1)}{\longrightarrow} \cdots \overset{(\delta^{m-1},\delta^{m-1})}{\longrightarrow} x_m \overset{(\delta^m,\delta^m)}{\longrightarrow} x_{m+1}$$

such that $x_i = (v_1^i, v_2^i, w_0 \circ \varphi(\langle [h_1^i], [h_2^i] \rangle)$, where $h_j^i = B_j(v_j^1) B_j(v_j^2) \ldots B_j(v_j^i)$, $1 \leq i \leq m$, $j = 1, 2$.

The proof is similar to that of Lemma 2.

Lemma 4. *Suppose π_1 and π_2 are reduced PDPs. Then $\pi_1 \sim_{\mathcal{F}} \pi_2$ holds iff Γ satisfies $(R1)$.*

Proof. Follows from Lemma 2 and $(C1)$ of a criterial system.

Lemma 5. *If π_1, π_2 are reduced PDPs then $(R1)$ implies $(R2)$.*

Proof. Suppose $(R1)$ is satisfied, but for some $u \in V_1$, $v \in V_2$ at least $k_0 + 1$ pairwise different vertices $y_1 = (u, v, w_1), \ldots, y_{k_0+1} = (u, v, w_{k_0+1})$ are accessible from the root of Γ. Since π_1 is the reduced PDP, the terminal node **exit** is accessible from u in π_1, i.e. **exit** $= T_1(\ldots T_1(T_1(u, \delta^1), \delta^2), \ldots, \delta^m)$ for some finite sequence of conditions $\delta_1, \delta_2, \ldots, \delta_m$, $m \geq 1$. Let us consider for every vertex y_i, $1 \leq i \leq k_0 + 1$, a path α_i

$$y_i \overset{(\delta^1,\delta^1)}{\longrightarrow} x_{1i} \overset{(\delta^2,\delta^2)}{\longrightarrow} \cdots \overset{(\delta^{m-1},\delta^{m-1})}{\longrightarrow} x_{mi} \overset{(\delta^m,\delta^m)}{\longrightarrow} z_i \ ,$$

whose arcs are marked with pairs $(\delta^1, \delta^1), (\delta^2, \delta^2), \ldots (\delta^m, \delta^m)$. Since Γ satisfies $(R1)$, the path α_i exists for every i, $1 \leq i \leq k_0 + 1$, and its final vertex z_i is one of the form $(\mathbf{exit}, \mathbf{exit}, e)$. Then, by Lemma 3, there exists a pair of $\mathcal{A}$-sequences h_1, h_2 such that $e = w_i \circ \varphi(\langle [h_1], [h_2] \rangle) \circ w^*$, $1 \leq i \leq k_0+1$. It means that each w_i is a solution of the equation $X \circ \varphi(\langle [h_1], [h_2] \rangle) \circ w^* = e$. Since $w_1, w_2, \ldots, w_{k_0+1}$ are pairwise different elements in coset $w^+ \circ U$, we arrive at the contradiction with condition $(C2)$ of k_0-criterial system K. □

Combining together Propositions 1,2 and Lemmas 4, 5, we complete the proof of Theorem 1. □

Note 1. Observing the proof of Theorem 1, one could notice that the constant c_1 is exponential of the cardinality of $\mathcal{P}$. It becomes of importance when the alphabet $\mathcal{P}$ of basic propositions generated from a first-order language of real programs is infinite, while each PDP uses only finitely many propositions for its conditions. Then the algorithm of Theorem 1 decides the equivalence problem in time which is polynomial of the number of program statements and exponential of the number of logical conditions.

Example 1. Let us consider a universal frame $\mathcal{U}$ and a semigroup W whose elements are truth-values $0, 1$, and a binary operation $\circ$ is a logical conjunction $\wedge$. Then $K = \langle W, W, 1, 1\rangle$ is 1-criterial system for $\mathcal{U}$. We assume that for every pair of actions a', a'' in $\mathcal{A}$, $\varphi(\langle [a'], [a'']\rangle) = 1$ if $a' = a''$ and $\varphi(\langle [a'], [a'']\rangle) = 0$ otherwise.

Corollary 1 ([18, 25]). *The equivalence problem w.r.t. the universal frames is decidable in time* $O(n^2 \log n)$.

Example 2. Let $\mathcal{F}_{fc}$ be a frame associated with a free commutative monoid generated by $\mathcal{A} = \{a_1, \ldots, a_N\}$. Consider a free Abelian group Z of the rank N generated by some elements $q_1, \ldots, q_N$. Then $K = \langle Z, Z, e, e\rangle$ is 1-criterial system for $\mathcal{F}_{fc}$. We assume that $\varphi(\langle [a_i], [a_j]\rangle) = q_i \circ q_j^{-1}$ for every pair of actions a_i, a_j.

Corollary 2 ([16]). *The equivalence problem w.r.t. the commutative frames is decidable in time* $O(n^2 \log n)$.

Example 3. Let $I \subseteq \mathcal{A} \times \mathcal{A}$ be a set of pairs of actions, and $\mathcal{F}_c^I$ be a frame associated with a free partially commutative monoid generated by $\mathcal{A}$ and specified by the identities $[a] * [b] = [b] * [a]$, $(a, b) \in I$. Consider a monoid $W = \langle \mathcal{E}(\mathcal{F}_c^I) \cup \{w^+, w^*\}, \circ\rangle$ whose binary operation $\circ$ is defined as follows:

$$w^+ \circ w^* = e, \quad \langle [g_1], [h_1]\rangle \circ \langle [g_2], [h_2]\rangle = \langle [g_1 g_2], [h_1 h_2]\rangle, \quad w^+ \circ \langle [a], [a]\rangle = w^+ ,$$

where $a \in \mathcal{A}$, $g_1, g_2, h_1, h_2 \in \mathcal{A}^*$. Then $K = \langle W, \mathcal{E}(\mathcal{F}_c^I), w^+, w^*\rangle$ is 1-criterial system for $\mathcal{F}_c^I$ having the identity map for the criterial homomorphism. In contrast to Example 2 it is not evident that K satisfies $(C2)$, but nevertheless this fact can be established by purely algebraic methods.

Corollary 3. *The equivalence problem w.r.t. the partially commutative frames is decidable in time* $O(n^2 \log n)$.

2.2 The Ordered Frames

Consider now the decidable cases of the equivalence problem w.r.t the ordered semigroup models.

Theorem 2. *Suppose an ordered semigroup frame $\mathcal{F}$ satisfies the following requirements:*

1. *The reachability problem "$[g] \preceq [h]$?" is decidable in time $t_1(m)$, where $m = \max(|g|, |h|)$;*
2. *$\mathcal{F}$ has a k_0-criterial system $K = \langle W, U, w^+, w^* \rangle$ such that the identity problem "$w_1 = w_2$?" on W is decidable in time $t_2(m)$, where $m = \max(|w_1|, |w_2|)$*

Then the equivalence problem "$\pi_1 \sim_{\mathcal{F}} \pi_2$?" is decidable in time $c_1(n^4(t_1(c_2n^2) + t_2(c_3n^2) + \log n)$, where $n = \max(|\pi_1|, |\pi_2|)$. The constants c_1, c_2, c_3 depend on k_0, $|\mathcal{A}|$, $|\mathcal{P}|$, and the homomorphism φ.

The proof of Theorem 2, though somewhat subtler and more complicated, follows the same way as that of Theorem 1.

Example 4. Consider a conservative substitution frame $\mathcal{F} = \langle Subst, \epsilon, R \rangle$ described in section 1.5. Let W be an extension of $\mathcal{F} \times \mathcal{F}$ by the elements w^+, w^* such that

$$\langle \mu, \nu \rangle \circ \langle \eta, \theta \rangle = \langle \eta\mu, \theta\nu \rangle, \;\; w^+ \circ \langle \tau, \tau \rangle = w^+, \;\; w^+ \circ w^* = e \tag{2}$$

where $\mu, \nu, \eta, \theta, \tau$ are in $Subst$. Then $K = \langle W, \mathcal{F} \times \mathcal{F}, w^+, w^* \rangle$ is 1-criterial system for $\mathcal{F}$. Clearly, $(C1)$ follows from the definition of K. It is worth noting also that an equation $X \circ \langle \eta, \theta \rangle = e$ has a solution in the coset $(\mathcal{F} \times \mathcal{F}) \circ w^*$ iff the substitutions η, θ are unifiable. Then $(C2)$ can be established by using the inherent properties of the most general unifiers [1] and the characteristic identities (2).

Corollary 4. *The equivalence problem w.r.t. the conservative frames is decidable in time $O(n^6 \log n)$.*

3 Conclusions and Acknowledgments

We proposed a new approach to the equivalence problem for propositional deterministic programs and show that sometimes our technique makes it possible to construct uniformly polynomial-time decision procedures. We have examples of k_0-criteria structures, $k_0 > 1$, applicable to some realistic dynamic frames, but their structure is a bit more sophisticated. The algebraic machinery of this paper may be rather well extended to some other computational models, e.g. monadic recursive programs [2].

The author would like to thank the anonymous referee whose comments helped him to improve the original version of the paper. This research was funded by RFBR Grant 97-01-00975.

References

1. K.Apt, From Logic Programming to Prolog, Prentice Hall, 1997.

2. E.Ashcroft, Z.Manna, A.Pnueli, A decidable properties of monadic functional schemes, **Journal of the ACM**, vol 20 (1973), N 3, p.489-499.
3. V.M.Glushkov, A.A.Letichevskii, Theory of algorithms and discrete processors, **Advances in Information System Science**, vol 1 (1969), N 1.
4. E.M.Gurari, O.H.Ibarra, The complexity of equivalence problem for simple programs, **Journal of the ACM**, vol 28 (1981), N 3, p.535-560.
5. E.M.Gurari, Decidable problems for the reinforced programs, **Journal of the ACM**, vol 32 (1985), N 2, p.466-483.
6. D.Harel, R.Sherman, Propositional dynamic logic of flowcharts, **Lecture Notes in Computer Science**, vol 158 (1982), p.195-206.
7. D.Harel, Dynamic logics, in **Handbook of Philosophical Logics**, D.Gabbay and F.Guenthner (eds.), (1984), p.497-604.
8. T.Harju, J.Karhumaki, The equivalence of multi-tape finite automata, **Theoretical Computer Science**, vol 78 (1991), p.347-355.
9. O.H.Ibarra, Reversal-bounded multicounter machines and their decision problems, **Journal of the ACM**, vol 25 (1978), N 1, p.116-133.
10. A.A.Letichevskii, On the equivalence of automata over semigroup, **Theoretic Cybernetics**, vol 6 (1970), p.3-71 (in Russian)
11. A.A.Letichevskii, To the practical methods for recognizing the equivalence of finite transducers and program schemata, **Kibernetika**, (1973), N 4, p.15-26 (in Russian).
12. A.A.Letichevskii, L.B.Smikun, On a class of groups with solvable problem of automata equivalence, **Sov. Math. Dokl.**, vol 17 (1976), N 2, p.341-344.
13. D.C.Luckham, D.M.Park, M.S.Paterson, On formalized computer programs, **J. Computer and System Sci.**, vol 4 (1970), N 3, p.220-249.
14. M.S.Paterson, Programs schemata, **Machine Intelligence**, Edinburgh: Univ. Press, vol 3 (1968), p.19-31.
15. M.S.Paterson, Decision problems in computational models, **SIGPLAN Notices**, vol 7 (1972), p.74-82.
16. R.I.Podlovchenko, V.A.Zakharov, On the polynomial-time algorithm deciding the commutative equivalence of program schemata, to be published in **Reports of the Soviet Academy of Science**, (1998).
17. M.O.Rabin, D.Scott, Finite automata and their decision problems, **IBM Journal of Research and Development**, vol 3 (1959), N 2, p.114-125.
18. J.D.Rutledge, On Ianov's program schemata, **J. ACM**, vol 11 (1964), N 1, p.1-9.
19. V.K.Sabelfeld, An algorithm deciding functional equivalence in a new class of program schemata, **Theoretical Computer Science**, vol 71 (1990), p.265-279.
20. G.Senizergues, The equivalence problem for deterministic pushdown automata is decidable, **Lecture Notes in Computer Science**, v.1256(1997), p.671-681.
21. M.A.Taiclin, The equivalence of automata w.r.t. commutative semigroups, **Algebra and Logic**, vol 8 (1969), N 5, p.553-600 (in Russian).
22. L.G.Valiant, Decision procedures for families of deterministic pushdown automata, Report N 7, Univ. of Warwick Computer Center, (1973)
23. L.G.Valiant, The equivalence problem for deterministic finite-turn pushdown automata, **Information and Control**, vol25 (1974), N 2, p.123-133.
24. L.G.Valiant, M.S.Paterson, Deterministic one-counter automata, **Journal of Computer and System Sci.**, vol 10 (1975), p.340-350.
25. Y.Yanov, To the equivalence and transformations of program schemata, **Reports of the Soviet Academy of Science**, vol 113 (1957), N 1, p.39-42 (in Russian).

On Branching Programs With Bounded Uncertainty (Extended Abstract)

Stasys Jukna *[12] and Stanislav Žák **[3]

[1] Department of Computer Science, University of Trier, D-54286 Trier, Germany
[2] Institute of Mathematics, Akademijos 4, LT-2600 Vilnius, Lithuania.
jukna@ti.uni-trier.de
[3] Institute of Computer Science, Academy of Sciences, Pod vodárenskou věží 2, 182 00 Prague 8, Czech Republic. stan@uivt.cas.cz

Abstract. We propose an information-theoretic approach to proving lower bounds on the size of branching programs (b.p.). The argument is based on Kraft-McMillan type inequalities for the average amount of uncertainty about (or entropy of) a given input during various stages of the computation. We first demonstrate the approach for read-once b.p. Then we introduce a strictly larger class of so-called 'gentle' b.p. and, using the suggested approach, prove that some explicit Boolean functions, including the Clique function and a particular Pointer function (which belongs to AC^0), cannot be computed by gentle program of polynomial size. These lower bounds are new since explicit functions, which are known to be hard for *all* previously considered restricted classes of b.p. (like $(1, +s)$-b.p. or syntactic read-k-times b.p.) can be easily computed by gentle b.p. of polynomial size.

1 Introduction

We consider the usual model of *branching programs* (b.p.) (see, e.g. [7] for the definitions). Despite considerable efforts, the best lower bound for unrestricted (nondeterministic) b.p. remains the almost quadratic lower bounds of order $\Omega(n^2/\log^2 n)$ proved by Nečiporuk in 1966 [5].

In this paper we describe one approach to proving lower bounds on the size of branching programs which is based on a more careful analysis of the 'amount of certainty' about single inputs during the computations on them.

Uncertainty. Given an input $a \in \{0,1\}^n$, the computation $comp(a)$ on it starts in the source-node with no knowledge about this input. At each step the computation makes a test "is $a(i) = 0$ or $a(i) = 1$?", and after each test one bit of information about the input a is obtained. However, this information about the $a(i)$ is lost at the node v if there is another input b such that $b(i) \neq a(i)$, the

* Research supported by the DFG grant Me 1077/10–1.

** Research supported by the Grant Agency ČR Grant No 201/98/0717 and partly by MŠMT ČR Grant No. OK-304 and by INCO-Copernicus Contract IP961095 ALTEC-KIT.

computation $comp(b)$ on b reaches the node v, and after the node v one of the following two events happen: either $comp(b)$ diverges from $comp(a)$ immediately after the test of x_i, or $comp(b)$ follows the computation $comp(a)$ until they both reach the same sink. In both cases the program is uncertain about the value $a(i)$: in the first case it tests this bit once more, whereas in the second - it forgets that bit forever.

We mark those bits $a(i)$, $i \in \{1,\ldots,n\}$ of the input a, for which at least one of these two events happen, and call the resulting (marked) string a 'window' of the input a at the node v. The total number $\mathcal{E}(a)$ of marked bits measures the entropy of (or uncertainty about) a at this node. This form to encode the uncertainty using windows was introduced by the second author in [8].

The approach. We suggest the following general frame to prove lower bounds for branching programs. If the program P is small then the computations on some large set F of inputs must meet at some node. Using Kraft-McMillan type inequalities we prove in Sect. 3 that then $size(P) \geq |F| \cdot 2^{-\mathcal{E}(F)}$ where $\mathcal{E}(F) = \frac{1}{|F|}\sum_{a\in F}\mathcal{E}(a)$ is the average entropy of inputs from F at this node. Thus, to get the desired lover bound on the size of P it is enough to show (using the properties of a given a Boolean function f) that if P computes f correctly, then the average entropy cannot be large.

The results. For read-once b.p. finding non-trivial upper bounds for the average entropy $\mathcal{E}(F)$ is an easy task. Looking for larger classes of b.p. where this task is still tractable, we define in Sect. 4 one general property of branching programs – the 'gentleness'. Roughly, a program P is gentle if at some its nodes some large set F of inputs is classified in a 'regular' manner, where the regularity requires that windows of inputs from F at these nodes have some special form. We then prove the following.

1. Read-once branching programs are gentle (Sect. 5).

2. Explicit functions, which are hard for *all* previously considered restricted models of b.p., can be easily computed by small gentle b.p. (Sect. 6). This fact is not surprising – it just indicates that 'gentleness' is a new type of restriction: if a function is easy to compute by an *unrestricted* b.p. and it has any combinatorial singularity hidden inside, then this singularity can be hardwired into the program to make it 'gentle'.

3. We isolate a new combinatorial property of Boolean functions – the 'strong stability', and (using the bounds on the average entropy $\mathcal{E}(F)$ established in Sect. 3) prove that any such function requires gentle b.p. of exponential size (Theorem 4). This criterion implies that some explicit Boolean function – the Clique function and a particular Pointer function (which belongs to AC^0) – cannot be computed by gentle programs of polynomial size.

2 Windows

Let P be a branching program and v be a node in P. Let $F \subseteq \{0,1\}^n$ be an arbitrary subset of inputs, each of which reach the node v. Let $comp_v(a)$ denote the part of the computation $comp(a)$ starting from the node v.

Definition 1. The *window* $w(a, v, F)$ of input $a \in F$ at the node v with respect to the set F is a string of length n in the alphabet $\{0, 1, +, \#\}$ which is defined according to the following three rules. Let $F(a)$ be the set of those inputs $b \in F$ for which $comp_v(b) = comp_v(a)$.

1. We assign a simple-cross (+) to the i-th bit of a if
   - either there is a $b \in F$ such that the first divergency of $comp_v(a)$ and $comp_v(b)$ is caused by a test on i (in this case we call that cross the *down-cross*),
   - or the bit i is not tested along any computation $comp(b)$ for $b \in F(a)$ (in this case we call that cross the *up-cross*).
2. We assign a *double-cross* (#) to the i-th bit of a if it was not crossed according to the first rule, and if $a(i) \neq b(i)$ for some input $b \in F(a)$.
3. The remaining bits of $w(a, v, F)$ are non-crossed (i.e. specified) and their values are the same as in a.

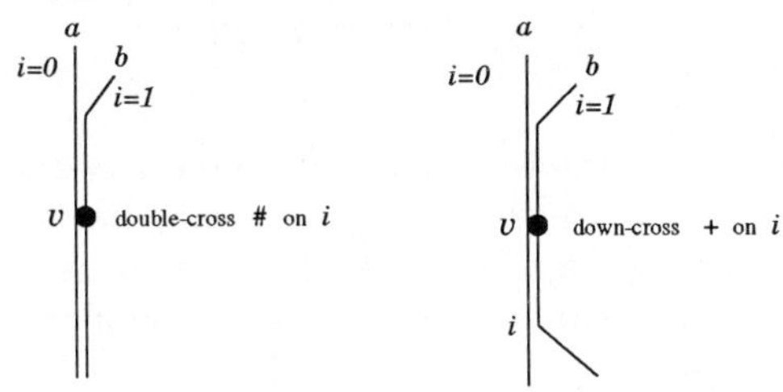

We have defined windows only at nodes but they can be easily extended to windows at edges as well. Let $e = (u, v)$ be an edge and $a \in F$ be an input, going through this edge. By a window $w(a, e, F)$ of a at the edge e with respect to F we mean the window $w(a, v, F_e)$ of a at v with respect to the set F_e of all those inputs from F, which go through the edge e. In this case we will also say that $w(a, v, F_e)$ is the window of a *immediately before* the node v (with respect to F).

Remark 1. If $a, b \in F$ and $comp_v(a) = comp_v(b)$ then the windows of a and b (at v with respect to F) have the same sets of down-crosses, of up-crosses (+) and of double-crosses (#), and all non-crossed bits and down-crossed bits have the same contents in both a and b.

This observation implies that double-crossed bits may be used to 'cut-and-paste' computations in the following sense. A *projection* of $a \in \{0, 1\}^n$ onto a subset $I \subseteq \{1, \ldots, n\}$ is a (partial) assignment $a\lceil_I : I \to \{0, 1\}$ which coincides with a on all the bits in I.

Proposition 1. *If $a, b \in F$ and $comp_v(a) = comp_v(b)$ then $P(b\lceil_I, a\lceil_{\overline{I}}) = P(a)$ where $I \rightleftharpoons D(a) = D(b)$.*

Proof. The fact that both a and b belong to F means, in particular, that the computations on these two inputs both reach the node v. Since after v these two computations do not diverge, we have that $P(a) = P(b)$. On the other hand, by Remark 1, we have that $comp(b\lceil_I, a\lceil_{\overline{I}}) = comp(b)$. Hence, $P(b\lceil_I, a\lceil_{\overline{I}}) = P(b) = P(a)$, as desired. □

3 General bounds for windows length

The number of crosses in the windows for inputs from $F \subseteq \{0,1\}^n$ measures the amount of uncertainty about these inputs when the corresponding computations meet in one node. The next theorem shows that the 'average uncertainty' is at least $\log_2 |F|$.

Theorem 1. *Let P be a branching program and v a node in it. Let $F \subseteq \{0,1\}^n$ be a set of inputs, each of which reaches the node v. For $a \in F$, let k_a be the number of bits which are crossed in the window of a at v with respect to F. Then*

$$\sum_{a \in F} 2^{-k_a} \leq 1 \tag{1}$$

and

$$\sum_{a \in F} k_a \geq |F| \cdot \log_2 |F|. \tag{2}$$

Proof. Our first goal is to establish a 1-1 connection between the inputs from F and branches in a particular binary tree. By a *binary tree* we mean a branching program, whose underlying graph is a tree. By a *branch* in such a tree we mean a path p from the root to a leaf; its *length* $|p|$ is the number of nodes in it minus 1 (i.e. the leaf is ignored).

Claim 1. There is a binary tree $T = T_{v,F}$ with $|F|$ leaves, and there is a 1-1 correspondence $F \ni a \mapsto p_a$ between the inputs from F and the branches of T such that $|p_a| \leq k_a$ for all $a \in F$.

Proof of Claim 1. Starting at the node v, we develop the program P into the tree rooted in v. In this tree we perform all computations starting from v which are given by the inputs from F. We delete from this tree all the nodes which are reachable by *no* of the inputs from F. After that we omit all non-branching edges. Observe that for every input $a \in F$, the bits tested along the corresponding branch of the resulting tree T_1 are exactly the bits which are down-crossed by (+) in $w(a, v, F)$. To capture the remaining crosses, we transform T_1 into a tree T_2, each leaf of which is reachable by only one input from F. At each leaf of T_1, which is reached by two or more inputs from F, we start a new subtree such that on each its branch there are tests on bits, which are up-crossed (+), and then on bits which are double-crossed (#) in the windows of corresponding inputs at v. This way, the length of every branch in T_2 is at most the total number of crossed bits in the windows of those inputs from F which follow this branch. Since, by Remark 1, non-crossed bits of inputs going to the same leaf of T_1, are the same and have the same value in all windows, each leaf of the transformed tree T_2 is reached by only one input from F, as desired. □

To get the first inequality (1), we combine this claim with the well-known Kraft-McMillan inequality from Information Theory about the codeword length for prefix codes: if $C = \{c_1, \dots, c_m\}$ are binary strings, no of which is a prefix of another, and l_i is the length of c_i, then $\sum_{i=1}^{m} 2^{-l_i} \leq 1$. Since the branches of $T = T_{v,F}$ clearly form a prefix code (each of them ends in the leaf) and are in 1-1 correspondence with the inputs from F, Kraft's Inequality immediately yields the desired estimate: $\sum_{a\in F} 2^{-k_a} \le \sum_{p\in T} 2^{-|p|} \le 1$.

To get the second inequality (2) (which was also derived in [8] using different argument), we relate the length of branches in a binary tree with the number of its leaves. For a binary tree T, let $|T|$ be the number of its leaves, and let $\lambda(T)$ be the total length of its branches, i.e. $\lambda(T) = \sum_p |p|$ over all branches p in T. By Claim 1, $\sum_{a\in F} k_a \ge \lambda(T)$, where $T = T_{v,F}$. Since $|F| = |T|$, inequality (2) follows directly from the following simple claim.

Claim 2. For any binary tree T, $\lambda(T) \ge |T| \cdot \log|T|$.

Proof of Claim 2. Induction on $|T|$. Basis ($|T| = 2$) is trivial. Take now a binary tree T with more than 2 leaves and let T_1 and T_2 be the subtrees of T, whose roots are immediate successors of the root of T. By inductive hypothesis,

$$\begin{aligned}\lambda(T) &= (\lambda(T_1) + |T_1|) + (\lambda(T_2) + |T_2|) \ge |T_1| \cdot \log|T_1| + |T_2| \cdot \log|T_2| + |T| \\ &\ge (|T_1| + |T_2|) \cdot \log\frac{|T_1| + |T_2|}{2} + |T| = |T| \cdot \log\frac{|T|}{2} + |T| = |T|\log|T|.\end{aligned}$$

This completes the proof of Claim 2, and thus, the proof of Theorem 1. □

The *length* of a window is the number of non-crossed bits in it. Theorem 1 can be used to estimate the 'average length' of windows in terms of program size.

Let P be a branching program, V is the set of its nodes and $A \subseteq \{0,1\}^n$ be a set of inputs. A *distribution* of A (among the nodes of P) is a mapping $\varphi : A \to V$ which sends each input $a \in A$ to some node of the computation *comp*(a). Given such a distribution, the *average length* of windows (of inputs from A) is the sum

$$H(A,\varphi) \rightleftharpoons \frac{1}{|A|}\sum_{a\in A} \ell_a,$$

where ℓ_a is the length of the window $w(a, v, F)$ of a at the node $v = \varphi(a)$ with respect to the set $F \rightleftharpoons \{b \in A : \varphi(b) = v\}$ of all those inputs, which are mapped to the same node; we call this set F the *class* of distribution at v. We can also distribute the inputs from A among the edges of P. In this case the average length of windows is defined in the same way with ℓ_a being the length of the window of a at the corresponding edge. The *size* of a program P is the number of its nodes, and is denoted by $|P|$.

Theorem 2. *Let P be a branching program, $A \subseteq \{0,1\}^n$ a set of inputs and φ be any distribution of these inputs among the nodes of P. Then*

$$H(A,\varphi) \le \log|P| + n - \log|A|.$$

If φ distributes the inputs from A among the edges of P then the same upper bound holds with $|P|$ replaced by $|E|$ where $E = \varphi^{-1}(A)$ is the set of edges to which at least one input is sent.

Proof. Let $v_1, \ldots, v_r$ be the nodes to which A is mapped by φ, and let F_j be the set of those inputs from A which are mapped to v_j. The sets $F_1, \ldots, F_r$ form a partition of A. For every $a \in A$, $n - \ell_a$ is the number of crossed bits in the window $w(a, v, F_j)$ of a at the node v_j with respect to the set F_j containing a. Thus, inequality (2) implies that $\sum_{a \in F_j} \ell_a \leq |F_j|(n - \log |F_j|)$ for every $j = 1, \ldots, r$. Hence,

$$H(A, \varphi) = \frac{1}{|A|} \sum_{j=1}^{r} \sum_{a \in F_j} \ell_a \leq \frac{1}{|A|} \sum_{j=1}^{r} |F_j|(n - \log |F_j|)$$

$$= n - \sum_{j=1}^{r} \frac{|F_j|}{|A|} \log \frac{|F_j|}{|A|} - \log |A| \leq n + \log r - \log |A|.$$

The last inequality here follows from the fact that, for $p_j \rightleftharpoons |F_j|/|A|$, the sum $-\sum_{j=1}^{r} p_j \log p_j$ is exactly the entropy of the partition of A into r blocks, and hence, does not exceed $\log r$, with the equality when blocks are of equal size. Since $|P| \geq r$, we are done. □

Theorem 2 suggest the following general frame to obtain lower bound on the size of P in terms of windows: if it is possible to distribute some large set of inputs $A \subseteq \{0,1\}^n$ among some nodes of P so that the average window-length is $\geq h$, then the program P must have size exponential in $\log |A| - n + h$.

In general, bounding the (average) window length is a hard task. On the other hand, for *read-once* branching programs (1-b.p.) this can be done easily. A Boolean function f is *m-mixed* if for any subset I of m bits and any two different assignments $a, b : I \to \{0,1\}$ we have that $f_a \neq f_b$; here, as usually, f_a denotes the subfunction of f obtained by setting the variables x_i with $i \in I$, to $a(i)$. It is well known (see, e.g. [2]) that any such function requires 1-b.p. of size 2^m. Most of exponential lower bounds for 1-b.p. were obtained using this criterion. Let us show how this result can be derived using the proposed frame in terms of windows.

Proof. Define the distribution φ of all inputs from $A \rightleftharpoons \{0,1\}^n$ among the nodes of P by sending each input a to the $(m+1)$-st node $v = \varphi(a)$ of the computation *comp*(a). Let $I(a)$ be the set of bits tested along the computation *comp*(a) until the node v; hence $|I(a)| = m$.

Claim 3. For every $a \in A$, no of the bits from $I(a)$ is crossed in the window of a at v with respect to the set $F = \varphi^{-1}(v)$.

To prove the claim, assume the opposite that some bit $i \in I \rightleftharpoons I(a)$ is crossed. Since i was tested before v, this cross cannot be an up-cross; since P is read-once, the bit i is not tested after v, and hence, this cross cannot be a down-cross. So, bit i is double-crossed, which means that some other input b such that $b(i) \neq a(i)$, also reaches the node v. Since P computes an m-mixed function, there must be an assignment $c : \overline{I} \to \{0,1\}$ such that $P(a\lceil_I, c) \neq P(b\lceil_I, c)$. But this is impossible because (due to read-once condition), no bit from I is tested along the computation *comp*(c) after the node v, and hence, the computations on both these two inputs reach the same sink. □

By the claim, $H(A, \varphi) \geq m$, which, together with Theorem 2, implies that $|P| \geq 2^{H(A,\varphi)-n+\log|A|} \geq 2^m$, as desired.

4 Gentle programs

We have seen that for 1-b.p., bounding the (average) window length is an easy task. In this section we describe one more general situation where it becomes tractable. This situation requires some additional knowledge about the *form* of windows.

Let P be a branching program and v be a node in P. Throughout this section, let $F \subseteq \{0,1\}^n$ be an arbitrary (but fixed) set of inputs which reach the node v, i.e. the computations on inputs from F go through the node v; in this case we say also that F is *classified at* v. We will always assume that the set F is *closed* in the following natural sense: $a \in F$, $b \in \{0,1\}^n$ and $comp(b) = comp(a)$ imply $b \in F$.

Let a be an input from F. Depending on what is the window $w(a, v, F)$ for this input a at the node v with respect to F, we define the following subsets of $\{1, \ldots, n\}$.

$N(a) \rightleftharpoons$ the set of all non-crossed bits;
$D(a) \rightleftharpoons$ the set of all double-crossed (#) bits;
$S(a) \rightleftharpoons$ the set of those bits $i \in D(a)$, which were non-crossed in the window for a *immediately before* the node v. i.e. which were non-crossed in the window for a at the corresponding edge, feeding into v.

Let also

$N \rightleftharpoons$ the set of all bits which are non-crossed and have the same value in the windows at v of *all* inputs from F (the *common specified part* of F), and
$D \rightleftharpoons$ the set of all bits which are double-crossed in the windows at v of *all* inputs from F (the *core* of F)

Definition 2. We say that F is classified at v *in a regular manner* with *fluctuation* γ and *deviation* δ if its core $D \neq \emptyset$ and, for every input $a \in F$, $|N(a) \setminus N| \leq \gamma$ and $max\,\{|D(a) \setminus D|, |D(a) \setminus S(a)|\} \leq \delta$.

The fluctuation tells that the "mixed" non-crossed part of $N(a)$ has at most γ bits, whereas the deviation ensures that at least $|D(a)| - \delta$ bits of a where double-crossed at the node v for the first time.

Definition 3. A branching program P is *gentle* on a set of inputs $A \subseteq \{0,1\}^n$ with fluctuation γ and deviation δ if there is a distribution $\varphi : A \to V$ of these inputs among the nodes of P such that each (non-empty) class $F = \{a \in A : \varphi(a) = v\}$ of this distribution is classified at the corresponding node v in a regular manner with the fluctuation γ and deviation δ. We also say that a program is α-*gentle* if it is such on some set of at least $2^{n-\alpha}$ inputs.

Parameters α, γ and δ range between 0 and n, and reflect the 'degree of gentleness': the smaller they are the more gentle the program is. In the next section we will show that read-once branching programs (1-b.p.) are very gentle: for them $\alpha \leq 1$ and $\gamma = \delta = 0$.

5 Read-once programs are gentle

Recall that a branching program is *read-once* (1-b.p.) if along every path every bit is tested at most once. Let $I(p)$ be the set of bits that are tested along some path p. A 1-b.p. is *uniform* if: (i) for a path p beginning at the source, the set $I(p)$ depends only on the terminal node v of p (accordingly, we denote it by $I(v)$), and (ii) for every sink v, $I(v)$ contains all variables. As observed in [6], the uniformity is actually not a serious restriction. Namely, by adding some "dummy tests" (i.e. tests where both out-going edges go to the same node), every 1-b.p. can be made uniform; the size increases by at most a factor of n.

Theorem 3. *Let P be a uniform read-once b.p. Then, for every set $A \subseteq \{0,1\}^n$, $|A| \geq 3$, the program P is gentle on all but two inputs from A with deviation $\delta = 0$ and fluctuation $\gamma = 0$. In particular, P is gentle with $\alpha \leq 1$.*

Proof. Let V be the set of nodes of P. Define the distribution $\varphi : A \to V$ inductively as follows: $\varphi(a) = v$ if v is the first node along the computation *comp*(a) at which *comp*(a) meets another computation *comp*(b) on some input $b \in A \setminus \{a\}$ which follows a different path from the source to v and which is still not mapped (by φ to a node before v).

Since P is uniform, each of the (two) sinks can be reached by at most one input which is not mapped to no of the nodes along its computation (including the sink). Hence the number of mapped inputs is at least $|A| - 2$.

We want to prove that each class of the distribution φ is classified at the corresponding node in a regular manner with the fluctuation 0 and deviation 0.

Let F be a class of the distribution at a node v. We are going to describe the window on each input from F (with respect to F at v). At first we see that there are no up-crosses since P is uniform. Let I be the set of bits tested along at least one computation *comp*(a), $a \in F$, on the path from the source to v. All bits outside I are down-crossed (in windows of all inputs from F) since P is uniform. No bit from I is tested at v and below v since P is read-once. Hence the bits in I can be only double-crossed or non-crossed.

Let us define $D \rightleftharpoons \{i \in I : \exists a, b \in F \; a(i) \neq b(i)\}$. By the definition of F, $D \neq \emptyset$. It is also clear that for any input from F the bits in $I \setminus D$ are non-crossed. We want to prove that for each input $a \in F$, D is the set of its double-crossed bits. For any $i \in D$ there must be a $b \in F$ such that $a(i) \neq b(i)$. Let us consider the combined input $c = (b\restriction_I, a\restriction_{\overline{I}})$. This input follows b from the source to v, hence is in F, too. After v, it follows the computation on a till the sink. Hence a has a double-cross on i. This shows that D is the (nonempty) core of F and that the fluctuation of F is 0 (since all inputs from F have the same set of noncrossed bits).

It remains to verify that the deviation of F is 0, i.e. that $S(a) = D(a)$ for all $a \in F$. This follows directly from the fact that the window on each $a \in F$ immediately before v has no double-crosses, since otherwise the computation on a would have to be met before v by the computation on some other input and therefore a would be distributed before v. □

6 Functions with small gentle programs

For a branching program to be gentle it is sufficient that it has some 'gentle enough' fragment – a node (or a set of nodes) at which some large set of inputs is classified in a regular enough manner. Assume that the function f can be represented in the form $f = g \wedge h$ (or $f = g \vee h$) so that h has a (unrestricted!) b.p. of size t whereas the first component g has a b.p. of size s which is gentle on some subset A of $g^{-1}(0)$ (resp., of $g^{-1}(1)$). Then, by connecting the 1-sink (resp., 0-sink) of the (gentle) b.p. for g to the source of the b.p. for h, we obtain a b.p. for the original function f which is α-gentle for $\alpha \leq n - \log|A|$, and has size $s+t$. Thus, to design the desired gentle b.p. for f, it is enough, by Theorem 3, that its first component g has small uniform 1-b.p. and the set $g^{-1}(0)$ (or $g^{-1}(1)$) is large enough.

These simple observations allow one to design small gentle b.p.'s for a lot of known functions. Due to space limitations, we show this only for *code functions.* Let $C \subseteq \{0,1\}^n$ be a linear code (i.e. a linear subspace of $GF[2]^n$), and let $f_C(x)$ be its characteristic function, i.e. $f_C(x) = 1$ iff $x \in C$. It is known that for some explicit linear codes $C \subseteq \{0,1\}^n$, their characteristic functions f_C require syntactic k-b.p. ([6]), syntactic k-n.b.p. ([3]) and $(1,+s)$-b.p. ([4]) of super-polynomial size, as long as $k = o(\log n)$ or $s = o(n/\log n)$. Thus, these functions are hard for *all* restricted models of branching programs, considered so far.

Proposition 2. *For every linear code $C \subseteq \{0,1\}^n$, the function $f_C(x)$ has an α-gentle branching program of size $O(n^2)$ with $\alpha \leq 2$ and $\gamma = \delta = 0$.*

Proof. Let $R \subseteq \{0,1\}^n$ be the set of rows in the parity-check matrix of C; hence $x \in C$ iff $\langle x, r\rangle = 0$ for all $r \in R$. Fix a row $r \in R$, and let $g \rightleftharpoons \langle x, r\rangle \oplus 1$. Since the scalar product $\langle x, r\rangle$ is just a parity function, it has a (standard) uniform 1-b.p. of linear size. Since $|g^{-1}(0)| = 2^{n-1}$, Theorem 3 implies that this program is α-gentle with $\alpha \leq 2$ and $\gamma = \delta = 0$. Since $f_C = g \wedge f_C$ and f_C has an obvious unrestricted b.p. of size $O(n^2)$, the combined program computes f_C and is also gentle, as desired. □

7 Stable functions are hard

What functions are hard for gentle programs? We have seen that functions, which were hard for previous restricted models of b.p., can be easily computed in a gentle manner. This is not surprising because for gentleness the presence of any 'gentle enough' singularity is sufficient. This fact just means that gentleness is a new property of b.p., and that combinatorial properties of Boolean functions, which make them hard for known restricted models of branching programs – like 'mixness' for 1-b.p. [2], 'degree' for 1-n.b.p. [2, 4], or 'density' and 'rareness' for (1,+s)-b.p. [4] and syntactic k-n.b.p. [3] – do not work for gentle b.p.

Mixness is quite universal property: it is known that almost all Boolean functions in n variables are m-mixed for $m = n - (1+\epsilon)\log n$. Besides mixness, a stronger property of 'stability' was introduced in [1, 2]. A function f is *m-stable* if for any subset I of m bits and for any bit $i \in I$ there is an assignment $c : \overline{I} \to \{0,1\}$ on the remaining bits and a constant $\epsilon \in \{0,1\}$ such that $f_c \equiv x_i \oplus \epsilon$, i.e. the subfunction f_c depends only on the i-th variable (and does not depend on variables x_j, $j \in I \setminus \{i\}$). Every m-stable function is also m-mixed, and hence, requires 1-b.p. of size 2^m.

In this section we prove that similar result holds also in the case of gentle branching programs with a somewhat stronger stability condition. Namely, we additionally require that the condition $f_c \equiv x_i \oplus \epsilon$ cannot be destroyed by toggling some small number of bits of c.

The *Hamming distance* $\mathrm{dist}(x, y)$ between two assignments $x : I \to \{0,1\}$ and $y : J \to \{0,1\}$ is the number of bits $i \in I \cap J$ for which $x(i) \neq y(i)$.

Definition 4. Say that f is *strongly (m, d)-stable* if for any subset of bits I with $|I| \leq m$ and any bit $i \in I$ there is an assignment $c : \overline{I} \to \{0,1\}$ and a constant $\epsilon \in \{0,1\}$ such that $f_{c'} \equiv x_i \oplus \epsilon$ for any assignment $c' : \overline{I} \to \{0,1\}$ of Hamming distance at most d from c.

Theorem 4. *If f is strongly (m, d)-stable for some $d \geq \gamma + \delta$, then any α-gentle branching program P computing f with fluctuation γ and deviation δ, has size larger than $2^{m-\alpha-\delta-1}$.*

Proof. Since P is α-gentle, there is a set of inputs $A \subseteq \{0,1\}^n$ of cardinality $|A| \geq 2^{n-\alpha}$ and a distribution $\varphi : A \to \{v_1, \ldots, v_r\}$ of these inputs among some nodes $v_1, \ldots, v_r$ of P such that every class $F_j \rightleftharpoons \{a \in A : \varphi(a) = v_j\}$ of this distribution is classified at the corresponding node v_j in a regular manner with fluctuation γ and deviation δ.

Let us first consider one of these classes $F \in \{F_1, \ldots, F_r\}$, and let $v \in \{v_1, \ldots, v_r\}$ be the corresponding node, at which this class is classified. Let also $N = N_F$ be the common specified part of F.

Claim 4. For every input $c \in \{0,1\}^n$ there is an input $w \in F$ which outside the set $D(w) \cup N$ differs from c in at most γ bits.

Proof. We construct the desired input w as follows. Starting at the node v, we develop the program into the tree rooted in v. In this tree we perform all computations starting from v which are given by the inputs from F. We delete from this tree all the nodes (together with corresponding subtrees) which are reachable by *no* of the inputs from F. Let T be the resulting tree. One branch p_c of this tree is consistent with c if we take into account only the tests made at outdegree-2 nodes (the branching nodes of T). Let $L \subseteq F$ be the set of all inputs from F which follow p_c. By Remark 1, these inputs have the same sets of double-crossed bits, of up-crossed bits, of down-crossed bits and of non-crossed bits. On down-crossed bits they have the same value as c has. Since up-crossed bits are free bits of these inputs and since F is closed, there is an input $w \in L$ which equals c also on up-crossed bits. Therefore, the inputs w and c may differ only on bits, which were either double-crossed or non-crossed (in the window of w at v with respect to F). Hence, outside the set $D(w) \cup N$, these inputs can differ in at most $|N(w) \setminus N| \leq \gamma$ bits. □

Let E be the set of edges entering the node v, and consider a new distribution $\psi : F \to E$ which sends every input $a \in F$ to the edge $\psi(a)$ which the input a goes through before it comes to v. Let $S(a)$ stand for the set of those bits in $D(a)$, which were non-crossed in the window of a immediately before the node v, i.e. in the window of a at the incoming edge $e = \psi(a)$. Let as before, $N = N_F$ be the common specified part of F. Since $S(a) \cap N = \emptyset$, $|S(a)| + |N|$ does not exceed the total length ℓ_a of the window of a at the corresponding edge e. This gives a lower bound $H(F, \psi) = \frac{1}{|F|} \sum_{a \in F} \ell_a \geq |N| + \frac{1}{|F|} \sum_{a \in F} |S(a)|$ on the average window length of inputs from F at edges feeding into the node v. We will use this to prove the following lower bound.

Claim 5. $H(F, \psi) > m - \delta$.

Proof. In fact, we will prove a stronger fact that *all* the windows are long enough, namely that $|S(a)| > m - \delta - |N|$, for every input $a \in F$. By the previous observation, this immediately gives the desired lower bound on $H(F, \psi)$.

Assume the opposite and take an input $a \in F$ for which $|S(a)| \leq m - \delta - |N|$. Consider the set of bits $I \rightleftharpoons D \cup N$ where $D = \bigcap_{a \in F} D(a)$ is the core of F. Since $S(a) \subseteq D(a)$ and $|D(a) \setminus S(a)|$ cannot exceed the deviation δ, we have that $|D(a)| \leq |S(a)| + \delta$. Hence, $|I| \leq |D(a)| + |N| \leq |S(a)| + \delta + |N| \leq m$. Since F is classified at v in a regular manner, its core D is non-empty. Take an arbitrary bit $i \in D$. Since $|I| \leq m$ and our function f is strongly (m, d)-stable, there must be an input $c \in \{0,1\}^n$ and a constant $\epsilon \in \{0,1\}$ such that $f(x, c'\lceil_{\overline{I}}) = x(i) \oplus \epsilon$ for any assignment $x : I \to \{0,1\}$ and any assignment $c' \in \{0,1\}^n$ such that $\mathrm{dist}(c\lceil_{\overline{I}}, c'\lceil_{\overline{I}}) \leq d$. By Claim 4, we can find in F an input w which outside the set $J \rightleftharpoons D(w) \cup N$ differs from c in at most γ bits. On the other hand, since the bit i belongs to the core D, it was double-crossed also in the window for the input w. Hence, there must be an input $b \in F$ such that $b(i) \neq w(i)$ and $comp_v(b) = comp_v(w)$. By Proposition 1, the program P must output the same value on both inputs w and $(b\lceil_J, w\lceil_{\overline{J}})$ (because inputs w and b coincide on N). But outside the set $I = D \cup N$ both these inputs differ from c in at most $\mathrm{dist}(w\lceil_{\overline{J}}, c\lceil_{\overline{J}}) + |D(w) \setminus D| \leq \gamma + \delta \leq d$ bits. This gives the desired contradiction because then, taking $c' = w$ and $c' = (b\lceil_{\overline{I}}, w\lceil_{\overline{I}})$, we have that $f(w) = w(i) \oplus \epsilon \neq b(i) \oplus \epsilon = f(b\lceil_I, w\lceil_{\overline{I}})$. □

Using this claim we complete the proof of the theorem as follows. Let $E_1, \ldots, E_r$ be the sets of edges, feeding into the nodes $v_1, \ldots, v_r$, and let $F_1, \ldots, F_r$ be the corresponding classes, distributed (by φ) to these nodes. Theorem 2 together with Claim 5 implies that $\log|E_j| > m - \delta - n + \log|F_j|$ for every $j = 1, \ldots, r$. Since the sets E_j of edges are mutually disjoint and $\sum_{j=1}^{r} |F_j| = |A| \geq 2^{n-\alpha}$, the desired lower bound on the total number $|P|$ of nodes in P follows: $2|P| \geq \sum_{j=1}^{r} |E_j| > 2^{m-\delta-n} \sum_{j=1}^{r} |F_j| \geq 2^{m-\alpha-\delta}$. □

The *clique function* $\text{Clique}_{n,k}$ has $\binom{n}{2}$ Boolean variables, encoding the edges of an n-vertex graph, and outputs 1 iff this graph contains at least one complete subgraph on k vertices. It is easy to show that this function is strongly (m,d)-stable for $d = k-2$ and any $m \leq \min\left\{\binom{k}{2} - k,\ (n-k^2)/2\right\}$. This, together with Theorem 4 yields

Corollary 1. *For $2 \leq k \leq \sqrt{n}/2$ and $\alpha \leq k^2/2$, any α-gentle program computing* $\text{Clique}_{n,k}$ *with parameters $\gamma + \delta \leq k - 2$, has size $2^{\Omega(k^2)}$. For maximal k, the bound is $2^{\Omega(n)}$ with $\alpha = \Omega(n)$ and $\gamma + \delta = \Omega(\sqrt{n})$.*

The Clique function is NP-complete. Bellow we describe an explicit strongly stable function which belongs to AC^0.

Let s and k be such that $ks^2 = n$ and $k \geq \log n$. Arrange the n variables $X = \{x_1, \ldots, x_n\}$ into a $k \times s^2$ matrix; split the i-th row $(1 \leq i \leq k)$ into s blocks $B_{i1}, B_{i2}, \ldots, B_{is}$ of size s each, and let ϵ_i be the OR of ANDs of variables in these blocks. The *pointer function* $\pi(X)$ is defined by: $\pi(X) = x_j$ where j is the number (between 1 and n), whose binary code is $(\epsilon_1, \ldots, \epsilon_k)$.

It is easy to show that $\pi(X)$ is strongly (m,d)-stable for any m and d such that $m + d \leq s - 1$. This, together with Theorem 4, implies the following

Corollary 2. *For $s = \lceil (n/\log n)^{1/2} \rceil$ any gentle program computing the function $\pi(X)$ with parameters $\alpha + \gamma + \delta \leq n^{1/2-\epsilon}$, has size* $\exp\left(\Omega(n/\log n)^{1/2}\right)$.

Acknowledgement. We thank anonymous referees for their stimulating criticism on the submitted version of this paper.

References

1. Dunne, P. E.: Lower bounds on the complexity of one-time-only branching programs. In: *Proc. of FCT'85*, Lect. Notes in Comput. Sci., **199** (1985), 90–99.
2. Jukna, S.: Entropy of contact circuits and lower bounds on their complexity. *Theoret. Comput. Sci.*, **57** (1988), 113–129.
3. ———: A note on read-k-times branching programs. *RAIRO Theoretical Informatics and Applications* **29**:1 (1995), pp. 75-83.
4. ———, Razborov, A. A.: Neither reading few bits twice nor reading illegally helps much. ECCC TR96-037 (1996). To appear in: *Discrete Appl. Math.*
5. Nečiporuk, E. I.: On a Boolean function. *Soviet Mathematics Doklady* **7**:4 (1966), 999–1000.
6. Okolnishnikova, E. A.: Lower bounds for branching programs computing characteristic functions of binary codes. *Metody discretnogo analiza* **51** (1991), pages 61–83.
7. Wegener, I.: *The complexity of Boolean functions*, Wiley-Teubner, 1987.
8. Žák, S.: A subexponential lower bound for branching programs restricted with regard to some semantic aspects. ECCC TR97-050 (1997).

CONS-Free Programs with Tree Input
(Extended Abstract)

Amir M. Ben-Amram[1] and Holger Petersen[2]

[1] The Academic College of Tel-Aviv
4 Antokolski Str., 64044 Tel Aviv, Israel
amirben@server.mta.ac.il

[2] Institute of Computer Science, University of Stuttgart
Breitwiesenstr. 20–22, 70565 Stuttgart, Germany
petersen@informatik.uni-stuttgart.de

Abstract. We investigate programs operating on LISP-style input data that may not allocate additional storage. For programs without a test of pointer equality we obtain a strict hierarchy of sets accepted by deterministic, non-deterministic, and recursive programs. We show the classes accepted by programs with the ability to test pointers for equality are closely related to well-known complexity classes where relationships are mostly open.

1 Introduction

1.1 Background

Programming paradigms and related features of programming languages are subjects of continuing interest within the computer science community.

While all general purpose programming languages provide Turing completeness, there are obvious differences with respect to ease of use and efficiency. One of the few results establishing such discrepancies in a precise sense is the recent separation of pure and impure (destructive) LISP programs by Pippenger [7], where the two language variants are separated with respect to efficiency. In the present work we consider a more restrictive setting of sub-recursive languages. Their study is mainly motivated by the observation that for such restricted languages, it is meaningful to compare language variants with respect to *expressive power*, regardless of efficiency. This kind of study has led in the past to fundamental results that characterize the expressive power of various types of automata, and show that important complexity classes can be captured by restricted languages.

1.2 Outline

We start by introducing CONS-free programs, programs in an imperative language operating on a LISP-style input tree, but without access to dynamic ("heap") storage. The trees accepted by programs of this kind can be put into correspondence with strings over a finite alphabet, e.g. via a preorder encoding. This makes it possible to compare the power of CONS-free programs with that of resource-bounded Turing machines and related models that operate on string input. In the special case where the input is a linear list the correspondence to string languages is close and has been studied intensively, see [5, 4].

Our results investigate the case of general input. In this setting, we have been able to separate the acceptance power of deterministic CONS-free programs from those of more powerful programs, for example non-deterministic ones. This stands in contrast with the situation found for string languages, where the analogous questions are long-standing open problems.

Some of our results make use of techniques for simulating bounded counters, building on known relationships of counter machines to other automata.

A question arising in programming languages is the kind of access that the programmer has to memory pointers. In our framework the question appears in the form of whether CONS-free programs gain power from an equality test of pointers. We have been able to show that this capability does add power to our non-deterministic CONS-free language, while for other language variants the problem is still open.

2 Technical Background

2.1 Preliminaries

We consider programs written in a simple "flow-chart" language, i.e., an imperative language without block structure and recursion, and with a LISP view of data. Such programs have been considered by Jones [4, 5] and Pippenger [7].

The instructions available include `car`, `cdr`, and assignments. The former two operate on a CONS-cell and return the value of its respective field, which is either an atom or a pointer to another cell. Every instruction carries a label that the program may use as the destination of an unconditional or conditional jump, where the latter tests a variable for `nil`. Note that we have excluded `cons`; this makes our language weaker than LISP, for it cannot allocate storage. We call our language CF, an abbreviation of CONS-Free.

The unstructured form of programs is convenient in proving facts about the expressive power of our model. Often we will however present code segments using structured constructs like "`while`" and "`if...then...else`" that readily translate into the more restricted language.

In order to eliminate unnecessary details, we assume our data to consist solely of CONS-cells (to whom we also refer as *nodes*) and the single atom `nil`. Clearly it is possible to represent any finite set of atoms by choosing a suitable encoding such as `nil`, `(nil.nil)` etc. We denote the set of binary trees, all of whose leaves are `nil`, by $\mathbb{D}$. For a non-atomic tree T, we refer to its two subtrees as `hd` T and `tl` T (we thus distinguish between `hd` T and `car` T, which denotes a pointer to the root of the subtree).

The input to a program is a single element of $\mathbb{D}$, i.e., a single tree. We will concentrate on recognition problems and assume that the program has a way of signaling acceptance, say with special `accept` and `reject` instructions. We define however "rejection" as non-acceptance, so that a program that fails to terminate is considered as rejecting its input. The interesting question of whether termination can be ensured is mentioned briefly in a later section.

As a programming convention, we allow Boolean values `true` and `false` in our programs. These will be represented by some non-`nil` value and `nil` respectively. There is a caveat here, since this requires the input to be non-`nil`. We will tacitly assume that a test takes care of the special case of an input `nil` before entering the main body of the program. By using k variables of this kind, a finite counter with values in $[0, 2^k - 1]$ can also be maintained.

A natural extension, from a programming point of view, is procedure calling and recursion. The language so extended will be called RCF. Extending our language in another direction we introduce non-determinism by a `choose` instruction that non-deterministically executes one of the operations supplied as its parameters. As usual we define acceptance by requiring that there be at least one successful sequence of choices. This variant will be called NCF.

Since we consider CONS-free programs, that cannot allocate any new cells, program variables act as pointers into the input structure. The capability of testing whether two variables point to the same node will be introduced as another extension that can be added to each of the above languages, obtaining respectively the variants ECF, RECF, and NECF.

We give an example of a program that falls into the most restricted class CF of deterministic CONS-free programs that cannot test pointers for equality. Note that block structure is indicated by indentation.

```
E := true; Y := X;
while Y do
  Y := cdr Y;
  if E then X := cdr X;
  E := not E
```

Considering the initial value of `X` as a LISP-style list, this program will move `X` to the middle of the list. This example shows an important programming technique whereby variables that point into the input tree can serve as counters, where here we have divided a counter by 2. The same technique has been used for counting by multihead automata. However, because the structure of the input tree can vary, more involved techniques will be necessary in order to simulate counters in our programs.

2.2 Classes of Sets Recognized by a Language

Since our languages are obviously sub-recursive, it is interesting to consider the class of sets of inputs that can be recognized by such a program. For a language L, We denote the class of sets that can be recognized by L-programs by a boldface **L**. We thus have the classes **CF**, **NCF** etc.

The fact that variables are constrained to point into the input structure brings to mind familiar computational models, in particular multihead automata.

The classes of sets of strings (string languages) recognized by such devices are well studied. It is thus natural to compare our classes to the classes of string languages. However our classes comprise sets of trees, not of strings. This discrepancy can be settled in two ways. The first is to restrict the trees to linear lists that in the obvious manner encode strings. This way our languages coincide with familiar automata, and the classes of lists recognized are then well-known classes of string languages. This treatment can be found in Jones [5, 4].

In our work we have adopted a different approach: we translate between trees and strings using an encoding function $c_{\mathbb{D}} : \mathbb{D} \to \{0,1\}^*$. The particular function we use is based on a preorder listing of the tree and is defined by $c_{\mathbb{D}}(\texttt{nil}) = 0$ and $c_{\mathbb{D}}(\texttt{d}_1.\texttt{d}_2) = 1c_{\mathbb{D}}(\texttt{d}_1)c_{\mathbb{D}}(\texttt{d}_2)$. Note that the set of strings that encode trees is obtained as the image set denoted by $c_{\mathbb{D}}(\mathbb{D}) \subseteq \{0,1\}^*$.

For any class $\mathcal{C}$ of subsets of $\{0,1\}^*$, we define the corresponding class of trees by tree-$\mathcal{C} = \{ c_{\mathbb{D}}^{-1}(A) : A \in \mathcal{C} \}$. Thus we consider, for instance, the class tree-LOGSPACE, which includes those sets of trees that, when transformed to strings, can be recognized by a logarithmic-space machine. For definitions of this class and other string classes such as NLOGSPACE and PTIME see [4]. The class of regular languages is denoted by REGULAR.

2.3 Counters as Storage Devices

In order to establish relations between our classes and string-language classes we will use simulations of *bounded counter machines*. We now briefly describe these machines and their relationship to Turing machines. Let $b(w)$ be a bound that depends on the input w. The counter machine has a read-only two-way input tape with one head and is equipped with a finite set of counters that can store a number in the range 0 to $b(w)-1$. A counter can be set to $b(w)-1$, decremented, and tested for zero. Note that an increment operation on a counter whose value is less than $b(w)-1$ can be simulated with the help of an auxiliary counter and a loop. Counter machines operate under the control of a finite program that may be deterministic, non-deterministic, or alternating. Taking a programming-language view, recursion can also be added (actually recursion has also been discussed in an automata-theory disguise of "machines with auxiliary pushdown store", see [2]).

The crucial fact that we exploit is the well-known correspondence of $b(w)$ bounded counters and Turing machines with space bound $\log b(w)$. The main example is the case of linearly bounded counters, $b(w) = \Theta(|w|)$, where deterministic, non-deterministic and alternating (or recursive) counter machines characterize the string-language classes LOGSPACE, NLOGSPACE, and PTIME, respectively. We refer to [4, 5] for a detailed discussion.

3 Programs without Test for Pointer Equality

We first summarize the basic inclusions between classes defined on trees and corresponding string representations.

Theorem 1. *The following relations hold:*

$$\mathbf{CF} \subseteq \text{tree-LOGSPACE}, \quad \mathbf{NCF} \subseteq \text{tree-NLOGSPACE}, \quad \mathbf{RCF} \subseteq \text{tree-PTIME}$$

Proof. The first two inclusions can be verified by a simple translation of CONS-free programs to Turing machines. The main points to note are that a pointer into the input can be represented in logarithmic space, and that logarithmic space suffices for the counter necessary for locating the `cdr` of a node in the string representation. For the third inclusion, the memoization technique of Cook is used [5]. □
We proceed to show that the first inclusion is strict.

Definition 1. *A node of a tree in* $\mathbb{D}$ *is called* even *if both of its children are* `nil`*, or both are non-*`nil`*. Otherwise the node is called* odd. EVEN *is the set of trees, all of whose internal nodes are even.*

EVEN has a very simple flavor, since it is defined by a local condition on each node; were the tree encoded as a string, a finite automaton would suffice for testing it.

Fact 1. EVEN $= c_{\mathbb{D}}^{-1}(0 + (1 + 100)^*) \in$ tree-REGULAR.

In contrast, we show that this test is beyond the capabilities of CONS-free programs.

Theorem 2. *No* CF *program can recognize* EVEN*. This statement remains true, even if it is guaranteed that in the input there is at most one odd node.*

To prove the theorem, we have to introduce some definitions. The *configuration* of program p at a certain instant during its computation is $(l, X_1, \ldots, X_k)$ where l is the label of the instruction to be executed next, and $X_1, \ldots, X_k$ are the values of the k variables of the program. These values are either `nil` or references to nodes of the input tree T. The set of possible configurations is turned into the *configuration graph* $G_C(\mathtt{p}, T)$ by adding the usual successor relation $C_1 \to C_2$. A *computation path* of p on input T is a path in this graph that starts with the initial configuration $(l_1, T, \mathtt{nil}, \ldots, \mathtt{nil})$, where l_1 is the first instruction of the program, and ends in a terminal configuration (one that bears the label of a stop instruction). Since the program is deterministic, every (non terminal) configuration has exactly one successor.

For a variable X_i, by the *tree value* of X_i we mean the *tree* (element of $\mathbb{D}$) referenced by X_i — in contrast with the "pointer value" which is a particular node of the input tree. We call two configurations *equivalent* if they agree on the instruction label and on the *tree values* of all variables. A *situation* is an equivalence class of configurations under this relation. Since the program semantics only depends on tree values (recall that the language does not allow pointers to be compared), the *successor* of a non-terminal situation is well defined, and we obtain the *situation graph* $G_S(\mathtt{p}, T)$.

Lemma 1. *For a configuration C_1 the following diagram commutes, where a horizontal arrow represents the successor relation and vertical arrows map configurations to their equivalence class.*

$$\begin{array}{ccc} C_1 & \longrightarrow & C_2 \\ \downarrow & & \downarrow \\ [C_1] & \longrightarrow & [C_2] \end{array}$$

Proof. The lemma is proved by looking at each of the instructions in the language, and verifying that its action on equivalent configurations yields equivalent successors. □

Definition 2. *For $T \in \mathbb{D}$, $\|T\|$ is the number of non-isomorphic subtrees of T.*

Lemma 2. *Let* p *be a CF program, using k variables. The length of any terminating computation of* p *on input T is bounded by $|\mathrm{p}| \cdot \|T\|^k$, where $|\mathrm{p}|$ is the number of instructions in* p.

Proof. A computation of length t corresponds to a path π of length t in the configuration graph. By Lemma 1 a corresponding path π', of the same length, exists in the situation graph. Because the program is deterministic (there is only one successor to a non-terminal configuration), the path π is simple, and we can use Lemma 1 to show that π' is simple too. Now, its length is bounded by the number of vertices in $G_S(\mathrm{p}, T)$, i.e., the number of situations, which is clearly bounded by $|\mathrm{p}| \cdot \|T\|^k$. □

We say that program p *inspects* a node of the input tree, if at some point during its computation a variable refers to this node. Clearly, if a node is never inspected, the values of its children cannot affect the behavior of the program.

Proof (of Theorem 2). Consider a CF program p that allegedly recognizes EVEN. Let n be a number of the form $2^h - 1$ and let T_n be the perfectly balanced tree of height h (T_n has n nodes). Correctness of p implies that on input T_n, it terminates and accepts. Lemma 2 shows that the length of p's computation on T_n is bounded by $|p| \cdot h^k$, where p has k variables. Thus during its computation on T_n, the program inspects $O((\log n)^k)$ nodes. It follows that for all n larger than some constant, there are internal nodes of T_n (nodes whose children are not `nil`) which are never inspected. Let T'_n be a tree obtained by choosing one such node and changing one of its children to `nil`; p accepts T'_n, failing to recognize that it is not in EVEN. □

The second inclusion of Theorem 1 is also strict.

Theorem 3. *No* NCF *program can recognize the set* EVEN, *but its complement can be recognized.*

Proof. The proof of the negative result is a simple extension of the proof for the deterministic case. We omit the details.

For the positive result, here is the outline of a program to recognize $\mathbb{D} \setminus$ EVEN.

Set `X` to the root of the tree.

Non-deterministically follow a path in the tree, by setting `X` either to `car X` or

to `cdr X`, until one of the children of `X` becomes `nil`.
If `X` also has a non-`nil` child, accept; else reject. □

Corollary 1. **CF** $\subsetneq$ **NCF** $\neq$ *co*-**NCF**

This result contrasts with the situation for the related string-language classes, where separation of LOGSPACE from NLOGSPACE is a notorious open problem, while closure under complement holds for the non-deterministic class [8, Chapter 7]. Finally we show that the third inclusion from Theorem 1 is strict.

Theorem 4. **RCF** $\subsetneq$ tree-PTIME.

Proof. Let $L \subsetneq \{1\}^*$ be a tally language that can be recognized in time $O(2^n)$ but not in polynomial time. Let S be the set of completely balanced trees of height i such that $1^i \in L$. Any RCF program running on a tree $T \in S$ of height i can be simulated by a deterministic Turing machine on input 1^i in time polynomial in i. By the choice of L, this proves that $S \notin$ **RCF**.

Now, the string encoding of T is a string of the form $1^i001\dots0$ and total length $2^{i+1}-1$; therefore, a polynomial-time DTM operating on this string can simulate an exponential-time DTM operating on 1^i. In particular it can check whether $1^i \in L$. Therefore, $S \in$ tree-PTIME. □

Recursion allows us (at last) to traverse a tree in preorder, and hence to simulate the action of a finite automaton on its preorder encoding; thus we have tree-REGULAR $\subseteq$ **RCF**. We present the procedure to simulate an automaton below. The procedure, `traverse`, calls auxiliary procedures `process0` and `process1` to simulate the action of the automaton when reading a 0 or a 1, respectively. The procedures will update the automaton's state, which they maintain as a finite counter. The result of the run (acceptance or rejection) will be determined from the state when the traversal is completed.

```
procedure traverse(T)
 if T ≠ nil then
   process1; traverse(car T); traverse(cdr T)
 else
   process0
```

An interesting extension of this technique allows for the simulation of Turing machines with $O(\log\log n)$ space.

Lemma 3. *For the input tree T of an RCF program let $t = \|T\|$. Then the program can simulate a finite number of counters bounded by t.*

Proof. We use the lexicographic ordering of trees according to their binary preorder encoding. This ordering can be checked by a recursive function `lexgt?` that returns `true` if its first parameter is strictly greater than its second. Let the decreasing sequence of subtrees of T be $t_{t-1} = T, \dots, t_0 = $ `nil`. A counter value i can be maintained by having a variable pointing to t_i. A counter is zero if and only if the corresponding variable is `nil`. Decrement can be implemented by finding the lexicographically preceding subtree (procedure `lexpred`). Setting a counter to the maximum value of $t-1$ is achieved with a recursive procedure `lexmax`.

We give a detailed description of `lexpred` only. It accesses two global variables `X` and `Y`, where `X` points to the old tree and `Y` receives the new one. Initially `Y` = `nil` and `lexpred` is called with the input tree.

```
procedure lexpred(Z)
 if lexgt?(X, Z) and lexgt?(Z, Y) then Y := Z;
 if Z ≠ nil then
   lexpred(car Z); lexpred(cdr Z)
```

□

Lemma 4. *For an input tree T with n nodes we have $\|T\| > \lceil \log n \rceil$.*

Proof. A binary tree with $n > 0$ nodes (CONS-cells) contains a path from its root to one of its leaves of length at least $\ell = \lceil \log_2(n+1) \rceil$. Thus there are $\ell + 1$ non-isomorphic subtrees in T rooted at the nodes of this path. □

We now show how the counters described in Lemma 3 can be used to simulate Turing machines.

Note: in the definition of acceptance by $O(\log\log n)$-space machines, we allow the weak mode of acceptance, where the space bound has to be obeyed only on accepted inputs. For a discussion of weak versus strong modes of space-bounded acceptance, see [8]; we will contend ourselves with citing the fact that the weak class strictly contains the strong class.

Theorem 5. tree-DSPACE($\log\log n$) $\subsetneq$ **RCF**.

Proof. First note that the inclusion must be strict, due to the deterministic space hierarchy (consider the restriction to lists). We proceed to show that the inclusion holds.

Let the number of nodes of T be n; then the length of its string representation is $2n+1$. According to the Lemma 3 we can maintain in the RCF programs a finite number of global variables that represent $\|T\|$ bounded counters. These counters can represent $O(\log \|T\|)$ bits of the Turing machine work tape. Since (by the last lemma) $\|T\| > \lceil \log n \rceil$, we can simulate any Turing machine whose space complexity is $O(\log\log n)$.

We enhance the `traverse` procedure shown above to simulate a bidirectional input head. We now assume that the `process` procedures—in addition to updating the representation of the machine's internal state and working storage—return the value "true" if the Turing machine's input head is to be moved to the right (forwards), and "false" if it is to move left (backwards). Similarly, we change `traverse` to accept a second parameter, `Dir`, indicating the direction in which traversal is to proceed.

Since Turing machines with read-only input tape are supposed to use endmarkers, we add procedures `process2` and `process3` to process the left and right endmarker, respectively. The simulation will be initiated by procedure `simulate`, which calls the recursive procedure `traverse2way`. We assume that the initial position of the input head is on the left endmarker, and that moving off an endmarker terminates the program.

```
procedure simulate(T)
  1:  if process2 then goto 2 else return
  2:  if traverse2way(T, true)  then goto 3 else goto 1
  3:  if process3 then return else goto 4
  4:  if traverse2way(T, false) then goto 3 else goto 1

procedure traverse2way(T,Dir)
  if T=nil then
    process0
  else
  if Dir then goto 1 else goto 5
  1:  if process1 then goto 2 else return
  2:  if traverse2way(car T, true)  then goto 3 else goto 1
  3:  if traverse2way(cdr T, true)  then return else goto 4
  4:  if traverse2way(car T, false) then goto 3 else goto 1
  5:  if traverse2way(cdr T, false) then return else goto 4
```

A further technical remark: we implement the operation of returning a value from a procedure by assigning it to a global variable that is reserved for this purpose. Therefore it is permissible for a function to return without explicitly defining a return value; the last return value rests unchanged. □

The simulation given in the preceding proof can be enhanced as follows. In an initial phase, when the input is not yet being traversed, it is possible to simulate non-deterministic and even alternating operation of the Turing machine by means of recursion (essentially changing non-deterministic search into deterministic backtracking). This extension uses the fact that our simulator can be forced to stop on every input (hence an unfortunate guess cannot cause it to run wild). We can thus simulate machines with "blind non-determinism" as well as "blind alternation" [6, 3, 1].

One consequence of the simulation is that Freivalds' result, that $\{a^p b^q \mid p, q \geq 0, p \neq q\} \in \mathrm{DSPACE}(\log\log n)$ [8, Lemma 4.1.3], can be adapted to show that the following set belongs to **RCF**: $\mathrm{BAL} = \{T \in \mathbb{D} : |\mathrm{hd}\ T| = |\mathrm{tl}\ T|\}$.

The counting technique of Lemma 3 can also be used to show the relationship between the classes **NCF** and **RCF**.

Theorem 6. **NCF** $\subsetneq$ **RCF**.

Proof. The inclusion follows by simulating non-determinism with recursion, as mentioned above. The classes are separated by the language EVEN. □

4 The Pointer Equality Test

Inspecting the proof of Theorem 2 reveals that it ceases to apply if the language is extended by the capability to test whether two pointers refer to the same node.

Thus it seems that the equality test, which we denote by `eq`, may affect the expressive power of the language (this is another feature which does not appear if the input is restricted to linear lists, where the test can be simulated with the help of an auxiliary variable and one loop). Recall that the basic language with equality test is named ECF, with the corresponding extensions NECF and RECF.

Theorem 7. *The following relations hold:*

$$\mathbf{ECF} \subseteq \text{tree-LOGSPACE}, \quad \mathbf{NECF} \subseteq \text{tree-NLOGSPACE}$$

$$\mathbf{RECF} \subseteq \text{tree-PTIME}$$

Proof. Analogous to the proof of Theorem 1. □

While we obtained a strict hierarchy for the classes of sets accepted by programs without a test for pointer equality, the situation is much more complex for the classes admitting this operation.

We have not been able to separate the class **ECF** from either **CF** or **NECF**. A separation from the latter class would probably require an argument exploiting the fact that the input is a tree. If the classes could be separated on linear input structures this would imply that LOGSPACE and NLOGSPACE can be separated, since on linear lists the inclusions of Theorem 7 are equalities.

In contrast with the case of **ECF**, for non-deterministic and recursive programs we have been able to extend the inclusions to equalities for general input.

Theorem 8. **NECF**= tree-NLOGSPACE.

Proof. As pointed out in Section 2.3 it suffices to show that an NECF program can simulate a non-deterministic counter program, whose counters have integer values bounded by a constant times the input size. Our construction achieves this with counters bounded by half the input size.

Let p be a non-deterministic $\lfloor |w|/2 \rfloor$-bounded counter program that operates on the string $w = c_{\mathbb{D}}(T)$. We translate it to an NECF program that operates on T by representing every counter as a pointer into the input tree, where the value of the counter is given by the preorder number of the node (note that this is a different method than used for programs without pointer comparison). In particular, the root of the tree represents the value zero. If T has n nodes, $|c_{\mathbb{D}}(T)| = 2n + 1$, so the desired counter size will be achieved.

Using this representation, testing a counter for zero is trivial, setting to $n-1$ is quite simple, so we will describe in more detail only the decrement operation.

Let ν be a node of the tree, and π its parent. We use the following facts:

1. If $\nu = \texttt{car}\,\pi$, the predecessor of ν in preorder is π.
2. If $\nu = \texttt{cdr}\,\pi$, the predecessor is the lowest node reachable by pursuing `cdr` pointers, starting at $\texttt{car}\,\pi$.

This gives the following procedure. Here non-determinism is used. The operation `choose` is the non-deterministic choice. The statement `fail` indicates that no answer is reached (this could be expressed by looping forever). The counter which we aim to decrement is Y; Z is a temporary variable. We assume that Y does not point to the root (which has preorder number zero).

```
Z := root     (* search for the parent of Y *)
while (cdr Z ≠ Y) and (car Z ≠ Y) and (Z ≠ nil)
  Z := choose(car,cdr) Z;
if Z = nil then
  fail
else
  if Y = car Z then    (* case 1 *)
    Y := Z
  else                 (* case 2 *)
    Y := car Z;
    while cdr Y ≠ nil
      Y := cdr Y
```

The input head is represented in much the same way as a pointer into the tree which can be moved forwards or backwards using a similar procedure. This completes the description of the translation and hence the proof. □

Theorem 9. RECF= tree-PTIME.

Proof. It is known (see for example [5]) that adding recursion to linearly-bounded counter programs gives a model that captures PTIME. Our theorem thus follows by showing how to compile linearly-bounded counter programs into RECF. The two languages have the same control structures: procedures, sequential execution and branching, so we only have to replace the instructions that manipulate the counters. As before, the involved operation is decrement, where we now use recursive traversal in order to find the predecessor of a node. Procedure pred below sets variable Y to the predecessor of X, which is again assumed to be different from the root. During the traversal the Boolean variable F (initially true) records whether the node references by X has already been discovered. The procedure is called with the input tree.

```
procedure pred(Z)
 if Z ≠ nil then
   if Z = X then F := false;
   if F then Y := Z;
   pred(car Z); pred(cdr Z)
```

□

5 Some Recent Results

In this abstract we have considered the classes of trees accepted by CONS-free programs with or without the pointer equality test, non-determinism and recursion. An extension that could not be included is alternating programs. It can be shown that for both our language variants, CF and ECF, alternation gives the same expressive power as recursion.

Further results about closure properties have been obtained. The classes **NECF** and **RECF** are known to be closed under complement because of Theorems 8 and 9. As known for Turing machines, closure under complement is related to the possibility of guaranteeing termination of the programs. Using various constructions, this has been shown possible for the classes **ECF**, **RCF** and **CF** (note that the question is non-trivial precisely because these classes do not seem to coincide with related complexity classes).

6 Conclusion

CONS-free programs, with input restricted to linear lists, can be equated with "conventional" types of automata, with the result that their expressive power can be nicely characterized. With general tree input, the situation is much different, and so far largely unexplored. In this work we have been able to identify many of the relations between classes accepted by such programs with different language features and compare them to related classes of string languages.

Many questions remain open, such as the relationship of **ECF** to LOGSPACE and to **CF**. The last relationship has to do with the interesting question of whether pointer comparison increases the power of a language. Another interesting direction is to consider non-tree inputs, for example by allowing shared CONS-cells.

References

1. G. Buntrock, F. Drewes, C. Lautemann, and T. Mossakowski. Some modifications of auxiliary pushdown automata. *Informatique théorique et Applications/Theoretical Informatics and Applications*, 25:545–556, 1991.
2. S. A. Cook. Characterizations of pushdown machines in terms of time-bounded computers. *Journal of the Association for Computing Machinery*, 18:4–18, 1971.
3. B. Jenner and B. Kirsig. *Alternierung und logarithmischer Platz.* PhD thesis, Universität Hamburg, 1989.
4. N. D. Jones. *Computability and Complexity — From a Programming Perspective.* MIT Press, Cambridge, Mass., London, England, 1997.
5. N. D. Jones. LOGSPACE and PTIME characterized by programming languages. 1997. Submitted.
6. I. Niepel. *Logarithmisch-platzbeschränkte Komplexitätsklassen—Charakterisierung und offene Fragen.* Diplomarbeit, Fachbereich Informatik der Universität Hamburg, 1987.
7. N. Pippenger. Pure versus impure Lisp. *ACM Transactions on Programming Languages and Systems*, 19:223–238, 1997.
8. A. Szepietowski. *Turing Machines with Sublogarithmic Space.* Number 843 in Lecture Notes in Computer Science. Springer, Berlin-Heidelberg-New York, 1994.

Concatenable Graph Processes: Relating Processes and Derivation Traces*

Paolo Baldan, Andrea Corradini, and Ugo Montanari

Dipartimento di Informatica - University of Pisa
Corso Italia, 40, 56125 Pisa, Italy
E-mail: {baldan, andrea, ugo}@di.unipi.it

Abstract. Several formal concurrent semantics have been proposed for graph rewriting, a powerful formalism for the specification of concurrent and distributed systems which generalizes P/T Petri nets. In this paper we relate two such semantics recently proposed for the algebraic double-pushout approach to graph rewriting, namely the *derivation trace* and the *graph process* semantics. The notion of *concatenable graph process* is introduced and then the category of concatenable derivation traces is shown to be isomorphic to the category of concatenable graph processes. As an outcome we obtain a quite intuitive characterization of events and configurations of the event structure associated to a graph grammar.

1 Introduction

Graph grammars (or *graph rewriting systems*) have been introduced as a generalization of string grammars dealing with graphs, but they have been quickly recognized as a powerful tool for the specification of concurrent and distributed systems [15]. The basic idea is that the state of many distributed systems can be represented naturally (at a suitable level of abstraction) as a graph, and (local) transformations of the state can be expressed as production applications. The appropriateness of graph grammars as models of concurrency is confirmed by their relationship with another classical model of concurrent and distributed systems, namely Petri nets, which can be regarded as graph rewriting systems that act on a restricted kind of graphs, i.e., discrete, labelled graphs (that can be considered as sets of tokens labelled by places). In this view, graph rewriting systems generalize Petri nets not only because they allow for arbitrary (also non-discrete) graphs, but also because they allow for the specification of context-dependent operations, where part of the state is read but not consumed.

In recent years, various concurrent semantics for graph rewriting systems have been proposed in the literature, some of which are based on the correspondence with Petri nets (see [2]). The aim of this paper is to relate two such semantics introduced recently by the last two authors in joint works with F. Rossi,

* Research partly supported by the EC TMR Network GETGRATS (General Theory of Graph Transformation Systems) and by the EC Esprit WG APPLIGRAPH (Applications of Graph Transformation).

H. Ehrig and M. Löwe: the *category of concatenable derivation traces* of [5], used there to obtain an event structure semantics, and the *graph processes* proposed in [6]. Both semantics are worked out, in the mentioned papers, for the algebraic, double-pushout approach to graph transformation [9, 7].

Derivation traces are equivalence classes of derivations with respect to two equivalences: a suitable refinement of the isomorphism relation (which makes use of *standard isomorphisms* to guarantee the concatenability of traces); and the *shift* equivalence, relating derivations that differ only for the order in which independent direct derivations are performed. Thus the concurrent semantics is obtained by collecting in equivalence classes all derivations that are conceptually indistinguishable. *Graph processes* are for graph grammars what deterministic, non-sequential processes [10] are for P/T Petri nets. A graph process of a graph grammar $\mathcal{G}$ is an "occurrence grammar" $\mathcal{O}$, i.e., a grammar satisfying suitable aciclicity constraints, equipped with a mapping from $\mathcal{O}$ to $\mathcal{G}$. This mapping is used to associate to the derivations in $\mathcal{O}$ corresponding derivations in $\mathcal{G}$, which can be shown to be *shift*-equivalent. Therefore a process can be regarded as an abstract representation of a class of *shift*-equivalent derivations, starting from the start graph of a grammar: as such it plays a rôle similar to *canonical derivations* [11]. The paper provides a bridge between processes and traces by introducing *concatenable graph processes*, which enrich processes with some additional information needed to be able to concatenate them, and showing that they are in bijective correspondence with *concatenable linear derivation traces*, a slight variation of the traces of [5].

The paper is structured as follows. Section 2 introduces the basics of *typed graph grammars* following the double pushout approach, and defines the category of *concatenable linear derivation traces*. After recalling in Section 3 the basics of graph processes as proposed in [6], Section 4 introduces the key notion of *concatenable graph process* and the corresponding category. Section 5 presents the main result of the paper, i.e., the fact that the category of concatenable linear derivation traces is isomorphic to the category of concatenable processes. In Section 6, exploiting the main result, we present a quite intuitive characterization of the configurations and events of the event structure of a grammar, as defined in [5], in terms of suitable classes of processes. Finally, Section 7 suggests some further directions of investigation.

2 Typed Graph Grammars

In this section we review the basic definitions about typed graph grammars as introduced in [6], following the algebraic double pushout approach [9]. Then a category $\mathbf{LTr}[\mathcal{G}]$ of concatenable linear derivation traces of a grammar $\mathcal{G}$ is introduced, by reformulating, in the typed framework, some notions of [5].

Recall that a *(directed, unlabelled) graph* is a tuple $G = \langle N, E, s, t \rangle$, where N is a finite set of *nodes*, E is a finite set of *arcs*, and $s, t : E \to N$ are the *source* and *target* functions. Sometimes we will denote by N_G and E_G the set of nodes and arcs of a graph G. A *graph morphism* $f : G \to G'$ is a pair of functions

$f = \langle f_N : N \to N', f_E : E \to E' \rangle$ such that $f_N \circ s = s' \circ f_E$ and $f_N \circ t = t' \circ f_E$; it is an *isomorphism* if both f_N and f_E are bijections; moreover, an *abstract graph* $[G]$ is an isomorphism class of graphs, i.e., $[G] = \{H \mid H \simeq G\}$. An *automorphism* of G is an isomorphism $h : G \to G$. The category having graphs as objects and graph morphisms as arrows is called **Graph**.

A typed graph, as introduced in [6], is a pair $\langle G, t_G \rangle$, where G is a graph and $t_G : G \to TG$ is a graph morphism, typing nodes and arcs of G over elements of a structure TG that is itself a graph. The category **TG-Graph** of graphs typed over a graph TG of types, is the comma category (**Graph** $\downarrow TG$).

Definition 1 (typed graph grammar). A *(TG-typed graph) production* is a span $(L \stackrel{l}{\leftarrow} K \stackrel{r}{\rightarrow} R)$ of injective typed graph morphisms. The typed graphs L, K, and R are called the *left-hand side*, the *interface*, and the *right-hand side* of the production. A *(TG-typed) graph grammar* $\mathcal{G}$ is a tuple $\langle TG, G_s, P, \pi \rangle$, where G_s is the *start (typed) graph*, P is a set of *production names*, and π maps each production name in P into a graph production. Sometimes we write $q : (L \stackrel{l}{\leftarrow} K \stackrel{r}{\rightarrow} R)$ for $\pi(q) = (L \stackrel{l}{\leftarrow} K \stackrel{r}{\rightarrow} R)$.

Since in this paper we work only with typed notions, when clear from the context we omit the word "typed" and the typing morphisms. Moreover, we will consider only *consuming* grammars, namely grammars where for each production $q : (L \stackrel{l}{\leftarrow} K \stackrel{r}{\rightarrow} R)$, morphism l is not surjective. This corresponds to the requirement of having non-empty preconditions in the case of Petri nets.

Definition 2 ((linear) direct derivation). Given a typed graph G, a production $q : (L \stackrel{l}{\leftarrow} K \stackrel{r}{\rightarrow} R)$, and an *occurrence* (i.e., a typed graph morphism) $g : L \to G$, a *(linear) direct derivation δ from G to H using q (based on g)* exists if and only if the diagram below can be constructed, where both squares are required to be pushouts in **TG-Graph**.

$$
\begin{array}{cccccc}
q: & L & \xleftarrow{\ l\ } & K & \xrightarrow{\ r\ } & R \\
 & \downarrow g & & \downarrow k & & \downarrow h \\
 & G & \xleftarrow[\ b\ ]{} & D & \xrightarrow[\ d\ ]{} & H
\end{array}
$$

In this case, D is called the *context* graph, and we write either $\delta : G \Rightarrow_q H$ or $\delta : G \stackrel{\langle g,k,h,b,d \rangle}{\Longrightarrow_q} H$, indicating explicitly all the involved morphisms. Since pushouts are defined only up to isomorphism, given isomorphisms $\kappa : G' \to G$ and $\nu : H \to H'$, also $G' \stackrel{\langle \kappa^{-1} \circ g,k,h,\kappa^{-1} \circ b,d \rangle}{\Longrightarrow_q} H$ and $G \stackrel{\langle g,k,h \circ \nu,b,d \circ \nu \rangle}{\Longrightarrow_q} H'$ are direct derivations, that we denote respectively by $\kappa \cdot \delta$ and $\delta \cdot \nu$.

Informally, the rewriting step removes (the image of) the left-hand side from the graph G and substitutes it by (the image of) the right-hand side R. The interface K (common part of L and R) specifies what is preserved.

Definition 3 ((linear) derivations). A *(linear) derivation* over $\mathcal{G}$ is a sequence of (linear) direct derivations (over $\mathcal{G}$) $\rho = \{G_{i-1} \Rightarrow_{q_{i-1}} G_i\}_{i \in \underline{n}}$, where $\underline{n}$ denotes the set of natural numbers $\{1, \ldots, n\}$. The derivation is written $\rho : G_0 \Rightarrow^*_{\mathcal{G}} G_n$ or simply $\rho : G_0 \Rightarrow^* G_n$. The graphs G_0 and G_n are called the *starting* and the *ending graph* of ρ, and are denoted by $\sigma(\rho)$ and $\tau(\rho)$, respectively. The derivation consisting of a single graph G (with $n = 0$) is called the *identity derivation* on G. The *length* $|\rho|$ of ρ is the number of direct derivations in ρ. Given two derivations ρ and ρ' such that $\tau(\rho) = \sigma(\rho')$, we define the *concrete* sequential composition $\rho; \rho' : \sigma(\rho) \Rightarrow^* \tau(\rho')$, as the derivation obtained by identifying $\tau(\rho)$ with $\sigma(\rho')$.

If $\rho : G \Rightarrow H$ is a linear derivation, with $|\rho| > 0$, and $\kappa : G' \to G$, $\nu : H \to H'$ are graph isomorphisms, then $\kappa \cdot \rho : G' \Rightarrow H$ and $\rho \cdot \nu : G \Rightarrow H'$ are defined in the expected way.

In the theory of the algebraic approach to graph grammars, it is natural to reason in terms of *abstract graphs* and *abstract derivations*, considering as equivalent graphs or derivations, respectively, which only differ for representation dependent details. However the definition of abstract derivations is a non-trivial task, if one wants to have a meaningful notion of sequential composition on such derivations. Roughly speaking, the difficulty is represented by the fact that two isomorphic graphs are, in general, related by more than one isomorphism, but to concatenate derivations keeping track of the flow of causality one must specify how the items of two isomorphic graphs should be identified. The problem is extensively treated in [4, 3], which propose a solution based on the choice of a uniquely determined isomorphism, named *standard isomorphism*, relating each pair of isomorphic graphs. Here we follow a slightly different technique: Inspired by the theory of Petri nets, and in particular by the notion of concatenable net process [8], and borrowing a technique proposed in [12], we choose for each class of isomorphic typed graphs a specific graph, named *canonical graph*, and we decorate the starting and ending graphs of a derivation with a pair of isomorphisms from the corresponding canonical graphs to such graphs. In such a way we are allowed to distinguish "equivalent"[1] elements in the starting and ending graphs of derivations and we can safely define their sequential composition.

Let Can denote the operation that associates to each (TG-typed) graph its *canonical graph*, thus satisfying $Can(G) \simeq G$ and if $G \simeq G'$ then $Can(G) = Can(G')$. The construction of the canonical graph can be performed by adapting to our slightly different framework the ideas of [12].

Definition 4 (decorated derivation). A *decorated derivation* $\psi : G_0 \Rightarrow^* G_n$ is a triple $\langle m, \rho, M \rangle$, where $\rho : G_0 \Rightarrow^* G_n$ is a derivation and $m : Can(G_0) \to G_0$, $M : Can(G_n) \to G_n$ are isomorphisms. We define $\sigma(\psi) = Can(\sigma(\rho))$, $\tau(\psi) = Can(\tau(\rho))$ and $|\psi| = |\rho|$. The derivation is called *proper* if $|\psi| > 0$.

Definition 5 (sequential composition). Let $\psi = \langle m, \rho, M \rangle$, $\psi' = \langle m', \rho', M' \rangle$ be two decorated derivations such that $\tau(\psi) = \sigma(\psi')$. Their *sequential composition* $\psi; \psi'$, is defined, if ψ and ψ' are proper, as $\langle m, \rho \cdot M^{-1}; m' \cdot \rho', M' \rangle$. Otherwise,

[1] With "equivalent" we mean here two items related by an automorphism of the graph, that are, in absence of further informations, indistinguishable.

if $|\psi| = 0$ then $\psi;\psi' = \langle m' \circ M^{-1} \circ m, \rho', M' \rangle$, and similarly, if $|\psi'| = 0$ then $\psi;\psi' = \langle m, \rho, M \circ m' \circ M^{-1} \rangle$.

The abstraction equivalence identifies derivations that differ only in representation details. As for $\equiv^{sh}$ and $\equiv^{c}$, introduced in the following, such equivalence is a reformulation, in our setting, of the equivalences defined in [5].

Definition 6 (abstraction equivalence). Let $\psi = \langle m, \rho, M \rangle$, $\psi' = \langle m', \rho', M' \rangle$ be two decorated derivations, with $\rho : G_0 \Rightarrow^* G_n$ and $\rho' : G'_0 \Rightarrow^* G'_{n'}$ (whose i^{th} step is depicted in the low rows of Fig. 1). Then they are *abstraction equivalent* if $n = n'$, $q_{i-1} = q'_{i-1}$ for all $i \in \underline{n}$, and there exists a family of isomorphisms $\{\theta_{X_i} : X_i \to X'_i \mid X \in \{G, D\},\ i \in \underline{n}\} \cup \{\theta_{G_0}\}$, between corresponding graphs in the two derivations, such that (1) the isomorphisms relating the starting and ending graphs commute with the decorations, i.e. $\theta_{G_0} \circ m = m'$ and $\theta_{G_n} \circ M = M'$; (2) the resulting diagram (step i is represented in Fig. 1) commutes.
Equivalence classes of decorated derivations w.r.t. $\equiv^{abs}$ are called *abstract derivations* and are denoted by $[\psi]_{abs}$, where ψ is an element of the class.

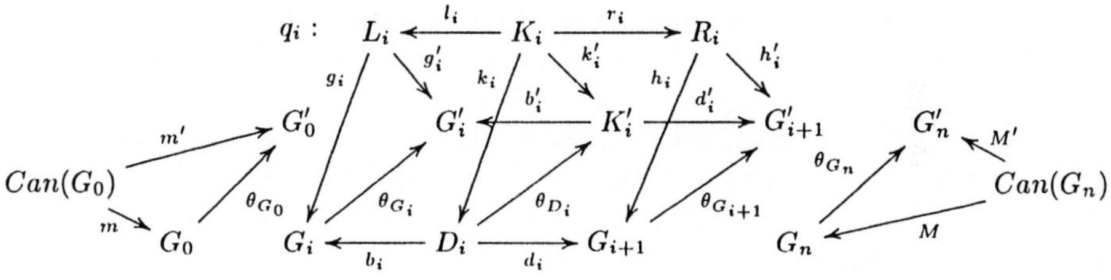

Fig. 1. Abstraction equivalence of decorated derivations.

From a concurrent perspective, two derivations which only differ for the order in which two independent direct derivations are applied, should not be distinguished. This is formalized by the classical shift equivalence on derivations.

Definition 7 (shift equivalence). Two direct derivations $\delta_1 : G \Rightarrow_{q_1,g_1} X$ and $\delta_2 : X \Rightarrow_{q_2,g_2} H$ (as in figure below) are *sequentially independent* if $g_2(L_2) \cap h_1(R_1) \subseteq g_2(l_2(K_2)) \cap h_1(r_1(K_1))$; in words, if the left-hand side of q_2 and the right-hand side of q_1 overlap only on items that are preserved by both steps.

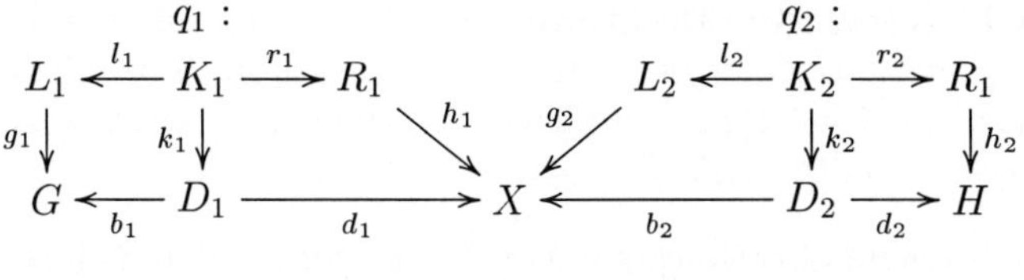

Given a derivation $\rho = G \Rightarrow_{q_1,g_1} X \Rightarrow_{q_2,g_2} H$, consisting of two sequentially independent direct derivations, there is a constructive way to obtain a new derivation $\rho' : G \Rightarrow_{q_2,g'_2} X' \Rightarrow_{q_1,g'_1} H$, where productions q_1 and q_2 are applied in the reverse order. We say that ρ' is a *switching* of ρ and we write $\rho \sim^{sh} \rho'$.

The *shift equivalence* $\equiv^{sh}$ on concrete derivations is the transitive and "context" closure of $\sim^{sh}$, i.e. the least equivalence, containing $\sim^{sh}$, such that if $\rho \equiv^{sh} \rho'$ then $\rho_1; \rho; \rho_3 \equiv^{sh} \rho_1; \rho'; \rho_3$. The same symbol denotes the equivalence on decorated derivations induced by $\equiv^{sh}$, i.e. $\langle m, \rho, M\rangle \equiv^{sh} \langle m, \rho', M\rangle$ if $\rho \equiv^{sh} \rho'$.

Definition 8 (ctc-equivalence). The *concatenable truly concurrent equivalence* (*ctc-equivalence*) $\equiv^{c}$ on derivations is the transitive closure of the union of the relations $\equiv^{abs}$ and $\equiv^{sh}$. Equivalence classes of decorated derivations with respect to $\equiv^{c}$ are denoted as $[\psi]_c$ and are called *concatenable linear (derivation) traces.*

It is possible to prove that sequential composition of decorated derivations lifts to composition of linear derivation traces.

Definition 9 (category of concatenable linear traces). The *category of concatenable linear traces* of a grammar $\mathcal{G}$, denoted by $\mathbf{LTr}[\mathcal{G}]$, has abstract graphs as objects and concatenable linear traces as arrows.

In [5] a category $\mathbf{Tr}[\mathcal{G}]$ of concatenable (parallel) traces is defined considering possibly parallel derivations and using standard isomorphisms instead of decorations. More precisely, a class of standard isomorphisms is fixed and abstraction equivalence on (parallel) derivations is defined as in Definition 6, but replacing condition 1 with the requirement for the isomorphisms θ_0 and θ_n, relating the starting and ending graphs, to be standard. Then the concatenable truly concurrent equivalence on parallel derivations is again defined as the least equivalence containing the abstraction and shift equivalences. Despite of these differences, the two approaches lead to the same category of traces.

Proposition 10. *The category of concatenable parallel traces* $\mathbf{Tr}[\mathcal{G}]$ *and the category* $\mathbf{LTr}[\mathcal{G}]$ *of concatenable linear traces are isomorphic.*

3 Graph Processes

Graph processes, introduced in [6], generalize the notion of (deterministic, non-sequential) process of a P/T net [10] to graph grammars. A graph process of a graph grammar $\mathcal{G}$ is an "occurrence grammar" $\mathcal{O}$, i.e., a grammar satisfying suitable acyclicity constraints, equipped with a mapping from $\mathcal{O}$ to $\mathcal{G}$.

Definition 11 (strongly safe grammar). A *strongly safe* graph grammar is a grammar $\mathcal{G} = \langle TG, G_s, P, \pi\rangle$ such that each graph H reachable from the start graph (i.e., $G_s \Rightarrow^* H$) has an injective typing morphism. We denote with $\mathit{Elem}(\mathcal{G})$ the set $N_{TG} \cup E_{TG} \cup P$.

Without loss of generality, injective morphisms can be seen as inclusions. Thus sometimes we identify a graph $\langle G, m\rangle$, reachable in a strongly safe grammar, with the subgraph $m(G)$ of TG. In the following, L_q (resp. K_q, R_q) denotes the graph L (resp., K, R) of a production $q : (L \stackrel{l}{\leftarrow} K \stackrel{r}{\rightarrow} R)$. When interested in the typing we assume $L_q = \langle LG_q, tl_q\rangle$, $K_q = \langle KG_q, tk_q\rangle$ and $R_q = \langle RG_q, tr_q\rangle$.

Definition 12 (causal relation). Let $\mathcal{G} = \langle TG, G_s, P, \pi \rangle$ be a strongly safe grammar, let $q \in P$ be a production, and let $x \in N_{TG} \cup E_{TG}$ be any arc or node of the type graph TG. We say that q *consumes* x if $x \in tl_q(LG_q - KG_q)$, that q *creates* x if $x \in tr_q(RG_q - KG_q)$ and that q *preserves* x if $x \in tk_q(KG_q)$.[2]

The *causal relation* of $\mathcal{G}$ is given by the structure $\langle Elem(\mathcal{G}), \leq \rangle$, where $\leq$ is the transitive and reflexive closure of the relation $<$ defined by the following clauses: for any node or arc x in TG, and for productions $q_1, q_2 \in P$

1. $x < q_1$ if q_1 consumes x;
2. $q_1 < x$ if q_1 creates x;
3. $q_1 < q_2$ if q_1 creates x and q_2 preserves x, or q_1 preserves x and q_2 consumes x.

The first two clauses of the definition of relation $<$ are obvious. The third one formalizes the fact that if an item is generated by q_1 and it is preserved by q_2, then q_2 cannot be applied before q_1, and, symmetrically, if an item is preserved by q_1 and consumed by q_2, then q_1 cannot be applied after q_2.

Definition 13 (occurrence grammar). An *(deterministic) occurrence grammar* is a strongly safe graph grammar $\mathcal{O} = \langle TG, G_s, P, \pi \rangle$ such that

1. its causal relation $\leq$ is a partial order, and for any $n \in N_{TG}, e \in E_{TG}$ such that $n = s(e)$ or $n = t(e)$, and for any $q \in P$, we have (i) if $q \leq n$, then $q \leq e$ and (ii) if $n \leq q$, then $e \leq q$;
2. consider the set Min of minimal elements of $\langle Elem(\mathcal{G}), \leq \rangle$ and $Min(\mathcal{O}) = \langle Min \cap N_{TG}, Min \cap E_{TG}, s_{|Min \cap N_{TG}}, t_{|Min \cap N_{TG}} \rangle$; then $G_s = Min(\mathcal{O})$;
3. for all $q \in P$, q satisfies the identification condition [9], i.e. there is no $x, y \in LG_q$ such that $tl_q(x) = tl_q(y)$ and $y \notin l(KG_q)$.
4. for all $x \in N_{TG} \cup E_{TG}$, x is consumed by at most one production in P, and it is created by at most one production in P.

For an occurrence grammar $\mathcal{O}$, denoted by Max the set of maximal elements in $\langle Elem(\mathcal{O}), \leq \rangle$, let $Max(\mathcal{O}) = \langle Max \cap N_{TG}, Max \cap E_{TG}, s_{|Max \cap N_{TG}}, t_{|Max \cap N_{TG}} \rangle$. Note that, since the start graph of an occurrence grammar $\mathcal{O}$ is determined as $Min(\mathcal{O})$, we often do not mention it explicitly.

Definition 14 (reachable sets). Let $\mathcal{O} = \langle TG, P, \pi \rangle$ be an occurrence grammar, and let $\langle P, \leq \rangle$ be the restriction of the causal relation to the productions of $\mathcal{O}$. For any $\leq$-left-closed $P' \subseteq P$, the *reachable set* associated to P' is the set of nodes and arcs $S_{P'} \subseteq N_{TG} \cup E_{TG}$ defined as

$$x \in S_{P'} \quad \text{iff} \quad \forall q \in P \,.\, (x \leq q \Rightarrow q \notin P') \wedge (x \geq q \Rightarrow q \in P').$$

We denote by $G(S_{P'})$ the structure $\langle S_{P'} \cap E_{TG}, S_{P'} \cap N_{TG}, s_{|S_{P'} \cap E_{TG}}, t_{|S_{P'} \cap E_{TG}} \rangle$.

For any reachable set $S_{P'}$, $G(S_{P'})$ is a graph and it is reachable from $Min(\mathcal{O})$ with a derivation which applies exactly once every production in P', in any order consistent with $\leq$.

[2] With abuse of notation, in $LG_q - KG_q$ or $RG_q - KG_q$ graphs are considered as sets of nodes and arcs.

As a consequence, in particular $Min(\mathcal{O}) = G(S_\emptyset)$ and $Max(\mathcal{O}) = G(S_P)$ are well-defined subgraphs of TG and $Min(\mathcal{O}) \Rightarrow_P^* Max(\mathcal{O})$, using all productions in P exactly once, in any order consistent with $\leq$. This makes clear why a graph process of a grammar $\mathcal{G}$, that we are going to define as an occurrence grammar plus a mapping to the original grammar, can be seen as a representative of a set of derivations of $\mathcal{G}$, where only independent steps may be switched.

Definition 15 (process). Let $\mathcal{G} = \langle TG, G_s, P, \pi\rangle$ be a typed graph grammar. A *process* p for $\mathcal{G}$ is a pair $\langle \mathcal{O}, \phi\rangle$, where $\mathcal{O} = \langle TG', P', \pi'\rangle$ is an occurrence grammar and $\phi = \langle mg, mp, \iota\rangle$, where (1) $mg : TG' \to TG$ is a graph morphism; (2) $mp : P' \to P$ is a function mapping each production $q' : (L' \leftarrow K' \to R')$ in P' to an isomorphic production $q = mp(q') : (L \leftarrow K \to R)$ in P and (3) ι is a function mapping each production $q' \in P'$ to a triple of isomorphisms $\iota(q') = \langle \iota^L(q') : L \to L', \iota^K(q') : K \to K', \iota^R(q') : R \to R'\rangle$, making the diagram in Fig. 2.(a) commute.
We denote with $Min(p)$ and $Max(p)$ the graphs $Min(\mathcal{O})$ and $Max(\mathcal{O})$ typed over TG by the corresponding restrictions of mg.

Notice that, unlike [6], we do not force processes to start from the *start graph* of the grammar. This is needed to define a reasonable notion of concatenable process.

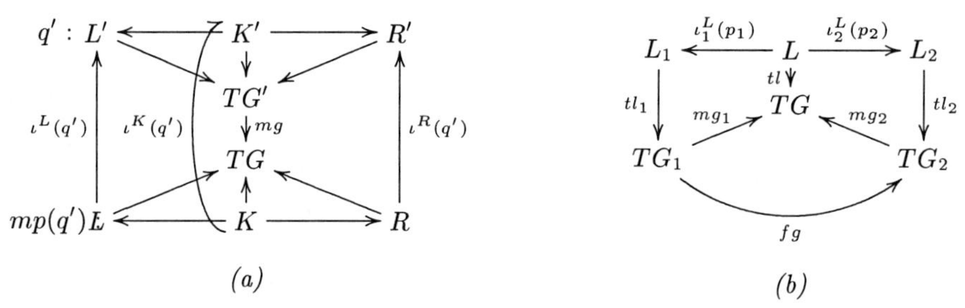

Fig. 2. Processes and isomorphisms of processes

Definition 16 (isomorphism of processes). Let $\mathcal{G} = \langle TG, G_s, P, \pi\rangle$ be a typed graph grammar and let $p_j = \langle \mathcal{O}_j, \phi_j\rangle$, with $\mathcal{O}_j = \langle TG_j, P_j, \pi_j\rangle$ and $\phi_j = \langle mg_j, mp_j, \iota_j\rangle$, for $j = 1, 2$, be two processes of $\mathcal{G}$. An *isomorphism* between p_1 and p_2 is a pair $\langle fg, fp\rangle : p_1 \to p_2$ such that

- $fg : \langle TG_1, mg_1\rangle \to \langle TG_2, mg_2\rangle$ is an isomorphism (of TG-typed graphs);
- $fp : P_1 \to P_2$ is a bijection such that $mp_1 = mp_2 \circ fp$;
- for each $q_1 : (L_1 \leftarrow K_1 \to R_1)$ in P_1, $q_2 = fp(q_1) : (L_2 \leftarrow K_2 \to R_2)$ in P_2, $q = mp_1(q_1) = mp_2(q_2) : (L \leftarrow K \to R)$ in P, the diagram in Fig. 2.(b) and the analogous ones for the interfaces and the right-hand sides, commute.

To indicate that p_1 and p_2 are *isomorphic* we write $p_1 \cong p_2$. This definition is slightly more restrictive than the original one in [6], since, guided by the notion of abstraction equivalence for decorated derivations, we require the commutativity of the diagrams like that in Fig. 2.(b) w.r.t. to fixed isomorphisms $\iota_j^L(p_j), \iota_j^K(p_j), \iota_j^R(p_j)$, which are here part of the processes, and not w.r.t. generic isomorphisms as in [6].

4 Concatenable Processes

Since processes represent (concurrent) computations and express explicitly the causal dependencies existing between single rewriting steps, it is natural to ask for a notion of sequential composition of processes consistent with causal dependencies. When trying to define such notion, the same problem described for traces arises, and we solve it in the same way, i.e., by decorating the source $Min(p)$ and the target $Max(p)$ of the process p with isomorphisms from the corresponding canonical graphs. Such isomorphisms play the same rôle of the ordering on maximal and minimal places of *concatenable processes* in Petri net theory [8]. In this view our *concatenable* graph processes are related to the graph processes of [6] in the same way as the concatenable processes of [8] are related to the classical Goltz-Reisig processes for P/T nets [10]. Essentially the same technique has been used in [12] to make *dynamic graphs* concatenable.

Definition 17 (concatenable process). Let $\mathcal{G} = \langle TG, G_s, P, \pi \rangle$ be a typed grammar. A *concatenable process (c-process)* for $\mathcal{G}$ is a triple $cp = \langle m, p, M \rangle$, where p is a process and $m : Can(Min(p)) \to Min(p)$, $M : Can(Max(p)) \to Max(p)$ are isomorphisms (of TG-typed graphs). We denote with $Min(cp)$ and $Max(cp)$ the graphs $Min(p)$ and $Max(p)$.

An *isomorphism* between two c-processes $cp_1 = \langle m_1, p_1, M_1 \rangle$ and $cp_2 = \langle m_2, p_2, M_2 \rangle$ is an isomorphism of processes $\langle fg, fp \rangle : p_1 \to p_2$ that "commutes" with the decorations, i.e., such that $fg \circ m_1 = m_2$ and $fg \circ M_1 = M_2$ (where fg denotes the restrictions of fg itself to $Min(cp_1)$ and $Max(cp_1)$ respectively). To indicate that cp_1 and cp_2 are *isomorphic* we write $cp_1 \cong cp_2$. An isomorphism class of c-processes is called *abstract c-process* and denoted by $[cp]$, where cp is a member of the class.

Given two c-processes cp_1 and cp_2 such that $Max(cp_1) \simeq Min(cp_2)$, we can concatenate them by gluing the *Max* graph of the first one with the *Min* graph of the second one. Formally, the type graph of the resulting process is obtained via a pushout construction and thus it is defined only up to isomorphism. However, when lifted to the abstract setting the operation turns out to be deterministic.

Definition 18 (sequential composition). Let $\mathcal{G} = \langle TG, G_s, P, \pi \rangle$ be a typed graph grammar and let $[cp_1]$ and $[cp_2]$ be two abstract c-processes for $\mathcal{G}$ (with $cp_j = \langle m_j, p_j, M_j \rangle$, $p_j = \langle \mathcal{O}_j, \phi_j \rangle = \langle \langle TG_j, P_j, \pi_j \rangle, \langle mg_j, mp_j, \iota_j \rangle \rangle$), such that $Max(cp_1) \simeq Min(cp_2)$. The *sequential composition* of $[cp_1]$ and $[cp_2]$, denoted by $[cp_1]; [cp_2]$ is the isomorphism class $[cp]$ of the c-process:

$$cp = \langle m, p, M \rangle,$$

where $p = \langle \mathcal{O}', \phi' \rangle = \langle \langle G'_s, TG', P', \pi' \rangle, \langle mg', mp' \rangle \rangle$, is defined as follows. The type graph TG', with the morphism $mg' : TG' \to TG$, is given by the following pushout diagram (in **TG-Graph**):

$$\begin{array}{ccccccc} Can(Max(cp_1)) & \xrightarrow{M_1} & Max(cp_1) & \hookrightarrow & TG_1 & \xrightarrow{g_1} & \\ \| & & & & & & TG' \\ Can(Max(cp_2)) & \xrightarrow[m_2]{} & Max(cp_2) & \hookrightarrow & TG_2 & \xrightarrow{g_2} & \end{array}$$

The set of production names is $P' = P_1 \uplus P_2$, with π' and mp' defined in the expected way. Finally $m = g_1 \circ m_1$, $M' = g_2 \circ M_2$ and $G'_s = g_1(Min(cp_1))$.

Definition 19 (category of (abstract) c-processes). Given a typed graph grammar $\mathcal{G} = \langle TG, G_s, P, \pi \rangle$, we denote by $\mathbf{CP}[\mathcal{G}]$ the category of *(abstract)* c-processes having abstract graphs typed over TG as objects and abstract c-processes as arrows.

5 Relating traces and processes

This section shows that the semantic model based on concatenable linear traces and the one based on concatenable graph processes are essentially the same. More formally we prove that the category $\mathbf{LTr}[\mathcal{G}]$ of concatenable linear traces (Definition 9) is isomorphic to the category of abstract c-processes $\mathbf{CP}[\mathcal{G}]$.

First, given an abstract c-process $[cp]$ we can obtain a derivation by "executing" the productions of cp in any order compatible with the causal order.

Definition 20 (from processes to traces). Let $\mathcal{G} = \langle TG, G_s, P, \pi \rangle$ be a typed graph grammar and let $[cp]$ be an abstract c-process of $\mathcal{G}$, where $cp = \langle m, p, M \rangle$, $p = \langle \mathcal{O}, \phi \rangle = \langle \langle TG', P', \pi' \rangle, \langle mg, mp, \iota \rangle \rangle$. Let $q'_0, \ldots, q'_{n-1}$ be an enumeration of the productions of P' compatible with the causal order of cp.

We associate to $[cp]$ the concatenable linear trace $\mathcal{L}_A([cp]) = [\psi]_c$, with

$$\psi = \langle m, \rho, M \rangle, \quad \text{where } \rho = \{G_{i-1} \Rightarrow_{q_{i-1}, g_{i-1}} G_i\}_{i \in \underline{n}}$$

such that $G_0 = Min(cp)$, $G_n = Max(cp)$, and for each $i = 0, \ldots, n-1$

- $q_i = mp(q'_i)$;
- $G_{i+1} = G(S_{\{q'_0, \ldots, q'_i\}})$, i.e. G_{i+1} is the subgraph of the type graph TG' of the process determined by the reachable set $S_{\{q'_0, \ldots, q'_i\}}$, typed by mg;
- each derivation step $G_i \Rightarrow_{q_i, g_i} G_{i+1}$ is as in Fig. 3.(a), where unlabelled arrows represent inclusions.

It can be shown that the mapping $\mathcal{L}_A$ is well defined. Moreover it preserves sequential composition of processes and identities, and thus it can be lifted to a functor $\mathcal{L}_A : \mathbf{CP}[\mathcal{G}] \to \mathbf{LTr}[\mathcal{G}]$ which acts as identity on objects.

The backward step, from concatenable linear traces to abstract c-processes, is performed via a colimit construction that, applied to a derivation in the trace, essentially constructs the type graph as a copy of the starting graph plus the items produced during the rewriting process. Productions of the process are occurrences of production applications.

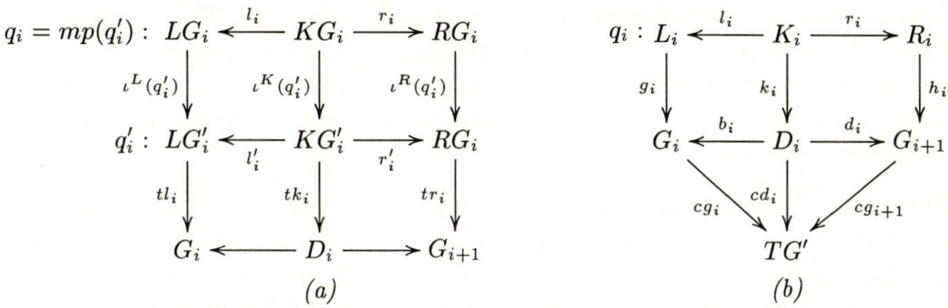

Fig. 3. From abstract c-processes to concatenable linear traces and backward.

Definition 21 (from traces to processes). Let $\mathcal{G} = \langle TG, G_s, P, \pi \rangle$ be a typed graph grammar and let $[\psi]_c$ be a concatenable linear trace, with $\psi = \langle m, \rho, M \rangle$. We associate to $[\psi]_c$ an abstract c-process $\mathcal{P}_A([\psi]_c) = [cp]$, with $cp = \langle m', p, M' \rangle$, $p = \langle \mathcal{O}, \phi \rangle = \langle \langle TG', P', \pi' \rangle, \langle mg, mp, \iota \rangle \rangle$, such that:

- $\langle TG', mg \rangle$ is the colimit object (in category **TG-Graph**) of the diagram representing derivation ψ, as depicted (for a single derivation step and without typing morphisms) in Fig. 3.(b);
- $P' = \{\langle q_i, i \rangle \mid q_i$ is used in step i, for $i = 0, \ldots, n-1\}$, and for all $i = 0, \ldots, n-1$, referring to Fig. 3.(b), $\pi'(\langle q_i, i \rangle) = (\langle LG_i, cg_i \circ g_i \rangle \overset{l_i}{\leftarrow} \langle KG_i, cd_i \circ k_i \rangle \overset{r_i}{\rightarrow} \langle RG_i, cg_{i+1} \circ h_i \rangle)$, $mp(\langle q_i, i \rangle) = q_i$ and $\iota(\langle q_i, i \rangle) = \langle id_{L_i}, id_{K_i}, id_{R_i} \rangle$.
- $m' = cg_0 \circ m$ and $M' = cg_n \circ M$;

It is possible to prove that $\mathcal{P}_A : \mathbf{Abs}[\mathcal{G}] \to \mathbf{LCP}[\mathcal{G}]$, obtained extending $\mathcal{P}_A$ as identity on objects, is a well defined functor, and that $\mathcal{L}_A$ and $\mathcal{P}_A$ are inverse each other.

Theorem 22. *Let $\mathcal{G}$ be a graph grammar. Then $\mathcal{L}_A : \mathbf{CP}[\mathcal{G}] \to \mathbf{LTr}[\mathcal{G}]$ and $\mathcal{P}_A : \mathbf{LTr}[\mathcal{G}] \to \mathbf{CP}[\mathcal{G}]$ are inverse each other, establishing an isomorphism of categories.*

6 Processes and events

The category of concatenable traces $\mathbf{Tr}[\mathcal{G}]$ is used in [5] to define the finitary prime algebraic domain (hereinafter *domain*) and the *event structure* of a grammar $\mathcal{G}$. Elements of the domain are suitable classes of concatenable traces. Proposition 10 implies that the same structure can be obtained starting from category $\mathbf{LTr}[\mathcal{G}]$.

Theorem 23. *For any graph grammar $\mathcal{G} = \langle TG, G_s, P, \pi \rangle$ the comma category $[G_s] \downarrow \mathbf{LTr}[\mathcal{G}]$ is a preorder $\mathbf{PreDom}[\mathcal{G}]$, i.e., there is at most one arrow between any pair of objects. Moreover the ideal completion of $\mathbf{PreDom}[\mathcal{G}]$ is a domain, denoted by $\mathbf{Dom}[\mathcal{G}]$.*

By results in [17], $\mathbf{Dom}[\mathcal{G}]$ is the domain of configurations of a uniquely determined PES $\mathbf{ES}[\mathcal{G}]$, which is proposed as the truly concurrent semantics of the grammar. Here, thanks to the close relation existing between concatenable processes and concatenable linear traces, stated in Theorem 22, we can provide a nice characterization of the finite configurations (finite elements of the domain $\mathbf{Dom}[\mathcal{G}]$) and of the events of $\mathbf{ES}[\mathcal{G}]$. The result resembles the analogous correspondence existing for P/T nets and is based on a similar notion of left concatenable process.

Definition 24 (abstract left c-process). Two c-processes cp_1 and cp_2 are *left isomorphic*, denoted by $cp_1 \equiv_l cp_2$, if there exists a pair of functions $f = \langle fg, fp \rangle$ satisfying all the requirements of Definition 16, but, possibly, the commutativity of the right triangle of Fig. 2. An *abstract left c-process* is a class of left isomorphic c-processes $[cp]_l$. It is *initial* if $Min(cp) \simeq G_s$. It is *prime* if the causal order $\leq$ of cp, restricted to the set P of its productions, has a maximum element.

The following result has a clear intuitive meaning if one think of the productions of (the occurrence grammar of) a process as instances of production applications in the original grammar $\mathcal{G}$, and therefore as possible events in $\mathcal{G}$.

Theorem 25. *There is a one to one correspondence between:*

1. *initial left c-processes and finite elements of* $\mathbf{Dom}[\mathcal{G}]$*;*
2. *prime initial left c-processes and elements of* $\mathbf{ES}[\mathcal{G}]$*.*

7 Conclusions

As recalled in the introduction, typed graph grammars can be seen as a proper generalization of P/T Petri nets and many concepts and results in the theory of concurrency for graph grammars manifest an evident similarity with corresponding notions for nets. The deepening and formalization of this analogy represents a direction for future research. In particular, we intend to continue the investigation of the relationship among the various notions of graph and net processes. Furthermore we are trying to extend to graph grammars the unfolding construction of [17, 13] (which generates the event structure associated to a net via the unfolded occurrence net) following, for what concern the handling of asymmetric conflicts, the ideas presented in [1]. Preliminary considerations suggest that graph processes of [6] are in precise correspondence with Goltz-Reisig processes [10]. On the other hand, our concatenable graph processes are not the exact counterpart of the concatenable processes of [8]. This is due to the fact that we have been mainly guided by the aim of unifying the various existing semantics for graph grammars: the equivalence with [5] has been formally proved in this paper and we are confident that a similar result can be obtained for the semantics proposed by Schied in [16]. Furthermore many variations of concatenable processes in the theory of nets exists, enjoying different properties. For instance, the *decorated processes* [14] generate the same domain produced by the unfolding construction. We are convinced that our concatenable graph processes correspond to a slight refinement of such net processes and, therefore, that the equivalence result between the process and unfolding semantics can be extended to the graph rewriting setting.

References

1. P. Baldan, A. Corradini, and U. Montanari. An event structure semantics for P/T contextual nets: Asymmetric event structures. *FoSSaCS '98*, *LNCS* 1378, pp. 63–80. Springer, 1998.
2. A. Corradini. Concurrent Graph and Term Graph Rewriting. *CONCUR'96*, *LNCS* 1119, pp. 438–464. Springer, 1996.
3. A. Corradini, H. Ehrig, M. Löwe, U. Montanari, and F. Rossi. Abstract Graph Derivations in the Double-Pushout Approach. *Dagstuhl Seminar 9301 on Graph Transformations in Computer Science*, *LNCS* 776, pp. 86–103. Springer, 1994.
4. A. Corradini, H. Ehrig, M. Löwe, U. Montanari, and F. Rossi. Note on standard representation of graphs and graph derivations. *Dagstuhl Seminar 9301 on Graph Transformations in Computer Science*, *LNCS* 776, pp. 104–118. Springer, 1994.
5. A. Corradini, H. Ehrig, M. Löwe, U. Montanari, and F. Rossi. An Event Structure Semantics for Graph Grammars with Parallel Productions. *5th International Workshop on Graph Grammars and their Application to Computer Science*, *LNCS* 1073. Springer, 1996.
6. A. Corradini, U. Montanari, and F. Rossi. Graph processes. *Fundamenta Informaticae*, 26:241–265, 1996.
7. A. Corradini, U. Montanari, F. Rossi, H. Ehrig, R. Heckel, and M. Löwe. Algebraic Approaches to Graph Transformation I: Basic Concepts and Double Pushout Approach. In [15].
8. P. Degano, J. Meseguer, and U. Montanari. Axiomatizing the algebra of net computations and processes. *Acta Informatica*, 33:641–647, 1996.
9. H. Ehrig. Tutorial introduction to the algebraic approach of graph-grammars. *3rd International Workshop on Graph-Grammars and Their Application to Computer Science*, *LNCS* 291, pp. 3–14. Springer, 1987.
10. U. Golz and W. Reisig. The non-sequential behaviour of Petri nets. *Information and Control*, 57:125–147, 1983.
11. H.-J. Kreowski. *Manipulation von Graphmanipulationen.* PhD thesis, Technische Universität Berlin, 1977.
12. A. Maggiolo-Schettini and J. Winkowski. Dynamic Graphs. In *MFCS'96*, *LNCS* 1113, pp. 431–442, 1996.
13. J. Meseguer, U. Montanari, and V. Sassone. On the semantics of Petri nets. In *CONCUR '92*, *LNCS* 630, pp. 286–301. Springer, 1992.
14. J. Meseguer, U. Montanari, and V. Sassone. Process versus unfolding semantics for Place/Transition Petri nets. *Theoret. Comput. Sci.*, 153(1-2):171–210, 1996.
15. G. Rozenberg, editor. *Handbook of Graph Grammars and Computing by Graph Transformation. Volume 1: Foundations.* World Scientific, 1997.
16. G. Schied. On relating Rewriting Systems and Graph Grammars to Event Structures. *Dagstuhl Seminar 9301 on Graph Transformations in Computer Science*, *LNCS* 776, pp. 326–340. Springer, 1994.
17. G. Winskel. Event Structures. In *Petri Nets: Applications and Relationships to Other Models of Concurrency*, *LNCS* 255, pp. 325–392. Springer, 1987.

Axioms for Contextual Net Processes*

F. Gadducci[1] and U. Montanari[2]

[1] Technical University of Berlin, Fach. 13 Informatik, gfabio@cs.tu-berlin.de.
[2] University of Pisa, Dipartimento di Informatica, ugo@di.unipi.it.

Abstract. In the classical theory of Petri nets, a *process* is an operational description of the behaviour of a net, which takes into account the causal links between transitions in a sequence of firing steps. In the categorical framework developed in [19, 11], processes of a P/T net are modeled as arrows of a suitable monoidal category: In this paper we lay the basis of a similar characterization for *contextual* P/T nets, that is, P/T nets extended with *read arcs*, which allows a transition to check for the presence of a token in a place, without consuming it.

1 Introduction

Petri nets [24] are probably the best studied and most used model for concurrent systems: Their range of applications covers a wide spectrum, from their use as a specification tool to their analysis as a suitable semantical domain. A recent extension to the classical model concerns a class of nets where transitions are able to check for the presence of a token in a place without actually consuming it. While the possibility of sensing for both presence *and absence* of a token yields very expressive nets equipped also with *inhibitory* arcs [14, 7, 4, 5], in the paper we focus our attention to nets extended with *read* arcs only, generically referred to as *contextual nets*, which have a richer theory and refer to several well-tailored applications. In fact, important constructions on ordinary nets can be extended to nets with read arcs, like those concerning non-sequential processes [22, 28] and event structures [1]. Moreover, these nets naturally model read-write access to shared memory, where readers are allowed to progress in parallel, with applications to transaction serializability in databases [25, 10], concurrent constraint programming [21, 3], asynchronous systems [27] and process algebras [20].

* Research partly supported by the EC TMR Network GETGRATS (General Theory of Graph Transformation Systems) through the Technical University of Berlin and the University of Pisa; by the Office of Naval Information Research Contracts N00014-95-C-0225 and N00014-96-C-0114; by the National Science Foundation Grant CCR-9633363; by the U.S. Army Contract DABT63-96-C-0096 (DARPA); and by the Information Technology Promotion Agency, Japan, as part of the Industrial Science and Technology Frontier Program "New Models for Software Architecture" sponsored by NEDO (New Energy and Industrial Technology Development Organization). Research carried out in part while the second author was on leave at Computer Science Laboratory, SRI International, Menlo Park, USA, and visiting scholar at Stanford University

The operational behaviour of Petri nets can be described either via firing sequences, or via non-sequential processes [13]. Even if tightly related, only the latter option fully exploits the ability of nets to describe concurrency. Processes are acyclic, deterministic safe nets whose transitions are occurrences of the transitions of the original net. A process thus defines a partial ordering of transition occurrences, and captures the abstract notion of concurrent computation, in the sense that all the firing sequences corresponding to linearizations of the partial ordering are considered equivalent. Most semantic and logic notions specifying the concurrent behavior of nets are based on the notion of process [23, 2].

Processes play an important role in the "Petri Nets are Monoids" approach to net theory [19, 11, 26]. In this approach, a net N is analogous to a signature Σ, and the symmetric monoidal category $\mathcal{P}(\mathcal{N})$ associated to N is analogous to the cartesian category $\mathcal{L}(\Sigma)$ of terms and substitutions freely generated by Σ. As the (tuples of) terms in $T_\Sigma(X)$ are the arrows of $\mathcal{L}(\Sigma)$, the processes[1] of N are the arrows of $\mathcal{P}(\mathcal{N})$. The construction of $\mathcal{P}(\mathcal{N})$ provides a concise, algebraic description of the concurrent operational semantics of P/T nets. Since $\mathcal{P}(\mathcal{N})$ can be finitely axiomatized [26], this construction provides a finite axiomatization of non-sequential processes. Moreover, the well-understood setting of monoidal categories allows for an easy comparison with related models, like linear logic [17].

The aim of this paper is to extend the above categorical approach to P/T nets with read arcs. Our results should enable a fully algebraic description and analysis of these nets and, as a consequence, of the concurrency paradigm based on shared memory they represent. To the best of our knowledge, the problem has been tackled only in [18]. The solution proposed there associates to a CP/T net N a monoidal category $\mathcal{P}'(\mathcal{N})$, where the monoid of objects is not freely generated from the class of places. Our solution is instead "more in line", so to say, with the approach, since the only axioms are on arrows: The results for processes of ordinary P/T nets can then be lifted to contextual processes.

The technical development presented in the paper is based on equipping a symmetric strict monoidal category with a transformation consisting of certain arrows, called *duplicators*. They are reminiscent of arrows of the same name which are obtained in cartesian categories as pairings of two instances of an identity. However they do not form a *natural* transformation as duplicators in cartesian categories. Besides duplicators, *gs-monoidal* categories [8] are equipped with *dischargers* and they differ from cartesian categories just for missing the naturality axioms on duplicators and dischargers. The arrows of the gs-monoidal category freely generated by a signature Σ represent the *term graphs* [8] on Σ. Symmetric strict monoidal categories equipped with duplicators (without naturality) are called *share* categories; *match-share*, if both them and their opposite are share categories. Those are the categories where processes of contextual nets live: The main result of the paper states that the category of processes of a contextual P/T net N is characterized as an inductively generated subcategory of the match-share category $\mathcal{CP}(\mathcal{N})$ associated via a free construction to N.

---

[1] Actually, a slightly extended version of the processes presented in [13], called *concatenable* processes, is needed to guarantee the uniqueness of sequential composition.

The paper is organized as follows. Section 2 defines contextual P/T nets and their processes, together with an algebra that allows for the derivation of all processes from some basic ones. Section 3 introduces symmetric monoidal categories and shows that the previously defined algebra of processes constitutes such a category. Match-share categories are then introduced. In Section 4 a lluf and faithful functor is defined from the category of processes of a net N to the match-share category $\mathcal{CP}(\mathcal{N})$ generated from N.

2 Contextual Nets Processes

Introduced in [25], along the line of the work for C/E systems [22], *contextual place/transition nets* are an extension of classical place/transitions (P/T) nets, in which a new relation, called *context relation*, is defined. A *read arc* between a place s and a transition t means that at least one token in s is needed in order to enable the firing of t and, when t is fired, no token in s is consumed.

Definition 1 (CP/T net). *A* contextual P/T net *(simply,* CP/T net*) N is a four-tuple (S_N, T_N, F_N, C_N) such that S_N and T_N are finite sets, whose elements are called* places *and* transitions, *respectively; $F_N = F_{1N} \cup F_{2N}$, and*

$$F_{1N} \subseteq (S_N \times T_N) \qquad F_{2N} \subseteq (T_N \times S_N) \qquad C_N \subseteq S_N \times T_N$$
$$F_{1N} \cap C_N = F_{2N} \cap (C_N)^{-1} = \emptyset$$

F_N and C_N are called the flow *and the* context relation, *respectively, while the "disjointness" property they must satisfy is called* no interference. □

For the sake of simplicity, we restrict our attention to the class of nets where the flow and the context relation are just partial functions: That is, in Petri nets terminology, in which each arc has weight 1. Hence, the no interference condition ensures us that no transition reads or consumes/creates more than one token from each place. Those restrictions would not affect the results of this chapter, but they simplify the categorical semantics described in Section 4.

In the following, we usually identify the various components of a net through their index. As for P/T nets, we associate a *pre-set* and a *post-set* with each transition $t \in T$, together with an additional third set, called *context-set.*

Definition 2 (pre-set, post-set and context-set). *Given a CP/T net N, we define for each $t \in T_N$ the sets*

$$^{\bullet}t = \{s \in S_N \mid (s,t) \in F_{1N}\} \qquad t^{\bullet} = \{s \in S_N \mid (t,s) \in F_{2N}\}$$
$$\widehat{t} = \{s \in S_N \mid (s,t) \in C_N\}$$

denoted respectively the pre-set, post-set *and* context-set *of t.* □

The no interference condition can now be reformulated as $^{\bullet}t \cap \widehat{t} = t^{\bullet} \cap \widehat{t} = \emptyset$ for each transition t.

Definition 3 (marking). *Given a CP/T net N,* a marking *M is a finite multiset of places in S.* □

The set of the markings of a net N coincides with $S_N^{\oplus}$, the free commutative monoid that has S_N as a set of generators [19]. Thus, a marking can be represented as a formal sum $\bigoplus_{s \in S} n_s s$, where the order of the summands is immaterial and $n_s \in \mathbb{N}$. The addition (disjoint union) $\oplus$ and subtraction $\ominus$ operators are defined pointwise (and note that $\ominus$ is actually a partial operation), and the partial order $\leq$ over markings is just multiset inclusion.

Definition 4 (net morphism). *Given two CP/T nets N and N', a* net morphism *$h : N \to N'$ is a pair of functions $\langle h_S : S_N \to S_{N'}^{\oplus}, h_T : T_N \to T_{N'} \rangle$, such that for each $t \in T_N$, the unique extension $h_S^{\oplus}$ satisfies $h_S^{\oplus}(\,{}^\bullet t) \oplus h_S^{\oplus}(\widehat{t}) = {}^\bullet h_T(t) \oplus \widehat{h_T(t)}$, $h_S^{\oplus}(t^\bullet) \oplus h_S^{\oplus}(\widehat{t}) = h_T(t)^\bullet \oplus \widehat{h_T(t)}$ and $h_S^{\oplus}(\widehat{t}) \subseteq \widehat{h_T(t)}$.*

A net morphism h is functional *if $h_S : S_N \to S_{N'}$. It is* strong *if the context-sets are preserved pointwise, namely $h_S^{\oplus}(\widehat{t}) = \widehat{h_T(t)}$ for each transition t.* □

Note that a net morphism may change the flow relation, in the sense that a place forming a loop may become part of the context relation. Note also that strong net morphisms actually preserve pointwise the pre-sets and post-sets, too; namely, ${}^\bullet h_T(t) = h_S^{\oplus}(\,{}^\bullet t)$ and $h_S^{\oplus}(t^\bullet) = h_T(t)^\bullet$ for each transition t.

A transitions t is *enabled* by a marking M if the union of the pre-set ${}^\bullet t$ and the context-set $\widehat{t}$ is contained in M. In this case a *firing step* may take place: It consumes the items in the pre-set and generates those in the post-set $t^\bullet$.

Definition 5 (firing step). *Given a* transition *t and a marking M, a* firing step *σ is a triple $M[t\rangle M'$ such that M* enables *t, that is $(\,{}^\bullet t \oplus \widehat{t}) \subseteq M$, and $M' = (M \ominus {}^\bullet t) \oplus t^\bullet$.* □

In general terms, the atomic consumption and regeneration of an element implies that the element is not present during the firing of the transition and, from a semantic point of view, it could be argued that to consume and regenerate a resource is different from accessing the resource without modifying it. Such a difference will be pivotal when defining the *causal* behaviour of a net, but it is immaterial with respect to the sequences of firing steps. In fact, it is easy to define a P/T net which can simulate the step-by-step behaviour of a CP/T net.

Definition 6 (net sequentialization). *A* P/T net *is a contextual P/T net such that the context relation is empty. Given a contextual CP/T net N, we denote with $\overline{N}$ the P/T net $\langle S_{\overline{N}}, T_{\overline{N}}, F_{\overline{N}} \rangle$ underlying N, i.e., such that $S_{\overline{N}} = S_N, T_{\overline{N}} = T_N$ and $F_{1\overline{N}} = F_{1N} \cup C_N$, $F_{2\overline{N}} = F_{2N} \cup (C_N)^{-1}$.* □

Roughly, for a CP/T net N, the associated P/T net $\overline{N}$ is defined by transforming each context into a loop. Conversely, starting from a P/T net, the associated CP/T net is simply obtained adding the empty context relation.

2.1 Defining processes

We present now a more concrete notion of behaviour for nets, *contextual processes*. A process (see for instance [11, 13, 22, 24]) provides a representation of a net behaviour which is "causally conscious", that is, which takes into account the causal relationship between transitions occurring in a sequence of firing steps.

Definition 7 (causal dependency). *Let N be a CP/T net. The causal dependency relation $\prec$ is the minimal transitive relation on $S_N \uplus T_N$ such that*

$$(s,t) \in F_{1N} \text{ implies } s \prec t \qquad (t,s) \in F_{2N} \text{ implies } t \prec s$$

$$t_1^\bullet \cap \widehat{t_2} \neq \emptyset \text{ or } \widehat{t_1} \cap {}^\bullet t_2 \neq \emptyset \text{ implies } t_1 \prec t_2$$

for each $s \in S_N$ and $t, t_1, t_2 \in T_N$ □

Alternative notions of precedence and causality have been considered in the literature [14, 28, 1]. Our solution ensures that the resulting processes are actually deterministic (in the sense that all choices all resolved, and the places of the underlying occurrence net represent the tokens of the net), a condition that results pivotal for obtaining their categorical characterization.

Definition 8 (contextual occurrence net). *A* contextual occurrence net *(or simply,* occurrence net*) P is a CP/T net such that*

1. *$\prec$ is irreflexive, and its reflexive closure $\preceq$ is a partial order;*
2. *${}^\bullet t \cap {}^\bullet t' = t^\bullet \cap t'^\bullet = \emptyset$ for $t, t' \in T_P$, $t \neq t'$.*

Given an occurrence net P, the set of minimal places *${}^\circ P$ is defined as $\{s \in S_P \mid s \notin T_P^\bullet\}$; the set of* maximal places *P° as $\{s \in S_P \mid s \notin {}^\bullet T_P\}$.* □

Since in a process the elements of an occurrence net P will be mapped onto the elements of a CP/T net N, via a net morphism π, in order to properly define the *concatenation* of two processes p_1, p_2 we need to impose a suitable ordering over those places in ${}^\circ P_2$ (resp. in P_1°) that are mapped to the same place.

Definition 9 (labeling ordering function). *Let A, B be sets, $f : A \to B$ a function and $f^{-1} : B \to A$ its inverse relation, such that $f^{-1}(b) = \{a \in A \mid f(a) = b\}$. A* (labeling) ordering function *α for A induced by f is a family $\{\alpha_b \mid b \in f(A)\}$ of bijective functions $\alpha_b : f^{-1}(b) \to [|f^{-1}(b)|]$.* □

Here and in the following, we denote with the expression $[n]$ the segment $\{1 \ldots n\}$ for $n \in \mathbb{N}$, equipped with the usual total ordering.

Definition 10 (process). *Let N be a CP/T net and P an occurrence net. A* concrete (contextual) process *p of N is a four-tuple (P, π, μ, ν) such that*

1. *$\pi : P \to N$ is a strong, functional net morphism;*
2. *μ is an ordering function for ${}^\circ P$, induced by $\pi_{|{}^\circ P}$;*
3. *ν is an ordering function for P°, induced by $\pi_{|P^\circ}$.*

Given two concrete processes p and p' of a net N, a concrete process morphism *$i : p \to p'$ is a net morphism $i : P \to P'$ such that $\pi' \circ i = \pi$ and for all $s_1, s_2 \in {}^\circ P$ satisfying $\pi(s_1) = \pi(s_2)$, then $\mu(s_1) \leq \mu(s_2)$ implies $\mu'(i(s_1)) \leq \mu'(i(s_2))$ (and the same for P° and ν, ν').*

A process *$[p]$ is an equivalence class of isomorphic concrete processes.* □

For a concrete process p, we define $Orig_p$ as the multiset $\pi({}^\circ P)$ and $Dest_p$ as the multiset $\pi(P^\circ)$. Since those multisets are preserved by net isomorphisms, the operators can be simply extended by $Orig_{[p]} = Orig_p$: We then usually drop the square brackets when denoting a process.

2.2 Decomposing processes

In this section we show a few properties of the class of processes of a net: Namely, that it forms a category, and that there exists a subclass of generators, from which all the other processes can be obtained through suitable operations. We start noting how to associate a process to a given transition: It is just an occurrence net with only one transition, where loops are, so to say, "unfolded".

Definition 11 (transition process). *Let N be a CP/T net. For a transition $t \in T_N$, the associated process p_t is the (equivalence class associated to the concrete) process (P, π, μ, ν), such that $T_P = \{t'\}$, $S_P = \{s_1 \mid s \in {}^\bullet t\} \cup \{s_2 \mid s \in t^\bullet\} \cup \{s' \mid s \in \widehat{t}\}$; furthermore, $\pi(s_1) = \pi(s_2) = \pi(s') = s, \pi(t') = t$, $F_{1P} = \{(s_1, t') \mid s \in {}^\bullet t\}$, $F_{2P} = \{(s_2, t') \mid s \in t^\bullet\}$ and $C_P = \{(s', t') \mid s \in \widehat{t}\}$.* □

Please note first that the definition is *not* incomplete: Simply, the ordering functions are trivial, since for all $s \in S_N$ we have $|\pi^{-1}(s) \cap {}^\circ P| \leq 1$ and $|\pi^{-1}(s) \cap P^\circ| \leq 1$. Roughly, the intended meaning of the definition is that the underlying occurrence net of the process p_t contains only one transition t', and as many places as there are elements of ${}^\bullet t \oplus \widehat{t} \oplus t^\bullet$.

For a given place s, we define now two processes, which intuitively denote basic computational features of the place: As in the following, we implicitly consider the equivalence class associated to the concrete processes we describe.

Definition 12 (place processes). *Let N be a CP/T net. For each $s \in P_N$, the process p_s is described by an occurrence net with no transitions and only one node, s', mapped to s. Similarly, the process $p_{s,s}$ is an occurrence net with no transitions and two nodes s_1, s_2, both mapped to s; moreover, the orderings are complementary: That is, $\mu(s_1) = \nu(s_2) = 1$ and $\mu(s_2) = \nu(s_1) = 2$.* □

Definition 13 (basic processes). *Let N be a CP/T net. We denote by $B(N)$ the class of* basic processes *of N, whose elements are the place and transition processes associated to N.* □

We introduce now two binary operators over the processes of a net.

Definition 14 (parallel composition). *Let N be a net, and p_1, p_2 processes. Their* union *or* parallel composition *is the process $p = p_1 \otimes p_2$, such that $P = P_1 \uplus P_2$, and the morphism and ordering functions are defined accordingly.* □

The disjoint union $P_1 \uplus P_2$ of CP/T nets is defined componentwise, while μ is described as $\mu(s) = \mu_1(s)$ if $s \in P_1$, $\mu_2(s) + |(\pi_1)^{-1}(\pi_2(s))|$ otherwise, and the same for ν. Let t be a transition with ${}^\bullet t = \{b, c\}$, $t^\bullet = \{c, e\}$ and $\widehat{t} = \{d\}$: Figure 1 shows the process associated to the expression $p_t \otimes p_b \otimes p_c$. Places and transitions are labeled with the corresponding places and transitions of the net they are mapped to; the labeling μ (resp. ν) of the places in ${}^\circ P$ (resp. P°) is displayed on the top (resp. bottom) of the circle representing the place.

We denote as *discrete* those processes containing no transitions, as the one described by $p_{a,a} \otimes p_b \otimes p_{b,b} \otimes p_c$. Any discrete process p such that $Orig_p = \bigoplus_{s \in S} n_s s$ identifies for each place s a bijection over $[n_s] = [|\pi^{-1}(s)|]$, defined by $\nu_s \circ \mu_s^{-1}$ and simply denoted by a list $(\nu_s(\mu_s^{-1}(1)) \ldots \nu_s(\mu_s^{-1}(n_s)))^s$: For example, the process given before corresponds to the family $[(2\,1)^a, (1\,3\,2)^b, (1)^c]$.

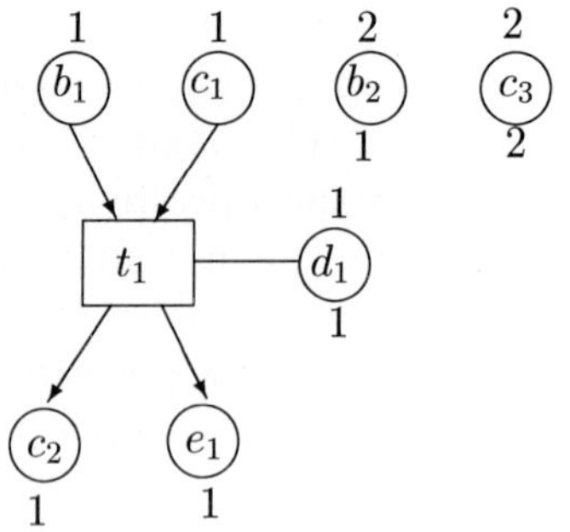

Fig. 1. the process $p_t \otimes p_b \otimes p_c$.

The sequential composition of p_1 and p_2, denoted by $p_1;p_2$, is a partial operation and it is defined only when the multiset of the origins of p_2 coincides with that of the destinations of p_1. The resulting process is obtained by "gluing" the maximal places of the first one to the minimal places of the second. Such a gluing is obtained through an equivalence relation that associates with each place in P_1° the place in ${}^\circ P_2$ that is mapped to the same element of the underlying net and has the same labeling number.

Definition 15 (sequential composition). *Let* $p_1 = (P_1, \pi_1, \mu_1, \nu_1)$ *and* $p_2 = (P_2, \pi_2, \mu_2, \nu_2)$ *be two processes such that* $Orig_{p_2} = Dest_{p_1}$. *Their* sequential composition *is the process* $p = p_1;p_2$, *such that* $P = (P_1 \uplus P_2)/_\approx$, *where* $\approx$ *is the minimal equivalence relation generated from* $x \approx y$ *if* $\pi(x) = \pi(y)$ *and* $\nu_1(x) = \mu_2(y)$; *and the morphism and ordering functions are defined accordingly, namely* $\pi = (\pi_1 \uplus \pi_2)/_\approx$, $\mu = \mu_1/_\approx$ *and* $\nu = \nu_2/_\approx$. □

The sequential composition of two processes is still a process. We introduce now two additional classes of discrete processes, *identities* and *permutations.*

Definition 16 (identity and permutation). *Let* N *be a CP/T net. Given a marking* $M = \bigoplus_{s \in S} n_s s$, *we define its* identity *as the discrete process* p_M, *such that* $S_P = \{s_i \mid s \in S_N$ *and* $1 \leq i \leq n_s\}$, $\pi(s_i) = s$ *and* $\mu(s_i) = \nu(s_i) = i$ *for* $1 \leq i \leq n_s$. *Given two markings* M, M', *we define their* permutation *as the discrete process* $p_{M,M'} = (P, \pi, \mu, \nu)$, *such that* $P = P_M \uplus P_{M'}$, *and the same for* π *and* μ, *while instead* ν *swaps its arguments.* □

Explicitly, while μ is described as in the case of parallel composition, for ν we have $\nu(s) = \nu_2(s)$ if $s \in P_2$, $\nu_1(s) + |(\pi_2)^{-1}(\pi_1(s))|$ otherwise.

Proposition 1 (properties of composition). *The sequential composition of processes is associative, that is,* $p_1;(p_2;p_3) = (p_1;p_2);p_3$. *Moreover, it has identities, since* $p_{Orig_p};p = p;p_{Dest_p} = p$. □

We will stress the categorical meaning of permutations and of parallel composition in the next section, and we just define $\mathbf{CP}(N)$ as the category whose objects are markings, and arrows are processes of N: In particular, a process p is an arrow from $Orig_p$ to $Dest_p$. We present now the main result of the section.

Theorem 1 (decomposing processes). *Let* N *be a CP/T net. Each process* p *of* N *can be obtained as the evaluation of an expression of the form* $p_1;p_2;\ldots;p_n$, *such that each* p_i *can be further decomposed as* $p_{M_i} \otimes p'_i \otimes p_{M'_i}$, *where* p'_i *is either a transition process* p_t *or a place process* $p_{s,s}$ *of* N. □

Theorem 1 says that each process can be decomposed into a sequence of firing steps. Such a sequence could be defined in a canonical way, but this is beyond the scope of the paper: See [22] for an analogous result on contextual C/E nets.

3 A Few Categorical Remarks

We introduce now *symmetric monoidal categories*: Since our presentation is tailored over the needs of our representation theorems, we refer the reader to [16].

Definition 17 (symmetric monoidal categories). *A* monoidal category $\mathbf{C}$ *is a triple* $\mathbf{C} = \langle \mathbf{C}_0, \otimes, e \rangle$ *where* $\mathbf{C}_0$ *is a category,* $e \in \mathbf{C}_0$ *is a distinguished object and* $\otimes : \mathbf{C}_0 \times \mathbf{C}_0 \to \mathbf{C}_0$ *is a functor, satisfying the coherence axioms* $(t \otimes t_1) \otimes t_2 = t \otimes (t_1 \otimes t_2)$ *and* $t \otimes e = e \otimes t = t$ *for all arrows* $t, t_1, t_2 \in \mathbf{C}_0$.[2]

A symmetric monoidal category *is a four-tuple* $\langle \mathbf{C}_0, \otimes, e, \rho \rangle$ *where* $\langle \mathbf{C}_0, \otimes, e \rangle$ *is a monoidal category, and* $\rho : \otimes \Rightarrow \otimes \circ X : \mathbf{C}_0 \times \mathbf{C}_0 \to \mathbf{C}_0$ *is a natural transformation*[3] *(X is the functor that swaps its two arguments) satisfying*

$$\begin{array}{ccc} a \otimes b \otimes c & \xrightarrow{a \otimes \rho_{b,c}} & a \otimes c \otimes b \\ & \searrow^{\rho_{a \otimes b, c}} & \downarrow \rho_{a, c \otimes b} \\ & & c \otimes a \otimes b \end{array} \qquad \begin{array}{ccc} a \otimes b & \xrightarrow{\rho_{a,b}} & b \otimes a \\ & \searrow^{a \otimes b} & \downarrow \rho_{b,a} \\ & & a \otimes b \end{array}$$

A monoidal functor $F : \mathbf{C} \to \mathbf{C}'$ *is a functor* $F : \mathbf{C}_0 \to \mathbf{C}'_0$ *such that* $F(e) = e'$ *and* $F(a \otimes b) = F(a) \otimes' F(b)$; *it is* symmetric *if* $F(\rho_{a,b}) = \rho'_{F(a),F(b)}$. **SM-Cat** *is the category of symmetric monoidal categories and their functors.* □

The class of arrows denoted by the transformation ρ are indicated as *symmetries*. The following result is lifted from [11, 26], and it shows the relationship between symmetries and discrete processes.

Lemma 1. *Let N be a CP/T net. The lluf subcategory* $\mathbf{DProc}(N)$ *of discrete processes of N is isomorphic to the symmetric monoidal category* $\mathbf{SM}(S_N)$, *freely generated from S_N, modulo the additional axiom* $\rho_{a,b} = a \otimes b$ *for each* $a, b \in S_N$ *such that* $a \neq b$. □

The term "lluf" denotes that the inclusion functor is an isomorphism for the class of objects. In fact, the axiom $\rho_{a,b} = a \otimes b$ actually implies that the objects of the category form a commutative monoid, and are in one-to-one correspondence with the markings of the generating net. Thanks to this result, we can provide our initial characterization for the category of processes of a net N.

Proposition 2 (process category). *Let N be a CP/T net. The four-tuple* $\langle \mathbf{CP}(N), \otimes, p_\emptyset, \{p_{M,M'} \mid M, M' \in S_N^\oplus\} \rangle$ *is a symmetric monoidal category.* □

The paradigm of *Petri nets are monoids* [19] can be summarized as: The concurrent behaviour of a (ordinary) net is described by the class of arrows of a monoidal category freely generated from the net itself. A similar correspondence result for CP/T nets is far more complex, due to the presence of contexts. Roughly: How to axiomatize the fact that the sequential composition of processes can be equivalent to a suitable instance of their parallel composition?

---

[2] We often denote the identity of an object by the object itself.

[3] Given functors $F, G : \mathbf{A} \to \mathbf{B}$, a *transformation* $\tau : F \Rightarrow G : \mathbf{A} \to \mathbf{B}$ is a family of arrows of $\mathbf{B}$ indexed by objects of $\mathbf{A}$, $\tau = \{\tau_a : F(a) \to G(a) \mid a \in |\mathbf{A}|\}$. Transformation τ is *natural* if for every arrow $f : a \to a'$ in $\mathbf{A}$, $\tau_a; G(f) = F(f); \tau_{a'}$.

3.1 Categories with duplications

In this section we just introduce the categorical definitions needed to extend the *Petri nets are monoids* framework to the general class of contextual P/T nets.

Definition 18 (share categories). *A* share category $\mathbf{C}$ *is a five-tuple* $\langle \mathbf{C}_0, \otimes, e, \rho, \nabla \rangle$ *where* $\langle \mathbf{C}_0, \otimes, e, \rho \rangle$ *is a symmetric monoidal category and* $\nabla : Id \Rightarrow \otimes \circ D : \mathbf{C}_0 \to \mathbf{C}_0$ *is a transformation (D is the diagonal functor), such that* $\nabla_e = id_e$ *and satisfying*

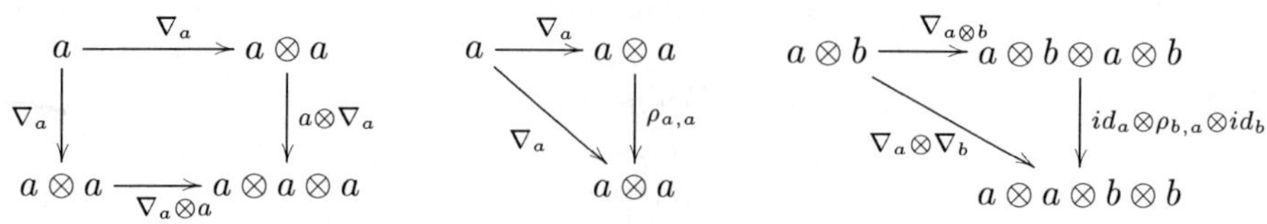

A share functor $F : \mathbf{C} \to \mathbf{C}'$ *is a symmetric monoidal functor such that* $F(\nabla_a) = \nabla'_{F(a)}$. **S-Cat** *is the category of share categories and their functors.* □

A share category is a monoidal category enriched with a transformation that allows a *local* way of duplicating information. If we consider an arrow $t : a \to b$ as a *data structure*, and the objects a, b as interfaces, then $\nabla_b : b \to b \otimes b$ represents a *duplication* of the pointer to b, and $t; \nabla_b$ a *shared* instance of t. This is confirmed by the expressiveness properties of similar structures, *gs-monoidal categories* [8], obtained adding an additional transformation (in order to discharge data).

Definition 19 (match-share categories). *A* match-share category $\mathbf{C}$ *is a six-tuple* $\langle \mathbf{C}_0, \otimes, e, \rho, \nabla, \Delta \rangle$ *where* $\langle \mathbf{C}_0, \otimes, e, \rho, \nabla \rangle$ *and* $\langle (\mathbf{C}_0)^{op}, \otimes, e, \rho^{op}, \Delta^{op} \rangle$ *are both share categories* ($(\mathbf{C}_0)^{op}$ *is the dual category of* $\mathbf{C}_0$*), and satisfying*

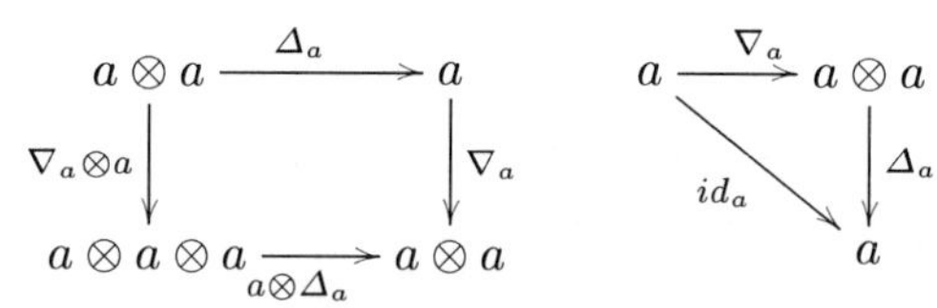

A match-share functor $F : \mathbf{C} \to \mathbf{C}'$ *is a share functor such that also* F^{op} *is so.* **MS-Cat** *is the category of match-share categories and their functors.* □

Match-share categories extend share categories with an operation Δ_a which intuitively corresponds to a *matching* of two pointers. To this extent, they are related to *dgs-monoidal categories* [12], which are their counterpart with respect to gs-monoidal structures. Equivalent presentations of dgs-monoidal categories surfaced in the literature along the years. In particular, a (bicategorical) presentation of them is used as a description of the (bi)category of relations already in [6], and it forms the basis for a categorical description of *circuits* [15].

An equivalence induced by the dgs-monoidal axioms on the sequential composition of two arrows is shown in Fig. 2 (∇^3_a denotes the arrow $\nabla_a; (a \otimes \nabla_a) = \nabla; (\nabla_a \otimes a)$, and similarly for Δ^3_a): It intuitively implies its correspondence to a suitable instance of the monoidal composition of the same arrows.

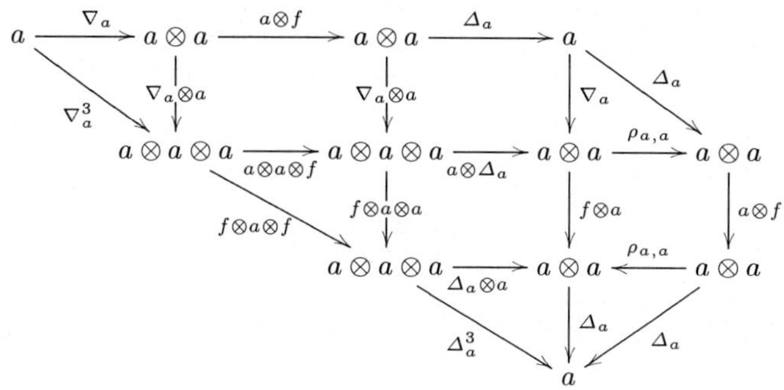

Fig. 2. a commuting diagram showing the equivalence between $\nabla^3_a; (f \otimes a \otimes f); \Delta^3_a$ and $\nabla_a; (a \otimes f); \Delta_a; \nabla_a; (a \otimes f); \Delta_a$ for $f : a \to a$.

4 Embedding Processes into Arrows

In this section we state the main result of the paper, namely, that for each contextual net N, the category of processes $\mathbf{CP}(N)$ defined in Section 2 can be embedded by a faithful functor into a suitable category $\mathcal{CP}(\mathcal{N})$, where processes live in. Along the *Petri nets are monoids* paradigm, this is (some kind of) a monoidal category, freely generated from the net itself.

Definition 20 (a free category for processes). *Let N be a CP/T net. $\mathcal{CP}(\mathcal{N})$ is the free match-share category obtained from the underlying P/T net $\overline{N}$, modulo the axiom $\rho_{a,b} = a \otimes b$ for each $a, b \in S_N$ such that $a \neq b$.* □

Given a CP/T net N, the objects of the category $\mathcal{CP}(\mathcal{N})$ are the markings of N, while its arrows are the equivalence classes of the concrete elements generated by the set of inference rules in Fig. 3, modulo the equation $\rho_{s,s'} = s \otimes s'$, for each $s, s' \in S_N$ such that $s \neq s'$, and the laws for match-share categories.

Proposition 3 (completeness). *Let N be a CP/T net. The function $\mathcal{C}_\mathcal{N}$ from the class of basic processes of N to the class of arrows of the free match-share category $\mathcal{CP}(\mathcal{N})$, defined by*

$$\mathcal{C}(p_s) = s \text{ and } \mathcal{C}(p_{s,s}) = \rho_{s,s} \text{ for } s \in S_N$$

$$\mathcal{C}(p_t) = ({}^\bullet t \otimes \nabla_{\widehat{t}}); (t \otimes \widehat{t}); (t^\bullet \otimes \Delta_{\widehat{t}}) \text{ for } t \in T_N$$

can be lifted to a symmetric monoidal functor $\mathcal{C}_N : \mathbf{CP}(N) \to \mathcal{CP}(\mathcal{N})$. □

Thanks to Theorem 1, $\mathcal{C}_N$ can be extended to a function from processes to arrows. Lemma 1 states that $\mathcal{C}_N$ is an isomorphic functor, when restricted to discrete processes. Once proved that $\mathcal{C}_N$ is a functor, Proposition 2 implies that it is symmetric monoidal. The difficult point is to show that $\mathcal{C}_N$ actually *is* a functor, that is, that it preserves the equivalence on processes induced by net isomorphism: The proof can be carried out by induction on the size of processes, namely, the number of places and transitions, preserved under isomorphism.

$$\frac{s \in S_N^{\oplus}}{s : s \to s \in \mathcal{CP}(\mathcal{N})} \qquad \frac{s, s' \in S_N^{\oplus}}{\rho_{s,s'} : s \oplus s' \to s' \oplus s \in \mathcal{CP}(\mathcal{N})}$$

$$\frac{s \in S_N^{\oplus}}{\nabla_s : s \to s \oplus s \in \mathcal{CP}(\mathcal{N})} \qquad \frac{s \in S_N^{\oplus}}{\Delta_s : s \oplus s \to s \in \mathcal{CP}(\mathcal{N})}$$

$$\frac{t \in T_N}{t : {}^{\bullet}t \oplus \widehat{t} \to t^{\bullet} \oplus \widehat{t} \in \mathcal{CP}(\mathcal{N})}$$

$$\frac{t : s \to s', t_1 : s' \to s_1 \in \mathcal{CP}(\mathcal{N})}{t; t_1 : s \to s_1 \in \mathcal{CP}(\mathcal{N})} \qquad \frac{t : s \to s', t_1 : s_1 \to s_1' \in \mathcal{CP}(\mathcal{N})}{t \otimes t_1 : s \oplus s_1 \to s' \oplus s_1' \in \mathcal{CP}(\mathcal{N})}$$

Fig. 3. the set of inference rules generating $\mathcal{CP}(\mathcal{N})$

The main difference with previous results for P/T nets lies in the equivalences induced on the sequential composition of processes sharing a context. The processes $p_1 = p_t \otimes p_b \otimes p_c$ of Fig. 1 and $p_2 = p_c \otimes p_e \otimes p_t$ can be sequentially composed, and the resulting process is described in Fig. 4: It corresponds to the simultaneous execution of two instances of the transition t.

According to the function $\mathcal{C}_N$, p_1 and p_2 are mapped (up to associativity) to

$$\mathcal{C}_N(p_1) = [(b \otimes c \otimes \nabla_d); (t \otimes d); (c \otimes e \otimes \Delta_d)] \otimes b \otimes c, \qquad \text{and}$$

$$\mathcal{C}_N(p_2) = c \otimes e \otimes [(b \otimes c \otimes \nabla_d); (t \otimes d); (c \otimes e \otimes \Delta_d)]$$

and their composition can be shown equivalent to

$$\mathcal{C}_N(p_1); \mathcal{C}_N(p_2) = (b \otimes c \otimes \nabla_d^3 \otimes b \otimes c); (t \otimes d \otimes t); (c \otimes e \otimes \Delta_d^3 \otimes c \otimes e).$$

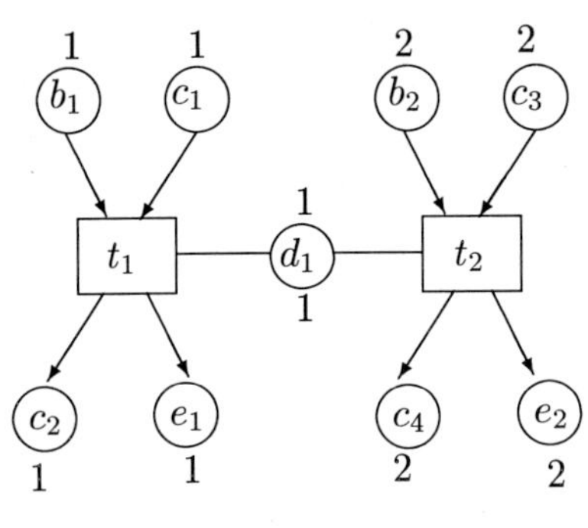

Fig. 4. the process $p_1; p_2$.

The structure of the resulting arrow mimics the spatial depiction of the process, as shown in Fig. 4. Note that p can be also decomposed as $p_2'; p_1' = (p_b \otimes p_c \otimes p_t); (p_t \otimes p_c \otimes p_e)$, since the two instances of t share the context d: The axioms ensure that $\mathcal{C}_N(p_1; p_2) = \mathcal{C}_N(p_2'; p_1')$. In fact, the laws for match-share categories reflect properties of the category of process, and the previous result can be strengthened: The functor *does not* identify processes that are not isomorphic.

Theorem 2 (soundness). *Let N be a CP/T net. The functor $\mathcal{C}_N$ is lluf and faithful.* □

Equivalently, the theorem states that, for all processes p_1, p_2, whenever $\mathcal{C}_N(p_1) = \mathcal{C}_N(p_2)$ is verified, also $[p_1] = [p_2]$ holds. The proof is carried out first by finding a suitable normal form for the arrows of the subcategory $\mathcal{C}_N(\mathbf{CP}(N))$, and then by induction on the length of normal forms, as in [11, 26, 9].

5 Conclusions

In this paper we provided a categorical characterization of the behaviour of contextual P/T nets. We first defined the class of contextual processes of a CP/T net (see Definition 10); then, we showed how these processes can be modeled as arrows of a suitable category, via a functor $\mathcal{C}_N$. In fact, the results of Section 4 imply that *the algebraic description* of the processes of the CP/T net N obtained through $\mathcal{C}_N$ *provides a sound and complete calculus* for proving process equivalence: Since $\mathcal{C}_N$ is a functor, all the equivalences between processes denoting the same process are preserved (completeness, Proposition 3); furthermore, since $\mathcal{C}_N$ is faithful, $\mathcal{C}_N(p_1)$ can be proved equivalent to $\mathcal{C}_N(p_2)$ if and only if the processes p_1 and p_2 actually denote the same process (soundness, Theorem 2).

We consider relevant the fact that our results fit smoothly in the categorical framework so far developed for P/T nets. In fact, if we denote as **P/T** the category of P/T nets (with arcs of weight 1), then the construction in Definition 6 can be lifted to an functor U_p between the category **CP/T** of contextual nets (with the no interference property and arcs of weight 1) and **P/T**. Such a functor admits a left adjoint F_p, that simply adds the empty context relation.

Since the "inclusion" functor U_c : **MS-Cat** → **SM-Cat** has an obvious left adjoint F_c, we end up in the situation described by the diagram

$$\mathbf{CP/T} \underset{F_p}{\overset{U_p}{\rightleftarrows}} \mathbf{P/T} \overset{\mathcal{P}}{\cdots\cdots} \mathbf{SM\text{-}Cat} \underset{U_c}{\overset{F_c}{\rightleftarrows}} \mathbf{MS\text{-}Cat}$$

$\mathcal{P}$ is a function associating to each P/T net N the category $\mathcal{P}(\mathcal{N})$, which is isomorphic, as recalled in the Introduction, to the category of processes of N. By construction $U_p(N) = \overline{N}$, so that we have a function $\mathcal{CP}(N) = F_c(\mathcal{P}(U_p(N)))$ associating to each contextual net the category $\mathcal{CP}(\mathcal{N})$ of its processes. Since $U_p(F_c(N)) = N$ for each P/T net N, we have that $\mathcal{CP}(F_p(N)) = F_c(\mathcal{P}(N))$: Hence, all the results on modelling through processes obtained for P/T nets can be lifted to the contextual setting, losing neither expressiveness nor granularity.

References

1. P. Baldan, A. Corradini, and U. Montanari. An event structure semantics for P/T contextual nets: Asymmetric event structures. In M. Nivat, editor, *Proceedings FoSSaCS'98*, LNCS, pages 63–80. Springer Verlag, 1998.
2. E. Best, R. Devillers, A. Kiehn, and L. Pomello. Fully concurrent bisimulation. *Acta Informatica*, 28:231–261, 1991.
3. F. Bueno, M. Hermenegildo, U. Montanari, and F. Rossi. Partial order and contextual net semantics for atomic and locally atomic CC programs. *Science of Computer Programming*, 30:51–82, 1998.
4. N. Busi and R. Gorrieri. A Petri semantics for the π-calculus. In I. Lee and S. A. Smolka, editors, *Proc. CONCUR'95*, volume 962 of *LNCS*. Springer Verlag, 1995.
5. N. Busi and M. Pinna. Non-sequential semantics for contextual P/T nets. In J. Billington and W. Reisig, editors, *Applications and Theory of Petri Nets 1996*, volume 1091 of *LNCS*. Springer Verlag, 1996.

6. A. Carboni and R.F.C. Walters. Cartesian bicategories I. *Journal of Pure and Applied Algebra*, 49:11–32, 1987.
7. S. Christensen and N. D. Hansen. Coloured Petri nets extended with place capacities, test arcs and inhibitor arcs. In M. Ajmone-Marsan, editor, *Applications and Theory of Petri Nets*, volume 691 of *LNCS*, pages 186–205. Springer Verlag, 1993.
8. A. Corradini and F. Gadducci. A 2-categorical presentation of term graph rewriting. In *Proceedings CTCS'97*, volume 1290 of *LNCS*. Springer Verlag, 1997.
9. A. Corradini and F. Gadducci. An algebraic presentation of term graphs, via gs-monoidal categories. *Applied Categorical Structures*, 1998. To appear.
10. N. De Francesco, U. Montanari, and G. Ristori. Modeling concurrent accesses to shared data via Petri nets. In E.-R. Olderog, editor, *Programming Concepts, Methods and Calculi*, IFIP Transactions A-56, pages 403–442. North Holland, 1994.
11. P. Degano, J. Meseguer, and U. Montanari. Axiomatizing the algebra of net computations and processes. *Acta Informatica*, 33:641–647, 1996.
12. G Gadducci and R. Heckel. An inductive view of graph transformation. In F. Parisi-Presicce, editor, *Recent Trends in Algebraic Development Techniques*, volume 1376 of *LNCS*. Springer Verlag, 1998.
13. U. Golz and W. Reisig. The non-sequential behaviour of Petri nets. *Information and Control*, 57:125–147, 1983.
14. R. Janicki and M. Koutny. Semantics of inhibitor nets. *Information and Computation*, 123:1–16, 1995.
15. P. Katis, N. Sabadini, and R.F.C. Walters. Bicategories of processes. *Journal of Pure and Applied Algebra*, 115:141–178, 1997.
16. S. Mac Lane. *Categories for the working mathematician.* Springer Verlag, 1971.
17. N. Martí-Oliet and J. Meseguer. From Petri nets to linear logic through categories: A survey. *Int. Journal of Foundations of Computer Science*, 4:297–399, 1991.
18. J. Meseguer. Rewriting logic as a semantic framework for concurrency: A progress report. In U. Montanari and V. Sassone, editors, *Proceedings CONCUR'96*, volume 1119 of *LNCS*, pages 331–372. Springer Verlag, 1996.
19. J. Meseguer and U. Montanari. Petri nets are monoids. *Information and Computation*, 88:105–155, 1990.
20. U. Montanari and G. Ristori. A concurrent functional semantics for a process algebra based on action systems. *Fundamenta Informaticae*, 31:1–21, 1997.
21. U. Montanari and F. Rossi. Contextual occurrence nets and concurrent constraint programming. In *Graph Transformations in Computer Science*, volume 776 of *LNCS*, pages 280–285. Springer Verlag, 1994.
22. U. Montanari and F. Rossi. Contextual nets. *Acta Informatica*, 32, 1995.
23. A. Rabinovich and B. A. Trakhtenbrot. Behaviour structures and nets. *Fundamenta Informaticae*, 11:357–404, 1988.
24. W. Reisig. *Petri Nets: An Introduction.* EACTS Monographs on Theoretical Computer Science. Springer Verlag, 1985.
25. G. Ristori. *Modelling Systems with Shared Resources via Petri Nets.* PhD thesis, University of Pisa - Department of Computer Science, 1994.
26. V. Sassone. An axiomatization of the algebra of Petri net concatenable processes. *Theoret. Comput. Sci.*, 170:277–296, 1996.
27. W. Vogler. Efficiency of asynchronous systems and read arcs in Petri nets. In *Proc. ICALP'97*, volume 1256 of *LNCS*, pages 538–548. Springer Verlag, 1997.
28. W. Vogler. Partial order semantics and read arcs. In *Proc. MFCS'97*, volume 1295 of *LNCS*, pages 508–518. Springer Verlag, 1997.

Existential Types: Logical Relations and Operational Equivalence

Andrew M. Pitts

Cambridge University Computer Laboratory
Pembroke Street, Cambridge CB2 3QG, UK

Abstract. Existential types have proved useful for classifying various kinds of information hiding in programming languages, such as occurs in abstract datatypes and objects. In this paper we address the question of when two elements of an existential type are semantically equivalent. Of course, it depends what one means by 'semantic equivalence'. Here we take a syntactic approach—so semantic equivalence will mean some kind of operational equivalence. The paper begins by surveying some of the literature on this topic involving 'logical relations'. Matters become quite complicated if the programming language mixes existential types with function types and features involving non-termination (such as recursive definitions). We give an example (suggested by Ian Stark) to show that in this case the existence of suitable relations is sufficient, but not necessary for proving operational equivalences at existential types. Properties of this and other examples are proved using a new form of operationally-based logical relation which does in fact provide a useful characterisation of operational equivalence for existential types.

1 Introduction

Type systems involving existentially quantified type variables provide a useful foundation for explaining and relating various features of programming languages to do with information hiding. For example, the classic paper by Mitchell and Plotkin (1988) popularised the idea that abstract data type declarations can be modelled by values of existential types; similarly, type-theoretic research into the foundations of object-oriented programming has made use of existential types, together with various combinations of function, record, and recursive types, to model objects and classes: see the recent paper by Bruce, Cardelli, and Pierce (1997) for a useful survey.

To establish the properties of such type-theoretic interpretations of information hiding requires a theory of semantic equivalence for elements of existential type. In this respect, the use of *relations* between types has proved very useful. Study of relational properties of types goes back to the 'logical relations' of Plotkin (1973) and Statman (1985) for simply typed lambda calculus and the notion of relational parametricity for polymorphic types due to Reynolds (1983). More relevant is Mitchell's principle for establishing the denotational equivalence of programs involving higher order functions and different implementations of an abstract datatype, in terms of the existence of a 'simulation' relation between the implementations (Mitchell 1991). This principle was extended to encompass all the (possibly impredicative) existential types of the Girard-Reynolds polymorphic lambda calculus by Plotkin and Abadi (1993). Their Theorem 7 shows that the principle gives a necessary and sufficient condition for equality at existential type in any model of their logic for parametric polymorphism.

One feature of the works mentioned above is that they develop proof principles for *denotational* models of programming languages—hence the relevance of such principles to the operational behaviour of programs relies upon 'goodness of fit' results (some published, some not) connecting operational and denotational semantics. A more serious shortcoming is that although they treat higher order functions, these works do not treat the use of general recursive definitions—hence the languages they consider are not Turing powerful. It is folklore that a proof principle for denotational equality at existential type, phrased in terms of the existence of certain simulation relations, is still valid in the presence of recursively defined functions of higher type, provided one imposes some 'admissibility' conditions on the notion of relation. Here we show that suitable admissibility conditions for relations and an associated proof principle for operational equivalence at existential type can be phrased directly, and quite simply, in terms of a programming language's syntax and operational semantics. The language we work with combines a call-by-value version of PCF (Plotkin 1977) with the polymorphic lambda calculus of Girard (1972) and Reynolds (1974). Of course, the ability to define functions by unrestricted fixpoint recursion necessarily entails the presence of non-terminating computations. In contrast to the result of Plotkin and Abadi (1993, Theorem 7) mentioned above, it turns out that in the presence of non-termination, the existence of a simulation relation is merely a sufficient, but not a necessary condition for operational equivalence at existential type (see Sect. 4). These results follow using the techniques for defining operationally-based logical relations developed in (Pitts 1998). The purpose of this paper is to explain the results and the background to them outlined above; more detailed proofs will appear elsewhere.

2 Why Consider Relations Between Types?

To begin with, we fix upon a particular syntax for expressions involving existentially quantified type variables. The reader can refer to the survey by Cardelli (1997), or the recent textbook by Mitchell (1996), for a formal treatment of both this and the other type systems we consider in this paper.

If $\tau(\alpha)$ is a type expression, possibly involving free occurrences of a type variable α, then we write $\exists\, \alpha \,.\, \tau(\alpha)$ for the corresponding existentially quantified type. Free occurrences of α in τ become bound in this type expression.[1] If τ' is a type and $M : \tau(\tau')$ (i.e. M is a term of type $\tau(\tau')$), then we can 'pack' the

[1] Throughout this paper we will always identify expressions, be they types or terms, up to renaming of bound variables.

type τ' and the term M together to get a term of type $\exists\,\alpha\,.\,\tau(\alpha)$, which we will write as

$$\texttt{pack}\,\tau', M\;\texttt{as}\;\exists\,\alpha\,.\,\tau(\alpha).$$

To eliminate such terms we use the form

$$\texttt{open}\,E\;\texttt{as}\;\alpha, x\;\texttt{in}\;M'(\alpha, x). \tag{1}$$

This is a binding construct: free occurrences of the type variable α and the variable x in $M(\alpha, x)$ become bound in the term. The typing of such terms goes as follows. If

$$E : \exists\,\alpha\,.\,\tau$$

and

$$M'(\alpha, x) : \tau', \quad \text{given } x : \tau(\alpha)$$

then

$$(\texttt{open}\,E\;\texttt{as}\;\alpha, x\;\texttt{in}\;M'(\alpha, x)) : \tau', \quad \textit{provided } \alpha \textit{ does not occur free in } \tau'. \tag{2}$$

The italicised restriction on free occurrences of α in τ' is what distinguishes an existential type from a type-indexed dependent sum, where there is free access both to the type component as well as the term component of a packed term: see (Mitchell and Plotkin 1988, p 474 *et seq*) for a discussion of this point. The evaluation behaviour of (1) is given by the rule

$$\frac{E \Downarrow (\texttt{pack}\,\tau', V\;\texttt{as}\;\exists\,\alpha\,.\,\tau(\alpha)) \quad M'(\tau', V) \Downarrow V'}{(\texttt{open}\,E\;\texttt{as}\;\alpha, x\;\texttt{in}\;M'(\alpha, x)) \Downarrow V'}$$

Because this paper is targeted at programming languages that adopt a strict, or 'call-by-value', evaluation strategy (such as the Standard ML of Milner, Tofte, Harper, and MacQueen 1997), we take the rule for evaluating pack terms to be

$$\frac{M \Downarrow V}{(\texttt{pack}\,\tau', M\;\texttt{as}\;\exists\,\alpha\,.\,\tau(\alpha)) \Downarrow (\texttt{pack}\,\tau', V\;\texttt{as}\;\exists\,\alpha\,.\,\tau(\alpha))}$$

Thus a closed term of the form $\texttt{pack}\,\tau', M\;\texttt{as}\;\exists\,\alpha\,.\,\tau(\alpha)$ is a value if and only if M is.

Example 2.1. Consider the existentially quantified record type

$$\texttt{cell} \stackrel{\text{def}}{=} \exists\,\alpha\,.\,\{\texttt{mk} : \alpha, \texttt{inc} : \alpha \to \alpha, \texttt{get} : \alpha \to \texttt{int}\}.$$

where int is a type of integers. (See Cardelli 1997, Sect. 3 for typing rules for function and record types.) Values of type cell consist of some type together with values of the appropriate types implementing mk, inc, and get. For example

$$\begin{aligned}
\texttt{Cell}_+ \stackrel{\text{def}}{=} \texttt{pack int}, \{\; & \texttt{mk} = 0, \\
& \texttt{inc} = \lambda\,x : \texttt{int}\,.\,x + 1, \\
& \texttt{get} = \lambda\,x : \texttt{int}\,.\,x \quad \}\;\texttt{as cell}
\end{aligned}$$

$$\begin{aligned}
\texttt{Cell}_- \stackrel{\text{def}}{=} \texttt{pack int}, \{\; & \texttt{mk} = 0, \\
& \texttt{inc} = \lambda\,x : \texttt{int}\,.\,x - 1, \\
& \texttt{get} = \lambda\,x : \texttt{int}\,.\,-x \quad \}\;\texttt{as cell}
\end{aligned}$$

are both values of type $\texttt{cell}$; and with either $? = +$, or $? = -$,

$$\texttt{open}\,\texttt{Cell}_?\ \texttt{as}\ \alpha, x\ \texttt{in}\ x.\texttt{get}(x.\texttt{inc}(x.\texttt{mk}))$$

is a term of type $\texttt{int}$ which evaluates to 1. By contrast the expression

$$\texttt{open}\,\texttt{Cell}_?\ \texttt{as}\ \alpha, x\ \texttt{in}\ x.\texttt{get}(x.\texttt{inc}(1))$$

evaluates to 2 in case $? = +$ and to 0 in case $? = -$, but neither expression is well-typed, because of the side condition in (2). Indeed, it is the case that *any* well-typed closed term involving occurrences of the term $\texttt{Cell}_+$ will exhibit precisely the same evaluation behaviour if we replace those occurrences by $\texttt{Cell}_-$. In other words, $\texttt{Cell}_+$ and $\texttt{Cell}_-$ are equivalent in the following sense.

Definition 2.2. *Two terms (of the same type τ) are called* contextually equivalent

$$M_1 =_{\mathrm{ctx}} M_2 : \tau$$

iff for all contexts $\mathcal{M}[- : \tau] : \texttt{gnd}$ where $\texttt{gnd}$ is a ground type ($\texttt{int}$, $\texttt{bool}$, $\texttt{char}$, etc) and for all values $V : \texttt{gnd}$

$$\mathcal{M}[M_1] \Downarrow V \quad \textit{iff} \quad \mathcal{M}[M_2] \Downarrow V.$$

This notion of program equivalence of course presupposes that the meaning of a program (= closed term of ground type) should only depend upon the final result (if any) of evaluating it. This is reasonable for deterministic and non-interactive programming. Certainly, contextual equivalence is a widely used notion of program equivalence in the literature and it is the one we adopt here.

For the terms in Example 2.1, it is the case that $\texttt{Cell}_+ =_{\mathrm{ctx}} \texttt{Cell}_- : \texttt{cell}$. But the quantification over all possible ground contexts which occurs in the definition of $=_{\mathrm{ctx}}$ makes a direct proof of this and similar facts rather difficult. Thus one is lead to ask whether there are useful proof principles for contextual equivalence at existential types. Since values of existential type are $\texttt{pack}$ed terms, given by pairs of data, as a first stab at such a proof principle one might try componentwise equality. Equality in the second component will of course mean contextual equivalence; but in the first component, where the expressions involved are types, what should equality mean? If we take it to mean syntactic identity up to alpha-conversion, $=_\alpha$, we obtain the following proof principle.

Principle 2.3 (Extensionality for $\exists$-types, Version I). *For each existential type $\varepsilon \stackrel{\text{def}}{=} \exists\,\alpha\,.\,\tau(\alpha)$, types τ_1, τ_2, and values V_1, V_2, if $\tau_1 =_\alpha \tau_2$ and $V_1 =_{\mathrm{ctx}} V_2 : \tau(\tau_1)$, then* $(\texttt{pack}\,\tau_1, V_1\ \texttt{as}\ \varepsilon) =_{\mathrm{ctx}} (\texttt{pack}\,\tau_2, V_2\ \texttt{as}\ \varepsilon) : \exists\,\alpha\,.\,\tau(\alpha)$.

The hypotheses of Principle 2.3 are far too strong to make it very useful. For example, it cannot be used to prove $\texttt{Cell}_+ =_{\mathrm{ctx}} \texttt{Cell}_- : \texttt{cell}$ in Example 2.1: for in this case $\tau_1 =_\alpha \texttt{int} =_\alpha \tau_2$, but

$$V_1 \stackrel{\text{def}}{=} \{\texttt{mk} = 0,\ \texttt{inc} = \lambda\,x : \texttt{int}\,.\,x + 1,\ \texttt{get} = \lambda\,x : \texttt{int}\,.\,x\} \tag{3}$$

$$V_2 \stackrel{\text{def}}{=} \{\texttt{mk} = 0,\ \texttt{inc} = \lambda\,x : \texttt{int}\,.\,x - 1,\ \texttt{get} = \lambda\,x : \texttt{int}\,.\,-x\} \tag{4}$$

are clearly not contextually equivalent values of the record type $\{\mathtt{mk}:\mathtt{int},\mathtt{inc}:\mathtt{int}\to\mathtt{int},\mathtt{get}:\mathtt{int}\to\mathtt{int}\}$. However, they do become contextually equivalent if in the second term we use a version of integers in which the roles of positive and negative are reversed. Such 'integers' are of course in bijection with the usual ones and this leads us to our second version of an extensionality principle for $\exists$-types—in which the use of syntactic identity as the notion of type equality is replaced by the more flexible one of bijection.

Principle 2.4 (Extensionality for $\exists$-types, Version II). *For each existential type $\varepsilon \stackrel{\text{def}}{=} \exists\,\alpha\,.\,\tau(\alpha)$, types τ_1,τ_2, and values V_1,V_2, if there is a* bijection $\mathtt{I}:\tau_1\cong\tau_2$ *such that $\tau[\mathtt{I}](V_1) =_{\mathrm{ctx}} V_2 : \tau(\tau_2)$, then*

$$(\mathtt{pack}\,\tau_1, V_1\ \mathtt{as}\ \varepsilon) =_{\mathrm{ctx}} (\mathtt{pack}\,\tau_2, V_2\ \mathtt{as}\ \varepsilon) : \exists\,\alpha\,.\,\tau(\alpha)\ .$$

Here a bijection $\mathtt{I}:\tau_1\cong\tau_2$ means a closed term $\mathtt{I}:\tau_1\to\tau_2$ for which there is a closed term $\mathtt{I}^{-1}:\tau_2\to\tau_1$ which is a two-sided inverse up to contextual equivalence: $\mathtt{I}^{-1}(\mathtt{I}\,x_1) =_{\mathrm{ctx}} x_1 : \tau_1$ and $\mathtt{I}(\mathtt{I}^{-1}\,x_2) =_{\mathrm{ctx}} x_2 : \tau_2$. Then given a type $\tau(\alpha)$, one can define an induced bijection $\tau[\mathtt{I}]:\tau(\tau_1)\cong\tau(\tau_2)$ (with inverse $\tau[\mathtt{I}^{-1}]$) by induction on the structure of $\tau(\alpha)$. For example, if

$$\tau(\alpha) \stackrel{\text{def}}{=} \{\mathtt{mk}:\alpha, \mathtt{inc}:\alpha\to\alpha, \mathtt{get}:\alpha\to\mathtt{int}\} \tag{5}$$

then

$$\begin{aligned}\tau[\mathtt{I}] \stackrel{\text{def}}{=} \lambda\,x:\tau(\tau_1)\,.\,\{\ & \mathtt{mk} = \mathtt{I}(x.\mathtt{mk}),\\ & \mathtt{inc} = \lambda\,x_2:\tau_2\,.\,\mathtt{I}(x.\mathtt{inc}(\mathtt{I}^{-1}x_2)),\\ & \mathtt{get} = \lambda\,x_2:\tau_2\,.\,x.\mathtt{get}(\mathtt{I}^{-1}x_2)\quad\}.\end{aligned}$$

We can use this second version of the extensionality principle for $\exists$-types to prove $\mathtt{Cell}_+ =_{\mathrm{ctx}} \mathtt{Cell}_- : \mathtt{cell}$ in Example 2.1: one uses the bijection $\mathtt{I} \stackrel{\text{def}}{=} \lambda\,x:\mathtt{int}\,.\,-x:\mathtt{int}\cong\mathtt{int}$, which does indeed satisfy $\tau[\mathtt{I}](V_1) =_{\mathrm{ctx}} V_2 : \mathtt{int}$ when V_1, V_2 and $\tau(\alpha)$ are defined as in (3)–(5). (Of course these contextual equivalences, and indeed the fact that this particular $\mathtt{I}$ is a bijection, all requires proof; but the methods developed in the next section render this straightforward.) However, the use of bijections between types is still too restrictive for proving many common examples of contextual equivalence of abstract datatype implementations, such as the following.

Example 2.5. Consider the existentially quantified record type

$$\mathtt{smph} \stackrel{\text{def}}{=} \exists\,\alpha\,.\,\{\mathtt{bit}:\alpha, \mathtt{flip}:\alpha\to\alpha, \mathtt{read}:\alpha\to\mathtt{bool}\}$$

and the following terms of type smph

$$\begin{aligned}\mathtt{Smph}_1 \stackrel{\text{def}}{=} \mathtt{pack}\,\mathtt{bool}, \{\ & \mathtt{bit} = \mathtt{true},\\ & \mathtt{flip} = \lambda\,x:\mathtt{bool}\,.\,\mathtt{not}\,x,\\ & \mathtt{read} = \lambda\,x:\mathtt{int}\,.\,x \qquad\}\ \mathtt{as}\ \mathtt{smph}\end{aligned}$$

$$\begin{aligned}\mathtt{Smph}_2 \stackrel{\text{def}}{=} \mathtt{pack}\,\mathtt{int}, \{\ & \mathtt{bit} = 1,\\ & \mathtt{flip} = \lambda\,x:\mathtt{int}\,.\,-2x,\\ & \mathtt{read} = \lambda\,x:\mathtt{int}\,.\,x>0\ \}\ \mathtt{as}\ \mathtt{smph}.\end{aligned}$$

There is no bijection $\texttt{bool} \cong \texttt{int}$, so one cannot use Principle 2.4 to prove $\texttt{Smph}_1 =_{\mathrm{ctx}} \texttt{Smph}_2 : \texttt{smph}$. Nevertheless, this contextual equivalence does hold. An informal argument for this makes use of the following relation $r : \texttt{bool} \leftrightarrow \texttt{int}$ between terms of type bool and of type int

$$r \stackrel{\mathrm{def}}{=} \{(\texttt{true}, (-2)^n) \mid 0 \leq n \text{ even}\} \cup \{(\texttt{false}, (-2)^n) \mid 0 \leq n \text{ odd}\} \ .$$

Writing V_1 and V_2 for the second components of $\texttt{Smph}_1$ and $\texttt{Smph}_2$, note that

- $V_1.\texttt{bit} \Downarrow \texttt{true}$, $V_2.\texttt{bit} \Downarrow 1$, and $(\texttt{true}, 1) \in r$;
- if $(B, N) \in r$, then $V_1.\texttt{flip}(B)$ and $V_2.\texttt{flip}(N)$ evaluate to a pair of values which are again r-related;
- if $(B, N) \in r$, then $V_1.\texttt{read}(B)$ and $V_2.\texttt{read}(N)$ evaluate to the same boolean value.

The informal argument goes: "if any ground context $\mathcal{M}[- : \texttt{smph}] : \texttt{gnd}$ makes use of a term placed in its hole $-$ at all, it must do so by opening it as an abstract pair α, x and applying the methods bit, flip, and read in some combination to get a term of ground type; therefore the above observations about r are enough to show that $\mathcal{M}[\texttt{Smph}_1]$ and $\mathcal{M}[\texttt{Smph}_2]$ always have the same evaluation behaviour." The assumptions this informal argument makes about the way a context can 'use' its hole need formal justification. Leaving that for the next section, at least we can state the relational principle a bit more precisely.

Principle 2.6 (Extensionality for $\exists$-types, Version III). *For each existential type $\varepsilon \stackrel{\mathrm{def}}{=} \exists\,\alpha\,.\,\tau(\alpha)$, types τ_1, τ_2, and values V_1, V_2, if there is a* relation *$r : \tau_1 \leftrightarrow \tau_2$ between terms of type τ_1 and of type τ_2, such that $(V_1, V_2) \in \tau[r]$, then* $(\texttt{pack}\,\tau_1, V_1\,\texttt{as}\,\varepsilon) =_{\mathrm{ctx}} (\texttt{pack}\,\tau_2, V_2\,\texttt{as}\,\varepsilon) : \exists\,\alpha\,.\,\tau(\alpha)$.

Here $\tau[r] : \tau(\tau_1) \leftrightarrow \tau(\tau_2)$ is a relation defined by induction on the structure of the type τ. It is the definition of this 'action' of types on term relations which is at the heart of the matter. It has to be phrased with some care in order for the above extensionality principle to be valid for languages involving non-termination of evaluation (through the presence of fixpoint recursion for example). We will give a precise definition in the next section (Fig. 2), for a language combining impredicative polymorphism with fixpoint recursion (Fig. 1).

Note. Principle 2.4 generalises Principle 2.3, because if $\tau_1 =_\alpha \tau_2$, then the identity function $\texttt{I} \stackrel{\mathrm{def}}{=} \lambda\,x : \tau_1\,.\,x$ is a bijection $\tau_1 \cong \tau_2$ satisfying $\tau[\texttt{I}](V) =_{\mathrm{ctx}} V$ (for any V)—so that $V_1 =_{\mathrm{ctx}} V_2$ implies $\tau[\texttt{I}](V_1) =_{\mathrm{ctx}} V_2$. Principle 2.6 generalises Principle 2.4, because each bijection $\texttt{I} : \tau_1 \cong \tau_2$ can be replaced by its *graph*

$$r_{\texttt{I}} \stackrel{\mathrm{def}}{=} \{(U_1, U_2) \mid \texttt{I}(U_1) =_{\mathrm{ctx}} U_2\}$$

which in fact has the property that $(V_1, V_2) \in \tau[r_{\texttt{I}}]$ iff $\tau[\texttt{I}](V_1) =_{\mathrm{ctx}} V_2 : \tau(\tau_2)$.

As mentioned in the Introduction, Principle 2.6 is an operational version of similar principles for the denotational semantics of abstract datatypes over simply typed lambda calculus (Mitchell 1991) and relationally parametric models of the polymorphic lambda calculus (Plotkin and Abadi 1993). It permits many examples of contextual equivalence at $\exists$-types to be proved rather easily. Nevertheless, we will see in Sect. 4 that in the presence of non-termination it is incomplete.

3 An Operationally-Based Logical Relation

The purpose of this section is to give a definition of an action $r \mapsto \tau[r]$ of type constructions $\tau(\alpha)$ on relations r (between terms) validating the extensionality Principle 2.6 for contextual equivalence at $\exists$-types. We will do this for a programming language combining a call-by-value version of Plotkin's PCF (1977) with record types and the polymorphic lambda calculus (Girard 1972; Reynolds 1974). The types, values (canonical forms), terms and frame stacks of the language are specified in Fig. 1. (The role of frame stacks is explained below.)

To simplify the definition of the language's operational semantics we are using a 'reduced' syntax in which all sequential evaluation has to be coded via `let`-expressions. For example, the general form of (call-by-value) function application is coded by

$$M_1\, M_2 \stackrel{\text{def}}{=} \mathtt{let}\, x_1 = M_1\, \mathtt{in}\, (\mathtt{let}\, x_2 = M_2\, \mathtt{in}\, (x_1\, x_2)).$$

As a further simplification, function abstraction and recursive function declaration have been rolled into the one form $\mathtt{fun}(f(x:\tau) = M : \tau')$ which corresponds to the Standard ML value

$$\mathtt{fn}\, x => (\mathtt{letfun}\, f(x{:}\tau) = (M{:}\tau')\, \mathtt{in}\, M\, \mathtt{end}).$$

Ordinary function abstraction $\lambda x : \tau \,.\, M$ can be coded as $\mathtt{fun}(f(x:\tau) = M : \tau')$ where f does not occur freely in M (and τ' is the type of M). See (Pitts and Stark 1998, pp 234–7) for further examples of this kind of reduced syntax. One slightly subtle aspect of the present language is that restricting the operation of polymorphic generalisation $\Lambda\,\alpha\,.\,(-)$ to apply only to values is a real restriction: one cannot define $\Lambda\,\alpha\,.\,M$ to be $\mathtt{let}\, x = M\, \mathtt{in}\, \Lambda\,\alpha\,.\,x$, since the latter will in general be an ill-typed term. In effect we are imposing an explicitly typed version of the 'value-restriction' on `let`-bound polymorphism which occurs in the 1996 revision of Standard ML (Milner, Tofte, Harper, and MacQueen 1997). It is convenient to do so, because then we do not have to consider evaluating 'under a Λ' and hence can restrict attention to the evaluation of closed terms of *closed* type. There is good evidence that this restriction is not important in practice (Wright 1995).

Note. The constructions

$$\forall\,\alpha\,.\,(-),\quad \exists\,\alpha\,.\,(-),\quad \mathtt{fun}(f(x:\tau) = (-) : \tau'),\quad \Lambda\,\alpha\,.\,(-),$$
$$\mathtt{open}\, V\, \mathtt{as}\, \alpha, x\, \mathtt{in}\, (-),\quad \mathtt{let}\, x = M\, \mathtt{in}\, (-),\quad \text{and}\quad S \circ (x)(-)$$

Types $\tau ::=$	α	type variables
	`bool`	type of booleans
	`int`	type of integers
	$\tau \to \tau$	function types
	$\{\ell : \tau, \ldots, \ell : \tau\}$	record types
	$\forall \alpha . \tau$	$\forall$-types
	$\exists \alpha . \tau$	$\exists$-types.

Values $V ::=$	f, x	variables
	$\mathtt{c}$	boolean and integer constants
	$\mathtt{fun}(f(x : \tau) = M : \tau)$	recursively defined functions
	$\{\ell = V, \ldots, \ell = V\}$	records
	$\Lambda \alpha . V$	polymorphic generalisations
	$\mathtt{pack}\ \tau, V\ \mathtt{as}\ \exists \alpha . \tau$	$\exists$-type constructors.

Terms $M ::=$	V	values
	$\mathtt{if}\ V\ \mathtt{then}\ M\ \mathtt{else}\ M$	conditionals
	$\mathtt{op}(V, \ldots, V)$	arithmetic and boolean operations
	$V\,V$	function applications
	$V.\ell$	record selections
	$V\,\tau$	polymorphic specialisations
	$\mathtt{open}\ V\ \mathtt{as}\ \alpha, x\ \mathtt{in}\ M$	$\exists$-type destructors
	$\mathtt{let}\ x = M\ \mathtt{in}\ M$	sequential evaluations.

Frame Stacks $S ::=$	Id	empty stack
	$S \circ (x)M$	non-empty stack.

Here α and x, f range over disjoint countably infinite sets of *type variables* and *variables* respectively; ℓ ranges over a countably infinite set of *labels*; c ranges over the constants `true`, `false`, and `n` (for $n \in \mathbb{Z}$); and `op` ranges over a fixed collection of arithmetic and boolean operations of various arities (such as $+$, $=$, `not`, etc).

Termination relation, $S \top M$ (S and M closed), is inductively defined by:

$$\mathit{Id} \top V \qquad \frac{S \top M(V/x)}{S \circ (x)M \top V} \qquad \frac{S \circ (x)M_2 \top M_1}{S \top \mathtt{let}\ x = M_1\ \mathtt{in}\ M_2} \qquad \frac{S \top M'}{S \top M}\ \text{if } M \to M'$$

where the relation $M \to M'$ of *primitive reduction* is directly defined, as follows:

$$\begin{aligned}
\mathtt{if\ true\ then}\ M_1\ \mathtt{else}\ M_2 &\to M_1, \\
\mathtt{if\ false\ then}\ M_1\ \mathtt{else}\ M_2 &\to M_2, \\
\mathtt{op}(\mathtt{c}_1, \ldots, \mathtt{c}_n) &\to \mathtt{c} \quad \text{if } c \text{ is the value of } op(c_1, \ldots, c_n), \\
F\,V &\to M(F/f, V/x) \quad \text{if } F = \mathtt{fun}(f(x : \tau) = M : \tau'), \\
R.\ell &\to V \quad \text{if } R = \{\ldots, \ell = V, \ldots\} \\
(\Lambda \alpha . V)\,\tau &\to V(\tau/\alpha), \\
\mathtt{open}\ V\ \mathtt{as}\ \alpha, x\ \mathtt{in}\ M &\to M(\tau'/\alpha, V'/x) \quad \text{if } V = \mathtt{pack}\ \tau', V'\ \mathtt{as}\ \exists \alpha . \tau.
\end{aligned}$$

Fig. 1. Syntax and operational semantics of the language

are binders and we will identify expressions up to renaming of bound variables and bound type variables. A type is *closed* if it has no free type variables; whereas a term or frame stack is closed if it has no free variables, whether or not it also has free type variables. The result of substituting a type τ for all free occurrences of a type variable α in e (a type, term, or frame stack) will be denoted $e(\tau/\alpha)$. Similarly, $e(V/x)$ denotes the result of substituting a value V for all free occurrences of the variable x in a term or frame stack e. Note that variables stand for unknown *values*—the substitution of a non-value term for a variable makes no sense syntactically, in that it may result in an ill-formed expression.

Termination

The operational semantics of the language can be specified in terms of an inductively defined evaluation relation $M \Downarrow V$ between closed terms M and closed values V; and this evaluation relation determines a notion of contextual equivalence for the language as in Definition 2.2. However, in this case (because evaluation is strict and the language has enough destructors of ground type) contextual equivalence can be phrased just in terms of the associated termination relation, $M\Downarrow$, which by definition holds iff $M \Downarrow V$ holds for some V. This is because two terms are contextually equivalent iff they yield the same termination behaviour when placed in any context (not necessarily of ground type). Therefore for our purposes, it suffices to define the termination relation. In fact, to define the action of types on relations we will need to define $\mathcal{E}[M]\Downarrow$ for any *evaluation context* $\mathcal{E}[-]$—a context with a unique hole, occurring in the place where the next step of evaluation will take place. In order to get a convenient, structural definition of termination, we will use a representation of evaluation contexts in terms of the auxiliary notion of *frame stack* given in Fig. 1. A typical frame stack

$$S = Id \circ (x_1)M_1 \circ \cdots \circ (x_n)M_n$$

corresponds to the evaluation context

$$\mathcal{E}[-] = \mathtt{let}\, x_1 = (\ldots(\mathtt{let}\, x_n = (-)\ \mathtt{in}\ M_n)\ldots)\ \mathtt{in}\ M_1$$

and under this correspondence it can be shown that $\mathcal{E}[M]\Downarrow$ holds iff $S \top M$, where the relation $(-) \top (-)$ is defined in the second half of Fig. 1.

Typing

We will only consider the termination relation $S \top M$ for terms and frame stacks which are *well-typed*. A term M is well-typed if a typing judgement

$$\Gamma \vdash M : \tau \tag{6}$$

can be derived for some type τ, where the typing environment

$$\Gamma = \alpha_1, \ldots, \alpha_m, x : \tau_1, \ldots, x_n : \tau_n$$

contains (at least) the free variables and type variables occurring in M and τ. The axioms and rules for inductively generating the valid judgements of the form (6) for this language are all quite standard and we will not give them here: see (Cardelli 1997), for example. The terms contain sufficient explicit type information to ensure that for any given Γ and M, there is at most one τ for which (6) holds. The judgement for typing frame stacks takes the form

$$\Gamma \vdash S : \tau \multimap \tau' \tag{7}$$

where, in terms of the corresponding evaluation contexts, τ is the type of the hole and τ' is the overall type of the context. The rules for generating this judgement are simply

$$\Gamma \vdash \mathit{Id} : \tau \multimap \tau \qquad \text{and} \qquad \frac{\Gamma \vdash S : \tau_2 \multimap \tau_3}{\Gamma \vdash S \circ (x)M : \tau_1 \multimap \tau_3} \text{ if } \Gamma, x : \tau_1 \vdash M : \tau_2 .$$

Unlike for terms, we have not included explicit type information in the syntax of frame stacks. For example, *Id* is not tagged with a type. However, it is not hard to see that, given Γ, S, and τ, there is at most one τ' for which $\Gamma \vdash S : \tau \multimap \tau'$ holds. This property is enough for our purposes, since the argument type of a frame stack will always be supplied in any particular situation in which we use it.

Definition 3.1. *Let Typ denote the set of closed types. Given $\tau \in \mathit{Typ}$, let*

- *$\mathit{Term}(\tau)$ denote the set of closed terms of type τ, i.e. those terms M for which $\emptyset \vdash M : \tau$ holds;*
- *$\mathit{Val}(\tau)$ denote the subset of $\mathit{Term}(\tau)$ whose elements are values;*
- *$\mathit{Stack}(\tau)$ denote the set of closed frame stacks whose argument type is τ, i.e. those terms S for which $\emptyset \vdash S : \tau \multimap \tau'$ holds for some $\tau' \in \mathit{Typ}$.*

Relations

We will be using binary relations between closed terms of closed type. However, the admissibility condition we consider on such relations involves the use of binary relations between frame stacks as well. Given closed types $\tau, \tau' \in \mathit{Typ}$, and referring to Definition 3.1, let

- $\mathit{Rel}(\tau, \tau')$ denote the set of all subsets of $\mathit{Term}(\tau) \times \mathit{Term}(\tau')$;
- $\mathit{Rel}^{\top}(\tau, \tau')$ denote the the set of all subsets of $\mathit{Stack}(\tau) \times \mathit{Stack}(\tau')$.

One can turn term relations into frame stack relations and *vice versa* using the Galois connection introduced in (Pitts 1998, Definition 4.7):

Definition 3.2. *If $r \in \mathit{Rel}(\tau, \tau')$, let $r^{\top} \in \mathit{Rel}^{\top}(\tau, \tau')$ be defined by*

$$(S, S') \in r^{\top} \quad \mathit{iff} \quad \forall (M, M') \in r \,.\, S \top M \Leftrightarrow S' \top M' \ .$$

If $s \in Rel^{\top}(\tau,\tau')$, *let* $s^{\top} \in Rel(\tau,\tau')$ *be defined by*

$$(M,M') \in s^{\top} \quad \textit{iff} \quad \forall\,(S,S') \in s\,.\,S \top M \Leftrightarrow S' \top M' \ .$$

Call a term relation $r \in Rel(\tau,\tau')$ valuable *if it satisfies* $r = (r^{val})^{\top\top}$, *where* r^{val} *indicates the restriction of the relation to values*

$$r^{val} \stackrel{\text{def}}{=} \{(V,V') \in Val(\tau) \times Val(\tau') \mid (V,V') \in r\} \ .$$

It is not hard to see that $r \mapsto (r^{val})^{\top\top}$ *is an idempotent operation, so that* r *is valuable iff it is of the form* $(r_1^{val})^{\top\top}$ *for some term relation* r_1.

The definition of the action of types on term relations is given in Fig. 2. It takes the following form: if $\tau(\vec{\alpha})$ is a type whose free type variables lie amongst the list $\vec{\alpha} = \alpha_1,\ldots,\alpha_n$, then given a corresponding list of term relations

$$r_1 \in Rel(\tau_1,\tau_1'),\ldots,r_n \in Rel(\tau_n,\tau_n')$$

we define a term relation $\tau[\vec{r}] \in Rel(\tau(\vec{\tau}/\vec{\alpha}),\tau'(\vec{\tau}/\vec{\alpha}))$. The definition is by induction on the structure of τ as in Fig. 2. (This definition should be compared with the corresponding one for call-by-name PCF plus polymorphism given in Pitts 1998, Fig. 5.)

We use the action defined in Fig. 2 to define a relation between open terms of the same type (cf. Pitts 1998, Definition 4.12).

Definition 3.3 (Logical relation). *Suppose* $\Gamma \vdash M : \tau$ *and* $\Gamma \vdash M' : \tau$ *hold, with* $\Gamma = \alpha_1,\ldots,\alpha_m, x:\tau_1,\ldots,x:\tau_n$ *say. Write*

$$\Gamma \vdash M \mathrel{\Delta} M' : \tau \tag{15}$$

to mean that for any $\sigma_i,\sigma_i' \in Typ$ *and* $r_i \in Rel(\sigma_i,\sigma_i')$ *(for* $i = 1,\ldots,m$*), and for any* $(V_j,V_j') \in \tau_j[\vec{r}]^{val}$ *(for* $j = 1,\ldots,n$*), it is the case that*

$$(M(\vec{\sigma}/\vec{\alpha},\vec{V}/\vec{x}),M'(\vec{\sigma}'/\vec{\alpha},\vec{V}'/\vec{x})) \in \tau[\vec{r}] \ .$$

Theorem 3.4 (Fundamental property of the logical relation). *The relation (15) is respected by all the term-forming operations of the language. So in particular, if (15) holds and* $\mathcal{M}[-]$ *is a context such that* $\Gamma' \vdash \mathcal{M}[M] : \tau'$ *and* $\Gamma' \vdash \mathcal{M}[M'] : \tau'$, *then* $\Gamma' \vdash \mathcal{M}[M] \mathrel{\Delta} \mathcal{M}[M'] : \tau'$ *also holds.*

The theorem can be proved by induction on the structure of terms. The hard induction step is that for recursively defined function values, where one needs an 'unwinding' property of such values with respect to the termination relation (cf. Pitts 1998, Theorem 4.8). One also needs the following substitution property:

$$\tau''[\vec{r}] = \tau[\tau'[\vec{r}],\vec{r}] \quad \text{when } \tau'' =_{\alpha} \tau(\tau'/\alpha), \quad \text{for any } \tau(\alpha,\vec{\alpha}) \text{ and } \tau'(\vec{\alpha}). \tag{16}$$

This is easily proved by induction on the structure of τ, using the fact that, by construction, each $\tau[\vec{r}]$ is valuable (i.e. $(\tau[\vec{r}]^{val})^{\top\top} = \tau[\vec{r}]$), whether or not the relations $\vec{r}$ are.

$$
\begin{aligned}
\alpha_i[\vec{r}] &\stackrel{\text{def}}{=} (r_i^{val})^{\top\top} && (8)\\
\texttt{bool}[\vec{r}] &\stackrel{\text{def}}{=} \{(\texttt{b},\texttt{b}) \mid \texttt{b} \in \{\texttt{true},\texttt{false}\}\}^{\top\top} && (9)\\
\texttt{int}[\vec{r}] &\stackrel{\text{def}}{=} \{(\texttt{n},\texttt{n}) \mid \texttt{n} \in \mathbb{Z}\}^{\top\top} && (10)\\
(\tau_1 \to \tau_2)[\vec{r}] &\stackrel{\text{def}}{=} \mathit{fun}(\tau_1[\vec{r}], \tau_2[\vec{r}])^{\top\top} && (11)\\
\{\ell_1 : \tau_1, \dots, \ell_n : \tau_n\}[\vec{r}] &\stackrel{\text{def}}{=} \{\ell_1 = \tau_1[\vec{r}], \dots, \ell_n = \tau_n[\vec{r}]\}^{\top\top} && (12)\\
(\forall\, \alpha \,.\, \tau)[\vec{r}] &\stackrel{\text{def}}{=} (\Lambda r \,.\, \tau[r, \vec{r}])^{\top\top} && (13)\\
(\exists\, \alpha \,.\, \tau)[\vec{r}] &\stackrel{\text{def}}{=} (\exists r \,.\, \tau[r, \vec{r}])^{\top\top} && (14)
\end{aligned}
$$

In addition to the $(-)^{\top\top}$ and $(-)^{val}$ operations on term relations of Definition 3.2, these definitions make use of the following operations for constructing *value* relations from term relations:

(11)
$$
\frac{r_1 \in \mathit{Rel}(\tau_1, \tau_1') \quad r_2 \in \mathit{Rel}(\tau_2, \tau_2')}{\begin{aligned}&\mathit{fun}(r_1, r_2) \in \mathit{Rel}(\tau_1 \to \tau_2, \tau_1' \to \tau_2')\\ &\quad\stackrel{\text{def}}{=} \{(F, F') \in \mathit{Val} \times \mathit{Val} \mid \forall\, (A, A') \in r_1^{val} \,.\, (F\, A, F'\, A') \in r_2\}\end{aligned}}
$$

(12)
$$
\frac{r_1 \in \mathit{Rel}(\tau_1, \tau_1') \quad \cdots \quad r_n \in \mathit{Rel}(\tau_n, \tau_n')}{\begin{aligned}&\{\ell_1 = r_1, \dots, \ell_n = r_n\} \in \mathit{Rel}(\{\ell_1 : \tau_1, \dots, \ell_n : \tau_n\}, \{\ell_1 : \tau_1', \dots, \ell_n : \tau_n'\})\\ &\quad\stackrel{\text{def}}{=} \{(R, R') \in \mathit{Val} \times \mathit{Val} \mid \\ &\qquad\qquad \forall\, i = 1, \dots, n \,.\, (R.\ell_i, R'.\ell_i) \in r_i\}\end{aligned}}
$$

(13)
$$
\frac{r \in \mathit{Rel}(\tau_2, \tau_2') \mapsto R(r) \in \mathit{Rel}(\tau_1(\tau_2/\alpha), \tau_1'(\tau_2'/\alpha)) \qquad (\tau_2, \tau_2' \in \mathit{Typ})}{\begin{aligned}&\Lambda r \,.\, R(r) \in \mathit{Rel}(\forall\, \alpha \,.\, \tau_1, \forall\, \alpha \,.\, \tau_1')\\ &\quad\stackrel{\text{def}}{=} \{(G, G') \in \mathit{Val} \times \mathit{Val} \mid \forall\, \tau_2, \tau_2' \in \mathit{Typ}, r \in \mathit{Rel}(\tau_2, \tau_2') \,.\\ &\qquad\qquad (G\, \tau_2, G'\, \tau_2') \in R(r)\}\end{aligned}}
$$

(14)
$$
\frac{r \in \mathit{Rel}(\tau_2, \tau_2') \mapsto R(r) \in \mathit{Rel}(\tau_1(\tau_2/\alpha), \tau_1'(\tau_2'/\alpha)) \qquad (\tau_2, \tau_2' \in \mathit{Typ})}{\begin{aligned}&\exists\, r \,.\, R(r) \in \mathit{Rel}(\exists\, \alpha \,.\, \tau_1, \exists\, \alpha \,.\, \tau_1')\\ &\quad\stackrel{\text{def}}{=} \{(\textsf{pack}\ \tau_2, V\ \textsf{as}\ \exists\, \alpha \,.\, \tau_1, \textsf{pack}\ \tau_2', V'\ \textsf{as}\ \exists\, \alpha \,.\, \tau_1') \mid \\ &\qquad\qquad \exists\, r \in \mathit{Rel}(\tau_2, \tau_2') \,.\, (V, V') \in R(r)\} \,.\end{aligned}}
$$

Fig. 2. Action of types on term relations

Note that if $\emptyset \vdash M \mathrel{\Delta} M' : \texttt{int}$, then from (10) we have that $(M, M') \in \{(\mathrm{n},\mathrm{n}) \mid \mathrm{n} \in \mathbb{Z}\}^{\top\top}$. Since $(\mathit{Id}, \mathit{Id}) \in \{(\mathrm{n},\mathrm{n}) \mid \mathrm{n} \in \mathbb{Z}\}^{\top}$, we have

$$M{\Downarrow} \quad \text{iff} \quad \mathit{Id} \top M \quad \text{iff} \quad \mathit{Id} \top M' \quad \text{iff} \quad M'{\Downarrow}.$$

From this observation (and a similar one for `bool`) and Theorem 3.4 we conclude that if $\Gamma \vdash M \mathrel{\Delta} M' : \tau$ holds, then M and M' are contextually equivalent (Definition 2.2). In fact the converse also holds (cf. Pitts 1998, Theorem 4.15) and so we obtain:

Corollary 3.5. *Given $\Gamma \vdash M : \tau$ and $\Gamma \vdash M' : \tau$, M and M' are contextually equivalent if and only if $\Gamma \vdash M \mathrel{\Delta} M' : \tau$.*

In particular, for an existential type $\exists\, \alpha \,.\, \tau \in \mathit{Typ}$, using (14) we have that contextual equivalence at this type coincides with the relation $(\exists\, r \,.\, \tau[r])^{\top\top}$. Since $\exists\, r \,.\, \tau[r]$ is always a subset of this latter relation, we have succeeded in validating the extensionality Principle 2.6 for this language.

4 Incompleteness of the Extensionality Principle for ∃-Types

For a closed type $\tau \in \mathit{Typ}$, writing $=_\tau \in \mathit{Rel}(\tau, \tau)$ for the relation of contextual equivalence at that type, we can summarise part of what was proved in the previous section by the following equations, which use the various constructions on relations from Fig. 2.

$$=_{\tau_1 \to \tau_2} = \mathit{fun}(=_{\tau_1}, =_{\tau_2})^{\top\top} \tag{17}$$

$$=_{\{\ell_1:\tau_1,\ldots,\ell_n:\tau_n\}} = \{\ell_1 = (=_{\tau_1}), \ldots, \ell_1 = (=_{\tau_n})\}^{\top\top} \tag{18}$$

$$=_{\forall\, \alpha \,.\, \tau(\alpha)} = (\Lambda\, r \,.\, \tau[r])^{\top\top} \tag{19}$$

$$=_{\exists\, \alpha \,.\, \tau(\alpha)} = (\exists\, r \,.\, \tau[r])^{\top\top} \;. \tag{20}$$

To understand what this tells us about the nature of contextual equivalence at function, record, ∀-, and ∃-types requires an analysis of the closure operation $(-)^{\top\top}$. We will not carry out that analysis here, other than to note what happens when we restrict these equations to values.

Simple calculations with the definitions in Fig. 2 reveal that for all term relations $\vec{r}$ it is the case that

$$(\tau_1 \to \tau_2)[\vec{r}]^{val} = \mathit{fun}(\tau_1[\vec{r}], \tau_2[\vec{r}]) \tag{21}$$

$$\{\ell_1 : \tau_1, \ldots, \ell_n : \tau_n\}[\vec{r}]^{val} = \{\ell_1 = \tau_1[\vec{r}], \ldots, \ell_n = \tau_n[\vec{r}]\} \tag{22}$$

$$(\forall\, \alpha \,.\, \tau)[\vec{r}]^{val} = (\Lambda\, r \,.\, \tau[r, \vec{r}]) \;. \tag{23}$$

This yields the following properties of contextual equivalence via Corollary 3.5.

$$(=_{\tau_1 \to \tau_2})^{val} = \mathit{fun}(=_{\tau_1}, =_{\tau_2}) \tag{24}$$

$$(=_{\{\ell_1:\tau_1,\ldots,\ell_n:\tau_n\}})^{val} = \{\ell_1 = (=_{\tau_1}), \ldots, \ell_1 = (=_{\tau_n})\} \tag{25}$$

$$(=_{\forall\, \alpha \,.\, \tau(\alpha)})^{val} = \Lambda\, r \,.\, \tau[r] \;. \tag{26}$$

Property (24) validates a familiar extensionality principle for functions (adapted to this call-by-value language):

> *given values* $F, F' \in Val(\tau_1 \to \tau_2)$, *then* $F =_{\mathrm{ctx}} F' : \tau_1 \to \tau_2$ *if and only if for all values* $A \in Val(\tau_1)$, $F\,A =_{\mathrm{ctx}} F'\,A : \tau_2$.

Similarly, (25) and (26) validate extensionality principles for values of record types and $\forall$-types. In fact (26) is far more powerful than a mere extensionality property: it tells us that, up to contextual equivalence, $\forall$-types are relationally parametric in the sense of Reynolds (1983); this can be exploited to easily establish many properties polymorphic types up to contextual equivalence (for example, encodings of datatypes—see Pitts 1998).

In contrast to these pleasant properties of function, record and $\forall$-types, if we restrict (20) to values all we obtain is the inclusion

$$(=_{\exists\,\alpha\,.\,\tau(\alpha)})^{val} \;=\; ((\exists\, r\,.\,\tau[r])^{\top\top})^{val} \supseteq \exists\, r\,.\,\tau[r]$$

but the inclusion is in general a proper one. In other words the converse of Principle 2.6 is not valid in general: *it can be the case that* $\mathtt{pack}\,\sigma, V\ \mathtt{as}\ \exists\,\alpha\,.\,\tau(\alpha)$ *is contextually equivalent to* $\mathtt{pack}\ \sigma', V'\ \mathtt{as}\ \exists\,\alpha\,.\,\tau(\alpha)$ *even though there is no* $r \in Rel(\sigma, \sigma')$ *with* $(V, V') \in \tau[r]$. The rest of this section is devoted to giving an example of this unpleasant phenomenon (based on a suggestion of Ian Stark arising out of our joint work on logical relations for functions and dynamically allocated names, Pitts and Stark 1993).

Example 4.1. Consider the following types and terms:

$$
\begin{aligned}
\mathtt{pp}(\alpha) &\stackrel{\text{def}}{=} (\alpha \to \mathtt{bool}) \to \mathtt{bool}\\
\mathtt{quant} &\stackrel{\text{def}}{=} \exists\,\alpha\,.\,\mathtt{pp}(\alpha)\\
\mathtt{null} &\stackrel{\text{def}}{=} \forall\,\alpha\,.\,\alpha\\
\mathtt{G} &\stackrel{\text{def}}{=} \mathtt{fun}(g(f : \mathtt{null} \to \mathtt{bool}) = (g\,f) : \mathtt{bool})\\
\mathtt{G}' &\stackrel{\text{def}}{=} \mathtt{fun}(g(f : \mathtt{bool} \to \mathtt{bool}) = \ \mathtt{if}\ (f\,\mathtt{true})\ \mathtt{then}\\
&\qquad\qquad \mathtt{if}\ (f\,\mathtt{false})\ \mathtt{then}\\
&\qquad\qquad\quad g\,f\\
&\qquad\qquad \mathtt{else}\ \mathtt{true}\\
&\qquad\quad \mathtt{else}\ (g\,f) \qquad\qquad : \mathtt{bool})\ .
\end{aligned}
$$

Thus `null` is a type with no values; `G` is a function which diverges when applied to any value of type $\mathtt{null} \to \mathtt{bool}$; and $\mathtt{G}'$ is a function which diverges when applied to any value of type $\mathtt{bool} \to \mathtt{bool}$ except ones (such as the identity function) which map `true` to `true` and `false` to `false`, in which case it returns `true`. We claim that

(i) there is no $r \in Rel(\mathtt{null}, \mathtt{bool})$ for which $(\mathtt{G}, \mathtt{G}') \in \mathtt{pp}[r]$ holds, but nevertheless

(ii) $\mathtt{pack}\,\mathtt{null}, \mathtt{G}\ \mathtt{as}\ \mathtt{quant} =_{\mathrm{ctx}} \mathtt{pack}\,\mathtt{bool}, \mathtt{G}'\ \mathtt{as}\ \mathtt{quant} : \exists\,\alpha\,.\,\mathtt{pp}(\alpha)$.

Proof of (i). Note that the definition of null implies that $\mathit{Val}(\texttt{null}) = \emptyset$. Therefore any $r \in \mathit{Rel}(\texttt{null}, \texttt{bool})$ satisfies that $(\alpha[r])^{val} = ((r^{val})^{\top\top})^{val} = \emptyset$. Therefore from (21) and the definition of $\mathit{fun}(-,-)$ in Fig. 2 we get

$$(\alpha \to \texttt{bool})[r]^{val} = \mathit{fun}(\alpha[r], \texttt{bool}[r]) = \mathit{Val}(\texttt{null} \to \texttt{bool}) \times \mathit{Val}(\texttt{bool} \to \texttt{bool}).$$

Now by Corollary 3.5, $\texttt{bool}[r] \stackrel{\text{def}}{=} \{(\texttt{b}, \texttt{b}) \mid \texttt{b} = \texttt{true}, \texttt{false}\}^{\top\top}$ is $=_{\texttt{bool}}$, contextual equivalence at type bool. Therefore

$$\begin{aligned} \texttt{pp}[r]^{val} &\stackrel{\text{def}}{=} \mathit{fun}((\alpha \to \texttt{bool})[r], \texttt{bool}[r]) \\ &= \{(G, G') \mid \forall F \in \mathit{Val}(\texttt{null} \to \texttt{bool}), F' \in \mathit{Val}(\texttt{bool} \to \texttt{bool}) \,. \\ &\qquad\qquad G\,F =_{\text{ctx}} G'\,F' : \texttt{bool}\}. \end{aligned}$$

But the values

$$\texttt{F} \stackrel{\text{def}}{=} \texttt{fun}(f(x:\texttt{null}) = f\,x : \texttt{bool}) \quad \text{and} \quad \texttt{F}' \stackrel{\text{def}}{=} \texttt{fun}(f(x:\texttt{bool}) = x : \texttt{bool})$$

satisfy

$$\texttt{G}\,\texttt{F} \not\Downarrow \quad \text{and} \quad \texttt{G}'\,\texttt{F}' \Downarrow \texttt{true}$$

so that $\texttt{G}\,\texttt{F} \neq_{\text{ctx}} \texttt{G}'\,\texttt{F}' : \texttt{bool}$. Hence $(\texttt{G}, \texttt{G}') \notin \texttt{pp}[r]^{val}$, as required.

Proof of (ii). The termination relation defined in Fig. 1 provides a possible strategy, if rather a tedious one, for proving contextual equivalences—by what one might call *termination induction*. For example, to prove (ii) it suffices to prove for all appropriately typed contexts $\mathcal{M}[-]$ that

$$\mathcal{M}[\texttt{pack null}, \texttt{G as quant}]\Downarrow \quad \text{iff} \quad \mathcal{M}[\texttt{pack bool}, \texttt{G}' \texttt{ as quant}]\Downarrow$$

or equivalently that

$$\mathit{Id} \top \mathcal{M}[\texttt{pack null}, \texttt{G as quant}] \quad \text{iff} \quad \mathit{Id} \top \mathcal{M}[\texttt{pack bool}, \texttt{G}' \texttt{ as quant}].$$

If one attempts to do this by induction on the definition of the $(-) \top (-)$ relation in Fig. 1, it is clear from the first of the three rules involved in that definition that one must attempt to prove a stronger statement, namely that for all contexts $\mathcal{M}[-]$ and frame stack contexts $\mathcal{S}[-]$

$$\begin{gathered} \mathcal{S}[\texttt{pack null}, \texttt{G as quant}] \top \mathcal{M}[\texttt{pack null}, \texttt{G as quant}] \\ \text{iff} \\ \mathcal{S}[\texttt{pack bool}, \texttt{G}' \texttt{ as quant}] \top \mathcal{M}[\texttt{pack bool}, \texttt{G}' \texttt{ as quant}]. \end{gathered}$$

It is indeed possible to prove this by induction on the definition of $(-) \top (-)$ (for all $\mathcal{M}[-]$ and $\mathcal{S}[-]$ simultaneously). The crucial induction step is that for the primitive reduction of a function application, where the following lemma is required. It lies at the heart of the reason why the contextual equivalence in Example 4.1(ii) is valid: if an argument supplied to $\texttt{G}'$ is sufficiently polymorphic (which is guaranteed by the existential abstraction), then when specialised to bool it cannot have the functionality ($\texttt{true} \mapsto \texttt{true}$, $\texttt{false} \mapsto \texttt{false}$) needed to distinguish $\texttt{G}'$ from the divergent behaviour of G.

Lemma 4.2. *With* $\mathtt{pp}(\alpha)$ *and* $\mathtt{G}'$ *as in Example 4.1, suppose* F *is any value satisfying* $\alpha, g : \mathtt{pp}(\alpha) \vdash F : \alpha \to \mathtt{bool}$*. Then* $\mathtt{G}'\, F(\mathtt{bool}/\alpha, \mathtt{G}'/g) \not\Downarrow$.

Proof. This can be proved quite easily using the logical relation of the previous section. Consider the following term relation in $Rel(\mathtt{bool}, \mathtt{bool})$:

$$r \stackrel{\text{def}}{=} \{(\mathtt{true}, \mathtt{true}), (\mathtt{false}, \mathtt{false}), (\mathtt{true}, \mathtt{false})\} .$$

Then one can calculate that $\mathtt{pp}[r] = \mathit{fun}(\mathit{fun}(r^{\top\top}, =_{\mathtt{bool}}), =_{\mathtt{bool}})$, from which it follows that $(\mathtt{G}', \mathtt{G}') \in \mathtt{pp}[r]$. So by Theorem 3.4 we have

$$(F(\mathtt{bool}/\alpha, \mathtt{G}'/g), F(\mathtt{bool}/\alpha, \mathtt{G}'/g)) \in (\alpha \to \mathtt{bool})[r] = \mathit{fun}(r^{\top\top}, =_{\mathtt{bool}}) .$$

Since $(\mathtt{true}, \mathtt{false}) \in r \subseteq (r^{\top\top})^{val}$, we get

$$(F(\mathtt{bool}/\alpha, \mathtt{G}'/g)\, \mathtt{true}, F(\mathtt{bool}/\alpha, \mathtt{G}'/g)\, \mathtt{false}) \in =_{\mathtt{bool}} .$$

Thus $F(\mathtt{bool}/\alpha, \mathtt{G}'/g)\, \mathtt{true}$ and $F(\mathtt{bool}/\alpha, \mathtt{G}'/g)\, \mathtt{false}$ are contextually equivalent closed terms of type $\mathtt{bool}$. So we certainly cannot have both

$$F(\mathtt{bool}/\alpha, \mathtt{G}'/g)\, \mathtt{true} \Downarrow \mathtt{true} \quad \text{and} \quad F(\mathtt{bool}/\alpha, \mathtt{G}'/g)\, \mathtt{false} \Downarrow \mathtt{false} .$$

Therefore by definition of $\mathtt{G}'$, it must be the case that $\mathtt{G}'\, F(\mathtt{bool}/\alpha, \mathtt{G}'/g) \not\Downarrow$. □

Note. The terms in Example 4.1 were formulated using *recursively* defined function values for convenience only: clearly there is an equivalent formulation using only ordinary (non-recursive) function abstraction combined with divergent terms of the appropriate types. Thus this shortcoming of Principle 2.6 comes about not so much from the presence of fixpoint recursion as from the presence of divergence in a language combining higher order functions and existential types.

5 Conclusion

We have seen that a familiar (to some) reasoning principle for semantic equivalence of terms of existential type can be formulated directly in terms of the syntax and operational semantics of a programming language combining impredicative polymorphism with recursively defined functions of higher type. One should not be too depressed by the nasty example in Sect. 4: Principle 2.6 seems very useful in practice for proving many examples of equivalent implementations of abstract datatypes—at least ones which can be phrased in the language considered in this paper. However, that language is limited in two important respects: it lacks recursively defined types and subtyping. These features are needed for applications to reasoning about object-oriented programs—for example, for proving properties of the object encodings considered by Bruce, Cardelli, and Pierce (1997). Recursively defined types provide a severe technical challenge for the method of operationally-based logical relations, since one looses the ability to define the relation by induction on the structure of types. One way round this is to develop syntactical versions of the use of projections for constructing recursively defined domains: see (Birkedal and Harper 1997), for example. It may be better in this case to replace the use of logical relations with methods based upon 'bisimilarity-up-to-context': see (Lassen 1998a; Lassen 1998b). We leave this, and the integration of subtyping into the picture, to the future.

References

Birkedal, L. and R. Harper (1997). Relational interpretation of recursive types in an operational setting (Summary). In M. Abadi and T. Ito (Eds.), *Theoretical Aspects of Computer Software, Third International Symposium, TACS'97, Sendai, Japan, September 23 - 26, 1997, Proceedings*, Volume 1281 of *Lecture Notes in Computer Science*. Springer-Verlag, Berlin.

Bruce, K. B., L. Cardelli, and B. C. Pierce (1997). Comparing object encodings. In M. Abadi and T. Ito (Eds.), *Theoretical Aspects of Computer Software, Third International Symposium, TACS'97, Sendai, Japan, September 23 - 26, 1997, Proceedings*, Volume 1281 of *Lecture Notes in Computer Science*. Springer-Verlag, Berlin.

Cardelli, L. (1997). Type systems. In *CRC Handbook of Computer Science and Engineering*, Chapter 103, pp. 2208–2236. CRC Press.

Girard, J.-Y. (1972). *Interprétation fonctionelle et élimination des coupures dans l'arithmetique d'ordre supérieur*. Ph. D. thesis, Université Paris VII. Thèse de doctorat d'état.

Lassen, S. B. (1998a). Relational reasoning about contexts. In A. D. Gordon and A. M. Pitts (Eds.), *Higher Order Operational Techniques in Semantics*, Publications of the Newton Institute, pp. 91–135. Cambridge University Press.

Lassen, S. B. (1998b). *Relational Reasoning about Functions and Nondeterminism*. Ph. D. thesis, Department of Computer Science, University of Aarhus.

Milner, R., M. Tofte, R. Harper, and D. MacQueen (1997). *The Definition of Standard ML (Revised)*. MIT Press.

Mitchell, J. C. (1991). On the equivalence of data representations. In V. Lifschitz (Ed.), *Artificial Intelligence and Mathematical Theory of Computation: Papers in Honor of John McCarthy*, pp. 305–330. Academic Press.

Mitchell, J. C. (1996). *Foundations for Programming Languages*. Foundations of Computing series. MIT Press.

Mitchell, J. C. and G. D. Plotkin (1988). Abtract types have existential types. *ACM Transactions on Programming Languages and Systems 10*, 470–502.

Pitts, A. M. (1998). Parametric polymorphism and operational equivalence (preliminary version). *Electronic Notes in Theoretical Computer Science 10*. Proceedings, 2nd Workshop on Higher Order Operational Techniques in Semantics, Stanford CA, December 1997. To appear.

Pitts, A. M. and I. D. B. Stark (1993). Observable properties of higher order functions that dynamically create local names, or: What's new? In *Mathematical Foundations of Computer Science, Proc. 18th Int. Symp., Gdańsk, 1993*, Volume 711 of *Lecture Notes in Computer Science*, pp. 122–141. Springer-Verlag, Berlin.

Pitts, A. M. and I. D. B. Stark (1998). Operational reasoning for functions with local state. In A. D. Gordon and A. M. Pitts (Eds.), *Higher Order Operational Techniques in Semantics*, Publications of the Newton Institute, pp. 227–273. Cambridge University Press.

Plotkin, G. D. (1973, October). Lambda-definability and logical relations. Memorandum SAI-RM-4, School of Artificial Intelligence, University of Edinburgh.

Plotkin, G. D. (1977). LCF considered as a programming language. *Theoretical Computer Science 5*, 223–255.

Plotkin, G. D. and M. Abadi (1993). A logic for parametric polymorphism. In M. Bezem and J. F. Groote (Eds.), *Typed Lambda Calculus and Applications*, Volume 664 of *Lecture Notes in Computer Science*, pp. 361–375. Springer-Verlag, Berlin.

Reynolds, J. C. (1974). Towards a theory of type structure. In *Paris Colloquium on Programming*, Volume 19 of *Lecture Notes in Computer Science*, pp. 408–425. Springer-Verlag, Berlin.

Reynolds, J. C. (1983). Types, abstraction and parametric polymorphism. In R. E. A. Mason (Ed.), *Information Processing 83*, pp. 513–523. North-Holland, Amsterdam.

Statman, R. (1985). Logical relations and the typed lambda calculus. *Information and Control 65*, 85–97.

Wright, A. K. (1995). Simple imperative polymorphism. *LISP and Symbolic Computation 8*, 343–355.

Optimal Sampling Strategies in Quicksort*

Conrado Martínez and Salvador Roura

Departament de Llenguatges i Sistemes Informàtics, Universitat Politècnica de Catalunya, E-08034 Barcelona, Catalonia, Spain. {conrado,roura}@lsi.upc.es

Abstract. It is well known that the performance of quicksort can be substantially improved by selecting the median of a sample of three elements as the pivot of each partitioning stage. This variant is easily generalized to samples of size $s = 2k + 1$. For large samples the partitions are better as the median of the sample makes a more accurate estimate of the median of the array to be sorted, but the amount of additional comparisons and exchanges to find the median of the sample also increases.

We show that the optimal sample size to minimize the average total cost of quicksort (which includes both comparisons and exchanges) is $s = a \cdot \sqrt{n} + o(\sqrt{n})$. We also give a closed expression for the constant factor a, which depends on the median-finding algorithm and the costs of elementary comparisons and exchanges. The result above holds in most situations, unless the cost of an exchange exceeds by far the cost of a comparison. In that particular case, it is better to select not the median of the samples, but the $(p+1)^{\text{th}}$ element. The value of p can be precisely determined as a function of the ratio between the cost of an exchange and the cost of a comparison.

1 Introduction

Quicksort with median–of–three [8, 10] is a well known variant of quicksort [3, 4, 9] whose benefits have been endorsed both by theoretical analysis and practical experiments. In this variant of quicksort, we select *pivots* in each recursive stage by taking a sample of 3 elements and using the median of the sample as the pivot. The idea is that it is more likely that no subarray is degenerate after the partitioning and hence, worst-case performance is less likely.

This variant is easily generalized to samples of size $s = 2k + 1$ elements, so that the $(k+1)^{\text{th}}$ element in the sample is selected as the pivot. Van Emden [11] analyzed this generalized variant of quicksort, showing that the average number of comparisons made to sort an array of size n is $q(k) \cdot n \ln n + o(n \log n)$, where the coefficient $q(k)$ steadily decreases with k, from $q(0) = 2$ to $q(\infty) = 1/\ln 2$. Thus, if the sample size is large enough, the main term in the average number of comparisons made by quicksort would be as close to the theoretical optimum $n \log_2 n$ as desired.

* This research was supported by the ESPRIT LTR Project ALCOM-IT, contract # 20244 and by a grant from CIRIT (Comissió Interdepartamental de Recerca i Innovació Tecnològica).

However, as the size of the sample increases, we need to invest more resources to compute the median of the samples. Thus the savings achieved by using large samples can easily get lost in practice. The time spent in finding the median of the samples shows up in larger lower order terms of the average performance, growing with the sample size, so that they cannot be disregarded unless n is impractically large.

As far as we know, McGeoch and Tygar [6] were the first authors that analyzed the performance of quicksort with sampling when the size of the samples is not fixed, but grows as a function of n. They considered several such strategies, and proved that samples of size $\Theta(\sqrt{n})$ are optimal over a class of possible strategies. They conjectured that the optimal sample size w.r.t. the number of comparisons is $\Theta(n^{0.56})$, by curve-fitting of the exact optimal sample sizes for various values of n.

The fundamental question studied in this paper is to find the optimal value of the sample size s as a function of n, taking into account comparisons and exchanges, both while selecting the pivot and while partitioning the array. We will study the general situation where we pick the $(p+1)^{\text{th}}$ element in the sample, $0 \le p < s$, not necessarily the median.

We provide the main order term for the average total cost (total cost includes both comparisons and exchanges) in quicksort with samples of fixed size, and when we select the $(p+1)^{\text{th}}$ element in the sample (Theorem 1). This analysis generalizes the former analysis of Van Emden of the average number of comparisons for quicksort with fixed size samples, picking the medians of the samples. As a consequence of our analysis, we prove that if exchanges were rather expensive compared to the cost of key comparisons, then the best strategy is not to pick the median of the samples but the $(p^* + 1)^{\text{th}}$ element, where p^* is the rank that minimizes the average total cost and which can be explicitly computed as a function of the relative cost of an exchange to that of a comparison.

Other new results include Theorem 3, where we prove that any sample size s such that $s = o(n)$ and $s = \omega(1)$, i.e., grows with n but is sublinear, has asymptotic near-optimal average performance, as the average number of comparisons in that case is $n \log_2 n + o(n \log n)$. This result is also the basis for Theorems 4 and 5, where we show that the optimal sample size – now taking care of lower order terms, not just the $n \log n$ term – is $a\sqrt{n} + o(\sqrt{n})$ and give an explicit formula for the constant a. Again, the relative cost of exchanges to the cost of comparisons makes a difference: if this relative cost is low, we should use the medians of the samples; otherwise, a different element must be used. These results disprove the conjecture of McGeoch and Tygar that the optimal sample sizes were $\Theta(n^{0.56})$.

The basic tools for our analysis are the continuous master theorem for divide-and-conquer recurrences (CMT, for short) and several related results [7]. A preliminary, but more complete version of this work is available in [5].

2 Preliminaries

We will assume that the input of quicksort is an array of $n > 0$ distinct integers. Furthermore, we shall assume —as is usual in the analysis of comparison-based sorting algorithms— that each permutation of the n items is equally likely.

We consider that the pivots are selected from samples of size $s \geq 1$ consisting of the first s elements in the (sub)array to be sorted. If $s = 1$ then we have standard quicksort. We assume that s, the size of the sample, is a function of the size of the current subarray, although we will not write down this dependence on n most of the time. We also assume $s(n) = o(n)$.

Let the selected pivot be the $(p+1)^{\text{th}}$ element $(0 \leq p < s)$ in the sample. We will denote $q = s - 1 - p$ the number of elements in the sample larger than the pivot. For the particular case where the sample is of odd size and the selected pivot is the median of the sample, we write $s = 2k + 1$, and hence $k + 1$ is the rank of the pivot, with $p = q = k$.

The following well known proposition will be used in all subsequent reasonings.

Proposition 1. *Let $\pi_{n,j}^{(s,p)}$ be the probability that the $(p+1)^{th}$ element of a sample of s elements, with $0 \leq p < s$, is the $(j+1)^{th}$ element of an array of size n, where $0 \leq j < n$. Then*

$$\pi_{n,j}^{(s,p)} = \frac{\binom{j}{p}\binom{n-1-j}{q}}{\binom{n}{s}} .$$

Note that for the plain variant of the algorithm (that is, $s = 1$ and $p = 0$) we have $\pi_{n,j}^{(1,0)} = 1/n$ for all $0 \leq j < n$.

Let $\mathsf{C}(n, s, p)$ denote the average number of comparisons to partition an array of size n when the sample has s elements. Analogously, let $\mathsf{X}(n, s, p)$ denote the average number of exchanges made by the partition.

The number of comparisons is $\mathsf{C}(n, s, p) = n + 1$ irrespective of s and p, since the pivot must be compared with every other element in the array, and two additional comparisons are performed at the end of the partition.

The following lemma gives the value of $\mathsf{X}(n, s, p)$ for any n, s and p, provided that $0 \leq p < s \leq n$. Its proof is not given here, but it can be found in [5].

Lemma 1. *The average number of exchanges to partition an array of size n when the pivot is the $(p+1)^{th}$ element of a sample of s elements is*

$$\mathsf{X}(n, s, p) = \frac{1}{(s+1)(s+2)(n-1)}\Big((p+1)(q+1)n^2$$
$$- ((p+1)^2 + (q+1)^2 - (p+1)(q+1) + s + 1)n + 2(p+1)(q+1)\Big),$$

where $q = s - 1 - p$.

Note that if the selection of the pivots is made in-place, then the first s components of the array would be arranged by the selection procedure and then it would probably not contain a random permutation, after the selection of the pivot is performed.

Hence, the computation of $\mathsf{X}(n, s, p)$ above is valid if and only if we assume that the selection of the pivot is performed in a separate area containing a copy of the s elements of the sample or we prove that the selection mechanism preserves randomness. However, it seems that, besides brute-force solutions, no such selection mechanism exists for general s.

Let $\mathsf{S}(s, p)$ denote the average total cost of the algorithm that selects the $(p+1)^{\text{th}}$ out of s elements. Here, we could include the cost to copy the sample in a separate area, though we will not do so.

Efficient selection algorithms work in linear time, at least on the average, so we may safely assume $\mathsf{S}(s, p) = \beta \cdot s + o(s)$ for some constant β that depends on the chosen algorithm, the unitary costs of a comparison u_c and of an exchange u_x, and typically on the ratio $(p+1)/(s+1)$. For example, the expected number of comparisons to select the median with standard quickselect [2, 4, 9] is $2(1 + \ln 2)s + o(s)$. Recall that the expected number of comparisons to select the $(p+1)^{\text{th}}$ out of s elements is bounded below [1] by $\left(\frac{3}{2} - \left|\frac{1}{2} - \frac{p+1}{s+1}\right|\right) s + o(s)$, and hence if $p = \lfloor (s-1)/2 \rfloor)$ then $\beta \geq 1.5 \cdot u_c$.

We now set up the recurrence for the average total cost of quicksort, valid for n large enough.

Lemma 2. *Let Q_n be the average cost of quicksort to sort an array of size n when we choose as the pivot of each partitioning stage the $(p+1)^{th}$ element of a sample of s elements. Then*

$$Q_n = \mathsf{S}(s, p) + \mathsf{C}(n, s, p) \cdot u_c + \mathsf{X}(n, s, p) \cdot u_x + \sum_{0 \leq j < n} \left(\pi_{n,j}^{(s,p)} + \pi_{n,n-1-j}^{(s,p)}\right) Q_j \ .$$

Finally, we define $\xi = u_x / u_c$ to be the cost of an exchange relative to that of a comparison. For the rest of the paper we will set $u_c = 1$, and thus $u_x = \xi$; in order words, we will measure the total cost in number of comparisons, where an exchange is worth ξ comparisons. If we set $\xi = 0$ then we only consider the number of comparisons.

3 Quicksort with Fixed-Size Samples

The analysis of quicksort with samples of fixed size is almost straightforward using the CMT. The first step in the analysis is to determine the value of the *toll function*, that is, the non-recursive cost in the recurrence. For n large enough, it is

$$\left(1 + \frac{(p+1)(q+1)}{(s+1)(s+2)} \cdot \xi\right) n + \mathcal{O}(1) \ . \tag{1}$$

Notice that $\mathsf{S}(s,p)$ and several other terms are accounted for in the $\mathcal{O}(1)$-term above, because we assume $s = \Theta(1)$.

Secondly, we have to compute the *shape function* associated to this problem; the shape function is essentially a continuous approximation to the discrete weights, which in our instance are (see Lemma 2)

$$\omega_{n,j}^{(s,p)} = \left(\pi_{n,j}^{(s,p)} + \pi_{n,n-1-j}^{(s,p)}\right) = \left(\pi_{n,j}^{(s,p)} + \pi_{n,j}^{(s,q)}\right) \quad . \tag{2}$$

Hence, the shape function is

$$\omega^{(s,p)}(z) = \frac{s!}{p!\,q!}\left(z^p(1-z)^q + z^q(1-z)^p\right) \quad . \tag{3}$$

Now we should compute the limiting const-entropy associated to this problem (in [7], the const-entropy is denoted $\mathcal{H}_n^{(1)}$ and its limit $\mathcal{H}^{(1)}$). In this case, the const-entropy is 0 for every s and p (we will not show the computation here). Hence, we need to compute the limiting log-entropy (denoted $\mathcal{H}^{(\ln)}$ in [7]), which is

$$\begin{aligned}\mathcal{H}(s,p) &= -(c+1)\int_0^1 \omega^{(s,p)}(z)\, z^b \ln z\, dz \\ &= -(c+1)\frac{s!}{p!\,q!}\int_0^1 \left(z^{p+b}(1-z)^q + z^{q+b}(1-z)^p\right)\ln z\, dz,\end{aligned}$$

with $b = 1$ and $c = 0$, as the toll function is $\Theta\left(n^1(\ln n)^0\right)$. A closed form for the integral above is not difficult to find, yielding $\mathcal{H}(s,p) = \mathrm{VE}(s,p)$, where

$$\mathrm{VE}(s,p) = H_{s+1} - \frac{(p+1)H_{p+1} + (q+1)H_{q+1}}{s+1} \quad . \tag{4}$$

The name of this function follows after Van Emden, who used it for the particular case where $p = q$. Recall that the harmonic number H_n admits the asymptotic expansion $H_n = \ln n + \gamma + o(1)$, where $\gamma = 0.577\ldots$ is Euler's constant.

The computations above give us the main order term in Q_n. It is possible to get more information about the lower order terms, by subtracting the main order term from Q_n and setting up a recurrence for the difference. In this case, we would find that the second order term is $\mathcal{O}(n)$, but no further information can be obtained using the CMT. We now summarize our findings in the following theorem.

Theorem 1. *The average total cost of quicksort with fixed-size samples is* $Q_n = q_\xi(s,p)\, n \ln n + \mathcal{O}(n)$, *where*

$$q_\xi(s,p) = \frac{1 + \frac{(p+1)(q+1)}{(s+1)(s+2)}\cdot\xi}{VE(s,p)} \quad .$$

Setting $s = 2k + 1$, $p = q = k$ and $\xi = 0$, we recover the original result of Van Emden [11, 4].

Let us shift our attention now to the constant factor $q_\xi(s,p)$ and study the values of s and p that minimize it.

If we only take into account comparisons ($\xi = 0$) then the best choice for p is $\lfloor (s-1)/2 \rfloor$. It is easy to show that $q_\xi(2k+1,k)$ is a strictly decreasing function of k, and hence we should get samples as large as possible and select the medians of the samples as pivots. This conclusion (in fact a stronger statement) was already proved by Sedgewick [8].

For moderately large values of ξ, like $\xi = 5$, nothing surprising occurs and the same conclusions hold.

But our intuition fails and leads us to a wrong conclusion when ξ is large. Using as pivots the medians of the samples is no longer the best choice. The best fixed-size strategy is certainly to have samples as large as possible, but the pivot should be the element of rank $p^* = p^*(s,\xi)$ in the sample, where p^* is the value that minimizes $q_\xi(s,p)$. It turns out that $p^* \neq \lfloor (s-1)/2 \rfloor$ when ξ is large (roughly, greater than 10).

For convenience, we will work with the quotients $\psi = \lim_{s\to\infty}(p/s)$ rather than with the actual ranks p for the rest of this section. What we have discussed so far could be then expressed by saying that $\psi^* = 1/2$ for small values of ξ, and $\psi^* \neq 1/2$ if ξ is large.

Consider, for instance, the case where $\xi = 30$. Then $q_\xi(s,p)$ is a "surface" with two valleys, symmetrically disposed with respect to the line defined by $\psi = 1/2$. In both valleys $q_\xi(s,p)$ is identical and minimum, and we should take the valley of smallest p to define ψ^*, which is clearly smaller than 1/2.

Let

$$q_\xi(\psi) = -\frac{1 + \psi(1-\psi)\xi}{\psi \ln \psi + (1-\psi)\ln(1-\psi)}, \tag{5}$$

for $0 < \psi < 1$. It is easy to see that $\lim_{s\to\infty} q_\xi(s, \psi \cdot s + o(s)) = q_\xi(\psi)$.

It is fairly easy to prove that $q_\xi(\psi)$ is symmetric around $\psi = 1/2$, with only one minimum located at $\psi^* = 1/2$ when $\xi \leq \tau$, whereas if $\xi > \tau$ we have a local maximum at $\psi = 1/2$ and two absolute minima at $\psi^* < 1/2$ and at $1 - \psi^* > 1/2$, respectively. The value τ is given by the solution of

$$\left.\frac{\partial^2 q_\xi(\psi)}{\partial \psi^2}\right|_{\psi=1/2} = 0,$$

which is $\tau = 4/(2\ln 2 - 1) \approx 10.35480$.

For $\xi > \tau$ the optimal ψ^* is the unique solution of the equation

$$\ln \psi + \xi\,\psi^2 \ln \psi = \ln(1-\psi) + \xi(1-\psi)^2 \ln(1-\psi) \tag{6}$$

in the interval $(0, 1/2)$. The solution of the equation above, $\psi^* = \psi^*(\xi)$, is 1/2 for $\xi \in [0,\tau)$, and $\psi^*(\xi)$ strictly decreases for $\xi > \tau$, tending to 0 as ξ grows.

For large samples the optimal value of p is $p^* \approx \psi^* \cdot s$. But now the question is whether taking large samples is the best choice. Informally speaking, the next theorem states just that.

Theorem 2. *For any s and p, $q_\xi(s,p) > q_\xi(\psi^*)$.*

Proof. Recall that for Q_n the shape function is

$$\omega^{(s,p)}(z) = \frac{s!}{p!\,q!} z^p (1-z)^q \ .$$

The key observation for our proof is the equality

$$q_\xi(s,p) = \frac{\int_0^1 \omega^{(s,p)}(z)\,(1 + z(1-z)\xi)\ dz}{\int_0^1 \omega^{(s,p)}(z)\,(-z\ln z - (1-z)\ln(1-z))\ dz} \ .$$

Now, let $f(z)$ and $g(z)$ be positive functions over the interval $[0,1]$, and let $0 < z^* < 1$ be the location of a minimum of $f(z)/g(z)$. Assume $g(z) > 0$ for $0 < z < 1$. Then, as $f(z) \geq g(z)f(z^*)/g(z^*)$ and $\omega^{(s,p)}(z)$ is also positive, we have

$$\frac{\int_0^1 \omega^{(s,p)}(z) f(z)\,dz}{\int_0^1 \omega^{(s,p)}(z) g(z)\,dz} \geq \frac{\int_0^1 \omega^{(s,p)}(z)\,[g(z)f(z^*)/g(z^*)]\ dz}{\int_0^1 \omega^{(s,p)}(z) g(z)\,dz} = \frac{f(z^*)}{g(z^*)} \ .$$

Taking $f(z) = 1 + z(1-z)\xi$ and $g(z) = -z\ln z - (1-z)\ln(1-z)$, which satisfy the assumptions, and since ψ^* is the minimum of $q_\xi(\psi) = f(\psi)/g(\psi)$, we have (almost) proved the statement of the theorem.

Notice that for any ξ there is always an interval $[\psi_1, \psi_2]$ with $0 \leq \psi_1 < \psi_2 \leq 1$ such that $q_\xi(\psi) > q_\xi(\psi^*(\xi))$ and $\omega^{(s,p)}(z) > 0$ for every ψ in $[\psi_1, \psi_2]$. Thus $q_\xi(s,p)$ is strictly greater than $q_\xi(\psi^*)$. □

The fact that ψ^* tends to 0 as ξ tends to ∞ can be informally described as a smooth transition from quicksort to selection sort. Recall that if we always select the smallest element in the array as the pivot, then quicksort behaves exactly as selection sort. And if exchanges are very expensive then selection sort is a good choice, as it minimizes the number of exchanges to sort the array.

On the other hand, we should be aware that the analysis of the case $\xi > \tau$ is mainly of theoretical interest, since in most practical situations we have $\xi \leq \tau$. If data movements were too expensive, we would sort an array of pointers to the actual records rather than sorting the records themselves.

Now we restrict our attention to the variants of quicksort that always take the median of a sample of fixed size as the pivot, irrespective of the value of ξ (and therefore are not the best theoretical alternatives when $\xi > \tau$). That is, we take $s = 2k+1$ and $p = k$ for some $k \geq 0$.

This time we have

$$q_\xi(k) = q_\xi(2k+1, k) = \frac{1 + \frac{k+1}{4k+6} \cdot \xi}{\frac{1}{k+2} + \cdots + \frac{1}{2k+2}}, \tag{7}$$

for every $\xi \geq 0$.[1]

It gives the constant of the main term of quicksort as a function of k, when we choose as pivot the median of samples of $2k+1$ elements.

As an example, for $\xi = 5$ and $\xi = 8$ the function $q_\xi(k)$ steadily decreases with k, in accordance with what we know. This behavior changes as soon as $\xi > \tau$. For values of ξ greater than τ the function $q_\xi(k)$ has one minimum at finite distance k^*. For instance, $k^* = 0$ if $\xi > 30$, and $k^* = 1$ if $\xi \in (20, 30)$.

The location of the minima k^* tends to 0 when ξ grows and to $+\infty$ when ξ decreases. Actually, there is a vertical asymptote as $\xi \to \tau^+$. For values of ξ larger than 30, we have $k^* = 0$; in other words, if we force choosing the median of the sample as pivot then the best alternative is plain quicksort (without sampling). Notice also that k^* is not well defined in some points: for instance, for $\xi = 20$ we have $q_\xi(1) = q_\xi(2)$, and both 1 and 2 compete as optimal choices for k.

The function

$$\xi^*(k) = \frac{4}{4(H_{2k} - H_k)\frac{k+1}{2k+3} - 1 + \frac{1}{2k+1}}$$

is the pseudoinverse of $k^* = k^*(\xi)$, in the sense that k is the optimal choice if ξ belongs to the open interval $(\xi^*(k+1), \xi^*(k))$. By convention, we take $\xi^*(0) = +\infty$. For instance, $\xi^*(2) = 20$ and $\xi^*(1) = 30$ and hence $k^* = 1$ if $20 < \xi < 30$. Because of the definition, for any $k > 0$, $q_{\xi^*(k)}(k) = q_{\xi^*(k)}(k-1)$.

4 Optimal Samples for Quicksort

In this section we study the asymptotic behavior of the optimal sample sizes of quicksort. We already know from Sect. 3 that picking the median of the sample as the pivot is not always the best choice. Therefore, we set p to equal $\psi \cdot s + o(s)$ for some fixed $0 < \psi \leq 1/2$ (the case $1/2 < \psi < 1$ is symmetrical). We do not assume $\psi = \psi^*(\xi)$.

We have the following theorem for the main term of the cost of quicksort when we make the size of the sample grow with the size of the input.

Theorem 3. *Let $p = \psi \cdot s + o(s)$, where $0 < \psi \leq 1/2$ and let $s = s(n)$ be any function such that $s = \omega(1)$ and $s = o(n)$. Then*

$$Q_n = q_\xi(\psi)\, n \ln n + o(n \log n) \ .$$

Proof. Let us first introduce the function

$$\nu_n(t, x) = \sum_{0 \leq j < n} \pi_{n,j}^{(t, x \cdot (t-1))} (j \ln j + (n-1-j)\ln(n-1-j)) ,$$

where t is any integer $1 \leq t \leq n$ and x is a real number, $0 < x \leq 1/2$. The weights $\pi_{n,j}^{(t,d)}$ are defined in terms of the Γ function in order to make sense for

[1] We overload the notation $q_\xi(\cdots)$ once again, this time $q_\xi(k) = q_\xi(2k+1, k)$.

real d ($d = x \cdot (t-1)$ in this case). Similarly, we extend the function $\mathrm{VE}(t,d)$ to real values of d by using the Ψ function instead of the harmonic numbers. We will stick to the same names for these extensions, though.

Now, since $j \ln j$ is a convex function, it is easy to see that $\nu_n(t,x_1) > \nu_n(t,x_2)$ if $0 < x_1 < x_2 \leq 1/2$, and $\nu_n(t_1,x) > \nu_n(t_2,x)$ if $t_1 < t_2$. Moreover, $\nu_n(t,x)$ is continuous on x.

Let $Q_n(t,x)$ be the average cost of quicksort when we use samples of fixed size t and select the $(d+1)^{\text{th}}$ item from the sample as the pivot, where $d = x \cdot (t-1)$. Then, according to the CMT, the log-entropy associated to $Q_n(t,x)$ is

$$\mathcal{H}_n(t,x) = \ln n - \frac{1}{n}\nu_n(t,x) + o(1),$$

and its limit $\mathcal{H}(t,x) = \lim_{n\to\infty} \mathcal{H}_n(t,x) = \mathrm{VE}(t,d)$ (see Sect. 3). Note that if d is not an integer number then this variant of quicksort makes no sense in practice, but the entropy and its limit are well-defined.

Fix any $0 < \delta < \psi$. Under the assumptions of the theorem, we have $s \geq t$ and $p \geq (\psi - \delta) \cdot (s-1)$ for large n. Therefore, the log-entropy associated to Q_n can be bounded by

$$\mathcal{H}_n \geq \ln n - \frac{1}{n}\nu_n(t, \psi - \delta) + o(1) \quad .$$

Hence, $\mathcal{H} = \lim_{n\to\infty} \mathcal{H}_n \geq \lim_{n\to\infty} \mathcal{H}_n(t, \psi-\delta) = \mathrm{VE}(t, (\psi-\delta)\cdot(t-1))$. This bound holds no matter how large we choose t or how small we choose δ. Hence, $\mathcal{H} \geq \lim_{t\to\infty} \lim_{\delta\to 0} \mathrm{VE}(t,(\psi-\delta)\cdot(t-1)) = -(\psi \ln \psi + (1-\psi)\ln(1-\psi))$.

On the other hand, a matching upper bound $\mathcal{H} \leq -(\psi \ln \psi + (1-\psi)\ln(1-\psi))$ can be easily derived using the probabilities

$$\pi_{n,j} = \begin{cases} 1 & \text{if } j = \lfloor \psi \cdot (n-1) \rfloor, \\ 0 & \text{otherwise.} \end{cases}$$

Thus $\mathcal{H} = -(\psi \ln \psi + (1-\psi)\ln(1-\psi))$. Using the CMT, we conclude the statement of the theorem, $Q_n = q_\xi(\psi)\, n \ln n + o(n \log n)$. □

If we only measure the number of comparisons ($\xi = 0$) then the theorem above states that *any* sample size $s = \omega(1)$ and $s = o(n)$ with $\psi = 1/2$ is asymptotically optimal w.r.t. the main term of quicksort. For any such sample size s, the expected number of comparisons is $Q_n \sim n \log_2 n$.

From now on we will take $p = \lceil \psi \cdot (s+1) \rceil - 1$, as similar discretizations yield similar results. To investigate the optimal sample size we need to consider the lower order terms and introduce a pseudoentropy

$$\mathcal{Q}(n,s,\psi) = -\left(H_n + \psi \ln \psi + (1-\psi)\ln(1-\psi)\right)\frac{n-1}{n} + \sum_{0\leq j<n} \left(\pi_{n,j}^{(s,p)} + \pi_{n,j}^{(s,q)}\right)\frac{jH_j}{n} \quad .$$

By Theorem 3 we know that we can decompose Q_n as $Q_n = q_\xi(\psi)\, nH_n + R_n$, where $R_n = o(nH_n)$. The recurrence for quicksort (Lemma 2) can be then rewritten as

$$Q_n = \mathsf{S}(s,\psi) + \mathsf{C}(n,s,\psi) + \mathsf{X}(n,s,\psi)\cdot\xi + \sum_{0\le j<n}\left(\pi_{n,j}^{(s,p)} + \pi_{n,j}^{(s,q)}\right) R_j \tag{8}$$
$$+ \Big(H_n + \psi\ln\psi + (1-\psi)\ln(1-\psi)\Big) q_\xi(\psi)\,(n-1) + \mathcal{Q}(n,s,\psi) q_\xi(\psi)\, n\ .$$

Let $\chi_\psi(s)$ be the oscillating factor induced by taking ceilings:

$$\chi_\psi(s) = \lceil \psi\cdot(s+1)\rceil - \psi\cdot(s+1)\ . \tag{9}$$

We have the following lemma for the asymptotic behavior of $\mathcal{Q}(n,s,\psi)$.

Lemma 3. *If $s=\omega(1)$, $s=o(n)$ and $p=\lceil\psi\cdot(s+1)\rceil-1$ for some ψ such that $0<\psi\le 1/2$, then*

$$\mathcal{Q}(n,s,\psi) = \frac{1}{2s} - \Big(\ln(1-\psi)-\ln\psi\Big)\frac{\chi_\psi(s)}{s} + \mathcal{O}\left(\max\left\{\frac{1}{n},\frac{1}{s^2}\right\}\right)\ .$$

Proof. Using a few elementary identities of discrete calculus yields

$$\sum_{0\le j<n}\left(\pi_{n,j}^{(s,p)} + \pi_{n,n-1-j}^{(s,p)}\right) jH_j = \left(H_n - H_{s+1} + \frac{p+1}{s+1}\cdot H_{p+1} + \frac{q+1}{s+1}\cdot H_{q+1}\right)(n-1)$$
$$+\frac{p+1}{s+1}(H_{p+1}-H_{q+1}) + \frac{q+1}{s+1}(H_{q+1}-H_{p+1}) + \frac{1}{p+1} + \frac{1}{q+1} - \frac{2}{s+1} - 1,$$

where $q=s-1-p$ as usual.

The last line above is $\mathcal{O}(1)$. On the other hand, from the equalities $p+1 = \psi\cdot(s+1)+\chi_\psi(s)$, $H_n = \ln n+\gamma+1/2n+\Theta(n^{-2})$ and $\ln(1+1/x) = 1/x+\Theta(x^{-2})$, it is not difficult to deduce

$$-H_{s+1} + \frac{p+1}{s+1}\cdot H_{p+1} + \frac{q+1}{s+1}\cdot H_{q+1}$$
$$= \psi\ln\psi + (1-\psi)\ln(1-\psi) + \frac{1}{2s} - \Big(\ln(1-\psi)-\ln\psi\Big)\frac{\chi_\psi(s)}{s} + \Theta\left(\frac{1}{s^2}\right),$$

and the lemma follows after a few simple manipulations. □

The factor $\ln(1-\psi)-\ln\psi$ in the statement of Lemma 3 is zero if and only if $\psi=1/2$. So the perturbation $\chi_\psi(s)/s$ has to be taken into account whenever we are not selecting the median of the sample as the pivot.

We also need the asymptotic properties of $\mathsf{X}(n,s,\psi)$, given in the next lemma, which easily follows from Lemma 1.

Lemma 4. *If $s=\omega(1)$, $s=o(n)$ and $p=\lceil\psi\cdot(s+1)\rceil-1$ for some ψ such that $0<\psi\le 1/2$, then*

$$\mathsf{X}(n,s,\psi) = \psi(1-\psi)\,n - \psi(1-\psi)\,\frac{n}{s} + (1-2\psi)\,\chi_\psi(s)\,\frac{n}{s} + \mathcal{O}\left(\max\left\{\frac{n}{s^2},1\right\}\right)\ .$$

We have already pointed out in Sect. 2 that $\mathsf{S}(s,p)$ is linear, with the constant of proportionality typically dependent on the quotient $(p+1)/(s+1)$. We assume thus, without loss of generality, that $\mathsf{S}(s,p) = \mathsf{S}(s,\psi) = \beta \cdot s + o(s)$ for some constant $\beta = \beta(\psi)$.

Consider (8). Since $R_n = o(Q_n)$, it is rather intuitive that the contribution of the sum of R_j's to the asymptotic location of s^* is irrelevant. The argument can be formalized as follows. Fix any $\delta > 0$. By hypothesis, there exists some N such that $|R_j| \leq \delta \cdot jH_j$ for every $j \geq N$. On the other hand, we are assuming $s = \omega(1)$, so $p = \psi \cdot s + o(s) \geq N$ and $q = (1-\psi) \cdot s + o(s) \geq N$ if n is large enough, and $\pi_{n,j}^{(s,p)} = \pi_{n,j}^{(s,q)} = 0$ for every $j < N$. Therefore,

$$\sum_{0 \leq j < n} (\pi_{n,j}^{(s,p)} + \pi_{n,j}^{(s,q)}) \, |R_j| \leq \delta \sum_{0 \leq j < n} (\pi_{n,j}^{(s,p)} + \pi_{n,j}^{(s,p)}) j \, H_j$$
$$= \delta \, \mathcal{Q}(n,s,\psi)\, n + \delta \, (H_n + \psi \ln \psi + (1-\psi)\ln(1-\psi))\,(n-1),$$

for large n. Thus

$$Q_n = \mathsf{S}(s,\psi) + \mathsf{C}(n,s,\psi) + \mathsf{X}(n,s,\psi) \cdot \xi \qquad (10)$$
$$+ E(n,\psi)\,(H_n + \psi \ln \psi + (1-\psi)\ln(1-\psi))\,(n-1) + E(n,\psi)\, \mathcal{Q}(n,s,\psi) n,$$

where we have the bounds $q_\xi(\psi) - \delta \leq E(n,\psi) \leq q_\xi(\psi) + \delta$.

Notice that the bounds for $E(n,\psi)$ do not depend on s, and hold for every $\delta > 0$, no matter how small we make it. Regarding the rest of terms, only $\mathsf{S}(s,\psi)$, $\mathsf{X}(n,s,\psi)$ and $\mathcal{Q}(n,s,\psi)$ depend on s—recall that $\mathsf{C}(n,s,\psi) = n+1$. For large n, the main term of the optimal sample size s^* can be found dismissing the $o(s)$, $\mathcal{O}(\max\{\frac{n}{s^2},1\})$ and $\mathcal{O}(\max\{\frac{1}{n},\frac{1}{s^2}\})$ terms in the asymptotic expansions of $\mathsf{S}(s,\psi)$, $\mathsf{X}(n,s,\psi)$ and $\mathcal{Q}(n,s,\psi)$, respectively.[2]

Thus, to obtain the main term of optimal sample size s^* it suffices to minimize w.r.t. s the expression

$$\beta \cdot s + \left(\frac{q_\xi(\psi)}{2} - \psi(1-\psi)\,\xi\right) \frac{n}{s}$$
$$+ \left[(1-2\psi)\,\xi - \left(\ln(1-\psi) - \ln\psi\right) q_\xi(\psi)\right] \chi_\psi(s)\, \frac{n}{s} \; . \qquad (11)$$

We will analyze two variants of quicksort with sample sizes depending on n: The first one is setting $\psi = \psi^*(\xi)$, i.e. choosing the optimal ratio p/s; the second one is setting $\psi = 1/2$ irrespective of ξ, that is, picking always the median of the sample. If $\xi \leq \tau$ both variants are identical as $\psi^* = 1/2$ for this case.

Fortunately, in any of these two variants the second line of (11) vanishes (because of (6)) and the next two theorems immediately follow.

Theorem 4. *Let s^* denote the optimal sample size w.r.t. Q_n when the $\lceil \psi^*(s+1) \rceil^{th}$ element of the sample is used as pivot. Then*

$$s^* = \sqrt{\left(\frac{q_\xi(\psi^*)}{2} - \psi^*(1-\psi^*)\xi\right) \frac{1}{\beta(\psi^*)}} \cdot \sqrt{n} + o\left(\sqrt{n}\right) \; .$$

[2] This can be rigurously proved, but it is rather lengthy and tedious.

The next theorem deals with the particular case where the medians of the samples are selected as pivots.

Theorem 5. *Let s^* denote the optimal sample size w.r.t. Q_n when the median of the sample is used as pivot and $\xi < \tau$. Then*

$$s^* = \sqrt{\left(\frac{4-(2\ln 2 - 1)\xi}{8\ln 2}\right)\frac{1}{\beta(1/2)}} \cdot \sqrt{n} + o\left(\sqrt{n}\right) \ .$$

Notice that when $\xi > \tau$ the result above makes no sense, as the factor multiplying $\sqrt{n}$ is the square root of a negative number. This provides a further check for the conclusions of Sect. 3, and is consistent with the observation that the optimal samples in that situation have constant size.

Because of space limitations, we cannot include here the comparison between the exact values of the optimal sample size (which can be obtained using dynamic programming, see [6]) and the optimal sample size as provided by the leading term of Theorem 5, but it might be found in [5].

References

[1] R.W. Floyd and R.L. Rivest. Expected time bounds for selection. *Communications of the ACM*, 18:165–173, 1975.

[2] C.A.R. Hoare. FIND (Algorithm 65). *Communications of the ACM*, 4:321–322, 1961.

[3] C.A.R. Hoare. Quicksort. *Computer Journal*, 5:10–15, 1962.

[4] D.E. Knuth. *The Art of Computer Programming: Sorting and Searching*, volume 3. Addison-Wesley, 1973.

[5] C. Martínez and S. Roura. Optimal sampling strategies in quicksort and quickselect. Technical Report LSI-98-1-R, LSI-UPC, 1998. Also available from `http://www.lsi.upc.es/dept/techreps/1998.html`.

[6] C.C. McGeoch and J.D. Tygar. Optimal sampling strategies for quicksort. *Random Structures & Algorithms*, 7:287–300, 1995.

[7] S. Roura. An improved master theorem for divide-and-conquer recurrences. In P. Degano, R. Gorrieri, and A. Marchetti-Spaccamela, editors, *Proc. of the 24th Int. Colloquium on Automata, Languages and Programming (ICALP'97)*, volume 1256 of *Lecture Notes in Computer Science*. Springer, 1997.

[8] R. Sedgewick. *Quicksort.* Garland, 1978.

[9] R. Sedgewick. *Algorithms in C*, volume 1. Addison-Wesley, 3rd edition, 1997.

[10] R.C. Singleton. Algorithm 347: An efficient algorithm for sorting with minimal storage. *Communications of the ACM*, 12:185–187, 1969.

[11] M.H. van Emden. Increasing the efficiency of quicksort. *Communications of the ACM*, 13:563–567, 1970.

A Genuinely Polynomial-Time Algorithm for Sampling Two-Rowed Contingency Tables

Martin Dyer and Catherine Greenhill

School of Computer Studies, University of Leeds
Leeds, LS2 9JT, United Kingdom

Abstract. In this paper a Markov chain for contingency tables with two rows is defined. The chain is shown to be rapidly mixing using the path coupling method. The mixing time of the chain is quadratic in the number of columns and linear in the logarithm of the table sum. Two extensions of the new chain are discussed: one for three-rowed contingency tables and one for m-rowed contingency tables. We show that, unfortunately, it is not possible to prove rapid mixing for these chains by simply extending the path coupling approach used in the two-rowed case.

1 Introduction

A *contingency table* is a matrix of nonnegative integers with prescribed positive row and column sums. Contingency tables are used in statistics to store data from sample surveys (see for example [3, Chapter 8]). For a survey of contingency tables and related problems, see [8]. The data is often analysed under the assumption of independence. If the set of contingency tables under consideration is small, this assumption can be tested by applying a chi-squared statistic to each such table (see for example [1, 7]). However, this approach becomes computationally infeasible as the number of contingency tables grows. Suppose that we had a method for sampling almost uniformly from the set of contingency tables with given row and column sums. Then we may proceed by applying the statistic to a sample of contingency tables selected almost uniformly.

The problem of almost uniform sampling can be efficiently solved using the Markov chain Monte Carlo method (see [13]), provided that there exists a Markov chain for the set of contingency tables which converges to the uniform distribution in polynomial time. Here 'polynomial time' means 'in time polynomial in the number of rows, the number of columns and the *logarithm* of the table sum'. If the Markov chain converges in time polynomial in the table sum itself, then we shall say it converges in *pseudopolynomial* time. Approximately counting two-rowed contingency tables is polynomial-time reducible to almost uniform sampling, as can be proved using standard methods. Moreover, the problem of exactly counting the number of contingency tables with fixed row and column sums is known to be $\#P$-complete, even when there are only two rows (see [11]).

The first Markov chain for contingency tables was described in [9] by Diaconis and Saloff-Coste. We shall refer to this chain as the Diaconis chain. For fixed dimensions, they proved that their chain converged in pseudopolynomial time. However, the constants involved grow exponentionally with the number of rows and columns. Some Markov chains for restricted classes of contingency tables have been defined. In [14], Kannan, Tetali and Vempala gave a Markov chain with polynomial-time convergence for the 0-1 case (where every entry in the table is zero or one) with nearly equal margin totals, while Chung, Graham and Yau [6] described a Markov chain for contingency tables which converges in pseudopolynomial time for contingency tables with large enough margin totals. An improvement on this result is the chain described by Dyer, Kannan and Mount [11]. Their chain converges in polynomial time whenever all the row and column sums are sufficiently large, this bound being smaller than that in [6].

In [12], Hernek analysed the Diaconis chain for two-rowed contingency tables using coupling. She showed that this chain converges in time which is quadratic in the number of columns and in the table sum (i.e. pseudopolynomial time). In this paper, a new Markov chain for two-rowed contingency tables is described, and the convergence of the chain is analysed using the path coupling method [4]. We show that the new chain converges to the uniform distribution in time which is quadratic in the number of columns and linear in the *logarithm* of the table sum. Therefore our chain runs in (genuinely) polynomial time, whereas the Diaconis chain does not (and indeed cannot). In the final section we discuss two extensions of the new chain. The first applies to three-rowed contingency tables and the second applies to general contingency tables with m rows. It is not known whether these chains converge rapidly to the uniform distribution, and it is quite possible that they do. However, we show that it is seemingly not possible to prove this simply by extending the path coupling approach used in the two-rowed case.

The structure of the remainder of the paper is as follows. In the next section the path coupling method is reviewed. In Section 3 we introduce notation for contingency tables and describe the Diaconis chain, which converges in pseudopolynomial time. We then outline a procedure which can perform *exact* counting for two-rowed contingency tables in pseudopolynomial time. A new Markov chain for two-rowed contingency tables is described in Section 4 and the mixing time is analysed using path coupling. The new chain is the first which converges in genuinely polynomial time for all two-rowed contingency tables. In Section 5 two extensions of this chain are introduced and discussed.

2 A review of path coupling

In this section we present some necessary notation and review the path coupling method. Let Ω be a finite set and let $\mathcal{M}$ be a Markov chain with state space Ω, transition matrix P and unique stationary distribution π. If the initial state of the Markov chain is x then the distribution of the chain at time t is given by $P_x^t(y) = P^t(x,y)$. The *total variation distance* of the Markov chain from π at time t, with initial state x, is defined by

$$d_{\mathrm{TV}}(P_x^t, \pi) = \frac{1}{2} \sum_{y \in \Omega} |P^t(x, y) - \pi(y)|.$$

A Markov chain is only useful for almost uniform sampling or approximate counting if its total variation distance can be guaranteed to tend to zero relatively quickly, given any initial state. Let $\tau_x(\varepsilon)$ denote the least value T such that $d_{\mathrm{TV}}(P_x^t, \pi) \leq \varepsilon$ for all $t \geq T$. Following Aldous [2], the *mixing time* of $\mathcal{M}$, denoted by $\tau(\varepsilon)$, is defined by $\tau(\varepsilon) = \max\{\tau_x(\varepsilon) : x \in \Omega\}$. A Markov chain will be said to be *rapidly mixing* if the mixing time is bounded above by some polynomial in $\log(|\Omega|)$ and $\log(\varepsilon^{-1})$, where the logarithms are to base e.

There are relatively few methods available to prove that a Markov chain is rapidly mixing. One such method is *coupling*. A *coupling* for $\mathcal{M}$ is a stochastic process (X_t, Y_t) on $\Omega \times \Omega$ such that each of (X_t), (Y_t), considered marginally, is a faithful copy of $\mathcal{M}$. The Coupling Lemma (see for example, Aldous [2]) states that the total variation distance of $\mathcal{M}$ at time t is bounded above by $\mathrm{Prob}[X_t \neq Y_t]$, the probability that the process has not *coupled*. The difficulty in applying this result lies in obtaining an upper bound for this probability. In the *path coupling* method, introduced by Bubley and Dyer [4], one need only define and analyse a coupling on a subset S of $\Omega \times \Omega$. Choosing the set S carefully can considerably simplify the arguments involved in proving rapid mixing of Markov chains by coupling. The path coupling method is described in the next theorem, taken from [10]. Here we use the term *path* to refer to a sequence of elements in the state space, which *need not* form a sequence of possible transitions of the Markov chain.

Theorem 1. *Let δ be an integer valued metric defined on $\Omega \times \Omega$ which takes values in $\{0, \ldots, D\}$. Let S be a subset of $\Omega \times \Omega$ such that for all $(X_t, Y_t) \in \Omega \times \Omega$ there exists a path*

$$X_t = Z_0,\ Z_1, \ldots, Z_r = Y_t$$

between X_t and Y_t where $(Z_l, Z_{l+1}) \in S$ for $0 \leq l < r$ and $\sum_{l=0}^{r-1} \delta(Z_l, Z_{l+1}) = \delta(X_t, Y_t)$. Define a coupling $(X, Y) \mapsto (X', Y')$ of the Markov chain $\mathcal{M}$ on all pairs $(X, Y) \in S$. Suppose that there exists $\beta < 1$ such that

$$\mathbf{E}\left[\delta(X', Y')\right] \leq \beta\, \delta(X, Y)$$

for all $(X, Y) \in S$. Then the mixing time $\tau(\varepsilon)$ of $\mathcal{M}$ satisfies

$$\tau(\varepsilon) \leq \frac{\log(D\varepsilon^{-1})}{1 - \beta}.$$

3 Contingency tables

Let $r = (r_1, \ldots, r_m)$ and $s = (s_1, \ldots, s_n)$ be two positive integer partitions of the positive integer N. The set $\Sigma_{r,s}$ of contingency tables with these row and column sums is defined by

$$\Sigma_{r,s} = \left\{ Z \in \mathbb{N}_0^{m \times n} : \sum_{j=1}^{n} Z_{ij} = r_i \text{ for } 1 \le i \le m, \sum_{i=1}^{m} Z_{ij} = s_j \text{ for } 1 \le j \le n \right\}. \tag{1}$$

The problem of approximately counting the number of contingency tables with given row and column sums is known to be $\#P$-complete even when one of m, n equals 2 (see [11, Theorem 1]). However the 2×2 problem can be solved exactly, as described below.

For 2×2 contingency tables we introduce the notation

$$T_{a,b}^{c} = \Sigma_{(a,c-a),(b,c-b)}$$

where $0 < a,\ b < c$. Now

$$T_{a,b}^{c} = \left\{ \begin{bmatrix} i & (a-i) \\ (b-i) & (c+i-a-b) \end{bmatrix} : \max\{0, a+b-c\} \le i \le \min\{a,b\} \right\}.$$

Hence

$$|T_{a,b}^{c}| = \begin{cases} \min\{a,b\} + 1 & \text{if } a+b \le c, \\ c - \max\{a,b\} + 1 & \text{if } a+b > c. \end{cases} \tag{2}$$

Choosing an element uniformly at random from $T_{a,b}^{c}$ is accomplished simply by choosing $i \in \{\max\{0, a+b-c\}, \ldots, \min\{a,b\}\}$ uniformly at random and forming the corresponding element of $T_{a,b}^{c}$; that is, the element of $T_{a,b}^{c}$ with i in the north-west corner.

For the remainder of the section, we consider two-rowed contingency tables. Here $m = 2$, and $r = (r_1, r_2)$, $s = (s_1, \ldots, s_n)$ are positive integer partitions of the positive integer N.

We now describe a well-known Markov chain for two-rowed contingency tables. In [9], the following Markov chain for two-rowed contingency tables was introduced. We refer to this chain as the *Diaconis* chain. Let $r = (r_1, r_2)$ and $s = (s_1, \ldots, s_n)$ be two positive integer partitions of the positive integer N. If the current state of the Diaconis chain is $X \in \Sigma_{r,s}$, then the next state X' is obtained using the following procedure. With probability $1/2$ let $X' = X$, otherwise choose two columns uniformly at random, choose $i \in \{1, -1\}$ uniformly at random and add the matrix

$$\begin{bmatrix} i & -i \\ -i & i \end{bmatrix}$$

to the chosen 2×2 submatrix of X. If $X' \notin \Sigma_{r,s}$ then let $X' = X$. It is not difficult to see that this chain is ergodic with uniform stationary distribution (see, for example [12]). This chain was analysed using coupling by Hernek [12]. She proved that the chain is rapidly mixing with mixing rate *quadratic* in the number of columns n and in the table sum N. Hence the Diaconis chain converges in pseudopolynomial time.

To close this section, we show that $|\Sigma_{r,s}|$ can be calculated *exactly* using $O(n\,N^2)$ operations. Hence exact counting is achievable in pseudopolynomial time, and approximate counting is only of value if it can be achieved in polynomial time.

Now $|\Sigma_{r,s}|$ can be calculated using

$$|\Sigma_{r,s}| = \sum_{x} |\Sigma_{(r_1-x, r_2+s_n-x),(s_1,\ldots,s_{n-1})}|, \tag{3}$$

where the sum is over all values of x such that $\max\{0, s_n - r_2\} \leq x \leq \min\{r_1, s_n\}$. This is a *dynamic programming* problem (see for example, [15]). We can evaluate $|\Sigma_{r,s}|$ exactly using (3), first by solving all the possible 2×2-dimensional problems, then using these results to solve the 2×3-dimensional problems and so on. This procedure costs $O(n N^2)$ integer additions, and so $|\Sigma_{r,s}|$ can be calculated exactly in pseudopolynomial time. Moreover, the cost of calculating $|\Sigma_{r,s}|$ in this manner is $O(n)$ lower than the best-known upper bound for the cost of *approximating* $|\Sigma_{r,s}|$ using the Diaconis chain.

4 A new Markov chain for two-rowed contingency tables

For this section assume that $m = 2$. A new Markov chain for two-rowed contingency tables will now be described. First we must introduce some notation. Suppose that $X \in \Sigma_{r,s}$ where $r = (r_1, r_2)$. Given (j_1, j_2) such that $1 \leq j_1 < j_2 \leq n$ let $T_X(j_1, j_2)$ denote the set $T^c_{a,b}$ where $a = X_{1,j_1} + X_{1,j_2}$, $b = s_{j_1}$ and $c = s_{j_1} + s_{j_2}$. Then $T_X(j_1, j_2)$ is the set of 2×2 contingency tables with the same row and column sums as the 2×2 submatrix of X consisting of the j_1th and j_2th columns of X. (Here the row sums may equal zero.) Let $\mathcal{M}(\Sigma_{r,s})$ denote the Markov chain with state space $\Sigma_{r,s}$ with the following transition procedure. If X_t is the state of the chain $\mathcal{M}(\Sigma_{r,s})$ at time t then the state at time $t+1$ is determined as follows:

1. choose (j_1, j_2) uniformly at random such that $1 \leq j_1 < j_2 \leq n$,
2. choose $x \in T_X(j_1, j_2)$ uniformly at random and let

$$X_{t+1}(k, j) = \begin{cases} x(k, l) & \text{if } j = j_l \text{ for } l \in \{1, 2\}, \\ X_t(k, j) & \text{otherwise} \end{cases}$$

for $1 \leq k \leq 2$, $1 \leq j \leq n$.

Clearly $\mathcal{M}(\Sigma_{r,s})$ is aperiodic. Now $\mathcal{M}(\Sigma_{r,s})$ can perform all the moves of the Diaconis chain, and the latter chain is irreducible (see for example [12]). Therefore $\mathcal{M}(\Sigma_{r,s})$ is irreducible, so $\mathcal{M}(\Sigma_{r,s})$ is ergodic. Given $X, Y \in \Sigma_{r,s}$ let

$$\phi(X, Y) = \sum_{j=1}^{n} |X_{1,j} - Y_{1,j}|.$$

Then ϕ is a metric on $\Sigma_{r,s}$ which only takes as values the even integers in the range $\{0, \ldots, N\}$. Denote by $\mu(X, Y)$ the minimum number of transitions of $\mathcal{M}(\Sigma_{r,s})$ required to move from initial state X to final state Y. Then

$$0 \leq \mu(X, Y) \leq \phi(X, Y)/2$$

using moves of the Diaconis chain only (see [12]). However, these bounds are far from tight, as the following shows. Let $K(X, Y)$ be the number of columns which differ in X and Y. The following result gives a bound on $\mu(X, Y)$ in terms of $K(X, Y)$ only.

Lemma 1. *If $X, Y \in \Sigma_{r,s}$ and $X \neq Y$ then*

$$\lceil K(X,Y)/2 \rceil \leq \mu(X,Y) \leq K(X,Y) - 1.$$

Proof. Consider performing a series of transitions of $\mathcal{M}(\Sigma_{r,s})$, starting from initial state X and relabelling the resulting state by X each time, with the aim of decreasing $K(X, Y)$. Each transition of $\mathcal{M}(\Sigma_{r,s})$ can decrease $K(X, Y)$ by at most 2. This proves the lower bound. Now $X \neq Y$ so $K(X, Y) \geq 2$. Let j_1 be the least value of j such that X and Y differ in the jth column. Without loss of generality suppose that $X_{1,j_1} > Y_{1,j_1}$. Then let j_2 be the least value of $j > j_1$ such that $X_{1,j} < Y_{1,j}$. Let $x = \min\{X_{1,j_1} - Y_{1,j_1}, Y_{1,j_2} - X_{1,j_2}\}$. In one move of $\mathcal{M}(\Sigma_{r,s})$ we may decrease X_{1,j_1} and X_{2,j_2} by x and increase X_{1,j_2} and X_{2,j_1} by x. This decreases $K(X, Y)$ by at least 1. The decrease in $K(X, Y)$ is 2 whenever $X_{1,j_1} - Y_{1,j_1} = Y_{1,j_2} - X_{1,j_2}$. This is certainly the case when $K(X, Y) = 2$, proving the upper bound. □

This result shows that the diameter of $\mathcal{M}(\Sigma_{r,s})$ is $(n-1)$, while the diameter of the Diaconis chain is $N/2$. In many cases, N is much larger than n, suggesting that the new chain $\mathcal{M}(\Sigma_{r,s})$ might be considerably more rapidly mixing than the Diaconis chain in these situations. The transition matrix P of $\mathcal{M}(\Sigma_{r,s})$ has entries

$$P(X,Y) = \begin{cases} \sum_{j_1<j_2} \left(\binom{n}{2}|T_X(j_1,j_2)|\right)^{-1} & \text{if } X = Y, \\ \left(\binom{n}{2}|T_X(j_1,j_2)|\right)^{-1} & \text{if } X, Y \text{ differ in columns } j_1, j_2 \text{ only}, \\ 0 & \text{otherwise.} \end{cases}$$

If all differences between X and Y are contained in the j_1th and j_2th columns only then $T_X(j_1, j_2) = T_Y(j_1, j_2)$. Hence P is symmetric and the stationary distribution of $\mathcal{M}(\Sigma_{r,s})$ is the uniform distribution on $\Sigma_{r,s}$. The Markov chain $\mathcal{M}(\Sigma_{r,s})$ is an example of a *heat bath* Markov chain, as described in [5]. We now prove that $\mathcal{M}(\Sigma_{r,s})$ is rapidly mixing using the path coupling method on the set S of pairs (X, Y) such that $\phi(X, Y) = 2$.

Theorem 2. *Let $r = (r_1, r_2)$ and $s = (s_1, \ldots, s_n)$ be two positive integer partitions of the positive integer N. The Markov chain $\mathcal{M}(\Sigma_{r,s})$ is rapidly mixing with mixing time $\tau(\varepsilon)$ satisfying*

$$\tau(\varepsilon) \leq \frac{n(n-1)}{2} \log(N\varepsilon^{-1}).$$

Proof. Let X and Y be any elements of $\Sigma_{r,s}$. It was shown in [12] that there exists a path

$$X = Z_0, Z_1, \ldots, Z_d = Y \tag{4}$$

such that $\phi(Z_l, Z_{l+1}) = 2$ for $0 \le l < d$ and $Z_l \in \Sigma_{r,s}$ for $0 \le l \le d$, where $d = \phi(X,Y)/2$. Now assume that $\phi(X,Y) = 2$. Without loss of generality

$$Y = X + \begin{bmatrix} -1 & 1 & 0 & \cdots & 0 \\ 1 & -1 & 0 & \cdots & 0 \end{bmatrix}.$$

We must define a coupling $(X,Y) \mapsto (X',Y')$ for $\mathcal{M}(\Sigma_{r,s})$ at (X,Y). Let (j_1,j_2) be chosen uniformly at random such that $1 \le j_1 < j_2 \le n$. If $(j_1,j_2) = (1,2)$ or $3 \le j_1 < j_2 \le n$ then $T_X(j_1,j_2) = T_Y(j_1,j_2)$. Here we define the coupling as follows: let $x \in T_X(j_1,j_2)$ be chosen uniformly at random and let X' (respectively Y') be obtained from X (respectively Y) by replacing the j_lth column of X (respectively Y) with the lth column of x, for $l = 1,2$. If $(j_1,j_2) = (1,2)$ then $\phi(X',Y') = 0$, otherwise $\phi(X',Y') = 2$.

It remains to consider indices (j_1,j_2) where $j_1 \in \{1,2\}$ and $3 \le j_2 \le n$. Without loss of generality suppose that $(j_1,j_2) = (2,3)$. Let $T_X = T_X(2,3)$ and let $T_Y = T_Y(2,3)$. Let $a = X_{1,2} + X_{1,3}$, $b = s_2$ and $c = s_2 + s_3$. Then

$$T_X = T^c_{a,b} \qquad \text{and} \qquad T_Y = T^c_{a+1,b}.$$

Suppose that $a + b \ge c$. Then, relabel the rows of X and Y and swop the labels of the second and third columns of X and Y. Finally interchange the roles of X and Y. Let a', b', c' denote the resulting parameters. Then

$$a' + b' = (c - a - 1) + (c - b) = c - (a + b - c) - 1 < c = c'.$$

Therefore we may assume without loss of generality that $a + b < c$. There are two cases depending on which of a or b is the greater.

Suppose first that $a \ge b$. Then

$$T_X = \left\{ \begin{bmatrix} i_X & (a - i_X) \\ (b - i_X) & (c + i_X - a - b) \end{bmatrix} : 0 \le i_X \le b \right\}$$

and

$$T_Y = \left\{ \begin{bmatrix} i_Y & (a + 1 - i_Y) \\ (b - i_Y) & (c + i_Y - a - b - 1) \end{bmatrix} : 0 \le i_Y \le b \right\}.$$

Choose $i_X \in \{0, \ldots, b\}$ uniformly at random and let $i_Y = i_X$. Let X' (respectively Y') be obtained from X (respectively Y) by replacing the j_lth column of X (respectively Y) with the lth column of x (respectively y) for $l = 1,2$. This defines a coupling of $\mathcal{M}(\Sigma_{r,s})$ at (X,Y) for this choice of (j_1,j_2). Here $\phi(X',Y') = 2$.

Suppose next that $a < b$. Then

$$T_X = \left\{ \begin{bmatrix} i_X & (a - i_X) \\ (b - i_X) & (c + i_X - a - b) \end{bmatrix} : 0 \le i_X \le a \right\}$$

and

$$T_Y = \left\{ \begin{bmatrix} i_Y & (a+1-i_Y) \\ (b-i_Y) & (c+i_Y-a-b-1) \end{bmatrix} : 0 \le i_Y \le a+1 \right\}.$$

Choose $i_X \in \{0, \ldots, a\}$ uniformly at random and let

$$i_Y = \begin{cases} i_X & \text{with probability } (a - i_X + 1)(a+2)^{-1}, \\ i_X + 1 & \text{with probability } (i_X + 1)(a+2)^{-1}. \end{cases}$$

If $i \in \{0, \ldots, a+1\}$ then

$$\begin{aligned} \mathrm{Prob}\,[i_Y = i] &= \mathrm{Prob}\,[i_X = i] \cdot (a - i + 1)(a+2)^{-1} \\ &\qquad + \mathrm{Prob}\,[i_X = i-1] \cdot ((i-1)+1)(a+2)^{-1} \\ &= (a+1)^{-1}\left((a-i+1)(a+2)^{-1} + i(a+2)^{-1}\right) \\ &= (a+2)^{-1}. \end{aligned}$$

Therefore each element of $\{0, \ldots, a+2\}$ is equally likely to be chosen, and the coupling is valid. Let x be the element of T_X which corresponds to i_X and let y be the element of T_Y which corresponds to i_Y. Let X', Y' be obtained from X, Y as above. This defines a coupling of $\mathcal{M}(\Sigma_{r,s})$ at (X, Y) for this choice of (j_1, j_2). Again, $\phi(X', Y') = 2$.

Putting this together, it follows that

$$\mathbf{E}\,[\phi(X', Y')] = 2\left(1 - \binom{n}{2}^{-1}\right) < 2 = \phi(X, Y).$$

Let $\beta = 1 - \binom{n}{2}^{-1}$. We have shown that $\mathbf{E}\,[\phi(X', Y')] = \beta\,\phi(X, Y)$, and clearly $\beta < 1$. Therefore $\mathcal{M}(\Sigma_{r,s})$ is rapidly mixing, by Theorem 1. Since $\phi(X, Y) \le N$ for all $X, Y \in \Sigma_{r,s}$ the mixing time $\tau(\varepsilon)$ satisfies

$$\tau(\varepsilon) \le \frac{n(n-1)}{2} \log(N\varepsilon^{-1}),$$

as stated. □

5 Two extensions of the two-rowed chain

In this section we describe two natural extensions of the Markov chain $\mathcal{M}(\Sigma_{r,s})$. The first is to three-rowed contingency tables and the second is to general m-rowed contingency tables. We show that the above path coupling approach cannot be successful for either of these chains without major modifications. This does not imply that a different argument might not be found to establish rapid mixing of either chain.

By analogy with the above, we will work with the metric

$$\psi(X, Y) = \sum_{i=1}^{m} \sum_{j=1}^{n} |X_{ij} - Y_{ij}|. \tag{5}$$

Note that, when $m = 2$ we have $\psi(X,Y) = 2\,\phi(X,Y)$ for all $X, Y \in \Sigma_{r,s}$. Also $\psi(X,Y) \geq 4$ whenever $X \neq Y$ and $X, Y \in \Sigma_{r,s}$. Consider the Markov chain which acts on $\Sigma_{r,s}$ by replacing a 2×2 submatrix of the current state, chosen uniformly at random, by another 2×2 matrix with the same row and column sums. This chain is not irreducible: for example, the chain cannot move from X to Y using any sequence of transitions, where

$$X = \begin{bmatrix} 1 & 0 & 0 \\ 0 & 1 & 0 \\ 0 & 0 & 1 \end{bmatrix}, \qquad Y = \begin{bmatrix} 0 & 0 & 1 \\ 1 & 0 & 0 \\ 0 & 1 & 0 \end{bmatrix}. \tag{6}$$

Therefore we must define different Markov chains for contingency tables with more than two rows. We shall use path coupling with respect to the metric ψ. The set S used in the path coupling is defined below.

Definition 1. *Let $S \subseteq \Sigma_{r,s} \times \Sigma_{r,s}$ be the set of all pairs $(X,Y) \in \Sigma_{r,s} \times \Sigma_{r,s}$ which satisfy both of the following conditions:*

1. *there exists $k \geq 2$ such that $\psi(X,Y) = 2k$,*
2. *there exist indices $1 \leq i_1, \ldots, i_k \leq m$, $1 \leq j_1, \ldots, j_k \leq n$ such that the $\{i_l\}$ are pairwise distinct, the $\{j_l\}$ are pairwise distinct,*

$$Y_{i_l,j_l} = X_{i_l,j_l} + 1 \text{ for } 1 \leq l \leq k, \qquad Y_{i_{l+1},j_l} = X_{i_{l+1},j_l} - 1 \text{ for } 1 \leq l < k,$$

and $Y_{i_1,j_k} = X_{i_1,j_k} - 1$.

5.1 A Markov chain for three-rowed contingency tables

Consider the following natural extension of the Markov chain $\mathcal{M}(\Sigma_{r,s})$ to the case of three-rowed contingency tables. Here $r = (r_1, r_2, r_3)$ and the state space is $\Sigma_{r,s}$. A transition of the extended chain is performed as follows: given a $3 \times n$ matrix X, choose *three* columns of X uniformly at random to give a 3×3 matrix with certain row and column sums. From the set of all 3×3 matrices with these row and column sums, choose a matrix uniformly at random and replace the three selected columns of X with this matrix.

It is not difficult to show that this Markov chain is ergodic and the stationary distribution is the uniform distribution on the set $\Sigma_{r,s}$ of $3 \times n$ contingency tables. Note that selecting an element uniformly at random from a set of 3×3 contingency tables can be easily achieved in polynomial time. Let us investigate the mixing time of this chain using path coupling. We use the metric ψ defined in (5) and the set S given in Definition 1 (where $m = 3$).

We now describe a case which is critical in designing a coupling of the extended chain on elements of S. Let $r = (r_1, r_2, r_3)$ and $s = (s_1, s_2, s_3)$ be two partitions of a positive integer, where the r_i are nonnegative and the s_i are positive. Let $\Sigma_X = \Sigma_{r,s}$ and let $\Sigma_Y = \Sigma_{(r_1+1, r_2-1, r_3), s}$. Suppose that we could define a joint probability distribution $f : \Sigma_X \times \Sigma_Y \to \mathbb{R}$ such that

$$C(f) = \sum_{x \in \Sigma_X} \sum_{y \in \Sigma_Y} f(x,y)\psi(x,y) \leq 2. \tag{7}$$

In order to establish rapid mixing of the extended chain using the path coupling method with the set S and the metric ψ, it suffices to establish (7). Conversely, if we cannot establish (7) then we cannot establish rapid mixing of the chain by path coupling using S and ψ. We do not prove this statement, but instead show that (7) fails.

A joint probability distribution f for $\Sigma_X \times \Sigma_Y$ corresponds to a solution of a related transportation problem, as described in [5]. A joint probability distribution f which minimises $C(f)$ corresponds to an optimal solution Z of the transportation problem. The coupling corresponding to f is called an *optimal coupling*, and $C(f)$ is referred to as the *cost* of an optimal coupling. (Note that an optimal coupling is not the same as a *minimal coupling* referred to in the literature.) The cost of an optimal solution of the related transportation problem is $|\Sigma_X||\Sigma_Y|$ times the cost of an optimal coupling.

We now give a concrete example of such a pair where the cost of the optimal coupling is greater than 2. Let Σ_X be the set of 3×3 contingency tables with row sums $(2,2,1)$ and column sums $(2,2,1)$, and let Σ_Y be the set of 3×3 contingency tables with row sums $(3,1,1)$ and column sums $(2,2,1)$. Then $|\Sigma_X| = 11$ and $|\Sigma_Y| = 8$. The cost of an optimal solution of the related transportation problem is 180, as can be verified by direct computation. Therefore the cost of an optimal coupling is 45/22, which is greater than 2. This example shows that we cannot easily prove that this chain for three-rowed contingency tables is rapidly mixing using path coupling on the set S with the metric ψ. We cannot conclude from this that the chain is not rapidly mixing or that it might not be possible to prove rapid mixing using another set of pairs S or another metric.

5.2 A Markov chain for m-rowed contingency tables

Here let $r = (r_1, \ldots, r_m)$ and $s = (s_1, \ldots, s_n)$ be two positive integer partitions of the positive integer N. Consider the Markov chain for $\Sigma_{r,s}$ with the following transitions: from current state X, choose two rows of X uniformly at random and replace them by a $2\times n$ matrix with the same row and column sums, chosen uniformly at random. It is not difficult to show that this chain is ergodic and that the stationary distribution is the uniform distribution on $\Sigma_{r,s}$.

We will investigate the mixing time of this chain using path coupling, using the metric ψ defined in (5) and the set S of pairs as given in Definition 1. As in the previous subsection, there is one case which is critical in defining a coupling on elements of S. Let $r = (r_1, r_2)$ and $s = (s_1, \ldots, s_n)$ be two partitions of a positive integer, where the r_i are positive and the s_i are nonnegative. Let $\Sigma_X = \Sigma_{r,s}$ and let $\Sigma_Y = \Sigma_{r,s'}$ where $s' = (s_1 + 1, s_2 - 1, s_3, \ldots, s_m)$. Suppose that we could define a joint probability distribution $f : \Sigma_X \times \Sigma_Y \to \mathbb{R}$ such that

$$C(f) = \sum_{x\in\Sigma_X} \sum_{y\in\Sigma_Y} f(x,y)\psi(x,y) \le 2. \tag{8}$$

If we cannot establish (8) then we cannot prove that the chain is rapidly mixing using path coupling on the set S and the metric ψ. We now demonstrate that

(8) fails. As above, a joint probability distribution f for $\Sigma_X \times \Sigma_Y$ corresponds to a solution of the related transportation problem.

We now present a concrete example where the cost of the optimal coupling is greater than 2. Consider the set Σ_X of contingency tables with row sums $(3,2)$ and column sums $(2,2,1)$, and the set Σ_Y of contingency tables with row sums $(3,2)$ and column sums $(3,1,1)$. Then $|\Sigma_X| = 5$ and $|\Sigma_Y| = 4$. It may be verified by direct computation that the cost of an optimal solution of the related transportation problem is 44. Therefore the cost of an optimal coupling is 11/5, which is greater than 2.

This example shows that it is not possible to prove that the Markov chain described in this subsection is rapidly mixing, using the path coupling method on the set S with the metric ψ. It may of course be possible to establish rapid mixing using path coupling with a different set S or a different metric. Note that transitions of this chain may be approximately performed using the Markov chain $\mathcal{M}(\Sigma_{r,s})$ to sample almost uniformly from two-rowed slices of m-rowed contingency tables. This introduces an uncertainty into the transition procedure which results in an increase in the mixing time. Whether this approach is of any practical use depends critically on whether the Markov chain is rapidly mixing, which remains to be seen.

References

1. Albert, J.H., Gupta, A.K.: Estimation in contingency tables using prior information. J. Roy. Statist. Soc. Ser. B **45** (1983) 60–69.
2. Aldous, D.: Random walks on finite groups and rapidly mixing Markov chains. In: Dold, A., Eckmann, B. (eds.): Séminaire de Probabilités XVII 1981/1982. Lecture Notes in Mathematics, Vol. 986. Springer-Verlag, New York (1983) 243–297.
3. Barlow, R.: Statistics. John Wiley and Sons, Chichester (1989).
4. Bubley, R., Dyer, M.: Path coupling: A technique for proving rapid mixing in Markov chains. In: 38th Annual Symposium on Foundations of Computer Science, IEEE, Miami Beach, Florida (1997) 223–231.
5. Bubley, R., Dyer, M., Greenhill, C., Beating the 2Δ bound for approximately counting colourings: A computer-assisted proof of rapid mixing. In: 9th Annual Symposium on Discrete Algorithms, ACM–SIAM, San Francisco, California (1998) 355–363.
6. Chung, F.R.K., Graham, R.L., Yau, S.T.: On sampling with Markov chains. Random Structures Algorithms **9** (1996) 55–77.
7. Diaconis, P., Effron, B.: Testing for independence in a two-way table: new interpretations of the chi-square statistic (with discussion). Ann. Statist. **13** (1985) 845–913.
8. Diaconis, P., Gangolli, A.: Rectangular arrays with fixed margins. In Aldous, D., Varaiya, P.P., Spencer, J., Steele, J.M. (eds.): Discrete Probability and Algorithms. IMA Volumes on Mathematics and its Applications, Vol. 72. Springer-Verlag, New York (1995) 15–41.
9. Diaconis, P., and Saloff-Coste, L.: Random walk on contingency tables with fixed row and column sums. Tech. rep., Department of Mathematics, Harvard University (1995).

10. Dyer, M., Greenhill, C.: A more rapidly mixing Markov chain for graph colourings. Preprint (1997).
11. Dyer, M., Kannan, R., Mount, J.: Sampling contingency tables. Random Structures Algorithms **10** (1997) 487–506.
12. Hernek, D.: Random generation and counting of rectangular arrays with fixed margins. Preprint (1997).
13. Jerrum, M., Sinclair, A.: The Markov chain Monte Carlo method: an approach to approximate counting and integration. In Hochbaum, D. (ed.): Approximation Algorithms for NP-Hard Problems. PWS Publishing, Boston (1996) 482–520.
14. Kannan, R., Tetali, P., Vempala, S.: Simple Markov chain algorithms for generating bipartite graphs and tournaments. In: 8th Annual Symposium on Discrete Algorithms. ACM–SIAM, San Francisco, California (1997) 193–200.
15. Kaufmann, A.: Graphs, Dynamic Programming and finite games. Academic Press, New York (1967).

A Modular Approach to Denotational Semantics

John Power[1,*] and Giuseppe Rosolini[2]

[1] Department of Computer Science, University of Edinburgh, King's Buildings, Edinburgh, EH9 3JZ, Scotland

[2] DISI, Università di Genova, via Dodecaneso 35, 16146 Genova, Italy

Abstract. We give an account of part of modularity in denotational semantics. We define a computational effect to consist of a category with algebraic structure together with a construction using that algebraic structure of a new denotational category together with an identity on objects functor to it from the original category. We make precise what we mean by algebraic structure and what constructions are allowable. Further, given two computational effects, we give a mathematical foundation for extending one along the other. We prove a theorem to show when such a extension is possible.

1 Introduction

We should like to consider a general approach to modularity in denotational semantics. A recent proposal [8] has been to consider (i) a category C with algebraic structure on it, and (ii) a construction, using the algebraic structure, of a category D and an identity on objects functor $j: C \longrightarrow D$. An example, which may be used to model nondeterminism, is given by (i) a category C together with a monad P on it, and (ii) making D the Kleisli category for P, with j the induced functor. Another example, which may be used to model side-effects, consists of (i) a symmetric monoidal category C together with a specified object S, and (ii) making $D(x, y) = C(S \otimes x, S \otimes y)$ with composition of D induced by that of C, and with j given on homs by $S \otimes -$. A third example, which may be used to model exceptions, is given by (i) a category C with finite coproducts and a specified object e, and (ii) making $D(x, y) = C(x, y + e)$, with composition induced by that of C, and j given by the first coprojection.

The notion of algebraic structure we use here was made precise in [8] by defining a category with algebraic structure to be an M-algebra for a 2-monad M on the 2-category Cat of small categories. General treatments of this idea, directed towards computer scientists, appear in [5, 10]. For instance, there is a 2-monad M for which an M-algebra (C, c) is precisely a small category C with finite products. There is another 2-monad for which an algebra is precisely a small symmetric monoidal category, another for which an algebra is precisely a small category with a monad on it; another for which it consists of a small

* This work has been done with the support of EPSRC grant GR/J84205: Frameworks for programming language semantics and logic.

symmetric monoidal category together with an object S; and yet another for which it is a small category with finite coproducts together with an object e.

The way modularity is supposed to be achieved is as follows: take two computational effects, the first involving an M-algebra (C, c) and a construction $j_{(C,c)}: C \longrightarrow D$, and the second involving an M'-algebra (C, c'); give conditions under which the M'-structure c' on C can be extended along $j_{(C,c)}$ to an M'-structure d on D. Then apply the construction given by the second computational effect to the M'-algebra (D, d), yielding an identity on objects functor $j'_{(D,d)}: D \longrightarrow E$. The composite $j'_{(D,d)} j_{(C,c)}: C \longrightarrow E$ is then regarded as the *lifting* of the second computational effect along the first.

For instance, given a powerdomain P on C to model nondeterminism, and given a symmetric monoidal structure $\otimes$ on C together with an object S of C in order to model side-effects as in our second example above, one can prove that the symmetric monoidal structure on C and its object S extend to the Kleisli category $Kl(P)$ for P, so one can apply the side-effects construction to $Kl(P)$. Thus the lifting of side-effects along nondeterminism yields the category E with objects those of C and with $E(x, y) = C(S \otimes x, P(S \otimes y))$. This was the leading example in [8].

For another example, consider the 2-monad for a small category with finite coproducts together with an object e. That structure, on any small category C, extends to $Kl(T)$ for any monad T. So the construction $Kl(- + j(e))$ may be made on the category $Kl(T)$, extending that given on C. So if, for example, T was given by a powerdomain P, then one could consider the category constructed by first moving to $Kl(P)$, then applying the construction $Kl(- + j(e))$ to it. This gives the category one seeks for modelling nondeterminism together with exceptions.

In order to validate the definition we shall make here of a construction using algebraic structure, we shall prove a theorem that allows us, given such a construction $j_{(C,c)}: C \longrightarrow D$ and an M'-structure (C, c') for a 2-monad M' on Cat, to lift the M'-structure along $j_{(C,c)}$ to D, thus allowing us to give a lifting of the second computational effect along the first. The condition of the theorem is necessarily nontrivial. For instance, there is a 2-monad for which an algebra is a small category with binary products, but binary products typically cannot be extended to the Kleisli category. The condition cited here, and the proof that it does the job, is the main result of the paper. The two leading examples for us are that for side-effects and nondeterminism, and in general, the composite of two monads, for instance those for nondeterminism and probabalistic nondeterminism.

Note that we only address a small aspect of modularity in denotational semantics here. Our examples, although in the spirit of a general approach to modularity, are crude, for instance not treating local variables or lack of snapback in accounting for side-effects, and not considering scoping of exceptions. Also, we are saying nothing at this point about control operators, but are restricting our attention to type constructors. Moreover, we are saying nothing about operational semantics and little about higher order structure. We do not imply that we cannot handle such considerations: we simply have not studied them yet. There have been axiomatic studies of several of these concerns, and we hope to incorporate them into this analysis in due course.

The work in this paper bears obvious relevance to the proposal to use monads to model computational effects by Moggi [3]. His proposal amounts to the special case of ours given by the 2-monad M on Cat for which an algebra is a small category with a monad on it, with the construction given by the Kleisli construction. As is well-known, the proposal in [3] is that monads be used to provide category theoretic models of computational effects. For instance, to model side-effects, one would use the side-effects monad $S \to (S \times -)$, and to model nondeterminism, one would use a powerdomain P: the three classical powerdomains all form monads. In order to account for modularity, Moggi and Cenciarelli defined a notion of monad transformer to be a function from the set of monads on a category C to itself, see [1,4]. For instance, the monad transformer for side-effects takes a monad T to the monad $S \to T(S \times -)$, assuming C is cartesian closed. To model the combination of nondeterminism with side-effects, one would apply the side-effects monad transformer to a powerdomain P, yielding the monad $S \to P(S \times -)$, see also [8].

Investigating how monad transformers arise, one sees that, in general, monad transformers do not arise from monads. On the contrary, the associated monad is derivable from the monad transformer by applying the monad transformer to the identity monad: for instance, the side-effects monad is given by applying the side-effects monad transformer to the identity monad. So monads cannot be taken as primitive, and whatever structure gives rise to monad transformers should therefore give rise to the associated monads too. So we start by considering what structures gives rise to monads. It is important to note that, in doing that, we can explain also how (the interesting cases of) monad transformers arise.

The paper is organized as follows. In Section 2, we make precise what we mean by a construction of an identity on objects functor $j: C \longrightarrow D$ from structure on C. In Section 3, we say what it means, given a 2-monad M on Cat and an M-algebra (C, c), for a constructor on C to be M-definable. Finally, in Section 4, we state and prove a theorem that gives conditions when one computational effect may lift along another: more specifically, when an M'-structure lifts along a construction of an identity on objects functor $j: C \longrightarrow D$ with right adjoint, thus allowing us to perform the second construction on D, yielding the desired composite.

2 The construction

In this section, we introduce the notion of a constructor on a category C. At first sight, the definition may look daunting, as it consists of four functors and six natural transformations, subject to six coherence axioms. As we mentioned in the introduction, we need something more sophisticated than a monad because monads do not, in general, support modularity for denotational semantics. A monad consists of one functor T and two natural transformations, subject to three coherence conditions. The Kleisli construction one builds from a monad is one sided, as one puts $Kl(T)(x,y) = C(x,Ty)$, with T only applied to the codomain. In order to model computational effects such as state, we need the freedom to make more balanced constructions, such as $D(x,y) = C(S\otimes x, S\otimes y)$, where a construction is applied to the domain as well as the codomain. Following this line of exposition leads one to consider not only more balanced constructions, but also more data with which one can make those constructions. This leads to the long list of data: in the examples, the data are simple and evident. We now give the definitions, then the examples.

2.1 Definition A *constructor* on a category C consists of endofunctors F, G, H and K, together with natural transformations $\alpha: Id \Rightarrow H$, $\beta: HG \Rightarrow KF$, $\gamma: KG \Rightarrow G$, $\delta: F \Rightarrow G$, $\mu: KK \Rightarrow K$, and $\eta: Id \Rightarrow K$, subject to the equations

$$\begin{array}{ccc} KKG & \xrightarrow{K\gamma} & KG \\ {\scriptstyle \mu G}\downarrow & & \downarrow{\scriptstyle \gamma} \\ KG & \xrightarrow[\gamma]{} & G \end{array} \qquad \begin{array}{ccc} HG & \xrightarrow{\beta} & KF \\ {\scriptstyle H\alpha G}\downarrow & & \downarrow{\scriptstyle \alpha KF} \\ HHG & \xrightarrow[H\beta]{} & HKF \end{array}$$

$$\begin{array}{ccccc} KG & \xrightarrow{K\alpha G} & KHG & \xrightarrow{K\beta} & KKF \\ {\scriptstyle \gamma}\downarrow & & & & \downarrow{\scriptstyle \mu F} \\ G & \xrightarrow[\alpha G]{} & HG & \xrightarrow[\beta]{} & KF \end{array} \qquad \begin{array}{ccc} G & \xrightarrow{\eta G} & KG \\ & {\scriptstyle Id}\searrow & \downarrow{\scriptstyle \gamma} \\ & & G \end{array}$$

$$\begin{array}{ccc} G & \xrightarrow{\eta G} & KG \\ {\scriptstyle \alpha G}\downarrow & & \uparrow{\scriptstyle K\delta} \\ HG & \xrightarrow[\beta]{} & KF \end{array} \qquad \begin{array}{ccc} F & \xrightarrow{\eta F} & KF \\ {\scriptstyle \alpha F}\downarrow & & \uparrow{\scriptstyle \beta} \\ HF & \xrightarrow[H\delta]{} & HG \end{array}$$

We call a constructor ***adjoint*** if F has a right adjoint.

For this paper, we shall focus almost solely on adjoint constructors. Our results generally hold for constructors too, but require more delicacy of description. So we refer the reader to [9] for the more general account.

2.2 Proposition *Given a constructor $\Gamma = (F,G,H,K,\alpha,\beta,\gamma,\delta,\mu,\eta)$ on a category C, the following data form a category $Con(\Gamma)$ and an identity on objects functor $j: C \longrightarrow Con(\Gamma)$:*

- $D(x,y) = C(Fx,Gy)$

– $\cdot : D(y,z) \times D(x,y) \longrightarrow D(x,z)$ *is defined by applying* H *to* $C(Fx,Gy)$, *applying* K *to* $C(Fy,Gz)$, *and applying* αF, β, *and* γ, *and using composition in* C *as follows*

$$\begin{array}{ccc}
D(x,y) \times D(y,z) & \xrightarrow{\qquad\qquad\qquad} & D(x,z) \\
\| & & \| \\
C(Fx,Gy) \times C(Fy,Gz) & & C(Fx,Gz) \\
{\scriptstyle H \times K}\Big\downarrow & & \Big\uparrow{\scriptstyle \circ} \\
C(HFx,HGy) \times C(KFy,KGz) & \xrightarrow{(\beta_y \circ - \circ \alpha_{Fx}) \times (\gamma_z \circ -)} & C(Fx,KFy) \times C(KFy,Gz)
\end{array}$$

– $j : C(x,y) \longrightarrow D(x,y)$ *is defined by sending* f *to* $\delta_y \circ Ff$.

2.3 Example Given a symmetric monoidal category C together with a specified object S, define $F = G = S \otimes -$, and $H = K = Id$, with all natural transformations the identities. The axioms all hold trivially. The category D is given by $D(x,y) = C(S \otimes x, S \otimes y)$, with composition determined by that in C; and $j : C \longrightarrow D$ is given on homs by $S \otimes -$. If C is closed, then F has a right adjoint.

2.4 Example Given a category C with a monad P on it, define $F = H = Id$, and $G = K = P$, with the natural transformations given by making α and β identities, putting γ and μ equal to the multiplication of the monad, and δ and η equal to the unit of the monad. All the axioms amount to either the monad laws or trivialities. The category D is the Kleisli category $Kl(P)$, and the functor $j : C \longrightarrow D$ is the canonical functor from C to $Kl(P)$.

2.5 Example We can put the above two examples together, as we would want in order to model side-effects together with nondeterminism, as follows: given a symmetric monoidal category C together with a monad P and an object S, define $F = S \otimes -$, $G = P(S \otimes -)$, $H = Id$, and $K = P$, with the natural transformations either identities or induced by the monad structure of P. The category D is given by $D(x,y) = C(S \otimes -, P(S \otimes -))$, with composition induced by the monad structure of P and by composition in C.

2.6 Proposition *Given an adjoint constructor* Γ *on a category* C, *the functor* $j : C \longrightarrow Con(\Gamma)$ *has a right adjoint.*

Proof. Suppose F has a right adjoint R, with counit $\epsilon : FR \Rightarrow Id$. Then j has a right adjoint whose object part is given by RG, and with counit the map in $Con(\Gamma)$ from RGx to x given by the map in C from $FRGx$ to Gx determined by ϵ. It is routine to verify that this is a universal map: one needs to use η and two of its axioms for both existence and unicity. $\square$

We let T_Γ denote the monad induced by an adjoint constructor. The significance of this result is that $Con(\Gamma)$ is the Kleisli category for T_Γ. So if Γ is adjoint, we may restrict our attention to those structures on C that lift along Kleisli constructions. This is a subtle point: it does not mean we can forget about our general account of constructions. For instance, there is no known way to account for the combination of side-effects and nondeterminism in terms of a construction on a pair of monads, as our object S of states must appear on either side of P in the functor $S \to P(S \otimes -)$. The point is that we lift the monoidal structure and object from C to $Kl(P)$ then build our side-effects constructor; and that is not the same as lifting the side-effects monad to $Kl(P)$. Our leading examples of constructors are adjoint.

For some general evidence, beyond the examples and the above result, that our notion of a constructor has reasonable category theoretic status, observe the following proposition.

2.7 Proposition *Any constructor Γ on a small category C lifts to a constructor on $[C^{op}, Set]$, the category of presheaves on C.*

Many of the constructions one makes on categories are given by the Yoneda embedding or a mild variant.

3 M-definable functors and natural transformations

One can extend the usual theory of universal algebra as given by operations and universally defined equations on a set, from sets to categories. In doing so, one can extend the equivalence between finitary monads on Set and universal algebra to an equivalence between finitary 2-monads on Cat and what can reasonably be called categories with algebraic structure [6]. These include categories with structures such as finite products, finite coproducts, symmetric monoidal structure, a monad, and other structures we shall introduce through the course of the paper. We simply assert that for each class of categories with algebraic structure that we introduce, there is a finitary 2-monad M for which the class forms the 2-category of M-algebras.

For the notion of M-definability, we first recall what a finite cotensor in a 2-category $\mathcal{K}$ is. Given a small category x, and an object A of $\mathcal{K}$, a *cotensor* of x with A is a representing object for the 2-functor $Cat(x, \mathcal{K}(-, A)) \colon \mathcal{K}^{op} \longrightarrow Cat$, *i.e.* an object A^x of $\mathcal{K}$ for which there is a natural isomorphism between the category of 1-cells from any B into A^x and the category $Cat(x, \mathcal{K}(B, A))$. A 2-category $\mathcal{K}$ is said to have finite cotensors if every object A has cotensors with all finitely presentable categories x.

A cotensor is a special sort of limit, see [2]. If we denote the 2-category of all (isomorphism classes of) finitely presentable categories by Cat_f, then Cat_f^{op} has finite cotensors given by the binary product of categories. (For simplicity of exposition, we shall assume Cat_f is a sub-2-category of Cat containing precisely one representative of each isomorphism class.) In the precise sense of their definition, cotensors play the same role for 2-categories as powers A^n do for ordinary categories, where n is a finite cardinal. And Cat_f plays the same role for 2-categories as the category Set_f of finite sets does for ordinary categories. In general, the notion of finitely presentable category is a better generalisation of the notion of finite set than the notion of finite category is, and Cat_f is thereby the appropriate generalisation of Set_f.

As, in the case of universal algebra, operations are defined on finite powers of the underlying set, so operations for algebraic theories at 2-level are given on cotensors of the underlying category. We are studying single-sorted theories here as we are interested in a single category with structure. So in defining Lawvere 2-theories, we need a precise way to state the single-sortedness, thus we use Cat_f just as Set_f is used in the definition of ordinary Lawvere theories.

3.1 Definition A *Lawvere 2-theory* consists of a small 2-category $\mathcal{M}$ with finite cotensors together with a bijective on objects finite cotensor preserving 2-functor $\iota: Cat_f^{op} \longrightarrow \mathcal{M}$. A *model* of a Lawvere 2-theory $\mathcal{M}$ is a finite cotensor preserving 2-functor from $\mathcal{M}$ to Cat.

The main result of [7], in the special case of enrichment in Cat, is

3.2 Theorem *To give a finitary 2-monad M on Cat is equivalent to giving a Lawvere 2-theory $\mathcal{M}$, and the 2-category of M-algebras is equivalent to the 2-category of $\mathcal{M}$-models.*

So, given any finitary 2-monad M on Cat, we could equivalently consider the corresponding Lawvere 2-theory $\mathcal{M}$, and that allows us to make the notion of functor and natural transformation determined by M precise. Given a 2-monad M, the 2-category $\mathcal{M}$ is the full sub-2-category of $Kl(M)^{op}$ determined by the finitely presentable categories, with $\iota: Cat_f^{op} \longrightarrow \mathcal{M}$ determined by the restriction of the canonical functor $J: Cat \longrightarrow Kl(M)$. Given an M-algebra (C, c), the corresponding model $L(c)$ of $\mathcal{M}$ is given by putting $L(c)(x) = Cat(x, C)$, with the functor $L(C)_{x,y}: \mathcal{M}(x, y) \longrightarrow Cat(Cat(x, C), Cat(y, C))$ given by the functor from $Cat(x, C) \times Cat(y, Mx)$ to $Cat(y, C)$ determined by

$$
\begin{array}{ccc}
Cat(x,C) \times Cat(y,Mx) & \longrightarrow & Cat(y,C) \\
{\scriptstyle M \times \mathrm{id}} \big\downarrow & & \big\uparrow {\scriptstyle c \circ -} \\
Cat(Mx,MC) \times Cat(y,Mx) & \xrightarrow[\mathrm{comp}]{} & Cat(y,MC)
\end{array}
$$

3.3 Example Let M be the 2-monad on Cat for which an M-algebra is a small symmetric monoidal category C together with a specified object S of C. Then $S \otimes -: C \longrightarrow C$ is in the image under $L(c)$ of a 1-cell in $\mathcal{M}$ from 1 to 1.

3.4 Example Let M be the 2-monad on *Cat* for which an M-algebra is a small category C with a monad T on it. Then T is in the image under $L(c)$ of a 1-cell in $\mathcal{M}$ from 1 to 1, and the natural transformations μ and η that form part of the data for the monad are in the image under $L(c)$ of 2-cells in $\mathcal{M}$ between 1-cells from 1 to 1.

The theorem provides the mathematical setting and these examples provide the motivation for our definition of an M-definable constructor.

3.5 Definition Given a finitary 2-monad M on *Cat* and an M-algebra (C, c), a constructor Γ on C is *M-definable* if it is the image under $L(c)$ of 1-cells $f, g, h, k: 1 \longrightarrow 1$ and 2-cells $a: id \Rightarrow h$, $b: hg \Rightarrow kf$, $\overline{c}: kg \Rightarrow g$, $d: f \Rightarrow g$, $m: kk \Rightarrow k$, and $n: id \Rightarrow k$, subject to equations corresponding to those in the definition of a constructor.

Finally, we need to recall a mild extension of Theorem 2. Given a 2-monad M, a *lax* map of M-algebras from (A, a) to (B, b) consists of a 1-cell $f: A \longrightarrow B$ together with a 2-cell $\overline{f}: b \cdot Mf \Rightarrow f \cdot a$ that respects the M-structure of the algebras. A *lax* transformation from a 2-functor $H: \mathcal{M} \longrightarrow Cat$ to $K: \mathcal{M} \longrightarrow Cat$ consists of, for each object x of $\mathcal{M}$, a functor $\phi_x: Hx \longrightarrow Kx$, and for each 1-cell $f: x \longrightarrow y$ of $\mathcal{M}$, a natural transformation $\phi_f: Kf \cdot \phi_x \Rightarrow \phi_y \cdot Hf$, with the natural transformations respecting the structure of the 2-functors. We thus have 2-categories $M\text{-}Alg_l$ of M-algebras and lax maps of algebras, and $Lax(\mathcal{M}, Cat)$ of 2-functors and lax transformations. Theorem 2 extends to the following.

3.6 Proposition *Given a 2-monad M on Cat, the equivalence $L: M\text{-}Alg \longrightarrow Mod(\mathcal{M})$ extends canonically to a 2-functor $L_l: M\text{-}Alg_l \longrightarrow Lax(\mathcal{M}, Cat)$.*

An explicit construction can be made routinely, by analysing the construction of $L(c)$.

4 Lifting the construction

Our paradigm for modularity is that we have a computational effect determining a constructor $\Gamma = (F, G, H, K, \alpha, \beta, \gamma, \delta, \mu, \eta)$, and hence the construction $j: C \longrightarrow Con(\Gamma)$, and we have an M'-algebra structure c' on C. We want to lift the M'-structure c' from C along j to an M'-structure on $Con(\Gamma)$, then apply the second construction to that.

4.1 Example Let Γ be the constructor for a powerdomain, so F and G are identities, H and K are given by a monad P, and the natural transformations are given by identities and the unit and multiplication of P. Then $Con(\Gamma)$ is $Kl(P)$ and $j: C \longrightarrow Con(\Gamma)$ is the canonical functor from C to $Kl(P)$. Let M' be an algebraic structure for side-effects, *i.e.* a symmetric monoidal structure and a specified object S. The symmetric monoidal structure on C together with the object S must lift along j to symmetric monoidal structure and an object on $Con(\Gamma)$. Thus we can apply our side-effects construction to $Con(\Gamma)$ together with its induced symmetric monoidal structure and object, and we obtain the category we want in order to model side-effects extended along nondeterminism, *i.e.* the category E with the same objects as C and with $E(x, y) = C(S \otimes x, P(S \otimes y))$. □

In order to provide a theorem to support this account of modularity, our central requirement is to seek conditions under which an M'-algebra structure on a small category C extends along a given construction $j: C \longrightarrow Con(\Gamma)$. Since we only consider adjoint constructors here, we may express the conditions in terms of M' and the monad T_Γ induced by a constructor Γ.

We need to define a functor $d': M'(Con(\Gamma)) \longrightarrow Con(\Gamma)$ that satisfies the equations required of an M'-algebra. In order to define such a functor, we need to know what the objects and arrows of the category $M'(Con(\Gamma))$ are in terms that are accessible to us. Given a constructor Γ and a 2-monad M', let $M'(\Gamma)$ denote the constructor on $M'(C)$ given by applying M' to each of the functors and natural transformations in Γ.

4.2 Definition A *distributive law* of a constructor Γ over a 2-monad M' is an isomorphism of categories between $M'(Con(\Gamma))$ and $Con(M'(\Gamma))$ that respects the monad structure of M', *i.e.* that respects the multiplication and unit of M'. We say that Γ *commutes* with M'.

See [8] for the relationship between this definition of distributive law and that between ordinary monads on a category C. In order to obtain a class of examples, Proposition 6 yields

4.3 Corollary *Let M' be a 2-monad on Cat that preserves bijective on objects functors, i.e. if $h: A \longrightarrow B$ is bijective on objects, then so is $M'(h): M(A) \longrightarrow M(B)$, and let Γ be an adjoint constructor. Then Γ commutes with M'.*

Proof. By Proposition 6, $Con(\Gamma)$ is $Kl(T_\Gamma)$. Since M' is a 2-monad, it preserves adjunctions; since it also preserves bijective on objects functors, it must preserve Kleisli constructions. Thus $M'(Kl(T))$ is isomorphic to $Kl(M'(T))$, coherently with respect to M'. So Γ commutes with M'. □

This provides a large class of examples for us. Every 2-monad we have considered in the paper preserves bijective on objects functors. All follow from fairly routine calculation: one must give a description of the free M'-algebra on a small category. For instance, an object in the free category with (strictly associative) finite products on an ordinary category X is a list of objects of X. That description is independent of the arrows in X; so the 2-monad with such algebras preserves bijective on objects functors. Similar proofs apply to monoidal categories, symmetric monoidal categories, and categories with finite coproducts. The proof for a small category with an object (such as S or e) is almost trivial, and putting that together with the above structures is routine. For a small category with a monad on it, it is again straightforward: one freely generates the objects by freely applying a monad T to each object of X, and continuing inductively; and again that is independent of the arrows of X.

4.4 Theorem *Suppose we have a 2-monad M' on Cat, an M'-algebra (C,c'), and an adjoint constructor Γ on C that commutes with M'. T_Γ underlies a lax map of M'-algebras that respects the monad structure of T_Γ if and only if $Kl(T_\Gamma)$ has and the canonical functor $j: C \longrightarrow Kl(T_\Gamma)$ preserves M'-structure.*

For a proof, see [8] or [9].

4.5 Corollary *Let M' be a 2-monad on Cat, let (C,c') be an M'-algebra, and let T be a monad on C. Suppose M' preserves bijective on objects functors. Then T underlies a lax map of M'-algebras that respects the monad structure of T if and only if $Kl(T)$ has and the canonical functor $j: C \longrightarrow Kl(T)$ preserves M'-structure.*

At the end of Section 3, we indicated how one can characterize lax maps of algebras and 2-cells between them directly in terms of algebraic structure, *i.e.* in terms of the primitive building blocks of M', such as the operations giving a symmetric monoidal structure and an object. So the conditions of the theorem are readily verifiable in elementary terms.

4.6 Example Let Γ be an adjoint constructor. Let M' be the 2-monad for a symmetric monoidal category together with a specified object S. Then M' preserves bijective on objects functors, so Γ commutes with it by Corollary 3. The other hypotheses of Theorem 4 are equivalent to giving a commutative strength to T_Γ. So, by Theorem 4, if T_Γ has a commutative strength, then side-effects can be extended from C to $Con(\Gamma)$. That holds, for instance, if T_Γ is the monad determined by any of the three powerdomains for modelling nondeterminism.

4.7 Example Let Γ be an adjoint constructor. Let M' be the 2-monad for a category with a monad T' on it. Then M' preserves bijective on objects functors, so Γ commutes with it by Corollary 3. The other hypotheses of Theorem 4 amount to giving a distributive law of T' over T_Γ. So, by Theorem 4, if there is a distributive law of T' over T_Γ, then T' extends from C to $Con(\Gamma)$. This holds for instance in combining two powerdomains, one for modelling inner nondeterminism, the other for modelling outer nondeterminism.

4.8 Example Let Γ be an adjoint constructor. Let M' be the 2-monad for finite coproducts together with a specified object e. Then M' preserves bijective on objects functors, so Γ commutes with it by Corollary 3. In this case, the other hypotheses of Theorem 4 are vacuous, essentially because finite coproducts and any object always lift along Kleisli constructions. So the exceptions construction lifts from C to $Con(\Gamma)$, yielding for instance models for exceptions combined with lifting or nondeterminism.

It should be clear how computational effects compose. Given a string of computational effects: first M, an M-algebra (C,c), and M-definable adjoint constructor $\Gamma = (F,G,H,K,\alpha,\beta,\gamma,\delta,\mu,\eta)$, then M', (C,c') and its M'-definable adjoint constructor, then M'', (C,c''), etcetera. One lifts M'-structure along $j: C \longrightarrow Con(\Gamma)$ provided the conditions are satisfied; then one applies the M'-definable constructor to $Con(\Gamma)$, yielding $Con'(Con(\Gamma))$. That is itself expressible as the result of a construction induced by a constructor as follows.

4.9 Theorem *Given an adjoint constructor Γ on C, a 2-monad M' on Cat, an M'-structure c' on C that extends along $j: C \longrightarrow Con(\Gamma)$, and an M'-definable constructor Γ' on C, then $Con'(Con(\Gamma))$ is of the form $Con(\overline{\Gamma})$ for a constructor $\overline{\Gamma}$ on C.*

Proof. First observe that since $j: C \longrightarrow Con(\Gamma)$ is an M'-algebra map, it respects the structure of the M'-definable constructor Γ'. So one can read off the definition of $Con'(Con(\Gamma))$ in terms of endofunctors and endonatural transformations on C as follows: $\overline{F} = F'$, $\overline{G} = T_\Gamma G'$, $\overline{H} = H'$, $\overline{K} = K'T_\Gamma$, with $\overline{\alpha}$ to $\overline{\eta}$ defined by use of the natural transformations required for Theorem 4: the central fact is that, for instance for T_Γ, taking T_Γ together with its associated natural transformation forms a lax map of M'-algebras from (C, c') to itself, hence, by Proposition 6, a lax transformation from $L(c')$ to itself, thus giving us a natural transformation $L(c')(r) \cdot G \Rightarrow G \cdot L(c')(r)$ for any 1-cell r in $\mathcal{M}$, hence in particular $F'T_\Gamma \Rightarrow T_\Gamma F'$, and so on. □

Thus, making the construction determined by a constructor is an iterative process. One can go further: given M and an M-definable adjoint constructor Γ, and M' and an M'-definable constructor Γ', such that M'-structure lifts along Γ, one can describe a 2-monad $\overline{M}$ such that the constructor $\overline{\Gamma}$ is $\overline{M}$-definable.

One may immediately observe that, given adjoint constructors Γ and Γ', then if $\overline{\Gamma}$ exists, it is adjoint too. Thus we see the shadow of the notion of monad transformer of [1] and [4]. Formally, we do not have a monad transformer, as we require a condition, namely that M'-structure lift along Γ. Moreover, the notion of monad transformer does not have the spirit of our analysis, as we consider Γ and $\overline{\Gamma}$ as primitive, rather than the monads generated by them. But this still explains why the notion of monad transformer arose in examples.

4.10 Example Given a powerdomain P on C to model nondeterminism, and symmetric monoidal structure with a specified object S for modelling side-effects, Theorem 9 shows that a model for side-effects extended with nondeterminism is determined by the constructor which has $F = S \otimes -$ and $G = P(S \otimes -)$, with the other structure evident. This constructor is an $\overline{M}$-definable constructor where $\overline{M}$ is the 2-monad for a small category with symmetric monoidal structure, an object S, and a commutative monad P.

References

1. P. Cenciarelli and E. Moggi. A syntactic approach to modularity in denotational semantics, 1993. CWI Tech. Report.

2. G.M. Kelly. *Basic concepts of enriched category theory*. Cambridge University Press, 1982.
3. E. Moggi. Notions of computation and monads. *Inform. and Comput.*, 93(1):55–92, 1991.
4. E. Moggi. Metalanguages and applications. Newton Institute Publications. Cambridge University Press, 1996.
5. A.J. Power. Why tricategories? *Inform. and Comput.*, 120:251–262, 1995.
6. A.J. Power. Categories with algebraic structure. In *Proc. CSL 97*, 1997. To appear.
7. A.J. Power. Enriched Lawvere theories. Submitted, 1997.
8. A.J. Power. Modularity in denotational semantics. *Electronic Notes in Theoretical Computer Science*, 6:#, 1997.
9. A.J. Power and G. Rosolini. Modularity in denotational semantics II. Draft, 1997.
10. E.P. Robinson. Variations on algebra: monadicity and generalisations of algebraic theories. To appear in Math. Structures in Computer Science.

Generalised Flowcharts and Games (Extended Abstract)

Pasquale Malacaria and Chris Hankin

Dept. of Computing
Imperial College
LONDON SW7 2BZ
pm5,clh@doc.ic.ac.uk

Abstract. We introduce a generalization of the classical notion of flowchart for languages with higher order and object-oriented features. These general flowcharts are obtained by an abstraction of the game semantics for Idealized Algol and as such rely on a solid mathematical basis. We demonstrate how charts may be used as the basis for data flow analysis.

1 Introduction

The objective of program analysis is to statically determine some aspect of a program's dynamic behaviour. Such information has traditionally been used in optimising compilers but it also can be used in program verification, providing an alternative to model checking that can deal with infinite state spaces, and formally-based debugging. Many of the traditional approaches to program analysis assume the existence of a control flow graph or flowchart of the program [3]. For first-order imperative languages, the construction of such a graph is relatively trivial. Unfortunately the same is not true for modern programming languages which combine object-oriented, higher-order and concurrency features. The first contribution of this paper is to develop a generalised notion of flowchart which does apply to these languages; our notion is based on an abstraction of game semantics [1]. We also discuss how these generalised flowcharts can be used as a basis for data flow analysis [3].

2 Idealised Algol

Idealised Algol(IA) is a synthesis of functional and imperative programming, originally proposed by Reynolds [12]. The basic types of IA are

$$B ::= \texttt{Exp}[X] \mid \texttt{Var}[X] \mid \texttt{com}$$

where X is a basic type `integer` or `boolean` . General types are constructed in the usual way:

$$T ::= B \mid T \rightarrow T$$

The syntax of the language is as follows:

$$x \in \mathit{Var} \qquad c \in \mathit{Const} \qquad e \in \mathit{Exp}$$
$$e ::= x \mid c \mid e_1\, e_2 \mid \lambda x.e$$

Integer constants: The basic integer constants are the numeral zero: $0 : \texttt{Exp[integer]}$ and the successor operation, predecessor operation and test for zero predicate:

$$\texttt{succ}, \texttt{pred} : \texttt{Exp[integer]} \to \texttt{Exp[integer]}$$
$$\texttt{iszero} : \texttt{Exp[integer]} \to \texttt{Exp[boolean]}$$

Boolean constants: The basic boolean constants are true and false and there is a conditional at each type:

$$\texttt{tt}, \texttt{ff} : \texttt{Exp[boolean]} \qquad \texttt{if} : \texttt{Exp[boolean]} \to T \to T \to T$$

Imperative constants: The basic imperative constant is the skip command: $\texttt{skip} : \texttt{com}$ In addition, commands can be sequentially composed using the sequencing operation: $\texttt{seq} : \texttt{com} \to \texttt{com} \to \texttt{com}$ and there are operations for generating local storage, dereferencing variables and assigning variables:

$$\texttt{new} : (\texttt{Var}[X] \to \texttt{com}) \to \texttt{com} \qquad \texttt{deref} : \texttt{Var}[X] \to \texttt{Exp}[X]$$
$$\texttt{assign} : \texttt{Var}[X] \to \texttt{Exp}[X] \to \texttt{com}$$

Finally, there is a fixed point operator at each type: $\texttt{Y} : (T \to T) \to T$. For our purposes we define $Y_T = \lambda f x_1 \ldots x_n.\mu_T(f)x_1 \ldots x_n$ where μ_T is a new constant whose operational rule is $\mu_T(f)$ evaluates to $f(\mu_T(f))$ for a variable f of type $T \to T$. This rule makes sense because we are using Linear Head Reduction (see later) which allows us to substitute one occurrence of f at the time.

Semantics. The small step operational semantics of IA we will refer to in this paper is the usual one for the constants of the language ([12]) and is *linear head reduction* for the lambda redexes [4]. Intuitively the linear head reduction of a term M can be described as follows: at each step consider the leftmost head variable x in the term M; replace (only) this occurrence of x with a copy of the corresponding argument N (correspondence given by λ binding); if this was the only occurrence of x then erase the original N and the corresponding λx. The semantics is defined in terms of *configurations*; a configuration is either a state, or a pair $< M, \sigma >$ where M is a term and σ is a state. A *redex* is a configuration to which a semantic rule applies; a *normal form* is a configuration to which no rule applies. We will require a *loose* semantics which associates a set of derivation sequences to a program; the set represents the usual operational semantics except that conditionals are interpreted as nondeterministic choice. We write $k \to^* k'$ to denote that the configuration k' is reachable from the configuration k using the loose semantics.

Here is an example of evaluation of an IA program (we use the standard infix notation for the imperative rules and write at each step the operational rule applied):

$$\begin{array}{llll}
< x := 2; y := (\lambda z.z + z)!x, \epsilon > & \to_{\text{seq},:=} & < y := (\lambda z.z + z)!x, [x \mapsto 2] > & \to_\lambda \\
< y := (\lambda z.!x + z)!x, [x \mapsto 2] > & \to_! & < y := (\lambda z.2 + z)!x, [x \mapsto 2] > & \to_\lambda \\
< y := 2 + !x, [x \mapsto 2] > & \to_! & < y := 2 + 2, [x \mapsto 2] > & \to \\
< y := 4, [x \mapsto 2] > & \to_{:=} & [x \mapsto 2, y \mapsto 4] &
\end{array}$$

where $!x$ is a shorthand for $\texttt{deref}(x)$. We define the *first occurence of a redex* (FOR in short) as a redex such that none of its subterms has been evaluated (e.g. in the example above $y := (\lambda z.z+z)!x$ is a FOR but $y := 2+2$ isn't). Given a program P the *execution trace* of P is defined as the sequence of FORs in the evaluation of P in the loose semantics. We write $r \leq r'$ if the FOR r precedes r' in the execution trace of P.

3 Object-Oriented Languages in IA

As Reynolds showed [11], Classes can be interpreted in IA by using higher order functions. Formally the statement

$$\texttt{DefineClass}\ C\ \texttt{as}\ \texttt{Decl}; \texttt{Init}; M_1, \ldots M_n$$

where $\texttt{Decl}; \texttt{Init}$ declare local variables and initialise them and the M_i are the methods defined in C can be translated as the term $\hat{C}$ where $\hat{C}$ is

$$\lambda c^{(\mu_1 \times \ldots \times \mu_n) \to \texttt{com}}.\texttt{Decl}; \texttt{Init}; c < M_1, \ldots M_n >$$

of type $((\mu_1 \times \ldots \times \mu_n) \to \texttt{com}) \to \texttt{com}$. Instantiation of classes as:

$$\texttt{newelement}\ x : C\ \texttt{in}\ P \text{ is translated by } \hat{C}(\lambda x^{(\mu_1 \times \ldots \times \mu_n)}.P)$$

A natural extension of Reynold's translation allows us to handle subclasses (with single inheritance). The translation of the statement

$$\texttt{DefineClass}\ C'\ \texttt{Subclassof}\ C\ \texttt{as}\ \texttt{Decl}; \texttt{Init}; M'_1, \ldots M'_l$$

is given by $\hat{C'}$ which is defined by

$$\lambda c^{\mu_1 \times \ldots \times \mu_n} c'^{(\mu_1 \times \ldots \times \mu_n \times \mu'_1 \times \ldots \times \mu'_l) \to \texttt{com}}.\texttt{Decl}; \texttt{Init}; c' < c.1, \ldots, c.n, M'_1, \ldots M'_l >$$

where $c.i$ is the $i-$th element of the tuple.

Instantiation of subclasses as in:

$$\texttt{newelement}\ y : C' < C\ \texttt{in}\ P \text{ is given by } \hat{C}(\lambda x^{(\mu_1 \times \ldots \times \mu_n)}.\hat{C'}\ x\ (\lambda y^{(\mu'_1 \times \ldots \times \mu'_l)}.P))$$

Overriding is implemented as follows: Suppose we want to override the $i-$th method of C in C' with M'_i. Then $\hat{C'}$ is:

$$\lambda c\ c'.\texttt{Decl}; \texttt{Init}; c' < c.1, \ldots, c.(i-1), M'_i, c.(i+1), \ldots, c.l, M_1, \ldots M_n >$$

where the types of the variables c, c' are as above.

A problem arising when using the translation for subclasses is that we get a type error if we try to implement subsumption. For example if we have defined a procedure $P(x)$ where x is a parameter of type Class C then subsumption should allow us to call $P(k')$ where k' is an instance of the subclass C'. However there is a type mismatch: According to the translation x has type $\mu_1 \times \ldots \times \mu_n$ whereas k' has type $\mu_1 \times \ldots \times \mu_n \times \mu'_1 \times \ldots \times \mu'_l$.

This problem is overcome by extending IA with a notion of subtyping whose base case is $A < A \times B$ and is then extended to arrow types by $A < A', B' < B$ implies $A' \rightarrow B' < A \rightarrow B$.

As far as our analysis is concerned subsumption is handled as follows: the type reconstruction algorithm associates more than one type to terms according to their subtyping instantiations (in the example above P is going to have the two possible types) specifying which one is appropriate for a particular program point; in the example above at the program point $P(k')$ the appropriate type for P will be $(\mu_1 \times \ldots \times \mu_n \times \mu'_1 \times \ldots \times \mu'_l) \rightarrow \texttt{com}$. Given this information the algorithm is then the usual one (i.e. the one for IA without subtyping).

4 The framework

We will be concerned with two player games [1]; we designate the two players by P, for Player, and O, for Opponent. The player represents the program and the opponent represents the environment. Players can make two kinds of moves: Questions and Answers. Formalising this, a game of type A is a triple, (M_A, λ_A, P_A), consisting of a set of moves, a labelling function (which specifies whether a move is a player/opponent question/answer move) and a set of valid positions.

The set of valid positions of a game of type A is a non-empty, prefix closed subset of the set of sequences of moves. In addition, elements of P_A satisfy the following three conditions: every valid position starts with an opponent move; moves alternate between player and opponent; there are at least as many questions as there are answers – this condition is called the *bracketing* condition.

Games correspond to types; the games corresponding to non-basic types are constructed according to the type constructors involved in the type. For example, the game for $A \multimap B$ is constructed from the games for A and B. The moves are the union of the moves from the two component games. The labelling function complements labels in A. The valid positions are constrained such that if we project over either A or B we get a valid position in the respective game, only the player is allowed to switch from A to B and answer moves correspond to the most recent unanswered question.

To model programs (of a particular type) we introduce the notion of *strategy* – a non-empty set of even length valid positions (the even length constraint ensures that any position ends with a P move). We further require that for any strategy, σ:

$$\overline{\sigma} = \sigma \cup \{sa \in P_A | \exists b.sab \in \sigma\}$$

is prefix closed. We can think of strategies as (infinite) trees – the trees may have infinite branches (assuming that answers are drawn from an infinite set) and infinite paths (if we allow fixed points – as we do).

The usual function space, $A \to B$, is constructed as the set of strategies in $(!A \multimap B)$ where $!A$ is the game for A repeated *ad libitum* (see [1] for details). For example, the strategy for a unary function, *f*, on natural numbers is:

$$\{\varepsilon, q_O q_P\} \cup \{q_O q_P \underline{n}\ \underline{m} \mid f(n) \to^* m\}$$

Both [1] and [6] define categories of games in which the games are objects and strategies are the morphisms. The categories are cartesian closed and thus provide a model for the standard denotational metalanguage.

Application of one program to another is modelled by parallel composition of the corresponding strategies, followed by hiding the interaction [1].

5 Generalized Flowcharts

For sake of simplicity in the following we are going to assume that the term to be analysed has the form, $M_1 \ldots M_n$, where each M_i is in normal form and the whole term is closed[1].

Given a normal form M (not containing the fixed point constant), its tree translation we are going to give is the tree M_0 obtained by collapsing the game interpretation $\mathcal{G}[\![M]\!]$ [2] of M according to the following rule: M_0 is $\mathcal{G}[\![M]\!]$ where justification pointers have been removed and every answer move has been replaced by the symbol $\star$. Notice that M_0 is always finite. If M is the fixed point constant then a graph (with cyclic paths) is required to finitize the game interpretation of M.

The rest of this section is devoted to explicitily define M_0

- `skip`, `assign`, `seq` and `deref` are represented as follows:

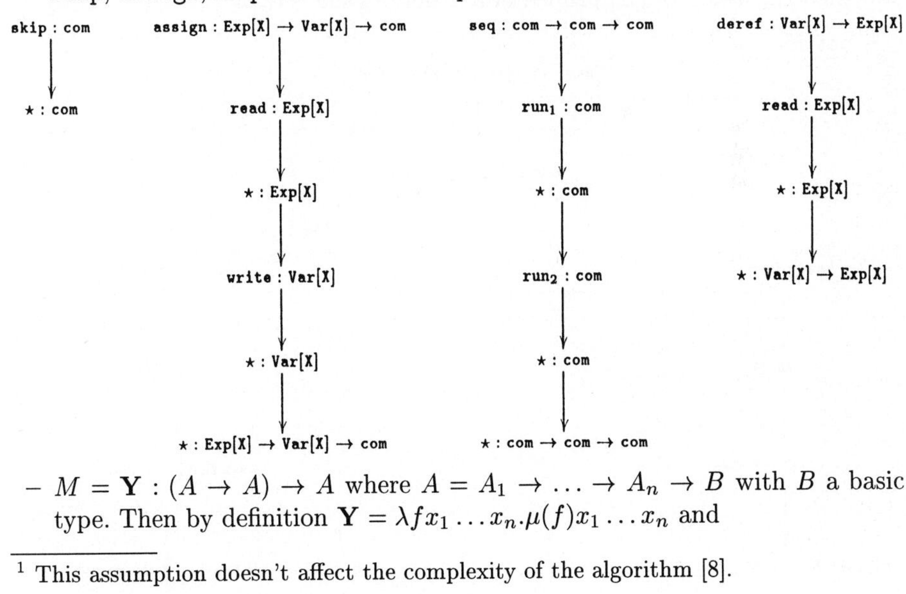

- $M = \mathbf{Y} : (A \to A) \to A$ where $A = A_1 \to \ldots \to A_n \to B$ with B a basic type. Then by definition $\mathbf{Y} = \lambda f x_1 \ldots x_n . \mu(f) x_1 \ldots x_n$ and

[1] This assumption doesn't affect the complexity of the algorithm [8].

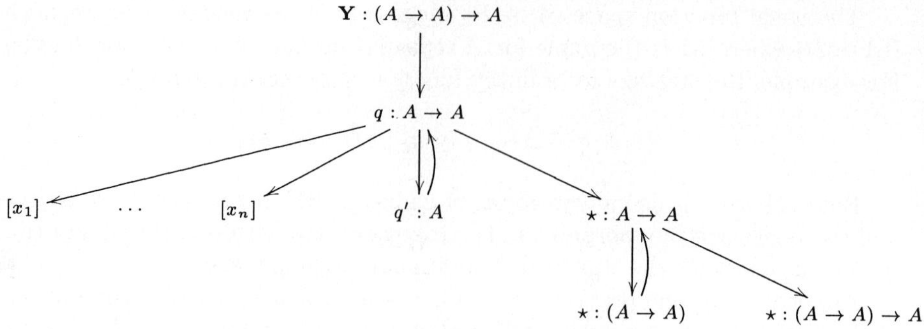

– $M = \lambda x_1 \dots x_m.yM_1 \dots M_n$ and $M = \lambda x_1 \dots x_m.\mathtt{cond}\ (yM_1 \dots M_n)\ N\ N'$ are

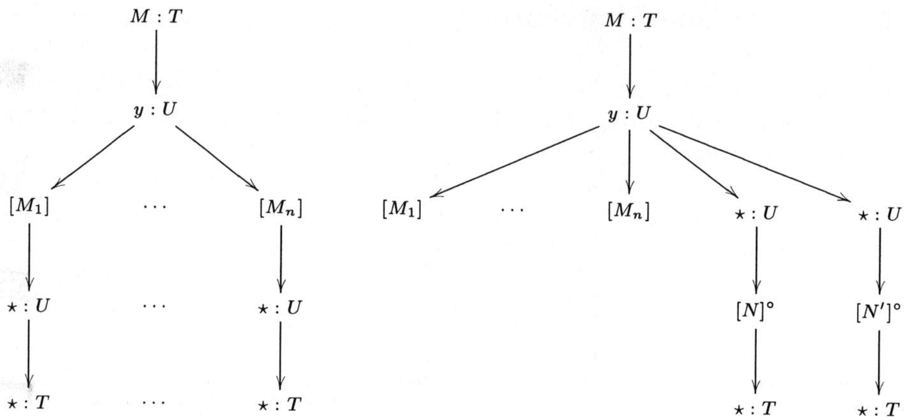

where T and U are the types of the term M and the variable y and $[H]^\circ$ is the translation of $[H]$ pruned of its root.

– new is

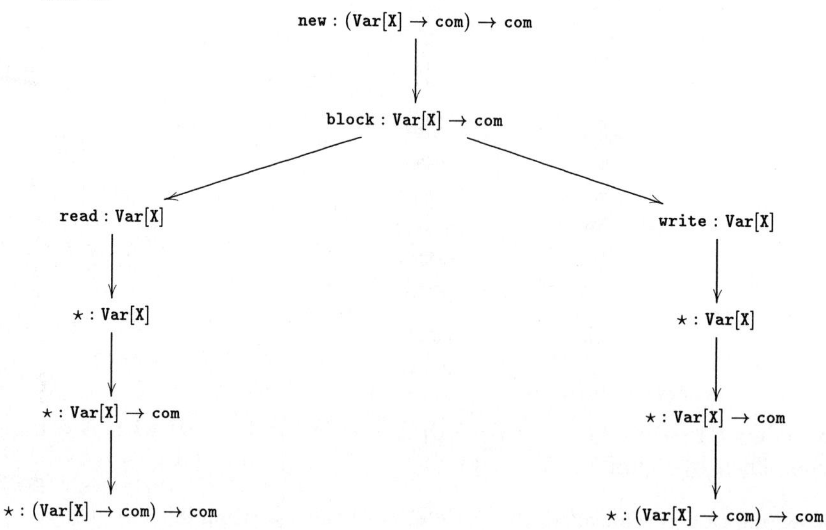

The other delta rules `succ`, `pred`, `iszero` are all interpreted by the same tree which is the obvious abstraction of the strategy discussed in the previous section.

In order to handle Object-Oriented features we need to interpret normal forms of product type. All graphs described so far have a root; products break this rule; for $< a, b >: A \times B$ its translation $[< a, b >]$ is given by the pair of graphs $[a][b]$.

To adjust the setting to cope with multiple roots we stipulate that in all the previous clauses of the translation, edges of the shape

are families of edges, one edge for each root of $[M]$.

Projections $\Pi_i : A_1 \times \ldots \times A_n \to A_i$ are interpreted by:

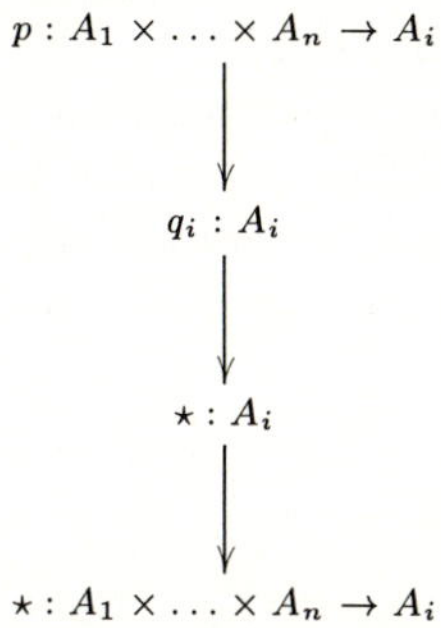

We will call *variables* the non $\star$ vertices at an even level of the tree and *subterms* the non $\star$ vertices at an odd level of the tree (the root of a tree is at level 1, for the fixpoint graph apply the convention erasing the looping (i.e. the upward) edge). $\star$ vertices are called answers; the ones at an even level of the tree are P-answers and the ones at an odd level are O-answers. This definition comes from the game interpretation of programs where variables (resp. subterms) are interpreted by Player (resp. Opponent) moves.

Interaction links. We are now going to connect the family of graphs $(M_1)_0 \ldots (M_n)_0$ generated by the previous section. These links between graphs of normal forms are called *dotted arrows* and are directed edges from variables to subterms and from P-answers to O-answers. It's enough to describe how links from variables to subterms are created because the ones from P-answers to O-answers are completely symmetric (each variable has associated a unique O-answer and each subterm has associated a unique P-answer).

- Notice first that by definition each variable and subterm in $M_1 \ldots M_n$ has associated a unique occurrence of a type. The difference between type and occurrence is essential in the analysis.
- Let $A_2 \to \ldots \to A_r \to B$ be the type of M_1 so that M_j $(j > 1)$ has type A_j. Mark as twin these two occurrences of A_j.
- For all M_i, $1 \leq i \leq n$ make the following associations of variable and subterms with occurrence of subtypes as follows:

0. Variables are associated with the occurrence of their types.
1. If x is associated with $A'_1 \rightarrow \ldots \rightarrow A'_m \rightarrow B$ and $N_1 \ldots N_h$ are arguments of x (i.e. $xN_1 \ldots N_h$ is a subterm) then N_j is associated with A'_j.
2. Moreover if $N_j = \lambda y_1 \ldots y_k.M''$ and $A'_j = C_1 \rightarrow \ldots \rightarrow C_h \rightarrow B$ Then y_l is associated with C_l.
3. Repeat the same process for each N_j in $1 \leq j \leq h$ going back to the step 1.

Given a variable x in M_1 (resp. a variable y in M_i, $i > 1$) which is associated with the occurrence of a subtype T of A_i, link x (resp. y) with the subterms in M_i $(i > 1)$(resp. the subterms in M_1) which are associated with the occurrence of the same subtype (in order for twin types to have all the "matching pairs" some η expansions may be needed).

We will say that $z \in \texttt{d-arr}(x)$ (i.e. there is a *dotted arrow* from x to z) if there is a link created by the previous procedure from x to z.

We have already noticed that there is a correspondence between question nodes (variables and subterms) and answers nodes. This translates to edges; a *question edge* is an edge leaving from a variable and an *answer edge* is one leaving from a P-answer. Notice that a given question edge has associated a unique answer edge (bracketing condition).

6 Charts and Flowcharts

Given a program define its *chart* as the graph defined in section 5; given nodes a, b in the chart we say that b is *reachable* from a if there is an alternating (dotted/solid arrows) path from a to b.

A *valid path* is a sequence $s_1 \ldots s_n$ such that each s_i is an alternating path and for $j < n$ the target of s_j is a variable node whose answer is the source of s_{j+1}.

A *1-valid path* is a valid path $s_1 \ldots s_n$ with no question edge repeated and for which there exists a (edge) well-bracketed alternating path completion, i.e. there exists $s'_1, \ldots, s'_n$ such that the sequence $s_1 s'_1 \ldots s_n s'_n$ is an alternating path which is edgewise well bracketed.

Given nodes a, b in the chart we say that b is *1-reachable* from a if there is a 1-valid path from a to b.

Given a *chart* of a program several kinds of information can be deduced: Given a subset N of nodes of a chart C define a *N-Flowchart* as the preorder $<_1$ on nodes in N defined by:

$$n <_1 n' \text{ iff the node } n' \text{ is 1-reachable from } n \text{ in } C$$

The worst case complexity for building an N-Flowchart is cubic in the size of the program; however this situation is rarely encountered; moreover for restricted languages N-Flowcharts are easier to build; for example the algorithm restricted to imperative programs has linear complexity.

Given a chart, a FOR is identified with the vertex which is the root for the translation of the leftmost term in the redex.

A *program* is an IA term of basic type. Our techniques are easily extended to terms of type $\sigma_1 \to \ldots \to \sigma_n$ (all σ_i of basic type) by applying the term to appropriate dummy arguments (of basic type). In the following, we use the term "program" to refer to these more general terms.

Theorem 1. *Let $P = TT_1 \ldots T_n$ be a (normalized) program and c, c' two nodes in the chart of P corresponding to two FORs of P; the following are equivalent:*

- $c <_1 c'$.
- *In the execution trace of P, $c \leq c'$*

In order to relate our general notion of Flowchart with the classic one proceed as follows. For a first-order program without procedure calls, P, take as subset N the nodes in the chart of P corresponding to the following program points: `cond`, `assign`. Note that we don't need any special node for `while` loops because of the lack of antisymmetry in the definition of preorder. We have then

Corollary 1. *For N and P as above the N-Flowchart of P and the usual Flowchart of P coincide (i.e. they are graph isomorphic).*

The proof of Theorem 1 relies on the relationship between composition in the category of Games and linear head reduction [4].

Our main theorem can be restated as follows (here $\sigma || \tau$ stands for the parallel composition of σ and τ [1]):

Theorem 2. *Let P and c, c' as in Theorem 1; the following are equivalent:*

- $c <_1 c'$.
- *In $\mathcal{G}[\![T]\!] || \mathcal{G}[\![T_1]\!] || \ldots || \mathcal{G}[\![T_n]\!]$ we have $s m_c s' m_{c'} s''$ for some s, s', s''.*
- *In the execution trace of P, $c \leq c'$*

An informal justification for this result is the following: $\mathcal{G}[\![T]\!] || \mathcal{G}[\![T_1]\!] || \ldots || \mathcal{G}[\![T_n]\!]$ is a play; erasing the justification part of moves we get a relation R between moves in correspondence with the copycat of composition; this is the same relation as the dotted arrow relation in the chart of the program. On the other side the same relation R can be translated (via the decomposition lemma) to a relation between variables and subterms of P which corresponds to linear head reduction. Once this is established the result follows rather easily.

7 Data Flow Analysis

Intra-procedural analysis. Data flow analyses are of two kinds: those that use some properties of the data that is being manipulated by the program and those that track the way in which data is used. An example of the former is constant propagation, whilst an example of the latter is reaching definitions [10]. The former class of analyses have been called first-order, whilst the latter have been called second-order. In order to present first-order analyses based on our approach, we would have to introduce some concrete answer moves into our abstract strategies and we will explore this in a forthcoming paper; however, our current framework is sufficient for second-order analyses.

We have already observed that our abstract strategies are generalised flow charts. From the point of view of data flow analysis, we are interested in certain nodes in the abstract strategy: questions corresponding to the roots of assignments, skips and the tests in conditionals. For each such node, we associate a pair of data flow equations which specify the data flow information present at the entry of the node and at the exit – the computation of this information requires access to the arguments of the nodes. For forward analyses, we require the notion of *immediate predecessor*. We write $n_1 <_i n_2$ if $n_1 < n_2$ and there is a path from n_1 to n_2 with no intervening nodes. The equations associated with a node are then:

$$\begin{aligned} n_\circ &= \bigcup_{n' <_i n} n'_\bullet \\ n_\bullet &= f_n(n_\circ) \end{aligned}$$

where $n_\circ$ specifies the data flow values at the entry to the node, $n_\bullet$ specifies the data flow values at the exit and f_n is the *transfer function.* The correctness of these equations follows from the correctness of $<$. The solution of such equations is straightforward using standard techniques such as those discussed in [10]. These solution procedures are independent of the underlying framework and thus the complexity is unaffected by the use of our framework.

Inter-procedural analysis. Given our earlier observations, extending these techniques to interprocedural analyses for first-order procedures is straightforward. We can use state-of-the-art algorithms from the literature. An interesting observation is that the common notion of "interprocedurally valid path" is the bracketing condition on valid positions in Game Semantics [1]. If we restrict attention to the nodes of interest, we immediately have an interprocedural flow graph from the abstract strategy. Once we have the flow graph, the analysis is independent of the underlying framework. For example, we can use the approach of Horwitz, Reps and Sagiv [5] and attain the same complexity that they do.

8 Higher-order Procedures

In the presence of higher-order procedures it is necessary to precede the data flow analysis by a closure analysis (to determine which procedures may be called at a particular call site). In an earlier paper, [8], we have demonstrated that charts may be used as the basis for a simple closure analysis which has the same (cubic) complexity as the state-of-the-art algorithms. Unfortunately, the 0-CFA is rather inaccurate – because it can not differentiate between different calls of a function. Consider the following term: $(\lambda f.(\lambda xy.x)(f(\lambda z.1))(f(\lambda z.2)))(\lambda a.a)$ After normalisation and η-expansion this becomes:

$$(\lambda rf.r\ (\lambda xy.x)(f(\lambda z.1))(f(\lambda z.2)))(\lambda cdeg.c\ d\ e\ g)(\lambda ab.ab)$$

The cache map of [8] effectively maps this term to: $\{\lambda g.1, \lambda g.2\}$. In fact the result of reducing the expression is the first term. The inaccuracy arises because the environment coalesces the bindings for a for the two different calls of f. This is a well-known property of the 0-CFA approach.

A number of solutions to this problem have been proposed in the literature (e.g. [9]). We will briefly consider polynomial k-CFA [7] – the k indicating the degree of differentiation that we can make between calls. The approach involves some form of labelling of call sites in the program – the dotted arrows introduced in our algorithm are also labelled with a string which records the last k calls according to the $<$ ordering. The environment ($\mathcal{V}$) and cache ($\mathcal{C}$) functions become (for conciseness we have omitted the conditional):

$$\mathcal{V}(x,\ell) \;= \bigcup_{z\in Z} \begin{cases} \{(\lambda x.M,\ell)\} & \text{if } z = [\lambda x.M] \\ \bigcup(\mathcal{V}'((\mathcal{V}(y,\ell:\ell'))^{\text{n-cut}},\ell:\ell')) & \text{if } z = [y^{\ell'} M_1 \ldots M_n] \\ \bigcup(\mathcal{V}'((\mathcal{V}(y,\ell))^{\text{n-cut}},\ell)) & \text{if } z = [y M_1 \ldots M_n] \end{cases}$$
$$\text{where } Z = \{y \mid y \in \text{d-arr}(x,\ell)\}$$

$$\mathcal{V}'(M,\ell) = \begin{cases} \{(\lambda x.N,\ell)\} & \text{if } M = [\lambda x.N] \\ \mathcal{V}'((\mathcal{V}(y,\ell:\ell'))^{\text{n+r-cut}},\ell:\ell') & \text{if } M = [(y^{\ell'} M_1 \ldots M_n)]^{\text{r-cut}} \\ \mathcal{V}'((\mathcal{V}(y,\ell))^{\text{n+r-cut}},\ell) & \text{if } M = [(y M_1 \ldots M_n)]^{\text{r-cut}} \end{cases}$$

$$(\lambda x.M)^{\text{n+1-cut}} = M^{\text{n-cut}}, \quad M^{\text{0-cut}} = M$$

$$\begin{aligned} \mathcal{C}(\lambda x.M,\ell) &= \{(\lambda x.M,\ell)\} \\ \mathcal{C}(M^{\ell'} M_1 \ldots M_r,\ell) &= \mathcal{V}'(\{M\}^{\text{r-cut}},\ell:\ell') \\ \mathcal{C}(x,\ell) &= \mathcal{V}(x,\ell) \end{aligned}$$

where d-arr(x,ℓ) is the set of links labelled ℓ which emanate from x and : concatenates a new label onto the end of the string ensuring that the length of the string does not exceed k – by dropping labels from the beginning of the string if necessary. The function $\mathcal{V}'$ is an auxiliary function that is used to follow dotted arrows transitively and n-cut removes head lambdas; we have defined these functions to operate on single terms – the extension to sets of terms is in the obvious way.
If we label the term: $(\lambda r\, f.r\ (\lambda xy.x)(f^1(\lambda z.1))(f^2(\lambda z.2)))^3(\lambda cdeg.c\ d\ e\ g)(\lambda ab.ab)$, a 1-CFA is sufficiently precise to give the accurate answer. The polynomial 1-CFA variant of our algorithm is $O(n^6)$, as are the state-of-the-art algorithms in the literature.

9 Conclusions

We have presented a generalised notion of flow charts. This new notion is sufficiently powerful to enable us to capture control flow information for a variety of modern programming language features, including higher-order procedures, object-orientation and concurrency. In this paper we have concentrated on imperative languages with higher-order procedures, which are sufficiently powerful to encode class-based object-oriented languages. We will consider concurrency in a sequel to this paper. We have shown how this framework can be used as a basis for program analysis; this continues a programme of work started in [8] which mainly considers control flow analysis for PCF. A major advantage of the approach is that the different programming language paradigms are handled in a uniform way within the same abstract game semantics framework. For future work, in addition to considering concurrent languages, we would like to see how the framework might be extended to support first-order data flow analysis.

Acknowledgements

We are grateful to our colleagues from the TCOOL project for their support and encouragement. Thanks also to the UK Engineering and Physical Sciences Research Council for funding TCOOL and supporting the first author through an Advanced Research Fellowship. Finally, we are grateful to Bernhard Steffen for his advice and encouragement.

References

1. Abramsky S., Jagadeesan R. and Malacaria P. Full abstraction for PCF (extended abstract). In *Proc. TACS'94*, LNCS 789, pp 1–15, Springer-Verlag, 1994.
2. Abramsky S. and McCusker G. Linearity, sharing and state: a fully abstract game semantics for Idealised Algol with active expressions. Draft manuscript, 1997.
3. Aho A. V., Sethi R. and Ullman J. D. *Compilers: Principles, Techniques, Tools.* Addison–Wesley, 1986.
4. V. Danos, H. Herbelin and L. Regnier. Game semantics and abstract machines. In *Proc. LICS'96*, IEEE Press, 1996.
5. Horwitz S., Reps T. and Sagiv M. Demand Interprocedural Dataflow Analysis. Proc. of the 3rd ACM SIGSOFT Symposium on Foundations of Software Engineering, ACM Press, 1995
6. Hyland M. and Ong L. On full abstraction for PCF: I, II and III. 130 pages, ftp-able at `theory.doc.ic.ac.uk` in directory `papers/Ong`, 1994
7. Jagannathan S. and Weeks S. A unified treatment of flow analysis in higher-order languages. In *Proc. POPL'95*, pp 393–407, ACM Press, 1995.
8. Malacaria P. and Hankin C. A New Approach to Control Flow Analysis. In *Proc. CC'98*, LNCS 1383, pp 95–108, Springer-Verlag, 1998.
9. Nielson F. and Nielson H. R. Infinitary Control Flow Analysis: a Collecting Semantics for Closure Analysis. In *Proc. POPL'97*, pp 332–345, ACM Press, 1997.
10. Nielson F., Nielson H. R. and Hankin C. *Principles of Program Analysis: Flows and Effects.* to appear, 1999.
11. Reynolds J. C. Syntactic control of interference. In *Proc. POPL'78*, pp 39–46, ACM Press, 1978.
12. Reynolds J. C. The essence of Algol. In J. W. de Bakker and J. C. van Vliet (eds), *Algorithmic Languages*, pp 345–372, North-Holland, 1981.

Efficient Minimization of Numerical Summation Errors

Ming-Yang Kao[1] and Jie Wang[2]

[1] Department of Computer Science Yale University, New Haven, CT 06520, USA. Email: kao-ming-yang@cs.yale.edu. Supported in part by NSF Grant CCR-9531028.
[2] Department of Mathematical Sciences, The University of North Carolina at Greensboro, Greensboro, NC 27402, USA. Email: wang@uncg.edu. Supported in part by NSF Grant CCR-9424164.

Abstract. Given a multiset $X = \{x_1, \ldots, x_n\}$ of real numbers, the *floating-point set summation* (FPS) problem asks for $S_n = x_1 + \cdots + x_n$, and the *floating point prefix set summation* problem (FPPS) asks for $S_k = x_1 + \cdots + x_k$ for all $k = 1, \ldots, n$. Let E_k^* denote the minimum worst-case error over all possible orderings of evaluating S_k. We prove that if X has both positive and negative numbers, it is NP-hard to compute S_n with the worst-case error equal to E_n^*. We then give the first known polynomial-time approximation algorithm for computing S_n that has a provably small error for arbitrary X. Our algorithm incurs a worst-case error at most $2(\lceil\log(n-1)\rceil + 1)E_n^*$.[1] After X is sorted, it runs in $O(n)$ time, yielding an $O(n^2)$-time approximation algorithm for computing S_k for all $k = 1, \ldots, n$ such that the worst-case error for each S_k is less than $2(\lceil\log(k-1)\rceil + 1)E_k^*$.
For the case where X is either all positive or all negative, we give another approximation algorithm for computing S_n with a worst-case error at most $\lceil\log\log n\rceil E_n^*$. Even for unsorted X, this algorithm runs in $O(n)$ time. Previously, the best linear-time approximation algorithm had a worst-case error at most $\lceil\log n\rceil E_n^*$, while E_n^* was known to be attainable in $O(n \log n)$ time using Huffman coding. Consequently, FPPS is solvable in $O(n^2)$ time such that the worst-case error for each S_k is the minimum. To improve this quadratic time bound in practice, we design two on-line algorithms that calculate the next S_k by taking advantage of the current S_k and thus reduce redundant computation.

1 Introduction

Summation of floating-point numbers is ubiquitous in numerical analysis and has been extensively studied (for example, see [2], [4], [5], [6], [7], [8], [10]). This paper focuses on the following two commonly encountered floating point arithmetic operations over a multiset $X = \{x_1, \ldots, x_n\}$ of real numbers:

- *Floating-Point Set Summation* (FPS): Evaluate $S_n = \sum_{i=1}^{n} x_i$.

[1] All logarithms log in this paper are base 2.

- *Floating-Point Prefix Set Summation* (FPPS): Evaluate all prefix sums $S_k = \sum_{i=1}^{k} x_i$ for $k = 1, \ldots, n$.

Without loss of generality, let $x_i \neq 0$ for all i throughout the paper. Here X may contain both positive and negative numbers. For such a general X, previous studies have discussed heuristic methods and obtained statistical or empirical bounds for their errors. We take a new approach by designing efficient algorithms whose worst-case errors are provably small.

Our error analysis uses the standard model of floating-point arithmetic with unit roundoff $\alpha \ll 1$:

$$\mathrm{fl}(x + y) = (x + y)(1 + \delta_{xy}), \text{where } |\delta_{xy}| \leq \alpha.$$

Since operator + is applied to two operands at a time, an ordering for adding X corresponds to a binary addition tree of n leaves and $n - 1$ internal nodes, where a leaf is an x_i and an internal node is the sum of its two children. Different orderings yield different addition trees, which may produce different computed sums $\hat{S}_n$ in floating-point arithmetic. We aim to find an optimal ordering that minimizes the error $E_n = |\hat{S}_n - S_n|$. Let $I_1, \ldots, I_{n-1}$ be the internal nodes of an addition tree T over X. Since α is very small even on a desktop computer, any product of more than one α is negligible in our consideration. Using this approximation,

$$\hat{S}_n \approx S_n + \sum_{i=1}^{n-1} I_i \delta_i.$$

Hence, $E_n \approx |\sum_{i=1}^{n-1} I_i \delta_i| \leq \alpha \sum_{i=1}^{n-1} |I_i|$, giving rise to the following definitions:

- The *worst-case error* of T, denoted by $E(T)$, is $\alpha \sum_{i=1}^{n-1} |I_i|$.
- The *cost* of T, denoted by $C(T)$, is $\sum_{i=1}^{n-1} |I_i|$.

Our task is to find a fast algorithm that constructs a binary addition tree T over X such that $E(T)$ is the minimum. Since $E(T) = \alpha \cdot C(T)$, minimizing $E(T)$ is equivalent to minimizing $C(T)$. We further adopt the following notations:

- E_n^* (respectively, C_n^*) is the minimum worst-case error (respectively, minimum cost) over all orderings of evaluating S_n.
- $T_{\min}$ denotes an optimal addition tree over X, i.e., $E(T_{\min}) = E_n^*$ or equivalently $C(T_{\min}) = C_n^*$.

In §2, we prove that if X contains both positive and negative numbers, it is NP-hard to compute a S_n with the minimum worst-case error E_n^*. In light of this result, we design an approximation algorithm in §3.1 that computes a binary addition tree T over X with $E(T) \leq 2(\lceil \log(n-1) \rceil + 1)E_n^*$. After X is sorted, this algorithm takes only $O(n)$ time. This is the first known polynomial-time approximation algorithm that has a provably small error for arbitrary X. Using this algorithm, we derive in §4 an $O(n^2)$-time approximation algorithm for computing S_k for all $k = 1, \ldots, n$ such that the worst-case error for each S_k is less than $2(\lceil \log(k-1) \rceil + 1) \cdot E_k^*$.

For the case where X is either all positive or all negative, we give another approximation algorithm in §3.2 for computing S_n. It computes a tree T with $E(T) \leq (1 + \lceil \log \log n \rceil) E_n^*$. This algorithm takes only $O(n)$ time even for unsorted X. Previously [5], the best linear-time approximation algorithm had a worst-case error at most $\lceil \log n \rceil E_n^*$. Using Huffman coding, it was known that E_n^* is attainable in $O(n \log n)$ time [9], which yields an algorithm for solving FPPS in $\Theta(n^2)$ time such that the worst-case error for each S_k is the minimum. To improve this quadratic time bound in practice, we design two on-line algorithms in §4 that calculate the next S_k by taking advantage of the current S_k and thus reduce redundant computation. While these algorithms may take quadratic time in the worst case, they require only linear time in the best case.

2 Minimizing the worst-case error is NP-hard

If X contains both positive and negative numbers, we prove that it is NP-hard to compute S_n with the minimum worst-case error E_n^*; i.e., it is NP-hard to find a $T_{\min}$. We first observe the following properties of $T_{\min}$.

Lemma 1. *Let z be an internal node in $T_{\min}$.*

1. *If $z > 0$, then z cannot have two positive children while z's sibling is negative and z's parent is nonnegative.*
2. *If $z < 0$, then z cannot have two negative children while z's sibling is positive and z's parent is nonpositive.*

For the purpose of proving that finding a $T_{\min}$ is NP-hard, we restrict all x_i to nonzero integers and consider the following optimization problem.

MINIMUM ADDITION TREE (MAT)

Input: A multiset X of n nonzero integers $x_1, \ldots, x_n$.

Output: Some $T_{\min}$ over X.

The following problem is a decision version of MAT.

ADDITION TREE (AT)

Instance: A multiset X of n nonzero integers $x_1, \ldots, x_n$, and an integer $k \geq 0$.

Question: Does there exist an addition tree T over X with $C(T) \leq k$?

Lemma 2. *If* MAT *is solvable in time polynomial in n, then* AT *is also solvable in time polynomial in n.*

In light of Lemma 2, to prove that MAT is NP-hard, it suffices to reduce the following NP-complete problem [3] to AT.

3-PARTITION (3PAR)

Instance: A multiset B of $3m$ positive integers $b_1, \ldots, b_{3m}$, and a positive integer K such that $K/4 < b_i < K/2$ and $b_1 + \cdots + b_{3m} = mK$.

Question: Can B be partitioned into m disjoint sets $B_1, \ldots, B_m$ such that for each B_i, $\sum_{b \in B_i} b = K$? (B_i must therefore contain exactly three elements from B.)

Given an instance (B, K) of 3PAR, let $W = 100(5m)^2 K$; $a_i = b_i + W$; $A = \{a_1, \ldots, a_{3m}\}$; $L = 3W + K$.

Lemma 3. *(A, L) is an instance of* 3PAR. *Furthermore, it is a positive instance if and only if (B, K) also is.*

Write $\epsilon = \frac{1}{400(5m)^2}$; $h = \lfloor 4\epsilon L \rfloor$; $H = L + h$.

Write $h = \beta_0 H$; $a_i = (\frac{1}{3} + \beta_i)H$; $a_i = (\frac{1}{3} + \epsilon_i)L$; $a_M = \max\{a_i : i = 1, \ldots, 3m\}$.

Lemma 4. *(1) For all a_i, $|\epsilon_i| < \epsilon$. (2) $0 < \beta_0 < 4\epsilon$, and for all a_i, $|\beta_i| < 4\epsilon$. (3) $3a_M < H$.*

To reduce (A, L) to an instance of AT, we consider a particular multiset

$$X = A \cup \{-H, \ldots, -H\} \cup \{h, \ldots, h\}$$

with m copies of $-H$ and h each. Given a node s in $T_{\min}$, let T_s denote the subtree rooted at s. For convenience, also let s denote the value of node s. Let $v(T_{\min})$ denote the value of the root of $T_{\min}$, which is always 0. For brevity, we use λ with or without scripts to denote the sum of at most $5m$ numbers in the form of $\pm\beta_i$. Then all nodes are in the form of $(N/3 + \lambda)H$ for some integer N and some λ. Since by Lemma 4, $|\lambda| \leq (5m)(4\epsilon) = (500m)^{-1}$, the terms N and λ of each node are uniquely determined. The nodes in the form of λH are called the *type*-0 nodes. Note that $T_{\min}$ has m type-0 leaves, i.e., the m copies of h in X.

Lemma 5. *In $T_{\min}$, type-0 nodes can only be added to type-0 nodes.*

Proof. Assume to the contrary that a type-0 node z_1 is added to a node z_2 in the form of $(\pm N/3 + \lambda)H$ with $N \geq 1$. Then $|z_1 + z_2| \geq (1/3 + \lambda')H$ for some λ'. Let z be the parent of z_1 and z_2. Since $v(T_{\min}) = 0$, z cannot be the root of $T_{\min}$. Let u be the sibling of z. Let r be the parent of z and u. Let t be the root of $T_{\min}$. Let p_r be the path from t to r in $T_{\min}$. Let m_r be the number of nodes on p_r. Since $T_{\min}$ has $5m - 1$ internal nodes, $m_r < 5m - 1$.

We rearrange $T_{\min}$ to obtain a new tree T' as follows. First, we replace T_z with T_{z_2}; i.e., r now has subtrees T_{z_2} and T_u. Let T'' be the remaining tree; i.e., T'' is $T_{\min}$ after removing T_{z_1}. Next, we create T' such that its root has subtrees T_{z_1} and T''. This tree rearrangement eliminates the cost $|z_1 + z_2|$ from T_r but may result in a new cost in the form of λH on each node of p_r. The total of these extra costs, denoted by C_λ, is at most $m_r(5m)(4\epsilon)H < (5m-1)(5m)(4\epsilon)H$. Then, $C(T') = C(T_{\min}) - |z_1 + z_2| + C_\lambda \leq C(T_{\min}) - (1/3 + \lambda')H + C_\lambda < C(T_{\min}) + (-1/3 + (5m)^2(4\epsilon))H = C(T_{\min}) + (-1/3 + 10^{-2})H < C(T_{\min})$, contradicting the optimality of $T_{\min}$. This completes the proof.

Lemma 6. *Let z be a node in $T_{\min}$. (1) If $z < 0$, then $|z| \leq H$. (2) If $z > 0$, then $z < H$.*

Proof. Statement 1. Assume that the statement is untrue. Then, since all negative leaves have values $-H$, some negative internal node z has an absolute value greater than H and two negative children z_1 and z_2. Since $v(T_{\min}) = 0$, some z

has a positive sibling u. We pick such a z at the lowest possible level of $T_{\min}$. Let r be the parent of z and u. By Lemma 1(2), $r > 0$. Then $u > |z| > H$. Since all positive leaves have values less than H, u is an internal node with two children u_1 and u_2. Since $u > 0$, $z < 0$, and $r > 0$, by Lemma 1(1), u must have a positive child and a negative child. Without loss of generality, let u_1 be positive and u_2 be negative. Then $u = u_1 - |u_2|$. Since z is at the lowest possible level, $|u_2| \leq H$, for otherwise we could find a z at a lower level under u_2. We swap T_z with T_{u_2}. Let T'_r be the new subtree rooted r. Let $u' = u_1 + z$. Since $u_2 + u' = r > 0$ and $u_2 < 0$, we have $u' > 0$. Since $|u_2| \leq H < |z|$, we have $u' = u_1 - |z| < u_1 - |u_2| = u$. Let $C_f = C(T_z) + C(T_{u_1}) + C(T_{u_2})$. Then, $C(T'_r) = r + u' + C_f < r + u + C_f = C(T_r)$, which contradicts the optimality of $T_{\min}$ because the costs of the internal nodes not mentioned above remain unchanged.

Statement 2. Assume that this statement is false. Then, since all positive leaves have values less than H, some internal node z has a value at least H as well as two positive children. Since $v(T_{\min}) = 0$, some such z has a negative sibling u. By Statement 1, $|u| \leq H$. Hence $z + u \geq 0$, contradicting Lemma 1(1).

The following lemma strengthens Lemma 6.

Lemma 7. *(1) Let z be a node in $T_{\min}$. If $z > 0$, then z is in the form of λH, $(1/3 + \lambda)H$, or $(2/3 + \lambda)H$. (2) Let z be an internal node in $T_{\min}$. If $z < 0$, then z is in the form of λH, $(-1/3 + \lambda)H$, or $(-2/3 + \lambda)H$.*

The following lemma supplements Statement 1 of Lemma 7.

Lemma 8. *Let z be a node in $T_{\min}$. If $z = (1/3 + \lambda)H$, then z is a leaf.*

The following lemma strengthens Statement 2 of Lemma 7.

Lemma 9. *Let z be an internal node in $T_{\min}$. If $z < 0$, then z can only be in the form of λH or $(-1/3 + \lambda)H$.*

Lemma 10. *$C(T_{\min}) \geq m(H + h)$. Moreover, $C(T_{\min}) = m(H + h)$ if and only if (A, L) is a positive instance of* 3PAR .

Proof. By Lemmas 5, 7, 8, and 9, each $a_i \in A$ can only be added to some $a_j \in A$ or to some $z_1 = (-1/3 + \lambda_1)H$. In turn, z_1 can only be the sum of $-H$ and some $z_2 = (2/3 + \lambda_2)H$. In turn, z_2 is the sum of some a_k and $a_l \in A$. Hence, in $T_{\min}$, $2m$ leaves in A are added in pairs. The sum of each pair is then added to a leaf node $-H$. This sum is then added to a leaf node in A. This sum is a type-0 node with value $-|\lambda'|H$, which can only be added to another type-0 node. Let $a_{p,1}, a_{p,2}, a_{p,3}$ be the three leaves in A associated with each $-H$ and added together as $((a_{p,1} + a_{p,2}) + (-H)) + a_{p,3}$ in $T_{\min}$. The cost of such a subtree is $2H - (a_{p,1} + a_{p,2} + a_{p,3})$. There are m such subtrees R_p. Their total cost is $2mH - \sum_{i=1}^{3m} a_i = mH + mh$. Hence, $C(T_{\min}) \geq mH + mh$.

If (A, L) is not a positive instance of 3PAR, then for any $T_{\min}$, there is some subtree R_p with $a_{p,1} + a_{p,2} + a_{p,3} \neq L$. Then, the value of the root r_i of R_p is $a_{p,1} + a_{p,2} + a_{p,3} - H \neq -h$. Since r_i is a type-0 node, it can only be added to a type-0 node. No matter how the m root values r_k and the m leaves h are added, some node resulting from adding these $2m$ numbers is nonzero. Hence, $C(T_{\min}) > mH + mh$.

If (A, L) is a positive instance of 3PAR, let $\{a_{p,1}, a_{p,2}, a_{p,3}\}$ with $1 \leq p \leq m$ form a 3-set partition of A; i.e., A is the union of these m 3-sets and for each p, $a_{p,1} + a_{p,2} + a_{p,3} = L$. Then each 3-set can be added to one $-H$ and one h as $(((a_{p,1} + a_{p,2}) + (-H)) + a_{p,3}) + h$, resulting in a node of value zero and contributing no extra cost. Hence, $C(T_{\min}) = mH + mh$. This completes the proof.

Let $f(B, K) = (X, mH + mh)$, then f is a desired reduction from 3PAR to AT. Hence, we have the following theorem.

Theorem 1. *It is NP-hard to compute an optimal addition tree over a multiset that contains both positive and negative numbers.*

3 Approximation algorithms for FPS

In light of Theorem 1, for X with both positive and negative numbers, no polynomial-time algorithm can find a $T_{\min}$ unless P = NP [3]. This motivates the consideration of approximation algorithms. We will focus on FPS in this section.

3.1 Linear-time approximation for general X

This section assumes that X contains at least one positive number and one negative number. We give an approximation algorithm whose worst-case error is at most $2(\lceil \log(n-1) \rceil + 1)E_n^*$. If X is sorted, this algorithm takes only $O(n)$ time.

In an addition tree, a leaf is *critical* if its sibling is a leaf with the opposite sign. Note that if two leaves are siblings, then one is critical if and only if the other is critical. Hence, an addition tree has an even number of critical leaves.

Lemma 11. *Let T be an addition tree over X. Let $y_1, \ldots, y_{2k}$ be its critical leaves, where y_{2i-1} and y_{2i} are siblings. Let $z_1, \ldots, z_{n-2k}$ be the noncritical leaves. Let $\Pi = \sum_{i=1}^{k} |y_{2i-1} + y_{2i}|$, and $\Delta = \sum_{j=1}^{n-2k} |z_j|$. Then $C(T) \geq (\Pi + \Delta)/2$.*

In view of Lemma 11, we desire to minimize $\Pi + \Delta$ over all possible T. Given $x_p, x_{p'} \in X$ with $p \neq p'$, $(x_p, x_{p'})$ is a *critical pair* if x_p and $x_{p'}$ have the opposite signs. A *critical matching* R of X is a set $\{(x_{p_{2i-1}}, x_{p_{2i}}) : i = 1, \ldots, k\}$ of critical pairs where the indices p_j are all distinct. For simplicity, let $y_j = x_{p_j}$. Let $\Pi = \sum_{i=1}^{k} |y_{2i-1} + y_{2i}|$ and $\Delta = \sum_{z \in X - \{y_1, \ldots, y_{2k}\}} |z|$. If $\Pi + \Delta$ is the minimum over all critical matchings of X, then R is called a *minimum critical matching* of X. Such an R can be computed as follows. Assume that X consists of l positive numbers $a_1 \leq \cdots \leq a_l$ and m negative numbers $-b_1 \geq \cdots \geq -b_m$.

Algorithm 1 1. If $l = m$, let $R = \{(a_i, -b_i) : i = 1, \ldots, l\}$.
2. If $l < m$, let $R = \{(a_i, -b_{i+m-l}) : i = 1, \ldots, l\}$.
3. If $l > m$, let $R = \{(a_{i+l-m}, -b_i) : i = 1, \ldots, m\}$.

Lemma 12. *If X is sorted, then Algorithm 1 computes a minimum critical matching R of X in $O(n)$ time.*

We now present an approximation algorithm to compute the summation over X.

Algorithm 2 1. Use Algorithm 1 to find a minimum critical matching R of X. The numbers x_i in the pairs of R are the critical leaves in our addition tree over X and those not in the critical pairs are the noncritical leaves.
2. Add each critical pair of R separately.
3. Construct a balanced addition tree over the resulting sums of Step 2 and the noncritical leaves.

Theorem 2. *Let T be the addition tree over X constructed by Algorithm 2. If X is sorted, then T can be obtained in $O(n)$ time and $E(T) \leq 2(\lceil \log(n-1) \rceil + 1)E(T_{\min})$.*

Proof. Steps 1 and 2 of Algorithm 2 both take $O(n)$ time. By Lemma 12, Step 1 also takes $O(n)$ time and thus Algorithm 2 takes $O(n)$ time. As for the error analysis, let T' be the addition tree constructed at Step 3. Then $C(T) = C(T') + \Pi$. Let h be the number of levels of T'. Since T' is a balanced tree, $C(T') \leq (h-1)(\Pi + \Delta)$ and thus $C(T) \leq h(\Pi + \Delta)$. By assumption, X has at least two numbers with the opposite signs. So there are at most $n-1$ numbers to be added pairwise at Step 3. Thus, $h \leq \lceil \log(n-1) \rceil + 1$. Next, by Lemma 11, since R is a minimum critical matching of X, we have $C(T_{\min}) \geq (\Pi + \Delta)/2$. In summary, $E(T) \leq 2(\lceil \log(n-1) \rceil + 1)E(T_{\min})$.

3.2 Improved approximation for single-sign X

This section assumes that all x_i are positive; the symmetric case where all x_i are negative can be handled similarly.

Let T be an addition tree over X. Observe that $C(T) = \sum_{i=1}^{n} x_i d_i$, where d_i is the number of edges on the path from the root to the leaf x_i in T. Hence, finding an optimal addition tree over X is equivalent to constructing a Huffman tree to encode n characters with frequencies $x_1, \ldots, x_n$ into binary strings [9].

Fact 3 *If X is unsorted, then a $T_{\min}$ over X can be constructed in $O(n \log n)$ time (see, e.g., [1]). If X is sorted, then a $T_{\min}$ over X can be constructed in $O(n)$ time [9].*

For the case where X is unsorted, many applications require faster running time than $O(n \log n)$. Previously, the best $O(n)$-time approximation algorithm used a balanced addition tree and thus had a worst-case error at most $\lceil \log n \rceil E_n^*$.

Here we provide an $O(n)$-time approximation algorithm to compute the sum over X with a worst-case error at most $\lceil \log \log n \rceil E_n^*$. More generally, given an integer parameter $t > 0$, we wish to find an addition tree T over X such that $C(T) \leq C(T_{\min}) + t \cdot |S_n|$.

Algorithm 3 1. Let $m = \lceil n/2^t \rceil$. Partition X into m disjoint sets $Z_1, \ldots, Z_m$ such that each Z_i has exactly 2^t numbers, except possibly Z_m, which may have less than 2^t numbers.

2. For each Z_i, let $z_i = \max\{x : x \in Z_i\}$. Let $M = \{z_i : 1 \leq i \leq m\}$.
3. For each Z_i, construct a balanced addition tree T_i over Z_i.
4. Construct a Huffman tree H over M.
5. Construct the final addition tree T over X from H by replacing z_i with T_i.

Theorem 4. *Assume that $x_1, \ldots, x_n$ are all positive. For any integer $t > 0$, Algorithm 3 computes an addition tree T over X in $O(n + m \log m)$ time with $C(T) \leq C(T_{\min}) + t|S_n|$, where $m = \lceil n/2^t \rceil$. Since $|S_n| \leq C(T_{\min})$, $E(T) \leq (1+t)E(T_{\min})$.*

Corollary 1. *Assume that $n \geq 4$ and all $x_1, \ldots, x_n$ are positive. Then, setting $t = \lfloor \log((\log n) - 1) \rfloor$, Algorithm 3 finds an addition tree T over X in $O(n)$ time with $E(T) \leq \lceil \log \log n \rceil E(T_{\min})$.*

4 Efficient solutions for FPPS

For X with both positive and negative numbers, we may repeatedly use Algorithm 2 to solve FPPS, which yields an $O(n^2)$ time approximation algorithm.

Next, we assume that all x_i are positive (or symmetrically, all x_i are negative). We will use the Huffman coding technique to derive fast algorithms. A binary addition tree over X satisfies the *sibling property* if the nodes can be numbered in the nondecreasing order of their values so that for $i = 1, \ldots, n-1$, nodes $2i-1$ and $2i$ are siblings and their parent is higher in the numbering. Denote by *node* i the node whose numbering is i. It is easy to see that for any X, there must be a Huffman tree that satisfies the sibling property, and any binary addition tree that satisfies the sibling property must be a Huffman tree.

Assume that X is sorted in nondecreasing order, then the following algorithm constructs a Huffman tree over X in $O(n)$ time [9].

Algorithm 4 1. Store the sorted numbers x_i in a sorted list L_1. Create another sorted list L_2, which is empty initially.

2. While L_1 is not empty, repeat the following: (1) Find the first two smallest numbers x and y in L_1 and L_2; (2) delete x and y from L_1 and L_2; (3) insert $x + y$ to the end of L_2.

Using Algorithm 4, we can solve FPPS with the minimum worst-case error in $O(n^2)$ time.

Algorithm 5 1. Sort the numbers $x_1, \ldots, x_n$ in nondecreasing order using a $O(n \log n)$-time sorting algorithm. Store the sorted numbers in a sorted list L.
2. Use Algorithm 4 to compute $\hat{S}_n$. Set $k \leftarrow n$.
3. While $k > 1$, repeat the following: (1) Set $L \leftarrow L - \{x_k\}$; (2) use Algorithm 4 over L to compute $\hat{S}_k$; (3) decrease k by 1.

Theorem 5. *Algorithm 5 evaluates all prefix sums S_k for $k = 1, \ldots, n$ with the minimum worst-case errors in $O(n^2)$ time.*

Using Algorithm 4, we can obtain a different algorithm that solves FPPS in $O(n^2)$ time with the minimum worst-case error as follows.

Algorithm 6 1. Set $k \leftarrow 1$. Create a sorted list L, which is empty initially.
2. While $k \leq n$, repeat the following: (1) Insert x_k into L and sort it; (2) use Algorithm 4 to compute $\hat{S}_k$; (3) increase k by 1.

Since both Algorithms 5 and 6 construct a Huffman tree over each X_i from scratch, the lower bound of these algorithms is also in the order of n^2, However, there are special cases where all S_k can be evaluated in $O(n)$ time with the minimum worst-case errors. For example, consider the following commonly used procedure that evaluates all S_k in $O(n)$ time: Set $S \leftarrow \emptyset$ and $k \leftarrow 1$; while $k \leq n$, set $S \leftarrow S + x_k$, output S and set $k \leftarrow k + 1$. If $x_k \geq S_{k-1}$ for all k, then this algorithm evaluates all S_k with the minimum worst-case errors, for the ordering for each S_k corresponds to a Huffman tree over X. To make use of the existing optimal ordering for S_k, we derive two algorithms in §4.1 and §4.2, respectively, to solve FPPS with the minimum worst-case errors in an *on-line* manner. Let k' denote the numbering of x_k in the Huffman tree for S_k. Then the running time of these algorithms is $O(\sum_{k=1}^{n}(2k - k'))$. So if $2k - k' = O(1)$ for all k, then the running time becomes $O(n)$. The first on-line algorithm evaluates S_k in the order of $S_n, S_{n-1}, \ldots, S_1$, which we refer to as the *decreasing order* of evaluating S_k. The second on-line algorithm evaluates S_k in the order of $S_1, S_2, \ldots, S_n$, which is called the *increasing order* of evaluating S_k.

4.1 Optimal on-line algorithms for FPPS in decreasing order

The key subroutine of our algorithm is to delete a leaf x from the existing Huffman tree T of n leaves in $O(2n - i)$ time such that the resulting tree is still Huffman, where i is the numbering of x in T.

We use doubly-linked lists to store trees so that there is a link from a parent to a child, and there is a link from a child to its parent. By doing so, we can move a subtree from one location to another by re-arranging the pointer of the root of the subtree, which only takes a constant number of pointer manipulations. We use a list A of size n to store pointers such that $A[i]$ points to the ith node in the tree. Following standard terminology, we denote by *weight* the numerical value of a node.

The idea of the deletion is to keep replacing the current node i, starting from the node to be deleted, by node j, where $j = i + 1$ if node $i + 1$ is not the parent of node i, or $j = i + 2$ otherwise. The weight of the parent of node i is updated accordingly. The following tow constant-time operations are useful.

1. Replace(i, j): Move the left child of node j to become the left child of node i, move the right child of node j to become the right child of node j, and assign w_j to w_i.
2. WeightUpdate(i, j, k): Set the weight of node i's parent to $w_j + w_k$.

The effect of calling Replace(i, j) moves the entire left (respectively, right) subtree of node j to become the left (respectively, right) subtree of node i. Node j may then be viewed as a dummy leaf. If we color the node to be replaced black, then the deletion can be viewed as the process of pushing the black node up until the root is found. The black node and the root will then be deleted from the tree. The following algorithm deletes node i_0 from a Huffman tree T of n leaves.

Algorithm 7 Set $i \leftarrow i_0$, and $m \leftarrow 2n - 1$.

Case A: Node i is a right child. We have the following three cases.

Case A1: Node $i + 1$ is the root.

Set $m \leftarrow m - 2$ and return $A[m]$. The algorithm ends. (*Remark:* Now root $m - 2$ is the root of the new tree.)

Case A2: Node $i + 1$ is the parent of node i.

First call WeightUpdate$(i, i - 1, i + 2)$, next call Replace$(i, i + 2)$. Then set $i \leftarrow i + 2$.

Case A3: Node $i + 1$ is not the root and it is not the parent of node i.

1. First call WeightUpdate$(i, i - 1, i + 1)$.
2. If $w_{i-1} \leq w_{i+1}$, call Replace$(i, i+1)$; otherwise, call Replace$(i, i-1)$ and then call Replace$(i - 1, i + 1)$.
3. Increase i by 1. Node i is now a left child, go to Case B.

Case B: Node i is a left child.

If $w_{i-1} \leq w_{i+1}$, then call Replace$(i, i+1)$; otherwise, call Replace$(i, i-1)$ and Replace$(i - 1, i + 1)$. Set $i \leftarrow i + 1$. Node i is now a right child, go to case A.

Lemma 13. *Let T be a Huffman tree of n leaves. Then deleting node i_0 from T using Algorithm 7 results in a Huffman tree T' of $n - 1$ leaves in $O(2n - i_0)$ time.*

The following on-line algorithm solves FPPS in decreasing order.

Algorithm 8 1. Construct a Huffman tree T_n over X_n. Set $k \leftarrow n$.

2. While $k > 1$, repeat the following: (1) Output the value of the root of T_k, and find x_k from the list A (by linear or binary search); (2) use Algorithm 7 to delete x_k and produce a Huffman tree T_{k-1} over X_{k-1}; (3) set $A \leftarrow A - \{A[2k - 2], A[2k - 1]\}$, and decrease k by 1.

Theorem 6. *Let the numbering of x_k in T_k be k', where $1 \leq k' \leq 2k-2$. Algorithm 8 solves FPPS in decreasing order with the minimum worst-case errors in $O(n \log n + \sum_{k=1}^{n}(2k-k'))$ time.*

Proof. It suffices to note that for each x_k, Step 2 takes $O(2k-k')$ time, which follows from Lemma 13.

Corollary 2. *If a Huffman tree over X is given, then we can use Step 2 of Algorithm 8 to solve FPPS in decreasing order with the minimum worst-case errors in $O(\sum_{k=1}^{n}(2k-k'))$ time. Hence, the running time is $O(n)$ if for all i, $2k-k'=O(1)$.*

4.2 Optimal on-line algorithms for FPPS in increasing order

The key subroutine of our algorithm is to insert a new leaf to an existing Huffman tree such that the resulting tree is still Huffman. Let T be a Huffman tree of n leaves. Let x be a new number to be inserted into T. Denote by $\mathsf{left}(i)$ the left child of node i, and $\mathsf{right}(i)$ the right child of node i. The following constant-time operation is useful.

$\mathsf{Swap}(i,j)$: Swap $\mathsf{left}(i)$ with $\mathsf{left}(j)$, $\mathsf{right}(i)$ with $\mathsf{right}(j)$, and w_i with w_j.

Algorithm 9 1. Copy T into the first $2n-1$ cells of a list A of $2n+1$ cells. Create two nodes, one being a new root with weight $x + w_{2n-1}$, and the other being a leaf with weight x.
2. Make the new root have T as the left child of and the leaf for x as the right child. Let $A[2n+1]$ point to the new root and $A[2n]$ to the leaf for x.
3. If $x \geq w_{2n-1}$, the algorithm ends. Otherwise, set $i \leftarrow 2n$. (*Remark:* Node i now holds value x; we want to find the first correct position in the tree for x that satisfies the sibling property.)
4. While $i > 1$ and $x < w_{i-1}$, repeat the following: (1) Call $\mathsf{Swap}(i, i-1)$; (2) set $i \leftarrow i-1$. (*Remark:* When this while loop terminates, node i is a leaf holding x and is the first correct position for x.)
5. Let $j = 2\lfloor (i+1)/2 \rfloor$. (*Remark:* Node j is the right sibling of node i if node i is a left child; otherwise, node j is node i.)
   While $j \leq 2n-2$, repeat the following: (1) Call $\mathsf{WeightUpdate}(j, j-1, j)$ (*Remark:* This updates the weight of node j's parent); if there are leaf nodes on the same level of the parent p of the x-node and on the left handside of p, then swap p, when necessary, with these leaf nodes so that their values are in increasing order; (2) increase j by 2.

Lemma 14. *Let T be a Huffman tree of n leaves. Let x be a new value. Then Algorithm 9 produces a new Huffman tree by inserting x into T as a new leaf in $O(2n - i_0)$ time, where i_0 is the numbering of the leaf for x in the new tree.*

The following on-line algorithm solves FPPS in increasing order.

Algorithm 10 1. Construct a binary addition tree T_2 over X_2. Set $k \leftarrow 2$.

2. While $k \leq n$, repeat the following: (1) Output the value of the root of T_k; (2) use Algorithm 9 to insert x_{k+1} to T_i to obtain a Huffman tree T_{k+1} over X_{k+1}; (3) increase k by 1.

Theorem 7. *Let the numbering of x_k in T_k be k', where $1 \leq k' \leq 2k-2$. Algorithm 8 solves FPPS in increasing order with the minimum worst-case errors in $O(\sum_{k=1}^{n}(2k-k'))$ time. Hence, the running time is $O(n)$ if for all k, $2k-k' = O(1)$.*

Acknowledgments. The authors wish to thank Tsan-Sheng Hsu, Don Rose, Hai Shao, Xiaobai Sun, and Steve Tate for helpful discussions.

References

1. T. H. Cormen, C. E. Leiserson, and R. L. Rivest, *Introduction to Algorithms*, McGraw Hill, 1990.
2. J. W. Demmel, *Underflow and the reliability of numerical software*, SIAM J. Sci. Statis. Comput., 5 (1984), pp. 887–919.
3. M. R. Garey and D. S. Johnson, *Computer and Intractability*, W. H. Freeman and Company, New York, 1979.
4. D. Goldberg, *What every computer scientist should know about floating-point arithmetic*, ACM Computing Surveys, 23 (1990), pp. 5–48.
5. N. J. Higham, *The accuracy of floating point summation*, SIAM Journal on Scientific Computing, 14 (1993), pp. 783–799.
6. N. J. Higham, *Accuracy and Stability of Numerical Algorithms*. SIAM Press, 1996.
7. D. E. Knuth, *The Art of Computer Programming II: Seminumerical Algorithms*, Addison–Wesley, Reading, Massachusetts, second ed., 1981.
8. U. W. Kulisch and W. L. Miranker, *The arithmetic of the digital computer: a new approach*, SIAM Review, 28 (1986), pp. 1–40.
9. J. V. Leeuwen, *On the construction of Huffman trees*, in Proceedings of the 3rd International Colloquium on Automata, Languages, and Programming, 1976, pp. 382–410.
10. T. G. Robertazzi and S. C. Schwartz, *Best "ordering" for floating-point addition*, ACM Transactions on Mathematical Software, 14 (1988), pp. 101–110.

Efficient Approximation Algorithms for the SUBSET-SUMS EQUALITY Problem*

Cristina Bazgan[1] Miklos Santha[2] Zsolt Tuza[3]

[1] Université Paris-Sud, LRI, bât.490, F–91405 Orsay, France, bazgan@lri.fr
[2] CNRS, URA 410, Université Paris-Sud, LRI, F–91405 Orsay, France, santha@lri.fr
[3] Computer and Automation Institute, Hungarian Academy of Sciences, H–1111 Budapest, Kende u.13–17, Hungary, tuza@sztaki.hu

Abstract. We investigate the problem of finding two nonempty disjoint subsets of a set of n positive integers, with the objective that the sums of the numbers in the two subsets be as close as possible. In two versions of this problem, the quality of a solution is measured by the ratio and the difference of the two partial sums, respectively.
Answering a problem of Woeginger and Yu (1992) in the affirmative, we give a fully polynomial-time approximation scheme for the case where the value to be optimized is the ratio between the sums of the numbers in the two sets. On the other hand, we show that in the case where the value of a solution is the positive difference between the two partial sums, the problem is not 2^{n^k}-approximable in polynomial time unless $P{=}NP$, for any constant k. In the positive direction, we give a polynomial-time algorithm that finds two subsets for which the difference of the two sums does not exceed $K/n^{\Omega(\log n)}$, where K is the greatest number in the instance.

1 Introduction

KNAPSACK is a well known problem which was shown to be NP-complete in 1972 by Karp [3]. It remains NP-complete even if the size of each object is equal to its value. This particular case is called the SUBSET-SUM problem. Ibarra and Kim [2], gave a fully polynomial-time approximation scheme for the optimization problem associated with KNAPSACK which, therefore, applies to SUBSET-SUM as well. The most efficient fully polynomial-time approximation scheme known for the SUBSET-SUM problem is due to Kellerer et al. [4]. The running time of their algorithm is $O(min\{n/\varepsilon, n + (1/\varepsilon)^2 log(1/\varepsilon)\})$, and the space required is $O(n + 1/\varepsilon)$, where n is the number of the integers and ε the accuracy.

The input to an instance of SUBSET-SUM is a set of n positive integers $a_1, \ldots, a_n$ and another positive integer b. The question is to decide if there

* This research was supported by the ESPRIT Working Group RAND2 n° 21726 and by the bilateral project Balaton, grant numbers 97140 (APAPE, France) and F-36/96 (TéT Alapítvány, Hungary)

exists a set of numbers (a subset of $\{a_1, \ldots, a_n\}$) whose sum is equal to b. In the optimization version the goal is to find a set of numbers whose sum is as large as possible under the constraint that it does not exceed b.

Woeginger and Yu [7] introduced a related problem, called SUBSET-SUMS EQUALITY. Given n positive integers, the question is to decide if there exist two disjoint nonempty subsets whose sums are equal. They also defined a related optimization problem that we call SUBSET-SUMS RATIO; it requires to find two disjoint subsets with the ratio of their sums being as close to 1 as possible. In the same paper they proved the NP-completeness of SUBSET-SUMS EQUALITY, and gave a polynomial-time 1.324-approximation algorithm for SUBSET-SUMS RATIO. They left as an open question to decide whether this problem has a polynomial-time approximation scheme.

In this paper we answer their question in the affirmative, by showing the stronger assertion that actually SUBSET-SUMS RATIO has a *fully polynomial-time* approximation scheme.

The problems defined by Woeginger and Yu have some interesting special instances. Consider the case where the sum of the n numbers is less than $2^n - 1$. It is immediately seen by the pigeonhole principle that there always exist two disjoint nonempty subsets whose sums are equal. Nonetheless, no polynomial-time algorithm is known so far to find two such subsets effectively. We call this latter problem PIGEONHOLE SUBSET-SUMS. This problem is a well known member of what Meggido and Papadimitriou [5,6] call the class $TFNP$ of total functions. This class contains function problems associated with languages in NP where, for every instance of the problem, a solution is guaranteed to exist. Other examples in the class are FACTORING, SECOND HAMILTONIAN CYCLE and HAPPYNET.

Many functions in $TFNP$ (like the examples quoted above) have a challenging intermediate status between FP and FNP, the function classes associated with P and NP. Although these problems are not NP-hard unless NP=*co*-NP, no polynomial-time algorithm is known for them.

Although the polynomial-time solvability of PIGEONHOLE SUBSET-SUMS still remains open, we will show that in a sense this problem is much better approximable in polynomial time than SUBSET-SUMS EQUALITY. For this purpose, we define a further related optimization problem that we call SUBSET-SUMS DIFFERENCE. Here the value of a solution is the positive difference between the sums of the two sets plus 1. The same problem, with the additional constraint that the sum of the numbers is less than $2^n - 1$, is called PIGEONHOLE SUBSET-SUMS DIFFERENCE.

The existence of a fully polynomial-time approximation scheme for SUBSET-SUMS RATIO implies that, for any constant k, there is a polynomial-time $2^n/n^k$-approximation algorithm for PIGEONHOLE SUBSET-SUMS DIFFERENCE. We will show an even stronger result, giving a polynomial-time $2^n/n^{\Omega(\log n)}$-approximation for this problem. This will follow from a more general theorem: we will show that SUBSET-SUMS DIFFERENCE has a polynomial-time $K/n^{\Omega(\log n)}$-approximation algorithm where K is the largest number in the input. On the other hand, we also present a negative result for SUBSET-SUMS DIFFERENCE, proving that it is not 2^{n^k}-approximable in polynomial time unless $P = NP$, for any constant k.

Showing that PIGEONHOLE SUBSET-SUMS (a total function) is better approximable than the corresponding NP search problem is somewhat analogous to the result we have obtained in [1]. There we have shown that there is a polynomial-time approximation scheme for finding another Hamiltonian cycle in cubic Hamiltonian graphs if a Hamiltonian cycle is given in the input (again a total function). On the other hand, finding the longest cycle is not even constant approximable in cubic Hamiltonian graphs, unless $P = NP$.

The paper is organized as follows. In Section 2 we give the necessary definitions. In Section 3 we describe a fully polynomial-time approximation scheme for SUBSET-SUMS RATIO, and in Section 4 we prove our results on SUBSET-SUMS DIFFERENCE.

2 Preliminaries

Let us recall a few notions concerning approximability. Given an instance I of an optimization problem A, and a feasible solution y of I, we denote by $m(I, y)$ the value of the solution y, and by $opt_A(I)$ the value of an optimum solution of I. The *performance ratio* of y is

$$R(I, y) = \max\left\{\frac{m(I, y)}{opt_A(I)}, \frac{opt_A(I)}{m(I, y)}\right\}.$$

For a constant $c > 1$, an algorithm is a *c-approximation* if, for any instance I of the problem, it returns a solution y such that $R(I, y) \leq c$. We say that an optimization problem is *constant approximable* if it admits a polynomial-time c-approximation for some $c > 1$. An optimization problem has a *polynomial-time approximation scheme* (a *ptas*, for short) if, for every constant $\varepsilon > 0$, there exists a polynomial-time $(1+\varepsilon)$-approximation for it. An optimization problem has a *fully polynomial-time approximation scheme* (an *fptas*, for short) if, for every constant $\varepsilon > 0$, there exists an $(1+\varepsilon)$-approximation algorithm for it which is polynomial both in the size of the input and in $1/\varepsilon$. The set of problems having an fptas is denoted by $FPTAS$.

An algorithm for a problem is called *pseudo-polynomial* if its running time is polynomial in the size of the input and in the unary representation of the largest number occurring in the input.

Let us now give the formal definitions of the problems to be investigated.

SUBSET-SUMS EQUALITY
Input: A set $\{a_1, \ldots, a_n\}$ of positive integers.
Question: Are there two disjoint nonempty subsets $S_1, S_2 \subseteq \{1, \ldots, n\}$ such that

$$\sum_{i \in S_1} a_i = \sum_{i \in S_2} a_i \ ?$$

PIGEONHOLE SUBSET-SUMS
Input: A set $\{a_1, \ldots, a_n\}$ of positive integers such that $\sum_{i=1}^{n} a_i < 2^n - 1$.
Output: Two disjoint nonempty subsets $S_1, S_2 \subseteq \{1, \ldots, n\}$ such that

$$\sum_{i \in S_1} a_i = \sum_{i \in S_2} a_i \ .$$

SUBSET-SUMS RATIO
Input: A set $\{a_1, \ldots, a_n\}$ of positive integers.
Output: Two disjoint nonempty subsets $S_1, S_2 \subseteq \{1, \ldots, n\}$ with

$$\sum_{i \in S_1} a_i \geq \sum_{i \in S_2} a_i$$

such that the ratio

$$\frac{\sum_{i \in S_1} a_i}{\sum_{i \in S_2} a_i} ,$$

termed the value of the output, is minimized.

SUBSET-SUMS DIFFERENCE
Input: A set $\{a_1, \ldots, a_n\}$ of positive integers.
Output: Two disjoint nonempty subsets $S_1, S_2 \subseteq \{1, \ldots, n\}$, with

$$\sum_{i \in S_1} a_i \geq \sum_{i \in S_2} a_i$$

such that the difference

$$\sum_{i \in S_1} a_i - \sum_{i \in S_2} a_i + 1 ,$$

the value of the output, is minimized.

Remark: The reason to add 1 in the value of the solution in the above problem is that otherwise the optimum value might be 0, and the performance ratio could not be defined in that case.

PIGEONHOLE SUBSET-SUMS DIFFERENCE
Input: A set $\{a_1, \ldots, a_n\}$ of positive integers such that $\sum_{i=1}^{n} a_i < 2^n - 1$.
Output: The same as for SUBSET-SUMS DIFFERENCE.

3 SUBSET-SUMS RATIO $\in$ FPTAS

In the first part of this section we give a pseudo-polynomial algorithm for the SUBSET-SUMS RATIO problem, that we use afterwards to construct an fptas.

3.1 A pseudo-polynomial algorithm

We assume that the n numbers are in increasing order, $a_1 < \cdots < a_n$, and we set $B = \sum_{i=1}^{n} a_i$. We are going to give an algorithm that finds an optimum solution in time $O(nB^2)$.

The main part of the algorithm will be a dynamic programming procedure. We will fill out (maybe partially) two tables, $t[0..n, 0..B]$ with values in $\{0,1\}$, and $c[0..n, 0..B]$ whose entries are *subsets* of $\{1, \ldots, n\}$. The completed parts of the tables will satisfy the following properties for $(i, j) \neq (0,0)$:

1. $t[i, j] = 1$ if and only if there exists a set $S \subseteq \{1, \ldots, n\}$ with $\sum_{k \in S} a_k = j$, $i \in S$, and $h \notin S$ for all $i < h \leq n$.
2. $c[i, j] = S$, where $S \subseteq \{1, \ldots, n\}$ is the (unique) subset satisfying the above conditions, if such an S exists; and $S = \emptyset$ otherwise.

We stop this procedure if, for some j, two integers $i_1 \neq i_2$ are found such that $t[i_1, j] = t[i_2, j] = 1$. Actually, the procedure will be stopped when the first (smallest) such j is found. Otherwise the tables will be filled out completely. The procedure is as follows:

```
t[0,0] := 1, c[0,0] := ∅;
for i = 1 to n do t[i,0] := 0, c[i,0] := ∅;
for j = 1 to B do t[0,j] := 0, c[0,j] := ∅;
for j = 1 to B do
    for i = 1 to n do
        if (j ≥ a_i and ∃ k ∈ {0,...,i−1} with t[k, j − a_i] = 1) then
            t[i,j] := 1, c[i,j] := c[k, j − a_i] ∪ {i};
        else t[i,j] := 0, c[i,j] := ∅;
    if (∃ i_1 ≠ i_2 with t[i_1,j] = t[i_2,j] = 1) then STOP.
```

If the optimum of the instance is 1, then the procedure is stopped when the smallest integer is found which is the sum of two different subsets. The minimality of the sum ensures that these subsets are in fact disjoint.

Otherwise the tables t and c will be completed and we continue the algorithm. We call an integer $j > 0$ *candidate* if it is the sum of some input elements; that is, if we have $t[i, j] = 1$ for some i. For each candidate j, let $i(j)$ be the (unique) integer with this property. Moreover, for every candidate j, let k_j be the greatest candidate less than j such that $c[i(j), j] \cap c[i(k_j), k_j] = \emptyset$, if there is any. Then the optimum solution is the couple $(c[i(j), j], c[i(k_j), k_j])$ for which j/k_j is minimized.

One can see that the above algorithm is pseudo-polynomial.

3.2 The fptas

Similarly to the previous algorithm, we start with sorting the input in increasing order; that is, after this preprocessing we have $a_1 < a_2 < \cdots < a_n$.

For $m = 2, \ldots, n$, let us denote by I_m the instance of SUBSET-SUMS RATIO which consists of the m smallest numbers $a_1, \ldots, a_m$. At the top level, the algorithm executes its main procedure on the inputs I_m, for $m = 2, \ldots, n$, and takes as solution the best among the solutions obtained for these instances.

Given any ε in the range $0 < \varepsilon < 1$, we set

$$k(m) = \varepsilon^2 \cdot a_m/(2m).$$

Let $n_0 \leq n$ be the greatest integer such that $k(n_0) < 1$. We now describe the algorithm on the instance I_m.

If $m \leq n_0$, then we apply the pseudo-polynomial algorithm of the previous subsection to I_m. Since $a_{n_0} \leq 2n/\varepsilon^2$, this will take polynomial time.

If $n_0 < m \leq n$, then we transform the instance I_m into another one that contains only polynomial-size numbers. Set $a'_i = \lfloor a_i/k(m) \rfloor$ for $i = 1, \ldots, m$. Observe that $a'_m = \lfloor 2m/\epsilon^2 \rfloor$ is indeed of polynomial size. Let us denote by I'_m the instance of SUBSET-SUMS RATIO that contains the numbers a'_i such that $a'_i \geq m/\varepsilon$. Suppose that I'_m contains t numbers, $a'_{m-t+1}, \ldots, a'_m$. Since $\varepsilon \leq 1$, we have $a'_m \geq m/\varepsilon$, and therefore $t > 0$. We will distinguish between two cases according to the value of t.

Case 1: $t = 1$. Let j be the smallest nonnegative integer such that $a_{j+1} + \ldots + a_{m-1} < a_m$. If $j = 0$, then the solution will be $S_1 = \{m\}$ and $S_2 = \{1, \ldots, m-1\}$. Otherwise the solution will be $S_1 = \{j, j+1, \ldots, m-1\}$ and $S_2 = \{m\}$.

Case 2: $t > 1$. We solve (exactly) I'_m, using the pseudo-polynomial algorithm which will take only polynomial time on this instance. Then we distinguish between two cases, depending on the value of the optimum of I'_m.

Case 2a: $opt(I'_m) = 1$. The algorithm returns the solution which realizes this optimum for I'_m.

Case 2b: $opt(I'_m) > 1$. In this case we generate a sufficiently rich collection of pairs of subsets in the following way. We consider 3^{t-1} pairs $P(\bar{v}, m), Q(\bar{v}, m)$ of disjoint sets,

$$P(\bar{v}, m), Q(\bar{v}, m) \subseteq \{m - t + 1, \ldots, m\},$$

parameterized by the vectors

$$\bar{v} = (v_1, \ldots, v_{t-1}) \in \{0, 1, 2\}^{t-1}.$$

The sets are defined according to the rule

$$\begin{array}{lllll} m - t + i \in P(\bar{v}, m) & \text{and} & m - t + i \notin Q(\bar{v}, m) & \text{if} & v_i = 1, \\ m - t + i \notin P(\bar{v}, m) & \text{and} & m - t + i \in Q(\bar{v}, m) & \text{if} & v_i = 2, \\ m - t + i \notin P(\bar{v}, m) & \text{and} & m - t + i \notin Q(\bar{v}, m) & \text{if} & v_i = 0, \end{array}$$

for $1 \leq i \leq t - 1$, and we put m into $P(\bar{v}, m)$. Define $R_1(\bar{v}, m) = P(\bar{v}, m)$ if $\sum_{i \in P(\bar{v}, m)} a_i > \sum_{i \in Q(\bar{v}, m)} a_i$, and $R_1(\bar{v}, m) = Q(\bar{v}, m)$ otherwise. Let $R_2(\bar{v}, m)$ be the other set.

The pair $S_1(\bar{v}, m), S_2(\bar{v}, m)$ is defined as follows. Let j be the smallest nonnegative integer such that

$$\sum_{i \in R_2(\bar{v}, m)} a_i + \sum_{i=j+1}^{m-t} a_i < \sum_{i \in R_1(\bar{v}, m)} a_i.$$

If $j = 0$, then $S_1(\bar{v}, m) = R_1(\bar{v}, m)$ and $S_2(\bar{v}, m) = R_2(\bar{v}, m) \cup \{1, \ldots, m - t\}$. Otherwise, if $m \in R_1(\bar{v}, m)$, then $S_1(\bar{v}, m) = R_2(\bar{v}, m) \cup \{j, \ldots, m - t\}$ and $S_2(\bar{v}, m) = R_1(\bar{v}, m)$. In the opposite case, where $m \in R_2(\bar{v}, m)$, we define $S_1(\bar{v}, m) = R_1(\bar{v}, m)$ and $S_2(\bar{v}, m) = R_2(\bar{v}, m) \cup \{j + 1, \ldots, m - t\}$. Finally, we choose a vector $\bar{v} \in \{0, 1, 2\}^{t-1}$ for which the ratio

$$\sum_{i \in S_1(\bar{v}, m)} a_i \Big/ \sum_{i \in S_2(\bar{v}, m)} a_i$$

is minimized. The solution given by the algorithm is then $S_1 = S_1(\bar{v}, m)$ and $S_2 = S_2(\bar{v}, m)$.

Theorem 1. *The above algorithm yields an* $(1+\varepsilon)$*-approximation, in time polynomial in* n *and* $1/\varepsilon$.

Proof. The algorithm clearly works in polynomial time whenever the number 3^{t-1} of vectors is polynomial in Case 2b. Since $opt(I'_m) > 1$ in that case, all the 2^t subsets of the set $\{a'_{m-t+1}, \ldots, a'_m\}$ make up mutually distinct sums. Since

$$a'_m \leq 2m/\varepsilon^2,$$

we have

$$\sum_{i=m-t+1}^{m} a'_i < 2m^2/\varepsilon^2.$$

Therefore

$$2^t \leq 2m^2/\varepsilon^2,$$

and thus $t \leq 2\log(m/\varepsilon) + 1$.

We will prove now that the algorithm indeed yields an $(1 + \varepsilon)$-approximation. Let m be an integer such that a_m is the greatest element occurring in an optimum solution. Then, clearly, this optimum solution for I_n is optimum for I_m as well. We prove that the algorithm yields an $(1 + \varepsilon)$-approximation on the instance I_m.

If $m \leq n_0$, then the pseudo-polynomial algorithm yields an optimum solution. Hence, let us suppose that $m > n_0$.

In Case 1, if $j = 0$, then the given solution is optimum, and if $j > 0$, then

$$\sum_{i \in S_1} a_i \Big/ \sum_{i \in S_2} a_i \leq 1 + a_j/a_m < 1 + \varepsilon.$$

In Case 2a, we have

$$\frac{\sum_{i \in S_1} a_i}{\sum_{i \in S_2} a_i} \leq \frac{\sum_{i \in S_1} k(m) \cdot (1 + a'_i)}{\sum_{i \in S_2} k(m) \cdot a'_i} = 1 + \frac{|S_1|}{\sum_{i \in S_2} a'_i} \leq 1 + \frac{t}{m/\varepsilon} < 1 + \varepsilon\,.$$

In Case 2b, let $S_1 = S_1(\bar{v}, m)$ and $S_2 = S_2(\bar{v}, m)$ for some $\bar{v} \in \{0, 1, 2\}^{t-1}$. If $j = 0$, then S_1, S_2 is an optimum solution. Otherwise, we have

$$\sum_{i \in R_2(\bar{v}, m)} a_i + \sum_{i=j+1}^{m-t} a_i < \sum_{i \in R_1(\bar{v}, m)} a_i \leq \sum_{i \in R_2(\bar{v}, m)} a_i + \sum_{i=j}^{m-t} a_i.$$

Therefore

$$\sum_{i\in S_1} a_i \,/ \sum_{i\in S_2} a_i \le 1 + a_j \,/ \sum_{i\in S_2} a_i \le 1 + a_j/a_m < 1+\varepsilon .$$

4 Subset-Sums Difference

Since Subset-Sums Ratio has a fptas, from the approximation point of view, we cannot distinguish Subset-Sums Equality from Pigeonhole Subset-Sums when the value of a solution is the ratio between the sums of the two sets. The situation changes drastically when a harder problem is considered, where the value of a solution is the difference between the two sums. In this section we show that Pigeonhole Subset-Sums Difference has a polynomial-time $2^n/n^{\Omega(\log n)}$-approximation, and on the other hand Subset-Sums Difference is not 2^{n^k}-approximable in polynomial time unless $P = NP$, for any constant k.

The fptas for Subset-Sums Ratio gives a polynomial-time $2^n/n^k$-approximation for Pigeonhole Subset-Sums Difference when we take $\varepsilon = 1/n^k$. But, in fact, one can do better than that.

Theorem 2. Subset-Sums Difference *has a polynomial-time* $K/n^{\Omega(\log n)}$-*approximation, where* K *is the greatest number in the instance.*

Proof. We will describe a polynomial-time algorithm that finds a solution of value at most $K/n^{\Omega(\log n)}$. Since the optimum value of each instance is at least 1 by definition, the assertion will follow.

Let $a_1 < a_2 < \cdots < a_n$ be an instance of Subset-Sums Difference, and let us define $a_0 = 0$. Consider the sequence

$$0 = a_0 < a_1 < a_2 < \cdots < a_n = K.$$

Notice that at most $n/3$ of the consecutive differences $a_i - a_{i-1}$ can be as large as $3K/n$; that is, at least $2n/3$ differences are smaller than $3K/n$. From these differences smaller than $3K/n$, we choose every second one (in the order of their occurrence), and create the sequence

$$a_1^{(1)} < a_2^{(1)} < \cdots < a_{n^{(1)}}^{(1)},$$

to which we adjoin $a_0^{(1)} = 0$. We also set $K^{(1)} = a_{n^{(1)}}^{(1)}$, where $K^{(1)} < 3K/n$ and $n^{(1)} \ge n/3$.

We repeat this type of "difference selection" $t = \lfloor \log_3 n \rfloor$ times, creating the sequences

$$0 = a_0^{(i)} < a_1^{(i)} < a_2^{(i)} < \cdots < a_{n^{(i)}}^{(i)} = K^{(i)}$$

for $i = 2, \ldots, t$, with $K^{(i)} < 3K^{(i-1)}/n^{(i-1)}$ and $n^{(i)} \ge n^{(i-1)}/3$. After that, we still have $n^{(t)} \ge n/3^t \ge 1$ numbers, from which we select the smallest one, namely $a_1^{(t)}$.

Observe that each number in each sequence represents a signed subset-sum, some of the input elements occurring with "+" and some with "−" (and some missing). The numbers with the same sign specify a subset, and the difference between the sum of the numbers of the "+" subset and of the "−" subset is at most the modified value of K.

We are going to show that $K^{(t)} = K/n^{\Omega(\log n)}$. We have

$$K^{(1)} < \frac{3K}{n},$$

and

$$K^{(i)} < \frac{3K^{(i-1)}}{n^{(i-1)}}$$

for $i = 2, \ldots, t$. Taking the product of these inequalities, we obtain

$$K^{(t)} < \frac{3^{t(t+1)/2} \cdot K}{n^t} = K/n^{\Omega(\log n)}.$$

Since the value of the solution is at most $K^{(t)}$, the statement follows.

Corollary 3. PIGEONHOLE SUBSET-SUMS DIFFERENCE *has a polynomial-time* $2^n/n^{\Omega(\log n)}$*-approximation.*

Finally, we show a simple non-approximability result for SUBSET-SUMS DIFFERENCE which is in strong opposition with the approximability of PIGEONHOLE SUBSET-SUMS DIFFERENCE.

Theorem 4. *If* $P \neq NP$*, then, for any constant* k*,* SUBSET-SUMS DIFFERENCE *is not* 2^{n^k}*-approximable in polynomial time.*

Proof. We prove that if SUBSET-SUMS DIFFERENCE were 2^{n^k}-approximable in polynomial time, then SUBSET-SUMS EQUALITY would admit a polynomial-time algorithm. Given an instance $I = \{a_1, a_2, \ldots, a_n\}$ of SUBSET-SUMS EQUALITY, we create (in polynomial time) an instance $I' = \{b_1, b_2, \ldots, b_n\}$ of SUBSET-SUMS DIFFERENCE where $b_i = 2^{n^k} \cdot a_i$. The size of I' is polynomial in the size of I, and clearly I is a positive instance if and only if the value of an optimum solution for I' is 1. Let q denote this optimum value, and let s be the value of the solution for I' given by the 2^{n^k}-approximation algorithm.

We claim that $q = 1$ if and only if $s = 1$. The "if" part is trivial. For the "only if" part, let us suppose that $s > 1$. We have

$$s \leq 2^{n^k} \cdot q,$$

because the solution was given by a 2^{n^k}-approximation algorithm. Since every element in I' is a multiple of 2^{n^k}, the value of a solution for I' is either 1 or greater than 2^{n^k}. Therefore, we also have

$$s > 2^{n^k},$$

and thus $q > 1$.

References

1. C. Bazgan, M. Santha and Zs. Tuza, *On the approximation of finding a(nother) Hamiltonian cycle in cubic Hamiltonian graphs*, 15th Annual Symposium on Theoretical Aspects of Computer Science, Lecture Notes in Computer Science, Vol. 1373 (1998), 276–286.
2. O. H. Ibarra and C. E. Kim, *Fast approximation algorithms for the Knapsack and Sum of Subset problems*, J. ACM, 22:4 (1975), 463–468.
3. R. M. Karp, *Reducibility among combinatorial problems*, in: Complexity of Computer Computations (R. E. Miller and J. W. Thatcher, eds.) (1972), 85–103.
4. H. Kellerer, R. Mansini, U. Pferschy and M. G. Speranza, *An efficient fully polynomial approximation scheme for the Subset-Sum problem*, manuscript, 1997.
5. N. Megiddo and C. Papadimitriou, *On total functions, existence theorems and computational complexity*, Theoretical Computer Science, 81 (1991), 317–324.
6. C. Papadimitriou, *On the complexity of the parity argument and other inefficient proofs of existence*, Journal of Computer and System Sciences 48 (1994), 498–532.
7. G. J. Woeginger and Z. Yu, *On the equal-subset-sum problem*, Information Processing Letters 42 (1992), 299–302.

Structural Recursive Definitions in Type Theory

Eduardo Giménez

INRIA-Rocquencourt
Eduardo.Gimenez@inria.fr

Abstract. We introduce an extension of the Calculus of Construction with inductive and co-inductive types that preserves normalisation, while keeping a relatively simple collection of typing rules. This extension considerably enlarges the expressiveness of the language, enabling a direct representation of recursive programs in type theory.

1 Introduction

The last twenty five years have seen an increasing development of different proof environments based on type theory. Several type theories have been proposed as a foundation of such proof environments [14, 5, 15], trying to find an accurate compromise between two criteria.

On the one hand, we search for extensions of type theory that preserve its conceptual simplicity of type theory (a few primitive constructions, a small number of typing rules) and meta-theoretical properties ensuring its soundness and a direct mechanisation (strong normalisation, decidability of type-checking, etc). On the other hand, we would like to provide a language with a high level of expressiveness. This is important if type theory is intended to be a language for describing programs and mathematical specifications as simply and directly as possible. These two criteria are sometimes in contradiction, and frequently it is necessary to find a good compromise.

An example of this situation is the representation of recursive definitions in type theory. Several approaches have been proposed to cope with them [16]. Maybe the oldest one consists in codifying each recursive definition in terms of a primitive-recursion operator, which represents the only authorised form of recursion of the theory [13–15]. This ensures the the expected meta-theoretical properties, and enables the representation of a large class of functions from a theoretical point of view. However, in practice, such codification introduces some rigidness in the language of type theory, and is quite far from the way we are used to program.

Looking for more flexible primitives for describing recursion, some recent works choose to separate recursion operators from pattern-matching, enabling fixpoint definitions in the style of the let-rec construction of functional programming languages [6, 8, 12]. Termination is ensured by a syntactical condition constraining the recursive calls occurring in the body of the definition. In this approach, the rule for typing recursive definitions looks like this:

$$\frac{\Gamma, f : A \to B \vdash e : A \to B}{\Gamma \vdash (\textbf{fix}\ f := e) : A \to B} \text{ when } \mathcal{C}(f, e)$$

where the side condition $\mathcal{C}(f, e)$ is defined by recursion on the set of untyped terms. A formal definition of such a condition can be found for example in [8]. Roughly speaking, if A is an inductive type, then f may occur only applied to those pattern variables issued from at least one pattern-matching on the formal argument of the function. If B is a co-inductive type, then any occurrence of f in e must be protected by at least one guarding constructor of B, and only by constructors.

Practice has shown that the use of a side condition $\mathcal{C}$ is a much more expressive and natural approach than the use of primitive recursion operators. However, it also poses some drawbacks in its turn. First of all, it is too restrictive. For example, in proof environments like Coq, there is no direct way of writing a recursive function as simple as the Euclidean division $\frac{x}{y+1}$, since its usual definition does not satisfy the side condition [11]. Moreover, even for simpler definitions, their acceptance is sometimes too sensitive to the way it is written down, i.e. to the syntactical shape of its body.

A second disadvantage of using a side condition concerns the development of efficient proof assistants to help us in the task of proof construction. In Coq, proofs are represented in the same way as programs. In particular, a recursively defined proof is represented by a fixpoint term (fix f := e). During the construction of such kind of proofs, the side condition $\mathcal{C}(f, e)$ required by its typing rule depends on the (still to be constructed!) body e of the definition, so it can be verified only when the pretended proof has been completed. This means that the user cannot be early prevented from doing a bad recursive call. This is particularly annoying for the introduction of some kind of automatic proof searching based on resolution techniques. Such techniques are based on type unification, and for efficiency reasons they do not care about the proof term they produce. Hence, they can lead the user into a dead-alley, where there is no way to complete the proof due to a uncared recursive call made by the proof assistant.

Finally, to our point of view, side conditions complicates the application of the usual proof techniques for establishing the meta-theory of the calculus, like for example Girard's *candidats de reductibilité* method for proving normalisation [7]. One of the keys steps of this method is the definition of an interpretation function from types to saturated sets of terms. However, in order to make sense of the typing rule of fix above, the occurrences of $(A \rightarrow B)$ at the left and right hand sides of the dash symbol cannot be both interpreted in the same way. Now, the information necessary to interpret them correctly does not appear *in the types* themselves, but in the side condition $\mathcal{C}(f, e)$ about its elements. Hence, it is difficult to define a sound interpretation for types simply by recursion on them, as is usual in the reducibility method.

This article introduces an alternative solution for the problem of typing recursive definitions. We present an extension of the Calculus of Constructions –that we call $\mathfrak{CCR}$– where recursion is still expressed using a let-rec style like in functional programming languages, but where termination is ensured only by typing conditions, as in traditional formulations of type theory. In this calculus the "global" condition $\mathcal{C}$ on pseudo-terms is split into local ones, associated to the primitives of the language. The calculus is sound, since it admits a model in terms of saturated sets [10]. This model entails that any well-typed term of $\mathfrak{CCR}$ is normalisable with respect to a lazy notion of computation.

2 Language and Forms of Judgement

The language of $\mathfrak{CCR}$ is defined by the following grammar:

T ::= *Type* | *Set* | x | $(T\ T)$ | $[x : T]T$ | $(x : T)T$	(CC)
| $\mathbf{Rec}_m(X, Y : T)\langle \boldsymbol{T} \rangle$	(recursive types)
| $\widehat{T}$	(guarded types)
| $T.i$	(i^{th} constructor of T)
| **Case** T **of** $\boldsymbol{T}$ **end**	(pattern-matching)
| **Law** $f : \forall X {\geq} T \cdot T := T$	(construction laws)
$\mathbf{Ind}_n$ $f : \forall X {\leq} T \cdot T := T$	(structural inductions)

The kernel of the language is the Calculus of Construction (CC) [5]. This language is extended with recursive types; a new type former $\widehat{T}$ for representing the type of constructor guarded terms; a pattern-matching expression; and two flavors of recursive definitions: laws for constructing infinite objects, and definitions by structural induction on finite ones.

The rules of the calculus enable to derive three forms of judgment :

a is an object of type A under Γ	: $\Gamma \vdash a : A$
Γ is a valid context	: Γ *valid*
A is a sub-type of B under Γ	: $\Gamma \vdash A \leq B$

The two first forms of judgement have the usual meaning. The order relation on types is introduced to enlarge the class of recursive definitions accepted by the calculus. On ground types, the informal meaning of $\Gamma \vdash A \leq B$ is that any object of type A is also an object of type B. This form of judgement depends on the context Γ because the typing rules for recursive definitions may introduce sub-typing constraints into Γ. Such constraints are of the form $X \leq \mathbf{R}$ or $X \geq \mathbf{R}$, where X is a type variable and $\mathbf{R}$ a recursive type.

3 Typing rules

This section presents the rules associated to the syntactical constructions extending CC and their informal justification.

3.1 Recursive Types.

Recursive types are types closed under a collection of introduction rules. *Closed* means here that their objects are constructed using the introduction rules of the type, and only these rules. The definition of a recursive type is synthesized into the expression $\mathbf{Rec}_m(X, Y : A)\langle \boldsymbol{C} \rangle$. The term A is the formation rule or *arity* of the type. Each C_i is the type of an introduction rule or *form of constructor*. The variables X and Y are both bound in all the forms of constructor, and they stand for the recursive type inside its own definition. The introduction rules of the type are referred selecting a form of constructor C_i of the declaration in this way: $\mathbf{Rec}_m(X : A)\langle \boldsymbol{C} \rangle.i$. The mark $m \in \{\phi, \iota\}$ indexing the type denotes whether the recursive type is *inductive* or *co-inductive*. Informally speaking, inductive types are recursive types whose elements are constructed only by a finite number of applications of its introduction rules —like natural numbers, for instance— while co-inductive types may also contain "infinite objects" –like for example the type of infinite streams. In order to make sense of this notation, a form of constructor must be an introduction scheme with respect to one of the variables abstracted, in the sense of the following definition.

Definition 1. ***Introduction scheme.*** *We say that C is an introduction scheme with respect to a free variable X if $C \equiv (x_1 : T_1) \dots (x_n : T_n)(X\ P_1 \dots P_n)$. When X does not occur free in any T_i then we say that C is a strict introduction scheme.* ■

In addition to this, the second variable Y bound in the definition must occur only negatively in the form of constructor. The choice of using two different variables to distinguish the rightmost occurrence of the type from the other ones simplifies the description of the typing rules. The following definitions formally define which occurrences of X and Y are allowed in a form of constructor.

Definition 2. ***Positiveness and negativeness.*** *Let X and Y be two different type variables. We define whether Y occurs negatively and X positively in a given term T (notation $T \in \mathcal{NP}\{Y, X\}$) by induction on T.*

1. *If $Z \neq Y$ then $Z \in \mathcal{NP}\{Y, X\}$, where Z is a variable.*
2. *If $M \in \mathcal{NP}\{Y, X\}$ and neither X nor Y occur free in N, then $(M\ N) \in \mathcal{NP}\{Y, X\}$*
3. *If $T_1 \in \mathcal{NP}\{X, Y\}$ and $T_2 \in \mathcal{NP}\{Y, X\}$, then $(x : T_1)T_2 \in \mathcal{NP}\{Y, X\}$*
4. *If $C_i \in \mathcal{NP}\{X, Y\}$ for all $i \in |\boldsymbol{C}|$ and X does not occur free in A, then $\boldsymbol{Rec}_m(W, Z : A)\langle \boldsymbol{C} \rangle \in \mathcal{NP}\{Y, X\}$, where $X, Y \neq W, Z$.* ■

Definition 3. ***Form of constructor.*** *We say that C is a form of constructor with respect to X and Y (notation $C \in \mathcal{FC}\{Y, X\}$) if C is a strict introduction scheme with respect to X such that $C \in \mathcal{NP}\{Y, X\}$. We write $C \in \mathcal{FC}\{X\}$ if there exists a term C' such that $C' \in \mathcal{FC}\{Y, X\}$ and $C \equiv C'\{Y{:=}X\}$.* ■

Example 1. **(Recursive types).** In order to fix ideas about this notation, let us introduce some examples of a recursive type: the type of natural numbers, and the type of infinite streams.

$$\begin{array}{lll} \mathit{Nat} \equiv \mathbf{Rec}_\phi(X, Y : \mathit{Set})\langle X \mid Y \to X \rangle & S \equiv \mathit{Nat}.2 & 0 \equiv \mathit{Nat}.1 \\ \mathit{Str} \equiv \mathbf{Rec}_\iota(X, Y : \mathit{Set})\langle \mathit{Nat} \to Y \to X \rangle & \mathit{Cons} \equiv \mathit{Str}.1 & \end{array}$$

■

The formation rule for a recursive type $\mathbf{Rec}_m(X, Y : A)\langle \boldsymbol{C} \rangle$ asserts that its type A must inhabit the universe *Type* (so the recursive type itself inhabit the universe *Set* of sets), and every C_i must be a well-typed form of constructor:

$$(\text{REC})\ \frac{\Gamma \vdash A : \mathit{Type} \quad \overset{\forall i \in |\boldsymbol{C}|}{C_i \in \mathcal{FC}\{Y, X\}} \quad \Gamma, X : A, Y : A \overset{\forall i \in |\boldsymbol{C}|}{\vdash} C_i : \mathit{Set}}{\Gamma \vdash \mathbf{Rec}_m(X, Y : A)\langle \boldsymbol{C} \rangle : A}$$

The inductive version of the recursive type corresponds to the least collection of objects closed under the introduction rules of the type, while the inductive version is the largest of such collections. This justifies the following type inclusion:

$$(\phi\iota) \qquad \frac{\Gamma \vdash \mathbf{R}_\iota : A}{\Gamma \vdash \mathbf{R}_\phi \leq \mathbf{R}_\iota}$$

In the following sections, $\mathbf{R}_m$ will stand for the term $\mathbf{Rec}_m(X, Y : A)\langle \boldsymbol{C} \rangle$. The letter A will denote the arity $A \equiv (\boldsymbol{x} : \boldsymbol{A})\mathit{Set}$ contained in the definition of $\mathbf{R}_m$ and $\boldsymbol{C}$ the list of its forms of constructor.

3.2 Guarded Types.

For each post-type P of $\mathbf{R}_\iota$ and pre-type of $\mathbf{R}_\phi$, we introduce the type $\widehat{P}$, obtained closing P under the introduction rules of $\mathbf{R}_m$. This gives rise to the following two formation rules:

$$(\mathrm{GRD}_\iota)\ \frac{\Gamma \vdash P : A \qquad \Gamma \vdash \mathbf{R}_\iota \leq P}{\Gamma \vdash \widehat{P} : A} \qquad \frac{\Gamma \vdash P : A \qquad \Gamma \vdash P \leq \mathbf{R}_\phi}{\Gamma \vdash \widehat{P} : A}\ (\mathrm{GRD}_\phi)$$

The type $\widehat{P}$ replace in our calculus the syntactical notion of "being a term guarded by constructors" used in [6, 8]. The introduction rule of this type ensures that the canonical terms of type $\widehat{P}$ contain at least one extra guarding constructor of $\mathbf{R}_m$ than those of P:

$$(\mathrm{CONS})\qquad \frac{\Gamma \vdash \mathbf{R}_m : \mathit{Set} \qquad \Gamma \vdash \mathbf{R}_\phi \leq P}{\Gamma \vdash \mathbf{R}_m.i : C_i\{Y{:=}P\}\{X{:=}\widehat{P}\}}$$

Notice that P can be instantiated both with $\mathbf{R}_\phi$, with $\mathbf{R}_\iota$, or with any pos-type of $\mathbf{R}_\iota$ – like for example a constrained variable $X{\geq}\mathbf{R}_\iota$ from the local context Γ. The intended meaning of the type $\mathbf{R}_m$ entails that this type is a fixpoint of the closure operator, and hence intensionally equal to $\widehat{\mathbf{R}}_m$.

3.3 Pattern-Matching and Case Analysis.

From the intuitive semantics given to guarded types, it seems natural to consider pattern-matching as the most basic elimination rule for them. Let us illustrate a definition by pattern-matching for a guarded type associated to natural numbers. That n is an object of such a type means that it was introduced using either *0* or *S* (which are different introduction rules). Therefore, an object **Case** n **of** $g_1\ g_2$ **end** in another type Q may be defined depending on which of these rules was used to introduce n. In a theory containing dependent types like CC, the type Q of the defined object may also depend on n. We speak in this case of *dependent* pattern-matching. A possible rule for typing definitions by dependent pattern-matching on natural numbers is the following one:

$$\frac{\begin{array}{c}\Gamma \vdash Q : \widehat{\mathit{Nat}} \to \mathit{Set} \\ \Gamma \vdash n : \widehat{\mathit{Nat}} \quad \Gamma \vdash g_0 : (Q\ \mathit{0}) \qquad \Gamma \vdash g_1 : (m : \mathit{Nat})(Q\ (S\ m))\end{array}}{\Gamma \vdash \mathbf{Case}\ n\ \mathbf{of}\ g_0\ \ g_1\ \mathbf{end} : (Q\ n)}$$

The second case in the definition is a function, whose formal argument m denotes the natural number that the constructor *S* was applied to. The use of functions to represent the cases simplifies the formulation of the computing and typing rules. The traditional pattern notation $(S\ m) \Rightarrow e$ used in programming languages can be seen just as a syntactic sugar for describing this function, and will be used in the examples of the sequel.

In general, the typing rule for pattern-matching on a guarded type $\widehat{P}$ associated to **R** is:

$$\text{(CASE)}\ \frac{\Gamma \vdash Q : (\boldsymbol{x} : \boldsymbol{A})(\widehat{P}\ \boldsymbol{x}) \rightarrow \mathit{Set} \qquad \Gamma \vdash e : (\widehat{P}\ \boldsymbol{p}) \quad \Gamma \vdash P \leq \mathbf{R}_\iota \quad \Gamma \overset{\forall i \in |\boldsymbol{C}|}{\vdash} g_i : C_i\{X \overset{\mathbf{R}.i}{:=} Q\}\{Y{:=}P\}}{\Gamma \vdash \mathbf{Case}\ e\ \mathbf{of}\ \boldsymbol{g}\ \mathbf{end} : (Q\ \boldsymbol{p}\ e)}$$

The type $(\boldsymbol{x} : \boldsymbol{A})\mathit{Set}$ denotes the arity of the guarded type $\widehat{P}$. The type of the i-th branch g_i is generated from the i-th form of constructor of $\mathbf{R}_\iota$ as follows. First, the variable Y is substituted by the type P. Second, and a special substitution operation $C_i\{X \overset{a}{:=} Q\}$ is performed for the variable X. If a is a term and $C_i \equiv (\boldsymbol{x} : \boldsymbol{B})(X\ q_1 \ldots q_n)$ is a strict introduction scheme with respect to X, then this operation is defined as $C_i\{X \overset{a}{:=} B\} \equiv (\boldsymbol{x} : \boldsymbol{B})(Q\ q_1 \ldots q_n\ (a\ \boldsymbol{x}))$.

3.4 Construction of Law-Like Infinite Objects.

Co-inductive types contain any object built up from the introduction rules of the type, even by an infinite application of them. Actually, the only infinite objects that we are able to write down are those whose process of generation is governed by a law. Laws of construction are described in $\mathfrak{CCR}$ by let-rec style definitions, like in lazy functional programming languages. Such laws are noted **Law** $f : \forall X{\geq}\mathbf{R}_\iota \cdot T$ **:=** e, where $\mathbf{R}_m$ is the co-inductive type that the infinite object belongs to; X is a bound variable standing for a post-type of $\mathbf{R}_m$ in both T and e; T is an introduction scheme with respect to X; and f is a variable bound in e which stands for the recursive method in its own definition. For example, the list $[0, 1, 2, 3, \ldots]$ containing all natural numbers can be represented by the term **Law** $nats : \forall X{\geq}\mathit{Nat} \cdot X$ **:=** $(\mathit{Cons}\ 0\ (\mathit{map}\ S\ nats))$, where *map* is the usual mapping function on streams. The rule for typing this construction is:

$$\text{(LAW)}\ \frac{T \in \mathcal{FC}\{X\} \quad \Gamma, \mathbf{R}_\iota{\leq}X, f : T \vdash e : T\{X{:=}\widehat{X}\} \quad \Gamma \vdash \mathbf{R}_\iota \leq P}{\Gamma \vdash \mathbf{Law}\ f : \forall X{\geq}\mathbf{R}_\iota \cdot T \mathrel{\mathbf{:=}} e : T\{X{:=}P\}}$$

From a syntactical point of view, the type $\widehat{X}$ is intended to be a set of terms guarded by some constructor of $\mathbf{R}_\iota$. Hence, the rule above asks for the body of the definition to be a guarded term, so that the recursive law outputs at least one constructor for each iteration.

The sub-typing relation serves to enlarge the class of definitions accepted by the typing rule above. The assumption $\mathbf{R}_\iota \leq X$ enables the description of laws that stop the iteration at a given moment and end returning some previously constructed object of $\mathbf{R}_m$. In order to accept definitions where e has more than one guarding constructor, we also allow to re-inject an object of type X into $\widehat{X}$ (cf. the rule (CONS)). This gives rise to the following sub-typing rule:

$$\text{(POST)} \qquad \frac{\Gamma \textit{ valid} \qquad \mathbf{R}_\iota \leq X \in \Gamma}{\Gamma \vdash \widehat{X} \leq X}$$

Finally, to take full advantage of law nesting, we authorise the introduction scheme of the law to be instantiated with any post-type P of $\mathbf{R}_\iota$. Consider for example the stream *nats* of all natural numbers introduced above. That law makes use of the mapping law on streams, which can be defined as follows:

$$\begin{array}{l}\textbf{Law } map : \forall Y{\geq}\mathit{Str} \cdot (\mathit{Nat} \to \mathit{Nat}) \to Y \to Y \textbf{ :=} \\ \quad [f : \mathit{Nat} \to \mathit{Nat}][x : \widehat{Y}]\textbf{Case } x \textbf{ of } (\mathit{Cons}\ n\ \underbrace{s}_{:Y}) \Rightarrow \overbrace{(\mathit{Cons}\ (f\ n)\ \underbrace{(map\ f\ s)}_{:Y})}^{:\widehat{Y}} \textbf{ end}\end{array}$$

To typecheck the definition of *nats*, the type scheme $\forall Y{\leq}\mathit{Str} \cdot (\mathit{Nat} \to \mathit{Nat}) \to (Y \to Y)$ given to *map* has to be instantiated with the type variable X introduced by *nats*:

$$\textbf{Law } nats : \forall X{\geq}\mathit{Nat} \cdot X \textbf{ :=} \overbrace{(\mathit{Cons}\ 0\ (\underbrace{\mathit{map}\ S}_{:X \to X}\ nats))}^{:\widehat{X}}$$

To our knowledge, our calculus is the first one where such a recursive definition can be typed without introducing some kind of "partial objects", like in LCF. Avoiding partial objects is crucial when the typing calculus is intended to be used as a proof system based on the propositions-as-types view of Logic. For this paradigm, truth amounts to type inhabitance, so the introduction of partial objects trivialises the logical system: every property would become true since it would contain at least the completely undefined object. Furthermore, definitions like $nats$ are frequently used in functional programming with streams [3] and in reactive programming [4], so it is important to be able to deal with them in proof environments.

3.5 Structural Recursion on Inductive Objects.

For inductive types, a form of elimination stronger than case analysis is allowed: structural induction. Structural inductions are noted $\mathbf{Ind}_n\ f : \forall X{\leq}\mathbf{R}_\phi \cdot T \mathbf{:=} e$. In this term, R is an inductive type;X is a bound variable which stands for a pre-type of R in T and e; and f is a variable bound in e standing for the recursive method in its own definition. The term T is an elimination scheme with respect to X at position $n+1$, in the sense of the following definition.

Definition 4. ***Elimination scheme.*** *We say that E is an elimination scheme with respect to a free variable X at position $n+1$ (notation $C \in \mathcal{E}\{X,n\}$) if $E \equiv (x_1 : T_1)\ldots(x_n : T_n)(y : (X\ P_1 \ldots P_m))T$, there exists a term E' such that $E' \in \mathcal{NP}\{X,Y\}$ and $E' \equiv E\{Y{:=}X\}$.* ■

The rule for typing structural inductions is the dual of the introduction of law-like objects:

$$(\text{IND})\ \frac{T \in \mathcal{E}\{X,n\} \quad \Gamma, X \leq \mathbf{R}_\phi, f : T \vdash e : T\{X{:=}\widehat{X}\} \quad \Gamma \vdash P \leq \mathbf{R}_\phi}{\Gamma \vdash \mathbf{Ind}_n\ f : \forall X{\leq}\mathbf{R}_\phi \cdot T := e : T\{X{:=}P\}}$$

Assuming that the function is already defined for a subset X of an inductive type $\mathbf{R}_\phi$, its body must extend the definition to the type $\widehat{X}$, that is, to any term containing at least one extra guarding constructor. To be able to apply the function f assumed, the nth formal argument $y : \widehat{X}$ of e must be decomposed by a pattern-matching (cf. the rule (CASE)). The assumption $X{\leq}\mathbf{R}_\phi$ enables to use any already defined function on $\mathbf{R}_\phi$ in the definition. The following sub-typing rule allows to re-inject an element of X into $\widehat{X}$, so that recursive calls can be also performed on deep components of the argument:

$$(\text{PRE})\qquad \frac{\Gamma\ \textit{valid} \qquad X \leq \mathbf{R}_\phi \in \Gamma}{\Gamma \vdash X \leq \widehat{X}}$$

In order to illustrate a definition by structural induction, we present a recursive function computing the Euclidean division $\frac{x}{y+1}$. We start introducing the subtraction of two natural numbers:

```
Ind minus : ∀Y≤Nat · Y → Nat → Y :=
 [x : Ŷ][y : Nat]Case x of
          0     ⇒ x
        | (S n) ⇒ Case y of 0 ⇒ x | (S m) ⇒ (minus n m) end
        end
```

```
(annotations: x : Ŷ;  n : Y;  x : Ŷ;  minus : Y→Nat→Y;  (minus n m) : Y ≤ Ŷ)
```

The following function computes the Euclidean division $\frac{x}{y+1}$:

```
Ind div : ∀X≤Nat · X → Nat → Nat :=
 [x : X̂][y : Nat]Case y of
          0     ⇒ x
        | (S n) ⇒ Case x of  0     ⇒ 0
                           | (S m) ⇒ (S (div (minus m n) y)) end
        end
```

```
(annotations: x : X̂ ≤ Nat;  minus : X→Nat→X;  (minus m n) : X)
```

3.6 Context Formation and Constrained Variables

In addition to type assumptions, the contexts of $\mathfrak{CCR}$ also contain sub-typing constraints, introduced by the rules for typing recursive definitions. Hence, the rules of context formation of the Calculus of Constructions have to be extended with the following two ones:

$$(\text{CONSTR}_\iota)\ \frac{\Gamma\ \mathit{valid} \qquad \Gamma \vdash \mathbf{R}_\iota : A}{\Gamma, \mathbf{R}_\iota \leq X\ \ \mathit{valid}} \qquad \frac{\Gamma\ \mathit{valid} \qquad \Gamma \vdash \mathbf{R}_\phi : A}{\Gamma, X \leq \mathbf{R}_\phi\ \ \mathit{valid}}\ (\text{CONSTR}_\phi)$$

The type of a constrained variable is the type of its bound:

$$(\text{VAR}_\iota)\ \frac{\mathbf{R}_\iota \leq X \in \Gamma \quad \Gamma \vdash \mathbf{R}_\iota : A}{\Gamma \vdash X : A} \qquad \frac{X \leq \mathbf{R}_\phi \in \Gamma \quad \Gamma \vdash \mathbf{R}_\phi : A}{\Gamma \vdash X : A}\ (\text{VAR}_\phi)$$

4 Type Inclusion

The intended meaning of the judgement $\Gamma \vdash A \leq B$ is that any object of type A is also an object of type B. This justifies the following rule, connecting this judgement with the typing one:

$$(\text{SUB}) \qquad \frac{\Gamma \vdash a : A \quad \Gamma \vdash B : s_2 \quad \Gamma \vdash A \leq B}{\Gamma \vdash a : B}$$

We turn now to some general rules for deriving type inclusions. The most basic ones that can be derived are the constraints of the context:

$$(\text{HYP}) \qquad \frac{\Gamma\ \mathit{valid} \qquad P \leq Q \in \Gamma}{\Gamma \vdash P \leq Q}$$

The intended meaning of $\Gamma \vdash A \leq B$ also entails that it is a transitive relation which subsumes intensional equality:

$$(\text{TRS})\ \frac{\Gamma \vdash T_1 \leq T_2 \quad \Gamma \vdash T_2 \leq T_3}{\Gamma \vdash T_1 \leq T_3} \qquad \frac{\Gamma \vdash Q : A \quad P = Q \quad \Gamma \vdash P : A}{\Gamma \vdash P \leq Q}\ (\text{EQ})$$

Finally, the rules below extend basic inclusions to the other type constructors:

$$(\text{GRD})\ \frac{\Gamma \vdash T_1 \leq T_2}{\Gamma \vdash \widehat{T_1} \leq \widehat{T_2}} \qquad \frac{\Gamma \vdash T_3 \leq T_1 \quad \Gamma, x : T_1 \vdash T_2 \leq T_4}{\Gamma \vdash (x : T_1)T_2 \leq (x : T_3)T_4}\ (\text{PROD})$$

$$(\text{APP}) \qquad \frac{\Gamma \vdash P_1 \leq P_2 \quad Q_1 = Q_2}{\Gamma \vdash (P_1\, Q_1) \leq (P_2\, Q_2)}$$

$$(\text{REC}) \qquad \frac{A = B \quad \Gamma, X : A, Y : A \overset{\forall i \in |\boldsymbol{C}|}{\vdash} C_i \leq C_i'}{\Gamma \vdash \mathbf{Rec}_m(X, Y : A)\langle \boldsymbol{C} \rangle \leq \mathbf{Rec}_m(X, Y : B)\langle \boldsymbol{C'} \rangle}$$

It is important to point out that the decidability of type inclusion depens only on the decidability of intensional equality. Let us call $<$ the relation obtained by dropping the rules (S-TRNS) and (S-EQ). It is not difficult to check that these two rules commute with all the other ones. Therefore, in order to decide if $\Gamma \vdash A \leq B$, it is sufficient to check if the respective normal forms A' and B' of A and B verify $\Gamma \vdash A' <^* B'$, where $<^*$ is the transitive closure of $<$. But $<^*$ is clearly decidable, since it is syntax-oriented.

4.1 Intensional Equality

The relation $A = B$ of intensional equality between two types is the minimal equivalent relation containing the notion of computation of the language. The notion of computation is defined as the minimal context stable relation satisfying the β rule of CC and the following computation rules associated to recursive types:

$$\widehat{\mathbf{R}}_m \longrightarrow \mathbf{R}_m \qquad (\hat{\ })$$

$$\mathbf{Case}\ (\mathbf{R}.i\ \ \boldsymbol{a})\ \mathbf{of}\ \boldsymbol{g}\ \mathbf{end} \longrightarrow (g_i\ \boldsymbol{a}) \qquad (\text{CASE})$$

$$\mathbf{Case}\ (\mathbf{L}\ \boldsymbol{a})\ \mathbf{of}\ \boldsymbol{g}\ \mathbf{end} \longrightarrow \mathbf{Case}\ (e\{X{:=}\mathbf{R}\}\{f{:=}\mathbf{L}\}\ \boldsymbol{a})\ \mathbf{of}\ \boldsymbol{g}\ \mathbf{end} \qquad (\text{LAW})$$

$$(\mathbf{I}\ \ \boldsymbol{p}\ \ (\mathbf{R}.i\ \boldsymbol{a})) \longrightarrow (e\{X{:=}\mathbf{R}\}\{f{:=}\mathbf{I}\}\ \ \boldsymbol{p}\ \ (\mathbf{R}.i\ \boldsymbol{a})),\ \text{if } |\boldsymbol{p}| = n \qquad (\text{IND})$$

where $I \equiv \mathbf{Ind}_n\ f : \forall X{\leq}\mathbf{R}_\phi \cdot T := e$ and $L \equiv \mathbf{Law}\ f : \forall X{\geq}\mathbf{R}_\iota \cdot T := e$. Notice that under this notion of computation, a law of construction is considered as a canonical term, and is only expanded in order to compute a pattern-matching on the object it introduces. If this notion of computation is adopted, then it is possible to construct a model of our calculus in terms of saturated sets [10]. The constuction of the model is based on a variant of Girard-Tait's reducibility method, and entails the normalisation property for the notion of computation.

5 Conclusions and Related Work

We have presented $\mathfrak{CCR}$, a sound extension of CC with recursive types which enables a direct representation of a large class of terminating recursive functions. We think that this calculus provides a better basis for implementing a proof environment than those calculus where terminating recursion is founded on syntactical side conditions. The next step of our research programme is the development of an efficient typechecking algorithm for it, and to explore its implementation as the core of a new version of the Coq system [2].

The calculus proposed here is directly inspired form a former version that we developed in [9]. It also shares some features with the one proposed by Mendler in [13], in particular the use of a sub-typing relation to improve the strength of recursive definitions. However, oppositely to [13], our calculus may type definitions containing recursive calls which are guarded by more than one constructor (or destructor), as well as nested recursive definitions.

Nested recursive definitions have been also studied by Amadio and Coupet in [1]. Starting from Coquand's notion of guarded definition for simple typed lambda calculus, they provide a semantics based on partial equivalent relations, and use ordinal iteration to interpret recursive types. This semantics lead them to a calculus closed to the one proposed in [9]. However, definitions like the stream *nats* of Section 3.4 cannot be typed in their calculus.

References

1. R. Amadio and S. Coupet. Analysis of a guard condition in type theory. Technical Report 3300, INRIA, October 1997. Extended abstract to appear in ETAPS 98 (FoSSaCS).
2. B. Barras, S. Boutin, C. Cornes, J. Courant, J.C. Filliatre, E. Giménez, H. Herbelin, G. Huet, C. Mu noz, C. Murthy, C. Parent, C. Paulin, A. Saïbi, and B. Werner. The Coq Proof Assistant Reference Manual – Version V6.1. Technical Report 0203, INRIA, 1997.
3. R. Bird and P. Wadler. *Introduction to Functional Programming*. Prentice-Hall, UK, 1988.
4. P. Caspi and M. Pouzet. Synchronous Kahn networks. In *ACM Sigplan International Conference of Functional Programming*, May 1996.
5. T. Coquand. Metamathematical Investigations of a Calculus of Constructions. In P. Odifreddi, editor, *Logic and Computer Science*, volume 31 of *The APIC series*, pages 91–122. Academic Press, 1990.
6. T. Coquand. Infinite objects in type theory. In H. Barendregt and T. Nipkow, editors, *Workshop on Types for Proofs and Programs*, number 806 in LNCS, pages 62–78. Springer-Verlag, 1993.
7. H. Geuvers. A short and flexible proof of strong normalisation for the Calculus of Constructions. In P. Dybjer, B. Nordström, and J. Smith, editors, *Workshop on Types of proofs and programs*, number 996 in LNCS, pages 14–38. Springer-Verlag, 1994.
8. E. Giménez. Codifying guarded definitions with recursive schemes. In *Workshop on Types for Proofs and Programs*, number 996 in LNCS, pages 39–59. Springer-Verlag, 1994.
9. E. Giménez. *A Calculus of Infinite Constructions and its application to the verification of communicating systems*. PhD thesis, Ecole Normale Supérieure de Lyon, 1996.
10. E. Giménez. A calculus for typing recursive definitions: rules and soundness. Technical report, INRIA, 1998.
11. E. Giménez. A tutorial on recursive types in coq. Technical report, INRIA, 1998. Electronically distributed with the system Coq.
12. Jean-Pierre Jouannaud and Mitsuhiro Okada. Inductive data type systems. *Theoretical Computer Science*, 173(2):349–391, February 1997.
13. F.P. Mendler. *Inductive Definitions in Type Theory*. PhD thesis, Cornell University, 1987.
14. B. Nordström, K. Petersson, and J. Smith. *Programming in Martin-Löf's Type Theory: An Introduction*, volume 7 of *International Series of Monographs on Computer Science*. Oxford Science Publications, 1990.
15. C. Paulin. Inductive Definitions in the System Coq - Rules and Properties. In M. Bezem and J.-F. Groote, editors, *Typed Lambda Calculi and Applications*, number 664 in LNCS. Springer-Verlag, 1993.
16. C. Paulin-Mohring. *Définitions Inductives en Théorie des Types d'Ordre Supérieur*. Habilitation à diriger les recherches, Université Claude Bernard Lyon I, December 1996.

A Good Class of Tree Automata. Application to Inductive Theorem Proving

D.Lugiez

Université de Provence. Lab. d'Informatique de Marseille,
CMI 39 av. Joliot Curie, 13453 Marseille Cedex, France.
and
Inria-Lorraine, 615 rue rue du Jardin Botanique, BP 101
54601 Villèrs les Nancy, France
e-mail lugiez@lim.univ-mrs.fr

Introduction

Automated proofs. Automated proofs play a growing role in the verification and certification of software. This task often leads to performing inductive proofs on first-order specification using automated theorem provers like NQTHM [BM88], RRL [KZ88] or Spike [BR95]. To guarantee that the deduction process has good properties, for instance it finds with a counter-example when we attempt to prove a false theorem, one must prove that the specifications enjoy some key properties. It must be *complete* and/or one must be able to compute *test-sets* or decide *ground reducibility.* These properties have been studied for a long time in the case of syntactical terms, but fewer results have been obtained when interpreted domains like integers, multisets, lists ... occur. Since actual applications always involve interpreted domains with *non-free constructors*, tools for deciding the above properties in these domains are strongly requested.

An example. For (non-empty) multisets, a definition of the membership predicate can be as follows.

$$\begin{array}{ll} x : Elt & \Rightarrow memb(x,\{x\}) \rightarrow True \\ x,y : Elt \wedge x \neq y & \Rightarrow memb(x,\{y\}) \rightarrow False \\ x : Elt \wedge E : MS & \Rightarrow memb(x,\{x\} \cup E) \rightarrow True \\ x,y : Elt \wedge E : MS \wedge x \neq y & \Rightarrow memb(x,\{y\} \cup E) \rightarrow memb(x,E) \end{array}$$

where *Elt* is the sort of elements and MS the sort of non-empty multisets. The completeness property states that each term $memb(\ldots,\ldots)$ without variable, i.e. *ground* term, can be rewritten at the top with the above rules. This is similar to the completeness test done in functional languages like ML. Almost all difficulties show up in this example: the definition uses *conditional* rules, it is *non-linear* (some variables occur more than once in a rule), it contains *interpreted* symbols involving axioms (associativity-commutativity of $\cup$ for instance). The *ground reducibility* property states that each ground term can be rewritten (not necessarily at the top).

The tree automata approach. Language theory and tree automata provide a general framework for stating and deciding the previous issues. Let $\mathcal{L}(memb(\alpha, \beta) \wedge \phi)$ denote the set of ground instances of $memb(\alpha, \beta)$ which satisfy ϕ, then the completeness of the definition of *memb* is equivalent to the following inclusion of language:

$$\begin{aligned}\mathcal{L}(memb(x,E) \wedge x : Elt \wedge E : MS) \subseteq\ & \cup\mathcal{L}(memb(x,\{x\}) \wedge x : Elt \wedge E : MS)\\ & \cup\mathcal{L}(memb(x,\{y\}) \wedge x \neq y \wedge x,y : Elt \wedge E : MS)\\ & \cup\mathcal{L}(memb(x,\{x\} \cup E) \wedge x : El \wedge E : MS)\\ & \cup\mathcal{L}(memb(x,\{y\} \cup E) \wedge x,y : Elt \wedge E : MS)\end{aligned}$$

This is equivalent to deciding if the intersection of $\mathcal{L}(memb(x, E) \wedge x : Elt \wedge E : MS$ and the complement of the union of the $\mathcal{L}(memb(\alpha, \beta) \wedge \phi)$'s is empty or not. Therefore, the problem is decidable if the languages $\mathcal{L}(\ldots)$ are accepted by a class of tree automata closed under union, intersection, complement and such that the emptiness of the language accepted by an automaton is decidable. Similarly, ground reducibility is equivalent to language inclusion. Both properties are undecidable, but interesting decidable classes of specifications have been defined and the tree automata approach has been quite successful in this task.

Content of this paper. We describe a constrained tree automata approach for the completeness problem and for the ground reducibility problem. Non-linearity and conditions are handled by constraints, and we set additional conditions on automata's rules to take the semantics of interpreted domains into account.

Comparison with previous works. Specifications involving interpreted domains are usually dealt with using ad-hoc approaches like in [KS96]. Several authors have considered automata handling AC axioms [NP93,Cou89], either for type checking or for classifying graph languages, but these automata don't use constraints and lack the expressive power needed for modeling specification. Constrained automata have been known for a long time, but have a severe drawback: the emptiness problem is undecidable. Several subclasses have been introduced to overcome this limitation ([BT92,CCC+94,DACJL95]. But the resulting classes are too limited or lack some closure property (under complementation or determinization) and the proofs for the decision of emptiness rely on a complex combinatorial reasoning. Furthermore, these automata can't be adapted to deal with interpreted domains. A first step towards a combination of constraints and interpreted domains was done in [LM94] which introduces constrained tree automata compatible with AC axioms. Unfortunately these automata can handle only non-linear terms such that all occurrences of non-linear variables occur under the same occurrence of an AC symbol, like in $g(x \cup x \cup a, y \cup y \cup a)$. Many useful specifications (like the *memb* specification) don't fall in this class.

Our contribution. We have extended constrained tree automata techniques to interpreted domains used in automated theorem proving. We have defined a new class of constrained tree automata which has nice properties. This provides a general framework for deciding properties like completeness of definition or ground reducibility. We are able to define new classes of specifications for which these problems are decidable. The proof techniques used in decision of emptiness are new and should be useful in other applications. The flexibility of the tree automata approach allows extensions to other domains (sets for instance) and combination of several domains (natural numbers, sets, multisets,...).

Plan of the paper. First, we recall some basic facts of term algebra (section 1), then we introduce a general class of tree automata enjoying basic properties: reduction of non-determinism and closure under the boolean operations (section 2). We give two specializations of this class, one for multisets (section3), one for natural numbers (section 4), and we prove the decidability of the emptiness of the language accepted by these automata for each case. Finally, we give the applications to inductive theorem proving in section 5. Because of lack of space, proofs are skipped and the reader is referred to the full paper available at `http://www.loria.fr/~lugiez`.

1 Definitions and notations

1.1 Terms

We consider terms built from a denumerable set of variables and a finite set of function symbols $\mathcal{F}$. Each function symbol $f \in \mathcal{F}$ has an arity $n \geq 0$. We assume that there is a symbol $\oplus$ which is *associative and commutative* (AC for short), i.e. $x \oplus y = y \oplus x$ and $x \oplus (y \oplus z) = (x \oplus y) \oplus z$ using infix notation. It is well known that terms can be flattened using rewrite rules $(x \oplus y) \oplus z \to x \oplus (y \oplus z)$ and then dropping parenthesis. From now on, we use flattened terms only, corresponding to the grammar $s, t ::= x \mid f(s_1, \ldots, s_n) \mid t_1 \oplus \ldots \oplus t_p$ where $f \in \mathcal{F}$ has arity n, $f \neq \oplus$ and $p \geq 2$. The equality relation $=$ on these terms is defined by $x = x$, $f(s_1, \ldots, s_n) = g(t_1, \ldots, t_m)$ iff $f = g$, $n = m$, $s_i = t_i$ for $i = 1, \ldots, n$ and $s_1 \oplus \ldots \oplus s_p = t_1 \oplus \ldots \oplus t_q$ iff $p = q$ and there is a permutation σ of $1, \ldots, p$ such that $s_{\sigma(i)} = t_i$ for $i = 1, \ldots, p$. We could have several AC symbols $\oplus_1, \ldots, \oplus_n$ but we use only one for simplicity. To model non-empty multisets, we should assume that $\oplus$ has also arity 1. This adds superfluous complications to the main proof of section 3.2, but it can be easily done. Since this is not an issue, we shall give examples with multisets. We take for granted all classical notions on terms like *ground* terms i.e. terms without variables, *linear* terms i.e. a variable may occur only once, or *non-linear* terms, *substitutions* and *instances* of terms,.... See [DJ90] for details. The set of terms is denoted by $T(\mathcal{F}, \mathcal{X})$ and the set of ground terms by $T(\mathcal{F})$. The notation $\sum_{i=1}^{i=n} s_i$ denotes $s_1 \oplus \ldots \oplus s_n$ and we may write $s \oplus t$ for terms s, t of the form $u_1 \oplus \ldots \oplus u_p$. Similarly, we write ns for $s \oplus \ldots \oplus s$, a sum of n occurrences of s. An important definition is the following one: a term x or $f(s_1, \ldots, s_n)$ is of *kind Free*, a term $t_1 \oplus \ldots \oplus t_p$ is of *kind* $\oplus$. Further on, we shall enrich the structure of terms using *sorts* and other theories like Presburger's arithmetic, i.e. the theory of natural numbers with addition.

1.2 Sufficient completeness

In many automated deduction systems, a function f is defined by a set R of rewrite rules of the form $Cond \Rightarrow l \rightarrow r$, called the *definition* of f. The *constructor-based* restriction states that $l = f(t_1, \ldots, t_n)$ where $f \in D$ with D a new set of function symbols such that $D \cap \mathcal{F} = \emptyset$, $t_i \in T(\mathcal{F}, \mathcal{X})$ for $i = 1, \ldots, n$ and similar restrictions on the conditional part $Cond$. The deduction process used for performing inductive proofs relies on rewriting and the *completeness* of definition is required to ensure properties like refutational completeness. This is defined as follows: a definition of a function $f \in D$ is (operationally [1]) *sufficiently complete* if for each ground term $f(s_1, \ldots, s_n)$ there is a substitution σ and a rule $Cond \Rightarrow l \rightarrow r$ of the definition such that $f(s_1, \ldots, s_n) = l\sigma$ and the condition $Cond\sigma$ holds. For unconditional rules and signature containing no AC constructors, the completeness of definition is a decidable property. For unconditional definitions and signature containing AC constructor, the problem is still open, although the linear case and some non-linear cases have been proved decidable. Our main result yields the decidability of this problem in useful non-linear cases. Our second main result yields the decidability of the problem when definitions involve Presburger's arithmetic. To prove these results we shall set strong restrictions on conditions $Cond$: they must be typing conditions, Presburger's formula or equalities or disequalities between variables.

Another key property in inductive automated theorem proving is *ground reducibility*. Given a rewrite system R, a term t is ground reducible if each ground instance of t can be rewritten (not necessarily at the top as in sufficient completeness). Again this property is decidable for unconditional rewrite systems [Pla85], but undecidable when AC symbols occur [KNRZ91]. In these cases, the property is decidable for left-linear and some restricted non-linear rewrite systems [LM94]. We give new decidable cases of this property.

Both properties are equivalent to tree language inclusion. Let $\mathcal{L}(t \wedge Cond)$ denote the set of ground instances of t satisfying the condition $Cond$ and $\mathcal{L}(C[t \wedge Cond])$ denote the set of terms containing an instance of t satisfying $Cond$. The definition of f is complete iff $\mathcal{L}(f(x_1, \ldots, x_n)) \subseteq_{i \in I} \mathcal{L}(l_i \wedge Cond_i)$ and t is inductively reducible iff $\mathcal{L}(t) \subseteq_{i \in I} \mathcal{L}(C[l_i \wedge Cond_i])$. The rest of the paper is devoted to defining good classes of tree automata accepting these languages.

1.3 Semilinear sets

Our approach strongly relies on arithmetics, like AC unification relies on solving diophantine equations. We use mainly properties of semilinear sets. Let $\mathbb{N}^n$ denote the set of n-tuples of elements of $\mathbb{N}$. A subset L of $\mathbb{N}^n$ is a *linear* set if there exists $a \in \mathbb{N}^n$ and $P = \{p_1, \ldots, p_l\}$ a finite subset of $\mathbb{N}^n$ such that $L = \{x \in \mathbb{N}^n \mid \exists n_1, \ldots, n_l \in \mathbb{N} \textit{ and } x = a + \sum_{i=1}^{i=l} n_i p_i\}$. L is denoted by $L(a, P)$. A *semilinear* set is a finite union of linear sets. Semilinear sets are

[1] semantical completeness is not needed for our purpose and is undecidable

closed under union, intersection and complementation. Moreover for each formula $\varphi(x_1,\ldots,x_n)$ of Presburger's arithmetic with free variables $x_1,\ldots,x_n$, the set of instances of the x_i's which validate φ is a semilinear set of $\mathbb{N}^n$ [GE66].

2 Abstract constrained automata

First, we describe a general class of constrained tree automata enjoying properties shared by the different kinds of automata used in the applications.

2.1 Constraints

Constraints are formulae with free variables in $\mathcal{X}_c \cup \mathcal{Y}_c$ with $\mathcal{X}_c = \{X_1, X_2, \ldots\}$ and $\mathcal{Y}_c = \{Y_1, Y_2, \ldots\}$ two distinct sets of variables. The set of constraints is $\mathcal{C} = \bigcup_{n\geq 0} \mathcal{C}_n$ where $\mathcal{C}_n$ is the set of constraints with free variables in $\{X_1,\ldots,X_n\} \cup \mathcal{Y}_c$. We assume that each $\mathcal{C}_n$ is closed under the boolean connectives $\wedge, \vee, \neg$. A domain $\mathcal{D}$ is used to interpret these constraints and there is a function $h : T(\mathcal{F},\mathcal{X}) \to \mathcal{D}$ to interpret terms in $\mathcal{D}$. The interpretation of a variable $Y \in \mathcal{Y}_c$ is restricted to some subset $\mathcal{D}_Y$ of $\mathcal{D}$. A term $t = f(t_1,\ldots,t_n)$ *satisfies* a constraint $c \in \mathcal{C}_n$ if the formula $c\{X_1 \leftarrow h(t_1),\ldots,X_n \leftarrow h(t_n), Y_1 \leftarrow y_1,\ldots,Y_m \leftarrow y_m\}$ is true for some $y_i \in D_{Y_i}$ for $i = 1,\ldots,m$ when $Y_1,\ldots,Y_m$ are the variables of $\mathcal{Y}_c$ occurring free in c. The satisfiability of c by t is denoted by $t \models c$. A constraint which is always true (resp. false) like $c \vee \neg c$ is denoted by $\top$ (resp. $\perp$).

Example 1. For automata with constraints between brothers [BT92], the set $\mathcal{Y}_c$ is empty and the set of constraints is closed under $\vee, \wedge, \neg$, contains the basic constraints $X_i = X_j$ with $i, j \in \mathbb{N}$, and the domain $\mathcal{D}$ is the set of ground terms with the syntactical equality on terms. For instance, the term $t = f(g(a), g(a))$ satisfies $X_1 = X_2$.

2.2 Constrained tree automata

Constrained tree automata are similar to tree automata but rules contain constraints which restrict the application of the rules, and the AC symbol $\oplus$ operator requires some compatibility conditions.

Definition 1. *A constrained tree automata is a tuple $(Q_{Free}, Q_\oplus, Q_{fin}, \mathcal{F}, R)$ where $\mathcal{F}$ is the signature, Q_{Free} is the set of states of kind Free, $Q_\oplus$ is the set of states of kind $\oplus$, $Q_{Free} \cap Q_\oplus = \emptyset$, $Q_{fin} \subseteq Q_{Free} \cup Q_\oplus$ is the set of final states, R is a set of rules of the form:*

- *$f(q_1,\ldots,q_n) \xrightarrow{c} q$ with f a free symbol of arity $n \geq 0$, and q a state of kind Free, c a constraint of $\mathcal{C}_n$,*
- *$q \to q'$ where q has kind Free and q' has kind $\oplus$or Free.*
- *$q_1 \oplus q_2 \to q_3$ where q_1, q_2, q_3 have kind $\oplus$.*

Moreover, the following consistency conditions hold: if $q_1 \oplus q_2 \rightarrow q_3$ *is in* R*, then* $q_2 \oplus q_1 \rightarrow q_3$ *is in* R*. If* $(q_1 \oplus q_2) \oplus q_3 \rightarrow q_4$ *is in* R*, then* $q_1 \oplus (q_2 \oplus q_3) \rightarrow q_4$ *is in* R *where* $(q \oplus q')$ *denotes any state* q'' *such that* $q \oplus q' \rightarrow q''$ *is in* R*.*

The last conditions ensure that equal terms reach the same states.

Example 2. Let $\mathcal{A} = (\{q_a, q_b, q, q_S\}, \{q_\oplus\}, \{a, b, f, \oplus\}, \{q_S\}, R)$ where $R = \{a \xrightarrow{\top} q_a, b \xrightarrow{\top} q_b, f(\_,\_) \xrightarrow{\top} q, f(q, q_\oplus) \xrightarrow{X_2 = X_1 \oplus Y_q \oplus Y_{q_a}} q_S, \_ \rightarrow q_\oplus, q_\oplus \oplus q_\oplus \rightarrow q_\oplus\}$ where _ stands for q_a, q_b,q or $q_\oplus$.

From now on, $\mathcal{A}$ denotes some constrained tree automaton. We define the reachability relation $\rightarrow_{\mathcal{A}}$ together with an auxiliary relation $\mapsto$.

Definition 2. *A ground term* t *reaches a state* q*, denoted by* $t \rightarrow_{\mathcal{A}} q$ *if* t *and* q *have the same kind and* $t \mapsto q$ *where* $\mapsto$ *is defined by:*

- *if* $q' \rightarrow q \in R$ *and* $t \mapsto q'$ *then* $t \mapsto q$*,*
- *if* $f(q_1, \ldots, q_n) \xrightarrow{c} q \in R$*,* $t_i \mapsto q_i$ *for* $i = 1, \ldots, n$*,* $f(t_1, \ldots, t_n) \models c$ *then* $f(t_1, \ldots, t_n) \mapsto q$*,*
- *if* $q' \oplus q'' \rightarrow q \in R$*,* $s \mapsto q'$*,* $t \mapsto q''$ *then* $s \oplus t \mapsto q$*.*

Example 3. Let $\mathcal{A}$ be the automaton of example 2, and assume that $f(t_1, t_2) \models X_2 = X_1 \oplus Y_q \oplus Y_{q_a}$ iff $t_2 = t_1 \oplus s_q \oplus s_{q_a}$ with $s_{q_a} \rightarrow_{\mathcal{A}} q_a, s_q \rightarrow_{\mathcal{A}} q$. Then $f(f(a, a), f(a, a) \oplus f(b, b) \oplus a) \rightarrow_{\mathcal{A}} q_S$.

We extend the relation to terms on $\mathcal{F} \cup Q_{Free} \cup Q_\oplus$, which allows to write $q_1 \oplus \ldots \oplus q_p \rightarrow_{\mathcal{A}} q$. The definition implies that $t \rightarrow_{\mathcal{A}} q$ if $s = t$ and $s \rightarrow_{\mathcal{A}} q$. A term is *accepted* or *recognized* if $t \rightarrow_{\mathcal{A}} q$ with $q \in Q_{fin}$. The language accepted by a constrained automaton is the set of terms accepted by the automaton. Such languages are called *constrained regular* tree languages. An automaton is *complete* if for each ground term t there is a state q such that $t \rightarrow_{\mathcal{A}} q$. It is *deterministic* if a ground term can reach at most one state.

Example 4. We define well-sorted terms, see [DJ90], from a finite set of sorts $\mathcal{S}$ containing the sort MS for multisets, sort inclusions $\tau \subseteq \tau'$ with $\tau' \neq MS$ and sort declarations $f : \tau_1, \ldots, \tau_n \rightarrow \tau$ with $\tau \neq MS$ if $f \neq \oplus$, and $\oplus : \tau, \tau' \rightarrow MS$ for any $\tau, \tau' \in \mathcal{S}$. Then the set of well-sorted terms of sort τ is a constrained regular tree language.

2.3 Basic properties

The next proposition states the basics properties of constrained tree automata.

Proposition 1. *The following properties holds for constrained tree automata.*

- *For each constrained tree automaton, there exists a complete constrained tree automaton accepting the same language.*
- *For each non-deterministic constrained tree automaton, there exists a deterministic tree automaton accepting the same language.*
- *The class of constrained regular tree language is closed under union, complement and intersection.*

Proof. Similar to the case of usual tree automata.

2.4 Semilinear sets and constrained tree automata

A specific property of constrained automata is that the set of terms reaching a state can be approximated by a semilinear set $\mathcal{L}(q)$ defined as follows.

Definition 3. *Let $\mathcal{A} = (Q_{Free}, Q_{\oplus}, Q_{fin}, \mathcal{F}, R)$ be a constrained automaton, let $q_1^F, \ldots, q_p^F$ be the states of kind Free. The set $\mathcal{L}(q)$ is a subset of $\mathbb{N}^p$ defined by*

- *if q is some q_i^F of kind Free then* $\mathcal{L}(q) = \{(0, \ldots, 0, \underbrace{1}_{i^{th}\ position}, 0 \ldots, 0)\}$
- *if q has kind $\oplus$ then* $L(q) = \{(n_1, \ldots, n_p) \mid \exists k \geq 1,\ q_1 \ldots, q_k\ of\ kind\ Free$
  $s.t.\ q_1 \oplus \ldots \oplus q_k \rightarrow_{\mathcal{A}} q$
  $n_i\ the\ number\ of\ occurrences\ of\ q_i^F\}$

Example 5. Let $\mathcal{A}$ be such that $Q_{Free} = \{q_1, q_2, q_3\}, Q_{\oplus} = \{q_{\oplus}, q'_{\oplus}\}$ and the rules involving $q_{\oplus}$ are $q_1 \rightarrow q_{\oplus}, q_{\oplus} \oplus q_{\oplus} \rightarrow q_{\oplus}, q_2 \rightarrow q'_{\oplus}, q'_{\oplus} \oplus q_{\oplus} \rightarrow q_{\oplus}, q_{\oplus} \oplus q'_{\oplus} \rightarrow q_{\oplus}$ then $\mathcal{L}(q_{\oplus}) = \{(n+1, m, 0) \mid n, m \in \mathbb{N}\}$.

These sets enjoy a nice property, as stated by the following theorem.

Theorem 1. *$\mathcal{L}(q)$ is a effectively computable semilinear set.*

Proof. Use either Parikh's theorem [Par66] or the characterization of flat feature trees using Presburger's formula given by [NP93].

Example 6. The set $\mathcal{L}(q_{\oplus})$ of the previous example is $L(a, \{p_1, p_2\})$ with $a = (1,0,0), p_1 = (1,0,0), p_2 = (0,1,0)$.

3 Equality constraints

We present now our first instance of constrained tree automata: constraints are equality constraints, which allows to use these automata for definitions involving multisets. The proof of the decidability of emptiness of the language accepted by such automata is the most difficult result of the paper.

3.1 Definition and basic properties

Applications leads us to define the basic constraints of $\mathcal{C}_n$ as

$$X_i = \sum_{j \in J} X_j \oplus \sum_{q \in K} Y_q \text{ where } K \subseteq Q_{Free} \cup Q_{\oplus} \text{ and } J \subseteq \{1, \ldots, n\}.$$

Therefore a term t satisfies $X_i = \sum_{j \in J} X_j \oplus \sum_{q \in K} Y_q$ iff $t = f(t_1, \ldots, t_n)$ and $t_i = \sum_{j \in J} t_j \oplus \sum_{q \in K} s_q$ with $s_q \rightarrow_{\mathcal{A}} q$. A first problem arising from this choice of constraints is that the $\rightarrow_{\mathcal{A}}$ relation and the satisfiability relation $\models$ are mutually recursive. Fortunately this recursion is well-founded, which is stated in the next proposition.

Proposition 2. *For each ground term t and state q it is decidable if $t \rightarrow_{\mathcal{A}} q$.*

A second problem arising from this definition of constraints is that the reduction of non-determinism yields an automaton where states are set of states of the non-deterministic automaton. But the variables Y_q's occurring in the constraints of the deterministic automaton still refer to states of the initial non-deterministic automaton. Fortunately, we can replace a constraint referring to old states by a disjunction of constraints referring to new states according to the following proposition.

Proposition 3. *Let $\mathcal{A}$ be a non-deterministic automaton, and let $\mathcal{A}_D$ be the deterministic automaton computed from $\mathcal{A}$. For each q state of $\mathcal{A}$, let Q_q be the set of states of $\mathcal{A}_D$ containing q. Then t satisfies $X_i = \sum_{j \in J} X_j \oplus \sum_{q \in K} Y_q$ iff t satisfies $X_i = \sum_{j \in J} X_j \oplus \sum_{\hat{q}' \in Q_q, q \in K} Y_{\hat{q}'}$ for some choice of $\hat{q}' \in Q_q$.*

Therefore the reduction of non-determinism is completed by an updating step which replaces constraints involving the original states by disjunctions of constraints involving the new states.

3.2 The emptiness decision algorithm

The most important and difficult result for tree automata with equality constraints is the following one.

Theorem 2. *Let $\mathcal{A}$ be a tree automata with equality constraints, then it is decidable if $\mathcal{L}(\mathcal{A}) = \emptyset$*

The proof is too complex to be given here and we simply sketch the main ideas. Without loss of generality, we can assume that we have a deterministic complete automaton.

The principle of the marking algorithm. The algorithm that we use for deciding emptiness is a variant of classical marking algorithms for tree automata. A state q is marked when we have computed enough terms reaching q. For classical tree automata, enough means one term, but this is not the case here. To reach q' using the rule $f(q, q) \xrightarrow{X_1 \neq X_2} q'$ we must have two distinct terms reaching q. The problem is to bound the number of terms required to mark a state. To get this bound we must solve the equality constraints occurring in the rules $f(q_1, \ldots, q_n) \xrightarrow{c} q$ which can't be done directly. As in AC unification, we transform constraint solving on terms into solving equations and disequations in $\mathbb{N}$.

Abstracting terms using arithmetics. The terms of kind $Free$ can be enumerated as $e_1, e_2, \ldots$ and any term can be written $\sum_i \lambda_i e_i$, a sum of terms e_i of kind $Free$ with $\lambda_i \in \mathbb{N}$. For instance if the enumeration is $a, b, g(a), g(b), g(a \oplus b), \ldots$ the term of component $0, 2, 0, 1, 0, 0 \ldots$ is $2b \oplus g(b)$ and the term of component $1, 0, 0, \ldots$ is a. To have a finite sum we abstract each e_i by the state reached by e_i in $\mathcal{A}$. Therefore each term is abstracted by a sum $\alpha^1.q_1^F + \ldots + \alpha^p.q_p^F$, i.e. by a p-tuple of natural numbers where p is the number of states of sort $Free$ in $\mathcal{A}$.

Solving abstracted constraints To apply a constrained rule, one must require that there are terms reaching the right states and that these terms satisfy some equalities and disequalities. For instance, $f(q_1, q_2) \xrightarrow{X_1=X_2} q$ is applicable iff there are terms X_1, X_2 such that $X_1 = X_2 \wedge X_1 \rightarrow_{\mathcal{A}} q_1 \wedge X_2 \rightarrow_{\mathcal{A}} q_2$. We replace this constraint by the arithmetical constraint $\mathcal{X}_1 = \mathcal{X}_2 \wedge \mathcal{X}_1 \in \mathcal{L}(q_1) \wedge \mathcal{X}_2 \in \mathcal{L}(q_2)$ where the $\mathcal{X}_i$'s are the p-tuples of integers abstracting the X_i's. By theorem 1, this is a Presburger's formula and the set of solutions is computable. But a solution of arithmetical constraint not necessarily yields a solution of the relevant term constraint. For instance, an arithmetical solution $(\mathcal{X}_1, \mathcal{X}_2) = (1,1)q_1^F + (1,1)q_2^F$ yields a term solution (X_1, X_2) only if there is at least one term reaching q_1^F and one term reaching q_2^F. A detailed study of the abstraction of terms allows to compute the minimal number required for each state, yielding a bound B suitable for all states and constraints. This study extensively uses semilinear sets [GE66] and the termination of the computation relies on Dickson's lemma.

The marking algorithm At each iteration, for each state q the algorithm computes $\#(q)$ the number of terms (up to the bound B) reaching q. Initially $\#(q) = 0$ for each state. The iteration stops either when we get $\#(q) > 0$ for a final state q or when no $\#(q)$ increases for any q. The key property for stating the correctness of the algorithm is that if B terms reach a state $q_i, i \in \{1, \dots, n\}$ occurring in a rule $f(q_1, \dots, q_n) \xrightarrow{c} q$, then the existence of one term reaching q with this rule implies that are at least B terms reaching q using this rule (this is similar to the proof in [BT92]) .

4 Automata with arithmetical constraints

Our second instance of constrained tree automata involves arithmetical constraints. In this section we consider well-sorted terms, see [DJ90], with two distinguished sorts Nat and MS. Conditions for MS are given in example 4. To construct terms of Nat, we have constructors $0 : Nat, s : Nat \rightarrow Nat, + : Nat, Nat \rightarrow Nat$. Moreover we prevent interleaving of terms of sort Nat and other sorts by imposing that there is no symbol $f : \tau_1, \dots, \tau_n \rightarrow Nat$ except $0, s, +$. For instance a symbol $cons : Nat, List \rightarrow List$ is allowed but not a symbol $remainder : Nat, Nat \rightarrow Nat$. This condition may seem very restrictive, but the reader should remind that we describe *constructor* terms here. In applications, we can have a *defined* function $remainder : Nat, Nat \rightarrow Nat$. We assume an interpretation function $IntNat$ to interpret terms of sort Nat in expressions with natural numbers. For instance, $IntNat(x + (s(0) + x)) = 2x + 1$.

Tree automata *with arithmetical constraints* contains a set Q_{Nat} of states of kind Nat besides Q_{Free} and $Q_{\oplus}$. Constraints are Presburger's arithmetic formulae and for each $f(q_1, \dots, q_n) \xrightarrow{c} q \in R$, the free variables of c are in $X_1, \dots, X_n$. Moreover, X_i may occur in c iff $q_i \in Q_{Nat}$. If $f = 0, s, +$ then c is built only from basic constraints $X_i \in L$ with L a semilinear set. We also require that if $f(q_1, \dots, q_n) \xrightarrow{c} q$ is a rule such that $q \in Q_{Nat}$ then $f = 0, s, +$

and all q_i's are in Q_{Nat}. A term $f(t_1,\ldots,t_n) \models c(X_{i_1},\ldots,X_{i_p})$ iff $c((X_{i_1} \leftarrow IntNat(t_{i_1}),\ldots,X_{i_p} \leftarrow IntNat(t_{i_p})))$ is true in $\mathbb{N}$.

Example 7. If $div : Nat, Nat \to Bool$, an automaton may contain the rule $div(q_{Nat}, q_{Nat}) \xrightarrow{\exists x,y\ X_1=x \wedge X_2=x+y} q_{div}$

The next result is needed in the emptiness decision algorithm.

Proposition 4. *For each $q \in Q_{Nat}$, the set $\{IntNat(t) \mid t \to_{\mathcal{A}} q\}$ is an effectively computable semilinear set.*

The algorithm to decide the emptiness of the language recognized by a constrained tree automaton is a simple adaptation of the classical marking algorithm, with the help of a decision procedure for Presburger's arithmetic to decide constraints.

Theorem 3. *It is decidable if the language accepted by a constrained tree automaton with arithmetical constraints is empty.*

Applications often requires *compatible* tree automata, i.e $s = t$ and $s \to_{\mathcal{A}} q$ implies $t \to_{\mathcal{A}} q$. Given a constrained tree automaton $\mathcal{A}$, we can compute an compatible tree automaton $\mathcal{A}_D$, i.e. $s \in \mathcal{L}(\mathcal{A})$ iff $s' \in \mathcal{L}(\mathcal{A}_D)$ for any s' such that $s' = s$.

A natural extension would be to allow equality constraints on rules involving $0, s, +$. The next example shows that the set of terms reaching $q \in Q_{Nat}$ is not necessarily semilinear, therefore the previous algorithm no longer works. Let $q_0, q_{pow(2)} \in Q_{Nat}$, and let the corresponding rules be $0 \xrightarrow{\top} q_0$, $s(q_0) \xrightarrow{\top} q_{pow(2)}$, $q_{pow(2)} + q_{pow(2)} \xrightarrow{X_1=X_2} q_{pow(2)}$. Then the set of interpretation of terms reaching $q_{pow(2)}$ is $2^0, 2^1, 2^2, \ldots$ which is not semilinear. Therefore constraints can't be solved using the decision procedure of Presburger's arithmetic.

5 Application to inductive theorem proving

The following theorem is a direct consequence of previous results.

Theorem 4. *The completeness of a constructor-based definition of a function f can be decided if for each rule $(Cond \Rightarrow l \to r)$ the set $\mathcal{L}(l \wedge Cond)$ is accepted by a constrained tree automaton with equality constraints (resp. arithmetical constraints)*[2].

To characterize syntactically the functions which are accepted by constrained automata results in complex or incomplete definitions. Roughly speaking, it covers non-linearity restricted to brother subterms and conditions are typing conditions, Presburger's formulae or equalities or disequalities on variables. This class strictly extends previously known classes except [LM94] (for instance all cases given in [KS96] fall in the class) and covers many useful definitions. We present here two significant examples. Both examples contain conditions involving typing condition, disequalities or interpreted predicates.

[2] in this case, f can have type $f : \tau_1, \ldots, \tau_n \to Nat$

Example 8. Let us consider the definition of *memb* given in the introduction for membership in non-empty multisets (replace $\{x\}$ by $\oplus(x)$ and $\cup$ by $\oplus$). Then the sets $\mathcal{L}(l_i \wedge Cond_i)$ for each rule $Cond_i \Rightarrow l_i \rightarrow r_i$ of the specification of *memb* is accepted by a constrained tree automaton, therefore the completeness of the definition can be checked automatically.

The second example is a definition involving arithmetics.

Example 9. Let us consider the following definition of *div*:

$$x_1 = 0 \Rightarrow div(x_1, y_1) \rightarrow \bot$$
$$x_2 > 0 \wedge y_2 = 0 \Rightarrow div(x_2, y_2) \rightarrow true$$
$$x_3 > 0 \Rightarrow div(x_3, x_3 + y_3) \rightarrow div(x_3, y_3)$$
$$y_4 > 0 \wedge x_4 > y_4 \Rightarrow div(x_4, y_4) \rightarrow false$$

Again the set of constrained ground instances of each left-hand side is accepted by a automaton with arithmetical constraints, therefore the completeness of the definition of *div* can be checked automatically using constrained tree automata.

Another key property needed in inductive theorem proving is ground reducibility, which we use to design test-sets in the Spike system.

Theorem 5. *The ground reducibility of a term t with respect to a rewrite system $Cond_i \Rightarrow l_i \rightarrow r_i$ is decidable if $\mathcal{L}(t)$ and $\mathcal{L}(C[l_i \wedge Cond_i])$ are accepted by a tree automaton with equality constraints (resp. arithmetical constraints).*

The theorems given in this section provide algorithms to deal with many specifications arising in practice. Moreover we can easily extend our results by combining these results together (handling specifications using multisets and natural numbers, several kinds of multisets,...).

The complexity of our approach is high (even for classical tree automata, the decision problems involved are EXPTIME-complete [Sei90]) but the specifications arising in practice are small and the constraints are quite simple. Moreover the results of [KNRZ91] show that the problem has a high complexity even for syntactical terms. They also show that that ground reducibility is undecidable for AC symbols, which limits what we can expect (but this doesn't prevent from looking for larger decidable classes).

6 Conclusion

We have presented a new class of tree automata which can deal with several interpreted domains and which extends previous works on constrained tree automata and automata dealing with AC axioms. The proof used for the decision of emptiness in the multiset case is new and may have other applications. This approach is complementary of the approach in [BJ97] which deals with specifications involving equations between constructors but doesn't handle the domains that we consider. Future work will be to embed the previous approach of [LM94] in our class and to look for efficient implementation of tree automata algorithms with AC symbols similar to [Mon97].

References

[BJ97] A. Bouhoula, J.-P. Jouannaud. Automata-driven automated induction. In *Proc. 12th IEEE Symp. on LICS*, p. 14–25. IEEE Comp. Soc. Press, 1997.

[BM88] R. S. Boyer and J. S. Moore. *A Computational Logic Handbook*. Academic Press inc., Boston, 1988.

[BR95] A. Bouhoula, M. Rusinowitch. Implicit induction in conditional theories. *J. of Automated Reasoning*, 14(2):189–235, 1995.

[BT92] B. Bogaert, S. Tison. Equality and disequality constraints on direct subterms in tree automata. In *Proc. of the 9th STACS*, vol. 577 of *LNCS*, p. 161–172, 1992.

[CCC+94] A.C. Caron, H. Comon, J.L. Coquidé, M. Dauchet, F. Jacquemard. Pumping, cleaning and symbolic constraints solving. In *Proc. 21st ICALP, Jerusalem (Israel)*, p. 436–449, 1994.

[Cou89] B. Courcelle. *On Recognizable Sets and Tree Automata*, in *Resolution of Equations in Algebraic Structures*. Academic Press, M. Nivat and Ait-Kaci editors, 1989.

[DACJL95] M. Dauchet, Caron A.-C., Coquidé J.-L. Reduction properties and automata with constraints. *J. of Symb. Comp.*, 20:215–233, 1995.

[DJ90] N. Dershowitz, J.-P. Jouannaud. *Handbook of Theoretical Computer Science*, vol. B, chapter 6: Rewrite Systems, p. 244–320. Elsevier Science Publishers B. V. (North-Holland), 1990.

[GE66] S. Ginsburg, E.H.Spanier. Semigroups, Presburger Formulas, and Languages. *Pacific J. Math.*, 16:285–296, 1966.

[KNRZ91] D. Kapur, P. Narendran, D. J. Rosenkrantz, H. Zhang. Sufficient completeness, ground-reducibility and their complexity. *Acta Informatica*, 28:311–350, 1991.

[KS96] D. Kapur, M. Subramaniam. New uses of linear arithmetic in automated theorem proving by induction. *J. of Automated Reasoning*, 16(1-2):39–78, March 1996.

[KZ88] D. Kapur, H. Zhang. RRL: A rewrite rule laboratory. In *Proc. 9th CADE, Argonne (Ill., USA)*, vol. 310 of LNCS, p 768–769. Springer-Verlag, 1988.

[LM94] D. Lugiez, J.-L. Moysset. Tree automata help one to solve equational formulae in AC-theories. *J. of Symb. Comp.*, 18(4):297–318, 1994.

[Mon97] B. Monate. Automates de forme normale et reductibilite inductive. Tech. Rep., LRI, Univ. Paris Sud, Bat 490, 91405 ORSAY, FRANCE, 1997.

[NP93] J. Niehren, A. Podelski. Feature automata and recognizable sets of feature trees. In *Proc. TAPSOFT'93*, vol. 668 of *LNCS*, p. 356–375, 1993.

[Par66] R.J. Parikh. On context-free languages. *J. of the ACM*, 13:570–581, 1966.

[Pla85] D. Plaisted. Semantic confluence and completion method. *Information and Control*, 65:182–215, 1985.

[Sei90] H. Seidl. Deciding equivalence of finite tree automata. *SIAM J. Comput.*, 19, 1990.

Locally Periodic Infinite Words and a Chaotic Behaviour [1]

Juhani Karhumäki, Arto Lepistö, and Wojciech Plandowski[2]

Department of Mathematics, University of Turku,
20014 Turku, Finland, and
Turku Centre for Computer Science

Abstract. We call a one-way infinite word w over a finite alphabet (ρ,p)-repetitive if all long enough prefixes of w contain as a suffix a repetition of order ρ of a word of length at most p. We show that each $(2,4)$-repetitive word is ultimately periodic, as well as that there exist nondenumerably many, and hence also nonultimately periodic, $(2,5)$-repetitive words. Further we characterize nonultimately periodic $(2,5)$-repetitive words both structurally and algebraically.

1 Introduction

One of the fundamental topics in mathematical research is to search for connections between local and global regularities. We consider such a problem in connection with infinite words, cf. [BePe]. The regularity is specified as a periodicity.

Our research is motivated by a remarkable result of Mignosi, Restivo and Salemi (cf. [MRS]) where they characterized one-way infinite ultimately periodic words: an infinite word w is ultimately periodic if and only if any long enough prefix of w contains as a suffix a repetition of order φ^2, i.e. a suffix of the form v^k , $v \neq 1$, k rational and $k > \varphi^2$ with φ being the golden ratio $(1+\sqrt{5})/2$. Moreover, they showed that the bound φ^2 is optimal meaning that it cannot be replaced by any smaller number without destroying the equivalence.

As a consequence any infinite word such that all except finitely many of its prefixes contain a cube at the end is ultimately periodic, while there exists a nonultimately periodic infinite word such that all except finitely many of its prefixes contain a square at the end. The famous Fibonacci word works as an example here. Now, let a "local regularity" mean that each long enough prefix of an infinite word contains as a suffix a repetition of a certain order and let the "global regularity" mean that the word is ultimately periodic. Then we have a nontrivial connections: the local regularity defined by cubes implies the global regularity, but that defined by squares does not do so!

Our goal here is to establish a sharpening of the above by taking into considerations also the lengths of words in the repetitions. We prove that a local

[1] Supported by Academy of Finland under the grant 14047

[2] On leave from Instytut Informatyki UW, Banacha 2, 02-047 Warszawa, Poland.

regularity defined by squares of words of length less than or equal to 4 implies global regularity. On the other hand, a local regularity defined using squares of words of greater length does not do so. In order to formalize this we say that an infinite word w over a finite alphabet is *(ρ, p)-repetitive*, where $\rho > 1$ is a real number and p is a positive integer, if all except finitely many prefixes of w contain as a suffix a repetition of order ρ of a word of length at most p, i.e. a word of the form v^k with $k \geq \rho$, k rational and $|v| \leq p$.

With the above notions we show that any $(2,4)$-repetitive word is ultimately periodic, while $(2,5)$-repetitive words need not be so. In fact, there exist nondenumerably many $(2,5)$-repetitive words, and we characterize all such nonultimately periodic binary words both structurally and algebraically. The former characterization tells how they can be built from simple blocks of words, while the latter tells how they are obtained using the Fibonacci morphism.

We also show that our result is optimal with respect to both of the parameters. Indeed, if ρ is fixed to be 2, then as we already said, the smallest value of p which does not require a (ρ, p)-repetitive word to be ultimately periodic is $p = 5$. Also if we fix $p = 5$, then the largest ρ which does not make an (ρ, p)-repetitive word ultimately periodic is $\rho = 2$. In other words, for any real $\rho' > 2$, each $(\rho', 5)$-repetitive word is necessarily ultimately periodic.

The paper is organized as follows. In Section 2 we fix our notation and introduce necessary notions. In Section 3 we prove a reduction result allowing us to restrict only to binary alphabets. Next, in Section 4, we prove that all $(2,4)$-repetitive words are ultimately periodic with a period not longer than 4. Section 5 is devoted to provide the description of the structure of nonultimately periodic $(2,5)$-repetitive words. Next, in Section 6, we show the optimality of our result also with respect to the first parameter, i.e. we show that there are no $(\rho, 5)$-repetitive nonultimately periodic words for ρ real number, $\rho > 2$. Finally, in Section 7, we note that our main result can be viewed, as a simple but illustrative example of a border between chaotic and predictable behaviour of infinite processes.

Some proofs are not presented here or are only partially presented here, for a full version we refer to [KLP].

2 Preliminaries

In this section we define formally our basic notions as well as fix the terminology, if necessary cf. [Lo] and [CK].

We consider *finite* and *one-way infinite words* over a finite alphabet A. The sets of such words are denoted by A^* and A^ω, respectively. A *factor* of a word is any consecutive sequence of its symbols. By $\mathrm{Pref}_k(w)$ we mean a prefix of w of length k. For a rational number $k \geq 1$, we say that a word w is a *kth power* if there exists a word v such that $w = v^k$, where v^k denotes the word $v'v''$ with $v' = v^{\lfloor k \rfloor}$ and $v'' = \mathrm{Pref}_{|v|(k-\lfloor k \rfloor)}v = \mathrm{Pref}_{(|w|-\lfloor k \rfloor |v|)}v$. Next we say that w contains a *repetition of order* $\rho \geq 1$ if it contains as a factor a kth power with $k \geq \rho$. Note that here ρ is allowed to be any real number ≥ 1.

Next we define our central notions. Let $\rho \geq 1$ be a real number and $p \geq 1$ an integer. We say that an infinite word w is *(ρ, p)-repetitive* if there exists an integer n_0 such that each prefix of w of length at least n_0 ends with a repetition of order ρ of a word of length at most p. Formally, the above means that, for each $n \geq n_0$, there exists a $k \geq \rho$ and words u and v, with $|v| \leq p$, such that

$$\mathrm{Pref}_n(w) = uv^k.$$

It is clear that (ρ, p)-repetitivity implies (ρ, p')-repetitivity for any $p' \geq p$ and (ρ', p)-repetitivity for any $\rho' \leq \rho$. Note that the above definition can be extended to the case where $p = \infty$. Our goal is to look for connections between (ρ, p)-repetitive and *ultimately periodic* words, i.e. words which are of the form uv^ω for some finite words u and v. If $w = uv^\omega$ we say that $|u|$ is a *threshold* and $|v|$ a *period* of w, and that v is a *word period* of w.

As another important notion we need that of the *Fibonacci morphism* τ, as well as its complementary version $\overline{\tau}$. These are morphisms from $A^* = \{a, b\}^*$ into itself defined by

$$\tau : \begin{array}{l} a \mapsto ab \\ b \mapsto a \end{array} \quad , \quad \overline{\tau} : \begin{array}{l} a \mapsto b \\ b \mapsto ba. \end{array}$$

Recall that the *Fibonacci word*

$$\alpha_F = \lim_{n \to \infty} \tau^n(a) \tag{1}$$

is the only fixed point (in A^ω) of τ.

In our terminology a remarkable result of Mignosi, Restivo and Salemi, cf. [MRS], can be stated as

Theorem 2.1. *An infinite word is ultimately periodic if and only if it is (φ^2, ∞)-repetitive, where $\varphi = (1 + \sqrt{5})/2$.*

As also shown in [MRS] the number φ, i.e. the number of *golden ratio*, plays an important role here. Indeed, Theorem 2.1 is optimal:

Theorem 2.2. *The infinite Fibonacci word (1) is (k, ∞)-repetitive for any $k < \varphi^2$, but not ultimately periodic.*

Our goal is to prove a similar result where the parameter p is finite.

3 A reduction to a binary alphabet

In this section we prove a reduction result which allows us to restrict ourselves to a binary alphabet.

Theorem 3.1. *For each nonultimately periodic (ρ, p)-repetitive word we can construct a nonultimately periodic (ρ, p)-repetitive word over a binary alphabet.*

Proof Let w be a (ρ, p)-repetitive word over an alphabet A such that it is not ultimately periodic. Let σ be a new letter, and define, for each $a \in A$, morphisms

$$h_a : A^* \to \{a, \sigma\}^*, \begin{cases} x \mapsto x, & \text{if } x = a; \\ x \mapsto \sigma, & \text{otherwise.} \end{cases}$$

We claim that at least one of the words $h_a(w)$ is (ρ, p)-repetitive and not ultimately periodic.

Clearly, as morphic images of a (ρ, p)-repetitive word by strictly alphabetic morphisms, all words $h_a(w)$ are (ρ, p)-repetitive as well. Suppose on the contrary that all of these words are ultimately periodic, say with a common period q (as a multiple of periods of words $h_a(w)$) and a common threshold t (as a maximum of thresholds of $h_a(w)$). Then, by the definition of h_a, the positions i of w, with $i \geq t$, such that they contain a letter a are located periodically in w with a period q. But this is true for all letters of A, and therefore w is ultimately periodic with threshold t and a period q. This contradiction proves our theorem. □

The importance of the above theorem is that now we can consider, without loss of generality, only words over a binary alphabet, say $A = \{a, b\}$. Indeed, for a fixed value of ρ or p, if there exist at all nonultimately periodic (ρ, p)-repetitive words, then there exists such a word over A. Consequently, to determine the smallest p for a fixed ρ, or the largest ρ for a fixed p, such that the (ρ, p)-repetitiveness does not require the word to be ultimately periodic, it is enough to study only binary words.

In the case where $\rho = 2$ and $p = 5$, which is the most important in our considerations, we can strengthen Theorem 3.1 to the following form, the proof can be found in [KLP].

Theorem 3.2. *Each nonultimately periodic* $(2, 5)$*-repetitive infinite word is in the form* vu *with* v *in* A^* *and* u *infinite and binary.*

4 (2,4)-repetitive words

In this section we consider $(2, 4)$-repetitive words, i.e. words whose all but finitely many prefixes end with a square of a word of length at most 4. To simplify our presentation we fix some terminology. In what follows we consider only those *finite words which contain as a suffix a square of a word of length at most* 4. Such words are called *legal.* We write

$$u \xrightarrow{c} v, \text{ with } u, v \in A^*, c \in A,$$

to denote that adding a letter c to a legal word containing u as a suffix leads to a legal word containing v as a suffix. Further if a letter c cannot be added preserving the legality we write

$$u \xrightarrow{c} \text{not possible.}$$

In order to define our third notation we agree that when we write "α" alone it means either of the letters of A, i.e. $\alpha = a$ or $\alpha = b$, and that when we write "α, β" together it means two distinct letters of A, i.e. either "$\alpha = a$ and $\beta = b$" or "$\alpha = b$ and $\beta = a$". With this convention we write

$$u \xrightarrow{*} S, \text{ with } u \in A^*, S \subseteq \{\alpha, \beta\}^*,$$

to denote that any infinite extension of a legal word containing u as a suffix leads to a periodic word, where the period is from the set S.

Using these notations we prove:

Theorem 4.1. *Each* $(2,4)$*-repetitive word is ultimately periodic.*

Proof By Theorem 3.1 it is enough to consider words over a binary alphabet $A = \{a, b\}$. We analyse how a given legal word u, i.e. a word containing as a suffix a square of a word of length at most 4, can be extended to a legal word. This is done in 5 cases depending on the suffix s of u of length 4. These 5 cases covers all possible suffixes of length 4 for a legal word.

Case I. $s = a^4$. Now the b-continuation does not produce a legal word and for the a-continuation we have

$$a^4 \xrightarrow{*} a^4,$$

which implies, in our earlier notations, that

$$a^4 \xrightarrow{*} \{\alpha\}.$$

Case II. $s = abab$. We construct the graph of Fig. 1 showing all possible extensions of the considered word u. A path in this graph may

- terminate to state $\{\alpha\}$ meaning that the word u extends to an ultimately periodic word with the word period α;
- terminate to the state "not possible" meaning that the extensions of u are finite; or
- run forever through the loop labelled by ab meaning that the word u extends to an ultimately periodic word with the word period ab.

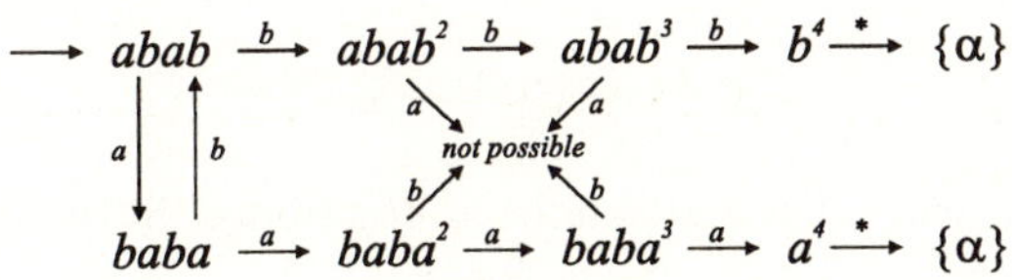

Fig. 1. Case $s = abab$

Consequently, we have

$$abab \xrightarrow{*} \{\alpha, \alpha\beta\}.$$

Note that an important feature of the graph of Fig. 1 is that it does not contain intersecting loops - a property which guaranties the ultimate periodicity!

Details of the other three cases $s = aabb$, $s = abba$ and $s = aaab$, which are similar to the previous cases, are not shown here because of lack of space. □

It is worth noticing that the proof of Theorem 4.1 (cf. [KLP]) says a bit more than stated, namely that all $(2,4)$-repetitive words are ultimately periodic with periods of length at most 4, i.e. with word periods from the set

$$\{\alpha, \alpha\beta, \alpha^2\beta, \alpha^2\beta^2, \alpha^3\beta\}.$$

In the next section we shall see that the situation changes drastically when the length of the repeated word is increased to 5.

5 (2,5)-repetitive words

In this section we consider $(2,5)$-repetitive words, and show contrary to Theorem 4.1 that they need not be ultimately periodic. Moreover, we give two characterizations of such words.

In this section a *legal* word means a word containing as a suffix a square of a word of length at most 5. As in the previous section we can assume also now that words are over a binary alphabet $A = \{a, b\}$. We need the following four lemmas, the proofs of which can be found in [KLP].

Lemma 5.1. *Each $(2,5)$-repetitive word $w \in A^\omega$ containing infinitely many occurrences of a factor ccc, with $c \in A$, is ultimately periodic.*

Lemma 5.2. *Each $(2,5)$-repetitive word $w \in A^\omega$ containing infinitely many occurrences of a factor $(\alpha\beta)^3$, with $\alpha, \beta \in A$, $\alpha \neq \beta$, is ultimately periodic.*

Lemma 5.3. *Let $w \in A^\omega$ be a $(2,5)$-repetitive word which is not ultimately periodic, $B=\{a, ab\}$ and $C = \{b, ba\}$. Then we can write $w = uv$, where $u \in A^*$ and*

$$v \in B^\omega \setminus A^*[a^3 + (ab)^3]A^\omega$$

or

$$v \in C^\omega \setminus A^*[b^3 + (ba)^3]A^\omega.$$

It is worth noticing that the condition describing the structure of the word v in Lemma 5.3 can be written in the form

$$v \in (\alpha\alpha\beta(1 + \alpha\beta))^\omega,$$

where $\{\alpha, \beta\} = \{a, b\}$.

Next lemma is crucial for our second characterization of $(2,5)$-repetitive words.

Lemma 5.4. *Let $v \in A^\omega$. Then v consists of only consecutive a- and ab-blocks such that a-blocks cannot appear twice consecutively and ab-blocks cannot appear three times consecutively if and only if*

$$\exists v' \in A^\omega : v = \tau^3(v').$$

Moreover, the sequence of lengths of consecutive blocks in v is ultimately periodic if and only if v' is ultimately periodic.

Now we are ready for our characterization of nonultimately periodic binary $(2,5)$-repetitive words.

Theorem 5.5. *Let $w \in A^\omega$. Then the following conditions are equivalent:*

(i) w is $(2,5)$-repetitive word without being ultimately periodic;

(ii) w has a suffix which consists of only consecutive α- and $\alpha\beta$-blocks such that the α-block cannot appear twice consecutively and $\alpha\beta$-block cannot appear three times consecutively and the lengths of blocks do not form an ultimately periodic sequence;

(iii) there exist words $u \in A^*, v \in A^\omega$ such that v is not ultimately periodic and $w = u\tau^3(v)$ or $w = u\overline{\tau}^3(v)$.

Proof First, the equivalence between the last two conditions follows from Lemma 5.4 and its symmetric formulation for b- and ba-blocks and the morphism $\overline{\tau}$.

The equivalence between the first two conditions is shown as follows. By Lemma 5.3 we conclude that (i) implies the first part of (ii). In order to prove that the latter part of (ii) also holds we assume that the lengths of blocks does form an ultimately periodic sequence. On the other hand, any word obtained from an ultimately periodic word by replacing letters with words is also ultimately periodic, so also w is ultimately periodic. A contradiction, so also the lengths of blocks have to form a nonultimately periodic sequence.

Now, if the second condition holds, then $w = uv$, where $u \in A^*$ and

$$v \in [B^\omega \setminus A^*(a^3 + (ab)^3)A^\omega] \cup [C^\omega \setminus A^*(b^3 + (ba)^3)A^\omega],$$

because a- and ab-blocks both have an a as a prefix. So, to prove the implication to the other direction we need to consider word v.

Let $B = \{a, ab\}$ and $t \in B^6 \setminus B^*[a^2 + (ab)^3]B^*$. All possible values of t are listed in Table 1. Here we use periods as separators for a- and ab-blocks. We also search for squares with a period less than or equal to 5, for all prefixes of t ending at a letter inside the last a- or ab-block.

As shown in Table 1 using upper- and underlinings the required squares can always be found. Consequently w is $(2,5)$-repetitive. Because $v \in B^\omega \cup C^\omega$ there exists a word $v' \in A^\omega$ such that

$$\tau(v') = v \quad \text{or} \quad \overline{\tau}(v') = v.$$

Table 1. Legality of words t

$$a.ab.\overline{a.ab.}\,\overline{\underline{a.}\,\underline{a}b} \quad a.ab.a.a\overline{b.a}\,\overline{b.a} \quad a.ab.\overline{ab.a.}\,\overline{ab.a}$$

$$a.ab.\underline{ab.a.}\,\underline{\overline{ab.}\,\overline{a}}\overline{b} \quad ab.a.\overline{ab.a.}\,\overline{ab.a} \quad ab.a.\underline{ab.a.}\,\underline{\overline{ab.}\,\overline{a}}\overline{b}$$

$$\overline{ab.a.ab.}\,\overline{ab.\underline{a.}\,\underline{a}b} \quad ab.ab.\overline{a.ab.}\,\overline{\underline{a.}\,\underline{a}b} \quad ab.ab.a.a\overline{b.a}\,\overline{b.a}$$

Furthermore, replacing in v' a's and b's by 2's and 1's, respectively, yields the sequence of lengths of blocks in v. Thus, this sequence of lengths of blocks is ultimately periodic if and only if v' is ultimately periodic. Now, because for the Fibonacci morphism a word is ultimately periodic if its image is ultimately periodic, we conclude that v cannot be ultimately periodic if v' is nonultimately periodic. This completes the proof. □

Theorem 5.5 has an immediate consequence.

Corollary 5.6. *There exist nondenumerably many* $(2,5)$*-repetitive words.*

Note that our above characterization of nonultimately periodic binary $(2,5)$-repetitive words does give, a characterization due to Theorem 3.2 for such words in an arbitrary alphabet, as well.

We finish this section by observing that our condition (ii) can be formalized in an equivalent form:

(ii′) w has a suffix which is built from $\alpha^2\beta$- and $\alpha^2\beta\alpha\beta$-blocks with $\alpha \neq \beta$ and such that the lengths of blocks does not form an ultimately periodic sequence.

6 Optimality

In this section we show that our result is optimal in the sense that each (ρ, p)-repetitive word with

$$(1) \qquad \rho > 2 \quad \text{and} \quad p = 5$$

or,

$$(2) \qquad \rho = 2 \quad \text{and} \quad p = 4$$

is ultimately periodic, while, as we saw, this is not true for $(2,5)$-repetitive words. Indeed, the latter case was proved in Section 4, and the former is proved in the next theorem.

Theorem 6.1. *Each* $(\rho, 5)$*-repetitive word with* $\rho > 2$ *is ultimately periodic.*

Proof Assume that w is $(2+\varepsilon, 5)$-repetitive. Then obviously, this word is also $(2,5)$-repetitive, and therefore the previous theorem and symmetry guarantee that it is sufficient to study how any word $t \in B^6 \setminus B^*[a^2 + (ab)^3]B^*$ can be extended with blocks a and ab such that the requirement of the legality is not violated. Again, by Theorem 5.5 and its proof, we conclude that all such ways to extend t can be found by considering which words in $B^6 \setminus B^*[a^2 + (ab)^3]B^*$ are suffixes of ta and tab. Thus we obtain the graph presented in Fig. 2. Let u and v be as in Theorem 5.5. Now, because the word $(aba)^2(ab)^2$ does not have a suffix being a repetition of order $2 + \varepsilon$ of a word of length less than 6, we conclude that any path corresponding to v could visit the node labelled by $(aba)^2(ab)^2$ only finitely many times. Thus, the word v, and so also w, is ultimately periodic with word period $abaab$ or aba. □

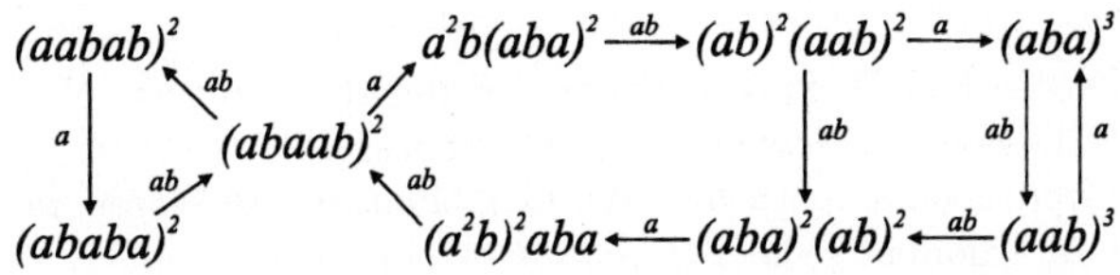

Fig. 2. Extensions of t's preserving the legality

7 Concluding remarks

We have established, in a very simple setting of words, a strict borderline where the amount of a local regularity stops to imply a global regularity. More formally, we proved that each infinite word w which satisfies a local regularity condition stating "any prefix of w contains as a suffix a repetition of order $\rho = 2$ of a word of length at most $p = 4$", is globally regular in the sense of being ultimately periodic. Similarly, if the local regularity is defined by the values $\rho > 2$ and $p = 5$, then the global regularity is forced, but this does not hold for the values $\rho = 2$ and $p = 5$. Indeed, there exist nondenumerably many words which are in the latter sense locally regular, but not globally, and moreover their distribution is completely chaotic.

To explain the above sentence it is useful to think about an infinite word as a dynamical process which extends finite words symbol by symbol. Then if the process is controlled by the assumption that the $(2,4)$-repetitiveness is preserved, then the process is completely predictable. On the other hand, if the assumption is made, as little as possible, weaker, then the process becomes completely unpredictable, that is chaotic. This follows, for example, from our structural characterization of $(2,5)$-repetitive words, see (ii′). Formally, denoting by $|w|_a$ the number of a's in the word w, this can be stated as follows:

Theorem 7.1. *For each real number* $\tau \in [\frac{1}{2}, \frac{2}{3}] \cup [\frac{3}{2}, 2] \cup \{0, \frac{1}{4}, \frac{1}{3}, 1, 3, 4, \infty\}$ *there exists a* $(2,5)$*-repetitive word* w_τ *such that*

$$\lim_{n \to \infty} \frac{|\mathrm{Pref}_n(w_\tau)|_a}{|\mathrm{Pref}_n(w_\tau)|_b} = \tau.$$

Note that Theorem 7.1 covers all possible values of the ratio. The discrete values are easy to verify by considering ultimately periodic words with periods at most 5.

We conclude this paper with two comments. First, we believe, that our results provide a very simple and clear example of predictable vs. chaotic behaviour. Second, and more importantly, it opens a lot of interesting questions. For example, what would be the values of p giving similar borderlines for values of ρ different from 2?

References

[BePe] J. Berstel and D. Perrin, Finite and infinite words, in: M. Lothaire, *Algebraic Combinatorics on Words* (to appear).

[CK] C. Choffrut and J. Karhumäki, Combinatorics of Words, in: G. Rozenberg and A. Salomaa (eds.), *Handbook of Formal Languages*, Vol. 1, Springer, 329–438, 1997.

[KLP] J. Karhumäki, A. Lepistö and W. Plandowski, Locally Periodic Infinite Words and a Chaotic Behaviour, *TUCS Report* **133**, 1997.

[Lo] M. Lothaire, *Combinatorics on Words*, Addison-Wesley, 1983.

[MP] F. Mignosi and G. Pirillo, Repetitions in the Fibonacci infinite word, *RAIRO Theor. Inform. Appl.* **26**, 199–204, 1992.

[MRS] F. Mignosi, A. Restivo and S. Salemi, A periodicity theorem on words and applications, *in MFCS'95*, Springer LNCS **969**, 337–348, 1995.

Bridges for Concatenation Hierarchies

Jean-Éric Pin

LIAFA, CNRS and Université Paris VII
2 Place Jussieu 75251 Paris Cedex O5, FRANCE
e-mail: Jean-Eric.Pin@liafa.jussieu.fr

Abstract. In the seventies, several classification schemes for the rational languages were proposed, based on the alternate use of certain operators (union, complementation, product and star). Some thirty years later, although much progress has been done, several of the original problems are still open. Furthermore, their significance has grown considerably over the years, on account of the successive discoveries of surprising links with other fields, like non commutative algebra, finite model theory, structural complexity and topology. In this article, we solve positively a question raised in 1985 about concatenation hierarchies of rational languages, which are constructed by alternating boolean operations and concatenation products. We establish a simple algebraic connection between the Straubing-Thérien hierarchy, whose basis is the trivial variety, and the group hierarchy, whose basis is the variety of group languages. Thanks to a recent result of Almeida and Steinberg, this reduces the decidability problem for the group hierarchy to a property stronger than decidability for the Straubing-Thérien hierarchy.

The reader is referred to [20] for undefined terms and a general overview of the motivations of this paper.

1 Introduction

In the seventies, several classification schemes for the rational languages were proposed, based on the alternate use of certain operators (union, complementation, product and star). Some thirty years later, although much progress has been done, several of the original problems are still open. Furthermore, their significance has grown considerably over the years, on account of the successive discoveries of surprising links with other fields, like non commutative algebra [7], finite model theory [34], structural complexity [4] and topology [11, 16, 19]. In this article, we solve positively a question left open in [11].

We are interested in hierarchies constructed by alternating union, complementation and concatenation products. All these hierarchies are indexed by half integers (i.e. numbers of the form n or $n+\frac{1}{2}$, where n is a non-negative integer) and follow the same construction scheme. The languages of level $n+\frac{1}{2}$ are the finite union of products of the form

$$L_0 a_1 L_1 a_2 \cdots a_k L_k$$

where $L_0, L_1, \dots, L_k$ are languages of level n and $a_1, \dots, a_k$ are letters. The languages of level $n+1$ are the boolean combinations[1] of languages of level $n+\frac{1}{2}$.

Thus a concatenation hierarchy $\mathcal{H}$ is fully determined by its level zero $\mathcal{H}_0$. For the sake of simplicity, levels of the form $\mathcal{H}_n$ will be called *full levels*, and levels of the form $\mathcal{H}_{n+\frac{1}{2}}$, *half levels.*

Three concatenation hierarchies have been intensively studied in the literature. The *dot-depth hierarchy*, introduced by Brzozowski [5], takes the finite or cofinite languages of A^+ as a basis. The *Straubing-Thérien hierarchy* [33, 28, 29] is based on the empty and full languages of A^*. The *group hierarchy*, considered in [11], is built on the group-languages, the languages recognized by a finite permutation automaton. It is the main topic of this paper.

These three hierarchies are infinite [6] and share another common feature : their basis is a variety of languages in the sense of Eilenberg [7]. It can be shown in general that, if the basis of a concatenation hierarchy is a variety of languages, then every level is a positive variety of languages, and in particular, is closed under intersection [2, 3, 22].

The main problems concerning these hierarchies are decidability problems : given a concatenation hierarchy $\mathcal{H}$, a half integer n and a rational language L, decide

(1) whether L belongs to $\mathcal{H}$,
(2) whether L belongs to $\mathcal{H}_n$.

The first problem has been solved positively for the three hierarchies [24, 11], but the second one is solved positively only for $n \leq \frac{3}{2}$ for the Straubing-Thérien hierarchy [25, 2, 3, 22] and for $n \leq 1$ for the two other hierarchies [9–11, 8]. It is still open for the other values of n although some partial results for the level 2 of the Straubing-Thérien hierarchy are known [21, 30, 32, 22, 36]. These problems are, together with the generalized star-height problem, the most important open problems on rational languages. Their logical counterpart is also quite natural : it amounts to decide whether a first order formula of Büchi's sequential calculus is equivalent to a Σ_n-formula on finite words models. See [14, 18] for more details.

Depending on the reader's favorite domain, a combinatorial, algebraic or logical approach of these problems is possible. The algebraic approach will be used in this paper. Since every level is a positive variety of languages, the variety theorem [7, 17] tells us there is a corresponding variety of finite ordered monoids (semigroups in the case of the dot-depth hierarchy) for each level. Let us denote these varieties by $\mathbf{V}_n$ for the Straubing-Thérien hierarchy, $\mathbf{B}_n$ for the dot-depth, and $\mathbf{G}_n$ for the group hierarchy (for any half integer n). Problem (2) now reduces to know whether the variety $\mathbf{V}_n$ (resp. $\mathbf{B}_n$, $\mathbf{G}_n$) is decidable. That is, given a finite ordered monoid (or semigroup) M decide whether it belongs to $\mathbf{V}_n$ (resp. $\mathbf{B}_n$, $\mathbf{G}_n$).

A nice connection between $\mathbf{V}_n$ and $\mathbf{B}_n$ was found by Straubing [29]. It is expressed by the formula

$$\mathbf{B}_n = \mathbf{V}_n * \mathbf{LI} \quad (n > 0) \tag{$*$}$$

[1] Boolean operations comprise union, intersection and complement.

which tells that the variety $\mathbf{B}_n$ is generated by semidirect products of the form $M * S$, where M is in $\mathbf{V}_n$ and S is a so-called "locally trivial" semigroup. Formula $(*)$ was established by Straubing for the full levels, but it still holds for the half levels.

In some sense, this formula reduces the study of the hierarchy $\mathbf{B}_n$ (the dot-depth) to that of $\mathbf{V}_n$ (the Straubing-Thérien's). Actually, things are not that easy, and it still requires a lot of machinery to show that $\mathbf{B}_n$ is decidable if and only if $\mathbf{V}_n$ is decidable [29]. Furthermore, this latter result is not yet formally proved for half levels.

A similar formula, setting a bridge between the varieties $\mathbf{G}_n$ and $\mathbf{V}_n$, was conjectured in [11] :

$$\mathbf{G}_n = \mathbf{V}_n * \mathbf{G} \quad (n \geq 0) \tag{$**$}$$

It tells that the variety $\mathbf{G}_n$ is generated by semidirect products of the form $M * G$, where M is in $\mathbf{V}_n$ and G is a group. The proof of this conjecture is the main result of this paper.

Actually, we show that a similar result holds for any hierarchy based on a group variety (such as commutative groups, nilpotent groups, solvable groups, etc.).

Does this result reduce the study of the group hierarchy to that of the Straubing-Thérien's? Yes and no. Formally, our result doesn't suffice to reduce the decidability problem of $\mathbf{G}_n$ to that of $\mathbf{V}_n$. However, a recent result of Almeida and Steinberg [1] gives a reduction of the decidability problem of $\mathbf{G}_n$ to a strong property of $\mathbf{V}_n$. More precisely, Almeida and Steinberg showed that if the variety of finite categories $\mathbf{gV}_n$ generated by $\mathbf{V}_n$ has a recursively enumerable basis of (pseudo)identities, then the decidability of $\mathbf{V}_n$ implies that of $\mathbf{G}_n$. Of course, even more algebra is required to use (and even state !) this result, but it is rather satisfactory for the following reason: although the decidability of $\mathbf{V}_n$ is still an open problem for $n \geq 2$, recent conjectures tend to indicate that a good knowledge of the identities of $\mathbf{gV}_n$ will be required to prove the decidability of $\mathbf{V}_n$. In other words, it is expected that the proof of the decidability of $\mathbf{V}_n$ will require the knowledge of the identities of $\mathbf{gV}_n$, giving in turn the decidability of $\mathbf{G}_n$.

2 Preliminaries and notations

2.1 Monoids

In this paper, all monoids are finite or free.

A relation $\leq$ on a monoid M is *stable* if, for all $x, y, z \in M$, $x \leq y$ implies $xz \leq yz$ and $zx \leq zy$. An *ordered monoid* is a monoid equipped with a stable order relation. An *order ideal* of M is a subset I of M such that, if $x \leq y$ and $y \in I$, then $x \in I$.

Note that every monoid, equipped with the equality relation, is an ordered monoid. This remark allows to consider any monoid as an ordered monoid.

Given two elements m and n of a monoid M, we put

$$m^{-1}n = \{x \in M \mid mx = n\}$$

Note that if M is a group, the set $m^{-1}n$ is equal to the singleton $\{m^{-1}n\}$, where this time m^{-1} denotes the inverse of m. This observation plays an important role in the proof of the main result.

Let M and N be monoids. A *monoid morphism* $\varphi : M \to N$ is a map from M into N such that $\varphi(xy) = \varphi(x)\varphi(y)$ for all $x, y \in M$. If M and N are ordered, φ is a morphism of ordered monoids if, furthermore, $x \leq y$ implies $\varphi(x) \leq \varphi(y)$ for all $x, y \in M$.

Let M and N be two ordered monoids. Then M is a *quotient* of N if there exists a surjective morphism of ordered monoids from N onto M. And M *divides* N if it is a quotient of a submonoid of N. Division is an order on finite ordered monoids (up to isomorphism).

A *variety of ordered monoids* is a class of finite ordered monoids closed under taking ordered submonoids, quotients and finite direct products. A *variety of monoids* is defined analogously.

Let M and N be ordered monoids. We write the operation of M additively and its identity by 0 to provide a more transparent notation, but it is not meant to suggest that M is commutative. A *left action* of N on M is a map $(t, s) \mapsto t{\cdot}s$ from $N \times M$ into M such that, for all $s, s_1, s_2 \in M$ and $t, t_1, t_2 \in N$,

(1) $(t_1t_2){\cdot}s = t_1(t_2{\cdot}s)$
(2) $1{\cdot}s = s$
(3) if $s \leq s'$ then $t{\cdot}s \leq t{\cdot}s'$
(4) $t{\cdot}(s_1 + s_2) = t{\cdot}s_1 + t{\cdot}s_2$
(5) $t{\cdot}0 = 0$
(6) if $t \leq t'$ then $t{\cdot}s \leq t'{\cdot}s$

The *semidirect product* of M and N (with respect to the given action) is the ordered monoid $M * N$ defined on $M \times N$ by the multiplication

$$(s, t)(s', t') = (s + t{\cdot}s', tt')$$

and the product order:

$$(s, t) \leq (s', t') \quad \text{if and only if } s \leq s' \text{ and } t \leq t'$$

Given two varieties of ordered monoids $\mathbf{V}$ and $\mathbf{W}$, denote by $\mathbf{V} * \mathbf{W}$ the variety of finite monoids generated by the semidirect products $M * N$ with $M \in \mathbf{V}$ and $N \in \mathbf{W}$.

The *wreath product* is closely related to the semidirect product. The wreath product $M \circ N$ of two ordered monoids M and N is the semidirect product $M^N * N$ defined by the action of N on M^N given by

$$(t{\cdot}f)(t') = f(t't)$$

for $f : N \to M$ and $t, t' \in N$. In particular, the multiplication in $M \circ N$ is given by

$$(f_1, t_1)(f_2, t_2) = (f, t_1t_2) \text{ where } f(t) = f_1(t) + f_2(tt_1) \text{ for all } t \in N$$

and the order on $M \circ N$ is given by

$$(f_1, t_1) \leq (f_2, t_2) \text{ if and only if } t_1 \leq t_2 \text{ and } f_1(t) \leq f_2(t) \text{ for all } t \in N$$

One can show that $\mathbf{V} * \mathbf{W}$ is generated by all wreath products of the form $M \circ N$, where $M \in \mathbf{V}$ and $N \in \mathbf{W}$.

2.2 Varieties of languages

Let A be a finite alphabet. The free monoid on A is denoted by A^* and the free semigroup by A^+. A language L of A^* is said to be *recognized* by an ordered monoid M if there exists a monoid morphism from A^* onto M and an order ideal I of M such that $L = \varphi^{-1}(I)$. In this case, we also say that L is recognized by φ. It is easy to see that a language is recognized by a finite ordered monoid if and only if it is recognized by a finite automaton, and thus is a rational (or regular) language. However, ordered monoids provide access to a more powerful algebraic machinery, that will be required for proving our main result. We start with an elementary result, the proof of which is omitted.

Proposition 1. *If a language L of A^* is recognized by M and if M divides N, then L is recognized by N.*

A set of languages closed under finite intersection and finite union is called a *positive boolean algebra*. Thus a positive boolean algebra always contains the empty language and the full language A^* since $\emptyset = \bigcup_{i \in \emptyset} L_i$ and $A^* = \bigcap_{i \in \emptyset} L_i$. A positive boolean algebra closed under complementation is a *boolean algebra*.

A *class of languages* is a correspondence $\mathcal{C}$ which associates with each finite alphabet A a set $\mathcal{C}(A^*)$ of languages of A^*.

A *positive variety of languages* is a class of recognizable languages $\mathcal{V}$ such that

(1) for every alphabet A, $\mathcal{V}(A^*)$ is a positive boolean algebra,
(2) if $\varphi : A^* \to B^*$ is a monoid morphism, $L \in \mathcal{V}(B^*)$ implies $\varphi^{-1}(L) \in \mathcal{V}(A^*)$,
(3) if $L \in \mathcal{V}(A^*)$ and if $a \in A$, then $a^{-1}L$ and La^{-1} are in $\mathcal{V}(A^*)$.

A *variety of languages* is a positive variety closed under complement.

To each variety of ordered monoids $\mathbf{V}$, is associated the corresponding positive variety of languages $\mathcal{V}$. For each alphabet A, $\mathcal{V}(A^*)$ is the set of all languages of A^* recognized by an ordered monoid of $\mathbf{V}$. Similarly, to each variety of monoids $\mathbf{V}$, is associated the corresponding variety of languages $\mathcal{V}$. For each alphabet A, $\mathcal{V}(A^*)$ is the set of all languages of A^* recognized by a monoid of $\mathbf{V}$, also called $\mathbf{V}$*-languages.*

The variety theorem [7,17] states that the correspondence $\mathbf{V} \to \mathcal{V}$ between varieties of ordered monoids and positive varieties of languages (resp. between varieties of monoids and varieties of languages) is one-to-one.

We refer the reader to [7,13,15,20] for more details on varieties.

3 Algebraic tools

The aim of this section is to introduce an ordered version of several standard algebraic tools. We start with power monoids.

3.1 Power monoids

Given a monoid M, denote by $\mathcal{P}(M)$ the monoid of subsets of M under the multiplication of subsets, defined, for all $X, Y \subseteq M$ by $XY = \{xy \mid x \in X \text{ and } y \in Y\}$. Then $\mathcal{P}(M)$ is not only a monoid but also a semiring under union as addition and the product of subsets as multiplication. Inclusion and reverse inclusion define two stable orders on $\mathcal{P}(M)$. For reasons that will become apparent in the next sections, we denote by $\mathcal{P}^+(M)$ the ordered monoid $(\mathcal{P}(M), \supseteq)$ and by $\mathcal{P}^-(M)$ the ordered monoid $(\mathcal{P}(M), \subseteq)$. The following proposition shows that the operator $\mathcal{P}$ preserves submonoids and quotients.

Proposition 2. *Let M be a submonoid (resp. a quotient) of N. Then $\mathcal{P}^+(M)$ is an ordered submonoid (resp. a quotient) of $\mathcal{P}^+(N)$.*

3.2 Schützenberger product

One of the most useful tools for studying the concatenation product is the *Schützenberger product* of n monoids, which was originally defined by Schützenberger for two monoids [24], and extended by Straubing [28] for any number of monoids. We give an ordered version of this definition.

Let $M_1, \ldots, M_n$ be monoids. Denote by M the product $M_1 \times \cdots \times M_n$ and by $\mathcal{M}_n$ the semiring of square matrices of size n with entries in the ordered semiring $\mathcal{P}^+(M)$. The *Schützenberger product* of $M_1, \ldots, M_n$, denoted by $\Diamond_n(M_1, \ldots, M_n)$, is the submonoid of the multiplicative monoid composed of all the matrices P of $\mathcal{M}_n$ satisfying the three following conditions:

(1) If $i > j$, $P_{i,j} = 0$

(2) If $1 \leq i \leq n$, $P_{i,i} = \{(1, \ldots, 1, s_i, 1, \ldots, 1)\}$ for some $s_i \in M_i$

(3) If $1 \leq i \leq j \leq n$, $P_{i,j} \subseteq 1 \times \cdots \times 1 \times M_i \times \cdots \times M_j \times 1 \cdots \times 1$.

The Schützenberger product can be ordered by simply inheriting the order on $\mathcal{P}^+(M)$: $P \leq P'$ if and only if for $1 \leq i \leq j \leq n$, $P_{i,j} \leq P'_{i,j}$ in $\mathcal{P}^+(M)$. The corresponding ordered monoid is denoted $\Diamond_n^+(M_1, \ldots, M_n)$ and is called the *ordered Schützenberger product* of $M_1, \ldots, M_n$.

Condition (1) shows that the matrices of the Schützenberger product are upper triangular, condition (2) enables us to identify the diagonal coefficient $P_{i,i}$ with an element s_i of M_i and condition (3) shows that if $i < j$, $P_{i,j}$ can be identified with a subset of $M_i \times \cdots \times M_j$. With this convention, a matrix of $\Diamond_3(M_1, M_2, M_3)$ will have the form

$$\begin{pmatrix} s_1 & P_{1,2} & P_{1,3} \\ 0 & s_2 & P_{2,3} \\ 0 & 0 & s_3 \end{pmatrix}$$

with $s_i \in M_i$, $P_{1,2} \subseteq M_1 \times M_2$, $P_{1,3} \subseteq M_1 \times M_2 \times M_3$ and $P_{2,3} \subseteq M_2 \times M_3$.

We first state without proof some elementary properties of the Schützenberger product. Let $M_1, \ldots, M_n$ be monoids and let M be their ordered Schützenberger product.

Proposition 3. *Each M_i is a quotient of M. Furthermore, for each sequence $1 \leq i_1 < \ldots < i_k \leq n$, $\Diamond_k^+(M_{i_1}, \ldots, M_{i_k})$ is an ordered submonoid of M.*

Proposition 4. *If, for $1 \leq i \leq n$, M_i is a submonoid (resp. a quotient, a divisor) of the monoid N_i, then M is an ordered submonoid (resp. a quotient, a divisor) of the ordered Schützenberger product of $N_1, \ldots, N_n$.*

Our next result gives an algebraic characterization of the languages recognized by a Schützenberger product. It is the "ordered version" of a result first proved by Reutenauer [23] for $n = 2$ and by the author [12] in the general case (see also [35]).

Theorem 1. *Let $M_1, \ldots, M_n$ be monoids. A language is recognized by the ordered Schützenberger product of $M_1, \ldots, M_n$ if and only if it is a positive boolean combination of languages recognized by one of the M_i's or of the form*

$$L_0 a_1 L_1 \cdots a_k L_k \tag{1}$$

where $k > 0$, $a_1, \ldots, a_k \in A$ and L_j is recognized by M_{i_j} for some sequence $1 \leq i_0 < i_1 < \cdots < i_k \leq n$.

Due to the lack of place, the proof is omitted, but follows the main lines of the elegant proof given by Simon [26].

3.3 The wreath product principle

Straubing's *wreath product principle* [27,31] provides a description of the languages recognized by the wreath product of two monoids. We extend here this result to the ordered case.

Let M and N be two ordered monoids and let $\eta : A^* \to M \circ N$ be a monoid morphism. We denote by $\pi : M \circ N \to N$ the morphism defined by $\pi(f, n) = n$ and we put $\varphi = \pi \circ \eta$. Thus φ is a morphism from A^* into N. Let $B = N \times A$ and $\sigma_\varphi : A^* \to B^*$ be the map defined by

$$\sigma_\varphi(a_1 a_2 \cdots a_n) = (1, a_1)(\varphi(a_1), a_2) \cdots (\varphi(a_1 a_2 \cdots a_{n_1}), a_n)$$

Observe that σ_φ is not a morphism, but a sequential function.

Theorem 2. *(Wreath product principle) Every language recognized by η is a finite union of languages of the form $U \cap \sigma_\varphi^{-1}(V)$, where U is a language of A^* recognized by φ and V is a language of B^* recognized by M.*

Conversely, every language of the form $\sigma_\varphi^{-1}(V)$ is recognized by a wreath product.

Proposition 5. *If V is a language of B^* recognized by M, then $\sigma_\varphi^{-1}(V)$ is recognized by $M \circ N$.*

Since we are working with concatenation hierarchies, we will encounter expressions of the form $\sigma_\varphi^{-1}\big(L_0(m_1,a_1)L_1\cdots(m_k,a_k)L_k\big)$. The inversion formula given below converts these expressions into concatenation products. It is the key result in the proof of our main result.

Define, for each $m \in N$, a morphism $\lambda_m : B^* \to B^*$ by setting $\lambda_m(n,a) = (mn,a)$. Then for each $u, v \in A^*$ and $a \in A$:

$$\sigma_\varphi(uav) = \sigma_\varphi(u)(\varphi(u),a)\lambda_{\varphi(ua)}(\sigma_\varphi(v)) \tag{2}$$

Let $m_1, \ldots, m_{k+1}$ be elements of N, $a_1, \ldots, a_k$ be letters of A and $L_1, \ldots, L_k$ be languages of B^*. Setting $n_0 = 1$ and $n_j = m_j\varphi(a_j)$ for $1 \le j \le k$, the following formula holds

Lemma 1. *(Inversion formula)*

$$\sigma_\varphi^{-1}\big(L_0(m_1,a_1)L_1\cdots(m_k,a_k)L_k\big) \cap \varphi^{-1}(m_{k+1}) = K_0a_1K_1\cdots a_kK_k$$

where $K_j = \sigma_\varphi^{-1}(\lambda_{n_j}^{-1}(L_j)) \cap \varphi^{-1}(n_j^{-1}m_{j+1})$ for $1 \le j \le k$.

Proof. Denote respectively by L and R the left and the right hand sides of the formula. If $u \in L$, then

$$\sigma_\varphi(u) = v_0(m_1,a_1)v_1(m_2,a_2)\cdots(m_k,a_k)v_k$$

with $v_j \in L_j$. Let $u = u_0a_1u_1\cdots a_ku_k$, with $|u_j| = |v_j|$ for $0 \le j \le k$. Then

$$\sigma_\varphi(u) = \underbrace{\sigma_\varphi(u_0)}_{v_0}\underbrace{(\varphi(u_0),a_1)}_{(m_1,a_1)}\underbrace{\lambda_{\varphi(u_0a_1)}(\sigma_\varphi(u_1))}_{v_1}\cdots$$

$$\underbrace{(\varphi(u_0a_1\cdots u_{k-1}),a_k)}_{(m_k,a_k)}\underbrace{\lambda_{\varphi(u_0a_1u_1\cdots u_{k-1}a_k)}(\sigma_\varphi(u_k))}_{v_k}$$

It follows $\sigma_\varphi(u_0) \in L_0$, $\lambda_{\varphi(u_0a_1)}(\sigma_\varphi(u_1)) \in L_1, \ldots, \lambda_{\varphi(u_0a_1u_1\cdots u_{k-1}a_k)}(\sigma_\varphi(u_k)) \in L_k$ and $(\varphi(u_0),a_1) = (m_1,a_1), \ldots, (\varphi(u_0a_1\cdots u_{k-1}),a_k) = (m_k,a_k)$. These conditions, added to the condition $\varphi(u) = m_{k+1}$, can be rewritten as

$$n_j\varphi(u_j) = m_{j+1} \text{ and } \lambda_{n_j}(\sigma_\varphi(u_j)) \in L_j \text{ for } 0 \le j \le k$$

and thus, are equivalent to $u_j \in K_j$, for $0 \le j \le k$. Thus $u \in R$.

In the opposite direction, let $u \in R$. Then $u = u_0a_1u_1\cdots a_ku_k$ with $u_0 \in K_0, \ldots, u_k \in K_k$. It follows $n_j\varphi(u_j) = m_{j+1}$, for $0 \le j \le k$. Let us show that $\varphi(u_0a_1\cdots a_ju_j) = m_{j+1}$. Indeed, for $j = 0$, $\varphi(u_0) = n_0\varphi(u_0) = m_1$, and, by induction,

$$\varphi(u_0a_1\cdots a_ju_j) = m_j\varphi(a_ju_j) = m_j\varphi(a_j)\varphi(u_j) = n_j\varphi(u_j) = m_{j+1}$$

Now, by formula (2):

$$\sigma_\varphi(u) = \sigma_\varphi(u_0)(m_1,a_1)\lambda_{n_1}(\sigma_\varphi(u_1))(m_2,a_2)\cdots(m_k,a_k)\lambda_{n_k}(\sigma_\varphi(u_k))$$

Furthermore, by the definition of K_j, $\sigma_\varphi(u_j) \in L_j$ and thus $u \in L$, concluding the proof.

4 Main result

Let $\mathbf{H}_0$ be a variety of groups and let $\mathcal{H}_0$ be the corresponding variety of languages. Let $\mathcal{H}$ be the concatenation hierarchy of basis $\mathcal{H}_0$. As was explained in the introduction, the full levels $\mathcal{H}_n$ of this hierarchy are varieties of languages, corresponding to varieties of monoids $\mathbf{H}_n$ and the half levels $\mathcal{H}_{n+\frac{1}{2}}$ are positive varieties of languages, corresponding to varieties of ordered monoids $\mathbf{H}_{n+\frac{1}{2}}$. Our main result can be stated as follows:

Theorem 3. *The equality* $\mathbf{H}_n = \mathbf{V}_n * \mathbf{H}_0$ *holds for any half integer* n.

The first step of the proof consists in expressing $\mathbf{H}_{n+\frac{1}{2}}$ in terms of $\mathbf{H}_n$. If $\mathbf{V}$ is a variety of monoids, and k is a positive integer, denote by $\Diamond_k(\mathbf{V})$ (resp. $\Diamond_k^+(\mathbf{V})$) the variety of (resp. ordered) monoids generated by the (resp. ordered) monoids of the form $\Diamond_k(M_1, \ldots, M_k)$ (resp. $\Diamond_k^+(M_1, \ldots, M_k)$), where $M_1, \ldots, M_k \in \mathbf{V}$. Finally, let $\Diamond(\mathbf{V})$ (resp. $\Diamond^+(\mathbf{V})$) be the union over k of all the varieties $\Diamond_k(\mathbf{V})$ (resp. $\Diamond_k^+(\mathbf{V})$). Theorem 1 and its non-ordered version give immediately

Theorem 4. *For every positive integer* n, $\mathbf{V}_{n+\frac{1}{2}} = \Diamond^+(\mathbf{V}_n)$ *and* $\mathbf{V}_{n+1} = \Diamond(\mathbf{V}_n)$. *Similarly,* $\mathbf{H}_{n+\frac{1}{2}} = \Diamond^+(\mathbf{H}_n)$ *and* $\mathbf{H}_{n+1} = \Diamond(\mathbf{H}_n)$.

The second step is to prove the following formula

Theorem 5. *For every variety of monoids* $\mathbf{V}$, $\Diamond^+(\mathbf{V} * \mathbf{H}_0) = \Diamond^+(\mathbf{V}) * \mathbf{H}_0$ *and* $\Diamond(\mathbf{V} * \mathbf{H}_0) = \Diamond(\mathbf{V}) * \mathbf{H}_0$.

The proof of Theorem 5 is given in the next section. Let us first derive the proof of Theorem 3 by induction on n. The case $n = 0$ is trivial, since $\mathbf{V}_0$ is the trivial variety. By induction, $\mathbf{H}_n = \mathbf{V}_n * \mathbf{H}_0$ and thus $\Diamond^+(\mathbf{H}_n) = \Diamond^+(\mathbf{V}_n * \mathbf{H}_0)$. It follows, by Theorem 4 and by Theorem 5,

$$\mathbf{H}_{n+\frac{1}{2}} = \Diamond^+(\mathbf{H}_n) = \Diamond^+(\mathbf{V}_n * \mathbf{H}_0) = \Diamond^+(\mathbf{V}_n) * \mathbf{H}_0 = \mathbf{V}_{n+\frac{1}{2}} * \mathbf{H}_0$$

and similarly,

$$\mathbf{H}_{n+1} = \Diamond(\mathbf{H}_n) = \Diamond(\mathbf{V}_n * \mathbf{H}_0) = \Diamond(\mathbf{V}_n) * \mathbf{H}_0 = \mathbf{V}_{n+1} * \mathbf{H}_0$$

5 Proof of Theorem 5

The proof is given in the ordered case, since the proof of the non-ordered case is similar and easier. We will actually prove a slightly more precise result:

Theorem 6. *Let* $\mathbf{U}_1, \ldots, \mathbf{U}_n$ *be varieties of monoids and let* $\mathbf{H}$ *be a variety of groups. Then* $\Diamond_n^+(\mathbf{U}_1, \cdots, \mathbf{U}_n) * \mathbf{H} = \Diamond_n^+(\mathbf{U}_1 * \mathbf{H}, \cdots, \mathbf{U}_n * \mathbf{H})$.

We treat this equality as a double inclusion. The inclusion from left to right is easier to establish and follows from a more general result

Theorem 7. *Let* $\mathbf{U}_1, \ldots, \mathbf{U}_n$ *and* $\mathbf{V}$ *be varieties of monoids. Then*

$$\Diamond_n^+(\mathbf{U}_1, \cdots, \mathbf{U}_n) * \mathbf{V} \subseteq \Diamond_n^+(\mathbf{U}_1 * \mathbf{V}, \cdots, \mathbf{U}_n * \mathbf{V})$$

Proof. Let $\mathbf{X} = \Diamond_n^+(\mathbf{U}_1, \cdots, \mathbf{U}_n) * \mathbf{V}$ and let $\mathbf{Y} = \Diamond_n^+(\mathbf{U}_1 * \mathbf{V}, \cdots, \mathbf{U}_n * \mathbf{V})$. It suffices to prove that the $\mathbf{X}$-languages are $\mathbf{Y}$-languages. By Theorem 2, every $\mathbf{X}$-language of A^* is a positive boolean combination of $\mathbf{V}$-languages and of languages of the form $\sigma_\varphi^{-1}(L)$, where $\varphi : A^* \to N$ is a morphism from A^* into some monoid $N \in \mathbf{V}$, $\sigma_\varphi : A^* \to (N \times A)^*$ is the sequential function associated with φ and L is a language of $\Diamond_n^+(\mathbf{U}_1, \cdots, \mathbf{U}_n)$. Since $\mathbf{V} \subseteq \mathbf{Y}$, the $\mathbf{V}$-languages are $\mathbf{Y}$-languages. Now, by Theorem 1, L is a positive boolean combination of languages of the form

$$L_0(m_1, a_1)L_1(m_2, a_2) \cdots (m_k, a_k)L_k \tag{3}$$

where $L_j \in \mathcal{U}_{i_j}((N \times A)^*)$, $(m_i, a_i) \in N \times A$ and $1 \leq i_0 < \cdots < i_k \leq n$. Since boolean operations commute with σ_φ^{-1}, it suffices to check that $\sigma_\varphi^{-1}(L)$ is a $\mathbf{Y}$-language when L is of the form (3). Furthermore

$$\sigma_\varphi^{-1}(L) = \bigcup_{m_{k+1} \in N} (\sigma_\varphi^{-1}(L) \cap \varphi^{-1}(m_{k+1}))$$

and by Lemma 1, $\sigma_\varphi^{-1}(L) \cap \varphi^{-1}(m_{k+1})$ can be written as $K_0 a_1 K_1 \cdots a_k K_k$, where $K_j = \sigma_\varphi^{-1}(\lambda_{n_j}^{-1}(L_j)) \cap \varphi^{-1}(n_j^{-1} m_{j+1})$ for $1 \leq j \leq k$.

Finally, L_j, and hence $\lambda_{n_j}^{-1}(L_j)$, is a $\mathbf{U}_{i_j}$-language. Now, $\varphi^{-1}(n_j^{-1} m_{j+1})$ is by construction a $\mathbf{V}$-language, and by Proposition 5, $\sigma_\varphi^{-1}(\lambda_{n_j}^{-1}(L_j))$ is a $(\mathbf{U}_{i_j} * \mathbf{V})$-language. It follows that K_j is also a $(\mathbf{U}_{i_j} * \mathbf{V})$-language and by Theorem 1 and formula 5, $\sigma_\varphi^{-1}(L)$ is a $\mathbf{Y}$-language.

Let us now conclude the proof of Theorem 6. We keep the notations of the proof of Theorem 7, with $\mathbf{V} = \mathbf{H}$. This theorem already gives the inclusion $\mathbf{X} \subseteq \mathbf{Y}$. To obtain the opposite inclusion, it suffices now to show that each $\mathbf{Y}$-language is a $\mathbf{X}$-language.

Let K be a $\mathbf{Y}$-language. Then K is recognized by an ordered monoid of the form $\Diamond_n^+(M_1 \circ G_1, \ldots, M_n \circ G_n)$, where $M_1, \ldots, M_n \in \mathbf{U}_n$ and $G_1, \ldots, G_n \in \mathbf{H}$. Let $G = G_1 \times \cdots \times G_n$. Then $G \in \mathbf{H}$, each G_i is a quotient of G, each $M_i \circ G_i$ divides $M_i \circ G$ and, thus by Proposition 4, $\Diamond_n^+(M_1 \circ G_1, \ldots, M_n \circ G_n)$ divides $\Diamond_n^+(M_1 \circ G, \ldots, M_n \circ G)$. By Proposition 1, K is also recognized by the latter ordered monoid, and, by Theorem 1, K is a positive boolean combination of languages of the form

$$K_0 a_1 K_1 \cdots a_k K_k$$

where $a_1, \cdots a_k \in A$, and K_j is recognized by $M_{i_j} \circ G$ for some sequence $1 \leq i_0 < i_1 < \cdots < i_k \leq n$. Now, by Theorem 2, K_j is a finite union of languages of the form $\sigma_\varphi^{-1}(L_j) \cap \varphi^{-1}(g_j)$ where $\varphi : A^* \to G$ is a morphism, $g_j \in G$, $\sigma_\varphi : A^* \to (G \times A)^*$ is the sequential function associated with φ and L_j is recognized by M_{i_j}. Using distributivity of product over union, we may thus suppose that $K_j = \sigma_\varphi^{-1}(L_j) \cap \varphi^{-1}(g_j)$ for $0 \le j \le k$. Set $n_0 = 1$, $m_1 = g_0$ and, for $1 \le j \le k$, $n_j = m_j\varphi(a_j)$ and $m_{j+1} = n_j g_j$.

Two special features of groups will be used now. First, if $g, h \in G$, the set $g^{-1}h$, computed in the monoid sense, is equal to $\{g^{-1}h\}$, where this time g^{-1} denotes the inverse of g. Next, each function λ_g is a bijection, and $\lambda_g^{-1} = \lambda_{g^{-1}}$. With these observations in mind, one gets

$$K_j = \sigma_\varphi^{-1}\Big(\lambda_{n_j}^{-1}(\lambda_{n_j^{-1}}^{-1}(L_j))\Big) \cap \varphi^{-1}(n_j^{-1}m_{j+1})$$

whence, by the inversion formula,

$$K = \sigma_\varphi^{-1}(L'_0(m_1, a_1)L'_1(m_2, a_2)\cdots(m_k, a_k)L'_k) \cap \varphi^{-1}(m_{k+1})$$

where $L'_j = \lambda_{n_j^{-1}}^{-1}(L_j)$. Now, L'_j is recognized by M_{i_j}, and by Theorem 1, the language $L'_0(m_1, a_1)L'_1(m_2, a_2)\cdots(m_k, a_k)L'_k$ is recognized by $\Diamond_n^+(M_1, \ldots, M_n)$. It follows, by Proposition 2, that K is a **X**-language. □

References

1. J. Almeida and B. Steinberg, *On the decidability of iterated semidirect products with applications to complexity*, preprint.
2. M. Arfi, Polynomial operations and rational languages, 4th STACS, Lect. Notes in Comp. Sci. **247**, Springer, (1987), 198–206.
3. M. Arfi, Opérations polynomiales et hiérarchies de concaténation, *Theoret. Comput. Sci.* **91**, (1991), 71–84.
4. B. Borchert, D. Kuske, F. Stephan, On existentially first-order definable languages and their relation to NP. *Proceedings of ICALP 1998, Lect. Notes in Comp. Sci.* , Springer Verlag, Berlin, Heidelberg, New York, (1998), this volume.
5. J. A. Brzozowski, Hierarchies of aperiodic languages, *RAIRO Inform. Théor.* **10**, (1976), 33–49.
6. J.A. Brzozowski and R. Knast, The dot-depth hierarchy of star-free languages is infinite, *J. Comput. System Sci.* **16**, (1978), 37–55.
7. S. Eilenberg, *Automata, languages and machines*, Vol. B, Academic Press, New York, 1976.
8. K. Henckell and J. Rhodes, The theorem of Knast, the *PG* = *BG* and Type II Conjectures, in J. Rhodes (ed.) *Monoids and Semigroups with Applications*, Word Scientific, (1991), 453–463.
9. R. Knast, A semigroup characterization of dot-depth one languages, *RAIRO Inform. Théor.* **17**, (1983), 321–330.
10. R. Knast, Some theorems on graph congruences, *RAIRO Inform. Théor.* **17**, (1983), 331–342.
11. S. W. Margolis and J.E. Pin, Product of group languages, FCT Conference, Lect. Notes in Comp. Sci. **199**, (1985), 285–299.
12. J.-E. Pin, Hiérarchies de concaténation, *RAIRO Informatique Théorique* **18**, (1984), 23–46.
13. J.-E. Pin, *Variétés de langages formels*, Masson, Paris, 1984; English translation: *Varieties of formal languages*, Plenum, New-York, 1986.

14. J.-E. Pin, Logic on words, *Bulletin of the European Association of Theoretical Computer Science* **54**, (1994), 145–165.
15. J.-E. Pin, Finite semigroups and recognizable languages: an introduction, in NATO Advanced Study Institute *Semigroups, Formal Languages and Groups, J. Fountain (ed.)*, Kluwer academic publishers, (1995), 1–32.
16. J.-E. Pin, **BG** = **PG**, a success story, in NATO Advanced Study Institute *Semigroups, Formal Languages and Groups, J. Fountain (ed.)*, Kluwer academic publishers, (1995), 33–47.
17. J.-E. Pin, A variety theorem without complementation, *Izvestiya VUZ Matematika* **39** (1995) 80–90. English version, *Russian Mathem. (Iz. VUZ)* **39** (1995) 74–83.
18. J.-E. Pin, Logic, semigroups and automata on words, *Annals of Mathematics and Artificial Intelligence*, (1996), **16**, 343–384.
19. J.-E. Pin, Polynomial closure of group languages and open sets of the Hall topology, *Theoretical Computer Science* **169**, (1996), 185–200.
20. J.-E. Pin, Syntactic semigroups, in *Handbook of language theory*, G. Rozenberg et A. Salomaa eds., vol. 1, ch. 10, pp. 679–746, Springer (1997).
21. J.-E. Pin and H. Straubing, 1981, Monoids of upper triangular matrices, *Colloquia Mathematica Societatis Janos Bolyai 39, Semigroups, Szeged*, 259–272.
22. J.-E. Pin and P. Weil, Polynomial closure and unambiguous product, *Theory Comput. Systems* **30**, (1997), 1–39.
23. Ch. Reutenauer, Sur les variétés de langages et de monoïdes, *Lect. Notes in Comp. Sci.* **67**, (1979) 260–265.
24. M.P. Schützenberger, On finite monoids having only trivial subgroups, *Information and Control* **8**, (1965), 190–194.
25. I. Simon, Piecewise testable events, *Proc. 2nd GI Conf., Lect. Notes in Comp. Sci.* **33**, Springer Verlag, Berlin, Heidelberg, New York, (1975), 214–222.
26. I. Simon, The product of rational languages, *Proceedings of ICALP 1993, Lect. Notes in Comp. Sci.* **700**, Springer Verlag, Berlin, Heidelberg, New York, (1993), 430–444.
27. H. Straubing, Families of recognizable sets corresponding to certain varieties of finite monoids, *J. Pure Appl. Algebra*, **15**, (1979), 305–318.
28. H. Straubing, A generalization of the Schützenberger product of finite monoids, *Theoret. Comp. Sci.* **13**, (1981), 137–150.
29. H. Straubing, Finite semigroups varieties of the form $\mathbf{U} * \mathbf{D}$, *J. Pure Appl. Algebra* **36**, (1985), 53–94.
30. H. Straubing, Semigroups and languages of dot-depth two, *Theoret. Comp. Sci.* **58**, (1988), 361–378.
31. H. Straubing, The wreath product and its application, in *Formal properties of finite automata and applications, J.-E. Pin (ed.), Lect. Notes in Comp. Sci.* **386**, Springer Verlag, Berlin, Heidelberg, New York, (1989), 15–24.
32. H. Straubing and P. Weil, On a conjecture concerning dot-depth two languages, *Theoret. Comp. Sci.* **104**, (1992), 161–183.
33. D. Thérien, Classification of finite monoids: the language approach, *Theoret. Comp. Sci.* **14**, (1981), 195–208.
34. W. Thomas, Classifying regular events in symbolic logic, *J. Comput. Syst. Sci* **25**, (1982), 360–375.
35. P. Weil, Closure of varieties of languages under products with counter, *J. Comput. System Sci.* **45**, (1992), 316–339.
36. P. Weil, Some results on the dot-depth hierarchy, *Semigroup Forum* **46**, (1993), 352–370.

Complete Proof Systems for Observation Congruences in Finite-Control π-Calculus*

H. Lin
Laboratory for Computer Science
Institute of Software, Chinese Academy of Sciences
E-mail: lhm@ox.ios.ac.cn

Abstract

Proof systems for weak bisimulation congruences in the finite-control π-calculus are presented and their completeness proved. This study consists of two major steps: first complete proof systems for *guarded* recursions are obtained; then sound laws sufficient to remove any unguarded recursions are formulated. These results lift Milner's axiomatisation for observation congruence in regular pure-CCS to the π-calculus. The completeness proof relies on the *symbolic bisimulation* technique.

1 Introduction

Axiomatisation for the π-calculus has received extensive studies since the infancy of this calculus. Different bisimulation equivalences in the recursion-free subset of the π-calculus have been successfully axiomatised: late ground bisimulation [9], late/early strong bisimulation congruences [10, 1, 4], open bisimulation [11], late/early weak bisimulation congruences [5]; styles of proof systems have been exploited: equational axiomatisation [10, 11] and *symbolic* inference systems [1, 4, 5]. To deal with recursion, [6] proposed a version of *Unique fixpoint induction*, thus obtained complete proof systems for both late and early strong bisimulation congruence in finite-control π-calculus with *guarded* recursions. The main contributions of the present paper are: (1) Presenting proof systems for weak bisimulation congruences in guarded finite-control π-calculus and proving their completeness; (2) Formulating sound axioms to transform unguarded recursions to guarded ones, thus extending these proof systems to the full language of finite-control π-calculus.

These results can be seen as "lifting" Milner's axiomatisation for observation congruence in regular pure-CCS ([8]) to the π-calculus. For the lifting to work three major problems must be tackled.

1. The proof of the complete axiomatisation in [8] relies on the finite-branching and finite-state properties of regular CCS. However in the π-calculus input actions may result in infinitely many outgoing transitions, and recursively defined processes are parameterised on names and therefore may have infinite states. Such infinity can be avoided by appealing to the *symbolic* approach, originally developed for general message-passing processes ([3]) and has been successfully adapted to the π-calculus in [1, 4, 5, 6].

2. The key inference rule to deal with recursion in [7, 8] is *unique fixpoint induction*:

$$\frac{P = Q[P/X]}{P = \mathbf{fix} X Q} \qquad X \text{ guarded in } Q$$

*Supported by grants from the National Science Foundation of China and the Chinese Academy of Sciences.

Here $[P/X]$ is a first order substitution: X is a process variable and P a process term. But in the π-calculus process variables may take name parameters, hence substitutions on process variables must cater for parameter-passing. This paper inherits the solution proposed in [6] of using ***second order substitution***. The syntactic form of the unique fixpoint induction will remain the same, but P, Q will be ***process abstractions***, namely functions from names to process terms, and X a process abstraction variable. In $Q[P/X]$, passing to P the actual parameters of the occurrences of X in Q is realized by β-conversion.

3. The last problem concerns unguarded recursions. Let us look at a simple example:

$$(\mathbf{fix}X(x,y,z)(\bar{x}y.0 + X(y,x,z) + X(x,z,y)))(a,b,c)$$

This process consists of a recursion abstraction with formal parameters (x,y,z), applied to the actual parameter (a,b,c). It contains two (immediate) unguarded recursions, $X(y,x,z)$ and $X(x,z,y)$. We can not use the law $\mathbf{fix}X(T+X) = \mathbf{fix}XT$, which is sound for pure-CCS [7, 8], to reduce the term to $\mathbf{fix}X(x,y,z)(\bar{x}y.0)(a,b,c)$, because, for instance, $X(y,x,z)$ may contribute to the behaviour of the original term by causing the transition $\xrightarrow{\bar{b}a}$ (resulted from unfolding the recursion once), and the combined effects of $X(y,x,z)$ and $X(x,z,y)$ may produce further transitions $\xrightarrow{\bar{c}a} \mathbf{0}$, $\xrightarrow{\bar{b}c} \mathbf{0}$ *etc.* General laws for eliminating immediate as well deeply nested unguarded recursions are formulated in Section 5, which also take care for conditions and restrictions.

Due to the presence of additional constructs in the π-calculus (more sophisticated actions, the conditional construct, name parameters, ...), it should not be surprising that proof of the completeness theorem is more complicated than in pure-CCS. However much of the complexity has been brought under control by the systematic employment of ***maximally consistent extensions*** of conditions.

The rest of the paper is organised as follows: The calculus and the symbolic semantics are introduced in the next section. Section 3 presents the inference system and summaries its properties, while the completeness proof is the subject of the subsequent section. The axioms for removing unguarded recursions are studied in Section 5, and the paper is concluded with Section 6.

2 The Language and Weak Bisimulations

We presuppose an infinite set $\mathcal{N}$ of ***names***, ranging over by a, b, x, $y, \ldots$, and a countably infinite set of ***process abstraction variables*** (or just ***process variables*** for short), *Var*, ranged over by $X, Y, Z, W, \ldots$. Each process abstraction variable is associated with an ***arity*** indicating the number of names it should take to form a process term. The language of the π-calculus we consider in this paper can then be given by the following BNF grammar

$$\begin{array}{lcl}
T & ::= & \mathbf{0} \mid \alpha.T \mid T+T \mid \phi T \mid \nu x T \mid F\tilde{x} \\
F & ::= & X \mid (\tilde{x})T \mid \mathbf{fix}XF \\
\alpha & ::= & \tau \mid a(x) \mid \bar{a}x \\
\phi & ::= & [x=y] \mid \phi \wedge \phi \mid \neg\phi
\end{array}$$

This language is the π-calculus analogue to *regular CCS*. By adding parallel composition while keeping it outside the scope of the **fix** operator we obtain the fragment known as "finite-control π-calculus" ([2]). We will concentrate on the regular subset in the main body of this paper, and will indicate how our results can be extended to the finite-control fragment at the end of Section 4.

Most of the operators are taken from [9]. The only construct worth mentioning is *abstraction* which is either a process variable, a process abstraction $(\tilde{x})T$ (where $\tilde{x}$ is a vector of distinct names), or a recursion abstraction $\mathbf{fix}XF$. Three constructs, input prefixing $a(x).T$, restriction νxT and process abstraction $(\tilde{x})T$, introduce bound names, and we use the customary notations $bn(T)$ and $fn(T)$ for bound and free names in T. For any expression e, $n(e)$ denotes the set of all names appearing in e. We shall only use name-closed abstractions, so in $(\tilde{x})T$ it is always required that $fn(T) \subseteq \{\tilde{x}\}$. A recursion abstraction $\mathbf{fix}XF$ binds X in F, and we use $FV(T)$ to denote the set of free process variables of T. We shall assume that all the expressions we write are syntactically well-formed. A recursion $\mathbf{fix}XF$ is *guarded* if each occurrence of X in F is within the scope of some prefix operator $\alpha.-$ with $\alpha \not\equiv \tau$.

Bound names and bound variables induce the notion of α-equivalence as usual. In the sequel we will not distinguish between α-equivalent terms and will use $\equiv$ for both syntactical equality and α-equivalence.

We use the customary notation for name substitution, ranged over by σ. $[F_i/X_i|1 \leq i \leq m]$, with X_i:s distinct, is a process substitution that sends X_i to F_i for $1 \leq i \leq m$. We will often simply write $T[F_i/X_i|i]$ when the range of i is clear from the context. In name and process substitutions bound names and bound variables will be renamed when necessary to avoid capture.

Conditions, ranged over by ϕ, ψ, are boolean expressions over *matches* of the form $[x = y]$. Sometimes we will abbreviate $\phi \wedge \psi$ as $\phi\psi$. *True* stands for $x = x$ and *false* for $\neg$*true*. We write $\sigma \models \phi$ if $\phi\sigma = true$, and $\phi \Rightarrow \psi$ if $\sigma \models \phi$ implies $\sigma \models \psi$ for any substitution σ. It is not difficult to see that the relation $\phi \Rightarrow \psi$ is decidable.

A condition ϕ is consistent if there are no $x,\ y \in \mathcal{N}$ such that $\phi \Rightarrow x = y$ and $\phi \Rightarrow x \neq y$. ϕ is *maximally consistent* on $V \subset \mathcal{N}$ if ϕ is consistent and for any $x,\ y \in V$ either $\phi \Rightarrow x = y$ or $\phi \Rightarrow x \neq y$.

Let the restriction of ϕ on V be

$$\phi|_V = \bigwedge\{x = y \mid x, y \in V, \phi \Rightarrow x = y\} \wedge \bigwedge\{x \neq y \mid x, y \in V, \phi \Rightarrow x \neq y\}$$

Lemma 2.1 *If ϕ is maximally consistent on V' and $V \subseteq V'$, then $\phi|_V$ is maximally consistent on V.*

$$\text{Pre}\ \frac{}{\alpha.P \xrightarrow{true,\alpha} P} \qquad \text{Cond}\ \frac{P \xrightarrow{\phi,\alpha} P'}{\psi P \xrightarrow{\phi\wedge\psi,\alpha} P'} \qquad \text{Rec}\ \frac{F\tilde{v}[\mathbf{fix}XF/X] \xrightarrow{\phi,\alpha} P'}{(\mathbf{fix}XF)\tilde{v} \xrightarrow{\phi,\alpha} P'}$$

$$\text{Sum}\ \frac{P \xrightarrow{\phi,\alpha} P'}{P + Q \xrightarrow{\phi,\alpha} P'} \qquad \text{Res}\ \frac{P \xrightarrow{\phi,\alpha} P'}{\nu xP \xrightarrow{\nu_x\phi,\alpha} \nu xP'}\ x \notin n(\alpha) \qquad \text{Open}\ \frac{P \xrightarrow{\phi,\bar{a}x} P'}{\nu xP \xrightarrow{\nu_x\phi,\bar{a}(x)} P'}\ x \neq a$$

Figure 1: π-Calculus Symbolic Transitional Semantics

ψ is a *maximally consistent extension* of ϕ on V, written $\psi \in MCE_V(\phi)$, if $n(\psi) \subseteq V$, $\psi \Rightarrow \phi|_V$ and ψ is maximally consistent on V. Up-to logical equivalence, the set of maximally consistent extensions of a given condition on a finite set of names V is finite. $MCE_V(true)$ will be abbreviated as MC_V.

Lemma 2.2 $\bigvee MCE_V(\phi) = \phi|_V$.

Due to space limitation we refer to the standard references of the π-calculus for the definitions of late ground weak bisimulation ($\approx_l$) and observation congruence ($\simeq_l$), and shall only give the ***symbolic*** versions of these equivalences. The symbolic transitional semantics of the π-calculus is reported in Figure 1, where ν_x is an operation on conditions defined thus ([1]):

$$\begin{array}{lll} \nu_x true = true & \nu_x[x = x] = true & \nu_x[x = y] = false \\ \nu_x[y = z] = [y = z] & \nu_x \neg\phi = \neg\nu_x\phi & \nu_x(\phi \wedge \psi) = \nu_x\phi \wedge \nu_x\psi \end{array}$$

Definition 2.3 The symbolic late double arrows are defined as the least relations satisfying the following rules: (1) $T \overset{true,\varepsilon}{\Longrightarrow}_L T$; (2) $T \overset{\phi,\alpha}{\longrightarrow}_L U$ implies $T \overset{\phi,\alpha}{\Longrightarrow}_L U$; (3) $T \overset{\phi,\tau}{\longrightarrow}_L \overset{\psi,\alpha}{\Longrightarrow}_L U$ implies $T \overset{\phi\psi,\alpha}{\Longrightarrow}_L U$; (4) If α does not have the form $a(x)$ then $T \overset{\phi,\alpha}{\Longrightarrow}_L \overset{\psi,\tau}{\longrightarrow}_L U$ implies $T \overset{\phi\psi,\alpha}{\Longrightarrow}_L U$.
We shall write $\overset{\phi,\hat{\tau}}{\Longrightarrow}_L$ for $\overset{\phi,\varepsilon}{\Longrightarrow}_L$, and $\overset{\phi,\hat{\alpha}}{\Longrightarrow}_L$ for $\overset{\phi,\alpha}{\Longrightarrow}_L$ when $\alpha \not\equiv \tau$. □

In the following definition of symbolic bisimulation we use $\alpha =^{\phi} \beta$ to mean

$$\begin{array}{ll} \text{if } \alpha \equiv \tau \text{ then } \beta \equiv \tau & \text{if } \alpha \equiv \bar{a}x \text{ then } \beta \equiv \bar{b}y \text{ and } \phi \Rightarrow a = b \wedge x = y \\ \text{if } \alpha \equiv \bar{a}(x) \text{ then } \beta \equiv \bar{b}(x) \text{ and } \phi \Rightarrow a = b & \text{if } \alpha \equiv a(x) \text{ then } \beta \equiv b(x) \text{ and } \phi \Rightarrow a = b \end{array}$$

Definition 2.4 A condition indexed family of symmetric relations $\mathcal{S} = \{S^{\phi}\}$ is a symbolic late weak bisimulation if $(T, U) \in S^{\phi}$ implies for each $\psi \in MCE_{fn(T,U)}(\phi)$ whenever $T \overset{\phi',\alpha}{\longrightarrow} T'$ with $bn(\alpha) \cap fn(T, U) = \emptyset$ and $\psi \Rightarrow \phi'$, then there is a $U \overset{\psi',\hat{\beta}}{\Longrightarrow}_L U'$ such that $\psi \Rightarrow \psi'$, $\alpha =^{\psi} \beta$, and

- If $\alpha \equiv a(x)$ then for each $\psi'' \in MCE_{fn(T,U)\cup\{x\}}(\psi)$ there is a $U' \overset{\phi''}{\Longrightarrow}_L U''$ such that $\psi'' \Rightarrow \phi''$ and $(T', U'') \in S^{\psi''}$.
- If $\alpha \equiv \bar{a}(x)$ then $(T', U') \in S^{\psi \cup \{x \neq y \mid y \in fn(\alpha.T', \beta.U')\}}$

$$\text{CHOICE}\ \frac{\phi \rhd T_i = U_i}{\phi \rhd T_1 + T_2 = U_1 + U_2} \qquad \text{COND}\ \frac{\phi \wedge \psi \rhd T = U \quad \phi \wedge \neg\psi \rhd \mathbf{0} = U}{\phi \rhd \psi T = U}$$

$$\text{TAU}\ \frac{\phi \rhd T = U}{\phi \rhd \tau.T = \tau.U} \qquad \text{RES}\ \frac{\phi \wedge \bigwedge_{y \in fn(\nu x T, \nu x U)} x \neq y \rhd T = U}{\phi \rhd \nu x T = \nu x U}\ x \notin n(\phi)$$

$$\text{INPUT}\ \frac{\phi \rhd T = U}{\phi \rhd a(x).T = b(x).U}\ \begin{array}{l}\phi \Rightarrow a = b \\ x \notin n(\phi)\end{array} \qquad \text{CUT}\ \frac{\phi_1 \rhd T = U \quad \phi_2 \rhd T = U}{\phi \rhd T = U}\ \phi \Rightarrow \phi_1 \vee \phi_2$$

$$\text{OUTPUT}\ \frac{\phi \rhd T = U}{\phi \rhd \bar{a}x.T = \bar{b}y.U}\ \begin{array}{l}\phi \Rightarrow a = b \\ \phi \Rightarrow x = y\end{array} \qquad \text{ABSURD}\ \frac{}{false \rhd T = U}$$

Figure 2: RP: The Inference Rules for Process Terms

- Otherwise $(T', U') \in S^{\psi}$

Let $\approx_L$ be the largest symbolic late weak bisimulation.
For abstractions, $F \approx_L^{true} G$ iff $F\tilde{x} \approx_L^{true} G\tilde{x}$ for any $\tilde{x}$. For process terms T, U with free process variables in $\tilde{X}$, $T \approx_L^{\phi} U$ iff $T[\tilde{F}/\tilde{X}] \approx_L^{\phi} U[\tilde{F}/\tilde{X}]$ for any vector $\tilde{F}$ of process-closed abstractions.

T, U are *symbolic late observation congruent* with respect to ϕ, written $T \simeq_L^\phi U$, if $T \approx_L^\phi U$, any initial τ move from T (U) is matched by at least one τ move from U (T), and the residuals are weak bisimilar. □

Notation We will write $(T,U)^\psi \in \mathcal{S}$ to mean that there is $S^\phi \in \mathcal{S}$ such that $(T,U) \in S^\phi$ and $\psi \Rightarrow \phi$.

The following theorem asserts that $\approx_L$ and $\simeq_L$ capture $\dot{\approx}$ and $\dot{\simeq}_l$, respectively:

Theorem 2.5 *1.* $T \approx_L^\phi U$ *iff* $T\sigma \dot{\approx}_l U\sigma$ *for any* $\sigma \models \phi$.

2. $T \simeq_L^\phi U$ *iff* $T\sigma \dot{\simeq}_l U\sigma$ *for every* $\sigma \models \phi$.

3 The Proof Systems

The proof system for $\simeq_L$ is presented as a set of inference rules (RP in Figure 2 for process terms, and RA in Figure 3 for abstractions), together with the standard equational axioms in Figure 4. The judgements are *conditional equations* of the form

$$\phi \rhd T = U$$

meaning "T and U are equal when their free names satisfying ϕ". $\vdash$ *true* $\rhd T = U$ is abbreviated as $\vdash T = U$.

Several subsets of this inference system are of interest. Let $\vdash^{fs} = RP \cup \{S1-S4, R1-R6\}$, $\vdash^{fw} = \vdash^{fs} \cup \{T1-T3\}$, $\vdash^{grs} = \vdash^{fs} \cup RA$, and $\vdash^{grw} = \vdash^{grs} \cup \{T1-T3\}$. $\vdash^{fs}$ ($\vdash^{fw}$) is sound and complete for late strong (weak) bisimulation congruence in recursion-free π-calculus ([4, 5]), and $\vdash^{grs}$ is sound and complete for late

$$\text{ABS}\ \frac{true \wedge T = U}{true \wedge (\tilde{x})T = (\tilde{x})U} \qquad \text{APP}\ \frac{true \wedge F = G}{true \wedge F\tilde{w} = G\tilde{w}}$$

$$\text{CONGR-fix}\ \frac{true \wedge F = G}{true \wedge \mathbf{fix}XF = \mathbf{fix}XG} \qquad \text{REC}\ \frac{}{true \wedge \mathbf{fix}XF = F[\mathbf{fix}XF/X]}$$

$$\text{UFI}\ \frac{true \wedge G = F[G/X]}{true \wedge G = \mathbf{fix}XF}$$

Figure 3: RA: The Inference Rules for Abstractions

strong bisimulation in guarded finite-control π-calculus ([6])[1]. In the next section we shall show that $\vdash^{grw}$ is sound and complete for $\simeq_L$ in guarded finite-control π-calculus. In Section 5 we will extend $\vdash^{grs}$ and $\vdash^{grw}$ to the full finite-control π-calculus. To simplify the notation, in this and next sections we will write $\vdash$ for $\vdash^{grw}$.

Some usefull properties of this proof system are summerised in the following propositions:

Proposition 3.1 *1.* $\vdash \phi \wedge \psi \rhd T = U$ *iff* $\vdash \phi \rhd \psi T = \psi U$.

2. If $\phi \Rightarrow \psi$ *and* $\vdash \phi \rhd T = U$ *then* $\vdash \phi \rhd \psi T = U$.

[1] By adding an "early" axiom (see Section 6), all these proof systems are extended to the corresponding early equivalences.

3. *If* $\phi \wedge \psi \Rightarrow$ *false then* $\vdash \phi \rhd \psi T = \mathbf{0}$.

4. $\vdash \psi(T + U) = \psi T + \psi U$.

5. $\vdash \nu x(\psi T) = (\nu_x \psi)\nu x T$.

Proposition 3.2 *Suppose* $fn(T,U) \subseteq V$. *If* $\vdash \psi \rhd T = U$ *for each* $\psi \in MCE_V(\phi)$ *then* $\vdash \phi \rhd T = U$.

Theorem 3.3 *(Soundness) If* $\vdash \phi \rhd T = U$ *then* $T \simeq_L^\phi U$.

4 Completeness of $\vdash$ over Guarded Terms

The structure of the completeness proof follows that of [8], but there are extra complications due to the presences of name parameters, the conditional construct, and bound actions. The first step is to demonstrate that any guarded process term can be proved to satisfy a standard set of equations. The next step is to show if two process terms are symbolically bisimilar then an equation set can be constructed which is provably satisfied by both. Finally we show that two process terms satisfying the same set of equations can be proved equal.

Let $\tilde{X} = \{X_1, X_2, ..., X_m\}$ and $\tilde{W} = \{W_1, W_2, ..., W_n\}$ be disjoint sets of process variables. Then

$$E : X_i(\tilde{x}_i) = H_i \qquad 1 \leq i \leq m,$$

S1 $T + \mathbf{0} = T$	S2 $T + U = U + T$	S3 $(T + U) + V = T + (U + V)$
S4 $T + T = T$		
R1 $\nu x \mathbf{0} = \mathbf{0}$	R2 $\nu x \alpha.T = \alpha.\nu x T$ $x \notin n(\alpha)$	R3 $\nu x \alpha.T = \mathbf{0}$ x is the port of α
R4 $\nu x \nu y T = \nu y \nu x T$	R5 $\nu x(T + U) = \nu x T + \nu x U$	R6 $\nu x T(\tilde{w}) = T(\tilde{w})$ $x \notin \{\tilde{w}\}$
T1 $\alpha.\tau.T = \alpha.T$	T2 $T + \tau.T = \tau.T$	T3 $\alpha.(T + \tau.U) + \alpha.U = \alpha.(T + \tau.U)$

Figure 4: The Equational Axioms

where $fn(H_i) \subseteq \{\tilde{x}_i\}$ and $FV(H_i) \subseteq \tilde{X} \cup \tilde{W}$, is a set of equations with formal process variables in $\tilde{X}$ and free process variables in $\tilde{W}$. E is *standard* if each H_i has the form

$$\sum_{\psi_{ik} \in MC_{\{\tilde{x}\}}} \psi_{ik}\Big(\sum_{p \in P_{ik}} \alpha_{ikp}.X_{f(i,k,p)}(\tilde{x}_{ikp}) + \sum_{p' \in P'_{ik}} \nu \tilde{w}'_{ikp'} W_{f'(i,k,p')}(\tilde{w}_{ikp'})\Big)$$

with $bn(\alpha_{ikp}) \cap \{\tilde{x}_i\} = \emptyset$ and $\{\tilde{w}'_{ikp'}\} \subseteq \{\tilde{w}_{ikp'}\}$. Given a standard equation set E we define the formal relations $\longrightarrow_F$ and $\succ_F$ by letting $X_i(\tilde{x}_i) \overset{\psi_{ik},\alpha_{ikp}}{\longrightarrow}_F X_{f(i,k,p)}(\tilde{x}_{ikp})$ and $X_i(\tilde{x}_i) \succ_F^{\psi_{ik}} \nu \tilde{w}'_{ikp'} W_{f'(i,k,p')}(\tilde{w}_{ikp'})$. Also write $\overset{\phi_1\phi_2 \ldots \phi_n}{\Longrightarrow}_F$ for $\overset{\phi_1,\tau}{\longrightarrow}_F \overset{\phi_2,\tau}{\longrightarrow}_F \ldots \overset{\phi_n,\tau}{\longrightarrow}_F$. E is *guarded* if there is no circle $X_i(\tilde{x}_i) \overset{\phi}{\Longrightarrow}_F X_i(\tilde{x}_i)$. E is τ-*saturated* if for all $1 \leq i \leq m$,

1. If α_{ikp} is a bound action, $X_i(\tilde{x}_i) \overset{\phi}{\Longrightarrow}_F \overset{\psi_{ik},\alpha_{ikp}}{\longrightarrow}_F X'(\tilde{x}')$ implies $X_i(\tilde{x}_i) \overset{\phi\psi_{ik},\alpha_{ikp}}{\longrightarrow}_F X'(\tilde{x}')$.
2. For other actions $X_i(\tilde{x}_i) \overset{\phi}{\Longrightarrow}_F \overset{\psi_{ik},\alpha_{ikp}}{\longrightarrow}_F \overset{\phi'}{\Longrightarrow}_F X'(\tilde{x}')$ implies $X_i(\tilde{x}_i) \overset{\phi\psi_{ik}\phi',\alpha_{ikp}}{\longrightarrow}_F X'(\tilde{x}')$.
3. $X_i(\tilde{x}_i) \overset{\phi}{\Longrightarrow}_F \succ_F^{\psi} \nu \tilde{w}' W(\tilde{w})$ implies $X_i(\tilde{x}_i) \succ_F^{\phi\psi} \nu \tilde{w}' W(\tilde{w})$.

A process term T provably $\tilde{\phi}$-satisfies an equation set E if there exist T_i with $fn(T_i) \subseteq \{\tilde{x}_i\}$, $1 \leq i \leq m$, and $T_1 \equiv T$ s.t.

$$\vdash \phi_i \rhd T_i = H_i[(\tilde{x}_k)\phi_k T_k / X_k | 1 \leq k \leq m] \qquad 1 \leq i \leq m$$

We will simply say "T provably satisfies E" when $\phi_i \equiv true$ for all i.

Lemma 4.1 *Any guarded process term T with free process variables in $\tilde{W}$ provably satisfies a standard, guarded and τ-saturated equation set E with free process variables in $\tilde{W}$.*

Proposition 4.2 *Suppose T, U are guarded process terms with free process variables in $\tilde{W}$. If $T \simeq_L^\phi U$ then there exists $\tilde{\phi}$ with $\phi_1 \equiv \phi$ and a set of guarded equations E with free process variables in $\tilde{W}$ such that both T and U provably $\tilde{\phi}$-satisfy E.*

Proof (Sketch) For simplicity we only consider the case $\{\tilde{W}\} = \emptyset$ here.

Let E_1, E_2 be the standard, guarded and τ-saturated equation sets provably satisfied by T, U, respectively:

$$E_1: \quad X_i(\tilde{x}_i) = \sum_{\phi_{ik} \in MC_{\{\tilde{x}_i\}}} \phi_{ik} \sum_{p \in P_{ik}} \alpha_{ikp}.X_{f(i,k,p)}(\tilde{x}_{ikp}) \qquad 1 \leq i \leq m$$

$$E_2: \quad Y_j(\tilde{y}_j) = \sum_{\psi_{jl} \in MC_{\{\tilde{y}_j\}}} \psi_{jl} \sum_{q \in Q_{jl}} \beta_{jlq}.Y_{g(j,l,q)}(\tilde{y}_{jlq}) \qquad 1 \leq j \leq n$$

Without losing generality we may assume that each $\tilde{x}_i$ is a vector over $\{\tilde{x}\}$, each $\tilde{y}_j$ a vector over $\{\tilde{y}\}$, $\{\tilde{x}\} \cap \{\tilde{y}\} = \emptyset$, and in E_1, E_2 all input and bound output prefixes use the same name $v \notin \{\tilde{z}\}$ where $\tilde{z} = \tilde{x}\tilde{y}$.

Thus there exist T_i, $1 \leq i \leq m$, with $fn(T_i) \subseteq \{\tilde{x}_i\}$, $T_1 \equiv T$, and U_j, $1 \leq j \leq n$, with $fn(U_j) \subseteq \{\tilde{y}_j\}$, $U_1 \equiv U$, such that

$$\vdash T_i = \sum_{\phi_{ik} \in MC_{\{\tilde{x}_i\}}} \phi_{ik} \sum_{p \in P_{ik}} \alpha_{ikp}.T'_{f(i,k,p)} \tag{1}$$

$$\vdash U_j = \sum_{\psi_{jl} \in MC_{\{\tilde{y}_j\}}} \psi_{jl} \sum_{q \in Q_{jl}} \beta_{jlq}.U'_{g(j,l,q)} \tag{2}$$

where $T'_{f(i,k,p)} \equiv T_{f(i,k,p)}[\tilde{x}_{ikp}/\tilde{x}_{f(i,k,p)}]$, $U'_{g(j,l,q)} \equiv U_{g(j,l,q)}[\tilde{y}_{jlq}/\tilde{y}_{g(j,l,q)}]$.

Since $T \simeq_L^\phi U$, there exists a symbolic late weak bisimulation S such that $(T, U)^\phi \in S$, and S has the properties stated in Definition 2.4, namely the first τ moves from T (U) are matched by proper τ moves from U (T). S will be used to guide the construction of the new equation set.

Our goal is to construct an equation set E, out of E_1 and E_2, satisfied by both T and U. Two factors complicate this task:

1. In general E will only be satisfied by T and U *conditionally*, over some vector of conditions $\tilde{\phi}$ with $\phi_1 = \phi$.
2. As T and U are observation congruent, we need to take special care of the first τ moves.

Our solution to the first complication is to find *the weakest* such $\tilde{\phi}$: For each pair of i, j, let

$$\Phi_{ij} = \{\, \psi \in MC_{\{\tilde{z}\}} \mid (T_i, U_j)^\psi \in S \,\}$$

and $\phi_{ij} = \bigvee \Phi_{ij}$. By construction ϕ_{ij} satisfies: $(T_i, U_j)^{\phi_{ij}} \in S$ and for any ϕ' s.t. $(T_i, U_j)^{\phi'} \in S$ it holds $\phi' \Rightarrow \phi_{ij}$.

By Lemma 2.1, for each $\psi \in \Phi_{ij}$, $\psi|_{\{\tilde{x}\}} \in MC_{\{\tilde{x}_i\}}$ and $\psi|_{\{\tilde{y}\}} \in MC_{\{\tilde{y}_j\}}$. Therefore there is a unique k and a unique l s.t. $\psi|_{\{\tilde{x}\}} = \phi_{ik}$ and $\psi|_{\{\tilde{y}\}} = \psi_{jl}$. To simplify the notation we will leave such choice of k and l implicit in the sequel.

In constructing E we need to treat four kinds of actions differently. Below we shall only consider τ and bound output, i.e. we assume in E_1 and E_2 α_{ikp} and β_{jlq} are either τ or bound output. The case for free output is straightforward, while the case for input is slightly more complicated and requires some auxiliary notation, but the basic idea is the same.

For each $\psi \in \Phi_{ij}$, let C_ψ be the equivalence classes on $\{\tilde{z}\}$ determined by ψ, namely $x, y \in \{\tilde{z}\}$ are in the same equivalence class if and only if $\psi \Rightarrow x = y$. Let $[e]$ range over C_ψ. Define

$$\begin{aligned} I_\psi^\tau &= \{\, (p,q) \mid \alpha_{ikp} \equiv \tau,\ \beta_{jlq} \equiv \tau,\ (T'_{f(i,k,p)}, U'_{g(j,l,q)})^\psi \in \mathcal{S} \,\} \\ I_\psi^1 &= \{\, q \mid \beta_{jlq} \equiv \tau,\ (T_i, U'_{g(j,l,q)})^\psi \in \mathcal{S} \,\} \\ I_\psi^2 &= \{\, p \mid \alpha_{ikp} \equiv \tau,\ (T'_{f(i,k,p)}, U_j)^\psi \in \mathcal{S} \,\} \\ I_\psi^{BO_{[e]}} &= \{\, (p,q) \mid \alpha_{ikp} =^\psi \beta_{jlq} =^\psi \overline{e}(v),\ (T'_{f(i,k,p)}, U'_{g(j,l,q)})^{\psi \cup \{ z' \neq v \mid z' \in \{\tilde{z}\} \}} \in \mathcal{S} \,\} \end{aligned}$$

The three cases for τ reflect the three different ways to matching a τ move: it can be matched by a proper τ move (I_ψ^τ), or by no move (I_ψ^1 and I_ψ^2) when it is not a first τ move. This is our solution to the second complication mentioned above. Note that $I_\psi^1 = I_\psi^2 = \emptyset$ for $\psi \in \Phi_{11}$.

Let $\{\, Z_{ij} \mid 1 \le i \le m,\ 1 \le j \le n \,\}$ be a set of new process variables and $\tilde{z}_{ij} = \tilde{x}_i\tilde{y}_j$. Consider the equation set

$$E: \ Z_{ij}(\tilde{z}_{ij}) = \sum_{\psi \in \Phi_{ij}} \psi(A_\psi^\tau + \sum_{[e]} A_\psi^{BO_{[e]}})$$

where

$$\begin{aligned} A_\psi^\tau &\equiv \sum_{(p,q) \in I_\psi^\tau} \tau.Z_{f(i,k,p)g(j,l,q)}(\tilde{x}_{ikp}\tilde{y}_{jlq}) + \sum_{q \in I_\psi^1} \tau.Z_{ig(j,l,q)}(\tilde{x}_i\tilde{y}_{jlq}) + \sum_{p \in I_\psi^2} \tau.Z_{f(i,k,p)j}(\tilde{x}_{ikp}\tilde{y}_j) \\ A_\psi^{BO_{[e]}} &\equiv \sum_{(p,q) \in I_\psi^{BO_{[e]}}} \alpha_{ikp}.Z_{f(i,k,p)g(j,l,q)}(\tilde{x}_{ikp}\tilde{y}_{jlq}) \end{aligned}$$

Informally, for each $\psi \in \Phi_{ij}$, the right-hand side of the ij^{th} equation of E consists of the summands in the ith equation of E_1 and the summands in the jth equation of E_2 which are bisimilar over ψ. Note that E is guarded because both $E1$ and $E2$ are. Set

$$V_{ij} \equiv T_i + \sum_{\psi \in \Phi_{ij}} \psi \sum_{q \in I_\psi^1} \tau.T_i$$

Then $V_{11} \equiv T_1 \equiv T$ because $I_\psi^1 = \emptyset$ for $\psi \in \Phi_{11}$. Also, for any $\psi \in \Phi_{ij}$

$$\vdash \psi \land V_{ij} = \begin{cases} T_i & \text{if } I_\psi^1 = \emptyset \\ \tau.T_i & \text{otherwise} \end{cases} \tag{3}$$

We claim that E is provably $\{\, \phi_{ij} \mid i, j \,\}$-satisfied by T when each Z_{ij} is instantiated with $(\tilde{z}_{ij})V_{ij}$ over ϕ_{ij}, i.e. for each i, j

$$\vdash \phi_{ij} \land V_{ij} = (\sum_{\psi \in \Phi_{ij}} \psi(A_\psi^\tau + \sum_{[e]} A_\psi^{BO_{[e]}}))\theta \tag{4}$$

where $[e]$ ranges over C_ψ and $\theta \equiv [(\tilde{z}_{ij})^{\phi_{ij}} V_{ij}/Z_{ij} | i, j]$. By Propositions 3.2 and 3.1, and the fact that the elements of Φ_{ij} are mutually disjoint, (4) can be reduced to: for each $\psi \in \Phi_{ij}$

$$\vdash \psi \land V_{ij} = A_\psi^\tau\theta + \sum_{[e]} A_\psi^{BO_{[e]}}\theta \tag{5}$$

By examining each summand of the right-hand side, one can show

$$\vdash \psi \wedge A^{\tau}_{\psi}\theta = \sum_{(p,q)\in I^{\tau}_{\psi}} \tau.T'_{f(i,k,p)} + \sum_{q\in I^{1}_{\psi}} \tau.T_i + \sum_{p\in I^{2}_{\psi}} \tau.T'_{f(i,k,p)} \quad (6)$$

$$\vdash \psi \wedge A^{BO[e]}_{\psi}\theta = \sum_{(p,q)\in I^{BO[e]}_{\psi}} \alpha_{ikp}.T'_{f(i,k,p)} \quad (7)$$

With (6) and (7) we go back to equation (5). If $I^1_\psi = \emptyset$, then, by (3), its left-hand side $V_{ij} = T_i$, and the right-hand side contains exactly the terms $\alpha_{ikp}.T'_{f(i,k,p)}$ and/or $\alpha_{ikp}.\tau.T'_{f(i,k,p)}$ (with possible repetitions), hence (5) follows from (1); Otherwise, the left-hand side $V_{ij} = \tau.T_i$, and the right-hand side additionally contains the terms $\tau.T_i$ and/or $\tau.\tau.T_i$ (rising from the second component of the right-hand side of (6)), therefore (5) also follows from (1) by axiom T2.

Symmetrically we can prove E is provably $\{\, \phi_{ij} \mid i,j \,\}$-satisfied by U. 2

Proposition 4.3 *Let $E : X_i(\tilde{x}_i) = H_i$, $1 \le i \le m$, be a guarded equation set with free process variables in $\tilde{W}$. If T, U both provably $\tilde{\tilde{\phi}}$-satisfy E then $\vdash \phi_1 \rhd T = U$.*

Putting Lemma 4.1 and Propositions 4.2, 4.3 together we obtain

Theorem 4.4 *For guarded process terms T and U, $T \simeq^{\phi}_{L} U$ implies $\vdash \phi \rhd T = U$.*

To extend this result to the finite-control π-calculus where parallel composition is allowed to combine regular processes, what needed is to add a version of expansion law ([10, 5]) to the proof system. Then Lemma 4.1 still holds, and the proofs of the other propositions are not affected.

5 Removing Unguarded Recursions

In [8] Milner formulated three elegant laws which are sufficient to remove all unguarded recursions in regular CCS:

R3 $\mathbf{fix}X(X+T) = \mathbf{fix}XT$
R4 $\mathbf{fix}X(\tau.X+T) = \mathbf{fix}X\tau.T$
R5 $\mathbf{fix}X(\tau.(X+T)+U) = \mathbf{fix}X(\tau.X+T+U)$

As has been illustrated by the example in Introduction, these laws can not be naively adopted to the π-calculus. To motivate the axioms to be formulated in the sequel, let us examine this example in more detail. The transition $(\mathbf{fix}X(x,y,z)(\overline{x}y.\mathbf{0} + X(y,x,z) + X(x,z,y)))(a,b,c) \xrightarrow{\overline{a}b} \mathbf{0}$ originates from the subterm $\overline{x}y.\mathbf{0}$ in the recursion body. On the other hand, the unguarded occurrences $X(y,x,z)$ and $X(x,z,y)$ can not contribute to the behaviours of the top-level term by generating transitions from themselves, but they can do so by permuting the recursion parameters appearing in the "real" action derived from $\overline{x}y.\mathbf{0}$. Thus $X(y,x,z)$ is responsible for the transition $\xrightarrow{\overline{b}a} \mathbf{0}$, and the transition $\xrightarrow{\overline{a}c} \mathbf{0}$ is also possible because of $X(x,z,y)$. Furthermore, the combined effects of $X(y,x,z)$ and $X(x,z,y)$ produce more transitions: $\xrightarrow{\overline{c}b} \mathbf{0}$ (first $X(y,x,z)$, followed by $X(x,z,y)$, then $X(y,x,z)$ again), ... As each of $X(y,x,z)$ and $X(x,z,y)$ may be travelled through arbitrary times before a transition is derived, it seems this process may have infinitely many transitions.

Fortunately this is not true. Each recursion unwinding amounts to a permutation of the formal parameter (x,y,z), and there are only finite many permutations over

(x, y, z) can be generated by composing the two permutations (y, x, z) and (x, z, y). So what is needed for this example is to generate the permutation closure from (y, x, z) and (x, z, y), applying every permutation in this closure to $\overline{x}y.\mathbf{0}$, and then removing the unguarded occurrences $X(y, x, z)$ and $X(x, z, y)$.

The actual formulation of the axioms below is complicated by the possible presence of *conditions* and *restrictions* before unguarded occurrences of process variables – a typical unguarded occurrence has the form $\phi\nu\tilde{x}'X(\tilde{x})$, not just $X(\tilde{x})$, but the basic idea remains the same.

Call $< \phi_i, \tilde{x}'_i, \tilde{x}_i >$ a *crp-triple over* $\tilde{x}$ if $\tilde{x}_i$ is a permutation of $\tilde{x}$, $\{\tilde{x}'_i\} \subseteq \{\tilde{x}\}$, and $n(\phi_i) \subseteq \{\tilde{x}\}$. The composition of two crp-triples over $\tilde{x}$, $< \phi_i, \tilde{x}'_i, \tilde{x}_i >$ and $< \phi_j, \tilde{x}'_j, \tilde{x}_j >$

$$\frac{}{\nu\tilde{w}'X(\tilde{w}) \succ^{true} \nu\tilde{w}'X(\tilde{w})} \qquad \frac{T \succ^{\phi} \nu\tilde{w}'X(\tilde{w})}{\tau.T \succ^{\phi} \nu\tilde{w}'X(\tilde{w})} \qquad \frac{T \succ^{\phi} \nu\tilde{w}'X(\tilde{w})}{T + U \succ^{\phi} \nu\tilde{w}'X(\tilde{w})}$$

$$\frac{U \succ^{\phi} \nu\tilde{w}'X(\tilde{w})}{T + U \succ^{\phi} \nu\tilde{w}'X(\tilde{w})} \qquad \frac{T \succ^{\phi} \nu\tilde{w}'X(\tilde{w})}{\psi T \succ^{\psi\phi} \nu\tilde{w}'X(\tilde{w})} \qquad \frac{T \succ^{\phi} \nu\tilde{w}'X(\tilde{w})}{(\tilde{x})T \succ^{\lambda\tilde{x}\phi} \lambda\tilde{x}\nu\tilde{w}'X(\tilde{w})}$$

$$\frac{F \succ^{\lambda\tilde{x}\phi} \lambda\tilde{x}\nu\tilde{w}'X(\tilde{w})}{F\tilde{x} \succ^{\phi} \nu\tilde{w}'X(\tilde{w})} \qquad \frac{F \succ^{\lambda\tilde{x}\phi} \lambda\tilde{x}\nu\tilde{w}'X(\tilde{w})}{\mathbf{fix}Y F \succ^{\lambda\tilde{x}\phi} \lambda\tilde{x}\nu\tilde{w}'X(\tilde{w})} \quad Y \not\equiv X$$

Figure 5: The Conditional Unguarded Relation

is defined as $< \phi_k, \tilde{x}'_k, \tilde{x}_k >$ where $\phi_k = (\nu_{\tilde{x}'_j}\phi_i)[\tilde{x}_j/\tilde{x}] \wedge \phi_j$, $\tilde{x}'_k = \tilde{x}'_j \circ (\tilde{x}_i[\tilde{x}_j/\tilde{x}])$, and $\tilde{x}_k = \tilde{x}_i \circ \tilde{x}_j$ ($\circ$ is permutation composition).

A set of crp-triples over $\tilde{x}$, K, is *closed* if the composition of any two elements of K is also in K. An arbitrary finite set of crp-triples over $\tilde{x}$ K can be closed up by repeatedly composing its elements, and this process will terminate in finite number of steps because only finite number of crp-triples over $\tilde{x}$ can be generated from K. We denote the closure of K by K^*.

Using the following axiom all "strongly" unguarded recursions can be removed:

$$\text{UNG1} \quad \mathbf{fix}X(\tilde{x})(\sum_{i \in I} \phi_i \nu\tilde{x}'_i X(\tilde{x}_i) + T) = \mathbf{fix}X(\tilde{x})(\sum_{<\phi_j, \tilde{x}'_j, \tilde{x}_j> \in K^*} \phi_j \nu\tilde{x}'_j T[\tilde{x}_j/\tilde{x}] + T)$$

where $K = \{ < \phi_i, \tilde{x}'_i, \tilde{x}_i > | \; i \in I \}$.

A similar axiom takes care for immediate τ-loops:

$$\text{UNG2} \quad \mathbf{fix}X(\tilde{x})(\sum_{i \in I} \phi_i \tau.\nu\tilde{x}'_i X(\tilde{x}_i) + T) = \mathbf{fix}X(\tilde{x})(\sum_{<\phi_j, \tilde{x}'_j, \tilde{x}_j> \in K^*} \phi_j \tau.\nu\tilde{x}'_j T[\tilde{x}_j/\tilde{x}] + T)$$

To deal with deep-nested τ-loops, we need an auxiliary relation. The conditional free-unguarded relation $\succ^{\phi}$ is defined by the rules in Figure 5, where λ notation is used as purly syntactic device. Intuitively $T \succ^{\phi} \nu\tilde{w}'X(\tilde{w})$ means $\nu\tilde{w}'X(\tilde{w})$ occurs free and unguarded in T with (accumulated) context condition ϕ. Now the last axiom for removing unguarded recursions:

$$\text{UNG3} \quad \mathbf{fix}X(\tilde{x})(\phi\tau.T + U) = \mathbf{fix}X(\tilde{x})(\phi\tau\psi.\nu\tilde{w}'X(\tilde{w}) + \phi\tau.T[\mathbf{0}] + U)$$

where $T \succ^{\phi} \nu\tilde{w}'X(\tilde{w})$ and $T[\mathbf{0}]$ denotes the term obtained by replacing this occurrence of $\nu\tilde{w}'X(\tilde{w})$ with $\mathbf{0}$.

Let $\vdash^{rw} = \vdash^{grw} \cup \{UNG1, UNG2, UNG3\}$. Given any term which contain unguarded recursions, we can first use UNG3 to "lift" deep-nested τ-loops to the top-level which can then be excised using UNG1 and UNG2. So we have

Proposition 5.1 *For any term T with $fn(T) \subseteq \{\tilde{x}\}$, there exists a guarded term T' with $fn(T') \subseteq \{\tilde{x}\}$, such that $\vdash^{rw} T = T'$.*

Combining this proposition with Theorem 4.4 gives the main result of this paper:

Theorem 5.2 *$T \simeq_L^{\phi} U$ implies $\vdash^{rw} \phi \rhd T = U$.*

6 Conclusions

We have presented complete proof systems for late weak observation congruence in the finite-control π-calculus. These results are achieved in two steps: First we work with guarded recursions and the proof system is obtained by combining that for weak congruence in finite π-calculus ([5]) and that for strong congruence in guarded finite-control π-calculus ([6]); We then formulate sound laws sufficient to remove arbitrary unguarded recursions, thus extend the result to the whole language of finite-control π-calculus.

Because of space limitation we have only discussed the proof system for late weak bisimulation. There are two ways to adopt it to the early weak equivalence: replacing the INPUT rule with the more general one:

$$\text{E-INPUT}\ \frac{\phi \rhd \sum_{i \in I} \tau.T_i = \sum_{j \in J} \tau.U_j \qquad \phi \Rightarrow a_i = b_j,\ i \in I,\ j \in J}{\phi \rhd \sum_{i \in I} a_i(x).T = \sum_{j \in J} b_j(x).U \quad x \notin n(\phi)}$$

or adding the following "early" axiom, due to Parrow and Sangiorgi [10]:

$$\text{EA} \quad a(x).T + a(x).U = a(x).T + a(x).U + a(x).([x = y]T + [x \neq y]U)$$

It is not difficult to see that EA can be derived from E-INPUT in the presence of the other rules.

References

[1] Michele Boreale and Rocco De Nicola. A symbolic semantics for the π-calculus. *Information and Computation*, 126(1):34–52, 1996.

[2] M. Dam. Model checking mobile processes. *Information and Computation*, 129:35–51, 1996.

[3] M. Hennessy and H. Lin. Symbolic bisimulations. *Theoretical Computer Science*, 138:353–389, 1995.

[4] H. Lin. Symbolic bisimulations and proof systems for the π-calculus. Report 7/94, Computer Science, University of Sussex, 1994.

[5] H. Lin. Complete inference systems for weak bisimulation equivalences in the π-calculus. In *TAPSOFT'95*, LNCS 915. Springer–Verlag, 1995.

[6] H. Lin. Unique fixpoint induction for the π-calculus. In *CONCUR'95*, LNCS 962. Springer–Verlag, 1995.

[7] R. Milner. A complete inference system for a class of regular behaviours. *J. Computer and System Science*, 28:439–466, 1984.

[8] R. Milner. A complete axiomatisation for observational congruence of finite-state behaviours. *Information and Computation*, 81:227–247, 1989.

[9] R. Milner, J. Parrow, and D. Walker. A calculus of mobile proceses, part I,II. *Information and Computation*, 100:1–77, 1992.

[10] J. Parrow and D. Sangiorgi. Algebraic theories for name-passing calculi. *Information and Computation*, 120(2):174–197, 1995.

[11] Davide Sangiorgi. A theory of bisimulation for the π-calculus. *Acta Informatica*, 33:69–97, 1996.

Concurrent Constraints in the Fusion Calculus
(Extended Abstract)

Björn Victor[1] and Joachim Parrow[2]

[1] Dept. of Computer Systems, Uppsala University, Sweden, Bjorn.Victor@DoCS.UU.SE
[2] Dept. of Teleinformatics, Royal Institute of Technology, Sweden, joachim@it.kth.se

Abstract. We use the fusion calculus, a generalization and simplification of the π-calculus, to model concurrent constraint programming. In particular we encode three basic variants of the ρ-calculus, which is a foundational calculus for the concurrent constraint programming language Oz. Using a new reduction-based semantics and weak barbed congruences for the fusion calculus we formally establish an operational correspondence between the ρ-calculi and their encodings. These barbed congruences are shown to coincide with the hyper-equivalences previously adopted for the fusion calculus.

1 Introduction

In this paper we use the fusion calculus to model concurrent constraint programming, thereby relating the paradigm of communicating processes to that of concurrent constraints. In the first, parallel agents interact with each other by sending and receiving data over named ports; in the second, agents produce constraints on the values of variables, which are combined to resolve queries about the values. Previous attempts at reconciling these paradigms have used one of two different lines: either extending a process calculus with logical variables [12] or encoding the variables as separate processes [15]. In the present paper our method is more direct, highlighting the fact that the fusion calculus serves as a basic underlying formalism. To establish correctness we explore the reduction semantics and weak, or observation, equivalences of the fusion calculus in detail.

Process Calculi: The fusion calculus is a calculus for mobile processes, in the sense that the communication structure of the involved processes may change over the execution of the system. The π-calculus [4] is the standard example of such a calculus. Here, the data sent and received over named ports are port names; there is no difference between ports and data, and they are collectively called *names*. An example of interaction in the π-calculus is:

$$\pi\text{-calculus:} \qquad \overline{u}\langle x\rangle \,.\, P \mid u(y) \,.\, Q$$

which can evolve into $P \mid Q\{x/y\}$ through communication over the name u.

The expressive power of mobile processes has been established by using the π-calculus for semantics of programming languages such as PICT [9] and of object-oriented programming [16], for encoding higher-order communications [10] and the λ-calculus [3]. Sequential logic programming [2] and simple concurrent constraint programming [15] have also been modelled: in both these cases, the major obstacle has been expressing logical variables, which can be updated from several processes and not only at their binding occurrence. The variables are modelled by separate processes which can be read, updated etc. by sending requests and receiving responses.

In a previous paper [7] we show how the π-calculus can be *simplified* into the fusion calculus while at the same time extending its expressiveness. The heart of the fusion calculus is the *fusion action*, which in interplay with the *scope* operator can express changes to names shared between several processes in the system. The changes amount to identifying, or *fusing*, previously distinct names. A sample interaction is:

$$\text{fusion calculus:} \qquad (y)(\overline{u}x\,.\,P \mid uy\,.\,Q \mid R)$$

which can evolve into $(P \mid Q \mid R)\{x/y\}$ by communication over the name u. In this example the communication has effect not only in Q, but in all the agents in the scope of y. Although the fusion calculus is a simplification, it gains considerable expressive power over the π-calculus, and we show in this paper that it is easy to model logical variables in a few basic constraint systems.

Concurrent Constraints: In concurrent constraints, the effect of computation consists of changes to a shared *constraint store* by adding variable constraints to it by *tell* operations. The store combines the constraints, and can subsequently be queried by *ask* operations to find out if a formula containing constrained variables is entailed. The store differs from a normal memory store, which holds *values* (such as 42) of variables; here a variable can have a *partial* value (such as "between 17 and x"). An example of a concurrent constraint computation is

$$\text{CC-program:} \qquad \mathit{ask}(x < y)\,.\,P \wedge \mathit{tell}(y > 17) \wedge \mathit{tell}(x < 11)$$

which can evolve into P with a store which entails $x < 11 \wedge y > 17$.

To relate mobile process calculi and concurrent constraints, we use the *ρ-calculus* of Niehren and Müller [6]. This is a calculus which serves as a foundation of the concurrent constraint programming language Oz, developed at DFKI in Saarbrücken. Oz incorporates constraints, functional, and object-oriented programming in a concurrent setting, and requires a richer foundational calculus than a pure constraint calculus as in, e.g., [11]. The process part of the ρ-calculus is a subcalculus of the π-calculus [6], and it is expressive enough to model functional and object-oriented programming. It can be extended by an arbitrary constraint system $\mathcal{CS}$, resulting in the calculus $\rho(\mathcal{CS})$. This takes the calculus beyond traditional process calculi and it thus cannot directly use the rich flora of associated theories and tools. An example of a term in $\rho(x = y, x \neq y)$, with constraints being equalities or inequalities, is

$$\rho(x = y, x \neq y): \quad x = u \;\wedge\; u \neq y \;\wedge\; \texttt{if } x = y \texttt{ then } E_1 \texttt{ else } (z = w \wedge E_2)$$

which can evolve into $x = u \;\wedge\; u \neq y \;\wedge\; z = w \;\wedge\; E_2$. The top-level equality and inequality conjuncts in this way represent the store and the `if`-conjunct corresponds to *ask*.

The main technical point of this paper is to represent $\rho(\mathcal{CS})$ for a few basic $\mathcal{CS}$ in the fusion calculus. The semantics of the ρ-calculus is given in [6] using reduction rules and a structural congruence resulting in an *unlabelled* transition system. (Term-rewriting systems such as the λ-calculus also have reduction semantics.) The semantics of the fusion calculus, on the other hand, is given in [7] using rules for *labelled* transitions (and a similar structural congruence), as traditionally has been done for process calculi such as CCS or the π-calculus. To relate the calculi we give a reduction semantics for the fusion calculus. The behaviour of an agent must then be considered together with an environment with which it can interact. We verify that the reduction semantics corresponds with the old labelled transition semantics, by defining appropriate equivalences between agents in the new semantics, and showing that it coincides with the equivalences of the old semantics.

Main Results and Overview: In the next Section, we review from [7] the syntax and labelled transition semantics of the fusion calculus, and the definition of (strong) hyperequivalence. We add a definition of *weak* hyperequivalence, and show that in the fusion calculus it is the weakest congruence which contains weak bisimulation. In Section 3 we give a reduction semantics to the fusion calculus, define strong and weak congruences in this semantics, based on *barbed bisimulation* [5, 10], and verify that they coincide with strong and weak hyperequivalence. In Section 4 we present the syntax and semantics of the ρ-calculus and show how to encode it in the fusion calculus for its instantiation to three basic constraint systems. We show that the encodings are correct by verifying an operational correspondence between reductions in the ρ-calculi and in the encodings. Finally in Section 5 we conclude and give some directions for future work.

Related work: The separation of binding and update in process calculi was, to our knowledge, first done independently by Fu [1] with his χ-calculus and by us [8] with the update calculus. The update calculus turned out not to generalize to a polyadic calculus (where more than one name at a time can be transmitted), and therefore we developed it further into the fusion calculus [7].

The Oz programming language is not only a concurrent constraint programming language, but also supports higher-order functional programming and concurrent objects, and requires a richer foundational calculus than a pure constraint calculus as in, e.g., [11]. The ρ-calculus [6] is more appropriate in this respect.

In [12], Smolka defined the γ-calculus and informally related it to a variant of the π-calculus with logical variables, equational constraints and a constraint elimination rule. Niehren and Müller in [6] defined the ρ-calculus, and related $\rho(\emptyset)$ (the ρ-calculus without constraints) to a subcalculus of the π-calculus, and $\rho(x = y)$ to a variant of the γ-calculus without constants. In [15], we related the π-calculus directly to the γ-calculus by an encoding which we proved correct. In the present paper we strengthen these results by relating the fusion calculus to both $\rho(x = y)$ and $\rho(x = y, C)$. (In [7] it is shown that the π-calculus is a subcalculus of the fusion calculus.) Compared to the encodings in this paper, the encoding of [15] was quite complex due to the difficulties of representing logical variables. Logical variables as part of Prolog were specified in [2], but no proofs of correctness were presented.

The theory of barbed bisimulation originated in [5], where CCS was treated, and was further developed in [10] for the π-calculus and the higher-order π-calculus.

2 The Fusion Calculus

In this section we first review the syntax and operational semantics of a version of the fusion calculus with match, mismatch and recursion. We then review the strong bisimulation equivalence and congruence from [7]. The novel contribution of the present paper begins by exploring the weak bisimulation equivalences. We show that the weak congruence, *weak hyperequivalence*, is the only reasonable congruence in the sense that it is the largest congruence contained in weak bisimulation.

2.1 Syntax and Semantics

We assume an infinite set $\mathcal{N}$ of *names* ranged over by $u, v, \ldots, z$. Like in the π-calculus, names represent communication channels, which are also the values transmitted. We write $\tilde{x}$ for a (possibly empty) finite sequence $x_1 \cdots x_n$ of names. φ ranges over total equivalence relations over $\mathcal{N}$ (i.e. equivalence relations with $\mathrm{dom}(\varphi) = \mathcal{N}$) with only finitely many non-singular equivalence classes. We write $\{\tilde{x} = \tilde{y}\}$ to mean the smallest such equivalence relation relating each x_i with y_i, and write $\mathbf{1}$ for the identity relation.

Definition 1. *The* free actions, *ranged over by* α, *and the* agents, *ranged over by* $P, Q, \ldots$, *are defined by*

$$\begin{array}{lll} \alpha ::= u\tilde{x} & \text{(Input)} \\ \quad\;\; \overline{u}\tilde{x} & \text{(Output)} \\ \quad\;\; \varphi & \text{(Fusion)} \end{array} \qquad \begin{array}{l} P ::= \mathbf{0} \;\mid\; \alpha\,.\,Q \;\mid\; Q+R \;\mid\; Q \mid R \;\mid \\ \quad (x)Q \;\mid\; [x=y]Q \;\mid\; [x \neq y]Q \;\mid\; A(\tilde{x}) \end{array}$$

The input and output actions above are collectively called *free communication* actions. In these, the names $\tilde{x}$ are the *objects* of the action, and the name u is the *subject*. We write a to stand for either u or $\overline{u}$, thus $a\tilde{x}$ is the general form of a communication action. We identify fusion actions not based on their concrete syntax, but based on their corresponding equivalence relations. Fusion actions have neither subject nor objects.

Prefixing an agent Q means that the agent must perform the action α before acting like Q. Performing a fusion here represents an obligation to treat all related names as identical. We often omit a trailing $\mathbf{0}$ and write α for $\alpha\,.\,\mathbf{0}$ if no confusion can arise. Like in the π-calculus, Summation $Q + R$ is alternative choice and Composition $Q \mid R$ lets agents act in parallel.

The Scope $(x)Q$ limits the scope of x to Q; no visible communication action of $(x)Q$ can have x as its subject, and fusion effects with respect to x are limited to Q. Restriction and input binding of the π-calculus can be recovered as special cases of Scope.

A Match $[x = y]Q$ acts like Q if x and y are the same name; a Mismatch $[x \neq y]Q$ acts like Q if x and y are *not* the same. We let M, N range over Match or Mismatch operators and A over a possibly infinite set of identifiers, each with an associated nonnegative arity k and agent definition $A(x_1, \ldots, x_k) \stackrel{def}{=} P$ with pairwise distinct x_i such that $\mathrm{fn}(P) \subseteq \{x_1, \ldots, x_k\}$.

The name x is said to be *bound* in $(x)P$. We write $(\tilde{x})P$ for $(x_1) \cdots (x_n)P$. The *free names* in P, denoted $\mathrm{fn}(P)$, are the names in P with a non-bound occurrence; here the names occurring in the fusion φ is defined to be the names in the non-singular equivalence classes, i.e. in the relation $\varphi - \mathbf{1}$. As usual we will not distinguish between alpha-variants of agents, i.e., agents differing only in the choice of bound names.

The action of a transition may be free or bound:

Definition 2. *The* actions, *ranged over by* γ, *consist of the fusion actions and of communication actions of the form* $(z_1) \cdots (z_n)a\tilde{x}$ *(written* $(\tilde{z})a\tilde{x}$*), where* $n \geq 0$ *and all elements in* $\tilde{z}$ *are also in* $\tilde{x}$. *If* $n > 0$ *we say it is a* bound *action.*

Note that there are no bound fusion actions. In the communication actions above, $\tilde{z}$ are the *bound objects* and the elements in $\tilde{x}$ that are not in $\tilde{z}$ are the *free objects.* We further write $\mathrm{n}(\gamma)$ to mean all names occurring in γ (i.e., also including the subject of communication actions and the names in non-singular equivalence classes in fusion actions).

For convenience we define $\varphi \backslash z$ to mean $\varphi \cap (\mathcal{N} - \{z\})^2 \cup \{(z,z)\}$, i.e., the equivalence relation φ with all references to z removed (except for the identity). For example, $\{x=y\}\backslash y = \mathbf{1}$, and $\{x=z, z=y\}\backslash z = \{x=y\}$.

We now define a structural congruence which equates all agents we will never want to distinguish for any semantic reason, and then use this when giving the transition semantics.

Definition 3. *The* structural congruence, $\equiv$, *between agents is the least congruence satisfying the abelian monoid laws for Summation and Composition (associativity, commutativity and* $\mathbf{0}$ *as identity), and the scope laws* $(x)\mathbf{0} \equiv \mathbf{0}$, $(x)(y)P \equiv (y)(x)P$, $(x)(P+Q) \equiv (x)P + (x)Q$, $(x)MP \equiv M(x)P$ *if* $x \notin \mathrm{n}(M)$ *and also the* scope extension *law* $P \mid (z)Q \equiv (z)(P \mid Q)$ *where* $z \notin \mathrm{fn}(P)$, *and the law for process identifiers:* $A(\tilde{y}) \equiv P\{\tilde{y}/\tilde{x}\}$ *if* $A(\tilde{x}) \stackrel{def}{=} P$.

Definition 4. *The family of* transitions $P \xrightarrow{\gamma} Q$ *is the least family satisfying the laws in Table 1. In this definition structurally equivalent agents are considered the same, i.e., if* $P \equiv P'$ *and* $Q \equiv Q'$ *and* $P \xrightarrow{\gamma} Q$ *then also* $P' \xrightarrow{\gamma} Q'$.

$$\text{PREF}\quad \frac{-}{\alpha\,.\,P \xrightarrow{\alpha} P} \qquad \text{SUM}\quad \frac{P \xrightarrow{\alpha} P'}{P+Q \xrightarrow{\alpha} P'} \qquad \text{PAR}\quad \frac{P \xrightarrow{\alpha} P'}{P \mid Q \xrightarrow{\alpha} P' \mid Q}$$

$$\text{COM}\quad \frac{P \xrightarrow{u\tilde{x}} P',\ Q \xrightarrow{\overline{u}\tilde{y}} Q',\ |\tilde{x}| = |\tilde{y}|}{P \mid Q \xrightarrow{\{\tilde{x}=\tilde{y}\}} P' \mid Q'} \qquad \text{SCOPE}\quad \frac{P \xrightarrow{\varphi} P',\ z\,\varphi\,x,\ z \neq x}{(z)P \xrightarrow{\varphi\backslash z} P'\{x/z\}}$$

$$\text{PASS}\quad \frac{P \xrightarrow{\alpha} P',\ z \notin \mathrm{n}(\alpha)}{(z)P \xrightarrow{\alpha} (z)P'} \qquad \text{OPEN}\quad \frac{P \xrightarrow{(\tilde{y})a\,\tilde{x}} P',\ z \in \tilde{x} - \tilde{y},\ a \notin \{z, \overline{z}\}}{(z)P \xrightarrow{(z\tilde{y})a\,\tilde{x}} P'}$$

$$\text{MATCH}\quad \frac{P \xrightarrow{\alpha} P'}{[x=x]P \xrightarrow{\alpha} P'} \qquad \text{MISMATCH}\quad \frac{P \xrightarrow{\alpha} P',\ x \neq y}{[x \neq y]P \xrightarrow{\alpha} P'}$$

Table 1. The Fusion Calculus: Laws of action.

The COM rule results in a fusion action rather than a substitution, and the SCOPE rule entails a substitution of the scoped name z for a nondeterministically chosen name x related to it by φ. For the purpose of the equivalence defined below it will not matter which such x replaces z. The only rule dealing with bound actions is OPEN. Using structural congruence, pulling the relevant scope to the top level, we can still infer e.g. $P \mid (x)ayx\,.\,Q \xrightarrow{(x)ayx} P \mid Q$ using PREF and OPEN (provided $x \notin \mathrm{fn}(P)$, otherwise an alpha-conversion is necessary). It is clear that for the purpose of the semantics, fusion prefixes can be regarded as derived forms since $\{\tilde{y} = \tilde{z}\} . P$ has exactly the same transitions as $(u)(\overline{u}\tilde{y} . \mathbf{0} \mid u\tilde{z} . P)$ when $u \notin \mathrm{fn}(P)$. (In the same way the τ prefix can be regarded as derived in CCS and in the π-calculus.)

For further examples and explanations we refer the reader to [7] and [14].

2.2 Equivalences

From [7] we recall the definition of strong bisimulation in the fusion calculus.

Definition 5. *A substitution σ* agrees with *the fusion φ if $\forall x, y : x \varphi y \Leftrightarrow \sigma(x) = \sigma(y)$. A* substitutive effect *of a fusion φ is a substitution σ agreeing with φ such that $\forall x, y : \sigma(x) = y \Rightarrow x \varphi y$ (i.e., σ sends all members of the equivalence class to one representative of the class). The only substitutive effect of a communication action is the identity substitution.*

Definition 6. *A* bisimulation *is a binary symmetric relation $\mathcal{S}$ between agents such that $P\, \mathcal{S}\, Q$ implies: If $P \xrightarrow{\gamma} P'$ with $\mathrm{bn}(\gamma) \cap \mathrm{fn}(Q) = \emptyset$ then $Q \xrightarrow{\gamma} Q'$ and $P'\sigma\, \mathcal{S}\, Q'\sigma$ for some substitutive effect σ of γ. P is bisimilar to Q, written $P \dot{\sim} Q$, if $P\, \mathcal{S}\, Q$ for some bisimulation $\mathcal{S}$.*

This definition differs from *ground* bisimulation only in the treatment of fusion actions. A fusion $\{x = y\}$ represents an obligation to make x and y equal everywhere. Therefore, if γ above is such a fusion, it only makes sense to relate P' and Q' when a substitution $\{y/x\}$ or $\{x/y\}$ has been performed. Note that it does not matter which substitution we choose, since $P\{x/y\} \dot{\sim} Q\{x/y\}$ implies $P\{y/x\} \dot{\sim} Q\{y/x\}$, by the simple fact that $P\{x/y\}\{y/x\} \equiv P\{y/x\}$ and that bisimulation is closed under injective substitutions.

The *weak* simulation, bisimulation and bisimilarity $\dot{\approx}$ are as usual defined by replacing $Q \xrightarrow{\gamma} Q'$ by $Q \xRightarrow{\gamma} Q'$ in Definition 6. For the case that γ is a fusion the definition of $\xRightarrow{\gamma}$ requires some care. The intuition is that $\xRightarrow{\varphi}$ represents a sequence of actions with "observable content" φ. But fusions are "observable" only through their substitutive effects. They have no subject and the environment cannot synchronize with them and keep track of, e.g., how many have been performed. Therefore we allow $\xRightarrow{\varphi}$ to be a sequence of fusions whose aggregated substitutive effect is the same as that of φ.

Definition 7. *Define the* composition *of two transitions, $\circ$, by $P(\xrightarrow{\gamma} \circ \xrightarrow{\gamma'})Q$ iff there exists an agent P' such that $P \xrightarrow{\gamma} P'$ and $P'\sigma_\gamma \xrightarrow{\gamma'} Q$, where σ_γ is a substitutive effect of γ. Define the* conjunction *of two fusions φ and ψ, written $\varphi \wedge \psi$, to be the least equivalence relation containing φ and ψ. Define the* weak transition *$\xRightarrow{\gamma}$ by the following: $P \xRightarrow{\gamma} Q$ means that for some $n \geq 0$, $P \xrightarrow{\gamma_1} \circ \cdots \circ \xrightarrow{\gamma_n} Q$ and either of*

1. *γ is a communication and $\gamma = \gamma_i$ for some i and $\gamma_j = \mathbf{1}$ for all $j \neq i$, or*
2. *γ and all γ_i are fusions and $\gamma = \gamma_1 \wedge \cdots \wedge \gamma_n$. Here we allow $n = 0$ where the empty conjunction is $\mathbf{1}$, in other words $P \xRightarrow{\mathbf{1}} P$ holds for all P.*

An illuminating exercise is to verify that

$$\{x = y\} . [x = y]\{v = w\} . P \quad \dot{\approx} \quad \{x = y\} . \{v = w\} . P \;+\; \{x = y, v = w\} . P$$

but not $\{x = y\} . \{v = w\} . P \dot{\approx} \{x = y, v = w\} . P$ since the RHS cannot simulate the transition $\xrightarrow{\{x=y\}}$. It is easy to prove that $\dot{\sim}$ and $\dot{\approx}$ are indeed equivalences (transitivity for $\dot{\approx}$ requires some care) and that they are not congruences. To find the congruences we close the bisimulations under arbitary substitutions:

Definition 8. *A* (weak) hyperbisimulation *is a substitution closed (weak) bisimulation, i.e., a (weak) bisimulation $\mathcal{S}$ with the property that $P\ \mathcal{S}\ Q$ implies $P\sigma\ \mathcal{S}\ Q\sigma$ for any substitution σ. Two agents P and Q are* (weakly) hyperequivalent, *written $P \sim Q$ ($P \approx Q$), if they are related by a (weak) hyperbisimulation.*

Theorem 9. [7] *Hyperequivalence is the largest congruence contained in bisimilarity.*

The corresponding relation does not quite hold for weak hyperequivalence. But we here show that it holds if we replace the summation operator by *guarded* summation $\sum \alpha_i . P_i$. (This is as expected, also in CCS and in the π-calculus weak bisimulation equivalence fails to be a congruence for the same reason.)

Theorem 10. *With guarded summation, weak hyperequivalence is the largest congruence in weak bisimilarity.*

This is proved the same way as the strong case in [7]: we construct a context which can perform any relevant substitutions at any time, and show that if two agents are equivalent in that context, which they must be if they are congruent, then they are also weakly hyperequivalent. The context used is the same as in [7]. Due to space limitations, we refer to the first author's PhD thesis [14] for the full proof.

3 The Barbed Congruences

We shall here provide a *reduction* semantics for the fusion calculus and prove that it in a precise way corresponds to the transition semantics. This lends credibility to our transition laws and equivalence definitions. A reduction semantics is also in some respects easier to comprehend, and facilitates a comparison with the ρ-calculus in the next section. We will here use the standard idea of *barbed bisimulation* [5] and prove that the largest congruence coincides with hyperequivalence.

The reduction semantics of the fusion calculus is given by the rules in Table 2, where again structurally equivalent agents are considered the same. We write $\tilde{M}, \tilde{N}$ for a sequence of match and mismatch operators. Here and in the following we use $\mathrm{dom}(\sigma) = \{u : \sigma(u) \neq u\}$ and $\mathrm{ran}(\sigma) = \{\sigma(u) : \sigma(u) \neq u\}$. The reductions of an appropriately scoped fusion prefix are obtained by viewing a fusion prefix $\{\tilde{x} = \tilde{y}\} . P$ as defined by $(u)(\overline{u}\,\tilde{x} \mid u\,\tilde{y} . P)$ where u is fresh.

Proposition 11. *$P \longrightarrow Q$ iff $P \xrightarrow{1} Q$.*

The implication to the right is a simple induction over the reduction rules; the implication to the left is an induction over transition rules using a slightly more general induction hypothesis.

We now want to construct a congruence relation based on a minimal power of observation, such that it coincides with the labelled bisimulation congruence. If there are *no* observables, the resulting *reduction congruence* is very weak, but turns out

$(\tilde{z})\Big(R \mid (\cdots + \tilde{M} u \tilde{x} . P) \mid (\tilde{N} \overline{u} \tilde{y} . Q + \cdots)\Big) \longrightarrow (R \mid P \mid Q)\sigma$ if $\lvert\tilde{x}\rvert = \lvert\tilde{y}\rvert$, $\tilde{M} \Leftrightarrow \tilde{N} \Leftrightarrow$ true, σ agrees with $\{\tilde{x} = \tilde{y}\}$, $\mathrm{ran}(\sigma) \cap \tilde{z} = \emptyset$, and $\mathrm{dom}(\sigma) = \tilde{z}$
$\dfrac{P \longrightarrow P'}{[x = x]P \longrightarrow P'}$ $\quad \dfrac{P \longrightarrow P',\ x \neq y}{[x \neq y]P \longrightarrow P'}$ $\quad \dfrac{P \longrightarrow P'}{P \mid Q \longrightarrow P' \mid Q}$ $\quad \dfrac{P \longrightarrow P'}{P + Q \longrightarrow P'}$ $\quad \dfrac{P \longrightarrow P'}{(x)P \longrightarrow (x)P'}$

Table 2. Reduction rules for the fusion calculus.

to be sufficient for divergence-free CCS [5]. For possibly divergent CCS processes, it is sufficient to be able to observe the possibility of communication [5], while in the π-calculus we must also observe the subject of the communication [10]. With the addition of fusion actions, you may suspect that these need to be observable. This is not the case: we can already observe fusions indirectly using the match and mismatch operators. The observation predicate below is thus the same as for the π-calculus.

Definition 12.

$x\tilde{y} . P \downarrow x$	$[x = x]P \downarrow y$ *if* $P \downarrow y$
$\overline{x}\tilde{y} . P \downarrow x$	$[x \neq z]P \downarrow y$ *if* $P \downarrow y$ *and* $x \neq z$
$(P \mid Q) \downarrow x$ *if* $P \downarrow x$ *or* $Q \downarrow x$	$(x)P \downarrow y$ *if* $P \downarrow y$ *and* $x \neq y$
$(P + Q) \downarrow x$ *if* $P \downarrow x$ *or* $Q \downarrow x$	$A(\tilde{y}) \downarrow z$ *if* $A(\tilde{x}) \stackrel{def}{=} P$, $\lvert\tilde{y}\rvert = \lvert\tilde{x}\rvert$ *and* $P\{\tilde{y}/\tilde{x}\} \downarrow z$

We repeat the standard definition of barbed bisimulation from [10]:

Definition 13. *A* barbed bisimulation *is a symmetric binary relation $\mathcal{S}$ between agents such that $P \mathcal{S} Q$ implies:*
1. If $P \longrightarrow P'$ then $Q \longrightarrow Q'$ and $P' \mathcal{S} Q'$.
2. If $P \downarrow x$ for some x, then $Q \downarrow x$.
P is barbed bisimilar to Q, written $P \dot{\sim}_b Q$, if $P \mathcal{S} Q$ for some barbed bisimulation $\mathcal{S}$.

We note that barbed bisimulation is a very weak equivalence: not only is $u . v . \mathbf{0} \dot{\sim}_b u . \mathbf{0}$, but in the fusion calculus also $\varphi . P \dot{\sim}_b \mathbf{0}$ for any P and φ different from $\mathbf{1}$, since a non-inert fusion prefix has neither reductions nor observations. By closing the bisimulation under contexts we obtain a more interesting relation:

Definition 14. *Two agents P and Q are* barbed congruent, *written $P \sim_b Q$, if for all contexts $C[\cdot]$, it holds that $C[P] \dot{\sim}_b C[Q]$.*

For CCS, the barbed congruence coincides with strong bisimulation [5]. For the π-calculus, it coincides with the early bisimulation congruence [10]. For the fusion calculus, we here show that it coincides with hyperequivalence:

Theorem 15. *$P \sim Q$ iff $P \sim_b Q$.*

Proof. *Every hyperbisimulation is clearly a barbed bisimulation, so $\sim \subseteq \dot{\sim}_b$, and $P \sim Q \Rightarrow C[P] \sim C[Q]$ for all contexts $C[\cdot]$, since $\sim$ is a congruence, so $C[P] \dot{\sim}_b C[Q]$, which means that $P \sim_b Q$. This means $\sim \subseteq \sim_b$. We know from [7] that $\sim$ is the largest congruence contained in bisimulation, so we need only show that barbed congruence is also contained in bisimulation to complete the proof. This is done in Lemma 16 below.* □

Lemma 16. *Barbed congruence is contained in bisimulation.*

The proof goes by constructing a context $C[\cdot]$ such that $\{(P,Q) : C[P] \sim_b C[Q]\}$ is a bisimulation. The context used is similar to (but simpler than) the one used for the weak case in Lemma 18 below; we omit the details.

To define the weak barbed bisimulation and congruence, we change $Q \longrightarrow Q'$ to $Q \longrightarrow^* Q'$ and $Q \downarrow x$ to $Q \longrightarrow^* \downarrow x$ (written $Q \Downarrow x$) in Definition 13. We write $P \dot{\approx}_b Q$ if P and Q are weak barbed bisimilar, and $P \approx_b Q$ if they are weak barbed congruent, again under the restriction to guarded summation.

Theorem 17. *$P \approx_b Q$ iff $P \approx Q$.*

The proof is just like that for Theorem 15, and needs Theorem 10 of Section 2 and Lemma 18 below.

Lemma 18. *Weak barbed congruence is contained in weak bisimulation.*

Proof. The proof is reminiscent of the corresponding proof for the π-calculus [10], but simpler. We construct a family of contexts $C^{\tilde{z}}_{n,k}[\cdot]$ such that

$$\mathcal{R} = \{(P,Q) : C^{\tilde{z}}_{n,k}[P] \approx_b C^{\tilde{z}}_{n,k}[Q], \text{fn}(P,Q) \subseteq \tilde{z}, n = |\tilde{z}|, k = \text{ma}(P,Q)\}$$

is a weak bisimulation, where $\text{ma}(P,Q)$ *is the maximal arity of communication actions in P and Q.*

In the definition below we postulate for each name u a fresh name u'; for each finite sequence of names $\tilde{y}$ a fresh name y''; and for each finite equivalence relation e on names a fresh name m_e. Furthermore, $\{c, s, in, out, d_n : n \geq 0\}$ contains fresh names, each M_e is a sequence of match and mismatch operators agreeing with the equivalence relation e, and $\text{eq}(\tilde{z})$ stands for the set of equivalence relations on names in $\tilde{z}$. The definition of $Count_n$ implictly uses an infinite number of arguments (remember that all free names must be in the argument list of the identifier). This can be avoided by parameterizing the context on the length r of the argument list and letting $\mathcal{R}$ include contexts for all r.

$$C^{\tilde{z}}_{n,k}[\cdot] \equiv (\tilde{z})(\cdot \mid V^k_n(\tilde{z}) \mid Count_n)$$
$$Count_n \stackrel{def}{=} d_n + c \,.\, Count_{n+1}$$
$$\begin{aligned} V^k_n(\tilde{z}) \stackrel{def}{=} & \sum_{u_i \in \tilde{z}, |\tilde{y}| \leq k} (\tilde{y}) u_i \tilde{y} \,.\, \overline{c} \,.\, (u'_i + out + y'' + \mathbf{1} \,.\, V^k_{n+1}(\tilde{z}\tilde{y})) \\ + & \sum_{u_i \in \tilde{z}, |\tilde{y}| \leq k} (\tilde{y}) \overline{u_i} \tilde{y} \,.\, \overline{c} \,.\, (u'_i + in + y'' + \mathbf{1} \,.\, V^k_{n+1}(\tilde{z}\tilde{y})) \\ + & \; s \\ + & \sum_{e \in \text{eq}(\tilde{z})} M_e m_e \end{aligned}$$

Now, for $(P,Q) \in \mathcal{R}$,

1. *If $P \stackrel{(\tilde{x})u\tilde{w}}{\longrightarrow} P'$, we must find a Q' such that $Q \stackrel{(\tilde{x})u\tilde{w}}{\Longrightarrow} Q'$ and $(P',Q') \in \mathcal{R}$. $C^{\tilde{z}}_{n,k}[P] \stackrel{1}{\longrightarrow} \stackrel{1}{\longrightarrow} (\tilde{z})(\tilde{x})(P' \mid W \mid Count_{n+1}) \equiv S$ where W is the appropriate derivative of $V^k_n(\tilde{z})$. Now, $S \downarrow d_{n+1}$, so for $C[Q]$ to simulate the reduction, it must reduce involving Q and V, but it cannot let Q communicate more than once. Furthermore, $S \downarrow u'_i$ and $S \downarrow in$, so $Q \stackrel{\alpha}{\Longrightarrow} Q'$ with $\text{subj}(\alpha) = u_i$, and $S \downarrow y''$, so $\text{obj}(\alpha) = \tilde{y} = \tilde{w}$,*

where $\tilde{x} \subseteq \tilde{w}$ is fresh. Then $C[Q] \overset{(\tilde{x})a\tilde{w}}{\Longrightarrow} (\tilde{z})(\tilde{x})(Q' \mid W \mid Count_{n+1}) \equiv T$. Finally the reduction $S \overset{1}{\longrightarrow} C^{\tilde{z}\tilde{x}}_{n+1,k}[P']$ must be simulated by $T \overset{1}{\longrightarrow} C^{\tilde{z}\tilde{x}}_{n+1,k}[Q']$ to preserve the observability of s and d_{n+1}.

2. *If $P \overset{(\tilde{x})\bar{u}\tilde{w}}{\longrightarrow} P'$ the argument is symmetric.*
3. *If $P \overset{\varphi}{\longrightarrow} P'$, then $C^{\tilde{z}}_{n,k}[P] \overset{1}{\longrightarrow} C^{\tilde{z}}_{n,k}[P']\sigma \downarrow m_e$ for σ agreeing with φ and m_e encoding the equivalence relation of names in $\tilde{z}$ agreeing with φ. To preserve this observation, it must be that $Q \overset{\varphi}{\Longrightarrow} Q'$, i.e., Q can perform a sequence of fusion actions which "sum up" to the same effect as φ, and then $C^{\tilde{z}}_{n,k}[Q] \overset{1}{\Longrightarrow} C^{\tilde{z}}_{n,k}[Q']\sigma \downarrow m_e$; if $Q \overset{\psi}{\Longrightarrow} Q'$ for some ψ different from φ, $m_f \neq m_e$ will be observable.*

Thus, the relation $\mathcal{R}$ is a weak bisimulation. □

4 Encoding constraint calculi

The ρ-calculus of Niehren and Müller [6] is a concurrent calculus parameterized by a constraint system, which serves as a foundation for the concurrent constraint language Oz [13]. Its development has been inspired by process calculi such as the π-calculus, but analysis methods such as equivalence checking or model checking have not been applied to it. This is partly because the calculus contains elements such as logical variables with no direct counterparts in other process calculi.

In the ρ-calculus, the constraint store can be seen as transparently distributed over the terms, in contrast with the monolithic constraint store of, e.g., [11]. The constraint store can be asked if a formula or its negation is entailed by using a conditional term, and a constraint is implicitly added when it is not guarded by a conditional or abstraction.

In this section we relate the fusion calculus to three basic instances of the ρ-calculus: $\rho(x = y)$, which uses constraints over name equations and conjunction; $\rho(x = y, \mathcal{C})$, which adds constants to the constraint system; and $\rho(x = y, x \neq y)$, which adds inequalities. We relate the calculi by giving a simple encoding of a term E in one of the instances of the ρ-calculus such that if E can reduce to another term F, then its encoding can reduce to the encoding of F, and vice versa. Correspondence between observations and of convergence properties is also shown.

4.1 The ρ-calculus

We give a brief presentation of the syntax and semantics of the ρ-calculus. For a fuller treatment we refer the reader to [6].

There are three basic entities in the ρ-calculus: *variables*, *constraints* and *terms*. Variables are ranged over by lower-case letters, constraints by $\phi, \varphi, \psi, \ldots$, and terms by $E, F, \ldots$. Their syntax is given by the following BNF equation:

$$E ::= \top \;\Big|\; E_1 \wedge E_2 \;\Big|\; \exists x E \;\Big|\; x\tilde{y} \;\Big|\; x{:}\,\tilde{y}/E \;\Big|\; \texttt{if } \varphi \texttt{ then } E_1 \texttt{ else } E_2 \;\Big|\; \phi$$

The terminology in the following explanation comes from [6]: Briefly, $\top$ represents an inactive term; each term in a *composition* $E_1 \wedge E_2$ can reduce in parallel; a *declaration* $\exists x E$ introduces a new variable x with scope E; an *abstraction* $x{:}\,\tilde{y}/E$ can communicate with an *application* $x\tilde{z}$, producing the new term $E\{\tilde{z}/\tilde{y}\}$. A *conditional* `if` φ `then` E_1 `else` E_2 tests if the current constraint store entails the condition φ or its negation. A *constraint* term ϕ is added to the current constraint store. We write $\phi \models \psi$ if $\phi \Rightarrow \psi$ is valid in all models of the constraint system. The constraint $\dot{\top}$ stands for logical truth, and conjunction of constraints is written $\dot{\wedge}$. The terms $\exists y E$ and $x{:}\,\tilde{y}/E$ bind y and $\tilde{y}$, respectively; we write $\text{fv}(E)$ for all names in E which are not bound.

The formal semantics of the ρ-calculus is given by a structural congruence in Table 3 and reduction rules in Table 4. Again structurally congruent terms are considered the same, i.e., if $E \equiv E'$ and $F \equiv F'$ and $E \longrightarrow F$ then also $E' \longrightarrow F'$.

$E \wedge \dot{\top} \equiv E$	$E \wedge \top \equiv E$	$E \wedge F \equiv F \wedge E$	$E \wedge (F \wedge G) \equiv (E \wedge F) \wedge G$
$\exists x\ \dot{\top} \equiv \dot{\top}$	$\exists x \top \equiv \top$	$\exists x \exists y E \equiv \exists y \exists x E$	$E \wedge \exists x F \equiv \exists x(E \wedge F)$ if $x \notin \text{fv}(E)$
$\phi \wedge \psi \equiv \phi \mathbin{\dot{\wedge}} \psi$	$\phi \equiv \varphi$ if $\phi \Leftrightarrow \varphi$		

Table 3. Structural congruence relation of the ρ-calculus.

$\phi \wedge x{:}\,\tilde{y}/E \wedge z\tilde{w} \longrightarrow \phi \wedge x{:}\,\tilde{y}/E \wedge E\{\tilde{w}/\tilde{y}\}$	if $\phi \models x = z$ and $\lvert\tilde{y}\rvert = \lvert\tilde{w}\rvert$	$\dfrac{E \longrightarrow F}{\exists x E \longrightarrow \exists x F}$
$\phi \wedge$ `if` ψ `then` E `else` $F \longrightarrow \phi \wedge E$	if $\phi \models \psi$	
$\phi \wedge$ `if` ψ `then` E `else` $F \longrightarrow \phi \wedge F$	if $\phi \models \neg\psi$	$\dfrac{E \longrightarrow E'}{E \wedge F \longrightarrow E' \wedge F}$

Table 4. Reduction rules of the ρ-calculus.

We say that a constraint is *guarded* if it occurs in the body of an abstraction or the clauses of a conditional. We show that a ρ-calculus term E can be written in a head normal form with all unguarded constraints merged together. For example, $x = y \wedge \exists z(z = w \wedge aw)$ has the head normal form $\exists z(x = y \mathbin{\dot{\wedge}} z = w \wedge aw)$.

Definition 19. *A ρ-calculus term E is in* head normal form *if E is of the form $\exists\tilde{x}(\phi \wedge E')$, where E' has no unguarded constraints and $\tilde{x} \subseteq \text{fv}(\phi)$.*

In this head normal form ϕ can be thought of as representing the store.

Proposition 20. *Any ρ-calculus term E is structurally congruent to a term F which is in head normal form.*

The proof is by structural induction on terms.

We further define the observation predicate of the ρ-calculus in a straightforward way:

Definition 21. $x\tilde{y} \downarrow x \qquad x{:}\,\tilde{y}/E \downarrow x$
$(E \mid F) \downarrow x$ *if* $E \downarrow x$ *or* $F \downarrow x$
$\exists x E \downarrow y \qquad$ *if* $E \downarrow y$ *and* $x \neq y$

4.2 Constraints over name equations

We first instantiate the constraint system in ρ with simple name equations and conjunction. This calculus is $\rho(x = y)$ of [6]. We give a simple encoding for it into the fusion calculus in Table 5. We here use the standard replication operator definable through recursion by $!P \stackrel{def}{=} P \mid !P$. For simplicity, we only describe the encoding where the condition of a conditional is of the form $x = y$. The general case can also be handled, e.g. by nesting conditionals. The encoding of a ρ-calculus name x is written $\underline{x}$. In Table 5 it suffices to define $\underline{x} = x$, assuming a unique name in the fusion calculus for each name in the ρ-calculus. Note that in $\rho(x = y)$, it is *never* the case that $\phi \models \neg(x = y)$ for any ϕ, so the "else" branch of a conditional can be completely ignored.

$$
\begin{aligned}
\underline{x} &\equiv x \\
[\![\top]\!] &\stackrel{def}{=} \mathbf{0} \\
[\![x\tilde{w}]\!] &\stackrel{def}{=} \overline{\underline{x}}\,\underline{\tilde{w}} \\
[\![x\!:\tilde{y}/E]\!] &\stackrel{def}{=} !\,(\underline{\tilde{y}})\underline{x}\,\underline{\tilde{y}}\,.\,[\![E]\!] \\
[\![x_1 = y_1 \mathbin{\dot\wedge} \cdots \mathbin{\dot\wedge} x_n = y_n]\!] &\stackrel{def}{=} \{\underline{x_1} = \underline{y_1}, \cdots, \underline{x_n} = \underline{y_n}\} \\
[\![E \wedge F]\!] &\stackrel{def}{=} [\![E]\!] \mid [\![F]\!] \\
[\![\exists x E]\!] &\stackrel{def}{=} (\underline{x})[\![E]\!] \\
[\![\texttt{if } x = y \texttt{ then } E \texttt{ else } F]\!] &\stackrel{def}{=} [\underline{x} = \underline{y}]\mathbf{1}\,.\,[\![E]\!]
\end{aligned}
$$

Table 5. The encoding of $\rho(x = y)$.

For the correctness of the encoding, we treat top-level constraints specially, and define $\mathcal{V}(\exists\tilde{u}(\phi \wedge E)) \stackrel{def}{=} (\underline{\tilde{u}})[\![E]\!]\sigma_\phi$ where $\exists\tilde{u}(\phi \wedge E)$ is in head normal form, σ_ϕ agrees with $[\![\phi]\!]$ and $\mathrm{ran}(\sigma_\phi) \cap \underline{\tilde{u}} = \emptyset$. In other words, the effect of the equations of the store is applied onto E. For example, $\mathcal{V}(\exists x(x = y \wedge axy))$ is $\overline{a}\,yy$.

The correctness is stated by the following theorem. The addition of scopes $\tilde{z}$ is a technical device, necessary to turn guarded fusions of free names in $\mathcal{V}(E)$ into reductions.

Theorem 22. *For E, F terms of $\rho(x = y)$ in head normal form,*

1. *If $E \longrightarrow F$, then for some $\tilde{z}$, $(\tilde{z})\mathcal{V}(E) \longrightarrow^+ P \approx \mathcal{V}(F)$.*
2. *For any $\tilde{z}$, if $(\tilde{z})\mathcal{V}(E) \longrightarrow^* P$, then $E \longrightarrow^* F$ and $P \approx (\tilde{z})\mathcal{V}(F)$.*
3. *$E \downarrow x$ iff $\mathcal{V}(E) \downarrow x'$, where $E = \phi \wedge E'$ and $\phi \models x = x'$.*
4. *If E converges to F, then for some $\tilde{z}$, $(\tilde{z})\mathcal{V}(E)$ converges to $P \approx \mathcal{V}(F)$.*
5. *For any $\tilde{z}$, if $(\tilde{z})\mathcal{V}(E)$ converges to P and P has no fusion transitions, then E converges to F with $P \approx (\tilde{z})\mathcal{V}(F)$.*

The proof is by inductions on the depths of inferences.

4.3 Adding constants

Adding constants to the constraint system of $\rho(x = y)$ gives a system which is closer to the γ-calculus of Smolka [12]. Here, the variables are divided into two families: normal variables and constants, and the axiom $\forall x, y \in C, x \not\equiv y : x \neq y$ is added to the constraint system, where C is the family of constants. This means that two constants which are not literally the same are always different. This instance of the ρ-calculus is called $\rho(x = y, C)$. Below we encode it into the fusion calculus. Here and in the following encoding, we write $[x = y](P, Q)$ for the fusion calculus agent $[x = y]P + [x \neq y]Q$.

As we have seen in the encoding of $\rho(x = y)$, variables of the ρ-calculus correspond directly to names in the fusion calculus. Constants, however, are explicitly encoded in the fusion calculus by adding a *handler process* for each constant, which can tell its environment that it is a constant. The encoding of a conditional can interrogate these handler processes to find out if $\neg\varphi$ is entailed. (Cf. [15], where the γ-calculus was encoded in the π-calculus using much more complex handler processes for constants, variables and updated variables.)

For each variable or constant u in $\rho(x = y, C)$ we introduce *two* names in the encoding: u and u_c. We redefine $\underline{u}$ to refer to these two together. u_c is used for communicating with a handler process for u, if it exists. A handler process for u can synchronize repeatedly on u_c, thereby signalling that u is a constant. We update the encoding in Table 5 by Table 6.

$$
\begin{array}{rll}
\underline{u} & \equiv u, u_c & \\
C(a_c) & \stackrel{def}{=} !\,\overline{a_c} & \\
[\![\exists a E]\!] & \stackrel{def}{=} (\underline{a})(C(a_c) \mid [\![E]\!]) & \text{if } a \in C \\
[\![\exists x E]\!] & \stackrel{def}{=} (\underline{x})[\![E]\!] & \text{if } x \notin C \\
[\![\texttt{if } x = y \texttt{ then } E \texttt{ else } F]\!] & \stackrel{def}{=} [x = y](1\,.\,[\![E]\!], x_c\,.\,y_c\,.\,[x = y](1\,.\,[\![E]\!], 1\,.\,[\![F]\!])) &
\end{array}
$$

Table 6. The encoding of $\rho(x = y, C)$.

The encoding of a conditional deserves a short explanation: If x and y are the same, we choose the E branch directly. Otherwise, to check if $\neg(x = y)$ is entailed, we must verify that both x and y are constants. Then we must *again* test if $x = y$ or not, for although they were not equal, a concurrent constraint may since have fused them.

For the correctness of this encoding, we must put the encoded terms in a context where all free a_c are scoped, and all free constants have a handler process. When I is a finite set we use $\prod_{i \in I} P_i$ to mean the Composition of all P_i for $i \in I$, and define $\mathcal{V}(\exists\tilde{u}(\phi \wedge E)) \stackrel{def}{=} (\underline{\tilde{u}})(\tilde{v}_c)((\prod_{a \in \tilde{a}} C(a_c) \mid [\![E]\!])\sigma_\phi)$ where $\exists\tilde{u}(\phi \wedge E)$ is in head normal form, $\tilde{v} = \text{fv}(\exists\tilde{u}(\phi \wedge E))$, $\tilde{a} = \tilde{v} \cap C$, σ_ϕ agrees with $[\![\phi]\!]$ and $\text{ran}(\sigma_\phi) \cap \underline{\tilde{u}} = \emptyset$. Theorem 22 holds for $\rho(x = y, C)$ with this definition of $\mathcal{V}$.

An inconsistent constraint store can be detected by redefining $C(a_c) \stackrel{def}{=} \overline{a_c}\,.\,C(a_c) + a_c\,.\,\mathit{fail}$. Then fail is a weak observation if the store gets inconsistent. Also, the *cell* construct of [12, 6] can be encoded by $\mathit{Cell}(x, u) \stackrel{def}{=} (w)x\,uw\,.\,\mathit{Cell}(x, w)$, nicely utilizing the free input of the fusion calculus.

4.4 Name inequations

Instead of constants, we here add explicit inequations to the constraint system, acquiring $\rho(x = y, x \neq y)$. Although $x \neq y$ could be encoded in $\rho(x = y, C)$ as $\exists a \exists b(x =$

$a \wedge y = b$), in $\rho(x = y, x \neq y)$ we avoid splitting the variables into constants and normal variables. In this encoding we also need additional names and processes, but the processes now explicitly encode inequations rather than constants.

$$
\begin{aligned}
\underline{x} &\equiv x, x_d \\
D(\underline{x}, \underline{y}) &\stackrel{def}{=} !\,(w,n)x_d\, wn \,.\, [w = y](\overline{n}, \overline{x_d}\, wn) \\
[\![\texttt{if } x = y \texttt{ then } E \texttt{ else } F]\!] &\stackrel{def}{=} (n)(\overline{x_d}\, yn \mid \overline{y_d}\, xn \mid ([x = y](1 \,.\, [\![E]\!], n \,.\, [\![F]\!]))) \\
[\![x_1 \neq y_1 \mathbin{\dot\wedge} \cdots \mathbin{\dot\wedge} x_n \neq y_n]\!] &\stackrel{def}{=} D(\underline{x_1}, \underline{y_1}) \mid \cdots \mid D(\underline{x_n}, \underline{y_n})
\end{aligned}
$$

Table 7. The encoding of $\rho(x = y, x \neq y)$.

The encoding in Table 7 updates the one in Table 5; note again the redefinition of $\underline{x}$. The presence of a process $D(\underline{x}, \underline{y})$ means that the inequation $x \neq y$ is present in the store. This process handles queries along x_d with objects w, n, meaning "is x different from w"? If $w = y$ it replies affirmatively by synchronizing on the supplied name n; otherwise it re-iterates the query to see if some other handler can decide it. This introduces divergence in the encoding, since the new query can be handled by the same process. We regard this as processing internal to the constraint system, which should not be a concern of the external observer. The encoding of a conditional simply asks both names in the equation if they are different.

The correctness again uses a context at top level, which scopes all free x_d. We redefine $\mathcal{V}(\exists\tilde{u}(\phi \mathbin{\dot\wedge} \psi \wedge E)) \stackrel{def}{=} (\underline{\tilde{u}})(\tilde{v}_d)[\![\psi \wedge E]\!]\sigma_\phi$ where $\exists\tilde{u}(\phi \mathbin{\dot\wedge} \psi \wedge E)$ is in head normal form, ϕ contains only positive constraints and ψ only negative, $\tilde{v} = \text{fv}(\exists\tilde{u}(\phi \mathbin{\dot\wedge} \psi \wedge E))$, σ_ϕ agrees with $[\![\phi]\!]$ and $\text{ran}(\sigma_\phi) \cap \underline{\tilde{u}} = \emptyset$. Theorem 22(1-3,5) holds for $\rho(x = y, x \neq y)$ with this definition of $\mathcal{V}$; case 4 holds if we disregard divergences introduced by D agents. The stronger form of case 5 where such divergences are ignored also holds.

By using $D'(\underline{x}, \underline{y}) \stackrel{def}{=} [x = y]\mathit{fail} \mid D(\underline{x}, \underline{y})$ in place of D, we can detect inconsistencies of the store.

5 Conclusion

We have explored the weak and barbed equivalences of the fusion calculus and used them to verify a model of the ρ-calculus. An interesting implication is that the ρ-calculus thereby may gain access to theories and tools developed for process calculi.

There are several lines of further work worth exploring. The correspondence between a ρ-calculus term and its encoding (Theorem 22) can probably be strengthened to imply that two terms are equivalent iff their encodings are equivalent. The question is which equivalence would be relevant in such a result. Convergence is of prime importance in the ρ-calculus and our equivalences do not currently take that into account. Refining the equivalences in that respect is probably necessary.

The fusion calculus as presented here is unsorted, while the ρ-calculus comes in a version where "constants" and "variables" are distinguished. An interesting question is if the sorting systems of the π-calculus can be adapted to accommodate this.

The question whether more complex constraint systems can be handled in the same way is largely open. Clearly the fusion calculus is geared particularly towards constraints on the identity of names. But it may be that unification can be represented cleanly, implying that ordinary logic programming has a good encoding.

Finally, simulation and verification tools for the π-calculus are currently being adapted for the fusion calculus. Using our encodings it is a straightforward task to derive tools also for the ρ-calculus.

References

[1] Y. Fu. A proof-theoretical approach to communication. In P. Degano, R. Gorrieri and A. Marchetti-Spaccamela, editors, *Proceedings of ICALP '97*, volume 1256 of *LNCS*, pages 325–335. Springer, 1997.

[2] B. Li. A π-calculus specification of Prolog. In D. Sannella, editor, *Proceedings of ESOP '94*, volume 788 of *LNCS*, pages 379–393. Springer, 1994.

[3] R. Milner. Functions as processes. *Journal of Mathematical Structures in Computer Science*, 2(2):119–141, 1992.

[4] R. Milner, J. Parrow and D. Walker. A calculus of mobile processes, Parts I and II. *Journal of Information and Computation*, 100:1–77, Sept. 1992.

[5] R. Milner and D. Sangiorgi. Barbed bisimulation. In W. Kuich, editor, *Proceedings of ICALP '92*, volume 623 of *LNCS*, pages 685–695. Springer, 1992.

[6] J. Niehren and M. Müller. Constraints for free in concurrent computation. In K. Kanchanasut and J.-J. Lévy, editors, *Asian Computer Science Conference*, volume 1023 of *LNCS*, pages 171–186. Springer, 1995.

[7] J. Parrow and B. Victor. The fusion calculus: Expressiveness and symmetry in mobile processes. In *Proceedings of LICS'98*. IEEE, Computer Society Press, June 1998. URL: `http://www.docs.uu.se/~victor/tr/fusion.html`.

[8] J. Parrow and B. Victor. The update calculus. In M. Johnson, editor, *Proceedings of AMAST'97*, volume 1349 of *LNCS*, pages 409–423. Springer, Dec. 1997.

[9] B. C. Pierce and D. N. Turner. Pict: A programming language based on the pi-calculus. In G. Plotkin, C. Stirling and M. Tofte, editors, *Proof, Language and Interaction: Essays in Honour of Robin Milner*, 1997. To appear.

[10] D. Sangiorgi. *Expressing Mobility in Process Algebras: First-Order and Higher-Order Paradigms.* PhD thesis, LFCS, University of Edinburgh, 1993.

[11] V. A. Saraswat, M. Rinard and P. Panangaden. Semantic foundations of concurrent constraint programming. In *Proceedings of POPL '91*, pages 333–352. ACM, 1991.

[12] G. Smolka. A foundation for higher-order concurrent constraint programming. In J.-P. Jouannaud, editor, *Constraints in Computational Logics*, volume 845 of *LNCS*, pages 50–72. Springer, Sept. 1994.

[13] G. Smolka. The Oz programming model. In J. van Leeuwen, editor, *Computer Science Today*, volume 1000 of *LNCS*, pages 324–343. Springer, 1995.

[14] B. Victor. *The Fusion Calculus: Expressiveness and Symmetry in Mobile Processes.* PhD thesis, Dept. of Computer Systems, Uppsala University, Sweden, June 1998. URL: `http://www.docs.uu.se/~victor/thesis.shtml`.

[15] B. Victor and J. Parrow. Constraints as processes. In U. Montanari and V. Sassone, editors, *Proceedings of CONCUR '96*, volume 1119 of *LNCS*, pages 389–405. Springer, 1996.

[16] D. Walker. Objects in the π-calculus. *Journal of Information and Computation*, 116(2):253–271, 1995.

On Computing the Entropy of Cellular Automata

Michele D'amico[1], Giovanni Manzini[2,3], Luciano Margara[4]

[1] Dipartimento di Matematica, Università di Bologna, Piazza di Porta S. Donato 5, 40127 Bologna, Italy
[2] Dipartimento di Scienze e Tecnologie Avanzate, Università di Torino, Via Cavour 84, 15100 Alessandria, Italy.
[3] Istituto di Matematica Computazionale, Via S. Maria, 46, 56126 Pisa, Italy.
[4] Dipartimento di Scienze dell'Informazione, Università di Bologna, Mura Anteo Zamboni 7, 40127 Bologna, Italy.

Abstract. We show how to compute the entropy of two important classes of cellular automata namely, *linear* and *positively expansive* cellular automata. In particular, we prove a closed formula for the topological entropy of D-dimensional ($D \geq 1$) linear cellular automata over the ring $\mathbf{Z}_m$ ($m \geq 2$) and we provide an algorithm for computing the topological entropy of positively expansive cellular automata.

1 Introduction

Cellular Automata (CA) are dynamical systems consisting of a regular lattice of variables which can take a finite number of discrete values. The global state of the CA, specified by the values of all the variables at a given time, evolves according to a global transition map F based on a *local rule* f which acts on the value of each single cell in synchronous discrete time steps. A CA can be viewed as a discrete time dynamical system (X, F) where $F: X \to X$ is the CA global transition map defined over the configuration space X. The *dynamical behavior* of CA can be analyzed — as that of any other dynamical system — in different frameworks. For example, in [2] the authors study measure theoretic properties of CA, while in [3, 11, 12] the authors investigate the topological behavior of CA. The classical problem in CA theory is the following: given a description of the local rule f, determine whether the global transition map F associated to f satisfies a certain property. In the case of general CA, this problem is algorithmically unsolvable for a number of important properties, e.g., surjectivity and injectivity are undecidable in any dimension greater than one [9], nilpotency is undecidable also for 1-dimensional CA [8], topological entropy of 1-dimensional CA is not even approximable [6]. Finally, it is a common belief that also topological properties such as sensitivity, equicontinuity, transitivity, and ergodicity are undecidable even if, to our knowledge, no formal proof of this fact has been produced so far. On the other hand, if we restrict to particular subclasses of CA, many of the above properties become decidable (often in polynomial time). For example, injectivity and surjectivity are decidable for 1-dimensional CA [1] and all topological properties are decidable for D-dimensional linear CA over $\mathbf{Z}_m$ [3, 7, 10–12]. Many questions concerning the asymptotic behavior of CA are still open, e.g., decidability of positive expansivity, computing the topological entropy for restricted classes of CA such as injective or linear CA, computing the Lyapunov exponents of 1-dimensional CA, and so on. In this paper we focus our attention on topological entropy which is one of the most studied properties of dynamical systems. Informally, topological entropy measures the *uncertainty* of the forward evolution of any dynamical system in the presence of incomplete description of initial configurations. As we already mentioned above, topological entropy of general CA cannot be algorithmically computed. Nevertheless it is important to investigate for which classes of CA topological entropy can be computed and how to accomplish this task. The main contribution of this paper is the solution to the two following open problems addressed in [6] and [2], respectively.

Problem 1. In [6] the authors prove the undecidability of topological entropy and conclude that "*... the undecidability question remains open if one restricts to a subclass of cellular automata such as linear rules ...*". In Theorems 2 and 3 we prove a closed formula for the topological entropy of D-dimensional linear CA over $\mathbf{Z}_m$ (in terms of the coefficients of the local rule associated to the CA) for $D = 1$ and for $D \geq 2$, respectively.

Problem 2. In [2] the authors review topological and metric properties of CA and prove that "*... the topological entropies of positively expansive cellular automata are log-integers ...*" leaving open the problem of computing the entropy for that class of CA. In Theorems 4 and 5 we show how to efficiently compute the entropy of positively expansive CA.

We also give a closed formula for the Lyapunov exponents of 1-dimensional linear CA over $\mathbf{Z}_m$ (Theorem 1).

2 Basic definitions

Cellular automata. For $m \geq 2$, let $\mathbf{Z}_m = \{0, 1, \ldots, m-1\}$. We consider the *space of configurations* $\mathcal{C}_m^D = \{c \mid c\colon \mathbf{Z}^D \to \mathbf{Z}_m\}$ which consists of all functions from $\mathbf{Z}^D$ into $\mathbf{Z}_m$. Each element of $\mathcal{C}_m^D$ can be visualized as an infinite D-dimensional lattice in which each cell contains an element of $\mathbf{Z}_m$. Let $s \geq 1$. A *neighborhood frame* of size s is an ordered set of distinct vectors $\boldsymbol{u}_1, \boldsymbol{u}_2, \ldots, \boldsymbol{u}_s \in \mathbf{Z}^D$. Given $f\colon \mathbf{Z}_m^s \to \mathbf{Z}_m$, a D-dimensional CA based on the *local rule* f is the pair $(\mathcal{C}_m^D, F)$, where $F\colon \mathcal{C}_m^D \to \mathcal{C}_m^D$, is the *global transition map* defined as follows.

$$[F(c)](\boldsymbol{v}) = f\left(c(\boldsymbol{v}+\boldsymbol{u}_1), \ldots, c(\boldsymbol{v}+\boldsymbol{u}_s)\right), \qquad \text{where} \qquad c \in \mathcal{C}_m^D,\ \boldsymbol{v} \in \mathbf{Z}^D. \quad (1)$$

In other words, the content of cell $\boldsymbol{v}$ in the configuration $F(c)$ is a function of the content of cells $\boldsymbol{v}+\boldsymbol{u}_1, \ldots, \boldsymbol{v}+\boldsymbol{u}_s$ in the configuration c. Note that the local rule f and the neighborhood frame completely determine F. For 1-dimensional CA we use a simplified notation. A local rule $f\colon \mathbf{Z}_m^{2r+1} \to \mathbf{Z}_m$ of *radius* r is denoted by $f(x_{-r}, \ldots, x_{-1}, x_0, x_1, \ldots, x_r)$. The associated global map $F\colon \mathcal{C}_m^1 \to \mathcal{C}_m^1$ is defined by $[F(c)](i) = f(x_{-r+i}, \ldots, x_{r+i})$ where $c \in \mathcal{C}_m^1$, $i \in \mathbf{Z}$. We assume that

f explicitly depends on at least one of the two variables x_{-r} and x_r. We say that f is *permutive* in the variable x_i, $-r \leq i \leq r$, if and only if, no matter which values are given to the other $2r$ variables, the modification of the value of x_i causes the modification of the output produced by f (for a formal definition of permutivity see Definition 6 of [5]). Throughout the paper, $F(c)$ will denote the result of the application of the map F to the configuration c, and $c(\boldsymbol{v})$ will denote the value assumed by c in $\boldsymbol{v}$. For $n \geq 0$, we recursively define $F^n(c)$ by $F^n(c) = F(F^{n-1}(c))$, where $F^0(c) = c$. Let $(\mathcal{C}_m^D, F)$ be a CA based on the local rule f. We denote by $f^{(n)}$ the local rule associated to F^n.

Linear CA over $\mathbf{Z}_m$. In the special case of linear CA the set $\mathbf{Z}_m$ is endowed with the usual sum and product operations that make it a commutative ring. In what follows we denote by $[x]_m$ the integer x taken modulo m. Linear CA have a local rule of the form $f(x_1, \ldots, x_s) = \left[\sum_{i=1}^{s} \lambda_i x_i\right]_m$ with $\lambda_1, \ldots, \lambda_s \in \mathbf{Z}_m$. Hence, for a linear D-dimensional CA Equation (1) becomes

$$[F(c)](\boldsymbol{v}) = \left[\sum_{i=1}^{s} \lambda_i c(\boldsymbol{v} + \boldsymbol{u}_i)\right]_m \qquad \text{where} \qquad c \in \mathcal{C}_m^D,\ \boldsymbol{v} \in \mathbf{Z}^D. \tag{2}$$

For linear 1-dimensional CA the local rule f can be written as $f(x_{-r}, \ldots, x_r) = \left[\sum_{i=-r}^{r} a_i x_i\right]_m$ where at least one between a_{-r} and a_r is nonzero. In this case Equation (1) becomes

$$[F(c)](i) = \left[\sum_{j=-r}^{r} a_j c(i+j)\right]_m \qquad \text{where} \qquad c \in \mathcal{C}_m^1,\ i \in \mathbf{Z}.$$

Note that if $\gcd(a_j, m) = 1$ then f is permutive in the j-th variable.

Topological entropy of CA. The topological properties of CA are usually defined with respect to the metric topology induced by the *Tychonoff distance* over the configuration space $\mathcal{C}_m^D$ (see for example [2]). With this topology $\mathcal{C}_m^D$ is compact and totally disconnected, and every CA is a (uniformly) continuous map. The definition of topological entropy $\mathcal{H}$ of a continuous map $F: X \to X$ over a compact space X can be found for example in [2]. The value $\mathcal{H}(X, F)$ is generally accepted as a measure of the complexity of the dynamics of F over X. In [6] it is shown that for 1-dimensional CA the general definition of topological entropy translates to the following simpler form. Let $R(w,t)$ denote the number of distinct rectangles of width w and height t occurring in a space-time evolution diagram of $(\mathcal{C}_m^1, F)$. Let r denote the radius of the local rule f associated to F, we have $m^w \leq R(w,t) \leq m^{w+2r(t-1)}$. Given w and t, $R(w,t)$ can be determined by computing the evolution of all blocks of length $w + 2r(t-1)$. The topological entropy of F is given by

$$\mathcal{H}(\mathcal{C}_m^1, F) = \lim_{w \to \infty} \left(\lim_{t \to \infty} \frac{\log R(w,t)}{t} \right). \tag{3}$$

From (3) it follows that the entropy of a 1-dimensional CA over $\mathcal{C}_m^1$ satisfies $\mathcal{H}(F) \leq 2r \log m$. For D-dimensional CA, we can still compute $\mathcal{H}$ using Equation (3) provided $R(w,t)$ is replaced by $R(w^{(D)}, t)$ which denotes the number of distinct $D+1$ dimensional hyperrectangles obtained as space-time evolution diagrams of $(\mathcal{C}_m^D, F)$. Now, w has to be interpreted as the side-length of a D-dimensional region of the lattice.

Lyapunov exponents for CA. We recall the definition of Lyapunov exponents for the special case of 1-dimensional CA given in [14]. There, the authors introduce quantities analogous to Lyapunov exponents of smooth dynamical systems with the aim of describing the *local instability* of orbits in CA. For every $x \in \mathcal{C}_m^1$ and $s \geq 0$ we set

$$W_s^-(x) = \{y \in \mathcal{C}_m^1 : \; y(i) = x(i) \text{ for all } i \leq -s\},$$
$$W_s^+(x) = \{y \in \mathcal{C}_m^1 : \; y(i) = x(i) \text{ for all } i \geq s\}.$$

We have that $W_i^+(x) \subset W_{i+1}^+(x)$ and $W_i^-(x) \subset W_{i+1}^-(x)$. For every $n \geq 0$ we define

$$\tilde{\Lambda}_n^-(x) = \min\{s \geq 0 : \; F^n(W_0^-(x)) \subset W_s^-(F^n(x))\},$$
$$\tilde{\Lambda}_n^+(x) = \min\{s \geq 0 : \; F^n(W_0^+(x)) \subset W_s^+(F^n(x))\}.$$

Intuitively, for the CA defined by F the value $\tilde{\Lambda}_n^+(x)$ $[\tilde{\Lambda}_n^-(x)]$ measures how far a perturbation front moves right [left] in time n if the front is initially located at $i=0$. Finally, we consider the following shift invariant quantities

$$\Lambda_n^-(x) = \max_{j \in \mathbf{Z}} \tilde{\Lambda}_n^-(\sigma^j(x)), \qquad \Lambda_n^+(x) = \max_{j \in \mathbf{Z}} \tilde{\Lambda}_n^+(\sigma^j(x)), \tag{4}$$

where σ denotes the shift map. Intuitively, the value $\tilde{\Lambda}_n^+(\sigma^j(x))$ $[\tilde{\Lambda}_n^-(\sigma^j(x))]$ measures how far a perturbation front moves right [left] in time n if the front is initially located at j. The values $\lambda^+(x)$ and $\lambda^-(x)$ defined by

$$\lambda^+(x) = \lim_{n\to\infty} \frac{1}{n}\Lambda_n^+(x), \qquad \lambda^-(x) = \lim_{n\to\infty} \frac{1}{n}\Lambda_n^-(x) \tag{5}$$

are called respectively the right and left Lyapunov exponents of the CA F for the configuration x. If F is linear then it is not difficult to see that $\lambda^-(x)$ and $\lambda^+(x)$ do not depend on x, i.e., there exist two constants λ^- and λ^+ such that for every $x \in \mathcal{C}_m^1$, $\lambda^-(x) = \lambda^-$ and $\lambda^+(x) = \lambda^+$. The following result is a simple corollary of Theorem 2, pag. 5, of [14]. For any CA F we have

$$\mathcal{H}(\mathcal{C}_m^1, F) \leq \mathcal{H}(\mathcal{C}_m^1, \sigma)(\lambda^+ + \lambda^-) \tag{6}$$

where $\mathcal{H}(\mathcal{C}_m^1, \sigma) = \log m$ is the entropy of the shift map.

3 Statement of new results

Our first result provides a closed formula for the Lyapunov exponents of 1-dimensional linear CA.

Theorem 1. *Let* $(\mathcal{C}_m^1, F)$ *be a 1-dimensional CA over* $\mathbf{Z}_m$ *with local rule*

$$f(x_{-r},\ldots,x_r) = \left[\sum_{i=-r}^{r} a_i x_i\right]_m ,$$

and let $m = p_1^{k_1} \cdots p_h^{k_h}$ *be the prime factor decomposition of* m*. For* $i = 1,\ldots,h$ *define* $P_i = \{0\} \cup \{j : \gcd(a_j, p_i) = 1\}$*,* $L_i = \min P_i$*, and* $R_i = \max P_i$*. Then, the left and right Lyapunov exponents of* $(\mathcal{C}_m^1, F)$ *are*

$$\lambda^- = \max_{1\le i\le h}\{R_i\} \qquad \text{and} \qquad \lambda^+ = -\min_{1\le i\le h}\{L_i\}\,.$$

In the next theorem we give a closed formula for the entropy of 1-dimensional linear CA which can be efficiently computed in terms of the coefficients of the local rule.

Theorem 2. *Let* $(\mathcal{C}_m^1, F)$ *be a 1-dimensional CA over* $\mathbf{Z}_m$ *with local rule*

$$f(x_{-r},\ldots,x_r) = \left[\sum_{i=-r}^{r} a_i x_i\right]_m ,$$

and let $m = p_1^{k_1} \cdots p_h^{k_h}$ *denote the prime factor decomposition of* m*. Let* L_i *and* R_i *be defined as in Theorem 1. Then*

$$\mathcal{H}(\mathcal{C}_m^1, F) = \sum_{i=1}^{h} k_i (R_i - L_i) \log(p_i). \tag{7}$$

In the next example we use the above theorems to compute the entropy and the Lyapunov exponents of a 1-dimensional linear CA.

Example 1. For $m = 1620 = 2^2 3^4 5$, consider the linear local rule

$$f(x_{-2},\ldots,x_4) = [(10x_{-2} + 15x_{-1} + 9x_0 + 18x_1 + 22x_2 + 4x_3 + 30x_4)]_{2^2 3^4 5}\,,$$

and let $(\mathcal{C}_{1620}^1, F)$ be the 1-dimensional linear CA associated with f. From Theorem 2 we have $L_1 = -1$, $L_2 = -2$, $L_3 = 0$, $R_1 = 0$, $R_2 = 3$, and $R_3 = 3$, and then $\mathcal{H}(\mathcal{C}_{1620}^1, F) = 2 + 20\log 3 + 4\log 5$. In addition, according to Theorem 1 we have $\lambda^+ = 2$ and $\lambda^- = 3$.

Finally, we determine the entropy of any linear D-dimensional CA with $D \ge 2$.

Theorem 3. *Let* $(\mathcal{C}_m^D, F)$ *be a* D*-dimensional linear CA over* $\mathbf{Z}_m$ *with* $D \ge 2$*. Then, either* F *is sensitive to initial conditions and* $\mathcal{H}(\mathcal{C}_m^D, F) = \infty$*, or* F *is equicontinuous and* $\mathcal{H}(\mathcal{C}_m^D, F) = 0$*.*

In what follows we show how to compute the topological entropy for positively expansive CA. Since positively expansive CA do not exist in any dimension greater than 1 (see [15]), in this section we consider only 1-dimensional CA.

However, in our proofs we only use the fact that each positively expansive CA is a surjective open map and is topologically conjugated to a one-sided full shift (see [13]).

We now introduce some notation we need in order to state the result of this section. To any CA F based on the local rule f (with radius r) we associate a directed labeled graph $G_F = (V, E)$ called *finite predecessor graph* (fp-graph) defined as follows. The vertex set $V = \{s \mid s \in \mathbf{Z}_m^{2r}\}$ is the set of all strings of length $2r$ from the alphabet $\mathbf{Z}_m$. The edge set E consists of all ordered pairs $(s_1, s_2) \in V \times V$ such that $s_1(i+1) = s_2(i)$, for $i = 1, \ldots, 2r-1$. The label a associated to (s_1, s_2) is $a = f(s_1(1), \ldots, s_1(2r), s_2(2r))$. As usual, we write $(s_1 \xrightarrow{a} s_2)$ to denote such edge.

Given any path $s_0 \xrightarrow{a_1} s_1 \xrightarrow{a_2} \cdots \xrightarrow{a_l} s_l$ of G_F we say that the sequence $s = s_0, \ldots, s_l$ is labeled by $a_1, \ldots, a_l$. From the definition of G_F we have that $s_0(1), \ldots, s_0(2r), s_1(2r), \ldots, s_l(2r)$ is a finite predecessor of $a_1, \ldots, a_l$ according to f, i.e., with a little abuse of notation,

$$f(s_0(1), \ldots, s_0(2r), s_1(2r), \ldots, s_l(2r)) = a_1, \ldots, a_l.$$

It is possible to prove that G_F has the following property: the cardinality of the set of finite predecessors of any given sequence s of length l is given by the number of distinct paths in G_F labeled by s.

Given a length-n string $\alpha \in (\mathbf{Z}_m)^n$ we denote by $\overline{\alpha}$ the 1-dimensional configuration consisting of the concatenation of infinitely many copies of α. Formally, for any $i \in \mathbf{Z}$, $\overline{\alpha}(i) = \alpha([i]_n + 1)$.

Example 2. Let $f\colon \{0,1\}^3 \to \{0,1\}$ be the radius 1 binary local rule defined by $f(x_{-1}, x_0, x_1) = [(x_{-1} + x_1)]_2$. Let F denote the global transition map associated to f. By Theorem 7 in [11] F is expansive. The fp-graph $G_F = (V, E)$ has vertex set $V = \{00, 01, 10, 11\}$, and edge set

$$\begin{aligned} E = \{&(00 \xrightarrow{0} 00), (00 \xrightarrow{1} 01), (01 \xrightarrow{0} 10), (01 \xrightarrow{1} 11), \\ &(10 \xrightarrow{1} 00), (10 \xrightarrow{0} 01), (11 \xrightarrow{0} 11), (11 \xrightarrow{1} 10)\}. \end{aligned}$$

In the next theorem we prove that using the fp-graph of a positively expansive CA $(\mathcal{C}_m^1, F)$ we can compute the number of predecessors of any $c \in \mathcal{C}_m^1$, that is, the cardinality of the set $F^{-1}(c)$.

Theorem 4. *Let $(\mathcal{C}_m^1, F)$ be a positively expansive CA and $a \in \mathbf{Z}_m$. F is a μ-to-one map, where μ is the sum of the lengths of all distinct cycles of $G_F = (V, E)$ labeled by sequences of type $s = a, \ldots, a$.*

Example 3. Consider the map F defined in Example 2. In the graph G_F there are 3 cycles labeled by sequences of type $0, \ldots, 0$ namely,

$$00 \xrightarrow{0} 00, \quad 01 \xrightarrow{0} 10 \xrightarrow{0} 01, \quad 11 \xrightarrow{0} 11.$$

We conclude that the number of predecessors of the configuration $\overline{0}$ is $1+2+1 = 4$. Indeed, they are $\overline{0}$, $\overline{10}$, $\overline{01}$, and $\overline{1}$. Since F is a μ-to-one mapping every other configuration has the same number of predecessors.

The following theorem, combined with Theorem 4, makes it possible to compute the topological entropy of any positively expansive CA.

Theorem 5. *The entropy of any positively expansive CA* $(\mathcal{C}_m^1, F)$ *is equal to* $\log \mu$, *where* μ *is the number of predecessors of any configuration* $c \in \mathcal{C}_m^1$ *and is given by Theorem 4.*

4 Proof of the main theorems

This section contains some of the proofs of the results stated in Section 3. The missing proofs are contained in [4].

Let $(\mathcal{C}_m^D, F)$ be a linear CA, and let q be any factor of m. For any configuration $c \in \mathcal{C}_m^D$, $[c]_q$ will denote the configuration in $\mathcal{C}_q^D$ defined by $[c]_q(\boldsymbol{v}) = [c(\boldsymbol{v})]_q$ for all $\boldsymbol{v} \in \mathbf{Z}^D$. Similarly, $[F]_q$ will denote the map $[F]_q : \mathcal{C}_q^D \to \mathcal{C}_q^D$ define by $[F]_q(c) = [F(c)]_q$.

Lemma 1. *Let* $(\mathcal{C}_{p^k}^1, F)$ *be a linear 1-dimensional CA over (p prime) with local rule* $f(x_1, \ldots, x_s) = [\sum_{i=1}^{s} a_i x_i]_{p^k}$. *Assume there exists* a_k *such that* $\gcd(a_k, p) = 1$, *and let* $\hat{P} = \{j : \gcd(a_j, p) = 1\}$, $\hat{L} = \min \hat{P}$ *and* $\hat{R} = \max \hat{P}$. *Then, there exists* $h \geq 1$ *such that the local rule* $f^{(h)}$ *associated to* F^h *has the form*

$$f^{(h)}(x_{-hr}, \ldots, x_{hr}) = \left[\sum_{i=h\hat{L}}^{h\hat{R}} b_i x_i \right]_{p^k} \qquad \textit{with} \quad \gcd(b_{h\hat{L}}, p) = \gcd(b_{h\hat{R}}, p) = 1.$$

Proof. See [4].

Proof of Theorem 1 (Sketch) We prove the thesis only for the left Lyapunov exponent λ^- since the proof for λ^+ is analogous. We know that, since F is a linear map, Lyapunov exponents are independent of the particular configuration considered. Hence, in the rest of the proof we can safely write λ^- and Λ_n^- instead of $\lambda^-(x)$ and $\Lambda_n^-(x)$.

We first consider the case $m = p^k$ with p prime. From Lemma 1 we know that there exist $h \geq 1$ and $\hat{R} \in \mathbf{Z}$ such that $f^{(h)}$ is permutive in the variable $x_{h\hat{R}}$ and does not depend on any other variable x_j with $j > h\hat{R}$. Let $\lambda_{F^h}^-$ denote the left Lyapunov exponent of the map F^h. If $\hat{R} \leq 0$ we have that $f^{(h)}$ does not depend on variables with positive index and then perturbation fronts never move left under iterations of F. We conclude that $\lambda_{F^h}^- = 0$. Assume now that $\hat{R} > 0$. Let x and x' be two configurations such that $x(i) = x'(i)$ for every $i < 0$ and $x(0) \neq x'(0)$ (i.e., x' is obtained from x by adding a perturbation front at position 0). From the rightmost permutivity of f we conclude that $[F(x)](i) = [F(x')](i)$ for every $i < -h\hat{R}$ and $x(-h\hat{R}) \neq x'(-h\hat{R})$, i.e., the perturbation front located at position 0 moves left of hR positions. As a consequence of this fact and from the linearity of F we conclude that $\lambda_{F^h}^- = h\hat{R}$.

We now prove that $\lambda^-_{F^h} = h\hat{R}$ implies $\lambda^-_F = \hat{R}$. From Equation (5) we have

$$\lambda^-_F = \lim_{n\to\infty} \frac{1}{n} \Lambda^-_n = \lim_{n\to\infty} \frac{1}{nh} \Lambda^-_{nh} = \frac{1}{h} \lim_{n\to\infty} \frac{1}{n} \Lambda^-_{nh} = \frac{1}{h} \lambda^-_{F^h}.$$

Since $R = \max\left(0, \hat{R}\right)$ then $\lambda^-_F = R$ and the thesis follows.

Consider now the general case $m = pq$, where $\gcd(p, q) = 1$. Since $\gcd(p, q) = 1$, the ring $\mathbf{Z}_m$ is isomorphic to the direct product $\mathbf{Z}_p \otimes \mathbf{Z}_q$. By the Chinese remainder theorem we know that F^n can be expressed as a linear combination of of $[F]_p^n$ and $[F]_q^n$ as follows

$$F^n = \alpha q \, [F]_p^n + \beta p \, [F]_q^n \tag{8}$$

where $[\alpha q]_p = 1$ and $[\beta p]_q = 1$. From Equation (8) we have that *perturbation fronts* move left under iterations of F at the maximum of the speeds at which perturbation fronts move under iterations of $[F]_p$ and $[F]_q$. This completes the proof. □

We now give two lemmas which enable us to compute the entropy of linear CA.

Lemma 2. *Let F be a linear D-dimensional CA over $\mathcal{C}_m^D$ with $m = pq$ and $\gcd(p, q) = 1$. Then $\mathcal{H}(\mathcal{C}_{pq}^D, F) = \mathcal{H}(\mathcal{C}_p^D, [F]_p) + \mathcal{H}(\mathcal{C}_q^D, [F]_q)$.*

Proof. See [4]

In view of the previous lemma, to compute the entropy of linear CA we can restrict our attention to linear CA defined over $\mathbf{Z}_{p^k}$ with p prime.

Lemma 3. *Let $f(x_{-r}, \ldots, x_r) = \left[\sum_{i=-r}^{r} a_i x_i\right]_{p^k}$ be any linear local rule defined over $\mathbf{Z}_{p^k}$ with p prime. Let F be the 1-dimensional global transition map associated to f. Let $P = \{0\} \cup \{j : \gcd(a_j, p) = 1\}$, $L = \min P$, and $R = \max P$. Then $\mathcal{H}(\mathcal{C}_{p^k}^1, F) = k(R - L)\log(p)$.*

Proof. From Equation (6) and Theorem 1 we have

$$\mathcal{H}(\mathcal{C}_{p^k}^1, F) \leq k(R - L)\log(p). \tag{9}$$

Let $f^{(n)}$ be the local rule associated to $(\mathcal{C}_{p^k}^1, F^n)$. In general, $f^{(n)}$ has radius rn, i.e., it depends on at most $2rn + 1$ variables. From Lemma 1 we have that there exist $h \geq 1$ and $\hat{L}, \hat{R} \in \mathbf{Z}$ such that F^h is permutive in the variables $x_{h\hat{L}}$ and $x_{h\hat{R}}$. In addition, F^h does not depend on variables x_j with $j < h\hat{L}$ or $j > h\hat{R}$. In other words, F^h is both leftmost and rightmost permutive. As a consequence of this fact, $\mathcal{H}(\mathcal{C}_{p^k}^1, F^h)$ can be given as a function of $\hat{L}$ and $\hat{R}$ as follows. If $\hat{R} \geq \hat{L} \geq 0$ then $\mathcal{H}(\mathcal{C}_{p^k}^1, F^h) = hk\hat{R}\log(p)$, if $\hat{L} \leq \hat{R} \leq 0$ then $\mathcal{H}(\mathcal{C}_{p^k}^1, F^h) = -hk\hat{L}\log(p)$, and if both $\hat{L} < 0$ and $\hat{R} > 0$ then $\mathcal{H}(\mathcal{C}_{p^k}^1, F^h) = hk(\hat{R} - \hat{L})\log(p)$. Note that topological entropy of leftmost and rightmost CA remains easy to compute also in the non-linear case. Since

$$L = \min\left(\hat{L}, 0\right) \qquad \text{and} \qquad R = \max\left(\hat{R}, 0\right), \tag{10}$$

we conclude that

$$\mathcal{H}(\mathcal{C}^1_{p^k}, F^h) = hk(R-L)\log(p). \tag{11}$$

From the definition of topological entropy we have

$$\begin{aligned}\mathcal{H}(\mathcal{C}^1_m, F) &= \lim_{w\to\infty}\left(\lim_{t\to\infty}\frac{\log R(w,t)}{t}\right) = \lim_{w\to\infty}\left(\lim_{t\to\infty}\frac{\log R(w,nt)}{nt}\right)\\ &\geq \frac{1}{n}\mathcal{H}(\mathcal{C}^1_m, F^n).\end{aligned} \tag{12}$$

From Equations (11) and (12) we have

$$\mathcal{H}(\mathcal{C}^1_{p^k}, F) \geq \frac{\mathcal{H}(\mathcal{C}^1_{p^k}, F^h)}{h} = k(R-L)\log(p). \tag{13}$$

Combining Equations (9) and (13) we obtain the thesis.

Proof of Theorem 2 The proof easily follows from Lemma 3 and Corollary 2. □

In order to compute the topological entropy for $D \geq 2$ we need a technical lemma which is the generalization of Lemma 1 to the case $D \geq 2$. Note that for $D \geq 2$ we do not have the concept of leftmost or rightmost permutivity, hence, we use a slightly different formulation. The common point between the two lemmas is that there exists $h \geq 1$ such that the coefficients of the local rule f which are multiple of p do not affect F^h.

Lemma 4. *Let $(\mathcal{C}^D_{p^k}, F)$ be a linear CA (p prime) with local rule $f(x_1,\ldots,x_s) = [\sum_{i=1}^{s}\lambda_i x_i]_{p^k}$, and neighborhood vectors $\boldsymbol{u}_1,\ldots,\boldsymbol{u}_s$. Define*

$$I = \{i \mid \gcd(\lambda_i, p) = 1\}, \qquad \hat{f} = \left[\sum_{i\in I}\lambda_i x_i\right]_{p^k},$$

and let $\hat{F}$ the global map associated to $\hat{f}$. Then, there exists $h \geq 1$ such that for all $c \in \mathcal{C}^D_{p^k}$, we have $F^h(c) = \hat{F}^h(c)$.

Proof. See [4]

Proof of Theorem 3 (Sketch) We know (see [11]) that a linear CA is either sensitive or equicontinuous. Since the entropy of any equicontinuous CA is zero (see for example [2]) we need only to prove that the entropy of a linear sensitive CA $(\mathcal{C}^D_m, F)$, $D \geq 2$, is unbounded. Let $\boldsymbol{u}_1,\ldots,\boldsymbol{u}_s$, $\lambda_1,\ldots,\lambda_s$ denote the neighborhood vectors and the corresponding coefficients of the map F (compare (2)). In [11] the authors prove that F is sensitive if and only if there exists a prime factor p of m such $p \nmid \lambda_i$ with $\boldsymbol{u}_i \neq \boldsymbol{0}$. Let k denote the power of p in the factorization of m. We now show that $\mathcal{H}(\mathcal{C}^D_{p^k}, [F]_{p^k}) = \infty$, which, by Lemma 2, proves the theorem. In [11] the authors prove that F $(\mathcal{C}^D_{p^k}, [F]_{p^k})$ is itself a sensitive CA. Hence, it suffices to show that every D-dimensional ($D \geq 2$) sensitive CA over

$\mathbf{Z}_{p^k}$ has unbounded entropy. For simplicity, we consider only the case $D = 2$. For $D > 2$ we only need to manage a more complex notation without introducing any new idea.

Let $(\mathcal{C}^2_{p^k}, F)$ denote a sensitive CA. We construct a set of 2-dimensional configurations whose evolutions according to F differentiate inside a space-temporal region of size $w \times w \times t$ Then we prove that the cardinality of this set of configurations grows with w and t at a rate that makes the entropy unbounded. We proceed as follows. Let $\boldsymbol{u}_1, \ldots, \boldsymbol{u}_s$, $\lambda_1, \ldots, \lambda_s$ denote the neighborhood vectors and the corresponding coefficients of the map F. Let h be defined as in Lemma 4. Let $f^{(n)}$ be the local rule associated to $(\mathcal{C}^2_{p^k}, F^n)$. Let $\boldsymbol{u}(F)$ and $\lambda(F)$ be a neighborhood vector of F of maximum norm and the corresponding coefficient, respectively. From the sensitivity of $(\mathcal{C}^2_{p^k}, F)$ and from Lemma 4 we conclude that $\gcd(\lambda(F^h), p) = 1$. Assume, without loss of generality, that $\rho = \boldsymbol{u}(F^h)(1) \geq \boldsymbol{u}(F^h)(2) \geq 0$.

We now show that given any set $\{z_{ij} \in \mathbf{Z}_{p^k} : i \in \mathbf{N},\ j \in \mathbf{Z}\}$ of elements of $\mathbf{Z}_{p^k}$ we can find a sequence $\{x_i \in \mathcal{C}^2_{p^k} : i \in \mathbf{N}\}$ of configurations such that

$$F^h(x_i) = x_{i+1} \qquad \text{and} \qquad x_i(0,j) = z_{ij}\ \forall j \in \mathbf{Z}. \tag{14}$$

In order to construct the above sequence we take advantage of the fact that the map F^h satisfies the property stated in Lemma 4 which is the extension of permutivity (defined for 1-dimensional CA) to the 2-dimensional case. We proceed as follows. Let $c_1 \in \mathcal{C}^2_{p^k}$ be any configuration such that $c_1(0,j) = z_{1j}$. We are not sure that $[F^h(c_1)](0,j) = z_{2j}$ for every $j \in \mathbf{Z}$. Since $\gcd(\lambda(F^h), p^k) = 1$ and $\boldsymbol{u}(F^h)(1) \geq \boldsymbol{u}(F^h)(2)$ we may find a configuration c_1' – obtained modifying c_1 at positions $(\rho h, j)$ with $j \in \mathbf{Z}$ – for which $[F^h(c_1')](0,j) = z_{2j}$ for every $j \in \mathbf{Z}$. Set $c_2 = F^h(c_1')$. Again, we may find a configuration c_1'' – obtained modifying c_1' at positions $(2\rho h, j)$ with $j \in \mathbf{Z}$ – for which $[F^h(c_1'')](0,j) = z_{1j}$ and $[F^{2h}(c_1'')](0,j) = z_{2j}$ for every $j \in \mathbf{Z}$. Set $c_2' = F^h(c_1'')$ and $c_3 = F^{2h}(c_1'')$.

By iterating the above described procedure we construct sequences of configurations of type $S_i = c_i, c_i', c_i'', \ldots$, $i \geq 1$. For every $i \geq 1$ let $l_i \in \mathcal{C}^2_{p^k}$ be the limit of S_i which exists since $\mathcal{C}^2_{p^k}$ is a compact space. It takes a little effort to verify that $\left\{l_i \in \mathcal{C}^2_{p^k} : i \in \mathbf{N}\right\}$ satisfies (14). We now show how to link the above constructed sequences (one for each set z_{ij}) of configurations to the computation of topological entropy. Let $Sqr(w,x) \in \mathbf{Z}^{w \times w}_{p^k}$ be the content of x at positions (i,j) with $-w < i \leq 0$ and $0 \leq j < w$. We have that $R(w^{(2)}, t)$ is equal to the number of distinct sequences $\langle Sqr(w,x), Sqr(w,F(x)), Sqr(w,F^2(x)), \ldots\rangle$ which can be obtained by varying $x \in \mathcal{C}^2_{p^k}$. It is not difficult to see that in view of (14) we can assign to the entries $(0,j)$, $0 \leq j < w$ of $Sqr(w, F^i(x))$ arbitrarily chosen elements of $\mathbf{Z}_{p^k}$ and still find a configuration x which realizes the sequence $\langle Sqr(w,x), Sqr(w,F(x)), Sqr(w,F^2(x)), \ldots\rangle$. Summarizing, we have that $R(w^{(2)}, ht) \geq p^{kwt}$ and then

$$\mathcal{H}(\mathcal{C}^2_{p^k}, F) = \lim_{w\to\infty} \lim_{t\to\infty} \frac{\log R(w^{(2)}, t)}{t} = \lim_{w\to\infty} \lim_{t\to\infty} \frac{\log R(w^{(2)}, ht)}{ht}$$

$$\geq \lim_{w\to\infty} \lim_{t\to\infty} \frac{\log(p^{kwt})}{ht} = \lim_{w\to\infty} \frac{kw}{h} = \infty.$$

□

We now prove Theorems 4 and 5 whose combination allows us to easily compute the topological entropy of positively expansive CA.

Proof of Theorem 4 (Sketch) Hedlund [5] proved that open CA are μ-to-one mappings, i.e., the cardinality of the set of predecessors of any configuration is μ. Since positively expansive CA are open, we conclude that they are also μ-to-one mappings. Let $a \in \mathbf{Z}_m$ be any element of the alphabet on which F is defined. Since every configuration has the same number of predecessors, in order to evaluate the constant μ for the map F it suffices to determine the number of predecessors of the configuration $\overline{a} \in \mathcal{C}_m^1$ which is such that $\overline{a}(i) = a$ for all $i \in \mathbf{Z}$. Since F is positively expansive it is surjective. We know that every predecessor of a spatially periodic configuration ($c \in \mathcal{C}_m^1$ is spatially periodic iff there exists $n \in \mathbf{N}$ such that $\sigma^n(c) = c$) according to a surjective CA is spatially periodic (see [3]). Thus, in order to count the number of predecessors of $\overline{a}$ it is sufficient to restrict our attention to spatially periodic configurations.

In what follows we prove that the number of spatially periodic predecessors of $\overline{a}$ is given by the sum of the lengths of all distinct cycles of the fp-graph G_F labeled by sequences of type $s = a, \ldots, a$. Consider any cycle $s = s_1 \xrightarrow{a} s_2 \xrightarrow{a} \cdots \xrightarrow{a} s_n \xrightarrow{a} s_1$ in the fp-graph G_F. Let $y_s = s_1(2r), s_2(2r), s_3(2r), \ldots, s_n(2r)$, where $s_i(j)$ denotes the j-th character of the node $s_i \in V$. By construction of y_s we have $F(\overline{y}_s) = \overline{a}$. In addition, we have the following two properties:
(i) every pair of distinct cycles of G_F are disjoint, i.e., they do not have common nodes. Assume by contradiction that there exist two distinct cycles t and s of length l_t and l_s, respectively, which share (without loss of generality) at least their first node. Let $\hat{y}_t$ denote the configuration obtained from $\overline{y}_t$ replacing the copy of y_t located at the origin of the lattice by l_s copies of y_s. We have that both $\hat{y}_t$ and $\overline{y}_s$ are predecessors of $\overline{a}$ according to F. Moreover, $\hat{y}_t$ and $\overline{y}_s$ differ in a finite number of positions which, in view of Theorem 9.3 in [5], is a contradiction.
(ii) every cycle of length l determines exactly l distinct predecessors of $\overline{a}$, one for each node of the cycle we choose to locate at the origin of the lattice.
The thesis easily follows from properties (i) and (ii). □

Proof of Theorem 5 Since F is positively expansive then it is topologically conjugated to a suitable defined one-sided full shift σ defined over the alphabet $\mathcal{B}$ (see [13]). As a consequence, $\mathcal{H}(\mathcal{C}_m^1, F) = \mathcal{H}(\mathcal{B}^{\mathrm{N}}, \sigma)$. Since the entropy of any one-sided full shift is the logarithm of the number of its predecessors and topological conjugations preserve the number of predecessors, we conclude that $\mathcal{H}(\mathcal{C}_m^1, F)$ is equal to the logarithm of the number of the predecessors of F. □

Note that for non-expansive CA $(\mathcal{C}_m^1, F)$ the logarithm of the number of the predecessors of F is not related to its topological entropy. As an example the logarithm of the number of predecessors of the shift CA is zero while its entropy is equal to $\log m$.

References

1. S. Amoroso and Y. N. Patt. Decision procedures for surjectivity and injectivity of parallel maps for tesselation structures. *Journal of Computer and System Sciences*, 6:448–464, 1972.
2. F. Blanchard, P. Kurka, and A. Maass. Topological and measure-theoretic properties of one-dimensional cellular automata. *Physica D*, 103:86–99, 1997.
3. G. Cattaneo, E. Formenti, G. Manzini, and L. Margara. Ergodicity and regularity for linear cellular automata over Z_m. *Theoretical Computer Science*. To appear.
4. M. D'amico, G. Manzini, and L. Margara. On computing the entropy of cellular automata. Technical Report B4-98-04, Istituto di Matematica Computazionale, CNR, Pisa, Italy, 1998.
5. G. A. Hedlund. Endomorphisms and automorphisms of the shift dynamical system. *Mathematical Systems Theory*, 3:320–375, 1969.
6. L. P. Hurd, J. Kari, and K. Culik. The topological entropy of cellular automata is uncomputable. *Ergodic Theory and Dynamical Systems*, 12:255–265, 1992.
7. M. Ito, N. Osato, and M. Nasu. Linear cellular automata over Z_m. *Journal of Computer and System Sciences*, 27:125–140, 1983.
8. J. Kari. The nilpotency problem of one-dimensional cellular automata. *SIAM Journal on Computing*, 21(3):571–586, June 1992.
9. J. Kari. Reversibility and surjectivity problems of cellular automata. *Journal of Computer and System Sciences*, 48(1):149–182, 1994.
10. G. Manzini and L. Margara. Invertible linear cellular automata over Z_m: Algorithmic and dynamical aspects. *Journal of Computer and System Sciences*. To appear.
11. G. Manzini and L. Margara. A complete and efficiently computable topological classification of D-dimensional linear cellular automata over Z_m. In *24th International Colloquium on Automata Languages and Programming (ICALP '97)*. LNCS n. 1256, Springer Verlag, 1997.
12. G. Manzini and L. Margara. Attractors of D-dimensional linear cellular automata. In *15th Annual Symposium on Theoretical Aspects of Computer Science (STACS '98)*. Springer Verlag, 1998.
13. M. Nasu. Textile systems for endomorphisms and automorphisms of the shift. *Memoirs of the Amer. Math. Soc.*, 114(546), 1995.
14. M. A. Shereshevsky. Lyapunov exponents for one-dimensional cellular automata. *Journal of Nonlinear Science*, 2(1):1, 1992.
15. M. A. Shereshevsky. Expansiveness, entropy and polynomial growth for groups acting on subshifts by automorphisms. *Indag. Mathem. N.S.*, 4:203–210, 1993.

On the Determinization of Weighted Finite Automata

Adam L. Buchsbaum[1], Raffaele Giancarlo[2], and Jeffery R. Westbrook[1]

[1] AT&T Labs, 180 Park Ave., Florham Park, NJ 07932, USA.
`{alb,jeffw}@research.att.com`,
`http://www.research.att.com/info/{alb,jeffw}`.

[2] Dipartimento di Matematica ed Applicazioni, Universitá di Palermo, Via Archirafi 34, 90123 Palermo, Italy. Work supported by AT&T Labs.
`raffaele@altair.math.unipa.it`,
`http://hpdma2.math.unipa.it/giancarl/source.html`.

Abstract. We study determinization of weighted finite-state automata (WFAs), which has important applications in automatic speech recognition (ASR). We provide the first polynomial-time algorithm to test for the *twins* property, which determines if a WFA admits a deterministic equivalent. We also provide a rigorous analysis of a determinization algorithm of Mohri, with tight bounds for acyclic WFAs. Given that WFAs can expand exponentially when determinized, we explore why those used in ASR tend to *shrink*. The folklore explanation is that ASR WFAs have an acyclic, multi-partite structure. We show, however, that there exist such WFAs that always incur exponential expansion when determinized. We then introduce a class of WFAs, also with this structure, whose expansion depends on the weights: some weightings cause them to shrink, while others, including random weightings, cause them to expand exponentially. We provide experimental evidence that ASR WFAs exhibit this weight dependence. That they shrink when determinized, therefore, is a result of favorable weightings in addition to special topology.

1 Introduction

Finite-state machines and their relation to rational functions and power series have been extensively studied [2, 3, 12, 16] and widely applied in fields ranging from image compression [9–11, 14] to natural language processing [17, 18, 24, 26]. A subclass of finite-state machines, the weighted finite-state automata (WFAs), has recently assumed new importance, because WFAs provide a powerful method for manipulating models of human language in automatic speech recognition (ASR) systems [19, 20]. This new research direction also raises a number of challenging algorithmic questions [5].

A *weighted finite-state automaton (WFA)* is a nondeterministic finite automaton (NFA), A, that has both an alphabet symbol and a weight, from some set K, on each transition. Let $R = (K, \oplus, \otimes, \overline{0}, \overline{1})$ be a semiring. Then A together with R generates a partial function from strings to K: the value of an accepted string is the semiring sum over accepting paths of the semiring product of the weights along each accepting path. Such a partial function is a *rational power series* [25]. An important example in ASR is the set of WFAs with the *min-sum semiring*, $(\Re^+ \cup \{0, \infty\}, \min, +, \infty, 0)$, which compute for each accepted string the minimum cost accepting path.

In this paper, we study problems related to the determinization of WFAs. A *deterministic*, or *sequential*, WFA has at most one transition with a given input symbol out of each state. Not all rational power series can be generated by deterministic WFAs. A *determinization algorithm* takes as input a WFA and produces a deterministic WFA that generates the same rational power series, if one exists. The importance of determinization to ASR is well established [17, 19, 20].

As far as we know, Mohri [17] presented the first determinization procedure for WFAs, extending the seminal ideas of Choffrut [7, 8] and Weber and Klemm [27] regarding string-to-string transducers. Mohri gives a determinization procedure with three phases. First, A is converted to an equivalent unambiguous, trim WFA A_t, using an algorithm analogous to one for NFAs [12]. (*Unambiguous* and *trim* are defined below.) Mohri then gives an algorithm, **TT**, that determines if A_t has the *twins property* (also defined below). If A_t does not have the twins property, then there is no deterministic equivalent of A. If A_t has the twins property, a second algorithm of Mohri's, **DTA**, can be applied to A_t to yield A', a deterministic equivalent of A. Algorithm **TT** runs in $O(m^{4n^2})$ time, where m is the number of transitions and n the number of states in A_t. Algorithm **DTA** runs in time linear in the size of A'. Mohri observes that A' can be exponentially larger than A, because WFAs include classical NFAs. He gives no upper bound on the worst-case state-space expansion, however, and due to weights, the classical NFA upper bound does not apply. Finally, Mohri gives an algorithm that takes a deterministic WFA and outputs the minimum-size equivalent, deterministic WFA.

In this paper, we present several results related to the determinization of WFAs. In Section 3 we give the first polynomial-time algorithm to test whether an unambiguous, trim WFA satisfies the twins property. It runs in $O(m^2n^6)$ time. We then provide a worst-case time complexity analysis of **DTA**. The number of states in the output deterministic WFA is at most $2^{n(2\lg n+n^2\lg|\Sigma|+1)}$, where Σ is the input alphabet. If the weights are rational, this bound becomes $2^{n(2\lg n+1+\min(n^2\lg|\Sigma|,\rho))}$, where ρ is the maximum bit-size of a weight. When the input WFA is acyclic, the bound becomes $2^{n\lg|\Sigma|}$, which is tight (up to constant factors) for any alphabet size.

In Sections 4–6 we study questions motivated by the use of WFA determinization in ASR [19, 20]. Although determinization causes exponential state-space expansion in the worst case, in ASR systems the determinized WFAs are often *smaller* than the input WFAs [17]. This is fortuitous, because the performance of ASR systems depends directly on WFA size [19, 20]. We study why such size reductions occur. The folklore explanation within the ASR community credits special topology—the underlying directed graph, ignoring weights—for this phenomenon. ASR WFAs tend to be multi-partite and acyclic. Such a WFA always admits a deterministic equivalent.

In Section 4 we exhibit multi-partite, acyclic WFAs whose minimum equivalent deterministic WFAs are exponentially larger. In Section 5 we study a class of WFAs, RG, with a simple multi-partite, acyclic topology, such that in the absence of weights the deterministic equivalent is smaller. We show that for any $A \in RG$ and any $i \leq n$, there exists an assignment of weights to A such that the *minimal* equivalent deterministic WFA has $\Theta(2^{i\lg|\Sigma|})$ states. Using ideas from universal hashing, we show that similar results hold when the weights are random i-bit numbers. We call a WFA *weight-dependent* if its expansion under determinization is strongly determined by its weights.

We examined experimentally the effect of varying weights on actual WFAs from ASR applications. In Section 6 we give results of these experiments. Most of the ASR examples were weight-dependent. These experimental results together with the theory we develop show that the folklore explanation is insufficient: ASR WFAs shrink under determinization because both the topology and weighting tend to be favorable.

Some of our results help explain the nature of WFAs from the algorithmic point of view, i.e., how weights assigned to the transitions of a WFA can affect the performance of algorithms manipulating it. Others relate directly to the theory of weighted automata.

2 Definitions and Terminology

Given a semiring $(K, \oplus, \otimes, \bar{0}, \bar{1})$, a *weighted finite automaton* (WFA) is a tuple $G = (Q, \bar{q}, \Sigma, \delta, Q_f)$ such that Q is the set of states, $\bar{q} \in Q$ is the initial state, Σ is the set of symbols, $\delta \subseteq Q \times \Sigma \times K \times Q$ is the set of transitions, and $Q_f \subseteq Q$ is the set of final states. We assume throughout that $|\Sigma| > 1$. A *deterministic*, or *sequential*, WFA has at most one transition $t = (q_1, \sigma, \nu, q_2)$ for any pair (q_1, σ); a *nondeterministic* WFA can have multiple transitions on a pair (q_1, σ), differing in target state q_2. The problems examined in this paper are motivated primarily by ASR applications, which work with the *min-sum semiring*, $(\Re^+ \cup \{0, \infty\}, \min, +, \infty, 0)$. Furthermore, some of the algorithms considered use subtraction, which the min-sum semiring admits. We thus limit further discussion to the min-sum semiring.

Consider a sequence of transitions $\boldsymbol{t} = (t_1, \ldots, t_\ell)$, such that $t_i = (q_{i-1}, \sigma_i, \nu_i, q_i)$; $\boldsymbol{t}$ *induces* string $w = \sigma_1 \cdots \sigma_\ell$. String w is *accepted by* $\boldsymbol{t}$ if $q_0 = \bar{q}$ and $q_\ell \in Q_f$; w is *accepted by* G if some $\boldsymbol{t}$ accepts w. Let $c(t_i) = \nu_i$ be the *weight* of t_i. The *weight of* $\boldsymbol{t}$ is $c(\boldsymbol{t}) = \sum_{i=1}^{\ell} c(t_i)$. Let $T(w)$ be the set of all sequences of transitions that accept string w. The *weight of* w is $c(w) = \min_{\boldsymbol{t} \in T(w)} c(\boldsymbol{t})$. The *weighted language* of G is the set of weighted strings accepted by G: $L(G) = \{(w, c(w)) \mid w \text{ is accepted by } G\}$. Intuitively, the weight on a transition of G can be seen as the "confidence" one has in taking that transition. The weights need not, however, satisfy stochastic constraints, as do the probabilistic automata introduced by Rabin [22].

Fix two states q and q' and a string $v \in \Sigma^*$. Then $c(q, v, q')$ is the minimum of $c(\boldsymbol{t})$, taken over all transition sequences from q to q' generating v. We refer to $c(q, v, q')$ as the *optimal cost* of generating v from q to q'. We generally abuse notation so that $\delta(q, w)$ can represent the set of states reachable from state $q \in Q$ on string $w \in \Sigma^*$. We extend the function δ to strings in the usual way: $q' \in \delta(q, v), v \in \Sigma^+$, means that there is a sequence of transitions from q to q' generating v.

The *topology* of G, *top*(G), is the projection $\pi_{Q \times \Sigma \times Q}(\delta)$: i.e., the transitions of G without respect to the weights. We also refer to *top*(G) as the *graph* underlying G.

A WFA is *trim* if every state appears in an accepting path for some string and no transition is weighted $\bar{0}$ (∞ in the min-sum semiring). A WFA is *unambiguous* if there is exactly one accepting path for each accepted string.

Determinization of G is the problem of computing a deterministic WFA G' such that $L(G') = L(G)$, if such a G' exists. We denote the output of algorithm **DTA** by *dta*(G). We denote the minimal deterministic WFA accepting $L(G)$ by *min*(G), if one exists. We say that G *expands* if *dta*(G) has more states and/or transitions than G.

Let $n = |Q|$ and $m = |\delta|$, and let the *size* of G be $n + m$. We assume that each transition is labeled with exactly one symbol, so $|\Sigma| \leq m$. Recall that the weights of G are non-negative real numbers. Let C be the maximum weight. In the *general case*, weights are incommensurable real numbers, requiring "infinite precision." In the *integer case*, weights can be represented with $\rho = \lceil \lg C \rceil$ bits. We denote the integral range $[a, b]$ by $[a, b]_Z$. The integer case extends to the case in which the weights are rationals requiring ρ bits. We assume that in the integer and rational cases, weights are normalized to remove excess least-significant zero bits.

For our analyses, we use the RAM model of computation as follows. In the general case, we charge constant time for each arithmetic-logic operation involving weights (which are real numbers). We refer to this model as the $\Re$-RAM [21]. The relevant parameters for our analyses are n, m, and $|\Sigma|$. In the integer case, we also use a RAM, except that each arithmetic-logic operation now takes $O(\rho)$ time. We refer to this model as the $\mathcal{CO}$-RAM [1]. The relevant parameters for the analyses are n, m, $|\Sigma|$, and ρ.

3 Determinization of WFAs

3.1 An Algorithm for Testing the Twins Property

Definition 1. *Two states, q and q', of a WFA G are* twins *if* $\forall (u, v) \in (\Sigma^*)^2$ *such that* $q \in \delta(\bar{q}, u)$, $q' \in \delta(\bar{q}, u)$, $q \in \delta(q, v)$, *and* $q' \in \delta(q', v)$, *the following holds:* $c(q, v, q) = c(q', v, q')$. *$G$ has the* twins property *if all pairs $q, q' \in Q$ are twins.*

That is, if states q and q' are reachable from $\bar{q}$ by a common string, then q and q' are twins only if any string that induces a cycle at each induces cycles of equal optimal cost. Note that two states having no cycle on a common string are twins.

Lemma 1 ([17, Lemma 2]). *Let G be a trim, unambiguous WFA. G has the twins property if and only if* $\forall (u, v) \in (\Sigma^*)^2$ *such that* $|uv| \leq 2n^2 - 1$, *the following holds: when there exist two states q and q' such that (i)* $\{q, q'\} \subseteq \delta(\bar{q}, u)$, *and (ii)* $q \in \delta(q, v)$ *and* $q' \in \delta(q', v)$, *then (iii)* $c(q, v, q) = c(q', v, q')$ *must follow.*

Definition 1 and Lemma 1 are analogous to those stated by Choffrut [7, 8] and (in different terms) by Weber and Klemm [27] to identify necessary and sufficient conditions for a string-to-string transducer to admit a sequential transducer realizing the same rational transduction. The proof techniques used for WFAs differ from those used to obtain analogous results for string-to-string transducers, however. In particular, the efficient algorithm we derive here to test a WFA for twins is not related to that of Weber and Klemm [27] for testing twins in string-to-string transducers.

We define $T_{\bar{q},\bar{q}}$, a multi-partite, acyclic, labeled, weighted graph having $2n^2$ layers, as follows. The root vertex comprises layer zero and corresponds to $(\bar{q}, \bar{q})$. For $i > 0$, given the vertices at layer $i - 1$, we obtain the vertices at layer i as follows. Let u be a vertex at layer $i-1$ corresponding to $(q_1, q_2) \in Q^2$; u is connected to u', corresponding to (q_1', q_2'), at layer i if and only if there are two distinct transitions $t = (q_1, a, c_1, q_1')$ and $t' = (q_2, a, c_2, q_2')$ in G. The arc connecting u to u' is labeled with $a \in \Sigma$ and has cost $c = c_1 - c_2$. $T_{\bar{q},\bar{q}}$ has at most $2n^4 - n^2 + 1$ vertices and $O(m^2 n^4)$ arcs.

Let $(q,q')_i$ be the vertex corresponding to $(q,q') \in Q^2$ at layer i of $T_{\bar{q},\bar{q}}$, if any. Let $RT \subseteq \{(q,q') \mid q \neq q'\}$ be the set of pairs of distinct states of G that are reachable from $(\bar{q},\bar{q})_0$ in $T_{\bar{q},\bar{q}}$. For each $(q,q') \in RT$, define $T_{q,q'}$ analogously to $T_{\bar{q},\bar{q}}$.

Fix two distinct states q and q' of G. Let $(q,q')_{i_1}, (q,q')_{i_2}, \ldots, (q,q')_{i_s}$, $0 < i_1 < i_2 < \cdots < i_s$, be all the occurrences of (q,q') in $T_{q,q'}$, excluding $(q,q')_0$. This sequence may be empty. A symmetric sequence can be extracted from $T_{q',q}$. We refer to these sequences as the *common cycles sequences* of (q,q'). We say that q and q' satisfy the *local twins property* if and only if **(a)** their common cycles sequences are empty or **(b)** zero is the cost of (any) shortest path from $(q,q')_0$ to $(q,q')_{i_j}$ in $T_{q,q'}$ and from $(q',q)_0$ to $(q',q)_{i_j}$ in $T_{q'q}$, for all $1 \leq j \leq s$.

Lemma 2. *Let G be a trim, unambiguous WFA. G satisfies the twins property if and only if (i) RT is empty or (ii) all $(q,q') \in RT$ satisfy the local twins property.*

Proof (Sketch). We outline the proof for the sufficient condition. The only nontrivial case is when some states in RT satisfy the local twins property and their common cycles sequences are not empty. Let RT' be such a set. Assume that G does not satisfy the twins property. We derive a contradiction. Since RT' is not empty, we have that the set of pairs of states for which (i) and (ii) are satisfied in Lemma 1 is not empty. But since G does not satisfy the twins property, there must exist two states q and q' and a string $uv \in \Sigma^*$, $|uv| \leq 2n^2 - 1$, such that (i) both q and q' can be reached from the initial state of G through string u; (ii) $q \in \delta(q,v)$ and $q' \in \delta(q',v)$; and (iii) $c(q,v,q) \neq c(q',v,q')$. Without loss of generality, assume that $p = c(q,v,q) - c(q',v,q') < 0$. Now, one can show that $(q,q') \in RT'$. Then, using the fact that G is unambiguous, one can show that there is exactly one path in $T_{q,q'}$ from the root to $(q,q')_{|v|}$ with cost $p < 0$. Therefore, (q,q') cannot satisfy the local twins property.

To test whether a trim, unambiguous WFA has the twins property, we first compute $T_{\bar{q},\bar{q}}$ and the set RT. For each pair of states $(q,q') \in RT$ that has not yet been processed, we need only compute $T_{q,q'}$ and $T_{q',q}$ and their respective shortest path trees.

Theorem 1. *Let G be a trim unambiguous WFA. In the general case, whether G satisfies the twins property can be checked in $O(m^2n^6)$ time using the $\Re$-RAM. In the integer case, the bound becomes $O(\rho m^2 n^6)$ using the $\mathcal{CO}$-RAM.*

3.2 The DTA Algorithm

In this section we describe the **DTA** algorithm. We then give an upper bound on the size of the deterministic machines produced by the algorithm. The results of Section 5 below show that our upper bound is tight to within polynomial factors.

Given WFA $G = (Q, \bar{q}, \Sigma, \delta, Q_f)$, **DTA** generalizes the classic power-set construction to construct deterministic WFA G' as follows. The start state of G' is $\{(\bar{q}, 0)\}$, which forms an initial queue P. While $P \neq \emptyset$, pop state $q = \{(q_1, r_1), \ldots, (q_n, r_n)\}$ from P, where $q_i \in Q$ and $r_i \in \Re^+ \cup \{0, \infty\}$. The r_i values encode path-length information, as follows. For each $\sigma \in \Sigma$, let $\{q'_1, \ldots, q'_m\}$ be the set of states reachable by σ-transitions out of all the q_i. For $1 \leq j \leq m$, let $\rho_j = \min_{1 \leq i \leq n; (q_i, \sigma, \nu, q'_j) \in \delta} \{r_i + \nu\}$ be the minimum of the weights of σ-transitions into q'_j from the q_i plus the respective

r_i. Let $\rho = \min_{1 \le j \le m}\{\rho_j\}$. Let $q' = \{(q'_1, s_1), \ldots, (q'_m, s_m)\}$, where $s_j = \rho_j - \rho$, for $1 \le j \le m$. We add transition (q, σ, ρ, q') to G' and push q' onto P if q' is new. This is the only σ-transition out of state q, so G' is deterministic.

Let $T_G(w)$ be the set of sequences of transitions in G that accept a string $w \in \Sigma^*$; let $\boldsymbol{t}_{G'}(w)$ be the (one) sequence of transitions in G' that accepts the same string. Mohri [17] shows that $c(\boldsymbol{t}_{G'}(w)) = \min_{\boldsymbol{t} \in T_G(w)}\{c(\boldsymbol{t})\}$, and thus $L(G') = L(G)$. Moreover, let $T_G(w, q)$ be the set of sequences of transitions in G from state $\bar{q}$ to state q that induce string w. Again, let $\boldsymbol{t}_{G'}(w)$ be the (one) sequence of transitions in G' that induces the same string; $\boldsymbol{t}_{G'}(w)$ ends at some state $\{(q_1, r_1), \ldots, (q_n, r_n)\}$ in G' such that some $q_i = q$. Mohri [17] shows that $c(\boldsymbol{t}_{G'}(w)) + r_i = \min_{\boldsymbol{t} \in T_G(w,q)}\{c(\boldsymbol{t})\}$. Thus, each r_i is a *remainder* that encodes the difference between the weight of the shortest path to some state that induces w in G and the weight of the path inducing w in G'. Hence at least one remainder in each state must be zero.

3.3 Analyzing DTA

We first bound the number of states in $dta(G)$, denoted $\#dta(G)$.

Theorem 2. *If WFA G has the twins property, then* $\#dta(G) < 2^{n(2\lg n + n^2 \lg|\Sigma| + 1)}$ *in the general case;* $\#dta(G) < 2^{n(2\lg n + 1 + \min(n^2 \lg|\Sigma|, \rho))}$ *in the integer (or rational) case; and* $\#dta(G) < 2^{n \lg|\Sigma|}$ *if G is acyclic, independent of any assumptions on weights. The acyclic bound is tight (up to constant factors) for any alphabet.*

Proof (Sketch). Let $\tilde{R}$ be the set of remainders in $dta(G)$. Let R be the set of remainders r for which the following holds: $\exists w \in \Sigma^*$, $|w| \le n^2 - 1$, and two states q_1 and q_2, such that $r = |c(\bar{q}, w, q_2) - c(\bar{q}, w, q_1)|$. The twins property implies that $\tilde{R} \subseteq R$. In the worst case, each i-state tuple from G will appear in $dta(G)$, and there are $|\tilde{R}|^i$ distinct i-tuples of remainders it can assume. (This over counts by including tuples without any zero remainders.) Therefore, $\#dta(G) \le \sum_{i=1}^{n} \binom{n}{i} |\tilde{R}|^i \le (2|\tilde{R}|)^n \le (2|R|)^n$.

General Case: Each string of length at most $n^2 - 1$ can reach a pair of (not necessarily distinct) states in G. Therefore, $|R| < n^2|\Sigma|^{n^2}$. **Integer Case**: The remainders in R are in $[0, (n^2 - 1)C]_Z$ implying $|R| < n^2 C$; but still $|R| < n^2|\Sigma|^{n^2}$. **Acyclic Case**: $\#dta(G)$ is bounded by the number of strings in the weighted language accepted by G, which is bounded by $|\Sigma|^n$. We discuss tightness in Section 5.

Processing each tuple of state-remainders generated by **DTA** takes $O(|\Sigma|(n + m))$ time, excluding the cost of arithmetic and min operations, yielding the following.

Theorem 3. *Let G be a WFA satisfying the twins property. In the general case,* **DTA** *takes* $O(|\Sigma|(n + m)2^{n(2\lg n + n^2 \lg|\Sigma| + 1)})$ *time on the* $\Re$*-RAM. In the (rational or) integer case,* **DTA** *takes* $O(\rho|\Sigma|(n + m)2^{n(2\lg n + 1 + \min(n^2 \lg|\Sigma|, \rho))})$ *time on the* $\mathcal{CO}$*-RAM. In the acyclic case,* **DTA** *takes* $O(|\Sigma|(n + m)2^{n \lg|\Sigma|})$ *time on the* $\Re$*-RAM and* $O(\rho|\Sigma|(n + m)2^{n \lg|\Sigma|})$ *time on the* $\mathcal{CO}$*-RAM.*

We can use the above results to generate hard instances for any determinization algorithm. A *reweighting function* (or simply *reweighting*) f is such that, when applied to a WFA G, it preserves the topology of G but possibly changes the weights. We want to determine a reweighting f such that $min(f(G))$ exists and $|min(f(G))|$ is maximized among reweightings for which $min(f(G))$ exists. We restrict attention to the integer case and, without loss of generality, we assume that G is trim and unambiguous.

Theorem 2 shows that for weights to affect the growth of $dta(G)$, it must be that $\rho \leq n^2 \lg |\Sigma|$. Set $\rho_{max} = n^2 \lg |\Sigma|$. To find the required reweighting, we simply consider all possible reweightings of G satisfying the twins property and requiring at most ρ_{max} bits. There are $(2^{\rho_{max}})^m = 2^{m\rho_{max}}$ possible reweightings, and it takes $2^{O(n(2\lg n+(n^2 \lg |\Sigma|)))}$ time to compute the expansion or decide that the resulting machine cannot be determinized, bounding the total time by $2^{O(n(2\log n+(n^2 \log |\Sigma|))+m\rho_{max})}$.

4 Hot Automata

This section provides a family of acyclic, multi-partite WFAs that are *hot*: when determinized, they expand independently of the weights on their transitions. Given some alphabet $\Sigma = \{a_1, \dots, a_n\}$, consider the language $L = \bigcup_{i=1}^{n} (\Sigma - \{a_i\})^n$; i.e., the set of all n-length strings that do not include all symbols from Σ. It is simple to obtain an acyclic, multi-partite NFA H of poly(n) size that accepts L. It is not hard to show that the minimal DFA accepting L has $\Theta(2^{n+\lg n})$ states. Furthermore, we can construct H so that these bounds hold for a *binary* alphabet. H corresponds to a WFA with all arcs weighted identically. Since acyclic WFAs satisfy the twins property, they can always be determinized. Altering the weights can only increase the expansion. Kintala and Wotschke [15] provide a set of NFAs that produces a hierarchy of expansion factors when determinized, providing additional examples of hot WFAs.

5 Weight-Dependent Automata

In this section we study a simple family of WFAs with multi-partite, acyclic topology. We examine how various reweightings affect the size of the determinized equivalent. This family shrinks without weights, so any expansion is due to weighting. This study is related in spirit to previous works on measuring nondeterminism in finite automata [13,15]. Here, however, nondeterminism is encoded only in the weights. We first discuss the case of a binary alphabet and then generalize to arbitrary alphabets.

5.1 The Rail Graph

We denote by $RG(k)$ the *k-layer rail graph*. $RG(k)$ has $2k + 1$ vertices, denoted $\{0, T_1, B_1, \dots, T_k, B_k\}$. There are arcs $(0, T_1, a)$, $(0, T_1, b)$ $(0, B_1, a)$, $(0, B_1, b)$, and then, for $1 \leq i < k$, arcs (T_i, T_{i+1}, a), (T_i, T_{i+1}, b), (B_i, B_{i+1}, a), and (B_i, B_{i+1}, b). See Fig. 1. $RG(k)$ is $(k + 1)$-partite and also has fixed in- and out-degrees. If we consider the strings induced by paths from 0 to either T_k or B_k, then the language of $RG(k)$ is the set of strings $L_{RG}(k) = \{a, b\}^k$. The only nondeterministic choice is at the state 0, where either the top or bottom rail may be selected. Hence a string w can be accepted by one of two paths, one following the top rail and the other the bottom rail.

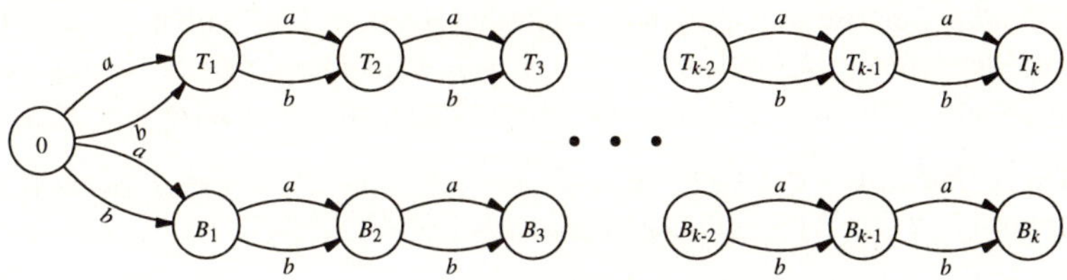

Fig. 1. Topology of the k-layer rail graph.

Technically, $RG(k)$ is ambiguous. We can disambiguate $RG(k)$ by adding transitions from T_k and B_k, each on a distinct symbol, to a new final state. Our results extend to this case. For clarity of presentation, we discuss the ambiguous rail graph.

The rail graph is weight-dependent. In Section 5.2 we provide weightings such that **DTA** produces the $(k+1)$-vertex *trivial series-parallel graph*: a graph on $k+1$ vertices, with transitions, on all symbols, only between vertices i and $i+1$, for $1 \leq i \leq k$. On the other hand, in Section 5.3 we exhibit weightings for the rail graph that cause **DTA** to produce exponential state-space expansions. We also explore the relationship between the magnitude of the weights and the amount of expansion that is possible. In Section 5.4, we show that random weightings induce the behavior of worst-case weightings. Finally, in Section 5.5 we generalize the rail graph to arbitrary alphabets.

5.2 Weighting $RG(k)$

Consider determinizing $RG(k)$ with **DTA**. The set of states reachable on any string $w = \sigma_1 \cdots \sigma_j$ of length $j \leq k$ is $\{T_j, B_j\}$. For a given weighting function c, let $c_T(w)$ denote the cost of accepting string w if the top path is taken; i.e., $c_T(w) = c(0, \sigma_1, T_1) + \sum_{i=1}^{j-1} c(T_i, \sigma_{i+1}, T_{i+1})$. Analogously define $c_B(w)$ to be the corresponding cost along the bottom path. Let $R(w)$ be the *remainder vector* for w, which is a pair of the form $(0, c_B(w) - c_T(w))$ or $(c_T(w) - c_B(w), 0)$. A state at layer $0 < i \leq k$ in the determinized WFA is labeled $(\{T_i, B_i\}/R(w))$ for any string w leading to that state. Thus, two strings w_1 and w_2 of identical length lead to distinct states in the determinized version of the rail graph if and only if $R(w_1) \neq R(w_2)$.

It is convenient simply to write $R(w) = c_T(w) - c_B(w)$. The sign of $R(w)$ then determines which of the two forms $(0, x)$ or $(x, 0)$ of the remainder vector occurs.

Let $r_i^T(\sigma)$ (rsp., $r_i^B(\sigma)$) denote the weight on the top (rsp., bottom) arc labeled σ into vertex T_i (rsp., B_i). Let $\delta_i(\sigma) = r_i^T(\sigma) - r_i^B(\sigma)$. Then $R(w) = \sum_{i=1}^{j} \delta_i(\sigma_i)$.

Theorem 4. *There is a reweighting f such that dta$(f(RG(k))) =$ min$(f(RG(k)))$, which consists of the $(k+1)$-vertex trivial series-parallel graph*

Proof. Any f for which $\delta_i(a) = \delta_i(b)$ for $i = 1$ to k suffices, since in this case $R(w_1) = R(w_2)$ for all pairs of strings $\{w_1, w_2\}$. In particular, giving zero weights suffices.

5.3 Worst-Case Weightings of $RG(k)$

Theorem 5. *For any $j \in [0, k]_Z$ there is a reweighting f such that layers 0 through j of dta$(f(RG(k)))$ form the complete binary tree on $2^{j+1} - 1$ vertices.*

Proof (Sketch). Choose any weighting such that $\delta_i(a) = 2^{i-1}$ and $\delta_i(b) = 0$ for $1 \leq i \leq j$, and let $\delta_i(a) = \delta_i(b) = 0$ for $j < i \leq k$. Consider a pair of strings w_1, w_2 of identical length such that $w_1 \neq w_2$. The weighting ensures that $R(w_1) \neq R(w_2)$.

Theorem 6. *For any $j \in [0, k]_Z$ there is a reweighting f such that layers 0 through $j-1$ of $min(f(RG(k)))$ form the complete binary tree on $2^j - 1$ vertices.*

Theorem 6, generalized by Theorem 10, shows that weight-dependence is not an artifact of **DTA** and that the acyclic bound of Theorem 2 is tight for binary alphabets.

We now address the sensitivity of the size expansion to the magnitude of the weights, arguing that exponential state-space expansion requires exponentially big weights for the rail graph. (This means that the size expansion, while exponential in the number of states, is only super-polynomial in the number of bits.)

Theorem 7. *Let f be a reweighting. If $|dta(f(RG(k)))| = \Omega(2^k)$, then $\Omega(k^2)$ bits are required to encode $f(RG(k))$.*

Proof (Sketch). There must be $\Omega(2^k)$ distinct remainders among the states at depth k in the determinized WFA, necessitating $\Omega(2^k)$ distinct permutations of the $\lceil \frac{k}{2} \rceil$ high-order bits among them. Thus $\Omega(k)$ weights must have similarly high-order bits set.

Corollary 1. *Let f be a reweighting. If $|min(f(RG(k)))| = \Omega(2^k)$, then $\Omega(k^2)$ bits are required to encode $f(RG(k))$.*

5.4 Random Weightings of $RG(k)$

Theorem 8. *Let G be $RG(k)$ weighted with numbers chosen independently and uniformly at random from $[1, 2^k - 1]_Z$. Then $E[|dta(f^R(RG(k)))|] = \Theta(2^k)$, where $E[X]$ denotes the expected value of the random variable X.*

Theorem 9. *Let G be $RG(k)$ weighted with logarithms of numbers chosen independently and uniformly at random from $[1, 2^k - 1]_Z$. Then $E[|dta(G)|] = \Theta(2^k)$.*

The proofs of Theorems 8 and 9 use the observation that the random functions defined by *RG* are essentially universal hash functions [6] to bound sufficiently low the probability that the remainders of two distinct strings are equal. Theorem 9 is motivated by the fact that the weights of ASR WFAs are negated log probabilities.

5.5 Extending $RG(k)$ to Arbitrary Alphabets

We can extend the rail graph to arbitrary alphabets, defining $RG(r, k)$, the *k-layer r-rail graph*, as follows. $RG(r, k)$ has $rk + 1$ vertices: vertex 0 and, for $1 \leq i \leq r$ and $1 \leq j \leq k$, vertex v_j^i. Assume the alphabet is $\{1, \ldots, r\}$. $RG(r, k)$ has arcs $(0, v_1^i, s)$ for all $1 \leq i, s \leq r$ and also arcs (v_j^i, v_{j+1}^i, s) for all $1 \leq i, s \leq r$ and $1 \leq j < k$.

The subgraph induced by vertex 0 and vertices v_j^i for some i and all $1 \leq j \leq k$ comprises *rail* i of $RG(r, k)$. The subgraph induced by vertices v_j^i for all $1 \leq i \leq r$ and some j comprises *layer* j of $RG(r, k)$. Vertex 0 comprises *layer* 0 of $RG(r, k)$. Thus, $RG(2, k)$ is the k-layer rail graph, $RG(k)$, defined in Section 5.1.

Let $c(i, j, s)$ be the weight of the arc labeled s into vertex v^i_j. Theorems 4 and 5 generalize easily to the k-layer r-rail graphs. Theorem 6 generalizes to $RG(r, k)$ as follows, showing that the acyclic bound of Theorem 2 is tight for arbitrary alphabets.

Theorem 10. *For any $j \in [0, k]_Z$ there is a reweighting f such that layers 0 through $j - 1$ of $min(f(RG(r, k)))$ form the complete r-ary tree on $\frac{r^j-1}{r-1}$ vertices.*

Proof (Sketch). Choose the following weighting. Set $c(i, \ell, s) = [(i + s) \mod r] \cdot r^\ell$ for all $1 \leq i, s \leq r$ and $1 \leq \ell \leq j$. Set $c(i, \ell, s) = 0$ for all $1 \leq i, s \leq r$ and $j < \ell \leq k$.

Given two strings, $w_1 \neq w_2$, such that $|w_1| = |w_2| = \ell < j$, we can show that w_1 and w_2 must lead to different vertices in *any* deterministic realization, D, of $RG(r, k)$. Assume that w_1 and w_2 lead to the same vertex in D. Let $c_d(w)$ be the cost of string w in D. Given any suffix s of length $k - \ell$, we can show that $c(w_1 s) - c(w_2 s) = c_d(w_1) - c_d(w_2)$. The right hand side is a fixed value, Δ.

Consider any position $i \leq \ell$ in which w_1 and w_2 differ. Denote the ith symbol of string w by $w(i)$. Consider two suffixes, s_1 and s_2, of length $k-\ell$, such that $s_1(j-\ell) = w_1(i)$ and $s_2(j - \ell) = w_2(i)$. Observe that the given weighting on $RG(r, k)$ forces the minimum cost path for any string with some symbol σ in position j to follow rail $(r-\sigma)$. Thus, $w_1 s_1$ and $w_2 s_1$ follow rail $r - w_1(i)$, and $w_1 s_2$ and $w_2 s_2$ follow rail $r - w_2(i)$. We can use this to show that $c(w_1 s_1) - c(w_2 s_1) \neq c(w_1 s_2) - c(w_2 s_2)$, a contradiction.

6 Experimental Observations on ASR WFAs

To determine whether ASR WFAs manifest weight dependence, we experimented on 100 WFAs generated by the AT&T speech recognizer [23], using a grammar for the Air Travel Information System (ATIS), a standard test bed [4]. Each transition was labeled with a word and weighted by the recognizer with the negated log probability of realizing that transition out of the source state; we refer to these weights as *speech weights*.

We determinized each WFA with its speech weights, with zero weights, and with weights assigned independently and uniformly at random from $[0, 2^i-1]_Z$ (for each $0 \leq i \leq 8$). One WFA could not be determinized with speech weights due to computational limitations, and it is omitted from the data.

Figure 2(a) shows how many WFAs expanded when determinized with different weightings. Figure 2(b) classifies the 63 WFAs that expanded with at least one weighting. For each WFA, we took the weighting that produced maximal expansion. This was usually the 8-bit random weighting, although due to computational limitations we were unable to determinize some WFAs with large random weightings. The x-axis indicates the open interval within which the value $\lg(|dta(G)|/|G|)$ falls.

The utility of determinization in ASR includes the reduction in size achieved with actual speech weights. In our sample, 82 WFAs shrank when determinized. For each, we computed the value $\lg(|G|/|dta(G)|)$, and we plot the results in Fig. 2(c).

In Fig. 2(d), we examine the relationship between the value $\lg(|dta(G)|/|G|)$ and the number of bits used in random weights. We chose the ten WFAs with highest final expansion value and plotted $\lg(|dta(G)|/|G|)$ against the number of bits used. For reference the functions i^2, $2^{\sqrt{i}}$, and 2^i are plotted, where i is the number of bits. Most

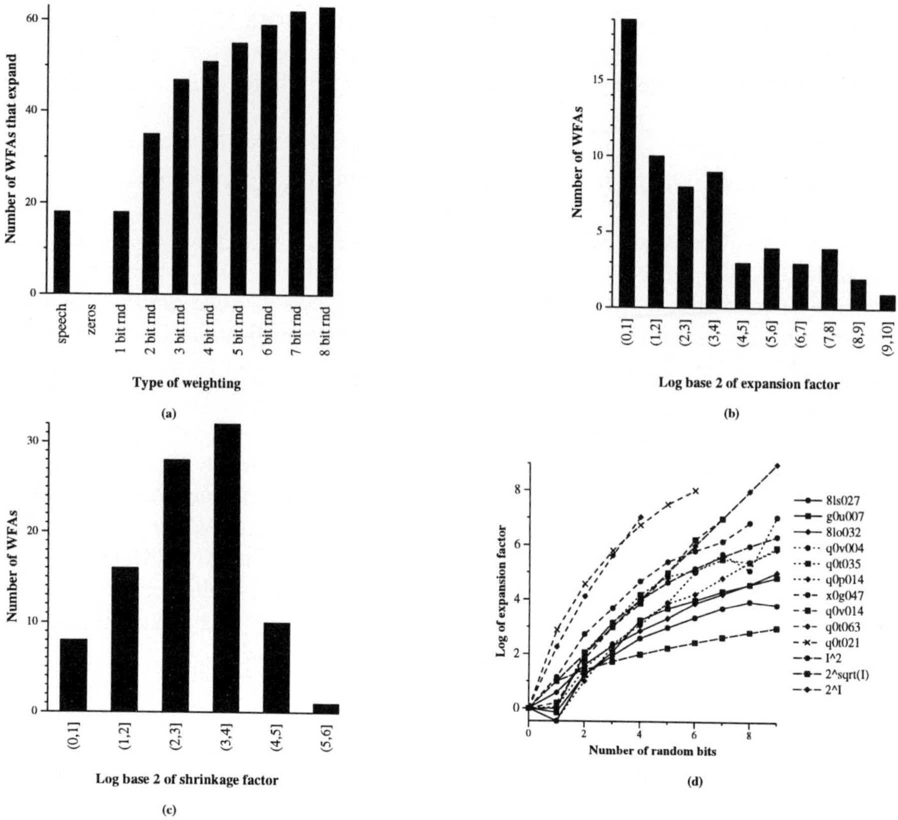

Fig. 2. Observations on ASR WFAs.

of the WFAs exhibit subexponential growth as the number of bits increases, although some, like `q0t063` have increased by 128 times even with four random bits.

The WFA that could not be determinized with speech weights was "slightly hot," in that the determinized zero-weighted variant had 2.7% more arcs than the original WFA. The remaining ninety-nine WFAs shrank with zero weights: none was hot. If one expanded, it did so due to weights rather than topology.

Figure 2(a) indicates that many of the WFAs have some degree of weight dependence. Figure 2(d) suggests that random weights are a good way to estimate the degree to which a WFA is weight dependent. Note that the expansion factor is some superlinear, possibly exponential, function of the number of random bits, suggesting that large, e.g., 32-bit, random weights should cause expansion if anything will. Analogous experiments on the minimized determinized WFAs yield results that are qualitatively the same, although fewer WFAs still expand after minimization. Hence weight dependence seems to be a fundamental property of these WFAs rather than an artifact of **DTA**.

Acknowledgements. We thank Mehryar Mohri, Fernando Pereira, and Antonio Restivo for fruitful discussions.

References

1. R. K. Ahuja, T. L. Magnanti, and J. B. Orlin. *Network Flows: Theory, Algorithms, and Applications*. Prentice-Hall, 1993.
2. J. Berstel. *Transduction and Context-Free Languages*. Springer-Verlag, 1979.
3. J. Berstel and C. Reutenauer. *Rational Series and Their Languages*. Springer-Verlag, 1988.
4. E. Bocchieri, G. Riccardi, and J. Anantharaman. The 1994 AT&T ATIS CHRONUS recognizer. In *Proc. ARPA SLT*, pages 265–8, 1995.
5. A. L. Buchsbaum and R. Giancarlo. Algorithmic aspects in speech recognition: An introduction. *ACM J. Exp. Algs.*, 2, 1997.
6. J. L. Carter and M. N. Wegman. Universal classes of hash functions. *JCSS*, 18:143–54, 1979.
7. C. Choffrut. Une caracterisation des fonctions sequentielles et des fonctions sous-sequentielles en tant que relations rationnelles. *Theor. Comp. Sci.*, 5:325–37, 1977.
8. C. Choffrut. *Contributions á l'étude de quelques familles remarquables de function rationnelles*. PhD thesis, LITP-Université Paris 7, 1978.
9. K. Culik II and J. Karhumäki. Finite automata computing real functions. *SIAM J. Comp.*, 23(4):789–814, 1994.
10. K. Culik II and P. Rajčáni. Iterative weighted finite transductions. *Acta Inf.*, 32:681–703, 1995.
11. D. Derencourt, J. Karhumäki, M. Latteux, and A. Terlutte. On computational power of weighted finite automata. In *Proc. 17th MFCS*, volume 629 of *LNCS*, pages 236–45. Springer-Verlag, 1992.
12. S. Eilenberg. *Automata, Languages, and Machines*, volume A. Academic Press, 1974.
13. J. Goldstine, C. M. R. Kintala, and D. Wotschke. On measuring nondeterminism in regular languages. *Inf. and Comp.*, 86:179–94, 1990.
14. J. Kari and P. Fränti. Arithmetic coding of weighted finite automata. *RAIRO Inform. Th. Appl.*, 28(3-4):343–60, 1994.
15. C. M. R. Kintala and D. Wotschke. Amounts of nondeterminism in finite automata. *Acta Inf.*, 13:199–204, 1980.
16. W. Kuich and A. Salomaa. *Semirings, Automata, Languages*. Springer-Verlag, 1986.
17. M. Mohri. Finite-state transducers in language and speech processing. *Comp. Ling.*, 23(2):269–311, 1997.
18. M. Mohri. On the use of sequential transducers in natural language processing. In *Finite-State Language Processing*. MIT Press, 1997.
19. F. Pereira and M. Riley. Speech recognition by composition of weighted finite automata. In *Finite-State Language Processing*. MIT Press, 1997.
20. F. Pereira, M. Riley, and R. Sproat. Weighted rational transductions and their application to human language processing. In *Proc. ARPA HLT*, pages 249–54, 1994.
21. F. P. Preparata and M. I. Shamos. *Computational Geometry: An Introduction*. Springer-Verlag, 1988.
22. M. O. Rabin. Probabilistic automata. *Inf. and Control*, 6:230–45, 1963.
23. M. D. Riley, A. Ljolje, D. Hindle, and F. C. N. Pereira. The AT&T 60,000 word speech-to-text system. In *Proc. 4th EUROSPEECH*, volume 1, pages 207–210, 1995.
24. E. Roche. *Analyse Syntaxique Transformationelle du Francais par Transducteurs et Lexique-Grammaire*. PhD thesis, LITP-Université Paris 7, 1993.
25. A. Salomaa and M. Soittola. *Automata-Theoretic Aspects of Formal Power Series*. Springer-Verlag, 1978.
26. M. Silberztein. *Dictionnaires électroniques et analise automatique de textes: le systéme INTEX*. PhD thesis, Masson, Paris, France., 1993.
27. A. Weber and R. Klemm. Economy of description for single-valued transducers. *Inf. and Comp.*, 118:327–40, 1995.

Bulk-Synchronous Parallel Multiplication of Boolean Matrices

A. Tiskin

Oxford University Computing Laboratory
Wolfson Building, Parks Rd., Oxford OX1 3QD, UK
email: tiskin@comlab.ox.ac.uk

Abstract

The model of bulk-synchronous parallel (BSP) computation is an emerging paradigm of general-purpose parallel computing. We study the BSP complexity of subcubic algorithms for Boolean matrix multiplication. The communication cost of a standard Strassen-type algorithm is known to be optimal for general matrices. A natural question is whether it remains optimal when the problem is restricted to Boolean matrices. We give a negative answer to this question, by showing how to achieve a lower asymptotic communication cost for Boolean matrix multiplication. The proof uses a deep result from extremal graph theory, known as Szemerédi's Regularity Lemma. Despite its theoretical interest, the algorithm is not practical, because it works only on astronomically large matrices and involves huge constant factors.

1 Introduction

The model of bulk-synchronous parallel (BSP) computation (see [19, 13, 14, 16]) provides a simple and practical framework for general-purpose parallel computing. Its main goal is to support the creation of architecture-independent and scalable parallel software. The key features of BSP are the treatment of the communication medium as an abstract fully connected network, and explicit and independent cost analysis of communication and synchronisation.

One of the basic BSP algorithms is the method suggested by McColl and Valiant for matrix multiplication (see [14, 16]). The algorithm works by a natural partitioning of the computation graph. For multiplication of matrices over a general semiring (without subtraction), the McColl–Valiant algorithm is provably optimal in all three BSP parameters: local computation, communication and synchronisation. Matrix multiplication over a commutative ring with unit can be performed by fast Strassen-type methods. The BSP implementation of Strassen's algorithm in [15] improves on the standard algorithm both in local computation and communication. It is also provably optimal.

In this paper we study the BSP multiplication of matrices over the semiring of Booleans, with operations $\vee$, $\wedge$ used as addition and multiplication respectively. A standard approach to multiplying $n \times n$ Boolean matrices is to embed the semiring of Booleans into the commutative ring of integers modulo $n+1$, and

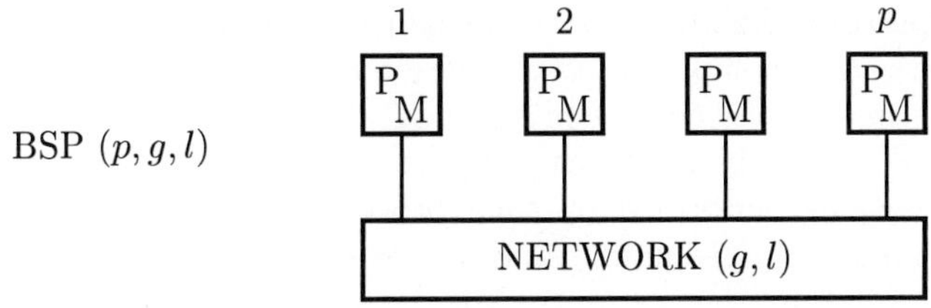

Figure 1: A BSP computer

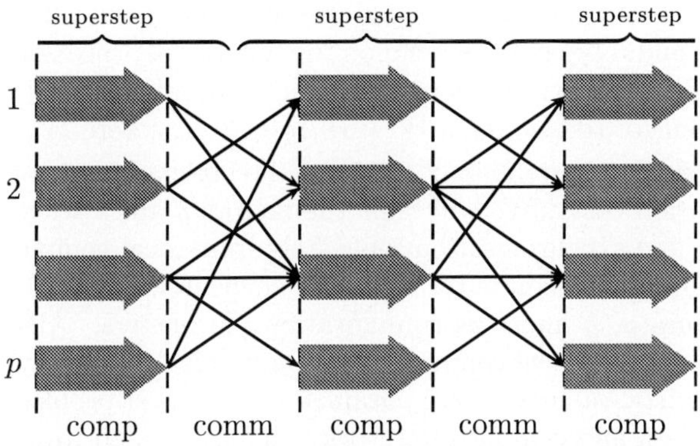

Figure 2: A BSP computation

then to use fast matrix multiplication. It is natural to ask whether this method is optimal, or it can be improved by using properties specific to Boolean matrices. This paper presents a method of achieving a significant reduction in the asymptotic communication cost of the straightforward Strassen-type method. We use a deep result from extremal graph theory, known as Szemerédi's Regularity Lemma.

The presented algorithm is not practical, because it works only for astronomically large matrices and involves huge constant factors. However, it answers an interesting theoretical question, relevant to optimality and lower bounds for BSP algorithms.

2 The BSP model

A *BSP computer*, introduced in [19, 20], consists of p *processors* connected by a communication network (see Figure 1). Each processor has a fast *local memory*. The processors may follow different threads of computation. A BSP computation is a sequence of *supersteps* (see Figure 2). A superstep consists of an *input phase*, a *local computation phase* and an *output phase*. In the input phase a processor receives data that were sent to it in the previous superstep; in the output phase it can send data to other processors, to be received in the next superstep. The processors are synchronised between supersteps. The computation within a superstep is asynchronous.

The *cost unit* is the cost of performing a basic arithmetic operation or a local memory access. If for a particular superstep w is the maximum number of local operations performed by each processor, h' (respectively h'') is the maximum number of data units received (respectively sent) by each processor, and $h = h' + h''$, then the cost of the superstep is defined as $w + h \cdot g + l$. Here g and l are parameters of the computer. The value g is the *communication throughput ratio* (also called "bandwidth inefficiency" or "gap"), the value l is the *communication latency* (also called "synchronisation periodicity"). We write BSP (p, g, l) to denote a BSP computer with the given values of p, g and l. The values of w and h typically depend on the number of processors p and on the problem size. If a computation consists of S supersteps with costs $w_s + h_s \cdot g + l$, $1 \leq s \leq S$, then its total cost is $W + H \cdot g + S \cdot l$, where $W = \sum_{s=1}^{S} w_s$ is the local computation cost, $H = \sum_{s=1}^{S} h_s$ is the communication cost, and S is the synchronisation cost. (We will omit the factors g and l when dealing with communication and synchronisation separately from local computation.)

In order to utilise the computer resources efficiently, a typical BSP program regards the values p, g and l as configuration parameters. Algorithm design should aim to minimise local computation, communication and synchronisation costs for any realistic values of these parameters. For most problems, a balanced distribution of data and computation work will lead to algorithms that achieve optimal cost values simultaneously. However, for some other problems a need to trade off the costs will arise.

An example of a communication-synchronisation tradeoff is the problem of broadcasting a single value from a processor: it can be performed with $H = S = O(\log p)$ by a balanced binary tree, or with $H = O(p)$ and $S = O(1)$ by sending the value directly to every processor (this was observed in [19]). On the other hand, a technique known as *two-phase broadcast* allows one to achieve perfect balance for the problem of broadcasting $n \geq p$ values from one processor. By dividing the values into p blocks of size n/p, scattering the blocks so that each one gets to a distinct processor, and then performing total exchange of the blocks, the problem can be solved with $H = O(n)$ and $S = O(1)$ — this is obviously optimal.

Algorithms presented in this paper, as well as many other BSP algorithms, are defined for input sizes that are sufficiently large with respect to the number of processors. This requirement is loosely referred to as *slackness*.

For the sake of simplicity, throughout the paper we ignore small irregularities that arise from imperfect matching of integer parameters. For example, when we write "divide an array of size n into p regular blocks", the value n may not be an exact multiple of p, and therefore the blocks may differ in size by ± 1. We use square bracket notation for matrices, referring to an element of an $n \times n$ matrix A as $A[i, j]$, $1 \leq i, j \leq n$. When the matrix is partitioned into regular blocks of size $m \times m$, we refer to each individual block as $A[[s, t]]$, $1 \leq s, t \leq n/m$.

The rest of this paper is organised as follows. Section 3 describes the McColl–Valiant algorithm for general matrix multiplication. Section 4 presents the proposed communication-efficient algorithm for Boolean matrix multiplication. Section 5 contains some concluding remarks.

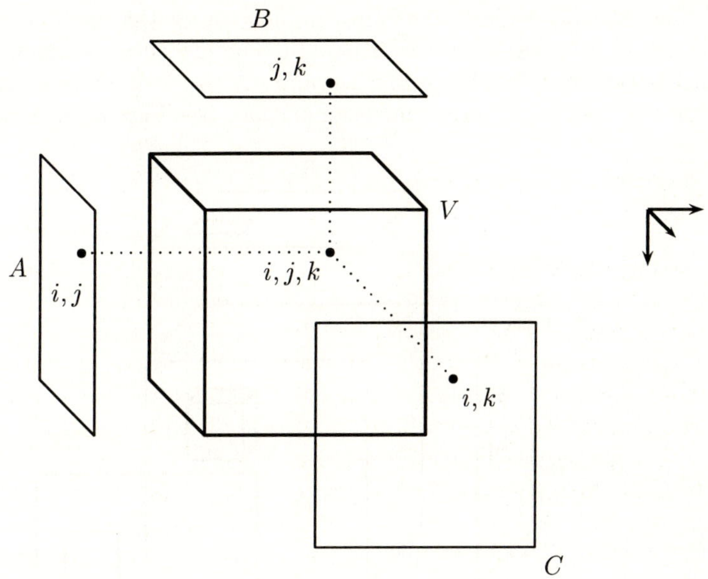

Figure 3: Matrix multiplication graph

3 General matrix multiplication

In this section we describe a BSP algorithm for one of the most common problems in scientific computation: dense matrix multiplication. We deal with the problem of computing the matrix product $AB = C$, where A, B, C are $n \times n$ matrices over a semiring. We assume that the matrices are distributed across the processors evenly, but otherwise arbitrarily.

We aim to parallelise the sequential $\Theta(n^3)$ method, asymptotically optimal for matrix multiplication over a general semiring (see [10]). The method consists in straightforward computation of the family of bilinear forms

$$C[i,k] = \sum_{j=1}^{n} A[i,j] \cdot B[j,k] \qquad 1 \le i,k \le n \tag{1}$$

Following (1), we need to set

$$C[i,k] \leftarrow 0 \quad \text{for } i,k = 1,\ldots,n \tag{2}$$

and then compute

$$V[i,j,k] \leftarrow A[i,j] \cdot B[j,k] \qquad C[i,k] \leftarrow C[i,k] + V[i,j,k] \tag{3}$$

for all i, j, k, $1 \le i, j, k \le n$. Computation (3) for different triples i, j, k is independent (although it requires concurrent reading from $A[i,j]$ and $B[j,k]$, and concurrent writing to $C[i,k]$), and therefore can be performed in parallel.

The McColl–Valiant algorithm implementing this method is described in [14, 16], and based on an idea from [1]. The algorithm works by a straightforward partitioning of the problem graph. Array V is represented as a cube of volume n^3 in integer three-dimensional space (see Figure 3). Arrays A, B, C are

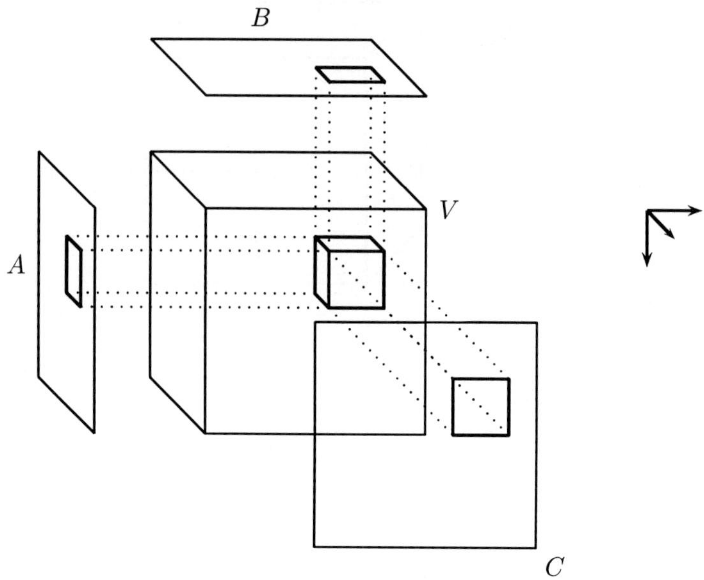

Figure 4: Matrix multiplication in BSP

represented as projections of the cube V onto the coordinate planes. Computation of the node $V[i, j, k]$ requires the input of its A and B projections $A[i, j]$ and $B[j, k]$, and the output of its C projection $C[i, k]$. In order to provide a communication-efficient BSP algorithm, the array V must be divided into p regular cubic blocks of size $n/p^{1/3}$ (see Figure 4). Such partitioning induces a partition of the matrices A, B and C into $p^{2/3}$ regular square blocks of size $n/p^{1/3}$,

$$A = \begin{pmatrix} A[[1,1]] & \cdots & A[[1,p^{1/3}]] \\ \vdots & \ddots & \vdots \\ A[[p^{1/3},1]] & \cdots & A[[p^{1/3},p^{1/3}]] \end{pmatrix} \quad (4)$$

and similarly for B and C (see Figure 4). Computation (2), (3) can be expressed in terms of blocks as

$$C[[i,k]] \leftarrow 0 \quad \text{for } i,k = 1,\ldots,p^{1/3} \quad (5)$$

and then

$$V[[i,j,k]] \leftarrow A[[i,j]] \cdot B[[j,k]] \qquad C[[i,k]] \leftarrow C[[i,k]] + V[[i,j,k]] \quad (6)$$

for all i, j, k, $1 \le i, j, k \le p^{1/3}$. Each processor computes a block product $V[[i,j,k]] = A[[i,j]] \cdot B[[j,k]]$ sequentially by (2), (3). The algorithm is as follows.

Algorithm 1. *Matrix multiplication.*

Input: $n \times n$ matrices A and B over a semiring.

Output: $n \times n$ matrix $C = A \cdot B$.

Description. We assume $n \ge p^{1/3}$.

After the initialisation step (5), the computation proceeds in one superstep. Each processor performs the computation (6) for a particular triple i, j, k. In the input phase, the processor receives the blocks $A[[i,j]]$ and $B[[j,k]]$. Then it computes the product $V[[i,j,k]] = A[[i,j]] \cdot B[[j,k]]$ by (2), (3). The block $V[[i,j,k]]$ is then written to $C[[i,k]]$ by sending it to the relevant processor. Concurrent writing is resolved by addition of the written blocks. The resulting matrix C is the product of A and B.

Cost analysis. The local computation, communication and synchronisation costs are

$$W = O(n^3/p) \qquad H = O(n^2/p^{2/3}) \qquad S = O(1) \quad \blacksquare$$

It can be shown that Algorithm 1 is an optimal BSP algorithm for matrix multiplication over a general semiring. The n^3 operations performed by the algorithm and their representation as a cube are essentially unique (see [10]). The lower bounds $W = \Omega(n^3/p)$ and $S = \Omega(1)$ are trivial. To prove the lower bound on H, we use the following fact, suggested for this proof by [18]. Let A be a finite set of points in $\mathbf{Z}^3$, and let A_1, A_2, A_3 be the orthogonal projections of A onto the coordinate planes. Then the *discrete Loomis–Whitney inequality* (see [12, 9, 6]) states that

$$|A| \le |A_1|^{1/2} \cdot |A_2|^{1/2} \cdot |A_3|^{1/2} \tag{7}$$

Since n^3 nodes are computed by p processors, there is a processor q that computes at least n^3/p nodes. We apply the discrete Loomis–Whitney inequality, and then the arithmetic-geometric mean inequality, to the set of nodes computed by processor q. Since the size of this set is at least n^3/p, one of the three projections of the set must contain at least $n^2/p^{2/3}$ nodes, therefore $H = \Omega(n^2/p^{2/3})$.

Paper [15] generalises Algorithm 1 to a BSP implementation of any fast bilinear algorithm, such as Strassen's. The method works for matrices over a commutative ring with unit. The BSP cost of this algorithm is $W = O(n^\omega/p)$, $H = O(n^2/p^{2/\omega})$, $S = O(1)$, where ω is the exponent of the bilinear algorithm (the best current value is 2.376 by [7]). For any particular bilinear algorithm these cost values are optimal. This can be shown by embedding the graph corresponding to general matrix multiplication to the graph corresponding to the bilinear algorithm, and then applying the Loomis–Whitney inequality (7).

4 Boolean matrix multiplication

We now turn to Boolean matrix multiplication. We consider the problem of multiplying two $n \times n$ Boolean matrices, using the operations $\wedge$ and $\vee$ as multiplication and addition respectively. The standard matrix multiplication algorithm has sequential complexity $O(n^3)$. Common subcubic methods for multiplying Boolean matrices include Kronrod's algorithm, also known as Four Russians' algorithm (see e.g. [2]), and a recent algorithm from [4]. However, the lowest exponent is achieved by fast multiplication of the matrices as $(0,1)$-matrices over the ring of integers modulo $n+1$ (see e.g. [17, 2] or [8, p. 747–748]).

As mentioned in the previous section, the fast matrix multiplication algorithm has BSP cost $W = O(n^\omega/p)$, $H = O(n^2/p^{2/\omega})$, $S = O(1)$. It is natural to ask whether the communication cost H is optimal, or it can be reduced by using properties specific to Boolean matrices. We require that the asymptotic cost of local computation W is not increased.

The problem of Boolean matrix multiplication differs from the problem of matrix multiplication over a general semiring in one important aspect: the algorithm can exploit the structure of the matrices to perform multiplication non-obliviously. One might expect that there exists a non-oblivious method for multiplying Boolean matrices that achieves a lower communication cost H than that of Algorithm 1. In this section we propose a method with $H = O(n^2/p)$. The proposed algorithm is not practical, since the required lower bound on n relative to p and the involved constant factors are astronomically large. However, the method is of theoretical importance, because it indicates that the lower bound $H = \Omega(n^2/p^{2/\omega})$, which is easy to prove for a general semiring, cannot be extended to the Boolean case.

We first give an intuitive explanation of the method. Let us consider the standard $\Theta(n^3)$ computation of the product $A \wedge B = C$, where A, B, C are square Boolean matrices of size n. As before, we assume that the matrices are distributed across the processors evenly, but otherwise arbitrarily. As in Section 3, we represent the n^3 computed Boolean products by a cube of volume n^3 in integer three-dimensional space. The basic idea is to perform communication only with matrices containing few ones, or few zeros. A matrix with m ones (or m zeros) can be communicated by sending m values — the indices of ones (zeros). If A contains at most n^2/p ones, the multiplication problem can be solved on a BSP computer in $W = O(n^3/p)$, $H = O(n^2/p)$, $S = O(1)$ by partitioning the cube into layers of size $n/p \times n \times n$, parallel to the coordinate plane representing the matrix A. Symmetrically, if B contains at most n^2/p ones, the problem can be solved at the same cost by a similar partitioning into layers of size $n \times n/p \times n$, parallel to the coordinate plane representing the matrix B. If both A and B are dense, we partition the cube into layers of size $n \times n \times n/p$, parallel to the coordinate plane representing the matrix C. Assuming for the moment that A and B are random matrices, it is likely that the partial product computed by each of the layers contains at most n^2/p zeros. Again, the problem can be solved in $W = O(n^3/p)$, $H = O(n^2/p)$, $S = O(1)$. The remaining case is when A and B have relatively many ones, but C still has relatively many zeros. We argue that in this case the triple A, B, C must have a special structure that allows one to decompose the computation into three matrix products corresponding to the three easy cases above. Computation of this structure requires no prior knowledge of C. Its cost is polynomial in n, but exponential in p.

The structure of a Boolean matrix product is best described in the language of graph theory. To expose the symmetry of the problem, let us slightly alter its formulation. For a Boolean matrix X, let $\overline{X}$ denote the Boolean complement to the transpose of X, i.e. $\overline{X}[i,j] = \overline{X[j,i]}$. We replace C by $\overline{C}$, and look for a C such that $A \wedge B = \overline{C}$. Boolean matrices A, B, C define a tripartite graph, if we consider them as adjacency matrices of the three bipartite connection subgraphs. We will denote this tripartite graph by $G = (A, B, C)$.

A simple undirected graph is called *triangle-free* if it does not contain a triangle (a cycle of length three). The graph G is triangle-free — existence of a triangle in G would imply that for some i, j, k, $A[i,j] = B[j,k] = C[k,i] = 1$, therefore $A[i,j] \wedge B[j,k] = 1$, but $\overline{C[k,i]} = \overline{1} = 0$. Note that the property of a graph G to be triangle-free is symmetric: the matrix C does not play any special role compared to A and B.

The following simple result is not necessary for the derivation of our algorithm, and is given only to illustrate the connection between Boolean matrix multiplication and triangle-free graphs. Let us call the factors A and B *maximal*, if changing a zero to a one in any position of A or B results in changing some zeros to ones in the product $\overline{C}$ (and therefore some ones to zeros in C). A triangle-free graph is called *maximal* if the addition of any new edge creates a triangle. When we consider tripartite triangle-free graphs, we call such a graph *maximal* if we cannot add any new edge so that the resulting graph is still tripartite and triangle-free. Note that by this definition, a maximal tripartite triangle-free graph may not be maximal as a general triangle-free graph. We have the following lemma.

Lemma 1. *Let A, B, C be arbitrary $n \times n$ Boolean matrices. The following statements are equivalent:*

(i) A and B are maximal matrices such that $A \wedge B = \overline{C}$;

(ii) $A \wedge B = \overline{C}$, $B \wedge C = \overline{A}$, $C \wedge A = \overline{B}$;

(iii) $G = (A, B, C)$ is a maximal 3-equipartite triangle-free graph.

Proof. Straightforward application of the definitions. ■

Lemma 1 shows that in the product $A \wedge B = \overline{C}$, the matrices A, B and C are in a certain sense interchangeable: any matrix which is a Boolean product can also be characterised as a maximal Boolean factor. It also gives a characterisation of such matrices by maximal triangle-free graphs.

One of the few references to maximal 3-equipartite triangle-free graphs was given in [5]. In particular, [5, p. 324–325] states the problem of finding the minimum possible density of such a graph; it is easy to see from the discussion above that this problem is closely related to Boolean matrix multiplication. In

[5, p. 324–325] it is noted that, as of time of writing, the minimum density problem was "completely unresolved". Since then, however, a general approach to problems of such kind has been developed. The basis of this approach is Szemerédi's Regularity Lemma (see e.g. [11]). Here we apply this lemma directly to the Boolean matrix multiplication problem; it might also be applied to similar extremal graph problems, including the minimum density problem above.

In most definitions and theorem statements below, we follow [11]. Let $G = (V, E)$ be a simple undirected graph. Let $v(G) = |V|$, $e(G) = |E|$. For disjoint $X, Y \subset V$ let $e(X, Y)$ denote the number of edges between X and Y, and define the *density* $d(X, Y) = e(X, Y)/(|X| \cdot |Y|)$. For disjoint $A, B \subset V$ we call (A, B) *an ϵ-regular pair*, if for every $X \subset A$, $|X| > \epsilon|A|$, and $Y \subset B$, $|Y| > \epsilon|B|$, we have $|d(X, Y) - d(A, B)| < \epsilon$. We say that G has *an (ϵ, d)-partitioning of size m*, if V can be partitioned into m disjoint subsets of equal size, called *clusters*, such that for any two clusters A, B the pair (A, B) is either an ϵ-regular pair of density at least d, or an empty graph. A *cluster graph* of an (ϵ, d)-partitioning is a graph with m nodes corresponding to the clusters, in which two nodes are connected by an edge if and only if the two corresponding clusters form a non-empty pair. If G is a 3-equipartite graph, then each cluster is a subset of one of the three parts, and the cluster graph is also 3-equipartite.

We will not apply the definition of an ϵ-regular pair directly. Instead, we will use the following theorem (in a slightly more general form, paper [11] refers to it as the Key Lemma).

Theorem 1. *Let $d > \epsilon > 0$. Let G be a graph with an (ϵ, d)-partitioning, and let R be the cluster graph of this partitioning. Let H be a subgraph of R with maximum degree $\Delta > 0$. If $\epsilon \leq (d - \epsilon)^\Delta/(2 + \Delta)$, then G contains a subgraph isomorphic to H.*

Proof. See [11]. ∎

Since we are interested in triangle-free graphs, we take H to be a triangle. We simplify the condition on d and ϵ, and apply Theorem 1 in the following form: if $d \leq 4/5$, $\epsilon \leq d^2/4$, and G is triangle-free, then its cluster graph R is also triangle-free.

Our main tool is Szemerédi's Regularity Lemma. Informally, it states that any graph can be transformed into a graph with an (ϵ, d)-partitioning by removing a small number of nodes and edges. Its precise statement, slightly adapted from [11], is as follows.

Theorem 2. *For every $\epsilon > 0$ there is an $M = M(\epsilon)$ such that for any d, $\epsilon \leq d \leq 1$, any arbitrary graph G contains a subgraph G_0 with an (ϵ, d)-partitioning of size at most M, and $e(G \setminus G_0) \leq (d + \epsilon)\big(v(G)\big)^2$.*

Proof. See [11]. ∎

Note that if $e(G) = o\big(v(G)^2\big)$, the statement of Theorem 2 becomes trivial. Also note that for any $d \geq \epsilon$, an (ϵ, d)-partitioning can be obtained from an (ϵ, ϵ)-partitioning by simply excluding the pairs with densities between ϵ and d.

For a 3-equipartite graph G of size $3n$, where $n \geq 2^{2^{12}\epsilon^{-18}}$, paper [3] gives an algorithm which finds the subgraph G_0 in sequential time $O\big(2^{2^{10}\epsilon^{-17}} \cdot n^\omega\big)$, where ω is the exponent of matrix multiplication (currently 2.376 by [7]). The size of the resulting (ϵ, d)-partitioning is at most $M = 2^{2^{10}\epsilon^{-17}}$.

We are now able to describe the proposed communication-efficient algorithm for computing $A \wedge B = \overline{C}$, where A, B, C are Boolean matrices of size n. Let $G = (A, B, C)$. We represent the n^3 elementary Boolean products as a cube of volume n^3 in the three-dimensional index space. The cube G is partitioned into p^3 regular cubic blocks of size n/p. Each block is local to a particular processor, and corresponds to a 3-equipartite triangle-free graph[1] $\mathsf{G} = (\mathsf{A}, \mathsf{B}, \mathsf{C})$, where $\mathsf{A} = A[[I, J]]$, $\mathsf{B} = B[[J, K]]$ for some $1 \leq I, J, K \leq p$, and $\overline{\mathsf{C}} = \mathsf{A} \wedge \mathsf{B}$. We shall identify the cubic block with its graph G.

Let us choose positive real numbers ϵ and d, such that $\epsilon \leq d^2/4$ (necessary as a condition of Theorem 1), and $d + \epsilon \leq 2/p^2$ (necessary to ensure that the communication cost $H = O(n^2/p)$ after the application of Theorem 2). We take $d = 1/p^2$, $\epsilon = d^2/4 = 1/(4p^4)$. By Theorem 2, we can find a large subgraph $\mathsf{G}_0 \subset \mathsf{G}$ with an (ϵ, d)-partitioning of size $3m \leq M(\epsilon)$. Let $\mathsf{G}_0 = (\mathsf{A}_0, \mathsf{B}_0, \mathsf{C}_0)$. Also let $\Delta\mathsf{G} = \mathsf{G} \setminus \mathsf{G}_0$, and $\Delta\mathsf{G} = (\Delta\mathsf{A}, \Delta\mathsf{B}, \Delta\mathsf{C})$. We have $e(\Delta\mathsf{G}) \leq (d+\epsilon)n^2/p^2$. Note that $\mathsf{A} = \mathsf{A}_0 \vee \Delta\mathsf{A}$, $\mathsf{B} = \mathsf{B}_0 \vee \Delta\mathsf{B}$, $\mathsf{C} = \mathsf{C}_0 \vee \Delta\mathsf{C}$, and $\overline{\mathsf{C}} = \mathsf{A} \wedge \mathsf{B} = \overline{\mathsf{C}'_0} \vee \overline{\Delta\mathsf{C}'}$, where $\overline{\mathsf{C}'_0} = \mathsf{A}_0 \wedge \mathsf{B}_0$, and $\overline{\Delta\mathsf{C}'} = (\Delta\mathsf{A} \wedge \mathsf{B}) \vee (\mathsf{A} \wedge \Delta\mathsf{B})$.

The (ϵ, d)-partitioning of the graph G_0 is, up to a permutation of indices, a partitioning of G_0 into m^3 regular cubic subblocks. Let us denote a subblock of G_0 by $\mathsf{G}_0[[i,j,k]] = (\mathsf{A}_0[[i,j]], \mathsf{B}_0[[j,k]], \mathsf{C}_0[[k,i]])$, $0 \leq i, j, k < m$. Let $\mathsf{G}[[i,j,k]]$ and $\Delta\mathsf{G}[[i,j,k]]$ denote similar subblocks of G and $\Delta\mathsf{G}$.

Consider an arbitrary subblock $\mathsf{C}_0[[k,i]]$. If $\mathsf{C}_0[[k,i]]$ is a zero matrix, then $\mathsf{C}[[k,i]] = \Delta\mathsf{C}[[k,i]]$, and $\overline{\mathsf{C}[[k,i]]} = \overline{\Delta\mathsf{C}[[k,i]]}$. If $\mathsf{C}_0[[k,i]]$ is non-zero, then for any j, $0 \leq j < m$, either $\mathsf{A}_0[[i,j]]$ or $\mathsf{B}_0[[j,k]]$ is a zero matrix by Theorem 1. Therefore, $\overline{\mathsf{C}'_0}[[k,i]]$ is a zero matrix, and $\overline{\mathsf{C}[[k,i]]} = \overline{\Delta\mathsf{C}'}[[k,i]]$. The two cases ($\mathsf{C}_0[[k,i]]$ zero or non-zero) can be distinguished by the cluster graph of G_0 alone. The product $\mathsf{A} \wedge \mathsf{B} = \overline{\mathsf{C}}$ can therefore be found by selecting each subblock of $\overline{\mathsf{C}}$ from $\overline{\Delta\mathsf{C}}$ or $\overline{\Delta\mathsf{C}'} = (\Delta\mathsf{A} \wedge \mathsf{B}) \vee (\mathsf{A} \wedge \Delta\mathsf{B})$, where the choice is governed by the cluster graph. The matrix $\overline{\mathsf{C}'_0} = \mathsf{A}_0 \wedge \mathsf{B}_0$ needs not to be computed.

In order to compute the (ϵ, d)-partitioning for all p^3 blocks of G at the communication cost $H = O(n^2/p)$, blocks must be grouped into p layers of size $n \times n \times n/p$, with p^2 blocks in each layer. The computation of the two Boolean matrix products in $\overline{\Delta\mathsf{C}'} = (\Delta\mathsf{A} \wedge \mathsf{B}) \vee (\mathsf{A} \wedge \Delta\mathsf{B})$ requires that the same p^3 cubic blocks are divided into p similar layers of sizes $n/p \times n \times n$ and $n \times n/p \times n$, respectively.

To obtain an algorithm with local computation cost $W = O(n^3/p)$, we require that the cost of computing all (ϵ, d)-partitions, bounded by $O\big(2^{2^{10}\epsilon^{-17}} \cdot n^\omega\big) = O\big(2^{2^{44}p^{68}} \cdot n^\omega/p\big)$, is at most $O(n^\omega/p)$. Therefore, it is sufficient to require that $n = \Omega\big(2^{2^{44}p^{68}}\big)$. This will also ensure that the computed cluster graphs can be exchanged between processors at the communication cost $H = O(n^2/p)$.

The algorithm is as follows.

---

[1] The sans-serif font is used for blocks, in order to reduce the number of subscripts.

Algorithm 2. *Boolean matrix multiplication.*

Input: $n \times n$ Boolean matrices A and B.

Output: $n \times n$ Boolean matrix C, such that $A \wedge B = \overline{C}$.

Description. We assume $n = \Omega(2^{2^{44} p^{68}})$. The Boolean matrix product $A \wedge B = \overline{C}$ is represented as a cube of size n in integer three-dimensional space. This cube is partitioned into p^3 regular cubic blocks.

The algorithm proceeds in three stages. We use the notation of Theorem 2 and of the subsequent discussion.

First stage. Matrix $\overline{C}$ is initialised with zeros. The cube is partitioned into layers of size $n \times n \times n/p$, each containing p^2 cubic blocks. Every processor picks a layer, reads the necessary blocks of matrices A and B, and for each cubic block G computes the graph G_0 and the decompositions $\mathsf{A} = \mathsf{A}_0 \vee \Delta\mathsf{A}$, $\mathsf{B} = \mathsf{B}_0 \vee \Delta\mathsf{B}$, $\mathsf{C} = \mathsf{C}_0 \vee \Delta\mathsf{C}$. Then for each block G the processor writes back the matrices $\Delta\mathsf{A}$, $\Delta\mathsf{B}$, $\Delta\mathsf{C}$, and the cluster graph of G.

Second stage. The Boolean products $\Delta\mathsf{A} \wedge \mathsf{B}$ and $\mathsf{A} \wedge \Delta\mathsf{B}$ are computed by partitioning the cube into layers of size $n/p \times n \times n$ and $n \times n/p \times n$, respectively, each containing p^2 cubic blocks. Then the Boolean sum $\overline{\Delta\mathsf{C}'} = (\Delta\mathsf{A} \wedge \mathsf{B}) \vee (\mathsf{A} \wedge \Delta\mathsf{B})$ is computed.

Third stage. The blocks of matrix $\overline{C}$ are partitioned equally among the processors. Every processor reads the necessary cluster graphs, and then computes each block $\overline{\mathsf{C}}$ by selecting its subblocks from $\overline{\Delta\mathsf{C}}$ or $\overline{\Delta\mathsf{C}'}$, as directed by the cluster graph.

The resulting matrix $\overline{C}$ is the Boolean matrix product of A and B.

Cost analysis. The local computation, communication and synchronisation costs are

$$W = O(n^\omega/p) \qquad H = O(n^2/p) \qquad S = O(1) \quad \blacksquare$$

Algorithm 2 is asymptotically optimal in communication, since the input of an $n \times n$ matrix already costs $H = \Omega(n^2/p)$.

5 Conclusions

We have demonstrated that the BSP complexity of Boolean matrix multiplication is $W = O(n^\omega/p)$ (where ω is the exponent of fast matrix multiplication), $H = \Theta(n^2/p)$, $S = \Theta(1)$. The communication cost H is asymptotically lower than in the straightforward application of the bilinear method, with $H = \Theta(n^2/p^{2/\omega})$. Indeed, the communication cost of our algorithm is optimal. Algorithm 2 can be used to obtain communication-efficient BSP algorithms for other problems, e.g. computation of the transitive closure of a directed graph.

Algorithm 2 is not practical, due to a huge problem size required, and enormous constant factors. The question remains whether a practical algorithm with optimal BSP cost exists. Such an algorithm may be either deterministic, or, more likely, randomised.

It also remains an open question whether the technique of Algorithm 2 can be extended for idempotent semirings other than the Booleans.

6 Acknowledgement

The author thanks Bill McColl for fruitful discussion, and Radu Calinescu for pointing out an error in an early version of the paper.

References

[1] A. Aggarwal, A. K. Chandra, and M. Snir. Communication complexity of PRAMs. *Theoretical Computer Science*, 71:3–28, 1990.

[2] A. V. Aho, J. E. Hopcroft, and J. D. Ullman. *The Design and Analysis of Computer Algorithms.* Addison-Wesley, 1976.

[3] N. Alon et al. The algorithmic aspects of the regularity lemma. *Journal of Algorithms*, 16:80–109, 1994.

[4] J. Basch, S. Khanna, and R. Motwani. On diameter verification and Boolean matrix multiplication. Technical Report STAN-CS-95-1544, Department of Computer Science, Stanford University, 1995.

[5] B. Bollobás. *Extremal Graph Theory.* Academic Press, 1978.

[6] Yu. D. Burago and V. A. Zalgaller. *Geometric Inequalities.* Number 285 in Grundl. der math. Wissenschaften. Springer-Verlag, 1988.

[7] D. Coppersmith and S. Winograd. Matrix multiplication via arithmetic progressions. *Journal of Symbolic Computation*, 9(3):251–280, March 1990.

[8] T. H. Cormen, C. E. Leiserson, and R. L. Rivest. *Introduction to Algorithms.* The MIT Electrical Engineering and Computer Science Series. The MIT Press and McGraw–Hill, 1990.

[9] H. Hadwiger. *Vorlesungen über Inhalt, Oberfläche und Isoperimetrie.* Number 93 in Grundl. der math. Wissenschaften. Springer-Verlag, 1957.

[10] J. E. Hopcroft and L. R. Kerr. On minimizing the number of multiplications necessary for matrix multiplication. *SIAM Journal of Applied Mathematics*, 20(1):30–36, January 1971.

[11] J. Komlós and M. Simonovits. Szemerédi's Regularity Lemma and its applications in graph theory. Technical Report 96-10, DIMACS, 1996.

[12] L. H. Loomis and H. Whitney. An inequality related to the isoperimetric inequality. *Bull. Amer. Math. Soc.*, 55:961–962, 1949.

[13] W. F. McColl. General purpose parallel computing. In A. Gibbons and P. Spirakis, editors, *Lectures on parallel computation*, volume 4 of *Cambridge International Series on Parallel Computation*, chapter 13, pages 337–391. Cambridge University Press, 1993.

[14] W. F. McColl. Scalable computing. In J. van Leeuwen, editor, *Computer Science Today: Recent Trends and Developments*, volume 1000 of *Lecture Notes in Computer Science*, pages 46–61. Springer-Verlag, 1995.

[15] W. F. McColl. A BSP realisation of Strassen's algorithm. In M. Kara, J. R. Davy, D. Goodeve, and J. Nash, editors, *Abstract Machine Models for Parallel and Distributed Computing*. IOS Press, 1996.

[16] W. F. McColl. Universal computing. In L. Bougé, P. Fraigniaud, A. Mignotte, and Y. Robert, editors, *Proceedings of Euro-Par'96–I*, volume 1123 of *Lecture Notes in Computer Science*, pages 25–36. Springer-Verlag, 1996.

[17] M. S. Paterson. Complexity of product and closure algorithms for matrices. In *Proceedings of the International Congress of Mathematicians*, pages 483–489, 1974.

[18] M. S. Paterson. Private communication, 1993.

[19] L. G. Valiant. A bridging model for parallel computation. *Communications of the ACM*, 33(8):103–111, August 1990.

[20] L. G. Valiant. General purpose parallel architectures. In J. van Leeuwen, editor, *Handbook of Theoretical Computer Science*, chapter 18, pages 943–971. Elsevier, 1990.

A Complex Example of a Simplifying Rewrite System

Hélène Touzet

Loria - Université Nancy 2
BP 239, 54506 Vandœuvre-lès-Nancy, France
touzet@loria.fr

Abstract. For a string rewriting system, it is known that termination by a simplification ordering implies multiple recursive complexity. This theoretical upper bound is, however, far from having been reached by *known* examples of rewrite systems. All known methods used to establish termination by simplification yield a primitive recursive bound. Furthermore, the study of the order types of simplification orderings suggests that the recursive path ordering is, in a broad sense, a maximal simplification ordering. This would imply that simplifying string rewrite systems cannot go beyond primitive recursion. Contradicting this intuition, we construct here a simplifying string rewriting system whose complexity is not primitive recursive. This leads to a new lower bound for the complexity of simplifying string rewriting systems.

Introduction

Rewriting systems serve as a model of computation in many fields of theoretical computer science, for instance automated theorem proving, algebraic specification, functional programming. A crucial question is that of termination, which has long been known to be undecidable. Several termination proof techniques have arisen, such as the recursive path orderings, the Knuth-Bendix orderings, polynomial interpretations etc. Those methods rely on a powerful combinatorial result, Kruskal's tree theorem, by establishing in fact termination by simplification. For practical purposes, termination is not enough. It is worth knowing the complexity of a given rewrite system, by measuring the number of necessary rewrite steps to reach a normal form. We call it the *derivation length.* For complexity of rewrite systems reducing with Kruskal's theorem, little is known. Weiermann proved in [13] that termination by simplification does not allow arbitrary high derivation length. However, there is a gap between the upper bound produced by Weiermann and the complexity of known examples of rewrite systems. The motivation for this research program is two-fold; firstly identifying the expressivity of Kruskal's theorem when applied in rewriting theory, secondly the evaluation of the possible limitations of existing reduction orderings that are used in termination proofs.

In this paper, we focus our attention on the complexity of string rewriting systems, or semi-Thue systems. We think that they provide a good insight into the general case of terms. For the general case of a simplifying string rewriting system, an upper bound is known: it corresponds to the multiple recursive functions. This is a consequence of a more general combinatorial result established by Cichon and Tahhan-Bittar [2] (see also [12] for an alternative proof).

Given a finite alphabet $\mathcal{A}$ and an integer k, there exists a multiple recursive function ϕ such that for all simplification ordering $\prec$ on $\mathcal{A}^*$ and for all decreasing sequence $(u_i)_{i\in\mathbb{N}}$ satisfying

$$\forall i \in \mathbb{N} \ |u_i| < |u_0| + k \times i$$

then the length of $(u_i)_{i\in\mathbb{N}}$ is bounded by $\phi(|u_0|)$.

Note, however, that the hypothesis used in obtaining this upper bound is rough. It does not take advantage of the structure of the rewrite relation, which is induced by a *finite* number of rules. The complexity of known examples of string rewrite systems is indeed much lower. All existing termination orderings seem to yield primitive recursive complexity.

- termination under the recursive path ordering implies primitive recursive derivation length (Hofbauer [8]),
- termination under the Knuth-Bendix ordering implies exponential derivation length (Lautemann and Hofbauer [7]),
- termination under polynomial interpretation implies exponential derivation length (Lautemann and Hofbauer [7]).

Another approach to complexity, considered by Dershowitz and Okada [5], or Martin and Scott [10], is concerned with the ordinal complexity of the reduction ordering used to establish termination. What does the study of the order type tell us? The lower upper bound for simplification orderings on strings was established by De Jongh and Parikh [3]. Given a simplification ordering $\prec$ defined an non-empty finite alphabet $\mathcal{A}$, the order type of $\prec$ is less than or equal to $\omega^{\omega^{|\mathcal{A}|-1}}$. Furthermore, this upper bound is attained by a well-known termination ordering: the recursive path ordering. So one may expect that the recursive path ordering, being of maximal order type, would also be of maximal complexity when considering derivation lengths and that it is not possible to go beyond primitive recursion with simplifying string rewrite systems. This question has been raised by Hofbauer and Frank [9], among others. The purpose of this article is to furnish a counterexample to the conjecture, by exhibiting a string rewriting system which reduces under simplification whose complexity is not primitive recursive. The construction relies on the encoding of a non-primitive recursive process over lists of natural numbers.

The paper is organised as follows: in the first section, we recall standard notions of term rewriting theory and termination. The second section is devoted to the description of the non-primitive recursive example on strings and the last section to the proof of termination by simplification.

1 Preliminary notions

This article assumes some familiarity with term rewriting theory. We recall here some useful basic notions. A comprehensive survey is to be found in Dershowitz-Jouannaud [4].

Let $\mathcal{A}$ be a finite alphabet. $\mathcal{A}^*$ denotes the set of strings built up on $\mathcal{A}$ and ε the empty string. Given a string u of $\mathcal{A}^*$, $|u|$ denotes the depth of u and, for all a in $\mathcal{A}$, $|u|_a$ denotes the number of occurrences of a in u.

A *string rewriting system* (abbreviated in SRS), $\mathcal{R}$, on $\mathcal{A}^*$ is a finite subset of $\mathcal{A}^* \times \mathcal{A}^*$. An element (l, r) of $\mathcal{R}$ is called a *rule* and is simply denoted $l \to r$. l is the *left hand side* and r the *right hand side* of the rule. The relation $(\mathcal{A}^*, \to_\mathcal{R})$ is defined as $u \to_\mathcal{R} v$ if and only if there exists a rule $l \to r$ of $\mathcal{R}$ and two strings w and z such that

$$u = wlz, \quad v = wrz.$$

The associated *rewrite relation*, denoted $\xrightarrow{+}_\mathcal{R}$, is the transitive closure of $\to_\mathcal{R}$. $\xrightarrow{*}_\mathcal{R}$ is the reflexive closure of $\xrightarrow{+}_\mathcal{R}$. The rewrite system $\mathcal{R}$ *terminates* if the rewrite relation $\xrightarrow{+}_\mathcal{R}$ is Nœtherian. We now introduce the *homeomorphic embedding* and Higman's lemma, which is the restricted version of Kruskal's theorem on strings.

Definition 1 (Homeomorphic embedding). Given a finite alphabet $\mathcal{A}$, define the *homeomorphic embedding* relation, $\trianglelefteq$, on $\mathcal{A}^*$ as the least preorder satisfying the following properties

- deletion property: $\forall a \in \mathcal{A}\ \varepsilon \lhd a$,
- monotonicity: $\forall u, v \in \mathcal{A}^* \forall a, b \in \mathcal{A} \cup \{\varepsilon\}\ \ u \trianglelefteq v \Rightarrow aub \trianglelefteq avb$.

Theorem 2 (Higman [6]). *Let $\mathcal{A}$ be a finite alphabet. The associated homeomorphic embedding $(\mathcal{A}^*, \trianglelefteq)$ is a well-quasi-ordering.*

In other words, every ordering extending homeomorphic embedding is a well-founded ordering. This result provides an obvious syntactic sufficiency condition for establishing termination.

Corollary 3. *Let $\mathcal{A}$ be a finite alphabet and $\mathcal{R}$ a SRS on $\mathcal{A}^*$. If*

$$\forall u, v \in \mathcal{A}^* \ \ u \xrightarrow{+}_\mathcal{R} v \Rightarrow \neg(u \trianglelefteq v)$$

then $\mathcal{R}$ is terminating.

The question of compatibility of a SRS with homeomorphic embedding is difficult, in fact, undecidable (Caron [1]). An interesting sub-class are the simplification orderings, which are *monotonic* orderings compatible with the homeomorphic embedding. The formulation we introduce here is due to Middeldorp and Zantema [11].

Definition 4 (Termination by simplification). Let $\mathcal{A}$ be a finite alphabet. Define the string rewrite system $\mathcal{E}mb(\mathcal{A})$ by the rules

$$\{a \to \varepsilon \ \ \forall a \in \mathcal{A}\}$$

A string rewriting system $\mathcal{R}$ of $\mathcal{A}^*$ *reduces by simplification* if $\mathcal{R} \cup \mathcal{E}mb(\mathcal{A})$ is terminating.

Remark 5. The rewrite relation associated with $\mathcal{E}mb(\mathcal{A})$ is the homeomorphic embedding relation, $\lhd$, of $\mathcal{A}^*$, which ensures that reduction under simplification implies termination.

We shall use a slightly different characterisation, which can easily be deduced from definition 4.

Proposition 6. *Let $\mathcal{A}$ be a finite alphabet and $\mathcal{R}$ a string rewriting system on $\mathcal{A}^*$. Define $\mathcal{A}' = \{a \in \mathcal{A}\ ;\ \exists l \to r \in \mathcal{R}\ |l|_a < |r|_a\}$. $\mathcal{R}$ reduces by simplification if and only if the string rewriting system $\mathcal{R} \cup \mathcal{E}mb(\mathcal{A}')$ is terminating.*

Proof. Let $\mathcal{R}' = \mathcal{R} \cup \mathcal{E}mb(\mathcal{A}')$. We assume $\mathcal{R}'$ is terminating and prove that $\mathcal{R} \cup \mathcal{E}mb(\mathcal{A})$ is terminating too. Define $\supseteq$ on $\mathcal{A}^*$ as

$$u \supseteq v \ \text{ iff } \forall a \notin \mathcal{A}'\ |u|_a \geq |v|_a$$

and $\supset$ as the strict part of $\supseteq$. The lexicographic combination of $\supset$ and $\xrightarrow{+}_{\mathcal{R}'}$ is a well-founded ordering which is compatible with the rewrite relation associated with $\mathcal{R} \cup \mathcal{E}mb(\mathcal{A})$. □

The third part of this article will involve the recursive path ordering on strings.

Definition 7 (Recursive path ordering on strings). Let $\mathcal{A}$ be a finite alphabet and $\prec$ a precedence on $\mathcal{A}$. The *recursive path ordering* $\prec_{\mathsf{rpo}}$ is the least ordering on $\mathcal{A}^*$ satisfying

- $\prec_{\mathsf{rpo}}$ is stable by context and by substitution,
- if $u \lhd v$, then $u \prec_{\mathsf{rpo}} v$,
- if $u \prec_{\mathsf{rpo}} bv$ and $a \prec b$, then $au \prec_{\mathsf{rpo}} bv$.

Proposition 8. *Let $\mathcal{A}$ be a finite alphabet. For any precedence $\prec$ on $\mathcal{A}$, the associated recursive path ordering is a simplification ordering.*

We conclude this section with the main question with which we are concerned: if a rewrite system is terminating, what can be said about the time of computation? We now define a complexity measure for rewrite systems: *derivation length* functions.

Definition 9 (Derivation length). Let $\mathcal{A}$ be a finite alphabet. For a terminating rewrite system $\mathcal{R}$ over $\mathcal{A}^*$, define the *derivation length* functions $dl_{\mathcal{R}}$ and $Dl_{\mathcal{R}}$:

$$\begin{aligned} dl_{\mathcal{R}} :\ & \mathcal{A}^* \to \mathbb{N} \\ & t \mapsto \max\{dl_{\mathcal{R}}(u),\ t \to_{\mathcal{R}} u\} + 1 \end{aligned}$$

$$\begin{aligned} Dl_{\mathcal{R}} :\ & \mathbb{N} \to \mathbb{N} \\ & m \mapsto \max\{n \in \mathbb{N},\ \exists\, t \in \mathcal{A}^*, dl_{\mathcal{R}}(t) = n\ \wedge\ |t| \leq m\} \end{aligned}$$

2 Construction of the SRS $\mathcal{R}$

We now come to the presentation of a string rewriting system, $\mathcal{R}$, whose derivation length function is not primitive recursive. The classical non-primitive recursive processes, such as the Ackermann function, are strongly related to nested recursion schemes involving binary function symbols. So they cannot be encoded directly by strings. We introduce here a process $\mathcal{P}$ of transformation on lists of natural numbers. This process was introduced by Hofbauer and Lautemann in [7], who used it to study the complexity of the Knuth-Bendix ordering. $\mathcal{P}$ is described by the two rules (A) and (B).

$$\begin{array}{ll} (A) & [\ldots, n+1, m, \ldots] \rightsquigarrow [\ldots, n, m+3, \ldots] \; n, m \in \mathbb{N} \\ (B) & [\ldots, n+1, m, k, \ldots] \rightsquigarrow [\ldots, n, k, m, \ldots] \quad k, n, m \in \mathbb{N}, m > 0. \end{array}$$

$\mathcal{P}$ allows us to build long derivations by considering lists of the form $[n, 0, \ldots, 0]$. Define the function ϕ by

$$\begin{aligned} \phi : \mathbb{N} \times \mathbb{N} &\to \mathbb{N} \\ (x, y) &\mapsto \max\{z \in \mathbb{N} \; ; \; [y+1, 0^{2x+1}] \xrightarrow{+} [0^{2x+1}, z+1]\}. \end{aligned}$$

where 0^{2x+1} denotes $2x+1$ occurrences of 0.

Proposition 10. *ϕ is not a primitive recursive function.*

Proof. We show that ϕ dominates the Ackermann function. By repeated applications of rule (A), we have $[y+1, 0] \rightsquigarrow [0, 3y+3]$ and $[1, 0, \ldots, 0] \rightsquigarrow [0, 2, 3, 0, \ldots, 0]$, which imply $\phi(0, y+1) \leq y+1$ and $\phi(x+1, 0) \leq \phi(x, 1)$. For the general case, we have by repeated applications of rule (A)

$$\begin{aligned} [y+2, 0, \ldots, 0] &\rightsquigarrow [1, 0, \ldots, 0, \phi(x+1, y)] \\ &\rightsquigarrow [0, 3, 0, \ldots, 0, \phi(x+1, y)] \\ &\rightsquigarrow [0, 2, \ldots 2, \phi(x+1, y) + 3] \end{aligned}$$

The use of rule (B) yields now

$$\begin{aligned} [0, 2, \ldots 2, \phi(x+1, y) + 3] &\rightsquigarrow [0, 2, \ldots 2, 1, \phi(x+1, y) + 3, 2] \\ &\rightsquigarrow [0, \phi(x+1, y) + 3, 1, \ldots, 1, 2] \end{aligned}$$

and so $\phi(x+1, y+1) > \phi(x, \phi(x+1, y))$. □

Thus, any rewrite system modelling $\mathcal{P}$ has a non-primitive recursive derivation length. The idea of our construction is to represent lists of natural numbers by strings on the two letter alphabet $\{s, []\}$. s allows us to denote an integer in unary representation and the symbol $[]$ is a separator. Each finite list $[a_0, \ldots, a_n]$ will be then represented by the string $s^{a_0} \, [] \, s^{a_1} \, [] \cdots [] \, s^{a_n}$. Hence our SRS should allow the following derivations

$$\begin{array}{lc} (A) & s[] \xrightarrow{+}_{\mathcal{R}} []sss \\ (B) & s \, [] \, s^m \, [] \, s^k \xrightarrow{+}_{\mathcal{R}} []s^k \, [] \, s^m \end{array}$$

(A) can be handled by a single rule. To simulate (B), we need to introduce two intermediate symbols, t and u, that will deal with the swapping of s^m and s^k.

On the alphabet $\{s, t, u, []\}$, define the SRS $\mathcal{R}$ by

$$\mathcal{R}\begin{cases} s[] \to []sss & (1)\\ s\,[]\,s \to []t & (2)\\ t[] \to []s & (3)\\ t\,[]\,s \to ut[] & (4)\\ []u \to []s & (5)\\ ts \to tt & (6)\\ tu \to ut & (7)\\ su \to ss & (8)\end{cases}$$

Proposition 11. *$\mathcal{R}$ simulates the process $\mathcal{P}$.*

Proof. One application of rule (1) simulates (A). The seven remaining rules, from (2) to (8), allow one to derive (B) as follows.

$$\begin{aligned} s\,[]\,s^m\,[]\,s^k &\to_{\mathcal{R}} []ts^{m-1}\,[]\,s^k && (2)\\ &\xrightarrow{*}_{\mathcal{R}} []t^m\,[]\,s^k && (6)^*\\ &\xrightarrow{*}_{\mathcal{R}} []t^{m-1}u^k t[] && (4)^*\\ &\xrightarrow{*}_{\mathcal{R}} []u^k t^m[] && (7)^*\\ &\xrightarrow{+}_{\mathcal{R}} []s^k t^m[] && (5)+(8)^*\\ &\xrightarrow{+}_{\mathcal{R}} []s^k\,[]\,s^m && (3)^+ \end{aligned}$$

□

Corollary 12. *$Dl_{\mathcal{R}}$ is not a primitive recursive function.*

Proof. Consequence of proposition 10. □

3 $\mathcal{R}$ terminates by simplification

Our aim is now to establish that $\mathcal{R}$ is simplifying. The termination of the process $\mathcal{P}$ is clear: at each step, the list reduces with respect to the lexicographic ordering. Unfortunately, this argument cannot be carried over the rewrite system $\mathcal{R}$, because of the rule $t\,[]\,s \to ut[]$. Moreover, note that $\mathcal{R}$ is not totally terminating. Indeed, assume there exists a relation $\sqsubset$, which is a monotonic well-order compatible with $\mathcal{R}$. Since $ts \to tt$ and $su \to ss$ belongs to $\mathcal{R}$, this ordering would satisfy $t \sqsubset s$ and $s \sqsubset u$. Hence

$$ts[] \sqsupset t\,[]\,sss \sqsupset uut\,[]\,s \sqsupset ts\,[]\,s.$$

So we cannot hope to produce a proof of termination using a total ordering.

We present a combinatorial proof, taking advantage of syntactic properties of $\mathcal{R}$. The outline of the proof is as follows. Following proposition 6, we aim to establish the termination of $\mathcal{R}'$, where

$$\mathcal{R}' = \mathcal{R} \cup \mathcal{E}mb\{s, t, u\}.$$

For that purpose, given a string w, we consider each possible derivation starting from w. We shall show that if $w \xrightarrow{+}_{\mathcal{R}'} w'$, then $\neg(w \trianglelefteq w')$. By Higman's lemma, this implies that any derivation is finite and so $\mathcal{R}'$ is terminating. We concentrate on w_1, w_1' in $\{u,s,t\}^*$ and w_2, w_2' in $\{u,s,t,[]\}^*$, defined by

$$\begin{aligned} w &= w_1 \, [] \, w_2, \\ w' &= w_1' \, [] \, w_2'. \end{aligned}$$

We shall consider three main cases and prove the following results:

(1) if w_1 ends with s or u, then $\neg(w_1 \trianglelefteq w_1')$,
(2) if w_1 ends with t and if this t is rewritten by the rules $t[] \to []s$ or $t \to \varepsilon$, then $\neg(w_1 \trianglelefteq w_1')$,
(3) if w_1 ends with t and if this t is not rewritten by the rules $t[] \to []s$, or $t \to \varepsilon$, then $\neg(w_2 \trianglelefteq w_2')$.

(1) and **(2)** will be dealt by lemma 15 and **(3)** by lemma 16. In all cases, this allows us to conclude $\neg(w \trianglelefteq w')$.

We now go into the technical details. We write $\natural\mathtt{t}$ for the function which counts the number of occurrences of t after the last occurrence of s in a string.

$$\begin{aligned} \natural\mathtt{t} : \{s,u,t\}^* &\to \mathbb{N} \\ w &\mapsto 0, && \text{if } w \in \{t,u\}^*, \\ w_1 s w_2 &\mapsto |w_2|_t, && \text{if } w_1 \in \{s,t,u\}^*,\ w_2 \in, \{t,u\}^*. \end{aligned}$$

Define $\psi : \{s,u,t\}^* \to \{s,t\}^*$, as the function which associates to each string its unique normal form with respect to the following rules:

$$\begin{cases} u \to \varepsilon \\ ss \to s \\ tt \to t \end{cases}$$

Define the ordering relation $(\{s,t,u\}^*, \preceq)$ by

$$\begin{aligned} w \preceq w' \iff & \psi(w) \lhd \psi(w'), \text{ or} \\ & \psi(w) = \psi(w') \text{ and } \natural\mathtt{t}(w) \le \natural\mathtt{t}(w'). \end{aligned}$$

ψ and $\preceq$ satisfy the following property.

Proposition 13.

$$\begin{aligned} &\text{(i) } \forall w, w' \in \{s,u,t\}^* \ w \trianglelefteq w' \Rightarrow \psi(w) \trianglelefteq \psi(w'), \\ &\text{(ii) } \forall w, w' \in \{s,u,t\}^* \ w \trianglelefteq w' \Rightarrow \neg(w \preceq w'). \end{aligned}$$

Proof. (i) is by induction on the depth of w. If $w = \varepsilon$, then $\psi(w) = \varepsilon$. If $|w| > 1$, let $x \in \{s,t,u\}$ and $z \in \{s,t,u\}^*$ such that $w = xz$. We examine each possibility for x.
$x = u$: $\psi(w) = \psi(z)$ and by induction hypothesis $\psi(z) \trianglelefteq \psi(w')$.

$x = s$: $\psi(sz) = \psi(s\psi(z))$. If $\psi(z)$ starts with s then $\psi(sz) = \psi(z)$ and the induction hypothesis yields $\psi(sz) \trianglelefteq \psi(w')$. If $\psi(z)$ begins with t, then $\psi(s\psi(z)) = s\psi(z)$. Since $s\psi(z) \trianglelefteq w'$, there exists z' such that $w' \in \{u,t\}^*s\{u,s\}^*tz'$ and $\psi(z) \trianglelefteq tz'$. The construction of ψ ensures $\psi(w') \in (\varepsilon \vee t)s\psi(tz')$. By induction hypothesis $\psi(z) \trianglelefteq \psi(tz')$, thus $\psi(sz) \trianglelefteq \psi(w')$.
$x = t$: the reasoning is the same as in the previous case, interchanging s and t.

For (ii), it remains to show that $\natural\mathtt{t}(w) \leq \natural\mathtt{t}(w')$ whenever $w \trianglelefteq w'$ and $\psi(w) = \psi(w')$. Let $z_1, z_1' \in \{s,t,u\}^*$ and $z_2, z_2' \in \{t,u\}^*$ be such that $w = z_1 z_2$ and $w' = z_1' z_2'$. The hypothesis $\psi(w) = \psi(w')$ ensures $\psi(z_1) = \psi(z_2)$. Assume now that $\natural\mathtt{t}(w) > \natural\mathtt{t}(w')$, that is, $|z_2|_t > |z_2'|_t$. Since $w \trianglelefteq w'$, this would imply $z_1 t \trianglelefteq z_2$, so with (i) $\psi(z_1 t) \trianglelefteq \psi(z_2)$ contradicting $\psi(z_1) = \psi(z_2)$. Thus $\natural\mathtt{t}(w) \leq \natural\mathtt{t}(w')$. □

The ordering $\prec$ will now allow us to establish **(1)** and **(2)**. For this purpose, we introduce the intermediate SRS $\mathcal{S}$, defined on $\{u,s,t,\Diamond\}^*$, where $\Diamond$ is a new symbol in the alphabet.

$$\mathcal{S} = \mathcal{E}mb\{s,t,u\} \cup \begin{cases} ts \to tt \\ tu \to ut \\ su \to ss \\ t\Diamond \to ut\Diamond \end{cases}$$

This allows us to study w_1 in the rewriting of $w_1 \,[]\, w_2$ by $\mathcal{R}$. The role of $\Diamond$ in $\mathcal{S}$ is to simulate the leftmost occurrence of $[]$ in a string. We have the following property:

$$\forall w_1, w_1' \in \{s,u,t\}^* \; \forall w_2, w_2' \in \{s,u,t,[]\}^* \quad w_1 \,[]\, w_2 \xrightarrow{+}_{\mathcal{R}} w_1' \,[]\, w_2' \;\Rightarrow\; w_1\Diamond \xrightarrow{+}_{\mathcal{S}} w_1'\Diamond.$$

Proposition 14.

$$\forall w, w' \in \{s,u,t\}^* \quad w\Diamond \xrightarrow{+}_{\mathcal{S}} w'\Diamond \;\Rightarrow\; w' \preceq w.$$

Proof. Since $\preceq$ is a transitive relation, it suffices to establish the result when w reduces to w' in one rewrite step. We examine each rule of $\mathcal{S}$. For the three embedding rules, the result follows from proposition 13-(ii). For the rules $tu \to ut$, $su \to ss$ and $t\Diamond \to ut\Diamond$, we have directly $\psi(w) = \psi(w')$ and $\natural\mathtt{t}(w) = \natural\mathtt{t}(w')$. There remains the rule $ts \to tt$. Let z and z' be such that $w = ztsz'$. We have $\psi(zttz') = \psi(ztz')$. Since $ztz' \triangleleft ztsz'$, proposition 13-(i) ensures $\psi(zttz') \trianglelefteq \psi(ztsz')$. In the case where $\psi(zttz') = \psi(ztsz')$, z' must contain at least one occurrence of s. Hence $\natural\mathtt{t}(zttz') = \natural\mathtt{t}(ztsz')$, which implies $zttz' \prec ztsz'$. □

$\mathcal{S}$ is clearly not simplifying. It is even not terminating, because of the last rule. Nevertheless it satisfies the following result.

Lemma 15. *Let w and w' be two strings of $\{s,u,t\}^*\Diamond$ such that $w \xrightarrow{+}_{\mathcal{S}} w'$. If one of the following two conditions is satisfied,*

(i) $w \in \{s,u,t\}^*(s \vee u)\Diamond$, *or*

(ii) $w \in \{s,u,t\}^*t\Diamond$ *and the rule $t \to \varepsilon$ was applied during the derivation on the suffix $t\Diamond$,*

then $\neg(w \trianglelefteq w')$.

Proof. Consider two strings w and w' of $\{s,u,t\}^*\Diamond$ such that $w \xrightarrow{+}_S w'$, as in the hypothesis of the lemma. First note that when the rule $t\Diamond \to ut\Diamond$ is not applied in the derivation, then we have directly $\neg(w \trianglelefteq w')$, since the other rules of $\mathcal{S}$ reduce under the recursive path ordering. From now on, we concentrate on derivations from w to w' where the rule $t\Diamond \to ut\Diamond$ is applied. We shall use the following consequence of proposition 13-(ii): $w' \prec w$ implies $\neg(w \trianglelefteq w')$.
Case 1: $w \in \{s,u,t\}^*t\{s,u\}^*s\{u\}^*\Diamond$. Let z_1 and z_2 such that $w \xrightarrow{+}_S z_1 \to_S z_2 \xrightarrow{+}_S w'$, where $z_1 \to_S z_2$ by the first application of the rule $t\Diamond \to ut\Diamond$ in the derivation. By construction of ψ, we have, by hypothesis on w,

$$\psi(w) \in \{s,t\}^*s\Diamond.$$

On the other hand, for the application of the rule $t\Diamond \to ut\Diamond$ on z_1, it is necessary that z_1 belong to $\{s,u,t\}^*t\Diamond$. This implies

$$\psi(z_1) \in \{s,t\}^*t\Diamond.$$

The property (ii) ensures that $z_1 \preceq w$, and so $z_1 \prec w$. Thus $w' \prec w$.
Case 2: $w \in \{s,u,t\}^*t\Diamond$ and the rule $t \to \varepsilon$ is applied to the last occurrence of t in w. Let z_1 and z_2 such that $w \xrightarrow{+}_S z_1 \to_S z_2 \xrightarrow{+}_S w'$ with $z_1 = zt\Diamond$ and $z_2 = z\Diamond$ ($z \in \{s,u,t\}^*$). By construction of $\prec$, we have

$$z\Diamond \prec zt\Diamond.$$

We therefore have $z_2 \prec z_1$, which leads to $w' \prec w$.
Case 3: $w \in \{s,u,t\}^*tu^+\Diamond$. Let z_1 and z_2 such that $w \xrightarrow{+}_S z_1 \to_S z_2 \xrightarrow{+}_S w'$, with $z_1 \to_S z_2$ by the first application of the rule $t\Diamond \to ut\Diamond$. There are two cases: either w' belongs to $\{s,u,t\}^*t\Diamond$, or it does not. If $w' \notin \{s,u,t\}^*t\Diamond$, the rule $t \to \varepsilon$ has been necessarily applied to the final occurrence of t in z_2. Case 2 yields $w' \prec z_2$, and so $w' \prec w$. If $w' \in \{s,u,t\}^*t\Diamond$, the interesting case is $\psi(w) = \psi(w')$. Let z such that $w' = zt\Diamond$. By definition of $\prec$, we have $z \prec w'$, which by (i) excludes $w \trianglelefteq z$. Therefore $\neg(w \trianglelefteq w')$. □

This last lemma is useful for establishing **(3)**.

Lemma 16. *Let* $w_1 \in \{s,u,t\}^*t$, $w_1' \in \{s,t,u\}^*$ *and* $w_2, w_2' \in \{s,t,u,[]\}$ *be such that* $w_1 \, [] \, w_2 \xrightarrow{+}_{\mathcal{R}'} w_1' \, [] \, w_2'$. *If the final occurrence of* t *in* w_1 *is not rewritten by* $t \to \varepsilon$ *or* $t[] \to []s$, *then* $sw_2 \xrightarrow{+}_{\mathcal{R}'} sw_2'$.

Recall that $\mathcal{R}' = \mathcal{R} \cup \mathcal{E}mb(\{s,t,u\})$.

Proof. In the derivation, the only rule that can be applied to t is $t\,[]\,s \to ut[]$. Since this rule does not affect the pattern $t[]$, it follows that $s\,[]\,s \to []t$ and $s[] \to []sss$ are never applied to the leftmost occurrence of $[]$. As a consequence, $[]w_2 \xrightarrow{+}_{\mathcal{R}'} []w_2'$. The only rule of $\mathcal{R}'$ which can be applied to the leftmost occurrence of $[]$ is $[]u \to []s$. This rewrite step can be simulated by the application of the rule $su \to ss$. Hence $sw_2 \xrightarrow{+}_{\mathcal{R}'} sw_2'$. □

Proposition 17. *The SRS $\mathcal{R}$ is simplifying.*

Proof. Following proposition 6, it is enough to establish the termination of the SRS $\mathcal{R}' = \mathcal{R} \cup \mathcal{E}mb(\{s,t,u\})$. For that, we prove that for all w, w' in $\{u,s,t,[]\}^*$, if $w \xrightarrow{+}_{\mathcal{R}'} w'$, then $\neg(w \trianglelefteq w')$. Higman's theorem leads then to the conclusion. The reasoning is by induction on $|w|_{[]}$, the number of occurrences of $[]$ in w.

$|w|_{[]} = 0$: Any derivation starting from w is a derivation by the subsystem $\{ts \to tt, tu \to ut, su \to ss, s \to \varepsilon, u \to \varepsilon, t \to \varepsilon\}$, which reduces under the recursive path ordering with the precedence $t \prec s \prec u$.

$|w|_{[]} > 0$: Define w_1, w_1' in $\{u,s,t\}^*$ and w_2, w_2' in $\{u,s,t,[]\}^*$ such that

$$w = w_1 \, [] \, w_2, \quad w' = w_1' \, [] \, w_2'.$$

Since $|w|_{[]} = |w'|_{[]}$, it is enough to prove that $\neg(w_1 \trianglelefteq w_1')$ or $\neg(w_2 \trianglelefteq w_2')$ to be able to deduce that $\neg(w \trianglelefteq w')$. We distinguish the four following cases.

Case 1: $w_1 \xrightarrow{+}_{\mathcal{R}'} w_1'$ or $w_2 \xrightarrow{+}_{\mathcal{R}'} w_2'$: the induction hypothesis leads directly to the conclusion.

Case 2: $w_1 \in \{s,u,t\}^*(s \vee u)$. This case is handled by lemma 15-(i): by construction of $\mathcal{S}$, $w_1 \Diamond \xrightarrow{+}_{\mathcal{S}} w_1' \Diamond$. It follows that $\neg(w_1 \trianglelefteq w_1')$.

Case 3: $w_1 \in \{s,u,t\}^* t$ and the final occurrence of t in w_1 is rewritten by at least one of the two rules $t[] \to []s$ or $t \to \varepsilon$. In both situations, this amounts to applying the rule $t \to \varepsilon$ to w_1. So lemma 15-(ii) ensures $\neg(w_1 \trianglelefteq w_1')$.

Case 4: $w_1 \in \{s,u,t\}^* t$ and the final occurrence of t in w_1 is not rewritten by either of the two rules $t[] \to []s$ or $t \to \varepsilon$. Lemma 16 guarantees $sw_2 \xrightarrow{+}_{\mathcal{R}'} sw_2'$, which by induction hypothesis implies $\neg(w_2 \trianglelefteq w_2')$. □

References

1. A.C. Caron, *Linear bounded automata and rewrite systems: influence of initial configuration on decision properties.* CAAP-Brighton, Lecture Notes in Computer Science 493 (1991), p. 74-89.
2. E.A. Cichon and E. Tahhan-Bittar, *Ordinal recursive bounds for Higman's theorem.* To appear in Theoretical Computer Science
3. D.H.J. De Jongh and R. Parikh, *Well-partial orderings and hierarchies.* Indagationes Mathematicae 14 (1977), p. 195-207.
4. N. Dershowitz and J.P. Jouannaud, *Rewrite systems.* Handbook of Theoretical Computer Science, J. Van Leeuwen Ed., North-Holland 1990, p.243-320.
5. N. Dershowitz and M. Okada, *Proof theoretic techniques for term rewriting theory.* 3rd Annual Symposium on Logic in Computer Science, IEEE (1988), p. 104-111.
6. G. Higman, *Ordering by divisibility in abstract algebras.* Bull. London Mathematical Society 3-2 (1952), p. 326-336.
7. D. Hofbauer and C. Lautemann, *Termination proofs and the length of derivations.* Proceedings of RTA-88, Lecture Notes in Computer Science 355.
8. D. Hofbauer, *Termination proofs with multiset path orderings imply primitive recursive derivation lengths.* Theoretical Computer Science 105-1 (1992), p.129-140.

9. D. Hofbauer and J. Frank, *On total simplification orderings on strings.* Proceedings of the Third International Workshop on Termination, University of Utrecht, p.11.
10. U. Martin and E.A. Scott, *The order types of termination orderings on monadic terms, strings and multisets.* 8th Annual Symposium on Logic in Computer Science, IEEE (1993), p. 356-363.
11. A. Middeldorp and H. Zantema, *Simple termination revisited.* CADE-12, Lecture Notes in Artificial Intelligence 814 (1994), p.451-465.
12. H. Touzet, *Propriétés combinatoires pour la terminaison de systèmes de réécriture.* Thèse de l'Université H. Poincaré – Nancy 1 (1997).
13. A. Weiermann, *Complexity bounds for some finite forms of Kruskal's theorem.* Journal of Symbolic Computation 18 (1994), p.463-488.

On a Duality Between Kruskal and Dershowitz Theorems

Paul-André Melliès
LFCS, University of Edinburgh
<paulm@dcs.ed.ac.uk>

Abstract. The article is mainly concerned with the Kruskal tree theorem and the following observation: there is a duality at the level of binary relations between well and noetherian orders. The first step here is to extend Kruskal theorem from orders to binary relations so that the duality applies. Then, we describe the theorem obtained by duality and show that it corresponds to a theorem by Ferreira and Zantema which subsumes Dershowitz's seminal results on recursive path orderings.

1 Introduction

1.1 A duality between well and noetherian relations

This paper investigates a duality between the two well-established concepts of well and noetherian order. An order $\preceq$ on a set $\mathbf{X}$ is *well* when in every sequence $(x_i)_{i \in \mathbb{N}}$ of elements of $\mathbf{X}$:

$$\exists (i,j) \in \mathbb{N}^2, \quad i < j \text{ and } x_i \preceq x_j \tag{1}$$

An order $\prec$ is *noetherian* on $\mathbf{X}$ when it induces no infinite descending chain ... $\prec x_2 \prec x_1$. In other words, letting $\prec^{\perp}$ denote the complement [1] of $\prec$, an order is noetherian when for every sequence $(x_i)_{i \in \mathbb{N}}$ of elements of $\mathbf{X}$:

$$\exists (i,j) \in \mathbb{N}^2, \quad i < j \text{ and } x_j \prec^{\perp} x_i \tag{2}$$

The similarity between the definitions (1) and (2) is striking. Letting $\prec^{\star}$ denote the reverse [2] of $\prec$'s complement $\prec^{\perp}$, the order $\prec$ is noetherian whenever

$$\prec^{\star} = (\prec^{\perp})^{op} = (\prec^{op})^{\perp}$$

is well. But we should be very careful here because the relation $\prec^{\star}$ need not be an order — only a binary relation.

In fact we are forced to consider binary relations instead of orders if we want to enjoy the duality sketched above. We declare that a binary relation $\preceq$ on a set $\mathbf{X}$ is *well* when it verifies an analogue of property (1) that for every sequence $(x_i)_{i \in \mathbb{N}}$ of elements of $\mathbf{X}$,

$$\exists (i,j) \in \mathbb{N}^2, \quad i < j \text{ and } x_i \preceq x_j \tag{3}$$

[1] By complement we mean its complement in $\mathbf{X} \times \mathbf{X}$, that is $\forall (x,y) \in \mathbf{X}^2, x \prec^{\perp} y \iff \neg(x \prec y)$.

[2] By reverse we mean the relation $\prec^{op}$ such that $\forall (x,y) \in \mathbf{X}^2, x \prec^{op} y \iff y \prec x$.

Similarly, a binary relation $\prec$ on a set $\mathbf{X}$ is declared *noetherian* when an analogue of property (2) holds that for every sequence $(x_i)_{i \in \mathbb{N}}$ of elements of $\mathbf{X}$,

$$\exists (i, j) \in \mathbb{N}^2, \quad i < j \text{ and } x_i \prec^\star x_j \tag{4}$$

The duality on binary relations can be expressed as follows (noting that the operator $(-)^\star$ is idempotent on binary relations):

A binary relation $\prec$ is noetherian if and only if its dual $\prec^\star$ is well.
A binary relation $\preceq$ is well if and only if its dual $\preceq^\star$ is noetherian.

We repeat here that this duality between well and noetherian relations is not visible on orders because the transformation $(\prec \mapsto \prec^\star)$ does not respect them.

1.2 A duality on Kruskal theorem extended to binary relations

Kruskal theorem states that the tree embedding extension of a well order on labels is also a well order. To justify our shift from orders to binary relations we extend Kruskal theorem to well binary relations — see section 3. Hence, we show that the tree embedding extension of a well binary relation on labels is a well binary relation on trees.

The immediate pay-off of this extension to binary relations is that Kruskal theorem can be *dualised* to another theorem on noetherian binary relations. It turns out that this new theorem — at least its restriction to orders — falls into a class of results developed by Nachum Dershowitz on recursive path orderings, see [2,3]. Here, we could oversimplify and write:

$$\text{Kruskal}^\star = \text{Dershowitz}$$

In fact, the duality is already (and secretly) at work in a series of paper [9,4,7] where Nash-Williams' proof of Kruskal theorem is *adapted* to establish noetherianity of various path orders.

2 Well Binary Relations (WBRs)

The section adapts some well-known order-theoretic notions and results to binary relations. In particular, lemma 6 establishes that every sequence in a well binary relation contains an increasing sequence.

Definition 1 (sequence, subsequence). Let $\mathbf{X}$ denote a set. A ***sequence*** over $\mathbf{X}$ is function from $\mathbb{N}$ to $\mathbf{X}$, where $\mathbb{N}$ denotes the set of natural numbers. We write $(x_i)_{i \in \mathbb{N}}$ the sequence which associates $x_i \in \mathbf{X}$ to $i \in \mathbb{N}$. A ***subsequence*** $g = (y_j)_{j \in \mathbb{N}}$ of $f = (x_i)_{i \in \mathbb{N}}$ is any sequence such that $g = f \circ \phi$ for ϕ a strictly monotone function from $\mathbb{N}$ to $\mathbb{N}$. We say that f ***contains*** g and write $(y_j)_{j \in \mathbb{N}} = (x_{\phi(i)})_{i \in \mathbb{N}}$.

Definition 2 (good, bad, perfect). Let $(\mathbf{X}, \preceq)$ be a set equipped with a binary relation $\preceq$. A sequence f over $\mathbf{X}$ is ***good*** w.r.t $\preceq$ when there exists two natural numbers i and j such that $i < j$ and $x_i \preceq x_j$. Otherwise it is ***bad***. The sequence f is ***perfect*** when every subsequence of it is good. An ***infinite increasing chain*** over $(\mathbf{X}, \preceq)$ is a sequence $(x_i)_{i \in \mathbb{N}}$ such that $\forall (i, j) \in \mathbb{N}^2, i < j \Rightarrow x_i \preceq x_j$.

Definition 3. The relation $\preceq$ is a ***well binary relation*** (WBR) on $\mathbf{X}$ when every sequence over $\mathbf{X}$ is good w.r.t $\preceq$.

Lemma 4. *Every sequence is perfect in a well binary relation.*

Lemma 5. *Every subsequence of a perfect sequence is perfect.*

Lemma 6. *Every perfect sequence over $(\mathbf{X}, \preceq)$ contains an infinite increasing chain.*

Proof We will show that any infinite sequence over $(\mathbf{X}, \preceq)$ contains an infinite subsequence which is either bad or infinitely increasing. Let the sequence be $f = (x_i)_{i \in Nn}$.

We consider the graph whose vertices are the natural numbers and edges $\{(i, j) \mid i < j\}$. An edge (i, j) is coloured red when $x_i \preceq x_j$ and blue otherwise.

From the infinite version of Ramsey theorem, see for instance pp.392 theorem 6.1 in [1], if there is a red-colored monochromatic countably infinite complete subgraph, this means the existence of an infinite increasing subsequence. If there is a blue-colored one, this means the existence of a bad subsequence. □

Lemma 7. *Suppose that $\preceq_1$ and $\preceq_2$ are two binary relations on $\mathbf{X}$. Every sequence perfect w.r.t $\preceq_1$ and $\preceq_2$ is also perfect w.r.t $(\preceq_1 \cap \preceq_2)$.*

Proof Let $f = (x_i)_{i \in \mathbb{N}}$ be perfect w.r.t $\preceq_1$ and $\preceq_2$. We show that every subsequence $g = (y_i)_{i \in \mathbb{N}}$ of f is good w.r.t $\preceq_1 \cap \preceq_2$. By lemma 4, g is perfect w.r.t $\preceq_1$. By lemma 6, g contains an increasing sequence w.r.t $\preceq_1$, viz. there is a strictly monotone function $\phi : \mathbb{N} \to \mathbb{N}$ such that

$$\forall (i, j) \in \mathbb{N}^2, i < j \Rightarrow y_{\phi(i)} \preceq_1 y_{\phi(j)}$$

As a subsequence of f, this sequence $(y_{\phi(i)})_{i \in \mathbb{N}}$ is good w.r.t $\preceq_2$. So, there is a couple of indexes $i < j$ such that $y_{\phi(i)} \preceq_2 y_{\phi(j)}$. We conclude with the observation that the two indices $I = \phi(i)$ and $J = \phi(j)$ verify $I < J$ and $y_I (\preceq_1 \cap \preceq_2) y_J$. Therefore, $g = (y_i)_{i \in \mathbb{N}}$ is good w.r.t $\preceq_1 \cap \preceq_2$. □

Lemma 8. *Suppose that $\preceq_1$ and $\preceq_2$ are WBRs on $\mathbf{X}$. Then $\preceq_1 \cap \preceq_2$ is a WBR on $\mathbf{X}$.*

Proof Let $f = (x_i)_{i \in \mathbb{N}}$ be any sequence over $\mathbf{X}$. We have to show that f is good w.r.t $\preceq_1 \cap \preceq_2$. By lemma 4, f is perfect w.r.t $\preceq_1$ and $\preceq_2$ and by lemma 7 it is perfect w.r.t $\preceq_1 \cap \preceq_2$ and a fortiori good. We conclude. □

3 Kruskal Theorem

This section is devoted to Kruskal theorem. Its proof is "abstract" in the sense that it does not proceed on the syntactical structure of the terms but on an abstract structure which mirrors them.

3.1 The abstract system

An abstract decomposition system is a 8-tuple $(\mathcal{T}, \mathcal{L}, \mathcal{V}, \preceq, \preceq_{\mathcal{L}}, \preceq_{\mathcal{V}}, \stackrel{\cdot}{\longrightarrow}, \vdash)$ where

- $\mathcal{T}$ is a set of *terms* noted $t, u, ...$, equipped with a binary relation $\preceq$,
- $\mathcal{L}$ is a set of *labels*, noted $f, g, ...$, equipped with a binary relation $\preceq_{\mathcal{L}}$,
- $\mathcal{V}$ is a set of *vectors*, noted $T, U, ...$, equipped with a binary relation $\preceq_{\mathcal{V}}$,
- $\stackrel{\cdot}{\longrightarrow}$ is a relation between terms, labels and vectors, for instance $t \stackrel{f}{\longrightarrow} T$,
- $\vdash$ is a relation between vectors and terms, for instance $t \vdash T$.

Example.— We briefly present the concrete structures we have in mind in the case of the (multiset) Kruskal theorem. In that case, $\mathcal{T}$ is the set of ground trees built on a signature $\mathcal{F}$, $\mathcal{L}$ is just $\mathcal{F}$, and $\mathcal{V}$ is the set of finite multisets of elements of $\mathcal{T}$. $\preceq_{\mathcal{L}}$ is a well order on $\mathcal{L} = \mathcal{F}$, $\preceq$ is the tree embedding of the order $\preceq_{\mathcal{L}}$, and $\preceq_{\mathcal{V}}$ is the multiset embedding of $\preceq$. The operator $\stackrel{\cdot}{\longrightarrow}$ is the tree deconstructor: if $t = f(s_1, ..., s_k)$, then $t \stackrel{f}{\longrightarrow} \{\{s_1, ..., s_k\}\}$. The operator $\vdash$ is the multi-set deconstructor: if $T = \{\{s_1, ..., s_k\}\}$, then $T \vdash s_i$ for every $i \in [1...k]$. A more detailed presentation is given in sections 3.4 and 3.5.

Definition 9. The binary relation $\rhd$ on $\mathcal{T}$ is defined as

$$t \rhd u \iff \exists (f, T) \in \mathcal{L} \times \mathcal{V}, t \stackrel{f}{\longrightarrow} T \vdash u$$

An *elementary term* t is a minimal term w.r.t $\rhd$, that is $\forall u \in \mathcal{T}, \neg(t \rhd u)$.

3.2 The axiomatics

Six axioms will be needed to prove our Kruskal theorem. We present them informally first, then formally.

- Axiom I asks that a term cannot be deconstructed for ever,
- Axiom II asks that every sequence $(t_i)_{i \in \mathbb{N}}$ of elementary terms contains a "comparable pair" $t_i \preceq t_j$ with $i < j$,
- Axioms III and IV are abstract adaptation of the syntactical requirements of the *subterm property*:
$$t \preceq u_i \Rightarrow t \preceq f(u_1, ..., u_m)$$
and of the *monotonicity* of the syntactical contexts $C[-]$:
$$\forall C[-], \quad t \preceq u \Rightarrow C[t] \preceq C[u]$$
- Axiom V is less traditional. We trace it back to [6,7]'s notion of lifting — here in its dual presentation. The axiom asks that $\preceq_{\mathcal{V}}$ is well on any subset $\mathcal{W}$ of $\mathcal{V}$ when $\preceq$ is well on the set $\mathcal{W}_{\vdash} \subset \mathcal{T}$ composed of the elements of the vectors of $\mathcal{W}$,
- Axiom VI asks that a term t has only a finite number of principal subterms.

Axiom I [well-foundedness] There is no infinite chain $t_1 \rhd t_2 \rhd ...$
Axiom II [elementary terms] The relation $\preceq$ is a WBR on the set of elementary terms.
Axiom III [subterm property] $\forall (t, u, u') \in \mathcal{T}^3, \forall (f, U) \in \mathcal{L} \times \mathcal{V}$,

$$\text{if } t \preceq u' \text{ and } u \xrightarrow{f} U \vdash u', \text{ then } t \preceq u.$$

Axiom IV [monotonicity] $\forall(t,u) \in \mathcal{T}^2, \forall(f,g) \in \mathcal{L}^2$ and $\forall(T,U) \in \mathcal{V}^2$, Suppose that $t \xrightarrow{f} T$ and $u \xrightarrow{g} U$ and $f \preceq_{\mathcal{L}} g$ and $T \preceq_{\mathcal{V}} U$.

$$\text{If } \forall t' \in \mathcal{T}, T \vdash t' \Rightarrow (t' \preceq u \text{ and } t' \neq u), \text{ then } t \preceq u.$$

Axiom V [lifting] Take any subset $\mathcal{W}$ of $\mathcal{V}$. Letting

$$\mathcal{W}_{\vdash} = \{t \in \mathcal{T} \mid \exists T \in \mathcal{W}, T \vdash t\}$$

we ask that $\preceq_{\mathcal{V}}$ is a WBR on $\mathcal{W}$ whenever $\preceq$ is a WBR on $\mathcal{W}_{\vdash}$.
Axiom VI [finitely branching] Take any vector T. We ask that the number of terms t such that $T \vdash t$ is finite.

3.3 The axiomatic Kruskal theorem

Theorem 10 (axiomatic Kruskal). *Suppose that* $(\mathcal{T}, \mathcal{L}, \mathcal{V}, \preceq, \preceq_{\mathcal{L}}, \preceq_{\mathcal{V}}, \longrightarrow, \vdash)$ *verifies the axioms I — VI. If* $\preceq_{\mathcal{L}}$ *is a WBR on* $\mathcal{L}$*, then* $\preceq$ *is a WBR on* $\mathcal{T}$.

Proof The proof in six steps uses Nash-Williams' minimal bad sequence argument and therefore is not constructive.
[Step 1]. Suppose that $\preceq$ is not a WBR on $\mathcal{T}$. By axiom I, there is a "minimal" bad sequence $t_0, ..., t_i, ...$ such that every sequence $u_0, ..., u_i, ...$ is good as soon as $\exists k \in \mathbb{N}$ such that $[t_0, ..., t_k] = [u_0, ..., u_k]$ and $t_{k+1} \rhd u_{k+1}$. By axiom II, there exists an index $M \in \mathbb{N}$ such that every term t_{M+k} decomposes into a vector T_k and a term u_k for $k \in \mathbb{N}$:

$$t_{M+k} \xrightarrow{f_k} T_k \vdash u_k$$

[Step 2]. Let ϕ be any function from $\mathbb{N}$ to $\mathbb{N}$ such that

$$\forall i \in \mathbb{N}, \quad \phi(i) \geq \phi(0) \tag{5}$$

Let $v_0, ..., v_i, ...$ any sequence of terms such that

$$\forall i \in \mathbb{N}, \quad t_{M+\phi(i)} \xrightarrow{f_{\phi(i)}} T_{\phi(i)} \vdash v_i \tag{6}$$

We claim that the sequence $(v_i)_{i \in \mathbb{N}}$ is good w.r.t $\preceq$. Indeed, by minimality of $(t_i)_{i \in \mathbb{N}}$ and $t_{M+\phi(0)} \rhd v_0$, the sequence

$$t_0, ..., t_{M+\phi(0)-1}, v_0, v_1, ..., v_i, ...$$

is good. This means that there is a "comparable pair" in that sequence. We show by case analysis that this pair occurs in $(v_i)_{i \in \mathbb{N}}$ and conclude:

1. Suppose that $t_i \preceq t_j$ for $0 \leq i < j < M + \phi(0)$. Then $(t_i)_{i \in \mathbb{N}}$ is good, which contradicts its construction.

2. Suppose that $t_i \preceq v_j$ for $i < M + \phi(0)$ and $j \in \mathbb{N}$. Then, $t_i \preceq t_{M+\phi(j)}$ by axiom III. Because $i < M + \phi(0) \leq M + \phi(j)$ by hypothesis (5), the relation $t_i \preceq t_{M+\phi(j)}$ contradicts the construction of $(t_i)_{i\in\mathbb{N}}$ as a bad sequence.
3. The cases 1. and 2. are impossible. The only remaining case is $v_i \preceq v_j$ for some $0 \leq i < j$ — hence $(v_i)_{i\in\mathbb{N}}$ is good.

[Step 3]. Let $\mathcal{W}$ be the set consisting of all the T_i's. We claim that $\preceq$ is well on the set

$$\mathcal{W}_\vdash = \{t \in \mathcal{T} \mid \exists T \in \mathcal{W}, T \vdash t\}$$

Take any sequence $w_0, ..., w_i, ...$ of terms in $\mathcal{W}_\vdash$. For every $i \in \mathbb{N}$, there is a minimum index $P(i) \in \mathbb{N}$ such that $T_{P(i)} \vdash w_i$. Let P be the minimum index among these $P(i)$'s, and $i_0 \in \mathbb{N}$ such that $P = P(i_0)$. We consider the subsequence $(v_i)_{i\in\mathbb{N}} = (w_{i_0+i})_{i\in\mathbb{N}}$ of $(w_i)_{i\in\mathbb{N}}$ and show that it is good. Indeed, the function $\phi : \mathbb{N} \to \mathbb{N}$ defined by $i \mapsto P(i_0 + i)$ verifies the two conditions 5 and 6 of [step 2]:

$$\forall i \in \mathbb{N}, \quad \phi(i) \geq \phi(0) \quad \wedge \quad t_{M+\phi(i)} \xrightarrow{f_{\phi(i)}} T_{\phi(i)} \vdash v_i$$

We deduce that $(v_i)_{i\in\mathbb{N}}$ is good, and a fortiori $(w_i)_{i\in\mathbb{N}}$ is good. We conclude that $\preceq$ is well on $\mathcal{W}_\vdash$.

[Step 4]. From this fact and axiom V, $\preceq_\mathcal{V}$ is well on $\mathcal{W}$. In particular, the sequence $(T_i)_{i\in\mathbb{N}}$ is perfect w.r.t $\preceq_\mathcal{V}$. The sequence $(f_0, T_0), ..., (f_i, T_i), ...$ being perfect w.r.t $\preceq_\mathcal{L} \times \mathcal{T}^2$ and $\mathcal{L}^2 \times \preceq_\mathcal{V}$ is also perfect w.r.t $(\preceq_\mathcal{L} \times \mathcal{T}^2) \cap (L^2 \times \preceq_\mathcal{V}) = \preceq_\mathcal{L} \times \preceq_\mathcal{V}$ by lemma 7.

From lemma 6, there exists a strictly monotone function $\psi : \mathbb{N} \to \mathbb{N}$ such that

$$(f_{\psi(0)}, T_{\psi(0)}), ..., (f_{\psi(i)}, T_{\psi(i)}), ...$$

is an increasing sequence w.r.t $\preceq_\mathcal{L} \times \preceq_\mathcal{V}$.

[Step 5]. The proof that there exists an index $j \in \mathbb{N}$ such that

$$\forall t' \in \mathcal{T}, T_{\psi(0)} \vdash t' \Rightarrow (t' \preceq t_{M+\psi(j)} \text{ and } t' \neq t_{M+\psi(j)})$$

is left as exercise. Note that it uses axiom VI.

[Step 6]. We conclude with axiom IV. Let $I = \psi(0)$ and $J = \psi(j)$. Here, the vector $T_{\psi(0)}$ can be rewritten as T_I and the index $M + \psi(j)$ as $M + J$. Step 1 shew that

$$t_{M+I} \xrightarrow{f_I} T_I \text{ and } t_{M+J} \xrightarrow{f_J} T_J$$

Step 4 established that

$$f_I \preceq_\mathcal{L} f_J \text{ and } T_I \preceq_\mathcal{V} T_J$$

Step 5 established that

$$\forall t' \in \mathcal{T}, T_I \vdash t' \Rightarrow (t' \preceq t_{M+J} \text{ and } t' \neq t_{M+J})$$

We apply axiom IV and derive $t_{M+I} \preceq t_{M+J}$, hence contradicting the construction of $(t_i)_{i\in\mathbb{N}}$ as a bad sequence. We conclude that $\preceq$ is a WBR on $\mathcal{T}$. □

Remark. — Axioms IV and VI appear as luxury from the point of view of Kruskal theorem. Indeed, they can be replaced by a simpler requirement:
Axiom IV[bis] $\forall(t,u) \in \mathcal{T}^2, \forall(f,g) \in \mathcal{L}^2$ and $\forall(T,U) \in \mathcal{V}^2$,
If $t \xrightarrow{f} T$ and $u \xrightarrow{g} U$ and $f \preceq_{\mathcal{L}} g$ and $T \preceq_{\mathcal{V}} U$, then $t \preceq u$.

In axiom IV[bis], the condition

$$\forall t' \in \mathcal{T}, T \vdash t' \Rightarrow (t' \preceq u \text{ and } t' \neq u) \tag{7}$$

disappears and [step 5] is not necessary in the proof of theorem 10. But duality is our reason to keep condition 7. In fact, the dual of condition (7) stands among the fundamentals of recursive path orderings — see section 4.1 for further discussion.

3.4 Application I: Higman theorem, in [8]

Let $\mathcal{L}$ be a set of labels equipped with a binary relation $\preceq_{\mathcal{L}}$. The set $\mathcal{T}$ is constructed as the set of finite strings on $\mathcal{L}$ equipped with the following binary relation $\preceq$.

$$(a_1, ..., a_m) \preceq (b_1, ..., b_n) \iff \exists \text{ an embedding } \phi : [1...m] \to [1...n] \\ \text{such that } \forall i \in [1...m], a_i \preceq_{\mathcal{L}} b_{\phi(i)}$$

where an (Higman) embedding $[1...m] \to [1...n]$ is a strictly monotone function.
Higman proved in [8] that $\preceq$ is a well order whenever $\preceq_{\mathcal{L}}$ is a well order.

Theorem 11 (Higman). *If $\preceq_{\mathcal{L}}$ is well on $\mathcal{L}$, then $\preceq$ is well on $\mathcal{T}$.*

We show that theorem 11 is an instance of our theorem 10. To do this, we identify the sets $\mathcal{V}$ and $\mathcal{T}$ and define $\vdash$ as the identity relation on $\mathcal{T}$. The relation $\xrightarrow{f}$ is defined as follows:

$$(a_1, ..., a_m) \xrightarrow{f} (b_1, ..., b_n) \iff (a_1, ..., a_m) = (f, b_1, ..., b_n)$$

Let us check that the decomposition system $(\mathcal{T}, \mathcal{L}, \mathcal{V}, \preceq, \preceq_{\mathcal{L}}, \preceq_{\mathcal{V}}, \longrightarrow, \vdash)$ verifies the axioms I — VI of section 3.2.

1. $t \rhd u$ implies that u's length is strictly smaller than t's length. In particular, there is no infinite sequence $t_1 \rhd t_2 \rhd ....$
2. the only elementary term is the empty string ϵ, and $\epsilon \preceq \epsilon$,
3. Letting $u' = (a_1, ..., a_n)$, $u \xrightarrow{f} u'$ means that $u = (f, a_1, ..., a_n)$. If $\phi : [1...m] \to [1...n]$ is an embedding corresponding to $t \preceq u'$, then $i \mapsto \phi(i)+1$ is an embedding $[1...m] \to [1...n+1]$ corresponding to $t \preceq u$. Therefore, $t \preceq u'$ implies $t \preceq u$.
4. Letting $T = (a_1, ..., a_m)$ and $U = (b_1, ..., b_n)$, $T \preceq_{\mathcal{V}} U$ means here that $T \preceq U$, hence that there is an embedding $\phi : [1...m] \to [1...n]$ such that $\forall i \in [1...m], a_i \preceq_{\mathcal{L}} b_{\phi(i)}$. Letting $\psi : [1...m+1] \to [1...n+1]$ be the function $1 \mapsto 1$ and $\forall i \in [1...m], 1+i \mapsto 1+\phi(i)$, ψ embeds $t = (f, a_1, ..., a_m)$ into $u = (g, b_1, ..., b_n)$ so that $t \preceq u$ — because $f \preceq_{\mathcal{L}} g$.

5-6. immediate.

This shows in six easy steps that Higman theorem is an instance of theorem 10. Simultaneously, it extends Higman theorem to binary relations.

3.5 Application II: Kruskal theorem, in [10]

We show here that the original Kruskal theorem is an instance of theorem 10.

A varyadic signature $(\mathcal{F}, \mathtt{arity})$ is a set $\mathcal{F}$ equipped with a function $\mathtt{arity} : \mathcal{F} \to \wp\mathbb{N}$. Intuitively, the set $\mathtt{arity}(f)$ contains the possible arities of f. Occurrences are finite strings of natural numbers which can be ordered by $\leq_{\mathcal{O}}$, the precedence order defined as follows: $o \leq_{\mathcal{O}} o'$ when the string o' extends the strings o.

Let $\mathcal{T}$ be the set of trees constructed from a varyadic signature $\mathcal{L}$. Every tree t in $\mathcal{T}$ is characterised by a function $o \mapsto t_o$ from its set $\mathcal{O}_t$ of occurrences to the set $\mathcal{L}$ of labels. Also, every tree t defines a function $o \mapsto [o]_t$ from $\mathcal{O}_t$ to $\mathbb{N}$ characterised by:

$$\forall i \in \mathbb{N}, \quad oi \in \mathcal{O}_t \iff i \in [1...[o]_t]$$

So, $[o]_t = 2$ means that $o1$ and $o2$ are occurrences of t, but not $o3$. And $[o]_t = 0$ means that o is a leaf occurrence of t.

An (Kruskal) embedding ϕ from $t \in \mathcal{T}$ to $u \in \mathcal{T}$ is a function from $\mathcal{O}_t$ to $\mathcal{O}_u$ such that:

1. $\forall (o, o') \in \mathcal{O}_t^2, \ o \leq_{\mathcal{O}} o' \Rightarrow \phi(o) \leq_{\mathcal{O}} \phi(o')$,
2. $\forall o \in \mathcal{O}_t$, there is a strictly monotone function $\psi_o : [1...[o]_t] \to [1...[\phi(o)]_u]$ such that $\forall i \in [1...[o]_t], \phi(o)\psi_o(i) \leq_{\mathcal{O}} \phi(oi)$.

Let $\mathcal{L}$ be equipped with a binary relation $\preceq_{\mathcal{L}}$. The binary relation $\preceq$ on $\mathcal{T}$ is constructed as follows:

$$t \preceq u \iff \text{there exists an embedding } \phi : \mathcal{O}_t \to \mathcal{O}_u \text{ such that } \forall o \in \mathcal{O}_t, t_o \preceq_{\mathcal{L}} u_{\phi(o)}$$

Theorem 12 (Kruskal). *If $\preceq_{\mathcal{L}}$ is well on $\mathcal{L}$, then $\preceq$ is well on $\mathcal{T}$.*

We show that theorem 12 is an instance of our theorem 10. To do this, we define the set $\mathcal{V}$ as the set of finite strings on $\mathcal{T}$ equipped with the Higman binary relation $\preceq_{\mathcal{V}}$ defined in section 3.4:

$$(t_1, ..., t_m) \preceq_{\mathcal{V}} (u_1, ..., u_n) \iff \exists \text{ a strictly monotone } \phi : [1...m] \to [1...n] \text{ such that } \forall i \in [1...m], t_i \preceq u_{\phi(i)}$$

The relation $\xrightarrow{f}$ for $f \in \mathcal{L}$ is the tree deconstructor:

$$f(t_1, ..., t_m) \xrightarrow{f} (u_1, ..., u_n) \iff (t_1, ..., t_m) = (u_1, ..., u_n)$$

The relation $\vdash$ is the string deconstructor:

$$\forall i \in [1...m], \quad (t_1, ..., t_m) \vdash t_i$$

The axiomatics of section 3.2 is checked on $(\mathcal{T}, \mathcal{L}, \mathcal{V}, \preceq, \preceq_{\mathcal{L}}, \preceq_{\mathcal{V}}, \longrightarrow, \vdash)$ as it is in section 3.4. Note that axiom V is theorem 11, and that axiom VI means that a finite string can only decompose to a finite number of elements.

So, Kruskal theorem is an instance of theorem 10 and as such extends to binary relations.

4 Dershowitz RPO theorems

In this section, we dualise the theorem 10 of section 3 and obtain a theorem on noetherian binary relations. To simplify the presentation, we write $\succ$ instead of $\prec^{op}$.

4.1 Axioms I—VI and theorem 10 dualised

We explain how to dualise the axioms and the theorem. Take a decomposition system $\Sigma = (\mathcal{T}, \mathcal{L}, \mathcal{V}, \prec, \prec_{\mathcal{L}}, \prec_{\mathcal{V}}, \longrightarrow, \vdash)$. Then, theorem 10 applied to the decomposition system $\Sigma' = (\mathcal{T}, \mathcal{L}, \mathcal{V}, \prec^\star, \prec^\star_{\mathcal{L}}, \prec^\star_{\mathcal{V}}, \longrightarrow, \vdash)$ reads as follows:

> If the decomposition system Σ' verifies the axioms I—VI and $\prec^\star_{\mathcal{L}}$ is a WBR on $\mathcal{L}$, then $\prec^\star$ is a WBR on $\mathcal{T}$.

By duality, we transform this assertion into:

> If the decomposition system Σ' verifies the axioms I—VI and $\prec_{\mathcal{L}}$ is noetherian on $\mathcal{L}$, then $\prec$ is noetherian on $\mathcal{T}$.

Now, we must express the conditions on Σ such that Σ' verifies the axioms I—VI. For instance, Σ' verifies axiom III when

$$\forall (t, u, u') \in \mathcal{T}^3, \forall (f, U) \in \mathcal{L} \times \mathcal{V}, \text{ if } t \prec^\star u' \text{ and } u \xrightarrow{f} U \vdash u', \text{ then } t \prec^\star u.$$

This is rephrased by contraposition as:

$$\forall (t, u, u') \in \mathcal{T}^3, \forall (f, U) \in \mathcal{L} \times \mathcal{V}, \text{ if } t \succ u \text{ and } u \xrightarrow{f} U \vdash u', \text{ then } t \succ u'.$$

Hence, Σ' verifies axiom III if and only if Σ verifies the previous assertion, called hereafter axiom III*. We list the "dualised" axioms we obtain:

Axiom I* [well-foundedness] There is no infinite chain $t_1 \rhd t_2 \rhd \ldots$

Axiom II* [elementary terms] There is no infinite chain $t_1 \succ t_2 \succ \ldots$ of elementary terms.

Axiom III* [subterm property] $\forall (t, u, u') \in \mathcal{T}^3, \forall (f, T) \in \mathcal{L} \times \mathcal{V}$,

$$\text{if } t \succ u \text{ and } u \xrightarrow{f} U \vdash u', \text{ then } t \succ u'.$$

Axiom IV* [decomposability] $\forall (t, u) \in \mathcal{T}^2, \forall (f, g) \in \mathcal{L}^2$ and $\forall (T, U) \in \mathcal{V}^2$, If $t \xrightarrow{f} T$ and $u \xrightarrow{g} U$ and $t \succ u$, then either:

1. $f \succ_{\mathcal{L}} g$,
2. or $T \succ_{\mathcal{V}} U$,
3. or $\exists t' \in \mathcal{T}$ such that $T \vdash t'$ and $t' \succ u$,
4. or $T \vdash u$.

Axiom V* [lifting] Take any subset $\mathcal{W}$ of $\mathcal{V}$. Letting $\mathcal{W}_\vdash = \{t \in \mathcal{T} \mid \exists T \in \mathcal{W}, T \vdash t\}$, we ask that $\succ_{\mathcal{V}}$ is noetherian on $\mathcal{W}$ whenever $\succ$ is noetherian on $\mathcal{W}_\vdash$.

Axiom VI* [finitely branching] Take any vector T. We ask that the number of terms t such that $T \vdash t$ is finite.

We obtain the following dual theorem:

Theorem 13 (Dual Kruskal). *Let $\Sigma = (\mathcal{T}, \mathcal{L}, \mathcal{V}, \prec, \prec_\mathcal{L}, \prec_\mathcal{V}, \overset{\cdot}{\longrightarrow}, \vdash)$ be a decomposition system which verifies the axioms I* — VI*. If $\succ_\mathcal{L}$ is noetherian on $\mathcal{L}$, then $\succ$ is noetherian on $\mathcal{T}$.*

Proof The previous discussion shows that Σ verifies the axioms I* — VI* if and only if Σ' verifies the axioms I — VI. We conclude with theorem 10. □

It is interesting that the dual of axiom IV is not a monotonicity requirement, but a decomposability one, as one could guess from the result of [7] and the last remark of section 1.2.

Monotonicity* = Decomposability

If we stop a moment and think of axiom IV[bis] at the end of section 3.3, we realise that its dual is just axiom IV* where disjunctions 3. and 4. disappear. This absence would have the disastrous effect to banish most recursive path orderings from the axiomatics!

4.2 Application III: Ferreira and Zantema's theorem, in [7]

We show that Ferreira and Zantema's theorem 16 in [7] is an instance of theorem 13.

Definition 14 (Ferreira-Zantema). Let $\mathcal{F}$ be a signature and $\mathcal{X}$ be a set of variables. Let the set $\mathcal{T}(\mathcal{F}, \mathcal{X})$ of trees on $\mathcal{F}$ and $\mathcal{X}$ be equipped with a partial order $\succ$. We define a *term lifting* to be a partial order $\succ^A$ such that the following holds: for every $A \subset \mathcal{T}(\mathcal{F}, \mathcal{X})$, if $\succ$ restricted to A is noetherian, then $\succ^A$ restricted to $\bar{A}$ is also noetherian, where $\bar{A} = \{f(t_1, ..., t_m) \mid f \in \mathcal{F}, n \in \text{arity}(f), \text{ and } \forall i \in [1...m], t_i \in A\}$

Ferreira and Zantema's theorem is then expressed as follows:

Theorem 15 (Ferreira-Zantema). *Let $\succ$ be a partial order on $\mathcal{T}(\mathcal{F}, \mathcal{X})$ and let $\succ^A$ be a term lifting of $\succ$. Suppose that $\succ$ has the subterm property:*

$$\forall f(t_1, ..., t_m) \in \mathcal{T}(\mathcal{F}, \mathcal{X}), \forall i \in [1...m], \quad f(t_1, ..., t_m) \succ t_i$$

And suppose that $\succ$ satisfies that for every term $f(t_1, ..., t_m)$ and $g(u_1, ..., u_n)$ in $\mathcal{T}(\mathcal{F}, \mathcal{X})$ with $m, n \in \mathbb{N}$:

If $s = f(s_1, ..., s_m) \succ g(t_1, ..., t_n) = t$, then either
- *$\exists i \in [1...m], s_i \succ t$ or $s_i = t$,*
- *or $s \succ^A t$.*

Then $\succ$ is noetherian on $\mathcal{T}(\mathcal{F}, \mathcal{X})$.

Ferreira and Zantema show in [7] that the noetherianity of the semantic path order [9] and of the general[3] path order [4] are direct consequences of their theorem 15.

We will qualify theorem 15 as an instance of theorem 13 by exhibiting the correct decomposition system Σ. Our solution is trivial but in a sense quite unexpected. The two sets $\mathcal{T}$ and $\mathcal{V}$ are identified as $\mathcal{T}(\mathcal{F}, \mathcal{X})$, and $\mathcal{L}$ is simply an arbitrary singleton $\{\clubsuit\}$. $\prec_\mathcal{L}$ is the empty relation (hence noetherian) on $\mathcal{L}$, $\prec_\mathcal{V} = \prec^A$ and our relation $\prec$ is Ferreira-Zantema's partial order $\prec$. The relation $\overset{\clubsuit}{\longrightarrow}$ is just the identity relation on $\mathcal{T} = \mathcal{V}$:

[3] Therefore of the original recursive path order defined in [2], see [4] for a detailed discussion.

$$t \xrightarrow{\clubsuit} T \iff t = T$$

The relation $\vdash$ is defined as the tree deconstructor:

$$T \vdash t \iff T = f(t_1, ..., t_m) \text{ and } \exists i \in [1...m], t = t_i$$

We check that the decomposition system Σ verifies axioms I*—VI* when the three hypothesis in theorem 15 are fulfilled:

1. $t \xrightarrow{\clubsuit} T \vdash u$ implies that u is a principal subterm of t. Hence axiom I*,
2. The constant and variable terms are the only elementary terms in $\mathcal{T}(\mathcal{F}, \mathcal{X})$. Note that the second hypothesis in theorem 13 implies that $(t \succ u \Rightarrow t \succ^{\Lambda} u)$ whenever t and u are elementary. We claim that $\succ^{\Lambda}$ is noetherian on the set of elementary terms and conclude. Indeed $\succ$ is trivially noetherian on the empty set $\emptyset$ whose completion $\bar{\emptyset}$ is the set of elementary terms. The term lifting $\succ^{\Lambda}$ is therefore noetherian on the elementary terms. We conclude that axiom II* holds.
3. Axiom III* is a consequence of transitivity of $\succ$ and subterm property hypothesis in theorem 15,
4. The second hypothesis of theorem 15 can be reformulated as:
   If $s = f(s_1, ..., s_m) \succ g(t_1, ..., t_n) = t$, $s \xrightarrow{\clubsuit} S$ and $t \xrightarrow{\clubsuit} T$, then either
   - $\exists s' \in \mathcal{T}$ such that $S \vdash s'$ and $s' \succ t$,
   - or $S \vdash t$,
   - or $S \succ_{\mathcal{V}} T$.

   Axiom IV* follows.
5. Axiom V* is a consequence of the first hypothesis of theorem 15 that $\succ^{\Lambda}$ is a term lifting,
6. Axiom VI* is immediate.

5 Conclusion

The axiomatic proof of Kruskal theorem originates from an attempt to extend the scope of the recursive path ordering (RPO) techniques to higher-order calculi like the λ-calculus. Two directions are suggested here to tackle the problem.

In [12], a proof of strong normalisation of the simply-typed λ-calculus is presented very close in spirit to Nash-Williams' minimal bad sequence argument: A "zoom-in" strategy is shown to be perpetual and terminating on every simply-typed λ-term, qed. Unfortunately, this proof does not transfer yet to a general RPO technique for higher-order calculi.

Also, the discovery of a duality between Dershowitz theorems on RPOs and Kruskal theorem on well-quasi-orderings conveys the hope for a similar dualisation of Robertson-Seymour "graph minor" theorem (see [16] for a survey) into a theorem on RPOs applicable to graphs. Since λ-terms are graphs, this is certainly another approach to a theory of RPOs for higher-order calculi,

I would like to conclude the article with two open problems. Is there a constructive proof like [15] of Kruskal theorem on binary relations? Is it possible to axiomatize Kruskal-Dershowitz theorems à la [5,14]?

Acknowledgement

I would like to thank Mizuhito Ogawa and the anonymous referee for relating lemma 6 to Ramsey theorem.

References

1. *Handbook of Mathematical Logic*, edited by J. Barwise, Studies in Logic and Foundations of Computer Science, North-Holland, 1977.
2. N. Dershowitz, "Orderings for term rewriting systems". Theoretical Computer Science 17, 3, pp.279-301, 1982.
3. N. Dershowitz, "Termination of rewriting". Journal of Symbolic Computation 3, 1 and 2, pp.69-116, 1987.
4. N. Dershowitz and C. Hoot, "Topics in termination". in Proceedings of the 5th conference on Rewriting Techniques and Applications, C. Kirchner ed., LNCS 690, Springer, pp.198-212, 1983.
5. A. Ehrenfeucht, D. Hausslet and G. Rozenberg, "On regularity of context-free languages", Theoretical Computer Science 27 (3), pp.311-332, 1983.
6. M. C. F. Ferreira and H. Zantema, "Syntactical Analysis of Total Termination", proceedings of the 4th International Conference on Algebraic and Logic Programming, editors G. Levi and M. Rodrigues-Artalejo, Springer Lecture Notes in Computer Science, volume 850, pages 204 - 222, 1994.
7. M. C. F. Ferreira and H. Zantema, "Well-foundedness of Term Orderings", in Conditional Term Rewriting Systems, proceedings fourth international workshop CTRS-94, editor N. Dershowitz, Springer Lecture Notes in Computer Science, volume 968, pages 106 - 123, 1995.
8. G. Higman, "Ordering by divisibility in Abstract Algebra", Proc. London Math. Soc, 3(2), 326-336, 1952.
9. S. Kamin and J. J. Lévy, "Two generalizations of the recursive path ordering", University of Illinois, 1980.
10. J. B. Kruskal, "Well-quasi-ordering, the tree theorem, and Vázsonyi's conjecture", Trans. Amer. Math. Soc. 95, pp.210-225, 1960.
11. P. Lescanne, "Well rewrite orderings", In Proceedings, Fifth Annual IEEE Symposium on Logic in Computer Science, pages 249-256, Philadelphia, Pennsylvania, 4-7 June 1990. IEEE Computer Society Press.
12. P.-A. Melliès, "Description abstraite des systèmes de réécriture", Thèse de l'Université Paris VII, Décembre 1996.
13. C. S. L. A. Nash-Williams, "On well-quasi ordering finite trees", Proceedings Cambridge Phil. Soc. 59, 833—382, 1963.
14. L. Puel, "Using unavoidable sets of trees to generalize Kruskal's theorem", Journal of Symbolic Computation 8 , 335-382, 1989.
15. M. Rathjen, A. Weiermann, "Proof-theoretic investigations on Kruskal's theorem", Annals of Pure and Applied Logic, 60, 1993.
16. C. Thomassen, "Embeddings and Minors", in *Handbook of Combinatorics*, Volume 1, R. L. Graham, M. Grötschel, L. Lovász editors, North-Holland, 1995.

A Total AC-Compatible Reduction Ordering on Higher-Order Terms

Daria Walukiewicz*

Institute of Informatics, Warsaw University
Banacha 2, 02-097 Warsaw, Poland
email: daria@mimuw.edu.pl

Abstract. The higher-order rewriting in presence of associative and commutative (AC) symbols is considered. A higher-order reduction ordering which allows to state the termination of a given rewriting system is presented. This ordering is an AC-extension of λ-RPO and is defined on simply-typed λ-terms in β-normal η-long form. It is total on ground terms.

1 Introduction

Automated methods of proving termination of rewrite systems are used in many theorem provers and specification development systems. Most of these methods are based on finding a suitable reduction ordering, i.e., a well-founded partial order which is stable under context and substitution. The most popular reduction ordering in first-order rewriting is RPO – *recursive path ordering*. Its principle is to generate recursively an ordering on terms from a given ordering on function symbols called *precedence*. The recursive definition of RPO allows to apply and to implement it easily.

Higher-order rewrite rules are used in the programming languages, like ML, Elf, or theorem provers, like Isabelle. Unfortunately, there are only few methods for proving termination of higher-order systems. In the case of first-order pattern matching it is known that a higher-order rewrite system has termination property when its rules follow a generalised form of a primitive recursive schema of higher type (see [5, 4]). In the general case of higher-order pattern matching one can use λ-RPO proposed by Jouannaud and Rubio [6].

λ-RPO is a *higher-order reduction ordering*, i.e., a well-founded ordering stable under ground contexts and substitutions and moreover compatible with the underlying typed λ-calculus. Since we are interested in higher-order pattern matching, compatibility with typed λ-calculus means compatibility with $\beta\eta$-conversions. This is easily achieved by defining λ-RPO on canonical representatives – terms in β-normal η-long form. Compared to RPO, λ-RPO needs not only a precedence on function symbols but also a precedence on types. Terms are compared first by type, then by top symbol, finally the comparison proceeds

* Partly supported by Polish KBN Grant 8 T11C 034 10.

recursively to subterms. Because of its recursive definition, λ-RPO is especially well suited for automation.

Practical applications often introduce AC-symbols (like +) into the signature. While rewriting terms with such symbols one has to have in mind that they satisfy the axioms of associativity ($x + (y + z) = (x + y) + z$) and commutativity ($x + y = y + x$). These axioms can't be just oriented and added to the system, because any orientation of commutativity yields an infinite reduction. The solution is to consider a new type of rewriting – rewriting modulo AC, rewriting of AC-equivalence classes (see [7]). In this case the ordering used to prove termination should be AC-compatible. An ordering is *AC-compatible* if the result of comparing of two AC-equivalence classes doesn't depend on representatives, i.e., $s' =_{AC} s > t =_{AC} t'$ implies $s' > t'$. The most intuitive method of making an order AC-compatible is *flattening* of terms (removing nested AC-symbols) before comparing them. Unfortunately, because of flattening monotonicity is lost. For example consider RPO with $f > g$, $f \in \mathcal{F}_{AC}$. We have $f(a, a) >_{rpo} g(a)$, but after flattening the terms $f(a, f(a, a))$, $f(a, g(a))$ we obtain $f(a, a, a) \not>_{rpo} f(a, g(a))$.

Recently Rubio and Nieuwenhuis showed a new method of making RPO AC-compatible [10]. Their method consists of computing interpretations of terms before comparing them in RPO. An interpretation of the term is a set of normal forms in the system containing flattening and the rules $f(u_1, \dots, g(v_1, \dots, v_n) \dots, u_m) \longrightarrow f(u_1, \dots, v_i \dots, u_m)$ for $i = 1 \dots n$, f an AC-symbol and any g smaller than f in the precedence.

The aim of this paper is to bring together two types of rewriting described above and construct an ordering which can be used to prove termination of higher-order rewrite systems modulo AC. The main idea is to apply the method of Rubio and Nieuwenhuis to λ-RPO. It is worth pointing out that our construction does not impose any restriction not already present in the definition of λ-RPO or Rubio and Nieuwenhuis's method. The obtained ordering is defined in a simple way by means of rewrite rules, and can be easily implemented since its main component is λ-RPO. Moreover, if there are no AC-symbols in the signature, AC-λ-RPO is just λ-RPO.

The paper is structured in the following way. Section 2 presents some preliminaries and definitions. In Sect.3 the ordering AC-λ-RPO is defined. Section 4 is devoted to the study of the properties of AC-λ-RPO which allow us to prove the main result. We present examples in Sect.5. The full version of this paper can be found at `http:\\zls.mimuw.edu.pl\~daria\papers`.

2 Definitions

We expect the reader to be familiar with the basic concepts and notations of term rewriting systems [3] and typed lambda calculi [1], [2].

2.1 Types and Terms

Let $\mathcal{S}$ denote the set of basic types and let $\mathcal{T}_{\mathcal{S}}$ denote the set of all types obtained from $\mathcal{S}$ using the type constructor $\rightarrow$.

An expression of the form $\sigma_1 \times \ldots \times \sigma_n \to \sigma$ is called the *type declaration.* $\sigma_1, \ldots, \sigma_n$ are input types, σ is the *output type*. We assume that the output type is always a basic type. Note that type declarations are not types.

A *signature* $\mathcal{F}$ is a set of function symbols subject to some restrictions. First, we assume that every function symbol $f \in \mathcal{F}$ comes with its type declaration. Next, we assume that there are only finitely many symbols of each output type and that for every type σ there is a symbol $\bot_\sigma : \sigma$ in $\mathcal{F}$. Finally there is a subset $\mathcal{F}_{AC} \subseteq \mathcal{F}$ of AC-symbols. Each $f \in \mathcal{F}_{AC}$ must have type declaration of the form $\sigma \times \sigma \to \sigma$ and satisfy the axioms of commutativity and associativity:

$$f(a, b) = f(b, a)$$
$$f(a, f(b, c)) = f(f(a, b), c)$$

In our reasonings we will often allow $f \in \mathcal{F}_{AC}$ to take an arbitrary, but not smaller than two, number of arguments. For example if we have $+ : int \times int \to int$ then we can have a term $+(a, b, c)$ and intuitively it is equivalent (among others) to $+(a, +(b, c))$.

We will denote by $\lambda\mathcal{F}$ the set $\mathcal{F}$ extended with symbols $\lambda_{\sigma\to\tau} : \tau \to (\sigma \to \tau)$ for each $\sigma, \tau \in \mathcal{T}_S$.

The set of *terms with types* $\mathcal{T}$ is generated from a denumerable set of variables $\mathcal{X} = \bigcup_{\sigma\in\mathcal{T}_S} \mathcal{X}_\sigma$, according to the grammar:

$$\mathcal{T} ::= \mathcal{X} \mid (\lambda\mathcal{X}.\mathcal{T}) \mid \mathcal{T}(\mathcal{T}) \mid \mathcal{F}(\mathcal{T}, \ldots, \mathcal{T})$$

This set is then restricted to *simply typed* λ*-terms* $\mathcal{T}(\mathcal{F}, \mathcal{X})$ by the following typing rules:

$$\textbf{(var)}\frac{}{x^\sigma : \sigma} \qquad \textbf{(abs)}\frac{u : \tau}{\lambda x^\sigma.u : \sigma \to \tau} \qquad \textbf{(app)}\frac{u : \sigma \to \tau \quad v : \sigma}{u(v) : \tau}$$

$$\textbf{(fun)}\frac{u_1 : \sigma_1, \ldots, u_n : \sigma_n}{f(u_1, \ldots, u_n) : \sigma} \quad \text{for } f : \sigma_1 \times \ldots \times \sigma_n \to \sigma$$

Terms are identified with finite labelled trees by considering $\lambda x.$ as an unary function symbol. *Positions* of a term are strings of positive integers. Λ denotes the empty string (root position), $\cdot$ denotes concatenation. The subterm of s at position p is denoted by $s|_p$, while $s[t]_p$ stands for the result of replacing $s|_p$ by t. The expressions $\langle s_1, \ldots s_n\rangle$ and $\boldsymbol{s}$ stand for ordered tuple of terms with and without specifying the elements of the tuple.

For convenience we assume that bound variables are all different, and are different from free ones.

Substitutions are written as in $\{x_1 \mapsto t_1, \ldots, x_n \mapsto t_n\}$, where t_i is assumed to be different from x_i. The substitution is called ground if all t_i are ground.

From now on, we will work only with terms in η-long β-normal form. This form is computed using the rules:

$$(\lambda x.v)(u) \longrightarrow_\beta u\{x \mapsto v\}$$

$$C[u]_p \longrightarrow_\eta C[\lambda x.u(x)]_p \text{ if } \begin{cases} u : \sigma \to \tau \\ x \notin Var(u) \\ u \text{ is not an abstraction} \\ C[u]|_q \text{ is not an application for } p = q \cdot 1 \end{cases}$$

The simply typed λ-calculus is confluent and terminating with respect to β-reductions and η-expansions. We write $u{\downarrow}$ for the unique normal form of u with respect to these rules. If $t = t{\downarrow}$ then t is called *normalised* and it is of the form $\lambda x_1 \ldots x_m.\, f(t_1, \ldots, t_n)$, where $m \geq 0$, $f \in \mathcal{F} \cup \mathcal{X}$, terms $t_1, \ldots t_n$ are normalised and $f(t_1, \ldots, t_n)$ is of basic type. In the sequel, $\mathcal{T}(\mathcal{F}, \mathcal{X}){\downarrow}$ stands for the set of normalised simply typed λ-terms.

2.2 Higher Order Rewriting modulo AC

A *higher-order term rewriting system* is a set of rewrite rules $R = \{l_i \to r_i\}_{i \in I}$, where for every $i \in I$, l_i, r_i are normalised terms of the same type. Given a system R, a term s rewrites modulo AC to a term t at a position p, with a rule $l \to r$ and a substitution γ if there is a term u such that $s =_{AC} u$, $u|_p = l\gamma{\downarrow}$ and $u[r\gamma{\downarrow}]_p =_{AC} t$. We denote this fact by $s \xrightarrow[l \to r/AC]{p} t$ or just $s \longrightarrow_R t$. A term s is in R-normal form if it can't be rewritten by R. We denote by $\longrightarrow_R^*$ the reflexive, transitive closure of $\longrightarrow_R$.

A rewrite system is said to be *confluent* if for any three terms s, u, t, $u \longrightarrow_R^* s$ and $u \longrightarrow_R^* t$, imply $s \longrightarrow_R^* v$ and $t \longrightarrow_R^* v$ for some v. A definition of *local confluence* is obtained when we replace $u \longrightarrow_R^* s$ and $u \longrightarrow_R^* t$ by $u \longrightarrow_R s$ and $u \longrightarrow_R t$.

A rewrite system is *terminating* (or *strongly normalising*) if there is no infinite rewriting sequence $s_1 \longrightarrow_R s_2 \longrightarrow_R \ldots \longrightarrow_R s_n \longrightarrow_R \ldots$.

2.3 Orderings

Throughout the paper we will make intensive use of orderings on λ-terms in η-long β-normal form.

A quasi-ordering $\geq$ is said to be *well-founded* if there is no infinite sequence $s_1 > s_2 \ldots > s_i > \ldots$, where $>$ is the strict part of $\geq$.

A quasi-ordering is *stable under ground contexts* if for all $s, t \in \mathcal{T}(\mathcal{F}, \mathcal{X}){\downarrow}$, $u \in \mathcal{T}(\mathcal{F}){\downarrow}$ and positions p, $s > t$ implies $u[s]_p > u[t]_p$. A quasi-ordering is *stable under ground substitutions* if for all $s, t \in \mathcal{T}(\mathcal{F}, \mathcal{X}){\downarrow}$ and for all ground substitutions γ, $s > t$ implies $s\gamma{\downarrow} > t\gamma{\downarrow}$.

A *higher order reduction ordering (reduction ordering on higher-order terms)* is a well-founded ordering stable under ground contexts and substitutions. Such an ordering is of principal significance in proving termination of rewrite system.

We can consider lexicographic ($\langle s_1, \ldots, s_n \rangle \geq^{lex} \langle t_1, \ldots, t_n \rangle$ iff $s_1 \geq t_1, \ldots s_{i-1} \geq t_{i-1}, s_i > t_i$) and multiset (transitive closure of $\{s_1, \ldots, s_i, \ldots, s_n\} \gg \{s_1, \ldots, t_1, \ldots, t_m, \ldots s_n\}$ for $s > t_i$ for all $i \in [1 \ldots m]$) extensions of a reduction ordering. These are reduction orderings.

A quasi-ordering is *total* if any two ground terms are comparable.

Dealing with rewriting modulo AC we have to assure AC-compatibility of orderings in use. This means that whenever $s' =_{AC} s > t =_{AC} t'$ then $s' > t'$.

Now we are going to define several useful notions.

Definition 1. *A* top symbol *of a term is defined by* $T(f(s_1,\dots,s_n)) = f$ *for* $f \in \mathcal{F} \cup \mathcal{X}$ *and* $T(\lambda x^\sigma.s) = \lambda_{\sigma\to\tau}$ *if* $\lambda x^\sigma.s : \sigma \to \tau$.

A term v *is an* immediate subterm *of a term* u *if* $v \in st_\lambda(u)$, *where*

$$st_\lambda(u) = \begin{cases} \langle u_1,\dots,u_n\rangle \text{ if } u = f(u_1,\dots,u_n),\ f \in \mathcal{F}\cup\mathcal{X} \\ v\{x \mapsto \bot_\sigma\} \text{ if } u = \lambda x^\sigma.v,\ u : \sigma \to \tau \end{cases}$$

The subterm relation, *denoted by* $\trianglerighteq$, *is the transitive closure of the immediate subterm relation. In order not to confuse these subterms with standard ones we will write* $s|_p^\lambda$ *for the subterm of* s *at the position* p *according to* $\trianglerighteq$.

We are now in a position to recall the definition of λ-RPO ordering from [6]. λ-RPO is based on:

- precedence on types : quasi-ordering $\geq_{\mathcal{T}s}$ on types, well-founded and compatible with term structure (i.e., for all $s:\sigma, t:\tau \in \mathcal{T}(\mathcal{F},\mathcal{X})\!\downarrow$, such that $s \trianglerighteq t$ we have $\sigma \geq_{\mathcal{T}s} \tau$; for details and examples see [6]).
- function *status* associating symbol *Lex* (for lexicographic) or symbol *Mul* (for multiset) to every function symbol and such that $status(f) = Mul$ if and only if $f \in \mathcal{F}_{AC}$ (the "only if" assumption is made for notational simplicity).
- precedence on function symbols : well-founded quasi-ordering $\geq_\mathcal{F}$ on function symbols from $\lambda\mathcal{F}$ of the same (modulo $=_{\mathcal{T}s}$) output type. If $\alpha =_{\mathcal{T}s} \beta$ we put $\bot_\alpha =_\mathcal{F} \bot_\beta$ and $\lambda_\alpha =_\mathcal{F} \lambda_\beta$. $\bot_\alpha$ is always minimal, position of λ_α is arbitrary. $\geq_\mathcal{F}$ may equalise the symbols of the same status and arity only. Variables are not comparable with any other symbol.

For $s,t \in \mathcal{T}(\mathcal{F},\mathcal{X})\!\downarrow$ we let $s:\sigma \geq_{\lambda rpo} t:\tau$ iff

1. $\sigma >_{\mathcal{T}s} \tau$, or
2. $\sigma =_{\mathcal{T}s} \tau$, and
   (a) $T(s) \notin \mathcal{X}$ and $s_i \geq_{\lambda rpo} t$ for some $s_i \in st_\lambda(s)$, or
   (b) $T(s) >_\mathcal{F} T(t)$ and $s >_{\lambda rpo} t_i$ for all $t_i \in st_\lambda(s)$, or
   (c) $T(s) = T(t) \in \mathcal{F}_{AC}$ and $st_\lambda(s) \geq^{mul}_{\lambda rpo} st_\lambda(t)$, or
   (d) $T(s) = T(t) \notin \mathcal{F}_{AC}$ and $st_\lambda(s) \geq^{lex}_{\lambda rpo} st_\lambda(t)$ and $s >_{\lambda rpo} t_i$ for all $t_i \in st_\lambda(s)$, or
   (e) $T(s) = T(t) \in \mathcal{X}$ and $st_\lambda(s) =^{lex}_{Mul} st_\lambda(t)$,

where $s >_{\lambda rpo} t$ iff $s \geq_{\lambda rpo} t$ and $t \not\geq_{\lambda rpo} s$; $\geq^{mul}_{\lambda rpo}$, $\geq^{lex}_{\lambda rpo}$ are multiset and lexicographic extensions of $\geq_{\lambda rpo}$; and $=_{Mul}$ means that both sides are equal modulo permutations of equivalent arguments below AC-symbol.

λ-RPO is a higher-order reduction ordering. It is total if $\geq_\mathcal{F}$, $\geq_{\mathcal{T}s}$ are total. It will serve as a basis in our construction of AC-compatible reduction ordering on λ-terms.

Finally we define a notion of embedding and well-order on type.

Definition 2 (Embedding). *We write* $\langle s_1, \ldots, s_n\rangle \hookrightarrow_e \langle t_1, \ldots t_m\rangle$ *if there are indexes* $1 \le j_1 < j_2 < \ldots < j_m \le n$ *such that* $s_{j_i} \,{}_e\!\!\geq t_i$ *for* $i=1\ldots m$. *A term t is* embedded *in s* ($s\,{}_e\!\!\geq t$) *iff:*

1. $s_i\,{}_e\!\!\geq t$, *for some* $s_i \in st_\lambda(s)$, *or*
2. $T(s) =_{\mathcal{F}} T(t)$ *and* $st_\lambda(s) \hookrightarrow_e st_\lambda(t)$.

A quasi-ordering $\geq$ is a *well-order on type* if for every infinite sequence $(t_i)_{i\in\mathbb{N}}$ of terms of the same type there are indexes $k > l$ such that $t_k \geq t_l$. We leave without proof that $\mathcal{T}(\mathcal{F})\!\downarrow^n$ and $\mathcal{T}(\mathcal{F})\!\downarrow^*$ (tuples and words over $\mathcal{T}(\mathcal{F})\!\downarrow$) are well-ordered on type by $\hookrightarrow_e$.

3 The ordering

As it was mentioned in the introduction, comparing terms in AC-λ-RPO consist of two phases. First we have to calculate the interpretations of the terms. These are sets of normal forms in the auxiliary system — system R. Then we compare the interpretations using $\geq_{\lambda rpo}$.

3.1 System *R*

Following the notation from [10] we distinguish some symbols from $\lambda\mathcal{F}$ and call them *interpreted*, $\mathcal{F}_\mathcal{I}$. We assume that $\mathcal{F}_{AC} \subseteq \mathcal{F}_\mathcal{I}$ and that no λ_α belongs to it. The possibility of having in $\mathcal{F}_\mathcal{I}$ some symbols not from $\mathcal{F}_{AC}$ enriches the obtained family of orderings.

System R comes in two parts: rules for flattening and rules for interpreted symbols. As the latter make the system R non confluent it is necessary to work with sets of normal forms. We will write $snf_R(u)$ for the set of normal forms of u with respect to R and $mnf(u)$ for its maximal, in λ-RPO, normal form, which is unique if $u \in \mathcal{T}(\mathcal{F})\!\downarrow$ and both precedences are total.

Let us introduce two useful notations. Suppose that $f, g \in \lambda\mathcal{F}$ have output types σ and τ respectively. We write $f >_{\mathcal{T_S},\mathcal{F}} g$ iff $\sigma >_{\mathcal{T_S}} \tau$ or $\sigma =_{\mathcal{T_S}} \tau$ and $f >_\mathcal{F} g$.

A set of *Subterms of the Same Type* is defined by:

$$SST(f(s_1, \ldots s_n)) = \begin{cases} \{s_i \mid \alpha_i =_{\mathcal{T_S}} \alpha\} & \text{if } f : \alpha_1 \times \ldots \times \alpha_n \to \alpha \\ & \text{and there is an } \alpha_i =_{\mathcal{T_S}} \alpha \\ \{\bot_\alpha\} & \text{if no such } \alpha_i \text{ exists} \end{cases}$$

$$SST(\lambda x^\sigma.s) \quad = \begin{cases} \{s\{x \mapsto \bot_\sigma\}\} & \text{if } \tau =_{\mathcal{T_S}} \sigma \to \tau \\ \{\bot_{\sigma\to\tau}\} & \text{otherwise} \end{cases}$$

System R:

(flat)

$$f(x_1, \ldots x_m, g(y_1, \ldots y_r), z_1, \ldots z_n) \longrightarrow_R f(x_1, \ldots x_m, y_1, \ldots y_r, z_1, \ldots z_n)$$

for $f \in \mathcal{F}_{AC}$ and $g =_\mathcal{F} f$,

(inter)

– $f(x_1, \ldots, x_m, g(y_1, \ldots, y_r), z_1, \ldots, z_n) \longrightarrow_R f(x_1, \ldots, x_m, a, z_1, \ldots, z_n)$ for $f \in \mathcal{F}_\mathcal{I}$, $f >_{T_S,\mathcal{F}} g$ and $a \in SST(g(y_1, \ldots, y_r))$,

– $f(x_1, \ldots, x_m, \lambda y^\sigma.Y y, z_1, \ldots, z_n) \longrightarrow_R f(x_1, \ldots, x_m, a, z_1, \ldots, z_n)$ for $f \in \mathcal{F}_\mathcal{I}$, $f >_{T_S,\mathcal{F}} \lambda_{\sigma\to\tau}$ and $a \in SST(\lambda y^\sigma.Y y)$.

The fact that we use the same constant $\bot$ both, in the subterm definition (cf. Definition 1) and in the definition of the system R is not essential to our work. All we need in the definition of the subterm is to prevent a variable that was bound from being substituted. For this purpose we could use any other constant instead of $\bot$. The other solution would be to syntactically separate free and bound variables and introduce loose bound variables (as it is done in [9]). In the definition of system R we really need $\bot$ as it is the smallest (in $\geq_\mathcal{F}$) element of the given output type (see the precedence on function symbols in the definition of λ-RPO).

Lemma 1. *The relation $\longrightarrow_R$ is included in $\geq_{\lambda rpo}$, hence terminating.*

Even though $\longrightarrow_R$ is not confluent we still have confluence for computing snf_R.

Lemma 2 (Confluence for computing snf_R).

$$snf_R(t[l\gamma]) = snf_R(t[r_1\gamma]) \cup \ldots \cup snf_R(t[r_n\gamma])$$

where γ is a substitution and $\{r_1, \ldots, r_n\}$ is the set of right-hand sides of all rules in R with left-hand side equal to l.

Proof. We begin by proving strong normalisation and confluence of the following rewriting of sets:

$$S \cup \{t[l\gamma]\} \longrightarrow_{SR} S \cup \{t[r_1\gamma], \ldots, t[r_n\gamma]\}$$

where γ, $r_1, \ldots, r_n$ are as above.

Strong normalisation of $\longrightarrow_{SR}$ is a consequence of the strong normalisation of $\geq_{\lambda rpo}$. Since by Newmann's lemma local confluence for terminating relation implies confluence, it remains to analyse all possible overlappings of redexes.

The proof is completed by showing that given term t, term s belongs to $snf_R(t)$ if and only if s belongs to SR-normal form of $\{t\}$. Both implications can be proved by a routine induction. □

3.2 Definition of AC-λ-RPO

For a given term u let us apply the rules of **(flat)** at the root position as long as possible. Call the result v. Then $st_\lambda(v)$ is the *top-flattening* of u (denoted by $tf(u)$).

Suppose we are given a λ-RPO with total precedences on types and function symbols. We define our AC-λ-RPO ordering ($\succ$) on $\mathcal{T}(\mathcal{F},\mathcal{X})\downarrow$ by $s \succ t$ iff

1. $\forall t' \in snf_R(t)\ \exists s' \in snf_R(s)$, such that $s' >_{\lambda rpo} t'$, or
2. $\forall t' \in snf_R(t)\ \exists s' \in snf_R(s)$, such that $s' \geq_{\lambda rpo} t'$, and
   (a) $T(s) \in F_{AC}$ and $tf(s) \succ^{mul} tf(t)$, or
   (b) $T(s) \notin F_{AC}$ and $tf(s) \succ^{lex} tf(t)$,

where $\succ^{mul}$, $\succ^{lex}$ are lexicographic and multiset AC-extensions of $\succ$ (it is left to the reader to verify that the case 2(b) is correct, i.e. the numbers of arguments of s and t are equal if s and t do not satisfy the case 1 and $T(s) \notin \mathcal{F}_{AC}$).

Note that if $s, t \in \mathcal{T}(\mathcal{F})\downarrow$, we can simply replace the first case of the above definition by $mnf(s) >_{\lambda rpo} mnf(t)$ and the second case by $mnf(s) \geq_{\lambda rpo} mnf(t)$.

4 Results

In this Section we show that AC-λ-RPO is an AC-compatible higher-order reduction ordering. To this end we proceed with the study of its properties.

It is easy to see that $\succ$ is irreflexive and transitive. The proof of AC-compatibility is little bit more involved. It is based on the observation that AC-equal terms have identical snf_Rs and AC-equal tfs (up to the permutation of arguments below AC-symbol). The desired conclusion is established by induction on term's size.

4.1 Subterm and deletion properties

Although subterm and deletion properties are not explicitly needed for our main result, it turns out that they will be extremely useful in all consecutive subsections. We begin by recalling that we have slightly modified the definition of subterm (cf. Definition 1).

We say that a quasi-ordering $\geq$ has the *subterm property* if for every $s_i \in st_\lambda(s)$ we have $s > s_i$. An easy verification shows that λ-RPO has the subterm property on $\mathcal{T}(\mathcal{F})\downarrow$. A subterm property of $\succ$ is an easy consequence of the following lemma.

Lemma 3. *For any $s \in \mathcal{T}(\mathcal{F})\downarrow$ and $t \in st_\lambda(s)$ we have $mnf(s) >_{\lambda rpo} mnf(t)$.*

Lemma 4 (Deletion property). *For each symbol $f \in \mathcal{F}_{AC}$, $f(v,t,u) \succ f(v,u)$.*

4.2 Monotonicity

Monotonicity is a basis of the stability under context and well-foundedness of AC-λ-RPO.

The unusual form of this property is due to the definition of subterm and the way λ-RPO treats an abstraction. Since when taking an immediate subterm of $\lambda x^\sigma.s$ we replace x by $\perp_\sigma$, we can reconstruct it while applying a context. The other reason for choosing such formulation is the simplicity of notation (see the definition of $c\langle - \rangle$ below).

Definition 3 (Closure by λ-context). *The* closure by λ-context *of the term s, denoted by $\lambda x^\sigma.\hat{s}$, is defined to be any term $\lambda x^\sigma.w$ such that $w\{x_\sigma \mapsto \bot_\sigma\} = s$. Note that all closures by λ-context of a given term are $=_{\lambda rpo}$ equal.*

Example 1. Set $s = f(\bot_\sigma, h(\bot_\sigma))$. Then $\lambda x^\sigma.f(\bot_\sigma, h(\bot_\sigma))$, $\lambda x^\sigma.f(x^\sigma, h(\bot_\sigma))$, $\lambda x^\sigma.f(\bot_\sigma, h(x^\sigma))$, $\lambda x^\sigma.f(x^\sigma, h(x^\sigma))$ are its closures by λ-context.

Definition 4 (Monotonicity). *Let $s,t \in \mathcal{T}(\mathcal{F})\!\downarrow$ be terms of the same type σ. We call an irreflexive and transitive relation $>$* monotone *if $s > t$ implies $f(\ldots s \ldots) > f(\ldots t \ldots)$ and $\lambda x^\sigma.\hat{s} > \lambda x^\sigma.\hat{t}$ for $f(\ldots s \ldots), f(\ldots t \ldots) \in \mathcal{T}(\mathcal{F})\!\downarrow$ and $\lambda x^\sigma.\hat{s}, \lambda x^\sigma.\hat{t}$ defined as in Definition 3.*

We write $c\langle u\rangle$ for the closure of u by either $\mathcal{F}$- or λ-context.

An easy computation shows that $>_{\lambda rpo}$ is monotone. To prove the monotonicity of $\succ$ we need to know when $>_{\lambda rpo}$ between *mnf*s is preserved under addition of a context.

Lemma 5. *Let $s,t \in \mathcal{T}(\mathcal{F})\!\downarrow$ be terms of the same type σ, and let $c\langle - \rangle$ be a ground $\mathcal{F}$- or λ-context. Then:*

$$mnf(s) \geq_{\lambda rpo} mnf(t) \Longrightarrow mnf(c\langle s\rangle) \geq_{\lambda rpo} mnf(c\langle t\rangle)$$
$$mnf(s) >_{\lambda rpo} mnf(t) \Longrightarrow mnf(c\langle s\rangle) >_{\lambda rpo} mnf(c\langle t\rangle) \quad \textit{if} \quad T(s) \geq_{T_S,\mathcal{F}} T(c)$$

Lemma 6. *$\succ$ is monotone.*

Proof. $s \succ t$ means that $mnf(s) \geq_{\lambda rpo} mnf(t)$. This implies, by the lemma above, that $mnf(c\langle s\rangle) \geq_{\lambda rpo} mnf(c\langle t\rangle)$. If this inequality is strict then $c\langle s\rangle \succ c\langle t\rangle$ obviously holds. So we are left with the case when $mnf(c\langle s\rangle) =_{\lambda rpo} mnf(c\langle t\rangle)$.

1. $T(c) \notin \mathcal{F}_{AC}$. Since $tf(c\langle s\rangle) = \langle u,s,v\rangle \succ^{lex} \langle u,t,v\rangle = tf(c\langle t\rangle)$ we conclude that $c\langle s\rangle \succ c\langle t\rangle$ by case 2(b) of the definition of $\succ$,
2. $T(c) \in \mathcal{F}_{AC}$ and $mnf(s) >_{\lambda rpo} mnf(t)$. If $T(s) \geq_{T_S,\mathcal{F}} T(c)$ then by Lemma 5 we get $mnf(c\langle s\rangle) >_{\lambda rpo} mnf(c\langle t\rangle)$. Otherwise $tf(c\langle s\rangle) = \langle u,s,v\rangle$, while $tf(c\langle t\rangle)$ is equal to either $\langle u,t,v\rangle$ or $\langle u,t_1\ldots t_k,v\rangle$, where t_i are proper subterms of t. In both cases $tf(c\langle s\rangle) \succ^{mul} tf(c\langle t\rangle)$ since $s \succ t$, $t \succ t_i$, $s \succ t_i$. Thus, by the case 2(a) of the definition of $\succ$, we have $c\langle s\rangle \succ c\langle t\rangle$,
3. $T(c) \in \mathcal{F}_{AC}$ and $mnf(s) =_{\lambda rpo} mnf(t)$. Note that this forces $T(s) =_{\mathcal{F}} T(t)$. If $T(s) \neq_{\mathcal{F}} T(c)$ we have $tf(c\langle s\rangle) = \langle u,s,v\rangle \succ^{mul} \langle u,t,v\rangle = tf(c\langle t\rangle)$. Otherwise $tf(c\langle s\rangle) = \langle u,s_1,\ldots s_n,v\rangle$ and $tf(c\langle t\rangle) = \langle u,t_1,\ldots t_k,v\rangle$. But $\{s_1\ldots s_n\} \succ^{mul} \{t_1\ldots t_k\}$ since $s \succ t$ and $mnf(s) =_{\lambda rpo} mnf(t)$. Hence $tf(c\langle s\rangle) \succ^{mul} tf(c\langle t\rangle)$ and consequently $c\langle s\rangle \succ c\langle t\rangle$. □

Using Lemma 6, by induction on the size of the context we get:

Corollary 7. *$\succ$ is stable under ground contexts.*

4.3 Well-foundedness

To show the well-foundedness of AC-λ-RPO we will formulate an analogue of Kruskal's theorem. This theorem states that the relation of embedding is a well-order on ground terms. In our case we have to replace well-order by well-order on type and ground terms by ground normalised terms, but the main idea remains the same.

Lemma 8. *Suppose that the precedences on types and function symbols are total and well-founded and that $\geq_{\mathcal{T}_S}$ is compatible with term structure. Then the relation of embedding $\,_{\scriptscriptstyle e}\!\!\geq$ is a well-order on type on $\mathcal{T}(\mathcal{F})\downarrow$.*

Lemma 9. *Let $s, t \in \mathcal{T}(\mathcal{F})\downarrow$. If $s \,_{\scriptscriptstyle e}\!\!\geq t$, then $s \succ t$ or $s =_{AC} t$.*

Proof. By induction on $|s| + |t|$ considering the way $s \,_{\scriptscriptstyle e}\!\!\geq t$ was shown: (cf. Definition 2 in Subsection 2.3)

- $s \,_{\scriptscriptstyle e}\!\!\geq t$ by the first part of the definition. Then there is an $s_i \in st_\lambda(s)$ such that $s_i \,_{\scriptscriptstyle e}\!\!\geq t$. By inductive hypothesis we have either $s_i \succ t$, or $s_i =_{AC} t$. The latter gives $s \succ t$ since $\succ$ is AC-compatible, the former does so by the subterm property ($s \succ s_i$) and transitivity of $\succ$.
- $s \,_{\scriptscriptstyle e}\!\!\geq t$ by the second part. Then for every $t_i \in st_\lambda(t)$ there is an $s_{j_i} \in st_\lambda(s)$ such that $s_{j_i} \,_{\scriptscriptstyle e}\!\!\geq t_i$ and $j_k < j_{k+1}$ for all k. Inductive hypothesis yields either $s_{j_i} \succ t_i$, or $s_{j_i} =_{AC} t_i$. Applying Lemma 6 (monotonicity) and Lemma 4 (deletion property — in case of different number of arguments) we obtain our claim. □

Corollary 10. *$\succ$ is well-founded on $\mathcal{T}(\mathcal{F})\downarrow$.*

Proof. Suppose that there is an infinite sequence $(u_i : \tau_i)_{i \in \mathbb{N}}$ decreasing in $\succ$. Since $s : \sigma \succ t : \tau$ implies $\sigma \geq_{\mathcal{T}_S} \tau$ the sequence $(\tau_i)_{i \in \mathbb{N}}$ is constant from a certain position, because $>_{\mathcal{T}_S}$ is well-founded. Considering $(u_i)_{i \in \mathbb{N}}$ from this position we can use Lemma 8 to obtain two indexes $k > l$ such that $u_k \,_{\scriptscriptstyle e}\!\!\geq u_l$. Previous lemma now yields $u_k \succ u_l$ or $u_k =_{AC} u_l$. Hence a contradiction. □

4.4 Stability under ground substitutions

Throughout this Subsection we consider only ground and normalised substitutions. Before we begin note that if $s >_{\lambda rpo} t$ or $s \succ t$ then $T(s) \notin \mathcal{X}$.

Lemma 11. *Let s, t be terms from $\mathcal{T}(\mathcal{F}, \mathcal{X})$ such that $s =_{AC} t$, and γ be a ground substitution. Then $s\gamma\downarrow =_{AC} t\gamma\downarrow$.*

Lemma 12. *Given $s, t \in \mathcal{T}(\mathcal{F}, \mathcal{X})\downarrow$ in R-normal form suppose that γ is a ground substitution. Then:*

$$s >_{\lambda rpo} t \Longrightarrow mnf(s\gamma\downarrow) >_{\lambda rpo} mnf(t\gamma\downarrow) \ .$$

Lemma 13. *Given $s, t \in \mathcal{T}(\mathcal{F}, \mathcal{X})\downarrow$ and a ground substitution γ, suppose that $s \succ t$. Then $s\gamma\downarrow \succ t\gamma\downarrow$.*

Proof. By induction on $|s|+|t|$ considering the proof of $s \succ t$.

1. $\forall t' \in snf_R(t)\ \exists s' \in snf_R(s)$ such that $s' >_{\lambda rpo} t'$. By Lemma 12 we have $mnf(s'\gamma\downarrow) >_{\lambda rpo} mnf(t'\gamma\downarrow)$, hence $mnf(s\gamma\downarrow) >_{\lambda rpo} mnf(t\gamma\downarrow)$ and $s\gamma\downarrow \succ t\gamma\downarrow$.
2. $\forall t' \in snf_R(t)\ \exists s' \in snf_R(s)$ such that $s' \geq_{\lambda rpo} t'$. Therefore $T(s) =_{\mathcal{F}} T(t)$ and $T(s) \notin \mathcal{X}$. By Lemma 12 we have $mnf(s'\gamma\downarrow) \geq_{\lambda rpo} mnf(t'\gamma\downarrow)$. Let $tf(s) = \langle s_1, \dots, s_n \rangle$, $tf(t) = \langle t_1, \dots, t_m \rangle$.
   (a) $T(s) \notin \mathcal{F}_{AC}$. Then $n = m$ and there is a k such that $s_k \succ t_k$ and $s_j =_{AC} t_j$ for $j = 1 \dots (k-1)$. By induction hypothesis and by Lemma 11 we have $s_k\gamma\downarrow \succ t_k\gamma\downarrow$ and $s_j\gamma\downarrow =_{AC} t_j\gamma\downarrow$ for $j = 1 \dots (k-1)$. This implies $s\gamma\downarrow \succ t\gamma\downarrow$.
   (b) $T(s) \in \mathcal{F}_{AC}$. Then for every $t_i \in tf(t)$ there is an $s_j \in tf(s)$ such that either $s_j =_{AC} t_i$ or $s_j \succ t_i$. It remains to determine dependences between rests of $s_j\gamma\downarrow$ and $t_i\gamma\downarrow$ in $tf(s\gamma\downarrow)$, $tf(t\gamma\downarrow)$. If $s_j =_{AC} t_i$ then these rests also are AC-equal. Otherwise $s_j \succ t_i$ and of course $T(s_j) \notin \mathcal{X}$. If also $T(t_i) \notin \mathcal{X}$ then in $tf(s\gamma\downarrow)$, $tf(t\gamma\downarrow)$ we have $s_j\gamma\downarrow$ and $t_i\gamma\downarrow$ which are obviously oriented by induction hypothesis. If $T(t_i) \in \mathcal{X}$ then $t_i\gamma\downarrow$ may give rise to many terms u_i in $tf(t\gamma\downarrow)$. But $\{s_j\gamma\downarrow\} \succ^{mul} \{u_i\}$ since $s_j\gamma\downarrow \succ t_i\gamma\downarrow$. Therefore $tf(s\gamma\downarrow) \succ^{mul} tf(t\gamma\downarrow)$ and $s\gamma\downarrow \succ t\gamma\downarrow$. □

4.5 Main Result

Having proved all the properties that make AC-λ-RPO an AC-compatible reduction ordering on higher-order terms in β-normal η-long form we can now formulate our main result.

Theorem 1. *Let H be a higher-order rewriting system modulo AC on normalised terms. If for every rule $l \to r$ of H we have $l \succ r$, then H is terminating.*

Proof. Suppose, on the contrary, that we have an infinite sequence $(u_i)_{i \in \mathbb{N}}$ in $\longrightarrow_H$. Substituting $\bot_\sigma$ for every free variable x^σ we can make $(u_i)_{i\in\mathbb{N}}$ ground. We now proceed to show that $(u_i)_{i\in\mathbb{N}}$ is decreasing with respect to $\succ$.

A rewrite step $s \xrightarrow[l \to r]{p} t$ means that $s|_p =_{AC} l\rho\downarrow$, $t =_{AC} s[r\rho\downarrow]_p$, and consequently that $s|_p^\lambda = l\rho\delta\downarrow$ where δ substitutes $\bot_\sigma$ for every free variable x^σ in $s|_p$. Note that $\rho\delta$ is a ground normalised substitution. We have $l\rho\delta\downarrow \succ r\rho\delta\downarrow$ by stability under ground substitutions (Lemma 13) and $s\langle l\rho\delta\downarrow\rangle_p \succ s\langle r\rho\delta\downarrow\rangle_p$ by stability under ground contexts (Corollary 7). As $s =_{AC} s\langle l\rho\delta\downarrow\rangle_p$ and $t =_{AC} s\langle r\rho\delta\downarrow\rangle_p$ we get by AC-compatibility $s \succ t$. Thus every infinite sequence in $\longrightarrow_H$ yields an infinite sequence decreasing in $\succ$ contradicting the well-foundedness of $\succ$ (Corollary 10). □

Finally let us note that AC-λ-RPO is a total ordering, that is for any $s, t \in \mathcal{T}(\mathcal{F})\downarrow$ one of $s =_{AC} t$, $s \succ t$, $t \succ s$ holds. Totality of AC-λ-RPO is a simple consequence of totality of λ-RPO which follows from the totality of precedences on types and function symbols.

5 Examples

5.1 Map on non empty sets

The following rewriting system implements the function *map* on non empty sets of integers; *map* takes a function from integers to integers and a set, and applies this function to every element of the set. There are two basic types: *Int* and *Set* and two constructors of sets: *union* and *sing* (singleton). Of course *union* is an AC-symbol. S is a variable of type *Set*, n of type *Int* and X of type $Int \to Int$.

$$map(\lambda x^{Int}.Xx, sing(n)) \longrightarrow sing(Xn)$$
$$map(\lambda x^{Int}.Xx, union(sing(n), S)) \longrightarrow union(sing(Xn), map(\lambda x^{Nat}.Xx, S)$$

To show the termination of this system consider RPO with $Set >_{\mathcal{T}_S} Int >_{\mathcal{T}_S} \to$ as a precedence on types and a precedence on function symbols where $map >_{\mathcal{F}} union >_{\mathcal{F}} sing$.

Analyse only the second rule. The $snf_{\mathcal{R}}$s of its left- and right-hand side are equal to $\{map(\lambda x^{Int}.Xx, union(\perp_{Set}, S))\}$ and $\{union(\perp_{Set}, map(\lambda x^{Int}.Xx, S)\}$ respectively. Applying case 2(b) of the definition of λ-RPO it remains to show

$$map(\lambda x^{Int}.Xx, union(\perp_{Set}, S)) >_{\lambda rpo} \perp_{Set}$$
$$map(\lambda x^{Int}.Xx, union(\perp_{Set}, S)) >_{\lambda rpo} map(\lambda x^{Int}.Xx, S)$$

Both inequalities hold, because $\perp_{Set}$ is a subterm of the right-hand side and the multiset $\{\lambda x^{Int}.Xx, union(\perp_{Set}, S)\}$ is strictly greater than $\{\lambda x^{Int}.Xx, S\}$.

5.2 Some Normalisation Procedures in First-Order Logic

We have two basic types: t (terms), f (formulae) and the constants: $\vee, \wedge, \neg, \exists, \forall$. Quantifiers take as an argument a function from terms to formulae and return a formula.

$$\mathcal{S} = \{t, f\} \qquad \begin{aligned} \mathcal{F}_{f\to f} &= \{\neg\} \\ \mathcal{F}_{f\times f\to f} &= \{\vee, \wedge\} \\ \mathcal{F}_{(t\to f)\to f} &= \{\forall, \exists\} \end{aligned} \qquad \begin{aligned} \mathcal{X}_f &= \{P, Q\} \\ \mathcal{X}_{t\to f} &= \{P', Q'\} \\ \mathcal{F}_{AC} &= \{\vee, \wedge\} \end{aligned}$$

We consider two rewriting systems from [8].

Negation Normal Form.

$$\begin{aligned} \neg\neg P &\longrightarrow P \\ \neg(P \wedge Q) &\longrightarrow \neg P \vee \neg Q \\ \neg(P \vee Q) &\longrightarrow \neg P \wedge \neg Q \\ \neg(\forall(\lambda x^t.P'x)) &\longrightarrow \exists(\lambda x^t.\neg(P'x)) \\ \neg(\exists(\lambda x^t.P'x)) &\longrightarrow \forall(\lambda x^t.\neg(P'x)) \end{aligned}$$

We choose the following precedences: all types are equal in $\geq_{\mathcal{T}_S}$ and $\{\vee, \wedge\} >_{\mathcal{F}} \{\neg\} >_{\mathcal{F}} \{\exists, \forall\} >_{\mathcal{F}} \{\lambda_{t\to f}\}$. We set $\mathcal{F}_{\mathcal{I}} = \mathcal{F}_{AC}$.

Let us consider only the second rule. The snf_Rs of its left- and right-hand side are equal to $\neg(P \wedge Q)$ and $P \vee Q$ respectively and the inequality $\neg(P \wedge Q) >_{\lambda rpo} P \vee Q$ holds because $\vee =_{\mathcal{F}} \wedge$.

Mini-Scoping.

$$\forall \lambda x^t.P \longrightarrow P$$
$$\forall \lambda x^t.(P'x \wedge Q'x) \longrightarrow (\forall \lambda x^t.P'x) \wedge (\forall \lambda x^t.Q'x)$$
$$\forall \lambda x^t.(P'x \vee Q) \longrightarrow (\forall \lambda x^t.P'x) \vee Q$$

To show the termination of this system we take the same $\geq_{\mathcal{T}_S}, \geq_{\mathcal{F}}$ as above. It is easy to verify that all left-hand sides of the rules are strictly greater than right-hand sides.

Acknowledgement

The paper was written during my DEA studies at the University of Paris-Sud. I would like to thank my supervisor, professor Jean-Pierre Jouannaud, for his helpful comments, critiques and suggestions.

References

1. Henk Barendregt *Handbook of Theoretical Computer Science*, volume B, chapter Functional Programming and Lambda Calculus, pages 321–364. North-Holland, 1990. J. van Leeuwen ed.
2. Henk Barendregt *Handbook of Logic in Computer Science*, chapter Typed lambda calculi. Oxford Univ. Press, 1993. eds Abramsky et al.
3. Nachum Dershowitz and Jean-Pierre Jouannaud. Rewrite systems. In J. van Leeuwen, editor, *Handbook of Theoretical Computer Science*, volume B, pages 243–309. North-Holland, 1990.
4. Jean-Pierre Jouannaud and Mitsuhiro Okada. Inductive data type systems. Technical report, Université de Paris Sud, 1996. submitted.
5. Jean-Pierre Jouannaud and Mitsuhiro Okada. Abstract data type systems. *Theoretical Computer Science*, 173(2):349–391, February 1997.
6. Jean-Pierre Jouannaud and Albert Rubio. A recursive path ordering for higher-order terms in η-long β-normal form. In Ganzinger H., editor, *Proc. 7th Rewriting Techniques and Applications, New-Jersey, LNCS 1103.* Springer-Verlag, 1996.
7. Dallas S. Lankford and A. M. Ballantyne. Decision procedures for simple equational theories with permutative axioms: Complete sets of permutative reductions. Research Report Memo ATP-37, Department of Mathematics and Computer Science, University of Texas, Austin, Texas, USA, August 1977.
8. Tobias Nipkow. Higher order critical pairs. In *Proc. IEEE Symp. on Logic in Comp. Science*, Amsterdam, 1991.
9. Tobias Nipkow. Functional Unification of Higher-Order Patterns. In *Proc. 8th IEEE Symp. Logic in Computer Science*, pages 64-74, 1993.
10. Albert Rubio and Robert Nieuwenhuis. A total AC-compatible ordering based on RPO. *Theoretical Computer Science*, 142(2):209–227, May 15, 1995.

Model Checking Game Properties of Multi-agent Systems

Thomas A. Henzinger

Electrical Engineering and Computer Sciences
University of California, Berkeley

Temporal logics are traditionally interpreted over Kripke structures, and model checking is traditionally performed by traversing Kripke structures. A Kripke structure represents the states and transitions of a system. In a multi-agent system, which consists of several processes or components, a single transition may result from simultaneous choices made by the individual agents of the system. Since the choices of agents are not represented within Kripke structures, the expressive power of traditional temporal logics is limited. These logics can express universal properties for the case that the agents interact adversarially (such as "no matter what any agent does, predicate p remains always true") and, in branching time, existential properties for the case that the agents cooperate (such as "all agents can collaborate to keep p true"). However, they cannot express properties about games between teams of agents, such as "agent SENDER and agent RECEIVER can collaborate to keep p true no matter what agent INTRUDER does." This property asserts that in a game in which SENDER and RECEIVER play together against INTRUDER, they have a strategy to keep the predicate p true.

We show how the ingredients of the traditional model-checking framework can be extended to game properties:

- Kripke structures are replaced by *alternating transition structures.* In an alternating transition structure, at every state, each agent suggests a set of possible successor states, and the next state is taken from the intersection of all suggestions.
- Traditional temporal logics are replaced by *alternating temporal logics.* Alternating temporal logics have quantifiers that assert the existence of winning strategies in games between teams of agents.
- In many interesting cases, model-checking algorithms can answer the question if a given state of an alternating transition structure satisfies a given formula of an alternating temporal logic. In particular, for the simple alternating temporal logic called ATL, model checking can be performed in linear time, as well as symbolically.

This talk is based on joint work with Rajeev Alur and Orna Kupferman. Some of the results can be found in [1].

[1] Rajeev Alur, Thomas A. Henzinger, Orna Kupferman, "Alternating-time temporal logic," *Proceedings of the 38th Annual IEEE Symposium on Foundations of Computer Science*, 1997, pp. 100–109.

Limited Wavelength Conversion in All-Optical Tree Networks

Luisa Gargano

Dipartimento di Informatica, Università di Salerno, 84081 Baronissi (SA), Italy.

Abstract. Let T be a symmetric directed tree, i.e., a tree with each edge viewed as two opposite directed links. We consider the problem of routing arbitrary sets of connection requests in T. In all-optical communication tree networks with WDM (wavelength-division multiplexing) this is equivalent to color a given set of directed paths so that no two directed paths of the same color use the same link of T. Let W be the number of available wavelengths. The load, that is, the maximum number of directed paths passing through a link of T cannot exceed W. If there is no wavelength conversion available then each request (directed path) is restricted to a single wavelength and it is known that the minimum number of colors needed to color any set of directed paths in a tree is lower bounded away from the load L of the paths on the tree; moreover, no algorithm is known that uses a number of colors less than $5L/3$. The presence of wavelength converters allows to overcome this limits. The complexity of converters is measured by the maximum degree, which represents the maximum number of possible conversions of any given wavelength. We show that it is possible to route any set of requests of load $L \leq W(1-\epsilon)$, where ϵ depends only on the degree of the converters. Moreover, we show that in any tree it is possible to route any set of requests of load $L \leq W$ with converters of degree $O(\sqrt{W})$. In case of trees containing at most one node of degree ≥ 4 we show that converters of degree 3 already allow to route any set of requests of load $L \leq W$.

1 Introduction

We consider the problem of efficiently routing arbitrary sets of connection requests in all–optical WDM-routed tree networks in which limited wavelength conversion is allowed.

Optical networks are emerging as key technology in communication networks and are expected to dominate many applications, such as video conferencing, scientific visualisation, real-time medical imaging, high–speed super-computing and distributed computing [14, 23, 26]. The books of Green [14] and McAulay [19] offer a comprehensive overview of the physical theory and applications of this emerging technology. Wavelength–division multiplexing (WDM) is used to exploit the high bandwidth of fiber–optic links which support the concurrent propagation of multiple laser beams through a single fiber–optic link provided that each laser beam uses a distinct optical wavelength. All–optical networks exploit photonic technology for the implementation of both switching and transmission functions, [?], and maintain the signal in optical form through the transmission, thus allowing for much higher data transmission rates. Such an approach allows the elimination of the "electronic bottleneck" of communications networks with electronic switching.

In routing in an all-optical network one needs to set up a number of communications (paths) between given pairs of nodes, with each path being assigned one particular wavelength, and all paths sharing a link having different wavelengths. Specifically, one is given a set of requests $(a_1, b_1), (a_2, b_2), \ldots, (a_k, b_k)$, and is required to connect each a_i to the corresponding b_i by a path P_i, and assign wavelengths to each P_i so that paths of the same wavelength do not share an optical link. The minimum number of wavelengths necessary for routing a set of requests is considered of importance in evaluating the competitiveness of the wavelength division multiplexing technology [20]. The problem of selecting the paths and assigning wavelengths is not trivial even in the simplest networks like trees and rings [11, 27]. A survey of graph theoretic problems associated with routing in optical networks can be found in [7].

The interest in trees is due to the fact tree-like networks are standard in the telecommunications industry [20]. Trees free us from one half of the problem - that of choosing the actual paths for connecting the required nodes (since in a tree these paths are unique). Let T be a symmetric directed tree. For each pair of nodes x, y in T, the *dipath* $P(x, y)$ is the only directed path joining x to y in T. One has to assign wavelengths to a set (or multiset) S of dipaths in T in such a way that two dipaths using the same optical link of T obtain different wavelengths. Let W_S denote the minimum possible number of wavelengths in such an assignment to the dipaths in S and let L_S denote the maximum number of dipaths in S which all pass through the same link of T. Clearly $L_S \leq W_S$ for every tree T and every set of requests S on T. It has been proved in [12] that if S is the set of all paths on T then $L_S = W_S$. Moreover, the equality $L_S = W_S$ holds for every S if and only if T has at most one node of degree larger than 2 [12]. The determination of W_S is NP-hard [11] and it is known that there are instances for which $W_S/L_S \geq 5/4$ [16]. Several authors [16, 15] have considered the problem of designing algorithms for minimizing the number of wavelengths used to route a set of requests of load L_S, the best bound known is $5L_S/3$. Therefore, if a dipath must employ the same wavelength on each of its links then it is possible to accommodate only requests which impose on the network a load which can be at most 5/3 the number of available wavelengths. This is a serious drawback since wavelengths are a costly and scarce resource.

Limited Wavelength Conversion. If the wavelength assigned to a path can change from one link to another it is possible to get a substantial improvement on the ratio between the maximum possible load and the number of available wavelengths.

In all-optical networks wavelength translation can be obtained by means of (optical) converters. A converter can be seen as a bipartite graph $G = (A \cup B, E)$ in which the two sets, A and B represent the input and output wavelengths, respectively; there is an edge between $a \in A$ and $b \in B$ if and only if a signal arriving in input on wavelength a can be send in output on the wavelength b.

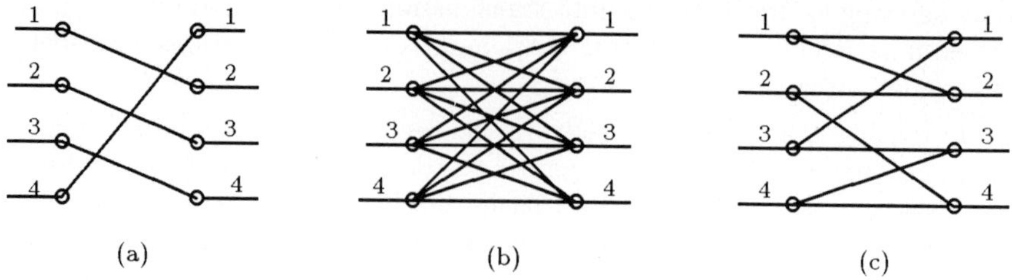

Figure 1: Examples of different types of converters on 4 wavelengths: (a) is a fixed converter, (b) is a full converter, (c) is converter of degree 2

It is known that for each network, if we use a sufficient number of full converters, in which every input wavelength can be translated into every output wavelength, then we can accommodate any set of requests whose load does not exceed the number of wavelengths [27]. However, the complexity and then the cost of the converters is strictly depending on its degree (intended in the usual sense of the maximum degree of the graph G that represents the converter). Networks with limited wavelength conversion will be less costly to implement than networks with full conversion capability. Moreover, in all-optical networks where the conversion is done without transforming the optical signal into electronic form, the conversion efficiency is a strong function of the input and output wavelengths, thus leading to limited conversion capability [22]. Different types of conversion are illustrated in Figure 1.

Related Work. Much work has been recently devoted to the problem of routing in all–optical networks, see for example [1, 4, 9, 11, 5, 21, 22]. A survey of graph theoretic problems associated with routing in optical networks can be found in [7]. Routing in all–optical tree-like networks has also received much attention [20, 15, 16, 12]. A good deal of work has been recently devoted to WDM-routing with converters, see for example [13, 22, 24, 27, 28]. WDM-routing with converters in trees has been considered in [2] and [3]. In these papers the authors mainly focus on binary trees. They show that the number of wavelengths n needed to route a request on a binary tree can be made near to the load L, i.e., $L(1+\epsilon) < n$, with converters of degree depending on ϵ; moreover, always in binary trees, they prove that the equality $L = n$ can be obtained using converters of degree logarithmic in L. For the case of general trees it is shown in [3] that it is possible to use $3L/2$ wavelengths if nodes have converters of degree poly–logarithmic in L,

Summary of results. We study the problem of efficiently routing any set of requests on a tree T with limited conversion capacity. Here and in the following, efficiency is intended as synonymous of polynomial time.

In Section 2 we introduce expander graphs and derive some results that will be useful to study the effectiveness of our routing algorithms.

In Section 3 we study the problem of routing requests on a general tree with converters of constant degree, that is, converters are independent both from the tree and the set of request, and their degree is independent from the number of available wavelengths. We show that in this setting it is possible to accommodate requests that induce on the tree a load arbitrary close to the number of available wavelengths. Namely, we prove that

Theorem 1.1 *For each $\epsilon > 0$ there exists k such that using (explicitly constructible) converters of degree k on n wavelengths, for any tree T it is possible to efficiently route any set of request of load L whenever $L \leq n(1-\epsilon)-1$.*

In Section 3.1 we show that the number of converters we use on the tree is almost minimum.

In Section 3.3 we consider the problem of minimizing the degree of the converters in case we want to accommodate any request of load equal to the number n of wavelength and show that $O(\sqrt{n})$ is sufficient.

In Section 4 we turn our attention to the special case of trees in which at most one node has degree greater than or equal to 4, we call them *quasi–binary trees.* We show that in any quasi–binary tree it is possible to route any set of requests of load equal to the number n of wavelength using constant degree converters. Namely,

Theorem 1.2 *Let T be any quasi–binary tree. Then converters of degree 3, allow to efficiently assign colors in to any set of request of load $L \leq n$, where n is the number of wavelengths available on each link.*

If explicitly constructible expanders are considered we get

Theorem 1.3 *Let T be any quasi–binary tree. Then explicitly constructible converters of any degree ≥ 9, allow to efficiently assign colors to any set of request of load $L \leq n$, where n is the number of wavelengths available on each link.*

Due to space limitations some proofs are omitted from this extended abstract.

2 Converters and Expanders

We give in this section some definitions and results which will be used to obtain the appropriate converters.

Definition 2.1 *A converter is a bipartite (undirected) graph $G = (A \cup B, E(G))$ with $|A| = |B| = n$. An input color $a \in A$ can be converted to an output color $b \in B$ iff $(a,b) \in E(G)$. In general a subset $X \subseteq A$ of colors in A can be converted to $Y \subseteq B$ iff there exists a matching between X and Y in G.*

The effectiveness of a converter G in minimizing the number of colors used in the routing will be shown to be related to the expansion capability of G. In the following we introduce expander graphs and derive some property that will be used for proving the feasibility of the routing algorithms.

Given a graph G, denote by $N(X)$ the neighbourhood of X in G, that is, the set of nodes which are connected by an edge to a node in X.

Definition 2.2 *A bipartite graph $G = (A \cup B, E(G))$ with $|A| = |B| = n$ is called an (α, β) expander if for each subset X of nodes with $|X| \leq \alpha n$ it holds $|N(X)| \geq \beta |X|$.*

The following Lemma states Tanner inequality [25] for bipartite graphs, see [10] for a proof.

Lemma 2.1 *If G is a k–regular bipartite graph on $2n$ nodes*

$$\frac{|N(X)|}{|X|} \geq \frac{k^2}{\lambda^2 + (k^2 - \lambda^2)|X|/n} \tag{1}$$

where λ is the smallest eigenvalue in absolute value of the adjacency matrix of G a part k and $-k$.

A special attention must be given to the class of Ramanujan graphs. These graphs have the property that the absolute value of each eigenvalue of the adjacency matrix, a part k and $-k$, is upper bounded by $2\sqrt{k-1}$, where k is the degree of the nodes. The interest in Ramanujan graphs is due to their good expansion property and to the fact that they are explicitly constructible [17, 18]. We will refer to bipartite k–regular Ramanujan graphs simply as Ramanujan graph of degree k. In case of Ramanujan graphs inequality (1) becomes

Corollary 2.1 *If G is a Ramanujan graph of degree k then*

$$\frac{|N(X)|}{|X|} \geq \frac{k^2}{4(k-1) + (k-2)^2|X|/n}.$$

From Definition 2.2 and Corollary 2.1 we get

Corollary 2.2 *For any $\beta > 1$, Ramanujan graphs of degree k are (α, β) expanders for $\alpha \leq (1 - 4(\beta - 1)(k-1)/(k-2)^2)/\beta$.*

Theorem 2.1 *Let $G = (A \cup B, E(G))$ be a (α, β) expander on $2n$ nodes, with $\alpha < 1 < \beta$. Let $Y_1, \ldots, Y_h \subset A$ with $h \leq \beta$ and $\sum_{i=1}^{h} |Y_i| \leq \lfloor \alpha n \rfloor \beta$. Then there exists $B' \subseteq B$ such that*

i) $|B'| = \sum_{i=1}^{h} |Y_i|$;

ii) for each $b \in B'$ there exists $a \in \cup_{i=1}^{h} Y_i$ such that $(a, b) \in E(G)$;

iii) $|\{i \mid 1 \leq i \leq h,\ a \in Y_i\}| = |\{(a, b) \in E(G) \mid b \in B'\}|$, for each $a \in \cup_{i=1}^{h} Y_i$

Proof. Omitted. □

3 General Trees

We show how to color (assign wavelengths to) any set P of dipaths on a tree T. If there are more connection requests for the same pair of nodes then some dipaths in P coincide on all links, however they are considered distinct for the coloring purpose. The load of P in T is the maximum number of dipaths in P using a same link of T.

We will call *segment* a dipath or any sequence of consecutive links of a dipath in P, formally, given a dipath $p = x_1x_2 \ldots x_\ell$ a segment of p is any dipath $x_ix_{i+1} \ldots x_{j-1}x_j$ with $1 \leq i < j \leq \ell$.

If we fix any node r as the root of T we can then call a link *ascending* (resp. *descending*) (with respect to r) if it is directed toward (resp. away from) the root. In the same way, we say that a segment is ascending (resp. descending) if all its links are ascending (resp. descending). Notice that any dipath $p = x_1x_2 \ldots x_\ell$ that has both ascending and descending links can be partitioned into one ascending segment $x_1x_2 \ldots x_i$ followed by one descending segment $x_i \ldots x_\ell$, for some $1 < i < \ell$; we indicate the ascending segment $x_1x_2 \ldots x_i$ as the *maximal ascending segment* of p (if p has only ascending links then p is ascending and the maximal segment of p is p itself).

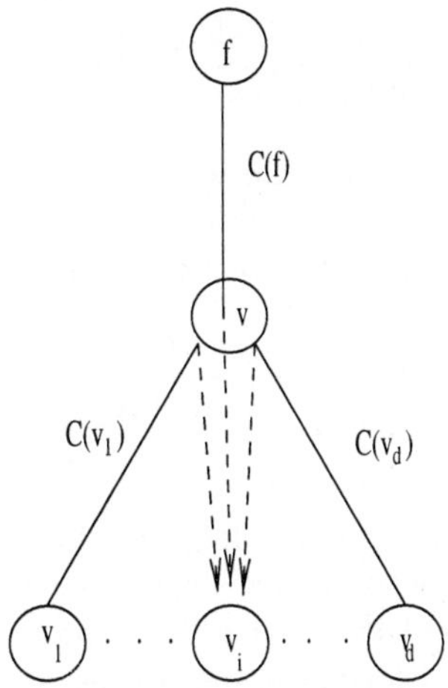

Figure 2: Bold lines denote the segments of paths crossing the link (v, v_i) where the colors are already fixed, dashed lines denote the segments where the colors must be assigned.

The algorithm [for the tree T and set of dipaths P of load L on T]
Step 1 Choose any node r as the root of T
Step 2 Color all maximal ascending segments of the paths in P. It is easy to see that this can be efficiently done using up to L colors.
Step 3 In order to complete the coloring we have to assign a color to all the descending segments. This must be done respecting the following
Constraint *If a dipath in P contains a link e_1 followed by a descending link e_2 then the color assigned to e_1 must be converted into the color assigned to e_2.*
We visit the nodes of T in BFS (Breadth–First Search) manner. For any node v visited we color all the descending segments consisting of a link going from v to a son of v; the coloring is done respecting the above Constraint. In general, suppose we have already considered all the nodes at level $l-1$ and we are considering a node v at level l. Indicate by f the parent of v and by $v_1, \ldots v_d$ the children of v. We have to assign colors to all the descending segments consisting of the links (v, v_i), for $i = 1, \ldots, d$.

Consider the link (v, v_i) and the paths that crosses this link. Since we have already fixed the colors of the set of segments crossing the links (f, v) and (v_ℓ, v), for $\ell \neq i$, each of these colors must be convertible into the color we will assign to the segment of the same dipath consisting of the link (v, v_i). As illustrated in Figure 2, let us denote by $C(v_j)$ the set of colors already fixed for the segments using the link (v_j, v), for $j \neq i$, and by $C(f)$ the set of colors already fixed for the segments using the link (f, v). Since all of the above segments belong to paths that also cross the link (v, v_i) we have

$$|C(f)| + \sum_{j\neq i} |C(v_j)| \leq L.$$

From Theorem 2.1 we know that if the converters have expansion at least d for any set of colors of size at most $(L + d - 1)/d$ then we can convert the set of colors $C(f)$ and $C(v_\ell)$, for $\ell \neq i$, into $|C(f)| + \sum_{j\neq i} |C(v_j)| \leq L$ different colors. By Corollary 2.2 this is possible if $((L + d - 1)/d) \leq (1 - (d - 1)4(k - 1)/(k^2 - 4k + 4)))/d$ which gives Theorem 3.1.

Theorem 3.1 *Let Δ be the maximum degree of T and n be the number of available wavelengths on each link. Using (constructible) converters of degree k, it is possible to assign color to any set of request of load L whenever*

$$L \leq n\left(1 - \frac{(\Delta - 2)4(k - 1)}{k^2 - 4k + 4}\right) - \Delta + 1. \qquad (2)$$

A drawback of inequality (2) is the dependency of its rightside on the maximum degree Δ of the tree. This implies that in order to obtain L close to n we have to use converters with degree depending on Δ. We show now how to eliminate the dependency of the converter degree k from Δ. This is obtained by making a more clever coloring of the ascending segments in Step 2 of the algorithm. To this aim we need the following result.

Definition 3.1 *Let T be a tree rooted in r. A set of dipaths is called almost-ascending in T if any descending segment of a dipath in P has length 1.*

Theorem 3.2 *Any set of almost-ascending dipaths of load L on a tree T can be efficiently colored (without converters) using exactly L colors.*

Proof. Omitted. □

The algorithm, for the tree T and set of dipaths P of load L on T, is as follows.
Step 1 Root T in any node r.
Step 2 Given P, we will assign a color to each maximal ascending segments of a path in P.
To this aim consider P' obtained as follows

i) P' contains all the ascending paths in P;
ii) for each $p \in P$, say $p = x_1 \ldots x_\ell$, having both ascending and descending links, P' contains the almost–ascending dipath $x_1 \ldots x_i x_{i+1}$, where $x_1 \ldots x_i$ is the maximal ascending segment of p.

Notice that the maximal ascending segments of P and P' coincide. Since the dipaths in P' are almost–ascending on T, we can apply Theorem 3.2 to color them. The desired coloring of the maximal ascending segments of dipaths in P is obtained by assigning to each of them the color given to the corresponding dipath in P'. Namely for each $p' \in P'$ let $c(p')$ be the color assigned to p' in coloring P': if p' is an ascending dipath, we assign to p' color $c(p')$; if $p' = x_1 \dots x_i x_{i+1}$, where (x_i, x_{i+1}) is a descending link, we assign to the maximal ascending segment $x_1 \dots x_i$ color $c(p')$.

Step 3 Is equal to the one given to prove Theorem 3.1. However, the coloring done in Step 2 allows the following simplification in the converters.

Suppose we are visiting a node w with parent f and children $v_1, \dots v_d$ and we want to color the segments using the link (w, v_i). Consider the set of colors $C(v_j)$, for $j \neq i$, already fixed for the segments using the link (v_j, v) (and belonging to a path that also uses the link (w, v_i)). The coloring of the ascending segments done in Step 2 assures that these sets are pairwise disjoint. This implies that we have only two sets on which we need to apply Theorem 2.1, namely $C = \cup_{j \neq i} C(v_j)$ and $C(f)$, the set of colors already fixed for the segments using the link (f, w), with $|C(f)| + |C| \leq L$.

Therefore, independently from d, we can apply Theorem 2.1 for $\beta = 2$ and, by Corollary 2.2 obtain that $L \leq n\left(1 - \frac{4(k-1)}{(k-2)^2}\right) - 1$, which gives Theorem 1.1.

3.1 Number of Converters

Previous papers [2, 3, 13, 22] made the general assumption that each node is provided with one converter for each pair of incoming/outgoing links. This means that if a node has degree $d+1$ it must contain $d^2 + d$ converters. However, the above algorithm does not need as many converters but only $2d$. Indeed, if we consider a node v with parent f and children v_i, for $i = 1 \dots, d$, we need in v only 2 converters for each outgoing link (v, v_i): one taking in input the signal arriving on (f, v) and the other taking in input the distinctly colored signals arriving on the links (v_j, v), with $j \neq i$.

Corollary 3.1 *The routing of Theorem 1.1 needs $2d$ converters in each node of degree $d \geq 2$.*

If in a node the number of converters is at most the number of children, then converters degree must be a poly-logarithmic function of the load [3].

3.2 Non-explicit Constructions.

It is worth mentioning that better bounds can be obtained if we do not ask for explicit constructions of expanders (converters) but use probabilistic methods. Bassalygo [6] proved that

Theorem 3.3 *[6] For real numbers $0 < \alpha < 1/\beta < 1$, let*

$$k > \frac{H(\alpha) + H(\beta\alpha)}{H(\alpha) - \alpha\beta H(1/\beta)}, \tag{3}$$

where $H(p) = -p\log_2 p - (1-p)\log_2(1-p)$ *is the binary entropy function. Then for any integer* n *there exists a* k*–regular bipartite* (α, β)*–expander on* $2n$ *nodes.*

Moreover, almost all random k–regular bipartite graphs on $2n$ satisfies Theorem 3.3, see [10]. For our purposes we need $\beta = 2$, therefore (3) becomes $k > \frac{H(\alpha)+H(2\alpha)}{H(\alpha)-2\alpha}$, for $\alpha < 1/2$, which allows to improve on Theorem 1.1.

3.3 Converters of Non-constant Degree

If we allow the degree of the converters to depend on the number n of wavelengths then we can route any set of requests of load up to n, namely

Theorem 3.4 *For any tree* T*, if* n *wavelengths are available on each link then using (constructible) converters of degree* $k > 2\sqrt{n}$*, it is possible to efficiently assign color to any set of request of load* L *whenever* $L \leq n$*.*

Proof. Omitted □

4 Quasi-Binary Trees

In this section we show that there is a class of trees in which constant degree converters allow to route any set of requests having load $L \leq n$, if n wavelengths are available.

We say that a tree is *quasi-binary* if at most one node has degree greater than or equal to 4.

Let T be a quasi–binary tree and P a set of dipaths on T. We assume that each node of degree 3 has one converter for each pair of incoming– outgoing links.

The algorithm

Step 1. Root the tree T in node r, where r is the unique node of degree larger than 3, if any.

Step 2. Consider the paths in P and assign colors to their segments consisting of links incident on r; this is equivalent to color dipaths on a star graph with center r and can be easily done in polynomial time [[12], Lemma 6].

Step 3. We continue visiting the nodes of T in BFS manner. Suppose we have already visited all the nodes at levels $\leq l-1$ (and, therefore, fixed the colors of all the segments of dipaths in P consisting of links incident on these nodes). Consider a node v at level l; we want to color the segments consisting of the links (v, w) and/or (w, v) where w is a son of v. If v has only one son this is immediately done. Suppose then that v has two children v_ℓ and v_r and indicate by f the parent of v. We show now that it is possible to set the converters so to have a coloring of the segments consisting of the links (v_ℓ, v) and/or (v, v_r) which is consistent with the previously fixed colors. (The segments consisting of the opposite links, (v_r, v) and/or (v, v_ℓ), can be colored independently in the same way.)

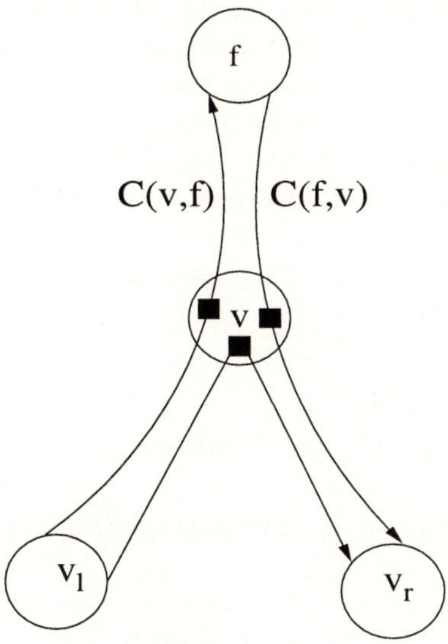

Figure 3

As indicated in Figure 3 we denote by $C(v,f)$ and $C(f,v)$ the set of already fixed colors on the links (v,f) and (f,v), respectively. Let the converters be bipartite graphs $G = (A \cup B, E(G))$, where $A = B$ is the set of colors available on each link, and assume that G is a $(\alpha, 2)$–expander with $\alpha \geq 1/3$. In order to assign colors to the segments consisting of links (v_ℓ, v) and (v, v_r), it is sufficient to determine a set $X \subset A$ such that the following two conditions hold:

1) G has a matching between the nodes in $X \subseteq A$ and those in $C(v,f) \subseteq B$;
2) G contains $|A \setminus X| + |C(f,v)| \leq n$ edges connecting nodes in $A \setminus X$ and nodes in $C(f,v)$ to different nodes in B so that for each $a \in (A \setminus X) \cup C(f,v)$

$$|\{(a,b) \in E(G) \mid b \in B\}| = \begin{cases} 2 & \text{if } a \in (A \setminus X) \cap C(f,v), \\ 1 & \text{otherwise.} \end{cases}$$

In order to determine a suitable $X \subset A$, we introduce the following bipartite graph $H = (U \cup V, E(H))$, where

- $|U| = n + |C(f,v)|$ and $|V| = n + |C(v,f)|$;
- for each $a \in A \setminus C(f,v)$, the set U contains one node denoted by a_1 and for each $a \in A \cap C(f,v)$, the set U contains two nodes denoted by a_1 and a_2;
- for each $b \in B \setminus C(v,f)$, the set V contains one node denoted by b_1 and for each $b \in B \cap C(v,f)$, the set V contains two nodes denoted by b_1 and b_2;
- $E(H)$ contains the edge (a_i, b_j), with $i,j \in \{1,2\}$, iff $a_i \in U$, $b_j \in V$, and $(a,b) \in E(G)$.

Following the lines of the proof of Theorem 2.1, it is possible to show that

Lemma 4.1 *H has a matching M_H of size $|M_H| = \min\{|U|,\ |V|\}$.*

We can then take $X = \{a \mid (a, b') \in M_H,\ b' \in C(f, v)\}$ and get that conditions 1) and 2) are satisfied. Notice that the routing can be done in a greedy manner, that is, the wavelength assignment/conversion is done at each node independently once it has been done by its father in the BFS tree. Hence, we can greedily route any set of requests with load $L \leq n$.
Using Theorem 3.3 with the required parameters we have that there exist converters of degree 3 which allow to efficiently route any set of request of load $L \leq n$, thus getting Theorem 1.2. If we are interested in explicit constructions, then by Corollary 2.2 constructible Ramanujan graphs assure that any $k \geq 9$ is suitable, thus giving Theorem 1.3.

5 Conclusions and Open Problems

We have considered the problem of routing in all-optical trees with wavelength converters.

We have shown that for each tree constant–degree converters are sufficient to route any set of requests with load arbitrarily close to the number of available wavelengths, that is, $L \leq W(1-\epsilon)$, where ϵ depends only on the degree of the converters. In case of trees of maximum degree 3 then there exist converters of degree 3 that allow to route any set of requests that pose on T a load $L \leq W$. Moreover, we have shown that in any tree it is possible to route any set of requests that pose on T a load $L \leq W$ if converters of degree $O(\sqrt{W})$ are used. It would be interesting to prove or disprove that there exist constant–degree converters that for any tree allow to route any set of requests with load $L \leq W$.

Acknowledgement Thanks are due to Ugo Vaccaro for his interest and advice.

References

1. A. Aggarwal, A. Bar-Noy, D. Coppersmith, R. Ramaswami, B. Schieber, M. Sudan, "Efficient Routing and Scheduling Algorithms for Optical Networks", in: *Proceedings of the 5th Annual ACM-SIAM Symposium on Discrete Algorithms (SODA'94)*, (1994), 412–423.
2. V. Auletta, I. Caraggiannis, C. Kaklamanis, G. Persiano, "Bandwidth Allocation Algorithms on tree–Shaped All-Optical Networks with Wavelength Converters" *SIROCCO'97*.
3. V. Auletta, I. Caraggiannis, C. Kaklamanis, G. Persiano, "Optimal and Nearly-Optimal Wavelength Routing with Low–Degree Converters", manuscript.
4. Y. Aumann and Y. Rabani, "Improved Bounds for All Optical Routing", in: *Proceedings of the 6th Annual ACM-SIAM Symposium on Discrete Algorithms (SODA'95)*, (1995), 567–576.
5. Y. Bartal, S. Leonardi, "On–Line Routing in All-Optical Networks", Proceedings of *24th International Colloquium on Automata, Languages, and Programming (ICALP 97)*, Bologna, Italy, July 1997.
6. L. A. Bassalygo, "Asymptotically Optimal Switching Circuits, *Problems of Information Transmission*, 1981, 206–211.

7. B. Beauquier, J.-C. Bermond, L. Gargano, P. Hell, S. Perennes, and U. Vaccaro, "Graph Problems Arising from Wavelength–Routing in All–Optical Networks", *2nd Workshop on Optics and Computer Science (WOCS)*, Geneve, Switzerland, April 1997,
8. C. Berge, *Graphs*, North–Holland.
9. J.–C.. Bermond, L. Gargano, S. Perennes, A.A. Rescigno, U. Vaccaro, "Efficient Collective Communication in Optical Networks", *Theoretical Compute Science*, to appear.
10. F.R.K. Chung, *Spectral Graph Theory*, CBMS 92, American Mathematical Society, 1997.
11. T. Erlebach and K. Jansen. "Scheduling of Virtual Connections in Fast Networks", *Proc. of 4th Workshop on Parallel Systems and Algorithms PASA '96*, (1996), 13–32.
12. L. Gargano, P. Hell, S. Perennes, "Colouring All Directed Paths in a Symmetric Tree with Applications to WDM Routing", Proceedings of *ICALP 97*.
13. O. Gerstel, S. Kutten, R. Ramaswami and G. Sasaki, "Wavelength Conversion in All-Optical Ring Networks", Proceedings of *6th Annual ACM SIGACT-SIGOPS Symposium on Principles of Distributed Computing (PODC'97)*.
14. P. E. Green, *Fiber-Optic Communication Networks*, Prentice–Hall, 1992.
15. K. Kaklamanis G. Persiano, T. Erlebach, K. Jansen, "Constrained Bipartite Edge Coloring with Applications to Wavelength Routing" Proceedings of *ICALP 97*.
16. E. Kumar, E. Schwabe, "Improved Access to Optical Bandwidth in Trees", *Proceedings of SODA'97*.
17. A. Lubotzky, R. Phillips, P. Sarnak, "Ramanujan Graphs", *Combinatorica*, vol. 8, 1988, 261–278.
18. G.A. Margulis, "Explicit Group–Theoretic Constructions of Combinatorial Schemes and their Applications for the Construction of Expanders and Concentrators", *Problemy Peredaci Informacii*, 1988.
19. A. D. McAulay, *Optical Computer Architectures*, John Wiley, 1991.
20. M. Mihail, K. Kaklamanis, S. Rao, "Efficient Access to Optical Bandwidth", in: *Proceedings of 36th Annual IEEE Symposium on Foundations of Computer Science (FOCS'95)*, (1995), 548–557.
21. P. Raghavan and E. Upfal, "Efficient Routing in All–Optical Networks", in: *Proceedings of STOC'94*, (1994), 133-143.
22. R. Ramaswami, G.H. Sasaki, "Multiwavelength Optical Networks with Limited Wavelength Conversion" *Proc. of IEEE Infocom 1997*.
23. R. Ramaswami, "Multi-Wavelength Lightwave Networks for Computer Communication", *IEEE Communication Magazine*, vol. 31, (1993), 78–88.
24. V. Sharma and E. A. Varvarigos, "Limited wavelength translation in all-optical WDM mesh networks", *IEEE Infocom'98*, to appear .
25. R.M. Tanner, "Explicit Construction of Concentrators from Generalized n-gons", *SIAM J. Alg. Discr. Meth.*, 5 (1984), 287–293.
26. R.J. Vetter and D.H.C. Du, "Distributed Computing with High-Speed Optical Networks", *IEEE Computer*, vol. 26, (1993), 8–18.
27. G. Wilfong, P. Winkler, "Ring Routing and Wavelength Translation", Proceedings of *SODA '98*, to appear.
28. J. Yates, J. Lacey, D. Everitt, M. Summerfield, "Limite Range Wavelength Translation in All–Optical Networks", *Proc. of IEEE Infocom 1996*, pp. 954-961.

Computing Mimicking Networks

Shiva Chaudhuri[1], K.V. Subrahmanyam[1],
Frank Wagner[2*], and Christos D. Zaroliagis[1,3**]

[1] Max-Planck-Institut für Informatik, Im Stadtwald, 66123 Saarbrücken, Germany
Email: {shiva,kv,zaro}@mpi-sb.mpg.de
[2] Institut für Informatik, Freie Universität Berlin, Takustr. 9, 14195 Berlin, Germany
Email: wagner@inf.fu-berlin.de
[3] Department of Computer Science, King's College, University of London,
Strand, London WC2R 2LS, UK

Abstract. A *mimicking network* for a k-terminal network, N, is one whose realizable external flows are the same as those of N. Let $S(k)$ denote the minimum size of a mimicking network for a k-terminal network. In this paper we give new constructions of mimicking networks and prove the following results (the values in brackets are the previously best known results): $S(4) = 5$ $[2^{16}]$, $S(5) = 6$ $[2^{32}]$. For bounded treewidth networks we show $S(k) = O(k)$ $[2^{2^k}]$, and for outerplanar networks we show $S(k) \leq 10k - 6$ $[k^2 2^{k+2}]$.

1 Introduction

Network flows is a problem domain of fundamental importance in computer science and other areas (e.g., operations research, engineering, etc.), having a wealth of theoretical and practical applications [1]. One of the central (and classical) problems in network flows is the characterization of the flow behavior of multiterminal networks, i.e., networks with $k > 2$ terminals, first motivated and solved by Gomory and Hu [6] and later improved and simplified by many others (see e.g., [4, 5, 10]). The Gomory-Hu approach, as well as its subsequent improvements and simplifications, deal mainly with the case where every vertex of the network is a potential candidate for being a terminal. However, there may be cases where the number of terminals is much smaller than the number of vertices in the network. For example, in computing max-flows/min-cuts on networks that can be decomposed into subnetworks that share a small number of vertices with the rest of the network; such a situation appears in hierarchical methods for integrated circuit layout problems [9].

Under this perspective, there is a recent, renewed interest on the problem of characterizing the flow behavior of networks with a small (usually constant) number of terminals [7]. More precisely, it was shown in [7] that for a k-terminal network G, there is a set of 2^k inequalities that characterize the feasible flow

* Supported by the Heisenberg program of the Deutsche Forschungsgemeinschaft.
** Partially supported by the EU ESPRIT LTR Project No. 20244 (ALCOM-IT).

values at the terminals (the external flows). Moreover, it was shown that there exists a network $M(G)$ with 2^{2^k} vertices, of which k are terminals, that has the same feasible external flows as G. The network $M(G)$ is called the *mimicking network* of G. For constant k this implies that the size of $M(G)$ is bounded by a (maybe large) constant. Mimicking networks constituted the main building block in the development of a linear time algorithm for computing a maximum s-t flow in a bounded treewidth network [7] and for obtaining an optimal solution to the all-pairs min-cut problem in the same class of networks [2].

A natural question is whether there are more efficient constructions of mimicking networks, i.e., constructions such that $|M(G)|$ does not depend double-exponentially on k. This question was partially answered for outerplanar networks. More precisely, in [2] it was proved that the mimicking network $M(G_o)$ of a k-terminal outerplanar network G_o has size $k^2 2^{k+2}$, and moreover $M(G_o)$ is also outerplanar. The outerplanarity of the resulting mimicking network was crucial in the development of better algorithms for computing an s-t min-cut and all-pairs min-cuts in planar networks [2].

In this paper, we make a step forward in constructing smaller mimicking networks. We have two types of results. The first result concerns the case of general undirected k-terminal networks for specific values of k; namely, for $k = 3, 4, 5$. We show that any 3-terminal network has a mimicking network consisting of 3 vertices, and any 4-terminal (resp. 5-terminal) network has a mimicking network consisting of 5 (resp. 6) vertices (Section 4). We also prove that these constructions are *optimal* by showing that, for any $k \geq 4$, there exists a k-terminal network for which the mimicking network must have at least one vertex in addition to the k terminals. We further provide necessary and sufficient conditions for a vector of min-cut values to be realizable, i.e., whether the values of a given vector represent min-cut values of a 3,- 4-, and 5-terminal network. Our methods are based on a result of independent interest (Section 3) concerning values of multisets of min-cuts in arbitrary k-terminal networks that seems to have further applications. In particular, it can be used to prove a conjecture by Lengauer [9, Sec. 6.1.5] regarding the problem of mimicking the cut properties of a hypergraph by a graph, a problem arising in circuit partitioning (Section 7).

The second result concerns the case of (directed or undirected) bounded treewidth networks. Informally, the treewidth t is a parameter that indicates how close the structure of the network is to a tree (see Section 2 for a formal definition). The class of bounded treewidth networks includes outerplanar networks ($t = 2$), series-parallel networks ($t = 2$), and networks with bounded bandwidth or cutwidth. For any k-terminal bounded treewidth network, we give a construction of a mimicking network of size $O(k)$, where the constant in the Big-O depends on the treewidth (Section 5). For the special case of outerplanar networks, we provide further improvements. We show that the size of the (outerplanar) mimicking network in this case is much smaller than the one we get with the general method of bounded treewidth networks (Section 6). For both the bounded treewidth and the outerplanar cases, our results are optimal up to constant factors.

2 Preliminaries

The treatment in this section follows that in [2]. A *network* is a (directed or undirected) graph $G = (V, E)$ with a nonnegative real capacity c_e associated with each edge $e \in E$. The *terminals* of G are the elements of a distinguished subset, $Q = \{q_1, q_2, \ldots, q_k\}$, of its vertices. A *flow* in G is an assignment of a nonnegative real value $f_e \leq c_e$ to each edge e such that the net flow out of each non-terminal vertex is zero, where the net flow out of a vertex is the sum of flows on edges leaving the vertex minus the sum of flows on edges entering the vertex. An *external flow* $x = (x_1, \ldots, x_k)$ is an assignment of a real value x_i to each terminal $q_i \in Q$, $1 \leq i \leq k$. A *realizable external flow* is an external flow such that there exists a flow in which the net flow out of each terminal q_i is x_i. A *cut* $(S, \overline{S})$ is a partition of the vertices of G into two subsets S and $\overline{S} = V \setminus S$; S is called the *defining subset* of the cut. The *capacity* of the cut $(S, \overline{S})$ is the sum of capacities of edges going from vertices in S to vertices in $\overline{S}$. For a subset R of Q, an *R-separating cut* is a cut $(S, \overline{S})$ where $Q \cap S = R$. A *minimum R-separating cut* (or just *min-cut* when R is well understood from the context) is an R-separating cut of minimum capacity. We denote the capacity of a minimum R-separating cut by b_R. The sum of the net flows out of the terminals in R is called the *R-value* of a flow. A *maximum R-flow* is a flow of maximum R-value. If $Q = \{s, t\}$, an *s-t max-flow* is a maximum $\{s\}$-flow, and an *s-t min-cut* is a minimum $\{s\}$-separating cut.

Let $(S_1, \overline{S_1})$ and $(S_2, \overline{S_2})$ be two min-cuts in a network G where $Q \cap S_1 = R_1$ and $Q \cap S_2 = R_2$. We call these min-cuts *equal* if $R_1 = R_2$, in the case where G is directed, or if $R_1 = R_2$ or $R_1 = Q \setminus R_2$, in the case where G is undirected. Two min-cuts that are not equal are called *distinct*. A k-terminal directed network has 2^k distinct min-cuts (two of which are trivial), and a k-terminal undirected network has $2^{k-1} - 1$ distinct min-cuts (since half of the $2^k - 2$ min-cuts are equal).

Let G be a network with terminal set Q. A network $M(G)$ with terminal set Q' is a *mimicking network* for G if there exists a bijection between Q and Q' such that every realizable external flow in G is also realizable in $M(G)$, and vice versa. The following lemma is a reformulation of the results in [7].

Lemma 1. *Let G and G' be two networks with the same terminal set Q. Then, every realizable external flow in G is also realizable in G' (and vice versa) iff the capacities of the minimum R-separating cuts are equal for all $R \subseteq Q$.*

To compute a mimicking network of a network G using either of the approaches in [2,7], as well as the approaches described in this paper, we have to find the 2^k minimum R-separating cuts. This is done by the standard method of solving 2^k s-t max-flow/min-cut problems in a network G' which consists of G augmented with two vertices s and t and edges of infinite capacity from s to every vertex in R and from every vertex in $Q \setminus R$ to t. However, G' may not preserve the structural properties (e.g., outerplanarity, planarity, bounded treewidth) that G may have and which may be desirable for reasons of efficiency.

In [2, Lemma 2.3] it was shown how to overcome this problem and find the 2^k minimum R-separating cuts by solving $k^2 2^k$ s-t max-flow/min-cut problems in G. Therefore, we assume henceforth that the 2^k minimum R-separating cuts are provided to us with the input.

A *separator* in a graph is a set of vertices which disconnects the graph. Let $G = (V(G), E(G))$ be a graph and $U \subseteq V(G)$ be a separator. Let V_1 and V_2 be a partition of $V(G)\backslash U$ such that in $G\backslash U$, there is no path from $v \in V_1$ to $w \in V_2$ for any v, w. Let G_1 and G_2 be graphs such that $V(G_1) = V_1 \cup U$, $V(G_2) = V_2 \cup U$, and $E(G_1) \cap E(G_2) = \emptyset$, $E(G_1) \cup E(G_2) = E(G)$. We say G_1 and G_2 are subgraphs obtained by *splitting* G *at* U.

Let $Q \subseteq V(G)$ be the set of terminals of G. Let $Q_1 = V_1 \cap Q$ and $Q_2 = V_2 \cap Q$. Suppose we construct mimicking networks $M(G_1)$ for G_1 at terminals $Q_1 \cup U$ and $M(G_2)$ for G_2 at terminals $Q_2 \cup U$. We join $M(G_1)$ and $M(G_2)$ by identifying, for each $u \in U$, the vertex in $M(G_1)$ corresponding to u with the vertex in $M(G_2)$ corresponding to u. It was shown in [7] that the resulting network is a mimicking network for G at terminals Q. We call this process *glueing* the mimicking networks together. The notions of *splitting* and *glueing* will be used extensively in Sections 5 and 6.

A *tree decomposition* of a (directed or undirected) graph $G = (V(G), E(G))$ is a pair (X, T), where $T = (V(T), E(T))$ is a tree, X is a family $\{X_i : i \in V(T)\}$ of subsets of $V(G)$ that cover $V(G)$, and the following conditions hold: (1) *Edge mapping*: $\forall (v, w) \in E(G)$, there exists an $i \in V(T)$ with $v \in X_i$ and $w \in X_i$. (2) *Continuity*: $\forall i, j, k \in V(T)$, if j lies on the path from i to k in T, then $X_i \cap X_k \subseteq X_j$, or equivalently: $\forall v \in V(G)$, the nodes $\{i \in V(T) : v \in X_i\}$ induce a connected subtree of T.

The *width* of the tree decomposition is $\max_{i \in V(T)} |X_i| - 1$. The *treewidth* of G is the minimum width over all possible tree decompositions of G.

Bodlaender [3] gave an $O(n)$ time algorithm that tests, for all constant $t \in \mathbb{N}$, whether a given n-vertex graph G has treewidth $\leq t$ and if so, computes a tree decomposition (X, T) of G of width $\leq t$, where $|V(T)| = n - t$. Furthermore, (X, T) can be converted into another tree decomposition (X', T') with width t, such that T' is binary and $|V(T')| \leq 2(n-t)$. We call such a tree decomposition a *binary tree decomposition.* Note that the edge mapping condition ensures that the endpoints of each edge in G appear together in at least one set $X_i \in X$, belonging to vertex i of T. For our purposes, we need to explicitly associate each edge of G with exactly one vertex of T. We do this by computing an *augmenting function* $h : E(G) \rightarrow V(T)$, satisfying the property that both endpoints of an edge are present in the set belonging to the vertex that the edge is mapped to by h, i.e., $\forall (v, w) \in E(G), \{v, w\} \subseteq X_{h(v,w)}$. Such an augmenting function can be easily computed by doing a traversal of T [2]. The resulting tree decomposition with the values $h(v, w), \forall (v, w) \in E(G)$, is called an *augmented tree decomposition.* The discussion above leads to the following result.

Lemma 2. *Given an n-vertex graph G of constant treewidth t, we can compute in $O(n)$ time an augmented binary tree decomposition of G of width t.*

3 A Fundamental Lemma

In the following, let $w(c)$ denote the capacity of a cut c belonging to a (multi)set C of cuts, and let $w(C) = \sum_{c \in C} w(c)$. The next lemma plays a central role in the paper.

Lemma 3. *Let $G = (V, E)$ be a network with k terminals $q_1, \ldots q_k$. Let $M = \{m_1, \ldots m_p\}$ be a multiset of min-cuts in G and let δ_{ij} be the number of m_i's, that separate q_i and q_j. Let N be a second multiset of min-cuts with $N = \{n_i^r \mid i \in \{1, \ldots, k\}, r \in \{1, \ldots, u_i\}\}$, where each n_i^r, $1 \leq r \leq u_i$, separates q_i from all other terminals. If for all i, j, $u_i + u_j \leq \delta_{ij}$, then $w(N) \leq w(M)$.*

Proof. The intersection of all min-cuts in M induce a partition of G into (disjoint) subsets U of V, which we call *parts*. We consider each such part U as a 0-1 vector of length p, where $U[i] = 1$ if U is a subset of the defining subset of m_i, and $U[i] = 0$ otherwise.

Let τ_i^1 be the part that contains q_i (such a part always exists). Define $\tau_i^r = \{U \mid H(\tau_i^1, U) \leq r - 1\}$, for $r \in \{1, \ldots, u_i\}$, where H is the Hamming distance of the two vectors (i.e., the number of bits in which they differ) corresponding to the parts. The sets τ_i^r satisfy the following two claims.

Claim 1: For every $1 \leq i \leq k$, $\tau_i^1 \subseteq \tau_i^2 \subseteq \ldots \subseteq \tau_i^{u_i}$.

Claim 2: For any $i \neq j$, any $r \in \{1, \ldots, u_i\}$ and any $s \in \{1, \ldots, u_j\}$, $\tau_i^r \cap \tau_j^s = \emptyset$.

The first claim follows directly from the definition of τ_i^r. For the second claim, assume that there is a pair τ_i^r and τ_j^s whose intersection is not the empty set. This means that there is a part from the partition induced by M which simultaneously has Hamming distance $r - 1 \leq u_i - 1$ from τ_i^1 and $s - 1 \leq u_j - 1$ from τ_j^1. By the triangle inequality this in turn implies that $H(\tau_i^1, \tau_j^1) \leq u_i + u_j - 2$. But this contradicts the fact that $H(\tau_i^1, \tau_j^1) = \delta_{ij} \geq u_i + u_j$. Hence, Claim 2 is also true.

To complete the proof of the lemma, it suffices to show that

$$w(N) \leq w(N') := w(\{\tau_i^r \mid i \in \{1, \ldots, k\}, r \in \{1, \ldots u_i\}\}) \leq w(M).$$

We first show $w(N) \leq w(N')$. It follows from Claim 2, that every τ_i^r contains only a single terminal, namely q_i. Thus, $w(\tau_i^r) \geq w(n_i^r)$, for all i and r, since n_i^r is a min-cut. Hence, $w(N) \leq w(N')$.

We now show $w(N') \leq w(M)$. By Claim 1, the set N' induces a partition of V into (disjoint) vertex sets ${\tau_i}^1, {\tau_i}^2 \setminus {\tau_i}^1, \ldots, {\tau_i}^{u_i} \setminus {\tau_i}^{u_i - 1}$, $i = 1, \ldots, k$, plus the set of the remaining vertices, say V^*. For convenience, we assume in the following that $\tau_i^0 = \emptyset$. There are three types of edges that are cut by the cuts in N'.

Type-1 edges: are those edges (x, y) with x in some $\tau_i^r \setminus \tau_i^{r-1}$ and y in some $\tau_i^s \setminus \tau_i^{s-1}$, $r \neq s$, $r, s \in \{1, \ldots, u_i\}$.

Type-2 edges: are those edges (x, y) with x in some $\tau_i^r \setminus \tau_i^{r-1}$ and y in some $\tau_j^s \setminus \tau_j^{s-1}$, where $i \neq j$, $r \in \{1, \ldots, u_i\}$, and $s \in \{1, \ldots, u_j\}$.

Type-3 edges: are those edges (x, y) with x in some $\tau_i^r \setminus \tau_i^{r-1}$ and y in V^*, where $i \in \{1, \ldots, k\}$ and $r \in \{1, \ldots, u_i\}$.

Let us count how many times the above edges are cut by (the cuts in) N' and M. A type-1 edge is cut by N' exactly $s-r$ times (assuming w.l.o.g. that $s>r$). By the triangle inequality we have $H(x,y) \geq H(y,q_i) - H(x,q_i) = s-r$. As $H(x,y)$ is exactly the number of times such an edge is cut by M, we have shown the desired inequality in this case. A type-2 edge is cut by N' exactly $u_i-(r-1)+u_j-(s-1) = u_i+u_j-r-s+2$ times, since it is cut only by those τ_i^a with $r \leq a \leq u_i$ and by those τ_j^b with $s \leq b \leq u_j$. By the generalized triangle inequality we have $H(x,y) \geq H(q_i,q_j) - H(q_i,x) - H(q_j,y) = \delta_{ij} - (r-1) - (s-1) = \delta_{ij} - r - s + 2 \geq u_i + u_j - r - s + 2$, where the last inequality follows by the assumption of the theorem. Therefore, the type-2 edges are cut by M at least as many times as they are cut by N'. For the type-3 edges, we can show (similarly to the type-1 edges) that they are cut by M at least as many times as they are cut by N'.

Hence, in total M cuts at least so many edges as N' does, and consequently $w(N') \leq w(M)$. □

4 Mimicking k-terminal networks for $k = 3, 4, 5$

Recall that a k-terminal undirected network has $2^{k-1}-1$ distinct min-cuts. Throughout this section, we shall use the following notation. The (at most 5 element) terminal set is denoted as $Q = \{A,B,C,D,E\}$. The capacities of the minimum R-separating cuts, for $R \subseteq Q$, will be denoted as: $\alpha := b_{\{A\}}$, $\beta := b_{\{B\}}$, $\gamma := b_{\{C\}}$, $\delta := b_{\{D\}}$, $\varepsilon := b_{\{E\}}$, $\alpha\beta := b_{\{A,B\}}$, $\alpha\gamma := b_{\{A,C\}}$, $\alpha\delta := b_{\{A,D\}}$, $\alpha\varepsilon := b_{\{A,E\}}$, $\beta\gamma := b_{\{B,C\}}$, $\beta\delta := b_{\{B,D\}}$, $\beta\varepsilon := b_{\{B,E\}}$, $\gamma\delta := b_{\{C,D\}}$, $\gamma\varepsilon := b_{\{C,E\}}$, and $\delta\varepsilon := b_{\{D,E\}}$.

For vertices X, Y of a mimicking network $M(G)$, we shall denote the capacity of the edge XY by $w(XY)$, and the capacity of a cut with defining subset S by $w(S \mid \overline{S})$.

4.1 3-terminal networks

Let G be a network with three terminals A, B, C. Note that G has three distinct min-cuts whose values are α, β and γ.

Theorem 1. *A 3-terminal network G with terminal set $\{A,B,C\}$ has a mimicking network $M(G)$ which is the complete graph on vertices $\{A,B,C\}$ with the following capacities on its edges:*
$w(AB) = \frac{\alpha+\beta-\gamma}{2}$, $w(BC) = \frac{\beta+\gamma-\alpha}{2}$, *and* $w(AC) = \frac{\alpha+\gamma-\beta}{2}$.

Proof. First we have to show that the edge capacities are nonnegative. To show that e.g., $w(AB) \geq 0$, it suffices to show that $\alpha+\beta \geq \gamma$. This is true, because $\alpha+\beta \geq \alpha\beta = \gamma$ (a cut separating A from $\{B,C\}$, and B from $\{A,C\}$ definitely separates C from $\{A,B\}$). Similarly, $w(BC) \geq 0$ and $w(AC) \geq 0$.

To complete the proof, we have to show that the conditions of Lemma 1 are satisfied. We have, $w(A \mid BC) = w(AB) + w(AC) = \frac{\alpha+\beta-\gamma}{2} + \frac{\alpha+\gamma-\beta}{2} = \alpha$. Similarly, $w(B \mid AC) = \beta$ and $w(C \mid AB) = \gamma$. Hence, the conditions of Lemma 1 are indeed satisfied and consequently $M(G)$ is a mimicking network of G. □

Let $\mathcal{M}$ be a vector with values $[a, b, c]$. It can be easily verified that these values are realizable min-cut values of a 3-terminal network iff the following inequalities are satisfied: $a + b \geq c$, $b + c \geq a$, and $c + a \geq b$.

4.2 4-terminal networks

Let G be a network with four terminals A, B, C, D. Note that G has seven distinct min-cuts whose values are α, β, γ, δ, $\alpha\beta$, $\alpha\gamma$, $\alpha\delta$.

Theorem 2. *A 4-terminal network G with terminal set $\{A, B, C, D\}$ has a mimicking network $M(G)$ which is the complete graph on vertices $\{A, B, C, D, Z\}$, where Z is an additional vertex, with the following capacities on its edges:* $w(AB) = \frac{\alpha+\beta-\alpha\beta}{2}$, $w(AC) = \frac{\alpha+\gamma-\alpha\gamma}{2}$, $w(AD) = \frac{\alpha+\delta-\alpha\delta}{2}$, $w(BC) = \frac{\beta+\gamma-\beta\gamma}{2}$, $w(BD) = \frac{\beta+\delta-\beta\delta}{2}$, $w(CD) = \frac{\gamma+\delta-\gamma\delta}{2}$, *and* $w(ZA) = w(ZB) = w(ZC) = w(ZD) = \Delta$, *where* $\Delta = \frac{(\alpha\beta+\alpha\gamma+\alpha\delta)-(\alpha+\beta+\gamma+\delta)}{2}$.

Proof. The capacities on the edges not incident on Z are all nonnegative as it was shown in the proof of Theorem 1. The nonnegativity of Δ follows by Lemma 3 with $M = \{\alpha\beta, \alpha\gamma, \alpha\delta\}$ and $N = \{\alpha, \beta, \gamma, \delta\}$. Hence, it remains to show that the conditions of Lemma 1 are satisfied.

It can be easily verified that $w(A \mid BCDZ) = \alpha$, $w(B \mid ACDZ) = \beta$, $w(C \mid ABDZ) = \gamma$, $w(D \mid ABCZ) = \delta$, and that $w(AB \mid CDZ) = w(ABZ \mid CD) = \alpha\beta$, $w(AC \mid BDZ) = w(ACZ \mid BD) = \alpha\gamma$, $w(AD \mid BCZ) = w(ADZ \mid BC) = \alpha\delta$. We must also ensure that any other cut that separates a subset of $\{A, B, C, D\}$ from the rest of terminals has value greater than or equal to these values. For example, we must have $w(AZ \mid BCD) \geq w(A \mid BCDZ)$, which is true since $w(AZ \mid BCD) = \alpha + 2\Delta \geq \alpha = w(A \mid BCDZ)$. The rest of the cuts can be checked in a similar way. Hence, the conditions of Lemma 1 are satisfied and consequently $M(G)$ is a mimicking network of G. □

Let $\mathcal{M}$ be a vector with values $[a, b, c, d, ab, ac, ad]$. It can be easily verified that these values are realizable min-cut values of a 4-terminal network iff the following inequalities are satisfied: $a + b \geq ab$, $a + c \geq ac$, $a + d \geq ad$, $b + c \geq ad$, $b + d \geq bd$, $c + d \geq ab$, $ab + ac + ad \geq a + b + c + d$.

4.3 5-terminal networks

Let G be a network with five terminals A, B, C, D, E. Note that G has 15 distinct min-cuts whose values are α, β, γ, δ, ε, $\alpha\beta$, $\alpha\gamma$, $\alpha\delta$, $\alpha\varepsilon$, $\beta\gamma$, $\beta\delta$, $\beta\varepsilon$, $\gamma\delta$, $\gamma\varepsilon$ and $\delta\varepsilon$.

Theorem 3. *A 5-terminal network G with terminal set $\{A, B, C, D, E\}$ has a mimicking network $M(G)$ which is the complete graph on 6 vertices $\{A, B, C, D, E, Z\}$, where Z is an additional vertex, with the following capacities on its edges:* $w(AB) = \frac{\alpha+\beta-\alpha\beta}{2}$, $w(AC) = \frac{\alpha+\gamma-\alpha\gamma}{2}$, $w(AD) = \frac{\alpha+\delta-\alpha\delta}{2}$, $w(AE) = \frac{\alpha+\varepsilon-\alpha\varepsilon}{2}$, $w(BC) = \frac{\beta+\gamma-\beta\gamma}{2}$, $w(BD) = \frac{\beta+\delta-\beta\delta}{2}$, $w(BE) = \frac{\beta+\varepsilon-\beta\varepsilon}{2}$,

$w(CD) = \frac{\gamma+\delta-\gamma\delta}{2}$, $w(CE) = \frac{\gamma+\varepsilon-\gamma\varepsilon}{2}$, $w(DE) = \frac{\delta+\varepsilon-\delta\varepsilon}{2}$,
$w(ZA) = \Delta_A = \frac{(\alpha\beta+\alpha\gamma+\alpha\delta+\alpha\varepsilon)-(2\alpha+\beta+\gamma+\delta+\varepsilon)}{2}$,
$w(ZB) = \Delta_B = \frac{(\alpha\beta+\beta\gamma+\beta\delta+\beta\varepsilon)-(2\beta+\alpha+\gamma+\delta+\varepsilon)}{2}$,
$w(ZC) = \Delta_C = \frac{(\alpha\gamma+\beta\gamma+\gamma\delta+\gamma\varepsilon)-(2\gamma+\alpha+\beta+\delta+\varepsilon)}{2}$,
$w(ZD) = \Delta_D = \frac{(\alpha\delta+\beta\delta+\gamma\delta+\delta\varepsilon)-(2\delta+\alpha+\beta+\gamma+\varepsilon)}{2}$,
and $w(ZE) = \Delta_E = \frac{(\alpha\varepsilon+\beta\varepsilon+\gamma\varepsilon+\delta\varepsilon)-(2\varepsilon+\alpha+\beta+\gamma+\delta)}{2}$.

Proof. As before, the capacities of the edges not incident on Z are all nonnegative as it was shown in the proof of Theorem 1. Hence, it remains to show that $\Delta_A \geq 0$, $\Delta_B \geq 0$, $\Delta_C \geq 0$, $\Delta_D \geq 0$, and $\Delta_E \geq 0$. The first inequality follows immediately by Lemma 3 with $M = \{\alpha\beta, \alpha\gamma, \alpha\delta, \alpha\epsilon\}$ and $N = \{\alpha, \alpha, \beta, \gamma, \delta, \epsilon\}$. The rest of the inequalities can be proved similarly.

Now, we have to satisfy the conditions of Lemma 1. Observe that $w(A \mid BCDEZ) = \alpha$ (as required) and $w(AZ \mid BCDE) = \alpha - \Delta_A + \Delta_B + \Delta_C + \Delta_D + \Delta_E$. Since it must hold that $w(AZ \mid BCDE) \geq w(A \mid BCDEZ)$, we have to show that

$$\Delta_B + \Delta_C + \Delta_D + \Delta_E \geq \Delta_A \quad (1)$$

Also, notice that $w(AB \mid CDEZ) = \alpha\beta$ (as required) and $w(ABZ \mid CDE) = \alpha\beta + (\Delta_C + \Delta_D + \Delta_E) - (\Delta_A + \Delta_B)$. We have to guarantee that $w(ABZ \mid CDE) \geq w(AB \mid CDEZ)$, i.e., we have to show that

$$\Delta_C + \Delta_D + \Delta_E \geq \Delta_A + \Delta_B \quad (2)$$

Note that (2) implies (1). By considering the rest of the cuts, we get a total of 10 inequalities symmetric to (2) (and which can be all proved in a similar way). Hence, to complete the proof of the theorem, it suffices to show that (2) holds. As before, this follows by Lemma 3 with $M = \{\gamma\delta, \gamma\epsilon, \delta\epsilon\}$ and $N = \{\alpha\beta, \gamma, \delta, \epsilon\}$. □

Let $\mathcal{M}$ be a vector with 15 values $[a, \ldots, e, ab, \ldots, ae, bc, \ldots, be, cd, ce, de]$. It can be easily verified that these values are realizable min-cut values of a 5-terminal network iff the following inequalities are satisfied:

$$\begin{array}{ll}
a+b \geq ab & \Delta'_C + \Delta'_D + \Delta'_E \geq \Delta'_A + \Delta'_B \\
a+c \geq ac & \Delta'_B + \Delta'_D + \Delta'_E \geq \Delta'_A + \Delta'_C \\
a+d \geq ad & \Delta'_B + \Delta'_C + \Delta'_E \geq \Delta'_A + \Delta'_D \\
a+e \geq ae & \quad\quad\quad\quad . \\
b+c \geq bc & \quad\quad\quad\quad . \\
b+d \geq bd & \quad\quad\quad\quad . \\
b+e \geq be & \quad\quad\quad\quad . \\
c+d \geq cd & \quad\quad\quad\quad . \\
c+e \geq ce & \quad\quad\quad\quad . \\
d+e \geq de & \Delta'_A + \Delta'_B + \Delta'_C \geq \Delta'_D + \Delta'_E
\end{array}$$

$\Delta'_A \geq 0, \Delta'_B \geq 0, \Delta'_C \geq 0, \Delta'_D \geq 0, \Delta'_E \geq 0$, where

$\Delta'_A = \frac{(ab+ac+ad+ae)-(2a+b+c+d+e)}{2}$, ... , and $\Delta'_E = \frac{(ae+be+ce+de)-(2e+a+b+c+d)}{2}$.

4.4 Optimality

We now show that the preceding constructions of mimicking networks are optimal. All we have to show is the next lemma.

Lemma 4. *There exists a k-terminal network for which the mimicking network must have at least one vertex in addition to the k terminals, for any $k > 3$.*

Proof. Assume that the network G to be mimicked is a star (i.e., a tree of depth one) where all vertices but the center Z (root of the tree) are the $k > 3$ terminals. Let Q denote the terminal set and let all k edges have capacity 1. Hence, every min-cut in G has a non-zero value.

Now assume contrary to the lemma that there is a mimicking network G' for G *without* additional vertices. Since there are no additional vertices in G', we must have that G' contains exactly k vertices, where each vertex is a terminal. Take any two vertices (terminals) in G', say A and B. Then, $w(AB \mid Q \setminus \{A, B\}) = w(A \mid Q \setminus \{A\}) + w(B \mid Q \setminus \{B\}) - 2w(AB)$, and since G' is a mimicking network, this gives that $\alpha\beta = \alpha + \beta - 2w(AB)$, or $w(AB) = \frac{\alpha+\beta-\alpha\beta}{2}$. Since $k > 3$, $\alpha\beta = w(AZ) + w(BZ) = 2$. Hence, $w(AB) = \frac{1+1-2}{2} = 0$.

But since A and B are any two terminals, this implies that every edge of the mimicking network has capacity zero, which, in turn, implies that the value of every cut in G' is also zero; this contradicts the fact that all min-cuts in G have non-zero value. □

5 Bounded Treewidth Networks

Let G be a network of bounded treewidth and (X, T) its augmented binary tree decomposition. For a subtree T' of T, we define the subgraph G' *spanned by* T', as follows. The vertices of G' are the vertices in the sets associated with the vertices of T', i.e., $V(G') = \cup_{i \in V(T')} X_i$. The edges of G' are those edges that the augmenting function maps to vertices in T', i.e., $E(G') = \{e \in E(G) : h(e) \in V(T')\}$. It is easy to check that vertex-disjoint subtrees span edge-disjoint subgraphs. (In fact it is only to ensure this property that we introduce the augmenting function.)

Theorem 4. *Let G be a n-vertex network of treewidth t. Let $Q \subseteq V(G)$ be the terminals of G and let $|Q| = k$. Then, we can construct a mimicking network for G at terminals Q that has size at most $k2^{2^{3(t+1)}}$.*

Proof (sketch). We use induction on k. If $k \leq 3(t+1)$, then the theorem follows from the result in [7]. Assume the theorem holds for $k' < k$. The idea to show that it holds for networks with k terminals is as follows.

Let (X, T) be an augmented binary tree decomposition of G. Root T at some arbitrary vertex of degree less than 3. For a vertex $x \in V(T)$, let T_x^- denote the subtree of T rooted at x, including the vertex x, and let T_x^+ denote the subtree $T \backslash T_x^-$. Define G_x^- and G_x^+ to be the subgraphs spanned by T_x^- and

T_x^+ respectively. Define $Q_x^- = Q \cap V(G_x^-)$ and $Q_x^+ = Q \cap V(G_x^+)$. Then, it can be shown that there exists a vertex, $v \in V(T)$, such that $|Q_v^+| < k$ and $|Q_v^-| \leq 3(t+1)$. Let w be the parent of v. The continuity condition of tree decompositions ensures that $X_v \cap X_w$ is a separator. *Split* the graph at $X_v \cap X_w$ into G_v^+ and G_v^-. By induction, we construct a mimicking network of size at most $(k-1)2^{2^{3(t+1)}}$ for G_v^+ at terminals Q_v^+. Using the algorithm of [7], we construct a mimicking network of size at most $2^{2^{3(t+1)}}$ for G_v^- at terminals Q_v^-. *Glueing* the two networks together yields a mimicking network for G at terminals Q of the required size. □

The above construction holds for both directed and undirected bounded treewidth networks.

6 Outerplanar networks

Outerplanar graphs have treewidth 2. Theorem 4 promises a mimicking network of size $2^{2^9}k$ for an outerplanar network with k terminals. By arguing more carefully for outerplanar networks, we can give a different construction for mimicking networks of much smaller size. The basic idea is as follows (details are omitted due to space limitations). Consider an embedding of the outerplanar network. Then, the endpoints of any edge not adjacent to the outer face are a separator. By working with the dual graph of the embedding (excluding the outer face), we can show how to *split* the network at a number of such separators to obtain $O(k)$ subgraphs with the property that each has either 3 or 4 terminals (including its separator vertices). Actually, the number of 3-terminal subgraphs is $k-2$ and that of 4-terminal subgraphs is $3(k-1)$. We can construct mimicking networks for each subgraph with 3 terminals using Theorem 1 and for each subgraph with 4 terminals using Theorem 2. However, we can also prove that this latter 4-terminal special subgraph has an outerplanar mimicking network of at most 12 vertices. Glueing the different mimicking networks together yields the desired mimicking network: start with one mimicking network and glue to it another that shares separator terminals with it. Then, since each separator has two vertices, every time we glue a new mimicking network with x vertices, we increase the total number of vertices by $x-2$. The first network has at most 5 vertices, after which we add one vertex for each 3-terminal mimicking network and (a) either three vertices for every 4-terminal mimicking network (Theorem 2) yielding a total of $5+(k-2)+3(3k-3) = 10k-6$, or (b) 10 vertices for every 4-terminal mimicking network yielding a total of $5+(k-2)+10(3k-3) = 31k-27$. It is easy to verify that the whole process takes $O(n)$ time.

Theorem 5. *Let G be an n-vertex undirected outerplanar network with terminal set Q, where $|Q| = k$. Then, in $O(n)$ time we can construct: (i) a mimicking network of G at Q with at most $10k-6$ vertices; (ii) an outerplanar mimicking network of G at Q with at most $31k-27$ vertices.*

In the case of directed outerplanar networks, we can show in a similar fashion that the outerplanar mimicking network has at most $80k-77$ vertices.

7 Extensions of Our Results

Another important area of research is to mimic the cut properties of a hypergraph H by a graph G. This is called modeling of a hypergraph by a graph with the same min-cut properties [8,9] and is of particular importance on partitioning circuits in layout problems. In this case, circuits are modeled as hypergraphs and the task is to partition them according to a minimum cut of the hypergraph. However, the existing partitioning algorithms are usually designed for (ordinary) graphs and become very inefficient when applied to hypergraphs [11], mainly because all interesting variants of the partitioning problem involving hypergraphs are NP-hard. Moreover, no approximation algorithm exists for any of the hypergraph partitioning problems. For this reason, an elegant and general method is to model hypergraphs by graphs with the same min-cut properties and then apply the graph partitioning algorithms to the resulting model [9, Sec. 6.1.5]. Note that in this case, it suffices to examine the existence of graphs that model a single hyperedge with capacity 1. For if this is true, then we can construct a model for an arbitrary hypergraph with positive hyperedge capacities by multiplying the edge capacities by appropriate factors and putting together the models for all the hyperedges.

A graph $G = (V \cup D, E)$, where $|V| = k$ and $|D| = d \geq 0$, is called a *min-cut model* for a hyperedge with capacity 1 and vertex set V', which is in 1-1 correspondence with V, if for every non-empty $U \subseteq V$ the capacity of any min-cut with defining subset $S \supseteq U$ is equal to 1. If $U = \emptyset$, then the capacity of the min-cut should be 0.

In [8] it is shown that there is no min-cut model for $k \geq 4$ if negative capacities on the edges of G are not allowed. But one can hope to find an approximate min-cut model with positive edge capacities that is as balanced as possible, i.e., the quotient between the capacity of the largest and the smallest min-cut that partitions V' is as small as possible. More formally:

A graph $G = (V \cup D, E)$, where $|V| = k$ and $|D| = d \geq 0$, with positive edge capacities is called a *b-approximate min-cut model* for a hyperedge with capacity 1 and vertex set V', which is in 1-1 correspondence with V, if the quotient between the capacity of the largest and the smallest min-cut separating a proper and non-empty subset U of V from $V \setminus U$ is b. The quotient b is called the *balance* of the model.

Lengauer conjectures in [9, Sec. 6.1.5] (see also [8, Conjecture 6]) that cliques without additional vertices (i.e., $d = 0$) are the best balanced approximate min-cut models. In the next theorem we show that Lengauer's Conjecture is true.

Theorem 6 (Lengauer's Conjecture). *For a hyperedge with capacity 1 and k vertices, there is no b-approximate min-cut model having a balance b smaller than that achieved by the complete graph on k vertices and all edge capacities equal to $1/(k-1)$.*

Proof. Take a best approximate min-cut model, i.e., a graph with $k + d$ vertices and positive edge capacities such that the quotient between the capacity $w(L)$ of the largest min-cut and the capacity $w(S)$ of the smallest min-cut is minimum.

Let M be the set of $\frac{\binom{k}{k/2}}{2}$ min-cuts separating $k/2$ of the terminals from the rest. Let N be the multiset of the k min-cuts separating a single terminal from the rest, where each one of the min-cuts is taken with multiplicity $\frac{k\binom{k}{k/2}}{8(k-1)}$. Now, invoke Lemma 3 with these two sets. It is not hard to verify that the conditions of Lemma 3 are fulfilled.

This implies that the capacity of the $\frac{\binom{k}{k/2}}{2}$ min-cuts in M is greater than or equal to the capacity of the $\frac{k^2\binom{k}{k/2}}{8(k-1)}$ min-cuts in N. Hence, the capacity of the largest min-cut in M, say $w(m)$, must be at least

$$\frac{k^2\binom{k}{k/2}/(8(k-1))}{\binom{k}{k/2}/2} = \frac{k^2}{4(k-1)}$$

times larger than the capacity of the smallest min-cut in N, say $w(n)$. Consequently, $\frac{w(L)}{w(S)} \geq \frac{w(m)}{w(n)} \geq \frac{k^2}{4(k-1)}$. But it can be easily verified that this is exactly the quotient achieved by a clique on k vertices and all edge capacities equal to $1/(k-1)$. □

References

1. R. Ahuja, T. Magnanti, and J. Orlin, *Network Flows* Prentice-Hall, 1993.
2. S. Arikati, S. Chaudhuri, and C. Zaroliagis, All-Pairs Min-Cut in Sparse Networks, *Journal of Algorithms*, to appear; preliminary version in *Found. of Software Technology and Theor. Comp. Science* – FSTTCS'95, Lecture Notes in Computer Science Vol. 1026, Springer-Verlag, 1995, pp.363-376.
3. H. Bodlaender, A Linear Time Algorithm for Finding Tree-decompositions of Small Treewidth, *SIAM Journal on Computing*, **25** (1996), 1305-1317.
4. C.K. Cheng and T.C. Hu, Maximum Concurrent Flows and Minimum Cuts, *Algorithmica*, **8** (1992), 233-249.
5. D. Gusfield, Very Simple Methods for All Pairs Network Flow Analysis, *SIAM Journal on Computing*, **19** (1990), 143-155.
6. R.E. Gomory and T.C. Hu, Multi-terminal network flows, *Journal of SIAM*, **9** (1961), 551-570.
7. T. Hagerup, J. Katajainen, N. Nishimura, and P. Ragde, Characterizations of k-Terminal Flow Networks and Computing Network Flows in Partial k-Trees, in *Proc. 6th ACM-SIAM Symposium on Discrete Algorithms (SODA'95)* ACM-SIAM, 1995, pp. 641-649.
8. E. Ihler, F. Wagner, and D. Wagner, Modeling hypergraphs by graphs with the same mincut properties, *Inform. Proc. Lett.*, **45** (1993), 171-175.
9. T. Lengauer, *Combinatorial Algorithms for Integrated Circuit Layout*, Teubner, Stuttgart and Wiley, Chichester, UK, 1990.
10. M.T. Shing and T.C. Hu, A Decomposition Algorithm for Multi-terminal Network Flows, *Discrete Applied Mathematics*, **13** (1986), 165-181.
11. A. Vanneli and S.W. Hadley, A Gomory-Hu cut tree representation of a netlist partitioning problem, *IEEE Trans. Circuits and Systems*, **37** (1990), 1133-1139.

Metric Semantics for True Concurrent Real Time

CHRISTEL BAIER[a], JOOST-PIETER KATOEN[b] AND DIEGO LATELLA[c]

[a] *Fakultät für Mathematik und Informatik, Universität Mannheim Seminargebäude A5, D-68159 Mannheim, Germany*

[b] *Lehrstuhl für Informatik VII, Friedrich-Alexander-Universität Erlangen-Nürnberg Martensstrasse 3, D-91058 Erlangen, Germany*

[c] *CNUCE Istituto del CNR, Via Santa Maria 36, I-56100 Pisa, Italy*

Abstract. This paper investigates the use of a complete metric space framework for providing denotational semantics to a real-time process algebra. The study is carried out in a non-interleaving setting and is based on a timed extension of Langerak's bundle event structures, a variant of Winskel's event structures. The distance function is based on the amount of time to which event structures do 'agree'. We show that this intuitive notion of distance is a pseudo metric (but not a metric) on the set of timed event structures. A generalisation to equivalence classes of timed event structures in which we abstract from event names and non-executable events (events that can never appear) is shown to be a complete ultra-metric space. We show that the resulting metric semantics is an abstraction of an existing cpo-based denotational and a related operational semantics for the considered language.

1 Introduction

In this paper we consider a metric denotational semantics for an algebraic specification language that besides concurrency, synchronisation, and non-determinism, encompasses the notion of real-time. The language that we consider is a real-time extension of a process algebra based on the standardised specification language LOTOS [7]. As semantic domain we take a timed extension (defined in [10]) of Langerak's bundle event structures, a variant of Winskel's event structures that has been shown to adequately deal with the operators of LOTOS (in particular, parallel composition and disruption) [11]. The suitability of this timed truly concurrent model for modelling time-critical systems is addressed in [10]. The metric approach of this paper can also be applied to timed variants of other brands of event structures, like prime and stable event structures.

The basic idea of this paper is to consider behaviours of event structures up to a certain time. This is in fact a continuous version of the idea in [12] to consider (untimed) event structures up to a certain depth (i.e. length of a causal chain). The distance function is based on the amount of time to which event structures do 'agree'. We show that this intuitive notion of distance is a pseudo metric (but not a metric) on TES, the set of timed event structures. As a first step towards obtaining a metric (rather than a pseudo metric), we consider TES modulo an isomorphism $\simeq_{iso}$ that abstracts from event names and from non-executable events, events that can never appear. Secondly, we refine this notion towards finitely approximable timed event structures module $\simeq_{iso}$ and show that this model is a complete ultra-metric space. The resulting domain is used as a semantic domain for time-guarded processes. A process is time-guarded if it cannot generate instantaneous recursive process instantiations. We show that the proposed metric semantics is an abstraction of the cpo-based semantics of [10].

2 A real-time process algebra

We assume a given set of observable actions Obs and an *invisible action* τ; $\tau \notin \mathsf{Obs}$. The action $\surd$ indicates the *successful termination* action of a process; $\surd \notin \mathsf{Obs}$ and $\surd \neq \tau$. In addition, let $\mathsf{Act} = \mathsf{Obs} \cup \{\tau, \surd\}$, $a \in \mathsf{Obs} \cup \{\tau\}$, $I \subseteq \mathbb{R}^+ \cup \{\infty\}$, $t \in \mathbb{R}^+ \cup \{\infty\}$, $A \subseteq \mathsf{Obs}$, $\lambda : \mathsf{Act} \longrightarrow \mathsf{Act}$ with $\lambda(\tau) = \tau$ and $\lambda(\surd) = \surd$, and Var a set of process variables with $x \in \mathsf{Var}$. The set of expressions defined in the following is denoted Expr.

$$P ::= \mathbf{0} \mid \mathbf{1} \mid a_I \,.\, P \mid P + P \mid P\,;\, P \mid P\,[\!> P \mid P \,||_A\, P \mid P \backslash A \mid P[\lambda] \mid P \rhd_t P \mid x.$$

$+$, $\backslash A$, and $[\lambda]$ are the usual process algebra operators choice, abstraction and relabelling, respectively.

- $\mathbf{1}$ represents the successful termination process; it can only perform action $\surd$ and then becomes $\mathbf{0}$, the process that cannot perform any action.
- $a_I \,.\, P$ denotes the prefix of a and P where a is allowed (but not forced) to occur at $t \in I$.
- $P\,;\,Q$ denotes the sequential composition of P and Q; the control is passed to Q by the termination of P as indicated by the occurrence of $\surd$.
- $P\,[\!> Q$ denotes the disruption of P by Q; i.e. P may at any point of its execution be disrupted by Q, unless P has terminated.
- $P \,||_A\, Q$ denotes the parallel composition of P and Q; P and Q execute actions not in A independently from each other, while actions in A (and successful termination actions) must be performed by both processes simultaneously.
- $P \rhd_t Q$ initially behaves like P, but if P does not perform an action before time t (since its enabling) then a timeout occurs and control is passed to Q.

Using these operators a timed interrupt, for instance, can easily be modelled: the process $P\,[\!> (\mathbf{0} \rhd_t Q)$ specifies that P is disrupted by Q at time t, unless P has terminated before. Various case studies have proven that the timed operators like $a_I \,.\, P$ and $P \rhd_t Q$ are convenient to specify practical real-time systems [1, 18].

Process variables are considered in the context of a set of process definitions of the form $x := P$, where P might contain occurrences of x or of other process variables. For process variable x let $decl(x)$ denote the body of x, i.e. $decl(x) = P$ for $x := P$. A *process* is a pair $\langle decl, P\rangle$ consisting of a declaration $decl : \mathsf{Var} \longrightarrow \mathsf{Expr}$ and an expression $P \in \mathsf{Expr}$. PA denotes the set of all processes.

3 Timed event structures

Event structures consist of *events* labelled with actions (an event modelling the occurrence of its action), together with relations of causality and conflict between events. We take Langerak's (extended bundle) event structures [11] and equip this with timing information. Event structures incorporate a *conflict* relation (denoted $\rightsquigarrow$) that—as opposed to what is common in other types of event structures—is not required to be symmetric and a *bundle* relation (denoted $\mapsto$) for modelling causality.

The meaning of $e \rightsquigarrow e'$ is that (i) if e' occurs it disables the occurrence of e, and (ii) if e and e' both occur in a single system run then e precedes e'. $e \rightsquigarrow e'$ and $e' \rightsquigarrow e$ is equivalent with $e \,\#\, e'$, the usual symmetric conflict in event structures. The reason for adopting $\rightsquigarrow$ rather than $\#$ is to model the disrupt operator $[>$ adequately.

Causality is represented by the bundle relation. For set X of events and an event e, $X \mapsto e$ means that if e happens in a system run, some event in X must have happened before. X is called the *bundle set* and we use $\mapsto$ to denote the set of bundles of an event structure. The reason for not having a binary causality relation between events (as in prime event structures [16]) is to model parallel composition $||_A$ in a less complex way.

Time is added to event structures in the following way [10]. Relative delays between events are attached to bundles, and delays relative to the start are attached to events. Delays determine when an event may happen, they do not specify that an event should happen at a particular time. For the latter purpose we use *urgent* events; an urgent event should happen as soon as it is enabled.

Definition 1. A *timed event structure* (tes) $\mathcal{E}$ is a tuple $(E, \rightsquigarrow, \mapsto, l, \mathcal{A}, \mathcal{R}, \mathcal{U})$ with E, a set of *events*, $\rightsquigarrow \subseteq E \times E$, the (irreflexive) *conflict* relation, $\mapsto \subseteq \mathcal{P}(E) \times E$, the *bundle* relation, $l : E \longrightarrow \mathsf{Act}$, the *labelling* function, $\mathcal{A} : E \longrightarrow \mathcal{P}(\mathrm{I\!R}^+ \cup \{\infty\})$, the *event delay* function, $\mathcal{R} : \mapsto \longrightarrow \mathcal{P}(\mathrm{I\!R}^+ \cup \{\infty\})$, the *bundle delay* function, and $\mathcal{U} \subseteq E$, the set of *urgent* events, such that:

(P1) $(X \times X) \setminus \mathrm{Id}_E \subseteq \rightsquigarrow$ for any bundle set X

and for all $e \in \mathcal{U}$:

(P2) $\forall e' \in E, X \subseteq E : ((e' \rightsquigarrow e \vee e \rightsquigarrow e') \wedge X \mapsto e) \Rightarrow (X \mapsto e' \vee X \rightsquigarrow e')$
(P3) $\exists t \in \mathrm{I\!R}^+ : (\mathcal{A}(e) \in \{\varnothing, \{t\}\}) \vee (\exists X : X \mapsto e \wedge \mathcal{R}(X, e) \in \{\varnothing, \{t\}\})$.

Here, $\mathcal{P}(\cdot)$ denotes the power-set function, $X \rightsquigarrow e'$ denotes $(\forall e'' \in X : e'' \rightsquigarrow e')$ and Id_E denotes the identity relation on set E. Note that $\varnothing \rightsquigarrow e'$ for all e'.

Event structures are depicted as follows. Events are denoted as dots; near the dot the action label is given. If no confusion arises we often use action labels rather than event identities to denote events. $e \rightsquigarrow e'$ is indicated by a dotted arrow from e to e'; if also $e' \rightsquigarrow e$, then a dotted line is drawn instead. A bundle $X \mapsto e$ is indicated by an arrow to which each event in X is connected via a line. Bundle and event delays are depicted near to a bundle and event, respectively. Urgent events are denoted by open dots, other events by closed dots. A bundle

$X \mapsto e$ with $\mathcal{R}(X,e) = I$ is denoted by $X \overset{I}{\mapsto} e$. Delays $[t, \infty)$ are simply denoted by t; delays $[0, \infty)$ are usually omitted. Figure 1(a) shows an example tes with e.g. $\{a\} \overset{[0,7]}{\mapsto} b$ and $\{a\} \overset{[0,5]}{\mapsto} c$, $b \rightsquigarrow \tau$ and $\tau \rightsquigarrow b$. $\mathcal{U} = \{\tau\}$ and $\mathcal{A}$ is 0 for all events.

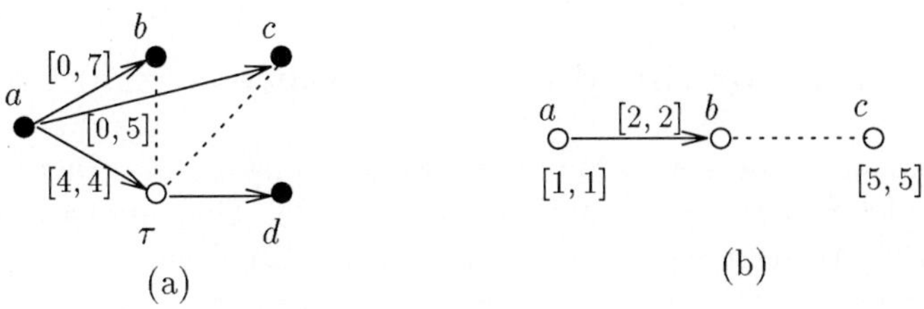

Fig. 1. A tes and a non-tes

The concept of a system run for tes's is captured by the notion of a *timed event trace*. For σ a sequence of distinct events let the set of events enabled in $\mathcal{E}$ after σ be defined as[1]

$$\mathsf{en}^{\mathcal{E}}(\sigma) \triangleq \{ e \in E \mid e \notin \sigma \,\wedge\, (\forall e_i \in \sigma : e \not\rightsquigarrow e_i) \,\wedge\, (\forall X \mapsto e : X \cap \sigma \neq \varnothing) \}.$$

The time instants at which an enabled event in $\mathcal{E}$ after $\sigma = (e_1, t_1) \ldots (e_n, t_n)$ could potentially happen is determined as

$$\mathsf{time}^{\mathcal{E}}_{\sigma}(e) \triangleq \mathcal{A}(e) \cap \bigcap_{e_i \rightsquigarrow e} [t_i, \infty) \cap \bigcap_{X \overset{I}{\mapsto} e,\, e_i \in X} t_i + I.$$

Definition 2. $\sigma = (e_1, t_1) \ldots (e_n, t_n)$ with $e_i \in E$ (all events being pairwise distinct) and $t_i \in \mathbb{R}^+$, is a *timed event trace* of $\mathcal{E} \in \mathsf{TES}$ iff for all $0 < i \leqslant n$:

1. $e_j \rightsquigarrow e_i \;\Rightarrow\; (j < i \,\wedge\, t_j \leqslant t_i)$ for all $0 < j \leqslant n$
2. $X \overset{I}{\mapsto} e_i \;\Rightarrow\; (\exists j : X \cap \{e_1, \ldots, e_{i-1}\} = \{e_j\} \,\wedge\, t_i \in t_j + I)$ for all $X \subseteq E$
3. $t_i \in \mathcal{A}(e_i)$
4. $(e_i \rightsquigarrow e \,\vee\, e \rightsquigarrow e_i) \;\Rightarrow\; t_i \leqslant \mathit{min}(\mathsf{time}^{\mathcal{E}}_{e_1 \ldots e_{i-1}}(e))$ for $e \in \mathcal{U} \cap \mathsf{en}^{\mathcal{E}}(e_1 \ldots e_{i-1})$.

The set of timed event traces of $\mathcal{E}$ is denoted by $\mathit{Traces}(\mathcal{E})$.

By convention we use $\mathit{min}\, \varnothing = \infty$. The last constraint takes care of the fact that urgent events may prevent the events that they disable (or by which they are disabled) to occur after a certain time. That is, event e_i can occur at time t_i provided there is no enabled urgent event e that disables e_i (or that is disabled by e_i) and that (if it occurs) must occur before t_i.

For example, for the following sequences of timed events the conditions are given under which they are timed event traces of Figure 1(a):

$$(a, t_a)(c, t_c)(b, t_b) \text{ if } 0 \leqslant t_a \leqslant t_c \leqslant t_b \,\wedge\, t_b \leqslant t_a + 4 \,\wedge\, t_c \leqslant t_a + 4$$
$$(a, t_a)(\tau, t_\tau)(d, t_d) \text{ if } 0 \leqslant t_a \leqslant t_\tau \leqslant t_d \,\wedge\, t_\tau = t_a + 4.$$

[1] Often the set of events of a sequence is identified with the sequence itself.

Note that Figure 1(a) models a typical timeout scenario: if after the occurrence of a neither b nor c happen within 4 time units, then a timeout (τ) is forced to occur. It τ would not be urgent, the conditions for t_a and t_b in the first case would be $t_b \leqslant t_a+7$ and $t_c \leqslant t_a+5$, since τ is not forced to occur and time does not resolve the choice.

4 Operators for timed event structures

In this section we present some operators on timed event structures that are needed to define a compositional semantics for PA. They are basically adopted from [9, 10]. We start with some basic notions. Let Events be a set such that for all actions $a \in \mathsf{Act}$ there is an event $e_a \in \mathsf{Events}$, and (i) if $e \in \mathsf{Events}$ then $(e,*), (*,e) \in \mathsf{Events}$, and (ii) if $e, e' \in \mathsf{Events}$ then $(e, e') \in \mathsf{Events}$. Let TES denote the set of tes's $\mathcal{E}$ with $E \subseteq \mathsf{Events}$. Let $init(\mathcal{E})$ be the set of initial events of $\mathcal{E}$ and $exit(\mathcal{E})$ its set of successful termination events, i.e. $init(\mathcal{E}) \triangleq \{ e \in E \mid \neg(\exists X \subseteq E : X \mapsto e) \}$ and $exit(\mathcal{E}) \triangleq \{ e \in E \mid l(e) = \surd \}$.

In the rest of this section let $\mathcal{E} \in \mathsf{TES}$ and $\mathcal{E}_1 = (E_1, \leadsto_1, \mapsto_1, l_1, \mathcal{A}_1, \mathcal{R}_1, \mathcal{U}_1)$, $\mathcal{E}_2 = (E_2, \leadsto_2, \mapsto_2, l_2, \mathcal{A}_2, \mathcal{R}_2, \mathcal{U}_2)$ such that w.l.o.g. $E_1 \cap E_2 = \varnothing$. Let $\hat{\tau}$ denote the urgent variant of τ.

Definition 3. For $a \in \mathsf{Obs} \cup \{ \tau, \hat{\tau} \}$ and $I \subseteq [0, \infty)$, $a_I \,.\, \mathcal{E}_1 \triangleq (E_1 \cup \{ e_a \}, \leadsto_1, \mapsto, l_1 \cup \{ (e_a, a) \}, \mathcal{A}, \mathcal{R}, \mathcal{U})$ where for $e \notin E_1$

- $\mapsto = \mapsto_1 \cup (\{ \{ e \} \} \times E_1)$
- $\mathcal{A} = \{ (e, I) \} \cup (E_1 \times \{ [0, \infty) \})$
- $\mathcal{R} = \mathcal{R}_1 \cup \{ ((\{ e \}, e'), \mathcal{A}_1(e)) \mid e' \in E_1 \}$
- $\mathcal{U} = \mathsf{if}\ a = \hat{\tau}\ \mathsf{then}\ \mathcal{U}_1 \cup \{ e \}\ \mathsf{else}\ \mathcal{U}_1$.

$\hat{\tau}_I \,.\, \mathcal{E}$ denotes the prefixing of τ_I and $\mathcal{E}$ where e is declared to be urgent. The possibility $\hat{\tau}_I \,.\, \mathcal{E}$ is used to define the semantics of the timeout operator $\rhd$ in a concise way. Notice that for $\hat{\tau}_I \,.\, \mathcal{E}$ set I must be either empty of equal to $[t, t]$ for some t in order to guarantee axiom (P3).

Definition 4. $\mathcal{E}_1 + \mathcal{E}_2 \triangleq (E_1 \cup E_2, \leadsto, \mapsto_1 \cup \mapsto_2, l_1 \cup l_2, \mathcal{A}_1 \cup \mathcal{A}_2, \mathcal{R}_1 \cup \mathcal{R}_2, \mathcal{U}_1 \cup \mathcal{U}_2)$ where $\leadsto = \leadsto_1 \cup \leadsto_2 \cup (init(\mathcal{E}_1) \times init(\mathcal{E}_2)) \cup (init(\mathcal{E}_2) \times init(\mathcal{E}_1))$.

Definition 5. Let $A \subseteq \mathsf{Obs}$. Then $\mathcal{E} \setminus A \triangleq (E, \leadsto, \mapsto, l', \mathcal{A}, \mathcal{R}, \mathcal{U})$ where $(l(e) \in A \Rightarrow l'(e) = \tau) \wedge (l(e) \notin A \Rightarrow l'(e) = l(e))$.

Definition 6. For $\lambda : \mathsf{Act} \longrightarrow \mathsf{Act}$ with $\lambda(\tau) = \tau$ and $\lambda(\surd) = \surd$ let $\mathcal{E}[\lambda] \triangleq (E, \leadsto, \mapsto, \lambda \circ l, \mathcal{A}, \mathcal{R}, \mathcal{U})$.

Definition 7. $\mathcal{E}_1 \,;\, \mathcal{E}_2 \triangleq (E_1 \cup E_2, \leadsto, \mapsto, l, \mathcal{A}, \mathcal{R}, \mathcal{U}_1 \cup \mathcal{U}_2)$ where

- $\leadsto = \leadsto_1 \cup \leadsto_2 \cup (exit(\mathcal{E}_1) \times exit(\mathcal{E}_1)) \setminus \mathrm{Id}_{E_1}$
- $\mapsto = \mapsto_1 \cup \mapsto_2 \cup (\{ exit(\mathcal{E}_1) \} \times E_2))$
- $l = ((l_1 \cup l_2) \setminus (exit(\mathcal{E}_1) \times \{ \surd \})) \cup (exit(\mathcal{E}_1) \times \{ \tau \})$
- $\mathcal{A} = \mathcal{A}_1 \cup (E_2 \times \{ [0, \infty) \})$

– $\mathcal{R} = \mathcal{R}_1 \cup \mathcal{R}_2 \cup \{ ((exit(\mathcal{E}_1), e), \mathcal{A}_2(e)) \mid e \in E_2) \}$.

As an example of how $\mathcal{E}_1 \,;\, \mathcal{E}_2$ is computed consider:

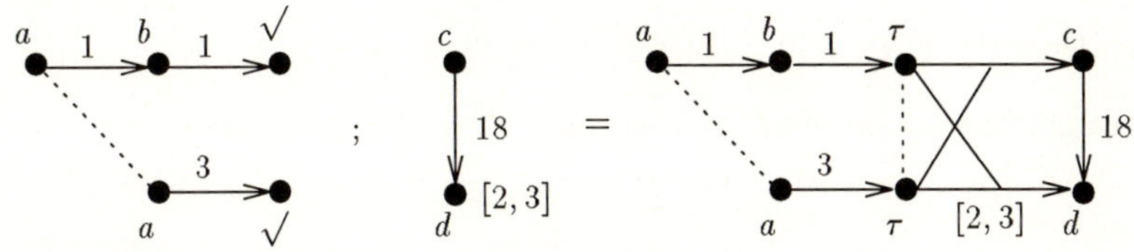

Notice that the delay of d in $\mathcal{E}_2$ now becomes relative to the termination of $\mathcal{E}_1$.

Definition 8. $\mathcal{E}_1 \,[\!> \mathcal{E}_2 \triangleq (E_1 \cup E_2, \rightsquigarrow, \mapsto_1 \cup \mapsto_2, l_1 \cup l_2, \mathcal{A}_1 \cup \mathcal{A}_2, \mathcal{R}_1 \cup \mathcal{R}_2, \mathcal{U}_1 \cup \mathcal{U}_2)$ where $\rightsquigarrow = \rightsquigarrow_1 \cup \rightsquigarrow_2 \cup (E_1 \times init(\mathcal{E}_2)) \cup (init(\mathcal{E}_2) \times exit(\mathcal{E}_1))$.

The events of $\mathcal{E}_1 \,||_A\, \mathcal{E}_2$ are constructed in the following way: an event e of E_i (i=1, 2) that does not need to synchronise is paired with the auxiliary symbol $*$, and an event which is labelled with $\surd$ or with an action in A is paired with all events (if any) in the other tes that are equally labelled. Two events are put in conflict if any of their components are in conflict, or if different events have a common component different from $*$ (such events appear if two or more events in one tes synchronise with the same event in the other tes). A bundle is introduced iff when we take the projection on the component $\mathcal{E}_i$ of the bundle-set we obtain a bundle in $\mapsto_i$. Let for $A \subseteq \mathsf{Obs}$, $E_i^s \triangleq \{ e \in E_i \mid l_i(e) \in A \cup \{ \surd \} \}$ be the set of synchronising events and $E_i^f \triangleq E_i \setminus E_i^s$ the set of 'free' events.

Definition 9. Let $A \subseteq \mathsf{Obs}$. Then $\mathcal{E}_1 \,||_A\, \mathcal{E}_2 \triangleq (E, \rightsquigarrow, \mapsto, l, \mathcal{A}, \mathcal{R}, \mathcal{U})$ where

– $E = (E_1^f \times \{ * \}) \cup (\{ * \} \times E_2^f) \cup \{ (e_1, e_2) \in E_1^s \times E_2^s \mid l_1(e_1) = l_2(e_2) \}$
– $(e_1, e_2) \rightsquigarrow (e_1', e_2')$ iff
  - $(e_1 \rightsquigarrow_1 e_1') \vee (e_2 \rightsquigarrow_2 e_2')$ or
  - $(e_1 = e_1' \neq * \wedge e_2 \neq e_2') \vee (e_2 = e_2' \neq * \wedge e_1 \neq e_1')$
– $X \mapsto (e_1, e_2)$ iff
  - $(\exists X_1 : X_1 \mapsto_1 e_1 \wedge X = \{ (e, e') \in E \mid e \in X_1 \})$ or
  - $(\exists X_2 : X_2 \mapsto_2 e_2 \wedge X = \{ (e, e') \in E \mid e' \in X_2 \})$
– $l(e_1, e_2) = \text{if } e_1 = * \text{ then } l_2(e_2) \text{ else } l_1(e_1)$
– $\mathcal{A}(e_1, e_2) = \mathcal{A}_1(e_1) \cap \mathcal{A}_2(e_2)$ with $\mathcal{A}_i(*) = [0, \infty)$.
– $\mathcal{R}(X, (e_1, e_2)) = \bigcap_{X_1 \in S_1} \mathcal{R}_1(X_1, e_1) \cap \bigcap_{X_2 \in S_2} \mathcal{R}_2(X_2, e_2)$ with
  - $S_1 = \{ X_1 \subseteq E_1 \mid X_1 \mapsto_1 e_1 \wedge X = \{ (e, e') \in E \mid e \in X_1 \} \}$ and
  - $S_2 = \{ X_2 \subseteq E_2 \mid X_2 \mapsto_2 e_2 \wedge X = \{ (e, e') \in E \mid e' \in X_2 \} \}$
– $(e_1, e_2) \in \mathcal{U}$ iff $e_1 \in \mathcal{U}_1 \vee e_2 \in \mathcal{U}_2$ with $* \notin \mathcal{U}_i$.

Parallel composition is illustrated by the following example where the left-hand tes is composed with the empty tes:

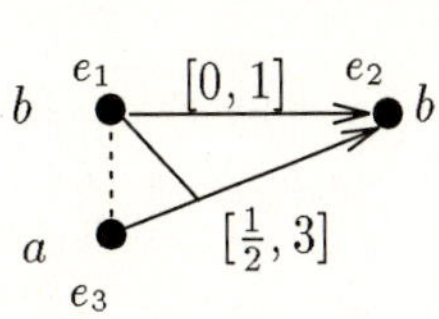

$||_a$ $=$

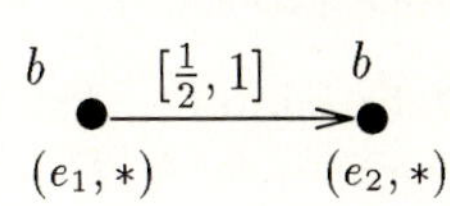

For $\mathcal{E}_1 \rhd_t \mathcal{E}_2$ a new urgent event e with delay $[t,t]$ is introduced that models the expiration of the timer. Since either the timer expires or $\mathcal{E}_1$ performs an initial event before (or at) t, e is put in mutual conflict with all initial events of $\mathcal{E}_1$.

Definition 10. For $t \in [0,\infty)$ let $\mathcal{E}_1 \rhd_t \mathcal{E}_2 \triangleq \mathcal{E}_1 + \hat{\tau}_{[t,t]} \cdot \mathcal{E}_2$.

By straightforward proof one can establish that TES is closed under the operators $a_I \cdot, +, \backslash A, [\lambda], ;, [>, ||_A$, and $\rhd_t$.

5 A metric denotational semantics

The approach. We only give a brief account of our approach; see [2] for a full treatment, and [15, 5, 6] for more information on the use of metrics for denotational semantics. The semantic domain S for PA is equipped with a set Op' of operators that reflect the operators Op of Expr. For any fixed declaration *decl*, the function $P \mapsto \mathcal{M}(\langle decl, P\rangle)$ is a homomorphism from (Expr, Op) to (S, Op') such that the meaning of process variable x is given by $decl(x)$. Function $\mathcal{M}$ satisfies these conditions iff, for any fixed declaration *decl*, the function $P \mapsto \mathcal{M}(\langle decl, P\rangle)$ is a fixed point of $F_{decl} : [\mathsf{Expr} \longrightarrow S] \longrightarrow [\mathsf{Expr} \longrightarrow S]$, defined (in our case) by:

$$\begin{aligned}
F_{decl}(\phi)(\mathbf{0}) &\triangleq \mathbf{0}' \\
F_{decl}(\phi)(\mathbf{1}) &\triangleq \mathbf{1}' \\
F_{decl}(\phi)(x) &\triangleq \phi(decl(x)) \\
F_{decl}(\phi)(op\ P) &\triangleq op'\ F_{decl}(\phi)(P) && \text{for } op \in \{\, a_I \cdot, \backslash A, [\lambda] \,\} \\
F_{decl}(\phi)(P\ op\ Q) &\triangleq F_{decl}(\phi)(P)\ op'\ F_{decl}(\phi)(Q) && \text{for } op \in \{\, +, ||_A, ;, [>, \rhd_t \,\}.
\end{aligned}$$

The semantics of PA is now obtained by $\mathcal{M}(\langle decl, P\rangle) = \phi_{decl}(P)$, where $\phi_{decl} : \mathsf{Expr} \longrightarrow S$ is the unique fixed point of F_{decl}. By Banach's fixpoint theorem, F_{decl} has a unique fixed point, provided that F_{decl} is contracting with respect to a distance function $\tilde{d}$ where $\langle [\mathsf{Expr} \longrightarrow S], \tilde{d}\rangle$ is a complete metric space (cms). $\tilde{d}$ is obtained from the cms $\langle S, d\rangle$ where

$$\tilde{d}(\phi_1, \phi_2) = sup\{\, d(\phi_1(P), \phi_2(P)) \mid P \in \mathsf{Expr} \,\}. \tag{1}$$

F_{decl} is contracting on $\langle [\mathsf{Expr} \longrightarrow S], \tilde{d}\rangle$ if its constituents $;$, $\rhd_t$ and so on, are non-distance increasing on $\langle S, d\rangle$ and contracting in certain arguments.

Time truncation. The basis of our distance function d is time truncation. The minimal time at which e can occur in $\mathcal{E}$ is defined by $mintime_{\mathcal{E}}(e) \triangleq inf\{\, t \in \mathbb{R}^+ \mid \exists \sigma \in Traces(\mathcal{E}) : (e,t) \in \sigma \,\}$, where $inf\, \varnothing \triangleq \infty$. For $t \in \mathbb{R}^+$ and $X \subseteq E$ let $X \upharpoonright t \triangleq \{\, e \in X \mid mintime_{\mathcal{E}}(e) < t \,\}$ and $X \upharpoonright \omega \triangleq \bigcup_{t \geqslant 0} X \upharpoonright t$. Event e is called *executable* iff $e \in E \upharpoonright \omega$, i.e. if $mintime_{\mathcal{E}}(e) < \infty$.

Definition 11. The *truncation* of $\mathcal{E}$ up to $t \in \mathbb{R}^+$ is defined by $\mathcal{E} \upharpoonright t \triangleq (E \upharpoonright t, \rightsquigarrow_t, \mapsto_t, l_t, \mathcal{A}_t, \mathcal{R}_t, \mathcal{U}_t)$ where $l_t(e) = l(e)$, $\mathcal{A}_t(e) = \mathcal{A}(e) \cap [0,t)$, $\mathcal{U}_t = \mathcal{U} \upharpoonright t$, and

- $\rightsquigarrow_t = \rightsquigarrow \cap (E \upharpoonright t \times E \upharpoonright t)$

- $X \mapsto_t e$ iff there exists $Y \mapsto e$ with $Y \upharpoonright t = X$
- $\mathcal{R}_t(X,e) = \bigcap \{ \mathcal{R}(Y,e) \mid Y \mapsto e, Y \upharpoonright t = X \}$.

It is not difficult to check that for $\mathcal{E} \in \mathsf{TES}$ we have $\mathcal{E} \upharpoonright t \in \mathsf{TES}$, for all $t \in \mathbb{R}^+$.

Example 1. Time truncation is illustrated by the following figure.

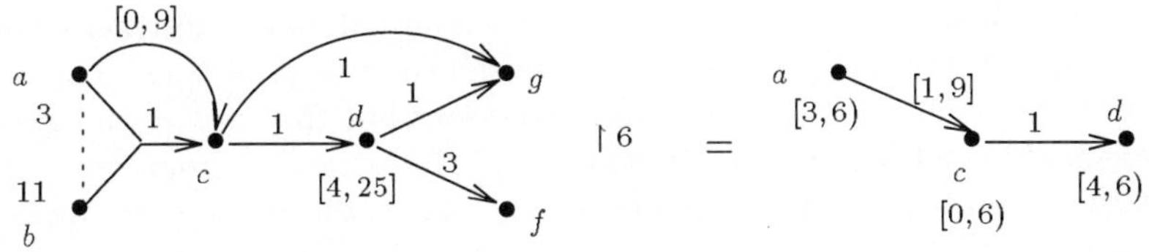

Events e_b, e_f and e_g are eliminated since the minimal time at which they can occur, time 11, 8 and 6, respectively, is at least 6. Note that $\{ e_a \} \overset{[1,9]}{\mapsto}_t e_c$ for t=6, since $\{ e_a, e_b \} \overset{1}{\mapsto} e_c$ and $\{ e_a \} \overset{[0,9]}{\mapsto} e_c$ and $[1, \infty) \cap [0, 9] = [1, 9]$.

Lemma 12. *Traces*$(\mathcal{E}) = \bigcup_{t \geqslant 0}$ *Traces*$(\mathcal{E} \upharpoonright t)$.

A complete ultra-metric space. The idea is to use time truncation as a basis for defining a distance d on TES. In particular, the distance between two tes's will be determined by the maximum amount of time they "agree", that is:

$$d(\mathcal{E}_1, \mathcal{E}_2) = inf\{ 2^{-t} \mid \mathcal{E}_1 \upharpoonright t = \mathcal{E}_2 \upharpoonright t \}. \tag{2}$$

Remark that $\mathcal{E} \upharpoonright 0$ is the empty tes, so each pair of tes's agrees at least up to time 0. Although this basic idea is rather intuitive, it is, unfortunately, too naive. The problem is that some distinct tes's cannot be distinguished according to d. This means that d is a pseudo-metric rather than a metric. For instance, the tes consisting of a single event e with an empty bundle pointing to e is indistinguishable from the empty tes, since their time truncations are all empty. That is, according to (2) their distance is 0. The problem with this example is that tes's may contain events that can never appear. Such events can, for instance, appear in the semantics for expressions that contain circular causal dependencies, like in $a \,.\, b \,.\, \mathbf{0} \,||_{\{a,b\}}\, b \,.\, a \,.\, \mathbf{0}$, or timing constraints that avoid certain actions from happening, like in $a_2 \,.\, \mathbf{0} \rhd_1 b \,.\, \mathbf{0}$ where a will never happen. (Such events can be removed by applying the transformations exposed in [11, 9] that preserve timed event traces.)

A solution to this problem is to impose an equivalence relation, $\simeq$ say, on TES, while aiming at $d(\mathcal{E}_1, \mathcal{E}_2) = 0 \Leftrightarrow \mathcal{E}_1 \simeq \mathcal{E}_2$. Stated in other words, where $\mathbf{d}$ is the equivalent of d on $\mathsf{TES}/\!\simeq$ and $\mathbf{E}_i$ denotes the equivalence class of $\mathcal{E}_i$ under $\simeq$, we aim at $\mathbf{d}(\mathbf{E}_1, \mathbf{E}_2) = 0 \Leftrightarrow \mathbf{E}_1 = \mathbf{E}_2$. In order to obtain $\simeq$, the example suggests to abstract from events that can never be executed:

Definition 13. The *normal form* of $\mathcal{E}$, denoted $NF(\mathcal{E})$, is defined as $NF(\mathcal{E}) \triangleq (E \upharpoonright \omega, \rightsquigarrow_\omega, \mapsto_\omega, l_\omega, \mathcal{A}_\omega, \mathcal{R}_\omega, \mathcal{U}_\omega)$ where $l_\omega(e) = l(e)$, $\mathcal{A}_\omega(e) = \mathcal{A}(e)$, $\mathcal{U}_\omega = \mathcal{U} \cap (E \upharpoonright \omega)$, $\rightsquigarrow_\omega = \rightsquigarrow \cap (E \upharpoonright \omega \times E \upharpoonright \omega)$ and

- $X \mapsto_\omega e$ iff $X \lceil t \mapsto e$ is a bundle in $\mathcal{E} \lceil t$ for all $t > mintime_{\mathcal{E}}(e)$
- $\mathcal{R}_\omega(X, e) = \bigcup_{t > mintime_{\mathcal{E}}(e)} \{ \mathcal{R}(X \lceil t, e) \mid X \lceil t \mapsto e \text{ is a bundle of } \mathcal{E} \lceil t \}$.

For $\mathcal{E} \in \mathsf{TES}$ it follows by straightforward verification that $NF(\mathcal{E}) \in \mathsf{TES}$.

Lemma 14. *Traces*$(NF(\mathcal{E})) =$ *Traces*$(\mathcal{E})$.

As in the untimed case [12] the metric approach also allows to abstract from the names of the events, i.e. to deal with isomorphism classes of tes's. The names of the events are only needed for technical reasons but they are meaningless for the semantics of a PA-process. The advantage of abstraction from event names is that the definitions of operators like +, [>, and so on, become less awkward.

Definition 15. $\mathcal{E}_i = (E_i, \rightsquigarrow_i, \mapsto_i, l_i, \mathcal{A}_i, \mathcal{R}_i, \mathcal{U}_i)$ for i=1, 2 are *isomorphic* if there exists a bijection $f : E_1 \lceil \omega \longrightarrow E_2 \lceil \omega$ such that $l_2 \circ f = l_1$, $\mathcal{A}_2 \circ f = \mathcal{A}_1$ and

1. $e_1 \rightsquigarrow_1 e_2$ iff $f(e_1) \rightsquigarrow_2 f(e_2)$ for all $e_1, e_2 \in E_1 \lceil \omega$,
2. $X \overset{I}{\mapsto}_1 e$ iff $f(X) \overset{I}{\mapsto}_2 f(e)$ for all $e \in E_1 \lceil \omega, X \subseteq E_1 \lceil \omega$, and
3. $e \in \mathcal{U}_1 \lceil \omega$ iff $f(e) \in \mathcal{U}_2$.

Let $\mathcal{E}_1 \simeq_{iso} \mathcal{E}_2$ iff there exists an isomorphism from $\mathcal{E}_1$ to $\mathcal{E}_2$. Note that $\mathcal{E} \simeq_{iso} NF(\mathcal{E})$.

For $\mathcal{E} \in \mathsf{TES}$ let $\mathbf{E}_{\mathcal{E}}$ denote the equivalence class of $\mathcal{E}$ under $\simeq_{iso}$. For $\mathbf{E} \in \mathsf{TES}/\simeq_{iso}$ let $\mathbf{E} \lceil t \triangleq \mathbf{E}_{\mathcal{E} \lceil t}$, where $\mathcal{E}$ is a representative of $\mathbf{E}$. The distance between equivalence classes (under $\simeq_{iso}$) of tes's is given by:

$$\mathbf{d}(\mathbf{E}_1, \mathbf{E}_2) \triangleq inf \{ 2^{-t} \mid \mathbf{E}_1 \lceil t = \mathbf{E}_2 \lceil t \}. \tag{3}$$

Remark that $\mathbf{d}(\mathbf{E}, \mathbf{E} \lceil t) \leqslant 2^{-t}$ for all $t \geqslant 0$.

Example 2. Let $\mathcal{E}_i = (E_i, \varnothing, \mapsto_i, E_i \times \{ a \}, \mathcal{A}_i, \mathcal{R}_i, \varnothing)$, for i=1, 2 where

- $E_1 = \{ (k, j) \mid j \geqslant 1, 0 < k \leqslant j \}$ and $E_2 = E_1 \cup \{ (k, 0) \mid k \geqslant 1 \}$
- $\{ (k, j) \} \mapsto_i (k{+}1, j)$ for $0 < k < j$ and $\{ (k, 0) \} \mapsto_2 (k{+}1, 0)$ for $k \geqslant 1$
- $\mathcal{A}_i(k, j) = [k, k]$ for all $(k, j) \in E_i$, and
- $\mathcal{R}_i(\{ (k, j) \}, (k{+}1, j)) = [1, 1]$.

Then, $\mathcal{E}_1 \not\simeq_{iso} \mathcal{E}_2$ while $\mathcal{E}_1 \lceil t \simeq_{iso} \mathcal{E}_2 \lceil t$ for all $t \geqslant 0$. If we now would define $\mathbf{d}$ as suggested in (3) on $\mathsf{TES}/\simeq_{iso}$ then $\mathbf{d}(\mathbf{E}_1, \mathbf{E}_2) = 0$, although $\mathcal{E}_1$ and $\mathcal{E}_2$ are not isomorphic, thus yielding a pseudo-metric.

The problem with this example is that both tes's allow an infinite number of events to occur in a finite amount of time. This is avoided by considering finitely approximable tes's, a timed analogon of approximable event structures [12].

Definition 16. $\mathcal{E}$ is called *finitely approximable* iff $E \lceil t$ is finite for all $t \in \mathbb{R}^+$.

Let $\mathsf{TES}_{fin}/\simeq_{iso}$ denote the isomorphism classes of finitely approximable tes's. The main result that we need in order to define a metric semantics for PA is:

Theorem 17. $\langle \mathsf{TES}_{fin}/{\simeq_{iso}}, \mathbf{d}\rangle$ *is a complete ultra-metric space.*

A metric semantics for PA. We now give a metric semantics for (a subset of) PA based on equivalence classes (under $\simeq_{iso}$) of tes's. The main difference with the standard (untimed) case is the notion of 'guardedness' which ensures the well-definedness of recursive programs. While in the untimed case [12] guardedness requires that each process instantiation is preceded by an action we use a notion of *time guardedness* (like in timed CSP [17]) which requires that a recursive process instantiation can only happen after a positive amount of time. Let functions $\surd_{min} : \mathsf{Expr} \longrightarrow [0, \infty)$ and $tg : \mathsf{Expr} \longrightarrow [0, \infty)$ be defined as in Table 1. For declaration *decl* let $tg(decl) \triangleq inf\{\, tg(decl(x)) \mid x \in \mathsf{Var}\,\}$. *decl* is called *time-guarded* iff $tg(decl) > 0$. We give a metric semantics to TGPA,

P	$\surd_{min}(P)$	$tg(P)$
$\mathbf{0}$	∞	∞
$\mathbf{1}$	0	∞
x	0	0
$a_I \,.\, P$	$inf(I) + \surd_{min}(P)$	$inf(I) + tg(P)$
$P[\lambda], P \setminus A$	$\surd_{min}(P)$	$tg(P)$
$P + Q, P\,[> Q$	$min\{\, \surd_{min}(P), \surd_{min}(Q)\,\}$	$min\{\, tg(P), tg(Q)\,\}$
$P \,\Vert_A\, Q$	$max\{\, \surd_{min}(P), \surd_{min}(Q)\,\}$	$min\{\, tg(P), tg(Q)\,\}$
$P\,;\,Q$	$\surd_{min}(P) + \surd_{min}(Q)$	$min\{\, tg(P), \surd_{min}(P) + tg(Q)\,\}$
$P \rhd_t Q$	$min\{\, \surd_{min}(P), t + \surd_{min}(Q)\,\}$	$min\{\, tg(P), t + tg(Q)\,\}$

Table 1. Auxiliary functions $\surd_{min}$ and tg .

the set of *time-guarded processes*, i.e. the set of pairs $\langle decl, P\rangle$ where *decl* is a time-guarded declaration and P an expression. For the definition of the meaning function $\mathcal{M}_{cms} : \mathsf{TGPA} \longrightarrow \mathsf{TES}_{fin}/{\simeq_{iso}}$ we lift the semantic operators of Section 4 to operators on $\mathsf{TES}_{fin}/{\simeq_{iso}}$. Given that all operators defined in Section 4 preserve $\simeq_{iso}$ and finitely approximability (as can be shown by straightforward proof) we may define for $\mathbf{E}$, $\mathbf{F} \in \mathsf{TES}_{fin}/{\simeq_{iso}}$:

$$op\ \mathbf{E} \triangleq \mathbf{E}_{op\ \mathcal{E}} \quad \text{for } op \in \{\, a_I\,.\,, \setminus A, [\lambda]\,\} \text{ and}$$
$$\mathbf{E}\ op\ \mathbf{F} \triangleq \mathbf{E}_{\mathcal{E}\ op\ \mathcal{F}} \text{ for } op \in \{\, +, \,;\, , \Vert_A\,, [>, \rhd_t\,\}$$

where $\mathcal{E}$, $\mathcal{F}$ are representatives of $\mathbf{E}$ and $\mathbf{F}$, respectively. Let $\mathbf{E_0}$ be the equivalence class of the empty tes and $\mathbf{E_1}$ the equivalence class of the tes

$$\mathcal{E}_1 \triangleq (\{\, e\,\}, \varnothing, \varnothing, \{\, (e, \surd)\,\}, \{\, (e, [0, \infty))\,\}, \varnothing, \varnothing).$$

Together with these semantic operators, $\mathsf{TES}_{fin}/{\simeq_{iso}}$ constitutes a PA-algebra.

Lemma 18. *For* $\mathbf{E}, \mathbf{E}', \mathbf{F}, \mathbf{F}' \in \mathsf{TES}_{fin}/{\simeq_{iso}}$ *we have*

1. $\mathbf{d}(a_I\,.\,\mathbf{E}, a_I\,.\,\mathbf{E}') = 2^{-inf(I)} \cdot \mathbf{d}(\mathbf{E}, \mathbf{E}')$

2. $\mathbf{d}(\mathbf{E}\, op\, \mathbf{F}, \mathbf{E}'\, op\, \mathbf{F}') \leqslant max\{\mathbf{d}(\mathbf{E},\mathbf{E}'), \mathbf{d}(\mathbf{F},\mathbf{F}')\}$ *for* $op \in \{+, ||_A, [>\}$
3. $\mathbf{d}(op\,\mathbf{E}, op\,\mathbf{E}') \leqslant \mathbf{d}(\mathbf{E},\mathbf{E}')$ *for* $op \in \{\backslash A, [\lambda]\}$
4. $\mathbf{d}(\mathbf{E}\,;\,\mathbf{F}, \mathbf{E}'\,;\,\mathbf{F}') \leqslant max\{\mathbf{d}(\mathbf{E},\mathbf{E}'), 2^{-\surd_{min}(\mathbf{E})} \cdot \mathbf{d}(\mathbf{F},\mathbf{F}')\}$
5. $\mathbf{d}(\mathbf{E} \rhd_t \mathbf{F}, \mathbf{E}' \rhd_t \mathbf{F}') \leqslant max\{\mathbf{d}(\mathbf{E},\mathbf{E}'), 2^{-t} \cdot \mathbf{d}(\mathbf{F},\mathbf{F}')\}$.

where $\surd_{min}(\mathbf{E}_\mathcal{E}) \triangleq inf\{mintime_\mathcal{E}(e) \mid e \in E, l(e) = \surd\}$.

Lemma 19. *For each decl and homomorphisms* $\phi_1, \phi_2 : \mathsf{Expr} \longrightarrow \mathsf{TES}_{fin}/{\simeq_{iso}}$*:*

$$\tilde{d}(F_{decl}(\phi_1), F_{decl}(\phi_2)) \leqslant 2^{-tg(decl)} \cdot \tilde{d}(\phi_1, \phi_2).$$

where $\tilde{d}$ *is defined in equation (1).*

This result says that F_{decl} is contracting with contraction coefficient $2^{-tg(decl)}$ provided that *decl* is time-guarded. Thus, for time-guarded declaration *decl*, F_{decl} has a unique fixed point, say ϕ_{decl}. The metric semantics $\mathcal{M}_{cms} : \mathsf{TGPA} \longrightarrow \mathsf{TES}_{fin}/{\simeq_{iso}}$ is now defined by $\mathcal{M}_{cms}(\langle decl, P\rangle) \triangleq \phi_{decl}(P)$.

6 Concluding remarks

Relation with untimed case. This paper defines a metric semantics $\mathcal{M}_{cms}$ for an expressive real-time process algebra PA that contains delay and timeout operators. The distance d measures the amount of time in which two processes coincide, i.e., $d(\mathcal{M}_{cms}(P_1), \mathcal{M}_{cms}(P_2)) \leqslant 2^{-t}$ iff P_1 and P_2 have the same behaviour upto time t. This notion of distance is a timed analogon of the distance proposed in [12] which is based on the number of steps processes coincide.

Consistency. [10] defines a cpo-based denotational semantics $\mathcal{M}_{cpo}$ and an (event-based) operational semantics for PA such that *Traces* $\circ\, \mathcal{M}_{cpo}$ are precisely the timed event traces that are generated operationally. The formal relationship between our cpo and metric semantics is as follows. Let TES_{fin} be the set of timed event structures that are finitely approximable. For time-guarded $\langle decl, P\rangle$ it follows that $\mathcal{M}_{cpo}(\langle decl, P\rangle)$ is finitely approximable. Function $f : \mathsf{TES}_{fin} \longrightarrow \mathsf{TES}_{fin}/{\simeq_{iso}}$ with $f(\mathcal{E}) \triangleq \mathbf{E}_\mathcal{E}$ is a homomorphism between the PA-algebras TES_{fin} and $\mathsf{TES}_{fin}/{\simeq_{iso}}$. Then, according to the results of [3], we obtain for any time-guarded process $\langle decl, P\rangle$: $f(\mathcal{M}_{cpo}(\langle decl, P\rangle)) = \mathcal{M}_{cms}(\langle decl, P\rangle)$. This entails that the presented metric semantics is significantly more abstract than the cpo-based, and consequently, the operational semantics of TGPA.

Related work. Several real-time extensions of process algebras have been proposed in the literature; for an overview see [14]. Usually, timed process algebras are provided with an operational semantics in the style of Plotkin that is based on some notion of (timed) transition system. Notably exceptions are the works on timed CSP by Reed & Roscoe [17] who use a metric denotational semantics based on timed refusals, and real-time LOTOS by Bryans, Davies & Schneider [8] who use a (non-standard) fixed point semantics based on an advanced form of timed refusals in order to deal with divergence. Both works provide an interleaving semantics. In the non-interleaving setting, related work has been done by

Murphy [13] on interval event structures in which events have a duration. Murphy uses time truncation—in a similar way as we do in the metric semantics—as a basis for obtaining limiting infinite objects using ideal completions.

References

1. A.F. Ates, M. Bilgic, S. Saito and B. Sarikaya. Using timed CSP for specification verification and analysis of multi-media synchronization. *IEEE J. on Sel. Areas in Comm.*, **14**(1):126–137, 1996.
2. C. Baier and M.E. Majster-Cederbaum. Denotational semantics in the cpo and metric approach. *Th. Comp. Sci.*, **135**:171–220, 1994.
3. C. Baier and M.E. Majster-Cederbaum. How to interpret consistency and establish consistency results for semantics of concurrent programming languages. *Fund. Inf.*, **29**:225–256, 1997.
4. C. Baier and M.E. Majster-Cederbaum. Metric semantics from partial order semantics. *Acta Inf.*, **34**:701–735, 1997.
5. J.W. de Bakker and J.I. Zucker. Processes and the denotational semantics of concurrency. *Inf. and Contr.*, **54**(1/2):70–120, 1982.
6. J.W. de Bakker and E.P. de Vink. *Control Flow Semantics.* MIT Press, 1996.
7. T. Bolognesi and E. Brinksma. Introduction to the ISO specification language LOTOS. *Comp. Netw. & ISDN Syst.*, **14**:25–59, 1987.
8. J. Davies, J.W. Bryans and S.A. Schneider. Real-time LOTOS and timed observations. In *Formal Description Techniques VIII.* Chapmann & Hall, 1995.
9. J-P. Katoen. *Quantitative and Qualitative Extensions of Event Structures.* PhD thesis, University of Twente, 1996.
10. J-P. Katoen, D. Latella, R. Langerak and E. Brinksma. On specifying real-time systems in a causality-based setting. In *Formal Techniques in Real-Time and Fault-Tolerant Systems*, LNCS 1135, pages 385–405. Springer-Verlag, 1996.
11. R. Langerak. Bundle event structures: a non-interleaving semantics for LOTOS. In *Formal Description Techniques V*, pages 331–346. North-Holland, 1993.
12. R. Loogen and U. Goltz. Modelling nondeterministic concurrent processes with event structures. *Fund. Inf.*, **14**(1):39–74, 1991.
13. D. Murphy. Time and duration in noninterleaving concurrency. *Fund. Inf.*, **19**:403–416, 1993.
14. X. Nicollin and J. Sifakis. An overview and synthesis on timed process algebras. In *Real-Time: Theory in Practice*, LNCS 600, pages 526–548. Springer-Verlag, 1992.
15. M. Nivat. Infinite words, infinite trees, infinite computations. In *Foundations of Computer Science III*, Mathematical Centre Tracts **109**, pages 3-52, 1979.
16. M. Nielsen, G.D. Plotkin and G. Winskel. Petri nets, event structures and domains, part 1. *Th. Comp. Sc.*, **13**(1):85–108, 1981.
17. G.M. Reed and A.W. Roscoe. A timed model for Communicating Sequential Processes. *Th. Comp. Sc.*, **58**:249–261, 1988.
18. J.J. Žic. Time-constrained buffer specifications in CSP+T and timed CSP. *ACM Transactions on Programming Languages and Systems*, 16(6):1661–1674, 1994.

The Regular Real-Time Languages*

T.A. Henzinger[1], J.-F. Raskin[2], and P.-Y. Schobbens[2]

[1] Electrical Engineering and Computer Sciences, University of California, Berkeley
[2] Computer Science Institute, University of Namur, Belgium

Abstract. A specification formalism for reactive systems defines a class of ω-languages. We call a specification formalism *fully decidable* if it is constructively closed under boolean operations and has a decidable satisfiability (nonemptiness) problem. There are two important, robust classes of ω-languages that are definable by fully decidable formalisms. The *ω-regular languages* are definable by finite automata, or equivalently, by the Sequential Calculus. The *counter-free ω-regular languages* are definable by temporal logic, or equivalently, by the first-order fragment of the Sequential Calculus. The gap between both classes can be closed by finite counting (using automata connectives), or equivalently, by projection (existential second-order quantification over letters).

A specification formalism for real-time systems defines a class of *timed* ω-languages, whose letters have real-numbered time stamps. Two popular ways of specifying timing constraints rely on the use of clocks, and on the use of time bounds for temporal operators. However, temporal logics with clocks or time bounds have undecidable satisfiability problems, and finite automata with clocks (so-called *timed automata*) are not closed under complement. Therefore, two fully decidable restrictions of these formalisms have been proposed. In the first case, clocks are restricted to *event clocks*, which measure distances to immediately preceding or succeeding events only. In the second case, time bounds are restricted to *nonsingular intervals*, which cannot specify the exact punctuality of events. We show that the resulting classes of timed ω-languages are robust, and we explain their relationship.

First, we show that temporal logic with event clocks defines the same class of timed ω-languages as temporal logic with nonsingular time bounds, and we identify a first-order monadic theory that also defines this class. Second, we show that if the ability of finite counting is added to these formalisms, we obtain the class of timed ω-languages that are definable by finite automata with event clocks, or equivalently, by a restricted second-order extension of the monadic theory. Third, we show that if projection is added, we obtain the class of timed ω-languages that are definable by timed automata, or equivalently, by a richer second-order extension of the monadic theory. These results identify three robust classes of timed ω-languages, of which the third, while popular, is not definable by a fully decidable formalism. By contrast, the first two classes are definable by fully decidable formalisms from temporal logic, from automata theory, and from monadic logic. Since the gap between these two classes can be closed by finite counting, we dub them the *timed ω-regular languages* and the *timed counter-free ω-regular languages*, respectively.

1 Introduction

A run of a reactive system produces an infinite sequence of events. A property of a reactive system, then, is an ω-language containing the infinite event sequences that satisfy the

* This work is supported in part by the ONR YIP award N00014-95-1-0520, the NSF CAREER award CCR-9501708, the NSF grant CCR-9504469, the ARO MURI grant DAAH-04-96-1-0341, the SRC contract 97-DC-324.041, the Belgian National Fund for Scientific Research (FNRS), the European Commission under WGs Aspire and Fireworks, the Portuguese FCT, and by Belgacom.

property. There is a very pleasant expressive equivalence between modal logics, classical logics, and finite automata for defining ω-languages [Büc62,Kam68,GPSS80,Wol82]. Let TL stand for the propositional linear temporal logic with next and until operators, and let Q-TL and E-TL stand for the extensions of TL with propositional quantifiers and grammar (or automata) connectives, respectively. Let ML_1 and ML_2 stand for the first-order and second-order monadic theories of the natural numbers with successor and comparison (also called S1S or the Sequential Calculus). Let BA stand for Büchi automata. Then we obtain the following two levels of expressiveness:

	Languages	Temporal logics	Monadic theories	Finite automata
1	*counter-free ω-regular*	TL	ML_1	
2	*ω-regular*	Q-TL = E-TL	ML_2	BA

For example, the TL formula $\Box(p \rightarrow \Diamond q)$, which specifies that every p event is followed by a q event, is equivalent to the ML_1 formula $(\forall i)(p(i) \rightarrow (\exists j \geq i)q(j))$ and to a Büchi automaton with two states. The difference between the first and second levels of expressiveness is the ability of automata to count. A counting requirement, for example, may assert that all even events are p events, which can be specified by the Q-TL formula $(\exists q)(q \wedge \Box(q \leftrightarrow \bigcirc\neg q) \wedge \Box(q \rightarrow p))$.

We say that a formalism is ***positively decidable*** if it is constructively closed under positive boolean operations, and satisfiability (emptiness) is decidable. A formalism is *fully decidable* if it is positively decidable and also constructively closed under negation (complement). All of the formalisms in the above table are fully decidable. The temporal logics and Büchi automata are less succinct formalisms than the monadic theories, because only the former satisfiability problems are elementarily decidable.

A run of a real-time system produces an infinite sequence of time-stamped events. A property of a real-time system, then, is a set of infinite time-stamped event sequences. We call such sets *timed ω-languages*. If all time stamps are natural numbers, then there is again a very pleasant expressive equivalence between modal logics, classical logics, and finite automata [AH93]. Specifically, there are two natural ways of extending temporal logics with timing constraints. The Metric Temporal Logic MetricTL (also called MTL [AH93]) adds time bounds to temporal operators; for example, the MetricTL formula $\Box(p \rightarrow \Diamond_{=5}\, q)$ specifies that every p event is followed by a q event such that the difference between the two time stamps is exactly 5. The Clock Temporal Logic ClockTL (also called TPTL [AH94]) adds clock variables to TL; for example, the time-bounded response requirement from above can be specified by the ClockTL formula $\Box(p \rightarrow (x := 0)\Diamond(q \wedge x = 5))$, where x is a variable representing a clock that is started by the quantifier $(x := 0)$. Interestingly, over natural-numbered time, both ways of expressing timing constraints are equally expressive. Moreover, by adding the ability to count, we obtain again a canonical second level of expressiveness. Let TimeFunctionML stand for the monadic theory of the natural numbers extended with a unary function symbol that maps event numbers to time stamps, and let TA (Timed Automata) be finite automata with clock variables. In the following table, the formalisms are annotated with the superscript $\mathbb{N}$ to emphasize the fact that all time stamps are natural numbers:

	Languages	Temporal logics	Monadic theories	Finite automata
1	*$\mathbb{N}$-timed counter-free ω-regular*	$\mathsf{MetricTL}^{\mathbb{N}} = \mathsf{ClockTL}^{\mathbb{N}}$	$\mathsf{TimeFunctionML}_1^{\mathbb{N}}$	
2	*$\mathbb{N}$-timed ω-regular*	$\mathsf{Q\text{-}MetricTL}^{\mathbb{N}} = \mathsf{Q\text{-}ClockTL}^{\mathbb{N}} = \mathsf{E\text{-}MetricTL}^{\mathbb{N}} = \mathsf{E\text{-}ClockTL}^{\mathbb{N}}$	$\mathsf{TimeFunctionML}_2^{\mathbb{N}}$	$\mathsf{TA}^{\mathbb{N}}$

Once again, all these formalisms are fully decidable, and the temporal logics and finite automata with timing constraints are elementarily decidable.

If time stamps are real instead of natural numbers, then the situation seems much less satisfactory. Several positively and fully decidable formalisms have been proposed, but no expressive equivalence results were known for fully decidable formalisms [AH92]. The previously known results are listed in the following table, where the omission of superscripts indicates that time stamps are real numbers:

Temporal logics	Monadic theories	Finite automata
	Fully decidable	
MetricIntervalTL [AFH96] EventClockTL [RS97]		
		EventClockTA [AFH94]
	Positively decidable	
TL^{+} + TA [Wil94]	$\mathcal{L}d^{\leftrightarrow}$ [Wil94]	TA [AD94]
	Fully undecidable	
MetricTL [AH93]		
ClockTL [AH94]	TimeFunctionML$_1$ [AH93]	
	TimeFunctionML$_2$	

On one hand, the class of Timed Automata is unsatisfactory, because over real-numbered time it is only positively decidable: $\mathbb{R}$-timed automata are not closed under complement, and the corresponding temporal and monadic logics (and regular expressions [ACM97]) have no negation operator. On the other hand, the classes of Metric and Clock Temporal Logics (as well as monadic logic with a time function), which include negation, are unsatisfactory, because over real-numbered time their satisfiability problems are undecidable. Hence several restrictions of these classes have been studied.

1. The first restriction concerns the style of specifying timing constraints using time-bounded temporal operators. The Metric-Interval Logic MetricIntervalTL (also called MITL [AFH96]) is obtained from MetricTL by restricting the time bounds on temporal operators to nonsingular intervals. For example, the MetricIntervalTL formula $\Box(p \to \Diamond_{[4,6]}\, q)$ specifies that every p event is followed by a q event such that the difference between the two time stamps is at least 4 and at most 6. The restriction to nonsingularity prevents the specification of the exact real-numbered time difference 5 between events.
2. The second restriction concerns the style of specifying timing constraints using clock variables. The Event-Clock Logic EventClockTL (also called SCL [RS97]) and Event-Clock Automata EventClockTA are obtained from ClockTL and TA, respectively, by restricting the use of clocks to refer to the times of previous and next occurrences of events only. For example, if y_q is a clock that always refers to the time difference between now and the next q event, then the EventClockTL formula $\Box(p \to y_q = 5)$ specifies that every p event is followed by a q event such that the difference between time stamps of the p event and the first subsequent q event is exactly 5. A clock such as y_q, which is permanently linked to the next q event, does not need to be started explicitly, and is called an *event clock*. The restriction to event clocks prevents the specification of time differences between a p event and any subsequent (rather than the first subsequent) q event.

Both restrictions lead to pleasing formalisms that are fully (elementarily) decidable and have been shown sufficient in practical applications. However, nothing was known about the relative expressive powers of these two independent approaches, and so the question which sets of timed ω-languages deserve the labels "$\mathbb{R}$-timed counter-free ω-regular" and "$\mathbb{R}$-timed ω-regular" remained open.

In this paper, we show that MetricIntervalTL and EventClockTL are equally expressive, and by adding the ability to count, as expressive as EventClockTA. This result is quite surprising, because (1) over real-numbered time, unrestricted MetricTL is known to be strictly less expressive than unrestricted ClockTL [AH93], and (2) the nonsingularity restriction (which prohibits exact time differences but allows the comparison of unrelated events) is very different in flavor from the event-clock restriction (which allows exact time differences but prohibits the comparison of unrelated events). Moreover, the expressive equivalence of Metric-Interval and Event-Clock logics reveals a robust picture of canonical specification formalisms for real-numbered time that parallels the untimed case and the case of natural-numbered time. We complete this picture by characterizing both the counter-free and the counting levels of expressiveness also by fully decidable monadic theories, called $\mathsf{MinMaxML_1}$ and $\mathsf{MinMaxML_2}$. These are first-order and second-order monadic theories of the real numbers with integer addition, comparison, and (besides universal and existential quantification) two first-order quantifiers that determine the first time and the last time at which a formula is true. Our results, which are summarized in the following table, suggest that we have identified two classes of ω-languages with real-numbered time stamps that may justly be called "$\mathbb{R}$-timed counter-free ω-regular" and "$\mathbb{R}$-timed ω-regular":

	Languages	Temporal logics	Monadic theories	Finite automata
		Fully decidable		
1	$\mathbb{R}$-*timed counter-free* ω-*regular*	MetricIntervalTL = EventClockTL	$\mathsf{MinMaxML_1}$	
2	$\mathbb{R}$-*timed* ω-*regular*	Q-MetricIntervalTL = Q-EventClockTL = E-MetricIntervalTL = E-EventClockTL	$\mathsf{MinMaxML_2}$	EventClockTA

Finally, we explain the gap between the $\mathbb{R}$-timed ω-regular languages and the languages definable by positively decidable formalisms such as timed automata. We show that the richer class of languages is obtained by closing the $\mathbb{R}$-timed ω-regular languages under projection. (It is unfortunate, but well-known [AFH94] that we cannot nontrivially have both full decidability and closure under projection in the case of real-numbered time.) The complete picture, then, results from adding the following line to the previous table (projection, or outermost existential quantification, is indicated by P-):

		Positively decidable		
3	*projection-closed* $\mathbb{R}$-*timed* ω-*regular*	P-EventClockTL	P-$\mathsf{MinMaxML_2}$ = $\mathcal{L}d^{\leftrightarrow}$	P-EventClockTA = TA

2 The Regular Timed ω-Languages

An *interval* $I \subseteq \mathbb{R}^+$ is a convex nonempty subset of the nonnegative reals. Given $t \in \mathbb{R}^+$, we freely use notation such as $t + I$ for the interval $\{t' \mid \text{exists } t'' \in I \text{ with } t' = t + t''\}$, and $t > I$ for the constraint "$t > t'$ for all $t' \in I$." Two intervals I and J are *adjacent* if the right endpoint of I is equal to the left endpoint of J, and either I is right-open and J is left-closed or I is right-closed and J is left-open. An *interval sequence* $\bar{I} = I_0, I_1, \ldots$ is a finite or infinite sequence of bounded intervals so that for all $i \geq 0$, the intervals I_i and I_{i+1} are adjacent. We say that the interval sequence $\bar{I}$ *covers* the interval $\bigcup_{i\geq 0} I_i$. If $\bar{I}$ covers $[0, \infty)$, then $\bar{I}$ partitions the nonnegative real line so that every bounded subset of $\mathbb{R}^+$ is contained within a finite union of elements from the partition.

Let P be a finite set of propositional symbols. A *state* $s \subseteq P$ is a set of propositions. Given a state s and a proposition p, we write $s \models p$ instead of $p \in s$. A *timed state sequence* $\tau = (\bar{s}, \bar{I})$ is a pair that consists of an infinite sequence $\bar{s}$ of states and an infinite interval sequence $\bar{I}$ that covers $[0, \infty)$. Equivalently, the timed state sequence τ

can be viewed as a function from $\mathbb{R}^+$ to 2^P, indicating for each time $t \in \mathbb{R}^+$ a state $\tau(t) \subseteq P$. In the introduction, we spoke of events rather than states. We do not formalize this distinction; it suffices to say that an event can be viewed as a change in state. A *timed ω-language* is a set of timed state sequences.

2.1 Recursive Event-Clock Automata

An event-clock automaton is a special case of a timed automaton [AD94], where the starting of clocks is determined by the input instead of by the transition relation. We generalize the definition of event-clock automata from [AFH94]. There, an automaton accepts (or rejects) a given timed state sequence τ. The automaton views the input sequence τ starting from time 0 by executing a transition relation that is constrained by conditions on clocks. There are two clocks for each proposition p. The history clock x_p always shows the amount of time that has expired since the proposition p has become false in τ, and the prophecy clock y_p always shows the amount of time that will expire until the proposition p will become true in τ. More precisely, if p has never been true, then the history clock has the undefined value $\perp$; if p was last true v time units ago during a right-closed interval, then the value of x_p is v; and if p was last true during a right-open interval whose right endpoint was v time units ago, then the value of x_p is the nonstandard real v^+, which is larger than v but smaller than all reals that are larger than v. Similar conventions apply to the prophecy clock y_p.

We have an automaton A accept (or reject) a given pair (τ, t) that consists of a timed state sequence τ and a time $t \in \mathbb{R}^+$. The automaton is started at time t and views the "past" of the input sequence τ by executing a ***backward*** transition relation, and the "future" by executing to a ***forward*** transition relation. If A accepts the pair (τ, t), we say that A accepts τ at time t. This allows us to associate a history clock and a prophecy clock with each automaton. The history clock x_A always shows the amount of time that has expired since the last time at which A accepted τ, and the prophecy clock y_A always shows the amount of time that will expire until the next time at which A will accept τ. This definition of event-clock automata is recursive. The base automata, whose transition relations are not constrained by clocks, are called floating automata. Formally, a ***floating automaton*** is a tuple $A = (Q, Q_0, \delta, \delta', P, \lambda, Q_F, Q'_F)$ such that

Q is a finite set of locations,
$Q_0 \subseteq Q$ is the set of starting locations,
$\delta \subseteq Q \times Q$ is the forward transition relation,
$\delta' \subseteq Q \times Q$ is the backward transition relation,
P is a finite set of propositional symbols,
λ: $Q \to \mathsf{BoolComb}(P)$ is a function that labels each location with a boolean combination of propositions,
$Q_F \subseteq Q$ is a set of forward accepting locations, and
$Q'_F \subseteq Q$ is a set of backward accepting locations.

Let τ be a timed state sequence whose propositional symbols contain all propositions in P. The floating automaton A ***accepts*** τ at time $t \in \mathbb{R}^+$, denoted $\mathsf{Accept}_\tau(A, t)$, iff there exist an infinite forward run $\rho = (\bar{q}, \bar{I})$ and an finite backward run $\rho' = (\bar{q}', \bar{I}')$ such that the following conditions are met.

Covering The forward run ρ consists of an infinite sequence $\bar{q}$ of locations from Q, and an infinite interval sequence $\bar{I}$ that covers $[t, \infty)$. The backward run ρ' consists of a finite sequence $\bar{q}'$ of locations and a finite interval sequence $\bar{I}'$, of the same length as $\bar{q}'$, which covers $[0, t]$.

Starting The forward and backward runs start in the same starting location; that is, $\rho(t) = \rho'(t)$ and $\rho(t) \in Q_0$.

Consecution The forward and backward runs respect the corresponding transition relations; that is, $(q_i, q_{i+1}) \in \delta$ for all $i \geq 0$, and $(q'_i, q'_{i-1}) \in \delta'$ for all $0 < i < |\bar{q}'|$.

Singularities We use the transition relations to encode the fact that a location may be transient, in the sense that the automaton control cannot remain in the location for any positive amount of time. For all $i \geq 0$, if $(q_i, q_i) \notin \delta$, then I_i is singular, and for all $0 \leq i < |\bar{q}'|$, if $(q'_i, q'_i) \notin \delta'$, then I'_i is singular.

Constraints The timed state sequence respects the constraints that are induced by the forward and backward runs; that is, $\tau(t') \models \lambda(\rho(t'))$ for all real times $t' \in [t, \infty)$, and $\tau(t') \models \lambda(\rho'(t'))$ for all real times $t' \in [0, t]$.

Accepting The forward run is Büchi accepting and the backward run ends in an accepting location; that is, there exist infinitely many $i \geq 0$ such that $q_i \in Q_F$, and $q'_0 \in Q'_F$.

A *recursive event-clock automaton of level* $i \in \mathbb{N}$ is a tuple $A = (Q, Q_0, \delta, \delta', P, \lambda, Q_F, Q'_F)$ that has the same components as a floating automaton, except that the labeling function $\lambda\colon Q \to \mathsf{BoolComb}(P \cup \Gamma_i)$ assigns to each location a boolean combination of propositions and level-i clock constraints. The set Γ_i of *level-i clock constraints* contains all atomic formulas of the form $x_B \sim c$ and $y_B \sim c$, where B is a recursive event-clock automaton of level less than i whose propositions are contained in P, where c is a nonnegative integer constant, and where $\sim \in \{<, \leq, =, \geq, >\}$. The clock x_B is called a *history clock*, and the clock y_B, a *prophecy clock*. In particular, the set of level-0 clock constraints is empty, and thus the level-0 event-clock automata are the floating automata. The level-1 event-clock automata have a history clock and a prophecy clock for each floating automaton, etc. If A contains a constraint on x_B or y_B, we say that B is a *subautomaton* of A.

The definition of when the recursive event-clock automaton A of level i accepts a timed state sequence τ at time t is as for floating automata, only that we need to define the satisfaction relation $\tau(t') \models (z \sim c)$ for every time $t' \in \mathbb{R}^+$ and every level-i clock constraint $(z \sim c) \in \Gamma_i$. This is done as follows. The timed state sequence τ *satisfies* the clock constraint $z \sim c$ at time t, written $\tau(t) \models (z \sim c)$, iff $\mathsf{Val}_\tau(z, t) \neq \bot$ and $\mathsf{Val}_\tau(z, t) \sim c$ for the following value of clock z at time t of τ (throughout this paper, v, v', and v'' range over the nonnegative reals):

$$\mathsf{Val}_\tau(x_B, t) = \begin{cases} v & \text{if } \mathsf{Accept}_\tau(B, t - v),\ v > 0, \\ & \quad \text{and for all } v',\ 0 < v' < v, \text{ not } \mathsf{Accept}_\tau(B, t - v') \\ v^+ & \text{if for all } v' > v, \text{ exists } v'',\ v < v'' < v' \text{ with } \mathsf{Accept}_\tau(B, t - v''), \\ & \quad \text{and for all } v',\ 0 < v' \leq v, \text{ not } \mathsf{Accept}_\tau(B, t - v') \\ \bot & \text{if for all } v,\ 0 < v \leq t, \text{ not } \mathsf{Accept}_\tau(B, t - v) \end{cases}$$

$$\mathsf{Val}_\tau(y_B, t) = \begin{cases} v & \text{if } \mathsf{Accept}_\tau(B, t + v),\ v > 0, \\ & \quad \text{and for all } v',\ 0 < v' < v, \text{ not } \mathsf{Accept}_\tau(B, t + v') \\ v^+ & \text{if for all } v' > v, \text{ exists } v'',\ v < v'' < v' \text{ with } \mathsf{Accept}_\tau(B, t + v''), \\ & \quad \text{and for all } v',\ 0 < v' \leq v, \text{ not } \mathsf{Accept}_\tau(B, t + v') \\ \bot & \text{if for all } v > 0, \text{ not } \mathsf{Accept}_\tau(B, t + v) \end{cases}$$

The recursive event-clock automaton A *defines* a timed ω-language, namely, the set of timed state sequences τ such that $\mathsf{Accept}_\tau(A, 0)$.

The following two theorems were proved in [AFH94] for the special case of level-1 event-clock automata. There, it was shown that every level-1 event-clock automaton can be determinized, because at all times during the run of an automaton, the value of each clock is determined solely by the input sequence and does not depend on nondeterministic choices made during the run. This crucial property, which fails for arbitrary timed automata, holds for all recursive event-clock automata.

Theorem 1. *The timed ω-languages definable by recursive event-clock automata are constructively closed under all boolean operations. In particular, for every recursive event-clock automaton we can construct a recursive event-clock automaton that defines the complementary timed ω-language.*

Theorem 2. *The emptiness problem for recursive event-clock automata is complete for* PSPACE.

It can be shown that level-$(i+1)$ event-clock automata, for all $i \in \mathbb{N}$, are strictly more expressive than level-i event-clock automata. It can also be shown that recursive event-clock automata are only partially closed under projection: only propositions that do not appear in subautomata can be projected. This partial-projection result will be used later to define decidable real-time logics with second-order quantification.

2.2 The Real-Time Sequential Calculus

In the sequel, we use p, q, and r for monadic predicates (second-order variables) over the nonnegative reals, and t, t_1, and t_2 for first-order variables over $\mathbb{R}^+$. The formulas of the *Second-Order Real-Time Sequential Calculus* $\mathsf{MinMaxML}_2$ are generated by the following grammar:

$$\begin{aligned}\Phi \;::=\;& p(t) \mid t_1 \sim t_2 \mid \\ & (\mathsf{Min}\ t_1)(t_1 > t_2 \wedge \Psi(t_1)) \sim (t_2 + c) \mid (\mathsf{Max}\ t_1)(t_1 < t_2 \wedge \Psi(t_1)) \sim (t_2 - c) \mid \\ & \Phi_1 \wedge \Phi_2 \mid \neg\Phi \mid (\exists t)\Phi \mid (\exists p)\Theta\end{aligned}$$

where $\Psi(t_1)$ is a $\mathsf{MinMaxML}_2$ formula that contains no free occurrences of first-order variables other than t_1, where Θ is a $\mathsf{MinMaxML}_2$ formula that contains no occurrences of p within the scope of a Min or Max quantifier, where c is a nonnegative integer constant, and where $\sim \in \{<, \leq, =, \geq, >\}$. The formulas of the *First-Order Real-Time Sequential Calculus* $\mathsf{MinMaxML}_1$ are defined as above, without the clause $(\exists p)\Theta$.

The truth value of a $\mathsf{MinMaxML}_2$ formula Φ is evaluated over a pair (τ, α) that consists of a timed state sequence τ whose propositional symbols contain all second-order variables of Φ, and a valuation α that maps each free first-order variable of Φ to a nonnegative real. By $\alpha_{[t \mapsto v]}$ we denote the valuation that agrees with α on all variables except t, which is mapped to the value v. We first define for each $\mathsf{MinMaxML}_2$ term θ a value $\mathsf{Val}_{\tau,\alpha}(\theta)$, which is either a nonstandard real or undefined. Intuitively, the term $(\mathsf{Min}\ t_1)(t_1 > t_2 \wedge \Psi(t_1))$ denotes the smallest value greater than t_2 that satisfies the formula Ψ. If there is no value greater than t_2 that satisfies Ψ, then the term $(\mathsf{Min}\ t_1)(t_1 > t_2 \wedge \Psi(t_1))$ denotes the undefined value $\bot$. If Ψ is satisfied throughout a left-open interval with left endpoint $v > t_2$, then the term $(\mathsf{Min}\ t_1)(t_1 > t_2 \wedge \Psi(t_1))$ denotes the nonstandard real v^+. Similarly, the term $(\mathsf{Max}\ t_1)(t_1 < t_2 \wedge \Psi(t_1))$ denotes the greatest value smaller than t_2 that satisfies Ψ:

$$\begin{aligned}&\mathsf{Val}_{\tau,\alpha}(t) = \alpha(t)\\ &\mathsf{Val}_{\tau,\alpha}(t+c) = \alpha(t) + c\\ &\mathsf{Val}_{\tau,\alpha}(t-c) = \begin{cases}\alpha(t) - c & \text{if } \alpha(t) \geq c\\ \bot & \text{otherwise}\end{cases}\\ &\mathsf{Val}_{\tau,\alpha}((\mathsf{Min}\ t_1)(t_1 > t_2 \wedge \Psi(t_1)) =\\ &\quad\begin{cases} v & \text{if } (\tau, \alpha_{[t_1 \mapsto v]}) \models (t_1 > t_2 \wedge \Psi(t_1)),\\ & \quad\text{and for all } v' < v, \text{ not } (\tau, \alpha_{[t_1 \mapsto v']}) \models (t_1 > t_2 \wedge \Psi(t_1))\\ v^+ & \text{if for all } v' > v, \text{ exists } v'' < v' \text{ with } (\tau, \alpha_{[t_1 \mapsto v'']}) \models (t_1 > t_2 \wedge \Psi(t_1)),\\ & \quad\text{and for all } v' \leq v, \text{ not } (\tau, \alpha_{[t_1 \mapsto v']}) \models (t_1 > t_2 \wedge \Psi(t_1))\\ \bot & \text{if for all } v \geq 0, \text{ not } (\tau, \alpha_{[t_1 \mapsto v]}) \models (t_1 > t_2 \wedge \Psi(t_1))\end{cases}\end{aligned}$$

$$\mathsf{Val}_{\tau,\alpha}((\mathsf{Max}\ t_1)(t_1 < t_2 \wedge \Psi(t_1)) = \begin{cases} v & \text{if } (\tau, \alpha_{[t_1 \mapsto v]}) \models (t_1 < t_2 \wedge \Psi(t_1)), \\ & \quad \text{and for all } v' > v, \text{ not } (\tau, \alpha_{[t_1 \mapsto v']}) \models (t_1 < t_2 \wedge \Psi(t_1)) \\ v^- & \text{if for all } v' < v, \text{ exists } v'' > v' \text{ with } (\tau, \alpha_{[t_1 \mapsto v'']}) \models (t_1 < t_2 \wedge \Psi(t_1)), \\ & \quad \text{and for all } v' \geq v, \text{ not } (\tau, \alpha_{[t_1 \mapsto v']}) \models (t_1 < t_2 \wedge \Psi(t_1)) \\ \bot & \text{if for all } v \geq 0, \text{ not } (\tau, \alpha_{[t_1 \mapsto v]}) \models (t_1 < t_2 \wedge \Psi(t_1)) \end{cases}$$

Now we can define the satisfaction relation for $\mathsf{MinMaxML}_2$ formulas:

$(\tau, \alpha) \models p(t)$ iff $p \in \tau(\alpha(t))$
$(\tau, \alpha) \models t_1 \sim t_2$ iff $\mathsf{Val}_{\tau,\alpha}(t_1) \sim \mathsf{Val}_{\tau,\alpha}(t_2)$
$(\tau, \alpha) \models \Phi_1 \wedge \Phi_2$ iff $(\tau, \alpha) \models \Phi_1$ and $(\tau, \alpha) \models \Phi_2$
$(\tau, \alpha) \models \neg\Phi$ iff not $(\tau, \alpha) \models \Phi$
$(\tau, \alpha) \models (\exists t)\Phi$ iff exists $v \geq 0$ with $(\tau, \alpha_{[t \mapsto v]})\Phi$
$(\tau, \alpha) \models (\exists p)\Theta$ iff $(\tau^p, \alpha) \models \Theta$ for some timed state sequence τ^p that agrees with τ on all propositions except p

A $\mathsf{MinMaxML}_2$ formula is *closed* iff it contains no free occurrences of first-order variables. Every closed $\mathsf{MinMaxML}_2$ formula Φ *defines* a timed ω-language, namely, the set of timed state sequences τ such that $(\tau, \emptyset) \models \Phi$.

Example 1. The $\mathsf{MinMaxML}_1$ formula

$$(\forall t_1)(p(t_1) \rightarrow (\exists t_2)(t_2 > t_1 \wedge q(t_2) \wedge (\mathsf{Min}\ t_3)(t_3 > t_2 \wedge r(t_3)) = t_2 + 5))$$

asserts that every p-state is followed by a q-state that is followed by an r-state after, but no sooner than, 5 time units. □

The following theorem shows that the second-order real-time sequential calculus defines the same class of timed ω-languages as the recursive event-clock automata. We call this class the *ω-regular real-time languages*.

Theorem 3. *For every* $\mathsf{MinMaxML}_2$ *formula we can construct a recursive event-clock automaton that defines the same timed ω-language, and vice versa.*

Corollary 1. *The satisfiability problem for* $\mathsf{MinMaxML}_2$ *is decidable.*

It is not difficult to embed the first-order fragment ML_1 of the sequential calculus into $\mathsf{MinMaxML}_1$ in linear time, which implies that the satisfiability problem for $\mathsf{MinMaxML}_1$ is nonelementary [Sto74].

3 The Counter-Free Regular Timed ω-Languages

3.1 Two Decidable Real-Time Temporal Logics

We recall the definitions of two real-time temporal logics that are known to have decidable satisfiability problems.

Event-Clock Temporal Logic The formulas of $\mathsf{EventClockTL}$ [RS97] are built from propositional symbols, boolean connectives, the temporal "until" and "since" operators, and two real-time operators: at any time t, the *history operator* $\lhd_I \phi$ asserts that ϕ was true last in the interval $t - I$, and the *prophecy operator* $\rhd_I \phi$ asserts that ϕ will be true next in the interval $t + I$. The formulas of $\mathsf{EventClockTL}$ are generated by the following grammar:

$$\phi \ ::= \ p \mid \phi_1 \wedge \phi_2 \mid \neg\phi \mid \phi_1 \mathcal{U} \phi_2 \mid \phi_1 \mathcal{S} \phi_2 \mid \lhd_I \phi \mid \rhd_I \phi$$

where p is a proposition and I is an interval whose finite endpoints are nonnegative integers. Let ϕ be an EventClockTL formula and let τ be a timed state sequence whose propositional symbols contain all propositions that occur in ϕ. The formula ϕ *holds* at time $t \in \mathbb{R}^+$ of τ, denoted $(\tau, t) \models \phi$, according to the following definition:

$(\tau, t) \models p$ iff $p \in \tau(t)$
$(\tau, t) \models \phi_1 \wedge \phi_2$ iff $(\tau, t) \models \phi_1$ and $(\tau, t) \models \phi_2$
$(\tau, t) \models \neg\phi$ iff not $(\tau, t) \models \phi$
$(\tau, t) \models \phi_1 \mathcal{U} \phi_2$ iff exists a real $t' > t$ with $(\tau, t') \models \phi_2$, and for all reals $t'' \in (t, t')$, we have $(\tau, t'') \models \phi_1 \vee \phi_2$
$(\tau, t) \models \phi_1 \mathcal{S} \phi_2$ iff exists a real $t' < t$ with $(\tau, t') \models \phi_2$, and for all reals $t'' \in (t', t)$, we have $(\tau, t'') \models \phi_1 \vee \phi_2$
$(\tau, t) \models \lhd_I \phi$ iff exists a real $t' < t$ with $t' \in (t - I)$ and $(\tau, t') \models \phi$, and for all reals $t'' < t$ with $t'' > (t - I)$, not $(\tau, t'') \models \phi$
$(\tau, t) \models \rhd_I \phi$ iff exists a real $t' > t$ with $t' \in (t + I)$ and $(\tau, t') \models \phi$, and for all reals $t'' > t$ with $t'' < (t + I)$, not $(\tau, t'') \models \phi$

Note that the temporal and real-time operators are defined in a strict manner; that is, they do not constrain the current state. Nonstrict operators are easily defined from their strict counterparts. We use the following abbreviations for additional operators: $\Diamond\phi \equiv \top\mathcal{U}\phi$, $\Box\phi \equiv \neg\Diamond\neg\phi$, and $\mathcal{J}\phi \equiv \bot\mathcal{U}\phi$. The EventClockTL formula ϕ *defines* the timed ω-language that contains all timed state sequences τ with $(\tau, 0) \models \phi$.

Example 2. The EventClockTL formula $\Box(p \rightarrow \Diamond(q \wedge \rhd_{[5,5]} r))$ defines the timed ω-language from Example 1. □

Theorem 4. [RS97] *The satisfiability problem for* EventClockTL *is complete for* PSPACE.

Metric-Interval Temporal Logic The formulas of MetricIntervalTL [AFH96] are built from propositional symbols, boolean connectives, and time-bounded "until" and "since" operators:

$$\phi \ ::= \ p \mid \phi_1 \wedge \phi_2 \mid \neg\phi \mid \phi_1 \mathcal{U}_I \phi_2 \mid \phi_1 \mathcal{S}_I \phi_2$$

where p is a proposition and I is a ***nonsingular*** interval whose finite endpoints are nonnegative integers. The formulas of the fragment $\mathsf{MetricIntervalTL}_{0,\infty}$ are defined as above, except that the interval I must either have the left endpoint 0, or be unbounded; in these cases I can be replaced by an expression of the form $\sim c$, for a nonnegative integer constant c and $\sim \in \{<, \leq, \geq, >\}$. The MetricIntervalTL formula ϕ *holds* at time $t \in \mathbb{R}^+$ of the timed state sequence τ, denoted $(\tau, t) \models \phi$, according to the following definition (the propositional and boolean cases are as for EventClockTL):

$(\tau, t) \models \phi_1 \mathcal{U}_I \phi_2$ iff exists a real $t' \in (t + I)$ with $(\tau, t') \models \phi_2$, and for all reals $t'' \in (t, t')$, we have $(\tau, t'') \models \phi_1$
$(\tau, t) \models \phi_1 \mathcal{S}_I \phi_2$ iff exists a real $t' \in (t - I)$ with $(\tau, t') \models \phi_2$, and for all reals $t'' \in (t', t)$, we have $(\tau, t'') \models \phi_1$

The MetricIntervalTL formula ϕ *defines* the timed ω-language that contains all timed state sequences τ with $(\tau, 0) \models \phi$.

Example 3. The MetricIntervalTL formula $\Box(p \rightarrow \Diamond_{[4,6]} q)$ asserts that every p-state is followed by a q-state at a time difference of at least 4 and at most 6 time units. Note that, by contrast, the EventClockTL formula $\Box(p \rightarrow \rhd_{[4,6]} q)$ asserts the stronger requirement that after every p-state, the *next* subsequent q-state occurs at a time difference of at least 4 and at most 6 time units. □

Theorem 5. [AFH96] *The satisfiability problem for* MetricIntervalTL *is complete for* EXPSPACE. *The satisfiability problem for* $\mathsf{MetricIntervalTL}_{0,\infty}$ *is complete for* PSPACE.

It is not difficult to see that the union of EventClockTL and MetricIntervalTL is still decidable in EXPSPACE, and that the union of EventClockTL and $\mathsf{MetricIntervalTL}_{0,\infty}$ is still decidable in PSPACE. These union logics are of practical interest, because the event-clock style and the metric-interval style of specification are orthogonal: for each style, there are properties that are more naturally specified in that style. Next we shall see that while the union enhances convenience in practical specification, it does not enhance the theoretical expressiveness of either logic.

3.2 Expressive-Equivalence Results

We show that all of EventClockTL, MetricIntervalTL, and $\mathsf{MetricIntervalTL}_{0,\infty}$ are expressively equivalent to the first-order real-time sequential calculus; that is, they all define the same class of timed ω-languages. We call this class the *counter-free ω-regular real-time languages*.

Theorem 6. *For every* $\mathsf{MinMaxML}_1$ *formula we can construct an* EventClockTL *formula that defines the same timed ω-language. For every* EventClockTL *formula we can construct an* $\mathsf{MetricIntervalTL}_{0,\infty}$ *formula that defines the same timed ω-language. For every* MetricIntervalTL *formula we can construct a* $\mathsf{MinMaxML}_1$ *formula that defines the same timed ω-language.*

Proof sketch. The following two examples present some of the main ideas behind the proof. First, the EventClockTL formula $\rhd_{[c,c]}\, p$ is equivalent to the MetricIntervalTL formula $\Box_{(0,c)}\neg p \wedge \Diamond_{(0,c]}\, p$. Second, the MetricIntervalTL formula $\Diamond_{(1,2)}\, p$ is equivalent to the disjunction of the three EventClockTL formulas (1) $\rhd_{[1,1]}\mathcal{J}p \vee \rhd_{(0,1)} \rhd_{[1,1]} \mathcal{J}p$, (2) $\rhd_{(0,1)} \rhd_{[1,1]}\, p$, and (3) $\neg\rhd_{(0,1]}\neg\rhd_{(0,1)}\, p$. Disjunct (1) corresponds to the case that the first p-state in interval $(1,2)$ occurs at least 1 time unit after the previous p-state, and is left-open; disjunct (2) corresponds to the left-closed case; and disjunct (3) corresponds to the case that the first p-state in interval $(1,2)$ occurs less than 1 time unit after the previous p-state. The translation of the more general MetricIntervalTL formula $\Diamond_{(c,c+1)}\, p$ is inductive and requires an exponential blow-up, which is unavoidable due to the lower complexity of EventClockTL satisfiability. □

3.3 From Counter-Free to Counting Regular Timed ω-Languages

The difference between the counter-free ω-regular real-time languages and the ω-regular real-time languages is the counting ability of automata (and of second-order quantification). This is demonstrated by the fact that if we add either automata connectives (in the style of [WVS83]) or quantification over propositions (in the style of [Sis83]) to either EventClockTL or MetricIntervalTL (or $\mathsf{MetricIntervalTL}_{0,\infty}$), we obtain a formalism that defines exactly the full class of the ω-regular real-time languages. These results complete the pleasant analogy to the untimed case.

Automata Connectives We define the *extended temporal logics* E-EventClockTL and E-MetricIntervalTL by adding to the definition of formulas the syntactic clause $\phi ::= A(\phi_1, \ldots, \phi_n)$, where A is a floating automaton whose propositions are replaced by the set $\{\phi_1, \ldots, \phi_n\}$ of formulas. In the definition of the satisfaction relation, add $(\tau, t) \models A(\phi_1, \ldots, \phi_n)$ iff $\mathsf{Accept}_\tau(A, t)$, using formula satisfaction $(\tau, t) \models \phi$ instead of proposition satisfaction $\tau(t) \models p$.

Theorem 7. *The satisfiability problems for* E-EventClockTL *and* E-MetricIntervalTL$_{0,\infty}$ *are complete for* PSPACE. *The satisfiability problem for* E-MetricIntervalTL *is complete for* EXPSPACE.

Theorem 8. *For every* MinMaxML$_2$ *formula we can construct an* E-EventClockTL *formula that defines the same timed ω-language. For every* E-EventClockTL *formula we can construct an* E-MetricIntervalTL$_{0,\infty}$ *formula that defines the same timed ω-language. For every* E-MetricIntervalTL *formula we can construct a* MinMaxML$_2$ *formula that defines the same timed ω-language.*

Propositional Quantification The *quantified temporal logics* Q-EventClockTL and Q-MetricIntervalTL are defined by adding to the definition of formulas the syntactic clause $\phi ::= (\exists p)\psi$, where p is a proposition which, inside the formula ψ, does not occur within the scope of a history or prophecy operator. Then, $(\tau, t) \models (\exists p)\psi$ iff $(\tau^p, t) \models \psi$ for some timed state sequence τ^p that agrees with τ on all propositions except p.

Theorem 9. *The satisfiability problems for* Q-EventClockTL *and* Q-MetricIntervalTL *are decidable.*

Since already the untimed quantified temporal logic Q-TL is nonelementary [Sis83], so are the satisfiability problems for Q-EventClockTL and Q-MetricIntervalTL$_{0,\infty}$.

Theorem 10. *For every* MinMaxML$_2$ *formula we can construct an* Q-EventClockTL *formula that defines the same timed ω-language. For every* Q-EventClockTL *formula we can construct an* Q-MetricIntervalTL$_{0,\infty}$ *formula that defines the same timed ω-language. For every* Q-MetricIntervalTL *formula we can construct a* MinMaxML$_2$ *formula that defines the same timed ω-language.*

4 Beyond Full Decidability

In our second-order formalisms MinMaxML$_2$ and Q-EventClockTL, we have prohibited quantified monadic predicates (propositions) from occurring within the scope of Min or Max quantifiers (history or prophecy operators). This restriction is necessary for decidability. If we admit only *outermost existential* quantification (projection) over monadic predicates (propositions) that occur within the scope of real-time operators, we obtain a positively decidable formalism (satisfiability is decidable, but validity is not) which is expressively equivalent to timed automata. Consequently, if we admit full quantification over monadic predicates (propositions) that occur within the scope of real-time operators, then both satisfiability and validity are undecidable, and the formalism is expressively equivalent to boolean combinations of timed automata.

A formula of the *Projection-Closed Real-Time Sequential Calculus* P-MinMaxML$_2$ has the form $(\exists q_1, \ldots, q_n)\Phi$, where $q_1, \ldots, q_n$ are monadic predicates and Φ is a formula of MinMaxML$_2$. A formula of the *Projection-Closed Event-Clock Logic* P-EventClockTL has the form $(\exists q_1, \ldots, q_n)\phi$, where $q_1, \ldots, q_n$ are propositions and ϕ is a formula of EventClockTL. A *projection-closed event-clock automaton* has the form $(\exists q_1, \ldots, q_n)A$, where $q_1, \ldots, q_n$ are propositions and A is a recursive event-clock automaton; it accepts all timed state sequences that agree with timed state sequences accepted by A on all propositions except $q_1, \ldots, q_n$. From Theorems 2, 3, and 4 it follows immediately that the satisfiability problem for P-MinMaxML$_2$ is decidable, and that the satisfiability problem for P-EventClockTL and the emptiness problem for projection-closed event-clock automata are complete for PSPACE. The dual problems of validity and universality, however, cannot be decided. This follows from the following theorem, which shows that by closing event-clock automata or event-clock logic under projection, we obtain timed automata, whose universality problem is undecidable [AD94].

Theorem 11. *For every timed automaton* [AD94] *we can construct a projection-closed event-clock automaton that defines the same timed ω-language, and vice versa.*

It follows that the formalisms of timed automata, projection-closed event-clock automata, P-EventClockTL, P-MinMaxML$_2$, and $\mathcal{L}d^{\leftrightarrow}$ [Wil94] define the same class of timed ω-languages. This class is closed under positive boolean operations, but not under complement [AD94].

Corollary 2. *The validity problems for* P-MinMaxML$_2$ *and* P-EventClockTL *and the universality problem for projection-closed event-clock automata are undecidable.*

A fully undecidable extension of MinMaxML$_1$ is obtained by relaxing the restriction that in every formula of the form $(\mathsf{Min}\ t_1)(t_1 > t_2 \wedge \Psi(t_1)) \sim (t_2 + c)$ or $(\mathsf{Max}\ t_1)(t_1 < t_2 \wedge \Psi(t_1)) \sim (t_2 - c)$, the subformula $\Psi(t_1)$ contains no free occurrences of first-order variables other than t_1. If we suppress this restriction, it can be shown that the real-time temporal logic MetricTL, which is MetricIntervalTL without the prohibition of singular intervals, can be embedded in MinMaxML$_1$. Since MetricTL is undecidable [AH93], so is the satisfiabilty problem for unrestricted MinMaxML$_1$.

References

[ACM97] E. Asarin, P. Caspi, and O. Maler. A Kleene theorem for timed automata. In *Proc. 12th IEEE Symp. Logic in Computer Science*, pp. 160–171, 1997.

[AD94] R. Alur and D.L. Dill. A theory of timed automata. *Theoretical Computer Science*, 126:183–235, 1994.

[AFH94] R. Alur, L. Fix, and T.A. Henzinger. A determinizable class of timed automata. In *Computer-aided Verification*, LNCS 818:1–13. Springer-Verlag, 1994.

[AFH96] R. Alur, T. Feder, and T.A. Henzinger. The benefits of relaxing punctuality. *J. ACM*, 43:116–146, 1996.

[AH92] R. Alur and T.A. Henzinger. Back to the future: towards a theory of timed regular languages. In *Proc. 33rd IEEE Symp. Foundations of Computer Science*, pp. 177–186, 1992.

[AH93] R. Alur and T.A. Henzinger. Real-time logics: complexity and expressiveness. *Information and Computation*, 104:35–77, 1993.

[AH94] R. Alur and T.A. Henzinger. A really temporal logic. *J. ACM*, 41:181–204, 1994.

[Büc62] J.R. Büchi. On a decision method in restricted second-order arithmetic. In *Proc. First Congress on Logic, Methodology, and Philosophy of Science* (1960), pp. 1–11. Stanford University Press, 1962.

[GPSS80] D. Gabbay, A. Pnueli, S. Shelah, and J. Stavi. On the temporal analysis of fairness. In *Proc. 7th ACM Symp. Principles of Programming Languages*, pp. 163–173, 1980.

[Kam68] J.A.W. Kamp. *Tense Logic and the Theory of Linear Order*. PhD thesis, University of California at Los Angeles, 1968.

[RS97] J.-F. Raskin and P.-Y. Schobbens. State clock logic: a decidable real-time logic. In *Hybrid and Real-time Systems*, LNCS 1201:33–47. Springer-Verlag, 1997.

[Sis83] A.P. Sistla. *Theoretical Issues in the Design and Verification of Distributed Systems*. PhD thesis, Harvard University, 1983.

[Sto74] L.J. Stockmeyer. *The Complexity of Decision Problems in Automata Theory and Logic*. PhD thesis, Massachusetts Institute of Technology, 1974.

[Wil94] T. Wilke. Specifying timed state sequences in powerful decidable logics and timed automata. In *Formal Techniques in Real-time and Fault-tolerant Systems*, LNCS 863:694–715. Springer-Verlag, 1994.

[Wol82] P.L. Wolper. *Synthesis of Communicating Processes from Temporal Logic Specifications*. PhD thesis, Stanford University, 1982.

[WVS83] P.L. Wolper, M.Y. Vardi, and A.P. Sistla. Reasoning about infinite computation paths. In *Proc. 24th IEEE Symp. Foundations of Computer Science*, pp. 185–194, 1983.

Static and Dynamic Low-Congested Interval Routing Schemes*

Serafino Cicerone[1] Gabriele Di Stefano[1] Michele Flammini[2]

[1] Department of Electrical Engineering, University of L'Aquila, Monteluco di Roio, I-67040 L'Aquila - Italy. Email: {cicerone,gabriele}@infolab.ing.univaq.it
[2] Department of Mathematics, University of L'Aquila, Via Vetoio loc. Coppito, I-67100 L'Aquila - Italy. Email: flammini@univaq.it

Abstract. In this paper we consider Interval Routing Schemes (IRS) that are optimal with respect to the congestion of the induced path system. We provide a general framework able to deal with the various congestion issues in IRS. In fact, it is possible to distinguish between static cases, in which the source-destination configurations are fixed, and dynamic cases, where they vary over time. All these situations can be handled in a unified setting, thanks to the notion of competitiveness introduced in this paper.
We first give some general results not related to specific traffic demands. Then, in the one-to-all communication pattern, we show that constructing competitive IRS for a given network is an intractable problem, both for the static and the dynamic case, that is respectively when the root vertex is fixed and when it can change along the time.
Finally, both for one-to-all and all-to-all communication patterns, we provide nicely competitive k-IRS for relevant topologies. Networks considered are chains, trees, rings, chordal rings and multi-dimensional grids and tori.
We consider both the directed congestion case, in which there are pairwise opposite unidirectional links connecting two neighbor processors, and the undirected congestion case, in which two neighbors are connected by a single bi-directional link.

1 Introduction

Interval Routing Schemes, or simply IRS, were introduced in [22, 24, 25] with the purpose of minimizing the memory requirements at the various processors of the interconnection network for the distributed representation of the (shortest) paths.

In IRS, vertex-labels belong to the set $\{1, \dots, n\}$, while link-labels are pairs of vertex-labels representing disjoint intervals of $[1..n]$. To send a message m from a source u to a destination v, m is transmitted by u on the (unique) link $e = (u, w)$ such that the label of v belongs to the interval associated with e.

As proved in [24, 25], for any network G there always exists an IRS which is *valid*, i.e. such that for all the vertices u and v of G, messages from u to v reach v correctly, not necessarily routing shortest paths. Moreover, in [22], [24], [25] it is shown how

* Work supported by the EU ESPRIT Long Term Research Project ALCOM-IT under contract N. 20244.

the IRS can be applied to route messages along shortest paths on particular network topologies, such as trees, rings, etc.

In order to enable shortest path routing for every network, in [25] the model has been extended to allow more than 1 interval to be associated with each link; in particular, a 2-IRS, i.e. a scheme associating at most 2 intervals per link, is proposed for 2-dimensional tori. Other characterization and computational complexity results related to k-IRS and compact routing schemes can be found in [5, 7, 8, 11, 14, 19] (see [13] for a survey).

Such results have emphasized that IRS seem effective for networks having particular regularities. In fact, it improves with respect to the trivial solution of storing, at each vertex v, a complete routing table which specifies, for each destination u, one incident link belonging to a shortest path between u and v. On the contrary, when no specific assumption about the topology of a network is made, IRS in general do not significantly reduce the space requirements [8, 14, 19].

In this paper we are concerned with the determination of IRS that are optimal with respect to the resulting congestion. In particular, given a communication pattern R, i.e. a set of source-destination pairs wishing to communicate, the congestion of the scheme with respect to R is defined as the maximum number of induced paths connecting pairs in R that share the same physical link.

Such an issue is crucial in parallel computation because good parallel models simulations and more in general efficient routing scheduling algorithms are strongly related to the congestion of the path system routed by the messages [4, 15, 20]. Besides its theoretical interest, the combination of congestion problems with interval routing is relevant also for parallel implementation, since k-IRS have been used in the last generation of INMOS Transputer C104 Router chips together with wormhole routing [18], that is very sensitive to congestion [4, 15]. Finally, this devising goal is important also from a fault-tolerance point of view, as a link failure should not disconnect too many source-destination pairs.

Interval Routing and congestion have been considered independently also in [21], where in the all-to-all case trade-offs between the number of intervals and the congestion of multi-dimensional IRS have been shown for bounded-degree networks, and low-congested multi-dimensional IRS are given for the cube-connected-cycle.

In general the congestion of the path systems has been extensively investigated in the literature. For instance, in the all-to-all case, it corresponds to the notion of *Edge Forwarding Index* introduced in [17]. A similar *Vertex Forwarding Index* measure taking into account the load of processors was defined in [2]. Various results on forwarding index issues can be found in [2, 17, 23].

In this paper we give a general framework able to deal with the various congestion issues in IRS. In fact, it is possible to distinguish between the static and the dynamic case. In the former, R is fixed in advance and the scheme is required to have a good performance with respect to R. In the latter, the scheme is fixed in advance, but R can vary over time within a family of communication requests $\mathcal{R}$; the scheme is required to behave efficiently with respect to each $R \in \mathcal{R}$. Static and dynamic situations can be faced in a unified setting, thanks to the notion of competitiveness introduced in this paper. Namely, a k-IRS is *c-competitive* if its performance ratio with respect to any other k-IRS is within a factor c, that is, for each $R \in \mathcal{R}$ its maximal link congestion is at most c times the one of the other k-IRS.

In such a framework, we first give some general results. i.e. not related to specific communication requests. Then, we focus on the one-to-all and all-to-all patterns. In the former, all processors have to communicate with a single root vertex and vice versa; in the static case the root is fixed in advance, while in the dynamic one it can vary over time. In the latter all processors want to communicate with all the others.

We first show that constructing one-to-all 1-competitive IRS for a given network is an intractable problem, both for static and dynamic cases.

Then, we provide nicely competitive k-IRS for relevant topologies, both for one-to-all and all-to-all communication patterns. Networks considered are chains, trees, rings, chordal rings and multi-dimensional grids and tori.

According to the congestion measures considered, it is possible to distinguish between the *directed* congestion and the *undirected* congestion cases. In the former the congestion of a link is defined as the maximum between the number of paths traversing the link in a given direction and the number of paths traversing it in the opposite one. In the latter, the congestion of a link is given by the number of all paths traversing the link, independent of their direction. We always consider first the directed congestion case, which is more restrictive, and then all results are extended to the undirected case.

The paper is organized as follows. The next section contains a description of the communication model used and some definitions. In Section 3 we give the general results concerning IRS and congestion. In Section 4 we show the NP-completeness results. In Section 5 and 6 we give efficient schemes for some relevant interconnection networks, respectively for the one-to-all and all-to-all communication patterns. Finally, in Section 7 we give some conclusive remarks and list some open problems.

Due to space constraints, technical details and proofs are omitted in this extended abstract and can be found in the full version of the paper [3].

2 The model

The model we use is the *point to point* communication model, where each processor in the network has access only to its own local memory and communicates by sending messages along bidirectional communication links to one of its neighbors. The network topology is modeled as a symmetric directed graph $G = (V, A)$ with vertex set V representing processors and arc set A representing the bidirectional links.

Each message has a header that includes its destination address. As a message reaches any given vertex, it is either evicted from the network (if it has reached its final destination) or it is forwarded through an outgoing arc. Such an arc is determined starting from the destination address according to the local information stored at the vertex.

The particular routing method considered in the paper is the *Interval Labeling Scheme* (ILS) [22, 24, 25], that is based on a suitable labeling of the vertices and of the arcs of the graph. Vertex labels belong to the set $N = \{1, 2, \ldots, n\}$, while arc labels represent disjoint intervals in N. An interval in N can be defined as $[a, b] = \{a, a+1, \ldots, b\}$. Intervals may *wrap-around*, that is if $a > b$ then $[a, b] = \{a, a+1, \ldots, n, 1, \ldots, b\}$. We denote as $l(v)$ the label of vertex v and as $I(u, v)$ the interval assigned to arc (u, v). The set of all intervals associated with the arcs leaving the same vertex forms a partition of the interval N. Messages to a destination vertex v are routed via the arc that is labeled with the interval $[a,b]$ containing $l(v)$. An ILS is *valid* if, for all the vertices u and v of G, messages sent from u to v always reach v correctly. A valid ILS is called an *Interval Routing Scheme* (*IRS* for short).

In a k-ILS each arc is labeled with up to k intervals in N, and again all the intervals associated with the arcs emanating from a same vertex form a partition of N. A message with destination v is then routed on the link such that one of its intervals contains the label of v. A valid k-ILS is also called a k-IRS.

Some restrictions of the classical k-IRS can be defined. For instance, in [1] a k-IRS is said *linear* if no interval wraps around, i.e. all intervals $[a,b]$ are such that $a \leq b$. Another restricted version of k-IRS, usually called *strict* k-IRS, was used in [11] and later formalized in [9]: at each vertex u, the intervals associated to its incident links must not contain the vertex-label $l(u)$.

Even if so far research activities on interval routing have focused on determining the minimum value of k such that a given network admits a shortest path k-IRS, as already remarked reducing the congestion of the induced path system in wormhole routing is a relevant design goal as well to yield good corresponding routing functions. The remaining part of this section is devoted to the definition of the framework combining interval routing and congestion.

Given two vertices u, v in G, let $p(u,v)$ denote the path used by a given routing strategy to route messages from u to v. A *path system* P in G is a set containing all possible n^2 paths in G, that is, $P = \{p(u,v) \mid (u,v) \in V \times V\}$. We denote as $\mathcal{P}(G)$ the set of all path systems in G.

A set of *communication requests* in G is a set $R \subseteq V \times V$ containing the source-destination pairs wishing to communicate. Given R, it is possible to define the restriction of P to R as $P_R = \{p(u,v) \in P \mid (u,v) \in R\}$, that is the set of paths in P connecting each communication request in R.

Definition 1. Given a set of communication requests R and a path system P in G, the congestion $\mathcal{C}(G,P,R,e)$ of an arc $e \in A$ is defined as the number of paths in P_R containing e, that is $\mathcal{C}(G,P,R,e) = |\{p(u,v) \in P_R \mid e \in p(u,v)\}|$. The congestion $\mathcal{C}(G,P,R)$ of P with respect to R is the maximum arc congestion, that is $\mathcal{C}(G,P,R) = \max_{e \in A} \mathcal{C}(G,P,R,e)$, and the minimal congestion with respect to R is $\mathcal{C}(G,R) = \min_{P \in \mathcal{P}(G)} \mathcal{C}(G,P,R)$.

As far as lower bounds on the congestion are concerned, a well-known relationship is established by the inequality $\mathcal{C}(G,P,R) \geq \frac{1}{|A|} \sum_{(u,v) \in R} dist_G(u,v)$ (see for instance [17]). Moreover, given a cut of s arcs which separates the graph into two maximal strongly connected components $G_1 = (V_1, A_1)$ and $G_2 = (V_2, A_2)$, trivially $\mathcal{C}(G,P,R) \geq \lceil \frac{p}{s} \rceil$ (see for instance [23]), where p is the number of source-destination pairs $(u,v) \in R$ such that $u \in V_1$ and $v \in V_2$, or analogously $p = |R \cap (V_1 \times V_2)|$. As a direct consequence, in the one-to-all case with $R = R^v = (\{v\} \times (V - \{v\})) \cup ((V - \{v\}) \times \{v\})$ for a specified vertex $v \in V$, $\mathcal{C}(G,P,R) \geq \lceil (n-1)/d \rceil$, where d is the degree of v, while in the all-to-all case with $R = V \times V$, $\mathcal{C}(G,P,R) \geq \lceil \lfloor n/2 \rfloor \lceil n/2 \rceil / b(G) \rceil = \lceil \lfloor n^2/4 \rfloor / b(G) \rceil$, where $b(G)$ is the bisection width of G, that is the minimum number of arcs that must be cut to split G in two maximal strongly connected components respectively of $\lfloor n/2 \rfloor$ and $\lceil n/2 \rceil$ vertices.

Any k-IRS of a network G induces a path system P in G in a trivial way. Then, it is possible to define $\mathcal{P}(G, k\text{-IRS}) \subseteq \mathcal{P}(G)$ as the subset containing all the possible path systems induced by k-IRS for G. The congestion in G due to k-IRS with respect to a set of communication requests R is denoted as $\mathcal{C}_k(G, R)$ and is given by $\mathcal{C}_k(G, R) = \min_{P \in \mathcal{P}(G,k-IRS)} \mathcal{C}(G, P, R)$.

The determination of path systems in $\mathcal{P}(G, k\text{-IRS})$ with congestion as close as possible to $\mathcal{C}_k(G, R)$ for a given R is a worth investigating issue and is one focus of this work. Moreover, another strictly related considered problem consists of finding the smallest possible k yielding good values of $\mathcal{C}_k(G, R)$ as compared to $\mathcal{C}(G, R)$.

As already observed, often a k-IRS has to fulfill the more challenging task of having a good behavior with respect to different communication patterns. The following parameter measures the behavior of P with respect to a family of sets of communication requests.

Definition 2. Given a family $\mathcal{R} \equiv \{R^i\}_{i \in I}$ of communication requests and a k-IRS for G with induced P, the k-IRS is said c-competitive with respect to $\mathcal{R}$ for a positive real number c if for any other k-IRS with induced path system P' $\max_{i \in I} \{\frac{\mathcal{C}(G,P,R^i)}{\mathcal{C}(G,P',R^i)}\} \leq c$.

The competitiveness factor c takes into account how well the k-IRS behaves with respect to any other scheme on all the sets of communication requests in $\mathcal{R}$. Notice that some graphs may have no 1-competitive k-IRS, since in order to perform better on a given R^i it might be necessary to increase the maximal congestion of another $R^{i'}$ and vice versa. For example, it is easy to see that in the ring of the four vertices 1, 2, 3 and 4 connected in a cycle, no c-competitive k-IRS (for any k) exists for $c < 2$ with respect to the family of the 3 sets of communication requests $R^1 = \{(1,2),(1,3)\}$, $R^2 = \{(1,2),(1,4)\}$ and $R^3 = \{(1,3),(1,4)\}$.

3 General results

In this section we show some general results concerning IRS and congestion. First of all, the natural question to ask is whether and how much one looses using k-IRS with respect to $(k+1)$-IRS and unrestricted path systems.

Lemma 3. *There exists a graph G and a set of requests R such that $\mathcal{C}_k(G, R) \geq \frac{n-2}{2}\mathcal{C}(G, R)$.*

Lemma 4. *For each fixed number of intervals $k \geq 2$, there exists a graph G and a set of requests R such that $\mathcal{C}_{k-1}(G, R) > \mathcal{C}_k(G, R)$.*

One natural question to ask is what is the maximum value of k such that $\mathcal{C}_{k-1}(G, R) > \mathcal{C}_k(G, R)$. A trivial upper bound is $k = \lfloor n/2 \rfloor + 1$, as $\lfloor n/2 \rfloor$ intervals are always sufficient to identify any subset of n vertices, so a higher number of intervals does not increase the representation power of the scheme.

A better lower bound is provided in the following lemma.

Lemma 5. *For each positive integer n there exists a graph G with $\Theta(n)$ vertices and $k = \Theta(n/\log n)$ such that, for a given set of requests R, $\mathcal{C}_{k-1}(G, R) > \mathcal{C}_k(G, R)$.*

Even if we don't put separate claims, Lemma 4 and Lemma 5 can be easily extended to prove that, for every positive integer c, $\mathcal{C}_{k-1}(G,R) > c + \mathcal{C}_k(G,R)$.

As far as competitiveness is concerned, the example of rings in the previous section shows that there are graph not admitting 1-competitive k-IRS for given families of communication requests. The following lemma shows that in some cases the best competitive ratio of any k-IRS grows as a function of the size of the graph.

Lemma 6. *There exists a graph G with n vertices and a family of communication requests $\mathcal{R}$ such that any k-IRS for G cannot be less than $\frac{n-1}{2}$-competitive.*

Lemma 7. *Given a graph G and any set of communication requests R, in a given k-IRS for G let e be an arc with maximum congestion with respect to R. Then, if there exists a cut of at most s arcs that splits G in two maximal strongly connected components G_1 and G_2 such that all the sources of the paths traversing e belong to G_1 and all the destinations to G_2, then the k-IRS is s-competitive with respect to any family of communication requests $\mathcal{R}$.*

This result clearly holds also with respect to a given family of communication requests $\mathcal{R}$, if each $R \in \mathcal{R}$ satisfies the conditions of the claim.

Concerning results for specific topologies, observe first that trivially chains and trees have dynamic 1-competitive 1-IRS with respect to any family of communication requests $\mathcal{R}$, as they have a unique simple (shortest) path connecting any source-destination pair and thus the path system induced by any k-IRS is the same. Moreover, as a direct consequence of Lemma 7, upper bounds on the competitive ratio can be determined for many interconnection networks.

Theorem 8. *For each of the following networks there exists a k-IRS c-competitive with respect to any set of communication requests $\mathcal{R}$, where*
- *$k = 1$ and $c = 2$ for any ring R_n of n vertices;*
- *$k = 1$ and $c = 2(1 + \sum_{i=1}^{h} l_i)$ for any n-vertex chordal ring $R_n(l_1, \ldots, l_h)$ having chords of length respectively $l_1, \ldots, l_h$ with $l_h \bmod n = 0$ and $l_j \bmod l_{j-1} = 0$, $1 < j < h$;*
- *$k = 1$ and $c = n$ for any $n \times n$ grid $G_{n\times n}$;*
- *$k = 2$ and $c = 2n$ for any $n \times n$ torus $T_{n\times n}$;*
- *$k = 1$ and $c = n/2$ for any hypercube H_d of $d = \log n$ dimensions.*

While the result for rings is optimal in the sense that there are families of communication requests for which there are not schemes with a competitive ratio less than 2, it would be worth to find suitable lower bounds on the competitive ratio for the other networks also.

4 The NP-completeness results

The problem of deciding the existence of a shortest path k-IRS for a graph has been shown to be NP-complete for non constant values of k on weighted graphs in [7]. Such a result has been extended in [6] by proving that it is NP-complete for $k = 2$ on unweighted graphs. The best NP-completeness result for shortest path 1-IRS on unweighted graphs has been proved in [5].

In this section we determine the computational complexity of the problem of devising IRS with a good competitive ratio. By exploiting ideas in [16], we prove that this problem is in general NP-complete both in the static and in the dynamic one-to-all cases. In particular, let $R^v = (\{v\} \times (V - \{v\})) \cup ((V - \{v\}) \times \{v\})$ for a given vertex $v \in V$. Then, in the *static* one-to-all case $\mathcal{R} = \{R^v\}$ for a fixed vertex $v \in V$, while in the *dynamic* one $\mathcal{R} = \{R^v\}_{v \in V}$, i.e., it includes all possible R^vs.

Since in order to obtain a low competitive ratio it is necessary to minimize the congestions with respect to the corresponding communication requests, the following problems naturally arise.

Definition 9. Minimum Static k-IRS Problem (Stat k-IRS):
INSTANCE: A symmetric digraph $G = (V, A)$, a root vertex r and an integer $C > 0$.
QUESTION: Is there a k-IRS for G whose induced path system P is such that $\mathcal{C}(G, P, R^r) \leq C$?

Definition 10. Minimum Dynamic k-IRS Problem (Dyn k-IRS):
INSTANCE: A symmetric digraph $G = (V, A)$ with $V = \{v_1, \ldots, v_n\}$ and a sequence of n positive integers $C_1, \ldots, C_n$.
QUESTION: Is there a k-IRS for G whose induced path system P is such that $\mathcal{C}(G, P, R^{v_i}) \leq C_i$ for each $v_i \in V$?

The NP-completeness of both the two problems can be shown by providing polynomial-time reductions from the 3-Partition problem [12].

Theorem 11. *Stat* 1*-IRS and Dyn* 2*-IRS are NP-complete.*

The NP-completeness of Stat 1-IRS holds also for linear 1-IRS and strict 1-IRS, and the problem is NP-complete for every fixed value of k. The NP-completeness of Dyn 2-IRS holds also for linear and/or strict 2-IRS, and the problem is NP-complete for every fixed value of $k \geq 2$.

Notice that, since the competitiveness of k-IRS is defined with respect to k-IRS themselves, often asking for the existence of c-competitive schemes does not make sense. For instance, in the static case there always exists a 1-competitive k-IRS and this holds also in the reductions provided in the proof of Theorem 11 ($k = 1$ and $k = 2$, respectively). This means that, even if we know in advance that a 1-competitive scheme exists, constructing it is anyway an NP-hard problem.

5 One-to-all: results for specific topologies

Starting from the hardness results shown in the previous section, we now provide efficient schemes for some commonly used interconnection networks, such as rings, grids and tori. The communication pattern is always assumed one-to-all.

Lemma 12. *(1) There exist a dynamic* 1*-competitive* 1*-IRS for rings R_n. (2) If a network G is Hamiltonian and every vertex of G has degree at most d, $d > 0$, then there exists a dynamic $d/2$-competitive* 1*-IRS for G.*

As a consequence of the previous lemma, 2-competitive 1-IRS can be determined for chordal rings $R_n(l)$, tori, De Bruijn graphs and other Hamiltonian networks of degree at most 4.

Lemma 13. *There exist a static* 1*-competitive* 1*-IRS for grids* $G_{n\times n}$ *and tori* $T_{n\times n}$.

Lemma 14. *There exist a dynamic* 2*-competitive* 1*-IRS for* $G_{n\times n}$.

Despite of its apparent simplicity, the task of devising better competitive schemes in the one-to-all directed case seems to be rather untrivial. We now show that in the less restrictive situation of an undirected congestion, better results can be found for networks like tori and chordal rings.

Undirected congestion case. In the undirected congestion case the network is modeled as an undirected graph and the congestion of an edge $\{u, v\}$ is given by the number of all paths traversing the edge, independently of their direction. Namely, the congestion of $\{u, v\}$ is given by the sum of the congestions of the directed arcs (u, v) and (v, u).

All definitions in Section 2 trivially extend to the undirected congestion case, and it is immediate to check that the same holds also for all the previous results, with the exception of the ones that we are going to list below.

The NP-completeness results still holds, but with respect to the static and dynamic *accumulation* problems, where we are interested only in the paths from all the nodes toward the route and not vice versa. Namely, for each node $v \in V$, we replace the sets R^v with $(V - \{v\}) \times \{v\}$.

Concerning results for specific topologies, all lower bounds derived by means of the cutting arguments double for undirected congestion, and the same trivially holds for the upper bounds, as a scheme with directed congestion C implies directly a scheme with undirected congestion $2C$. Hence, all optimal and nearly optimal results can be extended to the undirected congestion case.

First of all, a better result can be found for tori.

Theorem 15. *There exists a dynamic* $(1 + \frac{1}{n-1})$*-competitive* 1*-IRS for* $T_{n\times n}$.

The following theorem shows a similar result for chordal rings.

Theorem 16. *Let* $R_n(l)$ *be a chordal ring with* $l \bmod n = 0$. *There exists a dynamic* $(\frac{3}{2} + o(1))$*-competitive* 1*-IRS for* $R_n(l)$, *and a dynamic* $(1 + o(1))$*-competitive* 1*-IRS for* $R_n(l)$ *when* $l = \sqrt{n}$.

This theorem can be used whenever a chordal ring $R_n(l)$ is a subgraph of a n-node network G with degree at most d. In this case, there exists a dynamic $(\frac{3d}{8} + o(1))$-competitive 1-IRS for G, and a dynamic $(\frac{d}{4} + o(1))$-competitive 1-IRS for G when $l = \sqrt{n}$.

6 All-to-all: results for specific topologies

In this section we give optimal and nearly optimal results for some relevant interconnection networks, such as rings, chordal rings, and multi-dimensional grids and tori. The communication pattern is always assumed all-to-all, i.e. $R = V \times V$, and for the sake simplicity is always omitted from the notation.

Theorem 17. *There exist a* 1*-competitive* 1*-IRS for any ring* R_n.

We now consider the more general case of chordal rings. By the bisection width argument, $\mathcal{C}(R_n(l_1,\ldots,l_h)) \geq \lceil \lfloor n^2/4 \rfloor / 2(1+l_1+\ldots+l_h) \rceil$. However, if suitable restrictions on chord lengths are imposed, finer results can be determined.

Lemma 18. *Let $R_n(l_1,\ldots,l_h)$ be a chordal ring with $l_h \bmod n = 0$ and $l_j \bmod l_{j-1} = 0$, $1 < j < h$. Then*
$\mathcal{C}(R_n(l_1,\ldots,l_h)) \geq \max_{1\leq j\leq h}\{\left\lceil \frac{\lfloor n^2/4 \rfloor}{2(1+l_1+\ldots+l_h)} \right\rceil, n\frac{l_j-2}{8(1+l_1+\ldots+l_{j-1})}\}$*, and*
$\mathcal{C}_1(R_n(l_1,\ldots,l_h)) \leq \max_{1<j\leq h}\{\frac{n}{8}(\frac{n}{l_h}+2)+1, \frac{n}{4}(l_{j-1}+\frac{l_j}{2l_{j-1}}), \frac{n}{8}(l_1+2)\}$.

For chordal rings of type $R_n(l)$ with only one chord of length l such that $n \bmod l = 0$, the above results are very close, as they give $\max\{\left\lceil \frac{\lfloor n^2/4 \rfloor}{2(1+l)} \right\rceil, n\frac{l-2}{8}\} \leq \mathcal{C}_1(R_n(l)) \leq \max\{\frac{n}{8}(\frac{n}{l}+2)+1, \frac{n}{8}(l+2)\}$. As a consequence of the previous lemmas, optimal competitive schemes can be obtained under different assumptions.

Corollary 19. *There exist $(1+o(1))$-competitive 1-IRS for $R_n(l)$, when $l \bmod n = 0$ and $n/l = o(n)$, and for $R_n(l_1,\ldots,l_h)$, when $l_h \bmod n = 0$ and for each j, $1 \leq j < h$, $l_{j+1} \bmod l_j = 0$ and $l_j^2 = o(l_{j+1})$.*

In the remainder of this section, we consider grid and torus networks. These topologies belong to the more general class of the *Cartesian product* graphs, that includes other interconnection networks commonly used in parallel architectures, as for instance the hypercubes.

The Cartesian product $G \equiv G_1 \times G_2$ of two graphs $G_1 = (V_1, A_1)$ and $G_2 = (V_2, A_2)$ is the graph whose vertices are the pairs (u_1, u_2), where u_1 is a vertex of G_1 and u_2 is a vertex of G_2. Two vertices (u_1, u_2) and (v_1, v_2) of $G_1 \times G_2$ are adjacent if and only if $u_1 = v_1$ and (u_2, v_2) is an arc of G_2 or $u_2 = v_2$ and (u_1, v_1) is an arc of G_1. Many graphs can be defined in terms of Cartesian product of simpler graphs, like the hypercube H_d, defined from C_2 as $H_d = C_2 \times H_{d-1} = C_2 \times \ldots \times C_2$ d times, the grid $G_{n\times m}$, i.e. $C_n \times C_m$, and the torus $T_{n\times m} = R_n \times R_m$.

Lemma 20. *Let $G_1 = (V_1, A_1)$ and $G_2 = (V_2, A_2)$ be two networks with n_1 and n_2 vertices and bisection width $b(G_1)$ and $b(G_2)$, respectively. Then*
$\mathcal{C}(G_1 \times G_2) \geq \max\{\lceil n_1 \lfloor (n_2)^2/4 \rfloor / b(G_2) \rceil, \lceil n_2 \lfloor (n_1)^2/4 \rfloor / b(G_1) \rceil\}$.

Lemma 21. *Let G_1 and G_2 be two networks having n_1 and n_2 vertices, respectively. Then, $\mathcal{C}_{k+2}(G_1 \times G_2) \leq \max\{n_2 \cdot \mathcal{C}_k(G_1), n_1 \cdot \mathcal{C}_k(G_2)\}$.*

The $k+2$-IRS for $G_1 \times G_2$ constructed to prove Lemma 21 is obtained according to the construction given in [19]. As shown in [10], if G_1 and G_2 have respectively a strict k-IRS and a linear k-IRS then there exists a k-IRS for $G_1 \times G_2$ with the same induced path system, and consequently completely analogous argumentations as the ones in Lemma 21 show that if the strict k-IRS for G_1 is such that the induced path system P_1 satisfies $\mathcal{C}(G_1, P_1) = \mathcal{C}_k(G_1)$ and the linear k-IRS for G_2 is such that the induced path system P_2 satisfies $\mathcal{C}(G_2, P_2) = \mathcal{C}_k(G_2)$, then $\mathcal{C}_k(G_1 \times G_2) \leq \max\{n_2 \cdot \mathcal{C}_k(G_1), n_1 \cdot \mathcal{C}_k(G_2)\}$. Similarly, if G_1 has a strict k-IRS or G_2 has a linear k-IRS (not necessarily both) the product of G_1 and G_2 has a $k+1$-IRS obtained in the same way and if the two schemes match respectively $\mathcal{C}_k(G_1)$ and $\mathcal{C}_k(G_2)$ then $\mathcal{C}_{k+1}(G_1 \times G_2) \leq \max\{n_2 \cdot \mathcal{C}_k(G_1), n_1 \cdot \mathcal{C}_k(G_2)\}$.

By extending ideas in Lemmas 20 and 21, optimal results can be found for d-dimensional hypercubes, grids, tori and grid-tori, where grid-tori are the generalization of grids and tori obtained by Cartesian products of chains and rings.

Corollary 22. *There exists a $(1 + o(1))$-competitive 1-IRS for any d-dimensional grid $C_{n_1} \times C_{n_2} \times \cdots \times C_{n_d}$.*

Similarly, since $b(R_n) = 2$ and R_n admits a strict and linear 2-IRS with optimal congestion (it can be obtained directly from the strict 1-IRS in Theorem 17 by cutting wrap-around intervals in two linear intervals), in a completely analogous manner it is possible to prove the following corollary.

Corollary 23. *There exists a $(1 + o(1))$-competitive 2-IRS for any d-dimensional grid-torus $Q_{n_1} \times Q_{n_2} \times \cdots \times Q_{n_d}$, where for each i, $1 \leq i \leq d$, either $Q_{n_i} \equiv C_{n_i}$ or $Q_{n_i} \equiv R_{n_i}$.*

So far, we have given optimal results for Cartesian products of graphs. Namely, we have shown that $\mathcal{C}_{k+2}(G_1 \times G_2)$ can be bounded starting from $\mathcal{C}_k(G_1)$ and $\mathcal{C}_k(G_2)$. Now, a natural question arises: what about $\mathcal{C}_k(G_1 \times G_2)$ and $\mathcal{C}_{k+1}(G_1 \times G_2)$? We know how to give an optimal answer to this question only under particular assumptions, but in general proper bounds on $\mathcal{C}_k(G_1 \times G_2)$ have not been determined yet.

This problem is not trivial, even in the very simple case of a two dimensional torus. In fact, while an optimal congestion 2-IRS can be easily determined from the product theorem, no bound is known on the congestion achievable by 1-IRS.

By means of successive steps we are able to provide schemes with congestion $n^3/4 \approx 2\mathcal{C}(T_{n \times n})$, $3n^3/16$, and finally $3/20n^3 = 0.150n^3$, that is very close to the $\mathcal{C}(T_{n \times n}) \approx n^3/8 = 0.125n^3$ lower bound (from Lemma 20, when $G_1 \equiv G_2 \equiv R_n$ and $b(R_n) = 2$), thanks to two new techniques, called respectively halving and lightening (see [3]).

Theorem 24. $\mathcal{C}_1(T_{n \times n}) \leq 0.150n^3 + o(n^3)$.

Corollary 25. *There exists a $(1.2 + o(1))$-competitive 1-IRS for any torus $T_{n \times n}$.*

Undirected congestion case. Similarly as in the one-to-all communication pattern, in the undirected congestion case all lower bounds derived by means of the summation of distances and cutting arguments double, and the same holds for the upper bounds. Thus all optimal and nearly optimal results can be extended to the undirected congestion case, although little differences to yield exactly matching bounds might be necessary, due to integer rounding factors. For instance, the scheme for rings that assigns at each node i interval $[i + 1, i + \lfloor n/2 \rfloor]$ to edge $\{i, i + 1\}$ and interval $[i + \lfloor n/2 \rfloor + 1, i - 1]$ to $\{i, i - 1\}$ has congestion exactly $\mathcal{C}(R_n) = \lfloor n^2/4 \rfloor$, while the scheme proposed for the directed case might yield congestion $\mathcal{C}(R_n) + 1$, as two pairwise opposite arcs can have the same congestion $\lceil \lfloor n^2/4 \rfloor /2 \rceil$, while others congestion $\lfloor \lfloor n^2/4 \rfloor /2 \rfloor$.

7 Conclusion and open problems

In this paper we have considered the problem of devising Interval Routing Schemes with a low congestion per arc or per edge, both in the static and in the dynamic congestion cases.

Although we have not taken into account the length of the paths routed by the messages, all the proposed schemes exhibit also a good dilation, since they have a low constant stretch factor (the maximum ratio, over all the source-destination pairs, between the length of the path induced by the scheme and the distance).

Many questions are left open. First of all, what is the computational complexity of devising optimal (in terms of competitive ratio) all-to-all schemes? We observe here that to the best of our knowledge such a problem is still open even if we consider unrestricted path systems, i.e. not necessarily yielded by k-IRS. Moreover, what is the time-complexity of constructing efficient one-to-all k-IRS in the undirected congestion case? And in broadcasting (from the root toward the other processors and not vice versa) and permutation routing with directed and undirected congestion?

It would be worth to complete our results for particular network topologies, as for instance the $1 \div 2$ (one-to-all) gap on the competitive ratio of 1-IRS for grids and tori in the directed one-to-all case and the $1 \div 1.2$ gap of 1-IRS for tori in the directed all-to-all case. Furthermore, it would be nice to consider extensions to other possible communication patterns.

Apart from the specific results, another relevant contribution stands in the introduced framework, that enables to face all the different situations in a unified fashion. The competitive setting has actually more general applications than the ones tackled in this paper in "oblivious" routing schemes, when the induced path system must be checked versus different source-destination configurations. Here a scheme is said to be oblivious if the path followed by each message is just a function of the source and of the destination of the message. Besides the competitiveness definition, it might be possible to define a *strong*-competitive measure by comparing the performance of k-IRS with respect to unrestricted path systems, that is not necessarily yielded by k-IRS. We observe here that all the schemes proposed for specific topologies are strong competitive with the same factor.

References

1. E. Bakker, J. van Leeuwen, and R.B. Tan. Linear interval routing. *Algorithms Review*, 2(2):45–61, 1991.
2. F.R.K. Chung, E.G. Coffman, M.I. Reiman, and B.E. Simon. The forwarding index of communication networks. *IEEE Trans. on Inform. Theory*, 33:224–232, 1987.
3. S. Cicerone, G. Di Stefano, and M. Flammini. Low-congested interval routing schemes. Technical Report R.97-20, Dipartimento di Ingegneria Elettrica, Università di L'Aquila (L'Aquila, Italy), 1997.
4. R. Cypher, F. Meyer auf der Heide, C. Scheideler, and B. Vöcking. Universal algorithms for store-and-forward and wormhole routing. In *Proceedings of the 28th Annual ACM Symposium on Theory of Computing*, pages 356–365, Philadelphia, Pennsylvania, 22–24 May 1996.

5. T. Eilam, S. Moran, and S. Zaks. The complexity of characterization of networks supporting shortest-path interval routing. In *4th Colloquium on Structural Information and Communication Complexity (SIROCCO)*. Carleton University Press, 1997.
6. M. Flammini. On the hardness of devising interval routing schemes. *Parallel Processing Letters*, 7(1):39–47, 1997.
7. M. Flammini, G. Gambosi, and S. Salomone. Interval routing schemes. *Algorithmica*, 16(6):549–568, 1996.
8. M. Flammini, J. van Leeuwen, and A. Marchetti Spaccamela. The complexity of interval routing on random graphs. In *20th Symposium on Mathematical Foundation of Computer Science (MFCS)*, volume 969 of *Lecture Notes in Computer Science*, pages 37–49. Springer-Verlag, 1995.
9. P. Fraigniaud and C. Gavoille. A characterisation of networks supporting linear interval routing. In *13th Annual ACM Symposium on Principles of Distributed Computing (PODC)*, pages 216–224, 1994.
10. P. Fraigniaud and C. Gavoille. Interval routing schemes. Technical Report 94-04, Laboratoire de l'Informatique du Parallélisme, LIP, École Normale Supérieure de Lyon, 69364 Lyon Cedex 07, France, 1994. To appear in Algorithmica.
11. G.N. Frederickson and R. Janardan. Designing networks with compact routing tables. *Algorithmica*, 3:171–190, 1988.
12. M.R. Garey and D.S. Johnson. *Computers and Intractability. A Guide to the Theory of NP-completeness*. W.H. Freeman, 1979.
13. C. Gavoille. A survey on interval routing scheme. Research Report RR-1182-97, University of Bordeaux (France), October 1997.
14. C. Gavoille and S. Pérennès. Lower bounds for interval routing on 3-regular networks. In *3rd Colloquium on Structural Information and Communication Complexity (SIROCCO)*. Carleton University Press, 1996.
15. R. I. Greenberg and H.-C. Oh. Universal wormhole routing. *IEEE Transactions on Parallel and Distributed Systems (IEEE-TPDS)*, 8, 1997.
16. M.C. Heydemann, J.C. Meyer, J. Opatrny, and D. Sotteau. Forwarding indices of consistent routings and their complexity. *Networks*, 24(2):75–82, 1994.
17. M.C. Heydemann, J.C. Meyer, and D. Sotteau. On forwarding indices of networks. *Discrete Applied Math.*, 23:103–123, 1989.
18. *The T9000 Transputer Products Overview Manual*. INMOS, 1991.
19. E. Kranakis, D. Krizanc, and S.S. Ravi. On multi-label linear interval routing schemes. In *19th Workshop on Graph Theoretic Concepts in Computer Science (WG)*, volume 790 of *Lecture Notes in Computer Science*, pages 338–349. Springer-Verlag, 1993.
20. T. Leighton, B. Maggs, and S. Rao. Universal packet routing algorithms. In *29th Annual Symposium on Foundations of Computer Science*, pages 256–271, 1988.
21. P. Ruzicka and D. Stefankovic. On the complexity of multidimensional interval routing schemes. Manuscript, 1997.
22. N. Santoro and R. Khatib. Labeling and implicit routing in networks. *The Computer Journal*, 28:5–8, 1985.
23. P. Solé. Expanding and forwarding. *Discrete Applied Math.*, 58:67–78, 1995.
24. J. van Leeuwen and R.B. Tan. Routing with compact routing tables. In G. Rozemberg and A. Salomaa, editors, *The book of L*, pages 259–273. Springer–Verlag, 1986.
25. J. van Leeuwen and R.B. Tan. Interval routing. *The Computer Journal*, 30:298–307, 1987.

Low-Bandwidth Routing and Electrical Power Networks*

Doug Cook[1**], Vance Faber[2], Madhav Marathe[2], Aravind Srinivasan[3***], and Yoram J. Sussmann[4†]

[1] Department of Engineering, Colorado School of Mines, Golden CO 80401.
[2] P.O. Box 1663, MS B265, Los Alamos National Laboratory, Los Alamos NM 87545. Email: vxf,marathe@lanl.gov.
[3] Department of Information Systems and Computer Science, National University of Singapore, Singapore, 119260. Email: aravind@iscs.nus.edu.sg.
[4] Department of Computer Science, University of Maryland, College Park MD 20742. Email: yoram@cs.umd.edu.

Abstract. Given a graph G and a (multi-)set of pairs of vertices in it, the classical NP-hard *maximum edge-disjoint-paths problem* (MDP) is to connect as many of the given pairs as possible using pairwise edge-disjoint paths in G. We study a relative of this problem: we have a network with fixed link capacities that may have to service large demands when necessary. In particular, individual demands are allowed to exceed capacities, and thus flows for some request pairs necessarily have to be *split* into different flow-paths. This is the framework for computational problems arising from: (i) electrical power networks due to the proposed deregulation of the electric utility industry in the USA, and (ii) applications such as real-time Internet services (e.g., telephone, fax, video). We show that these problems come in a few variants, some efficiently solvable and many NP-hard; we also present approximation algorithms for many of the NP-hard variants presented. Some of our approximation algorithms benefit from certain improved tail estimates that we derive; the latter also yield improved approximations for a family of packing integer programs.

1 Introduction

The rapid growth of large-scale networks has spurred much attention on the classical NP-hard *maximum edge-disjoint-paths problem* (MDP): given a graph G and a (multi-)set of pairs of vertices in it, connect as many of the given pairs as possible using edge-disjoint paths in G [9]. The emergence of high-bandwidth networks supporting heterogeneous applications has also led to a

* This work has been supported by EPRI and Department of Energy under Contract W-7405-ENG-36.

** Work done while visiting Los Alamos National Laboratory, Los Alamos NM 87545.

*** Supported in part by National University of Singapore Academic Research Fund Grant RP970607.

† Part of this work was done while visiting Los Alamos National Laboratory, Los Alamos NM 87545. Supported in part by NSF CAREER Award CCR-9501355.

generalization of the MDP to the *unsplittable flow problem* (UFP): each network link has a capacity, each request pair has a demand, and to satisfy a request, *all* of its demand must be routed through a single path [10, 11, 16]. The usual assumption made here is that no single demand exceeds any capacity. What about the generalization of the MDP in the other direction to the *low bandwidth* case, where large demands must sometimes be serviced? Since some demands may exceed the link capacities, the flows for some request pairs will have to be split into different flow-paths. We study this framework here, motivated by two application domains: (a) Major telephone companies are devising protocols that subdivide audio and video signals into smaller packets and reassemble them at the destination, for real-time Internet services (e.g. phone, fax, etc.) [4, 12]; (b) New computational problems are arising in electrical flow networks due to the deregulation of the US electric utility industry. The results obtained reveal some striking differences between the problems considered here and the MDP/UFP.

Deregulation of the electric utility industry. The US electric utility industry is in the early stages of major structural changes driven by the move to deregulate the industry [5, 6, 19, 20]. A major consequence of deregulation is that consumers well as producers will eventually be able to negotiate prices to buy and sell electricity. See the comprehensive discussions by Wildberger [17–19]. Before formally defining the problems, we view the setting informally for now as a collection of request pairs (*contracts*) in a flow network wherein the flow for any pair can be *split into multiple paths.* In practice, deregulation is complicated by the fact that all power companies will have to share the same power network in the short term, with the network's capacity being just about sufficient to meet current demands. Under deregulation, most states are planning to set up an independent system operator (ISO), a governing body to arbitrate the use of the network. The basic questions facing the ISOs will be how to decide which contracts to deny (due to capacity constraints), and who is to bear the costs involved in such denials. Various policies for making these decisions are currently under consideration by the states [5, 18]; we focus here on the computational aspects of executing some of the proposed policies by the ISO. A more detailed discussion of the underlying issues and proposed policies can be found in [3].

Formal Problem Definitions. The variants of flow problems related to power transmission studied here are intuitively harder than some traditional multi-commodity flow problems, since although the flow out of and into resp. a given source-sink pair must be equal, we *cannot distinguish between* the flow "commodities" (power produced by different generators). See below and Section 2 for more on this. As a result, standard solution techniques used to solve single/multi-commodity flow problems are not directly applicable to the problems considered here. We will use a new rounding technique that gives good approximation bounds. We shall use power terminology throughout, but all results will hold for the message/voice-data routing domains discussed above. In particular, it is easy to modify our algorithms for such multi-commodity cases where the flows for the different commodities are *distinguishable.*

The basic setup is as follows. We are given a directed network $G = (V, E)$ with a capacity $c_f \geq 0$ for each edge f, and a (multi-)set $\{(s_1, t_1), \ldots, (s_k, t_k)\}$ of pairs of vertices. Each pair (s_i, t_i) has: (i) a *demand* reflecting the amount of power that s_i agrees to supply to t_i and (ii) a negotiated *cost* C_i of sending unit flow from s_i to t_i. We refer to the above as *a set of contracts*, defined by $R \subseteq (V \times V \times \Re \times \Re)$ so that $A = (v, w, \alpha, \beta) \in R$ denotes a contract between source v and sink w for α units of flow at a cost of β per unit flow. We denote $source(A) = v$, $sink(A) = w$, $flow(A) = \alpha$ and $cost(A) = \beta$. To handle the fact that flows for different pairs are indistinguishable, we model the problem as follows. Define two new vertices s and t; also $\forall A \in R$, define new vertices v_A and w_A. Let $S = \{v_A \mid A \in R\}$ and $T = \{w_A \mid A \in R\}$. Construct a digraph $H = (V \cup S \cup T \cup \{s, t\}, E')$ with source s, sink node t, capacities $u : E' \rightarrow \Re$ and costs $c' : E' \rightarrow \Re$ as follows. Each arc (x, y) from G is present in H with the same capacity as in G, and with cost 0. In addition, $\forall A = (v, w, \alpha, \beta) \in R$, we introduce: (i) arcs (v_A, v) and (w, w_A) with infinite capacity and 0 cost; (ii) arc (s, v_A) with capacity $flow(A)$ and cost 0; and (iii) arc (w_A, t) with capacity $flow(A)$ and cost equaling $cost(A)$.

A generic *flow* $f = (f_{x,y} \geq 0 : (x, y) \in E')$ in H is any non-negative flow that: (a) respects the arc capacities, (b) has s as the only source of flow and t as the only sink, and (c) satisfies, $\forall A \in R$, $f_{s,v_A} = f_{w_A,t}$ (we refer to this value as $f(A)$). Thus, $f(A) \in [0, flow(A)]$ follows, and this is the (unconstrained) *R-Version* of the problem. For some versions of our problems, additional constraints are imposed, including: (i) the *0/1-Version* in which $\forall A \in R$, $f(A) \in \{0, flow(A)\}$, (ii) the *I-Version* wherein $\forall A \in R$, $f(A) \in \{0, 1, 2, \ldots, flow(A)\}$. (The *I-version* is appropriate in the above-seen message/voice-data routing domains where data is split into atomic packets. Here, since we can also distinguish between the different commodities, the *I-version* can also require that the flow of any commodity on any arc be an integer.)

For many problems here, the complexity depends on the type of contract satisfaction used; we now define a few relevant ones. First, R-MAX-FLOW is the problem of deciding if R is feasible; this and its minimum cost versions can be solved in polynomial time. However, R usually does not form a feasible set; thus we are led to defining variants that deal with infeasible solutions. For instance, 0/1-MAX-FLOW and I-MAX-FLOW respectively ask for the maximum feasible amount of flow routable in the *0/1*- and *I*-versions. We denote the problems of decreasing the flow values by a minimum amount to make the residual flows feasible by (R-VERSION, MIN-#CONTRACTS), (I-VERSION, MIN-#CONTRACTS), and (0/1-VERSION, MIN-#CONTRACTS). We also let (0/1-VERSION, MAX-#CONTRACTS) denote the *0/1*-version where we seek to maximize the number of fulfilled contracts. A natural special case for these is where all the sources s_i are the same; we call this the single-source version of each of our problems.

Results Obtained and Related Work. For the first time in the literature, we study the complexity and approximability of several contract satisfaction problems. Where possible, we state the hardness results for the most restricted versions and approximation results for the most general versions of the problems. Given the flow network $G = (V, E)$, we let $n = |V|$ and $m = |E|$.

Our first main result is for the *single source* version of (0/1-VERSION, MAX-#CONTRACTS). We show that unless $NP = ZPP$, no polynomial-time algorithm can guarantee an approximation factor of $m^{\frac{1}{2}-\epsilon}$ for *any* fixed $\epsilon > 0$, even if all capacities are 1 and all demands integral. As mentioned before, this is in sharp contrast with the corresponding *single-source* versions of the MDP (polynomial-time solvable) and the UFP (NP-hard, but approximable to within $O(1)$ [10, 11]). We also show that for the *bounded-demands* version of this problem, there is a constant $\epsilon > 0$ such that we cannot approximate the problem to within $(1 + \epsilon)$ unless *P=NP*.

On the positive side, we consider the general weighted version of (0/1-VERSION, MAX-#CONTRACTS), where, given a profit w_A for each $A \in R$, we want a 0/1 solution that maximizes the profit of fulfilled contracts (this also generalizes 0/1-MAX-FLOW). We assume by scaling that $w_A \in [0, 1]$ for all $A \in R$, and show a nearly best-possible bicriteria approximation. Let OPT be the optimum value of this problem. Given $\epsilon > 0$ and a flow f, let us say that the flow $(1 - \epsilon)$-fulfills contract $A \in R$ iff $f(A) \geq (1 - \epsilon) \cdot flow(A)$. Then, in polynomial time, we can find a flow in which the total profit of the $(1-\epsilon)$-fulfilled contracts is at least: (i) $\Omega(\epsilon OPT^2/m)$ if $\epsilon \leq 1/2$, and (ii) $\Omega(OPT \cdot (OPT/m)^{(1-\epsilon)/\epsilon})$ if $\epsilon > 1/2$. (Note that if ϵ is "small", say 0.1, then we almost satisfy the demands of the $(1-\epsilon)$-fulfilled contracts, while still remaining close to the $m^{1/2-\epsilon'}$-hardness-of-approximation result. If ϵ is larger, i.e., if we are willing to satisfy a smaller fraction of the demands, the objective function gets even better: in particular, if $\epsilon = 1 - \Theta(1/\log n)$, we get to within a constant factor of OPT. This suggests that when possible, we can choose such a relatively large ϵ and conduct the routing in *rounds*, where the routing is feasible in each round. Even if ϵ is $1 - \Theta(1/\log n)$, we require only $O(\log^2 n)$ rounds to fully satisfy the demands of the $(1 - \epsilon)$-fulfilled contracts.)

This follows from a more general multi-source, multi-sink result that we derive. As sketched in Section 2, multi-source, multi-sink problems are somewhat complicated by the fact that we cannot distinguish between the flows for different pairs (e.g., there may be no (s_i, t_i)-path in the flow graph); we show how this issue can be handled, and derive the single-source result as a corollary. For the multi-source, multi-sink *I-version* of the problem where we wish to maximize the total weighted flow, we build on the previous algorithm to deliver a solution of value $\Omega(OPT^2/m)$. The approach of these algorithms is to conduct randomized rounding of a multi-commodity flow relaxation as in [16], with two main new ideas. First, it is well-known that adding valid constraints to relaxations is often crucial for optimization/approximation. Our solutions depend on a key valid constraint (see (2)) added to the "natural" LP relaxation. Next, our bounds above for the case $\epsilon \leq 1/2$ depend on an existentially optimal tail bound that we derive; in its absence, our analysis would have only yielded the bound we get for $\epsilon > 1/2$ for the case $\epsilon \leq 1/2$ (note the major difference between the two as $\epsilon \to 0+$). This tail bound also improves the approximation for a class of packing integer programs due to [15]; see Theorem 6. Further hardness results for various versions of our basic problems are mentioned at the end of Section 4.

To our knowledge, problems studied here have not been studied by previous researchers working in the area of power generation, operation and transimssion. Work done in electrical engineering has concentrated on addressing more traditional problems such as *unit commitment* and *economic dispatch* (see [2,3,13,14, 21] and the references therein). For want of space, the sequel presents illustrative examples and selected proof sketches; see [3] for a more detailed version.

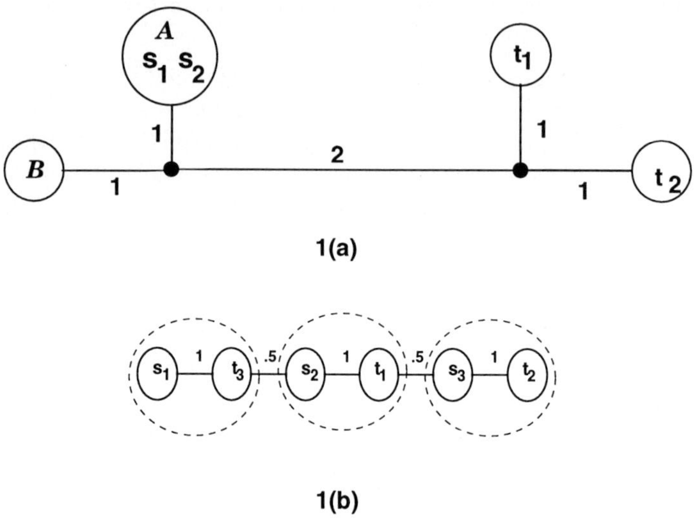

Fig. 1. Figures for Examples 1 and 2.

2 Illustrative Examples: Structure of Solutions

We now derive some insights into the structure of solutions to the problems at hand. The examples will illustrate contrasts between this problem and related flow problems from the literature.

Example 1. This example illustrates the issues encountered as a result of deregulation. Figure 1(a) shows an example in which there are two power plants A and B. Let us say that each consumer has a demand of 1. Before deregulation, say both A and B are owned by the same company. If we assume that the plants have identical operating and production costs, then the demands can be satisfied by producing 1 unit of power at each plant. Now assume that due to deregulation, A and B are owned by separate companies. Further assume that A provides power at a much cheaper rate and thus both the consumers sign contracts with A. It is clear that both the consumers cannot now be provided power by A alone.

Thus although the total production capacity available is more than total demand and it is possible to route that demand through the network under centralized control, it is not possible to route these demands in a deregulated scenario.

Example 2. Here, the graph consists of a simple line as shown in Figure 1(b). We have three contracts each with a demand of 1. The capacity of each edge is also 1. A feasible solution is $f(s_1, t_3) = f(s_2, t_1) = f(s_3, t_2) = 1$. The crucial point here is that *the flow originating at s_i may not go to t_i at all* — since power produced at the sources are indistinguishable, the flow from s_i joins a stream of other flows. If we look at the connected components induced by the edges with positive flow, we may have s_i and t_i in a different component. Thus we do not have a path or set of paths to round for the (s_i, t_i)-flow. This shows a basic difference between our problem and standard multi-commodity flow problems, and indicates that traditional rounding methods *may not be directly applicable.*

3 The hardness of (0/1-Version, Max-#Contracts)

Theorem 1. *Unless NP = ZPP, no polynomial-time algorithm can guarantee an approximation of $m^{\frac{1}{2}-\epsilon}$ for (0/1-Version, Max-#Contracts), for any fixed $\epsilon > 0$. This holds even when all edges have capacity 1, there is only one supplier node, and all contracts are integer-valued.*

Proof. We provide an approximation-preserving reduction from Independent Set (IS) to the problem. If n and m are the number of nodes and edges in the IS instance, the number of arcs in the problem will be $O(n+m)$. Now, IS is hard to approximate to within $n^{1-\epsilon}$ (and hence also hard to approximate to within $m^{1/2-\epsilon}$) [8]; hence the theorem will follow.

Let $H = (V, E)$ be the instance of IS. Create a graph $G' = (U \cup W, E')$ as follows. The set W will be a copy of V. We will abuse notation and refer to the copy of v in W as v. For every edge $e = \{u, v\} \in E$, create a node $x_e \in U$ and edges $\{x_e, u\}$ and $\{x_e, v\}$ in E'. Also create one "supply node" $s \in U$ and edges $\{\{s, x_e\} \mid e \in E\}$. All edges in G' have capacity 1. Each node in W has a contract with s with flow value equal to its degree in H (which is also its degree in G'). To satisfy the contract of any $w \in W$, there must be 1 unit of flow to w from each node in U adjacent to w. Since only 1 unit of flow can be sent to any node in $U \setminus \{s\}$, no other node in W adjacent to w in G can have its contract satisfied if w's contract is satisfied. So there is a bijection between feasible sets of contracts in G' and independent sets of the same size in H.

Next, a hardness result for the bounded-demands case (proof omitted):

Theorem 2. *The following hold for the bounded-demands version of (0/1-Version, Max-#Contracts), even when all edges have capacity 1, there is only one supplier, all vertices except the supplier have bounded degree, and all contracts have the same integer value. (a) The problem is NP-hard. (b) Unless P=NP, $\exists\epsilon > 0$ such that no polynomial-time algorithm can guarantee an approximation factor of less than $(1+\epsilon)$, where n is the number of nodes in G.*

4 Approximation algorithms

We now present algorithms for a general multi-source, multi-sink problem, and derive an algorithm for SINGLE SOURCE-(0/1-VERSION, MAX-#CONTRACTS) as a corollary. As seen above, flow indistinguishability needs some care in handling. By a *non-negative flow* f in a digraph $G = (V, E)$, our present context will simply mean a set of flow values $\{f_{u,v} \geq 0 : (u,v) \in E\}$; these values need not satisfy any conservation constraints etc., unless otherwise specified. Given f, the *net outflow* from $v \in V$, $f_{out}(v)$, is defined naturally to be $(\sum_{u:\ (v,u)\in E} f_{v,u}) - (\sum_{u:\ (u,v)\in E} f_{u,v})$. Similarly, the net inflow into v is $f_{in}(v) = -f_{out}(v)$. For any non-negative integer k, let $[k] \doteq \{1, 2, \ldots, k\}$.

We first define the exact multi-source, multi-sink problem we consider. We are given a digraph $G = (V, E)$ and *disjoint* subsets S (for "suppliers") and C (for "customers") of V. (If G is undirected, replace each edge $\{u, v\}$ by the arcs (u, v) and (v, u).) Each edge $(u, v) \in E$ has a *capacity* $c_{u,v} > 0$; each $s \in S$ has a *cost* $p(s) > 0$, and each $t \in C$ has a *demand* $d_t > 0$ and a *weight* $w_t > 0$. We are also given a *budget* B. We will assume that $|V| = n$ and $|E| = m$ throughout.

Informal problem description. Each $s \in S$ is a supplier who charges $p(s)$ per unit outflow from s; the weight w_t for $t \in C$ reflects the "importance" of customer t. We wish to construct a non-negative flow f in G and to choose an $A \subseteq C$, such that: (i) if $v \notin S$, then $f_{out}(v) \leq 0$ (i.e., no vertex outside of S can send out net positive flow) and if $v \notin C$, then $f_{in}(v) \leq 0$; (ii) for all $t \in A$, there is a net inflow of at least d_t (or, in a slightly relaxed setting, at least $d_t(1 - \epsilon)$ for some given $\epsilon > 0$), and (iii) no edge carries a flow more than its capacity.

We next discuss payment policy. Given f, note that $f_{out}(s)$ for any $s \in S$ can be viewed as the amount of flow contributed by s. Suppose s charges $p(s)$ per unit net outflow. Then, we can see that $\sum_{s\in S} f_{out}(s) = \sum_{t\in C} f_{in}(t)$, which equals some F, say. Thus, supplier s provides a fraction $f_{out}(s)/F$ of the total flow. Hence, each $t \in C$ can pay $f_{in}(t) \cdot p(s) \cdot f_{out}(s)/F$ to each supplier s. This way, each customer t pays an appropriate fraction to each supplier (i.e., divides up his payment in an appropriate way among the suppliers), and each supplier gets her rightful total amount of $(\sum_{t\in C} f_{in}(t) \cdot p(s) \cdot f_{out}(s)/F) = p(s)f_{out}(s)$. Thus, the total amount paid is $\sum_{s\in S} p(s)f_{out}(s)$, and our next constraint is that this should not exceed the budget B: (iv) $\sum_{s\in S} p(s)f_{out}(s) \leq B$. Finally, the objective is to maximize $\sum_{t\in A} w_t$ (the weighted sum of satisfied customers).

Formally, the problem $\mathcal{P}$ is to construct a non-negative flow f in G and to choose an $A \subseteq C$, such that: (A1) $\forall v \notin S$, $f_{out}(v) \leq 0$ and $\forall v \notin C$, $f_{in}(v) \leq 0$; (A2) $\forall t \in A$, $f_{in}(t) \geq d_t$; (A3) $\forall (u, v) \in E$, $f_{u,v} \leq c_{u,v}$, and (A4) $\sum_{s\in S} p(s)f_{out}(s) \leq B$. Subject to these constraints, we wish to maximize $\sum_{t\in A} w_t$. We shall mainly focus on the "ϵ-relaxed" variant of $\mathcal{P}$ wherein condition (A2) is weakened to "(A2'): $\forall t \in A,\ f_{in}(t) \geq d_t(1 - \epsilon)$". Setting $B = \infty$ in the ϵ-relaxed version of $\mathcal{P}$ yields the ϵ-relaxed version of a common generalization of (0/1-VERSION, MAX-#CONTRACTS) and 0/1-MAX-FLOW where, given a profit w_A for each $A \in R$, we want a 0/1 solution that maximizes the profit of fulfilled contracts. We now work toward an approximation algorithm for the ϵ-relaxed version of $\mathcal{P}$ given by Theorem 4.

A good LP relaxation for $\mathcal{P}$ (or its ϵ-relaxation) may not be immediate because of flow-indistinguishability; a little care helps. Suppose we have a non-negative flow f in a digraph $G = (V, E)$, such that for some given $h(\cdot)$,

$$\forall (u,v) \in E,\ f_{u,v} \leq c_{u,v},\ \text{and}\ \forall v \in V,\ f_{out}(v) = h(v). \quad (1)$$

Via appropriate "flow decomposition" ideas (see [1]; details omitted here), f can be efficiently transformed into a set of "path flows" that still essentially satisfy (1) in the following sense. We can efficiently construct a set of flow-paths $\{P_i : 1 \leq i \leq \ell\}$, where P_i is from some u_i to some v_i and has some flow value $a_i > 0$. Also, $\ell \leq m$ and we also have

(B1) $\forall v \in V$: (i) If $h(v) > 0$, then $v \neq v_i$ for any $i \in [\ell]$; also, $\sum_{i:v=u_i} a_i = h(v)$; (ii) if $h(v) < 0$, then $v \neq u_i$ for any $i \in [\ell]$; also, $\sum_{i:v=v_i} a_i = -h(v)$; (iii) if $h(v) = 0$, then $v \neq u_i$ and $v \neq v_i$ for any $i \in [\ell]$.

(B2) $\forall (u,v) \in E$, $\sum_{i:(u,v)\in P_i} a_i \leq c_{u,v}$.

4.1 An LP relaxation and its rounding

Consider the following LP related to our main problem. Let $C = \{t_1, t_2, \ldots, t_k\}$. The LP is to define k real variables $x_1, \ldots, x_k$ each lying in $[0, 1]$, and to construct k non-negative flows $f^{(1)}, f^{(2)}, \ldots f^{(k)}$ on G such that:

(C1) in each flow $f^{(i)}$, flow-conservation is satisfied at all nodes in $V - (S \cup \{t_i\})$, t_i is the only node allowed to have a positive in-flow, and $f^{(i)}_{in}(t_i) \geq d_i x_i$;

(C2) the total flow on any edge (u, v) is at most $c_{u,v}$, i.e., $\sum_{i\in[k]} f^{(i)}_{u,v} \leq c_{u,v}$;

(C3) $(\sum_{s\in S} p(s)(\sum_{i\in[k]} f^{(i)}_{out}(s))) \leq B$, and, crucially,

(C4)
$$\forall (u,v) \in E\ \forall i \in [k],\ f^{(i)}_{u,v} \leq c_{u,v} x_i. \quad (2)$$

Subject to these constraints, the objective is to maximize $\sum_{i\in[k]} w_i x_i$.

It is easy to check that the above can be written as an LP, and we now show that any optimal integral solution to our problem leads to a feasible solution to this LP. Given any optimal integral solution, define $x_i = 1$ if $i \in A$, and 0 otherwise. Do a flow-decomposition, and note from (B1) that only vertices in S can be the sources in the resulting flow paths, and that only vertices in A will be sinks. Now interpret the set of all the flow-paths that end in any given $t_i \in A$ as the flow $f^{(i)}$ for our LP. From (B2), we also see that the total flow on any edge (u, v) is at most $c_{u,v}$; the budget constraint of our LP (constraint (C3)) is also satisfied. Constraint (C4) will be crucial; we now check that (C4) is also satisfied (i.e., that it is a valid constraint). If $i \notin A$ in the given optimal integral solution, then note that no net positive in-flow will be sent to t_i in this integral solution; thus, if $x_i = 0$, then (C4) holds. On the other hand, if the given optimal integral solution sets $i \in A$, then we have $x_i = 1$ and (C4) holds since (C2) does.

Thus, any optimal integral solution leads to a feasible solution to our LP with the same objective function value; hence we indeed have a relaxation. Let OPT and y^* respectively denote the optimal values for our problem and for this LP relaxation; we have as usual that $OPT \le y^*$.

We now show how to round an optimal solution to our LP relaxation, to solve the "ϵ-relaxed" variant of our problem. Start with an optimal solution to the LP, and conduct a flow decomposition. For each $t_i \in C$, we get a set of flow-paths $P_{i,1}, P_{i,2}, \ldots$, each $P_{i,j}$ originating from some $s_{i,j} \in S$ and carrying a flow of value $z_{i,j} \ge 0$; (C1) shows that $\sum_j z_{i,j} = d_i x_i$. Let $\gamma > 1$ be a parameter that will be chosen below. Independently for each i, set a random variable Y_i to 1 with probability x_i/γ, and $Y_i := 0$ with probability $1 - x_i/\gamma$. If $Y_i = 1$, we will choose to satisfy an $(1-\epsilon)$-fraction of t_i's demand; i.e., for all j, we will multiply the flow values $z_{i,j}$ by $(1-\epsilon)/x_i$. If $Y_i = 0$, we will choose to have zero flow sent to t_i: i.e., we will reset all the $z_{i,j}$ to 0. This flow yields our final flow, and we set $A = \{t_i \in C : Y_i = 1\}$. We now analyze this rounding process and also select a suitable $\gamma > 1$ in the process.

4.2 Analysis of the Rounding

We start with an improved tail bound for a certain problem (Theorem 3). Let e denote the base of the natural logarithm. Recall a version of the Chernoff-Hoeffding bound: if X is a sum of independent random variables, each of which takes values in $[0,1]$, then for $\mu = E[X]$ and any $\delta \ge 0$,

$$Pr(X \ge \mu(1+\delta)) \le (e^{\delta}/(1+\delta)^{1+\delta})^{\mu} \le (e/(1+\delta))^{\mu(1+\delta)}. \tag{3}$$

Theorem 3. *Let $X_1, X_2, \ldots, X_\ell$ be* independent *random variables each taking values in $\{0,1\}$, and let $X = \sum_i r_i X_i$, where each r_i lies in $[0,1]$. Suppose $E[X] \le 1/\lambda$ for some $\lambda > 1$. Then, for any $\epsilon \in [0,1]$, $Pr(X > (1+\epsilon)) \le (e^2 + 2 + 2\epsilon^{-1})/\lambda^2$.*

This $O(\epsilon^{-1}\lambda^{-2})$ bound can be shown to be existentially optimal. To appreciate Theorem 3, think of $\lambda > 1$ as "large" and ϵ as a "small" positive constant such as 0.2; we want a tail bound that is $O(1/\lambda^2)$. Direct use of Markov's inequality and of (3) only yields the bounds $O(1/\lambda)$ and $O(\lambda^{-(1+\epsilon)})$ respectively.

We now return to analyze our randomized rounding process. For any edge $(u,v) \in E$, the "bad" event $E_{u,v}$ is that the final total flow $f_{u,v}$ on it is more than $c_{u,v}$. We can see that $f_{u,v} = \sum_{(i,j):(u,v)\in P_{i,j}} (z_{i,j}(1-\epsilon)/x_i) Y_i$; hence,

$$E[f_{u,v}] = \sum_{(i,j):(u,v)\in P_{i,j}} (z_{i,j}(1-\epsilon)/x_i)\cdot(x_i/\gamma) \le c_{u,v}(1-\epsilon)/\gamma, \tag{4}$$

since $\sum_{(i,j):(u,v)\in P_{i,j}} z_{i,j} \le c_{u,v}$ by (C2) and (B2). Since $Pr(f_{u,v} > c_{u,v})$ equals $Pr(\sum_{(i,j):(u,v)\in P_{i,j}} (z_{i,j}/(x_i c_{u,v})) Y_i > (1-\epsilon)^{-1})$, we have

$$Pr(f_{u,v} > c_{u,v}) \le Pr(\sum_{(i,j):(u,v)\in P_{i,j}} \frac{z_{i,j}}{x_i c_{u,v}} Y_i > 1+\epsilon). \tag{5}$$

Crucially, we can deduce from (C4) that for all (i,j) such that $(u,v) \in P_{i,j}$, $z_{i,j} \le x_i c_{u,v}$. Also, (4) shows that $E[\sum_{(i,j):(u,v)\in P_{i,j}} \frac{z_{i,j}}{x_i c_{u,v}} Y_i] \le 1/\gamma$. Thus, for any $(u,v) \in E$, Theorem 3 and (5) yield

$$Pr(f_{u,v} > c_{u,v}) \le Pr(\sum_{(i,j):(u,v)\in P_{i,j}} \frac{z_{i,j}}{x_i c_{u,v}} Y_i > 1+\epsilon) \le (e^2 + 2 + 2\epsilon^{-1})/\gamma^2. \quad (6)$$

Next, let TP denote the final payment. Due to the scaling down by γ, it is not hard to verify that $E[TP] \le B/\gamma$; thus, by Markov's inequality,

$$Pr(TP > B) \le 1/\gamma. \quad (7)$$

Now, as in [15], it is easily seen via the FKG inequality [7] that the events "$\{f_{u,v} \le c_{u,v} : (u,v) \in E\}$" and "$TP \le B$" are all "positive correlated". More precisely, we get that $Pr((TP \le B) \wedge (\bigwedge_{(u,v)\in E}(f_{u,v} \le c_{u,v})))$ is at least

$$Pr(TP \le B) \prod_{(u,v)\in E} Pr(f_{u,v} \le c_{u,v}) \ge (1-1/\gamma)\cdot(1-(e^2+2+2\epsilon^{-1})/\gamma^2)^m, \quad (8)$$

by (6) and (7). Next, since the objective function OBJ equals $\sum_{i\in[k]} w_i Y_i$ and has mean y^*/γ, we can see by a Chernoff bound that

$$Pr(OBJ \le y^*/(2\gamma)) \le e^{-y^*/(8\gamma)}. \quad (9)$$

There are now two cases, depending on the value of ϵ.

Case I: $0 < \epsilon \le 1/2$. Setting $\gamma = K_0 m/(\epsilon y^*)$ for a suitably large constant K_0, we have $(1-1/\gamma)\cdot(1-(e^2+2+2\epsilon^{-1})/\gamma^2)^m > e^{-y^*/(8\gamma)}$. Thus, $Pr((OBJ \ge y^*/(2\gamma)) \wedge (TP \le B) \wedge (\bigwedge_{(u,v)\in E}(f_{u,v} \le c_{u,v})))$, which is at least as big as

$$Pr((TP \le B) \wedge (\bigwedge_{(u,v)\in E} (f_{u,v} \le c_{u,v}))) - Pr(OBJ \le y^*/(2\gamma)),$$

is positive by (8) and (9); thus, with positive probability, we have satisfied all constraints **and** have the objective function value being $\Omega(y^*/\gamma) = \Omega(\epsilon(y^*)^2/m)$.

Case II: $\epsilon > 1/2$. The analog of (8) here, derived similarly, is that $Pr((TP \le B) \wedge (\bigwedge_{(u,v)\in E}(f_{u,v} \le c_{u,v})))$ is at least $(1-1/\gamma)\cdot(1-O(\gamma^{-(1+\epsilon)}))^m$. We now select $\gamma = K_0'(m/y^*)^{(1-\epsilon)/\epsilon}$; once again, we can now show that with with positive probability, we have satisfied all constraints and have objective function value $\Omega(y^*/\gamma)$. Finally, as in [15], this analysis can be turned into a deterministic polynomial-time algorithm. Thus we get

Theorem 4. *For the ϵ-relaxed version of problem $\mathcal{P}$, we can output, in polynomial time, a solution of value* $\Omega(\max\{\epsilon OPT^2/m,\ OPT\cdot(OPT/m)^{(1-\epsilon)/\epsilon}\})$.

In particular, we get a bicriteria result for the multi-source problem that is not far from the hardness threshold for the single-source case.

With some further steps in the algorithm, the above analysis also leads to

Theorem 5. *For the multi-source, multi-sink* I-version *where we wish to maximize the total weighted flow, we can deliver a solution of value $\Omega(OPT^2/m)$ in polynomial time.*

The proof is omitted. Another application of Theorem 3 is to improving certain approximation bounds shown in [15] for a family of packing integer programs (PIPs). Given $A \in [0,1]^{m \times n}$, $b \in [1, \infty)^m$ and $c \in [0,1]^n$ with $\max_j c_j = 1$, a PIP seeks to maximize $c^T \cdot x$ subject to $x \in Z_+^n$ and $Ax \leq b$. We also define $B = \min_i b_i$; we can take $B \geq 1$ without loss of generality [15]. PIPs model various NP-hard problems. A natural LP relaxation for a PIP is to relax "$x \in Z_+^n$" to "$x \in \Re_+^n$". The current-best approximation bound for general PIPs, due to [15], is as follows: in deterministic polynomial-time, we can output a solution of value $\Omega(y^* \cdot (y^*/m)^{1/(B-1)})$. We improve this to

Theorem 6. *Given a general packing integer program, we can in polynomial time output a solution of value* $\Omega(\max\{(B-1)(y^*)^2/(mB),\ y^* \cdot (y^*/m)^{1/(B-1)}\})$.

Note the significant improvement for the range $B \in (1, 2]$.

We can also show the following (proofs omitted). The problem (0/1-Version, Max-Feasible Flow) is *NP*-hard even for graphs with a single edge; (0/1-Version, Max-#Contracts) is polynomial-time solvable on graphs with a single edge. But (0/1-Version, Max-#Contracts) is *NP*-hard when each contract has a positive integral profit associated with it and the goal is to maximize the total profit. We can also show that (R-Version, Max-Feasible Flow) and (R-Version, Max-#Contracts) subject to step-wise linear production costs and a budget on the total costs are *NP*-hard. Also, (0/1-Version, Max-Feasible Flow) with capacity constraints on production units, and (R-Version, Max-Feasible Flow) with capacity constraints on production units and step-wise linear cost functions, are strongly *NP*-hard.

Acknowledgments: We thank Dr. Martin Wildberger (EPRI) for introducing us to the problems considered here. Much of this work would not have been possible without his support. We thank Dean Risenger (Los Alamos National Laboratory) for helping us with the experimental evaluation of the heuristics. We also thank Terence Kelly (University of Michigan), R. Ravi (CMU) and Riko Jacob (Los Alamos National Labs) for fruitful discussions.

References

1. R. K. Ahuja, T. L. Magnanti, and J. B. Orlin. *Network flows: theory, algorithms, and applications.* Prentice Hall, Englewood Cliffs, New Jersey, 1993.
2. D. Bertsekas, G. Lauer, N. Sandell and T.A. Posberg. Solution of large scale optimal unit commitment problems. *Transactions on Power Apparatus and Systems,* PAS 101(1), 1982.
3. D. Cook, V. Faber, M. Marathe, A. Srinivasan and Y. J. Sussmann. Combinatorial Problems in Production and Transmission of Electric Power: Theory and Experimental Results. Technical Report LAUR-97-2321, Los Alamos National Laboratory, Los Alamos, NM, 87545.

4. *The Economist*, Asian edition. From circuits to packets, in *Survey on Telecommunications*, pages 25–27, September 13th–19th, 1997.
5. EPRI-Workshop: Underlying Technical Issues in Electricity Deregulation, Technical report forthcoming, Electric Power Research Institute (EPRI), April 25-27, 1997.
6. The U. S. Federal Energy Regulatory Commission, Notice of Proposed Rulemaking ("NOPRA") (Docket No. RM95-8-000, March 29, 1995).
7. C. M. Fortuin, J. Ginibre, and P. N. Kasteleyn. Correlational inequalities for partially ordered sets. *Communications of Mathematical Physics*, 22:89–103, 1971.
8. J. Håstad. Testing of the long code and hardness for clique. In *Proc. ACM Symposium on the Theory of Computing*, pages 11–19, 1996.
9. J. Kleinberg. Approximation algorithms for disjoint paths problems. *PhD Thesis*, Department of EECS, MIT, 1996.
10. J. Kleinberg. Single-source unsplittable flow. In *Proc. IEEE Symposium on Foundations of Computer Science*, pages 68–77, 1996.
11. S. G. Kolliopoulos and C. Stein. Improved approximation algorithms for unsplittable flow problems. In *Proc. IEEE Symposium on Foundations of Computer Science*, 1997.
12. G. Lawton, In Search of Real-Time Internet Services. In *IEEE Computer*, pages 14–16, November 1997.
13. J. Muckstadt and S. Koenig. An application of Lagrangean relaxation to scheduling in power generation systems. *Operations Research*, 25(3):387–403, 1977.
14. C. Pang and H. Chen. Optimal short-term unit commitment. *Transactions on Power Apparatus and System*, 1976.
15. A. Srinivasan. Improved approximations of packing and covering problems. In *Proc. ACM Symposium on the Theory of Computing*, pages 268–276, 1995.
16. A. Srinivasan. Improved approximations for edge disjoint paths, unsplittable flow, and related routing problems. In *Proc. IEEE Foundations on Computer Science*, pages 416–425, 1997.
17. A.M. Wildberger. Issues associated with real time pricing. Unpublished Technical report, Electric Power Research Institute (EPRI), 1997.
18. A. M. Wildberger. Brief Overview of power systems operations, & Planning from the point of view of Mathematical Modeling, Simulation and Computation with Selected References to Books, EPRI Reports, Available Software & Web Sites. Unpublished Manuscript, Electric Power Research Institute (EPRI), 1997.
19. A.M. Wildberger. Autonomous adaptive agents for the distributed control of the power grid in a competitive electric power industry. Keynote Address, *IEEE Symposium on Knowledge Engineering and Systems, KES'97*, Adelaide, Australia, 1997.
20. Websites: http://www.magicnet.net/~metzler/page2d.html and http://www.enron.com/choice/dereg.fset.html (also see references therein).
21. A.J. Wood and B.F. Wollenberg. *Power Generation, Operation and Control.* John Wiley and Sons, 1996.

Constraint Automata and the Complexity of Recursive Subtype Entailment

Fritz Henglein and Jakob Rehof

DIKU, Department of Computer Science
Universitetsparken 1, DK-2100 Copenhagen Ø, Denmark
Electronic mail: {henglein,rehof}@diku.dk
Fax: +45 35321401

Abstract. We study entailment of structural and nonstructural recursive subtyping constraints. Constraints are formal inequalities between type expressions, interpreted over an ordered set of possibly infinite labeled trees. The nonstructural ordering on trees is the one introduced by Amadio and Cardelli for subtyping with recursive types. The structural ordering compares only trees with common shape. A constraint set *entails* an inequality if every assignment of meanings (trees) to type expressions that satisfies all the constraints also satisfies the inequality. In this paper we prove that nonstructural subtype entailment is PSPACE-hard, both for finite trees (simple types) and infinite trees (recursive types). For the structural ordering we prove that subtype entailment over infinite trees is PSPACE-complete, when the order on trees is generated from a lattice of type constants.
Since structural subtype entailment over finite trees has been shown to be coNP-complete these are the first complexity-theoretic separation results that show that, informally, nonstructural subtype entailment is harder than structural entailment, and recursive entailment is harder than nonrecursive entailment.

1 Introduction

1.1 Constraint entailment

Notions of *entailment* for subtype inequality constraints and set inclusion constraints are currently receiving much attention. Recent work in subtyping systems and in set constraints using notions of constraint entailment in the sense of the present paper includes [1, 5, 15, 22, 6, 2, 8, 13]. In subtyping systems, a program is typed under a set of *suptyping constraints* consisting of inequalities of the form $\tau \leq \tau'$, where τ and τ' are type expressions; the constraints express hypotheses about subtype relations which must hold between the types for the program to be well-typed. If C is a constraint set and ϕ is an inequality (such as a subtype inequality or a set inclusion), we say that C *entails* ϕ, written $C \models \phi$, if every assignment of meanings to expressions that satisfies all the constraints in C also satisfies ϕ; an inequality is satisfied under the assignment, if it is true in the intended model. The intended model for subtyping constraints consists of ordered labeled trees.

Constraint entailment and algorithms for deciding entailment have many important applications. Until now, perhaps the most important practical rôle of entailment has been to support, justify and reason about *constraint simplification*. Simplification removes redundant information, thereby making constraint sets more compact, more readable and algorithmically more manageable. If simplification is automated, then the simplification algorithm typically has to decide entailment problems in order to justify (or reject) a potential simplification step. It is therefore interesting to develop entailment algorithms and to know the computational complexity of deciding entailment. Works using entailment based simplification of set constraints include [1, 6, 2, 8]. In subtyping systems, quite similar problems are currently attacked using entailment for subtyping constraints; recent work includes [15, 22, 13], see also [17] for further references to previous work in subtype simplification.

1.2 Contribution and related work

The main objective of this paper is to understand the computational complexity of deciding the *entailment problem* for recursively constrained subtyping, both in the structural and the nonstructural version:

- Given a set of subtyping constraints C and type variables α, β, does $C \models \alpha \leq \beta$ hold in the set of ordered trees?

Here, C is a set of subtype inequalities between simple type expressions, where recursive type equations such as $\alpha = \alpha \to \beta$ have a solution.

The problem of finding a complete algorithm to decide recursive subtype entailment over nonstructurally ordered trees [3] remains open. However, no nontrivial lower bounds on the problem have been given up until now. Structural subtyping was introduced by Mitchell [14] and has been used in many subsequent subtyping systems, both with finite and recursive types. We study structural subtyping over a *lattice* of base types (*i.e.*, type constants such as, *e.g.*, `int`, `real`), because it is known [20] that even the satisfiability problem is PSPACE-hard for many nonlattices, but in PTIME for large classes of partial order, including lattices of base types, which are of practical interest. This makes subtyping over lattices of base types particularly interesting both from a practical and a complexity-theoretic (specifically, lower bound) point of view. Our results are summarized in the table:

	structural	nonstructural
finite types	$\frac{\text{coNP}}{\text{coNP}}$	$\frac{\text{PSPACE}}{?}$
infinite types	$\frac{\text{PSPACE}}{\text{PSPACE}}$	$\frac{\text{PSPACE}}{?}$

Here a complexity class above a line indicates a lower bound ("hard for ...") and above a line an upper bound ("contained in ..."). All the PSPACE–results are shown in this paper; the coNP-results have been reported before [10]. The results show that, unless NP = PSPACE, adding either recursive types or nonstructural subtyping to a basic setting with structural subtyping over finite types makes entailment strictly harder to solve. Note that our PSPACE-completeness result settles the complexity of entailment for structural subtyping over lattices of base types, for both finite and infinite types. Interestingly, nonstructural subtyping, adding just $\bot$ and $\top$, already makes entailment PSPACE-hard, even for finite types.

The study of entailment by Flanagan and Felleisen [8] is related to the present study, although they work in a different model of complete infinite trees labeled with sets of constructors, and their notion of entailment is different from ours. Even though the exact relation between their work and ours remains unclear, we have to some extent been inspired by their methods. Thus, Flanagan [7] proves PSPACE-hardness of their entailment predicate by reduction from the NFA containment problem (see [9].) However, the proof relies on a complicated (and impressive), complete axiomatization of entailment, whereas our proof uses nonsyntactic methods and a different reduction from a special form of the NFA universality problem (their reduction appears not to be directly applicable to our case.) Their axiomatization leads to a complete algorithm for entailment, but since it runs in exponential time and consumes exponential space they do not give a tight classification of complexity.

Due to space limitations, details of some proofs had to be left out. They can be found in [19, 18].

2 Preliminaries

Let Σ be the ranked alphabet of *constructors*, $\Sigma = B \cup \{\times, \rightarrow\}$; here $L = (B, \leq_B)$ is a lattice of *constants* (constructors of arity 0, to be thought of as base types such as, e.g., `int`, `real`) and $\times, \rightarrow$ are binary constructors. The order on L defines the subtype ordering on type constants in the standard way (see, e.g., [14] for a full introduction.) Let $\mathbf{A}$ be the alphabet $\mathbf{A} = \{f, s, d, r\}$, and let $\mathbf{A}^*$ denote the set of finite strings over $\mathbf{A}$; elements of $\mathbf{A}^*$ are called *addresses*. We consider types as *labeled trees* in the style of [12] to which the reader is referred for full information. A *tree* over Σ is a partial function $t : \mathbf{A}^* \rightarrow \Sigma$ with nonempty, prefix-closed tree domain $\mathcal{D}(t)$. The elements d,r select the domain and range, respectively, of a tree with root labeled $\rightarrow$, and f, s select the first and second component, respectively, of a tree with root labeled $\times$. Base types (constants) in L are ranged over by b, typical elements of $\mathbf{A}$ are ranged over by a, and typical elements of $\mathbf{A}^*$ are ranged over by w. (see, e.g., [12] for more information.) A tree t is *finite* (resp. *infinite*) if and only if $\mathcal{D}(t)$ is a finite (resp. infinite) set. If $w \in \mathcal{D}(t)$ and w is not a proper prefix of any string in $\mathcal{D}(t)$, then w is called a *leaf address* of t (i.e., $t(w) \in L$). If $w \in \mathcal{D}(t)$ and w is not a leaf address, then w is said to be an *interior address* of t. Whenever w is an interior address in t, then $t(w)$ is completely determined by $\mathcal{D}(t)$, e.g., $t(w) = \times$ if and only if $\{wf, ws\} \subseteq \mathcal{D}(t)$.

We let $\mathcal{T}_\Sigma$ denote the set of trees over Σ. For a partial order $\leq$, we let $\leq^0=\leq$ and $\leq^1=\geq$ (the reversed relation.) For $w \in \mathbf{A}^*$, we define the *polarity* of w, denoted πw, to be 0 if w contains an even number of d's and $\pi w = 1$ otherwise. We write $\leq^w$ as a shorthand for $\leq^{\pi w}$. The reversal of order in accordance with polarity captures contravariance of the subtype order with respect to the function space constructor $\rightarrow$ (see [12].) If Σ is equipped with a partial order $\leq_\Sigma$, we induce a partial order on $\mathcal{T}_\Sigma$ by setting

$$t \leq t' \text{ if and only if } \forall w \in \mathcal{D}(t) \cap \mathcal{D}(t').\ t(w) \leq^w_\Sigma t'(w)$$

Let $\mathcal{V}$ be a denumerable set of variables, distinct from elements of Σ. *Terms* or *type expressions* over Σ are *finite* trees in $\mathcal{T}_{\Sigma\cup\mathcal{V}}$, where elements of $\mathcal{V}$ are regarded as constructors of arity 0 (however, only members of Σ of arity 0 are called constants); terms are ranged over by τ. The set of terms is denoted $\mathcal{T}_\Sigma(\mathcal{V})$. A *constraint set* is a finite set of formal inequalities of the form $\tau \leq \tau'$, where τ and τ' are finite terms. We write $\mathsf{Var}(C)$ to denote the set of variables that occur in C. The notation $\leq^w$ may be extended to formal inequalities (denoting reversed formal inequality if $\pi w = 1$.) A constraint set C is said to be *closed* if and only if the following conditions are satisfied:

- (transitivity) $\tau_1 \leq \tau_2 \in C, \tau_2 \leq \tau_3 \in C \Rightarrow \tau_1 \leq \tau_3 \in C$
- (decomposition) $\tau_1 \times \tau_2 \leq \tau_3 \times \tau_4 \in C \Rightarrow \{\tau_1 \leq \tau_3, \tau_2 \leq \tau_4\} \subseteq C$
- (decomposition) $\tau_1 \rightarrow \tau_2 \leq \tau_3 \rightarrow \tau_4 \in C \Rightarrow \{\tau_3 \leq \tau_1, \tau_2 \leq \tau_4\} \subseteq C$

We define the *closure of* C to be the least closed constraint set containing C.

Nonstructural subtyping is obtained by fixing Σ to be the set $\{\times, \rightarrow, \top, \bot\}$ organized as a lattice by the order $\bot \leq \sigma$, $\sigma \leq \top$ for $\sigma \in \Sigma$. See [12] for further details. This organizes $\mathcal{T}_\Sigma$ as a complete lattice under the nonstructural order.

Structural subtyping over a lattice is obtained by extending the lattice $L = (B, \leq_B)$ to the partial order $(B \cup \{\times, \rightarrow\}, \leq_B)$; that is, by adding $\times$ and $\rightarrow$ as new, incomparable elements to L.

Let $\Sigma^\# = \{B, \times, \rightarrow\}$ be a ranked alphabet, where B is nullary and both $\times$ and $\rightarrow$ are binary. We can extend the *signature mapping* $\_^\#$ given by $b^\# = B$ for all $b \in B$, $\times^\# = \times$ and $\rightarrow^\# = \rightarrow$ to a mapping $\_^\#$ from $\mathcal{T}_\Sigma$ to $\mathcal{T}_{\Sigma^\#}$ in the following fashion:

$$t^\#(w) = (t(w))^\#$$

We call $t^\#$ the *shape* of t. This shape mapping can be extended to terms containing variables by adding $t^\#(w) = \alpha$ if $t(w) = \alpha$. The *shape constraints* $C^\#$ are the set of formal equalities (over $\mathcal{T}_{\Sigma^\#}(\mathcal{V})$) obtained from C by mapping every inequality $t_1 \leq t_2 \in C$ to $t_1^\# = t_2^\#$.

One can easily show that, in structural subtyping, we have $t \leq t'$ if and only if $\mathcal{D}(t) = \mathcal{D}(t')$, for every interior address w of t and t', one has $t(w) = t'(w)$, and for every leaf address w of t and t', one has $t(w) \leq^w_B t'(w)$. This implies that the set of structurally ordered trees is a disjoint union of lattices L_s, each lattice L_s consisting of the set of trees having the same shape s. See [20, 21] for more information. In particular, t and t' must have the same shape if $t \leq t'$.

As a standard consequence (which we will be very brief about here, see, e.g., [21, 14, 20] for more details) one has that any constraint set that is satisfiable over structurally ordered trees, must be *weakly unifiable*. This means that $C^{\#}$ is unifiable over $\mathcal{T}_{\Sigma^{\#}}(\mathcal{V})$. Let U_C be a most general unifier of $C^{\#}$. Let $\_^B$ be the mapping from $\mathcal{T}_{\Sigma^{\#}}(\mathcal{V})$ to $\mathcal{T}_{\Sigma^{\#}}$ that maps all variables in a shape tree to B. Each variable α in a satisfiable set C can be assigned a unique *shape* $s_C(\alpha)$ by defining $s_C(\alpha) = (U_C(\alpha))^B$.

Both structural and nonstructural subtyping have finite and infinite variants, according to whether variables range over finite or infinite trees; in the infinite case, we talk about *recursive* subtyping. We call a constraint set C *structural* (resp. *nonstructural*) if its intended interpretation is in structurally (resp. nonstructurally) ordered trees. A *valuation* is a ground substitution, *i.e.*, a map $v : \mathcal{V} \to \mathcal{T}_\Sigma$, extended canonically to $\mathcal{T}_\Sigma(\mathcal{V}) \to \mathcal{T}_\Sigma$. A valuation *satisfies* a constraint $\tau \leq \tau'$, written $v \models \tau \leq \tau'$, if $v(\tau) \leq v(\tau')$ is true in the (appropriate, structural or nonstructural) ordered structure $\mathcal{T}_\Sigma$. A constraint set C *entails* a constraint $\tau \leq \tau'$, written $C \models \tau \leq \tau'$, if every valuation satisfying all the constraints in C also satisfies the constraint $\tau \leq \tau'$.

3 Constraint automata

A constraint set can be regarded as a nondeterministic finite automaton: inequalities are viewed as ϵ-transitions and constructed types have transitions on elements of $\mathbf{A}$. For a given constraint set C, we first define a labeled digraph, called the *constraint graph* associated with C and denote it $\mathcal{G}_C = (V, E)$. The vertex set V is the set of subterms occurring in C. The edge relation E in $\mathcal{G}_C$ is a set of edges labeled with elements of $\mathbf{A} \cup \{\epsilon\}$; an edge from τ to τ' labeled with $a \in \mathbf{A} \cup \{\epsilon\}$ is written $\tau \mapsto_a \tau'$, for $\tau, \tau' \in V$. The set E of labeled edges is defined as the least relation $E \subseteq V \times (\mathbf{A} \cup \{\epsilon\}) \times V$ satisfying the following conditions:

- For all $\tau \in V$, $\tau \mapsto_\epsilon \tau$
- If $\tau \leq \tau' \in C$, then $\tau \mapsto_\epsilon \tau'$
- If $\tau = \tau_1 \times \tau_2$ is in V, then $\tau \mapsto_f \tau_1$ and $\tau \mapsto_s \tau_2$
- If $\tau = \tau_1 \to \tau_2$ is in V, then $\tau \mapsto_d \tau_1$ and $\tau \mapsto_r \tau_2$

The relation $\mapsto_\epsilon$ represents (the reflexive closure of) the inequalities in C, by the first two conditions. The next two conditions represent the syntactic structure of terms by the relations $\mapsto_a$, $a \in \mathbf{A}$. The constraint graph $\mathcal{G}_C$ can be directly regarded as a nondeterministic finite automaton (NFA) over the alphabet $\mathbf{A}$, where the labeled edge relation E defines the transition relation δ_N. The *nondeterministic constraint automaton* (NCA for short) associated with a set C and with a specified start state q_0, is denoted $\mathcal{A}_N^C(q_0) = (Q, \mathbf{A}, \delta_N, q_0, Q)$. The state set Q is V; the alphabet Σ is $\mathbf{A}$; every state is an accept state. The iterated transition relation, denoted $\widehat{\delta}_N$, is defined in the standard way (see [11]).

Let C be structural and weakly unifiable. A *C-shaped valuation* is one which maps every variable α in C to a tree of shape $s_C(\alpha)$. One can show (details in

[19], left out in this summary) that a structural set C is satisfiable if and only if it is satisfied by a C-shaped valuation. Moreover, one can show that, if C is satisfiable and $\alpha, \beta \in \mathsf{Var}(C)$ satisfy some easily (polynomial time) recognizable conditions (called *nontriviality conditions* in [19]) in C, then $C \models \alpha \leq \beta$ if and only if it holds for any C*-shaped* valuation v that $v \models \alpha \leq \beta$ whenever $v \models C$; and in case the nontriviality conditions are not satisfied, one can easily (in polynomial time) decide entailment. This amounts to saying that, in order to decide structural subtype entailment — over finite or infinite trees — it is sufficient to consider entailment restricted to C-shaped valuations.

A set C which does not mention the constructor $\rightarrow$ is called *monotone.* Any monotone, nonstructural set has a largest solution, and any monotone structural set has a largest C-shaped solution.

4 Nonstructural subtyping

An NFA (nondeterministic finite automaton) is called *prefix-closed*, if all its states are accept states. Thus, the only way a prefix-closed NFA can fail to accept a word w is by getting into a stuck state on input w. Let CLOSED-UNIV denote the computational problem:

- Given a *prefix-closed* NFA A over a nontrivial alphabet Σ, is it the case that $L(A) = \Sigma^*$?

By a construction due to Vaughan Pratt [16] we can show that CLOSED-UNIV is PSPACE-complete for any nontrivial alphabet, by reduction from the standard universality problem for NFA's [9].

Consider the two letter alphabet $\{f, s\} \subseteq \mathbf{A}$ and let ϵ denote the empty string. We will show that, for any closed NFA A over $\{f, s\}$, we can construct a constraint set C_A such that $L(A) = \{f, s\}^*$ if and only if $C_A \models \alpha_0 \leq \beta$, where α_0 and β are distinct variables used in the construction of C_A. The types in C_A will be built from variables and the pairing constructor only. The resulting construction will be a log-space reduction of CLOSED-UNIV to the entailment problem $C \models \alpha \leq \beta$, thereby proving the latter problem PSPACE-hard. The main idea is to simulate A by the constraint automaton $\mathcal{A}_N^{C_A}$.

We proceed to describe the construction of C_A. Assume we are given the closed NFA $A = (Q, \Sigma^\times, \delta, q_0, Q)$ (state set is Q, alphabet Σ is $\{f, s\}$, transition relation is δ, start-state is q_0, and — since the automaton is prefix-closed — the set of accept states is the entire set of states, Q.) We write $q_i \mapsto^w q_j$ to indicate that there is a w-transition from state q_i to state q_j in A. If $w \in \{f, s\} \cup \{\epsilon\}$, we say that a transition $q_i \mapsto^w q_j$ is *simple.* A is completely determined by its simple transitions, since these just define its transition relation.

Suppose that A has n simple transitions, and assume them to be ordered in some aritrary, fixed sequence. For the k'th simple transition $q_i \mapsto^w q_j$ we define a constraint set C_k; we associate a distinct variable α_i to each state q_i (so, in particular, the variable α_0 corresponds to the start state of A), and we associate a distinct variable δ_k to each k. The construction of C_k is as follows.

If the k'th simple transition in A is $q_i \mapsto^f q_j$, then $C_k = \{\alpha_i \leq \alpha_j \times \delta_k\}$; if the k'th simple transition in A is $q_i \mapsto^s q_j$, then $C_k = \{\alpha_i \leq \delta_k \times \alpha_j\}$; if the k'th simple transition in A is $q_i \mapsto^\epsilon q_j$, then $C_k = \{\alpha_i \leq \alpha_j\}$. Now define C_A to be

$$C_A = (\bigcup_{k=1}^{n} C_k) \cup \{\beta = \beta_1 \times \beta_2, \beta = \beta_1, \beta = \beta_2\}$$

where the notation $t = t'$ abbreviates the two inequalities $t \leq t'$ and $t' \leq t$. Notice that any solution to C_A must map β to the complete, infinite binary tree $t^\infty = \mu\gamma.\gamma \times \gamma$, hence β is just a name for that tree.

Theorem 1. *Nonstructural recursive subtype entailment is PSPACE-hard.*

Proof. By reduction from CLOSED-UNIV. We prove the following property. Let A be a prefix-closed NFA over $\{f, s\}$. Then

$$L(A) = \{f, s\}^* \text{ if and only if } C_A \models \alpha_0 \leq \beta$$

First notice that, by construction of C_A, there is a transition $q_i \mapsto^w q_j$ in A if and only if there is a transition $\alpha_i \mapsto^w \alpha_j$ in the constraint automaton $\mathcal{A}_N^{C_A}$. We first prove the implication

$$L(A) \neq \{f, s\}^* \Rightarrow C_A \not\models \alpha_0 \leq \beta$$

So assume that there exists a word $w \in \{f, s\}^*$ such that $w \notin L(A)$. Since we can assume w.l.o.g. that A has at least one state, and since A is prefix-closed, we have $\epsilon \in L(A)$, so $L(A) \neq \emptyset$. Then there is a prefix w' of w of maximal length such that $w' \in L(A)$; we can assume that w can be written as $w = w'fw''$ (the alternative case $w = w'sw''$ is similar.) Now, *because A is a prefix-closed automaton*, it follows that for *any* state q_k such that $q_0 \mapsto^{w'} q_k$, there can be no state q_l such that $q_k \mapsto^f q_l$; inspection of the construction of C_A then shows that, for any k such that $q_0 \mapsto^{w'} q_k$, the only nonvariable upper bounds in the transitive closure of C_A on α_k are of the form $\alpha_k \leq \delta_m \times \alpha_s$, where δ_m is unbounded in C_A; one can then show that the largest solution v^* to C_A (which is monotone) satisfies either $v^*(\alpha_0)(w') = \top$ or else $v^*(\alpha_0)(w'f) = \top$. In either case, $v^*(\alpha_0) \not\leq \beta$, thereby showing $C_A \not\models \alpha_0 \leq \beta$.

To prove the implication

$$L(A) = \{f, s\}^* \Rightarrow C_A \models \alpha_0 \leq \beta$$

let w be an arbitrary element in $\{f, s\}^*$. Then $w\ell \in L(A)$, $\ell \in \{f, s\}$, assuming the left hand side of the implication. Then there is a transition $q_0 \mapsto^w q_j \mapsto^\ell q_k$ for some q_j, q_k; by construction of C_A, there is a transition $\alpha_0 \mapsto^{wf} \alpha_k$ or $\alpha_0 \mapsto^{ws} \alpha_k$ in $\mathcal{A}_N^{C_A}$. Then, using the special form of C_A (only $\times$ and variables occur there), one can verify that $w \in \mathcal{D}(v^*(\alpha_0))$ with $v^*(\alpha_0)(w) = \times$, where v^* is the largest solution to C_A. It follows that, for any $w \in \{f, s\}^*$, one has $v(\alpha_0)(w) \leq \times$, whenever v is a solution to C_A, thereby showing $C_A \models \alpha_0 \leq \beta$.

4.1 PSPACE-hardness for finite subtyping

Entailment over finite, structural trees ordered over a lattice of type constants was shown to be coNP-complete in [10]. Intuitively, membership in coNP follows from the fact that the nonentailment problem $C \not\models \alpha \leq \beta$ has a succinct certificate in the form of a word $w \in \mathbf{A}^*$ of length at most n (size of constraint set) identifying a common leaf in $v(\alpha)$ and $v(\beta)$ for a possible solution v to C such that $v(\alpha)(w) \not\leq^w v(\beta)(w)$. It turns out that the corresponding problem with non–structural order is PSPACE-hard. The reason is that infinite trees can be approximated in the nonstructurally ordered space of finite trees. In order to prove PSPACE-hardness, we shall need to talk about approximations of infinite trees by finite trees. To this end, recall (from [4, 12]) the definition of the *level-k truncation* of a tree t, denoted $t\lceil_k$; it has domain $\mathcal{D}(t\lceil_k) = \{w \in \mathcal{D}(t) \mid |w| \leq k\}$ and is defined by

$$t\lceil_k(w) = \begin{cases} t(w) & \text{if } |w| < k \\ \bot & \text{if } |w| = k \end{cases}$$

This definition is simplified, since we shall restrict ourselves to the monotonic alphabet without $\rightarrow$. A monotone constraint set C is called *directed* if and only if every inequality in C has either one of the following forms: $\alpha \leq \alpha'$ or $\alpha \leq \alpha_1 \times \alpha_2$. Then it is easy to see that the sets C_A are directed, when the equations defining β are removed. Let $\mathcal{T}_\Sigma^{\mathrm{F}}$ denote the set of finite trees with nonstructural order. If v is a valuation in $\mathcal{T}_\Sigma$, we define for all $k \geq 0$ the valuation $v\lceil_k$ in $\mathcal{T}_\Sigma^{\mathrm{F}}$ by $v\lceil_k(\alpha) = v(\alpha)\lceil_k$.

We can now show that entailment over $\mathcal{T}_\Sigma^{\mathrm{F}}$ is PSPACE-hard. Given an NFA A, we define a constraint set C_A^{F}; it is defined exactly as C_A in Section 4, except that, instead of the equations $\beta = \beta_1 \times \beta_2, \beta = \beta_1, \beta = \beta_2$, we now take the single inequality $\beta \times \beta \leq \beta$.

Theorem 2. *Nonstructural subtype entailment over finite trees is PSPACE-hard.*

Proof. (Sketch) By reduction from CLOSED-UNIV, using the following property. Let C be directed, and let v be a valuation in $\mathcal{T}_\Sigma$ such that $v \models C$. Then one has

$$\forall k \geq 1.\ v\lceil_k \models C$$

in $\mathcal{T}_\Sigma^{\mathrm{F}}$. Using this property, one can show that, if A is a prefix-closed NFA over $\{f, s\}$, then

$$L(A) = \{f, s\}^* \text{ if and only if } C_A^{\mathrm{F}} \models \alpha_0 \leq \beta$$

holds over $\mathcal{T}_\Sigma^{\mathrm{F}}$. If $L(A) = \{f, s\}^*$ and $v \models C_A^{\mathrm{F}}$, then $v(\alpha_0) \leq t^\infty$ must hold in $\mathcal{T}_\Sigma$, as shown in the proof of Theorem 1. But $t^\infty \leq v(\beta)$ must hold, yielding $v(\alpha_0) \leq v(\beta)$ in $\mathcal{T}_\Sigma^{\mathrm{F}}$. If $L(A) \neq \{f, s\}^*$, then $v \models C_A^{\mathrm{F}}$ with $v(\alpha_0) \not\leq v(\beta)$ for some v in $\mathcal{T}_\Sigma$, by the argument in Theorem 1; by passing to $v\lceil_k$ for sufficiently large k (using the property above), one can then show $C_A^{\mathrm{F}} \not\models \alpha_0 \leq \beta$ in $\mathcal{T}_\Sigma^{\mathrm{F}}$. More details can be found in [19, 18].

The problem of giving an upper bound on nonstructural entailment remains open. In Section 5.2 we will show that structural recursive subtype entailment is in PSPACE. We believe that an elaboration of the ideas in the PSPACE–algorithm sketched there can be used to give a PSPACE decision procedure for nonstructural entailment also.

Conjecture 1. The problem of subtype entailment over nonstructural trees is PSPACE–complete, both in the finite and in the general case

5 Structural Recursive Subtyping

5.1 PSPACE-hardness

The reduction used to prove PSPACE-hardness for nonstructural recursive subtyping in Section 4 does not transfer directly to the structural case. To see the difference, let A be the NFA with all states accepting, start state q_0 and transitions $q_0 \mapsto^s q_1$, $q_1 \mapsto^f q_1$, $q_0 \mapsto^s q_2$, $q_2 \mapsto^s q_2$, $q_0 \mapsto^f q_3$, $q_3 \mapsto^f q_3$, $q_0 \mapsto^s q_4$, $q_4 \mapsto^s q_4$, and consider the constraint set C_A as defined in Section 4. A accepts (in addition to the empty string) just the strings over $\{f, s\}$ of either one of the forms ff^n, fs^n, ss^n, sf^n, $n \geq 0$. Thus, we certainly have $L(A) \neq \{f, s\}^*$. However, by unifying C_A (taking inequalities as equations under unification) the reader can easily verify that, due to the structural shape requirements on α_0 in C_A, any solution to C_A must map α_0 to the complete, infinite binary tree $t^\infty = \mu\gamma.\gamma \times \gamma$. What happens under unification in C_A corresponds to collapsing the states q_1, q_2, q_3, q_4 of A into a single state. This means that, for this particular set C_A, we have $C_A \models \alpha_0 \leq t^\infty$ but not $L(A) = \{f, s\}^*$, and our previous reduction is seen to be incorrect for the structural case. However, the previous reduction can be extended to cover the structural case, as we will now show.

The basic idea is to allow the start state α_0 to have one particluar, fixed shape, which will be compatible with all inequalities generated from A. As can be seen from our example, that shape must presumably be infinite. Define the infinite trees $t^\perp$ and $t^\top$ by

$$t^\perp = \mu\gamma.(\gamma \times \perp) \times (\gamma \times \perp) \text{ and } t^\top = \mu\gamma.(\gamma \times \top) \times (\gamma \times \top)$$

Our reduction, then, will be such that in all cases α_0 will satisfy

$$t^\perp \leq \alpha_0 \leq t^\top \tag{1}$$

The encoding of an automaton A will only depend upon whether or not the leaves in the value of α_0 must be $\perp$, in any solution to C_A. We now give the definition of a constraint set C_A constructible in logspace from a given NFA A. As before, we construct C_A from sets C_k corresponding to each k'th simple transition in A. The C_k are defined as follows. If the k'th simple transition in A is $q_i \mapsto^f q_j$, then $C_k = \{\alpha_i \leq (\alpha_j \times \perp) \times \gamma_k\}$; if the k'th simple transition in A is $q_i \mapsto^s q_j$, then $C_k = \{\alpha_i \leq \gamma_k \times (\alpha_j \times \perp)\}$; if the k'th simple transition in A is $q_i \mapsto^\epsilon q_j$, then $C_k = \{\alpha_i \leq \alpha_j\}$. Here the γ_k are fresh variables. The set C_A

is defined to be the inequality shown in (1) together with the union of all the C_k. In addition to the constraints above, we add the constraint (1) to C_A. The trees $t^\top$ and $t^\perp$ can be defined by regular sets of equations.) One can then show (details in [19, 18]) that, if A is a prefix-closed NFA over $\Sigma = \{f, s\}^*$, then

$$L(A) = \{f, s\}^* \text{ if and only if } C_A \models \alpha_0 \leq t^\perp$$

This leads to

Theorem 3. *Structural recursive subtype entailment is PSPACE-hard.*

5.2 PSPACE upper bound

Our PSPACE upper bound for deciding structural recursive subtype entailment proceeds by exhibiting a nondeterministic decision algorithm for nonentailment (*i.e.*, deciding $C \not\models \alpha \leq \beta$?) that runs in polynomial space. The PSPACE result follows, because PSPACE = NPSPACE = coNPSPACE by Savitch's Theorem. Our algorithm, in turn, is founded on a characterization theorem, which we proceed to present.

In order to state the characterization, we first define a relation R,

$$R \subseteq V \times V \times \{\downarrow, \uparrow\} \times \mathbf{A}^*$$

which intuitively captures properties of the closure of a constraint set. In order to define R we first define, for $a \in \mathbf{A}$, the operation a on $\{\downarrow, \uparrow\}$ by: for $a \neq d$, $a(\uparrow) = \uparrow$ and $a(\downarrow) = \downarrow$, and for $a = d$ we set $a(\uparrow) = \downarrow$ and $a(\downarrow) = \uparrow$. These operations will be used to make sure that contravariance is respected by the algorithm. Intuitively, the relation R holds of $(v, v', \uparrow, w)$ if there is a w-path in $\mathcal{G}_C$ from v to v' where ϵ-edges are followed in reversed direction according to the polarity of w. The relation R is defined by induction on $w \in \mathsf{A}^*$, as follows:

$$\begin{aligned}
&R(v, v', \uparrow, \epsilon) &&\Leftrightarrow v \mapsto_\epsilon v' \\
&R(v, v', \downarrow, \epsilon) &&\Leftrightarrow v' \mapsto v \\
&R(v, v', \uparrow, aw) &&\Leftrightarrow \exists v_1, v_2.\ v \mapsto_\epsilon v_1 \wedge v_1 \mapsto_a v_2 \wedge R(v_2, v', a(\uparrow), w) \\
&R(v, v', \downarrow, aw) &&\Leftrightarrow \exists v_1, v_2.\ v_1 \mapsto_\epsilon v \wedge v_1 \mapsto_a v_2 \wedge R(v_2, v', a(\downarrow), w)
\end{aligned}$$

Let $\uparrow_C^w (v) = \{v' \in V \mid R(v, v', \uparrow, w)\}$ and $\downarrow_C^w (v) = \{v' \in V \mid R(v, v', \downarrow, w)$ and define $\alpha \preceq_C^w \beta$ to hold if and only if there exists a prefix w' of w such that $\uparrow_C^{w'} (\alpha) \cap \downarrow_C^{w'} (\beta) \neq \emptyset$. Let $\bigwedge^w$ be the greatest lower bound operator in L, if $\pi w = 0$, and the lest upper bound operator if $\pi w = 1$; dually, let $\bigvee^w$ denote least upper bound in the first case and greatest lower bound in the second case. We can prove the following theorem which characterizes entailment over C-shaped valuations. The theorem is a (nontrivial) generalization of a similar theorem for atomic constraints over L, proved by the authors in [10]. A proof can be found in [19, 18].

Theorem 4. $C \models \alpha \leq \beta$ *(over C-shaped valuations) if and only if one of the following conditions holds for every address w of maximal length in the common shape of α and β in C:*

1. $\alpha \preceq_C^w \beta$ *or*
2. $\bigwedge^w \uparrow_C^w (\alpha) \leq_B^w \bigvee^w \downarrow_C^w (\beta)$

This theorem yields the central algorithmic idea for our algorithm: Given a weakly unifiable, consistent constraint set C in which α and β occur nontrivially, we guess a path $w \in \mathcal{D}(s_C(\alpha))$ and check that both conditions of Theorem 4 are violated. If so, we accept (which corresponds to reporting "not-entails"), otherwise we reject. More precisely, we iterate the following loop, with w initialized to ϵ:

1. If $\alpha \preceq_C^w \beta$, then reject; otherwise
2. If w is maximal and $\bigwedge^w \uparrow_C^w (\alpha) \leq_B^w \bigvee^w \downarrow_C^w (\beta)$, then reject; otherwise
3. If w is a maximal address then accept; otherwise
4. If w is not maximal, guess $a \in \{f, s, d, r\}$ such that $wa \in \mathcal{D}(s_C(\alpha))$, set $w := wa$ and go to Step 1.

What makes this a (nondeterministic) PSPACE algorithm for deciding nonentailment is that we do not actually need to store w, only $\uparrow_C^w (\alpha), \downarrow_C^w (\alpha), \uparrow_C^w (\beta)$ and $\downarrow_C^w (\beta)$ because both conditions of Theorem 4 require only $\uparrow_C^w (\alpha), \downarrow_C^w (\beta)$ and the $s_C(\alpha)$. Furthermore, $\uparrow_C^{wa} (\alpha), \downarrow_C^{wa} (\alpha), \uparrow_C^{wa} (\beta), \downarrow_C^{wa} (\beta)$ can be computed from a and $\uparrow_C^w (\alpha), \downarrow_C^w (\alpha), \uparrow_C^w (\beta), \downarrow_C^w (\beta)$ in polynomial time and space. Thus the algorithm requires only space for $\uparrow_C^w (\alpha), \downarrow_C^w (\alpha), \uparrow_C^w (\beta), \downarrow_C^w (\beta)$ and $s_C(\alpha)$, which is polynomial in the number of vertices in the constraint graph and thus also in the size of the input. Full details of the algorithm are given in [19, 18].

Theorem 5. *The problem of structural subtype entailment over infinite trees is PSPACE-complete.*

References

1. A. Aiken and E.L. Wimmers. Type inclusion constraints and type inference. In *Proceedings FPCA '93, Conference on Functional Programming Languages and Computer Architecture, Copenhagen, Denmark*, pages 31–42, June 1993.
2. A. Aiken, E.L. Wimmers, and J. Palsberg. Optimal representations of polymorphic types with subtyping. In *Proceedings TACS '97, Theoretical Aspects of Computer Software, Sendai, Japan*, pages 47–77. Springer Lecture Notes in Computer Science, vol. 1281, September 1997.
3. R. Amadio and L. Cardelli. Subtyping recursive types. In *Proc. 18th Annual ACM Symposium on Principles of Programming Languages (POPL), Orlando, Florida*, pages 104–118. ACM Press, January 1991.
4. R. Amadio and L. Cardelli. Subtyping recursive types. *ACM Transactions on Programming Languages and Systems*, 15(4):575–631, September 1993.
5. W. Charatonik and A. Podelski. The independence property of a class of set constraints. In *Conference on Principles and Practice of Constraint Programming*, pages 76–90. Springer-Verlag, 1996. Lecture Notes in Computer Science, Vol. 1118.
6. M. Fahndrich and A. Aiken. Making set-constraint program analyses scale. In *Workshop on Set Constraints, Cambridge MA*, 1996.
7. C. Flanagan. Personal communication, March 1997.

8. C. Flanagan and M. Felleisen. Componential set-based analysis. In *Proceedings of the ACM SIGPLAN '97 Conference on Programming Language Design and Implementation*. ACM, June 1997.
9. M. Garey and D. Johnson. *Computers and Intractability – A Guide to the Theory of NP-Completeness*. Freeman, 1979.
10. F. Henglein and J. Rehof. The complexity of subtype entailment for simple types. In *Proceedings LICS '97, Twelfth Annual IEEE Symposium on Logic in Computer Science, Warsaw, Poland*, pages 352–361. IEEE Computer Society Press, June 1997.
11. J. Hopcroft and J. Ullman. *Introduction to Automata Theory, Languages, and Computation*. Addison-Wesley, 1979.
12. Dexter Kozen, Jens Palsberg, and Michael Schwartzbach. Efficient recursive subtyping. In *Proc. 20th Annual ACM SIGPLAN-SIGACT Symp. on Principles of Programming Languages*, pages 419–428. ACM, ACM Press, January 1993.
13. S. Marlow and P. Wadler. A practical subtyping system for erlang. In *2nd International Conference on Functional Programming, Amsterdam*. ACM, June 1997.
14. J.C. Mitchell. Type inference with simple subtypes. *Journal of Functional Programming*, 1(3):245–285, July 1991.
15. F. Pottier. Simplifying subtyping constraints. In *Proceedings ICFP '96, International Conference on Functional Programming*, pages 122–133. ACM Press, May 1996.
16. V. Pratt. Personal communication, May 1997.
17. J. Rehof. Minimal typings in atomic subtyping. In *Proceedings POPL '97, 24th ACM SIGPLAN-SIGACT Symposium on Principles of Programming Languages, Paris, France*, pages 278–291. ACM, January 1997.
18. J. Rehof. The complexity of simple subtyping systems. Technical report, DIKU, Dept. of Computer Science, University of Copenhagen, Denmark. Available at http://www.diku.dk/research-groups/topps/personal/ rehof/publications.html, April 1998. Thesis submitted for the Ph.D. degree.
19. Jakob Rehof. Report on constraint automata and recursive subtype entailment. Technical report, DIKU, Dept. of Computer Science, University of Copenhagen, Denmark. Available at http://www.diku.dk/research-groups/topps/personal/ rehof/publications.html, 1998.
20. J. Tiuryn. Subtype inequalities. In *Proc. 7th Annual IEEE Symp. on Logic in Computer Science (LICS), Santa Cruz, California*, pages 308–315. IEEE Computer Society Press, June 1992.
21. J. Tiuryn and M. Wand. Type reconstruction with recursive types and atomic subtyping. In M.-C. Gaudel and J.-P. Jouannaud, editors, *Proc. Theory and Practice of Software Development (TAPSOFT), Orsay, France*, volume 668 of *Lecture Notes in Computer Science*, pages 686–701. Springer-Verlag, April 1993.
22. V. Trifonov and S. Smith. Subtyping constrained types. In *Proceedings SAS '96, Static Analysis Symposium, Aachen, Germany*, pages 349–365. Springer, 1996. Lecture Notes in Computer Science, vol.1145.

Reasoning about The Past with Two-Way Automata

Moshe Y. Vardi*

Rice University, Department of Computer Science, Houston, TX 77005-1892, USA

Abstract. The μ-calculus can be viewed as essentially the "ultimate" program logic, as it expressively subsumes all propositional program logics, including dynamic logics, process logics, and temporal logics. It is known that the satisfiability problem for the μ-calculus is EXPTIME-complete. This upper bound, however, is known for a version of the logic that has only forward modalities, which express weakest preconditions, but not backward modalities, which express strongest postconditions. Our main result in this paper is an exponential time upper bound for the satisfiability problem of the μ-calculus with both forward and backward modalities. To get this result we develop a theory of two-way alternating automata on infinite trees.

1 Introduction

The *propositional μ-calculus* is a propositional modal logic augmented with least and greatest fixpoint operators. It was introduced in [16], following earlier studies of fixpoint calculi in the theory of program correctness [3,23,27]. Over the past 15 years, the μ-calculus has been established as essentially the "ultimate" program logic, as it expressively subsumes all propositional program logics, including dynamic logics such as PDL, process logics such as YAPL, and temporal logics such as CTL* [7]. The μ-calculus has gained further prominence with the discovery that its formulas can be evaluated symbolically in a natural way [2], leading to industrial acceptance of computer-aided verification. More recently, the μ-calculus has found a new application domain in the theory of *description logics* in Artificial Intelligence [9]. As a result of this prominence, the μ-calculus has been the subject of extensive research; in particular, researchers focused on the truth problem and the satisfiability problem.

In the truth problem, we are asked to verify whether a given formula holds in a given state of a given Kripke structure (which is the essence of model checking). In spite of extensive research, the precise complexity of this problem is still open; it is known to be in NP$\cap$co-NP and PTIME-hard [1,6]. In contrast, the complexity of the satisfiability problem, where we are asked to decide if a given formula holds in some state of some Kripke structure, has been precisely

* Supported in part by NSF grants CCR-9628400 and CCR-9700061, and by a grant from the Intel Corporation. URL: `http://www.cs.rice.edu/~vardi`.

identified. An exponential time lower time bound follows from the lower bound for PDL in [8], and an exponential time upper time bound was shown in [4].

The exponential time upper bound for the μ-calculus was shown, however, only for a version of the logic that has only *forward* modalities. The formula $\langle a \rangle \varphi$ holds in a state s of a Kripke structure M when φ holds in some *a-successor* of s; in contrast, the "*backward*" formula $\langle a^- \rangle \varphi$ holds in s if φ holds in some *a-predecessor* of s. Here a^- describes the *converse* of the atomic program a. Essentially, forward modalities express weakest preconditions, while backward modalities express strongest postconditions. Backward modalities correspond to reasoning about the past. There is now a significant body of evidence of the usefulness of reasoning about the past in the context of program correctness [20]. For example, it is shown in [25] that past temporal connective can conveniently replace history variables in compositional verification. Backward modalities also have a counterpart in description logics, where they correspond to *inverse roles* [9].

The importance of backword modalities motivated the study of procedures for the satisfiability problem for logics that include them [11,18,24,30,34,35,38]. (Backward modalities do not, in general, pose any difficulty to truth-checking procedures.) The challenge in developing such decision procedures is that the interaction of backward modalities with other constructs of the logic can be quite subtle. For example, backward modalities interact with the *Repeat* construct of *Repeat-PDL*, posing a great difficulty to the development of decision procedures. The first elementary decision procedure for *Repeat-Converse-PDL* was octuply exponential [32]. This was improved later to a quadruply exponential procedure [30]. Finally, combining the techniques in [4] with the techniques in [34] lead to a singly exponential procedure.

Because of the subtlety of dealing with backward modalities, the satisfiability problem for the *full* μ-calculus, which has both forward and backward modalities, is still open. Our main result in this paper is an exponential time upper bound for the problem. The approach we take is the automata-theoretic approach advocated in [4,30,38]. We first show that even though the full μ-calculus does not have the finite-model property, it does have the *tree-model property*. (As argued in [37], the tree-model property, which asserts that if a formula is satisfiable then it is satisfiable by a bounded-degree infinite tree structure, offers an explanation for the robust decidability of many propositional program logics.) We then show how a formula φ can be translated to an automaton A_φ on infinite trees that accepts precisely the tree models of φ. To check whether φ is satisfiable it suffices then to solve the emptiness problem for A_φ.

Earlier papers that employed the automata-theoretic approach used nondeterministic tree automata [4,30,38]. The translation from formulas to nondeterministic automata is nontrivial; for example, the translation in [38] is exponential and consists of a sequence of successive translations. As demonstrated in [1,36], it is easier to translate formulas to *alternating* automata. Alternating tree automata generalize nondeterministic tree automata by allowing multiple successor states to go down along the same branch of the tree. It is known that while the translation from branching temporal logic formulas to nondeterministic tree automata is exponential, the translation to alternating tree automata is linear [1,21]. Similarly, there is a simple translation from μ-calculus formulas to alternating tree automata [1,5]. Alternating tree automata as defined in [22], however, cannot easily handle backwards modalities, since they are *one-way* automata. To deal with backward modalities we introduce *two-way* alternating automata on infinite trees, based on an analogous notion of two-way automata on *finite trees* in [29].

It remains then to solve the emptiness problem for two-way alternating tree automata. Alternating tree automata can be viewed as infinite games [22]; this holds for both one-way and two-ways automata. It is shown in [14] that under certains conditions, which hold here, the winning player has a *memoryless* strategy in these games. We use this to show that two-way alternating tree automata can be translated to equivalent one-way nondeterministic tree automata with an exponential blowup. The emptiness problem can then be solved by using known algorithms for emptiness of nondeterministic tree automata [4,19,26]. This yields an exponential time upper bound for the emptiness problem for alternating tree automata, resulting in a bound of the same complexity for satisfiability of the full μ-calculus.

2 Preliminaries

2.1 The μ-Calculus

The *propositional μ-calculus* is a propositional modal logic augmented with least and greatest fixpoint operators [16]. A *signature* Ξ for the μ-calculus consists of a set AP of atomic propositions, a set Var of propositional variables and a set Prog of atomic programs. In the *full* μ-calculus, we associate with each atomic program a its *converse* a^-. A *program* is either an atomic program or its converse. We denote programs by α.

A formula of the full μ-calculus over the signature Ξ is either:

- **true**, **false**, p or $\neg p$ for all $p \in \mathsf{AP}$;
- y for all $y \in \mathsf{Var}$;
- $\varphi_1 \wedge \varphi_2$ or $\varphi_1 \vee \varphi_2$, where φ_1 and φ_2 are μ-calculus formulas;
- $\langle\alpha\rangle\varphi$ or $[\alpha]\varphi$, where φ is a μ-calculus formula and α is a program;
- $\mu y.\varphi(y)$ or $\nu y.\varphi(y)$, where $y \in \mathsf{Var}$ and $\varphi(y)$ is a formula.

The only difference between the full μ-calculus and the *standard* μ-calculus is that in the full μ-calculus both atomic programs and their converse are allowed in the modalities $\langle\alpha\rangle\varphi$ and $[\alpha]\varphi$, while only atomic programs are allowed in such modalities in the standard μ-calculus. A *sentence* is a formula that contains no free propositional variables. We call μ and ν *fixpoint operators*. We say that a formula is a *μ-formula* (*ν-formula*), if it is of the form $\mu y.\varphi(y)$ $(\nu y.\varphi(y))$. We use λ to denote a fixpoint operator μ or ν. For a λ-formula $\lambda y.\varphi(y)$, the formula

$\varphi(\lambda y.\varphi(y))$ is obtained from $\varphi(y)$ by replacing each free occurrence of y with $\lambda y.\varphi(y)$. We call a formula of the form $\langle\alpha\rangle\varphi$ an *existential* formula.

The semantics of the full μ-calculus is defined with respect to a *Kripke structure* $K = \langle W, R, L\rangle$ over the signature Ξ, where W is a set of points, $R : \mathsf{Prog} \to 2^{W\times W}$ assigns to each atomic program a transition relation over W, and $L : \mathsf{AP} \to 2^W$ assigns to each atomic proposition a set of points. We now extend R to the converse of atomic programs. For each atomic program a, we define $R(a^-)$ to be the relational inverse of $R(a)$, i.e., $R(a^-) = \{(v,u) : (u,v) \in R(a)\}$.

Given a Kripke structure $K = \langle W, R, L\rangle$ and a set $\{y_1, \ldots, y_n\}$ of variables in Var, a *valuation* $\mathcal{V} : \{y_1, \ldots, y_n\} \to 2^W$ is an assignment of subsets of W to the variables $y_1, \ldots, y_n$. For a valuation $\mathcal{V}$, a variable y, and a set $W' \subseteq W$, we denote by $\mathcal{V}[y \leftarrow W']$ the valuation obtained from $\mathcal{V}$ by assigning W' to y. A formula φ with free variables among $y_1, \ldots, y_n$ is interpreted over the structure K as a mapping φ^K from valuations to 2^W. Thus, $\varphi^K(\mathcal{V})$ denotes the set of points that satisfy φ with the valuation $\mathcal{V}$. The mapping φ^K is defined inductively as follows:

- $\mathbf{true}^K(\mathcal{V}) = W$ and $\mathbf{false}^K(\mathcal{V}) = \emptyset$;
- For $p \in \mathsf{AP}$, we have $p^K(\mathcal{V}) = L(p)$ and $(\neg p)^K(\mathcal{V}) = W \setminus L(p)$;
- For $y_i \in \mathsf{Var}$, we have $y_i^K(\mathcal{V}) = \mathcal{V}(y_i)$;
- $(\varphi_1 \wedge \varphi_2)^K(\mathcal{V}) = \varphi_1^K(\mathcal{V}) \cap \varphi_2^K(\mathcal{V})$;
- $(\varphi_1 \vee \varphi_2)^K(\mathcal{V}) = \varphi_1^K(\mathcal{V}) \cup \varphi_2^K(\mathcal{V})$;
- $([\alpha]\varphi)^K(\mathcal{V}) = \{w \in W : \forall w' \text{ such that } (w,w') \in R(\alpha), \text{ we have } w' \in \varphi^K(\mathcal{V})\}$,
- $(\langle\alpha\rangle\varphi)^K(\mathcal{V}) = \{w \in W : \exists w' \text{ such that } (w,w') \in R(\alpha) \text{ and } w' \in \varphi^K(\mathcal{V})\}$,
- $(\mu y.\varphi(y))^K(\mathcal{V}) = \bigcap\{W' \subseteq W : f^K(\mathcal{V}[y \leftarrow W']) \subseteq W'\}$;
- $(\nu y.\varphi(y))^K(\mathcal{V}) = \bigcup\{W' \subseteq W : W' \subseteq f^K(\mathcal{V}[y \leftarrow W'])\}$.

Note that no valuation is required for a sentence. For a point $w \in W$ and a sentence φ, we say that φ holds at w in K, denoted $K, w \models \varphi$ iff $w \in \varphi^K$.

2.2 Alternating Tree Automata

For an introduction to the theory of automata on infinite trees see [33]. An *infinite tree* is a set $T \subseteq \mathbb{N}^+$, such that if $x \cdot c \in T$ where $x \in \mathbb{N}^*$ and $c \in \mathbb{N}$, then also $x \in T$, and, if the tree is *full*, then also $x \cdot c' \in T$ for all $0 < c' < c$, (Here we use $\mathbb{N}$ to denote the *positive* integers.) The elements of T are called *nodes*, and the empty word ε is the *root* of T. For every $x \in T$, the nodes $x \cdot c$ where $c \in \mathbb{N}$ are the *successors* of x. As a convention, we take $x \cdot 0 = x$ and $(x \cdot i) \cdot -1 = x$ ($\varepsilon \cdot -1$ is undefined). The *branching degree* $d(x)$ denotes the number of different successors x has. If $d(x) = k$ for all nodes x, then we say that the tree is k-ary. An *infinite path* P of T is a prefix-closed set $P \subseteq T$ such that for every $i \geq 0$, there exists a unique $x \in P$ with $|x| = i$. A *labeled tree* over an alphabet Σ is a pair (T, V) where T is a tree and $V : T \to \Sigma$.

Alternating automata on infinite trees generalize nondeterministic tree automata and were first introduced in [22]. Here we describe *two-way* alternating tree automata Let $\mathcal{B}^+(X)$ be the set of positive Boolean formulas over X (i.e., boolean formulas built from elements in X using $\wedge$ and $\vee$), where we also allow the formulas **true** and **false**, and, as usual, $\wedge$ has precedence over $\vee$. For a set $Y \subseteq X$ and a formula $\theta \in \mathcal{B}^+(X)$, we say that Y *satisfies* θ iff assigning **true** to elements in Y and assigning **false** to elements in $X \setminus Y$ makes θ true. on k-ary trees. Let $[k] = \{-1, 0, 1, \ldots, k\}$. A *two-way alternating automaton* over infinite k-ary trees is a tuple $A = \langle \Sigma, Q, \delta, q_0, F \rangle$, where Σ is the input alphabet, Q is a finite set of states, $\delta : Q \times \Sigma \to \mathcal{B}^+([k] \times Q)$ is the transition function, $q_0 \in Q$ is an initial state, and F specifies the acceptance condition.

A run of an alternating automaton A over a labeled tree $\langle T, V \rangle$ is a labeled tree $\langle T_r, r \rangle$ in which every node is labeled by an element of $T \times Q$. A node in T_r, labeled by (x, q), describes a copy of the automaton that is in the state q and reads the node x of T. Note that many nodes of T_r can correspond to the same node of T; there is no one-to-one correspondence between the nodes of the run and the nodes of the tree. The labels of a node and its successors have to satisfy the transition function. Formally, a run $\langle T_r, r \rangle$ is a Σ_r-labeled tree, where $\Sigma_r = T \times Q$ and $\langle T_r, r \rangle$ satisfies the following:

1. $\varepsilon \in T_r$ and $r(\varepsilon) = (\varepsilon, q_0)$.
2. Let $y \in T_r$ with $r(y) = (x, q)$ and $\delta(q, V(x)) = \theta$. Then there is a (possibly empty) set $S = \{(c_1, q_1), (c_1, q_1), \ldots, (c_n, q_n)\} \subseteq \{-1, 0, \ldots, k\} \times Q$, such that the following hold:
   - S satisfies θ, and
   - for all $1 \leq i \leq n$, we have $y \cdot i \in T_r$, $x \cdot c_i$ is defined, and $r(y \cdot i) = (x \cdot c_i, q_i)$.

Note that the automaton cannot go backwards from the root of the input tree, as we require that $x \cdot c_i$ be defined, but $\varepsilon \cdot -1$ is undefined.

A run $\langle T_r, r \rangle$ is *accepting* if all its infinite paths satisfy the acceptance condition. We consider here *parity* acceptance conditions [5]. A parity condition over a state set Q is a finite sequence $F = (G_1, G_2, \ldots, G_m)$ of subsets of Q, where $G_1 \subseteq G_2 \subseteq \ldots \subseteq G_m = Q$. Given a run $\langle T_r, r \rangle$ and an infinite path $P \subseteq T_r$, let $inf(P) \subseteq Q$ be such that $q \in inf(P)$ if and only if there are infinitely many $y \in P$ for which $r(y) \in T \times \{q\}$. That is, $inf(P)$ contains exactly all the states that appear infinitely often in P. A path P satisfies the condition F if there is an *even* i for which $inf(P) \cap G_i \neq \emptyset$ and $inf(P) \cap G_{i-1} = \emptyset$. (For *co-parity* acceptance condition we require i to be *odd*.) An automaton accepts a labeled tree if and only if there exists a run that accepts it. We denote by $\mathcal{L}(A)$ the set of all Σ-labeled trees that A accepts.

3 The Tree-Model Property

To determine the truth value of a Boolean formula it suffices to consider its subformulas. For modal formulas, one has to consider a bigger collection of formulas, the so called Fischer-Ladner closure [8]. The closure, $cl(\varphi)$, of a sentence φ is the smallest set of sentences that satisfies the following:

- $\varphi \in cl(\varphi)$.
- If $\varphi_1 \wedge \varphi_2 \in cl(\varphi)$ or $\varphi_1 \vee \varphi_2 \in cl(\varphi)$, then $\varphi_1 \in cl(\varphi)$ and $\varphi_2 \in cl(\varphi)$.
- If $\langle\alpha\rangle\psi \in cl(\varphi)$ or $[\alpha]\psi \in cl(\varphi)$, then $\psi \in cl(\varphi)$.
- If $\lambda y.\varphi(y) \in cl(\varphi)$, then $\varphi(\lambda y.\varphi(y)) \in cl(\varphi)$.

As proved in [16], for every sentence φ, the number of elements in $cl(\varphi)$ is linear in the length $||\varphi||$ of φ.

An *atom* $\mathbf{A}$ of φ is a set of formulas in $cl(\varphi)$ that satisfies the following properties:

- if $p \in \mathsf{AP}$, then, exclusively, either $p \in \mathbf{A}$ or $\neg p \in \mathbf{A}$,
- if $\varphi_1 \wedge \varphi_2 \in cl(\varphi)$, then $\varphi_1 \wedge \varphi_2 \in \mathbf{A}$ iff $\varphi_1 \in \mathbf{A}$ and $\varphi_2 \in \mathbf{A}$,
- if $\varphi_1 \vee \varphi_2 \in cl(\varphi)$, then $\varphi_1 \vee \varphi_2 \in \mathbf{A}$ iff $\varphi_1 \in \mathbf{A}$ or $\varphi_2 \in \mathbf{A}$,
- if $\lambda X.\psi(X) \in cl(\varphi)$, then $\lambda X.\psi(X) \in \mathbf{A}$ iff $\psi(\lambda X.\psi(X)) \in \mathbf{A}$.

Intuitively, an atom is a consistent subset of $cl(\varphi)$. The set of atoms of φ is denoted $at(\varphi)$. Clearly, the size of $at(\varphi)$ is at most exponential in the length of φ.

A *pre-model* (K, π) for φ is a pair consisting of a Kripke structure $K = \langle W, R, L\rangle$ and a labeling function $\pi : W \to at(\varphi)$ that satisfies the following properties:

- $\varphi \in \pi(u)$, for some $u \in W$,
- if $p \in \pi(u)$, then $u \in L(p)$, and if $\neg p \in \pi(u)$, then $u \notin L(p)$, for $p \in \mathsf{AP}$ and $u \in W$,
- if $\langle\alpha\rangle\psi \in \pi(u)$, for $u \in W$, then $\psi \in \pi(v)$, for some $v \in W$ such that $(u, v) \in R(\alpha)$.
- if $[\alpha]\psi \in \pi(u)$, for $u \in W$, then $\psi \in \pi(v)$, for all $v \in W$ such that $(u, v) \in R(\alpha)$.

A pre-model of φ is almost a model of φ except for fixpoint formulas that do not necessarily get the right semantics (that is, fixpoints are arbitrary rather than minimal or maximal as needed).

A *choice function* [31] ρ for a pre-model (K, π) of φ, where $K = \langle W, R, L\rangle$, is a partial function from $W \times cl(\varphi)$ to $W \cup cl(\varphi)$ such that for each $u \in W$: (a) for each disjunction $\varphi_1 \vee \varphi_2 \in \pi(u)$, we have that $\rho(u, \varphi_1 \vee \varphi_2)$ is either φ_1 or φ_2, and $\rho(u, \varphi_1 \vee \varphi_2) \in \pi(u)$, and (b) for each existential formula $\langle\alpha\rangle\psi \in \pi(u)$, we have that $\rho(u, \langle\alpha\rangle\psi)$ is some $v \in W$ such that $(u, v) \in R(\alpha)$ and $\psi \in \pi(v)$. Intuitively, a choice function identifies how a disjunctive formula or an existential formula is satisfied. An *adorned* pre-model (K, π, ρ) for φ consists of a pre-model (K, π) for φ and a choice function ρ.

We can now define formally the notion of *derivation* between occurrences of sentences in adorned pre-models. Let (K, π, ρ) be an adorned pre-model of φ, The derivation relation, denoted $\vdash$, is defined as follows:

- if $\varphi_1 \vee \varphi_2 \in \pi(u)$ then $(\varphi_1 \vee \varphi_2, u) \vdash (\rho(u, \varphi_1 \vee \varphi_2), u)$,
- if $\varphi_1 \wedge \varphi_2 \in \pi(u)$, then $(\varphi_1 \wedge \varphi_2, u) \vdash (\varphi_1, u)$ and $(\varphi_1 \wedge \varphi_2, u) \vdash (\varphi_2, u)$,
- if $\langle\alpha\rangle\psi \in \pi(u)$, then $(\langle\alpha\rangle\psi, u) \vdash (\psi, \rho(u, \langle\alpha\rangle\psi))$,
- if $\lambda X.\psi(X) \in \pi(u)$, then $(\lambda X.\psi(X), u) \vdash (\psi(\lambda X.\psi(X)), u)$.

A least-fixpoint sentence $\mu X.\psi(X)$ is said to be *regenerated* from point u to point v (u might be equal to v) in an adorned premodel (K, π, ρ) if there is a sequence $(\theta_1, u_1), \ldots, (\theta_k, u_k)$, with $k > 1$, such that $\theta_1 = \theta_k = \mu X.\psi(X)$, $u_1 = u$, $u_k = v$, $(\theta_l, u_l) \vdash (\theta_{l+1}, u_{l+1})$, for $0 < l < k$, and $\mu X.\psi(X)$ is a subsentence of each of the θ_i's. We say that (K, π, ρ) is *well-founded* if there is no fixpoint sentence $\mu X.\psi(X) \in cl(\varphi)$ and an infinite sequence $u_0, u_1, \ldots$ such that $\mu X.\psi(X)$ is regenerated from u_j to u_{j+1} for all $j \geq 0$.

The following theorem was shown for the standard μ-calculus, but the proof is insensitive to the direction of the modalities.

Theorem 1. [31] *A sentence φ of the full μ-calculus has a model K if and only if it has a well-founded adorned pre-model (K, π, ρ).*

We can now establish the tree-model property for the full μ-calculus. Note that it follows from [30] that the finite-model property does not hold for the full μ-calculus; in contrast, it does hold for the standard μ-calculus [17]. The tree-model property asserts that if a sentence is satisfiable then it is satisfiable by a bounded-degree infinite *tree structure*. A tree structure is a Kripe structure $\langle W, R, L\rangle$ where W is a tree and for each program α if $(u, v) \in R(\alpha)$, then either v is a successor of u or u is a successor of v.

The standard way of proving the tree-model property is to take a model and straightforwardly "unravel" it; see [37]. Special care, however, is needed to ensure that the number of successors at each node is bounded.

Theorem 2. *If a formula φ in the full μ-calculus is satisfiable, then it is satisfiable at the root of a tree structure whose branching degrees are bounded by $||\varphi||$.*

Note that the tree model constructed in the above proof is not a *full* tree; it is possible for xi to be a node in the tree without $x(i-1)$ being a node in the tree. It is technically more convenient to deal with full trees. To that end we add a new atomic proposition p_T. The intuition is that p_T is true only at nodes that belong to the tree (so nodes where p_T is false are dummy nodes). We now replace each modal subformula $\langle\alpha\rangle\psi$ by $\langle\alpha\rangle(p_T \wedge \psi)$ and each modal subformula $[\alpha]\psi$ by $[\alpha](p_T \rightarrow \psi)$. This transformation causes only a linear blow-up, It is easy to see that the if the original formula is satisfiable at the root of a tree structure whose branching degrees are bounded by $||\varphi||$, then the new formula φ' is satisfiable at the root of a $||\varphi'||$-ary tree (where p_T is true at the root). We call such formulas *uniform* formulas, and we can thus restrict attention to full trees. Since we need to represent the information about the transition function R, we introduce new atomic propositions to represent this information. For each atomic program a we introduce two atomic propositions: p_a holds at a node xj when $(x, xj) \in R(a)$ and p_a^- holds in xj when $(xj, x) \in R(a)$. We call tree structures that obey these constraints *well-behaved* tree structures,

We are now ready to describe the translation from formulas to two-way alternating tree-automata.

Theorem 3. *Given a uniform formula φ of the full μ-calculus, we can construct a two-way alternating parity automaton A_φ whose number of states is $O(||\varphi||)$, such that $\mathcal{L}(A_\varphi)$ is exactly the set of well-behaved $||\varphi||$-ary tree structures satisfying φ at the root.*

Proof Sketch: The automaton is obtained by taking the intersection of two automata (intersection is trivial for alternating automata [22]). The first automaton checks that the input tree is well-behaved. Constructing this automaton is an easy exercise. The second automaton checks that φ is satisfied at the root of the input tree. Take $A_\varphi = \langle 2^{\mathsf{AP}}, cl(\varphi), \delta, \varphi, F \rangle$. We need to define the transition function δ and the acceptance condition F. Let $n = ||\varphi||$. For all $\sigma \in 2^{\mathsf{AP}}$ and $a \in \mathsf{Prog}$ we define:

- $\delta(p, \sigma) = \mathbf{true}$ if $p \in \sigma$. • $\delta(p, \sigma) = \mathbf{false}$ if $p \notin \sigma$.
- $\delta(\neg p, \sigma) = \mathbf{true}$ if $p \notin \sigma$. • $\delta(\neg p, \sigma) = \mathbf{false}$ if $p \in \sigma$.
- $\delta(\varphi_1 \wedge \varphi_2, \sigma) = (0, \varphi_1) \wedge (0, \varphi 2)$.
- $\delta(\varphi_1 \vee \varphi_2, \sigma) = (0, \varphi_1) \vee (0, \varphi 2)$.
- $\delta(\lambda y.\varphi(y), \sigma) = (0, \varphi(\lambda y.\varphi(y)))$.
- $\delta(\langle a \rangle \psi, \sigma) = ((-1, \psi) \wedge (0, p_{\bar{a}})) \vee \bigvee_{c=1}^{n} ((c, \psi) \wedge (c, p_a))$.
- $\delta(\langle a^- \rangle \psi, \sigma) = ((-1, \psi) \wedge (0, p_a)) \vee \bigvee_{c=1}^{n} ((c, \psi) \wedge (c, p_{\bar{a}}))$.
- $\delta([a]\psi, \sigma) = ((-1, \psi) \vee (0, \neg p_{\bar{a}})) \wedge \bigwedge_{c=1}^{n} ((c, \psi) \vee (c, \neg p_a))$.
- $\delta([a^-]\psi, \sigma) = ((-1, \psi) \vee (0, \neg p_a)) \wedge \bigwedge_{c=1}^{n} ((c, \psi) \vee (c, \neg p_{\bar{a}}))$.

The translation here is by a straighfoward induction on the structure of φ. It simplifies the translation given in [1] (for the standard μ-calculus), since we allow the usage of ε-transitions (i.e., transitions to the direction 0).

It remains to define the parity acceptance condition F. This is done analogously to the construction in [6], which drew a tight relationship between model checking for the standard μ-calculus and one-way nondeterministic parity tree automata. □

Corollary 4. *A uniform formula φ of the full μ-calculus is satisfiable iff $\mathcal{L}(A_\varphi)$ is not empty.*

4 Emptiness of Two-Way Alternating Tree Automata

We solve the emptiness problem for two-way alternating tree automata, by reducing them to one-way nondeterministic tree automata. A run of a nondeterministic tree automaton is a tree with the same structure as the input tree but a different label set; the run tree is labeled by states. In contrast, a run of an alternating automaton is a tree whose structure can be quite different than that of the input tree. Thus, to reduce alternating automata to nondeterministic automata, we have to overcome this difficulty.

Let $A = \langle \Sigma, Q, \delta, q_0, F \rangle$ be a two-way alternating automaton on k-ary trees. A *strategy tree* for A is a mapping $\tau : \{1, \ldots, k\}^* \to 2^{Q \times [k] \times Q}$. Thus, each label in a strategy is an edge-$[k]$-labeled directed graph on Q. Intuitively, each label is a set of transitions. For each label ζ, we define $state(\zeta) = \{u : (u, i, v) \in \zeta\}$, i.e., $state(\zeta)$ is the set of sources in the graph ζ. The strategy tree τ is *on* a k-ary input tree $(\{1, \ldots, k\}^*, V)$ if $q_0 \in state(\tau(\varepsilon))$, and for each node $x \in \{1, \ldots, k\}^*$ and each state $q \in state(\tau(x))$, the set $\{(c, q') : (q, c, q') \in \tau(x)\}$ satisfies $\delta(q, V(x))$. Thus, each label can be viewed as a strategy of satisfying the transition function.

A *path* β in a strategy tree τ is a sequence $(u_1, q_1), (u_2, q_2), \ldots$ of pairs from $\{1, \ldots, k\}^* \times Q$ such that, for all $i > 0$, there is some $c_i \in [k]$ such that $(q_i, c_i, q_{i+1}) \in \tau(u_i)$ and $u_{i+1} = u_i \cdot c_i$. Thus, β is obtained by following transitions in the strategy tree. We define $inf(\beta)$ to be the set of states in Q that occur infinitely often in β. We say that an infinite path β satisfies a parity condition $F = (G_1, G_2, \ldots)$ if there is an even i for which $inf(\beta) \cap G_i \neq \emptyset$ and $inf(\beta) \cap G_{i-1} = \emptyset$. We say that τ is *accepting* if all infinite paths in τ satisfy F.

Proposition 5. *A two-way alternating parity automaton accepts an input tree iff it has an accepting strategy tree over the input tree.*

Proof Sketch: The "if" direction is immediate. For the "only if" direction, let $A = \langle \Sigma, Q, \delta, q_0, F \rangle$, $F = (G_1, G_2, \ldots)$, and let $(\{1, \ldots, k\}^*, V)$ be the input tree. Consider the following game between two players: the Protagonist and the Antagonist. Intuitively, the Protoganist is trying to show that A accepts the input tree, and the Antagonist is trying to challenge that. A *configuration* of the game is a pair in $\{1, \ldots, k\}^* \times Q$. The initial configuration is (ε, q_0). Consider a configuration (x, q). The Protagonist now chooses a set $\{(c_1, q_1), \ldots, (c_m, q_m)\}$ that satisfies $\delta(q, V(x))$; the Antagonist responds by choosing an element (c_i, q_i) of the set. The new configuration is then $(x \cdot c_i, q_i)$. If $x \cdot c_i$ is undefined or if $\delta(q, V(x)) =$ **false**, then the Antagonist wins immediately. Consider now an infinite play γ. Let $inf(\gamma)$ be the set of states in Q that repeat infinitely in the sequence of configurations in γ. The Protagonist wins if there is an even i for which $inf(\gamma) \cap G_i \neq \emptyset$ and $inf(\gamma) \cap G_{i-1} = \emptyset$. It is not difficult to see that the Protagonists *wins the game*, i.e., has a winning strategy against the Antagonist, iff A accepts the input tree.

The game as we described it meets the conditions in [14]. It follows that if the Protagonist wins then it as a *memoryless* strategy, i.e., a strategy whose moves do not depend on the history of the game, but only on the current configuration. Thus, A accepts the input tree iff it has a strategy tree over the input tree. □

We have thus succeeded in defining a notion of run for alternating automata that will have the same tree structure as the input tree. We are still facing the problem that paths in a strategy tree can go both up and down. We need to find a way to restrict attention to uni-directional paths.

Let $A = \langle \Sigma, Q, \delta, q_0, F \rangle$, $F = (G_1, G_2, \ldots, G_m)$, be a two-way alternating automaton on k-ary trees, and let $\tau : \{1, \ldots, k\}^* \to 2^{Q \times [k] \times Q}$ be a strategy tree for A. An *annotation* for A is a mapping $\eta : \{1, \ldots, k\}^* \to 2^{Q \times 2^{\{1, \ldots, m\}} \times Q}$. Thus, each label in an annotation is an edge-$2^{\{1, \ldots, m\}}$-labeled directed graph on Q. For each state $q \in Q$, let $index(q)$ be the minimal i such that $q \in G_i$. We say that η is an annotation *of* τ if some closure conditions hold for each node $x \in \{1,\ldots,k\}^*$. Intuitively, these conditions say that η contains all relevant information about finite paths in τ. The conditions are: (a) if $(q,H_1,q') \in \eta(x)$ and $(q',H_2,q'') \in \eta(x)$, then $(q,H_1 \cup H_2,q'') \in \eta(x)$, (b) if $(q,0,q') \in \tau(x)$ then $(q,index(q'),q') \in \eta(x)$, (c) if $x = yi$, $(q,-1,q') \in \tau(x)$, $(q',H,q'') \in \eta(y)$, and $(q'',i,q''') \in \tau(x)$, then $(q,H \cup \{index(q'),index(q''')\},q''') \in \eta(x)$, (d) if $y = xi$, $(q,i,q') \in \tau(x)$, $(q',H,q'') \in \eta(y)$, and $(q'',-1,q''') \in \tau(y)$, then $(q,H \cup \{index(q'),index(q''')\},q''') \in \eta(x)$.

A *downward path* κ in η is a sequence $(u_1,q_1,t_1),(u_2,q_2,t_2),\ldots$ of triples, where each u_i is in $\{1,\ldots,k\}^*$, each q_i is in Q, and each t_i is either an element of $\tau(u_i)$ or $\eta(u_i)$, such that: (a) either t_i is (q_i,c,q_{i+1}) for some $c \in \{1,\ldots,k\}$, and $u_{i+1} = u_i \cdot c$; in this case we define $index(t_i)$ to be $index(q_{i+1})$, or (b) t_i is (q_i,H,q_{i+1}), for $H \subseteq \{1,\ldots,m\}$, and $u_{i+1} = u_i$; in this case we define $index(t_i)$ to be $\min(H)$. We consider two kinds of downward paths: (a) infinite paths $\kappa = (u_1,q_1,t_1),(u_2,q_2,t_2),\ldots$, whose index, $index(\kappa)$ is defined as the minimal j such that $index(t_i) = j$ infinitely often, or finite paths $\kappa = (u_1,q_1,t_1),\ldots,(u_s,q_s,t_s)$, where $t_s = (q_s,H_s,q_s)$ (i.e., the path ends in a loop), whose index, $index(\kappa)$ is defined as $index(t_s)$. In either case we say that κ *violates* F if $index(\kappa)$ is odd. We say that η is *accepting* if no downward path in η violates F.

Proposition 6. *A two-way alternating parity automaton accepts an input tree iff it has a strategy tree over the input tree and an accepting annotation of the strategy tree.*

Proof Sketch: Let $A = \langle \Sigma, Q, \delta, q_0, F\rangle$, $F = (G_1, G_2, \ldots, G_m)$, and let $(\{1,\ldots,k\}^*, V)$ be the input tree. Suppose first that A accepts the input tree. By Proposition 5, there is an accepting strategy tree τ over $(\{1,\ldots,k\}^*, V)$. Consider two annotations η_1 and η_2 of τ. Their *intersection* $\eta_1 \cap \eta_2$, defined by $\eta_1 \cap \eta_2(x) = \eta_1(x) \cap \eta_2(x)$ for each $x \in \{1,\ldots,k\}^*$, is also an annotation of τ. Thus, there exists a *minimal* annotation η of τ. (That is, if η' is also an annotation of τ, then η must be *contained* in η', i.e., for each $x \in \{1,\ldots,k\}^*$ we have that $\eta(x) \subseteq \eta'(x)$.) It can be shown that since all paths in τ satisfies F, no downward path in η violates F. Conversely, suppose that τ is a strategy tree over $(\{1,\ldots,k\}^*, V)$ and η is an annotation of τ such that no downward path in η violates F. Let η' be the minimal annotation of τ; η' must be contained in η. It follows that no downward path in η' violates F. From this we can show that all paths in τ satisfy F. By Proposition 5, A accepts $(\{1,\ldots,k\}^*, V)$. □

Consider now *annotated trees* $(\{1,\ldots,k\}^*, V, \tau, \eta)$, where τ is a strategy tree for A on $(\{1,\ldots,k\}^*, V)$ and η is an annotation of τ. We say that $(\{1,\ldots,k\}^*, V, \tau, \eta)$ is *accepting* if η is accepting.

Theorem 7. *Let A be a two-way alternating parity tree automaton. Then there is a nondeterministic parity tree automaton A^n such that $\mathcal{L}(A) = \mathcal{L}(A^n)$. The number of states in A^n is exponential in the number of states of A, but the size of the acceptance condition of A^n is linear in the size of the acceptance condition of A.*

Proof Sketch: Let $A = \langle \Sigma, Q, \delta, q_0, F\rangle$, $F = (G_1, \ldots, G_m)$. The nondeterministic automaton A^n is the intersection of two automata. Given an annotated tree $(\{1,\ldots,k\}^*, V, \tau, \eta)$, the first automaton, A_1^n, checks that τ is a strategy tree on $(\{1,\ldots,k\}^*, V)$ and that η is an annotation of τ. Constructing A_1^n is a not-too-difficult exercise. The second automaton, A_2^n, checks that τ is accepting. We construct A_2^n in several steps.

Consider a downward path $\kappa = (u_1, q_1, t_1), (u_2, q_2, t_2), \ldots$. We define its *projection* to be the sequence $proj(\kappa) = (q_1, t_1), (q_2, t_2), \ldots$, which is is a sequence over the finite alphabet $Q \times ((Q \times [k] \times Q) \cup (Q \times 2^{\{1,\ldots,m\}} \times Q))$. We can construct a co-parity word automaton B that accepts projections of downward paths that violates F. The state set of B is $Q \times \{1,\ldots,m\}$. All that B does is check that (a) either t_i is (q_i, c, q_{i+1}) for some $c \in \{1,\ldots,k\}$, (b) t_i is (q_i, H, q_{i+1}) for some $H \subseteq \{1,\ldots,m\}$. In either case B also remembers $index(t_i)$. B accepts if there is some $t_i = (q_i, H_i, q_i)$ with an odd $index(t_i)$ or if the minimal index that repeats infinitely often is odd. The size of the acceptance condition of B is linear in the size of the acceptance condition of A. From B we construct another co-parity word automaton B'. This automaton reads a sequence of labels of τ or η and checks whether it contains a projection of a downward path that violates F. The state set of B' is still $Q \times \{1,\ldots,m\}$, though its alphabet is $2^{Q\times[k]\times Q} \cup 2^{Q\times 2^{\{1,\ldots,m\}}\times Q}$. The size of the acceptance condition of B' is still linear in the size of the acceptance condition of A. We now co-determinize B', i.e., determinize it and complement it in a singly-exponential construction [28,33] to obtain a deterministic parity word automaton B'' that rejects violating downward paths. The deterministic tree automaton B''' is obtained by simply running B'' in parallel over all branches of $(\{1,\ldots,k\}^*, V, \tau, \eta)$. Thus, its size is exponential in the size of A. The size of the acceptance condition of B''' is still linear in the size of the acceptance condition of A. Finally, A_2^n is obtained from B''' by projecting out the τ and η component of the inputs tree, so the input tree is of the form $(\{1,\ldots,k\}^*, V)$. □

We can now combine Theorem 3, Corollary 4, Theorem 7, and the tree automata emptiness algorithms in [4,19,26] (which are polynomial in the number of states, but exponential in the size of the acceptance condition) to obtain:

Theorem 8. *The satisfiability problem for the full μ-calculus is decidable in exponential time.*

Remark 9. One can extend the framework of the μ-calculus by allowing *deterministic* atomic programs. Such programs correspond to *functional roles* in description logics [10]. The mapping R in a Kripke structure $K = \langle W, R, L\rangle$ assigns to each deterministic atomic program a partial function over W. The results in this paper can be extended also to prove an exponential time upper bound for the full μ-calculus with deterministic programs. (See `http://www.cs.rice.edu/~vardi`.)

5 Concluding Remarks

Over the last few years there has been a significant interest in logics with bounded number of variables (see [15]). One surprising result in this line of research is that while FO^3, 3-variable first-order logic, is already undecidable, the satisfiability problem for FO^2, 2-variable first-order logic, is NEXPTIME-complete [12]. This lead researchers to consider extensions of FO^2. Unfortunately, fairly modest extensions of FO^2 by fixpoint constructs quickly lead to undecidability [13]. On the other hand, the full μ-calculus can be viewed as a fragment of 2-variable fixpoint logic [37]. Our main decidability result here for the full μ-calculus pushes the "decidability envelope" further. The key difference between the full μ-calculus and the fixpoint extensions of FO^2 seems to be the tree-model property, which was offered in [37] as an explanation for the robust decidability of propositional program logics.

References

1. O. Bernholtz, M.Y. Vardi, and P. Wolper. An automata-theoretic approach to branching-time model checking. In D. L. Dill, editor, *Computer Aided Verification, Proc. 6th Int. Conference*, volume 818 of *Lecture Notes in Computer Science*, pages 142–155, Stanford, June 1994. Springer-Verlag, Berlin.
2. J.R. Burch, E.M. Clarke, K.L. McMillan, D.L. Dill, and L.J. Hwang. Symbolic model checking: 10^{20} states and beyond. *Information and Computation*, 98(2):142–170, June 1992.
3. E.A. Emerson and E.M. Clarke. Characterizing correctness properties of parallel programs using fixpoints. In *Proc. 7th Int'l Colloq. on Automata, Languages and Programming*, pages 169–181, 1980.
4. E.A. Emerson and C. Jutla. The complexity of tree automata and logics of programs. In *Proc. 29th IEEE Symposium on Foundations of Computer Science*, pages 368–377, White Plains, October 1988.
5. E.A. Emerson and C. Jutla. Tree automata, Mu-calculus and determinacy. In *Proc. 32nd IEEE Symposium on Foundations of Computer Science*, pages 368–377, San Juan, October 1991.
6. E.A. Emerson, C. Jutla, and A.P. Sistla. On model-checking for fragments of μ-calculus. In *Computer Aided Verification, Proc. 5th Int. Conference*, volume 697, pages 385–396, Elounda, Crete, June 1993. Lecture Notes in Computer Science, Springer-Verlag.
7. E.A. Emerson and C.-L. Lei. Efficient model checking in fragments of the proposoitional Mu-calculus. In *Proc. 1st Symposium on Logic in Computer Science*, pages 267–278, Cambridge, June 1986.
8. M.J. Fischer and R.E. Ladner. Propositional dynamic logic of regular programs. *Journal of Computer and Systems Sciences*, 18:194–211, 1979.
9. G. De Giacomo and M. Lenzerini. Concept languages with number restrictions and fixpoints, and its relationship with μ-calculus. In *Proc. 11th European Conference on Artificial Intelligence (ECAI-94)*, pages 411–415. John Wiley and Sons, 1994.
10. G. De Giacomo and M. Lenzerini. Description logics with inverse roles, functional restrictions, and n-ary relations. In *Proc. 4th European Workshop on Logics in Artificial Intelligence (JELIA-94)*, number 838 in Lecture Notes In Artificial Intelligence, pages 332–346. Springer-Verlag, 1994.
11. G. De Giacomo and F. Masacci. Tableaux and algorithms for propositional dynamic logic with converse. In M. A. McRobbie and J.K. Slaney, editors, *Proc. 13th Int'l Conf. on Automated Deduction*, volume 1104 of *Lecture Notes in Artificial Intelligence*, pages 613–627. Springer-Verlag, 1996.

12. E. Grädel, Ph. G. Kolaitis, and M. Y. Vardi. The decision problem for 2-variable first-order logic. *Bulletin of Symbolic Logic*, 3:53–69, 1997.
13. E. Grädel, M. Otto, and E. Rosen. Undecidability results for two-variable logics. Unpublished manuscript, 1996.
14. C.S. Jutla. Determinization and memoryless winning strategies. *Information and Computation*, 133(2):117–134, 1997.
15. Ph.G. Kolaitis and M.Y. Vardi. On the expressive power of variable-confined logics. In *Proc. 11th IEEE Symp. on Logic in Computer Science*, pages 348–359, 1996.
16. D. Kozen. Results on the propositional μ-calculus. *Theoretical Computer Science*, 27:333–354, 1983.
17. D. Kozen. A finite model theorem for the propositional μ-calculus. *Studia Logica*, 47(3):333–354, 1988.
18. O. Kupferman and A. Pnueli. Once and for all. In *Proc. 10th IEEE Symposium on Logic in Computer Science*, pages 25–35, San Diego, June 1995.
19. O. Kupferman and M.Y. Vardi. Weak alternating automata and tree automata emptiness. In *Proc. 30th ACM Symposium on Theory of Computing*, Dallas, 1998.
20. O. Lichtenstein, A. Pnueli, and L. Zuck. The glory of the past. In *Logics of Programs*, volume 193 of *Lecture Notes in Computer Science*, pages 196–218, Brooklyn, June 1985. Springer-Verlag.
21. D.E. Muller, A. Saoudi, and P. E. Schupp. Weak alternating automata give a simple explanation of why most temporal and dynamic logics are decidable in exponential time. In *Proceedings 3rd IEEE Symposium on Logic in Computer Science*, pages 422–427, Edinburgh, July 1988.
22. D.E. Muller and P.E. Schupp. Alternating automata on infinite trees. *Theoretical Computer Science*, 54,:267–276, 1987.
23. D. Park. Finiteness is μ-ineffable. *Theoretical Computer Science*, 3:173–181, 1976.
24. S. Pinter and P. Wolper. A temporal logic for reasoning about partially ordered computations. In *Proc. 3rd ACM Symposium on Principles of Distributed Computing*, pages 28–37, Vancouver, August 1984.
25. A. Pnueli. In transition from global to modular temporal reasoning about programs. In K. Apt, editor, *Logics and Models of Concurrent Systems*, volume F-13 of *NATO Advanced Summer Institutes*, pages 123–144. Springer-Verlag, 1985.
26. A. Pnueli and R. Rosner. On the synthesis of a reactive module. In *Proc. 16th ACM Symposium on Principles of Programming Languages*, Austin, January 1989.
27. V.R. Pratt. A decidable μ-calculus: preliminary report. In *Proc. 22nd IEEE Symposium on Foundation of Computer Science*, pages 421–427, 1981.
28. S. Safra. On the complexity of ω-automata. In *Proc. 29th IEEE Symposium on Foundations of Computer Science*, pages 319–327, White Plains, October 1988.
29. G. Slutzki. Alternating tree automata. *Theoretical Computer Science*, 41:305–318, 1985.
30. R.S. Streett. Propositional dynamic logic of looping and converse. *Information and Control*, 54:121–141, 1982.
31. R.S. Streett and E.A. Emerson. An automata theoretic decision procedure for the propositional mu-calculus. *Information and Computation*, 81(3):249–264, 1989.
32. S.S. Streett. *A propositional dynamic logic for reasoning about program divergence*. PhD thesis, M.Sc. Thesis, MIT, 1980.
33. W. Thomas. Languages, automata, and logic. *Handbook of Formal Language Theory*, III:389–455, 1997.
34. M.Y. Vardi. The taming of converse: Reasoning about two-way computations. In *Logic of Programs Workshop*, volume 193, pages 413–424, Brooklyn, June 1985. Lecture Notes in Computer Science, Springer-Verlag.

35. M.Y. Vardi. A temporal fixpoint calculus. In *Proc. 15th ACM Symp. on Principles of Programming Languages*, pages 250–259, San Diego, January 1988.
36. M.Y. Vardi. Alternating automata – unifying truth and validity checking for temporal logics. In W. McCune, editor, *Proc. 14th International Conference on Automated Deduction*, volume 1249 of *Lecture Notes in Artificial Intelligence*, pages 191–206. Springer-Verlag, Berlin, july 1997.
37. M.Y. Vardi. What makes modal logic so robustly decidable? In *Descriptive Complexity and Finite Models*, pages 149–183. American Mathematical Society, 1997.
38. M.Y. Vardi and P. Wolper. Automata-theoretic techniques for modal logics of programs. *Journal of Computer and System Science*, 32(2):182–221, April 1986.

A Neuroidal Architecture for Cognitive Computation*

Leslie G. Valiant

Division of Engineering and Applied Sciences
Harvard University
Cambridge, MA 02138

Abstract. An architecture is described for designing systems that acquire and manipulate large amounts of unsystematized, or so-called commonsense, knowledge. Its aim is to exploit to the full those aspects of computational learning that are known to offer powerful solutions in the acquisition and maintenance of robust knowledge bases. The architecture makes explicit the requirements on the basic computational tasks that are to be performed and is designed to make these computationally tractable even for very large databases. The main claims are that (i) the basic learning tasks are tractable and (ii) tractable learning offers viable approaches to a range of issues that have been previously identified as problematic for artificial intelligence systems that are entirely programmed. In particular, attribute efficiency holds a central place in the definition of the learning tasks, as does also the capability to handle relational information efficiently. Among the issues that learning offers to resolve are robustness to inconsistencies, robustness to incomplete information and resolving among alternatives.

1 Introduction

We take the view that intelligence is a large scale computational phenomenon. It is associated with large amounts of knowledge, abilities to manipulate this knowledge to derive conclusions about situations not previously experienced, the capability to acquire more knowledge, and the ability to learn and apply strategies of some complexity. The large scale nature of the phenomenon suggests two prerequisites for constructing artificial systems with these characteristics. First, some theoretical basis has to be found within which the various apparent impediments to this endeavor that have been identified can be addressed systematically. Second, some large-scale experiments need to be conducted to validate the suggested basis – it is possible that the fundamental phenomena do not scale *down* and that small-scale experiments do not throw light on them.

Much effort has been devoted to identifying such a theoretical basis. One major thrust has been to develop definitions of capabilities that are functionally

* This research was supported in part by grants NSF-CCR-95-04436, ONR-N00014-96-1-0550, and ARO-DAAL-03-92-G-0115

adequate. Functionalities that, even if realized, would not go far towards achieving a significant level of performance are of little interest. Another thrust has been the search for capabilities that are demonstrably computationally feasible. Functionalities that are computationally intractable are again of little direct interest. A third viewpoint is that of biological plausibility. Perhaps an understanding of how cortex is constrained to perform these tasks would suggest specific mechanisms that the other viewpoints are not able to provide.

The hypothesis of this paper is that for intelligent systems to be realized the sought after theoretical basis has not only to be discovered, but needs to be embodied in an *architecture* that offers guidelines for constructing them. Composed as these systems will be of possibly numerous components, each performing a different function, and each connected to the others in a possibly complex overall design, there will need to be some unity of nature among the components, their interfaces, and the mechanisms they use.

We shall describe a candidate for such an architecture. This candidate emerged from a study that attempted to look at the issues of functional adequacy, computational feasibility and biological constraints together [52]. We call the architecture *neuroidal* since it respects the most basic constraints imposed by that model of neural computation. One feature of that study was that it was a "whole systems" study. It addressed a range of issues simultaneously insisting on biological and computational feasibility, plausible and simple interactions with the outside world, and adequate explanations about the internal control of the system. While definitions of intelligence, thinking and consciousness have all proved elusive, it appears that the basic computational substrate that neural systems have to support to realize these phenomena might be identified more easily. We believe that the functions and mechanisms associated with this substrate characterize an area and style of computation that is suitably referred to as *cognitive computation.*

In abstracting an AI architecture from that neural study, as we do here, we dispense with some of the most onerous constraints considered there to be imposed by biology. In the mammalian brain these constraints include, among others, the sparsity of the interconnections among the components, the inaccessibility of the separate components to an external teacher or trainer, and certain bounds on the weights of individual synapses. In artificial systems these constraints are not fundamental, and in order to maximize the computational power of the architecture we will free ourselves of them here.

Our purpose in describing the architecture is to suggest it as a basis for large scale experiments. The first critical question we ask is whether it is theoretically adequate: Can some of the obstacles that have been identified by researchers be solved, in principle, within the model? Are there further fundamental obstacles? The second critical question, which will need to be resolved empirically, is whether systems based on this architecture can indeed be constructed, that exhibit the phenomena outlined in our first paragraph to a more significantly extent than current systems.

As to the first question we observe that the McCulloch-Pitts model may be viewed as a valid architecture for intelligence, if one accepts threshold elements as representing the basic steps of cortical computation. Its shortcoming, clearly, is that it does not appear to offer useful guidelines for constructing systems.

Our architecture, in contrast, is designed to provide a design methodology. In particular, its main feature is that it comes with a set of associated algorithms and mechanisms. The basic constituents of the architecture are classical enough, being *circuit units* consisting of linear threshold elements, and short term memory devices called *image units.* The novelty is that for aggregates of such devices we can detail how the accompanying mechanisms can perform, at least in principle, a list of tasks that address significant problems. The bulk of this paper is devoted to enumerating these problems and describing how they can be addressed. Our purpose here is to point out that this broad variety of mechanisms can be supported on this single unified architecture, and that together, they go some way toward addressing an impressive array of problems.

There will remain the second question as to how to validate the architecture. As we shall suggest, this raises pragmatic issues that had previously received only limited attention. The mechanisms provided emphasize the centrality of learning for multiple purposes, from basic knowledge acquisition to ensuring robust behavior. To construct a system one would need to do a high level design as well as, possibly, some programming, although the main benefit of the architecture is the potential for *massive knowledge infusion* by learning.

If one is to realize a capability for massive knowledge infusion, we expect that there will be needed a significant new kind of effort directed towards the *preparation of teaching materials.* Ideally available resources such as dictionaries and annotated corpora of text should be usable. However, since the system will not operate identically to humans, the teaching materials needed cannot be expected to be identical to those that are effective for humans. The system and teaching materials need to be chosen so as to fit each other, and we believe that the development of these in tandem is a major challenge for future research. Although, clearly, there is much data available in natural language form, aside from the issue of natural language understanding, there is the independent question of whether these materials, without annotations, make explicit all the commonsense and other information that would be needed.

To summarize, the main feature of the architecture is that it brings learning to the heart of the general AI problem. Recent advances in machine learning help us to distinguish those aspects of learning that have very effective computational solutions, from those for which none is known. Thus in a learning task the problem of finding new compound features that are particularly effective is not one to which general effective solutions are known. In contrast, we know that the presence of irrelevant features can be tolerated in very large numbers, without degrading learning performance, for some classes of functions. Our proposal is that these insights be incorporated into the design of AI systems. We claim that this approach does offer a new view of some of the now traditional issues of AI. It also raises some new questions particularly with regard to the training of such systems.

On a historical note it is interesting to recall Turing's 1950 paper on "Computing Machinery and Intelligence" in which he describes his "Test". While he considers the possibility that a programmed system might be built to solve it, he appears to come out in favor of a learning machine. In the subsequent history of research on general intelligent systems, the overwhelming emphasis has been on programmed systems. We believe that this was largely because there existed a mathematical basis for following this avenue, namely mathematical logic. However, in the intervening years there has been much progress both on the theoretical foundations of machine learning, as well as in the experimental study of learning algorithms. It is, therefore, appropriate now to reexamine whether a synthesis can be found that resolves Turing's dilemma.

2 The Architecture

A system having the proposed architecture is composed of a number of *circuit units* and a number of *image units.* The image units can be thought of as the *working memory* of the system. During reasoning processes that is where the intermediate results of the reasoning computations are stored. The circuit units are the long term repositories of knowledge. Their behavior can be updated *by both inductive learning and explicit programming.*

The circuit units are defined so as to ensure that they provably have certain desirable learning capabilities. For this reason, we define them to consist of one layer of linear threshold gates or elements. The circuit units have one layer of inputs that are the inputs to these gates, and one layer of outputs that are the outputs of the gates themselves. The weights of the threshold elements can be either learned or programmed.

The intention is that each gate recognize some predicate. We say that it "fires" if such recognition has occurred in the sense that the output has taken value one or "true". The inputs may be Boolean or real valued. The latter is needed if some of the input devices or image units produce numerical values (or if we go outside the strict model by allowing, for example, the outputs, of gates to be numerical functions of the linear sums.).

The image units are short term repositories of information with unspecified format. Their outputs are regarded as preprogrammed *feature* detectors and the inputs include preprogrammed *inverse features.* For Boolean outputs, each output feature will have value one for some information contents and zero for others. As input the image may take information from a sensory device such as a camera. In addition the inputs to an image unit may be of the form of inverse features that modify the contents of the image so as to make some associated feature detectors fire. For example, the image unit may have a feature detector that fires if the image contains a depiction of an elephant, and it may also have an inverse feature that can create in the image the illusion of an elephant in the sense that the information it creates in the image makes the elephant feature detector fire. Thus image units can be used both to store information received from the outside world through sensory devices, as well as to store "imaginary constructs" that are useful for the system's internal computational processes. It is possible to have a number of such constructs in the image simultaneously in a novel combination. The system can then bring the power of its circuits to bear on a representation of a complex situation not previously represented in it. Both preprogrammed features and preprogrammed inverse features can be composed using the circuit units to create nodes that act as higher level features or inverse features. Thus the elephant instance may be more plausibly realized at a higher level in a hierarchy.

The circuit and image units will be composed together in a block diagram so that the outputs of some of the units are identified with the inputs of others. Typically image units will interface directly with circuit units, rather than other image units. Some inputs are identified with the outputs of input devices, and some outputs with the inputs of output devices. The block diagram may ultimately contain feedback or cycles.

Some rules are further specified for how the circuits can change in the process of knowledge acquisition. For the gates, linear threshold units in our case, some update rules are given, such as the perceptron algorithm [42] or Winnow [26], that specify the supervised inductive learning process. In addition some further rules are given to allow the acquisition of programmed knowledge. In particular new output gates may be added and the parameters or weights of that gate assigned appropriate values so that it fires under the intended conditions. These added gates can then also serve as targets for inductive learning or as inputs to other units. One method of adding to the circuit is to add gates to represent various fixed functions of existing nodes so as to enrich the feature space. Thus one may add nodes that compute the conjunction of all pairs from a certain set of existing nodes. Another method of programming a circuit is to change a weight between an existing pair of nodes. Thus, one can create a subcircuit to realize "grass $\Rightarrow$ green" by making the weight from the node representing "grass" to that representing "green" larger than the threshold.

2.1 Overview

We shall outline here the properties that are required for a device to be an image unit. In the section to follow we shall describe one particular realization of image units that is based on predicate calculus and highlights how our approach can be used to generalize the capabilities of logic based AI systems.

An image unit will at any instant contain some data that we call the *scene* S. The scene itself consists of a number of *objects* $a_1, \cdots, a_s$ as well as information about the properties of the objects and about the relationships amongst them. This information may be represented, in principle, in any number of ways, of which predicate calculus is one.

The computational *processes* that we describe are entirely in terms of interactions between the circuit units and the image units. Since we are free to limit the number of *objects* in the image units to some moderate number Ω, say equal to 10, we are able to limit *ab initio* the computational cost of the so-called binding problem, that grows with this number.

Even when we use standard logical notation to describe the contents of the image or to label circuit nodes, our interpretation of it is slightly different from the usual. In particular the objects in our architecture are best viewed as internal artifacts in the system. They are not intended to refer to the external world in the same direct way as in more familiar uses of the predicate calculus. Further, the primary *semantics* that we ascribe to nodes in the system are the PAC semantics described in the next section, rather than the standard semantics of predicate calculus.

Each node of a circuit unit is in some state. Most simply, it is in one of two states that indicates whether or not the predicate is true of the current scene in the image unit. However, it can contain further information, such as a real number that expresses a confidence level for the validity of the predicate. (c.f. neuroids in [52]).

Each node can be thought of as representing an existentially quantified relation, e.g.

$$\exists x_1 \, \exists x_2 \, \exists x_3 \; R(x_1, x_2, x_3)$$

where the existentially quantified variables range over the objects $a_1, \cdots, a_\Omega$ in the scene. The threshold will *fire*, in general, if this expression holds for the current scene. While no general assumptions are made about how R is represented, it is assumed that when this relation is recognized to hold for the current scene, a corresponding *binding*, or mapping θ from $\{x_1, x_2, x_3\} \rightarrow \{a_1, \cdots, a_\Omega\}$ is made explicit in the system. For brevity, where this leads to no ambiguity, we shall use R variously to refer to the predicate computed, the value of the predicate or to the node itself.

An aggregate of circuit units is a directed graph in which each pair of nodes that is connected is associated with a *weight*. Each node has an update function that updates its state as a function of its previous state, the states of nodes from which there are directed edges to it as well as the weights of these edges. More particularly each circuit unit is a directed graph of depth one (i.e. one layer of input nodes, one layer of output nodes, and no "hidden layer") and the update functions are linear threshold functions.

An important aspect of the circuits is that a directed edge from node representing R_1 to a node representing R_2 contains binding information called the *connection binding* $R_1 \rightarrow R_2$. If the nodes represent $\exists x_1 \exists x_2 \exists x_3 R_1(x_1, x_2, x_3)$ and $\exists y_1 \exists y_2 \exists y_3 R_2(y_1, y_2, y_3)$ then the binding information could specify, for example, that x_1 and y_2 have to represent the same object but that x_2, x_3, y_1 and y_3 may be objects arbitrarily different from each other. For this reason there may be *several* connections from R_1 to R_2, each one corresponding to a different connection binding and having a different weight. For example, if R_2 represents the notion of grandparent and R_1 that of parent then in the definition of the former one may wish to invoke the latter twice with different bindings.

The scene S in an image unit contains information about which relations hold for which object sets. An aggregate of circuit units can be evaluated for S node by node. For a node that represents relation $\exists x_1, \cdots, \exists x_i R(x_1, \cdots, x_i)$

the set of all bindings $\theta\{x_1, \cdots, x_i\} \to \{a_1, \cdots, a_\Omega\}$ that make R hold will be evaluated. If the node R has inputs from nodes R_1 and R_2, and the gate at R evaluates the threshold function $R_1 + R_2 \geq 2$, then R will fire for a binding θ if *there exist* bindings θ_1, θ_2 of the variables of R_1 and R_2 that respect the respective connection bindings $R_1 \to R$ and $R_2 \to R$, and make both R_1 and R_2 true. We shall expand on this in the next section.

2.2 An Implementation

We shall describe an implementation that is based on predicate calculus, but extends it in the direction advocated in this paper, so as to allow for effective learning, with attribute efficiency and error resilience. In particular, a programmed system in which knowledge is described as *Horn clauses*, and *modus ponens* is used as the rule of inference, can be embedded into this framework. The central role in AI systems of this language of description is discussed by Russell and Norvig ([45] pp 265-277). We are claiming, therefore, that in at least this one possible implementation of our architecture, it is the case that a significant class of existing programmed systems can be embedded. Systems so embedded would then have the addition benefits of a powerful learning capability.

Let us consider the following restriction of the language of predicate calculus (e.g. [45] p. 186). As constants we will choose the base objects $A_B = \{a_1, \cdots, a_\Omega\}$ of the image unit. We allow a set R_B of base relations of arities that are arbitrary but upper bounded by a constant α. We use no function symbols. We represent variable names by $\{x_1, \cdots, x_n\}$ and relations will be defined in terms of these.

The two features of predicate calculus that we exclude, therefore, are constants that refer directly to individuals in the world (e.g. Shakespeare), and functions that can be applied to them to refer to other individuals (e.g. Mother_of (Shakespeare).). In our system the only constants are the predefined base objects of the image, which are internal constructs of the systems. In order to refer to an individual like Shakespeare we shall use a unary predicate that can be applied to a base object. Thus Shakespeare(a_3) would express the fact that a_3 has the attributes of Shakespeare. Also, we dispense with function symbols by referring to the resulting object as a base object, and by expressing the necessary relation by an appropriate relation symbol. Thus instead of saying $x_1 =$ Mother_of(x_2) we would say Mother_of(x_1, x_2), where the latter is a binary relation. In these ways we ensure that the two linguistic restrictions, on constants and functions symbols, do not restrict what can be expressed.

A *term* will be therefore a base object a_i and an *atomic sentence* will be a single relation such as Mother_of $\in R_B$ applied to one or a collection of base objects (e.g. Mother_of(a_3, a_7).) A Horn *rule* will be an implication

$$R_{i_1}(x_{i_1,1}, \cdots x_{i_1,\delta(i_1)}) \wedge \cdots \wedge R_{i_r}(x_{i_r,1}, \cdots, x_{i_r,\delta(i_r)}) \Rightarrow R_{i_{r+1}}(x_{i_{r+1},1}, \cdots, x_{i_{r+1},\delta(i_{r+1})}). \quad (1)$$

where $R_{i_j} \in R_B$ and $\delta(k)$ is the arity of $R_k \in R_B$. We note that R_B may include the relation False that has zero arguments, that signifies logical impossibility and may be used meaningfully for $R_{i_{r+1}}$ on the right-hand side of an implication. Implications are to be interpreted as quantified universally over all the x variables that occur in them but these quantifiers are omitted for brevity.

A *binding* is a mapping from $\{x_1, \cdots, x_n\}$ to $\{a_1, \cdots, a_\Omega\}$. We say that a relation $R(x_1, x_2, x_3)$ is made true by θ if $R(\theta(x_1), \theta(x_2), \theta(x_3))$, or $R(\theta(\underline{x}))$ for short, holds. The derivation rule *modus ponens* is the following:

> "if $R_{i_1}(\underline{x}) \wedge \cdots \wedge R_{i_r}(\underline{x}) \Rightarrow R_{i_{r+1}}(\underline{x})$" is a rule,
> and if, for some binding θ, $R_{i_j}(\theta(\underline{x}))$ holds for $1 \leq j \leq r$,
> then $R_{i_{r+1}}(\theta(\underline{x}))$ also holds.

In a logic based system we would program a set of rules of the form (1) and consider the input to be a set of atomic sentences. We could then consider the output to be the set of all atomic sentences that can be deduced from the input by applying the rules using modus ponens in all possible ways. This output could be derived in the logical framework by means of forward chaining ([45]p. 273.).

Let us now describe the implementation of the neuroidal architecture into which this process embeds naturally. In this implementation the contents of the image will be simply the atomic sentences of the input. The circuits will implement the rules as follows: For each relation $R(\underline{x}) \in R_B$ there will be a gate in the circuit. We shall assume that each relation R occurs on the right-hand side in just one rule – otherwise we replace multiple occurrences of R on the right hand side by different names, say $R^1, R^2, \cdots, R^m$ and add a new rule $R^1 \vee R^2 \vee \cdots \vee R^m \Rightarrow R$.

For each Horn rule $R_{i_1} \wedge R_{i_2} \wedge \cdots \wedge R_{i_r} \Rightarrow R_{i_{r+1}}$ we shall make a *connection* to $R_{i_{r+1}}$ from each R_{i_j} $(1 \leq j \leq r)$. This connection will have the appropriate *connection binding*, defined below. At the $R_{i_{r+1}}$ node we shall implement the equivalent of an AND gate in terms of a threshold gate with threshold r. In other words, we regard the values of the R_{i_j} as Boolean $\{0, 1\}$, and have a gate that realizes.

$$R_{i_{r+1}} = 1 \quad \text{if and only if} \quad \sum_{j=1}^{r} R_{i_j} \geq r.$$

Executing this threshold gate will correspond, therefore, to performing one application of modus ponens.

To simulate OR gates, which are needed if multiple occurrences of the same relation occurs on the right hand side, we also use a threshold gate but have 1 as the threshold instead of r, i.e. $\sum R_{i_k} \geq 1$.

The further detail that needs to be clarified is the nature and meaning of the connection bindings. Each rule with r relations on the left defines r connections and connection bindings. Consider the following rule with $r = 2$:

$$R_1(x_1, x_2, x_3) \wedge R_2(x_3, x_4, x_5) \Rightarrow R_3(x_2, x_3, x_5). \tag{2}$$

This notation expresses the connection bindings implicitly. The binding of the connection from R_1 to R_3 says simply that the second parameter of R_1 binds with the first parameter of R_3 and the third parameter of R_1 with the second of R_3, and that there are no other constraints. The naming of the variables in each rule or gate can express this precisely. Note that in this example the implication is that any binding of x_1 that makes R_1 true can be combined with any binding for x_4 that makes R_2 true. For example, if elsewhere, we have the rules $R_4(x_7) \Rightarrow R_1(x_7, x_8, x_9)$ and $R_4(x_7) \Rightarrow R_2(x_{10}, x_7, x_{11})$, then it will be sufficient for these rules to be satisfied for distinct values of $\theta(x_7)$ since (2) did not require otherwise.

If *from* some R_i there is more than one connection, then for conceptual purposes it is simplest to think about a circuit in which the R_i is replicated so that each node has just one connection directed away from it and hence the circuit is a tree. In other words connection bindings restrict the multiple inputs to a node but never the multiple outputs. Note also that any correspondence between two variables occurring in two relations on the left hand side (i.e. x_3 in this example,) can be enforced only by having x_3 as an explicit variable in the right hand side relation, (i.e. R_3 in the example.) This can be circumvented by defining a node that represents a particular compound relation e.g. we could create a gate for computing $R_1(x_1, x_2, x_3) \wedge R_2(x_3, x_4, x_5)$, call it $R_5(x_2, x_5)$ and have an implication $R_5(x_2, x_5) \Rightarrow R_3(x_2, x_5)$ if we wish to avoid mentioning x_3 in R_3.

In this implementation we consider the network to evaluate for each gate all *possible* bindings $\theta : \{x_1, \cdots, x_n\} \rightarrow \{a_1, \cdots, a_\Omega\}$ so as to find all the ones, if any, that make the gate evaluate to one. To do this we shall, for simplicity, impose here the constraint that aggregates of circuit units are acyclic. We can then form a topological sort of their nodes (e.g. Knuth [23]) and for one such topologically sorted order evaluate each node in succession. The evaluation of each node is for all the Ω^d bindings θ, where $d < \alpha$ is the arity of the relation R at that node. (Allowing cycles would allow recursive rules to be expressed, but would make the evaluation mechanisms more complex. If the circuits express Horn rules, or other rules in which no negative weights occur, then evaluating circuits with cycles can still be done in time polynomial in Ω^α and the number of gates.)

In this graph the input nodes with no predecessors will represent relations themselves. To evaluate a gate at R, we simply enumerate all the Ω^d bindings of the d variables that appear in it. First we scan all the atomic sentences in the image that contain R and see which bindings make R true, before any rules are applied. Then for each binding, and for each predecessor node, if any, we determine whether that binding can make the predecessor true. Having done this for each predecessor, we can, for each binding compute the value of the gate at the current node, whether it is a disjunction, conjunction, or more generally, an arbitrary linear threshold gate. Note that the complexity of this task that is contributed by the binding problem is Ω^d. It is exponential in the *maximum arity* of the relations, and not in the number of base objects or the number of relations in a rule! (Note, however that this arity may be made larger by the restriction that all binding information is in the connections. This necessitates that if some correspondences among the variables need to be enforced on the left hand side of a rule, they must be made explicit on the right hand side. For example if we wish to represent father$(x, z) \wedge$ mother$(z, y) \Rightarrow$ grandfather(x, y) then in our representation grandfather will need to have a third argument, say t, that is to be identified with the two occurrences of z by the connection bindings.)

It is easy to verify that this evaluation algorithm computes all satisfying bindings for each relation that is represented at some node, in exactly the same way as would applying modus ponens in all possible ways to the rules.

From what has been said it should be clear that our architecture is expressive enough that programmed systems based on the Horn rules we have described and modus ponens can be embedded into it. What the architecture adds to such systems is a capability for learning. The point is that the gates we allow are not just Boolean conjunctions and disjunctions, but linear threshold functions. This allows a host of learning algorithms, discussed in later sections, that provide a provable learning capability that is not known to be available in strictly logical representations.

In conclusion we note that there are theoretical results that show for certain classes of Boolean functions that extending the representation of the learner to threshold functions makes the original class polynomial time learnable, while restricting the learner to the minimal representation needed for expressing these functions would make the task NP-compete [40]. Our richer representation, therefore, has not only the obvious advantage of being able to express more, but has the additional computational benefits of making Boolean domains potentially easier to learn. Also, while the quoted result discusses the polynomial time criterion for learning, as we shall discuss at length, we also desire and seek the further advantages that learning be achieved with attribute-efficiency and error-resilience.

3 Semantics

We cannot expect to develop a set of robust mechanisms for processing representations of knowledge without a robust semantics for the representation. The emphasis here is both on the necessity of *semantics*, that relates the representation to some reality beyond itself, as well as *robustness* to the many uncertainties, changes and errors in the world or in communications with the world, that the system will need to cope with.

The need for semantics has explained the attractiveness of formal logic in AI research. It is the need for robustness that forces us to look beyond logic, at notions centered on learning. The semantics we shall describe here, PAC *circuit semantics*, or PAC *semantics* for short, is based on the notion of computationally feasible learning of functions that are probably approximately correct [50].

To explain the contrast in viewpoints consider the situation calculus described in McCarthy and Hayes [30]. There, a situation is "the complete state of the world", and general facts are relations among situations. Thus $P \Rightarrow Q$ means that for all situations for which P holds Q holds also. This is an all embracing claim about the universe that is difficult to grade gracefully and becomes problematic in the real world where authoritative definitions of P and Q themselves may be difficult to identify.

In contrast, PAC semantics makes qualified behavioral assertions about the computational behavior of a particular system in a particular environment. In PAC semantics P and Q would be defined as functions computed by fixed algorithms or circuits within a system that takes input through a fixed feature set from a fixed but arbitrarily complex world. The inputs range over a set X that consists of all possible combinations of feature values that the input feature detectors can detect. There is a probability distribution D over this set X that summarizes the world in all the aspects that are discernible to the feature detectors of the system. The P and Q could correspond to nodes in a circuit. The relationship between P and Q would be typically of the following form: if a random example is taken from D that satisfies P, then it also satisfies Q with a certain probability. The latter would, at best, be known to be in some range with a certain confidence. Thus the semantics is relative to both the computational and sensory abilities of the system, and refers to an outside world about which direct observations can be made only one observation at a time. The claims that are made about the semantics do not go beyond what is empirically verifiable in a computational feasible way by the system operating in the world. In addition to making observations from D, the system can also acquire rules by being told them. It can then use these as working hypotheses, subject to subsequent empirical testing by the system in the PAC sense, and make deductions using them. The general goal of the system is to learn from D the invariants of the world.

In constructing an artificial system we envisage that each circuit unit can be trained separately. The unit will take as inputs the outputs of input devices or other circuit or image units to which it is connected. Thus it would see the world through a set of features that are themselves filtered through the input devices and circuits of the system. In contrast, the outputs of the unit being trained will be directly accessible to the trainer, who can venture to train each such output to behave as is desired. We note that if the system consists of a chain of circuit units trained in sequence in the above manner then the errors in one circuit do not necessarily propagate to the next. Each circuit will be accurate in the PAC sense as a function of the external inputs – the fact that intermediate levels of gates only approximate the functions that the trainer intended is not necessarily harmful. At each internal level these internal feature sets may permit accurate PAC learning at that next stage.

Since our architecture can perform computations via the image units that are more dynamic than the conventional view of circuits allows the terminology of circuits is best viewed as an analogy. The more general computational functions of the system, including those that use the image for reasoning as outlined in §4.8, for example, all need to be effective in the PAC sense.

The key advantage of PAC semantics is that it gives an intellectual basis for understanding learning and thereby validates empiricism and procedural views of knowledge. Inductive learning will be the key to overcoming the impediments that are to be enumerated in the next section. These will include defaults, non-monotonic reasoning, inconsistent data, and resolving among alternatives. Intelligent systems will inevitably meet the dilemmas that these issues raise but they will have a learned response to all but the rarer manifestations of them.

We mention that PAC learning, when offered as a basis for intelligent systems or cognitive science, suggests the following view. The world is arbitrarily complex and there is little hope that any system will ever be able to describe it in detail. Nevertheless by learning some simple computational circuits such systems can learn to cope, even in a world as complex as it is. Most often these circuits will be deterministic. It is the complexities of the world and the uncertainties in the system's interactions with it that force the framework of the semantics to be probabilistic.

Having circuits that have a probabilistic rather than a deterministic interpretation is an extension that may be considered, but this appears to make the learning task computationally less tractable [17]. There is little evidence that probabilistic processes are central to human reasoning [49]. While we do not exclude extensions to probabilistic representations, we do not consider them here.

4 Some Algorithmic Mechanisms

In this section we shall enumerate a series of algorithmic techniques for manipulating knowledge in a system having the described architecture. We claim that these mechanisms address issues that are inescapable for large scale learning based AI systems. The mechanisms described here arose in the main in studies of formal models of various specific phenomena. Our observation is that they can be brought together and adapted to provide an overall methodology within a single framework.

4.1 Conflict Resolution

The circuit units will contain large numbers of nodes. In general each one corresponds to a concept or action, that has some reference to the world or to the internal constructs of the image unit. The semantics of each node can be defined in the PAC sense. Let us suppose that each one when regarded separately, is highly accurate, correct say on 99% of the natural input distribution. The problem that arises is that because of the sheer number of nodes, perhaps in the hundreds of thousands, on almost any one input a large number of the nodes will be inaccurate.

In a natural scene we may expect a certain moderate number of predicates that are represented in the circuits to hold and the corresponding nodes to fire. However, the large numbers of remaining predicates will be represented with some inaccuracy, a certain number of these additional nodes that should not fire will do so also. Further some of these will be in semantic conflict with the correct ones. They may recommend inconsistent actions (e.g. "go left" as opposed to "go right") or inconsistent classifications (e.g. "horse" versus "dog".)

This is a fundamental and inescapable issue for which a technical solution is needed. A conventional approach is to suggest that each node be given a numerical "strength", and that in situations where several nodes fire in conflict the one with highest strength be chosen to be the operative one. This approach clearly needs some concrete technical mechanism for deriving the strengths. It also makes the assumption, which needs justification, that a single totally ordered set of numerical strengths is sufficient for the overall resolving process.

Our approach is the following: we have a large number of circuit nodes, computing functions $x_1, \cdots, x_n$, say, of the scene S. We assume that each x_i is correct in the PAC sense with high probability. Because of the sheer size of n, at any one time many of the x_i nodes will fire falsely, and we need a mechanism for resolving among them. The proposed solution is to have another set $y_1, \cdots, y_n$ of nodes where y_i corresponds to x_i. The purpose of y_i is the following: When y_i fires this will be taken to assert that x_i is true, and further that x_i is *preferred* over all the other x_j that may be firing. The implementation will have a circuit unit with x_j $(1 \leq j \leq n)$ as inputs and y_i $(1 \leq i \leq n)$ as outputs, and with a connection from each x_j to each y_i. Each y_i will be a linear threshold functions of the x_j. Thus if x_7, when firing, is to be preferred to all the x_j except for x_2, x_5 and x_8, whose firing should override that of x_7, then the appropriate linear inequality to be computed at y_7 will be

$$x_7 - x_2 - x_5 - x_8 \geq 1. \tag{3}$$

This will have the effect that y_7 will fire if and only if x_7 fires and none of x_2, x_5 or x_8 fires.

The force of this approach is two-fold. First, it is more expressive than the totally ordered strengths regime. For each x_i one can specify which x_j dominate it, independently of the other x_i. Second, the representation needed for expressing the preferences, namely linear threshold functions, are learnable in a very favorable sense as further discussed in subsection 4.2 below.

We are therefore suggesting that the conflict resolution problem can be solved by learning the correct resolutions from examples of past behavior. The justification of our architecture can be viewed as the possibility of repeated use of this same idea: that learning can resolve many otherwise fundamentally problematic issues, and that it can be realized effectively by the algorithms we describe. We chose to discuss the conflict resolution problem here, at the beginning, since it seems a particularly simple and convincing instance.

4.2 Learning From Few Cases

The problem with advocating systems based on massive knowledge bases is that one needs to specify mechanisms for coping with the issues of scale. In the previous section, for example, we suggested that a learning mechanism for linear threshold functions can address the issue of conflict resolution. As we shall invoke learning as the solution to a variety of other issues also, it is necessary to address the problem that the learning process itself has to face in the presence of a massive knowledge base.

The basic issue is fundamental and widely recognized. If there are n functions represented in the system, and each one can depend on any of the $n-1$ others, as a linear threshold (or some other) function, then there are potentially about n^2 parameters. Since n is large, say in the tens of thousands, n^2 is very large. With this backdrop it is a remarkable fact that biological learning systems appear to be able to learn from relatively few examples, certainly much fewer than reasonable estimates of the n (or n^2.) Some mechanism needs to be present to enable very high dimensional systems to learn from numbers of interactions with the world that are very small compared with this dimension.

The most relevant theory we know of how this can be done is that of *attribute-efficient learnability.* The phenomenon here is that for certain function classes of n variables one can *prove* that certain learning algorithms converge to a good hypothesis after a number of examples that depends on n not linearly, the canonical situation from dimensionality arguments, but much more slowly, sometimes *logarithmically.*

The phenomenon of efficient attribute efficient learning in the PAC sense was first pointed out by Haussler [13]. A striking and remarkable embodiment of this idea followed in the form of Littlestone's Winnow algorithm [26] for learning linear threshold functions. The algorithm is similar in form to the classical perceptron algorithm except that the updates to the weights are multiplicative rather than additive. The modification gives the algorithm the remarkable property that when learning a monotone k-variable Boolean disjunction over $\{x_1, \cdots, x_n\}$ the number of examples needed for convergence, whether in the PAC or mistake-bounded sense, is upper bounded by $ck \log_2 n$, where c is a small constant, [26, 27]. Thus the sample complexity is linear in k, the number of relevant variables, and logarithmic in the number of irrelevant ones.

Littlestone's Theorem 9 [26] adapted to the case when coefficients can be both positive and negative (his Example 6) has the following more general statement; For $X \subseteq \{0,1\}^n$ suppose that for the functions $g : X \to \{0,1\}$ there exist $\nu_1, \nu_2, \cdots, \nu_n \geq 0$ and $\bar{\nu}_1, \bar{\nu}_2, \cdots, \bar{\nu}_n \geq 0$ such that for all $(x_1, \cdots, x_n) \in X$

$$\textstyle\sum_{i=1}^n (\nu_i x_i + \bar{\nu}_i(1-x_i)) \geq 1 \quad \text{if} \quad g(x_1, \cdots, x_n) = 1$$

and

$$\textstyle\sum_{i=1}^n (\nu_i x_i + \bar{\nu}_i(1-x_i)) \leq 1 - \delta \ \text{ if } \ g(x_1, \cdots, x_n) = 0.$$

Then WINNOW2 with $\theta = 2n$ and $\alpha = 1 + \delta/2$ applied to the variable set $(x_1, \cdots, x_n, 1-x_1, \cdots, 1-x_n)$ makes at most the following number of mistakes:

$$\frac{16}{\delta^2}\frac{n}{\theta} + \left(\frac{5}{\delta} + \frac{14 ln\theta}{\delta^2}\right) \sum_{i=1}^n (\nu_i + \bar{\nu}_i). \tag{4}$$

Here θ and δ are parameters of the algorithm and δ, which quantifies the margin by which positive and negative examples are separated, is a parameter of the distribution of examples. For a monotone disjunction of k out of n variables, we can have $\nu_i = 1$ for the k variables in the disjunction, with all the other $\nu_i = 0$, and all $\bar{\nu}_i = 0$. Then clearly $\delta = 1$. Hence (4) becomes $O(k \log n)$. In all these cases the algorithm can be adapted so that it has similar bounds in the PAC model [27].

For linear inequalities of the form (3), we see that the particular example given is equivalent to $\frac{1}{4}(x_7 + (1 - x_2) + (1 - x_5) + (1 - x_8)) \geq 1$ so that $\delta = \frac{1}{4}$. In general if there were k negative terms then $\delta = 1/(k+1)$. In order to make the margin larger it is better to learn the negation of (3), namely $(1 - x_7) + x_2 + x_5 + x_8 \geq 1$ so that $\delta = 1$. The generalization of this to k terms would also give $\delta = 1$ and hence the $O(k \log n)$ bound.

It appears that some mechanism for attribute-efficiency is essential to any large scale learning system. The effectiveness of Winnow itself has been demonstrated in a variety of experiments. A striking example in the cognitive domain is offered in the work of Golding and Roth on spelling correction [11]. Even in the presence of tens of thousands of variables, Winnow is able to learn accurately from few examples, sometimes fewer than 100.

The question arises whether attribute efficient learning is possible for more expressive knowledge representations. Recently it has been found that this is indeed the case. Under a certain projection operation attribute-efficient learning algorithms can be composed to yield algorithms for a more expressive knowledge representation that are still attribute efficient. In subsection 4.4 we shall discuss this further.

Finally, we note that attribute-efficient learning is closely related to the issue of *relevance*, which has been widely discussed in the AI literature. Conventionally one would expect to preprocess data to identify the attributes that are relevant to the classification or action in question. One would then eliminate the irrelevant attributes, and apply a learning algorithm to a database containing only the relevant ones. There is, however, no evidence that biological systems have such an explicit preprocessing stage. Further, Winnow achieves the same overall effect implicitly, without explicitly identifying which variables are irrelevant in a preprocessing stage. What it offers therefore seems novel and important. (We note however that given an implicit method, such as Winnow, one can with some effort, explicitly identify the relevant variables by a binary search technique that needs about $k \log n$ applications of Winnow. This is an observation of A. Beimel.)

4.3 Learning Relations

The important point about our representation of a relation $R(x_1, \cdots, x_k)$ at a node is its duality of nature. It is Boolean in the sense that at any instant the node either fires or does not fire. On the other hand it is also relational in that at any instant it has some binding $\theta : \{x_1, \cdots, x_k\} \rightarrow \{a_1, \cdots, a_\Omega\}$, and the truth value taken depends on whether the relation holds for this particular binding of the variables to the objects in the image. This dichotomy exists also in other work on learning relations, such as inductive logic programming [45], but needs to be addressed in a different way here because of the circuit orientation. An overriding concern for us throughout is, of course, that the complexity of manipulating relations be controlled (c.f. [46]).

Suppose we have a connection. $R_1(x_1, \cdots, x_n) \to R_2(y_1, \cdots, y_k)$ and an associated connection binding that specifies $x_1 = y_2$ and $x_2 = y_3$. What does a strong weight on this connection mean? The interpretation of the semantics of circuit evaluation defined in § 2.1 and § 2.2 implies that a strong weight means that for any scene and any bindings of x_1, x_2 to objects for which R_1 is true, it is the case that R_2 should be "inclined" to be true also for *any* binding θ_2 s.t. $\theta_2(y_2)$ and $\theta_2(y_3)$ agree with the bindings of x_1, x_2. In other words, for any scene as far as the truth of R_2 is concerned for any one binding θ_2, the only influence of R_1 is via the question of whether there *exists* some θ_1 that makes R_1 true and agrees with θ_2 on the object pairs specified in the connection binding $R_1 \to R_2$.

Clearly we need to use the same semantics for learning as for evaluation. Further this is easy to do. If R is a node with connections from $R_1, \cdots, R_m$ and with m corresponding connection bindings, then during learning we shall for each *relational example* (i.e. a scene and a labelling of R for some or all bindings θ of its variables) evaluate $R_1, \cdots, R_m$ for each binding of their own variables. An example for the learning algorithm will then consist simply of truth values for $R_1, \cdots, R_m$ and a truth value for R. Hence the truth value taken of R is simply its truth value on θ. Also R_i will be taken to be true if and only if there exists *some* binding θ_i of the variables of R_i that makes R_i true and agrees with θ on the connection binding $R_i \to R$.

If the learning algorithm learns a function (of R in terms of $R_1, \cdots, R_m$,) that is consistent with the examples so presented, then the function that the resulting circuit evaluates will be consistent with these examples.

Given one relational example, the distribution of Boolean examples presented to the learning algorithm is not necessarily uniquely determined. The case in which all bindings of R are considered, and each given the same probability is only one choice, be it a natural one. If the vast majority of bindings give negative values for the truth of R, it may be advantageous for reasons of economy to sample from the negative examples. Also, in the case that cycles are allowed and the evaluation process recomputes a node several times, there are further choices to be made.

4.4 Learning More Complex Functions and Strategies

The previous section showed that the learning of linear inequalities with large margins can be done attribute efficiently, and therefore that mechanisms for doing that are ideal building blocks for our architecture. Clearly the intention of our architecture is that each new function that is learned or programmed be expressible in terms of old ones already represented in the system in a reasonably simple way. When discussing learning the crucial issue is *how far removed* the new function can be allowed to be from the old ones already represented, without necessitating a learning capability that is computationally intractable. In other words the issue is one of the *granularity* of the *relative* complexity of the successive functions that can be learned.

From what we have said linear threshold functions offer a level of granularity that is computationally attractive. The two questions raised therefore are: (1)

is this level of granularity sufficiently large to offer a convincing approach to building cognitive systems and (2) can this granularity be enlarged (i.e. to richer knowledge representations) while retaining attribute efficient learnability.

Even when a function class is expressible as lincar inequalities, this representation may be impractically large if many compound features need to be created. For example, for Boolean variables $\{x_1, \cdots, x_n\}$ each of the 2^{2^n} Boolean functions can be expressed as a disjunction of monomials over $\{x_1, \cdots, x_n, \bar{x}_1, \cdots \bar{x}_n\}$ and hence as a linear inequality, but this requires a variable for each potential monomial, and there are 3^n of these.

Examples of function classes that can be expressed as inequalities over just n variables are: disjunctions, conjunctions, and threshold-k functions. In the last case we would have

$$\sum_{i=1}^{n} z_i \geq k$$

where z_i is a variable over the reals that is given value 1 if $x_i = 1$, and zero otherwise. A further class that can be so expressed is that of 1-decision lists [41]. These test for a sequence of literals $y_{i_1}, \cdots, y_{i_m}$ where $y_{i_j} \in \{x_1, \cdots, x_n, \bar{x}_1, \cdots, \bar{x}_n\}$. If the literal y_{i_j} is true then the function is defined to be the constant c_j for $c_j \in \{0, 1\}$, otherwise $y_{i_{j+1}}$ is tested. Decision lists can be expressed as linear inequalities over n variable $z_1, \cdots, z_n$ corresponding to $x_1, \cdots, x_n$. The size of the coefficients grows exponentially, however, with n. In the special case that most of the c_j have one value, this growth is more limited. In particular, it is shown in [55] that if c_j has value 1 for d of the m values of j then the decision list can be expressed as a linear inequality with integer coefficients, where the magnitudes of the coefficients, and also their sum, is upper bounded by $(2m/d)^d$. If $d << m$ then this is much better than the general upper bound of 2^m. Also, we see that this inequality can be expressed so as to fit the requirements of expression 4.2 for Winnow. We then have $\delta = (2m/d)^{-d}$ and the sum of the magnitudes of the coefficients bounded by 1, so that the mistake bound is quadratic in $(2m/d)^d$ and logarithmic in n.

The question of characterizing the classes of linear inequalities that are learnable attribute efficiently remains unsettled. The possibility that decision lists can be so learned has not been excluded.

Another question is whether attribute efficient learning can be achieved by classes of functions beyond linear inequalities. A positive answer to this is provided by projection learning, which is is a technique that has been shown to extend the scope of attribute efficient learnability. It allows algorithms that are attribute efficient to be composed so as to obtain learning algorithms for more expressive representations that are still attribute efficient. Since Winnow is the paradigmatic attribute efficient algorithm currently known, the present applications of projection learning are based on Winnow itself.

The basic idea is that for Boolean variables $x_1, \cdots x_n$ we define a set $J = \{\rho_1, \cdots, \rho_r\}$ of *projections* that each map $\{0, 1\}^n$ to $\{0, 1\}$. For example, we could have $r = 2n$ and for each literal $\ell \in \{x_1, \cdots, x_n, \bar{x}_1, \cdots, \bar{x}_n\}$ we have a projection ρ_ℓ defined as $\rho_\ell(\underline{x}) = 1$ iff $\ell = 1$ on $\underline{x}$. This is the class of single variable projections. An alternative class has $r = 2^k$ with each member of J being a conjunction $l_1 l_2 \cdots l_k$ where $l_i \in \{x_i, \bar{x}_i\}$, i.e. if $\rho = x_1\bar{x}_2\bar{x}_3$ then $\rho(\underline{x}) = 1$ iff $x_1\bar{x}_2\bar{x}_3 = 1$.

For each $\rho \in J$ we consider the function $f(\underline{x})\rho(\underline{x})$. Clearly this equals zero for $\underline{x}$ s.t. $\rho(\underline{x}) = 0$, and it equals $f(\underline{x})$ otherwise. The hope is that for some of the restrictions ρ, the function $f(\underline{x})\rho(\underline{x})$ can be learned more accurately than $f(\underline{x})$ can directly, and that between the various choices of ρ, the $f(\underline{x})\rho(\underline{x})$ that are learned do cover the whole domain $\{0,1\}^n$ of $f(\underline{x})$.

Suppose that for the various choices of $\rho \in J$ the function learned that approximates $f(\underline{x})$ on $\rho(\underline{x}) = 1$ is $f'_\rho(\underline{x})$. Then $\sum f'_\rho(\underline{x})\rho(\underline{x})$ is taken as the approximation of f that has been learned. The main result in [55] states that if the $f(\underline{x})\rho(\underline{x})$ belong to a class that is learnable attribute efficiently on the restricted domain $\{\underline{x} \mid \rho((\underline{x}) = 1\}$ by an algorithm A say, and if a disjunction can be learned attribute efficiently by an algorithm B that shares certain specified properties with Winnow, then the function $\sum f_\rho(\underline{x})\rho(\underline{x})$ can be learned attribute efficiently, in the sense that the needed sample complexity depends linearly on the number of relevant $\rho's$ and the number of relevant variables in all the f_ρ, but only logarithmically on the total numbers r and n.

There is a variety of directions for which this can be used to extend attribute efficient learning beyond linear threshold functions.

First, suppose that we learn a function of the form $\sum_{\rho\in \bar{J}} f_\rho(\underline{x})\rho(\underline{x})$ where $\bar{J} \subseteq J$ for J the class of single variable projections, and f_ρ are conjunctions. Then if the conjunctions are assumed to be of length at most k, and the number of elements of $\bar{J}$ is at most m, then the sample complexity of learning these will be linear in m and k, and logarithmic in r and n. Furthermore, the circuit will need r nodes for the various f_ρ, n nodes for $x_1, \cdots, x_n$, and therefore rn weights to update, or $O(n^2)$ in the case of single variable projections. Thus we are learning somewhat economically a subclass of DNF formulae that have m monomials, each with at most $k+1$ literals. To learn these via general $(k+1)$-DNF learning methods [50] would be much more expensive, and intractable if r and n are both large. For example, if we constructed all the $(k+1)$-monomials we would have about n^{k+1} of them, which exceeds n^2 if $k > 1$.

A second class of functions is given by $\sum_{\rho\in R} f_\rho(\underline{x})\rho(\underline{x})$ where J is unchanged but f is the class of disjunctions. Here the disjunctions will be assumed to contain at most k literals, and the sum $\sum_\rho$ to contain at most m nonzero terms. The result will again be a subclass of DNF with at most 2 literals in each of the at most km terms. While the overall complexity of learning this as a 2-DNF is not too different, it would require an architecture with n^2 nodes, rather than the $O(n)$ nodes needed here.

A third way that projection learning can be used is best viewed as an application outside the architecture that is attribute efficient in a weaker sense. Consider a sequential covering algorithm, as in Rivest [41], for learning decision lists, or Khardon's extension to propositional production rule systems [19]. In the simplest case such a covering algorithm works as follows: it looks successively for a literal, say $\bar{x}_3$, that is the most predictive single literal, in some sense, of the function f being learned. For the case $\bar{x}_3 = 1$ it will predict the most likely Boolean outcome for the function. For the remaining subdomain, $x_3 = 1$ in this case, it will then repeat the process of finding the next most predictive literal. Proceeding in this way it will obtain a decision list or production system. We can extend these algorithms by projection learning as follows: Instead of looking for a best literal we look for a best projection ρ from a class J. Also, instead of predicting the most likely result on the subdomain where $\rho = 1$, we learn a new hypothesis for the subdomain $\rho = 1$, and in the decision list structure substitute the learned function, say a conjunction or disjunction instead of true and false, at that point in the list. The procedure is then repeated on the subdomain where either $\rho = 0$ or the last hypothesis is false. This learning procedure can be viewed as attribute efficient if the learning algorithm used in the subdomains are attribute efficient, and if J is chosen to be itself small. Thus a preliminary analysis, by, for example, simple Winnow may yield a candidate set of variables that are most relevant (e.g. have high weights) and this small set may be chosen as the set J of projections.

We note that the main motivation of projection learning is to learn more effectively in cases in which a representation more complex than linear thresholds is needed. In any one application domain we may have no *a priori* reason to believe that such a representation is necessary. What we expect to find is that projection learning will always yield at least as good results as simple Winnow, (possibly at the expense of more examples) and may yield better results when linear representations are insufficient.

An area in which complex representations may need to be learned is that of strategies and plans. Here production systems are widely believed to have useful expressivity [38]. Khardon has shown that a rich class of these can be learned using decision list algorithms [13]. The dilemma here is that no attribute-efficient learning algorithm is known for decision lists, unless the degree d is small, as explained in the previous section. Hence we may have to look at the flatter projective structures to find representations of such strategies that are learnable attribute efficiently.

4.5 Learning as an Approach to Robustness

Systems will acquire knowledge both by inductive learning as well as by explicit programming. Errors and inconsistencies may occur in either kind of input, and mechanisms are needed for coping with these.

In the case of inductive learning the issue of noise has been studied extensively. On the theoretical side a range of noise models have been considered, ranging from a malicious adversarial model [3] to the more benign random classification noise model, where the only noise is in the classification of the examples and this is random [3]. At least for the more benign models there are some powerful general techniques for making learning algorithms cope with noise in some generality [16].

For the problem of learning linear separators there exist theoretical results that show that there is no fundamental computational impediment to overcoming random classification noise [5, 8]. Currently somewhat complex algorithms are needed to establish this rigorously. In practice, fortunately, natural algorithms such as the perceptron algorithm and Winnow, or the linear discriminant algorithm, behave well on natural data sets which are often noisy, and for which there is no *a priori* reason to believe that linear thresholds should work at all. This empirical evidence lends credence to the use of linear threshold algorithms for complex cognitive data sets.

When knowledge is acquired by programming the issue of coping with noise also arises. The view we take here is that we use the same PAC semantics for programmed rules as for inductively learned rules. Thus the system would have high confidence in a rule that agreed with many examples. A programmed rule is therefore one which is treated as a working hypothesis, and easily discarded if evidence builds up against it.

In addition to the opportunity to discard rules there is also one for refining them. Thus we may have programmed rules $P \Rightarrow R$ and $Q \Rightarrow \neg R$ as working hypotheses, but discover that they do not hold in all cases. In particular, it may happen that in some relatively rare cases both P and Q hold and therefore the rules contradict each other. It may be that after sufficiently many observations it is found that $P \wedge Q \Rightarrow \neg R$ is a reliable rule. In that case we would refine $P \Rightarrow R$ to $P \wedge \neg Q \Rightarrow R$. The main point is that the dilemma that arises from two potentially contradictory rules is resolved by learning, even in the case that the original rules themselves are programmed rather than learned.

4.6 Learning as an Approach to the Problem of Context

It has been widely observed that rules that express useful commonsense knowledge often need qualification – they hold only in certain contexts. Thus a rule $Q \Rightarrow R$ may hold if context P is true, but not necessarily otherwise. Frames in the sense of Minsky [33] can be viewed as contexts that have a rich set of associated rules. The PAC semantics of such a rule is that on the subdomain in which P holds, $Q \Rightarrow R$ is the case, at least with high probability. In our architecture the simplest view to take is that it can cope easily with a context P if it has a node for recognizing whether an input satisfies P. If there is a node in a circuit unit that recognizes P, then a subcircuit that implements $P \wedge Q \Rightarrow R$ will implement exactly what is wanted, the rule $Q \Rightarrow R$ applying in the subdomain in which P holds. The question remains as to how domain sensitive knowledge can be learned. One answer is suggested immediately by projection learning; each concept R that is learned is also learned for the projections defined by every other concept P that has been previously learned or programmed. Thus if we have nodes for P and R then a complex set of conditions Q that guarantee R in the context of P can be learned from examples, for any P and R. This would be, of course, computationally onerous unless the choice of P is restricted somehow.

4.7 Learning as an Approach to Incomplete Information and Nonmonotonic Phenomena

Systems that attempt to describe the world declaratively run into methodological problems that arise from the fact that at any time there will be captured only incomplete knowledge about the world. The difficulty is that such systems need to take a generic view of how to treat incomplete information – they need a uniform theory, such as circumscription or the closed world assumption that takes positions on how to resolve the unknown [10, 29, 31].

PAC circuit semantics offers an advantage here – it resolves the unknown separately in each case by using information learned from past experience of cases where similar features to the case in hand were similarly unknown. A motivating observation here is that gates in a circuit take values at *all* times. Consider the paradigm of nonmonotonic reasoning exemplified by the widely discussed example of the bird called Tweety [10] . The system is invited to take positions on whether Tweety flies both before and after it is revealed to it that Tweety is, in fact, a penguin. Suppose that in a brain, for example, there is a two-valued gate intended to recognize penguins. This would take value 1 say, when a penguin is identified, in the PAC sense, and 0 when what is seen is identified in the PAC sense as not being a penguin. However, this gate must also take some value in cases where conventionally one would say that the system has not determined whether the object in question is a penguin or not. Suppose that in these cases the gate takes the value 0. Then we could say that a 1 value means {penguin} and a 0 means {not penguin, undetermined}. In this sense circuits represent internally the three cases {yes, no, undetermined} even if no explicit provision has been made for the third case. This means that learning and rule evaluations in the system are carried out with a semantics in which the undetermined value of each variable is represented. This is true both when a predicate is represented by a single gate having just two possible values (whether representing {yes, undetermined}/{no} or {yes}/{no,undetermined} by the two values) and also when there is a more explicit representation, say by a pair of binary gates whose four possible values do distinguish {yes}, {no}, and {undetermined}. Hence once the system has reached stability in learning it will cope with instances of incomplete information exactly as it does with ones with complete information [52]. One could say further that in natural learning systems instances of incomplete information are the natural ones, and usually the only ones available.

Pursuing this example further, suppose that the system has a rule "bird = 1 and penguin = 0 $\Rightarrow$ flies = 1". Suppose also that the gates "bird", "penguin", and "flies" all have value 0 if the truth of the corresponding predicate is undetermined in the system. Suppose further that this rule has been found to be consistent with most *natural cases* experienced by the system in accordance with the probability distribution D that describes the external world. It will then follow that for instances in which birdhood is confirmed but penguinhood is undetermined, it will be a reasonable conclusion that flies will be true and that the corresponding gate should indeed have value 1 to indicate that. This will be a valid inference since the same was true for past cases in the PAC sense. Thus the undefined is resolved here by learning from the real world distribution D, as seen through the feature set of the system. In this example D captured the fact that in the particular source of examples to which this system was exposed, in the majority of cases where a bird was identified but nothing was said about penguinhood, the bird did indeed fly.

In artificial systems, of course, the undefined value $*$ may be treated more explicitly. For example, gates may take three values $\{0, 1, *\}$, or, closer to the spirit of our architecture, the three values may be represented by a pair of binary gates.

Defaults may be viewed from this same perspective. Ignorance of the value of a predicate is rightly interpreted as not relevant to the value of another if in natural past cases of ignorance of the former, a certain consequence was true with high probability for the latter. We regard defaults as rules where certain predicates are assumed to have the undetermined value in the precondition. Their validity arises from the fact that they had proved accurate in the past, or that they could be deduced from those that had. Further examples are given in [43, 52, 53].

4.8 Reasoning

Much effort has been put into seeing whether the various formalisms that have been suggested for reasoning in AI, at least those outside the probabilistic realm, can be formulated within predicate calculus. The general answer found to this question is in the affirmative, in the sense that many of the various alternative formalisms, including those based on graph models, can be reexpressed in terms of the predicate calculus. Some of these alternative formalisms, and the necessary transformations are described by Russell and Norvig [45].

Instead of reformulating this body of work so as to fit in with our architecture, we will be content here to claim that a substantial part of it can be supported directly without change. In particular, we described an implementation of our architecture that can support modus ponens on Horn clauses. It follows that our architecture can do reasoning in all these frameworks whenever the translation results in Horn clauses. Further, it can do this by simple circuit evaluation of the contents of an image.

In addition, our architecture has capabilities for reasoning beyond those provided by circuit evaluations alone. In particular, the circuits and the image units can be used together more proactively within the reasoning process. The evaluation of a circuit may result in various actions on the image, such as the addition of further objects, the addition of statements of further relationships, or the deletion of an object. Thus a circuit may cause the execution of a step of a more complex reasoning strategy. In evaluating a scene, a circuit may add an object representing something already in the scene but at a later time, and add a relationship that expresses the future condition of the object. In other words the circuits may be able to depict a likely scenario following on from the current one. The way the future scenario is depicted can depend critically on the current one. In other words we need circuits that are able to make useful modifications to the scene in a highly content dependent manner.

The upshot is that the circuits will contain, in addition to information about the external world as implied in previous sections, further information that concerns the strategies that are to be used for the internal deliberations of the system. These deliberations will be seriously restricted, of course, by computational constraints, such as limits on the number of objects allowed in a scene.

4.9 System Design

It has been asked whether in our architecture one still has to design AI systems, exactly as in the old way, and all that is offered in addition are some mechanisms for the automatic adjustment of weights. While in some sense the answer to this is yes, the more important point is that the learning capability offers things that are qualitatively different. First it provides a behavioral semantics. Further it offers a unified methodology for dealing with conflict resolution, nonmonotonic phenomena, incomplete information, robustness, and the problem of context among others. Above all, it offers a viable approach for infusing knowledge into a system in bulk.

Clearly conventional design principles offer a start in designing systems in this domain also. In a programmed system one expects to construct various modules for various functionalities, and have these interface with each other. In particular, one may have a hierarchy of functions, lower level ones processing the inputs directly, and higher level ones processing the outputs of the lower level ones. Thus an acyclic graph of circuit units, in which some low level modules mimic the modules that would be used in, say, a language system, is one possible starting point.

There are also some design choices that are unique to the architecture. For creating new compound features there are various possibilities. Because of the centrality of attribute efficient learning algorithms, an obvious method is to generate large numbers of combinations in a systematic simple way. Any relevant ones so discovered will be valuable, and the irrelevant ones will do little harm. One approach is to generate for any variable set the set of conjunctions of all pairs of them. Another choice is to create conjunctions of just those pairs that occur with high correlation. More generally one can generate some set of *polynomialy generable* combinations [51]. The intention is that large numbers of variables, even if most are irrelevant, will not degrade performance in the presence of attribute efficient learning algorithms.

We are suggesting that the way to evaluate this architecture is by experimentation. In that connection we note here one aspect. Most general approaches to AI attempt to describe a uniform method for building a knowledge base starting from a blank slate. Facts and reasoning about the most universal concepts such as time and space are then formalized in the same framework as is more specialized knowledge (e.g. [25]). In the neuroidal framework there is room reserved for treating the universal concepts differently from the others. In particular, the features and inverse features of the image units can be used to implement efficiently certain universal knowledge, such as to do with low-level visual processing, and reasoning about time or space. These functions may be complex and specialized enough that implementing them directly in the same framework as the more general knowledge would introduce unnecessary difficulties. Thus interpreting a depiction of a three dimensional scene may be done in the first instance by computational mechanisms that are preprogrammed in the image units and expert at that task, and are possibly totally unrelated to the more general knowledge manipulation capability of the circuit units. This dichotomy may be analogous to that in biological systems between knowledge available at birth and acquired during evolution, and that learned during life. However, we expect that some circuit units will be programmed and do not exclude the possibility that some image unit functions are learned.

The choice of what features to implement in the input devices and image units poses significant questions. In current machine learning applications the choice of feature set is often critical to success. This phenomenon is probably accentuated when we scale up to more general cognitive problems. In particular, the training data may have to match the chosen feature set in some way. If, as is most likely, the feature set chosen is significantly different from that used by the human nervous system, the teaching materials that will succeed can be expected to be different from those that are effective for teaching humans.

5 Validating the Architecture

What we are claiming is that several of the generic difficulties that have been encountered in designing scalable AI systems are technically solvable within the described architecture. To give convincing evidence for this claim one would need to construct a system that uses general knowledge on the scale and with the success envisioned here. A first experimental question, therefore, is how this architecture might be bootstrapped to create a system whose performance in some cognitive area is indisputably superior to existing ones.

In designing a system important choices need to be made regarding the feature detectors of the images and of the input devices. If the main source of information for the system is visual, for example, then problems with interpreting visual inputs are likely to be inherited by the system. Our view is that the building of a database that would comprise the first level of internal knowledge in the system for such circumstance will have to be pursued in a careful and purposeful manner. It would have to acknowledge and compensate for the poverty of what we might be able to program currently as feature detectors. The Golding-Roth paper [11] is a good example, however, of how one might start. They take a linguistic corpus and create complex features out of single words, grammatical parts of speech of single words, and boolean conjunctions of these for sets of words that occur in close proximity in the text. Such features, though artificial, do capture useful information about meaning beyond what can be gleaned from examining each word in isolation. By using such a set of features they are able to learn to disambiguate certain pairs of words that humans often confuse. Although the feature set is imperfect and artificial, the system is able to create a useful level of knowledge that is a level of abstraction above the individual words.

By analogy one would hope to build a larger knowledge base in a succession of similar steps. This would be done by a managed combination of inductive training operations, and the use of programmed knowledge as contained, for example, in dictionaries. We believe that learning will need to play a large part of the overall task if we are to achieve the various kinds of robustness discussed in this paper. Purely programmed systems would appear to have an inherent limitation in this regard.

It is quite likely that if all this is to be achieved, natural language inputs will play a major role. Corpora suitably annotated with the appropriate levels of knowledge will have to be created. Substantial infrastructure will need to be manufactured to provide the teaching materials for these systems. This would compensate for any shortcoming in the range of preprogrammed features that we are able to realize. Although large amounts of reliable knowledge are already available in linguistic format, there are many obstacles to preparing or selecting useful linguistic teaching materials. Much commonsense knowledge is nowhere encoded, and much text produced by humans contains linguistic constructs that are currently difficult for machines to analyze. These facts make the preparation of the teaching materials challenging, but, we believe, not insurmountable

6 Conclusion

We have described a series of arguments that suggest that many of the problems that have been identified as obstacles to AI at a conceptual level, can be solved if one gives inductive learning a suitable central role. In this respect the proposed architecture differs from other general approaches to cognitive architectures that have been described, such as [1], [37], and [38], in which inductive learning plays a much smaller role.

We note that our use of PAC semantics suggests a modified Turing test. His basic criterion for whether a machine could think was that the performance of the machine should be indistinguishable from that of a human to an interrogator communicating via a teleprinter [47]. The significance of this informally stated criterion is that it is a purely *behavioral* one. What PAC semantics offers is a precise way of formulating such behavioral criteria. In particular it insists that both the task being learned, and the distribution of inputs over which learning is performed and performance measured, need to be identified.

The tasks in which we are interested here are those involving a large amount of knowledge that has not been systematized into an exact science. A possible area in which one might hope to test the performance of a system at such a task is that of intelligent word processing. One can imagine a word processor that not only detects misspelled words, but does a succession of more and more intelligent tasks, such as suggesting alternative words and phrasing, or noting confusions or inconsistencies, much as a teacher marking an essay might. There appears to be a continuum of tasks of increasing difficulty in this area. Even when restricted to the disambiguation tasks previously mentioned, systems could invoke more and more world knowledge in their suggestions, and their perceived performance would increase correspondingly. One can imagine experiments in which commentary to writers is provided variously by humans and machines, and the writers' task is to distinguish which one was the case. Such an instance of a modified Turing Test would therefore refer to a concrete real world distribution of cases generated, for example, by twelve year old students, and created independently of the context of the test. Each such distribution would define a different task and therefore a different test. For an empirical validation of our architecture one would need to show that systems can be built that pass such specific tests of ever higher levels of difficulty.

7 Acknowledgment

I am grateful to Roni Khardon, Dan Roth, and Rocco Servedio for their helpful comments on various versions of this paper.

References

1. J.R. Anderson. *The Architecture of Cognition.* Harvard University Press, 1983.
2. J.R. Anderson. *Rules of the Mind.* Erlbaum, Hillsdale, NJ, 1993.
3. D. Angluin and P. Laird. Learning from noisy examples. *Machine Learning*, 2(4):343–370, 1988.
4. A. Blum. Learning boolean functions in an infinite attribute space. *Machine Learning*, 9(4):373–386, 1992.
5. A. Blum, et al. A polynomial time algorithm for learning noisy linear threshold functions. In *Proc. 37th IEEE Symp. on Theory of Computing*, pages 330–338, 1996.
6. T. Bylander. Learning linear threshold functions in the presence of classification noise. In *Proc. 7th ACM Conference on Computational Learning Theory*, pages 340–347, 1994.
7. N. Cesa-Bianchi, et al. How to use expert advice. In *Proc. 25th ACM Symp. on Theory of Computing*, pages 382–39, 1993.
8. E. Cohen. Learning noisy perceptrons by a perceptron in polynomial time. In *Proc 38th IEEE Symp. on Foundation of Computer Science*, pages 514–523, 1997.
9. A. Ehrenfeucht, D. Haussler, M. Kearns, and L. Valiant. A general lower bound on the number of examples needed for learning. *Inf. and Computation*, 82(3):247–266, 1989.
10. M.L. Ginsberg. *Readings in Nonmonotonic Reasoning.* Morgan Kaufmann, Los Altos, CA, 1989.
11. A.R. Golding and D. Roth. Applying Winnow to context-sensitive spelling correction. In *Proc 13th Int. Conf. on Machine Learning*, pages 182–190, San Francisco, CA, 1996. Morgan Kaufmann.
12. J.Y. Halpern. An analysis of first-order logics of probability. In *Artificial Intelligence Journal*, volume 46, pages 311–350, 1990.

13. D. Haussler. Quantifying inductive bias: AI learning algorithms and Valiant's learning framework. *Artificial Intelligence*, 36:177–221, 1988.
14. D. Haussler. Learning conjunctive concepts in structural domains. *Machine Learning*, 4:7–40, 1989.
15. M. Kearns and M. Li. Learning in the presence of malicious errors. *SIAM Journal on Computing*, 22(4):807–837, 1993.
16. M.J. Kearns. Efficient noise-tolerant learning from statistical queries. In *Proc. 25th ACM Symp. on Theory of Computing*, New York, 392-401 1993. ACM Press.
17. M.J. Kearns and R.E. Schapire. Efficient distribution-free probabilistic concepts. *J. Comput. Syst. Sci.*, 48(3):464, 1994.
18. M.J. Kearns and U.V. Vazirani. *An Introduction to Computational Learning Theory.* MIT Press, 1994.
19. R. Khardon. Learning to take actions. In *Proc. National Conference on Artificial Intelligence*, pages 787–792. AAAI, 1996.
20. R. Khardon and D. Roth. Learning to reason. In *AAAI94*, pages 682–687. Morgan Kaufmann, 1994.
21. R. Khardon and D. Roth. Learning to reason with a restricted view. In *Proc. 8th ACM Conference on Computational Learning Theory*, pages 301–310, 1995.
22. J. Kivinen and M.K. Warmuth. The perceptron algorithm vs. Winnow: linear vs. logarithmic mistake bounds when few input variables are relevant. In *Proc. 8th ACM Conference on Computational Learning Theory*, pages 289–296, 1995.
23. D. Knuth. *The Art of Computer Programming*, volume 1. Addison Wesley, Reading, MA, 1973.
24. P. Langley, D. Klahr, and R Neches. *Production System Models of Learning and Development.* MIT Press, 1987.
25. D.B. Lenat, et al. CYC: Toward programs with common sense. In *CACM*, volume 33:8, pages 30–49, 1990.
26. N. Littlestone. Learning quickly when irrelevant attributes abound: a new linear-threshold algorithm. *Machine Learning*, 2:285–318, 1988.
27. N. Littlestone. From on-line to batch learning. In *Proc. 2nd Workshop on Computational Learing Theory*, pages 269–284, 1989.
28. J. McCarthy. Programs with commonsense. In *Proc. Teddington Conference on the Mechanization of Thought Processes*, London, 1959. HMSO.
29. J. McCarthy. Circumscription – a form of non-monotonic reasoning. *Artificial Intelligence*, 13:27–39, 1980.
30. J. McCarthy and P.J. Hayes. Some philosophical problems from the standpoint of artificial intelligence. In D. Michie, editor, *Machine Intelligence*, volume 4, New York, 1969. American Elsevier.
31. D. McDermott and J. Doyle. Nonmonotonic logic I. *Artificial Intelligence*, 13(1), 1980.
32. G.A. Miller. The magical number seven, plus or minus two: Some limits on our capacity for processing information. *Psychological Review*, 63:81–97, 1956.
33. M. Minsky. A framework for representing knowledge. In P.H. Winston, editor, *The Psychology of Computer Vision*, New York, 1975. McGraw Hill.
34. M. Minsky and S. Papert. *Perceptrons.* MIT Press, Cambridge, MA, 1969.
35. S. Minton. Quantitative results concerning the utility of explanation-based learning. *Artificial Intelligence*, pages 363–391, 1990.
36. S. Muggleton. Inductive logic programming: derivations, successes and shortcomings. *SIGART Bulletin*, 5(1):5–11, 1994. Also other articles in same volume.
37. A. Newell. *Unified Theories of Cognition.* Harvard University Press, 1990.

38. A. Newell and H.A. Simon. *Human Problem Solving.* Prentice-Hall, Englewood Cliffs, NJ, 1972.
39. J. Pearl. *Probabilistic Reasoning in Intelligent Systems: Networks of Plausible Inference.* Morgan Kaufmann, Los Altos, CA, 1988.
40. L. Pitt and L.G. Valiant. Computational limits on learning from examples. *J. ACM*, 35:965–984, 1988.
41. R.L. Rivest. Learning decision lists. *Machine Learning*, 2(3):229–246, 1987.
42. F. Rosenblatt. *Principles of Neurodynamics.* Spartan, New York, 1962.
43. D. Roth. Learning to reason: the non-monotonic case. *Proc. Int. Joint Conf. Art. Intl.*, pages 1178–118, 1995.
44. D. Roth. A connectionist framework for reasoning: Reasoning with examples. In *Proc. National Conference on Artificial Intelligence*, pages 1256–1261. AAAI, 1996.
45. S. Russell and P. Norvig. *Artificial Intelligence.* Prentice Hall, Upper Saddle River, NJ, 1995.
46. M. Tambe, A. Newell, and P.S. Rosenbloom. The problem of expensive chunks and its solution by restricting expressiveness. *Machine Learning*, 5:299–348, 1990.
47. A.M. Turing. Computing machinery and intelligence. *Mind 59*, pages 433–460, 1950. (Reprinted in Collected Works of A.M. Turing: Mechanical Intelligence, (D.C. Ince, ed.), North-Holland, 1992).
48. A.M. Turing. Solvable and unsolvable problems. *Science News*, 31:7–23, 1954. (Reprinted in Collected Works of A.M. Turing: Mechanical Intelligence (D.C. Ince, ed.) North-Holland 1992).
49. A. Tversky and D. Kahnemann. Causal schemata in judgments under uncertainty. In *Progress in Social Psychology*, Erlbaum, Hillsdale, NJ, 1977.
50. L.G. Valiant. A theory of the learnable. *Comm. of ACM*, 27(11):1134–1142, 1984.
51. L.G. Valiant. Learning disjunctions of conjunctions. In *International Joint Conference on Artificial Intelligence*, pages 560–566, Los Angeles, CA, 1985. Morgan Kaufmann.
52. L.G. Valiant. *Circuits of the Mind.* Oxford University Press, 1994.
53. L.G. Valiant. Rationality. In *Proc. 8th Ann. Conference on Computational Learning Theory*, pages 3–14. ACM Press, 1995.
54. L.G. Valiant. A neuroidal architecture for cognitive computation. Technical Report TR-11-96, Harvard University, 1996.
55. L.G. Valiant. Projection learning. Technical Report TR-19-97, Harvard University, 1997.

Deterministic Polylog Approximation for Minimum Communication Spanning Trees
(Extended Abstract)

David Peleg[1] * and Eilon Reshef[1] **

Department of Applied Mathematics and Computer Science, The Weizmann Institute, Rehovot 76100, Israel.

Abstract. This paper considers the problem of selecting a *minimum communication spanning tree (MCT)* for a given weighted network, namely, a tree that minimizes the total cost of transmitting a given set of communication requirements between n sites over the tree edges [8]. A slightly stronger formulation of the problem [1] is based on the concept of a *minimum average stretch spanning tree (MAST)* for weighted connected multigraphs. In particular, a ρ-solution for the MAST problem (namely, an algorithm for constructing a spanning tree with average stretch ρ) in the special case of *complete* weighted graphs implies an approximation algorithm for the MCT problem with approximation ratio ρ.

It is conjectured in [1] that for any given weighted multigraph there exists a spanning tree with average stretch $O(\log n)$ (which is the best possible, in view of the $\Omega(\log n)$ lower bound given therein). However, the (deterministic) construction presented (which is the best construction to date) yields only a bound of $\exp(O(\sqrt{\log n \log\log n}))$ on the average stretch. For the restricted case of complete weighted graphs, there is a better, albeit randomized, construction yielding average stretch $O(\log^2 n)$ [2]. This implies a randomized approximation algorithm for MCT with the same ratio.

This paper presents a *deterministic* algorithm that for every weighted complete multigraph constructs a spanning tree whose average stretch is bounded by $O(\log^2 n)$. This yields a deterministic polynomial-time approximation algorithm for MCT with ratio $O(\log^2 n)$. In addition, our solution approach confirms the conjecture of [1] in the special case of d-dimensional Euclidean complete multigraphs for fixed d, where our construction yields spanning trees with $O(\log n)$ average stretch.

1 Introduction

The problem of designing a communication network for a given set of requirements has been studied extensively in the literature, and many different variants of it were studied and given either exact solutions or heuristics (cf. [12]). The special case of the network design problem considered here involves selecting

* E-mail: peleg@wisdom.weizmann.ac.il. Supported in part by grants from the Israel Science Foundation and from the Israel Ministry of Science and Art.

** E-mail: eilon@wisdom.weizmann.ac.il.

an appropriate *spanning tree* for the network, on which all communication is to be performed. This problem can be formalized as follows. There are n sites, $V = \{v_1, \ldots, v_n\}$, with communication requirements specified by an $n \times n$ *requirement* matrix $\mathcal{R} = (r_{i,j})$, where $r_{i,j}$ is the amount of communication required from v_i to v_j. In addition, there are *distance weights* associated with each pair of sites, specified by a symmetric $n \times n$ matrix $\omega_{i,j}$. We make the reasonable assumption that the distances obey the triangle inequality, i.e., it is always cheaper to communicate over a direct edge than over an alternative route composed of a number of hops.

Connecting every pair of sites by a direct channel would make it possible for them to communicate directly, with a total communication cost of $C^* = \sum_{i,j} r_{i,j} \cdot \omega_{i,j}$. In contrast, communicating over the edges of a spanning tree may be more expensive. For any (weighted) graph G, let $dist(v_i, v_j, G)$ denote the distance between v_i and v_j in G, namely, the minimum sum of the edge weights along any path connecting v_i and v_j in G. A given spanning tree T specifies, for every two vertices v_i and v_j, a unique route $\rho^T_{i,j}$ of length $dist(v_i, v_j, T)$. The communication cost over the tree T is defined as

$$C(T) = \sum_{i,j} r_{i,j} \cdot dist(v_i, v_j, T).$$

This paper considers the *minimum communication spanning tree (MCT)* problem (listed as [ND7] in [7]), which requires us to select a spanning tree T for the network, minimizing the communication cost $C(T)$.

This problem has been introduced in [8], where two restricted variants of the problem were studied. The first was the *complete unweighted graph* version, in which $\omega_{i,j} = 1$ for every i and j. This version was given an exact solution. The second variant was the *uniform* version, in which the communication requirements between any two sites are equal (i.e., $r_{i,j} = 1$ for every i and j). Even this restricted problem is known to be NP-hard. In fact, this is shown in [11] for the unweighted uniform case, in which $\omega_{i,j} \in \{1, \infty\}$ for every i and j, namely, the tree has to be a spanning tree of some arbitrary (not necessarily complete) unweighted graph. Consequently, [8] proposed an algorithm for solving a restricted case of the uniform problem, in which the weights satisfy the following condition: For every $1 \le i, j, k \le n$ such that $\omega_{i,j} \le \omega_{i,k} \le \omega_{j,k}$, we have $(\omega_{j,k} - \omega_{i,j})/\omega_{i,k} \le (n-2)/(2n-2)$. (This can be thought of as a stronger version of the triangle inequality.) In fact, it is shown in [8] that in this case, the optimal tree is a star (composed of a root and $n-1$ leaves), hence the algorithm simply checks all n possible star trees. In [16] it is shown that the general uniform problem (without the additional restriction on weights) enjoys a polynomial time approximation scheme.

MCT is closely related to a problem studied in [1], where it was attempted to minimize the *average stretch* of the edges of a given multigraph over a spanning tree. Formally, let $G(V, E, \omega, m)$ be an undirected connected graph (V, E) with distance weights $\omega_{i,j} \ge 0$, multiplicities $m_{i,j} \ge 0$, for every edge $(v_i, v_j) \in E$. Let $\mathcal{M} = \sum_{i,j} m_{i,j}$. For a spanning tree T of G, the *stretch* over the vertex pair

v_i, v_j is defined as $dist(v_i, v_j, T)/\omega_{i,j}$, and the *average stretch* of T is

$$\bar{S}(T) = \frac{1}{\mathcal{M}} \sum_{(v_i,v_j)\in E} m_{i,j} \cdot \frac{dist(v_i, v_j, T)}{\omega_{i,j}} .$$

(Hence intuitively, an edge $e = (v_i, v_j)$ with $m_{i,j} = 0$ may be used in the constructed spanning tree, but its stretch is not taken into account in the average stretch computation.) dealing The *minimum average stretch spanning tree (MAST)* problem defined in [1] requires us to select a spanning tree T for G, minimizing $\bar{S}(T)$.

Despite the seemingly more general formulation of the MCT problem, it is easy to verify that it is in fact equivalent to a special case of the MAST problem on *complete* weighted graphs, in the sense that instances of MCT can be transformed into instances of MAST on complete graphs (and vice versa), so that for every tree T on V, $\bar{S}(T)$ and $C(T)$ are related by a factor of C^* (see [14, 16]). problem use This implies, in particular, that the optimal tree for MAST is also optimal for MCT, and similarly, that an approximation algorithm for the MAST problem entails also an algorithm for the MCT problem, with the same approximation ratio.

It is conjectured in [1] that for any given weighted multigraph there exists a spanning tree with average stretch $O(\log n)$ (which is the best possible, in view of the $\Omega(\log n)$ lower bound given therein). However, the (deterministic) construction presented (which is the best construction to date) yields only a bound of $\exp(O(\sqrt{\log n \log\log n}))$ on the average stretch. This implies a deterministic approximation algorithm with the same ratio for the MCT problem.

For the restricted case of MAST over complete weighted graphs, there is a better, albeit randomized, construction algorithm yielding average stretch $O(\log^2 n)$ [2]. This implies a randomized approximation algorithm for MCT with the same ratio [16].

This paper presents a *deterministic* algorithm that for every weighted complete multigraph constructs a spanning tree whose average stretch is bounded by $O(\log^2 n)$. In turn, this yields also a deterministic polynomial-time approximation algorithm for MCT with ratio $O(\log^2 n)$.

Our construction is given first for complete d-dimensional Euclidean networks, where the vertices have coordinates in d-dimensional Euclidean space, and distances are defined by the metric associated with the usual L_2 norm. For networks in this class with fixed d, our construction confirms the conjecture of [1], as it yields spanning trees with $O(\log n)$ average stretch. Then, we use the low-distortion embeddings of [4, 13, 9] to embed a given metric graph in $\log n$-dimensional Euclidean space, construct a tree for the embedded graph, and use it for the original graph. Finally, we present a direct method for constructing spanning trees with approximation ratio $O(\log^2 n)$.

We have recently learned that independently, in an upcoming paper, [5] use the techniques of [15, 6, 3] to construct an algorithm for MCT with an approximation ratio of $O(\log n \log\log n)$. Their technique is different from our first one, and more similar to our direct method. In particular, it does not seem to yield an $O(\log n)$ bound for the Euclidean case.

2 Overview of the Construction

Let $G(V, E, \omega, m)$ be a complete n-vertex weighted graph as before. For any subset of vertices $U \subseteq V$, let $Diam(U)$ denote the maximum distance between any two vertices in U. Let $D = Diam(V)$.

For any edge subset $F \subseteq E$, define

$$\mathcal{M}(F) = \sum_{(v_i,v_j)\in F} m_{i,j}$$

$$\psi(F) = \sum_{(v_i,v_j)\in F} \frac{m_{i,j}}{\omega_{i,j}}$$

A *partition* of the graph G is a collection $\mathcal{S} = \{S_1, \ldots, S_k\}$ of disjoint clusters (or sets) of vertices, such that $\bigcup_i S_i = V$. Let $\mathcal{C}(\mathcal{S})$ denote the set of inter-cluster edges of the partition $\mathcal{S}$, namely, those edges whose endpoints belong to different clusters.

Our construction applies the divide-and-conquer method to break G into a partition $\mathcal{S}$ (called an (α, β, γ)-separated partition) consisting of clusters with a small diameter, and in which $\mathcal{C}(\mathcal{S})$ contains only "few" light edges. After recursively constructing a spanning subtree for each of the clusters, the subtrees are assembled to form a spanning tree of G.

Formally, for a parameter γ, define the set of γ-*heavy* edges of a graph G as

$$H^\gamma(G) = \{(v_i, v_j) \in E \mid \omega_{i,j} \geq \frac{D}{\gamma \cdot n^3}\},$$

and let the set of γ-*light* edges be $L^\gamma(G) = E \setminus H^\gamma(G)$. We hereafter abbreviate $H^\gamma(G)$ and $L^\gamma(G)$ by H^γ and L^γ, respectively.

A partition $\mathcal{S} = (S_1, \ldots, S_k)$ of G is called an (α, β, γ)-separated partition if the following three properties hold:

1. $Diam(S_\ell) \leq \beta D$ for every $1 \leq \ell \leq k$,
2. $\psi(\mathcal{C}(\mathcal{S})) \leq \alpha \mathcal{M}(H^\gamma)/D$,
3. $\mathcal{C}(\mathcal{S}) \subseteq H^\gamma$,

where $\alpha > 0$, $0 \leq \beta < 1$ and $\gamma = O(1)$.

In Section 3 we show that given an algorithm $\mathcal{P}$ that breaks any graph G into an (α, β, γ)-separated partition $\mathcal{S}$, one can construct a spanning tree with an average stretch of $O(\alpha \ln n)$.

In Section 4 we describe an algorithm that breaks any 2-dimensional Euclidean graph into an (α, β, γ)-separated partition with $\alpha = O(1)$ and hence a spanning tree with an average stretch of $O(\ln n)$ can be constructed.

In Section 5 we generalize this algorithm to break any d-dimensional Euclidean graphs with an arbitrary dimension d into an (α, β, γ)-separated partition with $\alpha = O(d)$, and hence a spanning tree with an average stretch of $O(d \ln n)$ can be constructed.

Section 6 uses the low-distortion embeddings of [4, 13, 9] to embed a given metric graph in $\log n$-dimensional Euclidean space with an additional stretch of $\ln n$, giving a spanning tree with an average stretch of $O(\ln^3 n)$.

Finally, in section 7 we present an algorithm that breaks any graph into an (α, β, γ)-separated partition with $\alpha = O(\ln n)$, yielding a spanning tree with an average stretch of $O(\ln^2 n)$.

3 Constructing a Spanning Tree

Given an algorithm $\mathcal{P}$ that breaks any graph G into a (α, β, γ)-separated partition, let us describe a simple recursive algorithm for constructing a spanning tree T.

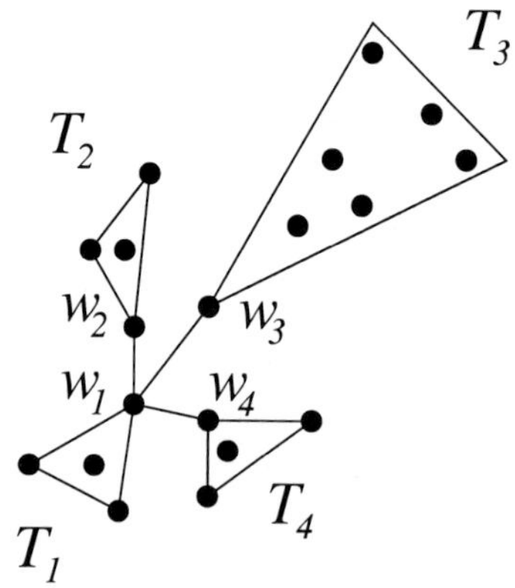

Fig. 1. Constructing the tree T. (Here $k = 4$.)

3.1 Algorithm

1. If the graph G consists of a single vertex, pick $T = G$.
2. Otherwise, apply the partitioning algorithm $\mathcal{P}$ to find an (α, β, γ)-separated partition $\mathcal{S} = \{S_1, \ldots, S_k\}$ for G. (If a cluster S_ℓ contains no vertices of G, then ignore it throughout the remainder of the construction.)
3. Proceed recursively to find the spanning trees T_ℓ $(1 \leq \ell \leq k)$ for $G(S_\ell)$, rooted at w_ℓ.
4. Without loss of generality suppose that S_1 is non-empty. Connect the trees into a single tree T by adding the edges (w_1, w_ℓ) for $2 \leq \ell \leq k$. (See Fig. 1.)

Since $D_\ell = Diam(S_\ell) \leq \beta D < D$ for every $1 \leq \ell \leq k$, at least one edge is added at each step of the algorithm and therefore the algorithm terminates after at most $n-1$ applications of $\mathcal{P}$, giving a spanning tree of G.

3.2 Analysis

To simplify the analysis of the algorithm, we describe an execution of the algorithm using its recursion tree $\mathcal{T}$, such that each node N in $\mathcal{T}$ corresponds to the subgraph examined at that stage. Let k be the maximum number of children of N over all nodes N of $\mathcal{T}$.

Let us label the nodes of $\mathcal{T}$ with strings over the alphabet $\Sigma = \{1, \ldots, k\}$ as follows:

1. Label the root of $\mathcal{T}$ with N_λ, where λ is the empty string.
2. Label the children of a node N_σ with $N_{\sigma 1}, \ldots, N_{\sigma k}$.

Define $G_\sigma = (V_\sigma, E_\sigma)$ to be the graph corresponding to N_σ, let $D_\sigma = Diam(G_\sigma)$, and let $H_\sigma^\gamma(G_\sigma)$ be its set of "heavy" edges with respect to D_σ and $n_\sigma = |V_\sigma|$. Furthermore, let $\mathcal{S}_\sigma$ be the partition used by the algorithm to separate G_σ into $(S_{\sigma 1}, \ldots, S_{\sigma k})$, and let T_σ be the spanning tree built for G_σ.

We observe that each $e = (v_i, v_j) \in E$ has a unique N_σ for which $e \in \mathcal{C}(\mathcal{S}_\sigma)$, and that T_σ contains the path from v_i to v_j.

By induction on the tree one can prove the following.

Lemma 1. *For each $\sigma \in \Sigma^*$, $Depth(T_\sigma) \leq \frac{1}{1-\beta} \cdot D_\sigma$.*

Theorem 2. *For every n-vertex graph $G(V, E, \omega, m)$ as above the algorithm generates a spanning tree T for G, with $\bar{S}(T) = O(\alpha \ln n)$.*

Proof. Since each $e = (v_i, v_j) \in E$ has a unique node N_σ for which $e \in \mathcal{C}(\mathcal{S}_\sigma)$,

$$\bar{S}(T) = \frac{1}{\mathcal{M}} \sum_{(v_i,v_j)\in E} m_{i,j} \cdot \frac{dist(v_i, v_j, T)}{\omega_{i,j}} = \frac{1}{\mathcal{M}} \sum_{\sigma} \sum_{(v_i,v_j)\in \mathcal{C}(\mathcal{S}_\sigma)} m_{i,j} \cdot \frac{dist(v_i, v_j, T)}{\omega_{i,j}}. \quad (1)$$

For $e = (v_i, v_j) \in \mathcal{C}(\mathcal{S}_\sigma)$, the path in T connecting v_i and v_j is contained in T_σ, and since T is a union of the subtrees T_σ, Lemma 1 guarantees that

$$dist(v_i, v_j, T) = dist(v_i, v_j, T_\sigma) \leq 2 \cdot Depth(T_\sigma) \leq \frac{2}{1-\beta} \cdot D_\sigma. \quad (2)$$

Combining (1) and (2) yields

$$\bar{S}(T) \leq \frac{1}{\mathcal{M}} \sum_{\sigma} \left(\frac{2}{1-\beta} \cdot D_\sigma \cdot \sum_{(v_i,v_j)\in \mathcal{C}(\mathcal{S}_\sigma)} \frac{m_{i,j}}{\omega_{i,j}} \right) = \frac{2}{1-\beta} \cdot \frac{1}{\mathcal{M}} \sum_{\sigma} (D_\sigma \cdot \psi(\mathcal{C}(\mathcal{S}_\sigma))). \quad (3)$$

Moreover, for every σ, Property (2) of the (α, β, γ)-separated partition S_σ guarantees that

$$\psi(\mathcal{C}(S_\sigma)) \leq \alpha \frac{\mathcal{M}(H_\sigma^\gamma)}{D_\sigma} .$$

Hence

$$\bar{S}(T) \leq \frac{2\alpha}{1-\beta} \cdot \frac{1}{\mathcal{M}} \sum_\sigma = \mathcal{M}(H_\sigma^\gamma). \tag{4}$$

Let $deg_H(v_i, v_j)$ denote the number of sets H_σ^γ to which (v_i, v_j) belongs. Thus, (4) can also be written as

$$\bar{S}(T) \leq \frac{2\alpha}{1-\beta} \cdot \frac{1}{\mathcal{M}} \sum_{(v_i,v_j)\in E} m_{i,j} \cdot deg_H(v_i, v_j) \leq \frac{2\alpha}{1-\beta} \cdot \max_{i,j} \{deg_H(v_i, v_j)\}. \tag{5}$$

Now suppose $e \in \mathcal{C}(\mathcal{S}_\sigma)$ for some σ. Clearly $e \in E_{\sigma'}$ if and only if $N_{\sigma'}$ is an ancestor of N_σ in $\mathcal{T}$, i.e., σ' is a prefix of σ. We will bound the number of nodes $N_{\sigma'}$ for which $e \in H_{\sigma'}^\gamma$, thus bounding $deg_H(e)$.

Let $e = (v_i, v_j)$, and let ξ denote the *depth* of N_σ in $\mathcal{T}$, i.e., $\xi = |\sigma|$. Since $e \in E_\sigma$, $\omega_{i,j} \leq D_\sigma$. Moreover, Property (1) of an (α, β, γ)-separated partition guarantees that for every ancestor $N_{\sigma'}$ of N_σ such that $|\sigma'| = \xi - \mu$,

$$D_\sigma \leq \beta^\mu \cdot D_{\sigma'} .$$

Fix $\mu_0 = \log_{1/\beta}(\gamma n^3)$. For $\mu > \mu_0$ we get

$$\omega_{i,j} \leq D_\sigma < \frac{D_{\sigma'}}{\gamma n^3} \leq \frac{D_{\sigma'}}{\gamma n_{\sigma'}{}^3}$$

and therefore $e \notin H_{\sigma'}^\gamma$. Thus, $e \in H_{\sigma'}^\gamma$ for at most $\mu_0 + 1$ nodes $N_{\sigma'}$, giving $deg_H(e) \leq \mu_0 + 1$. Combining this with (5) gives

$$\bar{S}(T) \leq \frac{2\alpha}{1-\beta} \cdot (1 + \log_{1/\beta}(\gamma n^3)) = O(\alpha \ln n) . \quad \blacksquare$$

Remark. Since $deg_H(e) \leq Depth(\mathcal{T})$ for all $e \in E$, it is possible to replace the $\ln n$ factor in the average stretch bound by $\ln \mathcal{D}$, where $\mathcal{D} = \max\{\omega_{i,j}\} \ / \ \min\{\omega_{i,j}\}$, yielding

$$\bar{S}(T) \leq \frac{2\alpha}{1-\beta} \cdot Depth(\mathcal{T}) = O(\alpha \ln \mathcal{D}).$$

4 Approximation in 2-Dimensional Euclidean Networks

In this section we consider the case where the network at hand is a complete 2-dimensional Euclidean network. Formally, let $G(V, E, \omega, m)$ be a complete n-vertex weighted graph as before, except that the vertices are embedded in 2-dimensional space, and the edge weights $\omega_{i,j}$ represent the Euclidean distance between the vertices (i.e., in the metric based on the L_2 norm).

Theorem 3. *For every n-vertex Euclidean graph $G(V, E, \omega, m)$ as above, there is an (α, β, γ)-separated partition $\mathcal{S} = \{S_1, \ldots, S_4\}$ with $\alpha = \gamma = 6(1 + \sqrt{2})$, $\beta = \sqrt{8/9}$.*

Corollary 4. *For every n-vertex 2-dimensional Euclidean graph $G(V, E, \omega, m)$ as above with diameter D there is a spanning tree T satisfying $Depth(T) = O(D)$ and $\bar{S}(T) = O(\ln n)$. This tree can be found deterministically in polynomial time.* ∎

Corollary 5. *For every n-vertex 2-dimensional Euclidean instance of the MCT problem with diameter D there is a spanning tree T satisfying $Depth(T) = O(D)$ and $C(T) = O(\ln n \cdot C^*)$. This tree can be found deterministically in polynomial time.* ∎

Proof. Denote the coordinates of a vertex v_i by (x_i, y_i). Without loss of generality assume that the network is placed in the first quadrant of the plane, so that $0 \le x_i \le D$ and $0 \le y_i \le D$ for every i. Define an (a,b)-*quad-partition* of G as a partition of the vertices into four clusters based on cutting the plane along the lines $x = a$ and $y = b$. (Vertices falling on the cutting line can be associated with one of the relevant clusters arbitrarily.)

Let $\mathcal{K} = D/3$, and let $q_k = \mathcal{K} + k/2$ for any integer k in the range $0 \le k \le 2\mathcal{K}$. Note that $D/3 \le q_k \le 2D/3$ for every k. For every integer $0 \le k \le 2\mathcal{K}$, let $\mathcal{S}_k = \{S_k^1, \ldots, S_k^4\}$ be the (q_k, q_k)-quad-partition of G. Observe that each such partition $\mathcal{S}_k$ satisfies the first property of an (α, β, γ)-separated partition for $\beta = \sqrt{8/9}$, as for every cluster S_k^ℓ, $1 \le \ell \le 4$, the width of the cluster along any dimension is at most $2D/3$, hence the maximum distance between any two vertices in S_k^ℓ is bounded by $\sqrt{2(2D/3)^2}$ (see Fig. 2).

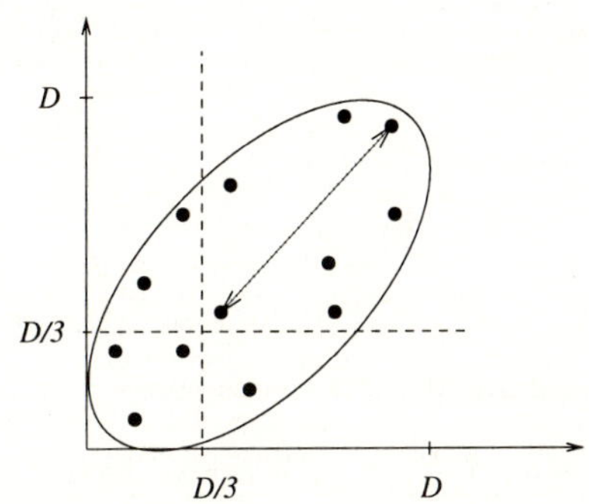

Fig. 2. Bounding the maximum cluster diameter in a (q_k, q_k)-quad-partition (here $k = 1$).

For every edge $e = (v_i, v_j)$, let $\delta_{i,j}$ denote the number of partitions $\mathcal{S}_k$ in which e occurs as an inter-cluster edge (i.e., $e \in \mathcal{C}(\mathcal{S}_k)$). Consider an edge $e = (v_i, v_j)$, and let $\Delta_x = |x_i - x_j|$ and $\Delta_y = |y_i - y_j|$. Observe that e will cross the vertical cut-line $x = q_k$ (respectively, the horizontal cut-line $y = q_k$) in at most $\lceil 2\Delta_x \rceil$ (resp., $\lceil 2\Delta_y \rceil$) partitions $\mathcal{S}_k$, and therefore $\delta_{i,j} \le \lceil 2\Delta_x \rceil + \lceil 2\Delta_y \rceil \le 2\Delta_x + 2\Delta_y + 2$. The sum $\Delta_x + \Delta_y$ maximizes (subject to $\Delta_x^2 + \Delta_y^2 = \omega_{i,j}^2$) when $\Delta_x = \Delta_y$, yielding $2\Delta_x + 2\Delta_y \le 2\sqrt{2} \cdot \omega_{i,j}$, and therefore

$$\delta_{i,j} \le 2\sqrt{2} \cdot \omega_{i,j} + 2 \le 2(1+\sqrt{2})\omega_{i,j}. \tag{6}$$

Let $\mathcal{G}$ be the class of "good" partitions, that do not intersect any light edge. Formally, $\mathcal{G}$ contains those partitions $\mathcal{S}_k$ that satisfy Property (3) of an (α, β, γ)-separated partition, i.e., $\mathcal{C}(\mathcal{S}_k) \subseteq H^\gamma$. Let $\mathcal{B}$ denote the class of remaining "bad" partitions. Since each partition in $\mathcal{B}$ contains a light edge $e \in L^\gamma$, the number of such partitions is bounded by

$$|\mathcal{B}| \le \sum_{(v_i,v_j)\in L^\gamma} \delta_{i,j} \le n^2 \cdot 2(1+\sqrt{2}) \max_{(v_i,v_j)\in L^\gamma} \{\omega_{i,j}\} \le \frac{2(1+\sqrt{2})}{\gamma \cdot n} \cdot D \le D/3$$

for $\gamma = 6(1+\sqrt{2})$, and hence $|\mathcal{G}| \ge \lfloor 2\mathcal{K} \rfloor + 1 - D/3 \ge D/3$.

For every edge $e = (v_i, v_j)$, let $\delta'_{i,j}$ denote the number of "good" partitions $\mathcal{S}_k$ in which e occurs as an inter-cluster edge. Let

$$Q = \sum_{\mathcal{S}_k \in \mathcal{G}} \psi(\mathcal{C}(\mathcal{S}_k)).$$

Note that this sum can also be written as

$$Q = \sum_{(v_i,v_j)\in E} \frac{\delta'_{i,j} m_{i,j}}{\omega_{i,j}}.$$

Since $\delta'_{i,j} \le \delta_{i,j}$ for all (v_i, v_j), and since $\delta'_{i,j} = 0$ for all $(v_i, v_j) \in L^\gamma$,

$$Q = \sum_{(v_i,v_j)\in H^\gamma} \frac{\delta'_{i,j} m_{i,j}}{\omega_{i,j}} \le \sum_{(v_i,v_j)\in H^\gamma} \frac{\delta_{i,j} m_{i,j}}{\omega_{i,j}}.$$

By inequality (6),

$$Q \le \sum_{(v_i,v_j)\in H^\gamma} \frac{2(1+\sqrt{2}) \cdot \omega_{i,j} \cdot m_{i,j}}{\omega_{i,j}} = 2(1+\sqrt{2})\mathcal{M}(H^\gamma).$$

Hence by an averaging argument there exists some partition $\mathcal{S}_k \in \mathcal{G}$ for which

$$\psi(\mathcal{C}(\mathcal{S}_k)) \le \frac{2(1+\sqrt{2})\mathcal{M}(H^\gamma)}{|\mathcal{G}|} \le \frac{2(1+\sqrt{2})\mathcal{M}(H^\gamma)}{D/3} \le \alpha\mathcal{M}(H^\gamma)/D$$

for $\alpha = 6(1+\sqrt{2})$. ∎

We remark that while the analysis refers to $\Theta(D)$ (q_k, q_k)-quad-partitions of G, there are at most $O(n)$ different partitions that need to be examined, and hence the construction is polynomial even if D is large.

5 Approximation in d-Dimensional Euclidean Networks

In this section we consider the case where the network $G(V, E, \omega, m)$ at hand is a complete weighted d-dimensional Euclidean network (with the vertices embedded in d-dimensional space and the edge weights representing distances in the L_2 norm). We assume $d \leq n$. The proof follows the lines of the 2-dimensional case (although some care is necessary to avoid a waste of a $\sqrt{d}$ factor), and is omitted from the extended abstract.

Theorem 6. *For every n-vertex d-dimensional Euclidean graph $G(V, E, \omega, m)$ as above, there is an (α, β, γ)-separated partition $\mathcal{S} = \{S_1, \ldots, S_k\}$ with $\alpha = O(d)$, $\beta = 1/2$, $\gamma = O(1)$.*

Corollary 7. *For every n-vertex d-dimensional Euclidean graph $G(V, E, \omega, m)$ as above with diameter D there is a spanning tree T satisfying $Depth(T) = O(D)$ and $\bar{S}(T) = O(d \ln n)$. This tree can be found deterministically in polynomial time.* ▮

Corollary 8. *For every n-vertex d-dimensional Euclidean instance of the MCT problem with diameter D there is a spanning tree T satisfying $Depth(T) = O(D)$ and $C(T) = O(d \cdot \ln n \cdot C^*)$. This tree can be found deterministically in polynomial time.* ▮

6 Approximation Using Embeddings in Low Dimension

In this section we consider the MAST problem on complete graphs with arbitrary (non-Euclidean) weights. Formally, the input to the problem is a complete weighted connected graph $G(V, E, \omega, m)$ (with arbitrary multiplicities $m_{i,j} \geq 0$).

Let $f_{p,p'}$ denote the Euclidean distance between points p and p' in d-dimensional space (according to the L_2 norm). An *embedding* of the graph G in d-dimensional Euclidean space is a mapping φ from the vertices of G into points in the Euclidean space. The *distortion* of the embedding is said to be $\rho \geq 1$ if for every two vertices v_i, v_j in G,

$$\omega_{i,j} \geq f_{\varphi(v_i),\varphi(v_j)} \geq \frac{1}{\rho} \cdot \omega_{i,j}. \tag{7}$$

We rely on the following result of [13, 9], giving a algorithmic version for an earlier existential result due to [4].

Proposition 9. **[13]** *There is a polynomial time algorithm for embedding any given n-vertex metric graph in an $O(\log n)$-dimensional Euclidean space with an $O(\log n)$ distortion.*

Using the proposition it is possible to prove the following (the proof is omitted from the extended abstract).

Theorem 10. *For every n-vertex graph $G(V, E, \omega, m)$ as above there is a spanning tree T for G with $Depth(T) = O(\ln n \cdot D)$ and $\bar{S}(T) = O(\ln^3 n)$.*

Remark. By Remark 3.2, the $\ln n$ factor in the average stretch bound can be replaced $\ln(\mathcal{D} \ln n)$, yielding a bound of $\bar{S}(T) = O(\ln^2 n(\ln \mathcal{D} + \ln\ln n))$.

Remark. Although the algorithm given in [13] for Proposition 9 is randomized, a different proof of the Johnson-Lindenstrauss lemma given in [9] can be derandomized by the method of conditional probabilities [10], yielding a *deterministic* algorithm for Theorem 10.

Corollary 11. *For every n-vertex instance of the MCT problem with diameter D, there is a spanning tree T satisfying $Depth(T) = O(\ln n \cdot D)$ and $C(T) = O(\ln^3 n \cdot C^*)$. This tree can be found in polynomial time.* ∎

7 Approximation Using Direct Partitioning

In this section we present a direct method to break any graph $G(V, E, \omega, m)$ into an (α, β, γ)-separated partition with $\alpha = O(\ln n)$.

Theorem 12. *Every graph $G(V, E, \omega, m)$ can be broken into an (α, β, γ)-separated partition with $\alpha = O(\ln n)$. The partition can be found deterministically in polynomial time.*

Corollary 13. *For every n-vertex graph $G(V, E, \omega, m)$ with diameter D there is a spanning tree T satisfying $Depth(T) = O(D)$ and $\bar{S}(T) = O(\ln^2 n)$. This tree can be found deterministically in polynomial time.* ∎

Corollary 14. *For every n-vertex instance of the MCT problem with diameter D there is a spanning tree T satisfying $Depth(T) = O(D)$ and $C(T) = O(\ln n \cdot C^*)$. This tree can be found deterministically in polynomial time.* ∎

Proof sketch. The crux of the proof is the observation that the partitioning algorithm used in [1] can be generalized for complete graphs.

For every cluster $S \subseteq V$, let $E(S)$ be the set of edges in or touching S, i.e. $E(S) = \{(v_i, v_j) \mid v_i \in S \text{ or } v_j \in S\}$, and let $\mathcal{C}(S)$ be the set of edges joining S and $V \setminus S$.

Analogous to the definitions in Section 2, we say that a cluster $S \subseteq V$ is an (α, β, γ)-separated cluster if:

1. $Diam(S) \leq \beta D$.
2. $\psi(\mathcal{C}(S)) \leq \alpha \cdot \frac{\mathcal{M}(E(S))}{D}$.
3. $\mathcal{C}(S) \subseteq H^\gamma$.

Given an algorithm that finds an (α, β, γ)-separated cluster one can easily generate an (α, β, γ)-separated partition, by repeatedly applying the cluster-finding algorithm, and by removing the found cluster from the graph at each iteration.

Let $B(v, r)$ denote the ball with radius r around vertex v, i.e. $B(v, r) = \{v_j \mid dist(v, v_j) \leq r\}$. We show that there exists a vertex v_i and a radius $r \leq D/2$, such that $B(v_i, r)$ is an (α, β, γ)-separated cluster with $\alpha = O(\ln n)$. (Such a pair (v_i, r) can thus be found deterministically in polynomial time.) The details are omitted from the extended abstract. ∎

References

1. N. Alon, R.M. Karp, D. Peleg, and D. West. A graph-theoretic game and its application to the k-server problem. *SIAM J. on Computing*, pages 78–100, 1995.
2. Y. Bartal. Probabilistic approximation of metric spaces and its algorithmic applications. In *Proc. 37th IEEE Symp. on Foundations of Computer Science*, pages 184–193, 1996.
3. Y. Bartal. On approximating arbitrary metrics by tree metrics. To appear in *Proc. 30th Annual ACM Symp. on Theory of Computer Science.*
4. J. Bourgain. On Lipschitz embeddings of finite metric spaces in Hilbert spaces. *Israel J. Math.*, pages 46–52, 1985.
5. M. Charikar, C. Chekuri, A. Goel, and S. Guha. Rounding via trees: deterministic approximation algorithms for group steiner trees and k-median. To appear in *Proc. 30th Annual ACM Symp. on Theory of Computer Science.*
6. G. Even, J. Naor, S. Rao, and B. Schieber. Divide-and-conquer approximation algorithms via spreading metrics. In *Proc. 36th IEEE Symp. on Foundations of Computer Science*, pages 62–71, October 1995.
7. M.R. Garey and D.S. Johnson. *Computers and Intractability: a Guide to the Theory of NP-Completness.* W. H. Freeman and Co., San Francisco, CA, 1979.
8. T.C. Hu. Optimum communication spanning trees. *SIAM J. on Computing*, pages 188–195, 1974.
9. P. Indyk, R. Motwani. Approximate nearest neighbors: towards removing the curse of dimensionality (preliminary version). To appear in *Proc. 30th Annual ACM Symp. on Theory of Computer Science.*
10. P. Indyk. *Private Communication.*
11. D.S. Johnson, J.K. Lenstra, and A.H.G. Rinnooy-Kan. The complexity of the network design problem. *Networks*, 8:275–285, 1978.
12. A. Kershenbaum. *Telecommunications network design algorithms.* McGraw-Hill Book Co., 1993.
13. N. Linial, E. London, and Y. Rabinovich. The geometry of graphs and some of its algorithmic applications. *Combinatorica*, 15:215–245, 1995.
14. D. Peleg. Approximating minimum communication spanning trees. In *Proc. 4th Colloq. on Structural Information & Communication Complexity*, July 1997.
15. P.D. Seymour. Packing directed circuites fractionally. *Combinatorica*, 15:2 281–288, 1995.
16. B.Y. Wu, G. Lancia, Y. Bafna, K.M. Chao, R. Ravi, and C.Y. Tang. A polynomial time approximation scheme for minimum routing cost spanning trees. In *Proc. 9th ACM-SIAM Symp. on Discrete Algorithms*, pages 21-32, January 1998.

A Polynomial Time Approximation Scheme for Euclidean Minimum Cost k-Connectivity *

Artur Czumaj[1] and Andrzej Lingas[2]

[1] Heinz Nixdorf Institute and Department of Mathematics & Computer Science
University of Paderborn, D-33095 Paderborn, Germany
E-mail: artur@uni-paderborn.de
[2] Department of Computer Science, Lund University
Box 118, S-22100 Lund, Sweden
E-mail: Andrzej.Lingas@dna.lth.se

Abstract. We present polynomial-time approximation schemes for the problem of finding a minimum-cost k-connected Euclidean graph on a finite point set in R^d. The cost of an edge in such a graph is equal to the Euclidean distance between its endpoints. Our schemes use Steiner points. For every given $c > 1$ and a set S of n points in $\mathbb{R}^d$, a randomized version of our scheme finds an Euclidean graph on a superset of S which is k-vertex (or k-edge) connected with respect to S, and whose cost is with probability $\frac{1}{2}$ within $(1 + \frac{1}{c})$ of the minimum cost of a k-vertex (or k-edge) connected Euclidean graph on S, in time $n \cdot (\log n)^{(\mathcal{O}(c\sqrt{d}k))^{d-1}} \cdot 2^{((\mathcal{O}(c\sqrt{d}k))^{d-1})!}$. We can derandomize the scheme by increasing the running time by a factor $\mathcal{O}(n)$. We also observe that the time cost of the derandomization of the PTA schemes for Euclidean optimization problems in $\mathbb{R}^d$ derived by Arora can be decreased by a multiplicative factor of $\Omega(n^{d-1})$.

1 Introduction

Connectivity problems are fundamental in graph theory and they have many important applications in computer science. There has been a lot of work done on the problems of finding subgraphs that meet given connectivity properties. The problem of finding a minimum-cost k-vertex or k-edge connected subgraph of an undirected graph belongs to the central algorithmic problems in this area. It is well-known that even if all edge weights are equal this problem is $\mathcal{NP}$-hard for $k \geq 2$ [4]. Therefore the research has concentrated on the design of polynomial-time approximation algorithms for the minimum-cost k-connectivity problems.

In this paper we consider the problems of finding a minimum-cost k-vertex or k-edge connected Euclidean graph on a finite point set in R^d. The cost of an edge in such a graph is equal to the Euclidean distance between its endpoints, and the cost of the whole graph is the total cost of its edges. We show that it is possible to approximate optimal solutions to these problems arbitrarily closely provided that additional points (i.e., Steiner points [5]) can be used.

A *polynomial-time approximation scheme* (*PTAS*) for an optimization problem is a family of algorithms $\{\mathcal{A}_\varepsilon\}$ such that for each fixed $\varepsilon > 0$, $\mathcal{A}_\varepsilon$ runs in time polynomial in the size of the input and produces a $(1 + \varepsilon)$-approximate solution [5].

* Research supported in part by ALCOM EU ESPRIT Long Term Research Project 20244 (ALCOM-IT), by DFG Grant Me872/7-1, and by TFR grant 96-278.

Our main results are the first PTA schemes (using Steiner points) for the Euclidean minimum-cost k-vertex connectivity and the Euclidean minimum-cost k-edge connectivity problems in $\mathbb{R}^d$ for all $k \geq 2$ and d such that $(\alpha\sqrt{d}k)^{d-1} \leq \beta\frac{\log\log n}{\log\log\log n}$ for some positive constants α and β. For every given c, we design a randomized algorithm running in time $n \cdot (\log n)^{(\mathcal{O}(c\sqrt{d}k))^{d-1}} \cdot 2^{((\mathcal{O}(c\sqrt{d}k))^{d-1})!}$ and producing with probability $\frac{1}{2}$ an Euclidean graph which is k-vertex (or, k-edge) connected with respect to the input point set and has cost within $(1+\frac{1}{c})$ of the minimum cost of a k-vertex (or k-edge) connected Euclidean graph on the input point set. We can derandomize the algorithm by increasing the running time by a factor $\mathcal{O}(n)$.

Our algorithms follow the general framework proposed recently by Arora [1–3] for designing PTAS for Euclidean versions of TSP, Minimum Steiner Tree, Min-Cost Perfect Matching, k-TSP, and k-MST. The aforementioned problems considered by Arora aim at the construction of simple graph structures (paths, trees or matchings) whereas our problem requires a construction of a k-connected graph. This adds several additional subproblems and crucial details in the design of our PTAS.

Similarly as Arora, we hierarchically partition the cube containing the input points into regions, and then show that there is an approximate solution to the problem which can cross the boundaries of each region only in prespecified points a bounded number of times (Structure Theorem). In order to combine optimal partial solutions within regions into an optimal global solution under the crossing restrictions we derive a k-connectivity characteristic of a spanning subgraph within a region solely in terms of the set of the prespecified points on the region boundary included in its vertex set. In our crucial theorem, we show that the connectivity characteristic of a union of two adjacent subgraphs can be computed from the connectivity characteristics of the subgraphs. This allows us to set up a dynamic programming procedure computing a minimum-cost Euclidean graph which is k-vertex or k-edge connected with respect to the input point set and obeys the crossing restrictions.

It is also worth mentioning that our Structure Theorem differs from those considered by Arora in [2]. First of all it relies on a more complicated (because of the k-connectivity requirement) so called Patching Lemma than those in [2]. Secondly, it uses a common random shift for all coordinates of the hierarchical partition whereas the Structure Theorems in [2] assume randomly picking an independent shift for each coordinate of the partition. The latter difference enables us to derandomize our PTA schemes by increasing the running time by a factor $\mathcal{O}(n)$ whereas Arora needs increase the running time of his PTA schemes by a factor $\mathcal{O}(n^d)$ in order to make them deterministic. Interestingly, we can easily modify the Structure Theorems in [2] by introducing the common shift and in this way improve the running times of the deterministic PTA schemes derived in [2] by a factor $\Omega(n^{d-1})$.

The structure of our paper is as follows. In Section 2, we precisely define the hierarchical partition, the so-called straight-line graphs that will be constructed by our dynamic programming procedure, the special crossing points, and the straight-line graphs using a bounded number of the crossing points. In Section 3, we derive our basic lemmata (Perturbation Lemma, Patching Lemma, and Charging Lemma) and derive our Structure Theorem from them. In Section 4, we prove the theorem on computing connectivity characteristic, present our dynamic programming procedure and estimate its time complexity. In Section 5, we present our main result on PTA schemes for the Euclidean minimum-cost k-vertex and k-edge connectivity problems and the possible improvement in the derandomization of PTA schemes presented in [2]. Because of space considerations, we present only the details of our PTAS for k-vertex connectivity and defer those for k-edge connectivity to the full version of the paper.

Related Works For an excellent survey presenting approximation algorithms for various minimum-cost k-connected spanning subgraph problems we refer the reader to the book edited by Hochbaum [5], and especially, to the chapter of Khuller [6]. As a byproduct of his PTAS for TSP, Arora presented a PTAS for the Euclidean Minimum Steiner Tree problem in [1–3]. The idea of a PTAS for Euclidean minimum-cost biconnectivity in $\mathbb{R}^2$ based on Mitchell's approach [8] is also outlined in a recent parallel work [7].

2 Preliminaries

We shall adhere to standard notation on approximation graph algorithms [5]. A set of paths in a graph will be called *internally vertex-disjoint* if each common vertex of any two paths in the set is an endpoint of both paths. We need introduce more specific notation on geometric graphs and partitioning.

Let U be a set of points in $\mathbb{R}^d$. A *straight-line graph* (SG for short) on U is a graph whose vertices are in one-to-one correspondence with the points in U, and whose edges are in one-to-one correspondence with the straight-line segments connecting the points corresponding to the incident vertices. The *cost* of an edge is the length of the corresponding segment, and the cost of the whole graph is the total cost of its edges. An SG on U is *k-vertex (or, k-edge) connected with respect to* a subset S of $\mathbb{R}^d$ if $S \subseteq U$ and for each pair of points in S there are at least k internally vertex-disjoint (or, edge-disjoint) paths connecting the corresponding vertices in the SG.

We shall find our approximation scheme for the minimum-cost straight-line graph that is k-connected with respect to the input n-point set in $\mathbb{R}^d$ by combing geometric partitioning with dynamic programming (we assume throughout the paper that $1 \leq k < n$ and that $d \geq 2$). To simplify the partitioning, we shall perform a perturbation of the input points that moves them to points of integral coordinates and guarantees the interpoint distance at least 8 (see the Perturbation Lemma). Some of the input points can have the same integral coordinates after the perturbation. For this reason and in order to facilitate the dynamic programming, the set of vertices in straight-line graphs will correspond to a multiset of points in $\mathbb{R}^d$ in general.

Let the *bounding cube* of the input multiset of points in $\mathbb{R}^d$ be the smallest axis-aligned cube W^d in $\mathbb{R}^d$ that contains it. Following [3], the geometric partitioning of the bounding cube can be defined as follows.

Definition 1. *A* (2^d-ary) dissection *of the bounding cube W^d is its recursive partitioning into sub-cubes, called* regions. *Each* region *U^d of volume > 1 is recursively partitioned into 2^d regions $(U/2)^d$. An* 2^d-ary tree *is a tree whose root corresponds to the bounding cube, and whose other non-leaf nodes correspond to the regions containing at least two points from the input multiset. For a non-leaf node v of the tree, the nodes corresponding to the 2^d regions partitioning the region corresponding to v are the children of v in the tree.*

Note that the dissection has $\mathcal{O}(W^d)$ regions and its recursion depth is $\mathcal{O}(\log W)$.

Definition 2. *For any a, where $0 \leq a < W$, the* a-shifted *dissection of the bounding cube W^d is defined by shifting all the coordinates of the hyperplanes forming the dissection by a, and then reducing them modulo W.*

Note that some of the regions of the shifted dissection are wrapped around. To simplify notation, we shall treat them as single regions (for more details see [3]). The *a-shifted 2^d-ary tree* is defined analogously.

Our *Structure Theorem* will assert that if the shift a is an integer chosen uniformly at random then with probability at least $\frac{1}{2}$ there exists SG which is k-vertex connected with respect to the input multiset, has cost within $(1 + \frac{1}{c})$ of the minimum cost of a k-connected SG on the multiset, crosses each facet of each region (corresponding to a node) in the a-shifted 2^d-ary tree $\mathcal{O}((c\sqrt{d}k)^{d-1})$ times only at prespecified points called *portals*, and has Steiner points only at some of the portals. It differs substantially from the original variants of Structure Theorems considered by Arora in [3] where the values of shifts for distinct coordinates are picked independently.

Definition 3. *An* m-regular *set of* portals *in a $d - 1$-dimensional cube N^{d-1} is an orthogonal lattice of m points in the cube where the spacing between the portals is* $\frac{N+1}{m^{\frac{1}{d-1}}}$.

Now, the restricted form of an SG considered in the Structure Theorem can be formalized as follows.

Definition 4. *An SG is* (m, r)-light *with respect to the shifted 2^d-ary tree if its edges cross each facet of each region of the tree at most r times, always through one of the m portals and all its Steiner points are at portals. (Its edges can cross a portal up to r times, possibly having (Steiner) endpoints at it).*

By the Structure Theorem, it will be sufficient to find a minimum-cost SG which is both (m, r)-light with respect to a shifted 2^d-ary tree and k-vertex connected with respect to the perturbed input multipoint set, in order to obtain a close approximation for our Euclidean minimum-cost k-connectivity problem for the perturbed instance.

3 Basic lemmata

A *well-rounded* instance of the minimum-cost k-vertex connectivity problem is one in which all input points have non-negative integral coordinates, the volume of the bounding box is $(\mathcal{O}(n\sqrt{d}))^d$, and the distance between any two points is at least 8 or is zero.

The proof of the following lemma is analogous to the proof of Proposition 1 in [1]. Additionally, it is important to observe that we may assume without loss of generality that the degree of any input point in a straight-line graph in $\mathbb{R}^d$ that is k-vertex connected with respect to the input points is k. (Otherwise, we could introduce k appropriately outerconnected and interconnected Steiner points overlapping with the input point and connected with it by only k zero-length edges.)

Lemma 1. (Perturbation Lemma) *Suppose there is a PTAS, using Steiner points, for well-rounded n-point instances of the minimum-cost k-vertex connectivity problem for straight-line graphs in $\mathbb{R}^d$. Then there is a PTAS, using Steiner points, for all n-point instances of the minimum-cost k-vertex connectivity problem for straight-line graphs in $\mathbb{R}^d$.*

The following *Patching Lemma* is crucial in the proof of the Structure Theorem. Because of the higher connectivity requirements, it is much complicated than the versions of patching lemmata considered by Arora [3].

Lemma 2. (Patching Lemma) *If G is a SG in $\mathbb{R}^d$ that is k-vertex connected with respect to the input multipoint set S and crosses a $(d-1)$-dimensional W^{d-1}-cube l times (where we assume that the border of the cube contains no point itself), then there exist straight-line graphs G^* and H, where G^* is a subgraph of G, and a positive constant α such that*

- *for any pair of vertices of G in S there are k internally vertex-disjoint paths connecting them in $G^* \cup H$,*
- *G^* does not cross the cube and H crosses the cube at most k times, and*
- *the sum of the costs of the edges in $G^* \cup H$ is at most $\alpha k W l^{1-\frac{1}{d-1}}$ plus the cost of the edges in G, where α is a positive constant.*

Proof. Since the lemma is trivial for $l \leq k$, we shall assume that $l > k$. We show only how G^* and H are constructed and that they satisfy the first (i.e., vertex-connectivity) requirement; the remaining requirements easily follow from our construction.

Let $x_1, \ldots, x_l$ be the points at which G crosses the $(d-1)$-dimensional W^{d-1}-cube C. For each i, $1 \leq i \leq l$, break the edge $\{y_i, z_i\}$ crossing C at x_i into two parts, one on each side of C; we assume that all vertices $y_1, \ldots, y_l$ are one the same side of C. We consider $2k+4$ copies of each x_i, denoted by $x^+_{i,j}$, and $x^-_{i,j}$ with $0 \leq j \leq k+1$, $k+2$ copies for each side of C.

Now we define straight-line graphs G^* and H. G^* is obtained from G by removing all the edges crossing C. H contains the vertex set $\{y_1, \ldots, y_l\} \cup \{z_1, \ldots, z_l\} \cup \bigcup_{1 \leq i \leq l \ \& \ 0 \leq j \leq k+1} \{x^+_{i,j}\} \cup \bigcup_{1 \leq i \leq l \ \& \ 0 \leq j \leq k+1} \{x^-_{i,j}\}$ and eight groups of edges:

(1) two halves of each edge crossing C in G in the form of the edges $\{y_i, x^+_{i,0}\}$ and $\{x^-_{i,0}, z_i\}$ for all $1 \leq i \leq l$,
(2) edges connecting $x^+_{i,0}$ with $x^+_{i,j}$ for all $1 \leq i \leq l, 1 \leq j \leq k$,
(3) edges connecting $x^-_{i,0}$ with $x^-_{i,j}$ for all $1 \leq i \leq l, 1 \leq j \leq k$,
(4) edges connecting $x^+_{i,k+1}$ with $x^-_{i,k+1}$ for all $1 \leq i \leq k$,
(5) edges connecting $x^+_{i,k+1}$ with $x^+_{i,j}$ for all $1 \leq i \leq l, 1 \leq j \leq k$,
(6) edges connecting $x^-_{i,k+1}$ with $x^-_{i,j}$ for all $1 \leq i \leq l, 1 \leq j \leq k$,
(7) edges of a traveling salesman path for $\bigcup_{1 \leq i \leq l} \{x^+_{i,j}\}$, for all $1 \leq j \leq k$,
(8) edges of a traveling salesman path for $\bigcup_{1 \leq i \leq l} \{x^-_{i,j}\}$, for all $1 \leq j \leq k$.

It is easy to see that the cost of the non-zero length edges in $G^* \cup H$ is bounded from above by the cost of the edges in G plus the cost of the $2k$ traveling salesman paths for the point sets $\bigcup_{1 \leq i \leq l} \{x^+_{i,j}\}$, $\bigcup_{1 \leq i \leq l} \{x^-_{i,j}\}$, $j = 1, \ldots, k$, respectively. We can always construct the traveling salesman paths within the $(d-1)$-dimensional cube so each of them has total length smaller than $\frac{\alpha}{2} \cdot W \cdot l^{1-\frac{1}{d-1}}$ by Proposition 12 in [3], where α is a positive constant. We conclude that the total additional cost is bounded by $\alpha \cdot k \cdot W \cdot l^{1-\frac{1}{d-1}}$.

It remains to show that $G^* \cup H$ satisfies the vertex-connectivity requirement. Let $v, u \in V(G)$ and let P be a set of k internally vertex-disjoint paths between v and u in

G. We show that there are k internally vertex-disjoint paths between v and u in $G^* \cup H$. We consider only the case when v and u are on the opposite sides of $\mathcal{C}$; the case when they are on the same side can be handled analogously.

Let $P_1, \ldots, P_k$ be the paths in P that cross $\mathcal{C}$. For every, $1 \le r \le k$, let $y_{\alpha(r)}$ be the head of the first edge in P_r that crosses $\mathcal{C}$, and let $z_{\beta(r)}$ be the tail of the last edge in P_i that crosses $\mathcal{C}$. For every $r = 1, \ldots, k$, we construct a path P_r^* from $y_{\alpha(r)}$ to $z_{\beta(r)}$ that goes through $x^+_{\alpha(r),0}$, $x^+_{\alpha(r),r}$, the fragment of the r-th traveling salesman path between $x^+_{\alpha(r),r}$ and $x^+_{r,r}$, $x^+_{r,r}$, $x^+_{r,k+1}$, $x^-_{r,k+1}$, $x^-_{r,r}$, the fragment of the $k+r$-th traveling salesman path between $x^-_{r,r}$ and $x^-_{\beta(r),r}$, $x^-_{\beta(r),r}$ and $x^-_{\beta(r),0}$. By our construction, the paths P_r^* are pairwise internally vertex-disjoint and they can be easily combined with the paths in P to obtain k internally vertex-disjoint paths between v and u in $G^* \cup H$.

To prove our Structure Theorem, we need also the so called *Charging Lemma.*

Lemma 3. (Charging Lemma) *If the minimum internode distance is at least* 4, *then the sum of the number of times a SG in* $\mathbb{R}^d$ *crosses the hyperplanes of the unit grid is at most* $\frac{5\sqrt{d}}{4}$ *times the cost of the SG.*

Now, we are ready to prove the Structure Theorem.

Theorem 1. (Structure Theorem) *Let* $c > 0$. *Let* W *be the size of its bounding cube in a well-rounded instance of the minimum-cost* k*-vertex connectivity problem in* $\mathbb{R}^d$. *Pick* $a \in \{0, \ldots, W-1\}$ *uniformly at random. With probability at least* $\frac{1}{2}$, *there is a SG that is both* k*-vertex connected with respect to the multiset in the instance and* (m, r)*-light with respect to the* a*-shifted dissection and has cost within* $(1 + 1/c)$ *of the minimum cost of a* k*-vertex connected SG on this multiset, where* $m = (\mathcal{O}(c\sqrt{d}k \log W))^{d-1}$ *and* $r = (\mathcal{O}(c\sqrt{d}k))^{d-1}$.

Proof. Let G be a minimum-cost k-vertex connected SG on the well-rounded input multiset. Our approach is to repeatedly modify G to make it (m, r)-light. We first apply the Patching Lemma to each region in the a-shifted dissection to decrease the number of crossings the facet of each region to at most r. Then we modify the graph by moving each crossing and each Steiner point to its nearest portal. In order to bound the increase of the cost of the modified SG we will charge each change in the cost to some grid hyperplanes.

Unit grid hyperplanes $\mathcal{H}_1, \ldots, \mathcal{H}_d$ are called *siblings* if there is a q, $0 \le q < W$, such that each $\mathcal{H}_j$ is defined by equation $X_j = q$. The *maximal level* of a grid hyperplane $\mathcal{H}$ is the level of the largest region of the a-shifted dissection that has its facet on $\mathcal{H}$. Let a, $0 \le a \le W-1$, be the random shift used to construct the shifted dissection. We note that for sibling hyperplanes $\mathcal{H}_1, \ldots, \mathcal{H}_d$ the maximal level of each of $\mathcal{H}_j$ is the same and it depends only on a. Therefore for every $1 \le i \le \log W$

$$\mathbf{Pr}_a(\text{maximal level of each of } \mathcal{H}_1, \ldots, \mathcal{H}_d \text{ is } i) = 2^i/W \ . \tag{1}$$

Let us fix i and sibling unit grid hyperplanes $\mathcal{H}_1, \ldots, \mathcal{H}_d$ with maximum level i. We use the Patching Lemma to modify G and decrease the number of crossings of $\mathcal{H}_1, \ldots, \mathcal{H}_d$ in adjacent regions in a bottom-up fashion. Successively, for $j = \log W, \log W - 1, \ldots, i$, if the SG crosses a facet of a region at level j adjacent to at least one of

$\mathcal{H}_1, \ldots, \mathcal{H}_d$ more than r times, then we apply the Patching Lemma to decrease the number of crossings to at most $k \cdot 2^d$. (The reason for the $k2^d$ crossings, instead of just k, is that after applying the a-shift a wrapped region may be a union of up to 2^d smaller regions, for all of which the Patching Lemma may have to be invoked separately.)

Let $c_j(\mathcal{H}_1, \ldots, \mathcal{H}_d)$ be the number of regions at level j adjacent to at least one of $\mathcal{H}_1, \ldots, \mathcal{H}_d$ for which the Patching Lemma is applied. Let $t(G; \mathcal{H}_1, \ldots, \mathcal{H}_d)$ denote the number of times graph G crosses $\mathcal{H}_1, \ldots, \mathcal{H}_d$. Since each invocation of the Patching Lemma replaces at least $r+1$ crossings by at most $k \cdot 2^d$, and since G crosses hyperplanes $\mathcal{H}_1, \ldots, \mathcal{H}_d$ only $t(G; \mathcal{H}_1, \ldots, \mathcal{H}_d)$ times, we obtain

$$\sum_{j=1}^{\log W} c_j(\mathcal{H}_1, \ldots, \mathcal{H}_d) = \sum_{j=i}^{\log W} c_j(\mathcal{H}_1, \ldots, \mathcal{H}_d) \le \frac{t(G; \mathcal{H}_1, \ldots, \mathcal{H}_d)}{r+1-k \cdot 2^d} . \qquad (2)$$

Let the sth ($1 \le s \le c_j(\mathcal{H}_1, \ldots, \mathcal{H}_d)$) invocation of the Patching Lemma at level j reduces the number of crossings of a region from $t_{j,s} \ge r+1$, to at most $k \cdot 2^d$ crossings. Then clearly

$$\sum_{j=1}^{\log W} \sum_{s=1}^{c_j(\mathcal{H}_1, \ldots, \mathcal{H}_d)} (t_{j,s} - k \cdot 2^d) \le t(G; \mathcal{H}_1, \ldots, \mathcal{H}_d) .$$

Thus we may upper bound the sum $\sum_{j=1}^{\log W} \sum_{s=1}^{c_j(\mathcal{H}_1, \ldots, \mathcal{H}_d)} t_{j,s}^{\lambda}$ for any $0 < \lambda \le 1$, by maximizing $\sum_{j=1}^{\log W} c_j(\mathcal{H}_1, \ldots, \mathcal{H}_d)$ and setting each $t_{j,s}$ to roughly $r+1$. Hence, by (2) we have

$$\sum_{j=1}^{\log W} \sum_{s=1}^{c_j(\mathcal{H}_1, \ldots, \mathcal{H}_d)} t_{j,s}^{1-\frac{1}{d-1}} \le 2 \cdot \frac{t(G; \mathcal{H}_1, \ldots, \mathcal{H}_d)}{r+1-k \cdot 2^d} \cdot (r+1)^{1-\frac{1}{d-1}} . \qquad (3)$$

As we have shown in the Patching Lemma, the increase of the cost by applying the Patching Lemma to $\mathcal{H}_1, \ldots, \mathcal{H}_d$ is bounded from above by

$$\sum_{j=i}^{\log W} \sum_{s=1}^{c_j(\mathcal{H}_1, \ldots, \mathcal{H}_d)} \alpha \cdot k \cdot t_{j,s}^{1-\frac{1}{d-1}} \cdot \frac{W}{2^j} .$$

Therefore we may combine this bound with equation (1), and inequalities (2) and (3) to upper bound the expected increase of the cost charged by $\mathcal{H}_1, \ldots, \mathcal{H}_d$ by

$$\sum_{i=1}^{\log W} \frac{2^i}{W} \sum_{j=i}^{\log W} \sum_{s=1}^{c_j(\mathcal{H}_1, \ldots, \mathcal{H}_d)} \alpha k \cdot t_{j,s}^{1-\frac{1}{d-1}} \frac{W}{2^j} \le 4\alpha k \frac{(r+1)^{1-\frac{1}{d-1}} \cdot t(G; \mathcal{H}_1, \ldots, \mathcal{H}_d)}{r+1-k2^d} .$$

This is at most $\frac{t(G; \mathcal{H}_1, \ldots, \mathcal{H}_d)}{5 \cdot c \cdot \sqrt{d}}$ for some $r = (\Theta(c \cdot \sqrt{d} \cdot k))^{d-1}$.

The next modification of the SG consists of moving each crossing and each Steiner point introduced by the Patching Lemma to the nearest portal. For sibling hyperplanes $\mathcal{H}_1, \ldots, \mathcal{H}_d$ with maximal level i, each of the crossings or Steiner points could have to be moved by a distance at most $\sqrt{d} \cdot \frac{W}{2^i} \cdot m^{\frac{-1}{d-1}}$. Each crossing eliminated by the

Patching Lemma induces $\mathcal{O}(k)$ Steiner points. Thus the expected cost of moving every crossing in $\mathcal{H}_1, \ldots, \mathcal{H}_d$ to its nearest portal point is at most

$$\mathcal{O}\left(\sum_{i=1}^{\log W} \frac{2^i}{W} k\, t(G; \mathcal{H}_1, \ldots, \mathcal{H}_d) \frac{\sqrt{d}W}{2^i m^{\frac{1}{d-1}}}\right) = \mathcal{O}\left(\frac{\sqrt{d}k}{m^{\frac{1}{d-1}}} \log W\, t(G; \mathcal{H}_1, \ldots, \mathcal{H}_d)\right)$$

The above cost is bounded by $\frac{t(G;\mathcal{H}_1,\ldots,\mathcal{H}_d)}{5 \cdot c \cdot \sqrt{d}}$ for some $m = (\mathcal{O}(c \cdot \sqrt{d} \cdot k \cdot \log W))^{d-1}$.

Therefore, the expected cost increase (over the choice of the random shift a) of modifying the SG at sibling hyperplanes $\mathcal{H}_1, \ldots, \mathcal{H}_d$ is at most

$$\frac{t(G; \mathcal{H}_1, \ldots, \mathcal{H}_d)}{\frac{5}{2} \cdot c \cdot \sqrt{d}} .$$

This yields by linearity of expectations that the expected increase in the cost of the SG is bounded by

$$\sum_{\substack{\text{sibling hyperplanes} \\ \mathcal{H}_1, \ldots, \mathcal{H}_d}} \frac{t(G; \mathcal{H}_1, \ldots, \mathcal{H}_d)}{\frac{5}{2} \cdot c \cdot \sqrt{d}} ,$$

which is at most $\frac{1}{2c}$OPT by the Charging Lemma. Now, Markov's inequality implies that with probability at least $\frac{1}{2}$ the cost of the best SG that is k-vertex connected with respect to the input multiset and (m, r)-light with respect to the shifted dissection is at most $(1 + \frac{1}{c}) \cdot$ OPT.

In the proof we ignored the fact that an application of the Patching Lemma can increase the number of times the modified G crosses some hyperplanes perpendicular to the patched facet. This difficulty can be handled analogously as the corresponding one in [3] by slightly increasing the constant factor in the definition of r.

4 Computing a minimum cost (m, r)-light SG

Let us fix a random shift a. By the Structure Theorem, it is sufficient to find a minimum-cost SG that is k-vertex connected with respect to S and (m, r)-light with respect to the shifted dissection in order to obtain a close approximation of a minimum cost k-vertex connected SG on S. To set up our dynamic programming procedure for such an SG, we need the following definition.

Definition 5. *An* SG within a region *is an SG on the part of the multiset S contained in the region of the shifted 2^d-ary tree and a multiset of some portals within the region such that its edges lie within the region. It is (m, r)-light if for each facet of the region it includes at most r vertices corresponding to its portals.*

We shall find a minimum-cost SG which is k-vertex connected with respect to S and (m, r)-light with respect to the shifted dissection by dynamic programming combining optimal (m, r)-light straight-line graphs within neighboring regions on the same level in bottom up manner. Note that generally the SG within regions do not have to be k-vertex connected with respect to the included subset of S as the "missing" connectivity can be added from the complementary SG outside a given region. We shall provide a *connectivity characteristic* of a SG within a region depending only on the multiset of portals used for outer connections. The characteristic expresses routing properties within the SG and requirements on the routing properties in the complementary SG from the point of view of portals in order to preserve the k-connectivity.

Our dynamic programming procedure will determine for each region, for each multiset P of at most $2dr$ portals of the region (at most r on each of the $2d$ facets), and for each possible connectivity characteristic of an (m,r)-light SG within the region, the cost of an optimal (m,r)-light SG within the region using P and having this characteristic. The efficiency of the procedure relies on the requirement of the (m,r)-lightness and our key lemma on efficiently computing the connectivity characteristic of a SG from the connectivity characteristics of two straight-line graphs within adjacent regions.

To derive this important lemma, we shall abstractly model the straight-line graphs within regions as subgraphs of a graph G on a superset of S with a distinguished set of vertices of degree two outside S, called *outer portal vertices*.

For a subgraph H of G, let $P(H)$ be the set of outer portal vertices in H that have degree one. (Note that in particular, H may contain edges connecting pairs of vertices in $P(H)$, modeling fragments of SG connections just passing through a region.) A *portal completion of* H is an augmentation of H by the edges in a matching of the complete graph on $P(H)$.

Definition 6. *For each pair of distinct vertices* v, u *of* H *in* S, *let* $Com_H(v,u)$ *be the set of portal completions which augment* H *to a graph with* k*-vertex disjoint paths between* v *and* u. $Com_H(\cdot,\cdot)$ *induces an* internal connectivity *equivalence relation for pairs of vertices of* H *in* S.

For each vertex v *of* H *in* S, *let* $Path_H(v)$ *be the set of pairs* (U,Q) *where* U *is a subset of* $P(H)$, *and* Q *is a subset of the set of pairs of distinct vertices in* $P(H)$ *outside* U *such that there are* $|Q|+|U|$ *internally vertex-disjoint paths in* H *connecting* v *with each vertex in* U, *and connecting each pair of vertices in* Q, *respectively. (In fact, only pairs* (U,Q) *where* $|U|\geq k$ *are essential.)* $Path_H(\cdot)$ *induces an* external connectivity *equivalence relation for vertices of* H *in* S. *Finally, let* $Path_H$ *be the set of subsets* Q *of the set of pairs of distinct vertices in* $P(H)$ *such that there are* $|Q|$ *internally vertex-disjoint paths connecting each pair of vertices in* Q.

Let $M(p)$ denote the number of matchings in a complete graph on p vertices. Note that $M(p) < 2^{p/2}\lceil p/2\rceil!$.

Remark 1. Let $p=|P(H)|$. There are at most $2^{M(p)}$ different values of $Com_H(v,u)$, at most $2^{M(p)+2^p}$ different values of $Path_H(v)$, and at most $2^{M(p)}$ different values of $Path_H$ for $v,\ u\in P(H)$.

Let us call the set of values of $Com_H(v,u)$, $Path_H(u)$ and $Path_H$, where u and v range over the set of vertices of H in S, the *connectivity characteristic of* H, and denote it by $Char(H)$.

Let F be the family of all subgraphs H of G such that after augmenting H with the edges of the clique on $P(H)$, for any pair of vertices of H is S there are k internally vertex-disjoint paths connecting this pair in the augmented graph. (Note that the members in F model straight-line graphs within regions that can be extended to a SG which is k-vertex connected with respect to S.)

Remark 2. If $H \in F$ then the empty set (of sets of pairs of vertices in $P(H)$) cannot belong to $Char(H)$.

Remark 3. For each pair of vertices $v,\ u$ of H in S there are k internally vertex-disjoint paths connecting v with u in H if and only if each element of $Char(H)$ which is a set of sets of pairs of vertices in $P(H)$ (i.e., corresponding to $Com(\cdot)$) contains the empty set.

Theorem 2. *Let $H,\ H'$ be subgraphs in F with disjoint non-empty sets of non-portal vertices. Let $p = P(H)$ and $p' = P(H')$. The connectivity characteristic of $H \cup H'$ can be determined on the basis of those for H and H' in time* $O(2^{M(p)+2^p} 2^{M(p')+2^{p'}} M(p+p')(p+p')^3)$.

Proof. We shall show only how $Char(H \cup H')$ can be constructed, leaving the proof of the correctness of the construction to the reader.

First, let us consider computing all the values of $Com_{H \cup H}(\cdot,\cdot)$. Suppose $v,\ u$ are vertices of $H \cup H'$ in S. If both are vertices of H then we can compute $Com_{H \cup H'}(v,u)$ on the basis of $Com_H(v,u)$ and $Path_{H'}$ as follows. For each $C \in Com_H(v,u)$ and each Q in $Path_{H'}$, compute the auxiliary graph A whose vertex set is $P(H) \cup P(H')$ and whose edge set is Q. Now, insert into $Com_H(v,u)$ any portal completion of $H \cup H'$ which augments A to a graph containing a set of vertex disjoint paths connecting the endpoints of pairs in C, respectively. Recall that the number of different Q in $Path_{H'}$ is bounded by $M(p')$ from above. If both $v,\ u$ are vertices of H', we can compute $Com_{H \cup H'}(v,u)$ symmetrically. We conclude via Remark 1 that all the values of $Com(v,u)$, where $v,\ u$ are both in H or both in H' can be computed in time $O((2^{M(p)}M(p') + 2^{M(p')}M(p))M(p+p')2^{p+p'}(p+p'))$. The term $M(p+p')$ corresponds to the number of portal completions of $H \cup H'$ whereas $2^{p+p'}(p+p')$ corresponds to the exponential time-cost of testing A augmented by such a completion for the inclusion of the desired paths (decide for each edge of A augmented by the completion whether it is on such a path and then verify whether the chosen edges form the desired paths in linear time).

Suppose in turn that v is a vertex of H and u is a vertex of H'. To compute $Com_H(v,u)$ in this case, for each $(U,P) \in Path_H(v)$ and each $(U',P') \in Path_{H'}(v)$, build the auxiliary graph B whose set of vertices consists of the vertices occurring in pairs in $P \cup P'$ and the vertices in $U \cup U'$, and two auxiliary vertices h and h'. The edge set of B consists of pairs in $P \cup P' \cup \{(h,w)|w \in U\} \cup \{(h',w')|w' \in U'\}$. Next, we insert into $Com_{H \cup H'}(v,u)$ each portal completion of $H \cup H'$ that augments the auxiliary graph B to a graph with k internally vertex-disjoint paths between h and h'. Again by Remark 1, we conclude that all the values of $Com(v,u)$, where v is in H and u is in H', and both $v,\ u$ are in S, can be computed in time $O(2^{M(p)+2^p} 2^{M(p')+2^{p'}} M(p+p')(p+p')^3)$. The term $M(p+p')$ corresponds to the number of all possible portal completions of $H' \cup H$, and the term $(p+p')^3$ corresponds to the asymptotic time-cost of testing (by network flow) the existence of k-vertex disjoint paths in the auxiliary graph B augmented by a portal completion of $H \cup H'$.

In turn, consider computing all values of $Path_{H \cup H'}(\cdot)$. Suppose v is a vertex of H in S. We can compute $Path_{H \cup H'}(v)$ on the basis of $Path_H(v)$ and $Path_{H'}$ as follows. For each $(U,P) \in Path_H(v)$ and Q in $Path_{H'}$, compute the auxiliary graph D on the set of portal vertices occurring in the pairs in $P \cup Q$, and in U, with the edge set equal to

$P \cup Q$. If D is a union of isolated vertices outside $P(H) \cup P(H')$ and simple paths which either have no endpoint in $P(H) \cap P(H')$ or exactly one endpoint in $P(H) \cap P(H')$ which belongs also to U then proceed as follows. Form the set W consisting of all isolated vertices in D (they belong to $U \setminus (P(H) \cap P(H'))$ and the other endpoints of the paths beginning at vertices in $P(H) \cap P(H') \cap U$. Furthermore, form the set R of all pairs of endpoints of the remaining paths into which D is decomposed. Insert (W, R) into $Path_{H \cup H'}(v)$. It follows from Remark 1, that all the values of $Path_{H \cup H'}(v)$ can be computed in time $\mathcal{O}((2^{M(p)+2^p} M(p') + 2^{M(p')+2^{p'}} M(p))(p + p'))$.

Finally, $Path_{H \cup H'}$ can be easily formed by computing the set of the transitive closures of the graphs induced by $P \cup Q$ where $P \in Path_H$ and $Q \in Path_{H'}$.

Corollary 1. *Let Q be a non-leaf region of the shifted 2^d-ary tree. For all multisets P of at most $2dr$ portals (at most r from each facet of Q), and all possible connectivity characteristics C for P, we can compute minimum costs of (m, r)-light straight-line graphs within Q using P and having the characteristics C, on the basis of the minimum costs of (m, r)-light straight-line graphs within the child regions of Q (for all possible outer portal multisets and connectivity characteristics) in total time $m^{\mathcal{O}(d2^d r)} \cdot 2^{\mathcal{O}(2^{d(r+1)}(dr)!)}$.*

Proof. There are 2^d child regions of Q. For each of them we can choose an outer portal multiset in $m^{\mathcal{O}(dr)}$ ways and the connectivity characteristic in $2^{\mathcal{O}(M(2dr))}$ ways by Remark 1. (By Remark 2, we can skip characteristics containing an empty set). There are at most $(m^{\mathcal{O}(dr)} 2^{\mathcal{O}(M(2dr))})^{2^d}$ combinations of the aforementioned parameters for the 2^d child regions. Given such a combination, we can compute the parameters for the union of the child regions (if possible) in time $\mathcal{O}(2^d 2^{\mathcal{O}(M(2dr))})$ by applying 2^d times Theorem 2. Then, we can update the candidate value for the minimum cost of an (m, r)-light SG within Q obeying the resulting parameters by taking the minimum of the current cost and the sum of the minimum costs of (m, r)-light straight-line graphs within the child regions under the combination of parameters. (Note however that in the majority of the cases, such a combination of the parameters for child regions is not compatible, leaving some portals inside accessed only from one side or leading to a connectivity characteristic containing an empty set). Now the corollary follows by straightforward calculations.

Theorem 3. *Let $n = |S|$. Let $m = (\mathcal{O}(c\sqrt{d}k \log W))^{d-1}$ and $r = (\mathcal{O}(c\sqrt{d}k))^{d-1}$. An SG which is k-vertex connected with respect to the well rounded S and (m, r)-light with respect to the shifted dissection and whose cost is within $1 + \epsilon$ of the minimum (cost of such an SG) can be computed in time $n \cdot (\log n)^{(\mathcal{O}(c\sqrt{d}k))^{d-1}} \cdot 2^{((\mathcal{O}(c\sqrt{d}k))^{d-1})!}$.*

Proof. The 2^d-ary tree for S has $\mathcal{O}(2^d n \log n)$ regions, and it can be constructed in time $\mathcal{O}(2^d n (\log n)^{\mathcal{O}(1)})$. For each leaf region of the tree, each possible multiset of at most $2dr$ of its portals and each connectivity characteristic, the minimum cost of an (m, r)-light SG within the region (containing at most one point in S and having potential locations of Steiner points only at its portals) could be arbitrarily closely approximated by a recursive invocation of an extension of our PTAS method in time polynomial in dr. A simpler, direct approach is to observe that the degrees of Steiner points, counting the overlapping edges, can be bounded by $\mathcal{O}(dr)$ and use this fact to restrict the number of possible locations of Steiner vertices in an approximate solution to a polynomial one in dr. For our purposes, it is sufficient to achieve such a $1 + \epsilon$ approximation in time which might be even double exponential in $\mathcal{O}(dr)$ and even polynomial in m, say in time $m^{\mathcal{O}(dr)}2^{\mathcal{O}(M(2dr))}$. We infer that the total time taken by a leaf region is $m^{\mathcal{O}(dr)} \cdot 2^{\mathcal{O}(2^{dr}\cdot(dr)!)}$. As Corollary 1 carries easily over to the $1 + \epsilon$-approximation of the minimum cost, we need spent $m^{\mathcal{O}(d2^d r)} \cdot 2^{\mathcal{O}(2^{d(r+1)}\cdot(dr)!)}$ time for a non-leaf region of the tree. By straightforward calculations, we conclude that we can find a $1 + \epsilon$ approximation of the minimum cost of a (m, r)-light SG whose connectivity characteristic guarantees k-connectivity with respect to S (see Remark 3) within the time stated in the theorem. We can also construct such an SG achieving this minimum cost by simple backtracking.

5 Main results

Our polynomial-time approximation scheme for the minimum cost k-connectivity problem in $\mathbb{R}^d$ starts from perturbing the input set S of n points to a well rounded one S'. By the Perturbation Lemma and its proof, it takes linear time and it is sufficient to obtain an $(1 + \Omega(\frac{1}{c}))$-approximation for the resulting well rounded set in order to obtain an $(1 + \frac{1}{c})$-approximation for S. In the next stage, our PTAS constructs the 2^d-ary tree for S' and shifts it by picking at random a in $\{0, \ldots, W - 1\}$ where W is the size of bounding cube of S'. The construction and shifting takes time $\mathcal{O}(2^d n \log^2 n)$. By combining the Structure Theorem with Theorem 3, we can find the desired $(1+\Omega(\frac{1}{c}))$-approximation for the minimum cost k-vertex connectivity problem for S' in the form of an SG with Steiner points in time $n \cdot (\log n)^{(\mathcal{O}(c\sqrt{d}k))^{d-1}} \cdot 2^{((\mathcal{O}(c\sqrt{d}k))^{d-1})!}$. We can replace each maximal path with internal vertices of degree two in the SG by straight-line segments in order to obtain not worse (by triangle inequality) approximation in the form of a straight-line graph. Note however that these shortcuttings will not eliminate the Steiner points introduced by the Patching Lemma. We can also derandomize our PTAS by trying all possible a in the range $\{0, \ldots, W - 1\}$ which increases the running time by a factor $\mathcal{O}(n)$. Putting everything together, we obtain our main result.

Theorem 4. *There is a polynomial-time approximation scheme for the minimum cost k-vertex connectivity problem in $\mathbb{R}^d$ using Steiner points. For a set of n-points in $\mathbb{R}^d$, and $c > 1$, the randomized version of the scheme finds a straight-line graph which is k-vertex connected with respect to S and is within $(1 + \frac{1}{c})$ of the minimum cost of a k-connected Euclidean graph on S in time $n \cdot (\log n)^{(\mathcal{O}(c\sqrt{d}k))^{d-1}} \cdot 2^{((\mathcal{O}(c\sqrt{d}k))^{d-1})!}$. The algorithm can be derandomized by increasing the running time by a factor $\mathcal{O}(n)$.*

By moderate modifications we can also obtain a PTAS for the minimum cost k-edge connectivity problem in $\mathbb{R}^d$, where the connecting paths need only be edge disjoint.

Theorem 5. *There is a polynomial-time approximation scheme for the minimum cost k-edge connectivity problem in $\mathbb{R}^d$ using Steiner points. For a set of n-points in $\mathbb{R}^d$, and $c > 1$, the randomized version of the scheme finds a straight-line graph which is k-edge connected with respect to S and is within $(1 + \frac{1}{c})$ of the minimum cost of a k-edge connected Euclidean graph on S in time $n \cdot (\log n)^{(\mathcal{O}(c\sqrt{d}k))^{d-1}} \cdot 2^{((\mathcal{O}(c\sqrt{d}k))^{d-1})!}$. The algorithm can be derandomized by increasing the running time by a factor $\mathcal{O}(n)$.*

Our Structure Theorem is based on a single random shift value which is common for all coordinates whereas the original Structure Theorems proved by Arora in [2] assume randomly picking independent values for distinct coordinates. By modifying the Structure Theorems in [2] along the lines of our Structure Theorem, we can significantly improve the derandomization of the randomized PTA schemes of Arora for Euclidean instances of TSP, Steiner Tree, Min-Cost Perfect Matching, k-TSP, and k-MST. Arora [2, Theorem 1] showed that each of these problems has a (deterministic) PTAS in Euclidean spaces $\mathbb{R}^d$ for constant d. The construction given in our Structure Theorem implies that the randomized PTAS algorithms presented in [2] can be derandomized by increasing the running time by a factor $\mathcal{O}(n)$ (instead of $\mathcal{O}(n^d)$), independently of d.

Theorem 6. *For each d such that $d^d = \mathcal{O}(\frac{\log n}{\log\log n})$, there is a* (deterministic) *PTAS on $\mathbb{R}^d$ instances of TSP, Steiner Tree, Min-Cost Perfect Matching, k-TSP, and k-MST. The running time of a $(1+\frac{1}{c})$-approximation for $\mathbb{R}^d$ instances of TSP, Steiner Tree, and Min-Cost Perfect Matching is $\mathcal{O}(n^2(\log n)^{(\mathcal{O}(\sqrt{d}c))^{d-1}})$, and the running time for $\mathbb{R}^d$ instances of k-TSP and k-MST is $\mathcal{O}(n^2k(\log n)^{(\mathcal{O}(\sqrt{d}c))^{d-1}})$.*

Final remark

We are currently working on the problem of eliminating Steiner points from our PTA schemes for the k-connectivity problems.

Acknowledgments

Thanks go to Christos Levcopoulos and Pawel Winter for helpful discussions.

References

1. S. Arora. Polynomial time approximation schemes for Euclidean TSP and other geometric problems. 37th FOCS'96, pp. 2–11.
2. S. Arora. Nearly linear time approximation schemes for Euclidean TSP and other geometric problems. 38th FOCS'97, pp. 554–563.
3. S. Arora. Polynomial time approximation schemes for Euclidean TSP and other geometric problems. Submitted for journal publication, June 1997. This is a full version combining [1] and [2].
4. M. R. Garey and D. S. Johnson. *Computers and Intractability: A Guide to the Theory of NP-completeness.* Freeman, New York, NY, 1979.
5. D. S. Hochbaum, editor. *Approximation Algorithms for $\mathcal{NP}$-Hard Problems.* PWS Publishing Company, Boston, MA, 1996.
6. S. Khuller. Approximation algorithms for finding connected subgraphs. Chapter 6 in [5].
7. D. Krznaric, C. Levcopoulos, G. Narasimhan, B. J. Nilsson, and M. Smid. The minimum 2-connected subgraph of a set of points. Manuscript, September 15, 1997.
8. J. S. B. Mitchell. Guillotine subdivisions approximate polygonal subdivisions: A simple polynomial-time approximation scheme for geometric TSP, k-MST, and related problems. To appear in *SIAM J. Comput.*, 1997.

Global/Local Subtyping and Capability Inference for a Distributed π-calculus

Peter Sewell

University of Cambridge

Peter.Sewell@cl.cam.ac.uk

Abstract

This paper considers how locality restrictions on the use of capabilities can be enforced by a static type system. A distributed π-calculus with a simple reduction semantics is introduced, integrating location and migration primitives from the Distributed Join Calculus with asynchronous π communication. It is given a type system in which the input and output capabilities of channels may be either global, local or absent. This allows compile-time optimization where possible but retains the expressiveness of channel communication. Subtyping allows all communications to be invoked uniformly. We show that the most local possible capabilities for internal channels can be inferred automatically.

1 Introduction

A central theme in programming language and system design is that of restricting access to resources to be in some sense *local*. This can support clean design, allow efficient implementation, and provide robustness against accidental errors and malicious attacks. The development of ubiquitous networking, particularly of systems in which executing agents or executable code are communicable, brings new kinds of resource and locality to the fore. One has resources such as the capability to input or output on a communication channel, to read or write a distributed reference cell, and to decrypt or encrypt with a cryptographic key pair. It may be desirable to restrict the use of these capabilities to, for example, a single agent, a group of trusted agents, a region of the network or a machine address space.

In this paper we consider how such restrictions, particularly the first, can be enforced by a static type system. We introduce a *distributed π-calculus*, with primitives for location, migration and π-calculus style channel communication, as an idealisation of a mobile agent programming language. It is given a type system in which the input and output capabilities for a communication channel can be either *global*, and therefore usable within any location, restricted to be *local*, and therefore usable only within the location where the channel is declared, or *absent*. The type system allows local communication to be implemented efficiently, while subtyping and subsumption ensure that, from the programmer's point of view, it is not unduly restrictive. The constructs for input and output along a channel are independent of whether its capabilities are global or local, thus facilitating programming. At the same time the programmer can distinguish between local and (potentially expensive) global communications via the typing of channel declarations. For the type system to be pragmatically usable it is essential that capability annotations can often be inferred automatically – one would like internal channels to be given the most local capabilities possible, to allow optimisation. We show that this can be done, by showing that typing is preserved by least upper bounds in a modified subtype order.

The distributed π-calculus used is introduced in Section 2. It is designed to allow the global/local type system to be presented clearly; it does not address other issues, such as name services, failure and administrative domains, that arise in mobile agent programming. It builds on the *π-calculus* of Milner, Parrow and Walker [MPW92]. The π-calculus is often described as a calculus of mobile processes. Strictly, however, this refers to the mobility of the scopes of channel declarations – channels are statically scoped, but their scopes may change over time as channel names are sent outside their current scopes. There is no other notion of locality or of identity of processes, so to directly model distributed phenomena, such as migration of agents, failure of machines or knowledge of agents, one must add primitives for grouping π-calculus processes, into units of migration, failure or shared knowledge respectively. This was done by Amadio and Prasad [AP94] in order to model an abstraction of the failure semantics of *Facile* [TLK96], an extension of ML with distribution primitives. More recently, Fournet et al have proposed the *Distributed Join Calculus* and a related programming language [FG96, FGL+96]. To model migrating agents one needs at least a two level hierarchy, with agents, each containing some processes, located at named virtual machines. The Distributed Join Calculus takes a generalisation of this, with primitive tree-structured *locations*. Immediate sublocations of the root model virtual machines; descendants of these represent hierarchically structured mobile agents. Locations are named; new locations can be created and their names can be scope-extruded by communication just as π-calculus channel names can be. Locations that are not immediate sublocations of the root may migrate, changing their parent location. The sublocations of a location thereby migrate with it. We adopt similar location and migration primitives (this choice gives a reasonably clean calculus, but it is not critical for the type system). For communication between agents a wide variety of primitives may be useful in practice. In this paper we adopt those of an asynchronous π-calculus [Bou92, HT92]. They are rather high level, operating independently of the physical locations of agents, and expressive, allowing any number of readers and writers on a channel. As in [AP94] channels have locations, giving the agents in which their queues of blocked writers or readers are stored.

The type system is introduced in Section 3. Generalising the Input/Output type system of Pierce and Sangiorgi [PS96], it has channel types annotated with capabilities. Here they are of the form $\updownarrow_{io} T$, with input and output capabilities i and o each taken from $\{-, \mathsf{L}, \mathsf{G}\}$. The intuition is that a G capability may be used at any location, an L capability may be used only at the location of the channel concerned and a $-$ capability may not be used at all. The types $\updownarrow_{--} T$ are replaced by a single top type $\top$, leaving the capabilities below.

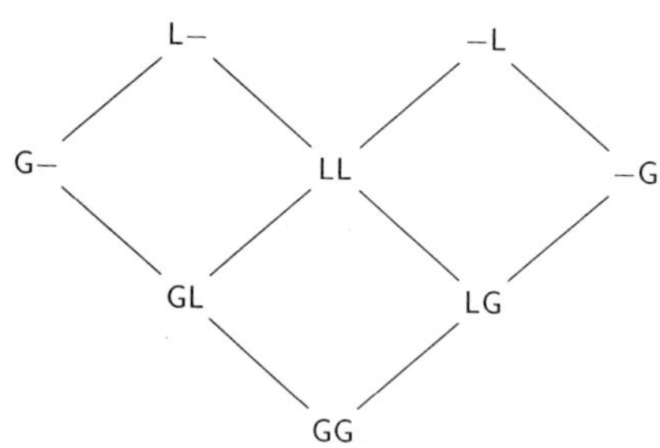

For example, consider a channel x of type $\updownarrow_{io} T$, which is located at a location named k. If $io = \mathsf{GG}$ then x is usable at any location, both for input and for output. If $io = \mathsf{LL}$ then x is usable only within location k, but still for both input and output. If $io = \mathsf{LG}$ then x can be used for output anywhere, but for input only within location k. Such a channel might be used for sending requests to a server located at k. Conversely, if $io = \mathsf{GL}$ then x can be used for input anywhere, but for output only at location k. Such a channel might be used for receiving results from servers, or for 'pushed' data from an information source. The tags $\pm, -, +$ of [PS96] correspond to the capabilities $\mathsf{GG}, \mathsf{G}-, -\mathsf{G}$, for global communication, and to $\mathsf{LL}, \mathsf{L}-, -\mathsf{L}$, for local communication.

A subtyping order is lifted from the tag ordering above (with $i-$ and $-o$ covariant and contravariant respectively), allowing subcapabilities to be communicated. For example if $x : \updownarrow_{\mathsf{LG}} T$ then x may be transmitted globally, along channels of type $\updownarrow_{\mathsf{GG}} \updownarrow_{-\mathsf{G}} T$, to readers that are guaranteed to use it only at type $\updownarrow_{-\mathsf{G}} T$.

The expressiveness of the system should aid programmers by detecting errors at compile time, including communications that inadvertently potentially involve network communication. In an implementation, channels with tags LL, L$-$ and $-$L can be implemented with data structures that are local to a single agent, and so always on the same (albeit possibly changing) machine. Their names need not be globally unique, but only unique within their location (note that this implies that equality testing of channel names should not be available) and need not be registered with global name services. Channels with tags GL (resp. LG) are subject to fewer optimizations, but still allow the references to the channel data structures by writers (resp. readers) to be local pointers.

The typing rules involve two novel features — the formation of certain types must be forbidden by kinding rules and the capabilities of channels must be compared with capabilities at which they can be used by readers. The main soundness result is subject reduction (Theorem 1); in addition one can see by examination of the typing rules that no well-typed process can immediately use a capability that it does not have.

In Section 4 we show that the most local possible capabilities for channels can be inferred (Theorem 2). Some related work and possible generalisations are discussed in Section 5. Proofs are omitted for lack of space. Further discussion of alternative calculi, and the proof of soundness for an extension of the type system with type variables and recursive types, may be found in [Sew97a].

2 A distributed π-calculus

In this section the syntax and operational semantics of our distributed π-calculus (dpi for short) are given. The operational semantics is a rather mild extension of that for the asynchronous π-calculus. It is a reduction semantics, defining reductions over process terms (no additional notion of configuration is required) using a structural congruence. It differs from an asynchronous π semantics in only two respects — there is a reduction rule for migration and the standard structural congruence and reduction rules are adapted to terms containing location information. Location and channel names are both subject to scope extrusion, just as π-calculus channel names are. The semantics and type system can therefore be simplified by treating new location and channel declarations similarly, taking a single binder $(\mathbf{new}\ x : @_l T)\_$ which declares x to be a sublocation of l (respectively a channel located at l) if the type T is the type loc of location names (respectively a channel type).

Types To the types of channels and locations introduced above we add *base types*, ranged over by B, for example a unit type 1 and Int, pairs, as a first step towards more interesting datatypes, and a type to be the top of the subtype order. The *pre-types*, ranged over by S, T, U, V, are given by

$$T \quad ::= \quad B \;\Big|\; T \times T \;\Big|\; \updownarrow_{io} T \;\Big|\; \mathrm{loc} \;\Big|\; \top$$

Only some pre-types will be considered well-formed. The syntax of processes involves types, and hence the reduction semantics does also. Its definition does not depend on them in any interesting way, however, so we defer the type formation rules to Section 3.

Processes We take an infinite set $\mathcal{X}$ of *names*, ranged over by a, j, k, l, x, y, z and containing a distinguished name top. We let m, n, p, q range over $\mathbb{N}$. *Values*, ranged over by u, v, w, are

$$v \quad ::= \quad b \;\Big|\; x \;\Big|\; \langle v, v \rangle$$

where b ranges over elements of the base types. There are two extremal possibilities for adding location information to terms. In one a locator applies to the largest possible unit, with all co-located subterms gathered into a single subterm. This is adopted, for example, in the *Ambient Calculus* of Cardelli and Gordon [CG98]. For dpi, however, communication is possible *across* the location tree structure, so to give a reduction semantics (in which writers and readers at different locations must be brought syntactically adjacent by a structural congruence) the other extreme is adopted, with each elementary subterm explicitly located. Accordingly, *processes*, ranged over by P, Q, R, are:

P ::=	$@_u\overline{v}w$	at location u, output value w on channel v
	$@_u v(y).P$	at u, input a value from channel v and bind it to y in P
	$@_u\, !\, v(y).P$	replicated input
	$@_u$ **migrate_to** v **then** P	migrate location u to become a sublocation of v
	$@_u$**let** $\langle y:T, y':T'\rangle = w$ **in** P	at u, bind the halves of the pair w to y and y' in P
	(**new** $y:@_uT)P$	declare a new channel or location named y, of type T, located at u and binding in P
	0	the null process
	$P \mid P$	parallel composition

The names y and y' above, which must be distinct in the **let** case, bind in the respective subterms P (in particular, in (**new** $y:@_uT)P$ the scope of y does not include u); we work up to alpha conversion of bound names. The free names of a value v and process P will be denoted by $\text{fn}(v)$ and $\text{fn}(P)$ respectively. The substitution of a value v for a name x in P will be written $\{v/x\}P$. Output values and input binders of type 1 will often be elided.

The syntax of processes includes some nonsensical terms, which the reduction semantics gives nonsensical reductions to. They will be formally excluded by the typing rules but two points are worth mentioning now. Firstly, in well-typed processes the u and v appearing in the grammar will always be names. They are allowed to be arbitrary values in the syntax so that substitution of values for names is always defined. Secondly, the syntax includes terms which can teleport after a prefix, e.g.

$$@_k x(y).@_l x(z).0 \qquad @_k x(y).@_y x(z).0$$

For conceptual simplicity we would like migration to be the *only* way in which processes may move, and so want locators $@_l\_$ to describe the locations of processes rather than cause them to move. Teleporting terms are excluded by considering the set of free inhabited locations $\text{fl}(P)$ of a process P. This is the set of the free location names that are inhabited in P by outputs, inputs, migrates, pair splits, channels or locations. It is the set of names which occur free in P within the argument u of a subterm $@_u\_$. For example, $\text{fl}((\textbf{new}\ j:@_l\text{loc})(@_j\overline{x} \mid @_l\overline{x} \mid @_k\overline{x})) = \{k, l\}$. The type system will require, in every prefix located at l with continuation P, that $\text{fl}(P) \subseteq \{l\}$.

Reduction semantics Structural congruence $\equiv$ is the least congruence relation over processes satisfying the following.

$$\begin{array}{rcll}
P \mid 0 & \equiv & P & (1)\\
P \mid Q & \equiv & Q \mid P & (2)\\
P \mid (Q \mid R) & \equiv & (P \mid Q) \mid R & (3)\\
(\textbf{new}\ x:@_uS)(\textbf{new}\ y:@_vT)P & \equiv & (\textbf{new}\ y:@_vT)(\textbf{new}\ x:@_uS)P \quad x \notin \text{fn}(v), y \wedge y \notin \text{fn}(u) & (4)\\
P \mid (\textbf{new}\ x:@_vT)Q & \equiv & (\textbf{new}\ x:@_vT)(P \mid Q) \quad x \notin \text{fn}(P) & (5)
\end{array}$$

The first three equations are standard, allowing parallel compositions to be treated as multisets. Equation 5 allows scope extrusion, both of channel names and of location names. Equation 4 allows new-binders to be permuted; the side condition ensures that the location tree structure, and the locations of channels, are preserved.

The reduction relation $\longrightarrow$ over processes is the least relation satisfying the following.

$$\begin{array}{rcl}
@_k\overline{x}v \mid @_l x(y).P & \longrightarrow & \{v/y\}P\\
@_k\overline{x}v \mid @_l\, !\, x(y).P & \longrightarrow & \{v/y\}P \mid @_l\, !\, x(y).P\\
@_l\textbf{let}\ \langle y_1:T_1, y_2:T_2\rangle = \langle v_1, v_2\rangle\ \textbf{in}\ P & \longrightarrow & \{v_1/y_1\}\{v_2/y_2\}P\\
(\textbf{new}\ l:@_jT)(\textbf{new}\ \Delta)(Q \mid @_l\textbf{migrate_to}\ k\ \textbf{then}\ P) & \longrightarrow & (\textbf{new}\ l:@_kT)(\textbf{new}\ \Delta)(Q \mid P)\\
\text{if } \{k,l\} \cap \text{dom}(\Delta) = \{\} \wedge k \neq l & &
\end{array}$$

$$\frac{P \longrightarrow Q}{P \mid R \longrightarrow Q \mid R} \qquad \frac{P \longrightarrow Q}{(\textbf{new}\ x:@_lT)P \longrightarrow (\textbf{new}\ x:@_lT)Q} \qquad \frac{P \equiv P' \quad P' \longrightarrow Q' \quad Q' \equiv Q}{P \longrightarrow Q}$$

where we define $(\mathbf{new}\ \Delta)P$, for lists of the grammar $\Delta ::= \bullet \ \big|\ \Delta, x : @_l T$, by $(\mathbf{new}\ \bullet)P = P$ and $(\mathbf{new}\ \Delta, x : @_l T)P = (\mathbf{new}\ \Delta)(\mathbf{new}\ x : @_l T)P$. The first two reduction rules are the standard communication rules for an asynchronous π-calculus; note that the communications can take place irrespective of the locations of the writer, reader and channel. The third is an unproblematic pair splitting reduction. The fourth is the only substantially new reduction rule. It allows location l to migrate from being a sublocation of j to become a sublocation of k. After the migration the continuation P is released. The additional context $(\mathbf{new}\ \Delta)(Q \mid \_)$, which is preserved by the reduction, is required as the scope of l may contain other location and channel declarations, and processes, that mention l. In particular, note that Q may contain other subterms $@_l \ldots$ that remain located at l as it migrates. Note also that the side condition means that the rule is not applicable if k is a sublocation of l. Such migrations, which would introduce a cycle into the location tree, are blocked, although later migrations may unblock them. The last three rules are standard.

The sublocation tree of a migrating location is unchanged, and so migrates with it. The unit of migration is thus a subtree of locations with all their processes and channels. The largest unit that is guaranteed to stay together (and so always be on the same machine), however, is not a subtree but just the processes and channels at a single location — its sublocations may migrate away. The tree structure is therefore essentially orthogonal to global/local typing.

Examples We give some simple example processes that will be well-typed in the empty context. First, a server that returns the result of some computation (in this trivial example it simply pairs the argument with itself):

$$
\begin{array}{l}
(\mathbf{new}\ \mathrm{pairServer} : @_{\mathrm{top}}\mathrm{loc})(\mathbf{new}\ \mathrm{client} : @_{\mathrm{top}}\mathrm{loc}) \\
\quad (\mathbf{new}\ \mathrm{pair} : @_{\mathrm{pairServer}} \updownarrow_{\mathsf{LG}}(\mathrm{Int} \times \updownarrow_{-\mathsf{G}}(\mathrm{Int} \times \mathrm{Int}))) \\
\qquad @_{\mathrm{pairServer}}\,!\,\mathrm{pair}(y).@_{\mathrm{pairServer}}\mathbf{let}\ \langle n : \mathrm{Int}, c : \updownarrow_{-\mathsf{G}}(\mathrm{Int} \times \mathrm{Int})\rangle = y\ \mathbf{in}\ @_{\mathrm{pairServer}}\overline{c}\langle n, n\rangle \\
\qquad | \\
\qquad (\mathbf{new}\ c : @_{\mathrm{client}} \updownarrow_{\mathsf{LG}}(\mathrm{Int} \times \mathrm{Int}))@_{\mathrm{client}}\overline{\mathrm{pair}}\langle 7, c\rangle \mid @_{\mathrm{client}}c(x).\cdots
\end{array}
$$

Note the use of subsumption for typing the output $@_{\mathrm{client}}\overline{\mathrm{pair}}\langle 7, c\rangle$. Secondly, a rudimentary tracker, that receives location names on a channel move (perhaps provided by an active badge system controller) and migrates to them:

$$
\begin{array}{l}
(\mathbf{new}\ \mathrm{l}_1 : @_{\mathrm{top}}\mathrm{loc}) \cdots (\mathbf{new}\ \mathrm{l}_3 : @_{\mathrm{top}}\mathrm{loc}) \\
(\mathbf{new}\ \mathrm{controller} : @_{\mathrm{top}}\mathrm{loc}) \\
\quad (\mathbf{new}\ \mathrm{move} : @_{\mathrm{controller}} \updownarrow_{\mathsf{GL}} \mathrm{loc}) \\
\\
\qquad @_{\mathrm{controller}}\overline{\mathrm{move}}\,\mathrm{l}_1 \mid \cdots \mid @_{\mathrm{controller}}\overline{\mathrm{move}}\,\mathrm{l}_3 \\
\qquad | \\
\qquad (\mathbf{new}\ \mathrm{follower} : @_{\mathrm{controller}}\mathrm{loc}) \\
\qquad\quad @_{\mathrm{follower}}\,!\,\mathrm{move}(l).@_{\mathrm{follower}}\mathbf{migrate\_to}\ l\ \mathbf{then}\ \cdots \\
\qquad\quad \mid @_{\mathrm{follower}} \cdots
\end{array}
$$

A more realistic tracker would have additional communications so that the moves could be sequentialised. As these examples show, the syntax of processes contains redundant location information. The design of a less verbose representation, allowing co-located processes to be gathered together at compile time, is discussed in [Sew97a]. Also discussed there is a calculus that is better suited to use by programmers, allowing locators to occur more freely. Both of these require a more complex operational semantics.

Action calculus semantics There is a rather large space of possible calculi with reduction semantics. One way of understanding it, particularly for comparing different calculi, is to put them into a common framework, such as the *Action Calculi* of Milner [Mil96]. This provides a well-understood structural congruence, with a graphical intuition, that has clarified the design of dpi. As an illustration, we give an action calculus presentation of the fragment of dpi without pairs or base type values. We take the arity monoid $(\mathbb{N}, +, 0)$, the names of arity 1 to be $\mathcal{X}$ and controls:

$$\mathbf{new}_T : 1 \to 1 \quad \mathbf{out} : 3 \to 0 \quad \frac{a : 1 \to 0}{\mathbf{in}(a) : 2 \to 0 \quad \mathbf{rep}(a) : 2 \to 0} \quad \frac{a : 0 \to 0}{\mathbf{mig}(a) : 2 \to 0}$$

Comparing with the action calculus for the π-calculus $\mathsf{AC}(\nu, \mathbf{out}, \mathbf{box}, \mathbf{rep})$, from [Mil96, §5.4], the arities of **new**, **out**, **in** and **rep** are obtained by adding one to the source of their corresponding arities; the name binding the new port on a control giving the location of that control. There is an obvious mapping taking processes in the fragment of dpi considered to actions of arity $0 \to 0$. Taking the reaction rules of the action calculus to be the translation of the first, second and fourth dpi rules, this is a bijection, up to structural congruence, that preserves one-step reaction.

3 Global/local subtyping

This section gives the global/local type system. It defines a judgement $\Gamma \vdash P : \mathrm{process}$ which should be read as 'under assumptions Γ the process P is well-formed'. As usual these contexts Γ contain assumptions on the types of names that may occur free in P. They must also contain assumptions on the locations of such names. *Pre-contexts* are therefore lists:

Γ	$::=$	$\bullet$	the empty context
		$\Gamma, x : @_l T$	Γ extended with name x, located at l, of type T

We now illustrate the three main phenomena that the type system must address. Firstly, a channel name must only be used (for input or output) if it has the appropriate capability, i.e. L or G for usages at its location; G for usages at other locations. For example, with respect to the context

$$\Gamma \stackrel{def}{=} k : @_{\mathrm{top}}\mathrm{loc},\ l : @_{\mathrm{top}}\mathrm{loc},\ w : @_l \updownarrow_{-\mathsf{G}} 1,\ z : @_l \updownarrow_{-\mathsf{L}} 1$$

we should have

$$\begin{array}{ll} \Gamma \vdash @_l\overline{w} : \mathrm{process} & \Gamma \vdash @_l\overline{z} : \mathrm{process} \\ \Gamma \vdash @_k\overline{w} : \mathrm{process} & \Gamma \not\vdash @_k\overline{z} : \mathrm{process} \end{array}$$

Secondly, local capabilities must not be sent outside their locations. Consider the context

Γ	$\stackrel{def}{=}$	$k : @_{\mathrm{top}}\mathrm{loc}$,	top level location
		$l : @_{\mathrm{top}}\mathrm{loc}$,	top level location
		$z : @_l \updownarrow_{\mathsf{LL}} 1$,	local channel carrying 1, at l
		$x : @_l \updownarrow_{\mathsf{GG}} \updownarrow_{\mathsf{LL}} 1$	global channel carrying names of local channels carrying 1, at l

and the process $P \stackrel{def}{=} @_l\overline{x}z \mid @_k x(y).@_k\overline{y}$. At first sight one might expect $\Gamma \vdash P : \mathrm{process}$, but the reduction

$$@_l\overline{x}z \mid @_k x(y).@_k\overline{y} \longrightarrow @_k\overline{z}$$

can send both L capabilities of z out of l — it is clear that $\Gamma \vdash @_k\overline{z} : \mathrm{process}$ should not hold, and hence that $\Gamma \vdash P : \mathrm{process}$ should not. It is prevented by restricting type formation, ruling out channel types, such as $\updownarrow_{\mathsf{GG}} \updownarrow_{\mathsf{LL}} 1$, that can be used to communicate local capabilities globally.

Thirdly, there must be a restriction on the mention of names outside their locations. This is a little delicate, as one cannot simply forbid all such mentions of the names of channels that are declared with some local capability. Suppose $x : \updownarrow_{\mathsf{LL}} \updownarrow_{-o} 1$ is located at l and $z : \updownarrow_{-o'} 1$, and consider when $@_l\overline{x}z$ should be well typed. If $o' = \mathsf{G}$ then z may be located anywhere, as its output capability is global. If $o = \mathsf{G}$ and $o' = \mathsf{L}$ then z is not a subtype of the expected value, so $@_l\overline{x}z$ should never be well typed. On the other hand, if $o = o' = \mathsf{L}$ then the output capability of z is local and may be used by a reader on x, so z must be located at l also. The essential point is whether the capabilities of z and the capabilities at which it can be used by readers (as determined by the type of x) share a local capability (either for input or for output). This will be captured by a relation of *colocality* over types. Note that if $x : \updownarrow_{\mathsf{LL}} \updownarrow_{-\mathsf{L}} 1$ and $z : \updownarrow_{\mathsf{LG}}$ was not located at l the output should still be well typed, despite the fact that both types have *a* local capability.

Kinds, Contexts, Types and Values We first define four mutually recursive judgements, $\vdash T : K$, read as 'type T is well-formed and has kind K', $\vdash \Gamma\ ok$, read as 'context Γ is well-formed', $\Gamma \vdash v : T$, read as 'value v has type T', and $\Gamma \vdash x@l$, read as 'name x is located at l'.

The *kinds*, ranged over by K, are $\mathrm{Type}_{\gamma\varepsilon}$ where γ and ε range over the 2-point lattices $\mathsf{G} \leqslant -$ and $\mathsf{E} \leqslant -$ respectively. They are ordered by the product order. The intuition is that types that have a kind $\mathrm{Type}_{\mathsf{G}\varepsilon}$ are *global*, with values of such types being freely communicable between locations. Types that have a kind $\mathrm{Type}_{\gamma\mathsf{E}}$ are *extensible*; new names at these types may be created by new-binders. We write $\sqcup$ for the least upper bounds in these lattices. The kinding rules for *types* are:

$$\frac{}{\vdash B : \mathrm{Type}_{\mathsf{G}-}} \qquad \frac{\vdash T : \mathrm{Type}_{\gamma\varepsilon} \quad \vdash T' : \mathrm{Type}_{\gamma'\varepsilon'}}{\vdash T \times T' : \mathrm{Type}_{(\gamma\sqcup\gamma')-}} \qquad \frac{}{\vdash \mathrm{loc} : \mathrm{Type}_{\mathsf{GE}}} \qquad \frac{}{\vdash \top : \mathrm{Type}_{\mathsf{GE}}}$$

$$\frac{\vdash T : \mathrm{Type}_{\mathsf{G}\varepsilon} \quad io \in \{\mathsf{GG}, \mathsf{G}-, -\mathsf{G}\}}{\vdash \updownarrow_{io} T : \mathrm{Type}_{\mathsf{GE}}} \qquad \frac{\vdash T : \mathrm{Type}_{\mathsf{G}\varepsilon} \quad io \in \{\mathsf{GL}, \mathsf{LG}\}}{\vdash \updownarrow_{io} T : \mathrm{Type}_{-\mathsf{E}}} \qquad \frac{\vdash T : \mathrm{Type}_{\gamma\varepsilon} \quad io \in \{\mathsf{LL}, -\mathsf{L}, \mathsf{L}-\}}{\vdash \updownarrow_{io} T : \mathrm{Type}_{-\mathsf{E}}} \qquad \frac{\vdash T : K \quad K \leqslant K'}{\vdash T : K'}$$

The rules for channel types prevent the formation of types that could be used to carry local capabilities between locations. For example, we have:

$$\vdash \updownarrow_{\mathsf{LL}} \updownarrow_{\mathsf{LL}} 1 : \mathrm{Type}_{-\mathsf{E}} \qquad \nvdash \updownarrow_{\mathsf{GG}} \updownarrow_{\mathsf{LL}} 1 : \mathrm{Type}_{--}$$

$$\vdash \updownarrow_{\mathsf{LL}} \updownarrow_{\mathsf{GG}} 1 : \mathrm{Type}_{-\mathsf{E}} \qquad \vdash \updownarrow_{\mathsf{GG}} \updownarrow_{\mathsf{GG}} 1 : \mathrm{Type}_{\mathsf{GE}}$$

and $\vdash \updownarrow_{io} \updownarrow_{i'o'} 1 : \mathrm{Type}_{-\mathsf{E}}$ iff $io \in \{\mathsf{GG}, \mathsf{G}-, -\mathsf{G}, \mathsf{GL}, \mathsf{LG}\} \Rightarrow i'o' \in \{\mathsf{GG}, \mathsf{G}-, -\mathsf{G}\}$, i.e. if io is at all global then $i'o'$ must be not at all local. Products are global only if both their components are global. Base types and $\top$ are global, as is loc, so location names may be communicated freely. The only extensible types are channel types, loc, and $\top$. The formation rules for *contexts* are:

$$\frac{}{\vdash \bullet\ ok} \qquad \frac{\vdash T : K \quad (\Gamma \vdash l : \mathrm{loc}) \vee (l = \mathrm{top}) \quad x \notin \mathrm{dom}(\Gamma) \cup \{\mathrm{top}\}}{\vdash \Gamma, x : @_l T\ ok}$$

Contexts thus contain location and type assumptions on free names. The rules ensure that locations are tree structured, with root top. The typing rules for values, and the rule for the location of names, are straightforward.

$$\frac{\vdash \Gamma, x : @_l T, \Delta\ ok}{\Gamma, x : @_l T, \Delta \vdash x : T} \qquad \frac{\vdash \Gamma\ ok \quad b \in |B|}{\Gamma \vdash b : B} \qquad \frac{\Gamma \vdash v : T \quad \Gamma \vdash v' : T'}{\Gamma \vdash \langle v, v' \rangle : T \times T'} \qquad \frac{\vdash \Gamma, x : @_l T, \Delta\ ok}{\Gamma, x : @_l T, \Delta \vdash x@l}$$

Subtyping The ordering on tags induces a subtype order on types — if $io \leqslant i'o'$ then a channel of type $\updownarrow_{io} T$ may be used as if it were a channel of type $\updownarrow_{i'o'} T$, which has weaker capabilities. As in [PS96], a tag io is covariant iff $o = -$, contravariant if $i = -$ and non-variant otherwise. The subtype order $\leqslant$ is the least binary relation over the pre-types such that

$$\frac{}{B \leqslant B} \qquad \frac{S_1 \leqslant T_1 \quad S_2 \leqslant T_2}{S_1 \times S_2 \leqslant T_1 \times T_2} \qquad \frac{io \leqslant i'o' \quad i' \neq - \Rightarrow S \leqslant T \quad o' \neq - \Rightarrow T \leqslant S}{\updownarrow_{io} S \leqslant \updownarrow_{i'o'} T} \qquad \frac{}{\mathrm{loc} \leqslant \mathrm{loc}} \qquad \frac{}{S \leqslant \top}$$

The replacement of the tag $--$ by a single top type ensures that subtyping is a partial order – otherwise names of types $\updownarrow_{--} T$ would be communicable but not usable, so we would have $\updownarrow_{--} S \leqslant \updownarrow_{--} T$ for all S and T. Note that the well-formed types are not up, down or convex-closed under the subtype order on pre-types.

Colocality We say that a tag is *local* if it contains an L capability and that two tags are *colocal* if they share a common L capability, i.e. $\text{local}(io) \overset{def}{\Leftrightarrow} i = \mathsf{L} \vee o = \mathsf{L}$ and $\text{colocal}(io, i'o') \overset{def}{\Leftrightarrow} (i = \mathsf{L} \wedge i' = \mathsf{L}) \vee (o = \mathsf{L} \wedge o' = \mathsf{L})$. The key properties of these definitions are that $\text{colocal}(io, io) \iff \text{local}(io)$ and that, if $io \leqslant i'o' \leqslant i''o''$ and $\text{colocal}(io, i''o'')$, then $\text{colocal}(io, i'o')$ and $\text{colocal}(i'o', i''o'')$. Note that the local tags are neither up, down or convex closed in the tag ordering. Further, colocal is a symmetric relation but is not reflexive or transitive, or closed under relational composition with the tag ordering. It does satisfy $\text{colocal}(io, i'o') \Rightarrow (io \leqslant i'o' \vee i'o' \leqslant io)$. Colocality is lifted from tags to a relation on well-formed types that are in the subtype relation as follows.

$$\frac{\begin{array}{l}(i = i' = \mathsf{L}) \vee (o = o' = \mathsf{L})\\ \vdash \updownarrow_{io} S : \text{Type}_{--}\\ \vdash \updownarrow_{i'o'} T : \text{Type}_{--}\\ \updownarrow_{io} S \leqslant \updownarrow_{i'o'} T\end{array}}{\text{colocal}(\updownarrow_{io} S, \updownarrow_{i'o'} T)} \qquad \frac{\begin{array}{l}\text{colocal}(S_i, T_i)\\ \vdash S_{1-i} : \text{Type}_{--}\\ \vdash T_{1-i} : \text{Type}_{--}\\ S_{1-i} \leqslant T_{1-i}\end{array}}{\text{colocal}(S_0 \times S_1, T_0 \times T_1)}\, i \in \{0,1\}$$

We define the colocal names of a value with respect to two types that are in the subtype relation:

$$\frac{\begin{array}{l}\Gamma \vdash x : S\\ \text{colocal}(S, T)\end{array}}{\Gamma \vdash x \in \text{colocaln}(x, S, T)} \qquad \frac{\begin{array}{l}\Gamma \vdash x \in \text{colocaln}(v_i, S_i, T_i)\\ \Gamma \vdash v_{1-i} : S_{1-i}\\ \vdash T_{1-i} : \text{Type}_{--}\\ S_{1-i} \leqslant T_{1-i}\end{array}}{\Gamma \vdash x \in \text{colocaln}(\langle v_0, v_1\rangle, S_0 \times S_1, T_0 \times T_1)}\, i \in \{0,1\}$$

The key properties lift as follows. If a value has any colocal names with respect to two types then those types are colocal, the types of the colocal names of a value are themselves local and the set of colocal names of a value varies contravariantly with the upper type.

Lemma 1 *If* $\Gamma \vdash x \in \text{colocaln}(v, V, T)$ *then* $\text{colocal}(V, T)$ *and there exists* U *such that* $\Gamma \vdash x : U$ *and* $\text{colocal}(U, U)$. *If in addition* $\vdash S : \text{Type}_{--}$ *and* $V \leqslant S \leqslant T$ *then* $\Gamma \vdash x \in \text{colocaln}(v, V, S)$.

Processes Finally the typing rules for processes can be given.

$$\textsc{Out}\ \frac{\begin{array}{l}\Gamma \vdash l : \text{loc}\\ \Gamma \vdash x : \updownarrow_{io} T\\ \Gamma \vdash v : T'\\ T' \leqslant T\\ o \leqslant \mathsf{L}\\ o = \mathsf{L} \Rightarrow \Gamma \vdash x@l\\ \forall a\,.\, \Gamma \vdash a \in \text{colocaln}(v, T', T) \Rightarrow \Gamma \vdash a@l\end{array}}{\Gamma \vdash @_l \overline{x} v : \text{process}} \qquad (\textsc{Rep-})\textsc{In}\ \frac{\begin{array}{l}\Gamma \vdash l : \text{loc}\\ \Gamma \vdash x : \updownarrow_{io} T\\ \Gamma, y : @_l T \vdash P : \text{process}\\ i \leqslant \mathsf{L}\\ i = \mathsf{L} \Rightarrow \Gamma \vdash x@l\\ \text{fl}(P) \subseteq \{l\}\end{array}}{\begin{array}{l}\Gamma \vdash @_l x(y).P : \text{process}\\ \Gamma \vdash @_l\, !\, x(y).P : \text{process}\end{array}}$$

$$\textsc{Let}\ \frac{\begin{array}{l}\Gamma \vdash l : \text{loc}\\ \Gamma \vdash v : T'\\ \Gamma, y_1 : @_l T_1, y_2 : @_l T_2 \vdash P : \text{process}\\ T' \leqslant T_1 \times T_2\\ \forall a\,.\, \Gamma \vdash a \in \text{colocaln}(v, T', T_1 \times T_2) \Rightarrow \Gamma \vdash a@l\\ \text{fl}(P) \subseteq \{l\}\end{array}}{\Gamma \vdash @_l \textbf{let}\ \langle y_1 : T_1, y_2 : T_2\rangle = v\ \textbf{in}\ P : \text{process}} \qquad \textsc{Mig}\ \frac{\begin{array}{l}\Gamma \vdash l : \text{loc}\\ \Gamma \vdash v : \text{loc}\\ \Gamma \vdash P : \text{process}\\ \text{fl}(P) \subseteq \{l\}\end{array}}{\Gamma \vdash @_l \textbf{migrate\_to}\ v\ \textbf{then}\ P : \text{process}}$$

$$\textsc{New}\ \frac{\begin{array}{l}\vdash T : \text{Type}_{-\mathsf{E}}\\ \Gamma, x : @_l T \vdash P : \text{process}\end{array}}{\Gamma \vdash (\textbf{new}\ x : @_l T) P : \text{process}} \qquad \textsc{Nil}\ \frac{\vdash \Gamma\ ok}{\Gamma \vdash 0 : \text{process}} \qquad \textsc{Par}\ \frac{\begin{array}{l}\Gamma \vdash P : \text{process}\\ \Gamma \vdash Q : \text{process}\end{array}}{\Gamma \vdash P \mid Q : \text{process}}$$

Most of the premises of these rules are routine; we discuss the others briefly.

OUT The first premise ensures that l is a location. The second through fifth premises are analogous to those of the OUT rule of [PS96]. Name x must be a channel, value v

must be of a subtype of the type carried by the channel, and the channel must have an output capability (either G or L). The fourth and fifth premises could be replaced by $\updownarrow_{io} T \leqslant \updownarrow_{-\mathsf{L}} T'$. The penultimate premise addresses the first phenomenon discussed at the beginning of this section, ensuring that if x has only a local output capability then it can only be used at its own location. The last premise addresses the third such phenomenon, ensuring that any transmitted channel names that have a local capability which can be used by receivers on x are located at l.

(REP-)IN This is very similar to OUT except for the premise $\mathrm{fl}(P) \subseteq \{l\}$, which prevents teleportation after the input. Note that for typing P it is assumed that y is located at l.

NEW This allows new-binding of names at channel types, loc, and $\top$.

LET This is similar to a combination of OUT and (REP-)IN (as, indeed, the reduction rule for LET is).

A few remarks: (1) The rules allow locations and channels, but not processes, to be located at top. This is consistent with the intuition that immediate sublocations of top model virtual machines. For other applications of the calculus different treatments of top are appropriate and should be straightforward. (2) Local channels can be sent outside their location (with reduced capabilities) and then back inside. Their local capabilities cannot then be used, however. (3) A name may be assumed to have a local type in a process P and still, if P is placed in a process context, engage in cross-location communication. (4) The let construct includes an explicit type for its pattern, which may be a supertype of the type of its value. Without this the set of typable processes would be unduly restricted. In the input construct the type of the pattern can be left implicit, as it is bounded by the type of the channel. (5) To add recursive types contexts must contain kind assumptions on type variables, type formation rules must be relativised to contexts, and enforce guardedness, subtyping must be defined coinductively, and type unfolding must be allowed in the value typing rules and definitions of subtyping and colocality. The details can be found in [Sew97a].

Soundness The main soundness result is that typing is preserved by reduction.

Theorem 1 (Subject reduction) *If* $\Gamma \vdash P : \mathrm{process}$ *and* $P \longrightarrow Q$ *then* $\Gamma \vdash Q : \mathrm{process}$.

To prove this it is necessary to show that typing is preserved by legitimate *context permutations*, by *relocation* (changes of location assumptions for names of non-local types), by *narrowing* (taking type assumptions of lower types, while keeping location assumptions constant) and by *substitution*. For reasons of space we state only the substitution lemma for processes.

Lemma 2 (Substitution — Processes) *The rule below is admissible.*

$$\frac{\begin{array}{l}\Gamma, z : @_j V \vdash P : \mathrm{process} \\ \Gamma \vdash u : U \\ U \leqslant V \\ \forall a \,.\, \Gamma \vdash a \in \mathrm{colocaln}(u, U, V) \Rightarrow \Gamma \vdash a@j \\ z \notin \mathrm{fl}(P)\end{array}}{\Gamma \vdash \{u/z\}P : \mathrm{process}}$$

The first three premises are standard. The fourth ensures that any names of the substituted value u are located at the same place as the substituted variable z was assumed to be at, if their actual and assumed types are colocal. The last premise ensures that no locators in P can be affected by the substitution.

In addition, it is easy to see from the typing rules that no well-typed process can immediately use a local capability outside its location. This can be made precise by immediate-soundness results such as the following.

Proposition 1 *If* $\Gamma \vdash (\mathbf{new}\ \Delta)(@_l \overline{x} v \mid Q) : \mathrm{process}$, $\Gamma, \Delta \vdash x : \updownarrow_{i\mathsf{L}} T$ *and* $\Gamma, \Delta \vdash x@k$ *then* $k = l$.

4 Capability Inference

One would like to be able to automatically infer the most local possible type for new-bound channels, to allow compile-time optimisation. Unfortunately, this is not possible in any straightforward sense based on the subtype order. Consider for example $k : @_{\text{top}}\text{loc}, z : @_k \updownarrow_{\mathsf{LL}} 1 \vdash (\mathbf{new}\ x : @_k T)(@_k \overline{x} z \mid @_k x(y).@_k \overline{y})$. This holds iff T is either $\updownarrow_{\mathsf{LL}} \updownarrow_{-\mathsf{L}} 1$ or $\updownarrow_{\mathsf{LL}} \updownarrow_{\mathsf{LL}} 1$; these types are not related by subtyping. We can, however, infer the most local possible top-level capabilities for T. Take the modified 'subtype' order $\sqsubseteq$ (with all channel type constructors covariant) to be the least relation over the pre-types such that

$$\frac{}{B \sqsubseteq B} \qquad \frac{S_1 \sqsubseteq T_1 \quad S_2 \sqsubseteq T_2}{S_1 \times S_2 \sqsubseteq T_1 \times T_2} \qquad \frac{\begin{array}{c} T \sqsubseteq T' \\ io \leqslant i'o' \end{array}}{\updownarrow_{io} T \sqsubseteq \updownarrow_{i'o'} T'} \qquad \frac{}{\text{loc} \sqsubseteq \text{loc}} \qquad \frac{}{\top \sqsubseteq \top} \qquad \frac{}{\updownarrow_{io} S \sqsubseteq \top}$$

and define $\simeq$ to be the least relation over the pre-types such that

$$\frac{}{B \simeq B} \qquad \frac{S_1 \simeq T_1 \quad S_2 \simeq T_2}{S_1 \times S_2 \simeq T_1 \times T_2} \qquad \frac{T \simeq T'}{\updownarrow_{io} T \simeq \updownarrow_{i'o'} T'} \qquad \frac{}{\text{loc} \simeq \text{loc}} \qquad \frac{}{\top \simeq \top} \qquad \frac{}{\begin{array}{c} \updownarrow_{io} S \simeq \top \\ \top \simeq \updownarrow_{io} S \end{array}}$$

relating any two types that have essentially the same shape, neglecting capabilities. Say a set of types $\tilde{T} = \{ T_n \mid n \in N \}$ is *compatible* if it is non-empty and $\forall m, n \in N \,.\, T_m \simeq T_n$. One can show that any compatible $\tilde{T}$ has a least upper bound, written $\sqcup\tilde{T}$, with respect to $\sqsubseteq$. Lifting $\sqsubseteq$, $\simeq$, compatibility and $\sqcup$ pointwise to pre-contexts and processes, one can show that the typing judgements are preserved by taking least upper bounds with respect to $\sqsubseteq$.

Theorem 2 (Capability Inference)

1. *If $\tilde{T}$ is compatible and $\forall n \in N \,. \vdash T_n : K_n$ then $\vdash \sqcup\tilde{T} : \sqcup\tilde{K}$.*
2. *If $\tilde{S}$ is compatible, $\tilde{T}$ is compatible and $\forall n \,.\, S_n \leqslant T_n$ then $\sqcup\tilde{S} \leqslant \sqcup\tilde{T}$.*
3. *If $\tilde{\Gamma}$ is compatible, $\tilde{S}$ is compatible, $\tilde{T}$ is compatible, $\forall n \,.\, \Gamma_n \vdash v : S_n$, $\forall n \,. \vdash T_n : \text{Type}_{--}$, $\forall n \,.\, S_n \leqslant T_n$ and $\sqcup\tilde{\Gamma} \vdash x \in \text{colocaln}(v, \sqcup\tilde{S}, \sqcup\tilde{T})$ then $\exists n \,.\, \Gamma_n \vdash x \in \text{colocaln}(v, S_n, T_n)$*
4. *If $\tilde{\Gamma}$ is compatible, $\tilde{P}$ is compatible and $\forall n \in N \,.\, \Gamma_n \vdash P_n : \text{process}$ then $\sqcup\tilde{\Gamma} \vdash \sqcup\tilde{P} : \text{process}$.*

For any pre-type S the set $\{ T \mid S \sqsubseteq T \}$ is finite. Given some $\Gamma \vdash P : \text{process}$ (perhaps with types containing only GG capabilities, inferred by an algorithm along the lines of [Gay93, VH93, Tur96]) one can therefore compute the least upper bound of $\{ P' \mid P \sqsubseteq P' \wedge \Gamma \vdash P' : \text{process} \}$. For the example above this gives $T = (\updownarrow_{\mathsf{LL}} \updownarrow_{-\mathsf{L}} 1) \sqcup (\updownarrow_{\mathsf{LL}} \updownarrow_{\mathsf{LL}} 1) = \updownarrow_{\mathsf{LL}} \updownarrow_{-\mathsf{L}} 1$. A more efficient algorithm will clearly be required in practice.

5 Conclusion

We conclude by briefly mentioning some related type systems and some possible future work. Capability-based type systems for process calculi have been given by De Nicola, Ferrari and Pugliese [DFP97], for a variant of Linda with localities, and by Riely and Hennessy [RH98], for a distributed π-calculus with site failure. Several authors have given type systems that enforce information flow properties, e.g. [HR98, SV98]. A type system that enforces secrecy and freshness for the Spi Calculus [AG97] has been proposed by Abadi in [Aba97]. In [Ste96] Steckler has given a static analysis technique for distributed Poly/ML with similar motivation to ours — to detect when channels are guaranteed to be local to a single processor. It incorporates also some reachability analysis, but does not separate input and output capabilities. Finally, Nielson and Nielson have studied static analysis techniques for CML, focussing on the number of usages of capabilities, in [NN95].

Special cases Three special cases of the type system may be of interest. In the Join Calculus the names introduced by a definition **def** D **in** P can only be used in P for output (to a first approximation D declares a single replicated reader on these names). For typing P, therefore, they are analogous to channels with capability $-\mathsf{G}$. One could allow the output capability to be local, taking the suborder of tags $-\mathsf{G} \leqslant -\mathsf{L}$. In some circumstances it may not be necessary to allow the input and output capabilities of channels to vary separately, cutting down to the suborder of tags $\mathsf{GG} \leqslant \mathsf{LL}$. This greatly reduces the complexity (although also the expressiveness) of the type system as all channel type constructors become nonvariant. It can be used to prevent the extrusion of local references from agents. A milder simplification is to omit the tags GL and LG, i.e. to take the product of the tags $\pm, -, +$ of [PS96] with the two-point lattice $\mathsf{G} \leqslant \mathsf{L}$. For such tags, if $io \leqslant i'o'$ then $\mathrm{colocal}(io, i'o') \iff \mathrm{local}(io) \wedge \mathrm{local}(i'o')$.

Linearity and Location Types In a distributed application one would expect many channels to be in some sense *linear*; in particular many servers will have a single replicated receiver (this observation motivates the introduction of join patterns in [FG96]). The integration of global/local typing with some form of linearity or receptiveness [Ama97, KPT96, San97] would allow more precise typing, and hence further optimizations, while retaining the expressiveness of general channel communication. One might also refine the system to allow location names to be local, with types loc_G and loc_L, enabling migration to locations to be restricted, and allow locations to be *immobile* or *mobile*, restricting the migration *of* locations. Linearity would again be useful — a common case is that of *one-hop* locations (c.f. Java Applets).

Behavioural equivalences In order to reason about dpi processes a labelled transition system and behavioural congruence are required, perhaps building on the bisimulation congruence results of Riely and Hennessy [RH97, RH98], together with an understanding of the appropriate extensional equivalence for a mobile agent programming language, building on [Sew97b].

Typing for secrecy properties The focus of this paper has been on locality information that can be used for implementation optimization. Very similar type systems should be applicable to the enforcement of secrecy properties for cryptographic keys or nonces. For this it would be desirable to take capabilities not just from $\{\mathsf{G}, \mathsf{L}, -\}$ but from the lattice of arbitrary sets of location names, lifted above a bottom element G. These (dependent) types would allow new names (modelling keys, for example, as in the Spi Calculus) to be created that are restricted to a dynamically calculated set of individuals. One would want a rather strong soundness result — the analogue of Theorem 1 would only show that secrecy is preserved by well-typed processes, whereas an attacker may perform some ill-typed computation.

Acknowledgements The author would like to thank Cédric Fournet, Robin Milner, Benjamin Pierce, Paweł Wojciechowski, and the Thursday group, for interesting discussions about this work, and to acknowledge support from EPSRC grant GR/K 38403 and Esprit Working group 21836 (CONFER-2).

References

[Aba97] Martín Abadi. Secrecy by typing in security protocols. In *TACS '97 (open lecture), LNCS 1281*, pages 611–638, September 1997.

[AG97] Martín Abadi and Andrew D. Gordon. A calculus for cryptographic protocols: The spi calculus. In *Proceedings of the Fourth ACM Conference on Computer and Communications Security, Zürich*, pages 36–47. ACM Press, April 1997.

[Ama97] R. M. Amadio. An asynchronous model of locality, failure, and process mobility. In *Proc. COORDINATION 97, LNCS 1282*, 1997.

[AP94] R. M. Amadio and S. Prasad. Localities and failures. In P. S. Thiagarajan, editor, *Proceedings of* 14th *FST and TCS Conference, FST-TCS'94. LNCS 880*, pages 205–216. Springer-Verlag, 1994.

[Bou92] Gérard Boudol. Asynchrony and the π-calculus (note). Rapport de Recherche 1702, INRIA Sofia-Antipolis, May 1992.

[CG98] Luca Cardelli and Andrew D. Gordon. Mobile ambients. In *Proc. of Foundations of Software Science and Computation Structures (FoSSaCS), ETAPS'98*, March 1998.

[DFP97] Rocco De Nicola, GianLuigi Ferrari, and Rosario Pugliese. Coordinating mobile agents via blackboards and access rights. In *Proc. COORDINATION '97, LNCS 1282*, 1997.

[FG96] Cédric Fournet and Georges Gonthier. The reflexive CHAM and the join-calculus. In *Proceedings of the 23rd POPL*, pages 372–385. ACM press, January 1996.

[FGL+96] Cédric Fournet, Georges Gonthier, Jean-Jacques Lévy, Luc Maranget, and Didier Rémy. A calculus of mobile agents. In *Proceedings of CONCUR '96. LNCS 1119*, pages 406–421. Springer-Verlag, August 1996.

[Gay93] Simon J. Gay. A sort inference algorithm for the polyadic π-calculus. In *Proceedings of the 20th POPL*. ACM Press, 1993.

[HR98] Nevin Heintze and Jon G. Riecke. The SLam calculus: Programming with secrecy and integrity. In *Proceedings of the 25th POPL*, January 1998.

[HT92] Kohei Honda and Mario Tokoro. On asynchronous communication semantics. In M. Tokoro, O. Nierstrasz, and P. Wegner, editors, *Object-Based Concurrent Computing. LNCS 612*, pages 21–51, 1992.

[KPT96] Naoki Kobayashi, Benjamin C. Pierce, and David N. Turner. Linearity and the pi-calculus. In *Proceedings of the 23rd POPL*, pages 358–371. ACM press, January 1996.

[Mil96] Robin Milner. Calculi for interaction. *Acta Informatica*, 33:707–737, 1996.

[MPW92] R. Milner, J. Parrow, and D. Walker. A calculus of mobile processes, Parts I + II. *Information and Computation*, 100(1):1–77, 1992.

[NN95] Hanne Riis Nielson and Flemming Nielson. Static and dynamic processor allocation for higher-order concurrent languages. In *Proceedings of TAPSOFT 95 (FASE). LNCS 915*, 1995.

[PS96] Benjamin Pierce and Davide Sangiorgi. Typing and subtyping for mobile processes. *Mathematical Structures in Computer Science*, 6(5):409–454, 1996.

[RH97] James Riely and Matthew Hennessy. Distributed processes and location failures. In *Proceedings of ICALP '97. LNCS 1256*, pages 471–481. Springer-Verlag, July 1997.

[RH98] James Riely and Matthew Hennessy. A typed language for distributed mobile processes. In *Proceedings of the 25th POPL*, January 1998.

[San97] Davide Sangiorgi. The name discipline of uniform receptiveness. In *Proceedings of ICALP '97. LNCS 1256*, pages 303–313, 1997.

[Sew97a] Peter Sewell. Global/local subtyping for a distributed π-calculus. Technical Report 435, University of Cambridge, August 1997. Available from `http://www.cl.cam.ac.uk/users/pes20/`.

[Sew97b] Peter Sewell. On implementations and semantics of a concurrent programming language. In *Proceedings of CONCUR '97. LNCS 1243*, pages 391–405. Springer-Verlag, 1997.

[Ste96] Paul Steckler. Detecting local channels in distributed Poly/ML. Technical Report ECS-LFCS-96-340, University of Edinburgh, January 1996.

[SV98] Geoffrey Smith and Dennis Volpano. Secure information flow in a multi-threaded imperative language. In *Proceedings of the 25th POPL*, January 1998.

[TLK96] Bent Thomsen, Lone Leth, and Tsung-Min Kuo. A Facile tutorial. In *Proceedings of CONCUR '96. LNCS 1119*, pages 278–298. Springer-Verlag, August 1996.

[Tur96] David N. Turner. *The Polymorphic Pi-calculus: Theory and Implementation*. PhD thesis, University of Edinburgh, 1996.

[VH93] Vasco Thudichum Vasconcelos and Kohei Honda. Principal typing schemes in a polyadic π-calculus. In *Proceedings of CONCUR '93. LNCS 715*, pages 524–538, 1993.

Checking Strong/Weak Bisimulation Equivalences and Observation Congruence for the π-Calculus*

(Extended Abstract)

Zhoujun Li, Huowang Chen

Department of Computer Science, Changsha Institute of Technology

Changsha, Hunan 410073, P.R. China

E-mail:zjli@csit.edu.cn

Abstract. *With efficiency motivations the notion of symbolic transition graph for the π-calculus is proposed along the lines of [4,7]. The single/double ground/symbolic arrows are given to such graphs. Based on them the strong/weak ground/symbolic bisimulation equivalences and observation congruences are defined and are shown to agree with each other. The notions of symbolic observation graph and symbolic congruence graph are also introduced. Finally algorithms for checking strong/weak bisimulation equivalences and observation congruence are presented together with their correctness proofs. These results lift and refine the techniques and algorithms for bisimulation checking of regular pure-CCS and value-passing process to the finite control π-calculus.*

1 Introduction

The π-calculus [10] is a widely studied process description language in which the interconnection topology of processes may be dynamically changed. It extends CCS by features of name-passing and scope restriction. Hence powerful expressiveness and practical usefulness are gained by this.

Since the infancy of the calculus, different bisimulation equivalences have been proposed for it[1,5,6,10,13].Moreover, different methods to check bisimulation equivalences have been exploited[3,11,12,14].But these methods are tedious and inefficient,especially when checking for weak bisimulation,hence cannot be used in practice.It is therefore important to exploit efficient characterisations and checking algorithms for the equivalences of the π-calculus along the lines of [4,7].

With such efficiency motivations, symbolic transition graph(STG for short) is introduced in this paper as an intuitive and compact representation for the

*This work is partially supported by 863 Hi-Tech Project and NSF of China.

π-calculus process. Based on such STGs,strong/weak ground/symbolic bisimulation and observation congruence are defined and algotithms are also developed to check these bisimulation equivalences, along the lines of [4,7]. These results lift and refine the techniques and algorithms for regular pure-CCS [2] and value-passing process to the more expressive setting of the finite-control π-calculus.

The rest of the paper is organised as follows: the π-calculus and the notion of symbolic transition graph are introduced in the next section. The late strong ground/symbolic operational semantics and late strong ground/symbolic bisimulation are defined in section 3. The late weak ground/symbolic bisimulation and observation congruence are given in section 4,and particularly equivalent characterisations of late weak symbolic bisimulation and observation congruence are established only in terms of late symbolic double arrows. The notions of symbolic observation graph and symbolic congruence graph are introduced in section 5,followed by some theorems ensuring the elimination of τ-cycles and τ-edges; Section 6 presents algorithms for checking late strong/weak bisimulations and observation congruence. The final section contains conclusions,comparisons with related work and suggestions for future research.

2 The π-calculus and Symbolic Transition Graphs

The language of π-calculus can be given by the following BNF grammar:

$$t ::= 0 \mid \alpha.t \mid [x=y]t \mid t+t \mid (x)t \mid \ t \mid t \ \mid A(y_1, ..., y_n)$$
$$\alpha ::= \tau \mid a(x) \mid \bar{a}x$$

We refer the readers to [5,10] for a detailed account on this subject.

The basic entities of the π-calculus are *names*. Let $\mathcal{N}$, ranged over by $x, y, z, \ldots$ be a countably infinite set of names. We always assume V is a finite subset of $\mathcal{N}$. We use $new(V)$ to denote the least name $x \in \mathcal{N}$ such that x is not in V.

The *boolean expressions* of $BExp$, ranged over by ϕ, ψ,..., can be given by the following BNF grammer:

$$\phi ::= true | x = y | \neg\phi | \phi \wedge \phi$$

Other connectives are just abbreviations.The evaluation Ev is a function from $BExp$ to $\{true,\ false\}$ defined inductively as expected.We will write $n(\phi)$ for the set of names occurring in ϕ. We say ϕ is a boolean expression on a name set V if $n(\phi) \subseteq V$. Boolean expressions are only used in our meta-theory.*Conditions*, finite conjunctions of equality or inequality tests on names,are part of the $\pi^{\neq}$-calculus(the version of π-calculus enriched with mismatch construction). *Matches*, special conditions consisting of only equality tests on names,are part of the π-calculus.We also represent a match (condition) as a finite set of name tests.

A *substitution* $\sigma \in Sub$ is a function σ from $\mathcal{N}$ to $\mathcal{N}$ which is almost everywhere identity.$[\bar{y}/\bar{x}]$ is the substitution sending $\bar{x}$ to $\bar{y}$ and is identity otherwise. If $\sigma = [\bar{y}/\bar{x}]$ then $n(\sigma)$=$\{\bar{x}\} \cup \{\bar{y}\}$.So for any $x \notin n(\sigma)$, $y\sigma = x$ iff $y = x$.$\emptyset$ is the empty substitution (identity). $\sigma[x \longmapsto z]$ denotes the substitution which differs from σ only in that it sends x to z. $\sigma\lceil V$ denotes the restriction of σ on V. Two substitutions σ and σ' are *equal* on V, written $\sigma =^V \sigma'$, if $x\sigma = x\sigma'$ for all $x \in V$.

A substitution σ satisfies a boolean expression ϕ, written $\sigma \models \phi$, if $Ev(\phi\sigma) = true$. We write $\phi \Rightarrow \psi$ to mean that $\sigma \models \phi$ implies $\sigma \models \psi$ for any substitution σ, and $\phi = \psi$ to mean that $\phi \Rightarrow \psi$ and $\psi \Rightarrow \phi$. A boolean expression ϕ is *consistent* if there are no $x, y \in \mathcal{N}$ such that $\phi \Rightarrow x = y$ and $\phi \Rightarrow x \neq y$. A boolean expression ϕ is *valid*, if $Ev(\phi) = true$. $\phi_1 \vee \phi_2 \vee ... \vee \phi_m$ is a *disjunction normal form* of a boolean expression ϕ (on V), if $\phi = \phi_1 \vee \phi_2 \vee ... \vee \phi_m$ and each ϕ_i is a consistent condition (on V).

Proposition 2.1 For any condition ϕ and ψ, the relation $\phi \Rightarrow \psi$ is decidable.

Corollary 2.2 For any boolean expressions ϕ and ψ, the relation $\phi \Rightarrow \psi$ is decidable.

A finite set of boolean expressions B is called a $\chi-partition$ if $\vee B = \chi$. A condition ϕ' is *maximally consistent* on V, if ϕ' is consistent, $n(\phi') \subseteq V$ and for any $x, y \in V$ either $\phi' \Rightarrow x = y$ or $\phi' \Rightarrow x \neq y$.Let ϕ be a consistent condition on V,then ϕ' is a *maximally consistent extension* of ϕ on V, if $\phi \subseteq \phi'$ and ϕ' is a maximally consistent condition on V. We will write $MCE_V(\phi)$ for the set of all maximally consistent extensions of ϕ on V. Let ϕ be a boolean expression on V, and $\phi_1 \vee \phi_2 \vee ... \vee \phi_m$ be a disjunction normal form of ϕ on V. We write $MCD_V(\phi)$ for $\bigcup_{1 \leq i \leq m} MCE_V(\phi_i)$.

Lemma 2.3 If ϕ is a consistent condition on V, then $\bigvee MCE_V(\phi) = \phi$.

Corollary 2.4 If ϕ is a boolean expression on V, then $\bigvee MCD_V(\phi) = \phi$.

Lemma 2.5 Suppose ϕ is a maximally consistent condition on V. If σ and σ' both satisfy ϕ, then there exists an injective substitution δ such that $\sigma' =^V \sigma\delta$.

Corollary 2.4 and lemma 2.5 shows two important properties of the notion of maximal consistence.By means of them, the proofs of the completeness theorems of symbolic bisimulation with respect to ground bisimulation have been simplified considerably.

Definition 2.6 A *symbolic transition graph*(STG for short) is a rooted directed graph where each node n is assciated with a finite set of free names $fn(n)$ and each edge is labelled by a guarded action such that if (ϕ,α) is the label of an edge from m to n, written $m \xmapsto{\phi,\alpha} n$, then $fn(\phi,\alpha) \subseteq fn(m)$ and $fn(n) \subseteq fn(m) \cup bn(\alpha)$.

A symbolic transition graph is simply an intuitive and efficient representation of the π-calculus process in a compact form. By means of the rules in [8],we can generate a finite STG for any process term t in the finite control π-calculus. Moreover, finite STGs are closed under parallel composition and scope restriction as shown in [7]. As examples we give two STGs in Figure 1.

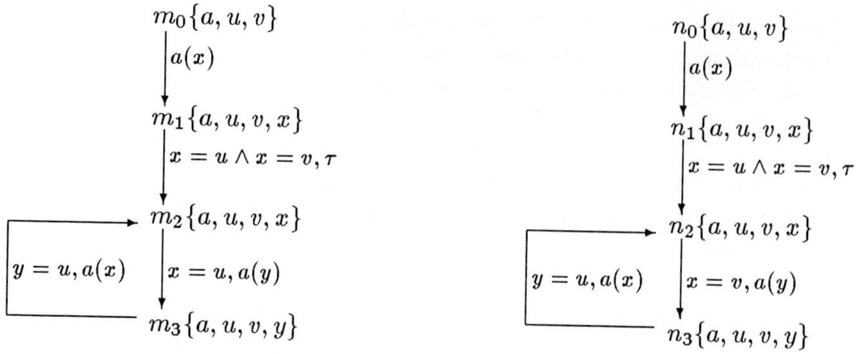

Figure 1. Two symbolic transition graphs

3 Late Strong Bisimulations

Given a STG, a *state* n_σ consist of a node n together with a substitution σ applying to free names of n (σ is restricted to $fn(n)$). One can use σ to evaluate the outgoing edge at n, resulting a ground transition. States are ranged over by p, q. If p is a state n_σ, we use $p[x \mapsto z]$ to denote the state $n_{\sigma[x \mapsto z]}$, $p\delta$ the state $n_{\sigma\delta}$ and $fn(p)$ the set $(fn(n))\sigma$ of free names.

Definition 3.1 The late strong ground operational semantics is defined as the least relation over states satisfying the following rules:

$$\frac{m \overset{\phi,\tau}{\longmapsto} n}{m_\sigma \overset{\tau}{\longrightarrow}_l n_\sigma} \quad \sigma \models \phi \qquad\qquad \frac{m \overset{\phi,\bar{a}x}{\longmapsto} n}{m_\sigma \overset{\overline{a\sigma}x\sigma}{\longrightarrow}_l n_\sigma} \quad \sigma \models \phi$$

$$\frac{m \overset{\phi,a(x)}{\longmapsto} n}{m_\sigma \overset{a\sigma(z)}{\longrightarrow}_l n_{\sigma[x \mapsto z]}} \quad \sigma \models \phi \quad z \notin fn(m_\sigma) \qquad \frac{m \overset{\phi,\bar{a}(x)}{\longmapsto} n}{m_\sigma \overset{\overline{a\sigma}(z)}{\longrightarrow}_l n_{\sigma[x \mapsto z]}} \quad \sigma \models \phi \quad z \notin fn(m_\sigma)$$

Thus the late strong ground bisimulation and late strong bisimilarity are defined as [5].

We can also give a more abstract operational semantics to STGs. Given a STG, a *term* n_σ also consists of a node n and a substitution σ(σ is restricted to $fn(n)$). Here σ applies only to the boolean guard and the action, resulting a symbolic transition as in STG. We use t, u to range over terms of π-calculus.

Definition 3.2 The late strong symbolic operational semantics is defined as the least relation over terms satisfying the following rules:

$$\frac{m \overset{\phi,\tau}{\longmapsto} n}{m_\sigma \overset{\phi\sigma,\tau}{\longrightarrow} n_\sigma} \qquad\qquad \frac{m \overset{\phi,\bar{a}x}{\longmapsto} n}{m_\sigma \overset{\phi\sigma,\overline{a\sigma}x\sigma}{\longrightarrow} n_\sigma}$$

$$\frac{m \overset{\phi,a(x)}{\longmapsto} n}{m_\sigma \overset{\phi\sigma,a\sigma(z)}{\longrightarrow} n_{\sigma[x \mapsto z]}} \quad z \notin fn(m_\sigma) \qquad \frac{m \overset{\phi,\bar{a}(x)}{\longmapsto} n}{m_\sigma \overset{\phi\sigma,\overline{a\sigma}(z)}{\longrightarrow} n_{\sigma[x \mapsto z]}} \quad z \notin fn(m_\sigma)$$

Definition 3.3 A boolean expression indexed family of symmetric relations over terms $S = \{S^{\phi}\}$ is a late strong symbolic bisimulation if $(t, u) \in S^{\phi}$ implies

whenever $t \xrightarrow{\psi,\alpha} t'$ with $bn(\alpha) \cap fn(t, u, \phi) = \emptyset$, then there exists a χ-partition B with the property that for each $\phi' \in B$ there is a $u \xrightarrow{\psi',\beta} u'$ such that $\phi' \Rightarrow \psi'$, $\alpha =^{\phi'} \beta$ and $(t', u') \in S^{\phi'}$, where

- If $\alpha \equiv \bar{a}(x)$ then $\chi = \phi \wedge \psi \wedge \bigwedge\{x \neq y | y \in fn(t, u, \phi)\}$ and $n(B) \subseteq fn(t, u, \phi) \cup \{x\}$.
- Otherwise $\chi = \phi \wedge \psi$ and $n(B) \subseteq fn(t, u, \phi)$.

We write $t \sim_L^{\phi} u$ if there is a late strong symbolic bisimulation S such that $(t, u) \in S^{\phi}$. Two STGs $\mathcal{G}$ and $\mathcal{G}'$ are late strong symbolic bisimilar over ϕ if $r_{\emptyset} \sim_L^{\phi} r'_{\emptyset}$ where r and r' are the root nodes of $\mathcal{G}$ and $\mathcal{G}'$, respectively.

The following theorem shows that symbolic bisimulation captures exactly ground bisimulation,which can be proved by means of the lammas in section 2.

Theorem 3.4 $t \sim_L^{\phi} u$ if and only if $t\sigma \dot{\sim}_l u\sigma$ for any substitution $\sigma \models \phi$.

4 Late Weak Bisimulations

Definition 4.1 The late symbolic double transitions are defined as the least relations over nodes satisfying the following rules:

- $m \overset{true,\varepsilon}{\Longmapsto}_L m$.
- $m \overset{\phi,\alpha}{\longmapsto} n$ implies $m \overset{\phi,\alpha}{\Longmapsto}_L n$.
- $m \overset{\phi,\tau}{\longmapsto}\overset{\psi,\alpha}{\Longmapsto}_L n$ implies $m \overset{\phi\wedge\psi,\alpha}{\Longmapsto}_L n$.
- If α is not of the form $a(x)$,then $m \overset{\phi,\alpha}{\Longmapsto}_L \overset{\psi,\tau}{\longmapsto} n$ implies $m \overset{\phi\wedge\psi,\alpha}{\Longmapsto}_L n$.

Definition 4.2 The late ground double arrows are defined as the least relations over states satisfying the following rules:

$$\frac{m \overset{\phi,\varepsilon}{\Longmapsto}_L n}{m_\sigma \overset{\varepsilon}{\Longrightarrow}_l n_\sigma} \quad \sigma \models \phi \qquad \frac{m \overset{\phi,\tau}{\Longmapsto}_L n}{m_\sigma \overset{\tau}{\Longrightarrow}_l n_\sigma} \quad \sigma \models \phi \qquad \frac{m \overset{\phi,\bar{a}x}{\Longmapsto}_L n}{m_\sigma \overset{\overline{a\sigma}\ x\sigma}{\Longrightarrow}_l n_\sigma} \quad \sigma \models \phi$$

$$\frac{m \overset{\phi,a(x)}{\Longmapsto}_L n}{m_\sigma \overset{a\sigma(z)}{\Longrightarrow}_l n_{\sigma[x\mapsto z]}} \quad \sigma \models \phi \quad z \notin fn(m_\sigma) \qquad \frac{m \overset{\phi,\bar{a}(x)}{\Longmapsto}_L n}{m_\sigma \overset{\overline{a\sigma}(z)}{\Longrightarrow}_l n_{\sigma[x\mapsto z]}} \quad \sigma \models \phi \quad z \notin fn(m_\sigma)$$

The late weak ground bisimulation,late weak bisimilarity and late ground observation congruence are then defined as [6]. To define the symbolic version of late weak bisimulations,we introduce the late symbolic double arrow relation.

Definition 4.3 The late symbolic double arrows are defined as the least relations satisfying the following rules:

$$\frac{m \overset{\phi,\varepsilon}{\Longmapsto}_L n}{m_\sigma \overset{\phi\sigma,\varepsilon}{\Longrightarrow}_L n_\sigma} \qquad \frac{m \overset{\phi,\tau}{\Longmapsto}_L n}{m_\sigma \overset{\phi\sigma,\tau}{\Longrightarrow}_L n_\sigma} \qquad \frac{m \overset{\phi,\bar{a}x}{\Longmapsto}_L n}{m_\sigma \overset{\phi\sigma,\overline{a\sigma}x\sigma}{\Longrightarrow}_L n_\sigma}$$

$$\frac{m \overset{\phi,a(x)}{\Longmapsto}_L n}{m_\sigma \overset{\phi\sigma,a\sigma(z)}{\Longrightarrow}_L n_{\sigma[x\mapsto z]}} \quad z \notin fn(m_\sigma) \qquad \frac{m \overset{\phi,\bar{a}(x)}{\Longmapsto}_L n}{m_\sigma \overset{\phi\sigma,\overline{a\sigma}(z)}{\Longrightarrow}_L n_{\sigma[x\mapsto z]}} \quad z \notin fn(m_\sigma)$$

Definition 4.4 A boolean expression indexed family of symmetric relations over terms $S = \{S^\phi\}$ is a late weak symbolic bisimulaion if $(t, u) \in S^\phi$ implies

whenever $t \xrightarrow{\psi,\alpha} t'$ with $bn(\alpha) \cap fn(t, u, \phi) = \emptyset$, then there exists a χ-partition B with the property that for each $\phi' \in B$ there is a $u \overset{\psi',\hat{\beta}}{\Longrightarrow}_L u'$ such that $\phi' \Rightarrow \psi'$, $\alpha =^{\phi'} \beta$ and

- If $\alpha \equiv a(x)$ then $\chi = \phi \wedge \psi$,$n(B) \subseteq fn(t, u, \phi)$, moreover,there exists a ϕ'-partition B' with $n(B') \subseteq fn(t, u, \phi) \cup \{x\}$ such that for each $\phi'' \in B'$ there is a $u' \overset{\psi'',\varepsilon}{\Longrightarrow}_L u''$ such that $\phi'' \Rightarrow \psi''$ and $(t', u'') \in S^{\phi''}$.
- If $\alpha \equiv \bar{a}(x)$,then $\chi = \phi \wedge \psi \wedge \bigwedge\{x \neq y \mid y \in fn(t, u, \phi)\}$,$n(B) \subseteq fn(t, u, \phi) \cup \{x\}$ and $(t', u') \in S^{\phi'}$.
- For other actions,$\chi = \phi \wedge \psi$,$n(B) \subseteq fn(t, u, \phi)$ and $(t', u') \in S^{\phi'}$.

We write $t \approx_L^\phi u$ if there is a late weak symbolic bisimulation S such that $(t, u) \in S^\phi$.Two STGs $\mathcal{G}$ and $\mathcal{G}'$ are late weak symbolic bisimilar over ϕ if $r_\emptyset \approx_L^\phi r'_\emptyset$,where r and r' are the root nodes of $\mathcal{G}$ and $\mathcal{G}'$,respectively.

Late symbolic observation congruence is defined in terms of $\approx_L$ as usual ,which is omitted here for limited space.The two versions(ground and symbolic) of late weak bisimulation and late observation congruence can be related as in the case of late strong bisimulation.

Theorem 4.5 (Soundness and Completeness of $\approx_L$ and $\simeq_L$)

1. $t \approx_L^\phi u$ if and only if $t\sigma \dot{\approx}_l u\sigma$ for any substitution $\sigma \models \phi$.
2. $t \simeq_L^\phi u$ if and only if $t\sigma \dot{\simeq}_l u\sigma$ for any substitution $\sigma \models \phi$.

To check late weak bisimulation,we give an equivalent characterization of late weak symbolic bisimulation only in term of late symbolic double arrows.

Theorem 4.6 Let $S = \{S^\phi\}$ be a boolean expression indexed family of symmetric relations over terms. S is a late weak symbolic bisimulaion, if and only if for any $(t, u) \in S^\phi$ and $\alpha \in \{\varepsilon, \bar{a}x, a(x), \bar{a}(x)\}$

whenever $t \overset{\psi,\alpha}{\Longrightarrow}_L t'$ with $bn(\alpha) \cap fn(t, u, \phi) = \emptyset$, then there exists a χ-partition B with the property that for each $\phi' \in B$ there is a $u \overset{\psi',\beta}{\Longrightarrow}_L u'$ such that $\phi' \Rightarrow \psi'$, $\alpha =^{\phi'} \beta$ and

- If $\alpha \equiv a(x)$ then $\chi = \phi \wedge \psi$,$n(B) \subseteq fn(t, u, \phi)$ and moreover,there exists a ϕ'-partition B' with $n(B') \subseteq fn(t, u, \phi) \cup \{x\}$ such that for each $\phi'' \in B'$ there is a $u' \overset{\psi'',\varepsilon}{\Longrightarrow}_L u''$ such that $\phi'' \Rightarrow \psi''$ and $(t', u'') \in S^{\phi''}$.
- If $\alpha \equiv \bar{a}(x)$,then $\chi = \phi \wedge \psi \wedge \bigwedge\{x \neq y \mid y \in fn(t, u, \phi)\}$,$n(B) \subseteq fn(t, u, \phi) \cup \{x\}$ and $(t', u') \in S^{\phi'}$.
- For other actions,$\chi = \phi \wedge \psi$,$n(B) \subseteq fn(t, u, \phi)$ and $(t', u') \in S^{\phi'}$.

To establish the equivalent characterization of late symbolic observation congruence, we must use the positive $\overset{\psi,\alpha}{\Longmapsto}_{+L}$ (resp.$\overset{\psi,\alpha}{\Longrightarrow}_{+L}$) which differs from $\overset{\psi,\alpha}{\Longmapsto}_L$ (resp.$\overset{\psi,\alpha}{\Longrightarrow}_L$) only in that it excludes the reflexive case.

Theorem 4.7 Two term t,u are late symbolic observation congruent with respect over ϕ,if and only if for any $\alpha \in \{\varepsilon, \bar{a}x, a(x), \bar{a}(x)\}$

whenever $t \overset{\psi,\alpha}{\Longrightarrow}_{+L} t'$ with $bn(\alpha) \cap fn(t,u,\phi) = \emptyset$, then there exists a χ-partition B with the property that for each $\phi' \in B$ there is a $u \overset{\psi',\beta}{\Longrightarrow}_{+L} u'$ such that $\phi' \Rightarrow \psi'$, $\alpha =^{\phi'} \beta$ and

• If $\alpha \equiv a(x)$ then $\chi = \phi \wedge \psi$,$n(B) \subseteq fn(t,u,\phi)$ and moreover,there exists a ϕ'-partition B' with $n(B') \subseteq fn(t,u,\phi) \cup \{x\}$ such that for each $\phi'' \in B'$ there is a $u' \overset{\psi'',\varepsilon}{\Longrightarrow}_L u''$ such that $\phi'' \Rightarrow \psi''$ and $t' \approx_L^{\phi''} u''$.

• If $\alpha \equiv \overline{a}(x)$,then $\chi = \phi \wedge \psi \wedge \bigwedge\{x \neq y \mid y \in fn(t,u,\phi)\}$,$n(B) \subseteq fn(t,u,\phi) \cup \{x\}$ and $t' \approx_L^{\phi'} u'$

• For other actions,$\chi = \phi \wedge \psi$,$n(B) \subseteq fn(t,u,\phi)$ and $t' \approx_L^{\phi'} u'$.

And similarly for u.

5 Symbolic Observation Graphs and Symbolic Congruence Graphs

Based on Theorem 4.6 and Theorem 4.7,we can generalize the notions of observation graph and congruence graph [2] to the symbolic level to check weak bisimulation equivalence and observation congruence for π-calculus processes with finite STGs.For a given STG $\mathcal{G}$,we will use $ND(\mathcal{G})$ to denote the set of nodes of $\mathcal{G}$,$E(\mathcal{G})$ the set of edges of $\mathcal{G}$ and $r_{\mathcal{G}}$ the root node of $\mathcal{G}$.For brevity,we simply write n for $n_\emptyset$ for any node n.

Late symbolic observation graph is based on the late symbolic double transition $\overset{\phi,\alpha}{\Longmapsto}_L$.The late symbolic observation graph transformation takes a symbolic transition graph and modifies the edges to reflect the late symbolic double transitions $\overset{\phi,\alpha}{\Longmapsto}_L$ where $\alpha \in \{\varepsilon, \overline{a}x, a(x), \overline{a}(x)\}$. Late symbolic congruence graph is a variation of late symbolic observation graph that records the possibility of initial τ-actions.Given a STG $\mathcal{G}$ with root node r,the late symbolic congruence graph of $\mathcal{G}$ can be constructed as [8].

As for STGs that contain a number of τ-cycles and τ-edges,their late symbolic observation graphs and late symbolic congruence graphs generated as above may increase too many edges than before.However, on certain conditions we can eliminate some τ-cycles and τ-edges of a given STG $\mathcal{G}$ to obtain an equivalent STG $\mathcal{G}'$ before generating its late symbolic observation graph and late symbolic congruence graph.For limited space, we only discuss how to eliminate τ-cycles.

In the sequel we assume C is a τ-cycle of $\mathcal{G}$ of the form: $m_1 \overset{\psi_1,\tau}{\longmapsto} m_2 \overset{\psi_2,\tau}{\longmapsto} \ldots\ldots m_{l-1} \overset{\psi_{l-1},\tau}{\longmapsto} m_l \overset{\psi_l,\tau}{\longmapsto} m_1$. we use $ND(C)$ to denote the set $\{m_1,\ldots,m_l\}$ and $E(C)$ the set $\{m_i \overset{\psi_i,\tau}{\longmapsto} m_{i+1} \mid i = 1,2,\ldots,l\}$,where $m_{l+1} = m_1$.Since $fn(m_{i+1)} \subseteq f(m_i)$ for any i,we have $fn(m_1) = fn(m_2) = \ldots = fn(m_l)$.

Definition 5.1 Suppose $\mathcal{G}$ is a STG with a τ-cycle C of the above form and $\psi = \psi_1 \wedge \cdots \wedge \psi_l$. C is *retractable*(as a point) in $\mathcal{G}$, if $\phi \Rightarrow \psi$ for any transition $n \overset{\phi,\alpha}{\longmapsto} m_i$ with $m_i \in ND(C)$ and $n \in ND(\mathcal{G}) - ND(C)$.We use $\mathcal{G}_0$ to denote the resulting STG by replacing C with a new node $m \notin ND(\mathcal{G})$ in $\mathcal{G}$ as follows:

i) $ND(\mathcal{G}_0) = ND(\mathcal{G}) \cup \{m\} - ND(C)$ and $fn(m) = fn(m_1)$

$$\begin{aligned} \text{ii) } E(\mathcal{G}_0) = \quad & E(\mathcal{G}) - \{m_i \overset{\phi,\alpha}{\longmapsto} n \in E(\mathcal{G}) \mid n \in ND(\mathcal{G})\} \\ & - \{n \overset{\phi,\alpha}{\longmapsto} m_i \in E(\mathcal{G}) \mid n \in ND(\mathcal{G})\} \\ & \cup \{m \overset{\phi,\alpha}{\longmapsto} m \mid m_i \overset{\phi,\alpha}{\longmapsto} m_j \in E(\mathcal{G}) - E(C)\} \\ & \cup \{m \overset{\phi,\alpha}{\longmapsto} n \mid m_i \overset{\phi,\alpha}{\longmapsto} n \in E(\mathcal{G}) \text{ and } n \notin ND(C)\} \\ & \cup \{n \overset{\phi,\alpha}{\longmapsto} m \mid n \overset{\phi,\alpha}{\longmapsto} m_i \in E(\mathcal{G}) \text{ and } n \notin ND(C)\} \end{aligned}$$

Such transformation is called a *τ-cycle retraction*.If $r_{\mathcal{G}} \notin ND(C)$ then $r_{\mathcal{G}_0} = r_{\mathcal{G}}$;otherwise let $r_{\mathcal{G}_0} = m$.For node $n \in ND(\mathcal{G}) - ND(C)$,we use $n_{\mathcal{G}}$ and $n_{\mathcal{G}_0}$ to denote its occurrences in $\mathcal{G}$ and $\mathcal{G}_0$,respectively.

Theorem 5.2 Suppose τ-cycle C is retractable in STG $\mathcal{G}$. Let $\mathcal{G}_0$ be the resulting STG by retracting C as a node m and $\psi = \psi_1 \wedge \psi_2 \wedge \cdots \wedge \psi_l$.Then

i) $n_{\mathcal{G}} \approx_L^{true} n_{\mathcal{G}_0}$ for any $n \in ND(\mathcal{G}) - ND(C)$,and $m_i \approx_L^{\psi} m$ for any $i \in \{1, 2, \ldots, l\}$.

ii) moreover,$n_{\mathcal{G}} \simeq_L^{true} n_{\mathcal{G}_0}$ for any $n \in ND(\mathcal{G}) - ND(C)$.

iii) if $r_{\mathcal{G}} \notin ND(C)$ then $r_{\mathcal{G}_0} = r_{\mathcal{G}}$ and $r_{\mathcal{G}_0} \simeq_L^{true} r_{\mathcal{G}}$.

iv) if $r_{\mathcal{G}} \in ND(C)$ and $\psi = true$,then $r_{\mathcal{G}_0} = m$.Let $\mathcal{G}_0^{\tau}$ be the STG by adding a new root node r' and the only new edge $r' \overset{true,\tau}{\longmapsto} m$ to $\mathcal{G}_0$.Then $r' \simeq_L^{true} r_{\mathcal{G}}$.

6 Computing Bisimulations for STGs

For value-passing processes,an algorithm to compute late strong symbolic bisimulation for a given pair of STGs was presented in [4].Since the algorithm halts when meeting the same pair of terms again,the soundness of the algorithm is not guaranteed for recursively defined processes as shown in [8].

For value-passing processes with STGAs,an algorithm,which returns a predicate equation system over a set of predicate variables,was proposed in [7].Due to space limitation, we refer readers to [7] for a detailed account on this subject.

We present an algorithm to check late symbolic bisimulation of the π-calculus processes, along the lines of [7], but the notions of *matching path*,*matching loop* and *matching loop entry* are different from those in [7], here they are based on terms,not on nodes. Let ζ be a sequence over alphabet Σ.We use $ind(\zeta)$ to denote the set of indices of ζ,$|\zeta|$ the length of ζ and $\zeta(i)$ the element at index i.

Definition 6.1 Suppose $\mathcal{G}$ and $\mathcal{H}$ are two STGs with root nodes r and r' respectively.Let $\xi \in ((BExp \times Act)^2)^*$ and $\zeta \in ((Node \times Sub)^2)^*$. $<(r,\emptyset),(r',\emptyset)> \overset{\xi,\zeta}{\Longrightarrow} <(m,\sigma),(n,\sigma')>$ is a *matching path*,if

i) when $\xi = \varepsilon$,then $\zeta = \varepsilon$,$(m,\sigma) = (r,\emptyset)$ and $(n,\sigma') = (r',\emptyset)$.

ii) otherwise there is a matching path $<(r,\emptyset),(r',\emptyset)> \overset{\xi_1,\zeta_1}{\Longrightarrow} <(m_1,\sigma_1),(n_1,\sigma_1')>$ such that $m_1 \overset{\psi,\alpha}{\longmapsto} m$,$n_1 \overset{\psi',\alpha'}{\longmapsto} n$, $\xi = \xi_1 \circ <(\psi,\alpha),(\psi',\alpha')>$,$\zeta = \zeta_1 \circ <(m_1,\sigma_1),(n_1,\sigma_1')>$ and

• if $\alpha \equiv \tau$ then $\alpha' \equiv \tau$, $\sigma = \sigma_1\lceil fn(m)$ and $\sigma' = \sigma_1'\lceil fn(n)$.

• if $\alpha \equiv \overline{a}x$ then $\alpha' \equiv \overline{b}y$, $\sigma = \sigma_1\lceil fn(m)$ and $\sigma' = \sigma_1'\lceil fn(n)$.

• if $\alpha \equiv a(x)$ then $\alpha' \equiv b(y)$, $\sigma = (\sigma_1\lceil fn(m))[x \mapsto z]$ and $\sigma' = (\sigma_1'\lceil fn(n))[y \mapsto z]$ where $z = new(fn(m_1)\sigma_1 \cup fn(n_1)\sigma_1')$.

• if $\alpha \equiv \overline{a}(x)$ then $\alpha' \equiv \overline{b}(y)$, $\sigma = (\sigma_1\lceil fn(m))[x \mapsto z]$ and $\sigma' = (\sigma_1'\lceil fn(n))[y \mapsto z]$ where $z = new(fn(m_1)\sigma_1 \cup fn(n_1)\sigma_1')$.

If there exists $i \in ind(\zeta)$ such that $\zeta(i) =< (m,\sigma),(n,\sigma') >$ and $\zeta(j) \neq \zeta(|\zeta| + j + 1 - i)$ for any $j \in \{1, \cdots, i-1\}$, then the matching path contains a *matching loop*,and $\zeta(i)$ is called the *entry of the matching loop.*

$$
\begin{array}{l}
bisim(\mathcal{G},\mathcal{H}) = \text{for each } < (m,\sigma),(n,\sigma') > \in LEntries \\
\qquad\qquad\qquad \text{return } X_{m,n}(\sigma,\sigma') = match(m,\sigma,n,\sigma') \\
match(m,\sigma,n,\sigma') = \bigwedge_{\gamma}\{match_{\gamma}((m,\sigma,n,\sigma') \mid \gamma \in NAType(m,n)\} \\
match_{\tau}(m,\sigma,n,\sigma') = \\
\quad \text{let} \quad M_{ij} = close(m_i, \sigma\lceil fn(m_i), n_j, \sigma'\lceil fn(n_j)) \\
\qquad\quad \text{for} \quad m \stackrel{\psi_i,\tau}{\longmapsto} m_i, n \stackrel{\psi_j',\tau}{\longmapsto} n_j \\
\quad \text{in} \quad \bigwedge_i(\psi_i\sigma \rightarrow \bigvee_j(\psi_j'\sigma' \wedge M_{ij})) \wedge \bigwedge_j(\psi_j'\sigma' \rightarrow \bigvee_i(\psi_i\sigma \wedge M_{ij})) \\
match_{fo}(m,\sigma,n,\sigma') = \\
\quad \text{let} \quad M_{ij} = close(m_i, \sigma\lceil fn(m_i), n_j, \sigma'\lceil fn(n_j)) \\
\qquad\quad \text{for} \quad m \stackrel{\psi_i,\overline{a_i}x_i}{\longmapsto} m_i, n \stackrel{\psi_j',\overline{b_j}y_j}{\longmapsto} n_j \\
\quad \text{in} \quad \bigwedge_i(\psi_i\sigma \rightarrow \bigvee_j(\psi_j'\sigma' \wedge a_i\sigma = b_j\sigma' \wedge x_i\sigma = y_j\sigma' \wedge M_{ij})) \wedge \\
\qquad\quad \bigwedge_j(\psi_j'\sigma \rightarrow \bigvee_i(\psi_i\sigma \wedge a_i\sigma = b_j\sigma' \wedge x_i\sigma = y_j\sigma' \wedge M_{ij})) \\
match_{in}(m,\sigma,n,\sigma') = \\
\quad \text{let} \quad z = new(fn(m)\sigma \cup fn(n)\sigma') \\
\qquad\quad M_{ij} = close(m_i, (\sigma\lceil fn(m_i))[x \mapsto z], n_j, (\sigma'\lceil fn(n_j))[y \mapsto z]) \\
\qquad\quad \text{for} \quad m \stackrel{\psi_i,a_i(x)}{\longmapsto} m_i, n \stackrel{\psi_j',b_j(y)}{\longmapsto} n_j \\
\quad \text{in} \quad \bigwedge_i(\psi_i\sigma \rightarrow \bigvee_j(\psi_j'\sigma' \wedge a_i\sigma = b_j\sigma' \wedge \forall z.M_{ij})) \wedge \\
\qquad\quad \bigwedge_j(\psi_j'\sigma' \rightarrow \bigvee_i(\psi_i\sigma \wedge a_i\sigma = b_j\sigma' \wedge \forall z.M_{ij})) \\
match_{bo}(m,\sigma,n,\sigma') = \\
\quad \text{let} \quad W = fn(m)\sigma \cup fn(n)\sigma' \\
\qquad\quad z = new(W) \\
\qquad\quad M_{ij} = close(m_i, (\sigma\lceil fn(m_i))[x \mapsto z], n_j, (\sigma'\lceil fn(n_j))[y \mapsto z]) \\
\qquad\quad \text{for} \quad m \stackrel{\psi_i,\overline{a_i}(x)}{\longmapsto} m_i, n \stackrel{\psi_j',\overline{b_j}(y)}{\longmapsto} n_j \\
\quad \text{in} \quad \bigwedge_i(\psi_i\sigma \rightarrow \bigvee_j(\psi_j'\sigma' \wedge a_i\sigma = b_j\sigma' \wedge \bigwedge\{z \neq c \mid c \in W\} \wedge M_{ij})) \wedge \\
\qquad\quad \bigwedge_j(\psi_j'\sigma' \rightarrow \bigvee_i(\psi_i\sigma \wedge a_i\sigma = b_j\sigma' \wedge \bigwedge\{z \neq c \mid c \in W\} \wedge M_{ij})) \\
close(m,\sigma,n,\sigma') = \ \text{if } < (m,\sigma),(n,\sigma') > \in LEntries \text{ then return } X_{m,n}(\sigma,\sigma') \\
\qquad\qquad\qquad\qquad\quad \text{else } match(m,\sigma,n,\sigma')
\end{array}
$$

Figure 2. The Algorithm for Late Strong Symbolic Bisimulation.

The algorithm for late strong symbolic bisimulation is presented in Figure 2,where $NAType(m,n)$ is the set of types of actions that appear in the next transitions from nodes m and n.The types of actions τ,$\overline{a}x$,$a(x)$,$\overline{a}(x)$ are τ,fo,in,bo, respectively.The algorithm takes as input a pair of STGs,$\mathcal{G}$ and $\mathcal{H}$,and uses the set *LEntries* of all matching loop entries which also includes the pair $<(r,\emptyset),(r',\emptyset)>$ where r and r' are root nodes of $\mathcal{G}$ and $\mathcal{H}$.The output is a predicate equation system.The function *bisim* introdues a predicate variable for each matching loop entry and creates an equation for each matching loop. The correctness of the algorithm is guaranteed by Theorem 6.2.

Theorem 6.2 Let $E = \{X_{m,n}(\sigma,\sigma') = \Lambda_{m,n}\}$ be the equation system returned by the algorithm on $\mathcal{G}$ and $\mathcal{H}$.

1. Suppose η is a symbolic solution of E and $<(m,\sigma),(n,\sigma')>\in$*LEntries*.If $\eta(X_{m,n})(\sigma,\sigma') = \phi$ then $m_\sigma \sim_L^\phi n_{\sigma'}$.

2. Suppose η is the greatest symbolic solution of E and $<(m,\sigma),(n,\sigma')>\in$ *LEntries*. If $m_\sigma \sim_L^\phi n_{\sigma'}$ then $\phi \Rightarrow \eta(X_{m,n})(\sigma,\sigma')$.

Theorem 6.3 Suppose $\phi \in BExp$,then there is $\psi \in BExp$ such that $\forall z.\phi = \psi$.

For example,consider $\phi = (z = u \wedge z = v) \vee (z \neq u \wedge z \neq v)$. Obviously we have $\forall z.\phi = (u = v)$.

By means of Proposition 2.1,Corollary 2.2 and Theorem 6.3,we can establish an oracle to simplify intermediate expressions and decide the implication problem for boolean expressions, even if $\forall$ is introduced by the function $match_{in}$. With the help of the oracle,the greatest solution(fixpoint) of such an equation system can be computed automatically by iteration,starting from the constant function η_0 which is defined by $\eta_0(X_{m,n})(\sigma,\sigma') = true$ for any matching loop entry $<(m,\sigma),(n,\sigma')>\in$ *LEntries*. This process will convergent after finite times of iteration.When $\eta_i(X_{m,n})(\sigma,\sigma') = \eta_{i+1}(X_{m,n})(\sigma,\sigma')$, η_i is the greatest solution(fixpoint) of the equation system.In most situations,we can obtain the greatest symbolic solution by only two or three iterations.

For instance,the simplified equation system returned by the algorithm for two STGs in Figure 1 is

$$X_{0,0} = \forall z_1(z_1 = u \wedge z_1 = v \rightarrow X_{2,2}[z_1/x, z_1/x])$$
$$X_{2,2}[z_1/x, z_1/x] = \quad z_1 \neq u \wedge z_1 \neq v \vee z_1 = u \wedge z_1 = v \wedge \forall z_2(z_2 = u \rightarrow \forall z_1 X_{2,2}[z_1/x, z_1/x])$$

We can compute its greatest symbolic solution as follows:

$$\eta_0(X_{2,2})[z_1/x, z_1/x] = true$$
$$\eta_1(X_{2,2})[z_1/x, z_1/x] = z_1 \neq u \wedge z_1 \neq v \vee z_1 = u \wedge z_1 = v$$
$$\eta_2(X_{2,2})[z_1/x, z_1/x] = z_1 \neq u \wedge z_1 \neq v \vee z_1 = u \wedge z_1 = v \wedge u = v$$
$$\eta_2(X_{0,0}) = (u = v)$$

So we have $m_0 \sim_L^{u=v} n_0$.

To check late weak symbolic bisimulation/late symbolic observation congruence of two given STGs $\mathcal{G}$ and $\mathcal{H}$,we first construct their late symbolic observation graphs/late symbolic congruence graphs $\mathcal{G}'$ and $\mathcal{H}'$.The algorithm for computing late weak symbolic bisimulation/late symbolic ovservation congruence is similar to the one presented in Figure 2 but working on $\mathcal{G}'$ and $\mathcal{H}'$.As Theorem 4.6/Theorem 4.7 indicates,we only need to modify the case dealing with input within function *match*:

$$
\begin{array}{ll}
\multicolumn{2}{l}{match_{in}(m,\sigma,n,\sigma') =} \\
\text{let} & z = new(fn(m)\sigma \cup fn(n)\sigma') \\
& M_{i,jk} = close(m_i, (\sigma\lceil fn(m_i))[x \mapsto z], n_{jk}, (\sigma\lceil fn(n_{jk}))[y \mapsto z]) \\
& \text{for} \quad m \overset{\psi_i, a_i(x)}{\Longmapsto}_L m_i, n \overset{\psi'_j, b_j(y)}{\Longmapsto}_L n_j \overset{\psi'_{jk}, \varepsilon}{\Longmapsto}_L n_{jk} \\
& M_{il,j} = close(m_{il}, (\sigma\lceil fn(m_{il}))[x \mapsto z], n_j, (\sigma'\lceil fn(n_j))[y \mapsto z]) \\
& \text{for} \quad m \overset{\psi_i, a_i(x)}{\Longmapsto}_L m_i \overset{\psi_{il}, \varepsilon}{\Longmapsto}_L m_{il}, n \overset{\psi'_j, b_j(y)}{\Longmapsto}_L n_j \\
\text{in} & \bigwedge\limits_i(\psi_i\sigma \rightarrow \bigvee\limits_j(\psi'_j\sigma' \wedge a_i\sigma = b_j\sigma' \wedge \forall z.(\bigvee\limits_k(\psi'_{jk}\sigma'[y \mapsto z] \wedge M_{i,jk}))))\wedge \\
& \bigwedge\limits_j(\psi'_j\sigma' \rightarrow \bigvee\limits_i(\psi_i\sigma \wedge a_i\sigma = b_j\sigma' \wedge \forall z.(\bigvee\limits_l \psi_{il}\sigma[x \mapsto z] \wedge M_{il,j}))))
\end{array}
$$

7 Conclusions and Related Work

We have presented a new approach to check late strong/weak bisimulation and observation congruence for the π-calculus on top of finite symbolic transition graphs,symbolic observation graphs and symbolic congruence graphs.The same has been done for early case as well,but due to space limitation, these and the proofs of theorems have to be omitted from this extended abstract.

Our results verify a conjecture posed in[1,3]:the notion of symbolic transition graph and the checking algorithm for value-passing processes can be refined to check bisimulation for the π-calculus.

The current paper inherits the main ideas from [2,4,7]. Our work has also strong connections with the papers[1,5,6].In[1] a symbolic semantics and proof systems have been proposed for the π-calculus.Our definition of symbolic bisimulation is very similar to theirs.But they only consider strong bisimulation on top of (syntactic) process terms.Neither symbolic transition graph nor checking algorithm is introduced.

In[5,6] proof systems for strong and weak bisimulation equivalences in the π-calculus are presented.The set of maximally consistent extensions of a condition is used as a canonical boolean partition of the condition in the definition of symbolic bisimulation.Such a definition is sufficient and suitable for proof systems,but it cannot be used to exploit checking algorithm and gain efficiency as ours.The notion of maximally consistence is inherited and refined in this paper only to simplify the proofs of the completeness theorems.

We believe that the techniques used in this paper may also be easily adapted to handle other semantic equivalences such as open bisimulation and to model check the π-calculus.We are engaged in implementing the algorithms in standard ML,and hope to establish a non-trivial automatic verification tool for the π-calculus, applying the theoretical results to practice.

Acknowledgements: Thanks to Huiming Lin for providing helpful articles,and to Binshan Wang, Jianqi Li and Guangjun Zhong for discussions on this subject.

References

[1] M.Boreale and R.De Nicola.A symbolic semantics for the π-calculus. In CONCUR'94,LNCS 836.Springer-Verlag,1994.

[2] R.Cleaveland,J.Parrow and B.Steffen.The concurrency workbench: A Semantics based verification tool for the verification of concurrent systems.ACM Transactions on Programming Language and Systems,Vol.15,No.1,1993.

[3] M.Dam.On the decidability of process equivalence for the π-calculus. Theoretical Computer Science,183:214-228,1997.

[4] M.Hennessy and H.Lin.Symbolic bisimulations.Theoretical Computer Science,138:353-389,1995.

[5] H.Lin.Symbolic bisimulations and proof systems for the π-calculus. Report 7/94,Computer Science,University of Sussex,1994.

[6] H.Lin.Complete inference systems for weak bisimulation equivalences in the π-calculus.In TAPSOFT'95.Spring-Verlag,1995.

[7] H.Lin.Symbolic transition graph with assignment.In CONCUR'96, LNCS 1119.Springer-Verlag,1996.

[8] Z.J.Li.Checking strong/weak bisimulation equivalences and observation congruence for value-passing processes and the π-calculus processes.Forthcoming Ph.D.thesis,Changsha Institute of Technology,1998.

[9] R.Milner.Communication and Concurrency.Prentice-Hall,1989.

[10] R.Milner.J.Parrow and D.Walker,A calculus of mobile processes, Part I,II.Information and Computation,100:1-77,1992.

[11] U.Montanari and M.Pistore.Checking bisimilarity for finitary π-calculus.In CONCUR'95,LNCS 962.Springer Verlag,1995.

[12] M.Pistore and D.Sangiorgi.A partition refinement algorithm for the π-calculus.In CAV'96,LNCS 1102.Spinger-Verlag,1996.

[13] D.Sangiorgi.A theory of bisimulation for the π-calculus. In CONCUR'93,LNCS 715.Springer-Verlag,1993.

[14] B.Victor and F.Moller.The mobility workbench–a tool for the π-calculus.In CAV'94,LNCS 818.Springer-Verlag,1994.

Inversion of Circulant Matrices over $\mathbf{Z}_m$

Dario Bini[1], Gianna M. Del Corso[2,3] Giovanni Manzini[2,4], Luciano Margara[5]

[1] Dipartimento di Matematica, Università di Pisa, 56126 Pisa, Italy.
[2] Istituto di Matematica Computazionale, CNR, 56126 Pisa, Italy.
[3] Istituto di Elaborazione dell'Informazione, CNR, 56126 Pisa, Italy.
[4] Dipartimento di Scienze e Tecnologie Avanzate, Università di Torino, 15100 Alessandria, Italy.
[5] Dipartimento di Scienze dell'Informazione, Università di Bologna, 40127 Bologna, Italy.

Abstract. In this paper we consider the problem of inverting an $n \times n$ circulant matrix with entries over $\mathbf{Z}_m$. We show that the algorithm for inverting circulants, based on the reduction to diagonal form by means of FFT, has some drawbacks when working over $\mathbf{Z}_m$. We present three different algorithms which do not use this approach. Our algorithms require different degrees of knowledge of m and n, and their costs range — roughly — from $n \log n \log\log n$ to $n \log^2 n \log\log n \log m$ operations over $\mathbf{Z}_m$. We also present an algorithm for the inversion of finitely generated bi-infinite Toeplitz matrices. The problems considered in this paper have applications to the theory of linear Cellular Automata.

1 Introduction

In this paper we consider the problem of inverting circulant and bi-infinite Toeplitz matrices with entries over the ring $\mathbf{Z}_m$. In addition to their own interest as linear algebra problems, these problems play an important role in the theory of linear Cellular Automata.

The standard algorithm for inverting circulant matrices with real or complex entries is based on the fact that any $n \times n$ circulant is diagonalizable by means of the Fourier matrix F (defined by $F_{ij} = \omega^{(i-1)(j-1)}$ where ω is a primitive n-th root of unity). Hence, we can compute the eigenvalues of the matrix with a single FFT. To compute the inverse of the matrix it suffices to invert the eigenvalues and execute an inverse FFT. The total cost of inverting an $n \times n$ circulant is therefore $O(n \log n)$ arithmetic operations.

Unfortunately this method does not generalize, not even for circulant matrices over the field $\mathbf{Z}_p$. The reason is that if $\gcd(p, n) > 1$ no extension field of $\mathbf{Z}_p$ contains a primitive n-th root of unity. As a consequence, $n \times n$ circulant matrices over $\mathbf{Z}_p$ are not diagonalizable. If $\gcd(p, n) = 1$ we are guaranteed that a primitive n-th root of unity exists in a suitable extension of $\mathbf{Z}_p$. However, the approach based on the FFT still poses some problems. In fact, working in an extension of $\mathbf{Z}_p$ requires that we find a suitable irreducible polynomial $q(x)$ and every operation in the field involves manipulation of polynomials of degree up to $\deg(q(x)) - 1$.

In this paper we describe three algorithms for inverting an $n \times n$ circulant matrix over $\mathbf{Z}_m$ which are not based on the reduction to diagonal form by means of FFT. Instead, we transform the original problem into an equivalent problem over the ring $\mathbf{Z}_m[x]$. Our first algorithm assumes the factorization of m is known and it requires $n \log^2 n + n \log m$ multiplications and $n \log^2 n \log\log n$ additions over $\mathbf{Z}_m$. Our second algorithm does not requires the factorization of m and its cost is a factor $\log m$ greater than in the previous case. The third algorithm assumes nothing about m but works only for $n = 2^k$. It is the fastest algorithm and it has the same asymptotic cost of a single multiplication between degree n polynomials in $\mathbf{Z}_m[x]$. Finally, we show that this last algorithm can be used to build a fast procedure for the inversion of finitely generated bi-infinite Toeplitz matrices.

The problem of inverting a circulant matrix with entries over an arbitrary commutative ring R has been addressed in [5]. There, the author shows how to compute the determinant and the adjoint of an $n \times n$ circulant matrix of the form $I + \sum_{i=1}^{l} \beta_i U^i$, (where $U_{ij} = 1$ for $i - j \equiv 1 \pmod n$ and 0 otherwise). A naive implementation of the proposed method takes $O(nl + 2^l)$ operations over R. Although the same computation can be done in $O(nl + M(l)\log n)$ operations, where $M(l)$ is the cost of $l \times l$ matrix multiplication (hence, $M(l) = l^\omega$, with $2 \le \omega < 2.376$), this algorithm is competitive only for very small values of l.

Due to limited space we omit the proof of some of the technical lemmas. Full details are given in [2].

2 Definitions and Notation

Circulant matrices. Let U denote the $n \times n$ cyclic shift matrix whose entries are $U_{ij} = 1$ if $j - i \equiv 1 \pmod n$, and 0 otherwise. A circulant matrix over $\mathbf{Z}_m$ can be written as $A = \sum_{i=0}^{n-1} a_i U^i$, where $a_i \in \mathbf{Z}_m$. Assuming $\det(A)$ is invertible over $\mathbf{Z}_m$, we consider the problem of computing a circulant matrix $B = \sum_{i=0}^{n-1} b_i U^i$, such that $AB = I$ (it is well known that the inverse of a circulant matrix is still circulant).

It is natural to associate with a circulant matrix $A = \sum_{i=0}^{n-1} a_i U^i$ the polynomial (over the ring $\mathbf{Z}_m[x]$) $f(x) = \sum_{i=0}^{n-1} a_i x^i$. Computing the inverse of A is clearly equivalent to finding a polynomial $g(x) = \sum_{i=0}^{r} b_i x^i$ in $\mathbf{Z}_m[x]$ such that

$$f(x)g(x) \equiv 1 \pmod{x^n - 1} . \tag{1}$$

The congruence modulo $x^n - 1$ follows from the equality $U^n = I$. Hence, the problem of inverting a circulant matrix is equivalent to inversion in the ring $\mathbf{Z}_m[x]/(x^n - 1)$.

Bi-infinite Toeplitz matrices. Let W, W^{-1}, W^0 denote the bi-infinite matrices defined by

$$W_{ij} = \begin{cases} 1, & \text{if } j - i = 1, \\ 0, & \text{otherwise;} \end{cases} \quad W^{-1}_{ij} = \begin{cases} 1, & \text{if } i - j = 1, \\ 0, & \text{otherwise;} \end{cases} \quad W^{0}_{ij} = \begin{cases} 1, & \text{if } j = i, \\ 0, & \text{otherwise;} \end{cases}$$

where both indices i, j range over $\mathbf{Z}$. If we extend in the obvious way the matrix product to the bi-infinite case we have $WW^{-1} = W^{-1}W = W^0$. Hence, we can define the algebra of finitely generated bi-infinite Toeplitz matrices over $\mathbf{Z}_m$ as the set of all matrices of the form $T = \sum_{i\in\mathbf{Z}} a_i W^i$ where $a_i \in \mathbf{Z}_m$ and only finitely many of them are nonzero. An equivalent representation of the elements of this algebra can be obtained using finite *formal power series* (fps) over $\mathbf{Z}_m$. For example, the matrix T above is represented by the finite fps $h_T(x) = \sum_{i\in\mathbf{Z}} a_i x^i$. In the following we use $\mathbf{Z}_m\{x\}$ to denote the set of finite fps over $\mathbf{Z}_m$. Instead of stating explicitly that only finitely many coefficients are nonzero, we write each element $f(x) \in \mathbf{Z}_m\{x\}$ as $f(x) = \sum_{i=-r}^{r} b_i x^i$ (where some of the b_i's can still be zero). Computing the inverse of a bi-infinite Toeplitz matrix T is clearly equivalent to finding $g(x) \in \mathbf{Z}_m\{x\}$ such that $h_T(x)g(x) \equiv 1 \pmod{m}$. Hence, inversion of finitely generated Toeplitz matrices is equivalent to inversion in the ring $\mathbf{Z}_m\{x\}$.

Connections with Cellular Automata theory. Cellular Automata (CA) are dynamical systems consisting of a finite or infinite lattice of variables which can take a finite number of discrete values. In the following we restrict our attention to linear CA, that is, CA which are based on a linear local rule. Despite of their apparent simplicity, linear CA may exhibit many complex behaviors (see for example [6–9]). Linear CA have been used for pattern generation, design of error correcting codes and cipher systems, generation of hashing functions, *etc.* (see [4] for a survey of recent applications).

An infinite one-dimensional linear CA is defined as follows. For $m \geq 2$, let $\mathcal{C}_m$ denote the *space of configurations* $\mathcal{C}_m = \{c \mid c\colon \mathbf{Z} \to \mathbf{Z}_m\}$, which consists of all functions from $\mathbf{Z}$ into $\mathbf{Z}_m$. Each element of $\mathcal{C}_m$ can be visualized as a bi-infinite array in which each cell contains an element of $\mathbf{Z}_m$. A local rule of *radius* r is defined by

$$f(x_{-r}, \ldots, x_r) = \sum_{i=-r}^{r} a_i x_i \mod m, \tag{2}$$

where the $2r+1$ coefficients $a_{-r}, \ldots, a_0, \ldots, a_r$ belong to $\mathbf{Z}_m$. The global map $F\colon \mathcal{C}_m \to \mathcal{C}_m$ associated to the local rule f is given by

$$[F(c)](i) = \sum_{j=-r}^{r} a_j c(i+j) \mod m, \qquad \forall c \in \mathcal{C}_m,\ \forall i \in \mathbf{Z}\ .$$

In other words, the content of cell i in the configuration $F(c)$ is a function of the content of cells $i-r, \ldots, i+r$ in the configuration c.

Finite one-dimensional additive CA (of size n) are defined over the configuration space $\mathcal{C}^*_{n,m} = \{c \mid c\colon \{0,1,\ldots,n-1\} \to \mathbf{Z}_m\}$, which can be seen as the set of all possible n-tuples of elements of $\mathbf{Z}_m$. To the local rule (2) we associate the global map $G\colon \mathcal{C}^*_{n,m} \to \mathcal{C}^*_{n,m}$ defined by

$$[G(c)](i) = \sum_{j=-r}^{r} a_j c(i+j \bmod n) \mod m, \qquad \forall c \in \mathcal{C}^*_{n,m},\ \forall i \in \{0,1,\ldots,n-1\}\ .$$

In other words, the new content of cell i depends on the content of cells $i - r, \ldots, i + r$, wrapping around the borders of the array.

Linear CA are often studied using formal power series. To each configuration $c \in \mathcal{C}_m$ we associate the infinite fps $P_c(x) = \sum_{i \in \mathbf{Z}} c(i)x^i$. The advantage of this representation is that the computation of a linear map is equivalent to power series multiplication. Let $F: \mathcal{C}_m \to \mathcal{C}_m$ be a linear map with local rule (2). We associate to f the finite fps $A(x) \in \mathbf{Z}_m\{x\}$ given by $A(X) = \sum_{i=-r}^{r} a_i x^{-i}$. Then, for any $c \in \mathcal{C}_m$ we have $P_{F(c)}(x) = P_c(x)A(x) \mod m$. For finite additive CA we use a similar representation. To each configuration $c \in \mathcal{C}^*_{n,m}$ we associate the polynomial of degree $n-1$ $P_c(X) = \sum_{i=0}^{n-1} c(i)x^i$. Then, for any configuration $c \in \mathcal{C}^*_{n,m}$ we have $P_{G(c)}(x) = [P_c(x)A(x) \pmod{x^n - 1}] \mod m$. The above results show that the inversion of F and G is equivalent to the inversion of $A(x)$ in $\mathbf{Z}_m\{x\}$ and $\mathbf{Z}_m[x]/(x^n - 1)$ respectively. Therefore they are also equivalent to the inversion of bi-infinite Toeplitz and circulant matrices.

Conditions for invertibility over $\mathbf{Z}_m\{x\}$ and $\mathbf{Z}_m[x]/(x^n - 1)$. A necessary and sufficient condition for the invertibility of an element in $\mathbf{Z}_m\{x\}$ has been given in [6] where the authors prove that a finite fps $f(x) = \sum_{i=-r}^{r} a_i x^i$ is invertible if and only if for each prime factor p of m there exists a unique coefficient a_i such that $p \not| a_i$. The following theorem (proved in [7]) provides an equivalent condition which does not require the knowledge of the factorization of the modulus m.

Theorem 1. *Let $f(x) = \sum_{i=-r}^{r} a_i x^i$ be a finite fps over $\mathbf{Z}_m$, and let $k = \lfloor \log_2 m \rfloor$. For $i = -r, \ldots, r$, define*

$$z_i = [\gcd(a_i, m)]^k, \qquad \text{and} \qquad q_i = \frac{m}{\gcd(m, z_i)}.$$

Then, $f(x)$ is invertible if and only if $q_{-r} \cdots q_r = m$. □

The following theorem states a necessary and sufficient condition for the invertibility of a circulant matrix over $\mathbf{Z}_m$.

Theorem 2. *Let $m = p_1^{k_1} p_2^{k_2} \cdots p_h^{k_h}$, denote the prime powers factorization of m and let $f(x)$ denote the polynomial over $\mathbf{Z}_m$ associated to a circulant matrix A. The matrix A is invertible if and only if, for $i = 1, \ldots, h$, we have $\gcd(f(x), x^n - 1) = 1$ in $\mathbf{Z}_{p_i}[x]$.* □

Review of bit complexity results. In the following we will give the cost of each algorithm in terms of number of *bit operations*. In our analysis we use the following well known results (see for example [1] or [3]). Additions and subtractions in $\mathbf{Z}_m$ take $O(\log m)$ bit operations. We denote by $\mu(d) = d \log d \log \log d$ the number of bit operations required by the Schönhage-Strassen algorithm [11] for multiplication of d-digits integers. Hence, multiplication between elements of $\mathbf{Z}_m$ takes $\mu(\log m) = \log m \log \log m \log \log \log m$ bit operations. Computing the inverse of an element $x \in \mathbf{Z}_m$ takes $\mu(\log m) \log \log m$ bit operations using a modified extended Euclidean algorithm (see [1, Theorem 8.20]). The same algorithm returns $\gcd(x, m)$ when x is not invertible.

The sum of two polynomials in $\mathbf{Z}_m[x]$ of degree at most n can be trivially computed in $O(n \log m)$ bit operations. The product of two such polynomials can be computed in $O(n \log n)$ multiplications and $O(n \log n \log\log n)$ additions/subtractions in $\mathbf{Z}_m$ (see [3, Theorem 7.1]). Therefore, the asymptotic cost of polynomial multiplication is $O(\Pi(m,n))$ bit operations where

$$\Pi(m,n) = n \log n \mu(\log m) + n \log n \log\log n \log m. \tag{3}$$

Given two polynomials $a(x), b(x) \in \mathbf{Z}_p[x]$ (p prime) of degree at most n, we can compute $d(x) = \gcd(a(x), b(x))$ in $O(\Gamma(p,n))$ bit operations, where

$$\Gamma(p,n) = \Pi(p,n) \log n + n\mu(\log p) \log\log p. \tag{4}$$

The same algorithm also returns $s(x)$ and $t(x)$ such that $a(x)s(x) + b(x)t(x) = d(x)$. The bound (4) follows by a straightforward modification of the polynomial gcd algorithm described in [1, Sec. 8.9] (the term $n\mu(\log p)\log\log p$ comes from the fact that we must compute the inverse of $O(n)$ elements of $\mathbf{Z}_p$).

3 Inversion in $\mathbf{Z}_m[x]/(x^n - 1)$. Factorization of m Known

In this section we consider the problem of computing the inverse of a circulant matrix over $\mathbf{Z}_m$ when the factorization $m = p_1^{k_1} p_2^{k_2} \cdots p_h^{k_h}$ of the modulus m is known. We consider the equivalent problem of inverting a polynomial $f(x)$ over $\mathbf{Z}_m[x]/(x^n - 1)$, and we show that we can compute the inverse by combining known techniques (Chinese remaindering, the extended Euclidean algorithm, and Newton-Hensel lifting). We start by showing that it suffices to find the inverse of $f(x)$ modulo the prime powers $p_i^{k_i}$.

Lemma 1. *Let $m = p_1^{k_1} p_2^{k_2} \cdots p_h^{k_h}$, and let $f(x)$ be a polynomial in $\mathbf{Z}_m[x]$. Given $g_1(x), \ldots, g_h(x)$ such that $f(x)g_i(x) \equiv 1 \pmod{x^n - 1}$ in $\mathbf{Z}_{p_i^{k_i}}[x]$ for $i = 1, 2, \ldots h$, we can find $g(x) \in \mathbf{Z}_m[x]$ which satisfies (1) at the cost of $O(nh\mu(\log m) + \mu(\log m)\log\log m)$ bit operations.*

Proof. The proof is constructive. Since $f(x)g_i(x) \equiv 1 \pmod{x^n - 1}$ in $\mathbf{Z}_{p_i^{k_i}}[x]$, we have

$$f(x)g_i(x) \equiv 1 + \lambda_i(x)(x^n - 1) \pmod{p_i^{k_i}}.$$

Let $\alpha_i = m/p_i^{k_i}$. Clearly, for $j \neq i$, $\alpha_i \equiv 0 \pmod{p_j^{k_j}}$. Since $\gcd(\alpha_i, p_i^{k_i}) = 1$, we can find β_i such that $\alpha_i \beta_i \equiv 1 \pmod{p_i^{k_i}}$. Let

$$g(x) = \sum_{i=1}^{h} \alpha_i \beta_i g_i(x), \qquad \lambda(x) = \sum_{i=1}^{h} \alpha_i \beta_i \lambda_i(x).$$

By construction, for $i = 1, 2, \ldots, h$, we have $g(x) \equiv g_i(x) \pmod{p_i^{k_i}}$ and $\lambda(x) \equiv \lambda_i(x) \pmod{p_i^{k_i}}$. Hence, for $i = 1, 2, \ldots, h$, we have

$$f(x)g(x) = \sum_{j=1}^{h} \alpha_j \beta_j f(x) g_j(x)$$

$$\equiv f(x)g_i(x) \pmod{p_i^{k_i}}$$
$$\equiv 1 + \lambda_i(x)(x^n - 1) \pmod{p_i^{k_i}}$$
$$\equiv 1 + \lambda(x)(x^n - 1) \pmod{p_i^{k_i}}.$$

We conclude that $f(x)g(x) \equiv 1 + \lambda(x)(x^n - 1) \pmod{m}$, or, equivalently, $f(x)g(x) \equiv 1 \pmod{x^n - 1}$ in $\mathbf{Z}_m[x]$. The computation of $g(x)$ consists in n (one for each coefficient) applications of Chinese remaindering. Obviously, the computation of α_i, β_i, $i = 1, \ldots, h$, should be done only once. Since integer division has the same asymptotic cost than multiplication, we can compute $\alpha_1, \ldots, \alpha_h$ in $O(h\mu(\log m))$ bit operations. Since each β_i is obtained through an inversion in $\mathbf{Z}_{p_i}^{k_i}$, computing the $\beta_1, \ldots, \beta_h$ takes $O\left(\sum_{j=1}^{h} \mu(\log p_j^{k_j}) \log\log p_j^{k_j}\right)$ bit operations . Finally, given $\alpha_1, \ldots, \alpha_h$, $\beta_1, \ldots, \beta_h$, $g_1(x), \ldots, g_h(x)$ we can compute $g(x)$ in $O(nh\mu(\log m))$ bit operations. The thesis follows using the inequality $\mu(\log a) \log\log a + \mu(\log b) \log\log b \leq \mu(\log ab) \log\log(ab)$. □

In view of Lemma 1 we can restrict ourselves to the problem of inverting a polynomial over $\mathbf{Z}_m[x]/(x^n - 1)$ when $m = p^k$ is a prime power. Next lemma shows how to solve this particular problem.

Lemma 2. *Let $f(x)$ be a polynomial in $\mathbf{Z}_{p^k}[x]$. If $\gcd(f(x), x^n - 1) = 1$ in $\mathbf{Z}_p[x]$, then $f(x)$ is invertible in $\mathbf{Z}_{p^k}[x]/(x^n - 1)$. In this case, the inverse of $f(x)$ can be computed in $O(\Gamma(p, n) + \Pi(p^k, n))$ bit operations, where $\Gamma(p, n)$ and $\Pi(p^k, n)$ are defined by (4) and (3) respectively.*

Proof. If $\gcd(f(x), x^n - 1) = 1$ in $\mathbf{Z}_p[x]$, by Bezout's lemma there exist $s(x), t(x)$ such that

$$f(x)s(x) + (x^n - 1)t(x) \equiv 1 \pmod{p}.$$

Next we consider the sequence

$$g_0(x) = s(x), \qquad g_i(x) = 2g_{i-1}(x) - [g_{i-1}(x)]^2 f(x) \bmod (x^n - 1).$$

It is straightforward to verify that $g_i(x)f(x) \equiv 1 + p^{2^i}\lambda_i(x) \pmod{x^n - 1}$. Hence, the inverse of $f(x)$ in $\mathbf{Z}_{p^k}[x]/(x^n - 1)$ is $g_{\lceil \log k \rceil}(x)$.

The computation of $s(x)$ takes $O(\Gamma(p, n))$ bit operations. For computing the sequence $g_1, \ldots, g_{\lceil \log k \rceil}$ we observe that it suffices to compute each g_i modulo p^{2^i}. Hence, the cost of obtaining the whole sequence is

$$O\left(\Pi(p^2, n) + \Pi(p^4, n) + \cdots + \Pi(p^{2^{\lceil \log k \rceil}}, n)\right) = O(\Pi(p^k, n))$$

bit operations. □

Note that from Lemmas 1 and 2, we get that the condition given in Theorem 2 is indeed a sufficient condition for invertibility of a circulant matrix. Combining the above lemmas we get Algorithm 1 for the inversion of a polynomial $f(x)$ over $\mathbf{Z}_m[x]/(x^n - 1)$. The cost of the algorithm is

$$T(m, n) = O\left(nh\mu(\log m) + \mu(\log m) \log\log m + \sum\nolimits_{j=1}^{h} \Gamma(p_j, n) + \Pi(p_j^{k_j}, n)\right)$$

```
Inverse1(f(x), m, n) → g(x)
{Computes the inverse g(x) of the polynomial f(x) in Z_m[x]/(x^n − 1)}

let m = p_1^{k_1} p_2^{k_2} ... p_h^{k_h};
for j = 1, 2, ···, h do
    if gcd(f(x), x^n − 1) = 1 in Z_{p_j}[x] then
        compute g_j(x) such that f(x)g_j(x) ≡ 1  (mod x^n − 1) in Z_{p_j^{k_j}}[x]
        using Newton-Hensel lifting (Lemma 2);
    else
        return "f(x) is not invertible";
    endif
endfor
compute g(x) using Chinese remaindering (Lemma 1).
```

Algorithm 1. Inversion in $\mathbf{Z}_m[x]/(x^n - 1)$. Factorization of m known.

bit operations. In order to get a more manageable expression, we bound h with $\log m$ and p_j with $p_j^{k_j}$. In addition, we use the inequalities $\Pi(a,n) + \Pi(b,n) \leq \Pi(ab,n)$ and $\Gamma(a,n) + \Gamma(b,n) \leq \Gamma(ab,n)$. We get

$$\begin{aligned} T(m,n) &= O(n \log m \mu(\log m) + \mu(\log m) \log\log m + \Gamma(m,n) + \Pi(m,n)) \\ &= O(n \log m \mu(\log m) + \Pi(m,n) \log n) . \end{aligned}$$

Note that if $m = O(n)$ the dominant term is $\Pi(m,n)\log n$. That is, the cost of inverting $f(x)$ is asymptotically bounded by the cost of executing $\log n$ multiplications in $\mathbf{Z}_m[x]$.

4 A General Inversion Algorithm in $\mathbf{Z}_m[x]/(x^n - 1)$

The algorithm described in Section 3 relies on the fact that the factorization of the modulus m is known. If this is not the case and the factorization must be computed beforehand, the increase in the running time may be significant since the fastest known factorization algorithms require time exponential in $\log m$. In this section we show how to compute the inverse of $f(x)$ without knowing the factorization of the modulus. The number of bit operations of the new algorithm is only a factor $O(\log m)$ greater than in the previous case.

Our idea consists in trying to compute $\gcd(f(x), x^n - 1)$ in $\mathbf{Z}_m[x]$ using the gcd algorithm for $\mathbf{Z}_p[x]$ mentioned in Section 2. Such algorithm requires the inversion of some scalars, which is not a problem in $\mathbf{Z}_p[x]$, but it is not always possible if m is not prime. Therefore, the computation of $\gcd(f(x), x^n - 1)$ may fail. However, if the gcd algorithm terminates we have solved the problem. In fact, together with the alleged[1] gcd $a(x)$ the algorithm also returns $s(x), t(x)$

[1] The correctness of the gcd algorithm has been proven only for polynomials over fields, so we do not claim any property for the output of the algorithm when working in $\mathbf{Z}_m[x]$.

```
Inverse2(f(x), m) → g(x)
{Computes the inverse g(x) of the polynomial f(x) in Z_m[x]/(x^n − 1)}

if gcd(f(x), x^n − 1) = 1 then
    let s(x), t(x) such that f(x)s(x) + (x^n − 1)t(x) = 1 in Z_m[x];
    return s(x);
else if gcd(f(x), x^n − 1) = a(x), deg(a(x)) > 0 then
    return "f(x) is not invertible";
else if gcd(f(x), x^n − 1) fails let d be such that d|m;
    let (m_1, m_2) ← GetFactors(m, d);
    if m_2 ≠ 1, then
        g_1(x) ← Inverse2(f(x), m_1);
        g_2(x) ← Inverse2(f(x), m_2);
        compute g(x) using Chinese remaindering (Lemma 1);
    else
        g_1(x) ← Inverse2(f(x), m_1);
        compute g(x) using Newton-Hensel lifting (Lemma 2);
    endif
    return g(x);
endif

GetFactors(m, d) → (m_1, m_2)

let m_1 ← gcd(m, d^⌊log m⌋);
if (m/m_1) ≠ 1 then
    return (m_1, m/m_1);
endif
let e ← m/d;
let m_1 ← gcd(m, e^⌊log m⌋);
if (m/m_1) ≠ 1 then
    return (m_1, m/m_1);
endif
let m_1 ← lcm(d, e);
return (m_1, 1);
```

Algorithm 2. Inversion in $\mathbf{Z}_m[x]/(x^n - 1)$. Factorization of m unknown.

such that $f(x)s(x) + (x^n - 1)t(x) = a(x)$ in $\mathbf{Z}_m[x]$. If $a(x) = 1$, then $s(x)$ is the inverse of $f(x)$. If $\deg(a(x)) \neq 0$, one can easily prove that $f(x)$ is not invertible in $\mathbf{Z}_m[x]/(x^n - 1)$. Note that we must force the gcd algorithm to return a monic polynomial.

If the computation of $\gcd(f(x), x^n - 1)$ fails, we use recursion. In fact, the gcd algorithm fails if it cannot invert an element $y \in \mathbf{Z}_m$. Inversion is done using the *integer* gcd algorithm. If y is not invertible, the integer gcd algorithm returns $d = \gcd(m, y)$, with $d > 1$. Hence, d is a non trivial factor of m. We use d to compute either a pair m_1, m_2 such that $\gcd(m_1, m_2) = 1$ and $m_1 m_2 = m$, or a single factor m_1 such that $m_1 | m$ and $m | (m_1)^2$. In the first case we invert $f(x)$ in $\mathbf{Z}_{m_1}[x]/(x^n - 1)$ and $\mathbf{Z}_{m_2}[x](x^n - 1)$, and we use Chinese remaindering to get the desired result. In the second case, we invert $f(x)$ in $\mathbf{Z}_{m_1}[x]/(x^n - 1)$ and we use one step of Newton-Hensel lifting to get the inverse in $\mathbf{Z}_m[x]/(x^n - 1)$. The computation of the factors m_1, m_2 is done by procedure `GetFactors` whose correctness is proven by Lemmas 3 and 4. Combining these ideas together we get Algorithm 2.

Lemma 3. *Let α, $\alpha > 1$, be a divisor of m and let $\alpha' = \gcd(m, \alpha^{\lfloor \log m \rfloor})$. Then, α' is a divisor of m and $\gcd(\alpha', m/\alpha') = 1$.*

Proof. Let $m = p_1^{k_1} \cdots p_h^{k_h}$ denote the prime factorization of m. Clearly, $\alpha^{\lfloor \log m \rfloor}$ contains every prime p_i which is in α, with an exponent at least k_i (since $k_i \le \lfloor \log m \rfloor$). Hence, α' contains each prime p_i which is in α with exponent exactly k_i. In addition, m/α' contains each prime p_j which is not in α with exponent exactly k_j, hence $\gcd(\alpha', m/\alpha') = 1$ as claimed. □

Lemma 4. *Let α, β be such that $\alpha\beta = m$, $m | \alpha^{\lfloor \log m \rfloor}$, and $m | \beta^{\lfloor \log m \rfloor}$. Then $\gamma = \mathrm{lcm}(\alpha, \beta) = m/\gcd(\alpha, \beta)$ is such that $\gamma | m$ and $m | \gamma^2$.*

Proof. Let $m = p_1^{k_1} \cdots p_h^{k_h}$ denote the prime factorization of m. By Lemma 3 we know that both α and β contain every prime p_i, $i = 1, \ldots, h$. Since $\alpha\beta = m$, each prime p_i appears in γ with exponent at least $\lfloor k_i/2 \rfloor$. Hence m divides γ^2 as claimed. □

Theorem 3. *If $f(x)$ is invertible in $\mathbf{Z}_m[x]/(x^n - 1)$, Algorithm 2 returns the inverse $g(x)$ in $O(\Gamma(m, n) \log m)$ bit operations.* □

5 Inversion in $\mathbf{Z}_m[x]/(x^n - 1)$ when $n = 2^k$

In this section we describe an algorithm for computing the inverse of an $n \times n$ circulant matrix over $\mathbf{Z}_m$ when n is a power of 2. Our algorithm is inspired by the method of Graeffe [10] for the approximation of polynomial zeros. The algorithm works by reducing the original problem to inversion of a circulant matrix of size $n/2$. This is possible because of the following lemma.

Lemma 5. *Let $f(x) \in \mathbf{Z}_m[x]$ and $n = 2^k$. If $f(x)$ is invertible over $\mathbf{Z}_m[x]/(x^n - 1)$ then $f(-x)$ is invertible as well. In addition, the product $f(x)f(-x)$ contains no odd power terms.*

Proof. Let $g(x)$ denote the inverse of $f(x)$. We have $f(-x)g(-x) \equiv 1$ modulo $(-x)^n - 1$. Since n is even, $(-x)^n = x^n$ and the thesis follows. Let $f(x) = \sum_{i=0}^{n-1} a_i x^i$. The k-th coefficient of the product $f(x)f(-x)$ is $\sum_{i+j=k} a_i a_j (-1)^j$. If k is odd, i and j must have opposite parity. Hence, the term $a_i a_j (-1)^j$ cancels with $a_j a_i (-1)^i$ and the sum is zero. □

Inverse3($f(x), m, n) \to g(x)$

{Computes the inverse $g(x)$ of the polynomial $f(x)$ in $\mathbf{Z}_m[x]/(x^n - 1)$, $n = 2^k$}

if $n = 1$ **then**
  if $\gcd(f_0, m) = 1$ **return** $g_0 \leftarrow f_0^{-1}$;
  else return "$f(x)$ is not invertible";
else
  let $F(x^2) \leftarrow f(x)f(-x) \bmod x^n - 1$;
  let $G(y) \leftarrow$ Inverse3($F(y), m, n/2$);
  let $S_e(x^2), S_o(x^2)$ be such that $f(-x) = S_e(x^2) + xS_o(x^2)$;
  let $T_e(y) \leftarrow G(y)S_e(y)$;
  let $T_o(y) \leftarrow G(y)S_o(y)$;
  return $g(x) \leftarrow T_e(x^2) + xT_o(x^2)$;
endif

Algorithm 3. Inversion in $\mathbf{Z}_m[x]/(x^n - 1)$. Requires $n = 2^k$.

The above lemma suggests that we can halve the size of the original problem by splitting each polynomial in its even and odd powers. Let $F(x^2) = f(x)f(-x) \bmod x^n - 1$. By Lemma 5, if $f(x)$ is invertible the inverse $g(x)$ satisfies

$$F(x^2)g(x) \equiv f(-x) \pmod{x^n - 1} . \tag{5}$$

Now we split $g(x)$ and $f(-x)$ in their odd and even powers. We get

$$g(x) = T_e(x^2) + xT_o(x^2), \qquad f(-x) = S_e(x^2) + xS_o(x^2).$$

From (5) we get

$$F(x^2)(T_e(x^2) + xT_o(x^2)) \equiv S_e(x^2) + xS_o(x^2) \pmod{x^n - 1}.$$

If $f(x)$ is invertible over $\mathbf{Z}_m[x]/(x^n - 1)$, $F(x^2)$ is invertible as well, its inverse being $g(x)g(-x)$. We can therefore retrieve $T_e(x^2)$ and $T_o(x^2)$ by solving the two subproblems

$$F(x^2)T_e(x^2) \equiv S_e(x^2) \pmod{x^n - 1}, \qquad F(x^2)T_o(x^2) \equiv S_o(x^2) \pmod{x^n - 1}.$$

Hence, to find $g(x)$ it suffices to compute the inverse of $F(x^2)$ and to execute two multiplications between polynomials of degree $n/2$. By setting $y = x^2$ inverting $F(x^2)$ reduces to an inversion modulo $x^{(n/2)} - 1$. Applying this approach recursively we get Algorithm 3 for the inversion over $\mathbf{Z}_m[x]/(x^n - 1)$.

Theorem 4. *Algorithm 3 takes $O(\Pi(m,n) + \mu(\log m) \log\log m)$ bit operations.*

Proof. The thesis follows observing that the number of bit operations $T(m,n)$ satisfies the following recurrence

$$T(m,n) = \begin{cases} \mu(\log m) \log\log m, & \text{if } n = 1, \\ \Pi(m,n) + T(m, n/2) + 2\Pi(m, n/2), & \text{otherwise.} \end{cases}$$

□

```
Inverse4(f(x), m) → g(x)
{Computes the inverse g(x) of f(x) = Σ_{i=-r}^{r} a_i x^i}

test if f(x) is invertible using Theorem 1;
if f(x) is invertible then;
    let M = 2^⌈2r log m⌉;
    let h(x) ← Inverse3(x^r f(x), m, M);
    return g(x) ← x^(r-M) h(x);
endif
```

Algorithm 4. Inversion in $\mathbf{Z}_m\{x\}$.

Note that Algorithm 3 assumes nothing about m. When $m = 2$ the ring $\mathbf{Z}_2$ does not contain the element -1. However, we can still apply Algorithm 3 replacing $f(-x)$ with $f(x)$ ($[f(x)]^2$ does not contain odd power terms).

6 Inversion in $\mathbf{Z}_m\{x\}$

In this section we describe an algorithm for inverting a finite fps $f(x) \in \mathbf{Z}_m\{x\}$. Our algorithm is based on the following observation which shows that we can compute the inverse of $f(x)$ inverting a polynomial over $\mathbf{Z}_m[x]/(x^n - 1)$ for a sufficiently large n.

Let $f(x) = \sum_{i=-r}^{r} a_i x^i$ denote an invertible finite fps. By Corollary 3.3 in [7] we know that the radius of the inverse is at most $R = (2\log m - 1)r$. That is, the inverse $g(x)$ has the form $g(x) = \sum_{i=-R}^{R} b_i x^i$. Let M be such that $M > R + r = 2r\log m$. Since $f(x)g(x) = 1$ we have

$$[x^r f(x)][x^{M-r} g(x)] = x^M [f(x)g(x)] = x^M \quad .$$

Hence, to compute the inverse of $f(x)$ it suffices to compute the inverse of $x^r f(x)$ over $\mathbf{Z}_m[x]/(x^M - 1)$. By choosing M as the smallest power of two greater than $2r\log m$, this inversion can be done using Algorithm 3 in

$$O(\Pi(m, 2r\log m) + \mu(\log m)\log\log m) = O(\Pi(m, 2r\log m))$$

bit operations. Verifying the invertibility of $f(x)$ takes $O(r\mu(\log m)\log\log m)$ bit operations (using Theorem 1), hence the cost of Algorithm 4 for inversion in $\mathbf{Z}_m\{x\}$ is $O(\Pi(m, 2r\log m))$ bit operations.

7 Conclusions and Further Works

We have described three algorithms for the inversion of an $n \times n$ circulant matrix with entries over the ring $\mathbf{Z}_m$. The three algorithms differ from the knowledge of m and n they require. The first algorithm assumes nothing about n but requires the factorization of m. The second algorithm requires nothing, while the third algorithm assumes nothing about m but works only for $n = 2^k$.

We believe it is possible to find new algorithms suited for different degrees of knowledge on m and n. A very promising approach is the following generalization of Algorithm 3. Suppose k is a factor of n and that $\mathbf{Z}_m$ contains a primitive k-th root of unity ω. Since $f(x)f(\omega x)\cdots f(\omega^{k-1}x) \bmod x^n - 1$ contains only powers which are multiples of k, reasoning as in Algorithm 3 we can reduce the original problem to a problem of size n/k. Since the ring $\mathbf{Z}_m$ contains a primitive p-th root of unity for any prime divisor p of $\varphi(m)$, we can iterate this method to "remove" from n every factor which appears in $\gcd(n, \varphi(m))$. From that point the inversion procedure may continue using a different method (for example, Algorithm 1).

Given the efficiency of Algorithm 3 it may be worthwhile even to extend $\mathbf{Z}_m$ adding an appropriate root of unity in order to further reduce the degree of the polynomials involved in the computation. This has the same drawbacks we outlined for the FFT based method. However, one should note that Algorithm 3 needs roots of smaller order with respect to the FFT method. As an example, for $n = 2^k$ Algorithm 3 only needs a primitive square root of unity, whereas the FFT method needs a primitive n-th root of unity.

References

1. A. V. Aho, J. E. Hopcroft, and J. D. Ullman. *The Design and Analysis of Computer Algorithms*. Addison-Wesley, Reading, Massachussets, 1974.
2. D. Bini, G. M. Del Corso, G. Manzini, and L. Margara. Inversion of Circulant Matrices over Z_m. Technical Report B4-97-14, Istituto di Matematica Computazionale, CNR, Pisa, Italy, 1997.
3. D. Bini and V. Y. Pan. *Polynomial and Matrix Computations, Fundamental Algorithms*, volume 1. Birkhäuser, 1994.
4. P. Chaudhuri, D. Chowdhury, S. Nandi, and S. Chattopadhyay. *Additive Cellular Automata Theory and Applications, Vol. 1*. IEEE Press, 1997.
5. P. Feinsilver. Circulants, inversion of circulants, and some related matrix algebras. *Linear Algebra and Appl.*, 56:29–43, 1984.
6. M. Ito, N. Osato, and M. Nasu. Linear cellular automata over Z_m. *Journal of Computer and System Sciences*, 27:125–140, 1983.
7. G. Manzini and L. Margara. Invertible linear cellular automata over Z_m: Algorithmic and dynamical aspects. *Journal of Computer and System Sciences*. To appear. A preliminary version appeared in Proc. MFCS '97, LNCS n. 1295, Springer Verlag.
8. G. Manzini and L. Margara. A complete and efficiently computable topological classification of D-dimensional linear cellular automata over Z_m. In *24th International Colloquium on Automata Languages and Programming (ICALP '97)*. LNCS n. 1256, Springer Verlag, 1997.
9. O. Martin, A. Odlyzko, and S. Wolfran. Algebraic properties of cellular automata. *Comm. Math. Phys.*, 93:219–258, 1984.
10. A. M. Ostrowski. Recherches sur la méthode de graeffe et les zéros des polynomes et des series de laurent. *Acta Math.*, 72:99–257, 1940.
11. A. Schönhage and V. Strassen. Schnelle Multiplikation grosse Zahlen. *Computing*, 7:281–292, 1971.

Application of Lempel-Ziv Encodings to the Solution of Word Equations

Wojciech Plandowski *[1] and **Wojciech Rytter** **[2]

[1] Turku Centre for Computer Science and Department of Mathematics, Turku University, 20 014, Turku, Finland

[2] Instytut Informatyki, Uniwersytet Warszawski, Banacha 2, 02–097 Warszawa, Poland, and Department of Computer Science, University of Liverpool, UK.

Abstract. One of the most intricate algorithms related to words is Makanin's algorithm solving word equations. The algorithm is very complicated and the complexity of the problem of solving word equations is not well understood. Word equations can be used to define various properties of strings, e.g. general versions of pattern-matching with variables. This paper is devoted to introduce a new approach and to study relations between Lempel-Ziv compressions and word equations. Instead of dealing with very long solutions we propose to deal with their Lempel-Ziv encodings. As our first main result we prove that each minimal solution of a word equation is highly compressible (exponentially compressible for long solutions) in terms of Lempel-Ziv encoding. A simple algorithm for solving word equations is derived. If the length of minimal solution is bounded by a singly exponential function (which is believed to be always true) then LZ encoding of each minimal solution is of a polynomial size (though the solution can be exponentially long) and solvability can be checked in nondeterministic polynomial time. As our second main result we prove that the solvability can be tested in polynomial deterministic time if the lengths of all variables are given in binary. We show also that lexicographically first solution for given lengths of variables is highly compressible in terms of Lempel-Ziv encodings.

1 Introduction

Word equations are used to describe properties and relations of words, e.g. pattern-matching with variables, imprimitiveness, periodicity, conjugation, see [5]. The main algorithm in this area is Makanin's algorithm for solving word equations, see [8]. The time complexity of the algorithm is too high, its most efficient version works in $2^{2^{p(n)}}$ nondeterministic time where $p(n)$ is the maximal index of periodicity of word equations of length n ($p(n)$ is a singly exponential function), see [6]. The descriptional complexity is also too high. As a side effect of our results we present a much simpler algorithm.

---

* On leave from Instytut Informatyki, Uniwersytet Warszawski, Banacha 2, 02–097 Warszawa, Poland. Email:`wojtekpl@mimuw.edu.pl`. Partially supported by Academy of Finland under grant 14047.

** Partially done while visiting University of Turku, Finland.

It is known that the solvability problem for word equations is NP-hard, even if we consider (short) solutions with the length bounded by a linear function and the right side of equations contains no variables, see [1].

The main open problem is to close the gap between NP and $2^{2^{p(d)}}$, and to show the following

Conjecture A: the problem of solving word equations is in NP.

Assume n is the size of the equation and N is the minimal length of the solution (if one exists). It is generally believed that another conjecture is true (at least no counterexample is known):

Conjecture B: N is at most singly exponential w.r.t. n.

Current estimation for the function N is $2^{2^{2^{p(n)}}}$. We strongly believe that the proper bound is singly exponential. If it is true then our construction would prove that the problem of solvability of word equations is NP-complete.
In this paper we introduce a new approach to deal with word equations: Lempel-Ziv (LZ) encodings of solutions of word equations. Recently many results for several variations of pattern-matching and other combinatorial problems for compressed texts were obtained, see [4, 9, 3]. Many words can be exponentially compressed using LZ-encoding. A motivation to consider compressed solutions follows from the following fact.

Lemma 1.
If we have LZ-encoded values of the variables then we can verify the word equation in polynomial time with respect to the size of the equation and the total size of given LZ-encodings.

Proof. We can convert each LZ-encoding to a context-free grammar generating a single word, due to the following claim.

Claim Let $n = |LZ(w)|$. Then we can construct a context-free grammar G of size $O(n^2 \log n)$ which generates w and which is in the Chomsky normal form.

Now we can compute the grammars corresponding to the left and right sides of the equations by concatenating some smaller grammars. The equality of grammars can be checked in polynomial time by the algorithm of [10].

Our first result is:

Theorem 2 (Main-Result 1).
Assume N is the size of minimal solution of a word equation of size n. Then each solution of size N can be LZ-compressed to a string of size $O(n^2 \log^2(N)(\log n + \log\log N))$.

As a direct consequence we have:

Corrolary 1. Conjecture B implies conjecture A.

Proof. If N is exponential then the compressed version of the solution is of a polynomial size. The algorithm below solves the problem in nondeterministic polynomial time. The first step works in nondeterministic polynomial time, the second one works in deterministic polynomial time due to Lemma 1.

ALGORITHM *Solving_by_LZ-Encoding* ; guess LZ-encoded solution of size $O(n^2 \log^2 N(\log n + \log\log N))$; verify its correctness using the polynomial time deterministic algorithm from Lemma 1.

Observation. Take $N = 2^{2^{2^{p(n)}}}$. Then the algorithm *Solving_by_LZ-Encoding* is probably the simplest algorithm solving word equations with similar time complexity as the best known (quite complicated) algorithms.

It was known before that there is a polynomial time deterministic algorithm if the lengths of all variables are given in unary. We strengthen this results allowing binary representations (changing polynomial bounds to exponential). Our second main result is:

Theorem 3 (Main-Result 2).
Assume the length of all variables are given in binary by a function f. Then we can test solvability in deterministic polynomial time, and produce polynomial-size compression of the lexicographically first solution (if there is any).

Let Σ be an alphabet of constants and Θ be an alphabet of variables. We assume that these alphabets are disjoint. A word equation E is a pair of words $(u, v) \in (\Sigma \cup \Theta)^* \times (\Sigma \cup \Theta)^*$ usually denoted by $u = v$. The *size* of an equation is the sum of lengths of u and v. A *solution* of a word equation $u = v$ is a morphism $h : (\Sigma \cup \Theta)^* \to \Sigma^*$ such that $h(a) = a$, for $a \in \Sigma$, and $h(u) = h(v)$. For example assume we have the equation

$$abx_1x_2x_2x_3x_3x_4x_4x_5 = x_1x_2x_3x_4x_5x_6,$$

and the length of x_i's are consecutive Fibonacci numbers. Then the solution is $h(x_i) = FibWord_i$, where $FibWord_i$ is the i-th Fibbonaci word.

We consider the same version of the LZ algorithm as in [3] (this is called LZ1 in [3]). Intuitively, LZ algorithm compresses the text because it is able to discover some repeated subwords. We consider here the version of LZ algorithm without *self-referencing*. The factorization of w is given by a decomposition: $w = c_1 f_1 c_2 \dots f_k c_{k+1}$, where $c_1 = w[1]$ and for each $1 \le i \le k+1$ $c_i \in \Sigma$ and f_i is the longest prefix of $f_i c_{i+1} \dots f_k c_{k+1}$ which appears in $c_1 f_1 c_2 \dots f_{i-1} c_i$. We can identify each f_i with an interval $[p, q]$, such that $f_i = w[p..q]$ and $q \le |c_1 f_1 c_2 \dots f_{i-1} c_{i-1}|$. If we drop the assumption related to the last inequality then it occurs a *self-referencing* (f_i is the longest prefix which appears before but not necessarily terminates at a current position). We assume (for simplicity) that this is not the case. We use simple relations between LZ-encodings and context-free grammars.

Example 1. The LZ-factorization of a word *aababbabbaababbabba#* is given by the sequence:

$$c_1\ f_1\ c_2\ f_2\ c_3\ f_3\ c_4\ f_4\ c_5 = a\ a\ b\ ab\ b\ abb\ a\ ababbabba\ \#.$$

After identifying each subword f_i with its corresponding interval we obtain the LZ encoding of the string. Hence

$$LZ(aababbabbababbabb\#) = a[1,1]b[2,3]b[4,6]a[2,10]\#.$$

As another example we have that the LZ-encoding of $FibWord_n$ is of size $O(n)$.

2 Relations on positions and intervals in the solutions

Let $\mathcal{V}$ be the set of variables. Assume the function $f : \mathcal{V} \to N$ gives the lengths of variables. The function f can be naturally extended to all words over $\mathcal{C} \cup \mathcal{V}$ giving lengths of them under the assumption that the lengths of words which are substituted for variables are defined by f. Let $e : u = v$ be the word equation to consider. Each solution of e in which the lengths of words which are substituted by variables are defined by f is called an f-solution of e. We consider a fixed equation $u = v$ with the lengths of the components of its solution h given by a function f.

We introduce the relation $\mathcal{R}'$ (defined formally below) on positions of the solution, two positions are in this relation iff they correspond to the same symbol in every f-solution ($\mathcal{R}'$ is implied by the structure of equation).

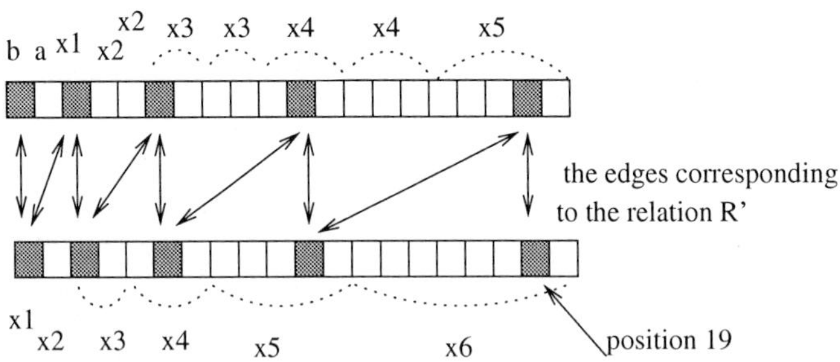

Fig. 1. Assume we have equation $abx_1x_2x_2x_3x_3x_4x_4x_5 = x_1x_2x_3x_4x_5x_6$ and the lengths of x_i's are consecutive Fibonacci numbers. Two positions are equivalent (contain always a same symbol) iff they are in the relation $\mathcal{R}$, which is a transitive closure of $\mathcal{R}'$. For example the 19th and the first positions are connected via pairs of positions which are in the relation $\mathcal{R}'$. Hence these positions are equivalent, so the 19th position is in the class corresponding to the constant b.

We use the identity $h(u) = h(v)$ in Σ^*, that is identify the corresponding letters on both sides of this identity, to define an equivalence relation $\mathcal{R}$ on positions of $h(u)$. The positions in the equivalence classes are to be filled by the same constant. The constant is uniquely determined if one of the positions in the class corresponds to a constant in an original equation. Otherwise the constant can be chosen arbitrarily. Moreover, the positions in such a class can be filled by any word.

Now, assume that we are given an equation $v_1 \dots v_k = u_1 \dots u_s$ over t variables and a function f such that $f(v) = f(u)$. Denote by $v(j)$ $(u(j))$ the variable or a constant from the left (right) hand of the equation and such that it contains a position j or in case of a constant occurs at position j under the assumption that the lengths of variables are given by the function f. Formally, $v(j) = v_{p+1}$ if $f(v_1 \dots v_p) < j \leq f(v_1 \dots v_{p+1})$. Denote also $l(j) = j - f(v_1 \dots v_p)$ $(r(j) = j - f(u_1 \dots u_p))$ the position in the variable $v(j)$ $(u(j))$ which correspond to j. We define a function $left$: $\{1, \dots, f(u)\} \to N \times (\Theta \cup \Sigma)$ in the following way:

$$left(j) = \begin{cases} (l(j), v(j)) & \text{if } v(j) \text{ is a variable} \\ (j, v(j)) & \text{otherwise.} \end{cases}$$

Similarly, we define the function $right$:

$$right(j) = \begin{cases} (r(j), u(j)) & \text{if } u(j) \text{ is a variable} \\ (j, u(j)) & \text{otherwise.} \end{cases}$$

The relation $\mathcal{R}'$ is defined as follows:

$$i\mathcal{R}'j \text{ iff } left(i) = right(j) \text{ or } left(i) = left(j) \text{ or } right(i) = right(j).$$

Finally, an equivalence relation $\mathcal{R}$ on positions $\{1 \dots f(u)\}$ is the transitive and symmetric closure of the relation $\mathcal{R}'$. We say that a position i *belongs* to a variable X if either $left(i) = (j, X)$ or $right(i) = (j, X)$, for some j. Let $\mathcal{C}$ be an equivalence class of the relation $\mathcal{R}$. We say that $\mathcal{C}$ *corresponds* to a constant a if there is a position i in $\mathcal{C}$ such that either $left(i) = (i, a)$ or $right(i) = (i, a)$. Now the following lemma is obvious.

Lemma 4. *Let $\mathcal{C}$ be an equivalence class of the relation $\mathcal{R}$ connected to an equation $e : u = v$ under the assumption that the lengths of variables are given by the function f. Then the following conditions are satisfied:*
1. If there is a class $\mathcal{C}$ corresponding to no constant then the solution is not of minimal length. The symbols at positions in $\mathcal{C}$ can be filled with a same arbitrary word, in particular by the empty word.
2. For any two positions i, $j \in \mathcal{C}$ and an f-solution h of e, $h(u)[i] = h(u)[j]$.
3. If $\mathcal{C}$ corresponds to a constant a and $i \in \mathcal{C}$, then for each f-solution h of e, $h(u)[i] = a$.
4. There is an f-solution of e iff no equivalence class contains positions of different constants of e.
5. A lexicographically first f-solution of e, if exists, can be obtained by filling all positions in all equivalence classes of $\mathcal{R}$ which do not contain a constant by lexicographically first letter of the alphabet.

The relation $\mathcal{R}$ is defined on positions of an f-solution of e. In our considerations we need an extension of this relation to length n segments of an f-solution of e.

$$left_n(j) = \begin{cases} (l(j), v(j)) & v(j) = v(j + n - 1) \\ (j, v(j)) & otherwise \end{cases}$$

$$right_n(t) = \begin{cases} (r(j), u(j)) & u(j) = u(j+n-1) \\ (j, u(j)) & otherwise \end{cases}$$

The functions $left_n$ and $right_n$ are used to define length n segments of solutions which have to be equal in each f-solution of e. They are defined by the relation $\mathcal{R}_n$ which is defined as a symmetric and transitive closure of the following relation $\mathcal{R}'_n$.

$i\mathcal{R}'_n j$ iff $left_n(i) = right_n(j)$ or $left_n(i) = left_n(j)$ or $right_n(i) = right_n(j)$.

Lemma 5. *Let h be an f-solution of a word equation $e : u = v$ and let $\mathcal{E}$ be an equivalence class of $\mathcal{R}_n$. If $i, j \in \mathcal{E}$ then $h(u)[i..i+n-1] = h(u)[j..j+n-1]$.*

3 Minimal solutions are highly LZ-compressible

Assume $h(u) = h(v) = \mathcal{T}$ is a solution of a given word equation E. A **cut** in $\mathcal{T}$ is a border of a variable or a constant in $\mathcal{T}$. There is a linear number of such cuts and they will be denoted by small Greek letters.

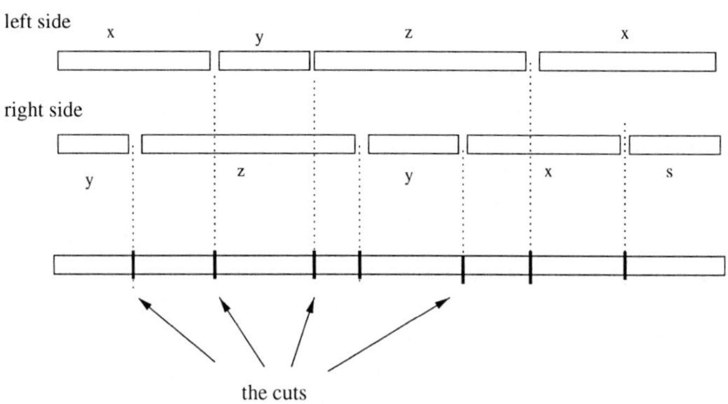

Fig. 2. The cuts for the equation $xyzx = yzyxs$ with fixed length of variables, corresponding to the figure.

We say that a subword w of $\mathcal{T}$ **overlaps** a cut γ iff an occurrence of w extends to the left and right of γ or γ is a border of an occurrence.

Lemma 6 (key lemma).
Assume $\mathcal{T}$ is the minimal length solution of the equation E. Then each subword of $\mathcal{T}$ has an occurrence which overlaps at least one cut in $\mathcal{T}$.

Proof. Assume that both sides of the equations are equal $\mathcal{T}$, where $\mathcal{T}$ is the minimal length solution of the equation E. Assume also that a subword $w = \mathcal{T}[i, j]$ of size t of $\mathcal{T}$ has no occurrence which overlaps at least one cut in $\mathcal{T}$. This implies that it never happens $i\ \mathcal{R}_t\ p$, for an interval $[p, q]$ overlapping a cut. It is easy to see that in this situation no position inside $[i, j]$ is in the relation $\mathcal{R}$ with any constant (since each constant is a neighbor of a cut, by definition). Hence in the equivalence class $\mathcal{C}$ corresponding to some position in $[i, j]$ there is no constant. Due to Lemma 4 we can delete all symbols on positions belonging to $\mathcal{C}$. In this way a new shorter solution is produced, which contradicts minimality of the initial solution $\mathcal{T}$. This completes the proof.

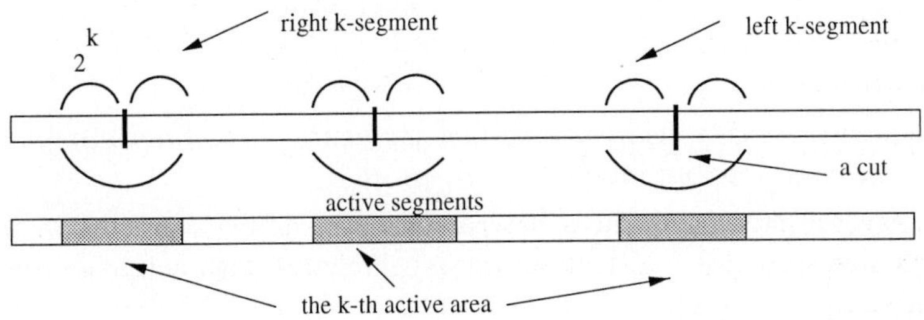

Fig. 3. Active segments and the k-th active area.

For $k = 0, 1, \ldots \log |\mathcal{T}|$ and each cut γ in $\mathcal{T}$ denote by $l_k(\gamma)$ and $r_k(\gamma)$ the subwords of length 2^k whose right (left) border is the cut γ. Denote also $segment_k(\gamma)$ to be the concatenation of $l_k(\gamma)$ and $r_k(\gamma)$. We say that $l_k(\gamma)$ and $r_k(\gamma)$ are respectively, left and right **characteristic words** of rank k and words $segment_k(\gamma)$ are **active segments**. The union of all active segments of rank k is denoted by **Active-Area**(k).

Theorem 7 (Main-Result 1).
Assume N is the size of minimal solution of a word equation of size n. Then each solution of size N can be LZ-compressed to a string of size $O(n^2 \log^2(N)(\log n + \log\log N))$.

Proof. For a given cut γ consider consecutive words $u_0(\gamma), u_1(\gamma), u_2(\gamma), \ldots$ whose lengths are 1, 1, 2, 4, ..., and which are on the left of γ. Similarly we define words $v_0(\gamma), v_1(\gamma), \ldots$ to the right of γ, see Figure 4. The sequences of these words continue maximally to the left (right) without hitting another cut. Then for $k \geq 0$

$$segment_{k+1}(\gamma) = u_{k+1}\ segment_k(\gamma)\ v_{k+1}$$

Claim 1. $\mathcal{T}$ is covered by a concatenation of a linear number of active segments.

It is easy to see that due to Lemma 6 we have.

Claim 2. Each of the words u_{k+1} and v_{k+1} is contained in $segment_k(\beta)$, $segment_k(\alpha)$ for some cuts α, β.

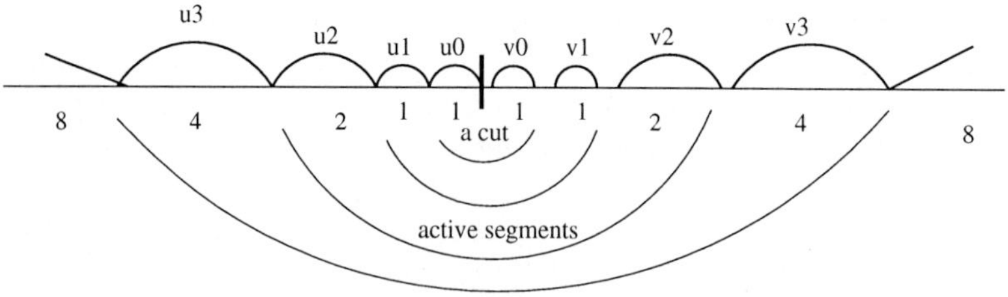

Fig. 4. The structure of active segments for the same cut.

We can write now:

$$segment_{k+1}(\gamma) = segment_k(\beta)[i..j]\ segment_k(\gamma)\ segment_k(\alpha)[p..q]$$

for some cuts α, β and intervals $[i..j]$, $[p..q]$.

In this way we have recurrences describing larger active segments in terms of smaller active segments (as their subwords). We start with active segments of a constant size.

Claim 3. Assume we have a set of m recurrences describing consecutive words in terms of previously defined words, as concatenations of finite number of subwords of these earlier words. Assume we start with words of constant size. Then the last described word has an LZ-encoding of size $O(m^2 \log m)$. This small LZ-encoding can be computed in deterministic polynomial time w.r.t. m if the recurrences are given.

Sketch of the proof of the Claim. Assume the words computed by recurrences are $z_1, z_2, \ldots, z_m$. Then we can create one long word $z = z_1 \cdot z_2 \cdot \ldots z_m$ which has the LZ-encoding of size $O(m)$ given by recurrences. We can transform this encoding to a context-free grammar of size $O(m^2 \log m))$ generating z as a single word, we refer to the claim in the proof of Theorem 11 in [4]. Next we construct a grammar of size $O(m^2 \log m)$ for z_m as a segment of z. Next we can transform this grammar to a LZ-encoding of similar size.

In our case we have $m = O(n \log N)$ as a bound for the number of possible $\log N$ segments for n cuts together with n subwords of segments, needed in Claim 1. Hence the resulting encoding is $O(m^2 \log m)$ which is $O(n^2 \log^2(N)(\log n + \log\log N))$.

4 Polynomial time algorithm for a given vector of lengths

We use again the idea of geometrically decreasing neighborhoods (active areas) of the cuts, which are the most essential in the solution. Let us fix the length of the variables and $h(u) = h(v) = \mathcal{T}$. We want to represent the relation between positions of $\mathcal{T}$ (implied by the equation) restricted to the k-th active areas, starting from large k and eventually finishing with $k = 0$, which gives the relation of a polynomial size which can be used directly to check solvability. So we compute consecutive structures like *shortcuts* in a graph corresponding to the relation on positions (identifying symbols on certain pairs of positions). The crucial point is to represent succinctly exponential sets of occurrences, this is possible due to the following fact.

Lemma 8.
The set of occurrences of a word w inside a word v which is exactly twice longer than w forms a single arithmetic progression.

Denote by $\mathcal{S}_k$ the relation $\mathcal{R}_{2^k}$ restricted to positions and intervals which are within the active area of rank k.
Our main data structure at the k-th iteration is the k-th *overlap structure* $\mathcal{OS}_k$, which is a collection:

$$\{Overlaps_k(w,\beta) \ : \beta \in CUTS(\mathcal{T})\}$$

where w is a characteristic word of rank k.
The sets in $\mathcal{OS}_k$ consist of overlaps of characteristic words against the cuts in $\mathcal{T}$. We consider only overlaps which fit inside $segments_k(\gamma)$, and which form arithmetic progressions and are implied by the structure of the equation, the relation $\mathcal{R}_{2^k}$. The overlap structure *Overlaps* has three features

- for each cut β and a characteristic word w of rank k the set $\{Overlaps_k(w,\beta) \ : \beta \in CUTS(\mathcal{T})\}$ forms single arithmetic progression,
- in each f-solution of the equation the words of length 2^k which start at positions in $Overlaps_k(w,\beta)$ are equal to w,
- the sum $Overlaps_k(w,\beta)$ which is taken over all cut points β is a union of some equivalence classes in $\mathcal{S}_k$.

The second and the third conditions gives us the following property of the set $\mathcal{OS}_0$ which deals with one-letter subwords of each f-solution.

Lemma 9. *The equation has an f-solution iff for each characteristic word w of rank 0 there is no set in $\bigcup_{\beta \in CUTS(\mathcal{T})} Overlaps_0(w,\beta)$ in $\mathcal{OS}_0$ which contains two different constants of the equation.*
If $\mathcal{OS}_0$ is given then solvability can be tested in polynomial time.

A *package* is a set of starting positions of some occurrences of some word w inside words which are twice longer than w. It is always an arithmetic progression and is stored as a pair (b,e) where b is the first number in the progression, e the last one. Since the distance between consecutive numbers in the progression will be the same for all packages it will be stored in one global variable *per*, which is a period of w. Each set $Overlaps_k(w,\beta)$ is represented as a package.
The algorithm works on graphs $G_k(w)$ where w is a characteristic word of rank k which is by definition of length 2^k. The vertices of the graph are the characteristic words of rank $k+1$ represented by two numbers: starting and ending positions of these words in an f-solution. There is an edge $u \to v$ labeled β in $G_k(w)$ if the set $Overlaps_{k+1}(u,\beta)$ is not empty and v is one of the words $l_{k+1}(\beta)$ or $r_{k+1}(\beta)$.

Each vertex v keeps a package $package(v)$ of occurrences of w in v. Initially, $package(v)$ is empty for all vertices except the vertex $v(w)$ which is $l_{k+1}(\beta)$ if

$w = l_k(\beta)$) or $r_{k+1}(\beta)$ if $w = r_k(\beta)$. The set $package(v(w))$ consists of one position which is the occurrence of w as the word $l_k(\beta)$ or $r_k(\beta)$ in $v(w)$. At the end the sets $package(v)$ contain all occurrences of w in v which can be deduced from the initial distribution of $package(v)$ and how the packages can move using the set $\mathcal{OS}_{k+1}$ of overlaps of characteristic words of rank $k+1$.

```
Algorithm Solvability_For_Given_Lengths
for k:=log T downto 0 do
        {invariant OS_{k+1} is known}
        for each characteristic word w of rank k do
            Close_Graph(G_k(w),v(w))
        compute OS_k on the basis of the closed graphs G_k(w)
        {invariant OS_k is computed}
test solvability using OS_0 and Lemma 8
```

Due to the fact that we operate on packages the set $package(v)$ may contain additional occurrences of w which cannot be deduced in a direct way from $\mathcal{OS}_k$, i.e. by simply moving the information on occurrences along the edges of G_k. Since the resulting set is to be a single progression we use operation *Join* for merging several packages of occurrences of w inside the same word into the smallest package containing all input packages. The legality of this operation is justified by the following fact.

Lemma 10. *Let p_1, p_2 be two packages of occurrences of a word w inside a twice longer word v. Then $Join(p_1, p_2)$ is also a package of occurrences of w in v.*

Example 2. The operation *Join* of joining packages can result in changing the distance between consecutive numbers in the input progressions *per* if the numbers in progressions do not synchronize as in the following case

$$Join(\{1,3\},\{6,8\}) = \{1,2,3,4,5,6,7,8\}.$$

To formalize the above we define the closure of a graph $G_k(w)$ as the smallest set of packages containing initial distribution of the packages and such that each edge $v \to u$ of the graph is *closed*, i.e. transferring a package $package(v)$ from a vertex v to u produces a package which is a subset of $package(u)$ (no new packets are produced). Transferring a package along the edge $v \to w$ labeled β consists in putting $package(v)$ in all occurrences of v in $Overlaps_{k+1}(v,\beta)$, joining them into one package, extracting those which drops into u and joining them with $packages(u)$.

Lemma 11. *Given closed graph $G_k(w)$, for each characteristic word w of rank k, the set $\mathcal{OS}_k$ can be computed in polynomial time.*

The algorithm for constructing an f-solution is more complicated. In this algorithm we have to compute a grammar which represents all characteristic words. A production for $l_{k+1}(\beta)$, which is now treated as a nonterminal in the created grammar, is of the form $l_{k+1}(\beta) \to l'_k(\beta) l_k(\beta)$ and the production for $r_{k+1}(\beta)$ is

$r_{k+1}(\beta) \to r_k(\beta)r'_k(\beta)$ where r' and l' are the halves of r_{k+1} and l_{k+1}. The productions for the words r' and l' are built on the basis of some of the occurrences of these words over some cut γ of the equation. We compute it using the same technique as for finding the occurrences of words l_k and r_k on the cuts. If such an occurrence does not exist the word l'_k and r'_k can be replaced with the word a^{2^k} which can be represented by a grammar of size $O(k)$. Otherwise the production for a word $r'_k(\beta)$ is of the form $r'_k(\beta) \to Suffix(t, l_k(\gamma))Pref(s, r_k(\gamma))$ where $Suffix(t, u)$ ($Pref(t, u)$) is a suffix (prefix) of length t of u. The application of the operations of $Suffix$ and $Pref$ generalizes context-free productions, and the whole construction is equivalent via a polynomial time/size transformation to a standard context-free grammar.

Theorem 12 (Main-Result 2).
Assume the length of all variables are given in binary by a function f. Then we can test solvability in polynomial time, and produce polynomial-size compression of the lexicographically first solution (if there is any).

5 Computing *Close_Graph*$(G_k(w), v(w))$

Assume w and k are fixed. The operation *Close_Graph*$(G_k(w),v(w))$ consists essentially in computing occurrences of w inside characteristic words of rank $k+1$. These occurrences are treated as packets. Initially we have one occurrence (initial packet) which is an occurrence of w in $v(w)$, then due to the overlaps of words of rank $k+1$ implied by the overlap structure OS_{k+1} the packets move and replicate. Eventually we have packages (changing sets of known occurrences) which are arithmetical progressions with difference *per* which is the currently known period (not necessarily smallest) of w.

A *meta-cycle* is a graph $(B, t \to s)$ which is composed of an edge $t \to s$ and an acyclic graph B such that each node of B belongs to some path from s (source) to t (target). A meta-cycle can be closed in polynomial time, see the full version of the paper [11].

Theorem 13. *The algorithm* Close_Graph *works in polynomial time.*

Sketch of the proof. Let n be the number of vertices of G. An acyclic version of the graph G is a graph *Acyclic*(G) which represents all paths of length n of G. The graph consists of n layers of vertices, each layer represents copies of the vertices of G. All edges join consecutive layers of *Acyclic*(G). If there is an edge $v \to w$ in G labeled β then there is an edge labeled β between the copies of v and w in all consecutive layers of *Acyclic*(G). There are also special edges which are not labeled and they go between copies of the same vertex in consecutive layers. The operation transfer of packages along these edges just copies the packages. It is not difficult to prove that transferring the packages in *Acyclic*(G) simulates transferring the packages n times in G using simultaneously all edges. In particular each package *package*(v) travels on all paths starting from v of length n. The restriction of *Acyclic*(G) to all vertices reachable from a copy of v from the first layer of *Acyclic*(G) is called *Path*(v). Similarly a graph *Simple_Paths*(u,v) is created from *Acyclic*(G) by removing all vertices which do not belong to a path from a copy of v in the first layer and some copy of u and by joining all copies of u into one vertex. The graph *Simple_Paths*(u,v) is acyclic and has one source u and target node v. Transferring a package from u to v in *Simple_Paths*(u,v) corresponds to transferring a package between u and v along all paths of length at most n in G in particular transferring packages along all simple paths (which do not contain a cycle) of G.

Algorithm *Close_Graph(G,source)*
G':=the vertex *source*;
T:=nonclosed edges going in G from *source*;
while $T \neq \emptyset$ **do**
  {*invariant* graph G' is closed}
  take an edge $u \to v$ from T and put it into G';
  construct the graph SP=*Simple_Paths*(v,u);
  if SP is not empty **then** Close_Meta-cycle(SP,$u \to v$);
  construct the graph *Paths*(v);
  transfer *package*(u) inside acyclic graph *Paths*(v);
  find edges in G which are nonclosed and put them into T

References

1. Angluin D., Finding patterns common to a set of strings, *J.C.S.S.*, **21(1)**, 46-62, 1980.
2. Choffrut, C., and Karhumäki, J., Combinatorics of words, *in* G.Rozenberg and A.Salomaa (eds), *Handbook of Formal Languages*, Springer, 1997.
3. Farah, M., Thorup M., String matching in Lempel-Ziv compressed strings, *STOC'95*, 703-712, 1995.
4. L. Gąsieniec, M. Karpiński, W. Plandowski and W. Rytter, *Randomized Efficient Algorithms for Compressed Strings: the finger-print approach.* in proceedings of the CPM'96, LNCS 1075, 39-49, 1996.
5. Karhumäki J., Mignosi F., Plandowski W., The expressibility of languages and relations by word equations, *in ICALP'97*, LNCS 1256, 98-109, 1997.
6. Koscielski, A., and Pacholski, L., Complexity of Makanin's algorithm, *J. ACM* **43**(4), 670-684, 1996.
7. A. Lempel, J. Ziv, On the complexity of finite sequences, *IEEE Trans. on Inf. Theory*, 22, 75-81, 1976.
8. Makanin, G.S., The problem of solvability of equations in a free semigroup, *Mat. Sb.*, Vol. 103,(145), 147-233, 1977. English transl. in *Math. U.S.S.R.* Sb. Vol 32, 1977.
9. Miyazaki M., Shinohara A., Takeda M., An improved pattern matching algorithm for strings in terms of straight-line programs, *in CPM'97*, LNCS 1264, 1-11, 1997.
10. W. Plandowski, Testing equlity of morphisms on context-free languages, in ESA'94
11. Plandowski W., Rytter W., Application of Lempel-Ziv encodings to the solution of word equations, TUCS report, Turku Centre for Computer Science, 1998.

Explicit Substitutitions for Constructive Necessity

Neil Ghani, Valeria de Paiva, and Eike Ritter*

School of Computer Science, University of Birmingham

This paper introduces a λ-calculus with explicit substitutions, corresponding to an S4 modal logic of constructive necessity. As well as being semantically well motivated, the calculus can be used (a) to develop abstract machines, and (b) as a framework for specifying and analysing *computation stages* in the context of functional languages. We prove several syntactic properties of this calculus, which we call xDIML, and then sketch its use as an interpretation of binding analysis and partial evaluation which respects execution of programs in stages.

1 Introduction

This paper introduces a λ-calculus with explicit substitutions, corresponding to an S4 modal logic of constructive necessity. As well as being semantically well motivated, the calculus can be used (a) to develop abstract machines, and (b) as a framework for specifying and analysing *computation stages* in the context of functional languages.

We first provide a full Curry-Howard isomorphism for the S4 constructive modal logic. This entails giving a calculus for annotating natural deduction proofs in the logic with typed λ-calculus terms. The annotations must be such that types correspond to propositions, terms correspond to proofs, and proof normalisation corresponds to term reduction. (The calculus we provide can be given a categorical model, but this is not described in this paper). We then add explicit substitutions to the calculus. Explicit substitutions are a theoretical way of making λ-calculi closer to their implementation through making substitution part of the calculus itself, rather than a meta-theoretical operation.

The first step, of providing the basic Curry-Howard isomorphism, uses the type theory developed by Barber and Plotkin [13] for Intuitionistic Linear Logic, adapting it to the modal logic by replacing the !-modality by the $\Box$-modality. We inherit the semantic foundations of Barber and Plotkin's calculus, and add to this a reduction calculus, for which we prove several syntactic properties required for developing an abstract machine.

The second step follows the approach of [6] in adding explicit substitutions to the calculus to provide the basis for an abstract machine. The addition is based on categorical techniques. Following [17] the categorical approach straightforwardly allows us to carry across, from the earlier calculus without explicit substitutions, proofs of desirable syntactic properties. Standard technology can then

* Research supported under the EPSRC project no. GR/L28296, **x-SLAM: The Explicit Substitutions Linear Abstract Machine**.

be applied to design an abstract machine from our modal calculus with explicit substitutions.

The main application of our modal calculus is as a framework for specifying and analysing *computation stages* in the context of functional languages. We use our constructive type theory to translate a variant of Nielson and Nielson's two-level functional language whose two levels correspond to compile-time and run-time (types and) programs. This gives rise to a compile-time and a run-time operational semantics. To show that this separation of types and terms into run-time and compile-time ones really works, we must show that any (closed) compile-time term c of ground type will reduce to a unique run-time term r in the compile-time operational semantics. Moreover, each closed run-time term r of ground type will reduce to a value, in the run-time operational semantics. A theorem asserting these two facts can be easily obtained from the metatheoretical results about our calculus, described in the paper.

Davies and Pfenning also discuss a modal logic and its application to binding analysis. Their operational semantics is motivated by the Kripke semantics of modal logics, whereas we use the standard operational semantics from the λ-calculus. Goubault-Larrecq [9] also presents a modal calculus with explicit substitutions, but it does not distinguish modal and intuitionistic contexts and is unsuitable for binding analysis using Nielson and Nielson's two-level functional language. Davies [3] uses a K-style modal logic to give a translation of a two-level λ-calculus into modal logic. In our approach the additional axioms of S4 are essential: the axiom $\Box A \to A$ is used for the evaluation of code at run-time.

This paper is organised as follows. First we describe a type theory for constructive modal logic S4, using a variant of Barber's Dual and Intuitionistic Linear Logic (DILL). We call this type theory Dual Intuitionistic and Modal Logic or DIML; we provide a reduction version of the calculus and sketch the proofs of the traditional syntactic requirements such as subject reduction, confluence and strong normalisation for DIML. In the next section we add explicit substitutions to DIML, obtaining xDIML. Again we discuss its reduction version and we prove that xDIML satisfies subject reduction. Then we prove the correctness of xDIML, by 'translating away' the explicit substitutions. Finally we discuss the application of our type-theory xDIML, by presenting its operational semantics and showing the preservation of execution in stages.

2 Dual Intuitionistic Modal Logic

This paper presents a proof system for constructive necessity called Dual Intuitionistic Modal Logic (DIML) which is based upon Barber's Dual Intuitionistic Linear Logic (DILL) [12] [13]. The typing judgements of DIML are of the form $\Gamma|\Delta \vdash t : A$ where Γ declares *modal variables* which may occur arbitrarily in a term, while Δ declares *intuitionistic* variables, which may not occur in any subterm of the form $\Box u$. DIML also contains *parallel* `let`-expressions of the form $\texttt{let}\ t_1, \ldots, t_n\ \texttt{be}\ \Box x_1, \ldots, \Box x_n\ \texttt{in}\ u$ which, in addition to being notationally more compact, are closer to the inherently parallel explicit substitutions of xDIML and hence simplify the correctness proof of xDIML.

2.1 The Typing Judgements of DIML

The types of DIML are ground types, function types $A \to B$ and box-types $\Box A$. Variables are tagged x_M or x_I to indicate whether they are *modal* or *intuitionistic* and the raw expressions of DIML are

$$t ::= x_M \mid x_I \mid \lambda x{:}\, A.t \mid tt \mid \Box t \mid \texttt{let}\ t_1, \ldots, t_n\ \texttt{be}\ \Box x_1, \ldots, \Box x_n\ \texttt{in}\ t$$

where the x's are variables. The tags on variables are sometimes omitted to increase legibility. We use standard abbreviations for parallel let-expressions, eg $\texttt{let}\ \bar{t}\ \texttt{be}\ \Box\bar{x}\ \texttt{in}\ v$, and identify α-equivalent terms. A context is a sequence of the form $x_1{:}\, A_1, \ldots, x_n : A_n$ where the x's are distinct variables and the A's are types. A DIML context consists of two contexts Γ and Δ containing disjoint sets of variables and is written $\Gamma|\Delta$. We call the variables in Γ *modal* and the variables in Δ *intuitionistic*. The typing judgements of DIML are of the form $\Gamma|\Delta \vdash t{:}\, A$ and are generated by the inference rules in Figure 1. Weakening for both kinds of variables is admissible because of the typing rule for these variables. Contraction of both kinds of variables follows from the additive way contexts are combined. Exchange is also admissible.

$$\Gamma, x{:}\, A, \Gamma'|\Delta \vdash x_M{:}\, A \qquad\qquad \Gamma|\Delta, x{:}\, A, \Delta' \vdash x_I{:}\, A$$

$$\frac{\Gamma|\Delta, x{:}\, A \vdash t{:}\, B}{\Gamma|\Delta \vdash \lambda x{:}\, A.t{:}\, A \to B}\ (\to I) \qquad \frac{\Gamma|\Delta \vdash t{:}\, A \to B \qquad \Gamma|\Delta \vdash u{:}\, A}{\Gamma|\Delta \vdash tu{:}\, B}\ (\to E)$$

$$\frac{\Gamma|\_ \vdash t{:}\, A}{\Gamma|\Delta \vdash \Box t{:}\, \Box A}\ (\Box I) \qquad \frac{\Gamma|\Delta \vdash t_i{:}\, \Box A_i \qquad \Gamma, x_i{:}\, A_i|\Delta \vdash u{:}\, B}{\Gamma|\Delta \vdash \texttt{let}\ t_1, \ldots, t_n\ \texttt{be}\ \Box x_1, \ldots, \Box x_n\ \texttt{in}\ u{:}\, B}\ (\Box E)$$

Fig. 1. Typing Judgements for DIML

The more complex nature of contexts in DIML results in a more subtle metatheory. Just as there are two rules for typing variables, so there are two substitution lemmas depending on the nature of the variable being substituted. As motivation for the following lemma, consider the special case where s is $\Box x_M$.

Lemma 1 (Substitution) *If* $\Gamma|\Delta \vdash t{:}\, A$ *and* $\Gamma|x_I{:}\, A, \Delta \vdash s{:}\, B$, *then* $\Gamma|\Delta \vdash s[t/x_I]{:}\, B$, *where* $[t/x_I]$ *denotes the traditional meta-level substitution. Similarly if* $\Gamma|- \ \vdash t{:}\, A$ *and* $\Gamma, x_M{:}\, A|\Delta \vdash s{:}\, B$ *then* $\Gamma|\Delta \vdash s[t/x_M]{:}\, B$.

Following the approach of [5], we can regard the introduction and elimination rules as being inverse and hence derive a β and an η-equality judgement for each type constructor. This then leads to a full full Curry-Howard correspondence for DIML. However, because of space concerns we do not expand upon these remarks and instead move directly to reduction in DIML.

2.2 The reduction calculus for DIML

As is customary, reduction in DIML consists only of β-redexes and is the least congruence on raw expressions containing the basic reductions

$$\begin{aligned} (\lambda x{:}\,A.t)u &\Rightarrow t[u/x] \\ \texttt{let}\ \bar{t}, \Box u, \bar{v}\ \texttt{be}\ \Box\bar{x}, \Box y, \Box\bar{z}\ \texttt{in}\ s &\Rightarrow \texttt{let}\ \bar{t}, \bar{v}\ \texttt{be}\ \Box\bar{x}, \Box\bar{z}\ \texttt{in}\ s[u/y] \end{aligned}$$

Two terms t and u which are equivalent in the equational theory generated by the DIML reduction relation are called DIML equivalent and this is written $t \cong u$. Subject reduction means that typing information is preserved by reduction and now we consider only those reductions whose redexes are well-typed terms — by subject reduction the reducts are also well-typed.

Two terms t and u which are equivalent in the equational theory generated by the DIML reduction relation are called DIML equivalent and this is written $t \cong u$. Subject reduction means that typing information is preserved by reduction and now we consider only those reductions whose redexes are well-typed terms — by subject reduction the reducts are also well-typed.

Lemma 2 (Subject Reduction) *If there is a typing judgement $\Gamma|\Delta \vdash t{:}\,A$ and a rewrite $t \Rightarrow t'$, then there is also a typing judgement $\Gamma|\Delta \vdash t'{:}\,A$.*

Theorem 3 *The relation $\Rightarrow$ is strongly normalising and confluent.*

Proof. Strong normalisation is proved by standard reducibility methods while confluence then follows from local confluence which may easily be checked.

3 Adding Explicit Substitutions to DIML

The traditional form of β-reduction $(\lambda x.t)u \Rightarrow t[u/x]$ substitutes the argument u into the body of the λ-abstraction t in one step. This is highly inefficient as each redex in u may be copied arbitrarily. Thus implementations usually evaluate terms in an environment and the contraction of a β-redex creates a new substitution which is added to the existing environment. In order to faithfully model implementations, Abadi et al. [1] proposed to make substitution part of the calculus. In this way they obtain a calculus with explicit substitution, the so-called $\lambda\sigma$-calculus, which has additional reduction rules corresponding to the inductive definition of reduction in the λ-calculus. The β-reduction of the λ-calculus is replaced by a rule which creates an explicit substitution.

We now apply this idea to DIML. In addition, just as the λ-calculus is contained in DILL, so the $\lambda\sigma$-calculus should be contained in xDIML. This containment should be such that every one-step reduction in the $\lambda\sigma$-calculus is mapped to a *one-step reduction* in xDIML. This is summarized by the following diagram in which inclusions of subcalculi are given by full lines, while the dotted lines refer to the embeddings involved in the proof that the explicit substitution calculus refines the corresponding calculus without explicit substitutions.

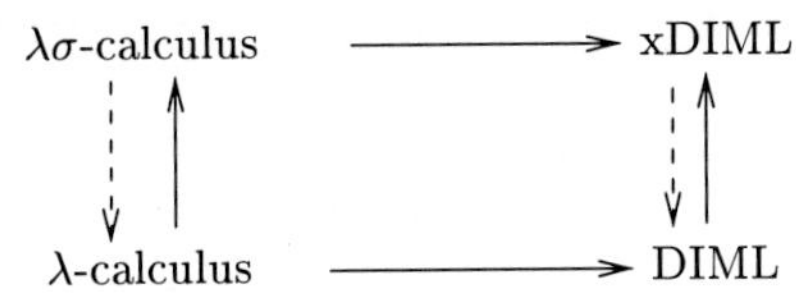

3.1 The Judgements of xDIML

In order to correctly add explicit substitutions to DIML we require not just terms of the form $\texttt{let}\ \overline{u}\ \texttt{be}\ \Box\overline{x}\ \texttt{in}\ t$ but also substitutions of the form $\texttt{let}\ \overline{u}\ \texttt{be}\ \Box\overline{x}\ \texttt{in}\ f$ where f is a substitution. This is equivalent to regarding the first half of a let-expression as an explicit substitution written $\langle\overline{u}/\Box\overline{x}\rangle$ — the above let-expressions are then $\langle\overline{u}/\Box\overline{x}\rangle * t$ and $\langle\overline{u}/\Box\overline{x}\rangle; f$. This replaces the notationally cumbersome let-expressions with "□"-substitutions whose behaviour is then governed by the $\Rightarrow_\sigma$-rewrite rules. Formally, the raw expressions of xDIML are:

$$t ::= x_I \mid x_M \mid \lambda x{:}\, A.t \mid tt \mid f * t \mid \Box t$$
$$f ::= \langle\rangle \mid \langle f, t/x_I\rangle \mid \langle f, t/x_M\rangle \mid \langle f, t/\Box x\rangle \mid f; f$$

The subscripts I and M in $\langle f, t/x_I\rangle$ and $\langle f, t/x_M\rangle$ indicate whether the substitution is for an intuitionistic or a modal variable but are sometimes omitted to increase legibility. We write $\langle t_1/x_1, \ldots, t_n/x_n\rangle$ for $\langle ..\langle\langle\rangle, t_1/x_1\rangle .., t_n/x_n\rangle$ and if $g = \langle t_1/p_1, \ldots, t_n/p_n\rangle$, we write $\langle f, g\rangle$ for $\langle f, t_1/p_1, \ldots, t_n/p_n\rangle$. A *pattern* is either x or $\Box x$, where x is a variable. A substitution $\langle t_1/p_1, \ldots, t_n/p_n\rangle$ is a *variable substitution* if each p_i is a variable pattern and a □*-substitution* if each p_i is a □-pattern. A *term substitution* is given by $s ::= \langle\rangle \mid \langle s, t/x_I\rangle, \mid \langle s, t/x_M\rangle \mid s; s$ where t is an arbitrary xDIML term. xDIML variables are bound by both λ-abstractions *and* the substitution operator $*$, *e.g.*, the variable x is bound in $\langle t/x\rangle * x$. Hence $\langle t/x\rangle * x$ is α-equivalent to $\langle t/y\rangle * y$. Consequently, the definition of bound variable is more complex than in the λ-calculus — see [16] for a full treatment. Henceforth, we identify α-equivalent terms and use Barendregt's variable convention that all bound variables are distinct from all free variables. xDIML term judgements are of the form $\Gamma|\Delta \vdash t : A$ and substitution judgements are of the form $\Gamma|\Delta \vdash f : \Gamma'|\Delta'$; these judgements are given in Figure 2. By replacing let-expressions by □-substitutions, we obtain an embedding of DIML into xDIML. In future, this embedding is left implicit and we regard DIML as a subcalculus of xDIML. xDIML satisfies *weakening*, *contraction* and *exchange* for both sorts of variables.

3.2 xDIML Reduction and Its Correctness

Reduction in the λσ-calculus consists of a modified form of β-reduction which creates an explicit substitution and a set of $\Rightarrow_\sigma$-rewrite rules which, amongst other functions, distribute substitutions over term constructors. In xDIML, such rewrite rules lead to a loss of subject reduction, eg if the rule $f * \Box u \Rightarrow_\sigma \Box f * u$ is instantiated with $f = \langle t/\Box x\rangle$ then the redex is well-typed but not the reduct.

Term Judgements

$$\Gamma, x{:}\, A, \Gamma'|\Delta \vdash x{:}\, A \qquad \Gamma|\Delta, x{:}\, A, \Delta' \vdash x{:}\, A$$

$$\frac{\Gamma|\Delta, x{:}\, A \vdash t{:}\, B}{\Gamma|\Delta \vdash \lambda x{:}\, A.t{:}\, A \to B} \qquad \frac{\Gamma|\Delta \vdash t{:}\, A \to B \qquad \Gamma|\Delta \vdash u{:}\, A}{\Gamma|\Delta \vdash tu{:}\, B}$$

$$\frac{\Gamma|\,\_ \vdash t{:}\, A}{\Gamma|\Delta \vdash \Box t{:}\, \Box A} \qquad \frac{\Gamma_1|\Delta_1 \vdash f{:}\, \Gamma_2|\Delta_2 \qquad \Gamma_2|\Delta_2 \vdash t{:}\, A}{\Gamma_1|\Delta_1 \vdash f * t{:}\, A}$$

Substitution Judgements: In the last three rules, $x \notin \mathtt{dom}(\Gamma'|\Delta')$

$$\frac{\Gamma' \subseteq \Gamma \qquad \Delta' \subseteq \Delta}{\Gamma|\Delta \vdash \langle\rangle : \Gamma'|\Delta'} \qquad \frac{\Gamma_1|\Delta_1 \vdash f{:}\, \Gamma_2|\Delta_2 \quad \Gamma_2|\Delta_2 \vdash g{:}\, \Gamma_3|\Delta_3}{\Gamma_1|\Delta_1 \vdash f; g{:}\, \Gamma_3|\Delta_3}$$

$$\frac{\Gamma|\Delta \vdash f : \Gamma'|\Delta' \quad \Gamma|\_ \vdash t{:}\, A}{\Gamma|\Delta \vdash \langle f, t/x_M\rangle{:}\, \Gamma', x{:}\, A|\Delta'} \qquad \frac{\Gamma|\Delta \vdash f : \Gamma'|\Delta' \qquad \Gamma|\Delta \vdash t{:}\, A}{\Gamma|\Delta \vdash \langle f, t/x_I\rangle{:}\, \Gamma'|\Delta', x{:}\, A}$$

$$\frac{\Gamma|\Delta \vdash f : \Gamma'|\Delta' \qquad \Gamma|\Delta \vdash t{:}\, \Box A}{\Gamma|\Delta \vdash \langle f, t/\Box x\rangle{:}\, \Gamma', x : A|\Delta'}$$

Fig. 2. xDIML Typing Judgements

Thus, in xDIML, certain $\Rightarrow_\sigma$-rewrite rules only apply to *term substitutions* and new rewrite rules are added to extract term substitutions. Firstly, there is a rewrite rule which separates $\Box$-substitutions from variable substitutions — if $g = \langle t_1/p_1, \ldots, t_n/p_n\rangle$ and @ is either ; or $*$, then $g@h \Rightarrow_\sigma g_\Box @ g_V @ h$ where $g_\Box$ is g restricted to $\Box$-patterns and similarly for g_V — definitions of $g_\Box$ and g_V can be found below. If f is a $\Box$-substitution then there are also new rewrites $(f; g)@h \Rightarrow_\sigma f@(g@h)$ and $\langle f; g, t/p\rangle \Rightarrow_\sigma f; \langle g, t/p\rangle$. These rules may seem counter-intuitive as there is a rewrite in the opposite direction if f is a term substitution. However, these rewrites have a natural explanation as examples of Ghani's η-expansions for `let`-expressions [5]. Formally, xDIML reduction is the least congruence on raw expressions containing the basic redexes of Figure 3. xDIML reduction satisfies subject reduction and so we restrict ourselves to reduction on well-typed terms.

If t is a term and f a variable substitution, then there is an xDIML reduction sequence $f*t \Rightarrow_\sigma^* t[f]$ where $t[f]$ denotes the result of applying f to t. In addition, every one-step $\lambda\sigma$-rewrite is a one-step xDIML rewrite so we have the desired embedding of the $\lambda\sigma$-calculus into xDIML.

The correctness proof for the $\lambda\sigma$-calculus constructs a reduction preserving embedding of the calculus into the subcalculus containing no explicit substitutions — this embedding essentially performs all explicit substitutions. The terms of this subcalculus are λ-terms and hence normalisation and confluence for the $\lambda\sigma$-calculus follow from strong normalisation and confluence for the λ-calculus.

Modified β-reduction: $\langle f, \Box t/\Box x\rangle \Rightarrow_\beta \langle f, t/x\rangle \qquad (\lambda x{:}\, A.t)u \Rightarrow_\beta \langle u/x\rangle * t$

σ-rewrite rules: Let @ be either ; or $*$, f be a $\Box$-sub. and g a term sub.

$$
\begin{array}{llll}
\langle\rangle @ h & \Rightarrow_\sigma h & (h; \langle\rangle) @ h' & \Rightarrow_\sigma h @ h \\
(f; h) @ h' & \Rightarrow_\sigma f @ h @ h' & \langle f; g, t/p\rangle & \Rightarrow_\sigma f; \langle g, t/p\rangle \\
\langle \bar{t}/\bar{p}\rangle @ h & \Rightarrow_\sigma \langle \bar{t}/\bar{p}\rangle_\Box @ \langle \bar{t}/\bar{p}\rangle_V @ h & & \\
 & & & \\
g @ h @ h' & \Rightarrow_\sigma (g; h) @ h' & g; \langle h, t/p\rangle & \Rightarrow_\sigma \langle g; h, (g * t)/p\rangle \\
g * (uv) & \Rightarrow_\sigma (g * u)(g * v) & g * \lambda x.t & \Rightarrow_\sigma \lambda y.\langle g, y/x\rangle * t \ \ (y \text{ fresh}) \\
\langle g, \bar{t}/\overline{x_M}\rangle * \Box t & \Rightarrow_\sigma g * \Box(\langle \bar{t}/\overline{x_M}\rangle * t) & \langle g, s/x_I\rangle * \Box t & \Rightarrow_\sigma g * \Box t \\
\langle g, t/x\rangle * x & \Rightarrow_\sigma t & \langle g, t/y\rangle * x & \Rightarrow_\sigma g * x
\end{array}
$$

Fig. 3. Reductions for xDIML

The correctness proof for xDIML is essentially the same as we construct a reduction preserving embedding from the terms of xDIML to the terms of DIML.

An xDIML term is called *canonical* iff it is a DIML term, while an xDIML substitution is called *canonical* iff all of its sub-terms are canonical. The key clause in the embedding of xDIML into DIML is the case of a canonical substitution f applied to a canonical term t. The translation of such a term is $f \star t$ and is defined recursively by case analysis. Firstly, $\langle\rangle \star t = t$, while $f \star t = f_R \star (f_\Box * t[f_V])$ if $f_\Box \neq \langle\rangle$ and $f \star t = f_R \star t[f_V]$ if $f_\Box = \langle\rangle$. The ancillary notions f_R, $f_\Box$ and f_V are defined as follows

$$
\begin{array}{rcrcrc}
\langle\rangle_R = \langle\rangle & & \langle\rangle_\Box = \langle\rangle & & \langle\rangle_V = \langle\rangle \\
\langle f, t/x\rangle_R = f_R & & \langle f, t/x\rangle_\Box = f_\Box & & \langle f, t/x\rangle_V = \langle f_V, t/x\rangle \\
\langle f, t/\Box y\rangle_R = f_R & & \langle f, t/\Box y\rangle_\Box = \langle f_\Box, t/\Box y\rangle & & \langle f, t/\Box\rangle_V = f_V \\
(f; g)_R = f; g_R & & (f; g)_\Box = g_\Box & & (f; g)_V = g_V
\end{array}
$$

One may easily verify that if f and t are canonical, then $f \star t$ is canonical and $f * t \Rightarrow_\sigma f \star t$. Arbitrary xDIML terms are mapped to canonical terms and arbitrary xDIML substitutions to canonical substitutions by the translation $[\![-]\!]$, which maps $f * t$ to $[\![f]\!] \star [\![t]\!]$ and respects all other term constructors. The key properties of $[\![-]\!]$ are

Proposition 4 *(i) There are reductions $f \Rightarrow_\sigma^* [\![f]\!]$ and $t \Rightarrow_\sigma^* [\![t]\!]$*
(ii) If there is a reduction $t \Rightarrow_\sigma t'$ in xDIML, then $[\![t]\!] = [\![t']\!]$.
(iii) If there is a reduction $t \Rightarrow_\beta t'$ in xDIML, then $[\![t]\!] \Rightarrow^* [\![t']\!]$.
(iv) If $t \Rightarrow t'$ in DIML, then also $t \Rightarrow^* t'$ in xDIML.

Finally we can prove confluence and normalisation:

Theorem 5 *The relation $\Rightarrow$ is confluent and every xDIML term rewrites to a unique DIML normal form.*

Proof. Given two terms u and v related in the xDIML equational theory, we have by proposition 4 that $[\![u]\!]$ and $[\![v]\!]$ are DIML equivalent. Because DIML is confluent these terms have a common reduct t and because each DIML-reduction gives rise to a sequence of xDIML-reductions both u and v reduce to t. A normal form for a term t can be computed by calculating the DIML normal form of $[\![t]\!]$ with uniqueness following from confluence.

The reduction strategy used in the normalisation proof is usually not used for abstract machines because this strategy executes all possible substitutions first and does β-reductions only afterwards. Mellies' counterexample [11] for strong normalisation of the $\lambda\sigma$-calculus applies to xDIML as well and shows that it is not strongly normalising either. Hence the termination of a particular reduction strategy needs to be shown separately. One way is to apply the reducibility method; see [18] for the proof that a wide range of reduction strategies terminate.

4 Analysis of Computation in Stages via Modal Logic

As an application of DIML we present an operational semantics for execution of functional programs in stages. Such an execution in stages is often called a *partial evaluation* of a program [10]. A program is executed in stages either because not all information is available at the same time or because we want to change the control flow of execution to execute early a part of a program that is used very often. In a functional language, this means that the variables are split into two kinds: one kind which is bound to values at compile-time, the so-called static or compile-time variables and the other kind of variables which is bound at run-time, the so-called dynamic or run-time variables. The process of separating the variables into compile-time or run-time variables is called binding analysis [2, 8, 15]. The aim of binding analysis is to identify variables as compile-time variables if they correspond to parts of the program which are guaranteed to terminate and which are arguments of needed redexes.

In this way one obtains a distinction between two kinds of function spaces: on the one hand, we have the function space $A \to B$ where the bound variable is a so-called *compile-time*-variable. Such a function is executed at compile-time. On the other hand, we have the function space $A \Rightarrow B$ where the bound variable is a so-called *run-time*-variable. Such a function is executed at run-time.

The standard presentation of this distinction uses a two-level λ-calculus [14, 15]. Such a calculus has two kinds of variables and two kinds of types. The two kinds of variables are the compile-time and run-time variables, and the types are separated into compile-time types and run-time types. Abstraction and application are defined for both compile-time types and run-time types. Redexes of compile-time type are to be reduced at compile-time, and redexes of run-time type at run-time. Run-time expressions may be encapsulated as code which the compiler may manipulate. Because normally code does not have any free variables this encapsulation must only be permitted if the run-time expression has no free run-time variables. Free compile-time variables will be bound during the compilation and are hence allowed.

There are several different versions of the two-level λ-calculus in the literature. Nielson and Nielson give only typing rules and do not specify how compile-time reductions should be performed. Palsberg defines a partial evaluator as a function who performs *all* compile-time reductions. This implies that compile-time reduction has to take place also under run-time λ-abstractions. We follow this approach as our view is that *all* compile-time reductions should be performed before any run-time execution takes place.

The distinction between compile-time and run-time has been modelled using modal logic [4]. A modal type $\Box A$ represents code of type A, and a term $\Box t$ represents a piece of code which is to be evaluated only at run-time *i.e.*, at a later stage. Davies and Pfenning also give an embedding of a two-level λ-calculus into a different modal λ-calculus which is motivated by the Kripke-semantics of modal logic where each application of the $\Box$-operator represents a new stage of the computation.

We model the execution in stages in a different way in modal logic. We use the distinction between intuitionistic and modal variables and function spaces to model the distinction between run-time and compile-time variables and function spaces respectively. The execution in stages is reflected by the separation of the operational semantics into compile-time and run-time semantics. The compile-time semantics and run-time semantics reduce only β-redexes with compile-time and run-time applications respectively. Now evaluation can proceed in stages: the compile-time operational semantics eliminates all compile-time redexes, and the run-time operational semantics eliminates all run-time redexes without re-introducing any compile-time redexes. Because in this operational semantics $\Box\Box A$ is operationally equivalent to $\Box A$, we can only model two stages of computation this way. If we want to model more stages, we have to add a new modality for each new stage. In this way we obtain the context stacks of Davies and Pfenning but with the standard operational semantics.

Our version of the two-level λ-calculus is a subcalculus of DIML. We partition the DIML-types into compile-time types C and run-time types R , given by

$$C ::= G \mid C \to^M C \mid \Box R \qquad\qquad R ::= G \mid R \to^I R$$

where $\to^I$ and $\to^M$ denote the intuitionistic and modal function space respectively, and G is any ground type. The DIML-terms are partitioned into compile-time terms c and run-time terms r with the judgements $\Gamma|_- \vdash c\colon C$ and $\Gamma|\Delta \vdash r\colon R$, where Γ is a context of compile-time variables and Δ a context of run-time variables, which are given by the grammar

$$\begin{array}{l} c ::= \texttt{const} \mid x_M \mid \lambda x^c\colon C.c \mid cc \mid \mathit{code}(r) \\ r ::= \texttt{const} \mid x_I \mid \lambda x^r\colon R.r \mid rr \mid \mathit{eval}(c) \end{array}$$

where `const` are the constants of ground type.

The compile-time terms stands for expressions which are evaluated at compile-time, with run-time expressions as potential values. Code is included via the constructor *code* (the DIML-term constructor $\Box$), but it is not evaluated, only copied. The run-time terms models expressions which are to be evaluated at run-time. The constructor *eval* (an abbreviation for `let` x `be` $\Box x$ `in` x) incorporates code as produced by the compiler into the run-time system for evaluation. The term $\lambda x_M : C.c$ is an abbreviation for the DIML-term $\lambda x_I : \Box C.$`let` x_M `be` $\Box x_I$ `in` c. Because our two-level λ-calculus is a subcalculus of DIML, a conservativity result in the sense of Davies and Pfenning trivially holds: a two level λ-term is well-formed if it is well-formed as a DIML-term by definition. This partitioning of terms follows the standard partitioning of DIML into intuitionistic and modal terms: A term $\Gamma|\_ \vdash t\colon A$ is a modal term (with only modal hypotheses), and a term $\Gamma|\Delta \vdash s\colon A$ is an intuitionistic term which has both intuitionistic and modal hypotheses.

Now we turn to the operational semantics. We use xDIML-expressions for the definition of the operational semantics because the step from an explicit substitution calculus to an abstract machines is small. We use the metatheory of xDIML, as developed earlier in the paper, to show the correctness of the operational semantics. The compile-time operational semantics is a call-by-value semantics for the compile-time terms together with the rule $eval(code(r)) \rightsquigarrow^c r$. We do not reduce intuitionistic applications, as these represent run-time redexes. As a consequence we must reduce under intuitionistic λ-abstractions. The values of this operational semantics of type $\Box A$ are the run-time terms with no compile-time terms as subexpressions, the values of type $C \to^M C$ are modal closures $h * \lambda x^M.t$, where h is some substitution $\langle \bar{t}/\bar{x}_M \rangle$, and the values of ground type are constants. The rules for this operational semantics are given in Figure 4.

Let h be any substitution $\langle \overline{c_v}/\overline{x}_M \rangle$ and c_v be any value.

$$
\begin{array}{llll}
(Var) & \langle h, t/x_M \rangle * x_M \rightsquigarrow_c t & & \langle h, t/y_M \rangle * x_M \rightsquigarrow_c h * x_M \\
(\lambda_I) & h * \lambda x_I \colon R.t \rightsquigarrow_c \lambda x_I \colon R.h * t & & h * x_I \rightsquigarrow_c x_I \\
(\beta_\Box) & h * \langle f, \Box t/\Box x \rangle * x_M \rightsquigarrow_c h * t & (\beta) & (h * \lambda x_M \colon A.t)c_v \rightsquigarrow_c \langle h, c_v/x_M \rangle * s \\
(app) & h * (ts) \rightsquigarrow_c (h * t)(h * s) & & \\
(\Box) & h * \Box t \rightsquigarrow_c \Box h * t & &
\end{array}
$$

$$
\frac{s \rightsquigarrow_c s'}{ts \rightsquigarrow_c ts'} \quad \frac{t \rightsquigarrow_c t'}{tc_v \rightsquigarrow_c t'c_v} \quad \frac{t \rightsquigarrow_c t'}{\Box t \rightsquigarrow_c \Box t'}
$$

plus congruence rules for all run-time constructors.

Fig. 4. Compile-time Operational Semantics

The operational semantics for the run-time terms is a standard call-by-value semantics together with the rule $eval(code(r)) \rightsquigarrow^c r$. Its values are the expected ones: constants for ground types, and intuitionistic λ-abstractions for function spaces. The rules are give in Figure 5, again for xDIML-expressions. In this way we achieve the separation of computation stages.

This staged operational semantics gives rise to a very natural abstract machines for the two-level λ-calculus: two standard abstract machines for the λ-

Let e be any substitution $\langle \overline{v}/\overline{x}_I \rangle$, and v be any value.

$$(\beta_\Box) \quad e * \langle f, \Box t/\Box x \rangle * x \leadsto_r e * t \qquad (\beta) \; (e * \lambda x_I \colon R.t)v \leadsto_r \langle e, v/x_I \rangle * t$$

$$(app) \qquad e * (ts) \leadsto_r (e * t)(e * s) \qquad \frac{s \leadsto_r s'}{ts \leadsto_r ts'} \quad \frac{t \leadsto_r t'}{tv \leadsto_r t' c_v}$$

Fig. 5. Run-time Operational Semantics

calculus; one for the modal (compile-time) β-redexes, and the other one for the intuitionistic (run-time) β-redexes. The compile-time machine needs an extension to treat run-time λ-abstractions not as values but to reduce under them. This is rather easy because the intuitionistic λ-abstraction never occurs as the function part in modal β-redexes.

The proof that the given operational semantics models the separation of execution stages relies on the meta-theoretic properties of our explicit substitution calculus xDIML. As already mentioned, we use the reducibility method applied to xDIML to show termination of the operational semantics.

Theorem 6 *(i) For each closed compile-time term c of ground type there exists a unique run-time term r such that $c \leadsto_c^* r$. Moreover, $c \Rightarrow^* r$ when we view c and r as xDIML-terms.*

(ii) For each closed run-time term r of ground type in the two-level λ-calculus there exists a unique value such that $r \leadsto_r^* v$. Moreover, $r \Rightarrow^* v$ when we view r and v as xDIML-terms.

Proof. To show the separation of stages one shows that any compile-time value of a compile-time function space is a term $\lambda x_M \colon C.c$. The uniqueness of v follows from confluence of reduction in xDIML. The existence of the value v follows from a reducibility argument similar to [18].

5 Conclusions and Further Work

This paper described a type theory xDIML associated with a modal logic for constructive necessity, that is suitable for an easy to prove correct implementation as an abstract machine. To obtain our type theory we used two processes, which seem to us generic enough to be applied to several logical systems. The first process consists of providing a Curry-Howard correspondence in the style of the dual contexts: this gave us the type theory DIML, which already satisfies most of the syntactic properties we wanted, such as subject reduction, confluence and strong normalisation. The second process is the adding of explicit substitutions to DIML to obtain xDIML. This was not as straightforward as we had hoped for, but it works and we obtain the desired syntactic results for xDIML. Is is pleasing to find that the type theory xDIML we obtain by using semantical methods (hidden way in this paper, but see [7]) can be used for practical applications such as abstract machines and binding analysis.

The implementation of the abstract machine based on this paper is the next step. This will give us means to compare different ways of doing binding analysis and partial evaluation. The semantic foundation of the machine should make it possible to give a slightly different machine for slightly different methods of binding analysis and partial evaluation, and also give a conceptual explanation of these differences.

Acknowledgements

We gratefully acknowledge discussions with Rowan Davies and Frank Pfenning about the subject of this paper.

References

1. M. Abadi, L. Cardelli, P.-L. Curien, and J.-J. Lévy. Explicit substitutions. *Journal of Functional Programming*, 1(4):375–416, 1991.
2. C. Consel. Binding time analysis for higher order untyped functional languages. In *Proc. ACM conference on Lisp and functional programming*, pages 264–272, 1990.
3. R. Davies. A temporal logic approach to binding-time analysis. In *Proc. of LICS'96*, pages 184–193, 1996.
4. R. Davies and F. Pfenning. A modal analysis of staged computation. In Guy Steele, Jr., editor, *Proc. of 23rd POPL*, pages 258–270. ACM Press, 1996.
5. N. Ghani. *Adjoint Rewriting.* PhD thesis, University of Edinburgh, 1995.
6. N. Ghani, V. de Paiva, and E. Ritter. Linear explicit substitutions. In *Proc. of Westapp'98*, 1998.
7. N. Ghani, V. de Paiva, and E. Ritter. Models for explicit substitution calculi. Technical report, School of Computer Science, University of Birmingham, 1998.
8. C.K. Gomard. Partial type inference for untyped functional programs. In *Proc. ACM conference on Lisp and functional programming*, pages 282–287, 1990.
9. J. Goubault-Larrecq. Logical foundations of eval/quote mechanisms, and the modal logic S4. Manuscript, 1996.
10. N.D. Jones, C.K. Gomard, and P. Sestoft. *Partial Evaluation and Automatic Program Generation.* Prentice Hall, 1993.
11. P.-A. Mellies. Typed λ-calculi with explicit substitution may not terminate. *Proc. of TLCA'95*, pages 328–334. LNCS No. 902, 1995.
12. A. Barber. *Linear Type Theories, Semantics and Action Calculi.* PhD-thesis, LFCS, University of Edinburgh, 1997.
13. A. Barber and G. Plotkin. Dual intuitionistic linear logic. Technical report, LFCS, University of Edinburgh, 1997.
14. F. Nielson and H.R. Nielson. *Two-Level Functional Languages.* CUP, 1992.
15. J. Palsberg. Correctness of binding-time analysis. *J. of Functional Programming*, 3(3):347–363, 1993.
16. E. Ritter and V. de Paiva. On explicit substitution and names (extended abstract). In *Proc. of ICALP'97*, LNCS 1256, pages 248–258, 1997.
17. Eike Ritter. Categorical abstract machines for higher-order lambda calculi. *Theoretical Computer Science*, 136(1):125–162, 1994.
18. Eike Ritter. Normalization for typed lambda calculi with explicit substitution. In *Proc. of CSL'93*, pages 295–304. LNCS 832, 1994.

The Relevance of Proof-Irrelevance

A Meta-Theoretical Study of Generalised Calculi of Constructions

Gilles Barthe

Institutionen för Datavetenskap, Chalmers Tekniska Högskola, Göteborg, Sweden,
gillesb@cs.chalmers.se
Departamento de Informatica, Universidade do Minho, Braga, Portugal,
gillesb@di.uminho.pt

Abstract. We propose a general technique, inspired from *proof-irrelevance*, to prove strong normalisation and consistency for extensions of the Calculus of Constructions.

1 Introduction

The Calculus of Constructions (CC) [12] is a powerful typed λ-calculus which may be used both as a programming language and as a logical framework. However, CC is *minimal* in the sense that the generalised function space $\Pi x{:}\, A.\, B$ is its only type constructor. The minimality of CC imposes strict limits to its applicability and has given rise to a spate of proposals to include new term/type constructors: algebraic types [3,7], fixpoints [1], control operators [6] and inductive types [21] to mention only the examples considered in this paper—some proposals are actually concerned with the more general setting of Pure Type Systems [4]. While most of these calculi, which we call *Generalised Calculi of Constructions* (GCCs), are known to enjoy meta-theoretical properties similar to CC itself, there are no general techniques to guide their meta-theoretical study. In particular, Subject Reduction, which is often the most intricate result in the meta-theory of GCCs, is usually proved by ad hoc means.

This paper is concerned with developing a general technique, inspired from *proof-irrelevance* [13], to prove strong normalisation and consistency results for GCCs without relying on Subject Reduction. In a nutshell, the technique proceeds in three steps: first, we define a family of *proof-irrelevant Calculi of Constructions* (PICCs), in which all *objects*—here the word object refers to an inhabitant of a type, as opposed to the word constructor which refers to an inhabitant of a kind—are identified in the conversion rule. Second, we prove that PICCs enjoy essentially the same properties as CC, including β-strong normalisation and, under suitable conditions, consistency. Third, we define a class of *sound* GCCs that may be viewed as subsystems of some PICC. By combining those steps, we conclude that sound GCCs are strongly normalising and, under suitable conditions, consistent. We can then show that several GCCs of interest, including the above mentioned ones, are sound. Applications are three-fold:

1. We prove strong normalisation for (1) CC with fixpoints (2) CC with first-order algebraic rewriting (3) CC with (some) inductive types.

2. We prove logical results such as (1) consistency of $0 =_{\mathsf{Nat}} 1$ in CC with inductive types but without large eliminations (2) consistency of $a =_\tau b$ for every closed algebraic terms $a, b : \tau$ in CC with algebraic rewriting (3) the axiom of choice and proof-irrelevance do not imply the excluded middle in CC.
3. We obtain a technique to prove strong normalisation of GCCs with non-left linear reduction rules. The technique may be used to prove strong normalisation of e.g. (1) CC with algebraic higher-order rewriting (2) CC with classical logic.

Disclaimers The paper *uses* proof-irrelevance as a technical tool but *does not intend to promote* proof-irrelevance as a desirable feature of type systems. Besides, this paper *is not meant to suggest* that one may develop a fully modular proof theory of type systems. Such a perspective seems indeed rather bleak. On the other hand, the proof-irrelevance technique yields modular proofs and seems genuinely useful in the framework of GCCs.

Contents The paper is organised as follows: Section 2 introduces the notion of generalised Calculus of Constructions. Section 3 is devoted to the definition and study of proof-irrelevant Calculi of Constructions. Section 4 is concerned with applications. We assess our method and conclude in Section 5.

Prerequisites The paper assumes some familiarity with the Calculus of Constructions [12]. Throughout the paper, a number of extensions are considered. We only give the syntax and refer readers to the literature for a more detailed presentation of these systems, including motivations.

As to notational conventions, we write $\twoheadrightarrow_i$ and $=_i$ for the reflexive-transitive and reflexive-symmetric-transitive closures of $\rightarrow_i$. In addition, we use $\rightarrow_{ij}$ to denote the union of two relations $\rightarrow_i$ and $\rightarrow_j$ and $\mathsf{SN}(i)$ to denote the set of terms that are strongly normalising with respect to $\rightarrow_i$. Finally, we write $a \downarrow_i b$ iff there exists c such that $a \twoheadrightarrow_i c$ and $b \twoheadrightarrow_i c$.

2 Generalised Calculi of Constructions

Throughout the paper, we assume disjoint, countably infinite sets V^* of *object variables* and $V^\Box$ of *constructor variables*; moreover we let $V = V^* \cup V^\Box$.

Definition 1 (Pseudo-terms, β-reduction).

1. *Let $\mathcal{B}$ be an arbitrary set. The set $\mathcal{T}$ of* pseudo-terms *(over $\mathcal{B}$) is given by the abstract syntax:*

$$\mathcal{T} = V \mid \mathcal{B} \mid * \mid \Box \mid \mathcal{T}\,\mathcal{T} \mid \lambda V{:}\mathcal{T}\,.\,\mathcal{T} \mid \Pi V{:}\mathcal{T}\,.\,\mathcal{T} \mid \bullet$$

(The pseudo-term $\bullet$ is introduced for purely technical reasons, see Section 3.)

2. *A pseudo-term M is* closed *if $\mathrm{FV}(M) = \emptyset$ where the set $\mathrm{FV}(M)$ of* free variables *of M is defined as usual. The set of closed terms is denoted by $\mathcal{T}_0$.*
3. *The β-reduction relation $\rightarrow_\beta$ is defined as the compatible closure of the rule*

$$(\lambda x{:}A\,.\,M)\,N \rightarrow_\beta M\{x := N\}$$

where $M\{x := N\}$ is obtained from M by substituting N for all free occurrences of x in M.

A generalised Calculus of Constructions is defined by a set of constants $\mathcal{B}$, a declaration map $\mathcal{D}$, that assigns to every constant its potential closed type, and an abstract conversion relation cnv, which is used in place of the usual β-equality in the (conversion) rule.

Definition 2 (Specifications). *A* specification *is a quadruple* $\mathrm{S} = (\mathcal{B}^*, \mathcal{B}^\square, \mathcal{D}, \mathsf{cnv})$ *where*

1. $\mathcal{B}^*$ *and* $\mathcal{B}^\square$ *are disjoint sets of* object constants *and* constructor constants *respectively. Below we let* $\mathcal{B} = \mathcal{B}^* \cup \mathcal{B}^\square$.
2. $\mathcal{D} : \mathcal{B} \to \mathcal{T}_0$ *is a* declaration map *such that for every* $f \in \mathcal{B}^*$, $\mathcal{D}(f) \equiv \Pi x_1{:}A_1.\ \ldots\ \Pi x_n{:}A_n.\ h\ P_1\ \ldots\ P_m$ *where* $h \in \{x_1, \ldots, x_n\} \cup \mathcal{B}^\square$ *and for every* $f \in \mathcal{B}^\square$, $\mathcal{D}(f) \equiv \Pi x_1{:}A_1.\ \ldots\ \Pi x_n{:}A_n.\ *$. *In both cases, we let* $n = \mathsf{ar}(f)$.
3. $\mathsf{cnv} \subseteq \mathcal{T} \times \mathcal{T}$ *is an* (abstract) conversion *relation.*

The triple $(\mathcal{B}^*, \mathcal{B}^\square, \mathcal{D})$ *is called a* declaration structure. *We sometimes write a specification as* $(\mathcal{DS}, \mathsf{cnv})$ *where* $\mathcal{DS}$ *is a declaration structure and* cnv *is an appropriate conversion relation.*

The notion of specification is very flexible, as illustrated below.

1. Specification $\mathbf{S}_{\mathsf{fix}} = (\mathcal{DS}_{\mathsf{fix}}, =_{\beta\phi})$ for fixpoints :

Constructor constants	
Object constants	Y
Constructor declarations	
Object declarations	$\mathcal{D}(Y) = \Pi\alpha{:}*.\ (\alpha \to \alpha) \to \alpha$
Reduction rules	$Y\ \alpha\ f \quad \to_\phi \quad f\ (Y\ \alpha\ f)$

2. Specification $\mathbf{S}_{(\Sigma,\mathcal{R})} = (\mathcal{DS}_\Sigma, \downarrow_{\beta\mathcal{R}})$ for a many-sorted term-rewriting system $\mathcal{R}$ over a many-sorted signature[1] $\Sigma = (\Lambda, \mathcal{F}, \mathsf{decl})$:

Constructor constants	$\sigma\ (\sigma \in \Lambda)$
Object constants	$f\ (f \in \mathcal{F})$
Constructor declarations	$\mathcal{D}(\sigma) = *$
Object declarations	$\mathcal{D}(f) = \sigma_1 \to\ \ldots\ \to \sigma_n \to \tau$ if $\mathsf{decl}(f) = ((\sigma_1, \ldots, \sigma_n), \tau)$
Reduction rules	$l \to_\mathcal{R} r$ if $(l, r) \in \mathcal{R}$

   Note that the presentation of PTSs suggests that one should take $=_{\beta\mathcal{R}}$ as abstract conversion relation but there is a caveat. If $\mathcal{R}$ is inconsistent, i.e. equates distinct variables, then $M =_{\beta\mathcal{R}} N$ for all $M, N \in \mathcal{T}$. In such cases the specification $(\mathcal{DS}_\Sigma, =_{\beta\mathcal{R}})$ is of no interest.

3. Specification $\mathbf{S}_{\mathsf{ac}} = (\mathcal{DS}_{\mathsf{ac}}, =_{\beta\pi})$ for Σ-types :

Constructor constants	Σ
Object constants	fst, snd, pair
Constructor declarations	$\mathcal{D}(\Sigma) = \Pi\alpha{:}*.\ (\alpha \to *) \to *$
Object declarations	$\mathcal{D}(\mathsf{fst}) = \Pi\alpha{:}*.\ \Pi\beta{:}\alpha \to *.\ (\Sigma\ \alpha\ \beta) \to \alpha$
	$\mathcal{D}(\mathsf{snd}) = \Pi\alpha{:}*.\ \Pi\beta{:}\alpha \to *.\ \Pi y{:}(\Sigma\ \alpha\ \beta).\ \beta\ (\mathsf{fst}\ \alpha\ \beta\ y)$
	$\mathcal{D}(\mathsf{pair}) = \Pi\alpha{:}*.\ \Pi\beta{:}\alpha \to *.\ \Pi y{:}\alpha.\ \beta\ y \to (\Sigma\ \alpha\ \beta)$
Reduction rules	$\mathsf{fst}\ A\ B\ (\mathsf{pair}\ A\ B\ x\ y) \to_\pi x$
	$\mathsf{snd}\ A\ B\ (\mathsf{pair}\ A\ B\ x\ y) \to_\pi y$

[1] A many-sorted signature consists of a set Λ of sorts, a set $\mathcal{F}$ of function symbols and a declaration map $\mathsf{decl} : \mathcal{F} \to \Lambda^w \times \Lambda$ where Λ^w is the set of finite lists over Λ. See e.g. [7] for a definition of many-sorted term-rewriting system.

4. Specification $\mathbf{S}_{\text{nat}} = (\mathcal{DS}_{\text{nat}}, =_{\beta\iota})$ for natural numbers :

Constructor constants Nat
Object constants 0, S, NatE
Constructor declarations $\mathcal{D}(\mathsf{Nat}) = *$
Object declarations $\mathcal{D}(0) = \mathsf{Nat}$
$\mathcal{D}(\mathsf{S}) = \mathsf{Nat} \to \mathsf{Nat}$

$$\mathcal{D}(\mathsf{NatE}) = \Pi P{:}\,\mathsf{Nat} \to *.\ (P\,0) \to (\Pi n{:}\,\mathsf{Nat}.\ (P\,n) \to (P\,(\mathsf{S}\,n))) \to \Pi n{:}\,\mathsf{Nat}.\ P\,n$$

Reduction rules $\mathsf{NatE}\ P\ H_0\ H_s\ 0 \to_\iota H_0$
$\mathsf{NatE}\ P\ H_0\ H_s\ (\mathsf{S}\ n) \to_\iota H_s\ n\ (\mathsf{NatE}\ P\ H_0\ H_s\ n)$

where n is a numeral, i.e. of the form $\mathsf{S}^p 0$. (A more general rule would allow for n to be arbitrary.)

5. Specification $\mathbf{S}_{\text{cl}} = (\mathcal{DS}_{\text{cl}}, =_{\beta\Delta})$ for classical logic :

Constructor constants $\perp$
Object constants Δ
Constructor declarations $\mathcal{D}(\perp) = *$
Object declarations $\mathcal{D}(\Delta) = \Pi\alpha{:}\,*.\ ((\alpha \to \perp) \to \perp) \to \alpha$
Reduction rules $\Delta\ (\Pi v{:}\,A.\ B)\ M \to_{\Delta_1} \lambda v : A.\ \Delta\ B\ (\lambda x : \neg B.\ M\ (\lambda w{:}(\Pi v{:}\,A.\ B)\,.\,x\,(w\,v)))$
$\Delta\ A\ (\lambda x : \neg A.\ x\ M) \to_{\Delta_2} M \quad \textit{if } x \notin \mathrm{FV}(M)$

$$\Delta\ A\ (\lambda x : \neg A.\ x\,(\Delta\ A\ (\lambda y : \neg A.\ M))) \to_{\Delta_3} \Delta\ A\ (\lambda y : \neg A.\ M\{y := x\})$$

where $\neg A \equiv A \to \perp$.

(axiom) $\quad \langle\rangle \vdash * : \square$

(start) $\quad \dfrac{\Gamma \vdash A : s}{\Gamma, x : A \vdash x : A}$ if $x \in V^s \setminus \mathrm{dom}(\Gamma)$

(weakening) $\quad \dfrac{\Gamma \vdash A : B \qquad \Gamma \vdash C : s}{\Gamma, x : C \vdash A : B}$ if $x \in V^s \setminus \mathrm{dom}(\Gamma)$

(constant) $\quad \dfrac{\langle\rangle \vdash A : s}{\langle\rangle \vdash^n F : A}$ if $\mathcal{D}(F) = A, \mathsf{ar}(F) = n$

(product) $\quad \dfrac{\Gamma \vdash A : s' \qquad \Gamma, x : A \vdash B : s}{\Gamma \vdash (\Pi x{:}\,A.\,B) : s}$

(application) $\quad \dfrac{\Gamma \vdash^n F : (\Pi x{:}\,A.\,B) \qquad \Gamma \vdash a : A \qquad \Gamma \vdash B\{x := a\} : s}{\Gamma \vdash^{n-1} F\,a : B\{x := a\}}$

(abstraction) $\quad \dfrac{\Gamma, x : A \vdash b : B \qquad \Gamma \vdash (\Pi x{:}\,A.\,B) : s}{\Gamma \vdash \lambda x{:}A\,.\,b : \Pi x{:}\,A.\,B}$

(conversion) $\quad \dfrac{\Gamma \vdash A : B \qquad \Gamma \vdash B' : s}{\Gamma \vdash A : B'}$ if B cnv B'

Fig. 1. TYPING RULES

The typing system is the one of the Calculus of Constructions, except for the (constant) rule which is new and for the (conversion) and (application) rules that have been modified—the former to account for the parameterized (conversion) rule, the latter to ensure Correctness of Types. For most GCCs of interest, the conversion relation is substitutive and one can prove that the extra premise in the (application) rule does not affect the set of derivable judgements. For proof-irrelevant Calculi of Constructions, the conversion relation is *not* substitutive and it is important to use this modified (application) rule.

Traditionally constants are *fully applied* in legal terms. In order to enforce this requirement, the derivability relation is indexed by a natural number n. In fact, this requirement is superfluous in all cases but to prove soundness of $\mathbf{S}_{(\Sigma,\mathcal{R})}$ for $(\Sigma, \mathcal{R})$ a many-sorted term-rewriting system.

Definition 3 (Generalized Calculi of Constructions).

1. *The* derivability *relation* $\vdash^n$ *induced by a specification* $\mathbf{S} = (\mathcal{B}^*, \mathcal{B}^\square, \mathcal{D}, \mathsf{cnv})$ *is defined in Figure 1. We write* $\vdash$ *for* $\vdash^0$ *and fix* $0 - 1 = 0$.
2. *If* $\Gamma \vdash M : A$ *then* Γ, M *and* A *are* legal.
3. *The* generalized Calculus of Constructions (GCC) *induced by a specification* $\mathbf{S} = (\mathcal{B}^*, \mathcal{B}^\square, \mathcal{D}, \mathsf{cnv})$ *is the quadruple* $\lambda\mathbf{S} = (\mathcal{T}, \mathcal{G}, \vdash, \mathsf{cnv})$.

Pseudo-terms of a GCC may be organized in the usual categories of objects, constructors and kinds.

Definition 4 (Pseudo-objects, pseudo-constructors and pseudo-kinds). *The classes* $\mathcal{O}$, $\mathcal{C}$ *and* $\mathcal{K}$ *of* pseudo-objects, pseudo-constructors *and* pseudo-kinds *are given by the abstract syntaxes:*

$$\begin{aligned}
\mathcal{O} &= V^* \mid \bullet \mid \mathcal{B}^* \mid \lambda V^*{:}\mathcal{C}\,.\,\mathcal{O} \mid \lambda V^\square{:}\mathcal{K}\,.\,\mathcal{O} \mid \mathcal{O}\,\mathcal{O} \mid \mathcal{O}\,\mathcal{C} \\
\mathcal{C} &= V^\square \mid \mathcal{B}^\square \mid \Pi V{:}\mathcal{C}.\,\mathcal{C} \mid \Pi V{:}\mathcal{K}.\,\mathcal{C} \mid \lambda V^*{:}\mathcal{C}\,.\,\mathcal{C} \mid \lambda V^\square{:}\mathcal{K}\,.\,\mathcal{C} \mid \mathcal{C}\,\mathcal{C} \mid \mathcal{C}\,\mathcal{O} \\
\mathcal{K} &= * \mid \Pi V{:}\mathcal{C}.\,\mathcal{K} \mid \Pi V{:}\mathcal{K}.\,\mathcal{K}
\end{aligned}$$

We write $M \sim N$ *if* $M \in \mathcal{D} \wedge N \in \mathcal{D}$ *for some* $\mathcal{D} \in \{\mathcal{O}, \mathcal{C}, \mathcal{K}\}$.

The fundamental observation behind this paper is that all the specifications considered above introduce reduction rules at the object level.

3 Proof-irrelevance

Proof-irrelevance, as introduced by N.G. de Bruijn in [13], is the thesis that all objects are equal. Proof-irrelevance may be understood in several ways, both at the syntactic and semantical level. In this paper, we enforce proof-irrelevance through an abstract conversion relation that identifies all objects.

3.1 Proof-irrelevant specifications

This subsection introduces a proof-irrelevant conversion relation $\simeq$ which is used to define the proof-irrelevant collapse $\tilde{\mathbf{S}}$ of an arbritrary specification $\mathbf{S}$.

Definition 5.

1. *The* proof-irrelevant skeleton $|.| : \mathcal{T} \to \mathcal{T}$ *is defined inductively as follows:*

$$\begin{aligned}
|M| &= \bullet && \text{if } M \in \mathcal{O} \\
|v| &= v && \text{if } x \in V^\square \cup \mathcal{B}^\square \cup \{*, \square\} \\
|M\,N| &= |M|\,|N| && \text{if } M\,N \notin \mathcal{O} \\
|\lambda x{:}A\,.\,M| &= \lambda x{:}|A|\,.\,|M| && \text{if } \lambda x{:}A\,.\,M \notin \mathcal{O} \\
|\Pi x{:}A.\,B| &= \Pi x{:}|A|.\,|B|
\end{aligned}$$

2. *The* proof-irrelevant conversion $\simeq$ *is defined by* $M \simeq N \Leftrightarrow |M| =_\beta |N|$.
3. *The* proof-irrelevant collapse *of* $\mathbf{S} = (\mathcal{B}^*, \mathcal{B}^\square, \mathcal{D}, \mathsf{cnv})$ *is the specification* $\tilde{\mathbf{S}} = (\mathcal{B}^*, \mathcal{B}^\square, \mathcal{D}, \simeq)$.

4. *A* proof-irrelevant specification *is a specification* $\mathbf{S}$ *of the form* $(\mathcal{B}^*, \mathcal{B}^\square, \mathcal{D}, \simeq)$. *A* proof-irrelevant Calculus of Constructions (PICC) *is a* GCC $\lambda\mathbf{S}$ *such that* $\mathbf{S}$ *is a proof-irrelevant specification. The* core proof-irrelevant Calculus of Constructions (cPICC) *is the* GCC $\lambda\mathbf{S}$ *where* $\mathbf{S} = (\emptyset, \emptyset, \epsilon, \simeq)$ *and* ϵ *is the empty map.*

3.2 Meta-theoretical properties of PICC

PICCs enjoy the same meta-theoretical properties as CC itself, except for consistency which may be destroyed by the introduction of logically inconsistent constants. Interestingly, the main difficulty in developing the meta-theory of PICCs is to show the Substitution Lemma. The proof of the Substitution Lemma relies on a Classification Lemma for which the following technical notion is required.

Definition 6. *A specification* $\mathbf{S} = (\mathcal{DS}, \mathsf{cnv})$ preserves sorts *if there is no* $A \in \mathcal{C}$ *and* $B \in \mathcal{K}$ *such that* A cnv B *or* B cnv A.

Before proving classification, we prove that the proof-irrelevant conversion preserves sorts.

Lemma 1. $\simeq$ *preserves sorts.*

Proof. Define $\mathcal{U} = V \mid \mathcal{B} \mid \mathcal{U}\mathcal{U} \mid \lambda V{:}\mathcal{T}.\mathcal{U} \mid \Pi V{:}\mathcal{T}.\mathcal{U}$ and $\mathcal{W} = * \mid \Pi V{:}\mathcal{T}.\mathcal{W}$. Clearly $\mathcal{U}$ and $\mathcal{W}$ are disjoint and closed under β-reduction. Hence $M \in \mathcal{U}$ and $N \in \mathcal{W}$ implies $M \neq_\beta N$. To conclude, observe that $M \in \mathcal{C} \Rightarrow M \in \mathcal{U} \Rightarrow |M| \in \mathcal{U}$ and $N \in \mathcal{K} \Rightarrow N \in \mathcal{W} \Rightarrow |N| \in \mathcal{W}$. Hence it follows from $M \in \mathcal{C}$ and $N \in \mathcal{K}$ that $M \not\simeq N$.

We now turn to the Classification Lemma.

Theorem 1 (Classification Lemma). *If* $\mathbf{S}$ *preserves sorts and* $\Gamma \vdash M : A$ *then exactly one of the three conditions hold: (1)* $M \in \mathcal{O}$ *and* $A \in \mathcal{C}$ *(2)* $M \in \mathcal{C}$ *and* $A \in \mathcal{K}$ *(3)* $M \in \mathcal{K}$ *and* $A \equiv \square$.

Proof. Uniqueness of the conditions follows from the fact that $\mathcal{O}$, $\mathcal{C}$ and $\mathcal{K}$ are pairwise disjoint. Satisfaction of one of the condition is proved by induction on the derivation of $\Gamma \vdash M : A$.

Next we prove the Substitution Lemma for a large class of specifications.

Definition 7. *A specification* $\mathbf{S} = (\mathcal{DS}, \mathsf{cnv})$ *that preserves sorts is* substitutive *if* $M\{x := N\}$ cnv $M'\{x := N\}$ *for every* $M, M', N \in \mathcal{T}$ *and* $x \in V$ *such that* M cnv M' *and* $N \sim x$.

Lemma 2. $\simeq$ *is substitutive.*

Proof. Prove for $M, M', N \in \mathcal{T}$:

1. If $x \in V^*$ and $N \sim x$ then $|M\{x := N\}| \equiv |M|$.
2. If $\alpha \in V^\square$ and $N \sim x$ then $|M\{\alpha := N\}| \equiv |M|\{\alpha := |N|\}$.
3. If $M \simeq M'$, $x \in V$ and $N \sim x$ then $M\{x := N\} \simeq M'\{x := N\}$.

The Substitution Lemma can now be proved as usual.

Lemma 3 (Substitution). *If* S *is substitutive,* $\Gamma, x : A, \Delta \vdash B : C$ *and* $\Gamma \vdash a : A$ *then* $\Gamma, \Delta\{x := a\} \vdash B\{x := a\} : C\{x := a\}$.

Proof. By induction on the derivation of $\Gamma, x : A, \Delta \vdash B : C$.

Once the Substitution Lemma is proved, Subject Reduction is proved as for CC itself.

Proposition 1. *If* S *is proof-irrelevant,* $\Gamma \vdash M : A$ *and* $M \twoheadrightarrow_\beta N$ *then* $\Gamma \vdash N : A$.

Proof. Using Correctness of Types (which holds for all GCCs), Substitution and the Key Lemma:

$$\Pi x{:}A.\, B \simeq \Pi x{:}C.\, D \quad \Rightarrow \quad A \simeq C \quad \wedge \quad B \simeq D$$

Before turning to strong normalisation, we need a technical result. We begin with preliminary definitions.

Definition 8 (Correct reduction).

1. *A* β*-redex* $(\lambda x{:}A.\, M)\, N$ *is* correct *if* $x \sim N$.
2. *A* β*-reduction step* $M \to_\beta N$ *is* correct, *written* $M \to_{\beta_c} N$, *if it contracts a correct* β*-redex.*
3. *A pseudo-term* $M \in \mathcal{T}$ *is* correct *if all its* β*-redexes are.*

The next result states some fundamental properties of correct reductions and correct terms.

Proposition 2.

1. *If* M *is correct and* $M \to_\beta N$ *then* $|M| \to_\beta |N|$.
2. *If* $|M| \to_{\beta_c} N$*, there exists* P *such that* $M \to_{\beta_c} P$ *and* $|P| \equiv N$.
3. *If* M *is correct and* $M \to_\beta N$ *then* N *is correct and* $M \to_{\beta_c} N$.
4. *If* M *is correct then* $|M|$ *is correct.*
5. *If* M *is legal then* M *is correct.*

Proof. (1)-(4). Induction on the structure M. (5) Induction on the structure of derivations.

Note that Proposition 2.1 is not true for incorrect reductions, e.g. take $M \equiv (\lambda x{:}\bot\,.\, \alpha\, x)\, \beta$ and $N \equiv \alpha\, \beta$ where $\alpha, \beta \in V^{\Box}$, $x \in V^*$ and $\bot \equiv \Pi \alpha{:}{*}.\, {*}$.

Corollary 1.

1. *If* $|M| \twoheadrightarrow_{\beta_c} N$*, there exists* P *such that* $M \twoheadrightarrow_{\beta_c} P$ *and* $|P| \equiv N$.
2. *If* M *is legal and* $|M| \twoheadrightarrow_\beta N$ *then* $|M| \twoheadrightarrow_{\beta_c} N$.

Proof. By induction on the number of reduction steps.

Proposition 3 (Factorising $\simeq$). *If* A *and* B *are legal and* $A \simeq B$*, then there exist* $C, D \in \mathcal{T}$ *that are legal and such that* $A \twoheadrightarrow_\beta C$, $B \twoheadrightarrow_\beta D$ *and* $|C| \equiv |D|$.

Proof. Assume $A \simeq B$. Then $|A|, |B| \twoheadrightarrow_\beta E$ for some $E \in \mathcal{T}$. By Corollary 1.2, $|A|, |B| \twoheadrightarrow_{\beta_c} E$. By Corollary 1.1, there exists $C, D \in \mathcal{T}$ such that

$$A \twoheadrightarrow_\beta C \qquad B \twoheadrightarrow_\beta D \qquad |C| \equiv E \qquad |D| \equiv E$$

We conclude by symmetry and transitivity of $\equiv$.

Recall that for any reduction relation ρ, we write $\lambda\mathsf{S} \models \mathsf{SN}(\rho)$ if every legal term in $\lambda\mathsf{S}$ is ρ-strongly normalising.

Theorem 2. *If* S *is proof-irrelevant then* $\lambda\mathsf{S} \models \mathsf{SN}(\beta)$.

Proof. The model construction in [16] carries over to PICCs *textually*, to the exception of the Adequacy Lemma, embodied in Fact 3.9 of [16], which states that "$=_\beta$-convertible types or kinds have equal interpretations". In our context, we consider $\simeq$ instead of $=_\beta$ in the conversion rule so we must modify the Adequacy Lemma appropriately, i.e. we must replace "$=_\beta$-convertible types or kinds have equal interpretations" by "$\simeq$-convertible types or kinds have equal interpretations". I.e. we need to prove that if A, B are legal, $(A, B) \in (\mathcal{C} \times \mathcal{C}) \cup (\mathcal{K} \times \mathcal{K})$ and $A \simeq B$ then $[\![A]\!] = [\![B]\!]$ where the function $[\![.]\!]$ is that of [16, Definition 3.7]. By Proposition 3, it is enough to prove:

1. if $A, B \in \mathcal{C} \cup \mathcal{K}$ and $|A| \equiv |B|$ then $[\![A]\!] = [\![B]\!]$;
2. if $A, B \in \mathcal{C} \cup \mathcal{K}$ are legal and $A \to_\beta B$ then $[\![A]\!] = [\![B]\!]$.

Both properties are proved by induction on the structure of A.

One can also prove strong normalisation along the lines of [17]. Again we only need to change the Adequacy Lemma, embodied in Remark 47 and Lemma 49 of [17].

Consistency is derived from normalization and subject reduction in the usual way. For the sake of brevity, we omit a more general consistency criterion and concentrate on cPICC. In the sequel we write $\mathsf{Con}(\lambda\mathsf{S})$ if there is no $M \in \mathcal{T}$ such that $\langle\rangle \vdash M : \Pi\alpha{:}*.\,\alpha$.

Lemma 4. $\mathsf{Con}(\mathsf{cPICC})$.

Proof. Show there cannot be any closed term M in β-normal form such that $\vdash M : \Pi\alpha{:}*.\,\alpha$.

3.3 Sound specifications

The notion of specification supports a natural notion of soundness. Intuitively, a specification is sound if its proof-irrelevant collapse types more terms. To avoid confusion, we use $\vdash_{\mathsf{S}}$ and $\vdash_{\tilde{\mathsf{S}}}$ instead of $\vdash$.

Definition 9. *A specification* $\mathsf{S} = (\mathcal{B}^*, \mathcal{B}^\square, \mathcal{D}, \mathsf{cnv})$ *is* sound *if*

$$(\Gamma \vdash_{\mathsf{S}} M : A \quad \wedge \quad \Gamma \vdash_{\mathsf{S}} B : s \quad \wedge \quad A \;\mathsf{cnv}\; B) \quad \Rightarrow \quad A \simeq B$$

The above definition ensures that $\tilde{\mathsf{S}}$ indeed types more terms than S itself.

Lemma 5. *If* S *is sound, then* $\Gamma \vdash_{\mathsf{S}} M : A \quad \Rightarrow \quad \Gamma \vdash_{\tilde{\mathsf{S}}} M : A$.

Proof. By induction on the structure of derivations. The only interesting case is when the last rule is (conversion), in which case the result follows from the definition of soundness.

Corollary 2. *Let* S *be a sound specification. Then (1)* $\lambda S \models \mathsf{SN}(\beta)$ *(2) If* $\mathsf{Con}(\lambda\tilde{S})$ *then* $\mathsf{Con}(\lambda S)$.

4 Applications

The purpose of this section is to consider applications of Theorem 2 and Corollary 2. We consider direct applications and results that require further work. Since we want to illustrate the use and generality of our method, we focus on the part of the proof where our method is used.

4.1 Fixpoints

Fixpoint operators enhance otherwise terminating typed λ-calculi with the possibility to define non-terminating expressions. The motivations for studying this calculus originate from partial type theory [1, 9] and dependently typed programming languages [2].

Theorem 3. $\lambda S_{\mathsf{fix}} \models \mathsf{SN}(\beta)$.

Proof. By Corollary 2, it is enough to show that the specification is sound. To this end, note that $\rightarrow_{\beta\phi}$ is confluent and hence $=_{\beta\phi}$ preserves sorts. Moreover λS_{fix} has the Subject Reduction property so we may conclude by proving

$$\Gamma \vdash M : A \ \wedge\ M \rightarrow_{\beta\phi} N \quad \Rightarrow \quad |M| \twoheadrightarrow_{\beta} |N|$$

The proof is by induction on the structure of derivations.

See [1] for a (non-modular) model-theoretic proof of a similar result.

4.2 Algebraic rewriting

Combinations of type theory and rewriting are of interest for higher-order programming and proof-checking. A central question in this field—see e.g. [3, 7, 8, 14, 20]—is whether the combination of CC and of a terminating rewriting system R is itself terminating. Most proofs of termination of a combination of a type theory and a rewriting system consist in redoing the proof of termination of the type theory. This is unsatisfactory and one would like to have a modular *proof* of these modularity *results*, i.e. a proof that *uses but does not re-prove* the facts that the type system and the term rewriting system are terminating. In [7], F. van Raamsdonk and the author exploit Dougherty's technique of normalisation by stability [14] to provide a modular proof of the following criterion.[2]

Proposition 4 ([7]). *Let* $\Sigma = (\Lambda, \mathcal{F}, \mathsf{decl})$ *be a first-order many-sorted signature and let* $\mathcal{R}$ *be a terminating term-rewriting system over* Σ*. Let* cnv *be an equivalence relation and set* $S = (\mathcal{D}S_{\Sigma}, \mathsf{cnv})$*. Suppose that*

[2] The proposition below combines Theorems 19 and 21 of [7] and assumes cnv to be an equivalence relation so as to simplify the last condition.

1. $\lambda\mathsf{S} \models \mathsf{SN}(\beta)$,
2. *If* $\Gamma \vdash M : A$ *and* $M \rightarrow_{\beta\mathcal{R}} N$ *then* $\Gamma \vdash N : A$,
3. *If* $\sigma, \tau \in \Lambda$, σ cnv $\tau \Rightarrow \sigma \equiv \tau$.

Then $\lambda\mathsf{S} \models \mathsf{SN}(\beta\mathcal{R})$.

To apply our main result, we set cnv to be $\simeq$ and prove that $\lambda\mathsf{S}_{(\Sigma,\mathcal{R})}$ is sound. We start with some preliminary definitions.

Definition 10 (Algebraically correct term).

1. *A term* $M \in \mathcal{T}$ *is* algebraically correct *if every function symbol* $f \in \mathcal{B}^*$ *occur in subterms of the form* $f\ t_1\ \dots\ t_n$ *where* $\mathsf{ar}(f) = n$ *and* $t_1, \ \dots\ , t_n \in \mathcal{O}$.
2. *A term* $M \in \mathcal{T}$ *is* AB-correct *(algebraically β-correct) if it is both correct and algebraically correct.*

AB-correct terms enjoy important properties.

Proposition 5.

1. *If M is AB-correct and* $M \rightarrow_{\beta\mathcal{R}} N$ *then* $|M| \twoheadrightarrow_\beta |N|$ *and N is AB-correct.*
2. *Legal terms are AB-correct.*

Proof. (1) Induction on the structure of terms. (2). Induction on the structure of derivations.

Corollary 3. $\mathsf{S}_{(\Sigma,\mathcal{R})}$ *is sound.*

Proof. Assume A and B are legal and $A \downarrow_{\beta\mathcal{R}} B$. Then A and B are AB-correct and so are all their reducts. Hence $|A| \downarrow_\beta |B|$ and hence $A \simeq B$.

We conclude:

Corollary 4. *Let Σ be a first-order many-sorted signature and let $\mathcal{R}$ be a terminating term-rewriting system over Σ. Then* $\lambda\mathsf{S}_{(\Sigma,\mathcal{R})} \models \mathsf{SN}(\beta\mathcal{R})$.

Proof. By soundness, we only need to prove $\lambda\tilde{\mathsf{S}}_{(\Sigma,\mathcal{R})} \models \mathsf{SN}(\beta\mathcal{R})$. By Theorem 2 and Proposition 4, it is enough to show

1. If $\Gamma \vdash_{\tilde{\mathsf{S}}_{(\Sigma,\mathcal{R})}} M : A$ and $M \rightarrow_{\mathcal{R}} N$ then $\Gamma \vdash_{\tilde{\mathsf{S}}_{(\Sigma,\mathcal{R})}} N : A$,
2. If $\sigma, \tau \in \Lambda$, $\sigma \simeq \tau \Rightarrow \sigma \equiv \tau$.

Property 1 is proved by induction on the structure of derivations. For Property 2, notice that $\sigma \simeq \tau$ iff $|\sigma| =_\beta |\tau|$ iff $\sigma =_\beta \tau$ iff $\sigma \equiv \tau$.

F. Barbanera, M. Fernández and H. Geuvers [3] have shown that strong normalisation is a modular property of the Calculus of Constructions with higher-order rewriting $\lambda C_{\mathcal{R}}$. Unfortunately, higher-order reduction rules may create β-redexes and thus we cannot apply normalisation by stability to derive the main result of [3]. However, the proof-irrelevance technique may be used to simplify the proofs of [3]. Indeed, one can prove—as for the first-order case—that $\lambda C_{\mathcal{R}}$ is sound, so one can derive $\beta\mathcal{R}$-strong normalisation of $\lambda C_{\mathcal{R}}$ from $\beta\mathcal{R}$-strong normalisation of $\lambda\tilde{C}_{\mathcal{R}}$; the latter may be proved *textually* as in [3], apart from minor modifications to the Adequacy Lemma, see Subsection 3.2. This is a simplification, since proving $\lambda\tilde{C}_{\mathcal{R}}$ and Property (3) of Proposition 4 is easy for $\lambda\tilde{C}_{\mathcal{R}}$ and hard for $\lambda C_{\mathcal{R}}$. (These properties are needed in the proof of strong normalisation in [3].)

We conclude this subsection by showing that one cannot distinguish between closed algebraic terms of the same type.

Lemma 6. *Let $\tau \in \Lambda$. The context $x : \tau, y : \tau, p : x =_\tau y$ is consistent in $\lambda\mathsf{S}_{(\Sigma,\mathcal{R})}$.*

Proof. The proposition $\Pi x{:}\tau.\, \Pi y{:}\tau.\, x =_\tau y$ is inhabited in $\lambda\tilde{\mathsf{S}}_{(\Sigma,\mathcal{R})}$ so by Corollary 2 we only need to show that $\mathsf{Con}(\lambda\tilde{\mathsf{S}}_{(\Sigma,\mathcal{R})})$. This is clear, since one can interpret $\lambda\tilde{\mathsf{S}}_{(\Sigma,\mathcal{R})}$ in cPICC by interpreting τ_i as $\Pi\alpha{:}*.\alpha \to \alpha$ and f_j as the constant function $z \mapsto \lambda\alpha{:}*\,.\,\lambda x{:}\alpha\,.\,x$.

4.3 Inductive Types

Inductive definitions are ubiquitous in programming languages and proof-assistant systems. In this subsection, we demonstrate how Theorem 2 yields immediate proofs of strong normalisation for extensions of CC with natural numbers and Σ-types.

Theorem 4. $\lambda\mathsf{S}_{\mathsf{ac}} \models \mathsf{SN}(\beta\pi)$.

Proof. The calculus may be interpreted in a reduction-preserving fashion in cPICC. Indeed, consider the usual impredicative definition of existential quantification:

$$\begin{aligned}
\exists &\equiv \lambda\alpha : *.\ \lambda\beta : \alpha \to *.\ \Pi\gamma : *.\ (\Pi x : \alpha.\ (\beta\ x) \to \gamma) \to \gamma \\
&: \Pi\alpha{:}*.\ (\alpha \to *) \to * \\
\mathsf{fst} &\equiv \lambda\alpha : *.\ \lambda\beta : \alpha \to *.\ \lambda H : (\exists\ \alpha\ \beta).\ H\ \alpha\ \beta\ \alpha\ (\lambda x : \alpha.\ \lambda H' : \beta\ x.\ x) \\
&: \Pi\alpha : *.\ \Pi\beta : \alpha \to *.\ (\exists\ \alpha\ \beta) \to \alpha \\
\mathsf{snd} &\equiv \lambda\alpha : *.\ \lambda\beta : \alpha \to *.\ \lambda H : (\exists\ \alpha\ \beta).\ H\ \alpha\ \beta\ (\beta\ (\mathsf{fst}\ \alpha\ \beta\ H))\ (\lambda x : \alpha.\ \lambda H' : \beta\ x.\ H') \\
&: \Pi\alpha : *.\ \Pi\beta : \alpha \to *.\ \Pi H : (\exists\ \alpha\ \beta).\ \beta\ (\mathsf{fst}\ \alpha\ \beta\ H)
\end{aligned}$$

Unlike in CC, the term snd is typeable in cPICC since for every $A : *$, $B : A \to *$ and $a, a' \in A$ we have $B\ a \simeq B\ a'$. The above terms enjoy the usual reduction rules for Σ-types.

Theorem 5. $\lambda\mathsf{S}_{\mathsf{nat}} \models \mathsf{SN}(\beta\iota)$.

Proof. The calculus may be interpreted in a reduction-preserving fashion in cPICC. Indeed, consider the usual impredicative definition of natural numbers and recursion:

$$\begin{aligned}
\mathsf{Nat} &\equiv \Pi\alpha{:}*.\ \alpha \to (\alpha \to \alpha) \to \alpha && : * \\
0 &\equiv \lambda\alpha{:}*\,.\,\lambda x{:}\alpha\,.\,\lambda f{:}\alpha \to \alpha\,.\,x && : \mathsf{Nat} \\
\mathsf{S} &\equiv \lambda n{:}\mathsf{Nat}\,.\,\lambda\alpha{:}*\,.\,\lambda x{:}\alpha\,.\,\lambda f{:}\alpha \to \alpha\,.\,f\ (n\ \alpha\ x\ f) && : \mathsf{Nat} \to \mathsf{Nat} \\
\mathsf{NatE} &\equiv \lambda P{:}\mathsf{Nat} \to *\,.\,\lambda B{:}P\ 0\,.\,\lambda H{:}\Pi n{:}\mathsf{Nat}.\ (P\ n) \to (P\ (\mathsf{S}\ n))\,.\,\lambda i{:}\mathsf{Nat}\,. \\
&\qquad \mathsf{NatR}\ (P\ i)\ B\ (H\ i) \\
&\ : \Pi P{:}\mathsf{Nat} \to *.\ (P\ 0) \to (\Pi n{:}\mathsf{Nat}.\ (P\ n) \to (P\ (\mathsf{S}\ n))) \to \Pi n{:}\mathsf{Nat}.\ P\ n
\end{aligned}$$

where NatR is the usual impredicative recursor $\mathsf{NatR} : \Pi\alpha{:}*.\ \alpha \to (\mathsf{Nat} \to \alpha \to \alpha) \to \mathsf{Nat} \to \alpha$ with the reduction rules:

$$\begin{aligned}
\mathsf{NatR}\ P\ H_0\ H_s\ 0 &\twoheadrightarrow_\beta H_0 \\
\mathsf{NatR}\ P\ H_0\ H_s\ (\mathsf{S}\ n) &\twoheadrightarrow_\beta H_s\ n\ (\mathsf{NatE}\ P\ H_0\ H_s\ n)
\end{aligned}$$

for n a numeral. Again the key observation is that NatE is typeable in cPICC because for every $P : \mathsf{Nat} \to *$ and $j, k : \mathsf{Nat}$ we have $P\,i \simeq P\,j$.

Our technique also proves that CC with small Σ-types and natural numbers is $\beta\iota\pi$-strongly-normalising. More generally, one can derive directly from Theorem 2 that the fragment of the Calculus of Inductive Constructions described in [21] extended with induction principles and their corresponding reduction rules is strongly normalising. However, the technique does not handle the so-called large eliminations since they introduce computational rules at the constructor level and hence are not sound.

We now turn to logical results. First, one can deduce that proof-irrelevance and the axiom of choice do not imply classical logic in CC.

Proposition 6. *The proposition $PI \to AC \to CL$ is not inhabited in* CC*, where* $\neg\, A \equiv A \to (\Pi\alpha{:}*.\,\alpha)$ *and*

$$\begin{aligned} AC &\equiv \Pi A{:}*.\,\Pi B{:}*.\,\Pi R{:}A \to B \to *. \\ &\qquad\qquad (\exists\, y{:}B.\ R\ x\ y) \to (\exists\, f{:}A \to B.\ \Pi x{:}A.\ \ R\ x\ (f\ x)) \\ PI &\equiv \Pi A{:}*.\,\Pi x{:}A.\,\Pi y{:}A.\,x =_A y \\ CL &\equiv \Pi A{:}*.\,(\neg\neg\, A) \to A \end{aligned}$$

Proof. CC is a subsystem of cPICC and both PI and AC are inhabited in cPICC hence it is enough to show that CL is not inhabited in cPICC. Since Strong Normalisation and Subject Reduction hold, we can restrict ourselves to inhabitants in normal form. By a case analysis on the possible shape of an inhabitant of CL.

Another application of Corollary 2 is to prove the independence of Peano's fourth axiom in the absence of large eliminations.

Proposition 7. *The context* $0 =_{\mathsf{Nat}} 1$ *is consistent in* $\lambda\mathsf{S}_{\mathrm{nat}}$.

Proof. The interpretation of $\lambda\mathsf{S}_{\mathrm{nat}}$ in cPICC validates $0 =_{\mathsf{Nat}} 1$. Since cPICC is consistent, we conclude.

4.4 Classical logic

Classical typed λ-calculi, i.e. typed λ-calculi enriched with control-like structures, have received much attention since Griffin's seminal work [18]. In [6], J. Hatcliff, M.H. Sørensen and the author propose a notion of Classical Pure Type System that allows for dependent types. Our last application is concerned with one specific Classical Pure Type System, namely the Classical Calculus of Constructions $\lambda\mathsf{S}_{\mathrm{cl}}$ for which the technique of this paper leads to a proof of Strong Normalisation from which one can derive Subject Reduction. For space constraints, the proof is merely sketched. The full proof of the theorem will be reported elsewhere.

Theorem 6. $\lambda\mathsf{S}_{\mathrm{cl}} \models \mathrm{SN}(\beta\Delta)$.

Proof. (Sketch) Prove that (1) $\lambda\mathsf{S}_{\mathrm{cl}}$ is sound (2) $\Delta_2\Delta_3$-reductions on legal terms may be postponed and are strongly normalising (3) $\lambda\tilde{\mathsf{S}}_{\mathrm{cl}} \models \mathrm{SN}(\beta\Delta_1)$ by a model construction based on a variant of saturated sets.

5 Assessment and Conclusion

Proof-irrelevance provides a general technique to prove strong normalisation of Generalised Calculi of Constructions. This paper presents some basic applications of the techniques: further applications include e.g. a proof of strong normalisation for CC with Streicher's K-operator [19]. It would be interesting to apply the techniques to other GCCs, such as CC with congruence types [5] or with pattern-matching [10], and to GCCs with $\beta\eta$-conversion [15].

This paper is concerned with CC but we conjecture that the proof-irrelevance technique scales up to the more general framework of *logical* Pure Type Systems [11]. Of course, the technique will only be able to handle extensions at the object level, as for CC. The notion of Classical Pure Type System [6] provides an important motivation for this work.

Acknowledgements This work has benefited from discussions with T. Altenkirch, T. Coquand, P. Dybjer, H. Geuvers, J. Hatcliff, F. van Raamsdonk, M.H. Sørensen and P. Thiemann. The author gratefully acknowledges financial support from a TMR fellowship of the European Union.

References

1. P. Audebaud. Partial objects in the calculus of constructions. In *Proceedings of LICS'91*, pages 86–95. IEEE Computer Society Press, 1991.
2. L. Augustsson. Cayenne: Spice up your programming with dependent types. Preliminary draft, 1998.
3. F. Barbanera, M. Fernández, and H. Geuvers. Modularity of strong normalisation and confluence in the algebraic λ-cube. *Journal of Functional Programming*, November 1997.
4. H. Barendregt. Lambda calculi with types. In S. Abramsky, D. Gabbay, and T. Maibaum, editors, *Handbook of Logic in Computer Science*, pages 117–309. Oxford Science Publications, 1992. Volume 2.
5. G. Barthe and H. Geuvers. Congruence types. In H. Kleine Buening, editor, *Proceedings of CSL'95*, volume 1092 of *Lecture Notes in Computer Science*, pages 36–51. Springer-Verlag, 1996.
6. G. Barthe, J. Hatcliff, and M.H. Sørensen. A notion of classical pure type system. In *Proceedings of MFPS'97*, volume 6 of *Electronic Notes in Theoretical Computer Science*. Elsevier, 1997.
7. G. Barthe and F. van Raamsdonk. Termination of algebraic type systems: the syntactic approach. In M. Hanus and J. Heering, editors, *Proceedings of ALP '97 - HOA '97*, volume 1298 of *Lecture Notes in Computer Science*, pages 174–193. Springer-Verlag, 1997.
8. V. Breazu-Tannen. Combining algebra and higher-order types. In *Proceedings of LICS'88*, pages 82–90. IEEE Computer Society Press, 1988.
9. R.L. Constable and S.F. Smith. Partial objects in constructive type theory. In *Proceedings of LICS'87*, pages 183–193. IEEE Computer Society Press, 1987.
10. T. Coquand. Pattern matching in type theory. In B. Nordström, editor, *Informal proceedings of LF'92*, pages 66–79, 1992.
11. T. Coquand and H. Herbelin. A-translation and looping combinators in pure type systems. *Journal of Functional Programming*, 4(1):77–88, January 1994.

12. T. Coquand and G. Huet. The Calculus of Constructions. *Information and Computation*, 76(2/3):95–120, February/March 1988.
13. N.G. de Bruijn. Some extensions of Automath: the AUT-4 family. In R. Nederpelt, H. Geuvers, and R. de Vrijer, editors, *Selected papers on Automath*, volume 133 of *Studies in Logic and the Foundations of Mathematics*, pages 283–288. North-Holland, Amsterdam, 1994.
14. D. Dougherty. Adding algebraic rewriting to the untyped lambda calculus. *Information and Computation*, 101(2):251–267, December 1992.
15. H. Geuvers. The Church-Rosser property for $\beta\eta$-reduction in typed λ-calculi. In *Proceedings of LICS'92*, pages 453–460. IEEE Computer Society Press, 1992.
16. H. Geuvers. A short and flexible proof of strong normalisation for the Calculus of Constructions. In P. Dybjer, B. Nordström, and J. Smith, editors, *Proceedings of TYPES'94*, volume 996 of *Lecture Notes in Computer Science*, pages 14–38. Springer-Verlag, 1995.
17. H. Geuvers and M.J. Nederhof. A modular proof of strong normalisation for the Calculus of Constructions. *Journal of Functional Programming*, 1(2):155–189, April 1991.
18. T. Griffin. A formulae-as-types notion of control. In *Proceedings of POPL'90*, pages 47–58. ACM Press, 1990.
19. M. Hofmann and T. Streicher. The groupoid model refutes uniqueness of identity proofs. In *Proceedings of LICS'94*, pages 208–212. IEEE Computer Society Press, 1994.
20. J.-P. Jouannaud and M. Okada. Abstract data type systems. *Theoretical Computer Science*, 173(2):349–391, February 1997.
21. F. Pfenning and C. Paulin. Inductively defined types in the calculus of constructions. In M. Main, A. Melton, M. Mislove, and D. Schmidt, editors, *Proceedings of MFPS'89*, volume 442 of *Lecture Notes in Computer Science*, pages 209–228. Springer-Verlag, 1989.

New Horizons in Quantum Information Processing

Gilles Brassard[1]*

Université de Montréal, brassard@iro.umontreal.ca

Abstract. This elementary talk will survey some of the striking new potential applications of quantum mechanics for information processing purposes. No previous acquaintance with quantum mechanics will be expected from the audience.

1 Introduction

Quantum mechanics, which is perhaps the most successful scientific theory of the 20th century, teaches us that things do not behave at the scale of elementary particles the way we are used to in our misleading macroscopic experience. Classical information theory is a very fruitful branch of mathematics, but it is as firmly rooted in classical physics as is computer science. This has prevented us from tapping the full potential of physical reality for information processing purposes. Quantum information is very different from its everyday classical counterpart: it cannot be read without disturbance, it cannot be copied or broadcast at all, but it can exist in superposition of classical states. Classical and quantum information can perform feats together that neither could achieve alone, such as quantum cryptography, quantum computing and quantum teleportation.

Quantum cryptography exploits the unavoidable disturbance caused by any attempt at measuring quantum information to implement a cryptographic system that allows two people to communicate in absolute secrecy under the nose of an eavesdropper equipped with unlimited computing power.

Quantum computers take advantage of the superposition principle to allow exponentially many computations to be performed simultaneously in a single piece of hardware. The use of constructive and destructive interference in computational patterns can be used to boost the probability of observing the desired result much faster than would be possible by a classical computing device. In particular, this technique threatens many of the classical cryptographic schemes currently in use to protect confidential information.

Quantum teleportation is a process that allows the transmission of quantum information over classical channels, provided sender and receiver have had previous access to a quantum channel. The technique can be made to work with arbitrarily high fidelity even if the prior quantum channel is imperfect, sometimes even if the quantum noise is too severe to allow using quantum error correction schemes for reliable quantum transmission.

---

* Supported in part by Canada's NSERC, Québec's FCAR and the Canada Council.

To the best of my knowledge, only one book has been published so far on quantum information processing [12], but several others are currently being written, including my own [7]. The availability of such books will make it much easier for motivated computer scientists to enter the field. In the mean time, you are encouraged to read some of the many survey papers that have been written on the subject [1,2,5,6, etc.] and browse the web at URL `http://xxx.lanl.gov/archive/quant-ph` if you wish to stay at the cutting edge.

2 Towards New Horizons

Until recently, most of the ideas behind quantum information processing were still the stuff of dreams. A notable exception is quantum cryptography, which has been known for years to work well in practice over tens of kilometres of optical fibre [8]. More recently, in an impressive new development, quantum cryptography has been shown to work over one kilometre of free space (no wave guides) outside the laboratory [11], and quantum cryptography by satellites is being seriously considered.

In the past year, a number of exciting experiments have shown that many of the other quantum dreams may also become reality faster than previously anticipated. Quantum teleportation has been implemented [4,3], although not yet over large distances and time scales. Small versions of some of the most important quantum algorithms have also been implemented in the laboratory, such as the Deutsch–Jozsa algorithm [10] and Grover's quantum search algorithm [9]. Effort is currently underway to implement other quantum algorithms on a small scale, such as Shor's factoring algorithm. The number of international laboratories dedicated to the study of various implementation approaches (ion traps, nuclear magnetic resonance, quantum electrodynamics, etc.) to quantum computation in particular and quantum information processing in general, as well as the sky-rocketing number of international conferences and workshops dedicated to the subject, are clear indication that the field is teeming with enthusiasm and optimism. Where does the horizon really lie? Future will tell.

References

1. Barenco, A., "Quantum physics and computers", *Contemporary Physics*, Vol. 38, 1996, pp. 357 – 389.
2. Berthiaume, A, "Quantum computation", in *Complexity Theory Retrospective II*, L. A. Hemaspaandra and A. L. Selman (editors), Springer–Verlag, New York, 1997.
3. Boschi, D., S. Branca, F. De Martini, L. Hardy and S. Popescu, "Experimental realization of teleporting an unknown pure quantum state via dual classical and Einstein-Podolsky-Rosen channels", *Physical Review Letters*, Vol. 80, no. 6, 9 February 1998, pp. 1121 – 1125.
4. Bouwmeester, D., Jian–Wei Pan, K. Mattle, M. Eibl, H. Weinfurter and A. Zeilinger, "Experimental quantum teleportation", *Nature*, Vol. 390, no. 6660, 11 December 1997, pp. 575 – 579.

5. Brassard, G., "A quantum jump in computer science", in *Computer Science Today*, Jan van Leeuwen (editor), Lecture Notes in Computer Science, Vol. 1000, Springer–Verlag, 1995, pp. 1 – 14.
6. Brassard, G., "New trends in quantum computing", *13th Annual Symposium on Theoretical Aspects of Computer Science - — STACS '96*, February 1996, Lecture Notes in Computer Science, Vol. 1046, Springer–Verlag, pp. 3 – 10.
7. Brassard, G., *Quantum Information Processing for Computer Scientists*, MIT Press, in preparation.
8. Brassard, G. and C. Crépeau, "25 years of quantum cryptography", *Sigact News*, Vol. 27, no. 3, pp. 13 – 24, 1996.
9. Chuang, I. L., N. Gershenfeld and M. Kubinec, "Experimental implementation of fast quantum searching", *Physical Review Letters*, Vol. 80, no. 15, 13 April 1998, pp. 3408 – 3411.
10. Chuang, I. L., L. M. K. Vandersypen, X. Zhou, D. W. Leung and S. Lloyd, "Experimental realization of a quantum algorithm", *Nature*, 1998, in press. Available on Los Alamos e-print archive as `quant-ph/9801037`.
11. Hughes, R. J., W. T. Buttler, P. G. Kwiat, S. K. Lamoreaux, G. G. Luther, G. L. Morgan, J. E. Nordholt, C. G. Peterson and C. M. Simmons, "Practical free-space quantum cryptography", *Proceedings of the First NASA Quantum Communications and Quantum Computation Conference*, February 1998, Lecture Notes in Computer Science, Springer–Verlag, in press; Los Alamos report LA-UR-98-1272. Earlier free-space experiment described in *Physical Review A*, Vol. 57, no. 4, pp. 2379 – 2382, April 1998.
12. Williams, C. P. and S. H. Clearwater, *Explorations in Quantum Computing*, Springer–Verlag, New York, 1998.

Sequential Iteration of Interactive Arguments and an Efficient Zero-Knowledge Argument for NP

Ivan Damgård[1] and Birgit Pfitzmann[2]

Abstract. We study interactive arguments, in particular their error probability under sequential iteration. This problem is more complex than for interactive proofs, where the error trivially decreases exponentially in the number of iterations.
In particular, we study the typical efficient case where the iterated protocol is based on a single instance of a computational problem. This is not a special case of independent iterations of an entire protocol, and real exponential decrease of the error cannot be expected. Nevertheless, for practical applications, one needs concrete relations between the complexity and error probability of the underlying problem and the iterated protocol. We formalize and solve this problem using the theory of proofs of knowledge. We also seem to present the first definition of arguments in a fully uniform model of complexity.
We also prove that in non-uniform complexity, the error probability of independent iterations of an argument does decrease exponentially – to our knowledge this is the first result about a strictly exponentially small error probability in a computational cryptographic security property.
To illustrate our first result, we present a very efficient zero-knowledge argument for circuit satisfiability, and thus for any NP problem, based on any collision-intractable hash function.

1 Introduction

1.1 Background

An interactive argument, also called a computationally convincing proof system, is a protocol in which a polynomial-time bounded prover tries to convince a verifier that a given statement is true, typically a statement of the form $x \in L$ for a word x and a language L. Interactive arguments were introduced in various conference papers finally merged into [1].

Compared to interactive proof systems [15, 16], arguments require only that polynomial-time provers cannot cheat with significant probability, whereas interactive proofs guarantee this for all provers. On the other hand they enjoy some advantages: Under reasonable computational assumptions, *perfect* zero-knowledge arguments can be constructed for any NP-language [1], i.e., the zero-knowledge property holds not only against polynomial-time verifiers; this is (probably) not possible for proof systems [11]. Moreover, in order to cheat in an argument, the prover must break the underlying computational assumption *before* the protocol ends, whereas the zero-knowledge property of a computational zero-knowledge proof system can also be broken at any later time.

Traditionally, e.g., in [1] (but see later for some exceptions), the notion of arguments seems to have been to modify the definition of proof systems from

[1] Aarhus University, BRICS (Basic Research in Computer Science, center of the Danish National Research Foundation)

[2] Universität des Saarlandes, Saarbrücken, Fachbereich Informatik

[15] by no longer allowing cheating provers unlimited computing resources, and to require that the success probability of cheating provers is *negligible*, i.e., decreases asymptotically faster than the inverse of any polynomial. Even this is not completely trivial to formalize (see Section 3), but we take it as a starting point for the moment.

Many constructions of interactive arguments and proofs start from an atomic step, in which the prover can cheat with at most some (large) probability ϵ, e.g., 1/2, under a computational assumption. This step is then iterated to reduce the error probability. For interactive proof systems, it is easy to see that the error probability of m such sequential iterations is ϵ^m. The same is true for parallel iterations, although this is somewhat less trivial to see [3]. For arguments, the problem is more complex. Bellare et al. show in [5] that parallel iteration for some types of what they call computationally sound protocols fails completely to reduce the error. On the positive side, they show that parallel iteration of arguments with at most 3 rounds reduces the error in the way one might expect: it goes down exponentially until it becomes negligible.

1.2 Our Work

The research reported here started by the observation that from the results of [9, 10, 1, 18], we could construct a very efficient statistical zero-knowledge argument for circuit satisfiability (see section 7). Its soundness can be based on any family of collision-intractable hash functions [7]. In typical practical cases, its complexity improves on the best previously known SAT protocols [6, 17]; moreover our intractability assumption is weaker. In practice, if we use a standard hash function and go for an error probability of 2^{-50}, the protocol can process 20000 binary gates per second on a standard PC. To the best of our knowledge, this makes it the computationally most efficient SAT protocol proposed.

The protocol consists of sequential iteration of a basic step, and to prove its soundness it seemed useful to consider sequential iteration of arguments generally. There are several reasons for doing this in some detail:

- The exact exponential decrease of the error probability for independent sequential iterations does extend from interactive proofs to arguments, but only if we allow cheating provers to be non-uniform. This is not hard to prove, but interesting because we are not aware of any previous proof that a computational security property has an exponentially (in contrast to just negligibly) small error probability (under the usual cryptologic assumptions). The uniform case is more complicated, as detailed below. No general sequential iteration lemma for arguments seems to have appeared in the literature.
- Although there are several definitions of arguments in the literature, it seems there is no previous treatment in a fully uniform model.
- Most iterated arguments in the literature (including [1] and ours) do not use *independent* iterations; instead the soundness of all iterations is based on a single instance of a computational problem. In practice this is more efficient than choosing a new instance for every step, and may even be the only option: if one wants to base a protocol on standard hash functions such as SHA-1 [19], there is only one instance. Note that this scenario is not a special case of independent iterations.

– For a practical application, asymptotic results are not enough. The basis for security is typically a concrete hard problem instance, such as a collision-intractable hash function or a large integer that should be hard to factor. The protocol designer is likely to ask "If I assume that this particular hash function cannot be broken in time T with probability ϵ, and I'm happy with error probability δ, how much time would an enemy need to break my protocol?" For this, the concrete complexity of reductions is important. We focus on this in the following.

In this version of the paper, several proofs have been omitted or sketched due to space limitations. A full version is available on-line [8].

2 Independent Iterations in the Non-uniform Model

Our model of uniform feasible computation is probabilistic polynomial-time interactive Turing machines [15]. For non-uniform computation, we use probabilistic polynomial-time interactive Turing machines with polynomial advice. This means that the machine obtains an additional "advice" input which is a function of the length n of the normal input, and whose length is polynomial in n. [3] For the non-uniform case, we use the following precise definition of arguments:

Definition 2.1 (Interactive arguments, non-uniform) *Let L be a language, (P, V) a pair of probabilistic polynomial-time interactive algorithms with a common input x, and $\epsilon : \{0,1\}^* \rightarrow [0,1]$ a function. We say that (P, V) is an* interactive argument for L in the non-uniform model with soundness error ϵ *if it has the following properties:*

- *Completeness: If $x \in L$ and P is given an appropriate auxiliary input (depending on x), the probability that V rejects is negligible in $|x|$.*
- *Soundness: For any non-uniform probabilistic polynomial-time algorithm P^* (a cheating prover), there is at most a finite number of values $x \notin L$ such that V accepts in interaction with P^* on input x with probability larger than $\epsilon(x)$.*

One can refine this definition by letting the level of security be determined by special security parameters, instead of the input length. One would typically use two such parameters, one for computational aspects and one for the tolerated error probability. This was omitted here for brevity and similarity with other definitions.

We now formally define sequential compositions and a view of them as game trees that will be used in most of the proofs.

Definition 2.2 (Iteration and proof trees) *If (P, V) is an interactive argument and $m : \mathbb{N} \rightarrow \mathbb{N}$ a polynomial-time computable function, the m-fold iteration or sequential composition is the pair of algorithms (P^m, V^m) which, on input x, execute P or V, respectively, $m(|x|)$ times sequentially and independently. V^m accepts if all its executions of V accept. Typically, m is a constant*

[3] It is well-known that this is equivalent to using circuit complexity. In particular, a polynomial-size circuit family can be simulated by a polynomial-time Turing machine with the description of the circuit for the given input length n as advice input.

or the identity function (i.e., the number of iterations equals the input length, which serves as the security parameter).

Cheating provers are denoted by P^{m*}*; this notation only means that this is a non-uniform probabilistic polynomial-time algorithm that can interact with* V^m*.*

The proof tree *for* V^m*, such a* P^{m*}*, and a fixed common input* x *has a node for each state that* P^{m*} *may be in just before an iteration of* V*. A node has an outgoing edge for each possible set of random choices that* P^{m*} *and* V *might make in the following iteration; if* V *rejects in the iteration with this set of random choices, we truncate off the corresponding edge.*

For this non-uniform case, we can show the following theorem about strictly exponential decrease of the error probability.

Theorem 2.3 *Let* (P, V) *be an interactive argument for a language* L *in the non-uniform model with soundness error* ϵ*, and* m *a polynomial-time computable function. Then* (P^m, V^m) *is an interactive argument for* L *with soundness error* ϵ^m*, i.e., the function that maps* x *to* $\epsilon(x)^{m(|x|)}$*.*

Proof (Sketch) Assume, for contradiction, that there were a non-uniform probabilistic polynomial-time prover P^{m*} and an infinite number of values $x \notin L$ such that V^m accepts in interaction with P^{m*} on input x with probability larger than $\epsilon(x)^{m(|x|)}$. Considering the proof tree corresponding to the interaction with P^{m*} on such an x, one can easily show that there must be a node where the number of not truncated sons is at least a fraction ϵ of the potential number of sons. We can then build a prover convincing V in one iteration with probability larger than ϵ by giving it this node as advice. □

3 Uniform Definitions

To get a definition of arguments involving uniform provers, it seems natural to take Definition 2.1 and replace the word "non-uniform" in the soundness by "uniform". We assume that this is what the authors of [1] had in mind, and it comprises the language-recognition case of [5]. The equivalence of several such definitions is proved in [4]. (In contrast, the similar-looking definitions for negligible and constant error in [12] are fully non-uniform because the cheating prover has an auxiliary input like the honest prover, which he can also use as advice function.) However, even to prove the seemingly uniform soundness where cheating provers have no auxiliary inputs, one will usually need a stronger, *non-uniform* complexity assumption. This is basically because the existence of a cheating prover contradicting the definition only guarantees that instances on which the verifier can be fooled *exist*, not that they can be *generated efficiently* to be exploited in a reduction proof. In other words, the common input itself can serve as advice function to break the underlying problem (see [8] and similar considerations for definitions of zero-knowledge in [13]).

Thus we propose a fully uniform definition. It contains a polynomial-time message finder like definitions of the secrecy in encryption schemes [14]. We can leave completeness unchanged for our purposes; in practice one might additionally require a probabilistic polynomial-time algorithm that generates instances together with the appropriate auxiliary input.

Definition 3.1 (Interactive arguments, uniform) *Let L be a language, (P, V) a pair of probabilistic polynomial-time interactive algorithms with a common input x, and $\epsilon : \mathbb{N} \to [0,1]$ a function. We say that (P, V) is an* interactive argument for L in the uniform model with soundness error ϵ *if it has the following properties:*

- *Completeness: If $x \in L$ and P is given an appropriate auxiliary input (depending on x), the probability that V rejects is negligible in $|x|$.*
- *Soundness: A cheating prover is modeled by two probabilistic polynomial-time algorithms M^* and P^*, called message finder and main prover. The input for M^* is a security parameter k, and its output should be a value $x \notin L$ of length k and a value $view_{M^*}$. We consider the joint probability distribution if first M^* is run on input k, and then V on input x interacts with P^* on input $(x, view_{M^*})$.*
  The soundness requirement is that for any such pair (M^*, P^*), there exists at most a finite number of integers k such that the probability (in the distribution just defined) that $|x| = k$, $x \notin L$, and that V accepts is larger than $\epsilon(k)$.

The definition and results in the following sections are all phrased in the uniform model. The results and proofs carry over easily to non-uniform provers, using essentially the same reductions.

4 Definition of Fixed-Instance Arguments

We now consider the case where the soundness of the entire iterated protocol is based on a single instance of a computational problem, which is chosen by the verifier initially. In this case, it is clear that the error probability cannot decrease strictly exponentially in the number of iterations, even in the non-uniform model, because it always suffices to break the one given instance.

The intuition behind the term "based on an instance of a problem" is that if a prover can convince the verifier on input $x \notin L$ with probability greater than some ϵ, the prover can solve the problem instance. We call such a definition *relative* (to the hardness of the underlying problem) and the definitions presented so far *absolute* in comparison. To capture what it means that the prover "can solve" the problem instance, we use the theory of proofs of knowledge. We do not claim that the resulting definition covers any conceivable argument where some part is iterated while another is kept constant, but it covers all known examples of what people have understood by basing an iteration on one problem instance.

We briefly recall the definition from [2] of a proof of knowledge, with minor modifications to match our context. For any binary relation R, let $R(z)$ be the set of y's such that $(z, y) \in R$, and $L_R = \{z | \; R(z) \neq \emptyset\}$.

Definition 4.1 (Proof of knowledge) *Let R be a binary relation, and $\kappa : \{0,1\}^* \to [0,1]$. Let V be a probabilistic polynomial-time interactive Turing machine. We say that V is a* knowledge verifier for R with knowledge error κ *if the following two conditions hold:*

- *Non-triviality (completeness): There is a prover P such that V always accepts in interaction with P for all inputs $z \in L_R$.*

– *Validity (soundness): There is a probabilistic oracle machine K (the universal knowledge extractor) and a constant c such that for every prover P^* and every $z \in L_R$, the following holds:*
  Let $p(z)$ be the probability that V accepts on input z in interaction with P^*. Now if $p(z) > \kappa(z)$, then on input z and access to the oracle P_z^* (P^* with fixed input z), the extractor K outputs a string in $R(z)$ within an expected number of steps bounded by

$$\frac{|z|^c}{p(z) - \kappa(z)}.$$

By having access to the oracle P_z^*, we mean the possibility to reset it to a previous state, including the state of the random tape. Cheating provers are not restricted to polynomial time in the soundness condition. However, their running time comes in as a linear factor in the time needed for extraction because each step of K might be an oracle call.

This definition makes no statement about the case $z \notin L_R$, e.g., it allows P to "convince" V that it knows a non-trivial factor of a prime. This is ok in our application where V will choose $z \in L_R$.

We now define soundness of an interactive argument based on the prover's presumed inability to solve a fixed instance of a computational problem. We model this problem by a relation R as described above, and the definition describes the idea that the prover can only argue something false by instead proving knowledge of a solution to the given problem instance from R. In order to get one uniform extractor, and not a different one for each value x, we include the values x in the relation.

Definition 4.2 (Interactive arguments, relative) *Let L be a language, R a binary relation, $\sigma : \{0,1\}^* \to [0,1]$, and (P, V) a pair of probabilistic polynomial-time interactive Turing machines, taking two common inputs x and z. We say that (P, V) is an* interactive argument for L with soundness error σ relative to R *if it has the following properties:*

– *Completeness: If $x \in L$ and $z \in L_R$, and P is given an appropriate auxiliary input (depending on x), the probability that V rejects on input (x, z) when interacting with P is negligible in the minimum of $|x|$ and $|z|$.*
– *Soundness relative to R: We require that V satisfies the validity condition of Definition 4.1 with knowledge error σ, considered as a knowledge verifier for the relation*
$$R' = \{((x, z), y) | x \notin L, (z, y) \in R\}.$$

We now show that this relative definition implies the absolute definition of soundness if the underlying problem is indeed hard.

Proposition 4.3 *Let (P, V) be an interactive argument for L relative to R with negligible soundness error σ. Let gen be a polynomial-time algorithm that, given a security parameter k, chooses an element $z \in L_R$ with $|z| \geq k$ and such that one assumes that no probabilistic polynomial-time algorithm F, on input (k, z), can find $y \in R(z)$ with more than negligible probability (in k).*

Let (P_1, V_1) be the protocol with common input x where the verifier first chooses z using gen$(|x|)$, and then (P, V) is run on input (x, z). Then (P_1, V_1) is an interactive argument for L according to Definition 3.1.

Proof (Sketch) Assume that a pair (M_1^*, P_1^*) contradicting soundness exists. Now, given an instance (k, z) of our hard problem, we first run M_1^* to obtain an input x where V_1 is hopefully fooled with non-negligible probability. Then we run the knowledge extractor guaranteed by Definition 4.2 for a certain polynomial number of steps, answering its oracle questions using P_1^* with input $(x, view_{M^*})$ and giving it z in the first step. Since the knowledge error is negligible and the success probability of P_1^* is not, we find a solution to z with more than negligible probability. □

5 Iteration in the Fixed-Instance Case

Bellare and Goldreich show in [2] that the knowledge error for a protocol iterated sequentially decreases almost exponentially with the number of iterations:

Theorem 5.1 *Let V be a knowledge verifier for relation R with soundness error κ. Assume that an element $y \in R(z)$ can be found in time $2^{l(z)}$ for any $z \in L_R$, where l is at most polynomial. Then the interactive algorithm V^m consisting of $m(|z|)$ independent sequential iterations of V on the same input z is a knowledge verifier for relation R with knowledge error $(1 + 1/l)\kappa^m$ (where l, κ, and m are all functions of z).*

By the relative definition of interactive arguments, this immediately implies that the soundness error of the m-fold iteration of such an argument on the same input (x, z), i.e., with a fixed instance, decreases in exactly the same way.

In [2], the question was raised of whether the factor $(1+1/l)$ can be removed. We show that this is possible in an important class of special cases. More importantly, we also provide a tighter reduction. The special cases are defined as follows:

Definition 5.2 (Sharp threshold extractor) *Let K be a knowledge extractor for knowledge verifier V and relation R. The machine K is called a* sharp threshold extractor *if the following is satisfied: for any deterministic prover P^* that on input z convinces V with probability larger than $\kappa(z)$, K using P_z^* as oracle runs in an expected number $f(|z|)$ of steps for some fixed polynomial f.*

Many, if not all known proofs of knowledge that one wants to iterate in practice have sharp threshold extractors. For example, consider a 3-round protocol where, in the second round, the verifier asks the prover one out of a polynomial number t of questions, and where the knowledge can be computed in polynomial time from correct answers to more than $g < t$ questions. Such a protocol has knowledge error g/t and a sharp threshold extractor, because any deterministic prover who convinces the verifier with probability greater than g/t must be able to answer at least $g + 1$ fixed questions, all of which can be found in polynomial time by rewinding the prover (at most t times). A related notion, but only for negligible error probabilities, has independently been proposed as "strong proofs of knowledge" in the updates of [12].

Theorem 5.3 *Let V be a knowledge verifier for relation R with knowledge error κ. Assume that there is a sharp threshold extractor for V. Then the interactive algorithm V^m consisting of $m(|z|)$ independent sequential iterations of V on the same input z is a knowledge verifier for relation R with knowledge error κ^m.*

Proof We fix an input z, so let $m(|z|) = m$ and $\kappa(z) = \kappa$. Let a be the maximum number of random bits consumed by V during one iteration and $t = 2^a$. Clearly, t is the maximal number of distinct interactions that could take place between V and any fixed deterministic prover. Let g be the maximal integer with $g/t \leq \kappa$.

Fix an arbitrary prover P^{m*} convincing V^m on input z with probability $p > \kappa^m$. Let $P^{m*}(r)$ denote P^{m*} with a specific random tape r and $p(r)$ the probability that $P^{m*}(r)$ convinces V^m.

We consider the proof tree for V^m, $P^{m*}(r)$, and z. The edges out of a node correspond to the t possible values of V's random choices in that execution, but those for which V rejects are deleted. A level i is the set of nodes at a fixed distance i from the root. The nodes in level m, which correspond to final acceptance by V, are called endnodes and their number is called *end*. In our case,

$$end = p(r)t^m. \qquad (1)$$

A node is said to be *good* (for the extractor) if it has more than g children. Let $Good_i$ be the number of good nodes in level i. We can show (by induction on the maximum i with $Good_i \neq 0$) that for all trees, the number of endnodes is

$$end \leq g^m + \sum_{i=0}^{m-1} (t-g)g^{m-i-1} Good_i. \qquad (2)$$

The overall strategy for the knowledge extractor is to find a good node as quickly as possible, basically by trying random nodes of random trees. Formula (2) gives a lower bound on the number of good nodes, except that the summation is weighted according to the level of the node. We will therefore not try levels uniformly, but choose each level i with a probability p_i that makes the most of the weighted sum: For $i = 0, ..., m-1$, let

$$p_i = t^i g^{m-i-1} p_{min}, \quad \text{where } p_{min} = \frac{t-g}{g^m((t/g)^m - 1)}.$$

It is easy to verify that these probabilities add up to 1. Now consider the following algorithm for a knowledge extractor for V^m:

Repeat the following loop until an element in $R(z)$ has been found:

1. Choose the random tape r for P^{m*} uniformly, and choose a level i, using the probability distribution $p_0, ..., p_{m-1}$.
2. Try to select a node in level i by simulating the protocol, i.e., running the algorithm V^m (with new random choices each time) and using the oracle $P_z^{m*}(r)$. If V^m rejects before we reach level i, go back to step 1. (This means selecting one of the t^i potential nodes in level i with uniform probability; it is reached iff it is in fact in the tree.)
3. Run the sharp threshold extractor K for this node, hoping that it is a good node. This means that we answer K's oracle queries by rewinding $P_z^{m*}(r)$ to the situation after step 2 each time. If K outputs an element in $R(z)$ within $2f(|z|)$ steps, where f is the polynomial guaranteed by Definition 5.2, output this element and stop. Else, go to step 1.

Let $p^*(r)$ be the probability that we reach step 3 with a good node for a specific r. We can bound $p^*(r)$ using formulas (1) and (2) and the definition of the p_i's (details omitted here):

$$p^*(r) \geq p(r) - \kappa^m.$$

The overall probability p^* that we reach step 3 with a good node is therefore at least $p - \kappa^m$.

If we reach step 3 with a good node, K succeeds in expected $f(|z|)$ steps, because running $P_z^{m*}(r)$ with a fixed starting state for one iteration is a valid oracle for K and V accepts in good nodes with probability at least $(g+1)/t \geq \kappa$. The probability that K runs for more than twice its expected number of steps is at most 1/2 by Markov's rule. Hence the expected number of times we restart the loop from step 1 is at most $2/(p - \kappa^m)$, and the number of steps each time is clearly polynomial. □

Corollary 5.4 *Let (P, V) be an interactive argument for language L with soundness error σ relative to R. Assume that there is a sharp threshold extractor for V, considered as knowledge verifier for the relation R' from Definition 4.2. Then the protocol (P^m, V^m) consisting of $m(|z|)$ independent sequential iterations of (P, V) on the same input (x, z) is an interactive argument for language L with soundness error σ^m relative to R.*

Let us elaborate a little on what this result means in practice. It does not say that a prover *cannot* cheat with probability better than σ^m. But we can say how much computing resources he would need to reach any given goal above σ^m: In the reduction in the above proof, doing the loop once corresponds to emulating at most one run of all m iterations, plus running the knowledge extractor for at most $2f(|z|)$ steps, which may include oracle calls. Hence we get:

Corollary 5.5 *With the notation and assumption as in Corollary 5.4: Any prover P^{m*} that makes the verifier accept all m iterations with probability $p(z) > \sigma(z)^m$ can be converted into an algorithm that finds an element in $R(z)$ in expected time*

$$2\frac{T_{P^{m*}}(z)(1 + 2f(|z|)) + mT_V(z)}{p(z) - \sigma(z)^m},$$

where $T_{P^{m*}}(\cdot)$ and $T_V(\cdot)$ are the running times of P^{m*} and V, respectively.

For the common case of protocols where the verifier only asks one out of a constant number t of questions, the factor $(1 + 2f(|z|))$ of $T_{P^{m*}}(z)$ in the denominator becomes $(1 + t)$. Thus the running time of P^{m*} contributes only by a linear term, implying a very tight connection between the time needed to cheat V^m and the time needed to break the computational assumption.

6 Independent Iterations in the Uniform Model

For completeness, we now briefly consider the remaining case, independent iterations in the uniform model.

Proposition 6.1 *Let (P, V) be an interactive argument for a language L (according to Definition 3.1) with constant soundness error $c < 1$. Then (P^m, V^m), the protocol consisting of $m(|x|) = |x|$ independent sequential iterations of (P, V) on the same input x, is an interactive argument for L with negligible soundness error.*

Proof (Sketch) The proof is very similar to the one for the fixed-instance case, and so is omitted here. □

7 An Efficient Zero-Knowledge Argument for NP

In this section we present an efficient statistical zero-knowledge argument for (Boolean) circuit satisfiability, and hence for any NP problem, by the NP completeness of circuit-SAT and standard reductions. The protocol can be based on the existence of collision-intractable hash functions, i.e., easily computable functions that map inputs of (in principle) any length to a fixed length output, and for which it is hard to find collisions, i.e., different inputs mapped to the same output. Our construction combines three ingredients:

- The unconditionally hiding multi-bit commitment scheme from [9, 10], based on any collision-intractable hash function family H. The receiver of the commitments chooses a hash function $h \in H$ with output length $k + 1$, where k is a security parameter. (The choice is made once and for all, and the functions have short descriptions.) An m-bit string can then be committed to by a non-interactive commitment of length $k + 1$ bits and opened by sending $10(k + 1)$ bits, plus the m bits of the string itself. The scheme guarantees that a commitment to x only reveals an exponentially small (in k) amount of Shannon information about x, and that any method for making a commitment and opening it in two different ways easily leads to a collision for h.
- The BCC protocol [1] for showing that a circuit is satisfiable. It works based on any bit commitment scheme for single bits and is a perfect/statistical zero-knowledge argument, if the commitments used are perfect/statistically hiding. The basic step of the protocol is that the prover commits to $O(m)$ bits, where m is the size of the circuit, and depending on a 1-bit challenge from the verifier, the prover either opens all the bits or a specific subset depending on the satisfying assignment.
- The method from [18] for using a multi-bit commitment scheme in any protocol of a type they call "subset-revealing", of which the BCC protocol is an example. This method works even if the commitment scheme does not allow opening individual bits in a multi-bit commitment. The method replaces each basic step of the original protocol by a new one which contains 2 commitments to $O(m)$ bits each instead of $O(m)$ commitments to 1 bit each. If making and opening commitments is non-interactive, it needs 5 rounds instead of 3, and the verifier only sends 1 bit each in round 2 and 4. If the prover could cheat in the old basic step with probability at most 1/2, he can cheat in the new one with probability at most 3/4 (without breaking the computational assumption).

Let (P, V) denote the protocol that takes as common input a circuit C and a hash function $h \in H$, and executes one basic step obtained by combining these three ingredients in the natural way. Iterations are then defined as (P^m, V^m) as usual. Finally, let (P_1^m, V_1^m) be the overall protocol constructed as in Proposition 4.3: V_1^m chooses a hash function of output length $|x|$ and then (P, V) is run for $|x|$ iterations.

Let R be the underlying computational problem of finding collisions, i.e., the relation $\{(h, (y, y'))|\ h \in H, h(y) = h(y'), y \neq y'\}$. The relation R' used in Definition 4.2 is then $\{((C, h), (y, y'))|\ C \text{ non-satisfiable}, (h, (y, y')) \in R\}$.

It is easy to see that V is a knowledge verifier for R' with knowledge error 3/4 and a sharp threshold extractor: In the protocol, V randomly chooses among 4 challenges, and given satisfactory answers to all of them for a non-satisfiable circuit, one can open a commitment in two ways and thus find a collision for h. A deterministic prover convincing V with probability larger than 3/4 for a certain input must know all these answers. By Definition 4.2, (P, V) is an interactive argument for circuit satisfiability with soundness error 3/4 relative to R. Hence, by applying Corollary 5.4 to the iterated protocol (P^m, V^m) and Proposition 4.3 to the overall protocol (P_1^m, V_1^m), we obtain the following theorem:

Theorem 7.1 *Assume that H is a family of collision-intractable hash functions. Then (P_1^m, V_1^m) is a statistical zero-knowledge argument for circuit satisfiability according to Definition 3.1 with the following properties: The protocol requires communicating $O(m^2)$ bits. The subprotocol (P^m, V^m) has soundness error $(3/4)^m$ relative to R. Concretely, if any probabilistic polynomial-time prover P^{m*} can cheat with probability $\epsilon(m) > (3/4)^m$ in expected time $T(m)$, there is a probabilistic algorithm that finds collisions for the hash function used in expected time dominated by the term $10T(m)/(\epsilon(m) - (3/4)^m)$.*

Based on a completely different method, an argument with $O(m^2)$ communication complexity appeared in [6]. For simplicity, we have here set the input size n and the output length k of the hash function equal to m. In practice, one should consider these parameters independently. We find that [6] is $O(n\max(m, k))$, while ours is $O(m(n + k))$. In a typical case we will have $n >> k > m$, whence our protocol is better by a factor of approximately k/m. On the other hand, [6] is perfect zero-knowledge and constant-round.

The computational complexity of [6] and our protocol are similar when based on the same assumption such as factoring. However, we can base our protocol on hash functions that are much more efficient than those obtained from the factoring assumption:

Using an independent choice of the three parameters, we can use the hash function SHA-1 [19], which has 160-bit outputs. Then a 10000-gate circuit could be proved satisfiable using about 3 Mbyte of communication with a soundness error of 2^{-50}. As to computation, it seems reasonable to assume that an implementation would spend almost all its time hashing (once for making or opening each string commitment). SHA-1 can be implemented on standard PC's at speeds around 6-8 Mbyte/sec. Thus, at a security level of 2^{-50}, an implementation should be able to handle around 20000 gates per second if the communication lines can keep up. For instance, a circuit part for proving that a secret value is a DES key encrypting a certain plaintext block into a certain ciphertext block can be handled in less than 2 seconds. To the best of our knowledge this is the most practical protocol proposed for circuit satisfiability.

Acknowledgments: We thank Oded Goldreich and Michael Waidner for helpful discussions.

References

1. G. Brassard, D. Chaum, and C. Crépeau, "Minimum Disclosure Proofs of Knowledge," *J. Computer and System Sciences*, vol. 37, pp. 156-189, 1988.
2. M. Bellare and O. Goldreich, "On Defining Proofs of Knowledge", in *Advances in Cryptology - Proc. CRYPTO '92*, Berlin: Springer-Verlag, 1993, pp. 390-420.
3. L. Babai and S. Moran, "Arthur-Merlin Games: A Randomized Proof System and a Hierarchy of Complexity Classes", *J. Computer and System Sciences*, vol.36, pp. 254-276, 1988.
4. M. Bellare, "A Note on Negligible Functions," *Technical Report CS97-529, Dept. of Comp. Sc. and Eng., UC San Diego*, 1997, and *Theory of Cryptography Library* 97-04, http://theory.lcs.mit.edu/ tcryptol/.
5. M. Bellare, R. Impagliazzo, and M. Naor, "Does Parallel Repetition Lower the Error in Computationally Sound Protocols?", in *Proc. 38th IEEE Symp. Foundations of Computer Science*, 1997.
6. R. Cramer and I. B. Damgård, "Linear Zero-Knowledge - A Note on Efficient Zero-Knowledge Proofs and Arguments", in *Proc. 29th Annual ACM Symp. Theory of Computing*, 1997, pp. 436-445.
7. I. B. Damgård, "Collision free hash functions and public key signature schemes," in *Advances in Cryptology - Proc. EUROCRYPT '87*, Berlin: Springer-Verlag, 1988, pp. 203-216.
8. I. B. Damgård and B. Pfitzmann, "Sequential Iteration of Interactive Arguments and an Efficient Zero-Knowledge Argument for NP," *BRICS report RS-97-50*, 1997, http://www.brics.dk.
9. I. B. Damgård, T. P. Pedersen, and B. Pfitzmann, "On the Existence of Statistically Hiding Bit Commitment Schemes and Fail-Stop Signatures," in *Advances in Cryptology - Proc. CRYPTO '93*, Berlin: Springer-Verlag, 1994, pp. 250-265.
10. I. B. Damgård, T. P. Pedersen, and B. Pfitzmann, "Statistical Secrecy and Multi-Bit Commitments," *BRICS report RS-96-45*, 1996, http://www.brics.dk. To appear in *IEEE Trans. Inform. Theory*, May 1998.
11. L. Fortnow, "The Complexity of Perfect Zero Knowledge," in *Proc. 19th Annual ACM Symp. Theory of Computing*, 1987, pp. 204-209.
12. O. Goldreich, *Foundations of Cryptography (Fragments of a Book)*, Dept. of Comp. Sc. and Applied Math., Weizmann Institute of Science, Rehovot, Israel, 1995, http://theory.lcs.mit.edu/ oded/ (with updates).
13. O. Goldreich, "A Uniform-Complexity Treatment of Encryption and Zero-Knowledge," *J. Cryptology*, vol. 6, no. 1, pp. 21-53, 1993.
14. S. Goldwasser and S. Micali, "Probabilistic encryption," *J. Computer and System Sciences*, vol. 28, pp. 270-299, 1984.
15. S. Goldwasser, S. Micali, and C. Rackoff, "The knowledge complexity of interactive proof systems," *SIAM J. Computing*, vol. 18, no. 1, pp. 186-208, 1989.
16. O. Goldreich, S. Micali, and A. Wigderson, "Proofs that Yield Nothing But Their Validity or All Languages in NP Have Zero-Knowledge Proof Systems," *J. ACM*, vol. 38, no. 1, pp. 691-729, 1991.
17. J. Kilian, "A Note on Efficient Zero-Knowledge Proofs and Arguments," in *Proc. 24th Annual ACM Symp. Theory of Computing*, 1992, pp. 723-732.
18. J. Kilian, S. Micali, and R. Ostrovsky, "Minimum resource zero-knowledge proofs," in *Proc. 30th IEEE Symp. Foundations of Computer Science*, 1989, pp. 474-479.
19. *Secure Hash Standard*, Federal Information Processing Standards Publication FIPS PUB 180-1, 1995.

Image Density Is Complete for Non-interactive-SZK
(Extended Abstract)

A. De Santis,[1] G. Di Crescenzo,[2] G. Persiano,[1] M. Yung[3]

[1] Dipartimento di Informatica ed Applicazioni, Università di Salerno, 84081 Baronissi (SA), Italy. E-mail: ads.giuper@cs.ucsd.edu

[2] Computer Science Department, University of Califonia San Diego, La Jolla, CA, 92093-0114. E-mail: giovanni@cs.ucsd.edu

[3] CertCo BTEC, NY. E-mail: moti@certco.com

Abstract. We show that the class NISZK of languages that admit *non-interactive* statistical zero-knowledge proof system has a natural complete promise problem. This characterizes statistical zero-knowledge in the public random string model without reference to the public random string or to zero knowledge.

Building on this result we are able to show structural properties of NISZK such as closure under OR composition and closure under complement.

1 Introduction

Completeness is a powerful tool in complexity theory. Having a complete language for class of languages provides us with an avenue to prove properties of the class by enabling one to study an entire class by focusing on a single problem. This tool has been exploited in various celebrated results of complexity theory.

Statistical Zero-Knowledge. In their seminal paper [15], Goldwasser, Micali and Rackoff introduced statistical zero-knowledge proofs (SZK), an important notion with practical as well as theoretical relevance. From a theoretical point of view, SZK proofs capture the intrinsic properties of the zero-knowledge concept, since they do not need further cryptographic assumptions, as it is the case for computational zero-knowledge (CZK) proofs. For CZK, all languages in NP [13] and in IP (=PSPACE) [18] (also [4]) are known to have a CZK proof system, while a precise characterization for the languages having SZK proof systems is not known. It is known that the class SZK is in AM $\cap$ co-AM [11, 1], and that NP-complete languages do not have such proofs unless the polynomial hierarchy collapses. Indeed today, exhibiting a statistical zero-knowledge proofs for a certain language seems the most effective way to give evidence that the language is not NP-complete.

The tool of completeness has proved to be very helpful for the theory of zero-knowledge and interactive proofs. In [13] it was showed that NP has computational zero-knowledge proofs by exhibiting such a proof system for a specific

NP-complete language and IP=PSPACE has been proved in [25] by giving an interactive proof system for a PSPACE-complete language. Recently, in [23] a complete promise problem has been given for the class of honest-verifier-SZK in the interactive setting.

Non-Interactive Statistical Zero-Knowledge. Blum et al. [5, 6] put forward the shared-string model for non-interactive zero-knowledge. Here, the prover and the verifier share a random string and the mechanism of the proof is mono-directional: the prover sends one message to the verifier. Non-interactive zero-knowledge proofs have found several applications in Cryptography (most notably the construction of cryptosystems secure against chosen-cyphertext attacks [20]) and can be employed in any setting in which communication is a precious and scarce resource. Thus, the shared-string model trades the need for interaction with the need for shared randomness. Since non-interactive zero-knowledge proofs from scratch can be obtained only for BPP languages ([14]), the shared-string model provides a minimal enough setting for non-interactive zero-knowledge. Statistical zero-knowledge in this setting has been investigated in [8, 9]. Unfortunately, the problem proposed in [23] for the interactive model is not known to have a statistical zero-knowledge proof system in the non-interactive setting. Indeed, due to the restrictions in the model, the design of non-interactive zero-knowledge protocols has often been a difficult task.

Our results. In this paper we identify a natural promise problem and show that it is complete for the class of languages having a non-interactive statistical zero-knowledge (NISZK) proof. We call such problem ID for Image Density. Roughly speaking (see next section for precise definitions), the set of 'yes' ('no') instances in ID is the set of almost regular and poly-time computable functions for which the density of the image in its range is large (small).

We also show many closure properties for the class NISZK. In particular, we show that NISZK is closed under complementation and under the OR of any polynomial number of statements. Due to lack of space, some proofs are omitted in this abstract.

2 Notations and definitions

In this section we introduce notations and basic definitions and recall the notion of non-interactive statistical zero-knowledge proofs.

Probabilistic algorithms. The notation $x \stackrel{D}{\leftarrow} S$ denotes the *random process* of selecting element x from set S according to distribution D; we only write $x \leftarrow S$ in the case D is the uniform distribution over S. Similarly, the notation $y \leftarrow A(x)$, where A is an algorithm, denotes the random process of obtaining y when running algorithm A on input x, where the probability space is given by the random coins (if any) of algorithm A. By $\{R_1; \ldots; R_n : v\}$ we denote the set of values v that a random variable V can assume, due to the distribution D determined by the sequence of random processes $R_1, \ldots, R_n$. By $\Pr[R_1; \ldots; R_n : E]$ we denote the probability of event E, after the execution of random processes

$R_1, \ldots, R_n$. If D is a distribution taking values in a set S, we call *collision probability* of D the probability $\Pr[x_1 \stackrel{D}{\leftarrow} S; x_2 \stackrel{D}{\leftarrow} S : x_1 = x_2]$. If A, B are distributions taking values in a set S, we call the *statistical difference* between A and B the quantity $\sum_x |\Pr[x_1 \stackrel{A}{\leftarrow} S : x_1 = x] - \Pr[x_2 \stackrel{B}{\leftarrow} S : x_2 = x]|$.

Basic definitions. A *language* L is a subset of $\{0,1\}^*$. We refer the reader to [12] for the notions of *polynomial-time reducibility* among problems and *completeness* of a problem in a class. A *promise problem* P is a pair $P = [P_Y, P_N]$ of disjoint subsets of $\{0,1\}^*$, where P_Y contains the 'yes' instances and P_N contains the 'no' instances. We note that the notions of reducibility and completeness naturally extend from languages to promise problems. For any two sets $Dom, Codom$, and a function $f : Dom \to Codom$, we denote by $Im(f)$ the *image set* under f, that is, $Im(f) = \{y \,|\, \exists x \text{ such that } f(x) = y\}$. A function f is *regular* if the quantity $|\{x : f(x) = y\}|$ is the same for all $y \in Im(f)$. A function $f : Dom \to Codom$ is *almost regular* if it holds that

$$\sum_{y \in Im(f)} \left| \frac{|\{x : f(x) = y\}|}{|Dom|} - \frac{1}{|Im(f)|} \right| \leq \frac{1}{|x|^c},$$

for all constants c. For any a, b, let $\text{REG}_{a,b,m}$ be the set of functions $\{f \,|\, f : \{0,1\}^a \to \{0,1\}^b, f \text{ is almost regular}, |f| = m\}$, where by $|f|$ we denote the size of the circuit evaluating function f. By $\mathcal{H}_{m,n}$ we denote a family of universal *hash functions* $h : \{0,1\}^m \to \{0,1\}^n$ [7]. We will use the family $\mathcal{H}_{m,n}$ of $m \times n$ boolean matrices H describing the function h defined as $h(x) = x \cdot H$, where $\cdot$ here denotes matrix multiplication.

Non-Interactive Zero-Knowledge. In the definition of non-interactive statistical zero-knowledge proof systems, we stress few parameters of interest in this paper; namely, the errors involved in the completeness, soundness, and zero-knowledge, and both cases of languages and promise problems.

Definition 1. Let P be a probabilistic Turing machine and V a deterministic Turing machine that runs in time polynomial in the length of its first input. We say that (P,V) is a NON-INTERACTIVE STATISTICAL ZERO-KNOWLEDGE PROOF SYSTEM WITH PARAMETERS $(c(\cdot), s(\cdot), z(\cdot))$ for the language L if there exists a constant a such that:

1. *Completeness.* $\forall x \in L$, $\Pr[\sigma \leftarrow \{0,1\}^{|x|^a}; \mathit{Proof} \leftarrow P(\sigma, x) \colon V(\sigma, x, \mathit{Proof}) = 1] \geq c(|x|)$.

2. *Soundness.* For all Turing machines P' returning pairs (x, Proof), where $x \notin L$,

$$\Pr[\sigma \leftarrow \{0,1\}^{|x|^a}; (x, \mathit{Proof}) \leftarrow P'(\sigma) \colon V(\sigma, x, \mathit{Proof}) = 1] \leq s(|x|).$$

3. *Statistical Zero-Knowledge.* There exists an expected polynomial time algorithm S, called the *Simulator* such that $\forall x \in L$,

$\sum_\alpha \Big|\Pr[\sigma \leftarrow \{0,1\}^{|x|^a}; \mathit{Proof} \leftarrow P(\sigma, x) \colon (\sigma, \mathit{Proof}) = \alpha] - \Pr[s \leftarrow S(x) : s = \alpha]\Big| < z(|x|)$.

Definition 2. We say that (P,V) is a NON-INTERACTIVE STATISTICAL ZERO-KNOWLEDGE PROOF SYSTEM for the language L if (P,V) is a non-interactive statistical zero-knowledge proof system for L with parameters $(c(\cdot), s(\cdot), z(\cdot))$, if for all n and for all constants d, it holds that $c(n) \geq 1 - n^{-d}$, $s(n) \leq n^{-d}$, and $z(n) \leq n^{-d}$.

We call the random string σ, input to both P and V, the *reference string.* The model considered in the above definitions requires that P and V share a public and uniformly distributed string, and is often called the *public-random-string model.* Analogue definitions of non-interactive statistical zero-knowledge proof systems for promise problems $\Pi = [\Pi_Y, \Pi_N]$ can be obtained from the above definitions for languages, by making the following modifications. The completeness and statistical zero-knowledge requirements hold for all input strings in set Π_Y (rather than in language L). The soundness requirement holds for all input strings in set Π_N (rather than for strings not in language L).

Non-Interactive Lower Bound Protocols. A lower bound protocol is a protocol between a prover and a polynomial-time bounded verifier who are given a set $S \subseteq \{0,1\}^m$ and an integer $n \leq m$, where the prover wants to prove the statement '$|S| \geq 2^n$'. If membership in S is verifiable in polynomial time then an interactive protocol for such a task has been given in [3] (also using a lemma from [24] for the analysis). Here we present this protocol in the public-random-string model, and recall its properties.
The lower bound protocol (P, V) for proving '$|S| \geq 2^n$'. Let σ be a reference string and let statement '$|S| \geq 2^n$' be chosen independently from σ. First P writes the reference string σ as $\sigma = h \circ z$, where $h \in \mathcal{H}_{m,n}$ and $z \in \{0,1\}^n$. Then P computes $c \in S$ such that $h(c) = z$ and sends it to V. Finally V accepts if and only if he received a string c' such that $c' \in S$ and $h(c') = z$.
Analysis of the lower bound protocol. The following lemma is proved in [3, 1].

Lemma 3. [3] *Let (P, V) be the above non-interactive lower bound protocol. Then* $1 - 2^n/|S| \leq \Pr[\text{V accepts}] \leq |S|/2^n$.

Leftover Hashing Lemma. The leftover hashing lemma analyzes a method based on universal hashing for extracting quasi-random strings given an unknown source of randomness. It was given in [17]; here, we recall a somewhat simplified version due to Rackoff (also appeared in [19]).

Lemma 4. *For any e, l, n, let $X \subseteq \{0,1\}^n$, $|X| \geq 2^l$, and let $h \in \mathcal{H}_{n,l-2e}$. The statistical difference between distributions $D_1 = \{h \leftarrow \mathcal{H}_{n,l-2e}; x \leftarrow X : (h, h(x))\}$ and $D_2 = \{h \leftarrow \mathcal{H}_{n,l-2e}; y \leftarrow \{0,1\}^{l-2e} : (h, y)\}$ is at most 2^{-e}.*

Proof. The proof is divided in the following two claims, proved in [19].

Claim 1 *The collision probability of D_1 is at most $(1+2/2^{2e})/(|\mathcal{H}_{n,l-2e}| \cdot 2^{l-2e})$.*

Claim 2 *Let D be a distribution taking values on a finite set S. If the collision probability of D is at most $(1 + 2\delta^2)/|S|$, then the statistical difference between D and the uniform distribution over S is at most δ.*

□

3 A promise problem complete for NISZK

We would like to show that the problem of deciding whether the image set of a polynomial-time computable and almost-regular function has high or low density in its range is complete for the class NISZK. We start by formally defining this problem, and variants of it, and then show that it is complete for NISZK.

The promise problem ID. Let a, b, m be polynomials and α, β be functions from $\mathcal{N}$ to $[0,1]$. Then for $n \geq 1$ we define

$$\mathrm{ID}_{Y,n,a,b,m}(\alpha) = \{(1^n, f) \mid f \in \mathrm{REG}_{a(n),b(n),m(n)}, |\mathrm{Im}(f)| \geq \alpha(n) \cdot 2^{b(n)}\}$$
$$\mathrm{ID}_{N,n,a,b,m}(\beta) = \{(1^n, f) \mid f \in \mathrm{REG}_{a(n),b(n),m(n)}, |\mathrm{Im}(f)| \leq \beta(n) \cdot 2^{b(n)}\}.$$

The promise problem ID (Image Density) is defined as ID=$\{\mathrm{ID}_{a,b,m}\}$ where $\mathrm{ID}_{a,b,m}$=$\mathrm{ID}_{a,b,m}(2/3, 1/2)$= $[\mathrm{ID}_{Y,a,b,m}(2/3)$,$\mathrm{ID}_{N,a,b,m}(1/2)]$, where $\mathrm{ID}_{Y,a,b,m}(\alpha) = \cup_n \mathrm{ID}_{Y,n,a,b,m}(\alpha)$ and $\mathrm{ID}_{N,a,b,m}(\beta) = \cup_n \mathrm{ID}_{N,n,a,b,m}(\beta)$. In the rest of the paper, we will drop the indices a, b, m, whenever they are clear from the context or immaterial. In this paper, we will also consider the promise problem ID(α, β)= $[\mathrm{ID}_Y(\alpha)$,$\mathrm{ID}_N(\beta)]$, for any α, β such that $\alpha \geq \beta(1 + n^c)$, for some constant c. In this section we obtain the following

Theorem 5. *ID is complete for NISZK.*

3.1 ID is NISZK-hard

We start by showing that any problem having a non-interactive statistical zero-knowledge proof system can be reduced to ID in polynomial time.

Lemma 6. *Let Π be a promise problem in NISZK; then Π is polynomial-time reducible to ID. Moreover, if Π has a non-interactive statistical zero-knowledge proof system with parameters $(c(\cdot), s(\cdot), z(\cdot))$, then Π is polynomial-time reducible to ID(α, β), for $\alpha = c(\cdot)(1 - z(\cdot))$ and $\beta = s(\cdot)$.*

Proof. Let $\Pi = (\Pi_Y, \Pi_N)$ be a promise problem belonging to NISZK. By the results of [9], there exists a a non-interactive statistical zero-knowledge proof system (A,B) for Π that admnits a simulator M that runs in strict polynomial-time. We denote by $t(n)$ and $r(n)$ the length of the random string used by (A,B) and the number of random bits needed by M on inputs of length n, respectively. We define the function f associated to problem ID as a modified version of the simulator M. Formally, for any x, $|x| = n$, let $a(n) = r(n)$ and $b(n) = t(n)$, and define function $f_x : \{0,1\}^{a(n)} \rightarrow \{0,1\}^{b(n)}$ as $f_x(R) = F_x(R)$, where F_x is the following algorithm:

Input to F_x: string $R \in \{0,1\}^{r(n)}$;

Instructions for F_x:

1. run algorithm M on input (x, R) and obtain pair $(\sigma, Proof)$.
2. if $B(\sigma, x, Proof) = 1$ then set $y = \sigma$, else set $y = 0^{t(n)}$;
3. output: y.

We can show that the pair $(1^{|x|}, f)$ is an instance of the promise problem $\mathrm{ID}(\alpha, \beta)$, for $\alpha = (1 - z(\cdot))c(\cdot)$ and $\beta = s(\cdot)$. The fact that function f_x is almost regular and the fact that, for $x \in \Pi_Y$, the function f_x has high density follow from the completeness and the statistical zero-knowledge property of (A,B). The fact that for $x \in \Pi_N$, function f_x has small range density follows from the soundness property of (A,B). □

3.2 ID is in NISZK

We now show that the promise problem ID has a non-interactive statistical zero-knowledge proof system. More formally, we obtain the following

Lemma 7. *ID is in NISZK. More precisely, for any polynomial $k(\cdot)$, and any α, β, the promise problem $\mathrm{ID}[\alpha, \beta]$ has a non-interactive statistical zero-knowledge proof system $[\Pi_Y, \Pi_N]$ with parameters $(c(\cdot), s(\cdot), z(\cdot))$, where $c(n) = 1 - 2^{-k(n)}$, $s(n) = 2^{-k(n)}$, $z(n) = n^{-c}$, for all n and all constants c.*

Proof. We describe a non-interactive statistical zero-knowledge proof system (A,B) for the promise problem $\mathrm{ID}[\alpha, \beta]$. Informally speaking, protocol (A,B) combines a first subprotocol in which the reference string is used in order to prove that the size of a set S is 'sufficiently large', and a second subprotocol which certifies that the set S is essentially a cartesian product of the image of function f associated to problem $\mathrm{ID}[\alpha, \beta]$. Moreover, the prover will choose the messages both in the first and in the second subprotocol according to a certain distribution, in order not to reveal knowledge. We note that some parameters of the lower bound subprotocol are chosen in such a way to take into account cheating provers who may choose function f after they are given the random string σ. Now we give a formal description of (A,B).

Input to A and B:

- $(1^n, f)$, where $f \in \mathrm{REG}_{a(n),b(n),m(n)}$, for polynomials $a(\cdot), b(\cdot), m(\cdot)$.
- A polynomial $k(\cdot)$ and functions $\delta(\cdot), l(\cdot)$ such that $\delta(n) = 2k(m(n))$ and $l(n) = 20k(m(n))$.
- A reference string $\sigma = h \circ z$, where $|z| = l(n)(b(n) - \log(1/\alpha)) - \delta(n)$, and $h \in \mathcal{H}_{l(n)b(n),|z|}$.

Instructions for A.

A.0 For each $v \in Im(f)$, define $Pre_v = \{u \mid f(u) = v\}$ and $p_v = |Pre_v|$.
A.1 Let $S = \{(v_1, \ldots, v_{l(n)}) \mid v_1, \ldots, v_{l(n)} \in Im(f); h(v_1 \circ \cdots \circ v_{l(n)}) = z\}$;
define the following distribution D over set S:
for each $(v_1, \ldots, v_{l(n)}) \in S$,
let $\Pr_D(v_1, \ldots, v_{l(n)}) = (p_{v_1} \cdots p_{v_{l(n)}})/|S|^{l(n)}$;
A.2 Choose $(v_1, \ldots, v_{l(n)}) \stackrel{D}{\leftarrow} S$;
for $i = 1, \ldots, l(n)$, uniformly choose u_i from set Pre_{v_i};
A.3 Send $(u_1, \ldots, u_{l(n)}, v_1, \ldots, v_{l(n)})$ to B.

Instructions for B.

B.0 Receive a string $(u_1,\ldots,u_{l(n)},v_1,\ldots,v_{l(n)})$, where $u_i \in \{0,1\}^{a(n)}$ and $v_i \in \{0,1\}^{b(n)}$, for $i = 1,\ldots,l(n)$.
B.1 For $i = 1,\ldots,l(n)$, verify that $f(u_i) = v_i$.
B.2 Verify that $h(v_1 \circ \cdots \circ v_{l(n)}) = z$.
B.3 If all verifications are satisfied then output: ACCEPT else output: REJECT.

We see that algorithm B can be executed in polynomial time since both functions f and h can be computed in polynomial time. Now we show that the requirements of completeness, soundness and perfect zero-knowledge are satisfied by (A,B).
Completeness. Assume $(1^n, f)$ belongs to $\mathrm{ID}_Y(\alpha)$. Then we observe that A can compute a proof $(u_1,\ldots,u_{l(n)},v_1,\ldots,v_{l(n)})$ which satisfies B's verifications if and only if the set S is not empty. The probability that set S is not empty can be written as the probability that there exists at least an $l(n)$-tuple in $Im(f)^{l(n)}$ satisfying $h(v_1 \circ \cdots \circ v_{l(n)}) = z$. Using Lemma 3, the latter probability is at least $1 - 2^{l(n)(b(n)-\log(1/\alpha))-\delta(n)}/|Im(f)^{l(n)}|$, which, by using the fact that $|Im(f)| \geq \alpha \cdot 2^{b(n)}$, is $\geq 1 - 2^{l(n)(b(n)-\log(1/\alpha))-\delta(n)}/2^{l(n)(b(n)-\log(1/\alpha))} = 1 - 2^{-\delta(n)}$.
Soundness. Let us first assume $(1^n, f)$ is a fixed pair belonging to $\mathrm{ID}_N(\beta)$. An algorithm A′ can compute a proof $(u_1,\ldots,u_{l(n)},v_1,\ldots,v_{l(n)})$ which satisfies B's verifications if and only if the set S is not empty. The probability that set S is not empty can be written as the probability that there exists at least a $l(n)$-tuple in $Im(f)^{l(n)}$ satisfying $h(v_1 \circ \cdots \circ v_{l(n)}) = z$. Using Lemma 3, the latter probability is at most $|Im(f)^{l(n)}|/2^{l(n)(b(n)-\log(1/\alpha))-\delta(n)}$, which is, by using the fact that $|Im(f)| \leq \beta \cdot 2^{b(n)}$, at most $2^{l(n)(b(n)-\log(1/\beta))}/2^{l(n)(b(n)-\log(1/\alpha))-\delta(n)}$. Since $\delta(n) = k(m(n))$ and $l(n) = 10k(m(n))$, and considering for simplicity the case $\alpha = 2/3$ and $\beta = 1/2$ (the general case is similar), we obtain that this quantity is at most $2^{-2k(m(n))}$.

Now, consider the most general case in which an infinitely powerful algorithm A' computes a pair $(1^n, f)$, where $|f| = m(n)$, for some polynomial $m(\cdot)$. Note that for any n, algorithm A' can choose an arbitrary polynomial $m(\cdot)$ and an arbitrary function f such that $|f| = m(n)$. For each such choice, the previous analysis shows that V accepts with probability at most $2^{-2k(m(n))}$ thus summing over all possible choiches of f we get that the overall probability that V accepts is at most $\sum_{m \geq n} 2^m \cdot 2^{-2k(m(n))} \leq \sum_{m \geq n} 2^{-k(m(n))} \leq 2^{-k(n)}$.
Statistical Zero-Knowledge. We give a simulator M such that, for each pair $(1^n, f) \in \mathrm{ID}_Y(\alpha)$, the output of M and the view of B in the protocol (A,B) are statistically indistinguishable. Now we formally describe M.

Input to M: A pair $(1^n, f)$, where $f \in \mathrm{REG}_{a(n),b(n),m(n)}$.

Instructions for M:

1. For $i = 1, \ldots, l(n)$, uniformly choose $u_i \in \{0,1\}^{a(n)}$ and compute $v_i = f(u_i)$.
2. Uniformly choose $h \in \mathcal{H}_{l(n)b(n),l(n)(b(n)-\log(1/\alpha))-\delta(n)}$;
   compute $z = h(v_1 \circ \cdots \circ v_{l(n)})$;
   set $\sigma = (h \circ z)$ and $Proof = (u_1, \ldots, u_{l(n)}, v_1, \ldots, v_{l(n)})$.
3. Output $(\sigma, Proof)$.

Clearly, M runs in polynomial time. Now we show that the pair $(\sigma, Proof)$ output by the simulator M is statistically indistinguishable from the pair $(\sigma, Proof)$ seen by the verifier B during an execution of protocol (A,B).

First of all, consider the output of the simulator M. Here, the string $Proof$ is made of $l(n)$ strings u_i uniformly chosen in $\{0,1\}^{a(n)}$, and $l(n)$ strings v_i satisfying $f(u_i) = v_i$. Then the string σ is made of a uniformly chosen hash function h and a string z such that $h(v_1 \circ \cdots \circ v_{l(n)}) = z$.

Now, consider an execution of protocol (A,B). We notice that strings $v_1, \ldots, v_{l(n)}$ are chosen by A with probability distribution D over the set S of strings in $Im(f)$ satisfying the equation $h(v_1 \circ \cdots \circ v_{l(n)}) = z$. The probability distribution D assigns a probability weight to each string $(v_1, \ldots, v_{l(n)})$ equal to the product of the number of preimages l_i of each string v_i under f. This implies that the probability assigned to string $(v_1, \ldots, v_{l(n)})$ is the same as in the output of the simulator, where such string is computed by first uniformly choosing strings $u_1, \ldots, u_{l(n)} \in \{0,1\}^{a(n)}$ and then computing $v_i = f(u_i)$, for $i = 1, \ldots, l(n)$. Moreover, the strings $u_1, \ldots, u_{l(n)}$ are uniformly distributed among the preimages of $v_1, \ldots, v_{l(n)}$ under function f both in the protocol and in the simulation. Finally, we need to show that the strings h and z are equally distributed in both spaces. In an execution of (A,B), the pair (h, z) is taken from the reference string and thus it is uniformly distributed. In the output of the simulator M, the pair (h, z) is clearly computed in a different way and its distribution may have a non-zero distance from the uniform one. In order to compute such distance, we use the Leftover Hashing Lemma. Following the analysis in [19] for such lemma, we first compute the collision probability of the distribution of pairs (h, z) output by the simulator M.

Claim 3 *For any n, let $m' = l(n)b(n)$ and $n' = l(n)(b(n) - \log(1/\alpha)) - \delta(n)$. Also, let D be the distribution $\{h \leftarrow \mathcal{H}_{m',n'}; u_1, \ldots, u_{l(n)} \leftarrow \{0,1\}^n, v_1 \leftarrow f(u_1), \ldots, v_{l(n)} \leftarrow f(u_{l(n)}); z \leftarrow h(v_1 \circ \cdots \circ v_{l(n)}) : (h, z)\}$, and let $c(D)$ be the collision probability of D. For all n, and all constants d, with probability at least $1-n^{-d}$, it holds that $c(D) \leq (1+2/2^{\delta(n)})/(|\mathcal{H}_{m',n'}| \cdot 2^{l(n)(b(n)-\log(1/\alpha))-\delta(n)})$.*

We now use Claim 2 in [19] (also reviewed in Section 2), and obtain that with probability at least $1 - n^{-d}$, for all constants d, the distance from the uniform distribution of the distribution of pair (h, z) in the output of M is at most $2^{-\delta(n)/2}$. Therefore, the distance between the output of M and the view of B is at most $2^{-k(m(n))} + n^{-d}$, which is smaller than n^{-d}, for all constants d. □

Remark. In the above proof we have assumed for simplicity that $\alpha = 2/3$ and $\beta = 1/2$. However, by a proper choice of parameters, the proof can work for any α, β such that $\alpha = \beta(1 + 1/n^c)$, for some constant c.

4 NISZK is closed under OR composition

In this section we show that the class NISZK is closed with respect to composition of a class of boolean formulae: those having an OR gate over any polynomial number of statements.

Theorem 8. *For any $n \geq 1$, any polynomial $t(\cdot)$, and any languages $L_1, \ldots, L_{t(n)}$, define the language $OR(L_1, \ldots, L_{t(n)}) = \{(x_1, \ldots, x_{t(n)}) \mid |x_1| = \ldots = |x_{t(n)}| = n$, and $\exists i \in [1, t(n)]$ such that $x_i \in L_i\}$. If $L_1, \ldots, L_{t(n)}$ are in NISZK then language $OR(L_1, \ldots, L_{t(n)})$ is in NISZK.*

The rest of the section is devoted to the proof of Theorem 8. We start with an amplification lemma and then present a protocol for our composed problem.

An amplification lemma. The size of the range of function f in the definition of problem ID is required to be at least 2/3 for ID_Y and at most 1/2 for ID_N. Here we show that using the results in Section 3, it is possible to amplify the gap between such two constants. We have the following

Lemma 9. *For any n and any polynomial $k(\cdot)$, the problem $ID(\alpha, \beta)$, for $\alpha \geq 1 - n^{-c}$, for all constants c, and $\beta = 2^{-k(n)}$ is complete for NISZK.*

Proof. We start from problem $\mathrm{ID}[2/3, 1/2]$, which is complete for NISZK, because of Theorem 5. Then, we apply Lemma 7 and obtain a non-interactive statistical zero-knowledge proof system (A,B) for $\mathrm{ID}[2/3, 1/2]$ having parameters $(1 - 2^{-k(n)}, 2^{-k(n)}, n^{-c})$, for any polynomial $k(\cdot)$ and all constants c. Now, we apply the transformation in Lemma 6 to protocol (A,B). Because of the values of the parameters of (A,B), this tranformation reduces problem $\mathrm{ID}[2/3, 1/2]$ to promise problem $\mathrm{ID}[1 - n^{-c}, 2^{-k(n)}]$, for all constants c. □

A protocol for the OR. Let n be an integer, let $t(\cdot)$ be a polynomial, let $t = t(n)$, and let $L_1, \ldots, L_t$ be languages in NISZK. Our goal is to construct a protocol for proving statement $T = (x_1 \in L_1) \vee \cdots \vee (x_t \in L_t)$, where $x_1, \ldots, x_t$ are n-bit input strings. Using Lemma 9, we have that for each $i = 1, \ldots, t$, each language L_i can be reduced in polynomial time to the promise problem $\mathrm{ID}(\alpha, \beta)$, where $\alpha = 1 - n^{-c}$, for all constants c, and $\beta = 2^{-k(n)}$, for any polynomial $k(\cdot)$. Therefore, proving statement $T_{1i} =$'$x_i \in L_i$' can be reduced in polynomial time into proving statement $T_{2i} =$'$(1^n, f_i) \in \mathrm{ID}_Y(1 - n^{-c})$', where $f_i \in \mathrm{REG}_{a_0(n), b_0(n), m_0(n)}$, for polynomials $a_0(\cdot)$, $b_0(\cdot)$, $m_0(\cdot)$ and all constants c (for simplicity we are considering the case all functions f_i have the same domain, codomain and circuit size; simple padding arguments show this is wlog). Clearly, the reduction implies that each statement T_{2i} is true if and only if statement T_{1i} is true. Now, let $a'(n) = ta_0(n)$, $a(n) = \lceil (b_0(n) - 1)/k(n) \rceil \cdot a'(n)$, $b'(n) = tb_0(n)$, and $b(n) = \lceil (b_0(n)-1)/k(n) \rceil \cdot b'_n$, and define function $g : \{0,1\}^{a'(n)} \rightarrow \{0,1\}^{b'(n)}$ as $g(u_1 \circ \cdots \circ u_t) = (f_1(u_1) \circ \cdots \circ f_t(u_t))$ and function $h : \{0,1\}^{a(n)} \rightarrow \{0,1\}^{b(n)}$ as $h(u_1 \circ \cdots \circ u_{b(n)/b_0(n)}) = (g(u_1) \circ \cdots \circ g(u_{b(n)/b_0(n)}))$.

It is not hard to show that (a) if statement T is true then it holds that $|Im(h)|/2^{b(n)} \geq 2^{-(t-1)(b_0(n)-1)-1}$, (b) if statement T is false then $|Im(h)|/2^{b(n)} \leq 2^{-t(b_0(n)-1)}$. Therefore, in order to show that statement T is true, it is enough to use a non-interactive statistical zero-knowledge proof system for the promise problem ID$[\alpha, \beta]$, where $\alpha = (2^{-(t-1)(b_0(n)-1)-1})$ and $\beta = 2^{-t(b_0(n)-1)}$. Finally, since $\alpha \geq 2\beta$, we observe that Lemma 7 implies the existence of such a protocol. □

5 NISZK is closed with respect to complement

We show that the class NISZK is closed with respect to complementation.

Theorem 10. *NISZK=co-NISZK.*

The proof of this result will use in a crucial way both the completeness result for the promise problem ID, and the result in Theorem 8. First we present a protocol for a variant of the problem ID and then show how to combine this protocol with the mentioned results in order to prove the above theorem.

A protocol for a variant of ID. We will consider the following promise problem, defined as k-ID$=$ (k-ID$_Y$, k-ID$_N$), where $k\text{-ID}_Y = \cup_n k\text{-ID}_{Y,n}$, $k\text{-ID}_N = \cup_n k\text{-ID}_{N,n}$, and

$k\text{-ID}_{Y,n} = \{(1^n, f) : f \in \text{REG}_{a(n),b(n),m(n)}, \text{ and } 2^k \leq |Im(f)| < 2^{k+1}\}$,

$k\text{-ID}_{N,n} = \{(1^n, f) : f \in \text{REG}_{a(n),b(n),m(n)}, 2^{k-1/2} < |Im(f)| \leq 2^{k+1/2}\}$,

where $a(\cdot), b(\cdot), m(\cdot)$ are polynomials. We describe a non-interactive statistical zero-knowledge proof system (A,B) for k-ID. Informally speaking, the idea behind protocol (A,B) is as follows. First of all the reference string is used in order to run a non-interactive lower bound protocol that convinces B that the size of set $Im(f)$ is at least 2^k. This protocols requires A to send an element $(v_1, \ldots, v_{l(n)})$ of $Im(f)^{l(n)}$ to B. Then another non-interactive lower bound protocol is executed in order to convince B that the size of set $Im(f)^{l(n)}$ is at most 2^{k+1}. Specifically, the lower bound protocol is executed on the preimage set of the element $(v_1, \ldots, v_{l(n)})$ (here, proving that an 'almost' randomly chosen element $(v_1, \ldots, v_{l(n)})$ of set $Im(f)^{l(n)}$ has a 'sufficiently large' preimage set is equivalent to proving that set $Im(f)^{l(n)}$ is sufficiently small). Let $\delta_1(\cdot), \delta_2(\cdot), l(\cdot)$ be some properly chosen polynomials. In the next page we give a formal description of (A,B). The proof that the protocol (A,B) is a non-interactive statistical zero-knowledge proof system for problem k-ID can be obtained by extending ideas in the proof of Lemma 7.

The protocol for the complement of ID. We present a protocol for the promise problem $\overline{ID}(\alpha, \beta)$ =[ID$_N$,ID$_Y$], where $\alpha = 1 - n^{-c}$, for all constants c, and $\beta = 2^{-k(n)}$, for some polynomial $k(\cdot)$. Since ID(α, β) is complete for NISZK, we obtain that NISZK is closed under complement.

A protocol for $\overline{ID}(\alpha,\beta)$. A protocol for the promise problem $\overline{ID}(\alpha,\beta)$ might be simply constructed as an 'upper bound' protocol (i.e., a protocol in which the prover proves that the size of a set is smaller than some bound 2^b). Specifically, it would be enough to prove that $|Im(f)|/2^{b(n)}$ is smaller than $2^{b(n)-k(n)}$, (for an appropriate choice of polynomial $k(\cdot)$). All known protocols for this task are interactive. Given the tools constructed in the previous sections in the paper, we are able to construct a non-interactive upper bound protocol. Then we obtain the following protocol (P,V) for the promise problem $\overline{ID}(\alpha,\beta)$:

P proves the statement $T = \vee_{i=1}^{b(n)-k(n)-1} [(1^n, f) \in i\text{-ID}_Y]$.

Notice that since the statement '$(1^n, f) \in i\text{-ID}_Y$' can be proved in non-interactive statistical zero-knowledge using the protocol for problem k-ID, then this is true also for the statement T, because of Theorem 8. The properties of completeness, soundness and statistical zero-knowledge of the resulting protocol follow from those of the subprotocols used. This concludes the proof of Theorem 10.

Input to A and B:

- $(1^n, f)$, where $f \in \text{REG}_{a(n),b(n),m(n)}, |f| = m(n)$, and $a(\cdot), b(\cdot), m(\cdot) = poly(\cdot)$.
- A reference string $\sigma = h_1 \circ z_1 \circ h_2 \circ z_2$, where $|z_1| = l(n)k - \delta_1(n)$, $|z_2| = l(n)(a(n) - k - 1) - \delta_2(n)$, $h_1 \in \mathcal{H}_{l(n)b(n),|z_1|}$, and $h_2 \in \mathcal{H}_{l(n)a(n),|z_2|}$.

Instructions for A.

A.0 For $v \in Im(f)$, let $Pre_v = \{u \mid f(u) = v\}$ and $p_v = |Pre_v|$.
A.1 Let $S_1 = \{(v_1, \ldots, v_{l(n)}) \mid v_1, \ldots, v_{l(n)} \in Im(f); h_1(v_1 \circ \cdots \circ v_{l(n)}) = z_1\}$;
define the following distribution D over set S_1:
for each $(v_1, \ldots, v_{l(n)}) \in S_1$,
let $\Pr_D(v_1, \ldots, v_{l(n)}) = (p_1 \cdots p_{l(n)})/|S_1|^{l(n)}$;
let $S_2 = \{(u_1, \ldots, u_{l(n)}) \mid f(u_i) = v_i$, for $i = 1, \ldots, l(n), h_2(u_1 \circ \cdots \circ u_{l(n)}) = z_2\}$;
A.2 Choose $(v_1, \ldots, v_{l(n)}) \stackrel{D}{\leftarrow} S_1$;
uniformly choose $(u_1, \ldots, u_{l(n)}) \in S_2$;
A.3 Send $(u_1, \ldots, u_{l(n)}, v_1, \ldots, v_{l(n)})$ to B.

Input to B: A string $(u_1, \ldots, u_{l(n)}, v_1, \ldots, v_{l(n)})$, where $u_i \in \{0,1\}^{a(n)}$ and $v_i \in \{0,1\}^{b(n)}$, for $i = 1, \ldots, l(n)$.

Instructions for B.

B.1 For $i = 1, \ldots, l(n)$, verify that $f(u_i) = v_i$.
B.2 Verify that $h_1(v_1 \circ \cdots \circ v_{l(n)}) = z_1$ and $h_2(u_1 \circ \cdots \circ u_{l(n)}) = z_2$.
B.3 If all verifications are satisfied then output: ACCEPT else output: REJECT.

References

1. W. Aiello and J. Håstad, *Statistical Zero Knowledge Can Be Recognized in Two Rounds,* Journal of Computer and System Sciences, 42, 1991, pp. 327–345.
2. W. Aiello, M. Bellare and R. Venkatesan, *Knowledge on the average - Perfect, Statistical and Logarithmic,* in Proc. of STOC 95.

3. L. Babai and S. Moran, *Arthur–Merlin Games: A Randomized Proof System and a Hierarchy of Complexity Classes*, Journal of Computer and System Sciences, vol. 36, 1988, pp. 254–276.
4. M. Ben-Or, O. Goldreich, S. Goldwasser, J. Håstad, J. Kilian, S. Micali, and P. Rogaway, *Everything Provable is Provable in Zero Knowledge*, in CRYPTO 88.
5. M. Blum, A. De Santis, S. Micali, and G. Persiano, *Non-Interactive Zero-Knowledge*, SIAM Journal of Computing, vol. 20, no. 6, Dec 1991, pp. 1084–1118.
6. M. Blum, P. Feldman, and S. Micali, *Non-Interactive Zero-Knowledge and Applications*, in STOC 88.
7. L. Carter and M. Wegman, *Universal Classes of Hash Functions*, Journal of Computer and System Sciences, vol. 18, 1979, pp. 143–154.
8. A. De Santis, G. Di Crescenzo, G. Persiano, *The Knowledge Complexity of Quadratic Residuosity Languages,* Theoretical Computer Science, vol. 132, (1994), pag. 291–317.
9. A. De Santis, G. Di Crescenzo, G. Persiano, *Randomness-Efficient Non-Interactive Zero-Knowledge,* in Proc. of ICALP 97.
10. A. De Santis, G. Di Crescenzo, P. Persiano, and M. Yung, *On Monotone Formula Closure of SZK*, in FOCS 94.
11. L. Fortnow, *The Complexity of Perfect Zero Knowledge*, in STOC 87.
12. M. Garey e D. Johnson, *Computers and Intractability: a Guide to the Theory of NP-Completeness,* W. H. Freeman & Co., New York, 1979.
13. O. Goldreich, S. Micali, and A. Wigderson, *Proofs that Yield Nothing but their Validity or All Languages in NP Have Zero-Knowledge Proof Systems*, Journal of the ACM, vol. 38, n. 1, 1991, pp. 691–729.
14. O. Goldreich and Y. Oren, *Definitions and Properties of Zero-Knowledge Proof Systems*, Journal of Cryptology, v. 7, n. 1, 1994.
15. S. Goldwasser, S. Micali, and C. Rackoff, *The Knowledge Complexity of Interactive Proof-Systems*, SIAM Journal on Computing, vol. 18, n. 1, February 1989.
16. S. Goldwasser and M. Sipser, *Private Coins versus Public Coins in Interactive Proof–Systems*, in STOC 1986.
17. J. Håstad, R. Impagliazzo, L. Levin, and M. Luby, *Construction of a Pseudo-Random Generator from One-Way Function*, to appear in SIAM J. on Computing.
18. R. Impagliazzo and M. Yung, *Direct Minimum Knowledge Computations*, in CRYPTO 87.
19. R. Impagliazzo and D. Zuckerman, *How to recycle random bits*, in FOCS 89.
20. M. Naor and M. Yung, *Public-Key Cryptosystems Provably Secure against Chosen Ciphertext Attack*, in STOC 90.
21. T. Okamoto, *On Relationships Between Statistical Zero-Knowledge Proofs*, in STOC 96.
22. R. Ostrovsky and A. Wigderson, *One-way Functions are Essential for Non-Trivial Zero-Knowledge*, in ISTCS 93.
23. A. Sahai and S. Vadhan, *A Complete Promise Problem for Statistical Zero-Knowledge*, in FOCS 97.
24. M. Sipser, *A Complexity Theoretic Approach to Randomness*, in STOC 83.
25. A. Shamir, *IP=PSPACE*, in FOCS 90.

Randomness Spaces

(Extended Abstract)

Peter Hertling[1] and Klaus Weihrauch[2]

[1] Department of Computer Science, University of Auckland, Private Bag 92019, Auckland, New Zealand, hertling@cs.auckland.ac.nz

[2] Theoretische Informatik I, FernUniversität Hagen, 58084 Hagen, Germany, klaus.weihrauch@fernuni-hagen.de

Abstract. Martin-Löf defined infinite random sequences over a finite alphabet via randomness tests which describe sets having measure zero in a constructive sense. In this paper this concept is generalized to separable topological spaces with a measure. We show several general results, like the existence of a universal randomness test under weak conditions, and a randomness preservation result for functions between randomness spaces. Applying these ideas to the real numbers yields a direct definition of random real numbers which is shown to be equivalent to the usual one via the representation of real numbers to some base. Furthermore, we show that every nonconstant computable analytic function preserves randomness. As a second example, by considering the power set of the natural numbers with its natural topology as a randomness space, we introduce a new notion of a random set of numbers. We characterize it in terms of random sequences. Surprisingly, it turns out that there are infinite co-r.e. random sets.

1 Introduction

Random infinite binary sequences have first been introduced by von Mises [17]. His motivation was to lay a foundation for probability theory. He considered sequences as random and called them "Kollektive" if the digits 0 and 1 appear with their expected limiting frequency not only in the sequence but also in any subsequence which could be obtained by applying certain "admissible place selection rules". His approach received a severe blow when Ville [16] showed that there exists a Kollektiv which does not satisfy the law of the iterated logarithm, which a random sequence should certainly satisfy.

A second approach is Martin-Löf's [11] definition of random sequences via typicalness. It is based on the idea that a sequence is typical or random, if it does not lie in any set which is in a constructive sense of measure 0. This idea is formalized by considering randomness tests, which are non–increasing computable sequences $(U_n)_n$ of open sets U_n whose measure tends to 0 with a prescribed convergence rate. The constructive set of measure 0 then consists of the intersection $\bigcap_n U_n$.

Another approach for defining random sequences is based on the idea to consider the program–size complexity of finite prefixes, defined via (certain) universal Turing machines. This idea has been proposed independently by Kolmogorov [8] and Chaitin [3, 4] in different versions (see also Solomonoff [15]) and further developed by Levin, Schnorr and others. It leads to the same notion of random infinite sequences as the second approach.

While the first and the third approach for defining randomness work naturally only for sequences, Martin-Löf's approach can be extended to much more general spaces which allow the formulation of computable sequences of open sets with fast decreasing measure. This was suggested already by Zvonkin and Levin [20]. We follow this idea and provide rigorous definitions of randomness spaces in Section 3. We prove the existence of a universal randomness test under rather weak conditions. Furthermore some examples of randomness spaces and random elements are given. In Section 4 we ask under which conditions a function between randomness spaces preserves randomness. Our main result gives sufficient conditions and corrects and extends a corresponding result by Schnorr [13]. In the following section we consider the real number space as a randomness space. The randomness preservation result is used to show that the resulting randomness notion is identical with the randomness notion for real numbers introduced via randomness of the b-ary representation of a number. This also gives a new proof of the result by Calude and Jürgensen [2] that randomness of a real number defined via randomness of its b-ary representation does not depend on the base b. Furthermore, we consider vectors and sequences of real numbers. The second main result in this section states that every nonconstant computable analytic function preserves randomness. In the last section we consider another randomness space: the power set of the natural numbers, endowed with its natural topology as a complete partial order. This point of view leads to a new notion of randomness for sets of natural numbers, which is different from the usual one defined via randomness of characteristic functions. The first main result of the section is a characterization of randomness for sets in terms of usual random sequences. The second main result is a theorem which implies that there are infinite random co-r.e. sets.

2 Notation

The power set $\{A \mid A \subseteq X\}$ of a set X, containing all subsets of X, is denoted by 2^X. By $f :\subseteq X \to Y$ we mean a (partial or total) function f with domain $\operatorname{dom} f \subseteq X$ and range $\operatorname{range} f \subseteq Y$. The notation $f : X \to Y$ indicates that the function is total, i.e. $\operatorname{dom} f = X$. We denote the set of natural numbers by $\mathbb{N} = \{0, 1, 2, \ldots\}$. We use the notions of a computable function $f :\subseteq \mathbb{N} \to \mathbb{N}$ and of an r.e. set $A \subseteq \mathbb{N}$ in the usual sense. A *sequence* is a mapping $p : \mathbb{N} \to X$ to some set X and usually written in the form $(p_n)_n$. The infinite product of X is the set of all sequences of elements in X, denoted by $X^\omega := \{p \mid p : \mathbb{N} \to X\}$. For any $k \in \mathbb{N}$ the finite product $X^k := \{w \mid w : \{1, \ldots, k\} \to X\}$ is the set of all vectors $w = w(1)w(2)\ldots w(k)$ over X of length k. We use the standard bijection

$\langle , \rangle : \mathbb{N}^2 \to \mathbb{N}$ defined by $\langle i,j \rangle := \frac{1}{2}(i+j)(i+j+1)+j$. Higher tupling functions are defined recursively by $\langle n \rangle := n$, $\langle n_1, n_2, \ldots, n_{k+1} \rangle := \langle \langle n_1, \ldots, n_k \rangle, n_{k+1} \rangle$. We also use the standard bijective numbering $D : \mathbb{N} \to \{E \subseteq \mathbb{N} \mid E \text{ is finite}\}$ of the set of all finite subset of $\mathbb{N}$, defined by $D^{-1}(E) := \sum_{i \in E} 2^i$.

We assume that the reader is familiar with basic mathematical notions like base and subbase of a topology (as usual, from a subbase we demand that the union of all of its elements is equal to the full space), σ–algebra generated by a class of subsets of a set, measure, σ–finite measure, finite measure, and probability measure.

3 Randomness Spaces

Zvonkin and Levin [20], pp. 110–111, observed that Martin–Löf's [11] definition of randomness tests and random elements can easily be generalized from the space of infinite sequences over a finite alphabet to any separable topological space with a given numbering of a base and with a measure. In this section we provide the necessary definitions and prove elementary results including the existence of a universal randomness test on a randomness space if its measure satisfies a weak effectivity condition. We construct product spaces of certain randomness spaces and give several examples of randomness spaces and random elements.

Definition 1. A *randomness space* is a triple (X, B, μ), where X is a topological space, $B : \mathbb{N} \to 2^X$ is a total numbering of a subbase of the topology of X, and μ is a measure defined on the σ-algebra generated by the topology of X (notation: $B_i := B(i)$).

Random points of a randomness space are defined via randomness tests. Before we define them we introduce the numbering B' of a base, derived from a numbering B of a subbase, and define and discuss computable sequences of open sets.

Definition 2. Let X be a topological space and $(U_n)_n$ be a sequence of open subsets of X.

1. A sequence $(V_n)_n$ of open subsets of X is called *U–computable*, iff there is an r.e. set $A \subseteq \mathbb{N}$ such that $V_n = \bigcup_{\langle n,i \rangle \in A} U_i$ for all $n \in \mathbb{N}$.
2. We define a sequence $(U'_n)_n$ of open sets, called the *sequence derived from* U, by $U'_i := U'(i) := \bigcap_{j \in D_{1+i}} U_j$, for all $i \in \mathbb{N}$.
3. We say that U satisfies the *intersection property*, iff there is an r.e. set $A \subseteq \mathbb{N}$ with
$$U_i \cap U_j = \bigcup_{\langle i,j,k \rangle \in A} U_k, \quad \text{for all } i,j.$$

One sees easily that U satisfies the intersection property, iff $(U'_n)_n$ is U–computable. If B is a total numbering of a subbase of the topology, then B' is a total numbering of a base. In general, we will deal mostly with B'–computable sequences of open sets. The next definition generalizes Martin–Löf's [11] definition of random sequences to points from arbitrary randomness spaces.

Definition 3. Let (X, B, μ) be a randomness space.

1. A *randomness test on* X is a B'–computable sequence $(U_n)_n$ of open sets with $\mu(U_n) \leq 2^{-n}$ for all $n \in \mathbb{N}$.
2. An element $x \in X$ is called *non–random*, iff $x \in \bigcap_{n\in\mathbb{N}} U_n$ for some randomness test $(U_n)_n$ on X. It is called *random*, iff it is not non–random.

If B satisfies the intersection property, then B is a numbering of a base itself and a sequence $(U_n)_n$ of open subsets of X is a randomness test iff it is B–computable and $\mu(U_n) \leq 2^{-n}$ for all n. In the following examples of randomness spaces the numberings B of subbases always satisfy the intersection property.

Examples 4. 1. The original randomness spaces are the spaces (Σ^ω, B, μ) of infinite sequences over a finite alphabet Σ with at least two elements (Martin-Löf [11]). The numbering B of a subbase of the topology is given by $B_i := \nu(i)\Sigma^\omega = \{p \in \Sigma^\omega \mid \nu(i) \text{ is a prefix of } p\}$, where $\nu : \mathbb{N} \to \Sigma^*$ is the length–lexicographical bijection between $\mathbb{N}$ and the set Σ^* of finite words over Σ. The measure μ is given by $\mu(w\Sigma^\omega) = |\Sigma|^{-|w|}$ for $w \in \Sigma^*$. It is easy to see that any computable sequence $p \in \Sigma^\omega$ is non–random.

2. For the set of real numbers $\mathbb{R}$ we consider the randomness space $(\mathbb{R}, B, \lambda)$, where λ is the usual Lebesgue measure and B is the numbering of a base of the real line topology defined by $B_{\langle i,j\rangle} := \{x \in \mathbb{R} \mid |x - \nu_{\mathbb{D}}(i)| < 2^{-j}\}$. Here $\nu_{\mathbb{D}} : \mathbb{N} \to \mathbb{D}$ is the total numbering of the set

$$\mathbb{D} := \{x \in \mathbb{R} \mid (\exists i, j, k \in \mathbb{N})\ x = (i - j) \cdot 2^{-k}\}$$

of dyadic rational numbers defined by $\nu_{\mathbb{D}}\langle i, j, k\rangle := (i - j)/2^k$. When we refer to *random real numbers* we mean random elements of this randomness space. As in the case of sequences, it is easy to see that computable real numbers (see Weihrauch [18]) are non–random.

3. For the unit interval $[0,1]$ we consider the randomness space $([0,1], \tilde{B}, \tilde{\lambda})$, where $\tilde{B}_i := B_i \cap [0,1]$ and $\tilde{\lambda}$ denotes the restriction of the Lebesgue measure to the unit interval. Later we shall prove that an element of the unit interval is a random element of the randomness space $([0,1], \tilde{B}, \tilde{\lambda})$ if and only if it is a random element of the randomness space $(\mathbb{R}, B, \lambda)$.

We note that one can assume without loss of generality that the sequence of sets $(U_n)_n$ defining a randomness test is non–increasing.

Proposition 5. *If $(V_n)_n$ is a randomness test, then $(U_n)_n$ with $U_n := \bigcap_{i\leq n} V_i$ is a randomness test with $U_{n+1} \subseteq U_n$ for all n and $\bigcap_{n=0}^\infty U_n = \bigcap_{n=0}^\infty V_n$.*

It is remarkable that the randomness space (Σ^ω, B, μ) from Example 4.1 has a universal randomness test (Martin-Löf [11]), i.e. a randomness test $(U_n)_n$ such that for each randomness test $(V_n)_n$ there exists a constant $c \in \mathbb{N}$ with $V_{n+c} \subseteq U_n$ for all n. We generalize the original definition as follows:

Definition 6. A randomness test $(U_n)_n$ on a randomness space (X, B, μ) is called *universal*, iff for any randomness test $(V_n)_n$ on (X, B, μ) there is an increasing, total computable function $r : \mathbb{N} \to \mathbb{N}$ with $V_{r(n)} \subseteq U_n$, for all n.

If $(U_n)_n$ is a universal randomness test, then the set $\bigcap_{n=0}^{\infty} U_n$ consists exactly of all non–random elements of the space. Any randomness space whose measure satisfies a certain weak effectivity condition possesses a universal randomness test. The measures of all examples of randomness spaces considered in this paper satisfy the following condition.

Definition 7. We call a measure μ of a randomness space (X, B, μ) *weakly bounded,* iff there are an increasing computable function $d : \mathbb{N} \to \mathbb{N}$ and an r.e. set $Z \subseteq \mathbb{N}$ with

$$\mu(B'_{i_1} \cup \ldots \cup B'_{i_k}) \leq 2^{-d(n)} \Longrightarrow \langle k, \langle i_1, \ldots, i_k \rangle, n \rangle \in Z \Longrightarrow \mu(B'_{i_1} \cup \ldots \cup B'_{i_k}) \leq 2^{-n}$$

for all $k, i_1, \ldots, i_k, n \in \mathbb{N}$.

Theorem 8. *On every randomness space (X, B, μ) with weakly bounded measure there exists a universal randomness test.*

The proof goes along the same lines as the proof of Martin–Löf's [11] original result. One produces an effective list of randomness tests on (X, B, μ) which contains all randomness tests $(S_n)_n$ satisfying $\mu(S_n) \leq 2^{-d(n)}$ for all n. Then the universal test is constructed by a diagonal argument.

Let $(X^{(0)}, B^{(0)}, \mu^{(0)})$, $(X^{(1)}, B^{(1)}, \mu^{(1)})$, ..., $(X^{(n)}, B^{(n)}, \mu^{(n)})$, for some $n \in \mathbb{N}$ be a finite list of randomness spaces with σ–finite measures $\mu^{(k)}$. One can in a canonical way define the *product randomness space*

$$\prod_{k=0}^{n} (X^{(k)}, B^{(k)}, \mu^{(k)}) := (X^{(0)} \times \ldots \times X^{(n)}, B^{(0)} \times \ldots \times B^{(n)}, \mu^{(0)} \times \ldots \times \mu^{(n)}).$$

It bears the product topology, its measure is the product measure (well–defined and a σ–finite measure because all $\mu^{(k)}$ are σ–finite), and the product numbering $B^{(0)} \times \ldots \times B^{(n)}$ of a subbase can be defined in a canonical way by using the tupling function $\langle , \rangle$. In a similar way one can also define the product space of an infinite sequence $((X^{(k)}, B^{(k)}, \mu^{(k)}))_k$ of randomness spaces with probability measures, i.e. $\mu^{(k)}(X^{(k)}) = 1$ for all $k \in \mathbb{N}$.

Straightforward proofs show that each component or subvector of a random element of a finite product of randomness spaces with finite measures must be random itself in the corresponding randomness space. The same is true for subvectors (or even subsequences which are obtained by recursively selecting a sequence of indices without repetitions) of random elements of the infinite product of randomness spaces with probability measures.

Since the Lebesgue measure λ on $\mathbb{R}$ is σ–finite we obtain in this way for example canonically the product randomness spaces $(\mathbb{R}^n, B^n, \lambda^n)$ of real vectors $(n \geq 1)$ by applying the construction to the randomness space of Example 4.2. Since the restriction $\tilde{\lambda}$ of the Lebesgue measure to the unit interval $[0, 1]$ is a probability measure, we obtain also the randomness space $([0, 1]^\omega, \tilde{B}^\omega, \tilde{\lambda}^\omega)$ of infinite sequences of real numbers in the unit interval.

We conclude this section with "concrete" examples of random elements of a randomness space. A sequence $(q_n)_n$ of dyadic rationals is called *computable,* iff there is a total computable function $f : \mathbb{N} \to \mathbb{N}$ with $q_n = \nu_{\mathbb{D}}(f(n))$ for all n (for $\nu_{\mathbb{D}}$ compare Example 4.2). A real number x is called *left–computable*, iff there is a computable increasing sequence $(q_n)_n$ of dyadic rationals with $\lim_{n\to\infty} q_n = x$, see Weihrauch [18, Ch. 3.8].

Examples 9. 1. Chaitin's [4] Ω–numbers are left–computable random real numbers contained in the unit interval.

2. Let $(U_n)_n$ be a universal randomness test on the space of real numbers $(\mathbb{R}, B, \lambda)$ of Example 4.2. Then, for any k, the open set U_k contains all non–random real numbers. This set is also the disjoint union of a countable set of open intervals. The boundaries of these intervals lie outside of U_k, hence they are random real numbers. It is well–known (e.g. Ko [7, Theorem 2.34]) that the right–hand boundary of any of these intervals is a left–computable real number. More on left–computable random numbers can be found in Calude, Hertling, Khoussainov, Wang [1].

4 Randomness Preserving Transformations

The main result of this section is a theorem giving conditions under which a computable function between randomness spaces preserves randomness. This corrects and extends a result by Schnorr [13].

Let Σ and $\tilde{\Sigma}$ be two finite alphabets. A function $g :\subseteq \Sigma^* \to \tilde{\Sigma}^*$ is called *monotonic*, iff $g(vw) \in g(v)\Sigma^*$ for all $v, vw \in \operatorname{dom} g$. The function $f :\subseteq \Sigma^\omega \to \tilde{\Sigma}^\omega$ *induced* by a monotonic function $g :\subseteq \Sigma^* \to \tilde{\Sigma}^*$ is defined by

1. $\operatorname{dom} f = \{p \in \Sigma^\omega \mid$ for each $n \in \mathbb{N}$ there exists a prefix $v \in \operatorname{dom} g$ of p with $|g(v)| \geq n\}$,
2. $f(p) \in g(v)\Sigma^\omega$ for any $p \in \operatorname{dom} f$ and for any prefix $v \in \operatorname{dom} g$ of p.

It is clear that f is well–defined by these conditions. A function $f :\subseteq \Sigma^\omega \to \tilde{\Sigma}^\omega$ is called a *computable functional*, iff there is a computable, monotonic function $g :\subseteq \Sigma^* \to \tilde{\Sigma}^*$ which induces f.

Schnorr claimed in [13, Satz 6.5]: *if* $f :\subseteq \{0,1\}^\omega \to \{0,1\}^\omega$ *is a computable functional satisfying* ($\exists$ *constant* $K > 0$) ($\forall$ *measurable* $A \subseteq \{0,1\}^\omega$) $\mu(f^{-1}(A)) \leq K\mu(A)$, *and if* $x \in \operatorname{dom} f$ *is random, then also* $f(x)$ *is random.* This, as well as Lemma 6.6 and Satz 6.7 in [13], is not completely correct, as was also observed by Wang, see Hertling and Wang [6]. The following proposition gives a counterexample. Note that the function f in the proposition satisfies the measure–theoretic condition above for any constant $K > 0$ since its domain has measure zero.

Proposition 10. *Consider the randomness space from Example 4.1 with* $\Sigma = \{0,1\}$. *There exists a random element* $r \in \{0,1\}^\omega$ *such that the function* $f :\subseteq \{0,1\}^\omega \to \{0,1\}^\omega$ *with* $\operatorname{dom} f = \{r\}$ *and* $f(r) = 0^\omega$ *is a computable functional.*

For the proof, let r be the binary representation of a left–computable random real number in the unit interval, compare Examples 9 and Theorem 15.

We wish to consider transformations from one randomness space to another one. For such transformations we need a computability notion. A direct and natural definition can be obtained by demanding that the transformation is continuous in an effective way.

Definition 11. Let (X, B) and (Y, C) be two topological spaces with total numberings B and C of subbases. We call a function $f :\subseteq X \to Y$ *computable*, iff there is a B'–computable sequence $(U_n)_n$ of open subsets of X with $f^{-1}(C_n) = U_n \cap \operatorname{dom} f$, for all n.

This definition generalizes the notion of a computable functional if one does not care about the precise domain of definition: if Σ and $\tilde{\Sigma}$ are two finite alphabets and B and C the corresponding numberings of bases of Σ^ω and $\tilde{\Sigma}^\omega$, respectively, considered in Example 4.1, then a function $f :\subseteq \Sigma^\omega \to \tilde{\Sigma}^\omega$ is computable if and only if there is a computable functional $g :\subseteq \Sigma^\omega \to \tilde{\Sigma}^\omega$ with $f(p) = g(p)$ for all $p \in \operatorname{dom} f$. For the case of T_0–spaces Definition 11 is equivalent to the definition of computable functions via standard representations by Kreitz and Weihrauch [9, 18, 19]. For real number functions the computability notion in Definition 11 derived from the numbering B from Example 4.2 is also the usual computability notion considered for example by Grzegorczyk [5], Pour-El and Richards [12], Weihrauch and Kreitz [9, 18, 19], Ko [7], and others; for more references see [18, 19].

Besides computability we need two additional conditions for a function in order to ensure that it preserves randomness: one saying that we can in some effective, measure-theoretical sense control its domain and one saying that it may not map too large sets to too small sets.

Definition 12. Let (X, B, μ) be a randomness space. A set $D \subseteq X$ is called *fast enclosable* if it is an element of the σ–algebra generated by the topology and if there is a B'–computable sequence $(U_n)_n$ of open sets with $D \subseteq U_n$ and $\mu(U_n \setminus D) \leq 2^{-n}$ for all n.

Definition 13. Let (X, B, μ) and $(Y, C, \tilde{\mu})$ be two randomness spaces. A function $f :\subseteq X \to Y$ is called *recursively measure–bounded* if $\operatorname{dom} f$ is an element of the σ–algebra generated by the topology and there is a total computable function $r : \mathbb{N} \to \mathbb{N}$ such that for all open sets $V \subseteq Y$ and all n:

$$\tilde{\mu}(V) \leq 2^{-r(n)} \Rightarrow \mu(f^{-1}(V)) \leq 2^{-n} .$$

Theorem 14. *Let (X, B, μ) and $(Y, C, \tilde{\mu})$ be randomness spaces. Let $f :\subseteq X \to Y$ be a computable, recursively measure–bounded function with a fast enclosable domain. If $x \in \operatorname{dom} f$ is a random element of X, then $f(x)$ is a random element of Y.*

Informally: a computable, recursively measure–bounded function with a fast enclosable domain preserves randomness. In our counterexample in Proposition 10 the set $\operatorname{dom}(f) = \{r\}$, r random, cannot be fast enclosable. For a randomness preservation result of a different kind, valid for infinite sequences, see Levin [10].

For the proof of Theorem 14 it is sufficient to show the following: if $(V_n)_n$ is a randomness test on $(Y, C, \tilde{\mu})$ then there is a randomness test $(U_n)_n$ on (X, B, μ) with $\bigcap_{n\in\mathbb{N}} U_n \supseteq f^{-1}\left(\bigcap_{n\in\mathbb{N}} V_n\right)$. Given $(V_n)_n$, an appropriate sequence $(U_n)_n$ can be constructed rather straightforwardly by using the three assumptions on f, which are all formulated in terms of sequences of open sets.

We mention one application of Theorem 14. Let Σ be a finite alphabet and $p, q \in \Sigma^\omega$ be two infinite sequences. From Theorem 14 one can easily deduce that the combined sequence $\langle p, q\rangle := p(0)q(0)p(1)q(1)p(2)q(2)\ldots \in \Sigma^\omega$ is random if and only if the pair $(p, q) \in (\Sigma^\omega)^2$ is random as an element of the product randomness space $((\Sigma^\omega)^2, B^2, \mu^2)$. The same is true for vectors and sequences in Σ^k for $k \in \{2, 3, \ldots\} \cup \{\omega\}$ if the tupling functions $\langle,\rangle$ are defined by $\langle p^{(1)}, \ldots, p^{(k)}\rangle := \langle\langle p^{(1)}, \ldots, p^{(k-1)}\rangle, p^{(k)}\rangle$ and by $\langle p^{(0)}, p^{(1)}, \ldots\rangle(\langle i, j\rangle) := p^{(i)}(j)$ for all i, j and for a sequence $(p^{(k)})_k$ of sequences.

5 Random Real Numbers

We show that considering the real number space as a randomness space leads to the same randomness notion for real numbers as the usual definition via representations to some base. Furthermore we show that every nonconstant computable analytic function preserves randomness.

Fix a natural number $b \geq 2$. The *b-ary representation* of the real numbers in the unit interval is based on the alphabet $\Sigma_b := \{0, 1, \ldots, b-1\}$ and defined by

$$\rho_b : \Sigma_b^\omega \to [0,1], \qquad \rho_b(p(0)p(1)p(2)\ldots) := \sum_{n=0}^{\infty} p(i)b^{-(i+1)}.$$

Only those rationals in $(0, 1)$ corresponding to sequences ending on 0's or on an infinite repetition of the digit $b - 1$ have two ρ_b–names; all other real numbers in $[0, 1]$ have exactly one ρ_b–name. This definition can directly be extended to the *b-ary representation* ρ_b^k of vectors in $[0, 1]^k$ by

$$\rho_b^k : \Sigma_b^\omega \to [0,1]^k, \qquad \rho_b^k\langle p^{(1)}, \ldots, p^{(k)}\rangle := (\rho_b(p^{(1)}), \ldots, \rho_b(p^{(k)})).$$

In the following theorem we consider the randomness spaces $(\mathbb{R}, B, \lambda)$ and $([0,1], \tilde{B}, \tilde{\lambda})$ introduced in Example 4 and their products according to the end of Section 3. For a vector $(x_1, \ldots, x_n)$ of reals the *fractional part* of $(x_1, \ldots, x_n)$ is the unique real vector $(y_1, \ldots, y_n) \in [0, 1)^n$ such that the difference $(x_1 - y_1, \ldots, x_n - y_n)$ is a vector of integers.

Theorem 15. *Let $n \geq 1$, $b \geq 2$. For a vector $(x_1, \ldots, x_n) \in \mathbb{R}^n$ the following conditions are equivalent.*

1. *It is a random element of the space $(\mathbb{R}^n, B^n, \lambda^n)$.*
2. *Its fractional part is a random element of the space $(\mathbb{R}^n, B^n, \lambda^n)$.*
3. *Its fractional part is a random element of the space $([0,1]^n, \tilde{B}^n, \tilde{\lambda}^n)$.*
4. *Its fractional part has a random ρ_b^n-name.*

All the equivalences follow by applying Theorem 14 to appropriate computable functions. For example for "3. ⇒ 4." one considers the inverse of ρ_b^n on vectors of irrational numbers (it is well–defined and computable) and uses the fact that all components of a random vector of real numbers are irrational.

From the equivalence of 3. and 4. in Theorem 15 one deduces the result by Calude and Jürgensen [2] that a real number $x \in [0,1]$ has a random ρ_b–name, iff it has a random ρ_c–name, for any integers $b, c \geq 2$. The equivalence of 3. and 4. in Theorem 15 can also be generalized to infinite sequences of real numbers in the unit interval if the b–ary representation $\rho_b^\omega : \Sigma^\omega \to [0,1]^\omega$ of such sequences is defined by $\rho_b^\omega \langle p^{(0)}, p^{(1)}, p^{(2)}, \ldots \rangle := (\rho_b(p^{(0)}), \rho_b(p^{(1)}), \rho_b(p^{(2)}), \ldots)$ for $p^{(0)}, p^{(1)}, p^{(2)}, \ldots \in \Sigma^\omega$.

It is well–known that a computable real number function preserves computability, that is, it maps computable real numbers to computable real numbers. Which real number functions preserve randomness? We give a sufficient condition which seems to cover all the functions commonly in use.

Theorem 16. *Let $n \geq 1$ and $f :\subseteq \mathbb{R}^n \to \mathbb{R}$ be a computable, continuously differentiable function with an open domain such that all zeros of its derivative f' are non–random elements of $\mathbb{R}^n$. If $x \in \operatorname{dom} f$ is random, then also $f(x)$ is random.*

We explain the idea for the case $n = 1$. Let $z \in \operatorname{dom} f$ be random. Then $f'(z) \neq 0$ by assumption. Since the derivative f' is continuous and the domain of f is open we can fix a rational interval $I \subseteq \operatorname{dom} f$ containing z such that for all $y \in I$ we have $|f'(y)| \geq c := \frac{1}{2}|f'(z)|$. We claim that the restricted function $g := f|_D$ satisfies all assumptions of Theorem 14. This, of course, implies that $f(z)$ is random. It is clear that g is computable and that its domain I is fast enclosable. By applying the Intermediate Value Theorem one can show that $\lambda(g^{-1}(U)) \leq \frac{1}{c}\lambda(U)$ for any open subset $U \subseteq \mathbb{R}$. Hence, g is recursively measure–bounded. The case $n > 1$ is treated similarly by additionally using Fubini's Theorem.

Let $n \geq 1$ and $U \subseteq \mathbb{R}^n$ be an open set. A function $f : U \to \mathbb{R}$ is *analytic* if for any point $z \in U$ there is a neighbourhood $V \subseteq U$ of z such that in this neighbourhood $f(x)$ can be written as an absolutely convergent power series $\sum_{k \in \mathbb{N}^n} a_k (x-z)^k$ where $y^k = y_1^{k_1} \cdot \ldots \cdot y_n^{k_n}$ for $y = (y_1, \ldots, y_n) \in \mathbb{R}^n$ and $k = (k_1, \ldots, k_n) \in \mathbb{N}^n$.

Theorem 17. *Let $n \geq 1$, let $U \subseteq \mathbb{R}^n$ be open, and let $f : U \to \mathbb{R}$ be a nonconstant analytic function which is computable on any compact subset of U. If $x \in \operatorname{dom} f$ is random, then also $f(x)$ is random.*

At least one of the partial derivatives of f, let us say $\frac{\partial f}{\partial x_k}$, is not identical to the constant zero function. Since it is an analytic function on U, its set of zeros has measure zero. Furthermore, one can show that $\frac{\partial f}{\partial x_k}$ is also computable on any compact subset of U, and by using this, that its set of zeros in a compact subset of U is constructively of measure zero. Hence, its zeros, and therefore the zeros of f', are non–random. The assertion follows now from Theorem 16.

We conclude that all the common arithmetic functions like addition, subtraction, multiplication, division, taking square roots or higher roots, exp, log, sin, cos, and so on preserve randomness. If for example (x, y) is a random pair of real numbers, then the sum $x + y$ is random as well. But it is important to note that it is insufficient to assume just that both components x and y are random. For example if x is random, then also $-x$ is random (by Theorem 16), but the sum $x + (-x) = 0$ is not random.

6 Random Sets

By considering the complete partial order $2^{\mathbb{N}}$ as a randomness space we introduce a new notion of random sets of numbers. We characterize it in terms of infinite random sequences and show that there exists an infinite random co-r.e. set. In this section Σ denotes the binary alphabet $\{0, 1\}$.

Which sets of natural numbers should be called random? One possibility to introduce randomness on $2^{\mathbb{N}}$ is to identify it with the usual randomness space (Σ^ω, B, μ) of Example 4.1 via the mapping $\chi : 2^{\mathbb{N}} \to \Sigma^\omega$ which maps a set $A \subseteq \mathbb{N}$ to its characteristic function χ_A (with $\chi_A(n) = 1$ if $n \in A$, $\chi_A(n) = 0$ if $n \notin A$). This mapping is a bijection. Then a set of numbers is random if and only if its characteristic function is random. But instead of using the topology τ_χ induced by χ on $2^{\mathbb{N}}$, that is, the topology on $2^{\mathbb{N}}$ with the base $\{\chi^{-1}(w\Sigma^\omega) \mid w \in \Sigma^*\}$, we wish to consider the topology on $2^{\mathbb{N}}$ viewed as a complete partial order, that is, the topology on $2^{\mathbb{N}}$ with the base $\{O_E \mid E \subseteq \mathbb{N}$ finite$\}$ where $O_E := \{A \subseteq \mathbb{N} \mid E \subseteq A\}$ for finite subsets E of $\mathbb{N}$. Let us call this topology τ. The topologies τ and τ_χ are not the same: τ is a proper subset of τ_χ. But their σ-algebras are the same. Hence, we can transfer the measure on Σ^ω via χ^{-1} to $2^{\mathbb{N}}$. We define a measure μ by $\mu(X) := \mu(\chi(X))$ for every set $X \subseteq 2^{\mathbb{N}}$ in the σ-algebra generated by τ (where the μ on the right-hand side of the equation denotes the usual product measure on Σ^ω, considered in Example 4.1). Notice that $\mu(O_E) = 2^{-|E|}$ for any finite set $E \subseteq \mathbb{N}$. Using the numbering O of basic τ-open sets defined by $O_i := O_{D_i}$ we obtain a randomness space $(2^{\mathbb{N}}, O, \mu)$.

Definition 18. A set $A \subseteq \mathbb{N}$ is called *random* iff it is a random element of the randomness space $(2^{\mathbb{N}}, O, \mu)$.

Which properties does this randomness space have? What are its random elements? It is clear that the numbering O satisfies the intersection property. The measure μ is weakly bounded. This implies by Theorem 8 that the space has a universal randomness test. Our first main result in this section characterizes randomness for sets in terms of randomness for sequences:

Theorem 19. *A set $A \subseteq \mathbb{N}$ is random if and only if there is a set $B \supseteq A$ such that χ_B is random.*

One can express this also negatively:

$$A \subseteq \mathbb{N} \text{ is non-random} \iff (\forall B \supseteq A)\ \chi_B \text{ is non-random.}$$

We conclude that every finite set $E \subseteq \mathbb{N}$ is random and every subset of a random set $A \subseteq \mathbb{N}$ is random also. Especially the first assertion might seem counterintuitive at first. But since the finite sets, considered as finite elements in the complete partial order $2^{\mathbb{N}}$, are in some sense very "rough" objects not having any property which is valid only for objects in an open set of very small measure, it makes sense to call them random. In contrast to the randomness space Σ^ω where one considers positive and negative information about a set, here we consider only positive information about sets, i.e. information telling us which numbers are in the set. This also gives an intuitive explanation for the second assertion.

Note that especially randomness of $p \in \Sigma^\omega$ implies randomness of $\chi^{-1}(p)$. The converse is not true: take a random sequence $p = p(0)p(1)p(2)p(3)\ldots \in \Sigma^\omega$. Then the sequence $q = p(0)0p(2)0\ldots$ is not random, but the set $\chi^{-1}(q) \subseteq \chi^{-1}(p)$ is random by Theorem 19.

Every finite set is random. How simple can infinite random sets be in terms of the arithmetical hierarchy? We know that there are random sequences $p \in \Sigma^\omega$ such that $\chi^{-1}(p)$ is in Δ_2 (for example the binary representations of the left–computable random real numbers mentioned in Examples 9). Thus, there are infinite random sets in Δ_2. But the set $\chi^{-1}(p)$ associated with a random sequence p cannot be in Σ_1 or Π_1. Are there infinite random sets even in Σ_1 or Π_1? A set is called *immune*, iff it is infinite and contains no infinite r.e. subset.

Theorem 20. *1. Every random set is either finite or immune.*
2. There is an infinite random co-r.e. set.

Hence, there are no infinite random sets in Σ_1, but there are infinite random sets in Π_1. The proof of the first part of the theorem is straightforward. The second part is based on the following theorem and on the existence of a universal randomness test on $(2^{\mathbb{N}}, O, \mu)$.

Theorem 21. *Let $A \subseteq \mathbb{N}$ be r.e. and $U := \bigcup\{O_{D_i} \mid i \in A\}$ have measure $\mu(U) < 1$. There exists an infinite co-r.e. set $B \notin U$.*

For the proof one uses a "movable marker" style construction, compare Soare [14]. The condition, when a marker should be moved, is of a measure–theoretic kind. In the correctness proof the notion of independence of events is used.

We deduce a corollary about random sequences. A set $A \subseteq \mathbb{N}$ is called *simple*, iff it is r.e. and its complement is immune.

Corollary 22. *There exist a simple set $A \subseteq \mathbb{N}$ and a random sequence $p \in \Sigma^\omega$ with $\chi^{-1}(p) \subseteq A$.*

Especially in view of Theorem 20.2 and the interesting proof of Theorem 21 the notion of a random set seems to deserve attention in its own right. Many questions about random sets arise. For example, is there a non–random sequence $p \in \Sigma^\omega$ such that both $\chi^{-1}(p)$ and $\mathbb{N} \setminus \chi^{-1}(p)$ are random? Another topic for which the randomness space $(2^{\mathbb{N}}, O, \mu)$ might be very useful and serve as a standard example besides the space of (finite or) infinite sequences is the problem to introduce and study randomness more generally on complete partial orders.

Acknowledgements

The first author was supported by the DFG Research Grant No. HE 2489/2-1. The authors thank Cristian Calude for stimulating discussions on randomness.

References

1. C. S. Calude, P. Hertling, B. Khoussainov, and Y. Wang. Recursively enumerable reals and Chaitin Ω numbers. In M. Morvan et al., editor, *STACS 98, Proceedings*, LNCS 1373, pages 596–606, Springer-Verlag, Berlin, 1998.
2. C. S. Calude and H. Jürgensen. Randomness as an invariant for number representations. In H. Maurer, J. Karhumäki, and G. Rozenberg, editors, *Results and Trends in Theoretical Computer Science*, pages 44–66. Springer-Verlag, Berlin, 1994.
3. G. J. Chaitin. On the length of programs for computing finite binary sequences. *J. of the ACM*, 13:547–569, 1966.
4. G. J. Chaitin. A theory of program size formally identical to information theory. *J. of the ACM*, 22:329–340, 1975.
5. A. Grzegorczyk. On the definitions of computable real continuous functions. *Fund. Math.*, 44:61–71, 1957.
6. P. Hertling and Y. Wang. Invariance properties of random sequences. *J. UCS*, 3(11):1241–1249, 1997.
7. K.-I. Ko. *Complexity Theory of Real Functions.* Birkhäuser, Boston, 1991.
8. A. N. Kolmogorov. Three approaches to the quantitative definition of information. *Problems of Information Transmission*, 1:1–7, 1965.
9. C. Kreitz and K. Weihrauch. Theory of representations. *Theor. Comp. Science*, 38:35–53, 1985.
10. L. A. Levin. Randomness conservation inequalities: information and randomness in mathematical theories. *Information and Control*, 61:15–37, 1984.
11. P. Martin-Löf. The definition of random sequences. *Information and Control*, 9(6):602–619, 1966.
12. M. B. Pour-El and J. I. Richards. *Computability in Analysis and Physics.* Springer-Verlag, Berlin, Heidelberg, 1989.
13. C.-P. Schnorr. *Zufälligkeit und Wahrscheinlichkeit*, volume 218 of *Lecture Notes in Mathematics.* Springer-Verlag, Berlin, 1971.
14. R. I. Soare. *Recursively Enumerable Sets and Degrees.* Springer–Verlag, Berlin, 1987.
15. R. J. Solomonoff. A formal theory of inductive inference I, II. *Information and Control*, 7:1–22, 224–254, 1964.
16. J. Ville. *Étude Critique de la Notion de Collectif.* Gauthier-Villars, Paris, 1939.
17. R. von Mises. Grundlagen der Wahrscheinlichkeitsrechnung. *Mathem. Zeitschrift*, 5:52–99, 1919.
18. K. Weihrauch. *Computability.* Springer–Verlag, Berlin, 1987.
19. K. Weihrauch. A foundation for computable analysis. In D. S. Bridges et al., editor, *Combinatorics, Complexity, and Logic, Proceedings of DMTCS'96*, pages 66–89, Springer-Verlag, Singapore, 1997.
20. A. K. Zvonkin and L. A. Levin. The complexity of finite objects and the development of the concepts of information and randomness by means of the theory of algorithms. *Russian Math. Surveys*, 25(6):83–124, 1970.

Totality, Definability and Boolean Circuits

Antonio Bucciarelli and Ivano Salvo

Università di Roma "La Sapienza", Dipartimento di Scienze dell'Informazione,
via Salaria, 113 - 00198 Rome (Italy)
e-mail:{buccia,salvo}@dsi.uniroma1.it

Abstract. In the type frame originating from the flat domain of boolean values, we single out elements which are hereditarily total. We show that these elements can be defined, up to total equivalence, by sequential programs. The elements of an equivalence class of the totality equivalence relation (totality class) can be seen as different algorithms for computing a given set-theoretic boolean function. We show that the bottom element of a totality class, which is sequential, corresponds to the most eager algorithm, and the top to the laziest one. Finally we suggest a link between size of totality classes and a well known measure of complexity of boolean functions, namely their sensitivity.
Keywords: Logical Relations, Scott's Model, PCF, Boolean Circuits.

1 Introduction

Adding parallel constants to a programming language strictly increase the expressive power of the language, in general. For instance, extending Scott's PCF with parallel-or, one can define any finite continuous function [7]. However, it is an open problem whether parallelism adds expressive power, if we restrict our attention to total functions. Totality is a natural notion in domain theory: a ground object (such as an integer or a boolean), is total if it is defined (i.e. different from $\perp$), and a function is total if it gives total values on total arguments. Hence totality is a logical predicate [6]. An equivalent definition of totality may be given in terms of a logical (partial) equivalence relation: at ground types, $x \sim^T y$ if x and y are equal and different from $\perp$; at higher types, $f \sim^T g$ if, whenever $x \sim^T y$ at the appropriate type, then $f(x) \sim^T g(y)$. It turns out that $f \sim^T f$ if and only if f is total in the previously defined sense. Parallel-or is total, and it is $\sim^T$-equivalent to the strict-or function, which is sequential (PCF-definable). Our original motivation for this work was to explore the following conjecture, due to Berger [2]: *For any total, parallel function f there exists a sequential function g such that $f \sim^T g$*, where "parallel" means definable by PCF$^+$ (PCF extended by parallel-or), "sequential" means PCF-definable and the type frame we refer to is the Scott hierarchy of continuous functions over the flat domains of integer and boolean values[1].

[1] Berger's conjecture is slightly complicated by the fact that, for infinite types, one has to take into account also the $\exists$ functional.

If the conjecture holds, then parallelism is inessential for defining total functions, since $f \sim^T g$ means intuitively that f and g "compute" the same total function. Since f and g are *functions*, this last statement deserves some explanations: whether Scott's semantics is concerned with functions or with algorithms is a matter of the intended source language. If, as in the case of PCF, the language has built-in divergence (e.g. via fixpoints operators), then partially defined object are first class, and two programs which provide the same results on all total arguments can be operationally different. But if we restrict ourselves to total objects, then the behaviour of a given function on non-total argument is irrelevant, and we can say, for instance, that the parallel-or and the strict-or are two algorithms computing the (total) logical disjunction (namely, the laziest and the most eager algorithm, respectively).

In order to make this intuition precise we define a (binary) heterogeneous logical relation between the Scott's type frame[2] and the one of set-theoretic functions over the set {true, false}, which, at the ground type, is the identity restricted to total elements. By this relation we can define a bijection between set theoretic functions and lattices of continuous functions "implementing" them: these lattices are exactly the equivalence classes of $\sim^T$ (*totality classes*). We can summarize the situation by saying that the set theoretic type frame is the collapse of the Scott's type frame by the totality partial equivalence relation.

Then we turn our attention to first order, set theoretic functions, i.e. to functions taking tuples of booleans as argument and giving a boolean as result. These are particular kind of boolean circuits, known as *formulae* in Complexity Theory [3]. Since our construction provides, for any formula, a lattice of continuous functions implementing it, it is natural to ask if there is any relation between the structure of this lattice and the complexity of the formula. For the time being, we are able to characterize the most eager (resp. the laziest) algorithm for a given formula as the bottom (resp. the top) of the totality class of the formula. We also suggest a relation between the size of totality classes and the *sensitivity* of formulae [10].

We assume some familiarity with the language PCF, its parallel extension PCF$^+$ and their continuous model [7].

1.1 Overview of the Results

In Sect. 2, we show that Berger's conjecture holds for finite types. Our proof is based on the semantic characterization of bottom elements of totality classes, which turn out to be PCF-definable, at any type. This is in fact an alternative proof of a (more general) result due to Plotkin [8], showing that the conjecture does hold at any type where ι (the type of integers) does not occur negatively. In Sect. 2.1, we discuss this result and argue about the relevance of our approach.

In Sect. 3, we define the "heterogeneous" logical relation between the Scott's and set theoretic type frames. This relation is a surjective partial function, and it

[2] To be precise, we consider only finite types, i.e. the type frame of Scott continuous functions over the flat domains of boolean values.

induces a partial equivalence relation on the Scott's type frame; we show that it is exactly the totality logical relation. Hence we have a bijection between totality classes and boolean functionals, at any type.

In Sect. 4 we turn our attention to first order functions: we show that the bottom and top elements of a totality class implement respectively the most eager and the laziest algorithm for the total (set-theoretic) function corresponding to that class, via the heterogeneous relations. We also provide two (families of) terms of PCF, $\mathcal{B}_n$ and $\mathcal{T}_n$ such that for any n-ary function f in a given totality class, $[\![\mathcal{B}_n]\!] f$ is the bottom and $[\![\mathcal{T}_n]\!] f$ the top element of that class. We relate the size of totality classes to the sensitivity of the corresponding boolean function, and we discuss the relationship between lazy and parallel computations for implementing a given boolean function.

We are not aware of previous attempts of using denotational semantics in order to study the complexity of boolean circuits. For the simple and tight connection it establishes between circuits and continuous function, this work seems to provide a solid ground for such investigation.

1.2 Related Works

We have already discussed the connections with Plotkin's work on totality [8]. As for the heterogeneous relation described in Sect. 3, it is reminiscent of two recent works of T. Ehrhard [5] and N. Barreiro and T. Ehrhard [1]. In the former, it was proved that strongly stable functions are the extensional collapse of Berry-Curien's sequential algorithms, in the latter, that the set-theoretic coherent model of intuitionistic linear logic is the extensional collapse of the multiset-theoretic one.

2 The Definability Result

Definition 1. *The* simple finite types *(SFT) are defined by*

$$\sigma = o \mid \sigma \to \sigma$$

Definition 2. *The* simple finite type hierarchy $\{D_\sigma\}_{\sigma \in SFT}$ *is inductively defined by:*

D_o *is the flat domain of boolean values.*

$D_{\sigma\to\tau}$ *is the set of monotone functions from* D_σ *to* D_τ*, ordered pointwise.*

Definition 3. *The* totality logical relation $\{\sim_\sigma^T\}_{\sigma\in SFT}$, $\sim_\sigma^T \subseteq D_\sigma \times D_\sigma$ *is inductively defined by:*

$x \sim_o^T y$ *if* $x = y \neq \perp$

$f \sim_{\sigma\to\tau}^T g$ *if for all* $x \sim_\sigma^T y$, $f(x) \sim_\tau^T g(y)$

An element $x \in D_\sigma$ which is invariant with respect to the totality relation (i.e. such that $x \sim_\sigma^T x$) is called a *total* element. For $x, y \in D_\sigma$, the notation "$x \uparrow y$" stands for: "x and y have a common upper bound".

Proposition 1. *For all $\sigma \in SFT$:*

1. *$\sim_\sigma^T$ is a partial equivalence relation over D_σ*
2. *if $x \sim_\sigma^T y$ then $x \wedge y \sim_\sigma^T y$*
3. *if $x, y \in D_\sigma$ are such that $x \sim_\sigma^T x$ and $x \leq y$; then $x \sim_\sigma^T y$*
4. *for all $x \in D_\sigma$ there exists $y \in D_\sigma$ such that $x \leq y$ and y is total.*
5. *if $x \sim_\sigma^T y$ then $x \uparrow y$*

Proof. Statements 1,2 and 3 are easily proved by induction on SFT. For the second one remark that all D_σ's are finite, bounded complete cpo's, hence any set of elements does have a greatest lower bound. As for statement 4, recall that all elements of D_σ are definable by Plotkin's parallel extension of PCF [7]. Let M_x be a term defining x, and M_y be the term obtained by replacing all occurrences of Ω in M_x by, say, *true*. We have that $[\![M_y]\!] \geq x$ and, by the Basic Lemma of logical relations, that $[\![M_y]\!]$ is total[3]. Statement 5 is an easy consequence of 4. □

Fact 1 *Let $\sigma \in SFT$, and $[x] \subseteq D_\sigma$ be an equivalence class of $\sim_\sigma^T$ (hereafter, a "totality class"), then $\bigwedge\{y \in D_\sigma \mid y \in [x]\} \in [x]$.*

This is a trivial consequence of the second statement of Prop. 1 and of finiteness of D_σ. We call *canonical elements* the greatest lower bounds of totality classes. If x is total (i.e. $x \sim_\sigma^T x$), then $\underline{x}$ stands for the canonical element of $[x]$, and we note $\mathrm{CAN}(\sigma)$ the set of canonical elements of D_σ. Totality classes are clearly (finite) lattices by the previous fact and by Prop. 1.3–5.

Lemma 1. *Let $c, d \in \mathrm{CAN}(\sigma)$; then either $c = d$ or $c \not\uparrow d$.*

Proof. Let us suppose that there exists $e \in D_\sigma$ such that $c, d \leq e$. By Prop. 1, $c \sim_\sigma^T e$ and $d \sim_\sigma^T e$, hence $c \sim_\sigma^T d$ and, by canonicity, $c \leq d$ and $d \leq c$. □

In the rest of this section, we prove that Berger's conjecture holds for SFT, by showing that canonical elements are sequential, at any type. First, we provide a semantic characterization of canonical elements in term of their *traces*.

Definition 4. *Let $f \in D_{\sigma \to \tau}$, we define the* trace *of f, notation $tr(f)$, by:*

$$tr(f) = \{(c, d) \mid c \in D_\sigma,\ d \in D_\tau,\ d \neq \perp_\tau,\ f(c) = d,\ \forall c' < c,\ f(c') < d\}\ .$$

The idea behind the definition of traces is that $tr(f)$ is what remains of the graph of f once we retire from it all the information that can be inferred by the monotonicity of f. In particular, $f(x) = \bigvee\{d \mid \exists (c, d) \in tr(f),\ c \leq x\}$.

As traces are subsets of cartesian products, we note $\pi_1(t)$ (resp. $\pi_2(t)$) the first (resp. second) projection of the trace t.

[3] This argument is due to Plotkin [8]. It relies on the fact that finite functions can be defined without using fixpoint operators, and that fixpoints and Ω are the only constants of PCF whose standard interpretation is non-total.

Remark that, for $f, g \in D_{\sigma\to\tau}$, $f \leq g$ if and only if for all $(c,d) \in tr(f)$ there exists $(c',d') \in tr(g)$ such that $c \geq c'$ and $d \leq d'$. Moreover, any subset T of $D_\sigma \times D_\tau$ such that, if $(c,d),(c'd') \in T$ then $c \leq c' \Rightarrow d \leq d'$ and $c \uparrow c' \Rightarrow d \uparrow d'$, is the trace of a monotone function.

Next two lemmas provide a characterization of the traces of canonical elements.

Lemma 2. *If $f \in D_{\sigma\to\tau}$ is total, and $f' : D_\sigma \to D_\tau$ is defined by:*

$$f'(x) = \begin{cases} \underline{f(\underline{x})} & \text{if } x \sim_\sigma^T x \\ \bot & \text{otherwise} \end{cases}$$

then $f' \in D_{\sigma\to\tau}$, $f \sim_{\sigma\to\tau}^T f'$ and $f' \leq f$.

Proof. First, f' is a monotone function, since if $x \leq y \in D_\sigma$ is such that $f'(x) \neq \bot$, then $xR_\sigma x$, hence by Prop. 1, $x \sim_\sigma^T y$ and $y \sim_\sigma^T y$. Since $\underline{x} = \underline{y}$, we get $f'(x) = f'(y)$. Let us now check that $f \sim_{\sigma\to\tau}^T f'$: if $x \sim_\sigma^T x'$, then

$$f(x) \sim_\tau^T f(\underline{x}) = f(\underline{x'}) \sim_\tau^T \underline{f(\underline{x'})} = f'(x')$$

Last, $f' \leq f$ holds trivially. □

Lemma 3. *A function $f \in D_{\sigma\to\tau}$ is canonical if and only if $\pi_1(tr(f)) = \mathrm{CAN}(\sigma)$ and $\pi_2(tr(f)) \subseteq \mathrm{CAN}(\tau)$.*

Proof. The "only if" part follows from the previous lemma, since the function f' defined above is clearly such that $\pi_1(tr(f')) = \mathrm{CAN}(\sigma)$ and $\pi_2(tr(f')) \subseteq \mathrm{CAN}(\tau)$. As for the "if" part, if f is such that $\pi_1(tr(f)) = \mathrm{CAN}(\sigma)$ and $\pi_2(tr(f)) \subseteq \mathrm{CAN}(\tau)$, then f is total, since $x \sim_\sigma^T y \Rightarrow f(x) = f(y) = f(\underline{x}) \in \mathrm{CAN}(\tau)$, by Lemma 1, and if $f \sim_{\sigma\to\tau}^T f'$, then for all $x \in D_\sigma$, $f(x) \neq \bot \Rightarrow x \sim_\sigma^T x$, hence $f(x) \sim_\tau^T f'(x)$; moreover $f(x)$ is canonical, again by Lemma 1, hence $f(x) \leq f'(x)$. □

An element $x \in D_\sigma$ is *definable* if there exists a closed PCF-term $M_x : \sigma$ such that $[\![M_x]\!] = x$.

Definition 5. *If $A \subseteq D_\sigma$, then A is*

- definable *if for all $x \in A$, x is definable.*
- testable *if for all $x \in A$, there exists a closed PCF-term $N_x : \sigma \to o$ such that*

$$[\![N_x]\!](y) = \begin{cases} tt & \text{if } x \leq y \\ ff & \text{if } \exists z \in A,\ z \neq x \text{ and } z \leq y \\ \bot & \text{otherwise} \end{cases}$$

Remark that if A is testable, then the elements of A are pairwise unbounded.

The next lemma shows that all canonical elements are definable. We use the following abbreviations: $TEST(\sigma)$ (resp. $DEF(\sigma)$) stands for "CAN(σ) is testable" (resp. "CAN(σ) is definable"). Moreover, if M, N $: \sigma_1 \to \ldots \to \sigma_n \to o$, and P $: o$, we write "**if** P **then** M **else** N" for "$\lambda x_1 : \sigma_1 \ldots x_n : \sigma_n$. **if** P **then** M$x_1 \ldots x_n$ **else** N$x_1 \ldots x_n$".

Lemma 4. *For all SFP-types σ and τ:*

1. $(\mathrm{TEST}(\sigma)$ *and* $\mathrm{DEF}(\tau)) \Rightarrow \mathrm{DEF}(\sigma \to \tau)$.
2. $(\mathrm{DEF}(\sigma)$ *and* $\mathrm{TEST}(\tau)) \Rightarrow \mathrm{TEST}(\sigma \to \tau)$.

Proof. 1) Let $f \in \mathrm{CAN}(\sigma \to \tau)$, $tr(f) = \{(c_1, d_1), \ldots, (c_k, d_k)\}$, and let TEST_1, $\ldots$, $\mathrm{TEST}_k : \sigma \to o$ be the test terms for $\mathrm{CAN}(\sigma)$ (TEST_i is a term testing c_i). Moreover, let $\mathrm{M}_1, \ldots, \mathrm{M}_k : \tau$ be terms defining $d_1, \ldots, d_k$, respectively. Define $\mathrm{M}_f : \sigma \to \tau$ by:

$$\begin{aligned}\mathrm{M}_f = \lambda x : \sigma.\ &\textbf{if } \mathrm{TEST}_1 x \textbf{ then } \mathrm{M}_1 \textbf{ else}\\ &\qquad\textbf{if } \mathrm{TEST}_2 x \textbf{ then } \mathrm{M}_2 \textbf{ else}\\ &\qquad\qquad\vdots\\ &\qquad\qquad\textbf{if } \mathrm{TEST}_k x \textbf{ then } \mathrm{M}_k \textbf{ else } \Omega\end{aligned}$$

In order to show that M_f defines f, remark that, by Lemma 1, $f(x) \neq \perp$ if and only if there exists a unique $c_i \in \mathrm{CAN}(\sigma)$ such that $c_i \leq x$, and in that case $f(x) = d_i$; hence $[\![\mathrm{M}_f]\!](x) = [\![\mathrm{M}_i]\!] = d_i$. It is easy to see that the converse does hold as well.

2) Let $\mathrm{CAN}(\sigma \to \tau) = \{f_1, \ldots, f_k\}$, $tr(f_i) = \{(c_1, d_1^i), \ldots, (c_l, d_l^i)\}$, where $l = \mid \mathrm{CAN}(()\sigma) \mid$, and $[\![M_1]\!] = c_1, \ldots, [\![M_l]\!] = c_l$. Moreover, for $1 \leq r \leq l$, $1 \leq s \leq k$, let TEST_r^s be a test term for d_r^s in $\mathrm{CAN}(\tau)$. Recall that this means:

$$[\![\mathrm{TEST}_r^s]\!](y) = \begin{cases} tt & \text{if } d_r^s \leq y \\ ff & \text{if } \exists x \in \mathrm{CAN}(\tau),\ d_r^s \neq x \text{ and } x \leq y \\ \perp & \text{otherwise} \end{cases}$$

A test term for f_i is then the following:

$$\mathrm{TEST}_i = \lambda f : \sigma \to \tau.\ \mathrm{AND}(\mathrm{TEST}_1^i(f(M_1)), \ldots, \mathrm{TEST}_l^i(f(M_l)))$$

where AND is a (sequential) l-ary conjunction.

First of all, remark that for all $g \in D_{\sigma \to \tau}$, $[\![\mathrm{TEST}_i]\!](g) \neq \perp$ if and only if for all $c_i \in CAN(\sigma)$ $g(c_i)$ is total, and this is the case if and only if g is total. Moreover, $[\![\mathrm{TEST}_i]\!](g) = tt$ if and only if $g \geq f_i$. □

The previous lemma, and the fact that $DEF(o), TEST(o)$ hold trivially, prove that all canonical elements are definable.

Corollary 1. *For all type σ and all $x \in \mathrm{CAN}(\sigma)$, x is definable.*

The main result of this section trivially follows, choosing canonical elements as sequential witnesses of totality classes:

Theorem 2. *Given $\sigma \in SFT$ and $x \in D_\sigma$ such that $x \sim_\sigma^T x$, there exists a definable $y \in D_\sigma$ such that $x \sim_\sigma^T y$.*

2.1 Beyond Finite Types

In this section, we give an overview of Plotkin's argument showing that, if a simple type σ does not have negative occurrences of ι, then Berger's conjecture holds at σ [8].

Definition 6. *Given two simple types σ and τ, $\sigma \lhd \tau$ if there exist two PCF-terms $M : \sigma \to \tau$ and $N : \tau \to \sigma$ such that:*

- *$[\![M]\!]$ and $[\![N]\!]$ are total.*
- *$[\![\lambda x^\sigma N(M(x))]\!] \sim^T_{\sigma\to\sigma} [\![\lambda x^\sigma x]\!]$*

It is easy to see that $\lhd$ is a preorder, and that if $\sigma \lhd \sigma'$ and $\tau \lhd \tau'$ then $(\sigma \to \tau) \lhd (\sigma' \to \tau')$.

Using the PCF-definability of the *fan functional*:$((\iota \to o) \to o) \to \iota$, computing the modulus of continuity of its argument, one can prove the following lemma:

Lemma 5. *If α is a type with no negative occurrences of ι, then $\alpha \lhd \iota$.*

The fact that Berger's conjecture holds at σ, whenever σ satisfies the hypothesis of the previous lemma, follows easily: let H be a total, PCF^{++}-definable[4] functional in D_σ, and let $M : \sigma \to \iota$, $N : \iota \to \sigma$ be the PCF-terms given by Def. 6. If P is a PCF^{++} term defining H, than $MP : \iota$ is PCF-definable, say by $n : \iota$, and $H' = [\![Nn : \sigma]\!]$ is a PCF-definable functional such that $H' \sim^T H$.

All this rests on the facts that, if σ does not contains negative occurrences of ι, then the total, PCF^{++}-definable elements of D_σ can be enumerated by PCF terms.

This result is stronger than the one we present in Sect. 2, but still we think that our proof provides new insights on totality for finite types: first, strictly speaking, Plotkin's argument cannot be formulated in the finite framework, since it is based on enumerations; second, and more important, we provide a semantic characterization of "sequential witnesses" in totality classes. In Sect. 4 we show that, at first order, we are able to characterize also maxima of totality classes.

The validity of Berger's conjecture is an open problem, in the general, infinite case.

3 Scott's Domain and Set Theoretic Boolean Functions

In this section we establish precise relationships between the Scott's type frame and boolean set-theoretic functions and we show that there is a one-to-one correspondence between the set of totality classes and the set of set-theoretic boolean functions. In order to do this first of all we define the hierarchy of set-theoretic functions and a heterogeneous logical relation between Scott's type frame and this hierarchy.

[4] PCF^{++} is a further extension of PCF^{+} with the second order $\exists : (\iota \to o) \to o$ functional, which tests whether its argument yields the value *tt* on some integer.

Definition 7. *The* set-theoretic boolean functions hierarchy $\{S_\sigma\}_{\sigma\in SFT}$ *is inductively defined by:*
S_o *is the set* {*true, false*}
$S_{\sigma\to\tau}$ *is the set of set-theoretic functions from* S_σ *to* S_τ*, usually written* $S_\tau^{S_\sigma}$.

Definition 8. *The* heterogeneous logical relation $\{\sim_\sigma^H\}_{\sigma\in SFT}$, $\sim_\sigma^H\subseteq D_\sigma\times S_\sigma$ *is inductively defined by:*
$tt \sim_o^H$ *true and* $ff \sim_o^H$ *false*
$f \sim_{\sigma\to\tau}^H \varphi$ if *for all* $x\sim_\sigma^H a$, $f(x)\sim_\tau^H \varphi(a)$

The heterogeneous relation $\sim^H$ induces in standard way [4] a partial equivalence relation $\sim_\sigma^S$ on each D_σ. The main result of this section is that this relation coincides with totality.

Definition 9. *The* extensional collapse *induced by* $\sim^H$ *is* $\{\sim_\sigma^S\}_{\sigma\in SFT}$, $\sim_\sigma^S\subseteq D_\sigma\times D_\sigma$*, defined by:*

$$f\sim_\sigma^S g \text{ if there exists } \varphi\in S_\sigma \text{ such that } f\sim_\sigma^H\varphi \text{ and } g\sim_\sigma^H\varphi$$

In order to prove that $\sim^T=\sim^S$, we introduce the following notions:

Definition 10. *A relation* $\sim\subseteq\bigcup_{\sigma\in SFT}D_\sigma\times D_\sigma$ *is* logical at σ *if either* σ *is ground or* $\sigma\equiv\sigma_1\to\sigma_2$ *and for all* $f,g\in D_\sigma$, $f\sim g$ *iff for all* $x,y\in D_{\sigma_1}$, $(x\sim y\Rightarrow f(x)\sim g(y))$.
Moreover $\sim$ *is* logical up to σ *if for all* τ *structurally smaller than* σ, $\sim$ *is logical at* τ.

The proof of the following theorem uses the fact that if two relations $R,S\subseteq\bigcup_{\sigma\in SFT}D_\sigma\times D_\sigma$ are such that R and S are equal at type o and are both logical up to σ, then they are equal up to σ.

Theorem 3. *For all* $\sigma\in SFT$ *the following statements hold:*

SPF$_\sigma$: $\sim_\sigma^H$ *is a surjective partial function from* D_σ *to* S_σ.
LUT$_\sigma$: $\sim^S$ *is logical up to* σ.

Proof. We prove SPF and LUT by simultaneous structural induction on SFT. As for SPF, which trivially holds for the ground type, let us show that it is preserved by arrow type constructor, i.e.:

1. $\forall\varphi\in S_{\sigma\to\tau}\,.\,\exists f\in D_{\sigma\to\tau}\,.\,f\sim_{\sigma\to\tau}^H\varphi$
2. $f\sim^H\varphi$ and $f\sim^H\psi\Rightarrow\varphi=\psi$

As for the first item, by LUT$_\tau$ we know that $\sim^S$ is logical up to τ, and hence $\sim^S=\sim^T$ up to τ. Consequently equivalence classes of $\sim_\tau^S$ are totality classes and by SPF$_\tau$ we conclude that the inverse image via $\sim_\tau^H$ of any given $b\in S_\tau$ is a lattice. Hence we are legitimate to define $k:S_\tau\mapsto D_\tau$ as follows:

$$k(b)=\bigvee\{y\in D_\tau \mid y\sim_\tau^H b\}$$

Let $\varphi \in S_{\sigma\to\tau}$ we define $f \in D_{\sigma\to\tau}$ as follows:

$$f(x) = \begin{cases} k(\varphi(a)) & \text{if } \exists a.\ x \sim^H_\sigma a \\ \bot_\tau & \text{otherwise} \end{cases}$$

Let us check that $f \in D_{\sigma\to\tau}$. Let $x \le y$ be elements of D_σ. If $f(x) = \bot$ we are done. Otherwise $\exists a \in S_\sigma$ such that:

$$x \sim^H_\sigma a \Rightarrow x \sim^S_\sigma x \Rightarrow^{(1)} x \sim^S_\sigma y \Rightarrow^{(2)} y \sim^H_\sigma a \Rightarrow f(x) = f(y)$$

where (1) follows from LUT_σ and Proposition 1.4 and (2) follows from SPF_σ. Finally, $f \sim^H_{\sigma\to\tau} \varphi$ easily follows from the construction of f.

As for the second item let $f \in D_{\sigma\to\tau}$ and $\varphi, \psi \in S_{\sigma\to\tau}$, such that $f \sim^H \varphi$ and $f \sim^H \psi$. In order to show that $\varphi = \psi$, let $a \in S_\sigma$. By SPF_σ, there exists $x \in D_\sigma$ such that $x \sim^H a$. Hence $f(x) \sim^H \varphi(a)$ and $f(x) \sim^H \psi(a)$. By SPF_τ, $\varphi(a) = \psi(a)$.

As for $\mathrm{LUT}_{\sigma\to\tau}$, we have to show that:

$$f \sim^S_{\sigma\to\tau} g \quad \text{iff} \quad \forall x \sim^S_\sigma y.\ f(x) \sim^S_\tau g(y)$$

($\Rightarrow$) Let $f \sim^S_{\sigma\to\tau} g$. By definition of $\sim^S$ there exists $\varphi \in S_{\sigma\to\tau}$ such that $f \sim^H \varphi$ and $g \sim^H \varphi$. Let $x, y \in D_\sigma$ be such that $x \sim^S_\sigma y$. By definition of $\sim^S$ there exist $a \in S_\sigma$ such that $x \sim^H a$ and $y \sim^H a$. Hence $\varphi(a)$ is such that $f(x) \sim^H \varphi(a)$ and $g(y) \sim^H \varphi(a)$ (since $\sim^H$ is a logical relation) and hence we have $f(x) \sim^S_\tau g(y)$.

($\Leftarrow$) Let f and g such that $\forall x \sim^S_\sigma y\ .\ f(x) \sim^S_\tau g(y)$. Then, by definition of $\sim^S$, $x \sim^S_\sigma y$ implies that there exists $b \in S_\sigma$ such that $x \sim^H_\sigma b$ and $y \sim^H_\sigma b$. Similarly $f(x) \sim^S_\tau g(y)$ implies that there exists $c \in S_\tau$ such that $f(x) \sim^H_\tau c$ and $g(y) \sim^H_\tau c$. Since $\sim^H_\sigma$ and $\sim^H_\tau$ are partial surjective function we are done. In fact given f and g as above, we can choose $\varphi : S_\sigma \mapsto S_\tau$ as follows: for all $b \in S_\sigma$ there exists $x \in D_\sigma$ such that $x \sim^H_\sigma b$. Furthermore for all $y \sim^S_\sigma x$, we have that $y \sim^H_\sigma b$. By hypothesis $f(x) \sim^S_\tau g(y)$ and then there exists $c \in S_\tau$ such that $f(x) \sim^H_\tau c$ and $g(y) \sim^H_\tau c$. Since $\sim^H_\tau$ is a function, this element c is uniquely determined. Clearly for the map φ, such that $b \overset{\varphi}{\mapsto} c$, we have $f \sim^H_{\sigma\to\tau} \varphi$ and $g \sim^H_{\sigma\to\tau} \varphi$. □

Corollary 2. *For all $\sigma \in SFT$ we have $\sim^S_\sigma = \sim^T_\sigma$*

Proof. It suffices to observe that at ground type o we have $\sim^S_o = \sim^T_o$ and that, by above theorem, both relations are logical. □

Now we are able to prove the existence of a bijection between totality classes and set-theoretic boolean functions.

Corollary 3. *For all $\sigma \in SFT$ there exists a bijection $\mathcal{I}_\sigma : D_{\sigma/\sim^T} \to S_\sigma$*

Proof. It suffices to show that $D_{\sigma/\sim^T} \to D_{\tau/\sim^T} \simeq D_{\sigma\to\tau/\sim^T}$.
Define $\mathcal{I}_{\sigma\to\tau}([f]_{\sim^T}) = \varphi$, where $f \sim^H \varphi$ and check that $\mathcal{I}_{\sigma\to\tau}$ is a bijection using Theorem 3. □

Corollary 3 essentially states that the extensional collapse of $\{D_\sigma\}$ by the totality relation yields exactly $\{S_\sigma\}$. We remark that this result cannot be extended to infinite types: in fact, if we add the type ι of integers to simple types, interpreted by the flat domain D_ι and the set S_ι of natural numbers, respectively, the following cardinality argument can be applied[5]. Each D_σ is an $\omega-$algebraic domain, that is the set of its compact elements is countable. This implies, by algebraicity that the cardinality of each D_σ is at most $2^{\aleph_0}$, whereas the cardinality of $S_{(\iota\to\iota)\to\iota}$ (pure type 2) is already $2^{2^{\aleph_0}}$. By the way it could be interesting to investigate the class of continuous functionals defined at type σ as the inverse image of $\sim^H_\sigma$. These functionals are total in natural sense.

4 First Order Boolean Functions

In this section we turn to first order set-theoretic functions, i.e. functions of type $\underbrace{o \to o \to \ldots \to o}_{n} \to o$ for some n[6]. These functions are known as *formulae* in complexity theory. Our goal is to use the totality class T_φ associated by $\sim^H$ to any formula φ as tool to study its computational properties. In particular any elements of T_φ is a parallel algorithm to compute φ, since elements of T_φ are PCF$^+$ definable and some of them are sequential (PCF definable). In Sect. 2 we have shown that the bottom element of T_φ is always sequential. A natural question arise about the degree of parallelism [9] of the top element of T_φ: is it the maximum degree of parallelism in T_φ? Without going into details about degrees of parallelism we can answer negatively providing an example of totality class which contains parallel elements, but whose top is sequential.

Example 1. Consider the two argument constantly true function $\kappa \in S_{o\to o\to o}$ and the following PCF$^+$ terms:

$$S_{true} = \lambda x^o, y^o.\ \mathbf{true}$$
$$P_{true} = \lambda x^o, y^o.\ \mathbf{por}(\mathbf{por}(x,y), \mathbf{por}(\mathrm{NOT}(x), \mathrm{NOT}(y)))$$

The first term is a PCF term, and one can show that no PCF term can define $[\![P_{true}]\!]$. It is easy to see, furthermore, that $[\![S_{true}]\!], [\![P_{true}]\!] \in T_\kappa$, and that $[\![S_{true}]\!]$ is the top element in T_κ.

However top elements of totality classes do have computational relevance as laziest algorithms: this means that the top element $\overline{f}$ of a given totality class $[f]_{\sim^T}$ yields a total result using only "needed" information. More formally, $\overline{f}x_1 \ldots x_n$ is defined whenever f is constant on maximal points of the principal ideal of $(x_1, \ldots, x_n)$. On the other hand, $\underline{f}$ is defined exactly on maximal point of D^n_o and this implies that $\underline{f}$ is not only sequential, but also definable in call-by-value PCF.

[5] The definitions of $\sim^H$ and $\sim^S$ go through this extension, definining $\sim^H_\iota = \{(n, \mathrm{n})\}$.

[6] Throughout this section we abbreviate this type by $o^n \to o$. We fell free of interchanging curried and uncurried versions of it.

We are able to define two families of PCF (resp. PCF$^+$) terms $\mathcal{B}_n$ (resp.$\mathcal{T}_n$) which transform a given total function f into $\underline{f}$ (resp. $\overline{f}$). We define them inductively on the arity of f:

$$\begin{array}{ll}\mathcal{B}_0 = \lambda x^o.x & \mathcal{T}_0 = \lambda x^o.x \\ \mathcal{B}_{n+1} = \lambda f^{o^{n+1}\to o}. & \mathcal{T}_{n+1} = \lambda f^{o^{n+1}\to o}. \\ \quad \lambda x^o.\lambda y^{o^n}.\ \textbf{if}\ x & \quad \lambda x^o.\lambda y^{o^n}.\ \textbf{pif}\ x \\ \quad\quad \textbf{then}\ \mathcal{B}_n(f\ \textbf{true})y & \quad\quad \textbf{then}\ \mathcal{T}_n(f\ \textbf{true})y \\ \quad\quad \textbf{else}\ \mathcal{B}_n(f\ \textbf{false})y & \quad\quad \textbf{else}\ \mathcal{T}_n(f\ \textbf{false})y \end{array}$$

where **pif** is the "parallel if" constant [7], as expressive as **por**, such that $[\![\,\textbf{pif\_then\_else\_}]\!](x,b,b) = b$ and $[\![\,\textbf{pif\_then\_else\_}]\!](b)=[\![\,\textbf{if\_then\_else\_}]\!](b)$ for $b \neq \perp$.

Since it is trivial to check that $[\![\,\mathcal{B}_n]\!](f) = \underline{f}$ (just remark that $[\![\,\mathcal{B}_n]\!](f)$ is defined exactly on total tuples), we restrict ourselves to prove the correctness of the definition of $\mathcal{T}_n$.

Proposition 2. *Let $f \in D_{o^n\to o}$ be a total function. Then the following statements hold:*

1. $\mathcal{T}_n f \sim^T f$
2. $\forall g.\ g \sim^T f.\ g \leq \mathcal{T}_n f$

Proof. Induction on n. (**0**) Obvious.
(**n + 1**) As for 1, it suffices to check the definition of $\mathcal{T}_{n+1}$. Let $g \sim^T f, g \in D_{o^{n+1}\to o}$ and $x \in D_{o^{n+1}}$. We show that $g(x) \leq (\mathcal{T}_{n+1}f)x$. We distinguish two cases:

– $x_1 \neq \perp$. Since $g(x_1) \sim^T f(x_1)$, the following holds:

$$g(x_1, x_2, \ldots, x_{n+1}) \stackrel{curry}{=} (gx_1)x_2 \ldots x_{n+1} \leq \stackrel{Ind.H}{\leq} \mathcal{T}_n(fx_1)x_2 \ldots x_{n+1} \stackrel{def}{=} (\mathcal{T}_{n+1}f)x_1x_2 \ldots x_{n+1}$$

– $x_1 = \perp$. Suppose that $g\perp x_2 \ldots x_{n+1} = b \neq \perp$ (otherwise the statements holds trivially). By monotonicity of g, $g(tt)x_2 \ldots x_{n+1} = g(ff)x_2 \ldots x_{n+1} = b \neq \perp$. By inductive hypothesis:

$$g(tt)x_2 \ldots x_{n+1} = \mathcal{T}_n(f(tt))x_2 \ldots x_{n+1}$$

and

$$g(ff)x_2 \ldots x_{n+1} = \mathcal{T}_n(f(ff)))x_2 \ldots x_{n+1}$$

and this implies that $\mathcal{T}_{n+1}f\,ff\,x_2 \ldots x_{n+1} = b$, by definition of **pif**.

□

In order to approach the issue of sensitivity, let us consider two classes of formulae: χ_n and κ_n computing respectively the n-ary parity function and the n-ary constant true function. We observe that T_{χ_n}, is a singleton for all n, whereas the size of T_{κ_n} grows exponentially in n. Intuitively the χ_n's are "difficult" to compute, whereas the κ_n's are "easy". This intuition is supported by the following definition of sensitivity [10].

Definition 11. *Let* $\varphi \in S_{o^n \to o}$ *and* $x \in S_o^n$. *Let* $x^{(i)} = (x_1, \ldots, \neg x_i, \ldots x_n)$. *The* sensitivity *of* φ *on* x *is*[7]*:*

$$s_x(\varphi) = \sum_{i=1}^{n} (\varphi(x) \ominus \varphi(x^{(i)}))$$

The sensitivity of φ *is:*

$$s(\varphi) = \sum_{x \in S_o^n} s_x(\varphi)$$

We remark that the sensitivity of χ_n is $2^n n$ and the sensitivity of κ_n is 0 for all n. Hence for these classes of formulae there is an inverse proportion between the size of totality classes and sensitivity. We believe that this phenomenon is general and we conjecture that the size of T_φ is functionally related to $s(\varphi)$. We checked this fact at type $o \to o \to o$, for which the following interesting relation holds:

$$2\lfloor \log_2 |T_\varphi| \rfloor + s(\varphi) = 2^2 2$$

Indeed the property we conjecture is not surprising since if φ has a low sensitivity w.r.t. some arguments, then there are many (inessentially) different ways to compute φ, taking decisions on evaluating them or not.

References

1. Barreiro, N., Ehrhard, T.: *Anatomy of an extensional collapse.* Submittend paper. (1997). Available from `http://hypatia.dcs.qmw.ac.uk/cgi-bin/sarah?q=ehrhard`.
2. Berger, U.: *Total Objects and Sets in domain Theory.* Annals of Pure and Applied Logic **60** (1993) 91–117
3. Boppana, R. B., Sipser, M.: *The Complexity of finite functions.* In: van Leeuwen, J. (ed.): Handbook of Theoretical Computer Science, vol. A. Elsevier (1990) 759–802
4. Bucciarelli, A.: *Logical Reconstruction of Bi-Domains.* Proc. of the 3rd Int. Conf. on Typed Lambda Calculi and Applications, LNCS 1210, Springer-Verlag (1997) 99–111
5. Ehrhard, T.: *A relative definability result for strongly stable functions, and some corollaries.* (1997) To appear in Information and Computation. Available from `http://hypatia.dcs.qmw.ac.uk/cgi-bin/sarah?q=ehrhard`.
6. Mitchell, J. C.: *Type Systems for Programming Languages.* In: van Leeuwen, J. (ed.): Handbook of Theoretical Computer Science, vol. B, Elsevier (1990) 365–458
7. Plotkin, G.: *LCF considered as a programming language.* Theoretical Computer Science **5** (1997) 223–256
8. Plotkin, G.: *Full Abstraction, Totality and PCF.* Available from `http://hypatia.dcs.qmw.ac.uk/authors/P/PlotkinGD/`
9. Sazonov, V. Y.: *Degrees of Parallelism in Computations.* Proc. Conference on Mathematical Foundations of Computer Science, LNCS 45, Springer-Verlag (1976)
10. Wegener, I.: *The Complexity of Boolean functions.* Wiley-Teubner Series in Comp. Sci., New York - Stutgart (1987)

[7] $\ominus : S_o^2 \to \{0, 1\}$ yields 0 if its arguments are equal and 1 otherwise.

Quantum Counting

Gilles Brassard [1]*, Peter Høyer [2]**, and Alain Tapp [1]***

[1] Université de Montréal, {brassard,tappa}@iro.umontreal.ca
[2] Odense University, u2pi@imada.ou.dk

Abstract. We study some extensions of Grover's quantum searching algorithm. First, we generalize the Grover iteration in the light of a concept called amplitude amplification. Then, we show that the quadratic speedup obtained by the quantum searching algorithm over classical brute force can still be obtained for a large family of search problems for which good classical heuristics exist. Finally, as our main result, we combine ideas from Grover's and Shor's quantum algorithms to perform approximate counting, which can be seen as an amplitude estimation process.

1 Introduction

Quantum computing is a field at the junction of theoretical modern physics and theoretical computer science. Practical experiments involving a few quantum bits have been successfully performed, and much progress has been achieved in quantum information theory, quantum error correction and fault tolerant quantum computation. Although we are still far from having desktop quantum computers in our offices, the quantum computational paradigm could soon be more than mere theoretical exercise [5, and references therein].

The discovery by Peter Shor [11] of a polynomial-time quantum algorithm for factoring and computing discrete logarithms was a major milestone in the history of quantum computing. Another significant result is Lov Grover's quantum search algorithm [9]. Grover's algorithm does not solve **NP**–complete problems in polynomial time, but the wide range of its applications compensates for this.

The search problem and Grover's iteration are reviewed in Section 2. It was already implicit in [6] that the heart of Grover's algorithm can be viewed as an amplitude amplification process. Here, we develop this viewpoint and obtain a more general algorithm.

When the structure in a search problem cannot be exploited, any quantum algorithm requires a computation time at least proportional to the square root of the time taken by brute-force classical searching [2]. In practice, the structure of

* Supported in part by Canada's NSERC, Québec's FCAR and the Canada Council.
** Supported in part by the ESPRIT Long Term Research Programme of the EU under project number 20244 (ALCOM-IT). Research carried out while this author was at the Université de Montréal.
*** Supported in part by postgraduate fellowships from FCAR and NSERC.

the search problem can usually be exploited, yielding deterministic or heuristic algorithms that are much more efficient than brute force would be. In Section 3, we study a vast family of heuristics for which we show how to adapt the quantum search algorithm to preserve quadratic speedup over classical techniques.

In Section 4, we present, as our main result, a quantum algorithm to perform counting. This is the problem of counting the number of elements that fulfill some specific requirements, instead of merely finding such an element. Our algorithm builds on both Grover's iteration [9] as described in [3] and the quantum Fourier transform as used in [11]. The accuracy of the algorithm depends on the amount of time one is willing to invest. As Grover's algorithm is a special case of the amplitude amplification process, our counting algorithm can also be viewed as a special case of the more general process of *amplitude estimation.*

We assume in this paper that the reader is familiar with basic notions of quantum computing [1, 4].

2 Quantum Amplitude Amplification

Consider the following search problem: Given a Boolean function $F : X \to \{0, 1\}$ defined on some finite domain X, find an input $x \in X$ for which $F(x) = 1$, provided such an x exists. We assume that F is given as a black box, so that it is not possible to obtain knowledge about F by any other means than evaluating it on points in its domain. The best classical strategy is to evaluate F on random elements of X. If there is a unique $x_0 \in X$ on which F takes value 1, this strategy evaluates F on roughly half the elements of the domain in order to determine x_0. By contrast, Grover [9] discovered a quantum algorithm that only requires an expected number of evaluations of F in the order of $\sqrt{N}$, where $N = |X|$ denotes the cardinality of X.

It is useful for what follows to think of the above-mentioned classical strategy in terms of an algorithm that keeps boosting the probability of finding x_0. The algorithm evaluates F on new inputs, until it eventually finds the unique input x_0 on which F takes value 1. The probability that the algorithm stops after exactly j evaluations of F is $1/N$ $(1 \le j \le N-2)$, and thus we can consider that each evaluation boosts the probability of success by an additive amount of $1/N$.

Intuitively, the quantum analog of boosting the probability of success would be to boost the *amplitude* of being in a certain subspace of a Hilbert space, and indeed the algorithm found by Grover can be seen as working by that latter principle [9, 3]. As discovered by Brassard and Høyer [6], the idea of amplifying the amplitude of a subspace is a technique that applies in general. Following [6], we refer to this as *amplitude amplification*, and describe the technique below. For this, we require the following notion, which we shall use throughout the rest of this section.

Let $|\Upsilon\rangle$ be any pure state of a joint quantum system $\mathcal{H}$. Write $|\Upsilon\rangle$ as a superposition of orthonormal states according to the state of the first subsystem:

$$|\Upsilon\rangle = \sum_{i \in \mathbb{Z}} x_i |i\rangle |\Upsilon_i\rangle$$

so that only a finite number of the states $|i\rangle|\Upsilon_i\rangle$ have nonzero amplitude x_i.

Every Boolean function $\chi : \mathbb{Z} \to \{0,1\}$ induces two orthogonal subspaces of $\mathcal{H}$, allowing us to rewrite $|\Upsilon\rangle$ as follows:

$$|\Upsilon\rangle = |\Upsilon^a\rangle + |\Upsilon^b\rangle = \sum_{i\in\chi^{-1}(1)} x_i|i\rangle|\Upsilon_i\rangle + \sum_{i\in\chi^{-1}(0)} x_i|i\rangle|\Upsilon_i\rangle. \quad (1)$$

We say that a state $|i\rangle|\cdot\rangle$ is *good* if $\chi(i) = 1$, and otherwise it is *bad*. Thus, we have that $|\Upsilon^a\rangle$ denotes the projection of $|\Upsilon\rangle$ onto the subspace spanned by the good states, and similarly $|\Upsilon^b\rangle$ is the projection of $|\Upsilon\rangle$ onto the subspace spanned by the bad states. Let $a_\Upsilon = \langle\Upsilon^a|\Upsilon^a\rangle$ denote the probability that measuring $|\Upsilon\rangle$ produces a good state, and similarly let $b_\Upsilon = \langle\Upsilon^b|\Upsilon^b\rangle$. Since $|\Upsilon^a\rangle$ and $|\Upsilon^b\rangle$ are orthogonal, we have $a_\Upsilon + b_\Upsilon = 1$.

Let $\mathcal{A}$ be any quantum algorithm that acts on $\mathcal{H}$ and uses no measurements. The heart of amplitude amplification is the following operator [6]

$$\mathbf{Q} = \mathbf{Q}(\mathcal{A}, \chi, \phi, \varphi) = -\mathcal{A}\mathbf{S}_0^\phi\mathcal{A}^{-1}\mathbf{S}_\chi^\varphi. \quad (2)$$

Here, ϕ and φ are complex numbers of unit norm, and operator $\mathbf{S}_\chi^\varphi$ conditionally changes the phase by a factor of φ:

$$|i\rangle|\cdot\rangle \longmapsto \begin{cases} \varphi|i\rangle|\cdot\rangle & \text{if } \chi(i) = 1 \\ |i\rangle|\cdot\rangle & \text{if } \chi(i) = 0. \end{cases}$$

Further, $\mathbf{S}_0^\phi$ changes the phase of a state by a factor of ϕ if and only if the first register holds a zero. The operator $\mathbf{Q}$ is a generalization of the iteration applied by Grover in his original quantum searching paper [9]. It was first used in [6] to obtain an exact quantum polynomial-time algorithm for Simon's problem. It is well-defined since we assume that $\mathcal{A}$ uses no measurements and, therefore, $\mathcal{A}$ has an inverse.

Denote the complex conjugate of λ by λ^*. It is easy to show the following lemma by a few simple rewritings.

Lemma 1. *Let $|\Upsilon\rangle$ be any superposition. Then*

$$\mathcal{A}\mathbf{S}_0^\phi\mathcal{A}^{-1}|\Upsilon\rangle = |\Upsilon\rangle - (1-\phi)\langle\Upsilon|\mathcal{A}|\mathbf{0}\rangle^*\mathcal{A}|\mathbf{0}\rangle.$$

By factorizing $\mathbf{Q}$ as $(\mathcal{A}\mathbf{S}_0^\phi\mathcal{A}^{-1})(-\mathbf{S}_\chi^\varphi)$, the next lemma follows.

Lemma 2. *Let $|\Upsilon\rangle = |\Upsilon^a\rangle + |\Upsilon^b\rangle$ be any superposition. Then*

$$\mathbf{Q}|\Upsilon^a\rangle = -\varphi|\Upsilon^a\rangle + \varphi(1-\phi)\langle\Upsilon^a|\mathcal{A}|\mathbf{0}\rangle^*\mathcal{A}|\mathbf{0}\rangle \quad (3)$$

$$\mathbf{Q}|\Upsilon^b\rangle = -|\Upsilon^b\rangle + (1-\phi)\langle\Upsilon^b|\mathcal{A}|\mathbf{0}\rangle^*\mathcal{A}|\mathbf{0}\rangle. \quad (4)$$

In particular, letting $|\Upsilon\rangle$ be $\mathcal{A}|\mathbf{0}\rangle = |\Psi^a\rangle + |\Psi^b\rangle$ implies that the subspace spanned by $|\Psi^a\rangle$ and $|\Psi^b\rangle$ is invariant under the action of $\mathbf{Q}$.

Lemma 3. *Let $\mathcal{A}|\mathbf{0}\rangle = |\Psi\rangle = |\Psi^a\rangle + |\Psi^b\rangle$. Then*

$$\mathbf{Q}\,|\Psi^a\rangle = \varphi((1-\phi)a-1)|\Psi^a\rangle + \qquad \varphi(1-\phi)a|\Psi^b\rangle \tag{5}$$
$$\mathbf{Q}\,|\Psi^b\rangle = -((1-\phi)a+\phi)|\Psi^b\rangle + (1-\phi)(1-a)|\Psi^a\rangle, \tag{6}$$

where $a = \langle\Psi^a|\Psi^a\rangle$.

From Lemmas 2 and 3 it follows that, for any vector $|\Upsilon\rangle = |\Upsilon^a\rangle + |\Upsilon^b\rangle$, the subspace spanned by the set $\{|\Upsilon^a\rangle, |\Upsilon^b\rangle, |\Psi^a\rangle, |\Psi^b\rangle\}$ is invariant under the action of $\mathbf{Q}$. By setting $\phi = \varphi = -1$, we find the following much simpler expressions.

Lemma 4. *Let $\mathcal{A}|\mathbf{0}\rangle = |\Psi\rangle = |\Psi^a\rangle + |\Psi^b\rangle$, and let $\mathbf{Q} = \mathbf{Q}(\mathcal{A}, \chi, -1, -1)$. Then*

$$\mathbf{Q}\,|\Psi^a\rangle = (1-2a)|\Psi^a\rangle - 2a|\Psi^b\rangle \tag{7}$$
$$\mathbf{Q}\,|\Psi^b\rangle = (1-2a)|\Psi^b\rangle + 2b|\Psi^a\rangle, \tag{8}$$

where $a = \langle\Psi^a|\Psi^a\rangle$ and $b = 1 - a = \langle\Psi^b|\Psi^b\rangle$.

The recursive formulae defined by Equations 7 and 8 were solved in [3], and their solution is given in the following theorem. The general cases defined by Equations 3–6 have similar solutions, but we shall not need them in what follows.

Theorem 1 (Amplitude Amplification—simple case). *Let $\mathcal{A}|\mathbf{0}\rangle = |\Psi\rangle = |\Psi^a\rangle + |\Psi^b\rangle$, and let $\mathbf{Q} = \mathbf{Q}(\mathcal{A}, \chi, -1, -1)$. Then, for all $j \geq 0$,*

$$\mathbf{Q}^j \mathcal{A}\,|\mathbf{0}\rangle = k_j|\Psi^a\rangle + \ell_j|\Psi^b\rangle,$$

where

$$k_j = \frac{1}{\sqrt{a}}\sin((2j+1)\theta) \quad \text{and} \quad \ell_j = \frac{1}{\sqrt{1-a}}\cos((2j+1)\theta),$$

and where θ is defined so that $\sin^2(\theta) = a = \langle\Psi^a|\Psi^a\rangle$ and $0 \leq \theta \leq \pi/2$.

Theorem 1 yields a method for boosting the success probability a of a quantum algorithm $\mathcal{A}$. Consider what happens if we apply $\mathcal{A}$ on the initial state $|\mathbf{0}\rangle$ and then measure the system. The probability that the outcome is a good state is a. If, instead of applying $\mathcal{A}$, we apply operator $\mathbf{Q}^m\mathcal{A}$ for some integer $m \geq 1$, then our success probability is given by $ak_m^2 = \sin^2((2m+1)\theta)$. Therefore, to obtain a high probability of success, we want to choose integer m such that $\sin^2((2m+1)\theta)$ is close to 1. Unfortunately, our ability to choose m wisely depends on our knowledge about θ, which itself depends on a. The two extreme cases are when we know the exact value of a, and when we have no prior knowledge about a whatsoever.

Suppose the value of a is known. If $a > 0$, then by letting $m = \lfloor \pi/4\theta \rfloor$, we have that $ak_m^2 \geq 1 - a$, as shown in [3]. The next theorem is immediate.

Theorem 2 (Quadratic speedup). *Let $\mathcal{A}$ be any quantum algorithm that uses no measurements, and let $\chi : \mathbb{Z} \to \{0,1\}$ be any Boolean function. Let the initial success probability a and angle θ be defined as in Theorem 1. Suppose $a > 0$ and set $m = \lfloor \pi/4\theta \rfloor$. Then, if we compute $\mathbf{Q}^m \mathcal{A}|\mathbf{0}\rangle$ and measure the system, the outcome is good with probability at least* $\max(1-a, a)$.

This theorem is often referred to as a quadratic speedup, or the square-root running-time result. The reason for this is that if an algorithm $\mathcal{A}$ has success probability $a > 0$, then after an expected number of $1/a$ applications of $\mathcal{A}$, we will find a good solution. Applying the above theorem reduces this to an expected number of at most $(2m+1)/(1-a) \in \Theta(\sqrt{1/a})$ applications of $\mathcal{A}$ and its inverse.

Suppose the value of a is known and that $0 < a < 1$. Theorem 2 allows us to find a good solution with probability at least $\max(1-a, a)$. A natural question to ask is whether it is possible to improve this to certainty, still given the value of a. It turns out that the answer is positive. This is unlike classical computers, where no such general de-randomization technique is known. We now describe two optimal methods for obtaining this, but other approaches are possible.

The first method is by applying amplitude amplification, not on the original algorithm $\mathcal{A}$, but on a slightly modified version of it. If $\tilde{m} = \pi/4\theta - 1/2$ is an integer, then we would have $\ell_{\tilde{m}} = 0$, and we would succeed with certainty. In general, $m_0 = \lceil \tilde{m} \rceil$ iterations is a fraction of 1 iteration too many, but we can compensate for that by choosing $\theta_0 = \pi/(4m_0+2)$, an angle slightly smaller than θ. Any quantum algorithm that succeeds with probability a_0 such that $\sin^2(\theta_0) = a_0$, will succeed with certainty after m_0 iterations of amplitude amplification. Given $\mathcal{A}$ and its initial success probability a, it is easy to construct a new quantum algorithm that succeeds with probability $a_0 \le a$: Let $\mathcal{B}$ denote the quantum algorithm that takes a single qubit in the initial state $|0\rangle$ and rotates it to the superposition $\sqrt{1-a_0/a}\,|0\rangle + \sqrt{a_0/a}\,|1\rangle$. Apply both $\mathcal{A}$ and $\mathcal{B}$, and define a good solution as one in which $\mathcal{A}$ produces a good solution, and the outcome of $\mathcal{B}$ is the state $|1\rangle$.

The second method is to slow down the speed of the very last iteration. First, apply $m_0 = \lfloor \tilde{m} \rfloor$ iterations of amplitude amplification with $\phi = \varphi = -1$. Then, if $m_0 < \tilde{m}$, apply one more iteration with complex phase-shifts ϕ and φ satisfying $\ell_{m_0}^2 = 2a(1 - \mathrm{Re}(\phi))$ and so that $\varphi(1-\phi)ak_{m_0} - ((1-\phi)a + \phi)\ell_{m_0}$ vanishes. Going through the algebra and applying Lemma 3 shows that this produces a good solution with certainty. For the case $m_0 = 0$, this second method was independently discovered by Chi and Kim [7].

Suppose now that the value of a is not known. In Section 4, we discuss techniques for finding a good estimate of a, after which one then can apply a weakened version of Theorem 2 to find a good solution. Another idea is to try to find a good solution without prior computation of an estimate of a. Within that approach, by adapting the ideas in Section 4 in [3] (Section 6 in its final version), we can still obtain a quadratic speedup.

Theorem 3 (Quadratic speedup without knowing a). *Let $\mathcal{A}$ be any quantum algorithm that uses no measurements, and let $\chi : \mathbb{Z} \to \{0,1\}$ be any Boolean* *function. Let the initial success probability a of $\mathcal{A}$ be defined as in Theorem 1. Then there exists a quantum algorithm that finds a good solution using an expected number of $\Theta(\sqrt{1/a}\,)$ applications of $\mathcal{A}$ and its inverse if $a > 0$, and otherwise runs forever.*

By applying this theorem to the searching problem defined in the first paragraph of this section, we obtain the following result from [3], which itself is a generalization of the work by Grover [9].

Corollary 1. *Let $F : X \to \{0,1\}$ be any Boolean function defined on a finite set X. Then there exists a quantum algorithm* **Search** *that finds an $x \in X$ such that $F(x) = 1$ using an expected number of $\Theta(\sqrt{|X|/t}\,)$ evaluations of F, provided such an x exists, and otherwise runs forever. Here $t = |\{x \in X \mid F(x) = 1\}|$ denotes the cardinality of the preimage of 1.*

Proof. Apply Theorem 3 with $\chi = F$ and $\mathcal{A}$ being any unitary transformation that maps $|0\rangle$ to $\frac{1}{\sqrt{|X|}} \sum_{x \in X} |x\rangle$, such as the Walsh–Hadamard transform. □

3 Quantum Heuristics

If function F has no useful structure, then quantum algorithm **Search** will be more efficient than any classical (deterministic or probabilistic) algorithm. In sharp contrast, if some useful information is known about the function, then some classical algorithm might be very efficient. Useful information might be clear mathematical statements or intuitive information stated as a probability distribution of the likelihood of x being a solution. The information we have about F might also be expressed as an efficient classical heuristic to find a solution. In this section, we address the problem of heuristics.

Search problems, and in particular **NP** problems, are often very difficult to solve. For many **NP**–complete problems, practical algorithms are known that are more efficient than brute force search on the average: they take advantage of the problem's structure and especially of the input distribution. Although in general very few theoretical results exist about the efficiency of heuristics, they are very efficient in practice.

We concentrate on a large but simple family of heuristics that can be applied to search problems. Here, by heuristics, we mean a probabilistic algorithm running in polynomial time that outputs what one is searching for with some nonzero probability. Our goal is to apply Grover's technique for heuristics in order to speed them up, in the same way that Grover speeds up black-box search, without making things too complicated.

More formally, suppose we have a family $\mathcal{F}$ of functions such that each $F \in \mathcal{F}$ is of the form $F : X \to \{0,1\}$. A *heuristic* is a function $G : \mathcal{F} \times R \to X$, for an appropriate finite set R. For every function $F \in \mathcal{F}$, let $t_F = |F^{-1}(1)|$ and $h_F = |\{r \in R \mid F(G(F,r)) = 1\}|$. We say that the heuristic is *efficient* for a given F if $h_F/|R| > t_F/|X|$ and the heuristic is *good* in general if

$$\mathrm{E}_{\mathcal{F}}\left(\frac{h_F}{|R|}\right) > \mathrm{E}_{\mathcal{F}}\left(\frac{t_F}{|X|}\right) .$$

Here $\mathrm{E}_{\mathcal{F}}$ denotes the expectation over all F according to some fixed distribution. Note that for some F, h_F might be small but repeated uses of the heuristic, with seeds r uniformly chosen in R, will increase the probability of finding a solution.

Theorem 4. *Given a search problem F chosen in a family $\mathcal{F}$ according to some distribution, if using a heuristic G, a solution to F is found in expected time T then, using a quantum computer, a solution can be found in expected time in $O(\sqrt{T})$.*

Proof. We simply combine the quantum algorithm **Search** with the heuristic G. Let $G'(r) = F(G(F,r))$, clearly $x = G(F, \mathbf{Search}(G'))$ is such that $F(x) = 1$. Thus, by Corollary 1, for each function $F \in \mathcal{F}$, we have an expected running time of $\Theta(\sqrt{|R|/h_F})$. Let P_F denote the probability that F occurs. Then $\sum_{F\in\mathcal{F}} P_F = 1$, and we have that the expected running time is of order $\sum_{F\in\mathcal{F}} \sqrt{|R|/h_F}\, P_F$, which can be rewritten as

$$\sum_{F\in\mathcal{F}} \sqrt{\frac{|R|}{h_F} P_F}\sqrt{P_F} \leq \left(\sum_{F\in\mathcal{F}} \frac{|R|}{h_F} P_F\right)^{1/2} \left(\sum_{F\in\mathcal{F}} P_F\right)^{1/2} = \left(\sum_{F\in\mathcal{F}} \frac{|R|}{h_F} P_F\right)^{1/2},$$

by Cauchy–Schwarz's inequality. □

4 Approximate Counting

In this section, we do not concentrate on finding one solution, but rather on counting them. For this, we complement Grover's iteration [9] using techniques inspired by Shor's quantum factoring algorithm [11].

Counting Problem: Given a Boolean function F defined on some finite set $X = \{0, \ldots, N-1\}$, find or approximate $t = |F^{-1}(1)|$.

Before we proceed, here is the basic intuition. From Section 2 it follows that, in Grover's algorithm, the amplitude of the set $F^{-1}(1)$, as well as the amplitude of the set $F^{-1}(0)$, varies with the number of iterations according to a periodic function. We also note that the period (frequency) of this association is in *direct* relation with the sizes of these sets. Thus, estimating their common period using Fourier analysis will give us useful information on the sizes of those two sets. Since the period will be the same if $F^{-1}(1)$ has cardinality t, as if $F^{-1}(1)$ has cardinality $N-t$, we will in the rest of this section assume that $t \leq N/2$.

The quantum algorithm **Count** we give to solve this problem has two parameters: the function F given as a black box and an integer P that will determine the precision of our estimate, as well as the time taken by the algorithm. For simplicity, we assume that P and N are powers of 2, but this is not essential. Our algorithm is based on the following two unitary transformations:

$$\mathbf{C}_F : |m\rangle \otimes |\Psi\rangle \rightarrow |m\rangle \otimes (\mathbf{G}_F)^m |\Psi\rangle$$

$$\mathbf{F}_P : |k\rangle \rightarrow \frac{1}{\sqrt{P}} \sum_{l=0}^{P-1} e^{2\pi\imath kl/P} |l\rangle.$$

Here $\imath = \sqrt{-1}$ and $\mathbf{G}_F = \mathbf{Q}(\mathbf{W}, F, -1, -1)$ denotes the iteration originally used by Grover [9], where $\mathbf{W}$ denotes the Walsh–Hadamard transform on n qubits that maps $|0\rangle$ to $2^{-n/2}\sum_{i=0}^{2^n-1}|i\rangle$.

In order to apply $\mathbf{C}_F$ even if its first argument is in a quantum superposition, it is necessary to have an upper bound on the value of m, which is the purpose of parameter P. Thus, unitary transformation $\mathbf{C}_F$ performs exactly P Grover's iterations so that P evaluations of F are required. The quantum Fourier transform can be efficiently implemented (see [11] for example).

Count(F, P)

1. $|\Psi_0\rangle \leftarrow \mathbf{W} \otimes \mathbf{W}\, |0\rangle|0\rangle$
2. $|\Psi_1\rangle \leftarrow \mathbf{C}_F\, |\Psi_0\rangle$
3. $|\Psi_2\rangle \leftarrow |\Psi_1\rangle$ after the second register is measured (*optional*)
4. $|\Psi_3\rangle \leftarrow \mathbf{F}_P \otimes \mathbf{I}\, |\Psi_2\rangle$
5. $\tilde{f} \leftarrow$ measure $|\Psi_3\rangle$ (if $\tilde{f} > P/2$ then $\tilde{f} \leftarrow (P - \tilde{f})$)
6. output: $N\sin^2(\tilde{f}\pi/P)$ (and $\tilde{f}$ if needed)

The following theorem tells us how to make proper use of algorithm **Count**.

Theorem 5. *Let $F : \{0, \dots, N-1\} \to \{0, 1\}$ be a Boolean function, $t = |F^{-1}(1)| \leq N/2$ and $\tilde{t}$ be the output of* **Count**(F, P) *with $P \geq 4$, then*

$$|t - \tilde{t}| < \frac{2\pi}{P}\sqrt{tN} + \frac{\pi^2}{P^2}N$$

with probability at least $8/\pi^2$.

Proof. Let us follow the state through the algorithm using notation from Section 2.

$$|\Psi_0\rangle = \frac{1}{\sqrt{PN}}\sum_{m=0}^{P-1}\sum_{x=0}^{N-1}|m\rangle|x\rangle$$

$$|\Psi_1\rangle = \frac{1}{\sqrt{P}}\sum_{m=0}^{P-1}|m\rangle\left(k_m \sum_{x\in F^{-1}(1)}|x\rangle \;+\; \ell_m \sum_{x\in F^{-1}(0)}|x\rangle\right).$$

We introduced Step 3 to make it intuitively clear to the reader why the Fourier transform in Step 4 gives us what we want. The result of this measurement is not used in the algorithm and this is why it is optional: the final outcome would be the same if Step 3 were not performed. Without loss of generality, assume that the state x observed in the second register is such that $F(x) = 1$. Then by replacing k_m by its definition we obtain

$$|\Psi_2\rangle = \alpha\sum_{m=0}^{P-1}\sin((2m+1)\theta)\,|m\rangle, \tag{9}$$

where α is a normalization factor that depends on θ.

Let

$$f = P\theta/\pi. \tag{10}$$

In Step 4, we apply the Fourier transform on a sine (cosine) of period f and phase shift θ. From $\sin^2(\theta) = t/N$ we conclude that $\theta \leq \pi/2$ and $f \leq P/2$. After we apply the Fourier transform, the state $|\Psi_3\rangle$ strongly depends on f (which depends on t). If f were an integer, there would be two possibilities: either $f = 0$ (which happens if $t = 0$ or $t = N$), in which case $|\Psi_3\rangle = |0\rangle$, or $t > 0$, in which case $|\Psi_3\rangle = a|f\rangle + b|P - f\rangle$, where a and b are complex numbers of norm $1/\sqrt{2}$.

In general f is not an integer and we will obtain something more complicated. We define $f^- = \lfloor f \rfloor$ and $f^+ = \lfloor f + 1 \rfloor$. We still have three cases. If $1 < f < P/2 - 1$, we obtain

$$|\Psi_3\rangle = a|f^-\rangle + b|f^+\rangle + c|P - f^-\rangle + d|P - f^+\rangle + |R\rangle$$

where $|R\rangle$ is an un-normalized error term that may include some or all values other than the desirable f^-, f^+, $P - f^-$ and $P - f^+$. The two other possibilities are $0 < f < 1$, in which case we obtain

$$|\Psi_3\rangle = a|0\rangle + b|1\rangle + c|P - 1\rangle + |R\rangle$$

or $P/2 - 1 < f < P/2$, in which case we obtain

$$|\Psi_3\rangle = a|P/2 - 1\rangle + b|P/2\rangle + c|P/2 + 1\rangle + |R\rangle\,.$$

In all three cases, extensive algebraic manipulation shows that the square of the norm of the error term $|R\rangle$ can be upper bounded by $2/5$,

$$\langle R|R\rangle < \frac{2}{5}\,.$$

In order to bound the success probability by $8/\pi^2$ (which is roughly 0.81 and therefore larger than $1 - 2/5 = 0.6$) as claimed in the statement of the Theorem, we could perform a complicated case analysis depending on whether the value x observed in Step 3 is such that $F(x) = 0$ or $F(x) = 1$. Fortunately, in the light of some recent analysis of Michele Mosca [10], which itself is based on results presented in [8], this analysis can be simplified. Since the information obtained by measuring the second register is not used, measuring it in a different basis would not change the behaviour of the algorithm. Measuring in the eigenvector basis of $\mathbf{G}_F$, one obtains this bound in an elegant way. Details will be provided in the final version of this paper.

Assuming that $\tilde{f}$ has been observed at Step 5 and applying Equation 10 and the fact that $\sin(\theta) = \sqrt{t/N}$, we obtain an estimate $\tilde{t}$ of t such that

$$|t - \tilde{t}| < \frac{2\pi}{P}\sqrt{tN} + \frac{\pi^2}{P^2}N\,.$$

□

Using a similar technique, it can be shown that the same quantum algorithm can also be used to perform amplitude estimation: Grover's algorithm [9] is to amplitude amplification what approximate counting is to amplitude estimation.

Theorem 6. *Replacing* $\mathbf{G}_F$ *in* $\mathbf{C}_F$ *of algorithm* **Count** *by* $\mathbf{Q} = \mathbf{Q}(\mathcal{A}, \chi, -1, -1)$ *and also modifying Step 6 so that the algorithm outputs* $\tilde{a} = \sin^2(\tilde{f}\pi/P)$, $\mathbf{Count}(F, P)$ *with* $P \geq 4$ *will output* $\tilde{a}$ *such that*

$$|a - \tilde{a}| < \frac{2\pi}{P}\sqrt{a} + \frac{\pi^2}{P^2}$$

with probability at least $8/\pi^2$.

In Theorems 5 and 6, parameter P allows us to balance the desired accuracy of the estimate with the running time required to achieve it. We will now look at different choices for P and analyze the accuracy of the answer. To obtain t up to a few standard deviations, apply the following corollary of Theorem 5.

Corollary 2. *Given a Boolean function* $F : \{0, \ldots, N-1\} \to \{0, 1\}$ *with* t *as defined above,* $\mathbf{Count}(F, c\sqrt{N})$ *outputs an estimate* $\tilde{t}$ *such that*

$$|t - \tilde{t}| < \frac{2\pi}{c}\sqrt{t} + \frac{\pi^2}{c^2}$$

with probability at least $8/\pi^2$ *and requires exactly* $c\sqrt{N}$ *evaluations of* F.

The above corollary states that some accuracy can be achieved with probability $8/\pi^2$. This means that, as usual, the success probability can be boosted exponentially close to 1 by repetition. We will denote by $\mathbf{Maj}(k, \mathbf{Count})$ an algorithm that performs k evaluations of **Count** and outputs the majority answer. To obtain an error probability smaller than $1/2^n$, one should choose k in $\Omega(n)$.

If one is satisfied in counting up to a constant relative error, it would be natural to call **Count** with $P = c\sqrt{N/t}$, but we need to use the following strategy because t is precisely what we are looking for.

$\mathbf{CountRel}(F, c)$

1. $P \leftarrow 2$
2. Repeat
   (a) $P \leftarrow 2P$
   (b) $\tilde{f} \leftarrow \mathbf{Maj}(\Omega(\log\log N), \mathbf{Count}(F, P))$
3. Until $\tilde{f} > 1$
4. Output $\mathbf{Count}(F, cP)$

Note that in the main loop the algorithm calls **Count** to obtain $\tilde{f}$ and not $\tilde{t}$.

Corollary 3. *Given* F *with* N *and* t *as defined above,* $\mathbf{CountRel}(F, c)$ *outputs an estimate* $\tilde{t}$ *such that*

$$|t - \tilde{t}| < t/c$$

with probability at least $\frac{3}{4}$, *using an expected number of* $\Theta((c + \log\log N)\sqrt{N/t})$ *evaluations of* F.

Proof. Suppose for the moment that in Step 2(b) we always obtain $\tilde{f}$ such that $|f - \tilde{f}| < 1$. Combining this with Equation 10 we see that to obtain $\tilde{f} > 1$, we must have $P\theta/\pi > 1$. Since $\sin(\theta)^2 = t/N$, then $P > 2\sqrt{N/t}$, so, by Theorem 5, $|t - \tilde{t}| < t\frac{\pi}{c}(1 + \frac{\pi}{c})$. Thus, the core of the main loop will be performed at most $\log(2\sqrt{N/t}\,)$ times before P is large enough. By using $\Omega(\log\log N)$ repetitive calls to **Count** in Step 2(b), we know that this will happen with sufficiently high probability, ensuring an overall success probability of at least 3/4.

The expected number of evaluations of F follows from the fact that $\sum_{i=1}^{\log(2\sqrt{N/t})}(\log\log N)2^i \in \Theta\big((\log\log N)\sqrt{N/t}\,\big)$. □

Of course, to obtain a smaller relative error, the first estimate can be used in order to call **Count** with P as large as one wishes. From Theorem 5, it is clear that by letting P be large enough, one can make the absolute error smaller than 1.

Corollary 4. *Given F with N and t as defined above, there is an algorithm requiring an expected number of $\Theta(\sqrt{tN}\,)$ evaluations of F that outputs an estimate $\tilde{t}$ such that $\tilde{t} = t$ with probability at least $\frac{3}{4}$ using only space linear in* $\log N$.

Proof. By Theorem 5, if $P > \pi(2 + \sqrt{6}\,)\sqrt{tN}$, the error in the output of **Count** is likely to be smaller than 1/2. Again we do not know t, but we already know how to estimate it. By calling first **Count**$(F, \sqrt{N}\,)$ a few times, we obtain an approximation $\tilde{t}$ such that $|t - \tilde{t}| < 2\pi\sqrt{t} + \pi^2$ with good probability. Now, assuming the first estimate was good, calling **Count**$(F, 20\sqrt{\tilde{t}N}\,)$ we obtain $\tilde{t}' = t$ with a probability of at least $8/\pi^2$. Thus, obtaining an overall success probability of at least 3/4. □

Note that successive applications of Grover's algorithm in which we strike out the solutions as they are found will also provide an exact count with high probability in a time in $O(\sqrt{tN}\,)$, but at a high cost in terms of additional quantum memory, that is $\Theta(t)$.

Acknowledgements

We are grateful to Joan Boyar, Harry Buhrman, Christoph Dürr, Michele Mosca, Barbara Terhal and Ronald de Wolf for helpful comments. The third author would like to thank Mélanie Doré Boulet for her encouragements throughout the realization of this work.

References

1. Barenco, Adriano, "Quantum physics and computers", *Contemporary Physics*, Vol. 38, 1996, pp. 357 – 389.
2. Bennett, Charles H., Ethan Bernstein, Gilles Brassard and Umesh Vazirani, "Strengths and weaknesses of quantum computing", *SIAM Journal on Computing*, Vol. 26, no. 5, October 1997, pp. 1510 – 1523.

3. BOYER, Michel, Gilles BRASSARD, Peter HØYER and Alain TAPP, "Tight bounds on quantum searching", *Proceedings of Fourth Workshop on Physics and Computation — PhysComp '96*, November 1996, pp. 36 – 43. Final version to appear in *Fortschritte Der Physik.*
4. BRASSARD, Gilles, "A quantum jump in computer science", in *Computer Science Today*, Jan van Leeuwen (editor), Lecture Notes in Computer Science, Vol. 1000, Springer–Verlag, 1995, pp. 1 – 14.
5. BRASSARD, Gilles, "New horizons in quantum information processing", *Proceedings of this ICALP Conference*, 1998.
6. BRASSARD, Gilles and Peter HØYER, "An exact quantum polynomial-time algorithm for Simon's problem", *Proceedings of Fifth Israeli Symposium on Theory of Computing and Systems — ISTCS '97*, June 1997, IEEE Computer Society Press, pp. 12 – 23.
7. CHI, Dong-Pyo and Jinsoo KIM, "Quantum database searching by a single query", Lecture at First NASA International Conference on Quantum Computing and Quantum Communications, Palm Springs, February 1998.
8. CLEVE, Richard, Artur EKERT, Chiara MACCHIAVELLO and Michele MOSCA, "Quantum algorithms revisited", *Proceedings of the Royal Society, London*, Vol. A354, 1998, pp. 339 – 354.
9. GROVER, Lov K., "Quantum mechanics helps in searching for a needle in a haystack", *Physical Review Letters*, Vol. 79, no. 2, 14 July 1997, pp. 325 – 328.
10. MOSCA, Michele, "Quantum computer algorithms and interferometry", Lecture at *BRICS Workshop on Algorithms in Quantum Information Processing*, Aarhus, January 1998.
11. SHOR, Peter W., "Polynomial-time algorithms for prime factorization and discrete logarithms on a quantum computer", *SIAM Journal on Computing*, Vol. 26, no. 5, October 1997, pp. 1484 – 1509.

On the Complexity of Deriving Score Functions from Examples for Problems in Molecular Biology

Tatsuya Akutsu[1] and Mutsunori Yagiura[2]

[1] Human Genome Center, Institute of Medical Science, University of Tokyo
4-6-1 Shirokanedai, Minato-ku, Tokyo 108-8639, Japan
takutsu@ims.u-tokyo.ac.jp
[2] Department of Applied Mathematics and Physics,
Graduate School of Informatics, Kyoto University
Sakyo-ku, Kyoto 606-8501, Japan
yagiura@kuamp.kyoto-u.ac.jp

Abstract. Score functions (potential functions) have been used effectively in many problems in molecular biology. We propose a general method for deriving score functions that are consistent with example data, which yields polynomial time learning algorithms for several important problems in molecular biology (including sequence alignment). On the other hand, we show that deriving a score function for some problems (multiple alignment and protein threading) is computationally hard. However, we show that approximation algorithms for these optimization problems can also be used for deriving score functions.

1 Introduction

Score functions (i.e., *potential functions*) have been used for solving many problems in molecular biology. For example, score functions were used for identification of transmembrane domains of amino acid sequences [10], comparison (alignment) of two or more amino acid sequences [5], prediction of RNA secondary structures [18], and prediction of 3D protein structures [4, 13, 14]. In those problems, the quality of outputs heavily depends on the quality of a score function. If we use a good score function, we can obtain biologically meaningful outputs. Therefore, using a good score function is very important. In some cases, score functions are derived from biological experiment or chemical theory. However, in most cases, score functions are derived via statistical methods such as Bayes' formula from example data. In most statistical methods, it is not guaranteed that a derived score function is consistent with example data (i.e., correct outputs can be obtained even if example data, which are used to derive a score function, are input). It is a crucial drawback of the previous statistical methods of deriving score functions.

By the way, there have been a lot of progress in learning theory since 1980's [11, 16]. In learning from examples, it is important to develop an algorithm which always outputs a hypothesis consistent with given examples [11, 16]. However, we do not know such results on deriving score functions. Thus, in this paper, we study methods and computational complexities of deriving score functions.

In this paper, we consider the following type of problems. We assume that the *original problem* is an optimization (minimization or maximization) problem and a score function is expressed by a set of parameters. For an instance $\mathcal{I}$ of the original optimization problem where a score function is not fixed, a set of positive examples (optimal solutions) $\mathcal{P} = \{POS_1, \cdots, POS_M\}$ and a set of negative examples (non-optimal solutions) $\mathcal{N} = \{NEG_1, \cdots, NEG_N\}$ are given. Then, we find a score function (i.e., a set of parameters) with which each POS_i becomes an optimal solution for $\mathcal{I}$ and any NEG_i does not become an optimal solution for $\mathcal{I}$. Note that we allow that multiple positive examples are included in an input since optimal solutions are not necessarily determined uniquely. This definition can be generalized for a case where examples for multiple instances are given: for a set of instances $\{\mathcal{I}^1, \mathcal{I}^2, \cdots, \mathcal{I}^L\}$, a family of pairs $\{(\mathcal{P}^1, \mathcal{N}^1), (\mathcal{P}^2, \mathcal{N}^2), \cdots, (\mathcal{P}^L, \mathcal{N}^L)\}$ are given as examples, where $\mathcal{P}^j = \{POS_1^j, \cdots, POS_{M_j}^j\}$ and $\mathcal{N}^j = \{NEG_1^j, \cdots, NEG_{N_j}^j\}$ are sets of positive and negative examples for $\mathcal{I}^j$ respectively.

For these problems, we propose a general method for deriving score functions using *linear programming* (in Sect. 2). In this method, the constraint that positive examples must have minimum (or maximum) scores is expressed by a set of *linear inequalities*, in which a score function is expressed by a set of unknown parameters. Then, by applying an LP (*linear programming*) solver to the set of linear inequalities, values of unknown parameters are determined and thus a score function is determined. Using this method, we can obtain polynomial time algorithms for deriving score functions consistent with example data for the following problems: identification of transmembrane domains, sequence alignment, and prediction of RNA secondary structures. The proposed method can be effectively applied to most problems whose optimal score can be calculated by using simple DP (*dynamic programming*) type algorithms. On the other hand, we show (in Sect. 3) that for *protein threading* [1, 12, 13] (a kind of 3D protein structure prediction problem) and *multiple sequence alignment* [6, 17], there is no polynomial time algorithm for deriving such a score function unless P=NP. However, we show (in Sect. 4) that approximation algorithms for these optimization problems can also be used for deriving score functions.

Here we briefly review previous work. As mentioned before, there are a lot of studies for deriving score functions based on statistical methods such as Boltzmann statistics approach, Baysian approach and EM (Expectation Maximization) approach. However, none of them does guarantee that a derived score function is consistent with examples. Maiorov and Crippen have already applied LP to deriving a score function for the protein structure prediction problem [14]. But, they did not make theoretical analysis. Gusfield *et al.* developed a parametric alignment algorithm for tuning a score function for sequence alignment [8]. However, only a few parameters of a score function can be determined by their method, while our method determines all parameters simultaneously.

Although this paper studies theoretical aspects of deriving score functions, the presented algorithms can be made practical with slight modifications. Indeed, we have successfully applied the modified algorithm to the identification of transmembrane domains and protein threading [2].

2 Deriving Score Functions for Sequence Alignment and Other Problems

In this section, we show an algorithm for deriving a score function for *sequence alignment*, and then we show that it can be generalized for problems whose original optimization problems can be solved by simple DP-type algorithms.

2.1 Sequence Alignment

Sequence alignment is well known and widely used in molecular biology [7]. It is used to measure the similarity of two (or more) sequences. Here we briefly review the alignment algorithm for two amino acid sequences. Although sequence alignment is defined as a maximization problem in most biological literatures, we follow a standard definition in computer science literatures [6, 7, 17] and we treat it as a minimization problem. Similar results hold if we define sequence alignment as a maximization problem.

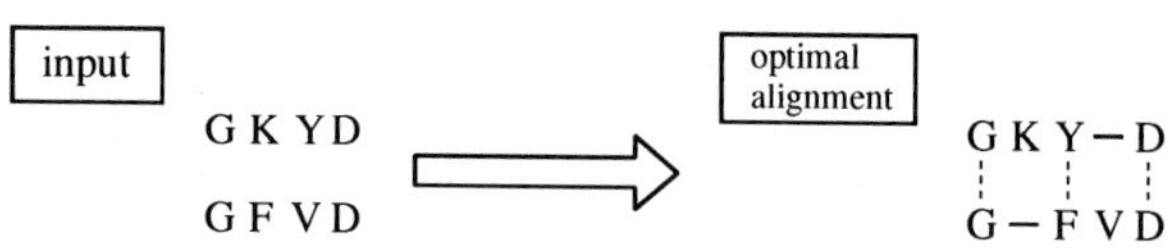

Fig. 1. Example of sequence alignment. In this case, the score of the obtained optimal alignment is $g(\mathrm{G},\mathrm{G}) + g(\mathrm{K},-) + g(\mathrm{Y},\mathrm{F}) + g(-,\mathrm{V}) + g(\mathrm{D},\mathrm{D})$.

Let $c = c_1 \ldots c_m$ and $d = d_1 \ldots d_n$ be two amino acid sequences (over Σ). An *alignment* of c and d is obtained by inserting *gap symbols* (denoted by '$-$') into or at either end of c and d such that the two resulting sequences c' and d' are of the same length l (see Fig. 1). Let $g(x, y)$ be a function from $\Sigma' \times \Sigma'$ to $\mathcal{R}$ that satisfies $g(x, y) \geq 0$, $g(x, y) = g(y, x)$ and triangle inequality $g(x, y) \leq g(x, z) + g(z, y)$ [7], where $\Sigma' = \Sigma \cup \{-\}$, and $g(x, y)$ denotes the dissimilarity (distance) between x and y. The score of an alignment is defined as $\sum_{i=1}^{l} g(c'_i, d'_i)$. It is well known that the score of an *optimal alignment* (i.e., an alignment with the minimum score) between c and d can be computed in $O(mn)$ time by the following simple DP procedure:

$$s(i, j) = \min\{s(i-1, j) + g(c_i, -),\ s(i, j-1) + g(-, d_j),\ s(i-1, j-1) + g(c_i, d_j)\},$$

where $s(0, 0) = 0$. The score of an optimal alignment is given by $s(m, n)$, and the dissimilarity between c and d is measured by $s(m, n)$.

2.2 Deriving Score Functions for Sequence Alignment

Here we define the problem of deriving score functions for sequence alignment. Since an optimal alignment is not necessarily uniquely determined, we assume that good alignments (positive examples) and bad alignments (negative examples) are given as example data (by experts in molecular biology, or by the results from structure alignment). Thus we define the problem in the following way:

Input: strings c and d over Σ, a set of good alignments $\mathcal{P} = \{POS_1, \cdots, POS_M\}$, a set of bad alignments $\mathcal{N} = \{NEG_1, \cdots, NEG_N\}$,
Output: values (real numbers) $g(x,y)$'s satisfying the following conditions:
- each POS_i is an optimal alignment between c and d,
- each NEG_i is not an optimal alignment between c and d,

'No' is output if there are no such values.

Although the recurrence for DP procedure is not linear (because of 'min' operator), we can solve this learning problem using LP.

Theorem 1. *Existence of a score function consistent with given alignments can be decided in polynomial time. Moreover, such a score function can be computed in polynomial time if it exists.*

Proof. We make the following instance of LP:

maximize $\sum_{i,j} s(i,j)$
subject to $s(i,j) \le s(i-1,j) + g(c_i,-), \quad s(i,j) \le s(i,j-1) + g(-,d_j),$
$s(i,j) \le s(i-1,j-1) + g(c_i,d_j), \quad s(0,0) = 0,$
$g(x,y) \ge 0, \ g(x,y) = g(y,x)$ (for all $x,y \in \Sigma'$),
$g(x,y) \le g(x,z) + g(z,y)$ (for all $x,y,z \in \Sigma'$),
$score(POS_i) = s(m,n)$ for all POS_i,
$score(NEG_i) > s(m,n)$ for all NEG_i.

(Practically, $g(x,y) \le B$ for all $x,y \in \Sigma'$ and $score(NEG_i) > C + s(m,n)$ should be appended for bounding the range of parameters, where B and C are appropriate constants.)

Note that $score(X)$ denotes the score of an alignment X, where $score(X)$ is represented by a linear combination of $g(x,y)$'s. Note also that $s(i,j)$'s and $g(x,y)$'s are unknown parameters in the above formulation.

It is easy to see that 'min' operations are executed by means of maximizing $\sum s(i,j)$ in the above formulation. Therefore, it is guaranteed that $s(m,n)$ is the optimal score. Since $score(POS_i)$ must be equal to $s(m,n)$ and $score(NEG_i)$ must be greater than $s(m,n)$, it is guaranteed that POS_i's are optimal alignments and NEG_i's are not optimal alignments.

Since the size of this LP instance is polynomially bounded and LP can be solved in polynomial time [9], a score function consistent with given examples can be found in polynomial time if it exists. □

The above method may be made more practical by weakening the condition in the following way: score of POS_i must not be greater than $\alpha\, OPT(c,d)$;

and score of NEG_i must be greater than $\beta OPT(c,d)$, where $OPT(c,d)$ denotes the score of an optimal alignment for sequences c and d. This modified version can be solved by replacing $score(POS_i) = s(m,n)$ with $score(POS_i) \leq \alpha\, s(m,n)$ and $score(POS_i) \geq s(m,n)$, and replacing $score(NEG_i) > s(m,n)$ with $score(NEG_i) > \beta\, s(m,n)$.

Corollary 1. *For any fixed α, β (≥ 1), a score function satisfying the constraint that $OPT(c,d) \leq score(POS_i) \leq \alpha OPT(c,d)$ and $score(NEG_i) > \beta OPT(c,d)$ (for all i) can be computed in polynomial time if it exists.*

The proposed learning method can be generalized for a case where multiple pairs of sequences are given. Let c^i's and d^i's ($1 \leq i \leq L$) be amino acid sequences. For each pair (c^i, d^i), a set of good alignments $\mathcal{P}^i = \{POS_1^i, \cdots, POS_{M_i}^i\}$, a set of bad alignments $\mathcal{N}^i = \{NEG_1^i, \cdots, NEG_{N_i}^i\}$ are given.

Corollary 2. *For any fixed α, β (≥ 1), a score function satisfying the constraint that $OPT(c^i, d^i) \leq score(POS_j^i) \leq \alpha OPT(c^i, d^i)$ and $score(NEG_j^i) > \beta OPT(c^i, d^i)$ (for all i, j) can be computed in polynomial time if it exists.*

Note that although we do not consider *affine gap costs* [7] in this section, the method can be modified for sequence alignment with affine gap costs.

2.3 Extensions

Note that the proposed LP-based method is simple and general. If an original optimization problem satisfies the following conditions (where we omit details), we can obtain a polynomial time algorithm for deriving a score function consistent with examples: (i) The optimal solution (score) can be computed in polynomial time by a dynamic programming procedure; (ii) The dynamic programming procedure consists of linear combinations of parameters, and 'max' and/or 'min' operators.

Since a lot of DP algorithms have been developed in molecular biology, the proposed method may be applied to many problems. For example, the proposed method can be applied for *RNA secondary structure prediction* [18]. The proposed method can also be modified for deriving a score function for the *identification of transmembrane domains* [10], although the original problem is not an optimization problem.

3 Hardness Results

For problems whose optimal scores can be computed by simple DP procedures in polynomial time, we can derive consistent score functions in polynomial time. But, if an optimal score can not be calculated by such a DP procedure in polynomial time, it may be difficult to derive a score function. In this section, we show such examples: *protein threading* and *multiple sequence alignment*, where the original optimization problems were already shown to be NP-hard [12, 17]. Note that *showing the hardness of the learning problem is not a trivial task even if the original optimization problem is NP-hard.*

3.1 Hardness Result for Protein Threading

In this subsection, we show that deriving a consistent score function for protein threading is hard. First, we briefly review the protein threading problem [1, 12, 13]. The protein threading problem is a kind of alignment problem. While an alignment between two sequences is computed in sequence alignment, an alignment between a sequence and a structure (a template structure) is computed in protein threading. In this paper, we consider the following very simple score functions (corresponding to *contact potentials*) [1, 12]. Let Σ be an alphabet corresponding to a set of types of residues. Let $g(x, y)$ be a function from $\Sigma \times \Sigma$ to $\mathcal{R}$ satisfying $g(x, y) = g(y, x)$. A score between two residues x and y is 0 if the interaction between residues is weak, otherwise it is $g(x, y)$.

Then we define the protein threading problem in the following way, which is a simplified version [1] of Lathrop and Smith's threading problem [12, 13]. Let $G(V, E)$ be an undirected graph, which represents interactions among residues in a template protein structure ($\{u, v\} \in E$ if the interaction between residues u and v is strong). We assume that elements of V are totally ordered, and $u \prec v$ denotes that u precedes v. Let $s = s_1 \dots s_n$ over Σ be an input sequence of amino acids, where we assume $n \geq |V|$.

A *threading* $\boldsymbol{t}$ for (s, G) is a *mapping* from V to $\{1, \cdots, n\}$, where $\boldsymbol{t}(u) < \boldsymbol{t}(v)$ if $u \prec v$. Note that in threading $\boldsymbol{t}$, amino acid of type $s_{\boldsymbol{t}(v)}$ is assigned to vertex (position) v. Score of threading $\boldsymbol{t}$ is defined by $score(\boldsymbol{t}) = \sum_{\{u,v\} \in E \,\wedge\, u \prec v} g(s_{\boldsymbol{t}(u)}, s_{\boldsymbol{t}(v)})$. A threading $\boldsymbol{t}$ is called an *optimal threading* if $score(\boldsymbol{t}) \geq score(\boldsymbol{t}')$ for any $\boldsymbol{t}'$.

Then, the protein threading problem is defined as a problem of, given $g(x, y)$, s and $G(V, E)$, finding an optimal threading $\boldsymbol{t}$ for (s, G). Note that although the protein threading problem is usually defined as a minimization problem, it is defined as a maximization problem here because usual score functions can take negative values and the minimum score can become negative [1].

Now we consider the learning problem for protein threading, which is formally defined as follows: given (s, G) and a set of good threadings $\mathcal{P} = \{\boldsymbol{t}_1, , \cdots, \boldsymbol{t}_M\}$ and a set of bad threadings $\mathcal{N} = \{\boldsymbol{t}'_1, \cdots, \boldsymbol{t}'_N\}$, find $g(x, y)$'s with which each $\boldsymbol{t}_i$ becomes an optimal threading for (s, G) and each $\boldsymbol{t}'_i$ does not become an optimal threading; 'No' is output if there are no such values. Note that, in protein threading, examples are generated from proteins whose three dimensional structures are known [2, 14].

In order to prove the hardness result for this learning problem, we consider the following problem (*optimality of an independent set*): given an undirected graph $G(V, E)$ and an independent set $U \subseteq V$, decide whether or not U is a maximum independent set of G. Recall that U is an *independent set* of G if there is no edge $\{v_i, v_j\}$ such that $v_i \in U$ and $v_j \in U$. The following lemma can be proved using some 'oracle' argument where we omit the proof here.

Lemma 1. *Optimality of a given independent set can not be decided in polynomial time unless P=NP. Moreover, this lemma holds even if an input graph is a 3-regular planar graph.*

Theorem 2. *Existence of a score function consistent with given threadings can not be decided in polynomial time unless P=NP.*

Proof. We prove that this theorem holds even if G is a planar graph of bounded degree 3.

We consider the case of $\Sigma = \{0,1\}$. Let $\alpha = g(1,1)$, $\beta = g(0,1)$, and $\gamma = g(0,0)$. Then, we construct the following examples from an instance $(G_0(V_0, E_0), U)$ of the optimality problem of an independent set, where we assume that G_0 is a 3-regular planar graph.

We construct $G(V,E)$ by $V = V_0 \cup \{v_a, v_b, v_c, v_d\}$ and $E = E_0 \cup \{\{v_a,v_b\},\{v_a,v_c\},\{v_b,v_c\},\{v_b,v_d\},\{v_c,v_d\}\}$ (we can assume arbitrary ordering of vertices), and s by $s = \overbrace{00\cdots0}^{m\text{-0's}}1\overbrace{00\cdots0}^{m\text{-0's}}1\cdots1\overbrace{00\cdots0}^{m\text{-0's}}$, where 1 appears $|U|+2$ times, and $m = |V|$. We construct two positive examples $(\boldsymbol{t}_1, \boldsymbol{t}_2)$ and one negative example $(\boldsymbol{t}'_1)$, where we only describe conditions that should be satisfied by each threading.

$\boldsymbol{t}_1$ (POS_1): $s_{\boldsymbol{t}_1(v_a)} = s_{\boldsymbol{t}_1(v_d)} = 0$, $s_{\boldsymbol{t}_1(v_b)} = s_{\boldsymbol{t}_1(v_c)} = 1$, $s_{\boldsymbol{t}_1(v)} = 1$ for all $v \in U$, and $s_{\boldsymbol{t}_1(v)} = 0$ for all $v \in V_0 - U$.
($\Longrightarrow$ $score(\boldsymbol{t}_1) = w_0 + 4\beta + \alpha$ where we let $w_0 = 3|U|(\beta-\gamma) + \frac{3}{2}|V_0|\gamma$).
$\boldsymbol{t}_2$ (POS_2): $s_{\boldsymbol{t}_2(v_a)} = s_{\boldsymbol{t}_2(v_d)} = 1$, $s_{\boldsymbol{t}_2(v_b)} = s_{\boldsymbol{t}_2(v_c)} = 0$, $s_{\boldsymbol{t}_2(v)} = 1$ for all $v \in U$, and $s_{\boldsymbol{t}_2(v)} = 0$ for all $v \in V_0 - U$. ($\Longrightarrow$ $score(\boldsymbol{t}_2) = w_0 + 4\beta + \gamma$)
$\boldsymbol{t}'_1$ (NEG_1): $s_{\boldsymbol{t}'_1(v_a)} = s_{\boldsymbol{t}'_1(v_c)} = 0$, $s_{\boldsymbol{t}'_1(v_b)} = s_{\boldsymbol{t}'_1(v_d)} = 1$, $s_{\boldsymbol{t}'_1(v)} = 1$ for all $v \in U$, and $s_{\boldsymbol{t}'_1(v)} = 0$ for all $v \in V_0 - U$. ($\Longrightarrow$ $score(\boldsymbol{t}'_1) = w_0 + 3\beta + \alpha + \gamma$)

Then, we can see that $\alpha = \gamma$ holds from $score(\boldsymbol{t}_1) = score(\boldsymbol{t}_2)$ and $\beta > \alpha = \gamma$ holds from $score(\boldsymbol{t}_1) > score(\boldsymbol{t}'_1)$. Hereafter, we assume $\beta > \alpha = \gamma$. Next, we prove the theorem by considering the following two cases, where we say that v has a label 1 if $s_{\boldsymbol{t}(v)} = 1$, and v has a label 0 otherwise.

(Case i) U is a maximum independent set:
First note that there are at most $|U|+2$ vertices having label 1 in G. If at least two vertices in $\{v_a, v_b, v_c, v_d\}$ have label 1, the score of a threading is at most $w_0 + 4\beta + \gamma$, where we let $w_0 = 3|U|(\beta-\gamma) + \frac{3}{2}|V_0|\gamma$. If at most one vertex in $\{v_a, v_b, v_c, v_d\}$ has label 1, the score of a threading is at most $w_0 + 4\beta + \gamma$ too because there is at least one edge in G_0 whose both endpoints have label 1. Therefore, $score(\boldsymbol{t}_1) = score(\boldsymbol{t}_2) \geq score(\boldsymbol{t})$ holds for any threading $\boldsymbol{t}$, and thus any score function satisfying $\beta > \alpha = \gamma$ is consistent.

(Case ii) U is not a maximum independent set:
In this case, there exists an independent set U' such that $|U'| = |U| + 1$. We consider a threading $\boldsymbol{t}$ satisfying the following: $s_{\boldsymbol{t}(v)} = 1$ for all $v \in U'$, $s_{\boldsymbol{t}(v)} = 0$ for all $v \in V_0 - U'$, $s_{\boldsymbol{t}(v_a)} = s_{\boldsymbol{t}(v_c)} = s_{\boldsymbol{t}(v_d)} = 0$, $s_{\boldsymbol{t}(v_b)} = 1$. Then, $score(\boldsymbol{t}) = w_0 + 6\beta - \gamma$. Since $score(\boldsymbol{t}) > score(\boldsymbol{t}_1) = score(\boldsymbol{t}_2)$, neither $\boldsymbol{t}_1$ nor $\boldsymbol{t}_2$ can be an optimal threading. Therefore, there exists no consistent score function.

From (Case i) and (Case ii), it is seen that if the existence of a score function can be decided in polynomial time, the optimality of an independent set can be decided in polynomial time. □

3.2 Hardness Result for Multiple Sequence Alignment

In this subsection, we prove that deciding the existence of a score function consistent with given examples of multiple (sequence) alignment is hard. *Multiple alignment* [7] is a natural generalization of sequence alignment considered in Sect. 2: two sequences are input in sequence alignment, whereas $K \geq 2$ sequences are input in multiple alignment (see Fig. 2(a)). In this case, an *alignment* is also obtained by inserting gap symbols into each sequence so that the resulting sequences have the same length l. In this paper, we assume *SP-score* (sum-of-pairs score) as in [6, 17]. That is, the score value of an alignment is the sum of the scores of all columns, and the score value of a column is the sum of scores of all (unordered) pairs of letters in the column. Then, the *multiple sequence alignment problem* (in short, multiple alignment) is, given K sequences, to find an alignment with the minimum score (i.e., an optimal alignment). In order to show a hardness result, we use the following theorem due to Wang and Jiang [17], giving a brief sketch of their proof here.

Theorem 3. *(Wang and Jiang 1994)*
The multiple sequence alignment problem is NP-hard.

Proof. The *shortest common supersequence* problem over a binary alphabet $\{0,1\}$ is reduced to a series of multiple alignment problems. Let a pair of $S = \{s_1, \cdots, s_K\}$ and m be an instance of the shortest common supersequence problem. That is, it asks whether or not there exists a common supersequence of S whose length is at most m. In the alignment problem, an alphabet $\Sigma = \{0, 1, a, b, -\}$ and a score function g_0 in Fig. 2(a) are used (note that a letter 'c' is not used here). From S, a series of instances $S_i = \{a^i, b^{m-i}\} \cup S$ $(0 \leq i \leq m)$ of multiple alignment is constructed, where x^i denotes $\overbrace{xx\ldots x}^{i}$.

Then, the following properties hold: the contribution of the scores among sequences in S is always the same value $(K-1)||S||$ where $||S|| = |s_1| + \cdots + |s_K|$; 0 must be aligned with an a and 1 must be aligned with a b in an optimal alignment. Therefore, there exists a common supersequence of S which consists of i 0's and $m - i$ 1's iff. the score of an optimal alignment for S_i is at most $(K-1)||S|| + (2K+1)m$. □

Lemma 2. *Optimality of a given alignment can not be decided in polynomial time unless P=NP.*

Proof. Middendorf reduced the *minimum node cover* problem to the *shortest common supersequence* problem over a binary alphabet $\{0,1\}$ [15]. From his reduction, Lemma 1 and the fact that complement of a node cover is an independent set, we can show that optimality of a given common supersequence can not be decided in polynomial time unless P=NP.

Let L be a set of sequences constructed in [15] and SS be a (not necessarily shortest) common supersequence ('S' in [15]) of L constructed from a given node cover. Let L' be a set of sequences obtained by replacing X_1^1 ($\in L$) with $X_1^1 \cdot 1$, where X_1^1 is a sequence appeared in [15] (we use the same notation), and $x \cdot y$ means a concatenation of x and y. Note that, from the construction of L in [15], the last letters of all sequences in L' except $X_1^1 \cdot 1$ is 0.

Now, we construct an instance of the optimality problem of multiple alignment (see Fig. 2). We use an alphabet $\Sigma = \{0, 1, a, b, c, -\}$ and a score function g_0 in Fig. 2(a). (it satisfies the triangle inequality). We construct a set of sequences $LL = L' \cup \{a^i \cdot c, b^j\}$, where i (resp. j) is the number of 0's (resp. 1's) in SS. From $SS \cdot 1$, we construct an (arbitrary) alignment $\mathcal{A}$ of LL such that each 0 is aligned with an a, each 1 except the last letter of $X_1^1 \cdot 1$ is aligned with a b, and the last letter of $X_1^1 \cdot 1$ is aligned with a c. Then, we can prove the following property (we omit details): $\mathcal{A}$ is an optimal alignment for LL under g_0 iff. SS is a shortest common supersequence of L. □

(a) score function g_0

	0	1	a	b	−	c
0	2	2	1	2	1	2
1	2	2	2	1	1	2
a	1	2	0	2	1	2
b	2	1	2	0	1	2
−	1	1	1	1	0	1
c	2	2	2	2	1	2

(b1) non-optimal alignment

```
− 0 0 1 − 0 1
1 − 0 1 − 0 −
− − 0 1 1 0 −
− a a − − a c
b − − b b − −
```

(b2) optimal alignment

```
0 − 0 1 0 1 −
− 1 0 1 0 − −
0 1 − 1 0 − −
a − a − a − c
− b − b − b −
```

Fig. 2. (a) Score function g_0 used in Theorem 3 and Lemma 2. (b) Relation between a common supersequence and a constructed alignment. From $L = \{0010, 1010, 0110\}$ ($X_1^1 = 0010$) and non-optimal common supersequence $SS = 100110$, non-optimal alignment (b1) for $LL = \{00101, 1010, 0110, a^3 \cdot c, b^3\}$ is constructed. In this case, (b2) is an optimal alignment for LL, which corresponds to a shortest common supersequence 01010 of L (i.e., a shortest common supersequence 010101 of L').

In order to prove the hardness for deriving a score function for multiple alignment, it is natural to try to impose a constraint (using examples) that a score function must be equal to g_0. Although it is impossible to do so (only from examples), we can still prove the hardness.

Theorem 4. *Existence of a score function consistent with given examples of multiple alignment can not be decided in polynomial time unless P=NP.*

Proof. From $\mathcal{A}$ and LL in Lemma 2, we construct positive and negative examples in the following way (Although multiple sets ($\mathcal{I}^i$'s) of sequences are used here, the proof can be modified for using only one set $\mathcal{I}$.)

For a set of sequences $\mathcal{I}^1 = \{110, 100\}$, we construct positive examples (i.e., optimal alignments) as in Fig. 3(a). For $\mathcal{I}^2 = \{1, 1, 1\}$, $\mathcal{I}^3 = \{01, aa, bb\}$ and

$\mathcal{I}^4 = \{01, cc, bb\}$, we construct positive examples and negative examples (i.e., non-optimal alignments) as in Fig. 3(b), Fig. 3(c) and Fig 3(d), respectively. For $\mathcal{I}^5 = LL$, we let $\mathcal{A}$ as a positive example.

Examples in Fig. 3(a)–(d) are used for imposing constraints on a score function. From examples (a), it is derived that $g(1,1) = 2g(1,-)$, $g(1,0) = g(0,-) + g(1,-)$, $g(0,0) = 2g(0,-)$. From examples (b), $g(-,-) = 0$ is derived. From the above equalities, as in Theorem 3, every alignment for the same sequences over $\{0,1\}$ must have the same score. From examples (c), in an optimal alignment, 0 must be aligned with an a and 1 (except the last letter in $X_1^1 \cdot 1$) must be aligned with a b. From examples (d), it is seen that if the last letter of $X_1^1 \cdot 1$ can be aligned with a b (not a c), an alignment better than $\mathcal{A}$ can be obtained.

Then, the following properties hold:

- g_0 satisfies the constraints imposed by examples (a)–(d),
- if $\mathcal{A}$ is not optimal under g_0, $\mathcal{A}$ is not optimal under the constraints imposed by examples (a)–(d).

Therefore, $\mathcal{A}$ is an optimal alignment for LL under g_0 iff. there exists a score function consistent with given examples. □

```
(a) positive examples:
    1 1 0    1 – 1 0    1 1 – 0    1 1 0 –
    1 0 0    – 1 0 0    1 – 0 0    1 0 – 0

(b) positive examples:
    1    – 1
    1    1 –
    1    1 –

(c) positive examples:
    0 1    0 – 1    0 1 –
    a a    a – a    a – a
    b b    – b b    b b –

    negative examples:
    0 – 1    0 1 –
    – a a    a a –
    b – b    b – b

(d) positive examples:
    – 0 1 –    0 – 1 –
    – c – c    – c – c
    b – b –    b – b –

    negative example:
    – 0 – 1
    – c – c
    b – b –
```

Fig. 3. Positive and negative examples of multiple alignment used in Theorem 4. These examples are used for imposing constraints on a score function.

4 Deriving Score Functions Using Approximation Algorithms for the Original Optimization Problems

Although we have shown hardness results, it does not necessarily mean that we can not develop practical learning algorithms for protein threading and multiple alignment. For example, we may utilize approximation algorithms which have been previously developed for for the original optimization problems. If there exist DP-type approximation algorithms, we may develop learning algorithms using the method in Sect. 2. In this section, we show such examples.

We assume that there exists an approximation algorithm *Appr* for a minimization problem which satisfies the following conditions (**Condition 1**):

- *Appr* is a DP-type algorithm to which the method in Sect. 2 can be applied,
- *Appr* always computes an approximate solution APR such that $score(APR) \leq \alpha\, score(OPT)$, where OPT denotes an optimal solution and α is a constant such that $\alpha > 1$.

Theorem 5. *If Appr for a minimization problem satisfies Condition 1 and there exists a score function consistent with given examples, we can find a score function in polynomial time such that* $score(POS_i) \leq \alpha\, score(OPT)$ *for all* i *and* $score(POS_i) < score(NEG_j)$ *for all* i, j*, where* POS_i*'s are positive (optimal) examples and* NEG_j*'s are negative (non-optimal) examples.*

Proof. From Condition 1, the score of an approximate solution can be represented by LP formula as in Theorem 1. Moreover, we add the following inequalities: $score(POS_i) \leq score(APR)$ for all i, $score(POS_i) < score(NEG_j)$ for all i, j, where $score(POS_i)$'s and $score(NEG_j)$'s are represented by linear combinations of parameters. Solving this LP instance, we can obtain a score function satisfying the required condition. □

The above theorem can be applied to an approximation algorithm with $\alpha < 2$ [6] developed for multiple alignment.

Although minimization problems are considered in Theorem 5, a similar result holds for maximization problems, and it can be applied to an approximation algorithm [1] developed for a special case of the protein threading problem.

5 Concluding Remarks

Although we studied theoretical aspects of the problem of deriving score functions in this paper, we have been developing a practical method for deriving a score function for protein threading. In this method, although there is no theoretical proof, inequalities are made from randomly generated incorrect threadings and LP is applied to these inequalities. Using this method, we could derive a score function for protein threading which was as good as previous score functions. Details of the method and the experimental results are reported in [2].

From a theoretical viewpoint, there are several open problems. **(i)** Although LP is used to solve inequalities in this paper, LP is not so efficient if the number of variables is large. Therefore, developing a learning method without LP, or reducing significantly the number of variables appearing in LP formula is an important open problem. **(ii)** We have shown two examples such that if the original optimization problem is NP-hard, deriving a score function for the problem is hard. However, we do not know whether this is always true. **(iii)** We have shown some algorithms to find a score function satisfying constraints approximately (in the sense of the score value). However, it is sometimes important to derive a score function with which most constraints must be satisfied but a small fraction of constraints can be violated. Although related theoretical studies (about LP) have been done [3] and we have developed a practical method [2], further studies should be done. **(iv)** We did not study PAC(*Probably Approximately Correct learning*)-type analysis [11, 16] because we did not know an appropriate statistical model for optimization problems treated in this paper. Developing such a model and making PAC-type analysis are important too.

References

1. Akutsu, T., Miyano, S.: On the approximation of protein threading. Proc. Int. Conf. on Computational Molecular Biology, ACM (1997) 3–8
2. Akutsu, T., Tashimo, H.: Linear programming based approach to the derivation of a contact potential for protein threading. Proc. Pacific Symp. Biocomputing'98, World Scientific (1998) 413–424
3. Amaldi, E., Kann, V.: On the approximability of finding maximum feasible subsystems of linear systems. LNCS, Vol. 775 (1994) 521–532
4. Bowie, J. U., Lüthy, R., Eisenberg, D.: A method to identify protein sequences that fold into a known three-dimensional structures. Science **253** (1991) 164–170
5. Dayhoff, M. O., Schwartz, R. M. and Orcutt, B C.: A model of evolutionary change in proteins. Atlas of protein sequence and structure **5** (1978) 345–352
6. Gusfield, D.: Efficient method for multiple sequence alignment with guaranteed error bounds. Bull. Math. Biol. **55** (1993) 141–154
7. Gusfield, D.: Algorithms on Strings, Trees, and Sequences. Computer Science and Computational Biology. Cambridge Univ. Press (1997)
8. Gusfield, D., Balasubramanian, K., Naor, D.: Parametric optimization of sequence alignment. Algorithmica **12** (1994) 312–326
9. Karmarkar, N. K.: A new polynomial-time algorithm for linear programming. Combinatorica **4** (1984) 373–395
10. Kyte, J., Doolittle, R. F.: A simple method of displaying the hydropathic character of a protein. J. Mol. Biol. **157** (1982) 105–132
11. Laird, P. D.: Learning from Good and Bad Data. Kluwer Academic Publishers (1988).
12. Lathrop, R. H.: The protein threading problem with sequence amino acid interaction preferences is NP-complete. Protein Eng. **7** (1994) 1059–1068
13. Lathrop, R. H., Smith, T. F.: Global optimum protein threading with gapped alignment and empirical pair score functions. J. Mol. Biol. **255** (1996) 641–665
14. Maiorov, V. N., Crippen, G. M.: Contact potential that recognizes the correct folding of globular proteins. J. Mol. Biol. **277** (1992) 876–888
15. Middendorf, M.: More on the complexity of common superstring and supersequence problems. Theoretical Computer Science **125** (1994) 205–228
16. Natarajan, B. K.: Machine Learning - A Theoretical Approach. Morgan Kaufmann (1991)
17. Wang, L., Jiang, T.: On the complexity of multiple sequence alignment. J. Comp. Biol. **1** (1994) 337–348
18. Zuker, M., Stiegler, P.: Optimal computer folding of large RNA sequences using thermodynamics and auxiliary information. Nucleic Acids Research **9** (1981) 133–148

A Hierarchy of Equivalences for Asynchronous Calculi
(extended abstract)

Cédric Fournet   Georges Gonthier

INRIA Rocquencourt *
{Cedric.Fournet,Georges.Gonthier}@inria.fr

Abstract. We generate a natural hierarchy of equivalences for asynchronous name-passing process calculi from simple variations on Milner and Sangiorgi's definition of weak barbed bisimulation. The π-calculus, used here, and the join-calculus are examples of such calculi.
We prove that barbed congruence coincides with Honda and Yoshida's reduction equivalence, and with asynchronous labeled bisimulation when the calculus includes name matching, thus closing those two conjectures. We also show that barbed congruence is coarser when only one barb is tested. For the π-calculus it becomes an odd limit bisimulation, but for the join-calculus it coincides with both fair testing equivalence and with the weak barbed version of Sjödin and Parrow's coupled simulation.

1 Introduction

There is a large number of proposals for the "right" equivalence for concurrent processes—see for instance [25] for an impressive overview. Choosing the proper equivalence to state a correctness argument often means striking a delicate balance between a simple, intuitively compelling statement, and a manageable proof. Although there are many effective, sometimes automated techniques for proving bisimulation-based equivalences, it can be quite hard to prove that two processes are *not* bisimilar—and to interpret this situation—because bisimulation does not directly correspond to an operational model. On the opposite, the proof that two processes are not testing equivalent is simply a failure scenario, but it can be quite hard to prove a testing equivalence.

In this paper we cast some of these diverse equivalences in a simple unifying hierarchy. In this framework, one can start a proof effort at the upper tier with a simple labeled bisimulation proof; if this fails, one can switch to a coarser equivalence by augmenting the partial proof; if the proof still fails for the testing equivalences in the last tiers then meaningful counter-examples can be found.

This hierarchy is backed by two new technical results: we close conjectures of Milner and Sangiorgi [17] and Honda and Yoshida [13] by showing that reduction-based equivalence coincides with barbed bisimulation, and we bridge the gap

* This work is partly supported by the ESPRIT CONFER-2 WG-21836

between bisimulation and testing equivalences by showing that fair testing [7, 19, 8] coincides with a form of coupled simulation [21]. Although our results were first obtained in the join-calculus, they are stated here in the more familiar asynchronous π-calculus [3], which enjoys similar properties in this respect, with one exception discussed in Section 5.

Our framework is based on abstract reduction systems $(\mathcal{P}, \rightarrow, \downarrow_x)$, where $\mathcal{P}$ is a set of processes, $\rightarrow \subseteq \mathcal{P} \times \mathcal{P}$ is a reduction relation on processes, and $\downarrow_x$ is a family of observation predicates on processes. The predicates $\downarrow_x$ are syntactic properties meant to detect the outcome of the computation (e.g., "success", convergence, ...). In process calculi based on labeled transition systems such as CCS or the π-calculus the reductions are the internal (τ) transitions and the predicates are the immediate communication capabilities—the barbs [17]. This style of definition is relatively independent of syntactic details, is adapted for higher-order settings, and is often used to compare different calculi.

The paper is organized as follows: in Section 2 we review the syntax of the asynchronous π-calculus, define evaluation contexts and barbs, and discuss may-testing equivalence; in Section 3 we present our results concerning bisimulation equivalences; in Sections 4 and 5 we discuss fair testing and coupled simulation equivalences, and we relate them; we conclude with a summary of our hierarchy. In an Appendix we give a proof sketch of our result on barbed congruence; all other proofs are omitted.

2 Barbs, contexts and testing

In this paper, we focus on the polyadic asynchronous π-calculus, with the grammar defined below:

$P ::=$	processes
$\quad \overline{x}\langle y_1, \dots, y_n \rangle$	asynchronous emission
$\mid\ x(y_1, \dots, y_n).P$	reception
$\mid\ 0$	null process
$\mid\ P \mid P'$	parallel composition
$\mid\ !P$	replication
$\mid\ \nu x_1, \dots, x_n.P$	scope restriction

We assume a countable set of names $x, y, \ldots \in \mathcal{N}$, and we use the operational semantics and the recursive sort discipline of [16]; in particular, this provides structural equivalence $\equiv$ and reduction $\rightarrow$ on processes.

We define a derived *internal choice* operator $\bigoplus_{i \in I} P_i \stackrel{\text{def}}{=} \nu t. \left(\overline{t}\langle\rangle \mid \prod_i t().P_i\right)$ where I is a finite set and t is a name that does not appear in any P_i. We note $P_1 \oplus \cdots \oplus P_n$ for $\bigoplus_{i=1 \ldots n} P_i$.

We define our notion of congruence for a particular class of contexts: an *evaluation context* is a context where the hole $[\cdot]$ occurs exactly once, and not under a guard— these contexts are called static contexts in [15]. Evaluation contexts describe environments that can communicate with the process being observed, but can neither replicate it nor prevent its internal reductions. In the asynchronous π-calculus, evaluation contexts are of the form $C[\cdot] = \nu\widetilde{x}.([\cdot] \,|\, P)$ modulo structural rearrangement.

We note $\mathcal{R}^\circ$ for the congruence of relation $\mathcal{R}$, i.e., $P \mathcal{R}^\circ Q$ iff $\forall C[\cdot], C[P] \mathcal{R} C[Q]$. We emphasize that an equivalence is not a congruence by using a dotted relation symbol (e.g., $\dot{\approx}$).

Our calculus is asynchronous in the sense of [6, 3]: emission on a name x can be detected by a reception on x that triggers a process but reception on x is not directly observable because emission is not a guard. Hence, the only way to distinguish processes is to look at their outputs on free names. We define our observation predicates accordingly:

Definition 1. *The basic observation predicate $\downarrow_x$—the strong barb on x—detects whether the process P emits on the name x: $P \downarrow_x$ iff $\exists C[\cdot], \widetilde{y}. P \equiv C[\overline{x}\langle\widetilde{y}\rangle]$ where $C[\cdot]$ is an evaluation context that does not bind x.*

The barbs only detect the superficial behavior of a process—for instance they do not separate $\overline{x}\langle y\rangle$ from $\overline{x}\langle z\rangle$—but in combination with the congruence property they provide a behavioral account of processes.

Definition 2. *The* may predicate *$\Downarrow_x$—the weak barb on x—detects whether a process can emit on x, possibly after performing some internal reductions.* May testing equivalence *$\simeq_{may}$ is the largest congruence that respects the barbs $\Downarrow_x$.*

$$P \Downarrow_x \stackrel{def}{=} \exists P'.P \rightarrow^* P' \downarrow_x$$
$$P \simeq_{may} Q \stackrel{def}{=} \forall C[\cdot], x.\ C[P] \Downarrow_x \textit{ if and only if } C[Q] \Downarrow_x$$

Testing semantics have a long history, which can be traced back to Morris equivalence for the λ-calculus [18]. As regards process calculi, they have been proposed for CCS in [9, 11, 15], extended to the π-calculus [5], then to the join-calculus [14]. In general, a test is an observer plus a way of observing; here, the set of observers is defined as the set of all evaluation contexts and the ways of observing are defined in terms of the barbs $\downarrow_x$. Testing semantics really make sense from a programming point of view; for instance barbs can be interpreted as print statements.

A typical example of may-testing equivalence is $\forall P.\ P \oplus 0 \simeq_{may} P$. May testing is most useful to prove safety properties: the specification of a program says that bad things should never happen. Thus suitable behaviors are characterized as those with no bad barbs. For example, it is adequate to specify security properties in cryptographic protocols [2]. Note, however, that it does not tell much about the presence of suitable behaviors.

3 Bisimulations and congruences

Bisimulation-based equivalences [15] are often preferred to testing semantics for the π-calculus. Independently of their intrinsic merits, they can be established by co-induction, by considering only a few single reduction steps instead of whole traces. Moreover, numerous sophisticated techniques lead to smaller candidate bisimulations, and to modular proofs (see [23] for some examples).

Barbed bisimilarity has been proposed in [17] as a uniform basis to define sensible behavioral equivalences on different process calculi:

Definition 3. *A relation $\mathcal{R}$ is a* (weak) barbed simulation *when for all processes P and Q, if $P \mathcal{R} Q$ then we have* (1) *if $P \to P'$ then $Q \to^* Q'$ and $P' \mathcal{R} Q'$, and* (2) *if $P \Downarrow_x$ then $Q \Downarrow_x$. A* barbed bisimulation *is a relation that is both a barbed simulation and the inverse of a barbed simulation. The largest barbed bisimulation is called* barbed bisimilarity, *and is denoted $\dot{\approx}$.*

This style of definition is not entirely unrelated to testing semantics; for instance, may testing is the congruence of the largest barbed simulation. Unlike may testing, however, barbed bisimulation reveals the internal branching structure of processes, and thus it induces congruences that are finer than testing semantics. Unfortunately, there are at least two sensible ways of ensuring the congruence property:

- either take the largest congruence $\dot{\approx}^\circ$ contained in barbed bisimilarity; this is the two-stage definition chosen for CCS and for the π-calculus [17, 24];
- or take the largest congruence $\approx$ that is a barbed bisimulation; this is the equivalence chosen for the ν-calculus in [12, 13] and in previous works on the join-calculus [10, 1].

By definition, the two congruences coincide if and only if $\dot{\approx}^\circ$ is a bisimulation, but this is not necessarily the case (cf. Section 5), and in general we only have $\approx \subseteq \dot{\approx}^\circ$. We detail the difference between the two definitions: for processes related by $\dot{\approx}^\circ$, the relation that is preserved in bisimulation diagrams after applying the congruence property is $\dot{\approx}$, and not $\dot{\approx}^\circ$; on the contrary, the congruence property of $\approx$ is preserved through repeated applications of bisimulation and congruence properties. Technically, the two definitions also induce different kinds of candidate relations in proofs of barbed congruence; as illustrated in this paper, $\approx$ seems easier to establish than $\dot{\approx}^\circ$. Fortunately, the two equivalences coincide in our setting (we give a proof sketch in appendix).

Theorem 1. *In the asynchronous π-calculus, we have $\dot{\approx}^\circ = \approx$.*

Checking barbed congruence still requires explicit quantification over contexts, as for instance in most proofs of [10, 1]. This is usually not the case for labeled bisimulations, where congruence is a derived property instead of a part of the definition. Thus, purely co-inductive proof techniques suffice to establish equivalences. We note $\approx_l$ for asynchronous labeled bisimulation; we refer to [3, 4] for various formulations of $\approx_l$ for asynchronous process calculi and their impact on proof techniques. Labeled bisimulation is usually finer than barbed congruence. In our case, the barb $\downarrow_x$ is present if and only if there is an output transition with a label of the form $(\widetilde{z})\overline{x}\langle\widetilde{y}\rangle$, the congruence property of $\approx_l$ is easily derived from [3], and thus we have the well-known inclusions $\approx_l \subseteq \approx \subseteq \dot{\approx}^\circ$. The first inclusion is strict because our contexts have less discriminating power than labels. For instance, the "equalizer" process $E \stackrel{\text{def}}{=} !x().\overline{y}\langle\rangle \,|\, !y().\overline{x}\langle\rangle$ can silently convert any message present on x to a message on y and vice-versa. Hence, the processes $E \mid \overline{z}\langle x\rangle$ and $E \mid \overline{z}\langle y\rangle$ are indistinguishable in any context, even though the labels $\overline{z}\langle x\rangle$ and $\overline{z}\langle y\rangle$ are not equated.

To remove this discrepancy, the usual approach is to supplement the syntax with a name-matching construct $[x = y].P$. Each label can then be tested by a particular context through a series of comparisons, and thus barbed congruence should coincide with some variant of labeled bisimulation. Note however that name-matching is not a primitive in higher-order settings. It breaks useful equations that are proper to asynchronous calculi, such as η-conversion.

In the π-calculus with matching, early bisimulation and barbed congruence coincide, but the proof is delicate—this is mentioned as an open question in [17]. To our knowledge, the only proof of the inclusion $\dot{\approx}^{\circ} \subseteq \approx_l$ appears in Sangiorgi's thesis [24], for both CCS and the monadic π-calculus; the technique consists of building contexts that test for all possible behaviors of a process under bisimulation, and that exhibit different barbs accordingly. This technique requires infinite contexts with infinitely many free names and recursive constants. These extended contexts are never considered in the usual congruence properties for the π-calculus, and they cannot be expressed using the simpler constructs of asynchronous calculi.

In other works, partial results are obtained for variants of the π-calculus [17, 3, 4]. The proof techniques are similar but only use finite contexts. As a result, the coincidence is established only for *image finite* processes. A process P is image finite when the set of its derivatives is finite. In the case of weak relations, this implies that $\{P', P \rightarrow^* P'\}$ is finite. This restriction is annoying, as many processes that use replication (or just replicated input) are not image-finite.

Theorem 2. *In the asynchronous π-calculus with name-testing we have $\dot{\approx}^{\circ} = \approx_l$.*

We actually prove the inclusion $\approx \subseteq \approx_l$, then we apply Theorem 1. A proof of this inclusion already appears at the end of [13] in a similar setting. Our proof, however, is significantly shorter, and illustrates the advantage of the congruence-and-bisimulation definition. Instead of capturing the whole synchronization tree in a huge context, we exhibit for every labeled transition a particular context that detects this particular transition, then disappears up to barbed congruence.

4 Fair testing and coupled simulation

In this section, we attempt to reconcile testing semantics and bisimulation-based semantics in an intermediate tier that hosts both kinds of equivalences.

We first refine may testing to capture the positive behavior of processes. The usual approach is to observe messages that are always emitted, independently of internal choices: the *must predicate* detects outputs that are present on all finite traces ($P \downarrow_{\Box x} \stackrel{\text{def}}{=} \forall P', P \rightarrow^* P' \not\rightarrow, P' \downarrow_x$) and can be used to define testing equivalences as in Definition 2. These relations, however, are unduly sensitive to diverging behaviors; they interpret all infinite computations in the same manner. Modifying the must predicate to incorporate a notion of "abstract fairness" yields an interesting testing equivalence that has been proposed for variants of CCS in [7, 19, 8].

Definition 4. *The* fair-must predicate $\Downarrow_{\Box x}$ *detects whether a process always has the possibility of emitting on* x. Fair Testing equivalence $\simeq_{fair}$ *is the largest congruence that respects the fair-must predicates* $\Downarrow_{\Box x}$.

$$P \Downarrow_{\Box x} \stackrel{def}{=} \forall P', P \rightarrow^* P' \textit{ implies } P' \Downarrow_x$$

$$P \simeq_{fair} Q \stackrel{def}{=} \forall C, x.\ C[P] \Downarrow_{\Box x} \textit{ if and only if } C[Q] \Downarrow_{\Box x}$$

For all processes P, $P \Downarrow_{\Box x}$ implies $P \Downarrow_x$, and if there are no infinite computations, $\downarrow_{\Box x}$ and $\Downarrow_{\Box x}$ coincide. Fairness is hidden in the fair-must predicate: $\Downarrow_{\Box x}$ succeeds if there is still a way to emit on x after any reduction. Intuitively, the model is the set of barbs present on all finite and infinite fair traces. For instance $\nu z.(\overline{z}\langle\rangle \mid z().\overline{x}\langle\rangle \mid !z().\overline{z}\langle\rangle) \simeq_{fair} \overline{x}\langle\rangle$, even if there is an infinite computation that never triggers $\overline{x}\langle\rangle$.

Fair testing is strictly finer than may testing ($\simeq_{fair} \subset \simeq_{may}$), as can be seen by using the contexts $C[\cdot] \stackrel{\text{def}}{=} \nu r, z.(\overline{r}\langle y\rangle \mid x().\overline{r}\langle z\rangle \mid r(u).\overline{u}\langle\rangle \mid [\cdot])$ to transform the presence of a barb $\Downarrow_x$ into the absence of the barb $\Downarrow_{\Box y}$. As we shall see, fair testing is also strictly coarser than barbed congruence. Similar inclusions are established in [7, 19]; the authors remark that weak bisimulation equivalences incorporate a particular notion of fairness, they identify sensitivity to the branching structure as an undesirable property of bisimulation, and they propose simulation-based sufficient conditions to establish fair-testing.

As regards discriminating power, fair testing is a reasonable equivalence to deal with asynchronous calculi; it detects deadlocks, but remains insensitive to livelocks. In [8], for instance, distributed communication protocols are studied using the fair-testing preorder as an implementation relation. Note however that "abstract fairness" is not enforced by practical scheduling policies.

Independently, *coupled simulation* has been proposed in [21] to address similar issues; this simulation-based equivalence does not require an exact correspondence between the internal choices, and thus abstracts some of the branching structure revealed by bisimulation. *Weakly-coupled simulation* is a variant that is insensitive to divergence [22]. It is used in [20] to establish the correctness of an encoding of the choice operator in the asynchronous π-calculus. Here we use barbed weakly-coupled simulation:

Definition 5. *Two relations* $\leqslant, \geqslant$ *form a pair of* barbed coupled simulations *when* $\leqslant$ *and* $\geqslant^{-1}$ *are barbed simulations that satisfy the coupling relations* (1) *if* $P \leqslant Q$, *then for some* Q', $Q \rightarrow^* Q'$ *and* $P \geqslant Q'$, *and* (2) *if* $P \geqslant Q$, *then for some* P', $P \rightarrow^* P'$ *and* $P' \leqslant Q$.

A relation $\mathcal{R}$ *is a* barbed coupled equivalence *when* $\mathcal{R} = \leqslant \cap \geqslant$ *for some coupled simulations* $(\leqslant, \geqslant)$. *The relation* $\lessgtr$ *is the largest barbed coupled equivalence; the relation* $\lessgtr$ *is the largest barbed coupled equivalence that is a congruence.*

By definition, coupled equivalences are coarser than the corresponding bisimulations; for instance we have $\overline{x} \oplus (\overline{y} \oplus \overline{z}) \lessgtr \overline{x} \oplus \overline{y} \oplus \overline{z}$ but these processes are not barbed bisimilar, because the choice between the three outputs is not performed atomically.

As for barbed bisimulations in Section 3, the problem of the two congruences arises, with a different situation here: we have $\lessgtr \subset \dot{\lessgtr}^{\circ}$, as can be seen from the processes $a().\bar{b}\langle\rangle \oplus a().\bar{c}\langle\rangle$ and $a().(\bar{b}\langle\rangle \oplus \bar{c}\langle\rangle)$. The discrepancy between these equivalences stems from internal choices that are spawned between visible actions.

The exact relation between fair testing and coupled simulation is intriguing. They are applied to the same problems, typically the study of distributed protocols where high-level atomic steps are implemented as a negotiation between distributed components, with several steps that perform a gradual commitment. Yet, their definitions are very different, and both have their advantages; fair-testing is arguably more natural than coupled simulations, but lacks efficient proof techniques.

Fair testing is strictly coarser than coupled congruence ($\simeq_{fair} \subset \dot{\lessgtr}^{\circ}$): by combining simulation, coupling, and barbed properties, we easily prove that every coupled barbed equivalence refines the fair-must predicates; conversely we have that $a() \simeq_{fair} a() \oplus 0$ but $\bar{a}\langle\rangle \mid a() \not\dot{\lessgtr} \bar{a}\langle\rangle \mid (a() \oplus 0)$. Nonetheless, the distance between fair testing and coupled congruence is rather small: as we shall see in the next section, both relations coincide in the join-calculus, and this result can be adapted to the π-calculus with a small restriction on the barbs.

5 More barbs

We conclude our extended abstract by a discussion of alternate definitions of observation. So far, we assumed a distinct predicate $\downarrow_x$ for every name, but there are other natural choices. We study the impact of two variations.

In the initial paper on barbed equivalences [17], and in most definitions of testing equivalences, a *single predicate* is used instead of an indexed family. Either there is a single observable action ω, or all barbs are collected by an existential predicate. Accordingly, for every family of observation predicates (e.g., $\Downarrow_x$), we define an existential observation predicate, that tests any of these predicates (e.g., $P \Downarrow \stackrel{\text{def}}{=} \exists x.P \Downarrow_x$), and we obtain existential variants (e.g., $\dot{\approx}_{\exists}^{\circ}$) for all previously defined equivalences.

Another variant is directly inspired by the join-calculus; since observation is supposed to occur after computation, the variant only considers strong barbs that are stable by reduction, which we call *committed barbs*—as opposed to ordinary, transient barbs. We define a predicate slightly stronger than $\downarrow_x$:

Definition 6. *The predicate $\downdownarrows_x$—the committed barb on x—detects whether P permanently emits on x: $P \downdownarrows_x \stackrel{\text{def}}{=} \forall P'.P \rightarrow^* P'$ implies $P' \downarrow_x$*

In the join-calculus, the locality property enforces the identity $\downdownarrows_x = \downarrow_x$ for all names. In the π-calculus, the situation is not so simple; for instance, the process $P = \bar{x}\langle\rangle \mid x()$ reduces to 0, and we have $P \downarrow_x$, $0 \not\downdownarrows_x$. Again, this induces variants for all our definitions (e.g., $\dot{\approx}_{\downdownarrows}$).

Fortunately, these two variations do not affect the discriminating power of our equivalences as long as congruence remains available. When present, the congruence property can be used to apply contexts that restrict all free names but one, and thus recover $\Downarrow_x$ from $\Downarrow$. The congruence property can also be used to encode weak committed predicates. It suffices to replace transient barbs by committed barbs that relay detection without further interaction with the process. We use $T_x[\cdot] \stackrel{\text{def}}{=} \nu x.(x().\bar{t}\langle\rangle \,|\, [\cdot])$ (where t is fresh.)

When simulation and congruence properties are not required at the same time, however, these variations may lead to significant differences. In our hierarchy, the question arises for the relations $\dot{\approx}^{\circ}$, $\dot{\lessapprox}^{\circ}$ and their variants.

In the full paper, we establish that Theorem 1 still applies with committed barbs only, and thus that we have $\dot{\approx}^{\circ}_{\Downarrow\!\!\downarrow} = \dot{\approx}^{\circ}$. On the contrary, we establish that, with a single barb, both equivalences $\dot{\approx}^{\circ}_{\exists}$ and $\dot{\approx}^{\circ}_{\exists,\Downarrow\!\!\downarrow}$ are strictly coarser than $\dot{\approx}^{\circ} = \approx = \approx_{\exists} = \approx_{\exists,\Downarrow\!\!\downarrow}$, which provides further examples of equivalences such that the two definitions of congruence in Section 3 make a difference. Rather surprisingly, the congruence of weak $\exists$-barbed bisimilarity ($\dot{\approx}^{\circ}_{\exists}$) is an *inductive*, or limit, bisimulation in the asynchronous π-calculus.

With a single committed barb, the situation is less exotic but perhaps more interesting: the bisimilarity $\dot{\approx}_{\exists,\Downarrow\!\!\downarrow}$ partitions the processes into the three classes $\Downarrow_{\Box}$, $\not\Downarrow$, and $\Downarrow \wedge \not\Downarrow_{\Box}$; its congruence yields fair testing ($\dot{\approx}^{\circ}_{\exists,\Downarrow\!\!\downarrow} = \simeq_{fair}$). In some sense, this identity completes our programme: we have a bisimulation-based characterization of fair-testing.

Next, we provide another, more useful characterization of this equivalence. We establish that, with committed barbs, we have $\dot{\lessapprox}^{\circ}_{\Downarrow\!\!\downarrow} = \simeq_{fair}$. To show this coincidence, we study the semantics of coupled simulation with committed barbs. We describe classes of processes that are entirely defined by the observation predicates $\Downarrow_x$ and $\Downarrow\!\!\downarrow_x$.

We first consider processes whose barbs $\Downarrow_x$ are all stable by reduction. This is the case for P if and only if for all name x we have $P \Downarrow_x = P \Downarrow\!\!\downarrow_x$. In some sense, P has converged to the set of names $\{x/P \Downarrow\!\!\downarrow_x\} = \{x/P \Downarrow_x\}$, which entirely captures its behavior. More generally, we associate to every process P the semantics $[\![P]\!]$ that collects these sets of names for all its stable derivatives:

$$[\![P]\!] \stackrel{\text{def}}{=} \{S \subseteq \mathcal{N} / \exists P', P \rightarrow^* P', S = \{x/P' \Downarrow\!\!\downarrow_x\} = \{x/P' \Downarrow_x\}\}$$

For example, $[\![0]\!]$ is the singleton $\{\emptyset\}$ and $[\![\bar{x}\langle\rangle \oplus \bar{y}\langle\rangle]\!]$ is $\{\{x\},\{y\}\}$. As is the case for weak barbs, $[\![P]\!]$ decreases by reduction; it is never empty. The predicates $\Downarrow_x$ and $\Downarrow_{\Box x}$ are easily recovered from our semantics: $P \Downarrow_x$ iff $x \in \bigcup [\![P]\!]$, and $P \Downarrow_{\Box x}$ iff $x \in \bigcap [\![P]\!]$.

Let $\dot{\simeq}_{\flat}$ be the equivalence defined as $P \dot{\simeq}_{\flat} Q \stackrel{\text{def}}{=} [\![P]\!] = [\![Q]\!]$. By definition of fair testing, we immediately obtain that $\dot{\simeq}_{\flat}^{\circ} \subseteq \simeq_{fair}$. This inclusion is actually an equality, as can be seen by using the following context T_S^N parameterized by two finite disjoint sets of names that do not contain t:

$$T^N_{\{x_1,\cdots,x_n\}}[\cdot] \stackrel{\text{def}}{=} \nu S, N.\left(\bar{t}\langle\rangle \mid \textstyle\prod_{y\in N} y().\bar{t}\langle\rangle \mid x_1().\cdots.x_n().t().0 \mid [\cdot]\right)$$

This context fair-tests exactly one set of names in our semantics: for all P such that $\mathsf{fv}[P] \subseteq S \cup N$, we have $T_S^N[P] \Downarrow_{\Box t}$ if and only if $S \notin [\![P]\!]$. The next result states that our semantics precisely captures barbed-coupled simulation, and thus provides an alternate, simulation-based characterization of fair-testing.

Theorem 3. *With committed barbs, $\dot{\simeq}_\flat$ is the largest coupled barbed equivalence; we have the identities $\dot{\lessgtr} = \dot{\simeq}_\flat$ and $\dot{\lessgtr}^{\circ} = \simeq_{fair}$.*

6 A family portrait

The diagram below gathers our results; we only mention the existential and committed variants when they differ from their original equivalence. An equivalence is above another when it is strictly finer. With name-matching, the two upper tiers coincide.

labeled bisimulation	$\approx_l$	
	$\vert$	– *name matching*
barbed congruence	$\approx = \dot{\approx}^\circ$	
	$\vert$	– *internal choice between visible actions*
coupled-barbed congruence	$\lessgtr$	
	$\vert$	– *internal choice interleaved with visible actions*
fair testing	$\simeq_{fair} = \dot{\lessgtr}^\circ_{\downdownarrows} = \dot{\approx}^\circ_{\exists,\downdownarrows}$	
	$\vert$	– *abstract fairness*
may testing	$\simeq_{may}$	

References

1. M. Abadi, C. Fournet, and G. Gonthier. Secure implementation of channel abstractions. In *Proceedings of LICS '98*, June 1998.
2. M. Abadi and A. D. Gordon. Reasoning about cryptographic protocols in the spi calculus. In *Proceedings of CONCUR '97*, pages 59–73, July 1997. LNCS 1243.
3. R. M. Amadio, I. Castellani, and D. Sangiorgi. On bisimulations for the asynchronous π-calculus. In *Proceedings of CONCUR '96*, Aug. 1996. LNCS 1119.
4. M. Boreale, C. Fournet, and C. Laneve. Bisimulations in the join-calculus. In *Proceedings of PROCOMET '98*. Chapman and Hall, June 1998.
5. M. Boreale and R. D. Nicola. Testing equivalence for mobile processes. *Information and Computation*, 120(2):279–303, Aug. 1995.
6. G. Boudol. Asynchrony and the π-calculus (note). Rapport de Recherche 1702, INRIA Sophia-Antipolis, May 1992.
7. E. Brinksma, A. Rensink, and W. Vogler. Fair testing. In *Proceedings of CONCUR '95*, pages 313–327, 1995. LNCS 962.
8. E. Brinksma, A. Rensink, and W. Vogler. Applications of fair testing. In *Formal Description Techniques IX: Theory, Applications and Tools*, volume IX. ch, 1996.
9. R. De Nicola and M. C. B. Hennessy. Testing equivalences for processes. *Theoretical Comput. Sci.*, 34:83–133, 1984.

10. C. Fournet and G. Gonthier. The reflexive chemical abstract machine and the join-calculus. In *Proceedings of POPL '96*, pages 372–385. ACM, Jan. 1996.
11. M. Hennessy. *Algebraic Theory of Processes.* The MIT Press, 1988.
12. K. Honda and M. Tokoro. On asynchronous communication semantics. In *Proceedings of the ECOOP '91 Workshop on Object-Based Concurrent Computing*, pages 21–51, 1992. LNCS 612.
13. K. Honda and N. Yoshida. On reduction-based process semantics. *Theoretical Comput. Sci.*, 151:437–486, 1995.
14. C. Laneve. May and must testing in the join-calculus. Technical Report UBLCS 96-04, University of Bologna, May 1996.
15. R. Milner. *Communication and Concurrency.* Prentice Hall, New York, 1989.
16. R. Milner. The polyadic π-calculus: a tutorial. In F. L. Bauer, W. Brauer, and H. Schwichtenberg, editors, *Logic and Algebra of Specification.* Springer-Verlag, 1993.
17. R. Milner and D. Sangiorgi. Barbed bisimulation. In *Proceedings of ICALP '92*, pages 685–695, 1992. LNCS 623.
18. J. H. Morris, Jr. *Lambda-Calculus Models of Programming Languages.* Ph. D. dissertation, MIT, Dec. 1968. Report No. MAC–TR–57.
19. V. Natarajan and R. Cleaveland. Divergence and fair testing. In *Proceedings of ICALP '95*, 1995. LNCS 944.
20. U. Nestmann and B. C. Pierce. Decoding choice encodings. In *Proceedings of CONCUR '96*, pages 179–194, Aug. 1996. LNCS 1119.
21. J. Parrow and P. Sjödin. Multiway synchronization verified with coupled simulation. In *Proceedings of CONCUR '92*, pages 518–533, 1992. LNCS 630.
22. J. Parrow and P. Sjödin. The complete axiomatization of CS-congruence. In *Proceedings of STACS '94*, pages 557–568, 1994. LNCS 775.
23. D. Sangiorgi. On the bisimulation proof method. Technical Report ECS–LFCS–94–299, University of Edinburgh, 1994. An extended abstract appears in *Proceedings of MFCS'95*, LNCS 969.
24. D. Sangiorgi. *Expressing Mobility in Process Algebras: First-Order and Higher-Order Paradigms.* Ph.D. thesis, University of Edinburgh, May 1993.
25. R. J. van Glabbeek. The linear time–branching time spectrum II; the semantics of sequential systems with silent moves (extended abstract). In *Proceedings of CONCUR '93*, pages 66–81, 1993. LNCS 715.

Appendix: Proof Sketch for Theorem 1

In order to establish that both congruences are equal, we use a series of internal encodings. We assume a continuation-passing-style encoding for boolean, integers, and their operations *is_zero*(·), *pred*(·), ... inside of the π-calculus. This encoding uses only a deterministic fragment of the π-calculus, see, e.g., [16]. We let n, m range over the representation of integers, when they occur in processes.

We fix two nullary names x and y; we note $\dot{\approx}_2$ for the largest weak bisimulation that refines $\Downarrow_x$ and $\Downarrow_y$. We are going to prove that $\dot{\approx}_2^\circ \subseteq \approx$. We first build a family of processes that are not $\dot{\approx}_2$-equivalent and retain this property by reduction.

Lemma 1. *Let $\mathcal{R}$ be a bisimulation relation, and $\mathcal{P}$ be a set of processes such that, if $P, Q \in \mathcal{P}$ and $P \rightarrow^* \mathcal{R}\ Q$, then $P = Q$. Then the set of processes $\oplus(\mathcal{P})$*

defined below (up-to the symmetry of $\oplus$) also has this property.

$$\oplus(\mathcal{P}) \stackrel{def}{=} \bigcup_{n\geq 2}\{P_1 \oplus \cdots \oplus P_n / P_i \in \mathcal{P} \wedge P_i = P_j \text{ implies } i = j\}$$

By iterating the lemma, we build an infinite family of processes $\mathcal{P}_\omega$ as follows:

$$\mathcal{P}_0 \stackrel{\text{def}}{=} \{\, 0,\ \overline{x}\langle\rangle,\ \overline{y}\langle\rangle \,\}, \qquad \mathcal{P}_{n+1} \stackrel{\text{def}}{=} \oplus(\mathcal{P}_n), \qquad \mathcal{P}_\omega \stackrel{\text{def}}{=} \bigcup_{n\geq 0} \mathcal{P}_n$$

The set $\mathcal{P}_\omega$ only contains processes that are not related by $\dot{\approx}_2$: if $P \in \mathcal{P}_n$ and $Q \in \mathcal{P}_{n+m}$, then for some $Q' \in \mathcal{P}_n, Q' \neq P$, we have $Q \rightarrow^m Q'$ and by construction this series of reduction cannot be matched by any reductions starting from P.

The next lemma says that a process can "communicate an integer" to the environment by using two barbs $\Downarrow_x$ and $\Downarrow_y$ in an exclusive, committed manner, thanks to the discriminating power of bisimulation. To every integer, we associate a distinct equivalence class of $\dot{\approx}_2$ in the hierarchy of processes $\mathcal{P}_\omega$, then we write a process that receives an integer and expresses it by reducing to its characteristic class. Thus, the context $N[\,\cdot\,]$ transforms integer-indexed barbs $\overline{int}\langle n\rangle$ (where *int* is a regular name of the π-calculus) into the barbs $\Downarrow_x$ and $\Downarrow_y$.

Lemma 2. *There is an evaluation context $N[\,\cdot\,]$ such that, for all integers n, m, if $N[\overline{int}\langle n\rangle] \rightarrow^* \dot{\approx}_2 N[\overline{int}\langle m\rangle]$, then $n = m$.*

Proof. We use the following context and we position its derivatives in $\mathcal{P}_\omega$.

$$\begin{aligned} I &\stackrel{\text{def}}{=} !c(u,x,y,z).\,\mathsf{if}\ is\_zero(u)\ \mathsf{then}\ \overline{x}\langle\rangle \\ &\qquad\qquad\qquad\qquad\quad \mathsf{else}\ (\overline{c}\langle(u-1),x,y,z\rangle \oplus \overline{c}\langle(u-1),y,z,x\rangle) \\ N[\,\cdot\,] &\stackrel{\text{def}}{=} \nu c,z.([\,\cdot\,] \,|\, I \,|\, int(u).(\overline{c}\langle u,x,y,z\rangle \oplus \overline{c}\langle u,y,z,x\rangle \oplus \overline{c}\langle u,z,x,y\rangle)) \end{aligned}$$

Every integer n yields a characteristic ternary sum in $\mathcal{P}_{n+1}$; all its derivatives are binary sums in $\bigcup_{i\leq n} \mathcal{P}_i$ that are distinct from any other ternary ones.

The next lemma applies this remark to restrict the class of contexts in use in congruence properties to contexts with at most two free (nullary) variables.

Lemma 3. *Let S be a finite set of names with $int \notin S$. There is an evaluation context $F_S[\,\cdot\,]$ such that for all processes P and Q, if $\mathsf{fv}[P] \cup \mathsf{fv}[Q] \subseteq S$ and $N[F_S[P]] \dot{\approx}_2 N[F_S[Q]]$ then $P \dot{\approx} Q$.*

Proof. Let $a, b \notin S$ and $[\![z]\!]$ be the integer encoding of z. We choose the context $F_S[\,\cdot\,] \stackrel{\text{def}}{=} \nu S,a,b.([\,\cdot\,] \,|\, \overline{a}\langle\rangle \,|\, \overline{b}\langle\rangle \,|\, \bigoplus_{x\in S\uplus\{a,b\}} x().\overline{int}\langle[\![x]\!]\rangle)$. and we establish that the relation that contains all pairs (P, Q) of the lemma is included in $\dot{\approx}$.

We also compile every process P into some integer representation $[\![P]\!]$. We define an interpreting process D_ε that takes (1) any integer representation $[\![P]\!]$ and (2) the encoding of an evaluation environment ρ that maps integers encodings $[\![z]\!]$ to names z for all names $z \in \mathsf{fv}[P]$. We omit the details from the extended abstract. The next lemma relates the source process P to its interpreted representation; this result is not surprising, since the π-calculus is Turing-complete.

Lemma 4. *For all processes P and environments ρ such that $\varepsilon, \rho \notin \mathsf{fv}[P]$ and $\forall x \in \mathsf{fv}[P], \rho([\![x]\!]) = x$, we have $\nu\varepsilon,\rho.(D_\varepsilon \mid \overline{\varepsilon}\langle [\![P]\!], \rho\rangle) \approx_l P$.*

In order to reduce quantification over evaluation contexts to quantification over integers, we remark that for every set of variables S represented in ρ, for every process P and evaluation context $C[\cdot]$ with $\mathsf{fv}[P] \cup \mathsf{fv}[C[\cdot]] \subseteq S$, there is an integer n such that $C[P] \approx_l \nu\widetilde{x}.\big(P \mid \nu\varepsilon,\rho.(D_\varepsilon \mid \overline{\varepsilon}\langle n, \rho\rangle)\big)$.

We are now ready to prove that $\approx$ and $\dot{\approx}_2^{\circ}$ coincide. By definition we have $\approx \subseteq \dot{\approx}_2^{\circ}$, and it suffices to show that $\dot{\approx}_2^{\circ}$ is a bisimulation to obtain the converse inclusion. To this purpose, we build a family of universal contexts $U_S[\cdot]$:

Lemma 5. *For all finite sets of names S with $x, y, int \notin S$, there is an evaluation context $U_S[\cdot]$ such that the relation*

$$\mathcal{R} \stackrel{def}{=} \{(P,Q) \mid \mathsf{fv}[P] \cup \mathsf{fv}[Q] \subseteq S \text{ and } U_S[P] \dot{\approx}_2 U_S[Q]\}$$

meets the properties (1) *for every evaluation context $C[\cdot]$ with $\mathsf{fv}[C[\cdot]] \subseteq \{x, y\}$ that binds all the names in S, if $P \mathcal{R} Q$, then $C[P] \dot{\approx}_2 C[Q]$, and* (2) *$\mathcal{R} \subseteq \approx$.*

Proof. Without loss of generality, we assume that $[\![x]\!] = 2$, $[\![y]\!] = 3$, and that processes and names in S are encoded by integers $n \geq 4$. We use the contexts defined as follows:

$$\begin{aligned} T_u &\stackrel{\text{def}}{=} \overline{int}\langle u\rangle \oplus \nu\varepsilon.\left(D_\varepsilon \mid \overline{\varepsilon}\langle u, \{([\![z]\!] \mapsto z)_{z \in S \uplus \{x,y\}}\}\rangle\right) \\ G &\stackrel{\text{def}}{=} \nu c.\left(\overline{c}\langle 4\rangle \mid c(u).T_u \mid !c(u).\overline{c}\langle u+1\rangle\right) \\ U_S[\cdot] &\stackrel{\text{def}}{=} N\left[F_{\{x,y\}}\left[\nu S.\left(G \,\|\, [\cdot]\right)\right]\right] \end{aligned}$$

The process T_u either reveals the choice of u or uses this choice to start the interpreter. The process G behaves like the infinite choice $T_4 \oplus (T_5 \oplus (T_6 \oplus \cdots))$.

Property (1) of the lemma is obtained by reasoning on the following bisimulation diagram for a given context $C[\cdot] \equiv \nu S.([\cdot] \mid R)$. The contexts $K[\cdot]$ and $K'[\cdot]$ are derivatives of $U_S[\cdot]$ after choosing $T_{[\![R]\!]} \approx_l \overline{int}\langle [\![R]\!]\rangle \oplus R$, and after starting the interpreter, respectively.

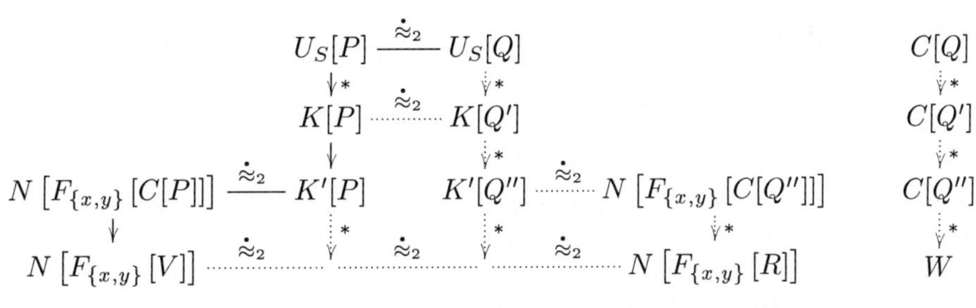

Property (2) relies on several instances of Property (1); for instance, we obtain the congruence property of $\mathcal{R}$ for a context $C'[\cdot]$ by choosing $C[\cdot] = U_S[C'[\cdot]]$. This concludes the proof of the theorem ($\mathcal{R} \subseteq \approx \subseteq \dot{\approx}^{\circ} \subseteq \dot{\approx}_2^{\circ} \subseteq \mathcal{R}$). The proof is not affected by committed barbs or name-matching.

On Asynchrony in Name-Passing Calculi

Massimo Merro   Davide Sangiorgi

INRIA Sophia-Antipolis, France

Abstract. We study an asynchronous π-calculus, called *Local* π (Lπ), where: (a) only the *output capability* of names may be transmitted; (b) there is no *matching* or similar constructs. We study the basic operational and algebraic theory of Lπ and show some applications: the derivability of *delayed input*; the correctness of an optimisation of the encoding of call-by-name λ-calculus; the validity of some laws for the Join-calculus.

1 Introduction

The *asynchronous π-calculus* (π_a) is a variant of the π-calculus where message emission is non-blocking. Formally, the output prefix $\overline{a}b.\,P$ of π-calculus is replaced with the simpler output particle $\overline{a}b$, which has no continuation. The asynchronous π-calculus has been first introduced by Honda and Tokoro [13], who showed that it is expressive enough to encode the (synchronous) π-calculus.

Asynchronous communications are interesting from the point of view of concurrent and distributed programming languages, because they are easier to implement and they are closer to the communication primitives offered by available distributed systems. The asynchronous π-calculus is considered the basis of experimental programming languages (or proposal of programming languages) like Pict [19], Join [9], and the Blue calculus [8]. However, at a closer inspection, these languages are based on an even simpler calculus, where:

(a) the recipient of a name may only use it in output actions; that is, only the *output capability* of names may be transmitted;
(b) there is no *matching* construct (or similar constructs like mismatching) for testing equality between names. (We may also view (b) as a consequence of (a), since testing the identity of a name requires more than the output capability.)

These restrictions are explicit in Join and in recent proposals of the Blue calculus. In Pict, (b) is explicit; (a) is not, but most Pict programs obey it.

We call *Local* π (Lπ) the asynchronous π-calculus with the additional simplifications (a) and (b). In this paper, we study the basic operational and algebraic theory of Lπ. We focus on bisimulation-based behavioural equivalences, precisely on *barbed congruence* [17].

Proof techniques for Lπ can be exploited to reason about languages such as Pict, Join, Blue and π_1, either by directly adapting the techniques to these languages, or by means of encodings into Lπ. The theory of Lπ should also be useful for giving the semantics to, and reasoning about, concurrent or distributed object-oriented languages. For instance, (a) can guarantee the fundamental property that an object has unique identity. In an object world, the name a of an object may be transmitted; the recipient may use a to access its methods, but he/she cannot create a new object called a. When representing objects in the π-calculus, this usually translates into the constraint that the recipient of a may only use it in output. Indeed, Lπ may also be seen as a simple calculus of objects. A restriction $\nu(a)P$ declares a new object called a. Constraint (a) ensures that all inputs at a are in P and can be statically detected. We may also say that restriction $\nu(a)$ defines the location of a, and see Lπ as a simple calculus of distributed objects.

Studies of bisimulation-based behavioural equivalences for asynchronous mobile calculi are [13, 14, 11, 2]. In these theories, the most important algebraic law that is not in the theory of the synchronous π-calculus is $!\,a(x).\,\overline{a}x = \mathbf{0}$. Although this law is useful, it seems fair to say that the restriction to asynchronous contexts does not affect much barbed congruence.

By contrast, asynchrony has strong semantic consequences under of simplifications (a) and (b). Consider these laws:

$$\overline{a}b \;=\; \nu(c)(\overline{a}c \mid c \triangleright b), \quad \text{where } c \triangleright b \stackrel{\text{def}}{=} !c(x).\,\overline{b}x \text{ and } c \neq b \tag{1}$$

$$\overline{a}b \mid c \triangleright b \mid b \triangleright c \;=\; \overline{a}c \mid c \triangleright b \mid b \triangleright c \tag{2}$$

$$\nu(c)(\overline{a}c \mid c(x)) \;=\; \nu(c)(\overline{a}c) \;=\; \nu(c)(\overline{a}c \mid \overline{c}b) \tag{3}$$

$$\nu(a)(!a(x).\,R \mid (P \mid Q)) = \nu(a)(!a(x).\,R \mid P) \mid \nu(a)(!a(x).\,R \mid Q) \tag{4}$$

where a does not appear free in input position in P, Q and R

These laws are valid in Lπ, but are false in π_{a} and in π-calculus. Laws 1 and 2 are false because they equate processes that may perform syntactically different outputs: in law 1 the process on the left makes the output of a global name, whereas that on the right the output of a local (i.e., private) name; in law 2 the two processes emit two different global names. In laws 3, the derivatives of the processes after the initial output are very different, and this difference is observable in π_{a} and in π-calculus. Law 4 is a distributivity law for replicated resources (a stronger[1] version of one of Milner's replication theorems [15]).

The main inconvenience of barbed congruence is that it uses quantification over contexts in the definition, and this can make proofs of process equalities heavy. Against this, it is important to find *direct* characterisations, without context quantification. In the synchronous π-calculus barbed congruence coincides with the closure under substitutions of *early* bisimilarity; in the asynchronous π-calculus it coincides with the closure under substitutions of *asynchronous early* bisimilarity (on image-finite processes) [2, 20].

We prove two characterisations of barbed congruence in Lπ (as usual, on image-finite processes). The first is based on an embedding of Lπ into a subcalculus where all names emitted are private. Barbed congruence between processes

---

[1] In Milner's original theorems name a may not be exported.

of Lπ coincides, on their images, with a variant of asynchronous early bisimulation. The second characterisation is based on a new labeled transition system (LTS). It modifies the standard LTS so to reveal what is observable in Lπ, that is, what an external observer that behaves like a Lπ process can see by interacting with a Lπ process. Barbed congruence in Lπ coincides with the standard asynchronous early bisimulation defined on the new LTS. The resulting coinductive proof method can be enhanced by means of "bisimulation up–to" techniques.

Technical differences of these characterisations of barbed congruence in Lπ w.r.t. those in π_a and π-calculus are: (i) the labeled bisimulations of Lπ are congruence relations and therefore do not have to be closed under substitutions to obtain barbed congruence; (ii) in Lπ the early labeled bisimulations coincide with their ground versions (which has no universal quantification on the received names); (iii) the characterisations in Lπ are proved without the matching construct (which is essential in the proofs in π_a and π-calculus).

In Section 6 we discuss some applications of the theory of Lπ. (i) We prove that in Lπ the *delayed input* (a form of non-blocking input prefixing) is derivable. (ii) We prove an optimisation of the encoding of call-by-name λ-calculus and, exploiting delayed input, we derive an encoding of *strong* call-by-name. (iii) We prove some laws for the Join-calculus. (iv) We prove some non-full abstraction and full abstraction results for the encoding used by Boreale [4] to compare the expressiveness of asynchronous mobility and internal mobility (where only private names may be passed).

Calculi similar to Lπ are discussed in [12, 4, 25]. Some of the techniques we use in Section 4 are inspired by techniques in [23]. Characterisations of barbed congruence on calculi for mobile processes include [2, 5]. However, in these bisimilarity, matching transitions of processes have the same labels, therefore the problems given by restrictions (a) and (b) do not appear. [6] studies barbed congruence in synchronous π-calculus with capability types and no matching, of which (a) and (b) are a special case. Our characterisations are simpler than those in [6], but the latter are more general, in that they can be applied to several π-calculus languages (although the extension to asynchronous languages is not straightforward). The technical approaches are different: in [6] bisimulations have a type environment (in fact, closures) whereas in this paper bisimulations are directly defined on processes.

Proofs are omitted or just sketched, so to leave space for the examples.

2 The calculus Lπ

The grammar of Lπ has operators of inaction, input prefix, asynchronous output, parallel composition, restriction and replicated input:

$$P ::= \mathbf{0} \;\big|\; a(x).\, P \;\big|\; \overline{a}b \;\big|\; P \mid P \;\big|\; \boldsymbol{\nu}(a)P \;\big|\; !a(x).\, P$$

where in $a(x).\, P$ name x may not occur free in P in input position (this constraint shows that only the output capability of names may be transmitted).

We use small letters $a, b, \ldots, x, y$ for *names*; capital letters P, Q, R for *processes*, σ for substitutions; $P\sigma$ is the result of applying σ to P, with the usual renaming convention to avoid captures. Parallel composition has the lowest precedence among the operators. The labeled transition system is the usual one (in the late style, [16, 23]). Transition are of the form $P \xrightarrow{\mu} P'$, where *action* μ can be: τ (interaction), $a(b)$ (input), $\overline{a}b$ (free output) and $\boldsymbol{\nu}(b)\overline{a}b$ (bound output, that is the emission of a private name b at a). In these actions, a is the *subject* and b the *object*. Free and bound names (fn, bn) of actions and processes are defined as usual. Relation $\Longrightarrow$ is the reflexive and transitive closure of $\xrightarrow{\tau}$; moreover, $\overset{\mu}{\Longrightarrow}$ stands for $\Longrightarrow\xrightarrow{\mu}\Longrightarrow$, and $\overset{\widehat{\mu}}{\Longrightarrow}$ for $\overset{\mu}{\Longrightarrow}$ if $\mu \neq \tau$, and for $\Longrightarrow$ if $\mu = \tau$.

2.1. Links A *link* process behaves as a name buffer receiving names at one end-point and retransmitting them at the other end-point (in the π-calculus literature, links are sometimes called forwarders [14]). Given two names a and b, we call *static link* the process $!a(x).\,\overline{b}x$, abbreviated $a \triangleright b$.

We sometimes use a more sophisticated form of link, which does not perform free outputs: the name sent at b is not x, but a link to x (this is the definition of links in calculi where all outputs are bound [22]). We call this a *dynamic link* process, written $a \to b$, and defined using recursion thus

$$a \to b \overset{\text{def}}{=} !a(x).\,\boldsymbol{\nu}(c)(\overline{b}c \mid c \to x).$$

Remark 1. The process $a \to b$ is not in Lπ, but it is synchronous early bisimilar (Definition 2) to a process of Lπ (using replication in place of recursion).

3 Some background on barbed congruence

Below, we define barbed congruence on a generic subset $\mathcal{L}$ of π-calculus processes (transitions between π-calculus processes are of the same form as for Lπ processes). A *$\mathcal{L}$-context* is a process of $\mathcal{L}$ with a single hole $[\cdot]$ in it. We write $P \downarrow_a$ if P can make an output action whose subject is a, that is if there exist P', b such that $P \xrightarrow{\overline{a}b} P'$ or $P \xrightarrow{\boldsymbol{\nu}(b)\overline{a}b} P'$. We write $P \Downarrow_a$ if $P \Longrightarrow P'$ and $P' \downarrow_a$.

Definition 1 (barbed bisimulation and congruence).[2] *Barbed bisimulation, written $\dot{\approx}$, is the largest symmetric relation on π-calculus processes s.t. $P \dot{\approx} Q$ implies:*

1. *If $P \xrightarrow{\tau} P'$ then $\exists Q'$ s.t. $Q \Longrightarrow Q'$ and $P' \dot{\approx} Q'$.*
2. *If $P \downarrow_a$ then $Q \Downarrow_a$.*

P and Q are barbed congruent *in $\mathcal{L}$, written $P \approx^{\mathcal{L}}_{bc} Q$, if for each $\mathcal{L}$-context $C[\cdot]$, it holds that $C[P] \dot{\approx} C[Q]$.*

[2] In π-calculus, the observability predicate normally checks also the possibility of input actions; observing only outputs does not affect the resulting barbed congruence.

In CCS barbed congruence coincides with observation congruence. In π_a with matching operator, barbed congruence coincides with the closure under substitutions of *asynchronous early bisimulation* [20, 2]. Similarly, in π-calculus with matching, it coincides with the closure under substitutions of *synchronous early bisimulation.* These two bisimulations only differ in the input clause.

Definition 2 (early bisimulations). *A symmetric relation $\mathcal{S}$ on π-terms is an $o\tau$-bisimulation if $P \; \mathcal{S} \; Q$, $P \xrightarrow{\mu} P'$, μ is not an input and* $\text{bn}(\mu) \cap \text{fn}(Q) = \emptyset$, *implies that there exists Q' s.t. $Q \stackrel{\widehat{\mu}}{\Longrightarrow} Q'$ and $P' \; \mathcal{S} \; Q'$.*

- synchronous early bisimulation *is the largest $o\tau$-bisimulation $\mathcal{S}$ on π-calculus s.t. $P \; \mathcal{S} \; Q$ and $P \xrightarrow{a(x)} P'$ implies that $\forall \, b$, $\exists \, Q'$ s.t. $Q \stackrel{a(x)}{\Longrightarrow} Q'$ and $P'\{b/x\} \; \mathcal{S} \; Q'\{b/x\}$.*
- asynchronous early bisimulation *is the largest $o\tau$-bisimulation $\mathcal{S}$ on π_a processes s.t. $P \; \mathcal{S} \; Q$ and $P \xrightarrow{a(x)} P'$ implies that $\forall \, b$, $\exists \, Q'$ s.t.:*
  1. *either $Q \stackrel{a(x)}{\Longrightarrow} Q'$ and $P'\{b/x\} \; \mathcal{S} \; Q'\{b/x\}$*
  2. *or $Q \Longrightarrow Q'$ and $P'\{b/x\} \; \mathcal{S} \; (Q' \mid \overline{a}b)$.*

The proofs of the above-mentioned characterisations are usually given on the class of the image finite processes (to which most of the processes one would like to write belongs) by exploiting the n-approximants of the labeled equivalences. We recall that the class of *image-finite processes* is the largest subset $\mathcal{I}$ of π-calculus process which is derivation closed and s.t. $P \in \mathcal{I}$ implies that, for all μ, the set $\{P' \; : \; P \stackrel{\mu}{\Longrightarrow} P'\}$, quotiented by alpha conversion, is finite. In the proofs of these characterisations, a central role is played by the *matching* construct. If matching is removed from the language, then (the closure under substitutions of) early bisimulation still implies barbed congruence, but the vice versa is false.

In the asynchronous π-calculus without matching, asynchronous early bisimulation coincides with its induced congruence and also with asynchronous *ground* bisimulation, which differs from the early one in that it has no universal quantification in the input clause.

Definition 3 (Asynchronous ground bisimulation). *The* asynchronous ground bisimulation *is the largest $o\tau$-bisimulation $\mathcal{S}$ on π_a processes s.t. $P \; \mathcal{S} \; Q$ and $P \xrightarrow{a(x)} P'$ implies that $\exists \, Q'$ s.t.:*

1. *either $Q \stackrel{a(x)}{\Longrightarrow} Q'$ and $P' \; \mathcal{S} \; Q'$*
2. *or $Q \Longrightarrow Q'$ and $P' \; \mathcal{S} \; (Q' \mid \overline{a}x)$.*

Remark 2. Also for the labeled bisimulations we shall study for Lπ, the early and the ground versions coincide. For this reason, in Lπ we shall simply present the ground versions.

4 Eliminating free output transitions

In this section we prove a characterisation for barbed congruence in Lπ by exploiting a compositional encoding $[\![\ ]\!]$ (essentially Boreale's [4]), which is an homomorphism on all operators except output, for which we have:

$$[\![\overline{a}b]\!] \stackrel{\text{def}}{=} \overline{a}[b] \quad \text{where } \overline{a}[b] \stackrel{\text{def}}{=} \boldsymbol{\nu}(d)(\overline{a}d \mid d \rightarrow b) \text{ with } d \notin \{a,b\}$$

Remark 3. The process $\overline{a}[b]$ is not in Lπ, but, by Remark 1, it is synchronous early bisimilar (Definition 2) to a process of Lπ.

Let $\approx_{\mathrm{L}}$ be the variant of asynchronous ground bisimulation in which the output $\overline{a}x$ is replaced by $\overline{a}[x]$ (clause 2, Definition 3). The proof technique for proving that two processes of Lπ are (or are not) barbed congruent consists in translating them, and then checking that their images are (or are not) in $\approx_{\mathrm{L}}$.

Lemma 1 (Boreale). *Let P and Q be two processes in* Lπ. *Then*

$$P \stackrel{\bullet}{\approx} Q \text{ iff } [\![P]\!] \stackrel{\bullet}{\approx} [\![Q]\!].$$

Theorem 1 (First characterisation of barbed congruence in Lπ). *Let P and Q be two processes in* Lπ. *Then*

1. $P \approx_{\mathrm{bc}}^{\mathrm{L}\pi} Q$ implies $[\![P]\!] \approx_{\mathrm{L}} [\![Q]\!]$, *for P and Q image finite processes*
2. $[\![P]\!] \approx_{\mathrm{L}} [\![Q]\!]$ implies $P \approx_{\mathrm{bc}}^{\mathrm{L}\pi} Q$.

Proof.

1. We prove that $[\![P]\!] \approx_{\mathrm{L}} [\![Q]\!]$ when for each $R \in \mathrm{L}\pi$ $[\![P \mid R]\!] \stackrel{\bullet}{\approx} [\![Q \mid R]\!]$ holds. By Lemma 1 we can conclude.
2. By proving that for each context $C[\cdot]$ in Lπ $[\![C[P]]\!] \approx_{\mathrm{L}} [\![C[Q]]\!]$. This implies $[\![C[P]]\!] \stackrel{\bullet}{\approx} [\![C[Q]]\!]$ and therefore, by Lemma 1, $C[P] \stackrel{\bullet}{\approx} C[Q]$.

5 A labeled bisimulation for Lπ

In this section we give a more powerful proof technique, in whose correctness proof, Theorem 1 is important. Table 1 gives a new Labelled Transition System (LTS) $\stackrel{\mu}{\longmapsto}$ for Lπ. We prove that asynchronous ground bisimulation defined on the new LTS coincides with barbed congruence in Lπ.[3] We recall that (the closure under substitution of) asynchronous early bisimulation on the original LTS $\stackrel{\mu}{\longrightarrow}$ coincides with barbed congruence in π_{a}. Therefore the difference between the two LTSs shows the difference between what is observable in Lπ, and in π_{a} (or π-calculus) with matching. The new LTS is defined on top of the original one, and transforms the output of a name b into the output of a fresh *pointer* p to b. We call p a pointer to b because a link $p \triangleright b$ is introduced through which any output along p is redirected onto b. The weak transitions $\stackrel{\mu}{\Longmapsto}$ and $\Longmapsto$ for the new LTS are defined from the strong transitions $\stackrel{\mu}{\longmapsto}$ and $\stackrel{\tau}{\longmapsto}$ in the usual way. We write $\stackrel{\mapsto}{\approx}_{\mathrm{a}}$ to denote the relation obtained by replacing, in Definition 3, arrow $\longrightarrow$ with $\longmapsto$ and arrow $\Longrightarrow$ with $\Longmapsto$.

[3] It also coincides with the early version, see Remark 2

$$\texttt{free-out:}\ \frac{P \xrightarrow{\overline{a}b} P' \qquad p \notin \mathrm{fn}(P)}{P \overset{\nu(p)\overline{a}p}{\longmapsto} (p \rhd b \mid P')} \qquad \texttt{bound-out:}\ \frac{P \xrightarrow{\nu(b)\overline{a}b} P' \qquad p \notin \mathrm{fn}(P)}{P \overset{\nu(p)\overline{a}p}{\longmapsto} \nu(b)(p \rhd b \mid P')}$$

$$\texttt{sync:}\ \frac{P \xrightarrow{\tau} P'}{P \overset{\tau}{\longmapsto} P'} \qquad \texttt{input:}\ \frac{P \xrightarrow{a(b)} P'}{P \overset{a(b)}{\longmapsto} P'}$$

Table 1. A new labeled transition system for Lπ

Theorem 2 (Second characterisation of barbed congruence in Lπ). *Let P and Q be two processes in* Lπ. *Then*

1. $P \approx_{\mathrm{bc}}^{\mathrm{L}\pi} Q$ implies $P \mathrel{\approx\!\!\!\!\sim}_{\mathrm{a}} Q$, *for P and Q image finite processes*
2. $P \mathrel{\approx\!\!\!\!\sim}_{\mathrm{a}} Q$ implies $P \approx_{\mathrm{bc}}^{\mathrm{L}\pi} Q$.

Proof. By proving that $P \mathrel{\approx\!\!\!\!\sim}_{\mathrm{a}} Q$ iff $[\![P]\!] \approx_{\mathrm{L}} [\![Q]\!]$, and then using Theorem 1.

Both the characterisation of barbed congruence in Lπ in Theorem 1 and the characterisation above are based on the use of links. In the former characterisation, links are added statically via an encoding (at "compile-time"); in the latter characterisation, they are added dynamically in the bisimulation game (at "run-time"). The advantage of the latter characterisation is that: (i) it uses simpler links $p \rhd b$ instead of links $p \to b$; (ii) links are not added in case of internal communications; (iii) in the input clause, it uses the particle $\overline{a}x$ instead of $\overline{a}[x]$ (that produces links). An even more important advantage of the latter characterisation is that the number of the added links may be further reduced using bisimulation up-to context and up-to *expansion* techniques [21] (the expansion relation is an asymmetric variant of the synchronous early bisimulation in Definition 2). For instance, under certain hypotheses on the occurrencies of b in P, the process $\nu(b)(p \rhd b \mid P')$ can be replaced by $P'\{p/b\}$ and the link added in rule `bound-out` can be removed. Similarly, it is easy to prove that $P \mathrel{\approx\!\!\!\!\sim}_{\mathrm{a}} Q$ holds when $p \rhd b | P \mathrel{\approx\!\!\!\!\sim}_{\mathrm{a}} p \rhd b | Q$ and $p \notin \mathrm{fn}(P \mid Q)$.

6 Applications

We report some applications of the theory of Lπ; the results we give fail in π_{a} and π-calculus. Further examples are reported in the full paper: for instance, other replication theorems in addition to that of law 4.

6.1. Some laws

Using either Theorem 1(2) or Theorem 2(2) it is simple to prove laws 1-4 in the introduction. Law 1 is a special case of the following law, where c is not free in P in input position and $b \neq c$:

$$P\{b/c\} = \nu(c)(P \mid c \rhd b) \tag{5}$$

We call law 5 *eta rule*. It is valid in Lπ but not in π_{a} and π-calculus. A similar law, but with the double link $c \rhd b \mid b \rhd c$ in place of $c \rhd b$, is given in [14].

$$\texttt{del-i:}\ \frac{}{a(b)P \xrightarrow{a(b)} P} \qquad \texttt{close:}\ \frac{P \xrightarrow{\sigma_b \overline{a}b} P' \quad Q \xrightarrow{a(b)} Q' \quad \mathrm{bn}(\sigma_b) \cap \mathrm{fn}(Q) = \emptyset}{P \mid Q \xrightarrow{\tau} \sigma_b(P' \mid Q')}$$

$$\texttt{self-com1:}\ \frac{P \xrightarrow{\overline{a}c} P'}{a(b)P \xrightarrow{\tau} \boldsymbol{\nu}(b)(P'\{c/b\})} \qquad \texttt{self-com2:}\ \frac{P \xrightarrow{\sigma_c \overline{a}c} P' \qquad b \notin \mathrm{n}(\sigma_c \overline{a}c)}{a(b)P \xrightarrow{\tau} \sigma_c(P'\{c/b\})}$$

$$\texttt{pass-i:}\ \frac{P \xrightarrow{\mu} P' \quad b \notin \mathrm{n}(\mu) \quad a \notin \mathrm{bn}(\mu)}{a(b)P \xrightarrow{\mu} a(b)P'} \qquad \texttt{open-i:}\ \frac{P \xrightarrow{\overline{a}b} P' \qquad b \neq a}{c(b)P \xrightarrow{c(b)\overline{a}b} P'}$$

$$\texttt{pass-}\boldsymbol{\nu}\texttt{:}\ \frac{P \xrightarrow{\mu} P' \quad b \notin \mathrm{n}(\mu)}{\boldsymbol{\nu}(b)P \xrightarrow{\mu} \boldsymbol{\nu}(b)P'} \qquad \texttt{open-}\boldsymbol{\nu}\texttt{:}\ \frac{P \xrightarrow{\mu} P' \quad [\mu = \overline{a}c \vee \mu = c(b)\overline{a}b] \quad a \neq c}{\boldsymbol{\nu}(c)P \xrightarrow{\boldsymbol{\nu}(c)\mu} P'}$$

Table 2. Inference rules for delayed input and restriction.

6.2. The delayed input In an asynchronous calculus message emission is non-blocking. Milner, Parrow, Victor and others have advocated also non-blocking message reception (which is among the motivations behind Fusion and Chi calculi [18, 10]). Such a *delayed input prefix*, written $a(x)P$, should allow the continuation P to evolve underneath the input guard, except for observable actions along x. The delayed input replaces *temporal precedencies*, imposed by plain input, with *causal dependencies*. This appears, for instance, in Abramsky's representation of Linear Logic proofs as π-calculus processes [1, 3]. Non-blocking message reception has been studied by Bellin and Scott [3], Boudol [7], Fu [10], Parrow and Victor [18], Yoshida [25] and van Breugel [24]. Bellin and Scott give a reduction semantics for a version of π-calculus, proposed by Milner, where both message emission and message reception are non-blocking; van Breugel defines a labelled transition system for such calculus and proves a correspondence with Bellin and Scott's reduction semantics.

Let DLπ be the calculus obtained by adding the delayed input construct $a(b)P$ to the grammar of Lπ (with the same constraint as plain input that b may not appear free in P in input position). In Table 2, we give the transition rules of delayed input in DLπ (we give also the rules of restriction because they are affected by the addition of delayed input). Our rules have two main differences w.r.t. van Breugel's [24]: (i) actions have a simpler syntax, because only the output capability of names may be transmitted; (ii) a restriction $\boldsymbol{\nu}(b)$ is added in rule `self-com1` to model *self communications*, as in $a(b)(\overline{a}b \mid P) \xrightarrow{\tau} \boldsymbol{\nu}(b)P$. We prove that the delayed input is a derived operator in Lπ.

Our actions are defined as follows:

$$\mu ::= \tau \;\Big|\; a(b) \;\Big|\; \overline{a}b \;\Big|\; \sigma_b\overline{a}b \quad \text{where} \quad \sigma_b ::= \boldsymbol{\nu}(b) \;\Big|\; c(b) \;\Big|\; \boldsymbol{\nu}(c)c(b)$$

σ_b represents the binding part of bound output actions. We set: $\mathrm{fn}(\boldsymbol{\nu}(b)\overline{a}b) = \{a\}$, $\mathrm{bn}(\boldsymbol{\nu}(b)\overline{a}b) = \{b\}$, $\mathrm{fn}(c(b)\overline{a}b) = \{c, a\}$, $\mathrm{bn}(c(b)\overline{a}b) = \{b\}$, $\mathrm{fn}(\boldsymbol{\nu}(c)c(b)\overline{a}b) = \{a\}$, $\mathrm{bn}(\boldsymbol{\nu}(c)c(b)\overline{a}b) = \{c, b\}$. We define an encoding $\{\!|\,|\!\}$, from DLπ to Lπ, and prove that it is fully abstract for barbed congruence. The encoding $\{\!|\,|\!\}$ is an homomorphism on all operators except delayed input:

$$\{\!|\, a(b)P \,|\!\} \stackrel{\text{def}}{=} \boldsymbol{\nu}(b)(a(c).\, c \rhd b \mid \{\!|\, P \,|\!\})$$

(A similar encoding, but with the double link $c \rhd b \mid b \rhd c$ in place of $c \rhd b$, is suggested by Yoshida [25]). In Lemma 2, $\approx$ is the synchronous early bisimulation of Definition 2; $[\![\ ]\!]$ is the extension of the encoding of Section 4 to DLπ which is an homomorphism also on the delayed input; $\{\!|\,|\!\}_{\mathcal{D}}$ is the variant of $\{\!|\,|\!\}$ with $\{\!|\, a(b)P \,|\!\}_{\mathcal{D}} \stackrel{\text{def}}{=} \boldsymbol{\nu}(b)(a(c).\, c \to b \mid \{\!|\, P \,|\!\}_{\mathcal{D}})$.

Lemma 2. *If* $P \in$ DLπ *then* $[\![P]\!] \approx \{\!|\, [\![P]\!] \,|\!\}_{\mathcal{D}}$.

Proof. $[\![P]\!]$ may perform only output actions of the form $\boldsymbol{\nu}(b)\overline{a}b$.

Theorem 3 (Full-abstraction of $\{\!|\,|\!\}$). *If* $P, Q \in$ DLπ *then:*

1. $P \approx_{\text{bc}}^{\text{DL}\pi} Q$ implies $\{\!|\, P \,|\!\} \approx_{\text{bc}}^{\text{L}\pi} \{\!|\, Q \,|\!\}$, *for* P *and* Q *image finite processes*
2. $\{\!|\, P \,|\!\} \approx_{\text{bc}}^{\text{L}\pi} \{\!|\, Q \,|\!\}$ implies $P \approx_{\text{bc}}^{\text{DL}\pi} Q$.

Proof.

1. $P \approx_{\text{bc}}^{\text{DL}\pi} Q \stackrel{1}{\Longrightarrow} [\![P]\!] \approx_{\text{L}} [\![Q]\!] \stackrel{2}{\Longrightarrow} \{\!|\, [\![P]\!] \,|\!\}_{\mathcal{D}} \approx_{\text{L}} \{\!|\, [\![Q]\!] \,|\!\}_{\mathcal{D}} \stackrel{3}{\Longrightarrow} [\![\{\!|\, P \,|\!\}]\!] \approx_{\text{L}} [\![\{\!|\, Q \,|\!\}]\!]$ $\stackrel{4}{\Longrightarrow} \{\!|\, P \,|\!\} \approx_{\text{bc}}^{\text{L}\pi} \{\!|\, Q \,|\!\}$. Step 1 uses an extension of Theorem 1(1) to DLπ processes, step 2 Lemma 2, step 3 the definition of the encodings, step 4 Theorem 1(1).
2. Similar to the previous case, using part (2) of Theorem 1.

6.3. Encodings of the λ-calculus (In this example, we use polyadicity, which is straightforward to accommodate in the theory of Lπ developed in the previous sections; we write $\overline{a}\langle b_1 \ldots b_n\rangle$ for outputs.) The following is Milner's encoding of call-by-name λ-calculus into π-calculus (more precisely, a variant of it, whose target calculus is Lπ).

$$\begin{aligned}
(\!|\, \lambda x.\, M \,|\!)_p &\stackrel{\text{def}}{=} \boldsymbol{\nu}(v)(\overline{p}\langle v\rangle \mid v(x,q).\, (\!|\, M \,|\!)_q) \\
(\!|\, x \,|\!)_p &\stackrel{\text{def}}{=} \overline{x}\langle p\rangle \\
(\!|\, MN \,|\!)_p &\stackrel{\text{def}}{=} \boldsymbol{\nu}(q)\Big((\!|\, M \,|\!)_q \mid q(v).\, \boldsymbol{\nu}(x)(\overline{v}\langle x,p\rangle \mid !x(r).\, (\!|\, N \,|\!)_r)\Big)
\end{aligned}$$

This is also an encoding into (polyadic) Lπ. Using the eta law 5 we can prove the following optimisation of the definition of application in the case when the argument is a variable (a tail-call-like optimisation):

$$(\!|\, My \,|\!)_p \stackrel{\text{def}}{=} \boldsymbol{\nu}(q)\Big((\!|\, M \,|\!)_q \mid q(v).\, \overline{v}\langle y,p\rangle\Big)$$

We can also exploit the delayed input operator, that is a derived operator in Lπ, to get an encoding of the *strong* call-by-name strategy, where reductions can also occur underneath an abstraction (i.e., the `Xi` rule, saying that if $M \longrightarrow M'$

then $\lambda x.\, M \longrightarrow \lambda x.\, M'$, is allowed). For this, we have to relax, in the translation of $\lambda x.\, M$, the sequentiality imposed by the input prefix $v(x, q)$ that guards the body $(\!|\ M\ |\!)_q$ of the function. Precisely, we have to replace this input with a delayed input:

$$(\!|\ \lambda x.\, M\ |\!)_p \stackrel{\text{def}}{=} \boldsymbol{\nu}(v)(\overline{p}\langle v\rangle \mid v(x,q)(\!|\ M\ |\!)_q) \tag{6}$$

Using the above encoding of delayed input, we get:

$$(\!|\ \lambda x.\, M\ |\!)_p \stackrel{\text{def}}{=} \boldsymbol{\nu}(v,x,q)\Big(\overline{p}\langle v\rangle \mid v(y,r).\,(x \triangleright y \mid q \triangleright r) \mid (\!|\ M\ |\!)_q\Big)$$

One can prove results of operational correspondence and validity of β-reduction for this encoding similar to those for the call-by-name λ-calculus. (The modelling of strong reductions is a major motivation behind Fusion and Chi; indeed both calculi allows us to encode strong call-by-name λ-calculus [18, 10]).

6.4. Some properties for the Join-calculus We apply the theory of Lπ to prove some behavioural equivalences of the Join-calculus. Fournet and Gonthier define the syntax of core Join thus [9]:

$$P ::= a\langle b\rangle \;\Big|\; P_1 \mid P_2 \;\Big|\; \mathtt{def}\ a\langle x\rangle \,|\, b\langle y\rangle = P_1\ \mathtt{in}\ P_2$$

A derived construct is $\mathtt{def}\ a\langle x\rangle = P_1\ \mathtt{in}\ P_2$ (with a single pattern). To explain the syntax above and study its expressiveness, Fournet and Gonthier give this encoding of the Join-calculus into the ordinary π-calculus:

$$\begin{array}{l} (\!|\, a\langle b\rangle\, |\!) \stackrel{\text{def}}{=} \overline{a}b \qquad\qquad (\!|\, P \mid Q\, |\!) \stackrel{\text{def}}{=} (\!|\, P\, |\!) \mid (\!|\, Q\, |\!) \\ (\!|\, \mathtt{def}\ a\langle x\rangle \,|\, b\langle y\rangle = P_1\ \mathtt{in}\ P_2\, |\!) \stackrel{\text{def}}{=} \boldsymbol{\nu}(a,b)(!a(x).\, b(y).\, (\!|\, P_1\, |\!) \mid (\!|\, P_2\, |\!)) \end{array}$$

This encoding, as an encoding of Join into π_{a} or π-calculus, is not full-abstract. To obtain full abstraction, Fournet and Gonthier have to add a layer of "firewalls" to the encoding. We believe that the above encoding is fully abstract as an encoding from Join to Lπ (a similar conjecture is made by Fournet and Gonthier [9]). It is easy to prove soundness, and this is sufficient for using the encoding and the theory of Lπ for proving properties of Join processes.

Theorem 4 (soundness of $(\!|\ |\!)$). *Let P and Q be two processes of core Join. Then $(\!|\, P\, |\!) \approx^{\mathrm{L}\pi}_{\mathrm{bc}} (\!|\, Q\, |\!)$ implies $P \approx^{\mathrm{J}}_{\mathrm{bc}} Q$ ($\approx^{\mathrm{J}}_{\mathrm{bc}}$ is barbed congruence in core Join).*

Using this theorem and the theory of Lπ we can prove laws for the Join-calculus, for instance:

(J1) $\mathtt{def}\ a\langle x\rangle = R\ \mathtt{in}\ P \mid Q \;\approx^{\mathrm{J}}_{\mathrm{bc}}\; (\mathtt{def}\ a\langle x\rangle = R\ \mathtt{in}\ P) \mid (\mathtt{def}\ a\langle x\rangle = R\ \mathtt{in}\ Q)$
(J2) $\mathtt{def}\ a\langle x\rangle = b\langle x\rangle\ \mathtt{in}\ P \;\approx^{\mathrm{J}}_{\mathrm{bc}}\; P\{^b\!/\!_a\}$
(J3) $\mathtt{def}\ a\langle x\rangle = P\ \mathtt{in}\ C[a\langle b\rangle] \;\approx^{\mathrm{J}}_{\mathrm{bc}}\; \mathtt{def}\ a\langle x\rangle = P\ \mathtt{in}\ C[P\{^b\!/\!_x\}]$
if context $C[\cdot]$ does not capture name a.

Laws (J1) and (J2) are the Join-calculus versions of laws 4 and 5 respectively. Law (J3) reminds us of *inline expansion*, an optimization technique for functional languages which replaces a function call with a copy of the function body. An instance of law (J3) is

$$\texttt{def}\ a\langle x\rangle = P\ \texttt{in}\ (Q \mid a\langle b\rangle)\ \approx^{\mathrm{J}}_{\mathrm{bc}}\ \texttt{def}\ a\langle x\rangle = P\ \texttt{in}\ (Q \mid P\{^{b}\!/\!_{x}\})$$

that shows a sort of insensitiveness to τ-actions (the process on the right is obtained from the process on the left by performing a τ-step). None of these laws can be proved using encoding $\langle\!|\ |\!\rangle$ and π_{a} or π-calculus (if the local name a is exported, the encodings of the processes in the laws can be distinguished both in π_{a} and π-calculus). In [5], a labeled bisimulation for the Join calculus is introduced. However, in this bisimulation the labels of the matching transitions must be syntactically the same. Therefore laws like (J2) cannot be proved.

6.5. Full abstraction of $[\![\ ]\!]$ Sangiorgi [22] introduces a subcalculus of the π-calculus, called πI, where only private names may be emitted, that is, output processes have the form $\boldsymbol{\nu}(c)(\overline{a}c.\,P)$. In [4] Boreale uses (a slight variant of) encoding $[\![\ ]\!]$ of Section 4 to show that any process in Lπ can be compiled onto πI. Boreale leaves as an open problem whether the encoding is fully abstract for some reasonable behavioural equivalence. We can prove that Boreale's encoding *is not* fully abstract as an encoding from Lπ to πI, assuming that the behavioural equivalence for both the source and the target calculus is barbed congruence. As a counterexample, take $P = !a(x).\,\overline{a}x$, $Q = \mathbf{0}$; then $P \approx^{\mathrm{L}\pi}_{\mathrm{bc}} Q$ but not $[\![P]\!] \approx^{\pi\mathrm{I}}_{\mathrm{bc}} [\![Q]\!]$. This is not surprising because the source language is asynchronous while the target language is synchronous. However, also if we considered as target language the asynchronous variant of πI (where output processes have the form $\boldsymbol{\nu}(c)(\overline{a}c \mid P)$), the encoding *is not* fully abstract (as a conterexample, take the same processes P and Q above). We can prove that (on image finite processes) the encoding *is* fully abstract if the target calculus is the asynchronous πI where only output capability of names may be transmitted. We denote by LπI (*Local* πI) this calculus.

Theorem 5 (Full-abstraction of $[\![\ ]\!]$). *Let P, Q be two processes in* Lπ. *Then*

$$P \approx^{\mathrm{L}\pi}_{\mathrm{bc}} Q \ \text{ iff } \ [\![P]\!] \approx^{\mathrm{L}\pi\mathrm{I}}_{\mathrm{bc}} [\![Q]\!].$$

Proof. As to completeness, by Theorem 2(2), we have $P \approx^{\mathrm{L}\pi}_{\mathrm{bc}} [\![P]\!]$ for each $P \in \mathrm{L}\pi$; hence $[\![P]\!] \approx^{\mathrm{L}\pi}_{\mathrm{bc}} [\![Q]\!]$. Because L$\pi$I $\subset$ Lπ, this implies $[\![P]\!] \approx^{\mathrm{L}\pi\mathrm{I}}_{\mathrm{bc}} [\![Q]\!]$. The soundness follows by Lemma 1 and by compositionality of $[\![\ ]\!]$.

Acknowledgements The authors were partially supported by France Télécom, CTI-CNET 95-1B-182 Modélisation de Systémes Mobiles. We thank Gérard Boudol, Ilaria Castellani, Silvano Dal-Zilio, Matthew Hennessy, Uwe Nestmann and Nobuko Yoshida for stimulating and insightful discussions. The anonymous referees provided useful suggestions.

References

1. S. Abramsky. Proofs as Processes. *Theoretical Computer Science*, 135(1):5–9, December 1994.

2. R. Amadio, I. Castellani, and D. Sangiorgi. On bisimulations for the asynchronous π-calculus. In *Proc. CONCUR '96*, LNCS 1119, Springer Verlag, 1996.
3. G. Bellin and P. Scott. On the π-calculus and Linear Logic. *Theoretical Computer Science*, 135(1):11–65, 1994.
4. M. Boreale. On the expressiveness of internal mobility in name-passing calculi. In *Proc. CONCUR '96*, LNCS 1119, Springer Verlag, 1996.
5. M. Boreale, C. Fournet, and C. Laneve. Bisimulations for the Join Calculus. Proc. IFIP Conference PROCOMET'98, 1997.
6. M. Boreale and D. Sangiorgi. Bisimulation in name-passing calculi without matching. To appear in *Proc. LICS'98*, IEEE Computer Society Press., 1998.
7. G. Boudol. Some Chemical Abstract Machines. LNCS 803, Springer Verlag, 1994.
8. G. Boudol. The pi-calculus in direct style. In *24th POPL*. ACM Press, 1997.
9. Fournet C. and Gonthier G. The Reflexive Chemical Abstract Machine and the Join calculus. In *Proc. 23th POPL*. ACM Press, 1996.
10. Y. Fu. A proof theoretical approach to communication. In *24th ICALP*, LNCS 1256, Springer Verlag, 1997.
11. M. Hansen, H. Hüttel, and J. Kleist. Bisimulations for asynchronous mobile processes. In *Proc. Tbilisi Symposium on Language, Logic, and Computation*, 1996. Also available as BRICS Report No. EP-95-HHK, BRICS, Aalborg.
12. K. Honda and M. Tokoro. A Small Calculus for Concurrent Objects. In *OOPS Messanger*, Association for Computing Machinery. 2(2):50-54, 1991.
13. K. Honda and M. Tokoro. An Object Calculus for Asynchronous Communication. In Proc. *ECOOP'91,* LNCS 512, Springer Verlag, 1991.
14. K. Honda and N. Yoshida. On reduction-based process semantics. *Theoretical Computer Science*, 152(2):437–486, 1995.
15. R. Milner. The polyadic π-calculus: a tutorial. Technical Report ECS–LFCS–91–180, LFCS, Dept. of Comp. Sci., Edinburgh Univ., October 1991.
16. R. Milner, J. Parrow, and D. Walker. A calculus of mobile processes, (Parts I and II). *Information and Computation*, 100:1–77, 1992.
17. R. Milner and D. Sangiorgi. Barbed bisimulation. In W. Kuich, editor, *19th ICALP*, LNCS 623, Springer Verlag, 1992.
18. J. Parrow and B. Victor. The fusion calculus: Expressiveness and symmetry in mobile processes. To appear in *Proc. LICS'98*, IEEE CSP, 1998.
19. B. C. Pierce and D. N. Turner. Pict: A programming language based on the pi-calculus. To appear in *Proof, Language and Interaction: Essays in Honour of Robin Milner*, MIT Press.
20. D. Sangiorgi. *Expressing Mobility in Process Algebras: First-Order and Higher-Order Paradigms.* PhD thesis CST–99–93, University of Edinburgh, 1992.
21. D. Sangiorgi. Locality and non-interleaving semantics in calculi for mobile processes. *Theoretical Computer Science*, 155:39–83, 1996.
22. D. Sangiorgi. π-calculus, internal mobility and agent-passing calculi. *Theoretical Computer Science*, 167(2):235–274, 1996.
23. D. Sangiorgi. The name discipline of receptiveness. In *24th ICALP*, LNCS 1256, Springer Verlag, 1997.
24. F. van Breugel. A Labelled Transition System for the $\pi\epsilon$-calculus. In *Proc. of TAPSOFT '97*, LNCS 1214. Springer Verlag, April 1997.
25. N. Yoshida. Minimality and Separation Results on Asynchronous Mobile Processes: representability theorem by concurrent combinators. Submitted, 1998.

Protection in Programming-Language Translations

Martín Abadi
ma@pa.dec.com

Digital Equipment Corporation
Systems Research Center

Abstract. We discuss abstractions for protection and the correctness of their implementations. Relying on the concept of full abstraction, we consider two examples: (1) the translation of Java classes to an intermediate bytecode language, and (2) in the setting of the pi calculus, the implementation of private channels in terms of cryptographic operations.

1 Introduction

Tangible crimes and measures against those crimes are sometimes explained through abstract models—with mixed results, as the detective Erik Lönnrot discovered [Bor74]. Protection in computer systems relies on abstractions too. For example, an access matrix is a high-level specification that describes the allowed accesses of subjects to objects in a computer system; the system may rely on mechanisms such as access lists and capabilities for implementing an access matrix [Lam71].

Abstractions are often embodied in programming-language constructs. Recent work on Java [GJS96] has popularized the idea that languages are relevant to security, but the relation between languages and security is much older. In particular, objects and types have long been used for protection against incompetence and malice, at least since the 1970s [Mor73,LS76,JL78]. In the realm of distributed systems, programming languages (or their libraries) have sometimes provided abstractions for communication on secure channels of the kind implemented with cryptography [Bir85,WABL94,vDABW96,WRW96,Sun97b].

Security depends not only on the design of clear and expressive abstractions but also on the correctness of their implementations. Unfortunately, the criteria for correctness are rarely stated precisely—and presumably they are rarely met. These criteria seem particularly delicate when a principal relies on those abstractions but interacts with other principals at a lower level. For example, the principal may express its programs and policies in terms of objects and remote method invocations, but may send and receive bit strings. Moreover, the bit strings that it receives may not have been the output of software trusted to respect the abstractions. Such situations seem to be more common now than in the 1970s.

One of the difficulties in the correct implementation of secure systems is that the standard notion of refinement (e.g., [Hoa72,Lam89]) does not preserve security properties. Ordinarily, the non-determinism of a specification may be intended to allow a variety of implementations. In security, the non-determinism may also serve for hiding sensitive data. As an example, let us consider a specification that describes a computer that displays an arbitrary but fixed string in a corner of a screen. A proposed implementation might always display a user's password as that string. Although this implementation may be functionally correct, we may consider it incorrect for security purposes, because it leaks more information than the specification seems to allow. Security properties are thus different from other common properties; in fact, it has been argued that security properties do not conform to the Alpern-Schneider definition of properties [AS85,McL96].

Reexamining this example, let us write P for the user's password, $I(P)$ for the proposed implementation, and $S(P)$ for the specification. Since the set of behaviors allowed by the specification does not depend on P, clearly $S(P)$ is equivalent to $S(P')$ for any other password P'. On the other hand, $I(P)$ and $I(P')$ are not equivalent, since an observer can distinguish them. Since the mapping from specification to implementation does not preserve equivalence, we may say that it is not fully abstract [Plo77]. We may explain the perceived weakness of the proposed implementation by this failure of full abstraction.

This paper suggests that, more generally, the concept of full abstraction is a useful tool for understanding the problem of implementing secure systems. Full abstraction seems particularly pertinent in systems that rely on translations between languages—for example, higher-level languages with objects and secure channels, lower-level languages with memory addresses and cryptographic keys.

We consider two examples of rather different natures and review some standard security concerns, relating these concerns to the pursuit of full abstraction. The first example arises in the context of Java (section 2). The second one concerns the implementation of secure channels, and relies on the pi calculus as formal framework (section 3). The thesis of this paper about full abstraction is in part a device for discussing these two examples.

This paper is rather informal and partly tutorial; its contributions are a perspective on some security problems and some examples, not new theorems. Related results appear in more technical papers [SA98,AFG98].

Full abstraction, revisited

We say that two expressions are equivalent in a given language if they yield the same observable results in all contexts of the language. A translation from a language L_1 to a language L_2 is equationally fully abstract if (1) it maps equivalent L_1 expressions to equivalent L_2 expressions, and (2) conversely, it maps nonequivalent L_1 expressions to nonequivalent L_2 expressions [Plo77,Sha91,Mit93]. We may think of the context of an expression as an attacker that interacts with the expression, perhaps trying to learn some sensitive information (e.g., [AG97a]).

With this view, condition (1) means that the translation does not introduce information leaks. Since equations may express not only secrecy properties but also some integrity properties, the translation must preserve those properties as well. Because of these consequences of condition (1), we focus on it; we mostly ignore condition (2), although it can be useful too, in particular for excluding trivial translations.

Closely related to equational full abstraction is logical full abstraction [LP98]. A translation from a language L_1 to a language L_2 is logically fully abstract if it preserves logical properties of the expressions being translated. Longley and Plotkin have identified conditions under which equational and logical full abstraction are equivalent. Since we use the concept of full abstraction loosely, we do not distinguish its nuances.

An expression of the source language L_1 may be written in a silly, incompetent, or even malicious way. For example, the expression may be a program that broadcasts some sensitive information—so this expression is insecure on its own, even before any translation to L_2. Thus, full abstraction is clearly not sufficient for security; however, as we discuss in this paper, it is often relevant.

2 Objects and Mobile Code

The Java programming language is typically compiled to an intermediate language, which we call JVML and which is implemented by the Java Virtual Machine [GJS96,LY96]. JVML programs are often communicated across networks, for example from Web servers to their clients. A client may run a JVML program in a Java Virtual Machine embedded in a Web browser. The Java Virtual Machine helps protect local resources from mobile JVML programs while allowing those programs to interact with local class libraries. Some of these local class libraries perform essential functions (for example, input and output), so they are often viewed as part of the Java Virtual Machine.

2.1 Translating Java to JVML

As a first example we consider the following trivial Java class:

```
class C {
    private int x;
    public void set_x(int v) {
      this.x = v;
    };
}
```

This class describes objects with a field `x` and a method `set_x`. The method `set_x` takes an integer argument `v` and updates the field `x` to `v`. The keyword **this** represents the self of an object; the keyword **public** indicates that any client or subclass can access `set_x` directly; the keyword **private** disallows a similar direct access to x from outside the class. Therefore, the field x can be written but never read.

The result of compiling this class to JVML may be expressed roughly as follows. (Here we do not use the official, concrete syntax of JVML, which is not designed for human understanding.)

```
class C {
    private int x;
    public void set_x(int) {
      .framelimits locals = 2, stack = 2;
      aload_0;        // load this
      iload_1;        // load v
      putfield x;     // set x
    };
}
```

As this example indicates, JVML is a fairly high-level language, and in particular it features object-oriented constructs such as classes, methods, and self. It differs from Java in that methods manipulate local variables, a stack, and a heap using low-level load and store operations. The details of those operations are not important for our purposes. Each method body declares how many local variables and stack slots its activation may require. The Java Virtual Machine includes a bytecode verifier, which checks that those declarations are conservative (for instance, that the stack will not overflow). If undetected, dynamic errors such as stack overflow could lead to unpredictable behavior and to security breaches.

The writer of a Java program may have some security-related expectations about the program. In our simple example, the field x cannot be read from outside the class, so it may be used for storing sensitive information. Our example is so trivial that this information cannot be exploited in any way, but there are more substantial and interesting examples that permit controlled access to fields with the qualifier **private** and similar qualifiers. For instance, a Java class for random-number generation (like `java.util.Random`) may store seeds in private fields. In these examples, a security property of a Java class may be deduced—or presumed—by considering all possible Java contexts in which the class can be used. Because those contexts must obey the type rules of Java, they cannot access private fields of the class.

When a Java class is translated to JVML, one would like the resulting JVML code to have the security properties that were expected at the Java level. However, the JVML code interacts with a JVML context, not with a Java context. If the translation from Java to JVML is fully abstract, then matters are considerably simplified—in that case, JVML contexts have no more power than Java contexts. Unfortunately, as we point out below, the current translation is not fully abstract (at least not in a straightforward sense). Nevertheless, the translation approximates full abstraction:

– In our example, the translation retains the qualifier **private** for x. The occurrence of this qualifier at the JVML level may not be surprising, but it cannot be taken for granted. (At the JVML level, the qualifier does not have the benefit of helping programmers adhere to sound software-engineering practices, since programmers hardly ever write JVML, so the qualifier might have been omitted.)

- Furthermore, the bytecode verifier can perform standard typechecking, guaranteeing in particular that a JVML class does not refer to a private field of another JVML class.
- The bytecode verifier can also check that dynamic errors such as stack overflow will not occur. Therefore, the behavior of JVML classes should conform to the intended JVML semantics; JVML code cannot get around the JVML type system for accessing a private field inappropriately.

Thus, the bytecode verifier restricts the set of JVML contexts, and in effect makes them resemble Java contexts (cf. [GJS96, p. 220]). As the set of JVML contexts decreases, the set of equivalences satisfied by JVML programs increases, so the translation from Java to JVML gets closer to full abstraction. Therefore, we might even view full abstraction as the goal of bytecode verification.

Recently, there have been several rigorous studies of the Java Virtual Machine, and in particular of the bytecode verifier [Coh97,SA98,Qia97,FM98]. These studies focus on the type-safety of the JVML programs accepted by the bytecode verifier. As has long been believed, and as Leroy and Rouaix have recently proved in a somewhat different context [LR98], strong typing yields some basic but important security guarantees. However, those guarantees do not concern language translations. By themselves, those guarantees do not imply that libraries written in a high-level language have expected security properties when they interact with lower-level mobile code.

2.2 Obstacles to full abstraction

As noted, the current translation of Java to JVML is not fully abstract. The following variant of our first example illustrates the failure of full abstraction. We have no reason to believe that it illustrates the only reason for the failure of full abstraction, or the most worrisome one; Dean, Felten, Wallach, and Balfanz have discovered several significant discrepancies between the semantics of Java and that of JVML [DFWB98].

```
class D {
    class E {
        private int y = x;
    };
    private int x;
    public void set_x(int v) {
      this.x = v;
    };
}
```

The class E is an inner class [Sun97a]. To each instance of an inner class such as E corresponds an instance of its outer class, D in this example. The inner class may legally refer to the private fields of the outer class.

Unlike Java, JVML does not include an inner-class construct. Therefore, compilers "flatten" inner classes while adding accessor methods. Basically, as far as compilation is concerned, we may as well have written the following classes instead of D:

```
class D {
    private int x;
    public void set_x(int v) {
      this.x = v;
    };
    static int get_x(D d) {
      return d.x;
    };
}

class E {
    ... get_x ...
}
```

Here E is moved to the top level. A method get_x is added to D and used in E for reading x; the details of E do not matter for our purposes. The method get_x can be used not just in E, however—any other class within the same package may refer to get_x.

When the classes D and E are compiled to JVML, therefore, a JVML context may be able to read x in a way that was not possible at the Java level. This possibility results in the loss of full abstraction, since there is a JVML context that distinguishes objects that could not be distinguished by any Java context. More precisely, a JVML context that runs get_x and returns the result distinguishes instances of D with different values for x.

This loss of full abstraction may result in the leak of some sensitive information, if any was stored in the field x. The leak of the contents of a private component of an object can be a concern when the object is part of the Java Virtual Machine, or when it is trusted by the Java Virtual Machine (for example, because a trusted principal digitally signed the object's class). On the other hand, when the object is part of an applet, this leak should not be surprising: applets cannot usually be protected from their execution environments.

For better or for worse, the Java security story is more complicated and dynamic than the discussion above might suggest. In addition to protection by the qualifier **private**, Java has a default mode of protection that protects classes in one package against classes in other packages. At the language level, this mode of protection is void—any class can claim to belong to any package. However, Java class loaders can treat certain packages in special ways, guaranteeing that only trusted classes belong to them. Our example with inner classes does not pose a security problem as long as D and E are in one of those packages.

In hindsight, it is not clear whether one should base any security expectations on qualifiers like **private**, and more generally on other Java constructs. As Dean et al. have argued [DFWB98], the definition of Java is weaker than it should be from a security viewpoint. Although it would be prudent to strengthen that definition, a full-blown requirement of full abstraction may not be a necessary addition. More modest additions may suffice. Section 4 discusses this subject further.

3 Channels for Distributed Communication

In this section, we consider the problem of implementing secure channels in distributed systems. As mentioned in the introduction, some systems for distributed programming offer abstractions for creating and using secure channels. The implementations of those channels typically rely on cryptography for ensuring the privacy and the integrity of network communication. The relation between the abstractions and their implementations is usually explained only informally. Moreover, the abstractions are seldom explained in a self-contained manner that would permit reasoning about them without considering their implementations at least occasionally.

The concept of full abstraction can serve as a guide in understanding secure channels. When trying to approximate full abstraction, we rediscover common attacks and countermeasures. Most importantly, the pursuit of full abstraction entails a healthy attention to the connections between an implementation and higher-level programs that use the implementation, beyond the intrinsic properties of the implementation.

3.1 Translating the pi calculus to the spi calculus

The formal setting for this section is the pi calculus [Mil92,MPW92,Mil93], which serves as a core calculus with primitives for creating and using channels. By applying the pi calculus restriction operator, these channels can be made private. We discuss the problem of mapping the pi calculus to a lower-level calculus, the spi calculus [AG97b,AG97c,AG97a], implementing communication on private channels by encrypted communication on public channels. Several low-level attacks can be cast as counterexamples to the full abstraction of this mapping. Some of the attacks can be thwarted through techniques common in the literature on protocol design [MvOV96]. Some other attacks suggest fundamental difficulties in achieving full abstraction for the pi calculus.

First we briefly review the spi calculus. In the variant that we consider here, the syntax of this calculus assumes an infinite set of names and an infinite set of variables. We let c, d, m, n, and p range over names, and let w, x, y, and z range over variables. We usually assume that all these names and variables are different (for example, that m and n are different names). The set of terms of the spi calculus is defined by the following grammar:

$L, M, N ::=$	terms
n	name
x	variable
$\{M_1, \ldots, M_k\}_N$	encryption ($k \geq 0$)

Intuitively, $\{M_1, \ldots, M_k\}_N$ represents the ciphertext obtained by encrypting the terms $M_1, \ldots, M_k$ under the key N (using a symmetric cryptosystem such as DES or RC5 [MvOV96]). The set of processes of the spi calculus is defined by the following grammar:

$P, Q ::=$	processes
$\overline{M}\langle N_1, \ldots, N_k\rangle$	output ($k \geq 0$)
$M(x_1, \ldots, x_k).P$	input ($k \geq 0$)
$\mathbf{0}$	nil
$P \mid Q$	composition
$!P$	replication
$(\nu n)P$	restriction
$[M\ \mathit{is}\ N]\ P$	match
$\mathit{case}\ L\ \mathit{of}\ \{x_1, \ldots, x_k\}_N\ \mathit{in}\ P$	decryption ($k \geq 0$)

An output process $\overline{M}\langle N_1, \ldots, N_k\rangle$ sends the tuple $N_1, \ldots, N_k$ on M. An input process $M(x_1, \ldots, x_k).Q$ is ready to input k terms $N_1, \ldots, N_k$ on M, and then to behave as $Q[N_1/x_1, \ldots, N_k/x_k]$. Here we write $Q[N_1/x_1, \ldots, N_k/x_k]$ for the result of replacing each free occurrence of x_i in Q with N_i, for $i \in 1..k$. Both $M(x_1, \ldots, x_k).Q$ and $\mathit{case}\ L\ \mathit{of}\ \{x_1, \ldots, x_k\}_N\ \mathit{in}\ P$ (explained below) bind the variables $x_1, \ldots, x_k$. The nil process $\mathbf{0}$ does nothing. A composition $P \mid Q$ behaves as P and Q running in parallel. A replication $!P$ behaves as infinitely many copies of P running in parallel. A restriction $(\nu n)P$ makes a new name n and then behaves as P; it binds the name n. A match process $[M\ \mathit{is}\ N]\ P$ behaves as P if M and N are equal; otherwise it does nothing. A decryption process $\mathit{case}\ L\ \mathit{of}\ \{x_1, \ldots, x_k\}_N\ \mathit{in}\ P$ attempts to decrypt L with the key N; if L has the form $\{M_1, \ldots, M_k\}_N$, then the process behaves as $P[M_1/x_1, \ldots, M_k/x_k]$; otherwise it does nothing.

By omitting the constructs $\{M_1, \ldots, M_k\}_N$ and $\mathit{case}\ L\ \mathit{of}\ \{x_1, \ldots, x_k\}_N\ \mathit{in}\ P$ from these grammars, we obtain the syntax of the pi calculus (more precisely, of a polyadic, asynchronous version of the pi calculus).

As a first example, we consider the trivial pi calculus process:

$$(\nu n)(\overline{n}\langle m\rangle \mid n(x).\mathbf{0})$$

This is a process that creates a channel n, then uses it for transmitting the name m, with no further consequence. Communication on n is secure in the sense that no context can discover m by interacting with this process, and no context can cause a different message to be sent on n; these are typical secrecy and integrity properties. Such properties can be expressed as equivalences (in particular, as testing equivalences [DH84,BN95,AG97a]). For example, we may express the secrecy of m as the equivalence between $(\nu n)(\overline{n}\langle m\rangle \mid n(y).\mathbf{0})$ and $(\nu n)(\overline{n}\langle m'\rangle \mid n(y).\mathbf{0})$, for any names m and m'.

Intuitively, the subprocesses $\overline{n}\langle m\rangle$ and $n(y).\mathbf{0}$ may execute on different machines; the network between these machines may not be physically secure. Therefore, we would like to explicate a channel like n in lower-level terms, mapping it to some sort of encrypted connection multiplexed on a public channel. For example, we might translate our first process, $(\nu n)(\overline{n}\langle m\rangle \mid n(x).\mathbf{0})$, into the following spi calculus process:

$$(\nu n)(\overline{c}\langle\{m\}_n\rangle \mid c(y).case\ y\ of\ \{x\}_n\ in\ \mathbf{0})$$

Here c is a distinguished, free name, intuitively the name of a well-known public channel. The name n still appears, with a restriction, but it is used for a key rather than for a channel. The sender encrypts m using n; the recipient tries to decrypt a ciphertext y that it receives on c using n; if the decryption succeeds, the recipient obtains a cleartext x (hopefully m).

This translation strategy may seem promising. However, it has numerous weaknesses; we describe several of those weaknesses in what follows. The weaknesses represent obstacles to full abstraction and are also significant in practical terms.

3.2 Obstacles to full abstraction

Leak of traffic patterns In the pi calculus, $(\nu n)(\overline{n}\langle m\rangle \mid n(x).\mathbf{0})$ is simply equivalent to $\mathbf{0}$, because the internal communication on n cannot be observed. On the other hand, in the spi calculus, $(\nu n)(\overline{c}\langle\{m\}_n\rangle \mid c(y).case\ y\ of\ \{x\}_n\ in\ \mathbf{0})$ is not equivalent to the obvious implementation of $\mathbf{0}$, namely $\mathbf{0}$. A spi calculus process that interacts with $(\nu n)(\overline{c}\langle\{m\}_n\rangle \mid c(y).case\ y\ of\ \{x\}_n\ in\ \mathbf{0})$ can detect traffic on c, even if it cannot decrypt that traffic.

The obvious way to protect against this leak is to add noise to communication lines. In the context of the spi calculus, we may for example compose all our implementations with the noise process $!(\nu p)\overline{c}\langle\{\}_p\rangle$. This process continually generates keys and uses those keys for producing encrypted traffic on the public channel c.

In practice, since noise is rather wasteful of communication resources, and since a certain amount of noise might be assumed to exist on communication lines as a matter of course, noise is not always added in implementations. Without noise, full abstraction fails.

Trivial denial-of-service vulnerability Consider the pi calculus process

$$(\nu n)(\overline{n}\langle m\rangle \mid n(x).\overline{x}\langle\rangle)$$

which is a small variant of the first example where, after its receipt, the message m is used for sending an empty message. This process preserves the integrity of m, in the sense that no other name can be received and used instead of m; therefore, this process is equivalent to $\overline{m}\langle\rangle$.

The obvious spi calculus implementations of $(\nu n)(\overline{n}\langle m\rangle \mid n(x).\overline{x}\langle\rangle)$ and $\overline{m}\langle\rangle$ are respectively

$$(\nu n)(\overline{c}\langle\{m\}_n\rangle \mid c(y).case\ y\ of\ \{x\}_n\ in\ \overline{c}\langle\{\}_x\rangle)$$

and $\overline{c}\langle\{\}_m\rangle$. These implementations can be distinguished not only by traffic analysis but also in other trivial ways. For example, the former implementation may become stuck when it interacts with $\overline{c}\langle p\rangle$, because the decryption $case\ y\ of\ \{x\}_n\ in\ \overline{c}\langle\{\}_x\rangle$ fails when y is p rather than a ciphertext. In contrast, the latter implementation does not suffer from this problem.

Informally, we may say that the process $\overline{c}\langle p\rangle$ mounts a denial-of-service attack. Formally, such attacks can sometimes be ignored by focusing on process equivalences that capture only safety properties, and not liveness properties. In addition, the implementations may be strengthened, as is commonly done in practical systems. For example, as a first improvement, we may add some replication to $(\nu n)(\overline{c}\langle\{m\}_n\rangle \mid c(y).case\ y\ of\ \{x\}_n\ in\ \overline{c}\langle\{\}_x\rangle)$, obtaining:

$$(\nu n)(\overline{c}\langle\{m\}_n\rangle \mid !c(y).case\ y\ of\ \{x\}_n\ in\ \overline{c}\langle\{\}_x\rangle)$$

This use of replication protects against $\overline{c}\langle p\rangle$.

Exposure to replay attacks Another shortcoming of our implementation strategy is exposure to replay attacks. As an example, we consider the pi calculus process:

$$(\nu n)(\overline{n}\langle m_1\rangle \mid \overline{n}\langle m_2\rangle \mid n(x).\overline{x}\langle\rangle \mid n(x).\overline{x}\langle\rangle)$$

which differs from the previous example only in that two names m_1 and m_2 are transmitted on n, asynchronously. In the pi calculus, this process is equivalent to $\overline{m_1}\langle\rangle \mid \overline{m_2}\langle\rangle$: it is guaranteed that both m_1 and m_2 go from sender to receiver exactly once.

This guarantee is not shared by the spi calculus implementation

$$(\nu n)\begin{pmatrix}\overline{c}\langle\{m_1\}_n\rangle \mid \overline{c}\langle\{m_2\}_n\rangle \mid \\ c(y).case\ y\ of\ \{x\}_n\ in\ \overline{c}\langle\{\}_x\rangle \mid \\ c(y).case\ y\ of\ \{x\}_n\ in\ \overline{c}\langle\{\}_x\rangle\end{pmatrix}$$

independently of any denial-of-service attacks. When this implementation is combined with the spi calculus process $c(y).(\overline{c}\langle y\rangle \mid \overline{c}\langle y\rangle)$, which duplicates a message on c, two identical messages may result, either $\overline{c}\langle\{\}_{m_1}\rangle \mid \overline{c}\langle\{\}_{m_1}\rangle$ or $\overline{c}\langle\{\}_{m_2}\rangle \mid \overline{c}\langle\{\}_{m_2}\rangle$.

Informally, we may say that the process $c(y).(\overline{c}\langle y\rangle \mid \overline{c}\langle y\rangle)$ mounts a replay attack. Standard countermeasures apply: timestamps, sequence numbers, and challenge-response protocols. In this example, the addition of a minimal challenge-response protocol leads to the following spi calculus process:

$$(\nu n)\begin{pmatrix}c(z_1).\overline{c}\langle\{m_1, z_1\}_n\rangle \mid c(z_2).\overline{c}\langle\{m_2, z_2\}_n\rangle \mid \\ (\nu p_1)(\overline{c}\langle p_1\rangle \mid c(y).case\ y\ of\ \{x, z_1\}_n\ in\ [z_1\ is\ p_1]\ \overline{c}\langle\{\}_x\rangle) \mid \\ (\nu p_2)(\overline{c}\langle p_2\rangle \mid c(y).case\ y\ of\ \{x, z_2\}_n\ in\ [z_2\ is\ p_2]\ \overline{c}\langle\{\}_x\rangle)\end{pmatrix}$$

The names p_1 and p_2 serve as challenges; they are sent by the subprocesses that are meant to receive m_1 and m_2, received by the subprocesses that send m_1 and m_2, and included along with m_1 and m_2 under n. This challenge-response protocol is rather simplistic in that the challenges may get "crossed" and then neither m_1 nor m_2 would be transmitted successfully; it is a simple matter of programming to protect against this confusion. In any case, for each challenge, at most one message is accepted under n. This use of challenges thwarts replay attacks.

Leak of message equalities In the pi calculus, the identity of messages sent on private channels is concealed. For example, an observer of the process

$$(\nu n)(\overline{n}\langle m_1\rangle \mid \overline{n}\langle m_2\rangle \mid n(x).\mathbf{0} \mid n(x).\mathbf{0})$$

will not even discover whether $m_1 = m_2$. (For this example, we drop the implicit assumption that m_1 and m_2 are different names.) On the other hand, suppose that we translate this process to:

$$(\nu n)\left(\begin{array}{l}\overline{c}\langle\{m_1\}_n\rangle \mid \overline{c}\langle\{m_2\}_n\rangle \mid \\ c(y).case\ y\ of\ \{x\}_n\ in\ \mathbf{0} \mid \\ c(y).case\ y\ of\ \{x\}_n\ in\ \mathbf{0}\end{array}\right)$$

An observer of this process can tell whether $m_1 = m_2$, even without knowing m_1 or m_2 (or n). In particular, the observer may execute:

$$c(x).c(y).([x\ is\ y]\ \overline{d}\langle\rangle \mid \overline{c}\langle x\rangle \mid \overline{c}\langle y\rangle)$$

This process reads and relays two messages on the channel c, and emits a message on the channel d if the two messages are equal. It therefore distinguishes whether $m_1 = m_2$. The importance of this sort of leak depends on circumstances. In an extreme case, one cleartext may have been guessed (for example, the cleartext "attack at dawn"); knowing that another message contains the same cleartext may then be significant.

A simple countermeasure consists in including a different confounder component in each encrypted message. In this example, the implementation would become:

$$(\nu n)\left(\begin{array}{l}(\nu p_1)\overline{c}\langle\{m_1, p_1\}_n\rangle \mid (\nu p_2)\overline{c}\langle\{m_2, p_2\}_n\rangle \mid \\ c(y).case\ y\ of\ \{x, z_1\}_n\ in\ \mathbf{0} \mid \\ c(y).case\ y\ of\ \{x, z_2\}_n\ in\ \mathbf{0}\end{array}\right)$$

The names p_1 and p_2 are used only to differentiate the two messages being transmitted. Their inclusion in those messages ensures that a comparison on ciphertexts does not reveal an equality of cleartexts.

Lack of forward secrecy As a final example, we consider the pi calculus process:

$$(\nu n)(\overline{n}\langle m\rangle \mid n(x).\overline{p}\langle n\rangle)$$

This process transmits the name m on the channel n, which is private until this point. Then it releases n by sending it on the public channel p. Other processes may use n afterwards, but cannot recover the contents of the first message sent on n. Therefore, this process is equivalent to

$$(\nu n)(\overline{n}\langle m' \rangle \mid n(x).\overline{p}\langle n \rangle)$$

for any m'. Interestingly, this example relies crucially on scope extrusion, a feature of the pi calculus not present in simpler calculi such as CCS [Mil89].

A spi calculus implementation of $(\nu n)(\overline{n}\langle m \rangle \mid n(x).\overline{p}\langle n \rangle)$ might be:

$$(\nu n)(\overline{c}\langle \{m\}_n \rangle \mid c(y).\mathit{case}\ y\ \mathit{of}\ \{x\}_n\ \mathit{in}\ \overline{c}\langle \{n\}_p \rangle)$$

However, this implementation lacks the forward-secrecy property [DvOW92]: the disclosure of the key n compromises all data previously sent under n. More precisely, a process may read messages on c and remember them, obtain n by decrypting $\{n\}_p$, then use n for decrypting older messages on c. In particular, the spi calculus process

$$c(x).(\overline{c}\langle x \rangle \mid c(y).\mathit{case}\ y\ \mathit{of}\ \{z\}_p\ \mathit{in}\ \mathit{case}\ x\ \mathit{of}\ \{w\}_z\ \mathit{in}\ \overline{d}\langle w \rangle)$$

may read and relay $\{m\}_n$, read and decrypt $\{n\}_p$, then go back to obtain m from $\{m\}_n$, and finally release m on the public channel d.

Full abstraction is lost, as with the other attacks; in this case, however, it seems much harder to recover. Several solutions may be considered.

- We may restrict the pi calculus somehow, ruling out troublesome cases of scope extrusion. It is not immediately clear whether enough expressiveness for practical programming can be retained.
- We may add some constructs to the pi calculus, for example a construct that given the name n of a channel will yield all previous messages sent on the channel n. The addition of this construct will destroy the source-language equivalence that was not preserved by the translation. On the other hand, this construct seems fairly artificial.
- We may somehow indicate that source-language equivalences should not be taken too seriously. In particular, we may reveal some aspects of the implementation, warning that forward secrecy may not hold. We may also specify which source-language properties are maintained in the implementation. This solution is perhaps the most realistic one, although we do not yet know how to write the necessary specifications in a precise and manageable form.
- Finally, we may try to strengthen the implementation. For example, we may vary the key that corresponds to a pi calculus channel by, at each instant, computing a new key by hashing the previous one. This approach is fairly elaborate and expensive.

The problem of forward secrecy may be neatly avoided by shifting from the pi calculus to the join calculus [FG96]. The join calculus separates the capabilities for sending and receiving on a channel, and forbids the communication of the latter capability. Because of this asymmetry, the join calculus is somewhat easier to map to a lower-level calculus with cryptographic constructs. This mapping is the subject of current work [AFG98]; although still impractical, the translation obtained is fully abstract.

4 Full Abstraction in Context

With progress on security infrastructures and techniques, it may become less important for translations to approximate full abstraction. Instead, we may rely on the intrinsic security properties of target-language code and on digital signatures on this code. We may also rely on the security properties of source-language code, but only when a precise specification asserts that translation preserves those properties. Unfortunately, several caveats apply.

- The intrinsic security properties of target-language code may be extremely hard to discover a posteriori. Languages such as JVML are not designed for ease of reading. Furthermore, the proof of those properties may require the analysis of delicate and complex cryptographic protocols. Certifying compilers [NL97,MWCG98] may alleviate these problems but may not fully solve them.
- Digital signatures complement static analyses but do not obviate them. In particular, digital signatures cannot protect against incompetence or against misplaced trust. Moreover, digital signatures do not seem applicable in all settings. For example, digital signatures on spi calculus processes would be of little use, since these processes never migrate from one machine to another.
- Finally, we still have only a limited understanding of how to specify and prove that a translation preserves particular security properties. This question deserves further attention. It may be worthwhile to address it first in special cases, for example for information-flow properties [Den82] as captured in type systems [VIS96,Aba97,ML97,HR98].

The judicious use of abstractions can contribute to simplicity, and thus to security. On the other hand, abstractions and their translations can give rise to complications, subtleties, and ultimately to security flaws. As Lampson wrote [Lam83], "neither abstraction nor simplicity is a substitute for getting it right". Concepts such as full abstraction should help in getting it right.

Acknowledgements

Most of the observations of this paper were made during joint work with Cédric Fournet, Georges Gonthier, Andy Gordon, and Raymie Stata. Drew Dean, Mark Lillibridge, and Dan Wallach helped by explaining various Java subtleties. Mike Burrows, Cédric Fournet, Mark Lillibridge, John Mitchell, and Dan Wallach suggested improvements to a draft. The title is derived from that of a paper by Jim Morris [Mor73].

References

[Aba97] Martín Abadi. Secrecy by typing in security protocols. In *Theoretical Aspects of Computer Software*, volume 1281 of *Lecture Notes in Computer Science*, pages 611–638. Springer-Verlag, 1997.

[AFG98] Martín Abadi, Cédric Fournet, and Georges Gonthier. Secure implementation of channel abstractions. In *Proceedings of the Thirteenth Annual IEEE Symposium on Logic in Computer Science*, June 1998. To appear.

[AG97a] Martín Abadi and Andrew D. Gordon. A calculus for cryptographic protocols: The spi calculus. Technical Report 414, University of Cambridge Computer Laboratory, January 1997. Extended version of both [AG97b] and [AG97c]. A revised version appeared as Digital Equipment Corporation Systems Research Center report No. 149, January 1998, and an abridged version will appear in *Information and Computation.*

[AG97b] Martín Abadi and Andrew D. Gordon. A calculus for cryptographic protocols: The spi calculus. In *Proceedings of the Fourth ACM Conference on Computer and Communications Security*, pages 36–47, 1997.

[AG97c] Martín Abadi and Andrew D. Gordon. Reasoning about cryptographic protocols in the spi calculus. In *Proceedings of the 8th International Conference on Concurrency Theory*, volume 1243 of *Lecture Notes in Computer Science*, pages 59–73. Springer-Verlag, July 1997.

[AS85] Bowen Alpern and Fred B. Schneider. Defining liveness. *Information Processing Letters*, 21(4):181–185, October 1985.

[Bir85] Andrew D. Birrell. Secure communication using remote procedure calls. *ACM Transactions on Computer Systems*, 3(1):1–14, February 1985.

[BN95] Michele Boreale and Rocco De Nicola. Testing equivalence for mobile processes. *Information and Computation*, 120(2):279–303, August 1995.

[Bor74] Jorge Luis Borges. La muerte y la brújula. In *Obras completas 1923–1972*, pages 499–507. Emecé Editores, Buenos Aires, 1974. Titled "Death and the compass" in English translations.

[Coh97] Richard M. Cohen. Defensive Java Virtual Machine version 0.5 alpha release. Web pages at `http://www.cli.com/`, May 13, 1997.

[Den82] Dorothy E. Denning. *Cryptography and Data Security.* Addison-Wesley, Reading, Mass., 1982.

[DFWB98] Drew Dean, Edward W. Felten, Dan S. Wallach, and Dirk Balfanz. Java security: Web browsers and beyond. In Dorothy E. Denning and Peter J. Denning, editors, *Internet beseiged: countering cyberspace scofflaws*, pages 241–269. ACM Press, 1998.

[DH84] Rocco De Nicola and Matthew C. B. Hennessy. Testing equivalences for processes. *Theoretical Computer Science*, 34:83–133, 1984.

[DvOW92] Whitfield Diffie, Paul C. van Oorschot, and Michael J. Wiener. Authentication and authenticated key exchanges. *Designs, Codes and Cryptography*, 2:107–125, 1992.

[FG96] Cédric Fournet and Georges Gonthier. The reflexive chemical abstract machine and the join-calculus. In *Proceedings of the 23rd ACM Symposium on Principles of Programming Languages*, pages 372–385, January 1996.

[FM98] Stephen N. Freund and John C. Mitchell. A type system for object initialization in the Java bytecode language. On the Web at `http://theory.stanford.edu/~freunds/`, 1998.

[GJS96] James Gosling, Bill Joy, and Guy L. Steele. *The Java Language Specification.* Addison-Wesley, 1996.

[Hoa72] C. A. R. Hoare. Proof of correctness of data representations. *Acta Informatica*, 1:271–281, 1972.

[HR98] Nevin Heintze and Jon G. Riecke. The SLam calculus: programming with secrecy and integrity. In *Proceedings of the 25th ACM Symposium on Principles of Programming Languages*, pages 365–377, 1998.

[JL78] Anita K. Jones and Barbara H. Liskov. A language extension for expressing constraints on data access. *Communications of the ACM*, 21(5):358–367, May 1978.

[Lam71] Butler W. Lampson. Protection. In *Proceedings of the 5th Princeton Conference on Information Sciences and Systems*, pages 437–443, 1971.

[Lam83] Butler W. Lampson. Hints for computer system design. *Operating Systems Review*, 17(5):33–48, October 1983. Proceedings of the Ninth ACM Symposium on Operating System Principles.

[Lam89] Leslie Lamport. A simple approach to specifying concurrent systems. *Communications of the ACM*, 32(1):32–45, January 1989.

[LP98] John Longley and Gordon Plotkin. Logical full abstraction and PCF. In Jonathan Ginzburg, Zurab Khasidashvili, Carl Vogel, Jean-Jacques Lévy, and Enric Vallduví, editors, *The Tbilisi Symposium on Logic, Language and Computation: Selected Papers*, pages 333–352. CSLI Publications and FoLLI, 1998.

[LR98] Xavier Leroy and François Rouaix. Security properties of typed applets. In *Proceedings of the 25th ACM Symposium on Principles of Programming Languages*, pages 391–403, 1998.

[LS76] Butler W. Lampson and Howard E. Sturgis. Reflections on an operating system design. *Communications of the ACM*, 19(5):251–265, May 1976.

[LY96] Tim Lindholm and Frank Yellin. *The Java Virtual Machine Specification.* Addison-Wesley, 1996.

[McL96] John McLean. A general theory of composition for a class of "possibilistic" properties. *IEEE Transactions on Software Engineering*, 22(1):53–66, January 1996.

[Mil89] Robin Milner. *Communication and Concurrency.* Prentice-Hall International, 1989.

[Mil92] Robin Milner. Functions as processes. *Mathematical Structures in Computer Science*, 2:119–141, 1992.

[Mil93] Robin Milner. The polyadic π-calculus: a tutorial. In Bauer, Brauer, and Schwichtenberg, editors, *Logic and Algebra of Specification.* Springer-Verlag, 1993.

[Mit93] John C. Mitchell. On abstraction and the expressive power of programming languages. *Science of Computer Programming*, 21(2):141–163, October 1993.

[ML97] Andrew C. Myers and Barbara Liskov. A decentralized model for information flow control. In *Proceedings of the 16th ACM Symposium on Operating System Principles*, pages 129–142, 1997.

[Mor73] James H. Morris, Jr. Protection in programming languages. *Communications of the ACM*, 16(1):15–21, January 1973.

[MPW92] Robin Milner, Joachim Parrow, and David Walker. A calculus of mobile processes, parts I and II. *Information and Computation*, 100:1–40 and 41–77, September 1992.

[MvOV96] Alfred J. Menezes, Paul C. van Oorschot, and Scott A. Vanstone. *Handbook of Applied Cryptography.* CRC Press, 1996.

[MWCG98] Greg Morrisett, David Walker, Karl Crary, and Neal Glew. From System F to Typed Assembly Language. In *Proceedings of the 25th ACM Symposium on Principles of Programming Languages*, pages 85–97, 1998.

[NL97] George C. Necula and Peter Lee. The design and implementation of a certifying compiler. To appear in the proceedings of PLDI'98, 1997.

[Plo77] Gordon Plotkin. LCF considered as a programming language. *Theoretical Computer Science*, 5:223–256, 1977.

[Qia97] Zhenyu Qian. A formal specification of Java(tm) Virtual Machine instructions (draft). Web page at `http://www.informatik.uni-bremen.de/~qian/abs-fsjvm.html`, 1997.

[SA98] Raymie Stata and Martín Abadi. A type system for Java bytecode subroutines. In *Proceedings of the 25th ACM Symposium on Principles of Programming Languages*, pages 149–160, January 1998.

[Sha91] Ehud Shapiro. Separating concurrent languages with categories of language embeddings. In *Proceedings of the Twenty Third Annual ACM Symposium on the Theory of Computing*, pages 198–208, 1991.

[Sun97a] Sun Microsystems, Inc. Inner classes specification. Web pages at `http://java.sun.com/products/jdk/1.1/docs/guide/innerclasses/`, 1997.

[Sun97b] Sun Microsystems, Inc. RMI enhancements. Web pages at `http://java.sun.com/products/jdk/1.2/docs/guide/rmi/index.html`, 1997.

[vDABW96] Leendert van Doorn, Martín Abadi, Mike Burrows, and Edward Wobber. Secure network objects. In *Proceedings 1996 IEEE Symposium on Security and Privacy*, pages 211–221, May 1996.

[VIS96] Dennis Volpano, Cynthia Irvine, and Geoffrey Smith. A sound type system for secure flow analysis. *Journal of Computer Security*, 4:167–187, 1996.

[WABL94] Edward Wobber, Martín Abadi, Michael Burrows, and Butler Lampson. Authentication in the Taos operating system. *ACM Transactions on Computer Systems*, 12(1):3–32, February 1994.

[WRW96] Ann Wollrath, Roger Riggs, and Jim Waldo. A distributed object model for the Java system. *Computing Systems*, 9(4):265–290, Fall 1996.

Efficient Simulations by Queue Machines*

Holger Petersen[1] and John Michael Robson[2]

[1] Institut für Informatik, Universität Stuttgart
Breitwiesenstraße 20–22
D-70565 Stuttgart, Germany
petersen@informatik.uni-stuttgart.de
[2] LaBRI, Université Bordeaux 1
351 cours de la Libération
33405 Talence Cedex, France
robson@labri.u-bordeaux.fr

Abstract. The following simulations by machines equipped with a one-way input tape and additional queue storage are shown:

- Every single-tape Turing machine (no separate input-tape) with time bound $t(n)$ can be simulated by one queue in $O(t(n))$ time.
- Every pushdown automaton can be simulated by one queue in time $O(n\sqrt{n})$.
- Every deterministic machine with a one-turn pushdown store can be simulated deterministically by one queue in $O(n\sqrt{n})$ time.
- Every Turing machine with several multi-dimensional tapes accepting with time bound $t(n)$ can be simulated by two queues in time $O(t(n)\log^2 t(n))$.
- Every deterministic Turing machine with several linear tapes accepting with time bound $t(n)$ can be simulated deterministically by a queue and a pushdown store in $O(t(n)\log t(n))$ time.

The former results appear to be the first sub-quadratic simulations of other storage devices such as pushdowns or tapes by one queue. The simulations of pushdown machines almost match the corresponding lower bounds.

1 Introduction

A classical result, essentially due to Post, says that a machine with a single queue is able to perform any computation a Turing machine can, see e.g. [12]. While the complexity of simulations between machines with pushdowns or tapes has been thoroughly investigated, fewer results have been obtained for the storage device queue. It is known that one-queue machines can simulate several tapes, pushdowns, and queues with quadratic slowdown [9, Theorem 3.1]. Nondeterministic two-queue machines can simulate any number of queues with linear time overhead, see [2, Theorem 4.5]

* Research supported in part by the French-German project PROCOPE.

for a simulation of linear time machines (which is even realtime) and [9, Theorem 4.2].

For deterministic devices with several queues Hühne gives a simulation of $t(n)$ time-bounded multi-storage Turing machines on $O(t(n)\sqrt[k]{t(n)})$ time-bounded machines with $k \geq 2$ queues [8]. He also reports almost matching lower bounds for online simulations of these storage devices.

Li and Vitányi report lower bounds for simulating one queue on other storages without the online restriction [10].

In the framework of formal languages, machines with one or more queues have been investigated e.g. in [15, 2].

Hartmanis and Stearns [5] showed that a k-dimensional tape machine with time bound $t(n)$ could be simulated by a linear tape machine in time $O(t^2(n))$. Pippenger and Fischer [14] improved the time to $O(t^{2-1/k}(n))$ and the result of Hennie [6] (with the correction from [3]) shows that this is optimal, at least for on-line deterministic simulation. Grigor'ev [4] and Loui [11] showed how to reduce the time when the simulating machine uses m-dimensional tapes ($m > 1$); they used nondeterministic and deterministic machines respectively. Monien [13] improved the result in case of nondeterministic simulation to use of linear tapes and time $O(t(n)\log^2 t(n))$. We show that this last result holds also for nondeterministic simulation by 2 queues.

2 Preliminaries

We adopt the concepts from [10, 9]. The simulated devices will be introduced below. Unless stated otherwise our simulating machines are nondeterministic and are equipped with a single one-way head on a read-only input tape. The machines can determine end-of-input, have access to one or more first-in-first-out queues storing symbols, and are able to signal acceptance of their input. Depending on the symbols read by the input head and at the front of the queues a finite control determines one or more of the following operations

- advance the input head to the next cell,
- dequeue the first symbols of some queues,
- enqueue at most one symbol per queue.

After these operations control is transferred to the next state.

A machine accepts in time $t(n)$ if, for all accepted inputs of length n, the machine admits a computation that ends with acceptance after at most $t(n)$ steps.

Simulation will be understood in the most general sense, i.e., machine A simulates B if both machines accept the same set of inputs. Note that other concepts of simulation are frequently used, notably step-by-step simulations or simulations of storages where some interface for transmitting information is specified and the simulator has to provide this information on demand.

3 Results

Theorem 1. *Every nondeterministic bi-infinite single-tape Turing machine accepting in $t(n)$ steps can be simulated by a nondeterministic one-queue machine in $O(t(n))$ steps.*

Proof. We call the Turing machine to be simulated S and the queue machine Q. Let the tape cells of S be labeled with consecutive integers, the first symbol of the input is labeled with 0. We assume without loss of generality that S moves its head in every step and that there is a single final state reachable only with right movements of the head.

Recall that a crossing sequence at the boundary between two adjacent tape cells consists of the chronological sequence of states the finite control of S transfers control to as the head crosses the boundary. Here we will denote by c_i the crossing sequence occurring in a computation between cell $i-1$ and i and we will also encode the direction when going to state q by $\overrightarrow{q}$ (right movement) and $\overleftarrow{q}$ (left movement). We adopt the convention that c_0 starts with the initial state of S moving right.

The computation of S in terms of crossing sequences can be divided into three phases:

- Involving cells to the left of the input ($i \leq 0$).
- Involving cells within the input w ($0 < i \leq |w|$).
- Involving cells to the right of the input ($i > |w|$).

Queue machine Q simulates the behaviour of S on every tape cell used by S, from left to right, i.e., generally not in chronological sequence. During a cycle corresponding to a tape cell Q keeps the symbol x currently in the cell in its finite control. The symbol x is initialised with a blank in the first and last case above and with the actual input symbol in the second case. This symbol is available to Q from Q's own input tape.

The idea of the simulation is to have a crossing sequence c_i on the queue and to guess c_{i+1} (which is separated from c_i by \$) in a manner consistent with S's finite control. More specifically, if the remaining suffix of c_i on the queue is c, we have the following cases, which are non-exclusive (c' is the part of the crossing sequence not affected by the step currently simulated):

- $c = \overrightarrow{q_1}\overleftarrow{q_2}c'$ and there is a transition from q_1 to q_2 reading x, writing some symbol y and moving the head left. Then Q dequeues $\overrightarrow{q_1}\overleftarrow{q_2}$ and replaces x with y.
- $c = \overrightarrow{q_1}c'$ and there is a transition from q_1 to q_2 reading x, writing some symbol y and moving the head right. Then Q dequeues $\overrightarrow{q_1}$, enqueues $\overrightarrow{q_2}$ and replaces x with y.
- $c = \overleftarrow{q_2}c'$ and there is a transition from q_1 to q_2 reading x, writing some symbol y and moving the head left. Then Q dequeues $\overleftarrow{q_2}$, enqueues $\overleftarrow{q_1}$ and replaces x with y.
- There is a transition from q_1 to q_2 reading x, writing some symbol y and moving the head right. Then Q enqueues $\overleftarrow{q_1}\overrightarrow{q_2}$ and replaces x with y.

If the last symbol of the current crossing sequence has been processed and no further operations according to the last case above occur, the marker symbol \$ is dequeued, enqueued and the next cycle starts.

Should the final state be reached, then no successor state is stored on the queue, but the fact that it has been encountered is recorded in the finite control of Q.

The simulation is initiated by guessing zero or more pairs of states according to the last case to be inserted into the queue with the initial tape symbol being a blank. It proceeds in phase 1 until Q guesses that c_{-1} is stored on the queue and phase 2 of the simulation is about to start. At this moment, S's initial state is inserted into the queue as the first element of c_0. After c_0 has been assembled, the input is read in every cycle, until the last symbol is consumed and $c_{|w|}$ has been formed. The simulation continues in phase 3 until the queue contains no symbol except \$. The machine Q eventually accepts when S's final state has been encountered during the simulation.

If S has an accepting computation, then the crossing sequences occurring in this computation give rise to an accepting computation of Q. Conversely, if Q accepts an input, then the contents of the queue after a full cycle of the simulation can be assembled into an accepting computation of S. The number of steps executed by S is equal to the sum of the lengths of all crossing sequences. For every element of a crossing sequence, Q executes a number of steps bounded by a constant. This shows the claimed time bound. □

A converse of the above simulation is not possible, showing that queue machines are stronger than single-tape Turing machines.

Observation 1. *The language $D^{\#} = \{w\#w \mid w \in \{0,1\}^*\}$ can be accepted in realtime by a deterministic one-queue machine but not by any nondeterministic single-tape Turing machine working in $o(n^2)$ time.*

Proof. Techniques due to Hennie and Barzdin show that $D^{\#}$ cannot be accepted in $o(n^2)$ time by a single-tape machine, see [16, Theorem 8.13]. On the other hand a queue machine stores all symbols up to the first $\#$ on the queue and compares them to the string following $\#$. The input is rejected if a mismatch is detected or no separator $\#$ is found, otherwise it is accepted. □

Theorem 2. *Every nondeterministic pushdown automaton can be simulated by one queue in $O(n\sqrt{n})$ time. Therefore every context-free language can be accepted by one queue in $O(n\sqrt{n})$ time.*

Proof. Without loss of generality we assume that the pushdown machine P works in linear time and accepts by empty stack. We assume that stack locations are addressed by integers in order increasing with push operations. We call a sequence of operations by P a *section* if its first stack operation is a push operation on a stack address a, it ends with a pop operation on a and it does not include any stack operations on stack addresses lower than a. The simulation depends on the existence of a set $s_1, \cdots, s_m$ of sections such that:

- every operation of the computation is in s_1
- any two sections are either disjoint or one embedded in the other
- $m = O(\sqrt{n})$
- the number of stack addresses used by the operations in s_j but not in any s_k embedded in s_j is $\leq \sqrt{n}$.

The existence of such a set of sections is easily seen by considering the $\lfloor\sqrt{n}\rfloor$ possible divisions of the stack into blocks, in each of which the first block has some positive size $i \leq \lfloor\sqrt{n}\rfloor$ and all others have size exactly $\lfloor\sqrt{n}\rfloor$; each of these divisions induces a set of sections starting at any instruction where P pushes a symbol in the first address of a block and ending at the next instruction which pops the same address (except that for the first block there is a single section s_1 which is the whole computation). Since each of the $O(n)$ push operations defines a section start for at most one of the $\lfloor\sqrt{n}\rfloor$ divisions, some division gives $O(\sqrt{n})$ sections.

The queue machine Q's simulation of P will proceed in two phases. In the first phase, Q guesses the computation of P and mimics the input reading and state changing operations of P; where P performs any stack related operations (push, pop or read (meaning that the guessed operation of P depends on the top of stack symbol)), Q will write symbols onto its queue for later consistency checking. By guessing when P's computation enters and leaves a section, Q writes all the records of stack operations in a given section (and not in any embedded section) in a contiguous section of its queue. If the guessed computation of P accepts, Q verifies the consistency of each queue block in a total of $O(\sqrt{n})$ cycles through the queue, accepting if it confirms consistency.

If the alphabet of the pushdown machine is X, then that of the queue machine is $\{(push, x)|x \in X\} \cup \{(read, x)|x \in X\} \cup \{*, \$, pop, finished\}$.

Phase 1 The queue blocks corresponding to sections are separated by \$ symbols and consist of symbols $(push, x)$, $(read, y)$ and *pop* possibly preceded by *finished.* The order of these blocks in the queue is the same as the order of entry into the corresponding sections (modulo cyclic rearrangements). In normal simulation the start of the active queue block is a $*$ symbol. When the guessed computation of P performs a stack operation, the corresponding symbol ($(push, x)$, $(read, y)$ or *pop*) is written to the back of the queue.

When Q guesses that the stack operation is the first of a section, it writes a \$ followed by a $*$ to create a new active block and cycles once through the queue, copying all symbols from the front of the queue to the back except the first $*$ (which is removed); when the second $*$ is found, normal simulation resumes.

When Q guesses that the stack operation just recorded was the last of a section other than s_1, it must find the last block corresponding to a non-finished section. It cycles through the queue copying all symbols and nondeterministically guesses the start of a previous block not starting with *finished*, marking it with a $*$; it then checks that the other block with a $*$ really is the next block not to start with *finished*, replaces this "old" $*$ by *finished*, and then continues copying all symbols until it reaches the remaining "new"$*$ again and then continues copying until the end of the immediately following block. If the section was (guessed to be) s_1, Q simply checks end-of-input, writes *finished* to the queue and enters phase 2. (Thus for this block the *finished* will follow the other symbols instead of preceding them but this will cause no problems in phase 2.)

This ensures that the symbols representing the stack operations of a given section are written in a queue block in the order of the execution of the operations.

By guessing a division of the computation into $O(\sqrt{n})$ sections Q can carry out phase 1 in time $O(n\sqrt{n})$.

Phase 2 In phase 2 Q must check that the guessed computation of P really accepted and that the records of stack operations correspond to a possible set of sections. To do this it checks that each queue block (the sequence of symbols between two \$ symbols)

- contains *finished*
- has the same number of *push* and *pop* symbols
- has no prefix with more *pop* than *push* symbols
- has every $(read, x)$ preceded by a $(push, x)$ with the intervening symbols having equal numbers of *push* and *pop* and no prefix with a majority of *pop* over *push*

This is achieved by $O(\sqrt{n})$ passes through the queue where each pass checks and removes (at least) every sequence of symbols starting with a $(push, x)$, ending *pop* and containing no intervening symbols except $(read, x)$. Since the number of stack addresses used in each section is $O(\sqrt{n})$, $O(\sqrt{n})$ passes will reduce every block to the single symbol *finished* unless an inconsistency is detected.

In more detail, Q continually copies symbols from the front of the queue to the back except for the following transformations:

- after $(push, x)$ any number of $(read, x)$ symbols are ignored
- if a *pop* follows a *push*, both are removed

If a pass through the queue (from one encounter with the single $*$ until the next) finds only \$ and *finished* symbols, Q accepts. Clearly the time taken by phase 2 is $O(n\sqrt{n})$ and it will lead to acceptance if and only if the guesses in phase 1 really did correspond to a valid accepting computation of P. □

The next machine to be simulated has a one-turn pushdown (in any computation the machine may switch from pushing to popping at most once). Machines in this class accept exactly the deterministic linear context-free languages.

Theorem 3. *Every deterministic machine equipped with a one-turn pushdown store can be simulated by a deterministic machine with one queue in $O(n\sqrt{n})$ time.*

Proof. Let P be a deterministic one-turn pushdown machine. Note that if P accepts, it does so in linear time.

Let Q be the queue machine with queue alphabet $X \cup \{\#, *, \$\}$ where X is the pushdown alphabet of P, the union is disjoint, and the length of the input is n.

The idea of the simulation is to divide Q's computation into three phases. In the first phase, Q simulates push operations of P by writing the pushed symbols into its queue. When P switches to popping the pushdown contents, Q suspends the simulation and prepares its storage in order to speed up the access to pushdown symbols. In the last phase of the simulation, Q simulates the pop operations of P, from time to time rearranging the queue contents. A more detailed description of the second and third phases follows.

Suppose v is the queue contents of Q when P reverses its access to the pushdown, $|v| \in O(n)$. First Q divides v into strings v_i with $|v_i| \in \Theta(\sqrt{|v|})$ except for the last string which may be shorter. To do so Q marks the end of the queue with \$ and in one pass writes the string $*\#$ after every symbol from X. As long as the number of $*$'s in the queue exceeds one, Q deletes every second $*$ starting with the first one and in every second pass also deletes every second #, except the one immediately before \$. Thus Q makes $\lfloor \log |v| \rfloor$ passes in $O(|v| \log |v|)$ steps and $\lfloor \lfloor \log |v| \rfloor / 2 \rfloor$ times approximately divides the number of #'s by 2. After these operations v is divided into k blocks v_i terminated by #. We have

$$|v_i| \leq 2^{\lfloor \frac{\lfloor \log |v| \rfloor}{2} \rfloor} \leq \sqrt{|v|}$$

and

$$k \leq \frac{|v|}{2^{\lfloor \frac{\lfloor \log |v| \rfloor}{2} \rfloor}} \leq 2\sqrt{|v|}.$$

Next, Q in one pass inserts a symbol $*$ before every #. Then it starts to reverse the blocks v_i by deleting a symbol $x \in X$ from the beginning of each block that is not yet completely reversed, keeping it in its finite control and inserting x after the $*$ in the same block. This process is repeated until all blocks start with $*$ and then the $*$'s are deleted in one pass. Each block $v_i\#$ has been transformed into $v_i^R\#$ in a total of $O(|v|\sqrt{|v|})$ steps.

The third phase of Q's operation requires a preparation that speeds up Q's access to the last block on the queue. In k cycles Q inserts a $*$ in front of every block that already contains a $*$ and of the first block that has not received a $*$ up to that point, until every block has received at least one $*$. The effect of these operations is that the blocks contain k,

$k-1, \ldots, 1$ symbols $*$. The preparation is $O(n\sqrt{n})$ time bounded. Now Q enters the third phase and simulates P's pushdown-reading operations by repeatedly rotating blocks to the rear of the queue until it finds the unique block with a single $*$. It deletes $*$ and reads this block of pushdown symbols while processing the next input segment until it encounters the trailing #, deletes this symbol, and rewrites \$ at the rear of the queue. Then in one cycle it deletes a single $*$ in every block. It repeats this sequence of operations until the input is exhausted. Emptiness of the pushdown store can easily be detected since then the \$ is the first symbol in the queue. Each rotation takes $O(|v|)$ time and there are $k \in O(\sqrt{|v|})$ blocks; therefore this phase is $O(|v|\sqrt{|v|})$ time-bounded. □

We remark that the previous simulation applies to the language $L = \{w\#w^R \mid w \in \{0,1\}^*\}$ investigated in [9, Section 3.2]. Our upper bound almost matches the lower bound $\Omega(n^{4/3}/\log n)$ from [9].

The proof of the next result uses ideas from [13].

Theorem 4. *Every nondeterministic Turing machine with several multi-dimensional work tapes accepting with time bound $t(n)$ can be simulated by two queues in $O(t(n)\log^2 t(n))$ time.*

Proof. For convenience we will describe a simulator that is equipped with a large number of queues. The linear-time simulation of machines with several queues with two queues [9, Theorem 4.2] will give the result.

Let the m work tapes of machine M that is to be simulated be d-dimensional. For tape i our simulator Q has $d+1$ queues. Queue $i(d+1)$ records the read-write operations on tape i, queues $i(d+1)+1$ through $i(d+1)+d$ contain binary counters that store the distance of M's head from its initial head position on tape i. More precisely, for a distance k, the reversal of the binary representation of k is written into the corresponding queue followed by a separator symbol #. If the sign of a distance changes this is recorded in Q's finite control. All counters are initially zero.

The simulation of M is divided into phases. In the first phase Q guesses step-by-step a computation of M, reading input symbols if necessary, and guessing a corresponding step of M. Let the symbol read by this step on tape i be x_i and the symbol written be y_i. The current distances for tape i are $k_1, \ldots k_d$. Then Q writes a record containing x_i, y_i, and $k_1, \ldots k_d$ (including signs) into queue $i(d+1)$. The distances are copied by rotating the binary representations stored in queues $i(d+1)+1, \ldots, i(d+1)+d$. Now Q updates the distances as indicated by the head move on tape i by adding or subtracting one if necessary. These operations are carried out for every tape and take $O(t(n)\log t(n))$ time. If eventually the simulation reaches an accepting state of M the second phase is started.

In the second phase the consistency of the guessed computation is checked. For every tape i the simulator uses queues $i(d+1)$ and $i(d+1)+1$ for sorting the records according to distances in a stable way. A suitable method is to use radix sort on their binary representations starting with the least significant bits and marking off used bits. First a new marker is appended to queue $i(d+1)$. Records containing 0 at the current position are put into queue $i(d+1)+1$, the others are moved to the rear of queue $i(d+1)$. If the marker is encountered the queues are appended and the next bit position is considered. In case all digits of a number are exhausted while there are still bits to be processed the symbol # is interpreted as a string of leading zeros. If all bits have been handled a final pass sorts according to signs. Sorting is done for all dimensions. Then Q checks for every run of records with equal distances that the first symbol read is a blank and that the symbol written by record j is equal to the symbol read by record $j+1$. If it detects an inconsistency it aborts the simulation, otherwise it accepts.

The number of records is $O(t(n))$, the length of each of these records is $O(\log t(n))$, and the number of passes required for sorting is $O(\log t(n))$. We obtain the required time bound $O(t(n) \log^2 t(n))$. □

We remark that tapes can simulate queues in linear time, see [16, Lemma 19.9].

Hühne states that his deterministic simulation of multi-storage Turing machines in time $O(t(n)\sqrt{t(n)})$ can be performed on a deterministic machine with a queue and a pushdown store [8]. He also mentions an $\Omega(t(n) \sqrt[4]{\log t(n)})$ lower bound. In the nondeterministic case a queue and a pushdown simulate any number of pushdown stores (and hence tapes) in linear time by adapting the technique of Book and Greibach [1]: Guess a sequence of partial configurations containing the state of the simulated machine, the topmost symbols of each pushdown store, the input symbol currently scanned, and the operations on input head and storage. This sequence is written onto the queue. Then the simulator checks that the sequence corresponds to a valid computation for each of the pushdown stores and the input.

We give a deterministic simulation of an arbitrary number of tapes on a queue and a pushdown store that almost matches the lower bound.

Theorem 5. *Any deterministic $t(n)$-time bounded multi-tape Turing machine can be simulated by a deterministic Turing machine accessing a queue and a pushdown store which is $O(t(n) \log t(n))$-time-bounded.*

Proof (sketch). We describe a modification of the simulation of multi-tape Turing machines on two-tape machines due Hennie and Stearns, see e.g. [7].

Recall that in the Hennie/Stearns simulation two-way infinite sequences of blocks of increasing length of storage cells are allocated on one of the tapes. These blocks are divided in two tracks. We first concatenate the tracks sequentially in the order the symbols would appear on the simulated tape. As in the simulation of a two-way infinite tape on a one-way infinite tape we bend the sequences around the center square and use separate tracks for the "halves" of the tapes. Note that blocks of corresponding length are stored on the tracks above each other. This tape will be simulated by the pushdown store, shorter blocks will be closer to the top of the pushdown. Initially only blocks of length one are stored on the pushdown store. Whenever a head of the simulated machine enters a tape segment it has not visited before, a new block of twice the length of the previous block is allocated. In order to simulate a step of the multi-tape machine our simulator unloads onto the queue the top segment of the pushdown store containing all blocks affected by the step, possibly introducing new blocks. Then it copies appropriate portions within the queue by rotating the queue contents. It uses its pushdown as a scratch memory always copying twice between pushdown and queue since the use of a last-in-first out memory reverses the strings stored. In the same way the simulator restores the pushdown by loading the queue onto the pushdown, unloading this topmost segment onto the queue, and finally loading it again onto the pushdown. The time bound for this simulation is of the same order as for the Hennie/Stearns technique. □

Acknowledgements

The first author would like to thank Jeff Shallit and Pierre McKenzie for comments on an earlier draft of this paper. We also thank Franz-Josef Brandenburg for useful remarks.

References

1. Ronald V. Book and Sheila A. Greibach. Quasi-realtime languages. *Mathematical Systems Theory*, 4:97–111, 1970.
2. Franz-Josef Brandenburg. Multiple equality sets and Post machines. *Journal of Computer and System Sciences*, 21:292–316, 1980.
3. D. Yu. Grigor'ev. Imbedding theorems for Turing machines of different dimensions and Kolmogorov's algorithms. *Dokl. Akad. Nauk SSSR*, 234:15–18, 1977. In Russian, translation in Soviet Math. Dokl., 18:588–592, 1977.

4. D. Yu. Grigor'ev. Time complexity of multidimensional Turing machines. *Zapiski Nauchnykh Seminarov Leningradskogo Otdelniya Matematicheskogo Instituta im. V. A. Steklova AN SSSR*, 88:47–55, 1979. In Russian, translation in J. Soviet Mathematics, 20:2290–2295, 1982.
5. Juris Hartmanis and Richard E. Stearns. On the computational complexity of algorithms. *Transactions of the American Mathematical Society*, 117:285–306, 1965.
6. Frederick C. Hennie. On-line Turing machine computations. *IEEE Transactions on Electronic Computers*, EC-15:35–44, 1966.
7. John E. Hopcroft and Jeffrey D. Ullman. *Introduction to Automata Theory, Languages, and Computation.* Addison-Wesley, Reading Mass., 1979.
8. Martin Hühne. On the power of several queues. *Theoretical Computer Science*, 113:75–91, 1993.
9. Ming Li, Luc Longpré, and Paul Vitányi. The power of the queue. *SIAM Journal on Computing*, 21:697–712, 1992.
10. Ming Li and Paul M. B. Vitányi. Tape versus queue and stacks: The lower bounds. *Information and Computation*, 78:56–85, 1988.
11. Michael C. Loui. Simulations among multidimensional Turing machines. *Theoretical Computer Science*, 21:145–161, 1982.
12. Zohar Manna. *Mathematical Theory of Computation.* McGraw-Hill, New York, 1974.
13. Burkhard Monien. About the derivation languages of grammars and machines. In M. Steinby, editor, *Proceedings of the 4th International Colloquium on Automata, Languages and Programming (ICALP), Turku, 1977*, Lecture Notes in Computer Science, pages 337–351, 1977.
14. Nicholas Pippenger and Michael J. Fischer. Relations among complexity measures. *Journal of the Association for Computing Machinery*, 26:361–381, 1979.
15. Roland Vollmar. Über einen Automaten mit Pufferspeicherung (On an automaton with buffer-tape). *Computing*, 5:57–70, 1970. In German.
16. Klaus Wagner and Gerd Wechsung. *Computational Complexity.* Mathematics and its Applications. D. Reidel Publishing Company, Dordrecht, 1986.

Power of Cooperation and Multihead Finite Systems *

Pavol Ďuriš[1], Tomasz Jurdziński[2], Mirosław Kutyłowski[2,**], and Krzysztof Loryś[2]

[1] Institute of Informatics, Comenius University, Bratislava
[2] Computer Science Institute, University of Wrocław

Abstract. We consider systems of finite automata performing together computation on an input string. Each automaton has its own read head that moves independently of the other heads, but the automata cooperate in making state transitions. Computational power of such devices depends on the number of states of automata, the number of automata, and the way they cooperate. We concentrate our attention on the last issue. The first situation that we consider is that each automaton has a full knowledge on the states of all automata (*multihead automata*). The other extreme is that each automaton (called also a *processor*) has no knowledge of the states of other automata; merely, there is a central processing unit that may "freeze" any automaton or let it proceed its work (so called *multiprocessor automata*). The second model seems to be severely restricted, but we show that multihead and multiprocessor automata have similar computational power. Nevertheless, we show a separation result.

1 Introduction

Many computing systems can be modeled by systems of cooperating finite automata. In fact, any existing physical device is finite, despite that we often think in terms of models with infinite memory.

The problem that we consider here is how finite automata may cooperate in order to perform complex computational tasks. We assume that an input is a string of characters from an alphabet Σ. The elements of the system are finite automata, each of them having a single head able to read input characters independently of other automata. Each automaton has the freedom to move its head arbitrarily. However, the automata perform their work together, and therefore the movements of different heads are coordinated.

Computational power of the system described depends on the number of finite automata involved, on the size of single automata (measured by the number of states), and finally on how the automata cooperate. We consider two extreme situations:

Multihead automaton: the state of each automaton is visible to all automata. So the transition function of a single automaton depends on the input symbol currently seen and the states of all automata. The value of the transition function determines a new state of the automaton and the move of its read head.
Equivalently, one may assume that a multihead automaton consists of a single processing unit with finitely many internal states and a number of read heads, which are moved as determined by the transition function of the processing unit.

* initially this research was supported by Polish KBN grant No. 2 P301 034 07.

** a part of this research has been done when this author was with Heinz Nixdorf Institute and Department of Mathematics & Computer Science, University of Paderborn

Multiprocessor automaton: finite automata, called *processors* [1], are coordinated by a central processing unit. Each processor is set by the central processing unit to be either *active* or *frozen* at a given moment. During a step of the multiprocessor automaton, each active processor performs one step according to its *internal* transition function depending on its internal state and the input symbol seen. A frozen processor is idle and preserves its position and its internal state. Afterwards, the central processing unit inspects the states achieved by all processors and determines which processors are frozen and active for the next step. (The name "multiprocessor automata" is a little bit controversial, but we preserve it for historical reasons.) We say that a multiprocessor automaton M accepts a word w, if there exists a computation of M on w starting from the initial configuration that reaches a state in which every processor is frozen.

Note that the processors of a multiprocessor automaton do not see each other and so the states reached by a given processor depend exclusively on the input and not on the computation performed by the other processors. Coordination is limited to timing through which the central unit lets some processors proceed. Obviously, a multiprocessor automaton with k processors may be simulated by a multihead automaton with k heads. On the other hand, the restrictions given on multiprocessor automata are so severe that one may expect them to be much weaker than multihead automata. In this paper, we inspect this quite intuitive conjecture and prove that it is false to certain extent.

Notation Multihead automata with k reading heads are called *k-head automata*. Similarly, we talk about *k-processor automata*. If the heads (processors) cannot move to the left and start on the leftmost input symbol we talk about *one-way* automata. If there are no such restrictions, we call them *two-way* automata.

We use notation s-xy(k) to denote types of automata: s=1 (s=2) stands for one-way (two-way) automata, x=d (x=n) stands for deterministic (nondeterministic) automata, y=p (y=h) stands for multiprocessor (multihead) automata, k is the number of heads or processors, respectively. So, for instance, 1-dh(4) means *one-way deterministic 4-head automaton*. To denote the family of languages recognized by automata of type s-xy(k) we replace lower case letters by capital letters (e.g. 1-DP(k) is the family of languages recognized by one-way deterministic k-processor automata).

Previous results Multihead automata have been studied quite intensively for over thirty years. They have been considered, for instance, in complexity theory, due to the fact that many important classes are characterizable via multihead machines. For example, LOGSPACE= $\bigcup_k$ 2-DH(k). For some recent characterizations of this kind, see [3].

The structural properties of multihead automata are pretty well understood. For instance, it is generally known that $k+1$ heads can do more than k heads. Yao and Rivest [7] show this for one-way multihead automata by considering languages

$$L_m = \{w_1 * \ldots * w_{2m} | w_i \in \{0,1\}^* \text{ for } 1 \le i \le 2m, w_i = w_{2m-i+1} \text{ for } 1 \le i \le m\}.$$

Namely, they show that $L_{\binom{k}{2}} \in$ 1-DH(k) $\setminus$ 1-NH($k-1$). Monien [6] proves a hierarchy result for two-way multihead automata.

Regardless of long research, there are some open problems concerning structural properties of multihead automata. One such difficult question is about computational power of *sensing* (a multihead automaton is sensing, if each two of its heads may recognize whether they stand at the same input position). Some recent results on this topic may be found in [2]. Some questions still remain open.

Certain specific computational problems received much attention for multihead automata. Perhaps the most challenging one was whether one-way deterministic multihead automata can do string matching. This problem, stated by Galil and Seiferas, was open for several years and finally was solved by Jiang and Li [4]. We are not aware of any solution of this question for multihead sensing automata.

Multiprocessor automata have been introduced by Buda [1]. He shows that for some constant l, 1-DP(k) $\subsetneq$ 1-DP($k+l$). This can be improved to 1-DP(k) $\subsetneq$ 1-DP($k+1$) by considering the language $L_{\binom{k+1}{2}}$. Since $L_{\binom{k+1}{2}} \notin$ 1-NH(k) ([7]), also holds $L_{\binom{k+1}{2}} \notin$ 1-DP(k). On the other hand, the $k+1$-head deterministic automaton recognizing $L_{\binom{k+1}{2}}$ may be modified so that it becomes a $k+1$-processor automaton. No further results on relationship between multihead and multiprocessor automata has been known.

New results It is obvious that every multiprocessor automaton with k processors may be simulated by a multihead automaton with k heads. One may expect the inverse inclusion to be false. However, this is not the case for nondeterministic automata:

Theorem 1. *1-NP(k) = 1-NH(k) and 2-NP(k) = 2-NH(k) for every $k \in \mathbb{N}$.*

For the deterministic case, we show that the heads may be replaced by processors if we increase their number slightly:

Theorem 2. *1-DH(k) $\subseteq$ 1-DP($k+2$) for any $k \geq 1$.*

Theorem 3. *2-DH(k) $\subseteq$ 2-DP($k+2$) for any $k \geq 1$.*

Using Kolmogorov complexity analysis, we show the deepest result of this paper:

Theorem 4. *1-DP(2) $\subsetneq$ 1-DH(2).*

In Section 4, we discuss closure properties of the classes of languages recognized by multiprocessor automata.

2 Simulation Results

In Section 2, we prove Theorems 1, 2 and 3.

First, we introduce a more formal definition of multiprocessor automata. A 2-dp(k) automaton is a structure $M = (Q, \Sigma, g, h, v_0)$, where Q is a finite set of states, Σ is an input alphabet (with $\cent, \$ \notin \Sigma$), g is the *transition function*, $g : Q \times (\Sigma \cup \{\cent, \$\}) \longrightarrow Q \times \{-1, 0, 1\}$ (with the restriction that for $p, q \in Q$, $g(p, \cent) = (q, d)$ implies that $d \geq 0$ and $g(p, \$) = (q, d)$ implies that $d \leq 0$), h is the *switching function*, $h : \{1, 2, \ldots, k\} \times Q^k \longrightarrow \{0, 1\}$, and $v_0 \in Q^k$ is the k-tuple of initial states.

If processors $P_1, \ldots, P_k$ are in states $q_1, \ldots, q_k$, scan the symbols $a_1, \ldots, a_k$ on the input tape and $g(q_i, a_i) = (q'_i, d_i)$, then each processor P_i such that $h(i, q_1, \ldots, q_k) = 1$ must enter state q'_i and move its read head d_i squares to the right on the tape; if $h(i, q_1, \ldots, q_k) = 0$, then processor P_i is idle during this step. (For the sake of simplicity, we have assumed that each processor runs the same program. We do not lose generality, since every processor starts in its own initial state.)

We may modify the definition above as follows: If g maps $Q \times (\Sigma \cup \{\cent, \$\})$ into *subsets* of $Q \times \{-1,0,1\}$, then M is a two-way *nondeterministic* k-processor automaton. M is a *one-way* deterministic [nondeterministic] k-processor automaton, if g maps $Q \times (\Sigma \cup \{\cent, \$\})$ into $Q \times \{0,1\}$ [into the subsets of $Q \times \{0,1\}$].

A configuration C of M on an input $u \in \Sigma^*$ is a $2k$-tuple $(q_1, \ldots, q_k, j_1, \ldots, j_k)$, where $q_i \in Q$ denotes the state of processor P_i and $1 \leq j_i \leq |u| + 2$ denotes the position of the reading head of processor P_i, for $1 \leq i \leq k$.

2.1 Nondeterministic Automata

In this section, we prove Theorem 1 for two-way automata. (The proof for one-way automata is analogous.) Since obviously 2-NP(1) = 2-NH(1), we assume that $k \geq 2$.

Let M be a two-way nondeterministic k-head automaton and let Q, Σ, g be its set of states, the alphabet and the transition function, respectively. We construct a multiprocessor automaton $M' \in$ 2-np(k), $M' = (Q \cup P, \Sigma, g', h, v_0)$, where $P = Q \times (\Sigma \cup \{\cent, \$\}) \times Q \times \{-1,0,1\}$. M' simulates one step of M in two steps. Within the first step, M' guesses a candidate for a next step of M, and in the second step, M' verifies (by h) whether the guessed step is legitimate for M. If it is so, then M' makes the step transition as M. If not, then the processors of M' desynchronize, what prevents M' from freezing all processors. We set $v_0 = (q_0, \ldots, q_0)$, where $q_0 \in Q$ is the initial state of M.

We define g' and h as follows: For all $q, q' \in Q$, $a \in \Sigma \cup \{\cent, \$\}$, $d \in \{-1,0,1\}$, such that $d \neq -1$ if $a = \cent$ and $d \neq 1$ if $a = \$$, we define:

(a) $([q,a,q',d],0) \in g'(q,a)$,
(b) $(q',d) \in g'([q,a,q',d],a)$.

For all $q, q_1, \ldots, q_k \in Q$, $a_1, \ldots, a_k \in \Sigma \cup \{\cent, \$\}$, $d_1, \ldots, d_k \in \{-1,0,1\}$, $s_1, \ldots, s_k \in Q \cup P$, we define the switching function as follows:

(c) $h(i,q,q,\ldots,q) = 1$ for $i = 1,2,\ldots,k$, if $q \in Q$ is not an accepting state of M,
(d) $h(i,q,q,\ldots,q) = 0$ for $i = 1,2,\ldots,k$, if $q \in Q$ is an accepting state of M,
(e) if $q_1 = \cdots = q_k$ and $(q_1,d_1,\ldots,d_k) \in g(q,a_1,\ldots,a_k)$, then
$h(i,[q,a_1,q_1,d_1],\ldots,[q,a_k,q_k,d_k]) = 1$ for $i = 1,2,\ldots,k$, else
$h(1,[q,a_1,q_1,d_1],\ldots,[q,a_k,q_k,d_k]) = 1$ and
$h(i,[q,a_1,q_1,d_1],\ldots,[q,a_k,q_k,d_k]) = 0$ for $i = 2,3,\ldots,k$,
(f) $h(i,s_1,s_2,\ldots,s_k) = 1$ for $i = 1,2,\ldots,k$ if $s_j \in Q$ and $s_l \in P$ for some $1 \leq j,l \leq k$.

Suppose that M is in a configuration $(q,i_1,\ldots,i_k)$ on an input u, q is not an accepting state of M, M' is in a corresponding configuration $(q,\ldots,q,i_1,\ldots,i_k)$ on u, and a_j is the symbol scanned by the jth head of M (and also by the jth head of M') for $j = 1,2,\ldots,k$. By (a) and (c), the ith processor must enter a state $r_i = [q,a_i,q_i,d_i]$ with $q_i \in Q$, $d_i \in \{-1,0,1\}$, for $i = 1,2,\ldots,k$.

Let $q_1 = \cdots = q_k$ and $(q_1,d_1,\ldots,d_k) \in g(q,a_1,\ldots,a_k)$, i.e. the step guessed is a possible next step of M. By (e) and (b), M enters the configuration $(q_1, i_1+d_1, \ldots, i_k+d_k)$ and M' enters the corresponding configuration $(q_1,\ldots,q_1,i_1+d_1,\ldots,i_k+d_k)$. It follows that if there is a computation of M on u leading from the initial configuration C_0 to an accepting configuration C_t, then there is a corresponding computation of M' on u leading from the corresponding initial configuration C'_0 to the corresponding configuration C'_t in which all processors of M' become frozen and thereby M' accepts (see (d)).

Let $q_j \neq q_l$ for some $1 \leq j,l \leq k$ or $q_1 = \cdots = q_k$ and $(q_1,d_1,\ldots,d_k) \notin g(q,a_1,\ldots,a_k)$, i.e. the guess of a step is not correct. By (e), $h(1,r_1,\ldots,r_k) = 1$ and $h(i,r_1,\ldots,r_k) = 0$ for all $i \geq 2$. By (b), the first processor enters the state $q_1 \in Q$ but the ith processor, for $i \geq 2$, remains in the state $r_i \in P$. Hence, by (f), at any time during the rest of the computation, either the first processor is in some state of Q and the other processors are in some states of P, or vice versa.

This completes the proof that 2-NH(k) $\subseteq$ 2-NP(k). The opposite inclusion is obvious.

2.2 One-way Deterministic Automata

In this section, we prove Theorem 2. Suppose that M is 1-dh(k) automaton with alphabet $\Sigma = \{a_1,\ldots,a_l\}$ and the set of states $Q_M = \{q_1,\ldots,q_s\}$ (q_1 is the initial state). W.l.o.g. we may assume that during each step of M at least one of its heads moves.

We construct a 1-dp($k+2$) automaton M', which recognizes the same language as M. The first k processors of M', denoted by $P_1,\ldots P_k$, correspond to the heads of M. The remaining processors, denoted by R_1,R_2, store the current state of M and coordinate the process of simulation. Define the set of states of M' as $Q' = Q_P \cup Q_R$, where

$$Q_P = \{q_0\} \cup (\Sigma \times \{0,1,2\}) \quad \text{and} \quad Q_R = Q \cup \{q' \mid q \in Q\}$$

In the initial configuration, processors R_1,R_2 are in state q_1 and $P_1,\ldots,P_k$ are in state q_0. Then the processors work as follows:

(a) processor R_1 changes its states in a cycle $q_1 \to q_2 \to q_3 \to \ldots \to q_s \to q'_1 \to \ldots \to q'_s \to q_1$, without moving on input word,
(b) processor R_2 changes its states in a cycle $q_1 \to q_2 \to \ldots \to q_s \to q_1$, without moving on input word,
(c) processors $P_1,\ldots P_k$ work according to the transitions:
$$g(q_0,x) = ([x,0],0), \qquad g([x,0],x) = ([x,1],1)$$
$$g([x,1],y) = ([x,2],0), \quad g([x,2],y) = ([y,0],0), \quad \forall_{x\in\Sigma, y\in\Sigma\cup\{\$\}}, \text{ and}$$
$$g([\$,0],\$) = ([\$,0],0)$$
Thus each P_i stores every scanned letter for its three consecutive steps.

Let w be an input for M, and let $w(i)$ denote the ith letter of w. Our simulation runs in stages that correspond to steps of M. If after t steps M reaches a configuration $(q,j_1,\ldots,j_k)$ (j_i's denote heads positions), then the stage t ends in the configuration $([w(j_1),0],\ldots,[w(j_k),0],q,q,j_1,\ldots,j_k,1,1)$, in which the heads of processors $P_1,\ldots,P_k$ scan the same cells as the corresponding heads of M and store the letters read in their states.

To perform such simulation we use the following switching function: To start the first stage, the processors $P_1,\ldots,P_k$ of M' have to put the first letter of w into their states. Thus we set

$$h(P_i,q_0,\ldots,q_0,q_1,q_1) = 1, \quad \text{for } i = 1,\ldots k,$$

$$h(R_i,q_0,\ldots,q_0,q_1,q_1) = 0, \quad \text{for } i = 1,2.$$

For every transition $g(q_u,b_1,\ldots,b_k) = (q_v,d_1,\ldots,d_k)$ of M, we assign the value 1 to h in the following situations (otherwise, h has value 0):

- $\forall_{1 \leq j \leq s}\ h(R_1, [b_1, 0], \ldots [b_k, 0], q_j, q_u) = 1$
  $\forall_{1 \leq j < v}\ h(R_1, [b_1, 0] \ldots [b_k, 0], q'_j, q_u) = 1$
  Together with (a), this implies that R_1 enters state q'_v, which is a "copy" of the new state of M. Note that R_2 still "stores" q_u, the previous state of M.
- $\forall_{1 \geq i \geq k}\ h(P_i, [b_1, 0] \ldots [b_k, 0], q'_v, q_u) = 1 \iff d_i = 1$
  This assures that only these processors will move, which correspond to the heads moving right during this step. We shall call them *running processors*. By (c), all running processors enter states of the form $[*, 1]$, where the wildcard "*" stands for an arbitrary input letter.
- The information on the previous state of M is no longer needed, so R_2 changes its state for q_v:

$$\forall_{l=1,..s; l \neq v} \forall_{x_1,\ldots,x_k \in Q_P} \text{ if } \exists_{1 \leq i \leq k}\, x_i = [*, 1], \text{ then } h(R_2, x_1, \ldots, x_k, q'_v, q_l) = 1.$$

- When the above process ends, all running processors change the second coordinate of their states for 2:

$$\forall_{i=1,\ldots k;\, x_1,\ldots x_k \in Q_P}\ x_i = [*, 1] \Rightarrow h(P_i, x_1, \ldots, x_k, q'_v, q_v) = 1.$$

- At this moment, there is a state of the form $[*, 2]$. This is a signal to perform a process of removing the apostrophe from the state of R_1:

$$\forall_{j=1,\ldots,s}\ h(R_1, x_1, \ldots, x_k, q'_j, q_r) = 1 \quad \text{if } x_i = [*, 2] \text{ for some } i = 1, \ldots, k,$$

$$\forall_{j<r}\ h(R_1, x_1, \ldots, x_k, q_j, q_r) = 1 \quad \text{if } x_i = [*, 2] \text{ for some } i = 1, \ldots, k.$$

- To finish the stage, the running processors have to put new letters into their states. This is forced by (c) and by the condition that $h(P_i, x_1, \ldots, x_k, q_r, q_r) = 1$ for $x_i = [*, 2]$.

It is easy to see that the automaton M' stops in the same state as M for every input word (more precisely, state of processor R_1 will be the same as the state of M). It remains to guarantee that the automaton M' enters an infinite loop whenever M stops in a rejecting state. We omit the details.

2.3 Two-way Deterministic Automata

In this section, we discuss main ideas of the proof of Theorem 3. Now our task is more complicated than in the one-way case, since the heads get information from the finite control in which direction they should move. This information cannot be used to control the movements of processors, since their moves are predefined.

As before, the simulating machine has k processors $P_1, \ldots, P_k$ which correspond to the heads of the simulated automaton M and two auxiliary processors R_1 and R_2. Each step of automaton M is simulated in one stage consisting of two phases. At the beginning of the first phase, each P_i stores (q, a_i), that is, the current state and the symbol seen by the corresponding head of M. Then:

Phase 1: processor R_1, with the set of states $Q \times \Sigma^k$, changes its state to $(q, a_1, \ldots, a_k)$.

Phase 2: all processors P_i update their positions. In this process, we use processor R_2 that traverse the input word twice making $2n$ moves. Simultaneously, the central processing unit activates processors P_i appropriately, so that each processor corresponding to the left moving head performs $2n-1$ moves. First it goes to the right until endmarker, then back to the left endmarker and again to the right, so after $2n-1$ moves it stops at the cell left to the initial one. In a similar way, the processors corresponding to non moving heads can perform $2n$ moves. This can be necessary, since all processors have to be tuned to store the new state of M.

Note that R_1 is used exclusively for storing information used by transition function of M. Processor R_2 is used to measure the distance $2n$ and to coordinate the phases.

3 Separation for Two-Head Automata

In this section, we prove Theorem 4. The language which separates classes 1-DP(2) and 1-DH(2) is the language L_P defined below.

Definition 5. Let $\# \notin \Sigma$ and $z(i)$ denote the ith symbol of word z. Then $L_P = \{x\#y: \ x,y \in \Sigma^*, \ |x| = |y|, \ p(x,y) = 1\}$, where

$$p(x,y) = \begin{cases} 1, & \text{when } |\{i: x(i) \neq y(i)\}| \text{ is odd,} \\ 0, & \text{when } |\{i: x(i) \neq y(i)\}| \text{ is even.} \end{cases}$$

It is easy to construct a 1-dh(2) automaton which recognizes L_P. The rest of this section presents a proof of the following lemma which immediately implies Theorem 4.

Lemma 6. *$L_P \notin$ 1-DP(2) for every alphabet Σ of size greater than two.*

Surprisingly, if $|\Sigma| = 2$, then $L_P \in$ 1-DP(2). Indeed, for any $v \in \{0,1\}^*$ define $ones(v) = |\{i: \ v_i = 1\}|$. It is easy to see that $p(x,y) = 1$ for $x,y \in \{0,1\}^n$ if and only if the numbers $ones(x)$ and $ones(y)$ have different parities. So, to recognize L_P we have only to check that x and y have equal length and different parities of the number of ones.

Let us assume that Lemma 6 is false and the language L_P is recognized by a 1-dp(2) automaton $M = (Q, \Sigma \cup \{\#\}, g, h, v_0)$, $q = |Q|$, $|\Sigma| = 3$. W.l.o.g. we may assume that transition function g enables both processors to loop on every input word at the right endmarker \$.

Let the processors of M be denoted by P_1 and P_2, where P_1 is the processor which first reaches symbol #. An *Border Event* of the automaton M on word $x\#y$ is the first configuration of M in which processor P_1 is on symbol #.

Definition 7 (Configuration Difference). For any configuration $C = (q_1, q_2, j_1 + |x| + 1, j_2)$ $(j_1, j_2 > 0)$ of automaton M on word $x\#y$, we define *configuration difference* $R(C)$ as:

- undefined, if both processors are on y,
- $-k$, where k is the number of steps that processor P_1 has to make in order to reach position $|x| + 1 + j_2$, if $j_1 \leq j_2$,
- the number of steps that processor P_2 has to make in order to reach position j_1, if $j_2 < j_1$.

Definition 8 (Computation map). A *computation map* of a finite deterministic one-way automaton A over words $w_1, w_2, \ldots, w_k$ is a sequence of states $(q_0, q_1, \ldots, q_k)$ such that automaton A, when started in state q_0, reaches state q_i immediately after reading w_i on input word $= w_1 w_2 \ldots w_k$.

Our proof exploits the notion of Kolmogorov complexity (cf. [5]). Recall that Kolmogorov complexity of a word x (denoted by $K(x)$), is the length of the shortest program that prints x. The conditional Kolmogorov complexity of x with respect to y, $K(x|y)$, is the length of the shortest program which prints x using information y.

The main idea of the proof is to show that there exists a set of words

$$\{w''x_1x_2\ldots x_l\#w''b^l \ : \ x_i \in \{a_1,a_2\},\ |b| = |a_1| = |a_2| = n \text{ and } p(a_1,b) \neq p(a_2,b)\}$$

for which processors of M cannot keep track of the parity of the number of copies a_1 and a_2. However, this is indispensable to decide if the input word belongs to L_P. Using Kolmogorov complexity arguments and appropriate a_1, a_2, we show that automaton M has to compare the corresponding words before and after symbol # almost synchronously, i.e., configuration difference cannot be too large. On the other hand, we show that the only possibility to "remember" the present value of parity of number of differences is to increase or decrease configuration difference. For this reason, the configuration difference may grow too much.

Applying techniques used to prove Moving Lemma from [4], one may guarantee that before Border Event processor P_2 remains almost stationary for all input words considered.

Lemma 9. *There exists a word w, a state p and a position $k < |w|$, such that for every $v \in \Sigma^*$, during computation on the word $wv\#$, processor P_2 is in state p and position k at the Border Event.*

Definition 10. Let $[q_1,q_2,n]_A$ or shortly $[q_1,q_2,n]$ be the set of words of length n for which deterministic one-way finite automaton A starting computation at state q_1 finishes at state q_2.

We can construct a deterministic one-way finite automaton F_M associated with M which simulates work of both processors on the input word (disregarding the switching function). The set of states of F_M is Q^2; the initial state of F_M is the vector v_0. The head of automaton F_M moves right at every step, the state of F_M at a given position is the pair of states of automaton M reached by the processors while entering this position.

Using counting arguments we restrict the set of inputs considered:

Lemma 11. *There is a constant α such that for any $n \in \{\alpha \cdot i | i \in \mathbb{N}\}$, there exists a set of words*

$$W_n = \{w''x_1x_2\ldots x_l\#w''y_1y_2\ldots y_l,\ l \in \mathbb{N}\}$$

satisfying the following conditions:

1. *There exist a state p and a position $k < |w''|$ such that at the Border Event processor P_2 is in state p at position k regardless of $x_1x_2\ldots x_l$.*
2. *$|w''| \leq n/3$ and $\forall_{i=1,2,\ldots l}\ |x_i| = |y_i| = n$.*
3. *For every word $w''x_1x_2\ldots x_l\#w''y_1y_2\ldots y_l \in W_n$ the computation map of automaton F_M on words $w'',x_1,x_2,\ldots,x_l,\#,w'',y_1,y_2,\ldots,y_l$ has the form $v_0s^{l+1}v_0't^{l+1}$ for some $v_0',s,t \in Q^2$. So, $x_i \in [s,s,n]_{F_M}$ and $y_i \in [t,t,n]_{F_M}$ for every $i \in \{1,\ldots l\}$.*
4. *For some constant e independent of n, we have $|X_n| \geq \frac{3^n}{e}$ and $|Y_n| \geq \frac{3^n}{e}$, where $X_n = [s,s,n]_{F_M}$ and $Y_n = [t,t,n]_{F_M}$.*

The construction of W_n ensures that both processors of automaton M have the same computation map on words $w'',x_1,x_2,\ldots,x_l,\#,w'',y_1,y_2,\ldots,y_l$ for every word $w''x_1x_2\ldots x_l\#w''y_1y_2\ldots y_l$ from W_n. In the next lemma, we show that $W_n \cap L_P \neq \emptyset$ and $W_n \backslash L_P \neq \emptyset$. An important step in this direction is the following proposition:

Proposition 12. *For any $n \in \mathbb{N}$, alphabet Σ of size greater than two and words $x \neq y \in \Sigma^n$, there exist words $z,v \in \Sigma^n$ such that $p(x,z) = p(y,z)$ and $p(x,v) \neq p(y,v)$. So, for every word $x \in \Sigma^n$, the set $\{y : p(x,y) = 0\}$ uniquely identifies x.*

Proof. Let $x \neq y$ be arbitrary words of length n. Let $x(i) \neq y(i)$, $c \in \Sigma \setminus \{x(i),y(i)\}$. Take an arbitrary $z \in \Sigma^n$. Assume that $p(x,z) = p(y,z)$ (the case $p(x,z) \neq p(y,z)$) is analogous). Then $p(x,v) \neq p(y,v)$ for $v = z(1)\ldots z(i-1)c\, z(i+1)\ldots z(n)$ if $z(i) = x(i)$ or $z(i) = y(i)$, and $v = z(1)\ldots z(i-1)x(i)z(i+1)\ldots z(n)$, if $z(i) = c$. □

Lemma 13. *For infinitely many n and arbitrary sets W_n, X_n, Y_n defined as in Lemma 11, there exist words a_1, $a_2 \in X_n$ and $b \in Y_n$ such that $K(a_i|b) \geq n - O(\log n)$, $K(b|a_i) \geq n - O(\log n)$ for $i = 1,2$ and $p(a_1,b) \neq p(a_2,b)$.*

Proof. Let d be constant, $d \gg q$, $\alpha | d$. Using simple counting arguments, we can show that for some constants c and c_1 and n large enough, $d|n$, there exist $b \in Y_n$ such that the set $X'_{b,c_1} = \{x : x \in X_n \text{ and } K(x|b) \geq n - c_1 \log n,\ K(b|x) \geq n - c_1 \log n\}$ has size at least $\frac{3^n}{c}$. It remains to show that for some b satisfying these conditions, there are words $a_1, a_2 \in X'_{b,c_1}$ such that $p(a_1,b) \neq p(a_2,b)$. Assume conversely that this is false:

$$\forall_{c,c_1>0} \exists_{n_0} \forall_{n>n_0} \forall_{b \in Y_n} \forall_{a_1,a_2 \in X'_{b,c_1}}\ |X'_{b,c_1}| \geq 3^n/c \Rightarrow p(a_1,b) = p(a_2,b) \qquad (1)$$

We show that in this case $|X'_{b,c_1}| = o(3^n)$ for every $b \in Y_n$, contradicting our previous observation. Take any $b \in Y_n$, $c, c_1 > 0$ for which $|X'_{b,c_1}| \geq 3^n/c$. Divide b into blocks of length d, $b = b_1 b_2 \ldots b_{n/d}$. Let $q_0 q_1 \ldots q_{n/d}$ be the computation map of automaton F_M on $b_1, b_2, \ldots, b_{n/d}$, where q_0 is the pair of states in which processors P_1 and P_2 start computation on b (on words from W_n). Let B_i be the set of words of length d for which computation beginning in q_i finishes in q_{i+1}, $X'_{b,c_1,i} = \{w : \exists_{x \in X'_{b,c_1}} x[(i-1)d+1, id] = w\}$, where $x[e,f]$ denotes the word $x(e)x(e+1)\ldots x(f)$ (recall that $x(k)$ is the kth symbol of x).

Due to incompressibility of b, most sets B_i have at least two elements. Indeed, otherwise we could encode b by the sequence $q_0 q_1 \ldots q_{n/d}$, automaton M, and those parts of b that correspond to all B_i with $|B_i| \geq 2$. This would yield a word of length at most $n/d \cdot \log q + n/2 + O(1)$.

We show that $|X'_{b,c_1,i}| \leq 3^d - 1$, if $|B_i| \geq 2$. (Hence $|X'_{b,c_1}| \leq (3^d)^{n/2d}(3^d - 1)^{n/2d} = o(3^n)$ for n large enough, what finishes the proof.) Take B_i such that $|B_i| \geq 2$, $b_i, b'_i \in B_i$ ($b_i \neq b'_i$). Let b' be equal b with block b_i replaced by b'_i, so $b' \in Y_n$. According to (1), for some γ, $p(b,x) = p(b,y) = \gamma$ for any $x, y \in X'_{b,c_1}$. Since b and b' are different only on a part of a constant length, it can be shown using Kolmogorov complexity that for some c'_1 independent of n holds: $X'_{b,c_1} \subseteq X'_{b',c'_1}$. So according to (1), $p(b',x) = p(b',y) = \gamma'$, for every $x, y \in X'_{b,c_1}$ and some fixed γ'. Assume that $\gamma = \gamma'$ (for $\gamma \neq \gamma'$ the proof is analogous). Then $p(b_i, x_i) = p(b'_i, x_i)$ for any $x_i \in X'_{b,c_1,i}$, since b and b' differ only on the ith block. By Proposition 12, this implies that $X'_{b,c_1,i}$ does not contain all words of length d, i.e. $|X'_{b,c_1,i}| \leq 3^d - 1$. □

Assume that words a_1, a_2 and b are given by Lemma 13. For every $n \in \mathbb{N}$, let

$$V_n = \{w''x_1x_2\ldots x_l\#w''b^l \in W_n \ : \ x_i \in \{a_1,a_2\} \text{ for } i = 1,\ldots l\}.$$

Let C_0 be a configuration of M at Border Event for an input in V_n. By C_i we denote the first configuration in which P_2 is observing x_i and P_1 is observing the ith copy of b. If such an event does not occur at all, by C_i we mean the last configuration in which processor P_1 is observing the ith copy of b (when the configuration difference is positive) or the last configuration in which P_2 is observing x_i (when the configuration difference is negative).

We show that a big configuration difference on the words from V_n cannot occur:

Lemma 14 (Difference Lemma). *Assume that for some n large enough, $l = O(n)$ and word $w = w''x_1x_2\ldots x_l\#w''b^l \in V_n \cap L_P$, there exists a configuration C_i of automaton M with $|R(C_i)| > qn$. Then automaton M does not recognize L_P.*

Proof. By properties of W_n, we get the same value of $R(C_i)$ for words $w''x_1x_2\ldots x_l\#w''b^l$ and $w''x_1x_2\ldots x_i\#w''b^i$. So, we may examine computation of automaton M on input word $w''x_1x_2\ldots x_i\#w''b^i$. Consider two possibilities:
Case 1: $R(C_i) < 0$. In this case, processor P_1 is on the left side of the last copy of b, when P_2 finishes scanning x_i. Let C be a configuration in which processor P_1 reaches the first symbol of the last copy of b. The configuration C uniquely identifies the word $x_i \in \{a_1,a_2\}$. Indeed, if we replace the last copy of b by any word, then automaton M will have to decide if this word differs on even or odd number of positions from x_i. By Proposition 12, this uniquely identifies x_i. So if we know b, we can encode x_i using w'', configuration C, number i and automaton M which gives $n/3 + K(C) + K(M) + K(i) \leq n/3 + O(\log n)$ length string for n large enough. This contradicts the assumption that $K(x_i|b) \geq n - O(\log n)$.
Case 2: $R(C_i) > 0$. So P_1 reaches the right endmarker \$, while P_2 has not read x_i yet. When P_1 scans x_i, processor P_2 does not move (Lemma 9). Similarly, during scanning x_i by P_2, processor P_1 does not move (processor P_1 can only loop on \$). So, behavior of automaton M on x_i can be described by behavior of some deterministic one-way finite automaton F'. Using Pumping Lemma for finite automata, we can "pump" the word x_i so that automaton M does not distinguish words in L_P and their "pumped" versions, which do not belong to L_P. □

We show now that in some situations the configuration difference measured at $C_1, C_2, \ldots$ has to change strictly monotonically.

Lemma 15 (Difference Growth Lemma). *For infinitely many $n \in \mathbb{N}$, $l = O(n)$, there exists a word $w = w''x_1x_2\ldots x_l\#w''b^l$ in $V_n \cap L_P$ such that $|R(C_i)| > qn$ for some configuration C_i.*

Proof. Without loss of generality assume that $p(a_1,b) = 1$. We construct a word w in the following way: we put $x_1 = a_1$, $x_2 = a_1, \ldots, x_i = a_1$ until $R(C_i) = R(C_{i+1})$ or $|R(C_i)| > qn$. This situation eventually happens, as shown by the following proposition:

Proposition 16. *Let* $x_j = x_{j+1} = x_{j+2} = x$. *If* $R(C_j) \geq R(C_{j+1})$, *then* $R(C_{j+1}) \geq R(C_{j+2})$. *If* $R(C_j) \leq R(C_{j+1})$, *then* $R(C_{j+1}) \leq R(C_{j+2})$.

Proof of Proposition 16. Assume that during computation on w processor P_1 (P_2) starts computation on b (x) in state t_0 (s_0), and $t_0, t_1, \ldots, t_m$ ($s_0, s_1, \ldots, s_p$) is the sequence of states reached by P_1 (P_2) during computation on b (x). So $t_m = t_1$ and $s_p = s_1$, since $b \in [t,t,n]$ and $x \in [s,s,n]$.

We prove the first claim of the proposition (the proof of the second part is analogous). We describe a history of a computation of automaton M between configurations C_j and C_{j+1} using a geometrical representation. Every configuration is described as a point with integer coordinates on the plane. A point with coordinates (k_1,k_2) represents the configuration in which processor P_1 made k_1 steps on the ith copy of b and processor P_2 made k_2 steps on $x_i = x$, if $k_1 \leq m$ and $k_2 \leq p$. Value $k_1 > m$ ($k_2 > p$) means that processor P_1 (P_2) has already reached the end of the current copy of b (x_{i+1}) and afterwards made $k_1 - m$ ($k_2 - p$) steps.

The history of computation between configurations C_j and C_{j+1} is a broken line, denoted by L_j, consisting of segments connecting points describing consecutive configurations of M. The start point of L_j is (k_1,k_2) with $k_1 = 0$ or $k_2 = 0$ and endpoint (k'_1,k'_2) with $k'_1 = m$ or $k'_2 = p$. Assume that $R(C_{j+1}) \geq R(C_j)$. Consider two cases:
Case 1: $R(C_{j+1}) = R(C_j)$. Then $R(C_{j+2}) = R(C_{j+1})$, since M is deterministic.
Case 2: $R(C_{j+1}) > R(C_j)$. Suppose that $R(C_{j+2}) < R(C_{j+1})$. This implies that L_j and L_{j+1} cross. By definition of L_k, if (a,b) and (a',b') are consecutive points on L_k corresponding to consecutive configurations, then $a' = a+1$ or $b' = b+1$. So, the common point of L_j and L_{j+1} has integer coordinates and denotes some configuration. Starting from this point, broken lines L_j and L_{j+1} are identical, since M is deterministic. So $R(C_{j+2}) = R(C_{j+1})$. (Proposition 16) □

Proposition 16 implies that configuration difference measured at $C_1, C_2, \ldots$ changes monotonically. So either $R(C_i) = R(C_{i+1})$ or $|R(C_i)| > qn$ will occur for some $2qn > i > 0$. If $|R(C_i)| > qn$, then the proof of Lemma 15 is finished. In the case $R(C_i) = R(C_{i+1})$, we assign $x_{i+1} = a_2, x_{i+2} = a_2, \ldots$. By Proposition 16, the value of configuration difference changes monotonically starting from $R(C_i)$. We claim that it changes strictly monotonically (which gives $|R(C_l)| \geq qn$, for some $l \leq 4qn$). If not, then there exists $4qn \geq l > i$ such that $R(C_l) = R(C_{l+1})$. Then automaton M accepts or rejects both words $w''a_1^i a_2^{l-i+1} \# w'' b^{l+1}$ and $w'' a_1^{i+1} a_2^{l-i} \# w'' b^{l+1}$. But exactly one of these words is in L_P, contrary to the assumption that M recognizes L_P. □

Applying Difference Growth Lemma we know that for n large enough, $l = O(n)$ and some word w from $V_n \cap L_P$, automaton M reaches a configuration C with $|R(C)| \geq qn$ during a computation on w. So, by Difference Lemma, automaton M does not recognize the language L_P. This completes the proof of Lemma 6 and thereby of Theorem 4.

4 Closure Properties

Buda [1] shows that the families of languages recognized by the multiprocessor finite automata are closed under union and intersection. By equivalence of multihead- and multiprocessor automata, shown by Theorems 1, 2 and 3, and known results on multihead automata, one may show the following properties:

1. $\bigcup_{k=1}^{\infty}$ 2-NP(k) and $\bigcup_{k=1}^{\infty}$ 2-DP(k) are closed under complement.
2. $\bigcup_{k=1}^{\infty}$ 1-NP(k) is not closed under complement.

We prove yet another property of this kind:

Theorem 17. *1-DP(k) is closed under complement, for $k > 2$.*

Proof. Let M be a 1-dp(k) automaton. We construct a 1-dp(k) automaton M' recognizing the complement of the language L accepted by M. For this purpose, we change the program of processors so that every step of M is simulated in five phases. To this end we extend the set of states to $Q \cup (Q \times \Sigma \times \{0,1,2,3,4\})$. Every transition $g(q,a) = (q',d)$ after which a processor sees a cell containing b is now replaced by a sequence of transitions that forces the processor to enter consecutively the states $[q,a,0]$, $[q,a,1]$, $[q,a,2]$, $[q,a,3]$, $[q,a,4]$, $[q',b,0]$, called later *switching sequence*.

W.l.o.g. we may assume that g is defined on the whole domain. To ensure that M' halts for every word w from $\bar{L}$, we have to set the switching function to 0 for all configurations being a part of an infinite loop of M. Since the heads do not move during such loops, these configurations may be detected easily. On the other hand, we must guarantee that M' loops infinitely for $w \in L$. For this purpose, we apply technique of desynchronization. We say that some processor P precedes processor P' by k phases, if P and P' are in states $[q,a,i]$, $[s,b,j]$, respectively, and $k = (i-j) \bmod 4$. We change the switching function so that configuration in which processor P_3 precedes by two phases processors P_1 and P_2 causes M' to fall into an infinite loop.

When we start simulating a step of M, all processors of M' have states of the form $[*,*,0]$. Then the processors that are active at this step of M go simultaneously through their switching sequences. However, in such a way we may fall unwillingly into an infinite loop, when, for example, processor P_3 makes the next step (of M) and processors P_1 and P_2 are frozen. We allude this problem by letting processor P_1 start and finish simulation of a step of M in a state of the form $[*,*,1]$. In any configuration, in which M halts, automaton M' synchronizes P_1 and P_2 and lets P_3 perform three phases. □

Open problems By an involved analysis, we have shown that 1-dp(2) automata are weaker than 1-dh(2) automata. It is a challenging problem to show such a separation for a number of heads bigger than 2. However, it is not sure that the answer is affirmative for every k. At the moment, we are unaware of any separation result of this kind for two-way automata, for $k > 1$.

References

1. A.O. Buda, *Multiprocessor automata*, IPL 25 (1987), 257-161.
2. P. Ďuriš, Z. Galil, *Sensing versus nonsensing automata*, in Proc. ICALP'95, LNCS 944, Springer-Verlag 1995, pp. 455-463.
3. M. Holzer, Multi-head finite automata: data-independent *versus* data-dependent computations, in Proc. MFCS'97, LNCS 1295, Springer-Verlag 1995, pp. 299-308.
4. T. Jiang, M. Li, *k one-way heads cannot do string-matching*, in Proc. STOC '93, pp. 62–70.
5. M. Li, P. Vitanyi, *An Introduction to Kolmogorov Complexity and its Applications*, Springer-Verlag 1993.
6. B. Monien, *Two-way multihead automata over a one-letter alphabet*, R.A.I.R.O. Informatique théorique 14 (1980), 67-82.
7. A.C. Yao, R.L. Rivest, $k+1$ *heads are better than* k, JACM 25 (1978), 337-340.

A Simple Solution to Type Specialization

Olivier Danvy

BRICS
Department of Computer Science
University of Aarhus
Building 540, Ny Munkegade, DK-8000 Aarhus C, Denmark
E-mail: danvy@brics.dk
Home page: http://www.brics.dk/~danvy

Abstract. Partial evaluation specializes terms, but traditionally this specialization does not apply to the type of these terms. As a result, specializing, e.g., an interpreter written in a typed language, which requires a "universal" type to encode expressible values, yields residual programs with type tags all over. Neil Jones has stated that getting rid of these type tags was an open problem, despite possible solutions such as Torben Mogensen's "constructor specialization." To solve this problem, John Hughes has proposed a new paradigm for partial evaluation, "Type Specialization," based on type inference instead of being based on symbolic interpretation. Type Specialization is very elegant in principle but it also appears non-trivial in practice.
Stating the problem in terms of types instead of in terms of type encodings suggests a very simple type-directed solution, namely, to use a projection from the universal type to the specific type of the residual program. Standard partial evaluation then yields a residual program without type tags, simply and efficiently.

1 The Problem

1.1 An example

Say that we need to write an evaluator in a typed language, such in Figure 1. To this end we use a "universal" data type encoding all the expressible values. As witnessed by the type of the evaluator, evaluating an expression yields a value of the universal type.

```
- eval (LAM ("x", ADD (VAR "x", LIT 1))) Env.init;
val it = FUN fn : univ
-
```

We can visualize the text of this universal value by using *partial evaluation* [3, 10], i.e., by specializing the evaluator of Figure 1 with respect to the expression above. In that, specializing an interpreter with respect to a program provides

```
datatype exp = LIT of int
             | VAR of string
             | LAM of string * exp
             | APP of exp * exp
             | ADD of exp * exp

datatype univ = INT of int
              | FUN of univ -> univ

exception TypeError

(* eval : exp -> univ Env.env -> univ *)
fun eval (LIT i) env
    = INT i
  | eval (VAR x) env
    = Env.lookup (x, env)
  | eval (LAM (x, e)) env
    = FUN (fn v => eval e (Env.extend (x, v, env)))
  | eval (APP (e0, e1)) env
    = (case (eval e0 env) of
           (FUN f) => f (eval e1 env)
         | _ => raise TypeError)
  | eval (ADD (e1, e2)) env
    = (case (eval e1 env, eval e2 env) of
           (INT i1, INT i2) => INT (i1 + i2)
         | _ => raise TypeError)

signature ENV
= sig
    type 'a env
    exception UndeclaredIdentifier
    val extend : string * 'a * 'a env -> 'a env
    val init : 'a env
    val lookup : string * 'a env -> 'a
  end
```

Fig. 1. An example evaluator in Standard ML

a mechanized solution to the traditional exercise in denotational semantics of exhibiting the denotation of a program [13, Exercises 1 and 2, Chapter 5].

A simple partial evaluator would perform the recursive descent and the environment management of the evaluator, and yield a residual term such as the following one.

```
FUN (fn v => (case (v, INT 1) of
                  (INT i1, INT i2) => INT (i1 + i2)
                | _ => raise TypeError))
```

A slightly more enterprising partial evaluator would propagate the constant 1 and fold the corresponding computation, essentially yielding the following residual term.

```
FUN (fn (INT i1) => INT (i1 + 1)
       | _ => raise TypeError)
```

In both cases, the residual program is cluttered with the type tags `FUN` and `INT`.

1.2 The problem

Obtaining a residual program without type tags by specializing an interpreter expressed in a typed language has been stated as an open problem for about ten years now [8, 9]. This problem has become acute with the advent of partial evaluators for typed languages, such as SML-Mix [2].

We note that this problem does not occur for *command* interpreters, which essentially have the functionality `cmd -> sto -> sto`. No matter which command such an interpreter is specialized with respect to, the result is of type `sto`.

The problem only arises for *expression* interpreters, whose codomain *depends* on their domain. Indeed, the type of an expressible value depends on the type of the corresponding source expression.

2 A Sophisticated Solution: "Type Specialization"

Partial evaluation is traditionally performed by non-standard interpretation [3, 10]: during specialization, part of the source term is interpreted, and the rest is reconstructed, yielding a residual term.

Recently, John Hughes has proposed to shift perspective and to perform partial evaluation by non-standard type inference instead of by non-standard interpretation [6]. In doing so, he has achieved both term and type specialization. His new approach has been favorably met in the functional-programming community [7].

The resulting type specialization is very elegant in principle but so far it appears non-trivial in practice. Like all other partial evaluators in their infancy, in its current state, it requires expert source annotations to work. Correspondingly, no efficient implementations seem to exist yet, despite recent progress [14].

3 A Simpler Solution: Projecting from the Universal Type

Let us go back to the example of Section 1.1. There is an obvious embedding/projection between the native types of ML and the universal type `univ`. Noting ε for the embedding and π for the projection, it reads as follows.

$$
\begin{cases}
\varepsilon_{\text{int}}\, i = \texttt{INT}\ i \\
\varepsilon_{t_1 \to t_2}\, f = \texttt{FUN}\ \lambda v.\varepsilon_{t_2}\, (f\, (\pi_{t_1}\, v)) \\
\\
\pi_{\text{int}}\, (\texttt{INT}\ i) = i \\
\pi_{t_1 \to t_2}\, (\texttt{FUN}\ f) = \lambda v.\pi_{t_2}\, (f\, (\varepsilon_{t_1}\, v))
\end{cases}
$$

Thus equipped, we can project the expressible value of Section 1.1 from the universal type to the type of the original expression, i.e., `int -> int`. In doing so, we obtain

1. a value of type `int -> int` by evaluation; and
2. a residual program without type tags by partial evaluation, that reads:

```
fn v => v + 1
```

Our simple solution thus amounts to composing the projection with the interpreter prior to partial evaluation. In effect, the projection specializes the type, and in practice, the partial evaluator specializes the term, including its projection.

4 A Case Study

We have paired the embedding/projection described above with type-directed partial evaluation [4], both in Scheme and in ML. Here is a typical measure in Standard ML of New Jersey, Version 0.93, on a 150Mhz Pentium running Linux. The ML measures are more significant than the Scheme measures because they do not depend on our particular tagged representation of typed values. For lack of an interactive timer, we are not able to report similar measures in Caml [1].

For this measure, we have extended the interpreter of Figure 1 to handle a more substantial language including booleans, conditional expressions, recursive functions, and extra numerical operations.

We repeated the following computations 1000 times. The resulting numbers should thus be divided by 1000. They include garbage collection.

We consider the functional F associated to the factorial function (but using addition instead of multiplication, to avoid numeric overflow).

Term overhead and type overhead: Let m denote the result of applying the interpreter to F. The value m has type `univ`. Applying the fixed point of m to 100 and projecting its result, i.e.,

$$\pi_{\text{int}}\, (\text{fix}_{\texttt{univ}}\, m\, (\varepsilon_{\text{int}}\, 100))$$

(repeated 1000 times) yields 5050 in 4.1 seconds.

Term overhead and type overhead, plus the projection: We then project m, obtaining a value of type `(int -> int) -> int -> int`. Applying the fixed point of this value to 100, i.e.,

$$\text{fix}_{(\text{int}\to\text{int})\to\text{int}\to\text{int}}\,(\pi_{(\text{int}\to\text{int})\to\text{int}\to\text{int}}\,m)\,100$$

(repeated 1000 times) yields 5050 in 4.9 seconds.

The projection slows down the computation by about 20%.

No term overhead, but type overhead: We now consider M, the result of specializing the interpreter with respect to F. The meaning of M has type `univ`. Applying the fixed point of this meaning to 100 and projecting its result, i.e.,

$$\pi_{\text{int}}\,(\text{fix}_{\texttt{univ}}\,[\![M]\!]\,(\varepsilon_{\text{int}}\,100))$$

(repeated 1000 times) yields 5050 in 0.5 seconds.

No term overhead and no type overhead: We now consider M', the result of specializing the projected interpreter with respect to F. The meaning of M' is of type `(int -> int) -> int -> int`. Applying the fixed point of this meaning to 100, i.e.,

$$\text{fix}_{(\text{int}\to\text{int})\to\text{int}\to\text{int}}\,[\![M']\!]\,100$$

(repeated 1000 times) yields 5050 in 0.3 seconds.

Overhead of type-directed partial evaluation: specializing the projected denotation of F (repeated 1000 times) takes 0.4 seconds.

Analysis: Specializing the interpreter removes the term overhead: the residual computation is about 88% faster than the original one. Specializing the projected interpreter removes both the term and the type overhead: the residual computation is about 94% faster than the original one with the projection and about 92% faster than the original one without the projection. Finally, the type overhead slows down the residual code by about 67%.

As for the cost of specialization, it is immediately amortized since the time spent running the residual code plus the time spent for partial evaluation is less than the time spent running the source code.

Using Standard ML, we were not able to measure the time spent compiling the residual code. However, we could estimate it using Caml and Chez Scheme. Our Caml implementation combines type-directed partial evaluation and run-time code generation [1], and Chez Scheme offers run-time code generation through `eval` [11]. In both cases, the time spent specializing, compiling the residual code, and running it is vastly inferior to the time spent running the source code.

```
local datatype 'a Fix = FIX of 'a Fix -> 'a
in fun fix_univ (FUN f)
       = let fun g (FIX x)
                 = f (FUN (fn a => let val (FUN h) = x (FIX x)
                                   in h a
                                   end))
         in g (FIX g)
         end
end
```

Fig. 2. Universal fixed-point operator

```
structure Ep
= struct
    datatype 'a ep
        = EP of ('a -> univ) * (univ -> 'a)

    val ep_int
        = EP (fn e => (INT e), fn (INT e) => e)

    fun ep_fun (EP (embed1, project1), EP (embed2, project2))
        = EP (fn f => FUN (fn x => embed2 (f (project1 x))),
              fn (FUN f) => fn x => project2 (f (embed1 x)))
  end

fun ts (Ep.EP (embed, project)) x = project x
fun tg (Ep.EP (embed, project)) x = embed x

val int = Ep.ep_int
infixr 5 -->; val op --> = Ep.ep_fun;
```

Fig. 3. Embeddings and projections in ML (after Andrzej Filinski and Zhe Yang)

5 Implementation

We have specified and implemented the embedding/projection of Section 3 to make it handle unit, booleans, products, disjoint sums, lists, and constructor specialization [12]. Except for constructor specialization, the embedding/projection is trivial since ML supports unit, booleans, products, disjoint sums and lists. Constructor specialization is handled with an encoding in ML. Other type constructs that are not native in ML would be handled similarly, i.e., with an encoding. Recursion is handled through a fixed-point operator (see Figure 2).

It is not completely immediate to implement embedding/projection pairs in ML. We did it using a programming technique due to Andrzej Filinski (personal communication, Spring 1995) and Zhe Yang (personal communication, Spring 1996) [15], originally developed to implement type-directed partial evaluation in ML. The technique works in two steps:

1. defining a polymorphic constructor of embedding/projection pairs for each type constructor; and
2. constructing the corresponding pair, following the inductive structure of the type.

Given such a pair, one can achieve type specialization with its projection part, and type generalization with its embedding part, as defined in Figure 3 and illustrated in the following interactive session.

```
- tg (int --> int) (fn x => x + 1);
val it = FUN fn : univ
- ts (int --> int) (FUN (fn (INT x) => INT (x + 1)));
std_in:22.24-22.48 Warning: match nonexhaustive
          INT x => ...

val it = fn : int -> int
-
```

And along the same lines, one can add a polymorphic component to `univ`.

6 An Improvement

With its pairs of type-indexed functions reify and reflect [4], type-directed partial evaluation is defined very similarly to the embedding/projection pairs considered in this article. It is therefore tempting to compose them, to specialize the interpreter at the same time as we are projecting it.

The results are two-level versions of the embedding/projection pairs:

$$\begin{cases} \varepsilon_{t_1 \to t_2}\, \mathtt{f} = \mathtt{FUN}\ \lambda v.\varepsilon_{t_2}\,(\mathtt{APP}\ \mathtt{(f,}\ \pi_{t_1}\, v\mathtt{)}) \\ \\ \pi_{\mathrm{int}}\,(\mathtt{INT}\ i) = \mathtt{LIT}\ i \\ \pi_{t_1 \to t_2}\,(\mathtt{FUN}\ f) = \mathtt{LAM}\ \mathtt{(x,}\ \pi_{t_2}\,(f\,(\varepsilon_{t_1}\,(\mathtt{VAR}\ \mathtt{x}))) \mathtt{)} \qquad \text{where } \mathtt{x} \text{ is fresh.} \end{cases}$$

Each projection now maps a universal value into the text of its normal form (if it exists), and each embedding maps a text into the corresponding universal value. As usual in offline type-directed partial evaluation, one cannot embed a dynamic integer. (Base types can only occur positively in the source type [5].)

The following ML session illustrates how to residualize universal values, using the two-level embedding/projection pairs defined just above.

```
- residualize (a --> a) (FUN (fn x => x));
val it = LAM ("x1",VAR "x1") : exp
- residualize ((int --> a) --> a) (FUN (fn (FUN f) => f (INT 42)));
std_in:53.14-53.37 Warning: match nonexhaustive
          FUN f => ...

val it = LAM ("x1",APP (VAR "x1",LIT 42)) : exp
- residualize (a --> int) (FUN (fn x => INT (1+1)));
val it = LAM ("x1",LIT 2) : exp
-
```

The last interaction illustrates the normalization effect of residualization (`1+1` was calculated at residualization time).

7 Conclusion and Issues

Traditionally, partial evaluators have mostly been developed for untyped languages, where type specialization is not a concern. Type specialization, however, appears to be a real issue for typed languages [9]. The point is that to be satisfactory, partial evaluation of typed programs must specialize both terms and types, and traditional partial evaluators specialize only terms. Against this shortcoming of traditional partial evaluation, John Hughes has proposed an elegant new paradigm to specialize both terms and types [6, 7]. We suggest the simpler and more conservative solution of (1) using a projection to achieve type specialization, and (2) reusing traditional partial evaluation to carry out the corresponding term specialization. This solution requires no other insight than knowing the type of the source program and, in the case of definitional interpreter, its associated type transformer.[1] In combination with type-directed partial evaluation, it also appears to be very efficient in practice.

Given a statically typed functional language such as ML or Haskell, and using Andrzej Filinski and Zhe Yang's inductive technique, it is very simple to write embedding/projection pairs. This simplicity, plus the fact that, as outlined in Section 6, they mesh very well with type-directed partial evaluation, counterbalance the fact that one needs to write such pairs for every new universal type one encounters.

[1] For example, the type transformation associated to an interpreter in direct style is the identity transformation, the type transformer associated to an interpreter in continuation style is the CPS transformation, etc.

As several anonymous referees pointed out, using embedding/projection pairs is not as general as John Hughes's approach. It however has the advantage of being directly usable since it builds on all the existing partial-evaluation technology.

But getting back to the central issue of type specialization, i.e., specializing both terms and types, and how it arose, i.e., to specialize expression interpreters, the author is struck by the fact that such interpreters are dependently typed. Therefore, he conjectures that either the partial-evaluation technology we are building will prove useful to implement dependently typed programs, or that conversely the wealth of work on dependent types will provide us with guidelines for partially evaluating dependently typed programs – probably a little of both.

Acknowledgements

This work is supported by BRICS (Basic Research in Computer Science, Centre of the Danish National Research Foundation).

Thanks to Neil D. Jones for letting me present this simple solution to type specialization at DIKU in January 1998, and to the whole TOPPS group for the ensuing lively discussion. Thanks also to the organizers of the CLICS lunch, at BRICS, for letting me air this idea at an early stage.

I am grateful to Belmina Dzafic, Karoline Malmkjær, and Zhe Yang for their benevolent ears in the fall of 1997, and to the anonymous referees for their pertinent reviews.

And last but not least, many thanks are due to Andrzej Filinski and Zhe Yang for their beautiful programming technique!

References

1. Vincent Balat and Olivier Danvy. Strong normalization by type-directed partial evaluation and run-time code generation (preliminary version). Technical Report BRICS RS-97-43, Department of Computer Science, University of Aarhus, Aarhus, Denmark, October 1997. To appear in the proceedings of TIC'98.
2. Lars Birkedal and Morten Welinder. Partial evaluation of Standard ML. Master's thesis, DIKU, Computer Science Department, University of Copenhagen, August 1993. DIKU Rapport 93/22.
3. Charles Consel and Olivier Danvy. Tutorial notes on partial evaluation. In Susan L. Graham, editor, *Proceedings of the Twentieth Annual ACM Symposium on Principles of Programming Languages*, pages 493–501, Charleston, South Carolina, January 1993. ACM Press.
4. Olivier Danvy. Type-directed partial evaluation. In Guy L. Steele Jr., editor, *Proceedings of the Twenty-Third Annual ACM Symposium on Principles of Programming Languages*, pages 242–257, St. Petersburg Beach, Florida, January 1996. ACM Press.
5. Olivier Danvy. Online type-directed partial evaluation. In Masahiko Sato and Yoshihito Toyama, editors, *Proceedings of the Third Fuji International Symposium on Functional and Logic Programming*, pages 271–295, Kyoto, Japan, April 1998.

World Scientific. Extended version available as the technical report BRICS RS-97-53.

6. John Hughes. Type specialisation for the lambda calculus; or, a new paradigm for partial evaluation based on type inference. In Olivier Danvy, Robert Glück, and Peter Thiemann, editors, *Partial Evaluation*, number 1110 in Lecture Notes in Computer Science, Dagstuhl, Germany, February 1996. Springer-Verlag.
7. John Hughes. An introduction to program specialisation by type inference. In *Functional Programming*, Glasgow University, July 1996. Published electronically.
8. Neil D. Jones. Challenging problems in partial evaluation and mixed computation. In Dines Bjørner, Andrei P. Ershov, and Neil D. Jones, editors, *Partial Evaluation and Mixed Computation*, pages 1–14. North-Holland, 1988.
9. Neil D. Jones. Relations among type specialization, supercompilation and logic program specialization. In Hugh Glaser and Herbert Kuchen, editors, *Ninth International Symposium on Programming Language Implementation and Logic Programming*, number 1292 in Lecture Notes in Computer Science, Southampton, UK, September 1997. Invited talk.
10. Neil D. Jones, Carsten K. Gomard, and Peter Sestoft. *Partial Evaluation and Automatic Program Generation.* Prentice Hall International Series in Computer Science. Prentice-Hall, 1993.
11. Richard Kelsey, William Clinger, and Jonathan Rees, editors. Revised^5 report on the algorithmic language Scheme. *LISP and Symbolic Computation*, 1998. To appear.
12. Torben Æ. Mogensen. Constructor specialization. In David A. Schmidt, editor, *Proceedings of the Second ACM SIGPLAN Symposium on Partial Evaluation and Semantics-Based Program Manipulation*, pages 22–32, Copenhagen, Denmark, June 1993. ACM Press.
13. David A. Schmidt. *Denotational Semantics: A Methodology for Language Development.* Allyn and Bacon, Inc., 1986.
14. Per Sjörs. Type specialization of a subset of Haskell. Master's thesis, Chalmers University, June 1997.
15. Zhe Yang. Encoding types in ML-like languages. Draft, Department of Computer Science, New York University, April 1998.

Multi-Stage Programming: Axiomatization and Type Safety*

Walid Taha, Zine-El-Abidine Benaissa, and Tim Sheard

Oregon Graduate Institute

Abstract. Multi-stage programming provides a new paradigm for constructing efficient solutions to complex problems. Techniques such as program generation, multi-level partial evaluation, and run-time code generation respond to the need for general purpose solutions which do not pay run-time interpretive overheads. This paper provides a foundation for the formal analysis of one such system.
We introduce a multi-stage language and present its axiomatic and reduction semantics. Our axiomatic semantics is an extension of the call-by-value λ-calculus with staging constructs. We show that staged-languages can "go Wrong" in new ways, and devise a type system that screens out such programs. Finally, we present a proof of the soundness of this type system with respect to the reduction semantics.

1 Introduction

Recently, there has been significant interest in various forms of multi-stage computation, including program generation [12], multi-level partial evaluation [4], and run-time code generation [11]. Such techniques combine both the software engineering advantages of general purpose systems and the efficiency of specialized ones.

Because such systems execute generated code *never inspected by human eyes* it is important to use formal analysis to guarantee properties of this generated code. We would like to guarantee statically that a program generator synthesizes only programs with properties such as: type-correctness, global references only to names in scope, and local names which do not inadvertently hide global references.

In previous work [13], we introduced a multi-stage programming language called MetaML. In that work we introduced four staging annotations to control the order of evaluation of terms. We argued that staged programs are an important mechanism for constructing general purpose systems with the efficiency of specialized ones, and addressed engineering issues necessary to make such systems usable by programmers. We introduced an operational semantics and a type system to screen out bad programs, but we were unable to prove the soundness of the type system.

* The research reported in this paper was supported by the USAF Air Materiel Command, contract # F19628-93-C-0069, and NSF Grant IRI-9625462.

Further investigation revealed important subtleties that were not previously apparent to us. In this paper, we report on work rectifying some of the limitations of our previous work. In contrast to our earlier work that focused on implementations and problem solving using multi-stage programs, this paper reports on a more abstract treatment of MetaML's foundations. The key results reported in this paper are as follows:

1. An axiomatic semantics and a reduction semantics for a core of MetaML.
2. A characterization of the new ways in which staged programs "go Wrong".
3. A type system to screen out such programs.
4. A soundness proof for the type system with respect to the reduction semantics using the syntactic approach to type-soundness [7, 8, 14].

These results form a strong, tightly-woven foundation which gives us both a better understanding of MetaML, and more confidence in the well-foundedness of the multi-stage paradigm.

1.1 What are Staged Programs?

In staging a program, the user has control over the order of evaluation of terms. This is done using staging annotations. In MetaML the staging annotations are Brackets <>, Escape ~ and **run**. An expression <*e*> defers the computation of *e*; ~*e* splices the deferred expression obtained by evaluating *e* into the body of a surrounding Bracketed expression; and **run** *e* evaluates *e* to obtain a deferred expression, and then evaluates this deferred expression. It is important to note that ~*e* is only legal within lexically enclosing Brackets. To illustrate, consider the script of a small MetaML session below:

```
-| val pair = (3+4,<3+4>);
val pair = (7,<3+4>) : (int  * <int>)

-| fun f (x,y) = < 8 - ~y >;
val f = fn : ('a  * <int>) -> <int>

-| val code = f pair;
val code = <8 - (3+4)> : <int>

-| run code;
val it = 1 : int
```

The first declaration[1] defines a variable pair. The first component of the pair is evaluated, but the evaluation of the second component is deferred by the Brackets. Brackets in types such as <int> are read *"Code of int"*, and distinguish values such as <3+4> from values such as 7. The second declaration illustrates

[1] Such top-level declarations are let-bindings. Let-bindings are type-checked as textual substitutions.

that code can be abstracted over, and that it can be spliced into a larger piece of code. The third declaration applies the function `f` to `pair` performing the actual splicing. And the last declaration evaluates this deferred piece of code.

To give a feel for how MetaML is used to construct larger pieces of code at run-time consider:

```
-| fun mult x n = if n=0 then <1> else < ~x * ~(mult x (n-1)) >;
val mult = fn  : <int> -> int -> <int>

-| val cube = <fn y => ~(mult <y> 3)>;
val cube = <fn a => a * (a * (a * 1))> : <int -> int>

-| fun exponent n = <fn y => ~(mult <y> n)>;
val exponent = fn  : int  -> <int -> int>
```

The function `mult`, given an integer piece of code `x` and an integer `n`, produces a piece of code that is an `n`-way product of `x`. This can be used to construct the code of a function that performs the `cube` operation, or generalized to a generator for producing an exponentiation function from a given exponent `n`. Note how the looping overhead has been removed from the generated code. This is the purpose of program staging and it can be highly effective as discussed elsewhere [4, 13]. In this paper we move away from how staged languages are used and address their foundations.

2 The λ-R Language

The λ-R language represents the core of MetaML. It has the following syntax:

$$e := i \mid x \mid e\,e \mid \lambda x.e \mid <e> \mid \tilde{}e \mid \texttt{run}\ e$$

which includes the normal constructs of the λ-calculus, integer constants, and the three additional staging constructs.

To define the semantics of Escape, which is dependent on the surrounding context, we choose to explicitly annotate all terms with their level. The *level* of a term is the (non-negative) number of Brackets minus the number of Escapes surrounding that term. We define *level-annotated* terms as follows:

$$\begin{array}{ll} a^0 & := i^0 \mid x^0 \mid (a^0\,a^0)^0 \mid (\lambda x.a^0)^0 \mid <a^1>^0 \mid (\texttt{run}\ a^0)^0 \\ a^{n+1} & := i^{n+1} \mid x^{n+1} \mid (a^{n+1}\,a^{n+1})^{n+1} \mid (\lambda x.a^{n+1})^{n+1} \mid \\ & \quad <a^{n+2}>^{n+1} \mid (\tilde{}a^n)^{n+1} \mid (\texttt{run}\ a^{n+1})^{n+1} \end{array}$$

Note that Escape never appears at level 0 in a level-annotated term. We define a λ-R program as a closed term a^0. Hence, example programs are $(\lambda x.x^0)^0$ and $<<((\lambda x.(x^2\,x^2)^2)^2\,5^2)^2>^1>^0$.

2.1 Values

It is instructive to think of values as the set of terms we consider to be acceptable results from a computation. Values are defined as follows:

$$\begin{array}{ll} v^0 & := i^0 \mid x^0 \mid (\lambda x.a^0)^0 \mid \texttt{<}v^1\texttt{>}^0 \\ v^1 & := i^1 \mid x^1 \mid (v^1\ v^1)^1 \mid (\lambda x.v^1)^1 \mid \texttt{<}v^2\texttt{>}^1 \mid (\texttt{run}\ v^1)^1 \\ v^{n+2} & := i^{n+2} \mid x^{n+2} \mid (v^{n+2}\ v^{n+2})^{n+2} \mid (\lambda x.v^{n+2})^{n+2} \mid \\ & \quad \texttt{<}v^{n+3}\texttt{>}^{n+2} \mid ({\tilde{}}v^{n+1})^{n+2} \mid (\texttt{run}\ v^{n+2})^{n+2} \end{array}$$

The set of values for λ-R has three notable points. First, values can be bracketed expressions. This means that computations can return pieces of code representing other programs. Second, values can contain applications such as $(\lambda y.y^1)^1\ (\lambda x.x^1)^1$. Third, there are no level 1 Escapes in values. We take advantage of this important property of values in many proofs and propositions in our present work.

2.2 Contexts

We generalize the notion of contexts [1] to a notion of *annotated contexts*:

$$\begin{array}{ll} c^0 & := [\,]^0 \mid (c^0\ a^0)^0 \mid (a^0\ c^0)^0 \mid (\lambda x.c^0)^0 \mid \texttt{<}c^1\texttt{>}^0 \mid (\texttt{run}\ c^0)^0 \\ c^{n+1} & := [\,]^{n+1} \mid (c^{n+1}\ a^{n+1})^{n+1} \mid (a^{n+1}\ c^{n+1})^{n+1} \mid (\lambda x.c^{n+1})^{n+1} \mid \\ & \quad \texttt{<}c^{n+2}\texttt{>}^{n+1} \mid ({\tilde{}}c^n)^{n+1} \mid (\texttt{run}\ c^{n+1})^{n+1} \end{array}$$

where $[\,]$ is a *hole*. When instantiating an annotated context $c^n[\,]^m$ to a term e^m we write $c^n[e^m]$.

2.3 Promotion and Demotion

The axioms of MetaML remove Brackets from level-annotated terms. To maintain the consistency of the level-annotations we need an inductive definition for incrementing and decrementing all annotations on a term. We call these operations *promotion* and *demotion*.

Promotion	**Demotion**
$x^n \uparrow\ = x^{n+1}$	$x^{n+1} \downarrow\ = x^n$
$(a_1\ a_2)^n \uparrow\ = (a_1 \uparrow\ a_2 \uparrow)^{n+1}$	$(a_1\ a_2)^{n+1} \downarrow\ = (a_1 \downarrow\ a_2 \downarrow)^n$
$(\lambda x.a)^n \uparrow\ = (\lambda x.a \uparrow)^{n+1}$	$(\lambda x.a)^{n+1} \downarrow\ = (\lambda x.a \downarrow)^n$
$\texttt{<}a\texttt{>}^n \uparrow\ = \texttt{<}a \uparrow\texttt{>}^{n+1}$	$\texttt{<}a\texttt{>}^{n+1} \downarrow\ = \texttt{<}a \downarrow\texttt{>}^n$
$({\tilde{}}a)^{n+1} \uparrow\ = ({\tilde{}}a \uparrow)^{n+2}$	$({\tilde{}}a)^{n+2} \downarrow\ = ({\tilde{}}a \downarrow)^{n+1}$
$(\texttt{run}\ a)^n \uparrow\ = (\texttt{run}\ a \uparrow)^{n+1}$	$(\texttt{run}\ a)^{n+1} \downarrow\ = (\texttt{run}\ a \downarrow)^n$
$i^n \uparrow\ = i^{n+1}$	$i^{n+1} \downarrow\ = i^n$

Promotion is a total function over level-annotated terms and is defined by a simple inductive definition. Demotion is a partial function over level-annotated terms. Demotion is undefined on terms Escaped at level 1, and on level 0 terms in general.

An important property of demotion is that while it is partial over level-annotated terms it is total over level-$(n+1)$ values. Proof of this is a simple induction on the structure of values.

2.4 Substitution

The definition of substitution is standard for the most part. In this paper we are concerned only with the substitution of values for variables. When the level of a value is different from the level of the term in which it is being substituted, promotion (or demotion, whichever is appropriate) is used to correct the level of the subterm.

$$
\begin{aligned}
i^n[x^n := v^n] &= i^n \\
x^n[x^n := v^n] &= v^n \\
y^n[x^n := v^n] &= y^n && x \neq y \\
(a_1\ a_2)^n[x^n := v^n] &= ((a_1[x^n := v^n])\ (a_2[x^n := v^n]))^n \\
(\lambda x.a_1)^n[x^n := v^n] &= (\lambda x.a_1)^n \\
(\lambda y.a_1)^n[x^n := v^n] &= (\lambda y'.(a_1[y^n := y'^n][x^n := v^n]))^n \\
& \quad\ y' \notin FV(v^a, a_1) && x \neq y \\
<a_1>^n[x^n := v^n] &= <a_1[x^{n+1} := v^n \uparrow]>^n \\
(\tilde{}a_1)^{n+1}[x^{n+1} := v^{n+1}] &= (\tilde{}(a_1[x^n := v^{n+1} \downarrow]))^{n+1} \\
(\texttt{run}\ a_1)^n[x^n := v^n] &= (\texttt{run}\ (a_1[x^n := v^n]))^n
\end{aligned}
$$

This function is total because both promotion and demotion are total over values (of the relevant level). A richer notion of demotion is needed to perform substitution of a variable by any expression. This generalization is beyond the scope of this paper.

2.5 Axiomatization and Reduction Semantics of λ-R

The axiomatic semantics describes an equivalence between two level-annotated terms. Axioms can be thought of as pattern-based equivalence rules, and are applicable in a context-independent way to any subterm that they match. The three axioms we will introduce can each be given a natural orientation or direction, reducing "bigger" terms to "smaller" terms. This provides a reduction semantics.

Axiomatic	Reduction
$((\lambda x.e^n)^n v^n)^n = e^n[x^n := v^n]$	$((\lambda x.e^n)^n v^n)^n \xrightarrow{\beta} e^n[x^n := v^n]$
$(\texttt{run}\ <v^{n+1}>^n)^n = v^{n+1} \downarrow$	$(\texttt{run}\ <v^{n+1}>^n)^n \xrightarrow{run} v^{n+1} \downarrow$
$(\tilde{}<e^{n+1}>^n)^{n+1} = e^{n+1}$	$(\tilde{}<e^{n+1}>^n)^{n+1} \xrightarrow{esc} e^{n+1}$

We write $\lambda\text{-R} \vdash M = N$ when $M = N$ is provable by the above axioms and the classical inference rules of an equational theory, and we write $\xrightarrow{*}$ for the reflexive, transitive, context closure of $\longrightarrow$.

Theorem 1 (Confluence). *The reduction semantics is confluent.*

Proof. Using a notion of parallel reduction and a Strip Lemma, following closely the development in [1, pages 277–283].

Corollary 1 (Church-Rosser). *The axiomatic semantics is Church-Rosser.*

3 Faulty Terms

Under the reduction semantics, when a term has been sufficiently reduced, we would like such a term to be a *value*, but this is not always the case. If no rules apply, and the term is not a value, we say that such a term is *stuck* [10, 14]. There are four contexts in which such terms can arise:

1. A non-λ value in a function position in an application (at level 0). This is the familiar form of undesirable behavior arising whenever the pure λ-calculus is extended with constants. For example, $(<5^1>^0\ 3^0)^0$ is stuck because $<5^1>^0$ is a piece of code, not a λ-abstraction. This term is not a value and contains no redex.
2. A variable appears at a level lower than the level at which it was bound. This is the key, distinguishing form of undesirable behavior in multi-stage computation [13]. For example: $<(\lambda x.\tilde{}(x^0)^1)^1>^0$ is stuck since x is used at level 0 but bound at level 1.
3. A non-Bracket value is the argument to Run. For example: $(\texttt{run}\ \ 7^0)^0$ is stuck since 7^0 is an integer and not a piece of code.
4. A non-Bracket value is the argument to Escape. For example: $<(4^1+\tilde{}(7^0)^1)^1>^0$.

We wish to consider as *faulty*, terms in the form above. We will show that if a term is typable, then it is not faulty, and neither can it reduce to a faulty term. We formalize this notion in the next sections.

We can now define the set of faulty terms F as the least set containing all expressions of the form $c[((<e^{n+1}>)^n\ \ e')^n]$, $c[(i^n\ \ e')^n]$, $c[(\lambda x.c'[x^n])^m]$ where $m > n$, $c[(\texttt{run}\ \ (\lambda x.e)^n)^n]$, $c[(\texttt{run}\ \ i^n)^n]$, $c[(\tilde{}(\lambda x.e)^n)^{n+1}]$, and $c[(\tilde{}(i^n))^{n+1}]$.

The success of our specification of faulty expressions depends on whether they help us characterize the behavior of our reduction semantics. The following lemma is an example of such a characterization, and is needed for our proof of type soundness.

Lemma 1 (Uniform Evaluation). *Let e^n be a closed term. If e^n is not faulty then either it is a value or it contains a redex.*

Proof: By induction on the structure of e^n.

4 Type System

The main obstacle to defining a sound type system for our language is the interaction between Run and Escape. While this is problematic, it adds significantly to the expressiveness of a staged language [13], so it is worthwhile overcoming the difficulty. The problem is that Escape allows Run to appear inside a Bracketed λ-abstraction, and it is possible for Run to "drop" that λ-bound variable to a level lower than the level at which it is bound. The following example illustrates the phenomenon:

$$<(\lambda x.(\tilde{}(\texttt{run}\ \ <x^1>^0)^0)^1)^1>^0 \rightarrow <(\lambda x.(\tilde{}x^0)^1)^1>^0$$

To avoid this problem, for each λ-abstraction we need to count the number of surrounding Runs for each occurrence of its bound variable (here x^1) in its body. We use this count to check that there are enough Brackets around each formal parameter to execute all surrounding Runs without leading to a faulty term.

The type system for λ-R is defined by a judgment $\Delta \vdash e^n : \tau, m$, where e^n is our well-typed expression, τ is the type of the expression, m is the number of the surrounding Run annotations of e^n and Δ is the environment assigning types to term variables.

Syntax

types	τ	$::= \tau \to \tau \mid <\tau> \mid \mathtt{int}$
type assignments	Δ	$::= x \mapsto (\tau, j)^i ; \Delta \mid \{\}$
judgments	J	$::= \Delta \vdash t : \tau, m$

Type System

$$\frac{\Delta(x) = (\tau, j)^i \quad i + m \leq n + j}{\Delta \vdash x^n : \tau, m}\text{Var} \qquad \frac{}{\Delta \vdash i^n : \mathbf{int}, m}\text{Int}$$

$$\frac{\Delta \vdash e^n : <\tau>, m+1}{\Delta \vdash (\mathrm{run}\ e^n)^n : \tau, m}\text{Run}$$

$$\frac{\Delta \vdash e^{n+1} : \tau, m}{\Delta \vdash <e^{n+1}>^n : <\tau>, m}\text{Bra} \qquad \frac{\Delta \vdash e^n : <\tau>, m}{\Delta \vdash (\tilde{\ } e^n)^{n+1} : \tau, m}\text{Esc}$$

$$\frac{\Delta \vdash e_2^n : \tau', m \quad \Delta \vdash e_1^n : \tau' \to \tau, m}{\Delta \vdash (e_1^n\ e_2^n)^n : \tau, m}\text{App} \qquad \frac{(x \mapsto (\tau', m)^n ; \Delta) \vdash e^n : \tau, m}{\Delta \vdash (\lambda x.e^n)^n : \tau' \to \tau, m}\text{Lam}$$

The type system employs a number of mechanisms to reject terms that either are, or can reduce to faulty terms. The **App** rule has the standard role, and rejects non-functions applied to arguments.

The **Escape** and **Run** rules require that their operand must have type Code. This means terms such as $\mathtt{run}\ 5$ and $<\lambda x.\tilde{\ }5>$ are rejected. But while this restriction in the **Escape** and **Run** rules rejects faulty terms, it is not enough to reject all terms that can be reduced to faulty terms. The first example of such a term is $<\lambda x.\tilde{\ }(\mathtt{run}\ <x>)>$ which would be typable if we use only the restrictions discussed above, but reduces to the term $<\lambda x.\tilde{\ }x>$ which would not be typable. The second examples involves an application $(\lambda f.<\lambda x.\tilde{\ }(f<x>)>)(\lambda x.\mathtt{run}\ x)$ which would also be typable, and also reduces to the untypable $<\lambda x.\tilde{\ }x>$. To reject such terms we need the **Var** rule.

The **Var** rule is instrumented with the condition $i + m \leq n + j$. Here i is the number of Bracket's surrounding the λ-abstraction where the variable was bound, m is the number of Runs surrounding this occurence of the variable, n is the number of Brackets surrounding this occurence of the variable, and j is the number of Runs surrounding the λ-abstraction where it was bound. The condition ensures that there are more explicit Brackets than Runs between the binding and each occurance of a variable. This way, our estimate of level is always conservative, even though the levels of a some subterms may be affected by Run.

In previous work, we have attempted to avoid these two kinds of problems using two distinct mechanisms: First, the argument of Run cannot contain free variables, and second, we prohibit the λ-abstraction of Run. We used unbound polymorphic type variable names in a scheme similar to that devised by Launchbury and Peyton Jones for ensuring the safety of state in Haskel [5]. It turns out that not allowing any free variables is too strong, and that using polymorphism was too weak. It is better to simply take account of the number of surrounding occurrences of Run in the **Var** rule. This way we ensure that if Run is ever in a λ-abstraction, it can only strip away Brackets that are explicitly apparent in that λ-abstraction.

5 Type Soundness of the Reduction Semantics

The type soundness proof closely follows the subject reduction proofs used by Nielson [7,8] and promoted by Wright and Felliesen [14]. Once the reduction semantics and type system have been defined, the syntactic type soundness proof proceeds as follows: 1) show that reduction in the standard reduction semantics preserves typing. This is called *subject reduction*, and 2) show that faulty terms are not typable.

If programs are well-typed, then the two results above can be used as follows: By (1), evaluation of a well-typed program will only produce well-typed terms. By Lemma 1, every such term is either faulty, or a value, or contains a redex. The first case is impossible by (2). Thus the program either reduces to a well-typed value or it diverges.

5.1 Subject Reduction

The Subject Reduction Lemma states that a well-typed term remains well-typed under reduction. The proof relies on the Demotion, Promotion and Substitution Type Preservation Lemmas. First we need to introduce two operations on the environment assigning types to term variables:

$$\Delta \uparrow_{(q,p)} (x) = (\tau, j+q)^{i+p} \text{ iff } \Delta(x) = (\tau, j)^i$$
$$\Delta \downarrow_{(q,p)} (x) = (\tau, j)^{i} \text{ iff } \Delta(x) = (\tau, j+q)^{i+p}$$

These two operations map environments to environments. They are needed in the Promotion and Demotion Lemmas. They provide an environment necessary to derive a valid judgement for a promoted or demoted well-typed value. Notice that we have the following two properties:

$$(\Delta \uparrow_{(q,p)}) \uparrow_{(i,j)} = \Delta \uparrow_{(q+i,p+j)} \text{ and } (\Delta \uparrow_{(q+i,p+j)}) \downarrow_{(i,j)} = \Delta \uparrow_{(q,p)}$$

We write $v \uparrow^p$ and $v \downarrow^p$, respectively, for an abbreviation of p applications of $\uparrow$ and $\downarrow$ to v. Note that this operation is different from $\uparrow_{(q,p)}$ and $\downarrow_{(q,p)}$ which is a function on environments assigning types to term variables.

Lemma 2 (Demotion). *If* $q \leq p$ *and* $\Delta_2 \downarrow_{(q,p)}$ *is defined and* $\Delta_1 \cup \Delta_2 \vdash v^{n+p} : \tau, m+q$ *then* $\Delta_1 \cup (\Delta_2 \downarrow_{(q,p)}) \vdash v^{n+p} \downarrow^p : \tau, m$.

Proof. By induction on the structure of v^{n+p}. We develop only the variable case $v^{n+p} = x^{n+p}$. There are only two possible sub-cases, which are:

$$\frac{\Delta_1(x) = (\tau, j)^i \quad i + m + q \leq n + j + p}{(\Delta_1 \cup \Delta_2) \vdash x^{n+p} : \tau, m+q} \text{(Var)}$$

By hypothesis $q \leq p$ implies $m+i \leq n+j$. Hence $(\Delta_1 \cup (\Delta_2 \downarrow_{(q,p)})) \vdash v^{n+p} \downarrow^p : \tau, m$.

$$\frac{\Delta_2(x) = (\tau, j+q)^{i+p} \quad i + m + 2q \leq n + j + 2p}{(\Delta_1 \cup \Delta_2) \vdash x^{n+p} : \tau, m+q} \text{(Var)}$$

Similar to the above sub-case.

Lemma 3 (Promotion). *Let* $q \leq p$. *If* $\Delta_1 \cup \Delta_2 \vdash v^n : \tau, m$ *then* $\Delta_1 \cup (\Delta_2 \uparrow_{(q,p)}) \vdash v^n \uparrow^p : \tau, m+q$.

Proof. By induction on v^n.

Lemma 4 (Substitution). *If* $j \leq m$ *and* $\Delta_1 \cup (x \mapsto (\tau', j)^i; \Delta_2) \vdash e^n : \tau, m$ *and* $\Delta_1 \vdash v^i : \tau', j$ *then one of the following three judgments holds.*

1. $\Delta_1 \vdash e^n[x^n := v^i \uparrow^{n-i}] : \tau, m$ *if* $n > i$.
2. $\Delta_1 \vdash e^n[x^n := v^i \downarrow^{i-n}] : \tau, m$ *if* $n < i$
3. $\Delta_1 \vdash e^n[x^n := v^n] : \tau, m$, *otherwise*

Proof. By induction on the structure e^n. If $e^n = x^n$ then we have:

$$\frac{\Delta(x) = (\tau, j)^i \quad m + i \leq n + j}{\Delta_1 \cup (x \mapsto (\tau, j)^i; \Delta_2) \vdash x^n : \tau, m}$$

- If $n < i$ and by the hypothesis $j \leq m$ then $m + i > n + j$. Consequently, the judgement $\Delta_1 \cup (x \mapsto (\tau, j)^i; \Delta_2) \vdash x^n : \tau, m$ is not possible.
- if $n > i$ then $m - j < n - i$ and the Promotion Lemma 3 applies.
- $i = n$ and by hypothesis $j \leq m$ and $m + i \leq n + j$ then $j = m$. Then, $\Delta_1 \vdash e^n[x^n := v^n] : \tau, m$.

Corollary 2 (β Rule). *If* $\Delta \vdash ((\lambda x.e^n)^n\ v^n)^n : \tau, m$ *then* $\Delta \vdash e^n[x^n := v^n] : \tau, m$.

Lemma 5 (Escape Rule). *If* $\Delta \vdash ({\char`~}\texttt{<}e^{n+1}\texttt{>}^n)^{n+1} : \tau, m$ *then* $\Delta \vdash e^{n+1} : \tau, m$.

Proof. Straightforward from the type system.

Lemma 6 (Run Rule). *If* $\Delta \vdash (\textbf{run}\ \texttt{<}v^{n+1}\texttt{>}^n)^n : \tau, m$ *then* $\Delta \vdash v^{n+1} \downarrow : \tau, m$.

Proof. If $\Delta \vdash (\textbf{run}\ \texttt{<}v^{n+1}\texttt{>}^n)^n : \tau, m$ then $\Delta \vdash v^{n+1} : \tau, m+1$ is valid. By Demotion Lemma 2, $\Delta \vdash v^{n+1} \downarrow : \tau, m$ is valid.

Proposition 1. *If* $\Delta \vdash e_1^n : \tau, m$ *and* $e_1^n \rightarrow e_2^n$ *then* $\Delta \vdash e_2^n : \tau, m$.

Proof. By induction on the structure of e_1^n. If the rewrite is at the root then use Lemmas 5 and 6, and Corollary 2. If e_1^n contains a redex then apply induction hypothesis.

Proposition 2 (Subject Reduction). *If* $\Delta \vdash e_1^n : \tau, m$ *and* $e_1^n \xrightarrow{*} e_2^n$ *then* $\Delta \vdash e_2^n : \tau, m$.

Proof. By induction on the length of the derivation.

5.2 Faulty Terms

Lemma 7 (Faulty Terms are Not Typable). *If* $e \in F$ *then there is no* Δ, t, a *such that* $\Delta \vdash e : t, a$.

Proof. By case analysis over the structure of e. Let $e = c_1[(\lambda x.c_2[x^n])^i]$ such that $n < i$, that is, $i = n + k_1 + 1$. Assume that $\Delta \vdash e : \tau, m$. This implies that $x \mapsto (\tau', j)^i \Delta' \vdash x^n : \tau', p$. This means that $i + p \leq n + j$. Because $p = j + k_2$ then $j \leq p$. This implies that $n + k + 1 + 1 + j + k_2 \leq n + j$ which is impossible. The other cases are straight-forward.

6 Related Work

Multi-stage programming techniques have been used in a wide variety of settings [13], including run-time specialization of C programs [11].

Nielson and Nielson present a seminal detailed study into a two-level functional programming language [9]. This language was developed for studying code generation. Davies and Pfenning show that a generalization of this language to a multi-level language called $\lambda^\Box$ gives rise to a type system very related to a modal logic, and that this type system is equivalent to the binding-time analysis of Nielson and Nielson [3]. Intuitively, $\lambda^\Box$ provides a natural framework where LISP's quote and eval can be present in a language. The semantics of our Bracket and Run correspond closely to those of quote and eval, respectively.

Glück and Jørgensen study partial evaluation in the generalized context where inputs can arrive at an arbitrary number of times rather than just two (namely, specialization-time and run-time) [4], and demonstrate that binding-time analysis in a multi-level setting can be done with efficiency comparable to that of two-level binding time analysis. Our notion of level is very similar to that used by Glück and Jørgensen.

Davies extended the Curry-Howard isomorphism to a relation between modal logic and the type system for a multi-level language [2]. Intuitively, $\lambda^\bigcirc$ provide a good framework for formalizing the presence of quote and quasi-quote in a language. The semantics of our Bracket and Escape correspond closely to those of quote and quasi-quote, respectively. Previous attempts to combine the $\lambda^\Box$ and $\lambda^\bigcirc$ systems have not been successful [3, 2, 13]. To our knowledge, our work is the first successful attempt to define a sound type system combining Brackets, Escape and Run in the same language.

Moggi advocates a categorical approach to two-level languages, and and uses indexed categories to develop models for two languages similar to $\lambda^{\Box}$ and $\lambda^{\bigcirc}$ [6]. He points out that two-level languages generally have not been presented along with an equational calculus. Our paper has eliminated this problem for MetaML, and to our knowledge, is the first presentation of a multi-level language using axiomatic and reductions semantics.

7 Conclusion

In this paper, we have presented an axiomatic and reduction semantics for a language with three staging constructs: Brackets, Escape, and Run. Arriving at the axiomatic and reduction semantics was of great value to enhancing our understanding of the language. In particular, it helped us to formalize an accurate syntactic characterization of faulty terms for this language. This characterization played a crucial role in leading us to the type system presented here. Finally, it is useful to note that our reduction semantics allows for β-reductions inside Brackets, thus giving us a basis for verifying the soundness of the safe-β optimization that we discussed in previous work [13].

MetaML currently exists as a prototype implementation that we intend to distribute freely on the web. The implementation supports the three programming constructs, higher-order datatypes (with support for Monads), Hindley-Milner polymorphism, recursion, and mutable state. The system has been used for developing a number of small applications, including a simple term-rewriting system, monadic staged compilers, and numerous small bench-mark functions.

We are currently investigating the incorporation of an explicit recursion operator and Hindley-Milner polymorphism into the type system presented in this paper. In practice, the type system presented here seems to work with polymorphism. However, it is limited in that it does not admit expressions like $\lambda x.\texttt{run}\ x$. We continue to look for type systems admitting such terms, but todate, all such systems do not seem to integrate naturally with polymorphism.

Acknowledgements: We would like to thank Frederick Smith, John Matthews and Matt Saffell for comments on a draft of this paper. We benefited from discussions with Koen Claessen, John Launchbury, Erik Meijer, Amr Sabry, and Phil Wadler, and their encouragement to investigate the small-step semantics. We would also like to thank the referees for many helpful comments and pointers.

References

1. Henk . P. Barendregt. *The Lambda-Calculus, its syntax and semantics.* Studies in Logic and the Foundation of Mathematics. North-Holland, Amsterdam, 1984. Second edition.
2. Rowan Davies. A temporal-logic approach to binding-time analysis. In *Proceedings, 11th Annual IEEE Symposium on Logic in Computer Science*, pages 184–195, New Brunswick, New Jersey, July 1996. IEEE Computer Society Press.

3. Rowan Davies and Frank Pfenning. A modal analysis of staged computation. In *23rd Annual ACM Symposium on Principles of Programming Languages (POPL'96)*, St.Petersburg Beach, Florida, January 1996.
4. Robert Glück and Jesper Jørgensen. An automatic program generator for multi-level specialization. *Lisp and Symbolic Computation*, 10(2):113–158, 1997.
5. John Launchbury and Simon L. Peyton-Jones. State in haskell. *Lisp and Symbolic Computation*, 8(4):293–342, December 1995.
6. Eugenio Moggi. A categorical account of two-level languages. In *MFPS 1997*, 1997.
7. Flemming Nielson. A formal type system for comparing partial evaluators. In D Bjørner, Ershov, and Jones, editors, *Proceedings of the workshop on Partial Evaluation and Mixed Computation (1987)*, pages 349–384. North-Holland, 1988.
8. Flemming Nielson. The typed λ-calculus with first-class processes. In K. Odijk, M. Rem, and J.-C. Syre, editors, *PARLE '89: Parallel Languages and Architectures Europe, volume 1*, pages 357–373. Springer-Verlag, New York, NY, 1989. Lecture Notes in Computer Science 365.
9. Flemming Nielson and Hanne Rijs Nielson. *Two-Level Functional Languages.* Number 34 in Cambridge Tracts in Theoretical Computer Science. Cambridge University Press, 1992.
10. Gordon D Plotkin. A Structural Approach to Operational Semantics. Tech. Rep. FN-19, DAIMI, Univ. of Aarhus, Denmark, September 1981.
11. Calton Pu, Andrew Black, Crispin Cowan, and Jonathan Walpole. Microlanguages for operating system specialization. In *Proceedings of the SIGPLAN Workshop on Domain-Specific Languages*, Paris, January 1997.
12. Walid Taha and Jim Hook. The anatomy of a component generation system. In *International Workshop on the Principles of Software Evolution*, Kyoto, Japan, April 1998.
13. Walid Taha and Tim Sheard. Multi-stage programming with explicit annotations. In *Proceedings of the ACM-SIGPLAN Symposium on Partial Evaluation and semantic based program manipulations PEPM'97, Amsterdam*, pages 203–217. ACM, 1997.
14. Andrew K. Wright and Matthias Felleisen. A syntactic approach to type soundness. *Information and Computation*, 115(1):38–94, 15 November 1994.

Author Index

Springer and the environment

At Springer we firmly believe that an international science publisher has a special obligation to the environment, and our corporate policies consistently reflect this conviction.

We also expect our business partners – paper mills, printers, packaging manufacturers, etc. – to commit themselves to using materials and production processes that do not harm the environment. The paper in this book is made from low- or no-chlorine pulp and is acid free, in conformance with international standards for paper permanency.

Springer

Lecture Notes in Computer Science

For information about Vols. 1–1361

please contact your bookseller or Springer-Verlag

Vol. 1362: D.K. Panda, C.B. Stunkel (Eds.), Network-Based Parallel Computing. Proceedings, 1998. X, 247 pages. 1998.

Vol. 1363: J.-K. Hao, E. Lutton, E. Ronald, M. Schoenauer, D. Snyers (Eds.), Artificial Evolution. XI, 349 pages. 1998.

Vol. 1364: W. Conen, G. Neumann (Eds.), Coordination Technology for Collaborative Applications. VIII, 282 pages. 1998.

Vol. 1365: M.P. Singh, A. Rao, M.J. Wooldridge (Eds.), Intelligent Agents IV. Proceedings, 1997. XII, 351 pages. 1998. (Subseries LNAI).

Vol. 1366: Z. Li, P.-C. Yew, S. Chatterjee, C.-H. Huang, P. Sadayappan, D. Sehr (Eds.), Languages and Compilers for Parallel Computing. Proceedings, 1997. XII, 428 pages. 1998.

Vol. 1367: E.W. Mayr, H.J. Prömel, A. Steger (Eds.), Lectures on Proof Verification and Approximation Algorithms. XII, 344 pages. 1998.

Vol. 1368: Y. Masunaga, T. Katayama, M. Tsukamoto (Eds.), Worldwide Computing and Its Applications — WWCA'98. Proceedings, 1998. XIV, 473 pages. 1998.

Vol. 1370: N.A. Streitz, S. Konomi, H.-J. Burkhardt (Eds.), Cooperative Buildings. Proceedings, 1998. XI, 267 pages. 1998.

Vol. 1371: I. Wachsmuth, M. Fröhlich (Eds.), Gesture and Sign Language in Human-Computer Interaction. Proceedings, 1997. XI, 309 pages. 1998. (Subseries LNAI).

Vol. 1372: S. Vaudenay (Ed.), Fast Software Encryption. Proceedings, 1998. VIII, 297 pages. 1998.

Vol. 1373: M. Morvan, C. Meinel, D. Krob (Eds.), STACS 98. Proceedings, 1998. XV, 630 pages. 1998.

Vol. 1374: H. Bunt, R.-J. Beun, T. Borghuis (Eds.), Multimodal Human-Computer Communication. VIII, 345 pages. 1998. (Subseries LNAI).

Vol. 1375: R. D. Hersch, J. André, H. Brown (Eds.), Electronic Publishing, Artistic Imaging, and Digital Typography. Proceedings, 1998. XIII, 575 pages. 1998.

Vol. 1376: F. Parisi Presicce (Ed.), Recent Trends in Algebraic Development Techniques. Proceedings, 1997. VIII, 435 pages. 1998.

Vol. 1377: H.-J. Schek, F. Saltor, I. Ramos, G. Alonso (Eds.), Advances in Database Technology – EDBT'98. Proceedings, 1998. XII, 515 pages. 1998.

Vol. 1378: M. Nivat (Ed.), Foundations of Software Science and Computation Structures. Proceedings, 1998. X, 289 pages. 1998.

Vol. 1379: T. Nipkow (Ed.), Rewriting Techniques and Applications. Proceedings, 1998. X, 343 pages. 1998.

Vol. 1380: C.L. Lucchesi, A.V. Moura (Eds.), LATIN'98: Theoretical Informatics. Proceedings, 1998. XI, 391 pages. 1998.

Vol. 1381: C. Hankin (Ed.), Programming Languages and Systems. Proceedings, 1998. X, 283 pages. 1998.

Vol. 1382: E. Astesiano (Ed.), Fundamental Approaches to Software Engineering. Proceedings, 1998. XII, 331 pages. 1998.

Vol. 1383: K. Koskimies (Ed.), Compiler Construction. Proceedings, 1998. X, 309 pages. 1998.

Vol. 1384: B. Steffen (Ed.), Tools and Algorithms for the Construction and Analysis of Systems. Proceedings, 1998. XIII, 457 pages. 1998.

Vol. 1385: T. Margaria, B. Steffen, R. Rückert, J. Posegga (Eds.), Services and Visualization. Proceedings, 1997/1998. XII, 323 pages. 1998.

Vol. 1386: T.A. Henzinger, S. Sastry (Eds.), Hybrid Systems: Computation and Control. Proceedings, 1998. VIII, 417 pages. 1998.

Vol. 1387: C. Lee Giles, M. Gori (Eds.), Adaptive Processing of Sequences and Data Structures. Proceedings, 1997. XII, 434 pages. 1998. (Subseries LNAI).

Vol. 1388: J. Rolim (Ed.), Parallel and Distributed Processing. Proceedings, 1998. XVII, 1168 pages. 1998.

Vol. 1389: K. Tombre, A.K. Chhabra (Eds.), Graphics Recognition. Proceedings, 1997. XII, 421 pages. 1998.

Vol. 1390: C. Scheideler, Universal Routing Strategies for Interconnection Networks. XVII, 234 pages. 1998.

Vol. 1391: W. Banzhaf, R. Poli, M. Schoenauer, T.C. Fogarty (Eds.), Genetic Programming. Proceedings, 1998. X, 232 pages. 1998.

Vol. 1392: A. Barth, M. Breu, A. Endres, A. de Kemp (Eds.), Digital Libraries in Computer Science: The MeDoc Approach. VIII, 239 pages. 1998.

Vol. 1393: D. Bert (Ed.), B'98: Recent Advances in the Development and Use of the B Method. Proceedings, 1998. VIII, 313 pages. 1998.

Vol. 1394: X. Wu. R. Kotagiri, K.B. Korb (Eds.), Research and Development in Knowledge Discovery and Data Mining. Proceedings, 1998. XVI, 424 pages. 1998. (Subseries LNAI).

Vol. 1395: H. Kitano (Ed.), RoboCup-97: Robot Soccer World Cup I. XIV, 520 pages. 1998. (Subseries LNAI).

Vol. 1396: E. Okamoto, G. Davida, M. Mambo (Eds.), Information Security. Proceedings, 1997. XII, 357 pages. 1998.

Vol. 1397: H. de Swart (Ed.), Automated Reasoning with Analytic Tableaux and Related Methods. Proceedings, 1998. X, 325 pages. 1998. (Subseries LNAI).

Vol. 1398: C. Nédellec, C. Rouveirol (Eds.), Machine Learning: ECML-98. Proceedings, 1998. XII, 420 pages. 1998. (Subseries LNAI).

Vol. 1399: O. Etzion, S. Jajodia, S. Sripada (Eds.), Temporal Databases: Research and Practice. X, 429 pages. 1998.

Vol. 1400: M. Lenz, B. Bartsch-Spörl, H.-D. Burkhard, S. Wess (Eds.), Case-Based Reasoning Technology. XVIII, 405 pages. 1998. (Subseries LNAI).

Vol. 1401: P. Sloot, M. Bubak, B. Hertzberger (Eds.), High-Performance Computing and Networking. Proceedings, 1998. XX, 1309 pages. 1998.

Vol. 1402: W. Lamersdorf, M. Merz (Eds.), Trends in Distributed Systems for Electronic Commerce. Proceedings, 1998. XII, 255 pages. 1998.

Vol. 1403: K. Nyberg (Ed.), Advances in Cryptology – EUROCRYPT '98. Proceedings, 1998. X, 607 pages. 1998.

Vol. 1404: C. Freksa, C. Habel. K.F. Wender (Eds.), Spatial Cognition. VIII, 491 pages. 1998. (Subseries LNAI).

Vol. 1405: S.M. Embury, N.J. Fiddian, W.A. Gray, A.C. Jones (Eds.), Advances in Databases. Proceedings, 1998. XII, 183 pages. 1998.

Vol. 1406: H. Burkhardt, B. Neumann (Eds.), Computer Vision – ECCV'98. Vol. I. Proceedings, 1998. XVI, 927 pages. 1998.

Vol. 1407: H. Burkhardt, B. Neumann (Eds.), Computer Vision – ECCV'98. Vol. II. Proceedings, 1998. XVI, 881 pages. 1998.

Vol. 1409: T. Schaub, The Automation of Reasoning with Incomplete Information. XI, 159 pages. 1998. (Subseries LNAI).

Vol. 1411: L. Asplund (Ed.), Reliable Software Technologies – Ada-Europe. Proceedings, 1998. XI, 297 pages. 1998.

Vol. 1412: R.E. Bixby, E.A. Boyd, R.Z. Ríos-Mercado (Eds.), Integer Programming and Combinatorial Optimization. Proceedings, 1998. IX, 437 pages. 1998.

Vol. 1413: B. Pernici, C. Thanos (Eds.), Advanced Information Systems Engineering. Proceedings, 1998. X, 423 pages. 1998.

Vol. 1414: M. Nielsen, W. Thomas (Eds.), Computer Science Logic. Selected Papers, 1997. VIII, 511 pages. 1998.

Vol. 1415: J. Mira, A.P. del Pobil, M.Ali (Eds.), Methodology and Tools in Knowledge-Based Systems. Vol. I. Proceedings, 1998. XXIV, 887 pages. 1998. (Subseries LNAI).

Vol. 1416: A.P. del Pobil, J. Mira, M.Ali (Eds.), Tasks and Methods in Applied Artificial Intelligence. Vol.II. Proceedings, 1998. XXIII, 943 pages. 1998. (Subseries LNAI).

Vol. 1417: S. Yalamanchili, J. Duato (Eds.), Parallel Computer Routing and Communication. Proceedings, 1997. XII, 309 pages. 1998.

Vol. 1418: R. Mercer, E. Neufeld (Eds.), Advances in Artificial Intelligence. Proceedings, 1998. XII, 467 pages. 1998. (Subseries LNAI).

Vol. 1419: G. Vigna (Ed.), Mobile Agents and Security. XII, 257 pages. 1998.

Vol. 1420: J. Desel, M. Silva (Eds.), Application and Theory of Petri Nets 1998. Proceedings, 1998. VIII, 385 pages. 1998.

Vol. 1421: C. Kirchner, H. Kirchner (Eds.), Automated Deduction – CADE-15. Proceedings, 1998. XIV, 443 pages. 1998. (Subseries LNAI).

Vol. 1422: J. Jeuring (Ed.), Mathematics of Program Construction. Proceedings, 1998. X, 383 pages. 1998.

Vol. 1423: J.P. Buhler (Ed.), Algorithmic Number Theory. Proceedings, 1998. X, 640 pages. 1998.

Vol. 1424: L. Polkowski, A. Skowron (Eds.), Rough Sets and Current Trends in Computing. Proceedings, 1998. XIII, 626 pages. 1998. (Subseries LNAI).

Vol. 1425: D. Hutchison, R. Schäfer (Eds.), Multimedia Applications, Services and Techniques – ECMAST'98. Proceedings, 1998. XVI, 532 pages. 1998.

Vol. 1427: A.J. Hu, M.Y. Vardi (Eds.), Computer Aided Verification. Proceedings, 1998. IX, 552 pages. 1998.

Vol. 1430: S. Trigila, A. Mullery, M. Campolargo, H. Vanderstraeten, M. Mampaey (Eds.), Intelligence in Services and Networks: Technology for Ubiquitous Telecom Services. Proceedings, 1998. XII, 550 pages. 1998.

Vol. 1431: H. Imai, Y. Zheng (Eds.), Public Key Cryptography. Proceedings, 1998. XI, 263 pages. 1998.

Vol. 1432: S. Arnborg, L. Ivansson (Eds.), Algorithm Theory – SWAT '98. Proceedings, 1998. IX, 347 pages. 1998.

Vol. 1433: V. Honavar, G. Slutzki (Eds.), Grammatical Inference. Proceedings, 1998. X, 271 pages. 1998. (Subseries LNAI).

Vol. 1434: J.-C. Heudin (Ed.), Virtual Worlds. Proceedings, 1998. XII, 412 pages. 1998. (Subseries LNAI).

Vol. 1435: M. Klusch, G. Weiß (Eds.), Cooperative Information Agents II. Proceedings, 1998. IX, 307 pages. 1998. (Subseries LNAI).

Vol. 1436: D. Wood, S. Yu (Eds.), Automata Implementation. Proceedings, 1997. VIII, 253 pages. 1998.

Vol. 1437: S. Albayrak, F.J. Garijo (Eds.), Intelligent Agents for Telecommunication Applications. Proceedings, 1998. XII, 251 pages. 1998. (Subseries LNAI).

Vol. 1438: C. Boyd, E. Dawson (Eds.), Information Security and Privacy. Proceedings, 1998. XI, 423 pages. 1998.

Vol. 1439: B. Magnusson (Ed.), Software Configuration Management. Proceedings, 1998. X, 207 pages. 1998.

Vol. 1441: W. Wobcke, M. Pagnucco, C. Zhang (Eds.), Agents and Multi-Agent Systems. Proceedings, 1997. XII, 241 pages. 1998. (Subseries LNAI).

Vol. 1443: K.G. Larsen, S. Skyum, G. Winskel (Eds.), Automata, Languages and Programming. Proceedings, 1998. XVI, 932 pages. 1998.

Vol. 1444: K. Jansen, J. Rolim (Eds.), Approximation Algorithms for Combinatorial Optimization. Proceedings, 1998. VIII, 201 pages. 1998.

Vol. 1445: E. Jul (Ed.), ECOOP'98 – Object-Oriented Programming. Proceedings, 1998. XII, 635 pages. 1998.

Vol. 1446: D. Page (Ed.), Inductive Logic Programming. Proceedings, 1998. VIII, 301 pages. 1998. (Subseries LNAI).

Vol. 1448: M. Farach-Colton (Ed.), Combinatorial Pattern Matching. Proceedings, 1998. VIII, 251 pages. 1998.

Vol. 1456: A. Drogoul, M. Tambe, T. Fukuda (Eds.), Collective Robotics. Proceedings, 1998. VII, 161 pages. 1998. (Subseries LNAI).